James Henderson

CARIBBEAN
& THE BAHAMAS

'Every fan of the Caribbean pursues the Green Flash. It is one of the islands' most ephemeral but satisfying moments, best sought on a palm-backed beach, rum punch in hand, with just the wash of the waves to disturb the evening calm.'

CADOGANguides

1 Marigot Bay, St Lucia

4

5 Emerald Pool, Dominica
6 Saut d'Eau pilgrimage, Haiti
7 Pineapples, Martinique

8 Puerto Plata, Dominican Republic
9 Banana shack, Dominican Republic
10 Carnival, Dominican Republic
11 Puerto Plata market, Dominican Republic

12 Traditional cottage, Bahamas

13 14

15

17 Exuma Cays, Bahamas

18 American classic car, Cuba

About the Author

For almost two decades, **James Henderson** has studied the Caribbean, from the window of tiny island-hopping planes, through scuba-diving masks and from some of the smartest hotels in the region. He travels there as much as possible, braving flash tropical downpours and droughts, *coups d'état*, jerk, drunken bus drivers and posses of mad Californians; dodging safari buses of cruise-ship passengers and the attentions of over-zealous aloe masseurs, jumbies and machete-flourishing coconut salesmen. To stop himself going soft on so much luxury, he takes part in some of the most arduous endurance events in the world. He has lingered longest in the Caribbean, still watching for the Green Flash and writing features for the UK newspapers. James is also founder editor of *Definitive Caribbean*, a free online guide found at *www.definitivecaribbean.com*.

About the Updaters

Kay Showker has been a writer, photographer and lecturer on travel for almost three decades. Following a 10-year tenure at *Travel Weekly*, she became a freelance writer, authoring 13 guidebooks and America On Line's 'Cruise Critic/Caribbean Ports of Call'. She has also appeared on CNN, ABC, CBS, NBC, and The Travel Channel.

David Orkin updated the Cuba chapter. Prior to his current career as a travel writer, David worked in the travel industry for 15 years, first for Trailfinders, and then as a Director of Quest Worldwide Travel. In recent years, he has travelled extensively in North and Latin America (and, of course, Cuba).

Contents

Maps

Cadogan Guides
2nd Floor, 233 High Holborn,
London WC1V 7DN
info@cadoganguides.co.uk
www.cadoganguides.com

The Globe Pequot Press
246 Goose Lane, PO Box 480, Guilford,
Connecticut 06437–0480

Copyright © James Henderson 1990, 1992, 1994,
1997, 2001, 2005

Cover photographs by © James Henderson and
© John Miller
Photo essay: © James Henderson, © John Miller,
© Beth Evans
Art direction: Sarah Rianhard-Gardner
Maps © Cadogan Guides,
drawn by Maidenhead Cartographic Services
Managing Editor: Natalie Pomier
Editor: James Alexander
Editorial Assistant: Nicola Jessop
Proofreading: Elspeth Anderson and
Anna Amari-Parker
Indexing: Isobel McLean

Printed in Italy by Legoprint
A catalogue record for this book is available from
the British Library
ISBN 1–86011–212–9

Introduction

When you first arrive in the Caribbean you might find that people walk rather slowly. But then, after a few days, as the island atmosphere gets to work on you and the concerns of daily life at home gradually fade, you will notice that they begin to catch up with you. The Caribbean is an ideal place to wind down and relax. It's an easy life in the islands: with reliable warmth and sun, strikingly new and beautiful tropical scenery and, of course, magnificent sea and sand.

The Caribbean has an enchanting atmosphere, and for centuries it has captivated travellers from the temperate zones. It is a wonderful experience to be surrounded by islands; they sit serenely on the sea horizon and the glare of the sun makes the surface of the sea glint as though it were sprinkled with diamonds. You will be bombarded by vibrant unfamiliar sensations: the sweet flavours of ripened fruits – mango, soursop or sweet banana – and the fragrance of jasmine and frangipani on the night air. Only the strongest colours stand out in the glare of the Caribbean sun – the impossibly bright plumage of a scarlet ibis and the shimmering fluorescence of a hummingbird. And rhythms familiar from elsewhere – reggae, steel pan and Latin salsa – suddenly take on a different feel in their element.

The Caribbean is known as a hedonist's destination, the place for an all-over body holiday. You can simply lie back and absorb the sun's warmth; scuba dive in euphoric suspension, feasting your eyes on a glittering seascape of corals and tropical fish; savour the taste of piña colada; take a trip on a catamaran; or feel the surge of a windsurfer beneath you as you race off on the trade winds – it's the 21st century's ultimate rest cure. There are beach bars from paradise here, made of just a few rickety struts and a deck standing on the sand.

But beyond the beach and body culture, the coconut oil and ganja, you will discover a West Indies that pulses to a different beat, a land of creole, callaloo and calypso, rhythmic, vibrant and compelling. There is such variety on the islands, a hundred variations on the tropical theme. The pace of life is carefree and laid-back. At times it is too laid-back. It can feel shambolic, even infuriating – service can be so absurdly slow that you feel like an unwitting player in a farce. If you make a fuss, expect the islanders simply to look on in bemusement at the worries of a slave to the minute hand.

Caribbean life is also demonstrative and always lively. There is a theatre of the street which turns a bus trip or a visit to the market into an adventure. The West Indians are masters of street talk and you can expect to be on the receiving end of a 'limers'' quip or two. It is difficult for a visitor even to understand at first, let alone respond in kind, but, whatever your reaction, you can guarantee peals of distinctive West Indian laughter all around you. Music is played all the time, everywhere and usually at high volume. People set up vast speakers in the road and dance just for the hell of it. Practically every island has its own rhythm – soca, salsa, ska. The Caribbean is an easy place to travel: if you want company, you simply stop and talk to somebody.

Since its discovery and colonization by the Europeans, the Caribbean has become an extraordinary mixing bowl of cultures, with echoes from all over the world: Parisian chic, parish churches from rural England, American-style cable TV and large cruising cars, Hindu prayer flags and Muslim minarets, and of course the strongest reminders of Africa in the faces, the spirit religions and the relentless drum-based rhythms. And yet the flashes are only momentary, because they have metamorphosed, creolized into something new and uniquely West Indian – Christmas carols to a reggae or calypso beat, faces with Dutch features and ebony black skin, Martinican creole, which sounds so like French, but which evaporates as soon as you think you have understood it. Each island has its distinctive characteristics and the variety is striking, even across just a few miles of sea. If you are island-hopping, it is interesting to work out the common strains across the islands.

It is only in the fortresses and plantation houses that you can see how wealthy the Caribbean was two hundred years ago. These fertile islands were turned into sugar factories – the wealth of the West Indies was enough to kick-start the Industrial Revolution – and imperial armies would come thousands of miles to fight over them. But that time is long past. In the 21st century the Caribbean must struggle along with everyone else to keep financially afloat. The economic mainstay is tourism, an industry which has changed the face of the islands over the last twenty years – many islands are now highly developed, and most are continuing to build.

There is amazing variety in the Caribbean. Something, somewhere, is just right for you. With a bit of luck you'll find it and, once you've settled into the pace of Caribbean life, you'll be captivated by the place just as generations of travellers have been before you.

A Little Geography

To get a mental picture of the Caribbean islands, imagine a dinosaur skeleton, standing between the North and South American continents, facing left. The body is made of the Greater Antilles, perched in the middle of the Caribbean Sea, its trunk at Hispaniola, supported by feet in Jamaica and stretching out its head and neck (Cuba) towards the Gulf of Mexico. In the east, the arc of the Lesser Antilles makes up the links of its prehensile tail, of which the final vertebra, Trinidad, is firmly embedded in South America.

The area has a variety of names: 'Caribbean' comes from the indigenous tribe of American Indians, the Caribs (see p.19) , who inhabited the Lesser Antilles until the arrival of the Europeans; the origin of the term 'West Indies' lies with Columbus himself, who found the islands while trying to find a route to India via the west; and the 'Greater' and 'Lesser Antilles' derive from Antillia, supposedly a corruption of 'Atlantis', the lost continent that was presumed to lie beyond the Azores. The string of islands encloses the Caribbean Sea, separating it from the Atlantic Ocean, and over the millennia active volcanoes have sprouted along the rift between the Atlantic and Caribbean tectonic plates. The Tropic of Cancer cuts through the middle of the Bahamas, passing just a few miles north of Havana in Cuba.

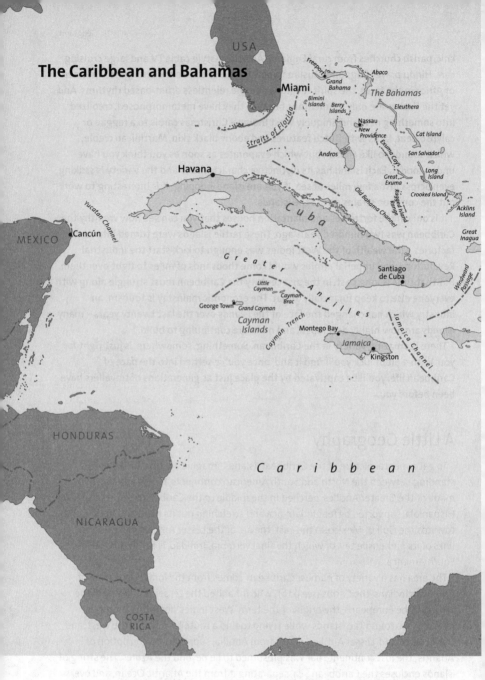

The Caribbean and Bahamas

USA

Freeport
Grand Bahama
Abaco
Miami
Bimini Islands
Berry Islands
The Bahamas
Eleuthera
Nassau
New Providence
Cat Island
San Salvador
Straits of Florida
Andros
Exuma Cays
Havana
Great Exuma
Long Island
Crooked Island
Yucatan Channel
Old Bahama Channel
Ragged Island Range
Acklins Island
MEXICO
Cancún
Cuba
Great Inagua
Greater Antilles
Santiago de Cuba
Little Cayman
Cayman Brac
Windward Passage
George Town
Grand Cayman
Cayman Islands
Cayman Trench
Montego Bay
Jamaica
Jamaica Channel
HONDURAS
Kingston
Caribbean
NICARAGUA
COSTA RICA

There are 28 different political units in the Caribbean and the Bahamas, among them independent countries, crown colonies, overseas departments, a territory and a commonwealth. This guidebook approaches them in a rough geographical order, tracking along the island chain from the southeast to the northwest, but collecting

them according to language and political allegiance, according to the old groupings of the colonial administration. For convenience and in order to emphasize their cultural unity, the French West Indies are treated as one group (even though they are scattered among other islands and spread over 300 miles), as are the two groups of the Netherlands Antilles, which are separated by some 600 miles of the Caribbean Sea. Strictly speaking, the archipelago of the Bahamas is not geographically in the Caribbean itself, but it is included in this book as the islands and their people have a similar heritage, and visitors of course have much the same reasons for going there as they do to the Caribbean.

A Guide to the Guide

o6 Barbados

The gentleman of Caribbean tourism and second home to a crowd of English sophisticates; it has some of the Caribbean's best-known hotels and restaurants along the west coast. The south coast offers a lower-key atmosphere with riotous nightlife. Barbados boasts excellent beaches, and it is easily accessible. It caters well for all tastes, making it a good option for a first visit to the Caribbean. The Bajans are among the most charming people in the West Indies.

o7 Trinidad and Tobago

Trinidad is industrialized, crowded, and strong on culture – lively home to carnival, steel pan and calypso. There's also spectacular natural life, with over 400 species to be found in the rainforest and the coastal swamps. There are some quiet coastal retreats in the east.

Partnered with Trinidad, **Tobago** is a lovely, low-key tropical island. Tourism, which has developed rapidly over the last few years, is concentrated in the southwest, but elsewhere idyllic spots are still to be found in isolated coves beneath the tumbling rainforests.

o8 The Windward Islands

Grenada has volcanic peaks and rainforests, fruit and spice plantations and easy-going islanders. It is less developed than St Lucia and has good beaches in the south of the island. It is easy to reach, with some good small hotels: a full range from luxury to budget.

St Vincent is an unspoilt, quite poor, English-speaking island; it has grand natural fertility and just a few comfortable, family-run hotels. It is a good starting point for a tour of the Grenadines.

Strung between St Vincent and Grenada, the **Grenadines** boast fantastic sea, beaches and sailing. There's a good mix of attractive tourist islands – including island-enclaves of super-luxury – and accessible West Indian life. Island-hopping is possible.

The most developed of the volcanic Windwards, **St Lucia** has some very smart and comfortable hotels along its good beaches. It is lively in the main centres, but alsohas some lovely and luxurious hideaways to stay in among the coves of the leeward coastline.

Least developed of the Windwards, **Dominica** has a natural charm of its own. It has supreme natural life above and below the waterline – a rainforest with over 100 species of birds, whale-watching in season and excellent scuba. There are just a few golden-sand beaches and life is extremely low-key.

09 The French Caribbean

Martinique is the most developed French Caribbean island. Martinicans are chic and their restaurants excellent – in town and in the resorts. The beaches are best in the south, where most of the tourist industry is concentrated. **Guadeloupe** is also a developed island, with a large tourist industry, particularly on Grande-Terre in the east (for the beaches). Less crowded, Basse-Terre has golden sand beaches in the northwest, but also rainforest for trekking. The charming offshore islands, Marie Galante and La Désirade, are very low key; Terre de Haut in Les Saints is pretty and well developed.

St Martin is the larger and (marginally) less-developed French half of the island shared with Dutch Sint Maarten. Quite expensive, it has good beaches, some smart hotels, a number of nice (if expensive) guest houses and excellent restaurants, all with a Gallic atmosphere.

St Barts is a champagne playground, as only the French could conceive. It has some charming hotels and fine restaurants, and is very expensive. There is barely any West Indian culture to distract you from the essentials of gourmet dining, sunning and posing.

10 The Leeward Islands

Antigua does have some smart hotels and some laid-back retreats for independent travellers, but also has a large package-tourism industry. It is fairly expensive, but is easy to reach and has some busy beaches with watersports as well as countless miles of undisturbed, superb sand. Antigua is known for its sailing, out of English Harbour and Falmouth Harbour in the south. Attached to Antigua, tiny **Barbuda** is one of the least-known islands in the Caribbean. It has superb sand, a couple of outrageously expensive hotels and a lazy Caribbean life that has remained unchanged for about fifty years.

Poor **Montserrat**. It is a charming, slow and sedate island, but is being held to ransom by its angry volcano for the moment, making it hard to recommend.

The larger and marginally more developed partner of Nevis, **St Kitts** has an easy-going West Indian atmosphere. Its beaches and the traditional Caribbean resort hotels are in the south; the north has some of the Caribbean's best plantation hotels. A gradually developing island, **Nevis** is just waking up from its slow and gentle small-island life. It has only a few bars and restaurants, with some excellent beaches, several classic Caribbean plantation hotels, and a plush resort hotel that American visitors consistently put on the Caribbean's top ten list.

With an ultimately laid-back atmosphere and magnificent beaches, **Anguilla** is still uncrowded and has a string of excellent places to stay, some at the very top of the range, others affordably cheaper. The restaurants are excellent, if a little pricey, and you can eat in serious gourmet style or in rickety beachfront shacks on superb sand.

11 The Dutch Caribbean

Sint Maarten is the more developed (Dutch) half of an island shared with French St Martin, with a large tourist industry. It has excellent beaches and good sports facilities, casinos and shops. There are also great restaurants (with an endless choice of others in the French half) and bars. It is strong on package tourism and too developed for some, but the locals swear by the island. A tiny outcrop, whose heyday was really two centuries ago, **Sint Eustatius** is a very peaceful, writer's retreat. **Saba** is also a tiny outcrop, with gentle, easy-going islanders. There is not much to do, but the diving is a good option. Development continues, but without beaches it is a quiet, reliable retreat.

Easily accessible and extremely cosmopolitan, **Curaçao** is the senior Dutch Caribbean island and has a string of good bars and restaurants and a lively crowd. The beaches are not brilliant, but there is good diving and a decent range of hotels.

A slumberstruck coral outcrop with a quiet life and excellent diving, **Bonaire** has great diving lodges to stay in and a surprising string of good restaurants. **Aruba** has fantastic beaches, developed in very American style, with a string of high-rise hotels, big names such as Holiday Inn and Hyatt Regency. It's not the place for a quiet, off-beat holiday, but it has American standards of comfort and is well organized with cabarets and casinos. Aruba is easily accessible from the USA (although it is more difficult from the UK).

12 The Virgin Islands

The British Virgin Islands are easy-going and pretty expensive islands with the feel of a sophisticated playground. There are good restaurants and bars on **Tortola** (the main island) and all the passing yachts give it a nautical feel – the Virgin Islands have excellent sailing. Across Francis Drake Channel is the second island, **Virgin Gorda**, with a string of excellent hotels and beaches, and the nearly deserted **Norman Island** and **Cooper Island** (nothing but a beach bar). **Jost van Dyke** and **Anegada** are low-key to the point of somnolence.

Of the US Virgin Islands, **St Thomas** is highly developed and easily reached from mainland USA. There are big hotels and endless shopping in Charlotte Amalie. The island gets crowded, but it has great restaurants and bars and is a good transit point. **St Croix** is larger and less developed, but still has some nice hotels and restaurants. **St John** is the least developed of the US Virgins – much of it is National Park. There are good bars and restaurants on the coasts. The island is also frequented by passing yachties.

13 Puerto Rico

The smallest of the Greater Antilles (but still a large island by Caribbean standards), Puerto Rico is a Spanish-speaking American territory (English is also spoken). It has a large tourist industry on the northern shore, with good bars and restaurants in the capital San Juan, National Parks, mountains and rainforest. There are also delightful offshore islands, **Vieques** and **Culebra**.

14 The Dominican Republic

Spanish-speaking, the Dominican Republic is one of the largest Caribbean countries. It has a huge tourist industry (around two and a half million visitors each year), but beyond the tourist ghettos are cool coastal towns on superb beaches and lively island life. It is also relatively cheap.

15 Haiti

Haiti is hardly a typical tourist island, as politics prevent it. For the traveller, however, Haiti is quite simply one of the most compelling countries in the world, with its French and African influences, naïve art, markets, tap-taps and voodoo.

16 Cuba

Cuba is selling its tourism hard at the moment. If you are prepared to be a dutiful package tourist, spending your time in the resorts and on packaged bus tours, then the island offers a typical Caribbean beach holiday. As an independent traveller's destination, Cuba can be frustrating but very rewarding.

17 Jamaica

The largest of the former British Islands, Jamaica is easily accessible and has a full range of tourist hotels (super-luxury to friendly guest houses), good bars and restaurants. Beyond the coastal resorts, it offers a glimpse of a fascinating island life, and vibrant music and culture.

18 The Cayman Islands

Grand Cayman is highly developed and fairly American in style – some of the hotels are big and modern, and many are condominium-style with housekeeping facilities. It is a well-organized rest-cure, easily accessible from the USA, with charming islanders and superb scuba diving. The Caymanians are a charming people. **Cayman Brac** and particularly **Little Cayman** have a castaway-island atmosphere, good small hotels and more excellent diving.

19 The Bahamas

New Providence and **Grand Bahama** are the principal tourist resorts; they are crowded and upbeat, but they have lively bars and good restaurants and everything you might want in the way of watersports. Most package holidays end up here.

The **Out Islands** consist of hundreds of cays and sandbars. They are some of the least explored islands in the whole area – scattered with occasional hotels, each isolated on its own magnificent strip of sand. They have superb sailing, deep-sea fishing, bonefishing and scuba diving.

20 The Turks and Caicos Islands

At the southeastern limit of the Bahamas, the Turks and Caicos Islands lie in two groups. **Providenciales**, the most developed and accessible, is also the gateway to several posh, private-island resorts; the rest are in varying states of underdevelopment and are ideal for a lazy retreat. There are spectacular beaches throughout and the diving is superb.

Topics

Flora

Columbus himself was the first European to be captivated by the extraordinary beauty of the West Indies. The volcanic islands of the Lesser Antilles and the windward coasts of the Greater Antilles are incredibly fertile, watered by constant showers from the Atlantic winds. There are many rainforests among the Caribbean islands. A gardener's most useful tool is a machete, to keep back what used to be known as 'the green hell'. Growth is so rampant that fences turn into hedges and even telegraph wires fur up in no time.

Trees and Plants

There are many varieties of palm tree in the Caribbean and you will see **coconut palms** everywhere, including the beaches of course – beware of sitting under them, though, because people have been killed by falling coconuts.

In Caribbean gardens you will often find the **golden palm**, which looks like a spray of greenery similar to a fountain, and the **sago palm**, on a brown stump of a trunk, with scratchy, dark green fronds like a comb. In St Barts they use the **sabal palm** (*latanier* in French) for weaving rushwork. There are also some **date palms** in the islands and the odd curious one like the **fish-tail palm**, with ragged fronds looking like torn fish-tails, but the most impressive of all are the tall **cabbage palm**, and particularly the **royal palm**, both of which grow to over 100ft in height and cast off a spike that points directly upwards. The royal palm is cultivated for the heart of palm that is put into salads.

There are many trees that come out in a riot of colourful blooms: the **flamboyant** turns scarlet in May, June and July; the African **tulip tree** (or flame of the forest) comes out in rich red blooms between December and May; and the **immortelle** tree (or *madre de cacao* in Spanish because it was used to protect cocoa trees) bursts into orange blooms in January and February. Yellow and pink **pouis** are called so for obvious reasons, and they leave the ground smothered in their colourful blooms. **Frangipani** have blooms of yellow and white, and *Lignum vitae* and **jacaranda** bloom a lilac colour. The **cannonball tree** has huge wooden fruits like cannonballs and yet small and delicate flowers. They drop to earth at dusk, unlike the night-blooming **cereus** (a flower), which dies with the daylight.

In the forests you will see clumps of **bamboo** (brought to the Caribbean from the Far East for its versatility as a farm material) that reach up to 60ft, sometimes grown in alleys. Gourds are made from the orange- to football-sized fruits of the bushy and spiky-branched **calabash tree**. The **bearded fig tree** has a shaggy collection of aerial roots that hang from branches like a beard. In the dry ABC islands look out for the lopsided **divi-divi tree**, whose branches blow over and grow downwind.

In lowlands and mid-range forests you will find **gommiers** (used by the Caribs to construct their canoes), **mahoe** and **mahogany** as well as more exotic species such as the spiky-trunked **sandbox tree**, **locust trees** and **silk cotton**, also known as kapok, whose trunk has buttresses.

In the branches of higher trees you will find **mosses**, **cycads**, **bromeliads**, **creeping vines** and **lianas** on an endless cycle moving from the forest floor up into the top branches, and **ferns** as much as 10ft long that explode out of the treetops. Back at sea level you will find **silver-backed ferns** which will leave their pattern like a stencil when you slap them on your skin.

Many of the fruit-bearing trees that grow so well in the islands' fertile soil were imported during the 18th century, mainly intended as a commercial proposition, or else to provide food for the slaves. The **banana** and some of its many relatives, the **plantain** and **green fig**, came from the Indian Ocean area.

In the southern Caribbean they still grow **nutmeg** and **cocoa** (*see* 'The Spice Isle of the Caribbean', pp.150–1), which was made fashionable in Europe by Marie-Thérèse d'Espagne when she became Queen of France.

Breadfruit, with fruits like vast green cannonballs (also its relation the breadnut), was unpopular with the slaves at first, but has since become a staple. The fruit of the **ackee** tree tastes a bit like scrambled egg and is eaten at breakfast. **Christophene** (known in some islands as chow chow), a crisp and light green vegetable the shape of a pear, grows on a creeping vine.

'Ground provisions', staple vegetables grown locally, include **yam**, **tannia**, **eddo**, **sweet potato**, **'Irish' potato** and **cassava** (dried and used by the Arawaks to make bread), all of which you will see at markets.

Flowers

The Caribbean is perhaps most famous for its flowers and gardens, and you will see explosions of tropical colours all year round: the orange, pink and purple blooms of **bougainvillea** grow in long spindly fingers; there are some 200 species of brightly coloured **hibiscus** (one of which is known as *choublac* in Haiti, and is used to blacken shoes); and then there's **poinsettia**, whose green leaves turn bright red at Christmas time.

More exotic flowers are **passionflowers**; **heliconia**, shaped like a lobster claw; the **chenille plant** (also called red-hot cat tail because of its shape); and the **bird of paradise flower**, like a bird's face with topknot plumage. You will see the plastic-looking **anthurium** everywhere.

There are also hundreds of **orchids** in the Caribbean, one of which is grown commercially to produce vanilla. The local names for plants vary of course from island to island and between the languages, but there are some colourful names: **mother-in-law's tongue** grows in a sprout of fearsome twisted green spikes.

Botanical Gardens

There are botanical gardens throughout the islands. Originally they were used for the propagation of food and of important medicinal and commercial plants (quinine, arrowroot, camphor and spices such as cinnamon, clove, allspice). The oldest and most famous are the gardens in **St Vincent**, but there were gardens in most islands at one stage; many can be visited and a few of them are still in commercial use.

Fauna

The animal life of the Caribbean is relatively limited and all the domestic animals that you see were imported by the colonists – including the ubiquitous goat. Only a few indigenous land animals survive and it is rare to see an **armadillo**, an **agouti** or a **jutia** (a rat-like creature). Reptiles of all sorts exist, from the tiny little **tree frogs** that keep you awake at night with their chirruping and **toads** that croak so loud that they sound like a generator, to the prehistoric, tank-like 5ft **iguanas** and the **crocodiles** that live in the swamplands.

There are a few snakes, but only one or two of them are poisonous – if you see a pair of eyes glowing at night in Martinique or St Lucia watch out, because it will be the venomous **fer-de-lance**.

There are plenty of insects, including **mosquitoes**, marching columns of **termites** and on the beaches irritating tiny **sandflies** that appear towards dusk. **Fireflies**, which flash bright green, on for a second, off for a second, can be seen all over the islands. Trinidad has much the widest selection of animals and particularly birds because of its proximity to South America.

Birdlife

The birds of the Caribbean are spectacular and incredibly varied. Not only are there plenty of indigenous species, many with plumage of startling tropical colours, but the islands are on migratory routes and so other species pass through as they escape from the winter cold (both north and south). In the gardens you will find small and daring **tanagers** and **bananaquits** (which will have a go at the food on your table if you look away) as well as the **yellow orioles** and noisy characters called **grackles**. There are also a large number of **hummingbirds** (Trinidad alone has about 15 species) and you will see these beautiful creatures in the rainforests and gardens. The 'doctor bird' or **red-billed streamertail** (it has a long double tail) is the Jamaican national bird.

Many of the Windward Islands have their own **parrots** that hide high up in the rainforest; sadly these have been hunted nearly to extinction and exported as pets. Other forest dwellers are the black and yellow **trogons** and fluorescent green **honey creepers**. There are **woodpeckers**, **cuckoos** and **warblers** in the larger islands. Shore birds include **pelicans**, which you will see offshore, perched on a rock digesting their meal; **boobies**; **terns**; scissor-tailed red-billed **tropicbirds**; and magnificent, sleek and speedy **frigate birds**.

Swamps have the greatest diversity of birdlife and here you will find many sorts of **herons**, **waders** and **ducks** as well as **sandpipers** and the odd tiny **water-tyrant**. Oddest of all are the **purple gallinule** and the **wattled jacana**, with overlong toes that allow it to walk over lilies.

One of the most spectacular sights that you can witness in the West Indies is the evening flight of the **scarlet ibis**, which only takes place in the Caroni Swamp in Trinidad. Another fine sight is the **pink flamingo**, which nests only in Great Inagua in the Bahamas and on Bonaire in the ABC islands.

For birdlife, Trinidad is undoubtedly the most exciting island to visit (it supposedly has more species than Canada, which is not that unlikely because most Canadian birds probably spend the winter here), but all the Greater Antilles also have an excellent variety. Over the last few years there has been an increase in awareness of the natural habitat in the countries of the Caribbean, along with the establishment of natural parks or increased powers for those that already exist. There should be some excellent opportunities for enthusiasts, but not all islands have the organization to cope well with visitors. The best islands to visit for a general impression of the flora and birdlife are Trinidad (rainforest and swamplands), Dominica (rainforest) and Puerto Rico.

The Green Flash

Every fan of the Caribbean pursues the Green Flash. It is one of the islands' most ephemeral but satisfying moments, best sought on a palm-backed beach, rum punch in hand with just the wash of the waves to disturb the evening calm. The Green Flash occurs only over uninterrupted sea, and then only during a totally cloudless sunset, at the very moment when the last of the sun's globe disappears over the sea horizon. It usually lasts for just half a second and never for more than a second and a half: a green strip that appears on the sea's surface.

In scientific terms it is caused by refraction of the sun's light as it passes through the earth's atmosphere (and at this angle of view it is passing through more of the atmosphere than when the sun is directly above). Green light is refracted more than red light. As the sun descends to the horizon it runs through the spectrum: orange to yellow (the normal sunsets that we know), to pale green and finally to emerald green. In less scientific terms, people might say that if you stare straight at the sun for long enough you can persuade yourself that you have seen anything. If you're still up at dawn, it is sometimes possible to see the same effect as the sun appears over the sea horizon in the east.

Music

People joke that the West Indians change the roll of their gait as they walk along the street, switching rhythm to each successive stereo system that they pass. A bit of an exaggeration, but music has been central to Caribbean life since slave days, when it was the principal form of recreation. You will hear it everywhere, all day, every day. You'll see three-year-olds in the first throes of dancing and sixty-year-olds who will take a turn on the living-room floor with lightning footwork and an easy grace. In Santo Domingo in the Dominican Republic, the shoeshine boys will strike up on their boxes with brushes and tins of polish. Buses are like mobile discotheques. At Carnival, people dance for days. There are almost as many beats as there are islands in the Caribbean and they go on changing and developing over time. The roots are audible in many cases – you will see marching bands dressed in their red tunics playing 'Oh, when the Saints' reggae style, Indian flourishes appear in Trinidadian calypso, the Latin beat is clear in Cuban and Puerto Rican salsa, and the vocals of rap appear in calypso and Jamaican dancehall. But in all the Caribbean sounds, the rhythm is relentlessly fast and the beat is as solid as the African drums from which it is derived.

The West Indians will use anything to make music. At Carnival, the crowds shuffle along to the sound of a couple of drums, a car wheel-rim, a cheese-grater and a cowbell. Even garden forks have been tuned up in Curaçao. But the best example of them all is the steel drum in Trinidad, which was invented in the yards of Port of Spain after the Second World War. Discarded biscuit tins and oil drums were bashed out and then tuned up and an orchestra was created.

As you travel around the islands, you will see speakers set up in the street just for the hell of it. Cars practically bulge with the beat and they can often be heard before they can be seen coming along the road. If you are invited to a fête, go, because they are a wild side of West Indian life. Dance is all lower-carriage movement, shuffle-stepping and swaying hips, and is incredibly energetic.

Any of the Caribbean Carnivals is worth attending if you happen to be on the island. You can often join in, if you do go, by asking around (usually for a small fee to cover the cost of the costume). It is worth crossing half the world to get to the Trinidad Carnival (many Trinidadians do), which takes place at the beginning of Lent and hosts steel band and calypso competitions. Other music festivals include the various jazz festivals and the Merengue Festival in Santo Domingo, Dominican Republic, in July. At around the same time, reggae fans see some of the best bands in concert at Reggae Sumfest in Montego Bay, Jamaica.

The rhythms of one island often spread to another. Just a few of the popular musical styles and their country of origin are as follows:

Bachata – Dominican Republic. Has recently been revived and grown popular. Generally songs of unrequited love, with a slower and more melodic rhythm than *merengue*.

Calypso – Trinidad. Witty, satirical, political or just gossipy songs, with as many styles as there are calypsonians (*see* 'Carnival, Calypso and Steel Pan', p.100). The songs were probably first sung in French creole during the 19th century. After the Second World War the calypsos were often backed by *steel pan* but in the late 1970s this was replaced by *soca* music.

Compas – Haiti. A rawer rhythm, but not dissimilar to the *zouk* of the French Antilles, also with echoes of West Africa but strongly influenced by *merengue*.

Dancehall – Jamaica. Developed during the mid-1980s and early 90s. A compulsive and monotonous rap grafted onto a hard *reggae* beat. Its rhythm makes it danceable, but, as with all Jamaican music, it's the lyrics, rude and controversial, that make it popular.

Merengue – Dominican Republic. A Latin beat, relentless, bustling and compulsive. Popular merengue is played on modern instruments now, but you may still see a traditional *perico ripiao* band: a drum, an accordion, a *güira* (a cheese-grater scratched with a metal stick) and sometimes a *bajo* (a sit-on bass-box with metal teeth that the player strums).

Parang – Trinidad. Sung in the run-up to Christmas, parang is Spanish in origin but has absorbed influences from Venezuela and is set to a Trinidadian rhythm, with instruments such as guitar, cuatro, maracas, violin and bass-box.

Reggae – Jamaica. Developed during the late 1960s and introduced the chaka-chaka lilt to existing rhythms, such as those of *ska*. Made internationally famous by Bob Marley.

Salsa – two different sorts, one each from Cuba and Puerto Rico, the latter influenced by the 'Neo-Riceñans' (Puerto Ricans in New York). Cuban salsa is distinctly Latin and grew out of *son*.

Ska – Jamaica. A riotous and compulsive beat, developed during the early 1960s, overtaken by rhythms such as *reggae*.

Soca (soul-calypso) – Trinidad. A much faster beat than *calypso*, played on more conventional modern instruments, with influences from European rock to Indian and Chinese music. Barbados and other islands nearby also produce their own soul-calypsonians, some of them very good.

Son – Cuba. Son is typically performed with a guitar, washboard and heavy drum backing. Other Cuban rhythms include rumba, danzón, cha-cha-cha and, of course, Cuban jazz.

Steel Pan – Trinidad. Played on the stretched lids of discarded oil drums and invented in the poorest areas of Port of Spain at the end of the Second World War. The beat is energetic and compulsive.

Zouk – Martinique and Guadeloupe. A bustling double beat, with echoes of West Africa.

Historical Topics

Caribbean Indians

Virtually no indigenous Caribbean Indians survive today, but when the Europeans first arrived in the New World there were two principal races of Amerindians living in the islands. In the north were the tribes of the **Arawaks**, spread over the Greater Antilles and the Bahamas, and to the south the islands of the Eastern Caribbean were inhabited by the **Carib Indians**, who were working their way up along the chain of the Lesser Antilles from South America as far as the Leeward Islands.

The Amerindians are thought to have made their way over from Asia to the American continent about 40,000 years ago, fanning out into different areas to become Eskimos, the North American Indians and the settled tribes of South America. The first settlers on the islands, the **Ciboneys**, are thought to have come to the islands about four or five thousand years ago, but the Arawaks began their hopping up the islands just a few hundred years BC. They settled the Windwards and the Leewards in turn, and eventually the Greater Antilles. The Arawaks were to live in peace on the islands for a thousand years or so, until the Caribs, a belligerent tribe who originated in the Amazon jungle, started to follow them up the chain and force them out. When Columbus arrived, the Caribs had got as far as the northernmost of the Lesser Antilles and were just starting to make raids on Puerto Rico. If the Spaniards had not arrived and set about killing the Arawaks, the Caribs would probably have done so.

Arawaks

The Spaniards found different tribes of Arawaks: on Puerto Rico the Borinquens; in Hispaniola, Jamaica and Cuba the Tainos (the Indians shouted this word, supposedly meaning 'peace' in their language, when they first saw the Spanish ships); and in the Bahamas the Lucayans. A tribe called the Guanahatabeyes had already found their way to Cuba, probably from Florida, and lived in the caves inland, but very little is known about them.

The Arawaks were the first to discover the tropical island idyll. They led a very peaceable existence in their hammocks, fishing occasionally and snorting tobacco at three-day dance parties. They lived off the food they could catch – fish, manatee, doves and parrots, animals like iguana, and fruits – and grew a few crops like cassava and maize. They were adept hunters. To catch ducks they would allow gourds (fruits like wooden footballs) to float downriver into a flock so that it would become used to them, and then they would swim down with gourds on their heads, grabbing the ducks by the feet and pulling them under as they floated past. They also used to attach a cord to a remora, a little suckerfish with a grip so tight that it could hang on to a turtleshell while they pulled it in.

The height of beauty in an Arawak was a pointed skull with hair worn in a topknot, and so babies' heads were pressed with slats of wood, giving them huge foreheads. This reputedly made their heads so hard that they could stop a Spanish sword. Like the Caribs, Arawaks had thick and glossy black hair which they oiled and wore long. They wore few clothes but they decorated themselves with feathers, tattoos and beads. Only married women would cover themselves at all. Their only domestic animal was a little dog, an *alcos*, that could not bark. Possessions meant little to them, so they happily gave away what they had to the early Spanish visitors. In their simplicity they were fascinated by the mirrors and bells that they were given in return. Theft was regarded as the worst of crimes and those caught were slowly skewered to death with a pole.

They lived in small communities near the sea, in conical thatched shelters, and they were led by a *cacique* or chieftain. The *cacique*, who was also the spiritual leader, would preside over the religious ceremonies, calling his people together on a conch shell and then forcing himself to vomit so that he would be pure enough to communicate with the gods. Then began day-long sessions of dance, stupor and games (some played with a shuttlecock and others like volleyball), all fired by maize alcohol and the Arawak drug, a powder blasted up the nostrils through a metre-long, double-pronged tube called a *tabaco*. The Arawak for tobacco was '*cohiba*', and the habit of smoking comes from them – the Spaniards were terrified to see these people with firebrands hanging out of their mouths. Tobacco, syphilis, the hammock, the potato and maize are some of the Arawak bequests to the Europeans.

All the tribes had similar spiritual beliefs, in a male and a female god. They worshipped them in the form of *zemes*, figures of animals or humans carved in wood and stone, which also represented the forces in their lives – rain, wind, fire and hurricanes. They believed that after death they went on to *coyaba*, a plentiful land without sickness or hurricanes, where they feasted and danced all day long.

Columbus noted that the Arawaks were gentle, generous and honest. Today there is nothing left of them, except a few Arawak features in the faces of the Cubans and the Dominicans. In their search for gold, the Spaniards managed to wipe them out within 50 years. They took them off to work in their gold mines and in the pearl beds off South America. The Arawaks, who believed firmly in an afterlife, preferred to commit suicide.

Caribs

History has been pretty mean to the Caribs (the European powers had to justify their act of genocide), but these people were hardly liberal or philanthropic towards their fellow Indians, the Arawaks or the Europeans. They were widely accused of being cannibals (for which there is in fact not really much evidence, and if there was any eating it was probably more ceremonial than for nourishment). Their love for alcohol, however, was so great that they would have no qualms about killing the crew of a ship which might have brandy aboard. And they were a fearsome enemy – in their *piragua* canoes, which could hold as many as 100 men, they could paddle as fast as a sailing ship and they would attack on the high seas.

The Caribs never harmed women, merely taking them to live with them, but for men they reserved a special ceremony – the barbecue. They would prepare the unfortunate captive by slitting his legs and back, stuffing the cuts with pimentoes and herbs before despatching him with a club and putting him on the spit. A Carib victim would insult his captors by saying that he had done for so many of the others' relatives that barbecuing him was tantamount to cooking up their own flesh and blood. There was actually reckoned to be a pecking order of tastiness among the Europeans. The French were regarded as the most delicate and tasty, followed by the English and Dutch, but Spaniards were so stringy and disgusting as to be almost inedible (a rumour presumably put about by the Spaniards themselves).

On land the men were expert hunters and excellent shots with bows and arrows. They could split a coin at 100 yards and astonished early visitors by the speed with which they fired arrow after arrow in succession. They would capture parrots by burning hot pepper beneath them until they suffocated and they could entrance an iguana out of its hole by whistling monotonously. Fish were shot or poisoned with dogwood bark and simply collected when they floated to the surface.

The Carib features were similar to those of other South American Indians and they were stocky. They painted their skin bright red and adorned themselves with parrot feathers and necklaces strung with the teeth of their victims. But their pride was their long blue-black hair which was oiled by the women after breakfast.

While men fished and hunted, the women worked around the *carbet*, a round palm-thatch house and living area. They tended crops such as *yucca* (cassava) and sweet potato. Many of the women were Arawak captives and so they spoke a different language among themselves. The Caribs had a hazy concept of good and evil spirits in the world but were completely uninterested in religious matters. Missionaries gave up in the end – the Caribs got baptized simply for the presents that they would receive.

Columbus

Columbus is famous as the discoverer of America. One Caribbean calypso singer objected in song that this view was simply Eurocentric arrogance because American Indians clearly beat him to it by several thousands of years. However, his voyages were to have an importance that changed the world. Certainly he gave the West Indies their name. In fact he was sailing for India, Cathay (China) and Cipango (Japan), as mentioned by Marco Polo, to reopen the spice trade with the East. Discovery of other islands – the existence of islands in the Atlantic, including Antillia (later used in the word Antilles), had been suspected since biblical times – was a secondary concern for him. Strictly speaking, he failed in his quest, but it was clear to all, even by the time that he died, how significant his discoveries in the New World were.

Cristoforo Colombo (or Cristobal Colon in Spanish) was born in the 1450s in Genoa, the son of a weaver, but he chose his career as a sailor while still a young man and travelled throughout the Mediterranean on trading voyages. Eventually he sailed further afield, to Iceland and along the coast of West Africa.

Columbus was largely self-taught. He was obviously an intelligent and forceful man, but he was inflexible and jumped to illogical geographical conclusions. He decided at one stage that the world was pear-shaped. All the same, he was a bold and accomplished explorer and a fine navigator. He was persuasive and even charismatic in court, impressing Queen Isabella so much that she helped him despite the advice of her courtiers. But he was vain and domineering in authority and this was his downfall. He may have carried it off on board ship, persuading his lieutenants to 'see' land and re-assure a potentially mutinous crew, but he was a hopeless administrator of the colonies.

If he was a visionary, and he stuck to his plan for years before he was granted the opportunity to carry it out, his dreams also tipped into fantasy and self-delusion. He considered himself chosen by God, with a mission to bring Christianity to the New World, and he was paranoid about others encroaching on what he considered his domain. But he fulfilled the dreams of the age: the world had outgrown its Mediterranean confines. With the ancient spice routes to the east closed after the fall of Constantinople in the 1450s they were beginning to look west. Columbus, the master mariner who had sailed all the seas and was acquainted with all available maps, gradually evolved his plan. He would try to reach the east by sailing west.

He petitioned all the major European kings for sponsorship and had to attend the Spanish court for six years before Ferdinand and Isabella granted him a commission to sail. Freed of the last of the Moors and in confident mood in 1492, they gave him three caravels, the *Santa Maria*, the *Niña* and the *Pinta*. On 3 August 1492 Columbus set off from Palos, touching the Canaries and then heading off into the ocean, navigating due west. According to his calculations (which he had massaged to his favour), he expected to come to Japan or China after about 2,500 miles (about where America is). They sailed with the wind behind for over a month, through the Sargasso Sea, into the unknown. Steadily the crew became more rebellious, fearing they might not get home. On 12 October 1492, they sighted land, one of the Bahamian islands.

Columbus called the island San Salvador in honour of the Saviour, but clearly he had not found Japan, so after a few days he set off in search of it, asking along the way for gold. He touched Cuba and then his flagship was wrecked off Hispaniola (now the Dominican Republic and Haiti). He was forced to leave about 40 men behind when he sailed for Spain, where he announced that he had reached Asia. On Palm Sunday 1493 Columbus was received with all the pomp and glory that he craved. He was treated almost as an equal to the monarchs in court. He insisted on huge public honour in reward for his service to the Crown of Spain. He was ennobled, granted the titles of Admiral of the Ocean Sea and Viceroy of the Indies, as well as huge financial rewards from any future trading with the area. A second expedition was sent the same year, with 1,500 settlers to colonize the island of Hispaniola. Administrative problems began almost at once and were compounded when Columbus left his brother Diego in charge during his exploration of Cuba and Jamaica.

Columbus led a third voyage in 1498, arriving in Trinidad in the south, narrowly missing the continent of South America. From here he sailed to Hispaniola by dead reckoning (no mean feat: a journey of 800 miles through uncharted waters). He found the colony in disarray and was forced to treat with the rebels. Eventually his viceregal authority was revoked and he was shipped back to Spain in chains.

He was treated kindly by Ferdinand and Isabella and eventually he was permitted to return to the New World on a fourth journey in 1502, on the express understanding that he was not to set foot on Hispaniola. In some ways his last trip was the most successful – he made contact for the first time with the more developed Indian cultures of the Central American seaboard and he discovered gold in larger quantities there (the shape of things to come). However, he was shipwrecked on the coast of Jamaica and had to wait a year before he was rescued and made it back to Spain.

Columbus died in Spain in 1506, faintly ridiculed because of all his problems in the Indies, his eccentric behaviour and his excessive claims against the Crown. Though his experience as a seaman had probably told him otherwise, he maintained to his death that he had discovered the Far East. Columbus (his remains at least) made yet more journeys after his death. He was brought to Santo Domingo in 1544 by his daughter-in-law and then removed (or not, as the case may be; *see* 'Santo Domingo' in **The Dominican Republic**, p.617) to Spanish soil (Cuba) at the time of the Haitian invasion in 1796, perhaps returning to Seville a century later. In honour of the 500th anniversary of the discovery, Columbus has possibly made yet another journey to a specially constructed crypt in the enormous Faro a Colon, a megalithic lighthouse in the shape of a cross in Santo Domingo.

Pirates, Buccaneers and Privateers

The Papal edicts or 'Bulls' that quickly followed the discovery of the New World by Columbus ordained that all land, discovered or undiscovered, west of a line 100 leagues beyond the Azores, should be an exclusive Spanish preserve (the line cuts off the eastern tip of Brazil and so the Portuguese were allowed to settle there). No peace beyond the line was declared, and any ships found in American waters were regarded by the Spaniards as pirates. The crews would be killed if captured. But this did not stop sea-rovers from other European nations, who had heard of the massive riches that the Spaniards were pillaging from the Indian settlements on the Spanish main. Already by 1540 many of these 'privateers', working under contracts to their governments, had started to creep into the Caribbean.

Jack Hawkins (son of a seafaring father who had brought an Indian chief from South America to the English court) made three voyages to the Caribbean in the second half of the 16th century. On his final voyage he took the young Francis Drake. Hawkins was working a trade route via Africa that was later to become very familiar – he collected Africans to sell to the Spaniards in the New World as slaves. Others, including French pirates Pie de Palo (Timberleg) and Jacques Sores, were less interested in trade as privateers and more interested in what they could seize by besieging and ransoming Spanish settlements. Drake returned at the end of the 16th century, as did Walter Raleigh, on his search for the Golden King, El Dorado.

In the early 1600s large numbers of pirate ships operated in the Caribbean and some of the sailors ended up settling the north coast of Hispaniola (now Haiti and the Dominican Republic), killing cattle and curing it for sale to passing ships. They were called buccaneers, because of the *boucan*, the oven in which they smoked the meat. Sea-rovers, misfits and deserters came to join them, jumping ship or deserting from their indentureships on the plantations. They lived in small groups, sharing all their property (even wives if they had them) and wore loose clothes with a leather belt that was slung with knives. They were renowned for their shooting. As the century progressed they moved across to the island of Tortuga off the north coast of Haiti, overlooking the Windward Passage between Cuba, Hispaniola and the Bahamas, which became their stronghold and from where they would set off in search of Spanish ships.

They called themselves the Brethren of the Coast and they took to sea as pirates, ranging as far afield as Madagascar and the Indian Ocean. The lure of this life on the edge was, of course, easy money, and when the money from the previous expedition ran out, they were ruthless and cunning about getting more, attacking any ships that they could find, taking the loot and selling it in their ports at St Thomas in the Virgin Islands, Port Royal in Jamaica and later Nassau in the Bahamas. They were fearsome fighters, putting the fright into professional soldiers and sailors, and they were renowned for their cruelty. They worked in small crews, with laws amongst themselves.

Père Labat tells of a French filibuster, a privateer rather than a pirate, for whom he said Mass in 1694. During the service, the privateers fired a salvo of cannons at the Elevation of the Holy Sacrament and at the Benediction and then contributed handsomely to Labat's coffers from the profits of their latest venture. These privateers divided the prizes equally amongst themselves, with a slightly larger share for the captain, quartermaster, surgeon and pilot, and a bonus for the man who first sighted the prize. Money was put aside for a wounded member of the crew and compensation was paid – 600 ecus for a limb, 300 for a finger or an eye – and they were cared for out of captured loot.

Henry Morgan was one of the most colourful of the privateers/pirates and he worked out of Port Royal at the height of its infamy in the late 1600s. He soon became the 'admiral' of the buccaneers (elected by them). He developed a strategy of attacking towns far inland and he even took the most fortified Spanish city, Puerto Bello (by using a human shield of monks and nuns to storm the walls). His men would then loot, ransack and rape their way through the town and, loaded down with pieces of eight, they would return to Port Royal for more revelry. Morgan was notoriously cruel and became hugely wealthy. Eventually he switched sides, double-crossing many of his buccaneers. As Lieutenant Governor of Jamaica he had a hand in stamping out piracy in the region.

Edward Teach or Blackbeard was the most notorious pirate of the 1700s and one of the 'sweet trade's' greatest showmen. He dressed outrageously and cultivated a monstrous appearance with a huge black beard and fuses fizzing in his hair when he went into battle. At one stage he led a whole squadron of boats around the islands. He was known occasionally to fire on his companions just to keep them guessing, while quaffing his favourite drink rumfustion, a mix of beer, gin, sherry, rum and gunpowder.

Stede Bonnet was a gentleman and a man of letters of Barbados, a Justice of the Peace who actually bought his own ship and provided for his family before taking to the seas. Jack Rackham had two women in his crew, Anne Bonney and Mary Read, who were reputed to be just as violent as their male colleagues. A man could be killed for cowardice and the captain could lose his command if the crew thought he had failed in attacking a prize, so the pirates were always bold and brave, and they would regularly take on ships larger than their own. One Captain Moidore loaded up his cannons with gold coins when he ran out of shot. L'Ollonois, a Frenchman, executed the whole crew of a ship at one point, licking their blood off his sword, and then tore out the heart of a man and ate it. He himself was dismembered and roasted in the end.

The Slave Trade

The slave trade in the Caribbean grew from Europe's voracious appetite for sugar during the 18th century. Sugar was an alternative to honey, was readily available in almost limitless quantity, and was suitable for use as a sweetener in the newly fashionable hot drinks such as tea and coffee. As the sugar industry developed, there was a massive demand for labour to work the cane fields. Indentured servants from Europe were tried but did not cope well in the heat, and so the planters decided on Africans instead: slaves were shipped across the Atlantic in hundreds of thousands.

The slave trade to the Caribbean began as early as 1517, when a friar in Hispaniola, Bartoleme de las Casas, suggested bringing Africans to the Caribbean to replace the Arawak Indians, who were dying out alarmingly quickly. At that time, slavery was established throughout Europe and the Arab world. Prisoners of war could usually expect to be sold into slavery and sometimes people actually sold themselves into slavery in order to pay off their debts. But plantation slavery of the sort that developed during the 18th century was something new. It involved vast numbers and it was more systematized and far more brutal. It also entrenched racist views that had not existed before that time, but which still linger today. It grew into a huge transatlantic business called the triangular trade. Ships would leave their home ports in the metropolitan countries with manufactured goods, arms and liquor for the African slave traders; slaves would be shipped from Africa to the colonies; then sugar and rum would be transported from the Caribbean to the metropolitan countries. The notorious 'Middle Passage', from the African coast to the West Indies, during which the slaves were packed into holds so tightly that they could not sit up, lasted anything from three weeks to three months.

The majority of slaves were tribespeople from the Guinea coast, in the bight of West Africa. They were generally captured from their villages by slave-raiding parties spon-sored by the local African leaders, and were sold to the 'factors' of the slave trading companies, bartered in return for drink, weapons and other goods. The captives were tied together by the neck and driven to the coast, where they were branded and then held in corrals or in the cells of the vast fortresses that dotted the coast. At the moment of departure on the transatlantic crossing, the crew stood by with lighted torches, threatening to set the ship and all the people on board alight if the slaves rebelled.

Most of the captives had never seen the sea before, so the ocean journey was terrifying as well as appallingly uncomfortable. They were chained by the feet and packed in the hold, sometimes so tightly that there was only enough room for them to lie on their side. The air was foul – people died of suffocation – and there were no sanitary arrangements. With meagre amounts of food and limited spells on deck, chained together in pairs, it is hardly surprising that an average of 12% of the slaves died on these transatlantic trips. Some slaves even committed suicide by jumping overboard to certain drowning in their pairs.

When they neared land the slaves would be fed and 'oiled' so that they looked healthier (open wounds were sometimes disguised with an application of rust) and then as the ship came into harbour its arrival would be announced with a gunshot. The exhausted slaves (who often thought they were being sold to cannibals to be eaten) would be paraded through the streets on the way to the market where they were auctioned.

The first year on a plantation, called the 'seasoning', was known to be the hardest for a newly arrived slave. Cut off from family and their homeland, they had to learn a new language and accustom themselves to the harsh regime of plantation life. There was also a deliberate effort to sever their connections with their former life. Slaves of the same tribe and language would be separated because it was thought that singly they would be more compliant. Life expectancy was only seven years for imported slaves, but many died within the first twelve months.

Punishment was brutal in an already brutal age. Slaves – like soldiers and sailors – could expect to be flogged within an inch of their life for misdemeanours, and mutilations were also common. Repeat offenders would often have their tongue and nose slit, or even limbs amputated to stop them running away. There was no law against killing a black man in the British colonies until the early 1800s. Meanwhile, the wealth of the planters was immense and often expressed in ostentatious luxury and lavish entertainment.

The estates were run on the basis of mutual fear. The planters maintained their law with a rod of iron and with a liberal use of the whip, while always living in the fear that the slaves would rebel, which from time to time they did. Many slave revolts were rumbled before they started and their ringleaders executed, but, if they got going, they could hold an island to ransom for months. For example, the most successful revolt on Jamaica came to be known as Tacky's Rebellion, which took place in 1760 when a band of slaves broke into a fort and stole arms and ammunition, attacked a few plantations and then took to the hills. There were numerous revolts in the other islands, always put down ruthlessly by the authorities. The French Revolution wrought havoc in the French Caribbean and caused bloody armed uprisings – *égalité* could not be reconciled with slavery. In Guadeloupe the slaves were emancipated in 1794, only for slavery to be reintroduced in 1802.

During the early 18th century there was little moral debate in the metropolitan countries about slavery, but from the 1770s there was a rising tide of anti-slavery feeling in Europe. In 1787 the Society for the Abolition of the Slave Trade was established in England by men such as William Wilberforce. They raised public awareness of the maltreatment of slaves through a campaign of pamphlets and lectures. But for abolition to be made law it had to be passed in Parliament, where the West Indian planters were well represented. Eventually the pressure was strong enough and in 1807 laws were passed outlawing the trade in slaves in British ships. A number of other European countries followed suit soon afterwards (Denmark had banned the trade six years before) and Britain sent her ships out against the remaining traders. The demand for slaves was still there, of course, and the price went up; despite its illegality (and not all countries had banned it) the slave trade flourished. There was a good deal of smuggling, and blind eyes were turned because the profits were so large. Eventually it became clear that the trade would not be prevented until slavery itself was abolished.

A massive revolt in Jamaica in 1831 (led by Sam 'Daddy' Sharpe) led to turmoil and the burning of sugar estates. Parliament in London was compelled to force through the Emancipation Act in 1834 for all the British colonies in the West Indies. There was a period of 'apprenticeship' for four years, in which the slaves were tied to the plantations, but in 1838 the slaves were set free unconditionally. This situation was by no means universal, however. The French islands did not liberate their slaves until 1848, and the Dutch not until 1863. Puerto Rico abolished slavery in 1873. Cuba was still importing slaves right up to 1865; slavery itself was not abolished there until 1888.

On most islands, freed slaves bought plots of land and turned to subsistence farming. The plantation owners had lost their workforce and so on some islands they encouraged fresh immigration, such as the indentured East Indians who sailed to the French Antilles and Trinidad. On small islands such as Barbados, Antigua and St Kitts, there simply was no unowned land, so freed slaves either emigrated or continued to work on the plantations. Following Emancipation, the sugar industry declined in the Caribbean, partly due to the cultivation of sugar beet in Europe. On many islands it was not until the late 20th-century advent of tourism that any industry developed to replace it.

Food and Drink

When visiting the Caribbean on his trip to write *The Traveller's Tree*, Patrick Leigh Fermor decided that: 'Hotel cooking in the island [Trinidad in this case, but Trinidad is usually better than most] is so appalling that a stretcher may profitably be ordered at the same time as dinner'. Admittedly this was in the late 1940s, but until very recently Caribbean food was unadventurous and had a universal and lacklustre 'international' style, particularly in hotels. A former British colonial influence might just have something to do with it, but responsibility should probably be shared by the Americans, who make up the majority of visitors and who were happy to put up with this.

On the restaurant circuit things have improved radically in the last ten years (with looser immigration patterns and more reliable sources of supply), and there are some serious chefs in the islands. You will find several good and often adventurous restaurants in every island now, and even the hotels have made great improvements. Some chefs and restaurateurs have taken the best of West Indian traditions and applied Continental or Asian techniques (and often imported ingredients too) to produce a sophisticated and satisfying Caribbean cuisine. You will find an eclectic mishmash of tastes (there was even a case of 'Thairibbean' food a while ago). Such is the popularity of certain restaurants that, in order to make sure of their favourite table, people will fax their reservations months in advance. You can expect to pay as much (or more) to eat in these restaurants as you would at home.

Have no doubt, running a restaurant in the Caribbean is hard work. There are problems of supply, particularly if the fishermen decide that they just don't want to go out that day, or if Customs decides that they're holding onto today's delivery of food for inspection. Then there is the traditional island inertia (chefs who go for training abroad are as frustrated by this when they return as metropolitan visitors). A few restaurants import their food fresh on a daily basis, but the majority of local restaurants serve frozen food (people will tell you jokingly that the lengthy delays are because they only start unfreezing it when you place your order; it's often true).

Islands with the best cuisine include: **St Barts** and French **St Martin** for their French heritage, which is then tailored to the climate. Of the former British islands, **Barbados** is in excellent form (there is even a string of wine bars there, serving such unlikely Caribbean fare as deep-fried Camembert); and, unexpectedly, there are some superb restaurants in **Anguilla**, which has the advantage of importing fresh French and American ingredients daily from Dutch **Sint Maarten**; this too can offer some good restaurants, serving mainly international fare. **Martinique** and **Guadeloupe** stand in their own right for their indigenous creole food, and **Trinidad** is interesting for its Indian influences. **Puerto Rico**, meanwhile, has a growing number of restaurants run by a crop of innovative young chefs.

Restaurant Generalities

Dress codes for dinner have almost entirely died out in the Caribbean and only a couple of hotel dining rooms will request that men wear even a jacket and tie. Many will expect long trousers and a shirt with a collar for dinner. Service, on the other hand, is often a problem. It is one of the hardest things to get right and often the most noticeable difference between the islands and home. Even in quite smart restaurants and hotel dining rooms it can be haphazard and sometimes it will border on the macabre. There seems little point in complaining in most cases. The settings, though, are magnificent. Wine is available in the smartest restaurants, but it does not take well to the heat (nor does it complement West Indian food too well) and not all restaurants have cooled cellars. *See* **Practical A–Z**, p.52, for prices used in this guide.

Local Food

A week's worth of curry goat or stew fish might be more than any newcomer could take, but it is worth getting out in search of West Indian food. It has its own distinctive flavours, it is cheaper and the restaurants are often more fun. It is also worth seeking out the beach bars, where you will have barbecued local fish and vegetables.

Gastronomes should aim for the French islands, where there is a strong tradition of creole cookery with luxurious sauces, served with meticulous attention to detail both in preparation and service. Like their metropolitan counterparts, the French Antilleans treat their food with a little more ceremony than other West Indians. You will have a surprise in the Dutch Caribbean islands (particularly in the ABC islands), where there are echoes of Holland in dishes made with Edam cheese, but more curiously Indonesian food (Dutch West Indies meets Dutch East Indies) in *rijstafel*. The tastes of India emerge strongest in Trinidad, but curry goat and *roti* (an envelope of dough with a meat or vegetable filling) have reached everywhere now. The Spanish islands are known for their aromatic sauces and stews.

Caribbean food is traditionally quite spicy. Beware of bottles marked 'Hot Pepper'. Fish is abundant, and often delicious, as are seafoods such as lobster and crab and an island favourite, conch. Other foods that have become popular are made of ingredients that were originally hardship foods, often fed to the slaves, because they were cheap at the time. The Jamaican national dish is ackee and saltfish; now that there is refrigeration and food is no longer salted in order to preserve it, salted cod is expensive and difficult to get hold of. Rice 'n' peas (or peas 'n' rice depending on which island you are in) is another standard meal in the cheaper restaurants in the British islands and is particularly good when made with coconut milk. Callaloo is a traditional West Indian soup made from pumpkin (which is often excellent) or a leafy green vegetable similar to Swiss chard. Oil-dunk, more frequently called 'rundown', is a pot of vegetables cooked in coconut oil.

West Indian food is universally heavyweight, with stews and rice or a volley of tropical vegetables, or 'ground provisions' which are mostly starchy and often sweet. Try breadfruit, yam, fried plantain, cassava and the delicious christophene. Then of course there are the more familiar 'Irish' and sweet potatoes and avocados. The Caribbean is famous for its fruits, which taste especially good in the ice creams.

Caribbean Fruits and Nuts

Perhaps the most striking thing about the tropics is the strength and variety of new sensations – the smells of trees in bloom; reds, greens and yellows of plants reflected in the setting sun; the evening warmth. But tastes too have a fascinating newness and the best of these can be found in the sweet and exotic Caribbean fruits and nuts. A good idea is to go down to the market and collect a box of all the fruits in season and then gorge yourself on the new tastes.

Perhaps the best-known fruit (or nut, if you prefer) in the Caribbean is **coconut**, which grows everywhere in the islands. Coconut is extremely versatile: the milk can be drunk or used for flavouring in cooking, and the inner flesh is turned into desiccated coconut for flavouring in confectionery. It can also be used as soap and as oil to burn. The fronds of the palm are used for weaving and palm thatch. A fruit that fascinated early Caribbean visitors was the **pineapple**, which grows on a stem at the centre of an explosion of leaves. So exotic was it considered in the 17th century that it became a symbol of welcome (you had to be generous to give your guests pineapple from the Caribbean) and people placed stone pineapples on their gateposts.

The taste of **soursop** is both sweet and slightly tart, and at moments it can seem like a cross between a citrus fruit and a banana. Soursops are large and irregularly shaped, with dark hooks on their leathery green skin. Inside, the sweet white flesh is filled with big black pips. Of the many 'bush teas' drunk by the West Indians, soursop tea is one of the most popular. **Sweetsop** (also known as sugar apple) is smaller and shaped like a green pine cone. It is so full of sugar that when it is ripe the sweetness feels almost crystalline. **Mango** is perhaps the most exotic and luxurious of them all. Fist-sized, mangos start off green and ripen to startling yellows, oranges and flushing pinks. There are many different sorts of mango, including the Julie and the Number 11 (the sweetest around). Eating a mango from the skin is a hands-on business – the juice runs everywhere and the strands from the flesh get stuck in your teeth and can stay there for days – but the taste is of course uniquely delicious. The **papaya** (also known as pawpaw) is widespread around the Caribbean. Green papaya is used in cooking; it steadily ripens and sweetens to a bright orange colour and a more fruit-like taste. Another well-known Caribbean fruit is of course the **banana** (see 'Bananas', p.143), which comes in many different varieties, only a few of which are found in Europe and the States. Look out for the tastiest, small variety called the sweet banana. **Watermelons** grow huge around the Caribbean.

Lesser-known fruits seen around the islands include **guava**, a pip-filled mush of sweetness with a hard skin, often used in jams; the distinctively shaped **carambola** or star apple (in cross-section it looks like a five-pointed star), which has a crisp, juicy flesh usually yellow in colour; the **golden apple**, a small, round and slightly golden-coloured fruit which looks not dissimilar to a pomegranate and has an aromatic flavour; and the **guinep**, a hard green lump just smaller than a golf ball, with a large pip covered in sweet white flesh, not unlike a lychee. Yet more exotic varieties include **tamarind**, with a slightly bitter taste, extracted from a pod like a brown, knobbly broad bean and used to flavour sauces and drinks; and **jackfruit**, foot-long fleshy lumps of fruit covered in hooks. You can even eat **sea grape**, found along the beach, best once they have turned purple, although these are something of an acquired taste. Finally, if you see someone selling **cocoa pods** at the roadside, stop and get one. Inside, the delicious white flesh is both sweet and tart, silky and sticky.

There are many **citrus fruits**: oranges (often green here), lemons, grapefruits, tangerines and nectarines. There are even some citrus crosses: the **ortanique** is a mix of orange and tangerine, and the **ugli fruit**, whose name derives from its unfortunate bumpy skin, is a cross between a grapefruit, an orange and a tangerine. But perhaps the finest of the Caribbean citrus fruits is the small, green **lime**, which is used in cooking and in many of the best Caribbean drinks. British sailors became known as Limeys because of their daily ration of lime juice, given to them to keep away scurvy.

Drinks

Cocktails

The Caribbean is famous for its cocktails and many were invented here, making the best use of the exotic fruits. The piña colada (pineapple, coconut cream and rum) supposedly originated in Puerto Rico, and the daiquiri (crushed ice, rum and fruit syrup whisked up like a slushy sorbet) in Havana. The Cuba libre, first mixed after the Spanish-American War in 1898, is made of rum with lemon and cola, and Hemingway's mojito is made with white rum, fresh mint and Angostura bitters. The planter's punch, traditionally drunk all over the Caribbean, is made from rum and water with a twist of lime and sugar, topped with ground nutmeg. Unfortunately there's a rumour that all a tourist ever wants is something bright red and sticky, so barmen often use over-liberal dashes of sticky, sweet Grenadine syrup. Blue Bols, which finds its way into cocktails all over the world, is actually made in Curaçao.

Rum and Red Stripe

Rum is the Caribbean 'national' drink; 50 years ago bars kept their bottles of rum on the counter free of charge and it was the water you had to pay for. Distilled from sugar molasses, rum is produced all over the islands and, though it often tastes like rocket fuel, it gives the West Indians their energy for dancing, so it cannot be all bad. The most popular local variety of rum and the quickest to produce is 'white rum', which is drunk in the rum bars and at local dances. Gold rums are a little mellower; their colour comes from caramel which is introduced as they age in wooden barrels; some are blended. As you would expect, the French West Indians treat their rums with admirable solemnity and seriousness. The *petit ponch* is drunk as an apéritif: brown sugar is heaped into a measure of white rum, a lime is squeezed within an inch of destruction, and then it is downed in one; chilled water is used as a chaser. Alternatively, some restaurants hold a series of *ponch à fruits* in which fruits are steeped in bottled rum, giving it their flavour. After dinner (in the French islands), older rums are drunk as a *digestif*, in much the same way as brandies are in Europe; they are laid down to mature for years and there are even vintages (*see* Martinique and Guadeloupe).

Look out for the following brands of rum: Appleton's in Jamaica, Mountgay in Barbados, Barbancourt in Haiti, and the varieties of Trois Rivières, Rhum Bally and Rhum St James in Martinique. Guadeloupe also has plenty of home-grown rums.

Far more than wine, the West Indians prefer a cool beer to combat the heat and nowadays almost every island brews its own. The best known is Red Stripe, from Jamaica, but you may also recognize Banks from Barbados and Stag and Carib from Trinidad. Cuban beers include Hatuey. St Vincent has been brewing Hairoun and EKU, passable but not brilliant, for many years, and St Lucia now produces Piton ('La Bière Sent Lisi'), which is good, while Dominica offers Kubuli. Antigua's contribution is a mediocre brew, Wadadli, and the Cayman Islands went for the unlikeliest idea, a dark beer called Stingray, which is probably best left untouched. Perhaps the best of all the Caribbean beers is produced in the Dominican Republic, a light lager called Presidente. Heineken and American beers such as Bud are almost universally available.

Soft Drinks

Caribbean fruits make excellent non-alcoholic drinks: fruit punches are particularly good in Barbados, and in the Windward Islands you will find that they make the best of their fruit juices; often they are spiced. In the Dominican Republic they also make *bastidas*, which are delicious fresh-fruit concoctions with ice, rather like milkshakes.

Life in the Caribbean sun is hot work, and so, besides the bottled drinks available in the shops, the West Indians have an array of drinks on sale in the street. Snow cones and sky juice are made with crushed ice (scraped off a huge block), water and a dash of fruit concentrate and put into a bag or cup. You swill it around with a straw and the effect is something like a cold Ribena. You have to be careful not to drink the water and the concentrate too quickly otherwise you are just left with a mound of crystals. In some of the islands you'll also be offered weird and wonderful toppings with condensed milk and crushed peanuts. Each island has its own system. In Jamaica the vendors walk around pushing brightly painted handcarts and they present the drink to you in a little plastic goldfish bag rather than a cup. In Trinidad they use silver carts like mobile soup kitchens and they crush the ice by machine, and in the Dominican Republic and Haiti they have tricycles mounted with an ice-box and a whole armoury of concentrate bottles (the water is often dodgy here, so you might be better off going for a *bastida* instead). Gradually these traditions are dying out, as people settle for canned and bottled drinks instead. The usual international soft drinks, Coke, Fanta, Sprite, etc., are sold all over the Caribbean, alongside some more Caribbean ones like Ting. A particularly good Trinidadian drink is a Bentley: lemon and lime with a dash of bitters. Other popular West Indian drinks are sorrel, the red Christmas drink not unlike Ribena, ginger beer and mauby juice, a disgusting, bitter concoction made from tree bark. If in doubt, fresh lime juice is always an excellent choice for a soft drink.

Another option available in all the islands is coconuts, which are often sold in the street. When you approach, don't be alarmed if the vendor pulls out a 2ft machete... He will deftly top the coconut with a few strokes, leaving just a small hole through which you can drink. Get an older coconut if you can, because the milk will be sweeter. Once you have drunk the milk, hand it back to the vendor, who will split it for you so that you can eat the delicious coconut slime that lines the inside (it eventually turns into the white coconut flesh). You will also be offered sugar-cane juice, either as a liquid, or in the sticks themselves, which you bite off and chew to a pulp.

Travel

04

Getting There

Package or Independent Travel?

The first thing to consider about getting to the Caribbean is whether to travel independently or on a package. Most visitors from the UK and Europe do buy a 'package', and Caribbean packages can be exclusive, personally tailored and extremely expensive. Basically though, tour operators will put together the whole trip for you, including flights, airport transfers, accommodation for the duration of your stay and often a variety of meal plans and other optional extras. Their fee will be less than the rate you would pay if you were to arrange the whole thing yourself.

If you style yourself a traveller rather than a tourist, you might want to consider whether to travel independently, by buying a seat to the region and arranging your own accommodation. There are opportunities for savings here too because airline seats are often discounted to travel agencies and of course there are many cheaper hotels in the islands that are not available through tour operators. Independent travel is much more flexible and offers possibilities for island-hopping and exploration. Most importantly, it enables you to reach places that most operators do not offer. Some charming hotels are too small or too inexpensive to have arrangements with a tour operator.

You might even use the advantages of the package format by buying one at a knock-down price, staying at the hotel for a couple of nights, and then taking off independently.

In the USA and Canada, packages are available from tour operators in the same way as in Britain but there is a much larger market for independent travellers because of the greater flexibility in flights to the Caribbean and because the package cost is not drastically cheaper.

For details of package operators, see 'Tour Operators', pp.38–41. For information on pre-booking accommodation only, see 'Where to Stay', p.62.

Sourcing Information

The single most vital ingredient of any successful holiday is an informed choice. The Caribbean has amazing variety. This book will provide leads, but there are many other sources of information and it is best to use them in combination. If you are going to travel with a tour operator on the basis of details published in a brochure, do not be scared to ring them up and quiz them (even if a travel agency is handling the actual booking for you). Of course they're only going to sell you the hotels in their brochure, but you'll soon discover their level of knowledge. Also look at newspapers and magazines.

There is an increasing amount of information, some of it more than electronic brochures, on the Internet (see p.46). Of course, email has made it many times easier to contact Caribbean hoteliers in order to ask specific questions about their hotel.

By Air

Further details on flights to and between individual islands are listed under 'Getting There' in each island chapter. See also 'By Air' under 'Getting Around', below.

From the UK

The Caribbean is quite well served from the UK, by both scheduled and charter flights. The transatlantic flight takes 8 or 9 hours and so with the time change (chasing the sun round the earth) you usually arrive in good time to catch onward flights to almost all the Caribbean islands or just to settle down and watch the sunset. There is no reason to fly via the States unless you particularly want to. Fares are at their peak in the weeks around Christmas (when it is very difficult to get a seat so you are advised to book well in advance), and between July and September. This is slightly curious because it does not coincide with the Caribbean's own high season (winter in the northern hemisphere), which runs from about mid-Jan to mid-April.

The main hubs for travel from the UK are Antigua, Barbados, Trinidad and Jamaica, but many other islands do have direct flights on either scheduled or charter services.

Scheduled fares have come down over the past few years and it is now possible to get to the Caribbean in the winter season (an economy return) from £500. Prices do not vary much according to your destination.

The UK

Scheduled Flights

Air Jamaica: t (020) 8570 7999, *www.air jamaica.com*. Several weekly flights from London to Kingston and Montego Bay.

BMI: t 0870 607 0222, *www.flybmi.com*. Runs weekly flights from Edinburgh, Glasgow, London Heathrow and Manchester to Antigua, Barbados and St Lucia.

British Airways: t 0870 850 9850, *www.britishairways.com*. The widest range of services from the UK, with direct flights to Antigua, Barbados, Grenada, St Lucia, Jamaica, the Cayman Islands, Turks and Caicos, Cuba, and Nassau in the Bahamas.

BWIA: t 0870 499 2942, *www.bwee.com*. Has a number of flights from London Heathrow to Trinidad, often touching Barbados, St Lucia, Grenada or Antigua en route.

Virgin Atlantic: t (01293) 562 345, *www.virgin atlantic.com*. Flights departing from Gatwick to Antigua, Barbados and St Lucia.

Charter Flights

Britannia: *www.britanniaairways.com*; or book through Thomson Direct, **t** 0870 165 0079, *www.thomson-holidays.com*; First Choice, **t** 0870 850 3999, *www.firstchoice.co.uk*; or Airtours, **t** 0870 238 7788, *www.airtours.com*.

jmc: t 0870 750 5711, *www.jmc.com*; 'seats only' tickets are generally booked through Golden Lion Travel, **t** (01293) 567 800.

Flight Clubs

There are a few flight clubs for regular Caribbean visitors. You join for a minimal fee and then are sent information about special offers. Contact:

BWIA's Sunjet Reunion Club: Central House, Lampton Rd, Hounslow, Middlesex TW3 1HY, **t** (020) 8570 4446.

Caribbean Reunion Club: 93 Newman St, London W1T 3EZ, **t** (020) 7344 0101. Run by tour operator Caribbean Connection.

Travel Agencies

Caribjet: 141 North Hyde Road, Hayes, Middlesex UB3 4NS, **t** (020) 8581 2317, *sales@caribjet.com*, *www.caribjet.com*.

Diamond Travel: 178 Dudley Rd, Edgbaston, Birmingham B18 7QX, **t** (0121) 454 6990.

Newmont Travel: t (020) 8920 1155. In Shepherds Bush and Dalston.

Stoke Newington Travel: 168 Stoke Newington Rd, London N16 7UY, **t** (020) 7254 0136.

Europe

Scheduled Flights

Air France: t 08 20 82 08 20, UK **t** 0870 142 4343, *www.airfrance.com*. From Paris to Martinique, Guadeloupe and Sint Maarten.

Condor, t (810) 576 7757, *www.condor.de*. Flies from a number of German cities.

Iberia, Spain **t** 90 24 00 500, UK **t** 0870 609 0500, *www.iberia.com*. Flies from Madrid to San Juan (Puerto Rico), Santo Domingo (the Dominican Republic) and Havana in Cuba.

KLM, Holland **t** (0204) 747 747, UK **t** 08705 074 074, *www.klm.com*. Flies from Amsterdam daily to Curaçao and Aruba, and twice weekly to Bonaire and Sint Maarten.

Martinair, Holland **t** (0206) 011 222, *www.martinair.com*. Flies from Amsterdam weekly to the Dutch Antilles, Cuba, Aruba, Puerto Rico and to the Dominican Republic.

The USA

Scheduled Flights

Air Jamaica: t 1 800 523 5585, *www.airjamaica.com*. Has flights from a number of major

These fares may require 7 days' or 21 days' advance booking and sometimes have a minimum length of stay. There are also penalties for changing reservations. Fully flexible fares cost from £1,000. Lower fares are almost always on offer as the airlines sell off block-bookings of seats.

Charter airlines are probably your best bet for a cheap ticket and most now sell seats on a flight-only basis. Generally restrictions are tight. You can reach all the main Caribbean hubs – Barbados, Antigua, Puerto Rico and Jamaica – but they also fly to other islands which are less accessible by scheduled flights, such as Cuba, Tobago, Grenada, St Lucia and the Dominican Republic. With luck and a bit of shopping around, you can find a return fare to the Caribbean for as little as £200.

cities around the USA (Atlanta, Miami, New York, Newark, New Jersey, Baltimore, Philadelphia, Chicago, Orlando, Los Angeles and Fort Lauderdale) into Kingston and Montego Bay. The latter is the hub for flights connecting to the islands in the Eastern Caribbean (Barbados, St Lucia, Grenada, Bonaire, Curaçao), making it a good alternative to American Airlines. Also routes some flights out of New York to St Lucia and Barbados.

American Airlines: t 1 800 433 7300, *www.aa.com*. Has the most extensive service from the States to the Caribbean. It flies direct to all the Greater Antilles and a few of the smaller Eastern Caribbean islands, originating in New York (JFK) and Miami, from where there are often two flights a day. Smaller islands that are not served by direct flights are reached via American Airlines' hub in San Juan, Puerto Rico, from where its subsidiary, American Eagle, has onward flights. You can usually get to your destination on the same day.

BWIA: t 1 800 538 2942, *www.bwee.com*. Flights from New York, Miami, Washington and Atlanta to Port of Spain in Trinidad, some of them touching Antigua, St Lucia and Barbados en route.

Continental Airlines: t 1 800 231 0856, *www.continental.com*. Flies from Newark to Antigua, Sint Maarten, St Thomas (Virgin Islands), San Juan (Puerto Rico) and Santo Domingo (Dominican Republic).

Delta: t 1 800 241 4141, *www.delta.com*. Flies regularly from Atlanta (with other services from Orlando) to Nassau (Bahamas), San Juan (Puerto Rico), St Thomas and St Croix (in the USVI), Jamaica, Aruba, Antigua and the Cayman Islands.

US Airways: t 1 800 428 4322, *www.usairways.com*. Flies from a variety of cities on the east coast (Baltimore, Boston, Philadelphia, Charlotte, Ft. Lauderdale, Pittsburgh, New York/La Guardia, Washington/Dulles,) to Grand Cayman, San Juan (Puerto Rico), Montego Bay (Jamaica), St Thomas and St Croix (USVI), Aruba, Santo Domingo (Dominican Republic), Sint Maarten, five islands in the Bahamas, Antigua, Barbados, Freeport, La Romana, St Kitts & Nevis, St Lucia, Turks & Caicos, Grand Bahama Island, and Washington Reagan National. US Airways also has cooperative marketing with Caribbean Star Airlines, Caribbean Sun, WINAIR and Bahamasair.

JetBlue: *www.jetblue.com*. Flies from New York (JFK) to San Juan and Aguadilla (Puerto Rico), Nassau (Bahamas) and Santiago (Dominican Republic).

Spirit Airlines: *www.spiritairlines.com*. Fort Lauderdale to Nassau, San Juan, Santo Domingo; Orlando to San Juan; New York/La Guardia (via Fort Lauderdale).

Canada

Scheduled Flights

Air Canada: t 1 800 268 7240, *www.aircanada.ca*. Flies direct, usually out of Toronto but occasionally Montreal, to destinations in the Caribbean including Jamaica (Montego Bay and Kingston), Antigua, Guadeloupe, St Lucia, Barbados, Port of Spain in Trinidad, and Nassau in the Bahamas.

BWIA: t (905) 676 8382, t 1 800 538 2942, *www.bwee.com*. Flies from Toronto in Canada to Port of Spain in Trinidad, stopping over in Antigua and Barbados.

Charter Flights

Canada 3000: t (416) 916 3000, *www.canada3000.com*.

From the USA

Fares from the USA vary according to seat availability and what deals are being offered. The seasons are strictly observed: mid-December–mid-April is high season, late June–mid-September is the summer peak, and the rest of the year is low season. In the winter season **scheduled** return fares from Miami to Jamaica start at US$350 and to Antigua US$450, from New York to Jamaica US$500 and to Antigua US$650. From the Midwest add around US$200, and from the West Coast around US$350. These fares require advance booking and there is often a minimum stay of a week; supplements are payable for weekend travel and cancellations. New competition from low-cost airlines is likely to see these prices dipping in the near future. *See* the box opposite for scheduled airlines.

Charter flights are also available through travel agencies and this may mean as much as a third off the scheduled price. Check the newspapers and with your travel agency.

From Canada

As well as the scheduled and charter airlines listed in the box opposite, another alternative is to connect with American or Caribbean carriers in New York or Miami.

By Sea

From the UK

The possibilities of independent travel from the UK to the Caribbean by sea are limited, and also take a long time. However, many cargo ships make the crossing to the Caribbean and Central and South America and some of them do take passengers. Transatlantic passages are quite expensive; reckon on at least UK£1,000 each way. It no longer seems possible to work a passage out to the islands, even swabbing the decks, unless you have a merchant marine card. An agency with details of a large number of ships to the Caribbean, anything from cruise ships to banana boats, is:

The Cruise People, 88 York St, London W1H 1QT, t (020) 7723 2450/ 0800 526 313, *home@ cruisepeople.co.uk www.cruisepeople.co.uk*.

A large number of **yachts** make the Atlantic crossing to the Caribbean towards the end of the year, arriving in time for the winter sailing season. You might be able to pick up a yacht on the south coast of Britain, in the south of France, in Gibraltar, or even in the Canaries any time from September (just after the hurricane

---

Cruises

A popular way of travelling around the Caribbean is by cruise liner, which enables you to visit as many as four or five different islands in a week, without the hassle of delayed flights or even packing your suitcase. The big cruise ships have a pretty bad reputation around the islands (except with taxi drivers and on-island tour operators) as the less acceptable side of mass tourism. Some are truly massive, with as many as 2,500 passengers. Most depart from Miami or Fort Lauderdale and a few are based in San Juan, Puerto Rico. They sail all year round. There are, however, a number of smaller ships, with up to 300 or 400 passengers, which sail the islands, are much more personal and can reach shallower bays on smaller islands. These cruises can be arranged through a tour operator, travel agency or sometimes direct.

Celebrity Cruises, UK t 0845 456 1520, *www.celebritycruises.co.uk*; USA t 1 800 437 3111, *www.celebritycruises.com*.

Cunard, UK t 0845 071 0300, USA t 1 800 221 4770, *www.cunardline.com*. Has some ships in the Caribbean.

Norwegian Cruise Lines, UK t 0845 658 8010, USA t 1 800 327 7030, *www.ncl.com*.

Seabourn Cruises, 5901 Sun Bd, Suite 201, Tierra Verde, Florida 33715, t (1727) 906 0444, t 1 888 313 8883, *sailinluxury@mail.com*, *www.seabourncruiseweb.com*.

Star Clipper, Ermanno Palace, 27 Bd Albert Premier, 98000 Monaco, t (00 377) 97 97 84 00, *info@starclippers-ltd.mc*, *www.star-clippers.com*; 4101 Salzedo Avenue, Coral Gables, Florida 33146, t (1 305) 442 0550, *info@starclippers.com*. They have three sailing ships, including the magnificent *Royal Clipper*, the largest sailing ship in the world, which has over thirty sails when they are fully deployed.

Swan Hellenic, Richmond House, Terminus Terrace, Southampton SO13 3PN, t 0845 355 5111, *reservations@swanhellenic.com*, *www.swanhellenic.com*; 631 Commack Rd, Suite 1A, Commack, NY 11725, t 1 877 219 4239, *kainyc@att.net*, *www.swanhellenic.com*. Offers a Caribbean cruise with a programme of guest speakers on arts, culture and historical topics.

Windstar Cruises, UK t (020) 7940 4480, *windstaruk@carnival.com*, US t 1 800 258 7245, *info@windstarcruises.com*, *www. windstarcruises.com*. They operate three ships, the *Windstar*, the *Windspirit* and the *Windsurf*.

Tour Operators

Most holidays to the Caribbean are sold as packages, and with these you can get anything from a two-week, two-destination package at two different luxury resorts at opposite ends of the Caribbean Sea, with transatlantic legs in First Class, through the proliferation of wedding and honeymoon packages (complete with nuptial underwear if you want), to the charter holidays that take advantage of the low-season rates and give you a return flight and two weeks' accommodation for less than the price of a normal scheduled return air fare.

Many of the tour companies include obligatory insurance in their packages, but travel agencies will always sell you a policy. Check your existing policies – it is worth insuring against medical problems, cancelled flights and lost luggage.

In the UK

General Packages

The following companies cover a broad range of prices and products. Some of the smaller, less well-known companies offer the advantages of more personal service and perhaps more unusual deals. The less expensive deals are generally, but not always, with the big, worldwide companies.

Airtours, Wavell House, Holcombe Rd, Helmshore, Rossendale, Lancs BB4 4NB, t 0870 238 7788, *www.airtours.co.uk*. One of the most inexpensive package operators to the Caribbean.

British Airways Holidays, travel shops throughout the UK, t 0870 243 3407, *www.baholidays.co.uk*. A broad selection of upper-end and mid-range hotels in their 'Worldwide' brochure, including a number of all-inclusives.

ITC Classics, Concorde House, Canal St, Chester CH1 4EJ, t 0870 751 9300, brochure line t 0870 751 9400, *info@itc-uk.com*, *www.itc-classics.co.uk*. A wide-ranging selection of hotels in most of the Caribbean islands at a range of prices, including all-inclusives, some villas, yachting and cruising, plus some special-interest trips including test matches.

Caribbean Expressions, 104 Belsize Lane, London NW3 5BB, t (020) 7433 2610, *info@expressionsholidays.co.uk*, *www.expressionsholidays.co.uk*. A relative newcomer to the Caribbean scene with a good variety of top hotels and other suggestions in their brochure.

Caribtours, Kiln House, 210 New Kings Rd, London SW6 4NZ, t (020) 7751 0660, *escapes@caribtours.co.uk*, *www.caribtours.co.uk*. A small and friendly operator whose 'Caribbean Escapes' brochure offers a broad range of hotels in different categories, with special programmes for children, spa and boutique hotels, crewed yacht charters, villas and all-inclusives.

Carrier, Church St, Wilmslow, Cheshire SK9 1AX, t (01625) 547 020, *aspects@carrier.co.uk*, *www.carrier.co.uk*. Formerly of African fame, they offer a small number of élite properties in their 'Carrier Caribbean' brochure (which also covers Florida), including yacht charter.

Complete Caribbean, St James House, 36 James Street, Harrogate, HG1 1RF, t (01423) 531 031, *reservations@completecaribbean.co.uk*, *www.completecaribbean.co.uk*. A broad selection of top-of-the-range and some less expensive hotels.

Elegant Resorts, The Old Palace, Chester CH1 1RB, t 01244 897 999, *enquiries@elegantresorts.co.uk*, *www.elegantresorts.co.uk*. Top-of-the-range packages to the Caribbean's smartest hotels, with special details on spas, boutique hotels, weddings

---

season). Try the yacht club noticeboards and yachting magazines. Experience is not necessarily required. Most yachts will charge you just enough to cover food, or nothing at all, but there are one or two sharks around making outrageous charges for what can be quite a hard three-week sail. Catamarans are more comfortable.

The return journey eastwards across the Atlantic generally takes place at the end of April, fairly soon after Antigua Race Week. Antigua is the best place to look, but yachts also leave from other places, such as St Lucia and Sint Maarten. Contact:

The Cruising Association, CA House, 1 Northey St, Lime House Basin, London E14 8BT, t (020)

and honeymoons, golf, yacht charter and cruising. Special villa brochure.

Harlequin Worldwide Travel, 2 North Rd, South Ockendon, Essex RM15 6AZ, **t** (01708) 850 300, *info@harlequinholidays.co.uk*, *www.harlequinholidays.co.uk*. Their 'Connoisseurs' Collection' brochure has an excellent selection of top-end hotels but also some offbeat gems.

Hayes and Jarvis, The Atrium, London Road, Crawley, West Sussex RH10 9SR, **t** 0870 366 1636, *res@hayesandjarvis.co.uk*, *www. hayesandjarvis.co.uk*. A mid- to upper-end tour operator.

Journey Latin America, 12–13 Heathfield Terrace, Chiswick, London W4 4JE, **t** (020) 8747 8315, *sales@journeylatinamerica.co.uk*, *www.journeylatinamerica.co.uk*. Covers a small number of islands around the region, particularly in tandem with Central America.

Just Grenada, The Barns, Woodlands End, Mells, Frome, Somerset BA11 3QD, **t** (01373) 814 214, *mail@justgrenada.co.uk*. Specializes exclusively in holidays to Grenada.

Kuoni, Kuoni House, Dorking, Surrey RH5 4AZ, **t** (01306) 747 733, *www.kuoni.com*. A broad selection of mid-range properties in a good selection of islands.

Silk Cut Travel, Meon House, Petersfield, Hants GU32 3JN, **t** (01730) 265 211. Focuses on small hotels, some top of the range, others less so.

The Caribbean Centre, 6 Heasewood, Haywards Heath, West Sussex RH16 4TJ, **t** 01444 455 993, *jan@caribean.itsnet.co.uk*, *www.caribbeancentre.co.uk*. Will book hotels with good savings, either for a two-week period or for a three-day (min) stay before you set off travelling; also some private homes (mainly Jamaica, St Lucia, Grenada and Antigua). They don't sell flights.

The Owners' Syndicate, 6 Port House, Plantation Wharf, London SW11 3TY, **t** (020) 7801 9801, *caribbean@ownerssyndicate.com*, *www.ownerssyndicate.com*. Originally a villa company which has released a separate brochure with a number of smaller and more charming hotels as well as some of the Caribbean stalwarts.

Thomas Cook Holidays, travel shops throughout the UK, **t** 0870 750 5711, *www.thomascook.com*. Mid- and upper-range hotels around the islands.

Thomson Holidays, Greater London House, Hampstead Road, London NW1 7SD, brochure line **t** 0870 550 2046, reservations **t** 0870 165 0079. Reaches most of the major Caribbean islands, departing Heathrow, Gatwick and Manchester.

Trips Worldwide, 14 Frederick Place, Clifton, Bristol BS8 1AS, **t** (0117) 311 4400, *info@ tripsworldwide.co.uk*, *www.tripsworld wide.co.uk*. Small brochure, 'Alternative Caribbean', which offers tailor-made trips to a number of Caribbean islands, including unexpected ones such as Haiti, Guadeloupe and the Dominican Republic.

Western and Oriental Travel, 1st Floor 38–44 Gillingham Street, London SW1V 1HV, **t** 0870 499 1111, *info@westernoriental.com*, *www.westernoriental.com*. Exclusive tailored service to top hotels throughout the islands.

Birdwatching

Barefoot Traveller, 204 King St, London W6 0RA, **t** (020) 8741 4319, *dive@barefoot-traveller.com*, *www.barefoot-traveller.com*. In Trinidad and Tobago.

Cricket

When the England cricket team tours the West Indies, a number of companies offer tours, often with former players as guides.

Fred Rumsey Travel, 26a Main Street, Burton under Needwood, Burton on Trent, Staffs, **t** (01283) 712 233.

7537 2828, *office@cruising.org.uk*, *www. cruising.org.uk*. Has a crewing service, connecting skippers and crew in a monthly newsletter. It costs £29 to put your name on the list, after which you negotiate with the skipper. The service is free to members of the Cruising Association (though membership currently costs £116/annum.

From the USA

The American yachting community migrates down to the Caribbean over the winter. Try yacht club noticeboards, the yachting magazines and the ports on the eastern seaboard. Experience is not necessarily required. Most yachts will charge you just enough to cover food, or nothing at all.

Gullivers Sports Travel, Fiddington Manor, Tewkesbury, Gloucester GL20 7BJ, **t** (01684) 293 175, *gullivers@gulliversports.co.uk*, *www.gulliversports.co.uk*.

Honeymoons and Weddings

Honeymoon packages (with wedding included if you want) get ever more popular and most of the general tour operators above will arrange one for you.

Sailing

There are two options: 'crewed yachts', in which there is a captain and usually a crew (some are massive gin palaces with chefs to prepare your personal menu, on-board Renoirs and troops of flunkies in white shorts who communicate by whistle), and 'bareboats', in which you look after yourself (though it is possible to have the yacht provisioned and if you lack confidence you can have a skipper for a day or two to get you started).

Crewed yachts are usually handled by brokers, who have the details of a number of yachts and crews on their books, though some own and manage their own yachts. It is a personal business. The brokers know the owners and crew and then match you to the right yacht. Mostly you are left to arrange your own flights. Crewed yachts (generally over 100 feet) are available through:

Camper & Nicholsons, 25 Bruton St, London W1 6QH, **t** (020) 7491 2950, *info@lon.cnyachts. com*, *www.cnconnect.com*. A long-standing broker with a large range of extremely luxurious and expensive yachts.

Cavendish White, Lutidine House, Newark Lane, Ripley, Surrey GU23 6BS, **t** (020) 7381 7600, *yachts@cavendishwhite.com*, *www.cavendishwhite.com*.

Crestar Yachts Ltd, 16–17 Pall Mall, London SW1Y 5LU, **t** (020) 7766 4331, *crestar@ nigelburgess.com*, *www.crestar.co.uk*.

Yachting Partners International, 28–9 Richmond Place, Brighton BN2 2NA, **t** (01273) 571 722, *ypi@ypi.co.uk*, *www.ypi.co.uk*. A large range of incredibly luxurious yachts.

For less expensive yachts (both motor and sailing yachts, generally under 100ft):

Liz Fenner Yachting Holidays, 35 Fairfax Place, London NW6 4EJ, **t** (020) 7328 1033.

Tenrag, Tenrag House, Preston, Canterbury, Kent CT3 1EB, **t** (01227) 721 874, *info@ tenrag.com*, *www.tenrag.com*.

Yacht Connections, The Wheelhouse, Main Road, East Boldre, near Lymington, Hants SO42 7WU, **t** (01590) 626 291, *ac@yacht-connections.co.uk*, *www.yacht-connections. co.uk*. Arranges lots of stay-and-sail holidays.

For a **bareboat** you can contact one of the following or go through the big UK general package tour operators above, any of whom will put together a complete package, including flights, yacht and possibly time ashore. Contact:

Stardust Marine, *info@saltyseas.com*, *www.saltyseas.com/stardust.html*. With bases in Cuba, Puerto Rico, the British Virgin Islands, Sint Maarten, Martinique and Union Island in the Grenadines.

Sunsail, The Port House, Port Solent, Portsmouth, Hants PO6 4TH, **t** 0870 777 0313, *sales@sunsail.com*, *www.sunsail.com*.

The Moorings, Middle Wall, Bradstowe House, Whitstable, Kent CT5 1BF, **t** (01227) 776 677, *yacht-charter@moorings.co.uk*, *www. moorings.com*.

Scuba Diving

Barefoot Traveller, 204 King St, London W6 0RA, **t** (020) 8741 4319, *dive@barefoot-traveller.com*, *www.barefoot-traveller.com*. Covers Tobago, Cayman, Bonaire, Curaçao, Grand Turk and the Bahamas.

Dive Worldwide, Crown House, 28 Winchester Road, Romsey, Hants SO51 8AA, **t** 0845 130

Entry Formalities

As a British, US or Canadian citizen travelling as a tourist you do not need a visa to any of the Commonwealth Caribbean countries or the French or Netherlands Antilles. To enter Cuba, the Dominican Republic and Haiti you must have a tourist card, which can be bought in advance but also at the point of entry. Citizens of other countries do not usually need a visa, except sometimes for Puerto Rico and the US Virgin Islands (which have the same regulations as USA) and if you are flying to the Caribbean via Miami of course. Business visitors should consult the embassy before departure.

6980, *info@diveworldwide.com*, *www.dive worldwide.com*. Wide variety of islands.

Harlequin Worldwide Travel, 2 North Rd, South Ockendon, Essex RM15 6AZ, t (01708) 850 330, *info@harlequinholidays.co.uk*, *www. harlequinholidays.co.uk*.

Hayes and Jarvis, The Atrium, London Road, Crawley, West Sussex RH10 9SR, t 0870 366 1636, *res@hayesandjarvis.co.uk*, *www. hayesandjarvis.co.uk*. Grenada, St Kitts, Tobago, Antigua, Barbados, the Cayman Islands, Cuba and more.

Regal Dive, 58 Lancaster Way, Ely, Cambs CB6 3NW, t 0870 220 1777, *info@regal-diving. co.uk*, *www.regal-diving.co.uk*.

In the USA

General Packages

Alken Tours, 1661 Norstrand Av, 2nd Floor, Brooklyn, New York, NY 11226, t (718) 856 7711, t 1 800 221 6686, *res@alkentours.com*. Has a number of offices around the States.

American Express Vacations, t 1 800 241 1700, *travel.americanexpress.com*.

Air Jamaica Vacations, t 1 800 568 3247, *www.airjamaicavacations.com*.

Apple Vacations, 7 Campus Blvd., Newtown Square, PA 19073, *www.applevacations.com*. One of the main Caribbean tour companies, with 35 years' experience.

American Airlines Vacations, t 1 800 321 2121, *www.aavacations.com*.

Caribbean Concepts, 649 Strander Bd, Suite F, Seattle WA 98188, t 1 800 777 0907, *www.caribbeanconcepts.com*. A small operator for the upper end of the market.

Cheap Caribbean, t 1 800 915 2322, *www.cheapcaribbean.com*. A fairly new company claiming up to 70% off published prices to the Caribbean.

Classic Custom Vacations, 1 North First St, San Jose, California 95113-1215, t (408) 287 4550, *www.classiccustomvacations.com*. They arrange trips to top-of-the-range hotels in a good selection of the islands.

GoGo Worldwide Vacations, t (201) 934 3500, t 1 800 526 0405, *www.gogowwv.com*.

Inter Island Tours, t 1 800 245 3434, *www.inter islandtours.com*. Wide range of packages.

Island Resort Tours, t 1 800 351 5656, *www.islandresorttours.com*. A well-established tour company.

Travel Impressions, t 1 800 284 0044, *www.travelimpressions.com*.

Birdwatching

Caligo Ventures, 156 Bedford Rd, Armonk, NY 10504, t (914) 273 6333, *info@caligo.com*, *www.caligo.com*. Arranges birding trips and natural-history tours of Trinidad and Tobago centred on the Asa Wright Nature Centre.

Honeymoons and Weddings

Most of the general tour companies above will arrange a Caribbean honeymoon for you.

Sailing

For a **crewed yacht** try:

Camper & Nicholsons, 450 Royal Palm Way, Palm Beach, FL 33480, t (561) 655 2121, *info@pal.cnyachts.com*, *www.cnconnect.com*. With three offices in Florida – Palm Beach, Fort Lauderdale and Miami.

Yachting Partners International, t 1 800 626 0019, *ypi@ypi.co.uk*, *www.mycharter.com*.

For a **bareboat**, in which you largely look after yourself, try:

The Moorings, PO Box 9064, Clearwater, Florida, FL 34618-9064, t (1727) 535 1446, t 800 535 7289, *yacht@moorings.com*, *www.moorings.com*.

Sunsail, Landing Marina, 908 Awald Rd, Annapolis, MD 21403, t 1 800 327 2276, t (410) 280 2553, *sunsailusa@sunsail.com*, *www.sunsail.com*.

The Caribbean may be known for being laid-back, but their immigration authorities are generally not so. Often they will demand to see an onward ticket and they will hold your passport until you produce one. Some islands may require proof of funds. On the immigration form you will also be asked to give a local address: this is almost a formality, but it eases entry to put something down. Addresses of hotels and guest houses are in each chapter.

Customs

Drugs not issued on prescription are illegal in the Caribbean and people do occasionally end up in prison for possession of user quantities. Customs officials operate a strict policy against them and do occasionally search bags on arrival and departure.

Alcohol and tobacco allowances vary.

Departure Tax

It is worth remembering to keep some change for when you leave, because most countries levy a departure tax, usually payable in US dollars. The amount of departure tax payable on each island is listed under 'Getting There' in individual island sections.

Getting Around

Island-hopping is one of the great pleasures of a Caribbean holiday and the Lesser Antilles particularly has a grand variety of islands near one another. In the chain of the Eastern Caribbean islands (which are visible one from the next for the 500 miles from Grenada in the south to Anguilla in the north, and then again from the Virgin Islands to Puerto Rico), 20 minutes' flying can get you from a French overseas *département* or a Spanish-speaking island to independent islands that have a strong British heritage, from busy, developed countries to tiny, comatose blips with just a few shacks and palm trees.

Most of the big Caribbean tour operators will arrange an island-hopping itinerary for you, with flights between hotels. If you wish to travel more independently you can take off on your own with one of the island-hopper tickets issued by the local Caribbean airlines (*see* box below). If you do not want to arrange an actual island-hopping itinerary, it is perfectly possible to visit other islands nearby by making short day or weekend tours (some by sailboat, others by plane, bookable on the islands themselves with local tour operators). Barbados, St Lucia and Martinique offer many trips to the Grenadines, and there are endless trips to the islands around Sint Maarten – Saba, Statia, St Barts and Anguilla.

Travel is very easy from the USVI to the BVI and vice versa. Frequent ferries operate between St Thomas and Tortola and onward to Virgin Gorda.

Island-Hopper Air Passes

Air Jamaica offers hopper fares from its hub in Jamaica, from where – as long as you travel on with Air Jamaica – you can cross to their Caribbean destinations (Barbados, Grand Cayman, Nassau, St Lucia, Bonaire, Cuba, Grenada and Turks & Caicos) for US$399.

American Eagle offer a *Caribbean Explorer* pass, which allows travellers from the US and Canada to fly via the San Juan hub and then on to 23 Caribbean destinations.

BWIA offer the *Intra-Caribbean Airpass*, which allows you up to ten stops at BWIA destinations in the Caribbean (Jamaica, Antigua, Barbados, Grenada, Guyana, Sint Maarten, St Lucia, Caracas, St Vincent, Trinidad and Tobago), connections allowed (maximum stay 24 hours), over a 30-day period, with return to the original point of departure (US$399 economy, or US$599 first class). This is particularly interesting because it includes Jamaica, which is not covered by LIAT.

Caribbean Star offer a *Starpass*, which allows passengers to make up to four flights for a total of US$299 (in conjunction with an international ticket).

LIAT (*see* 'Caribbean Airlines' for their destinations) has three hopper tickets which are ideal for people travelling extensively around the Caribbean. The *Caribbean Super Explorer* ticket allows you unlimited stops in one direction (though you are permitted to return to a destination to make a connection) for a period of a month, with return to point of origin (US$575). The *Caribbean Explorer* lasts for a 21-day period and allows three stops (none repeated except for connections), with return to point of origin (US$300). Those flying from Europe, meanwhile, can buy the *Eastern Caribbean Airpass*, which allows stops at between three and six LIAT destinations over a 21-day period, each leg being charged at US$98. This ticket comes with restrictions – for example, it can only be bought in conjunction with an international return ticket to the Caribbean. *Super Caribbean Explorer* tickets may be bought once you are out in the Caribbean, but the other two must be bought before departure from your country of residence, in conjunction with a ticket to the Caribbean (any carrier will do, despite what some airlines assure you).

Caribbean Airlines

As well as those airlines listed below, many companies link the British Virgin Islands to the US Virgin Islands and to San Juan, Puerto Rico, plus the French islands of St Barts and St Martin to Guadeloupe and San Juan. For details, *see* the separate islands.

Air Antilles, t 42 16 71, *www.airantilles.com*.

Air Calypso, t 89 27 77, *air.calypso@ wanadoo.fr*.

Air Caraïbes, t 27 61 90, *info@aircaraibes. com*, *www.aircaraibes.com*. Flies between Martinique, Dominica, Guadeloupe, St Martin and St Barts.

Air Jamaica, UK t (020) 8570 7999, US t 1 800 523 5585, *www.airjamaica.com*. Flies from Jamaica to Barbados, Bonaire, Cuba, Grand Cayman, Grenada, Nassau (Bahamas), St Lucia, and between St Lucia and Grenada.

Air Martinique/Air Caraibes, t 42 16 60.

BonairExpress, t 599 717 0707.

BWIA, UK t (020) 8577 1100, US t 1 800 538 2942, *www.bwee.com*. The Trinidad and Tobago airline, pronounced Beewee and also known as 'Best Wait in the Airport', 'Best West Indian Airline', 'But Will It Arrive?', 'Better Walk If Able'. BWIA destinations are Antigua, Barbados, Caracas, Grenada, Guyana, Jamaica, St Vincent, Sint Maarten, Trinidad and Tobago.

Carib Aviation, t (1268) 462 3147, *carib@candoo. com*, *www.candoo.com/carib*. Flies out of Antigua to the smaller islands to the north (mainly St Barts and Anguilla). A charter airline offering an almost scheduled service (a 'shared charter' service).

Caribbean Star, t (1268) 461 7827, *www.fly caribbeanstar.com*. Opened up services in 2000, flying north and south from Antigua to most of the former British islands. There are no acronyms yet for this airline. Please send them in.

Caribbean Sun Airlines, t 1 800 866 6272, *www.flycsa.com*.

Cayman Airways, t 1 800 422 9626, *www.caymanairways.com*.

LIAT, t (1268) 480 5600, *reservations@ liatairline.com*, *www.liatairline.com*. The biggest carrier in the Eastern Caribbean. Officially LIAT means Leeward Islands Air Transport, but the number of acronyms it has gives an idea of how fondly it is thought of: 'Leave Island Any Time', 'Lost in Air Transit', 'Luggage in Another Town', 'Likely to Irritate Another Tourist'! Many LIAT flights originate in Antigua and destinations include Anguilla, Barbados, Dominica, Grenada, Guadeloupe, Guyana, Martinique, Nevis, Puerto Rico, St Croix, St Kitts, St Lucia, St Thomas, St Vincent, Sint Maarten, Tortola (BVI) and Trinidad.

Mustique Airways, UK t (01602) 604 030, US t (570) 595 7863, Mustique t (1784) 458 4380, *info@mustique.com*, *www.mustique. com*. A shared charter service that connects Barbados and the Grenadines.

TIA, t (246) 418 1654, *reservations@tia2000. com*, *www.tia2000.com*. Connects Barbados with the Grenadines. Another shared charter airline that offers an almost sched-uled service.

SVG Grenadine Air, t (1784) 457 5124.

Winair, t (599) 545 4237, *reservations@fly-winair.com*, *www.fly-winair.com*. The airline of the Dutch Windward Islands, based in Sint Maarten and flying to all the neigh-bouring islands.

Cuba has also opened up for weekend hops to and from the surrounding islands: Jamaica, the Bahamas and the Cayman Islands.

By Air

Most island-hopping nowadays is by aero-plane (often Twin Otters or Islanders and increasingly DASH 8s). Some of these planes, the smaller ones at least, do look a bit like coffins with wings on and when they take off they have so much lift that it feels almost alarming, but they are very safe and reliable. The pilot will position the plane at the start of the runway and run the engines hard until the control panel becomes a blur and the plane thrums like an outsized tuning fork. Then he lets off the brakes and rams the props in drive. Flight can be a bit of a novelty (some people actually pay for rides like this in the funfairs). In calmer moments the views of the islands and the sea from 3,000ft are fantastic.

Island-hopper planes are affectionately known as the islands' bus service. They tend to run along the island chain and will simply miss out a destination if nobody wants to get on or off.

Generally, island-hopping by plane is a good and reliable way of travelling. A couple of words of warning, however. Booking can be a little haphazard. Planes are sometimes over-sold, and those booked in advance may well leave half-empty. Travelling stand-by often works. And it is worth reconfirming obsessively (local numbers for airlines are listed under 'Getting There' in the relevant island chapters). If you miss one flight you may find the whole itinerary is cancelled. Most airlines are usually quite amenable when it comes to excess luggage if the plane is not full.

The Caribbean has some pretty hairy airstrips. Some are very short – you will know about this just after landing when the whole plane shudders because the pilot applies reverse thrust. Others are hairy because there is an obstacle course on the approach to landing. The most spectacular of them all is the strip on Saba, just 400 yards long (shorter than any self-respecting aircraft carrier) and with a 100ft drop at either end. Taking off is exciting; landing has a stress quotient. People say, 'They only use half the runway.' Just pray that it's the first half.

In the UK, the specialist Caribbean travel agencies (see 'By Air' under 'Getting There', above) are very knowledgeable and they will make suggestions and book for you.

Another option is to charter a small plane, which can work out at a good price if there are enough of you. All Caribbean airports have a charter company (five-seaters, nine-seaters and sometimes helicopters) on call (see Mustique Airways, TIA and Carib Aviation, under 'Caribbean Airlines', p.43, and the separate island chapters).

By Sea

Until 30 years ago all the islands of the Caribbean were linked by elegant old sloops and schooners once or twice a week. These have mostly gone now, but it is still sometimes possible to hitch a ride on the **freighters** which bring provisions and manufactured goods into the islands. Go to the dock and ask around and they might sign you on as 'crew'. There is a regular service out of Barbados to St Vincent, Trinidad and South America. If you are travelling between Grenada and Trinidad, you might be able get a lift on one of the magnificent sloops that tie up in St George's harbour, Grenada. Boats from the Grenadines go as far north as Sint Maarten, though they won't necessarily stop at other islands.

Ferries connect all the Virgin Islands; Grenada, the Grenadines and St Vincent; the French island of Guadeloupe to Martinique (via Dominica) with the occasional onward trip to St Lucia; the Guadeloupean mainland to all its small offshore islands; and some of the islands around Sint Maarten. See 'Getting There' or 'Getting Around' under individual island sections for more details.

Another possibility is to travel by hitching a ride on a **yacht**, which you can catch at the main centres (British Virgin Islands, US Virgin Islands, Sint Maarten, Antigua, Guadeloupe, Martinique, St Lucia and some of the Grenadines). If you go down to the marina and ask around, you may come up with something: the crews are often happy to take along the occasional passenger who is prepared to help out.

By Road

For details of buses, car and bike hire, taxis, guided tours etc., see 'Getting Around' in each individual island section.

Practical A–Z

Beaches

If modern times' ultimate quest is the finest sun-drenched, palm-fringed curve of satin-soft, ankle-deep sand, washed by warm waves and set in an aquamarine sea, all of course with a perfect sunset view, then the Caribbean offers happy hunting grounds. The best sand tends to be on the low-lying islands like the Bahamas and the Leeward and Grenadine Islands, which because of their coral base have the bright white sand, but you will also find magnificent, often secluded coves tucked between the vast headlands of the mountainous islands in the Eastern Caribbean and the Greater Antilles. Swimming is safe in most places, but do not swim alone, and beware the undertow on the Atlantic side of the Lesser Antilles.

If all you want from the Caribbean on your holiday is a beach, then the best islands for being alone on uninterrupted miles of sand are Anguilla, Antigua and Barbuda, the Out Islands in the Bahamas and the Caicos Islands in the Turks and Caicos. A bit better known, and often more crowded, are the British Virgin Islands, Barbados and the Grenadines. As a general rule, beaches in the Caribbean are usually public up to the high-water mark (basically the top of the sand) and so, as long as there is access, you are permitted onto them. However you get there, you will find that facilities are often limited to hotel guests. This means that there are not that many 'public beaches', but most islands will have at least one popular beach with facilities, water-sport shops and beach bars. Only a few islands have any system of lifeguards and rangers.

You should note that not every Caribbean hotel is set on a picture-postcard beach, particularly at the lower end of the price range, and that not every beach is necessarily that nice. If the most important ingredient of your holiday is the beach, you should ensure that it is good enough by quizzing the tour operator on its nature and facilities. Even brochure pictures and the Internet pictures can be quite clever in disguising shortcomings. Most hotels of any size will have some water-sports but, as this is not necessarily the case, find out if in doubt. For more details, *see* 'Best Beaches' in the individual island sections.

Bookshops

In the UK

The following London shops have a wide selection of travel books with special sections for the Caribbean:

Daunt's Bookshop, 83–4 Marylebone High St, London W1U 4QW, t (020) 7224 2295. They will send you a reading list.

Nomad Books, 781 Fulham Rd, London SW6 5HA, t (020) 7736 4000.

Stanfords, 12–14 Longacre, London WC2E 9LP, t (020) 7836 1321, *www.stanfords.co.uk*. This is also a specialist map shop.

The Travel Bookshop, 13 Blenheim Crescent, London W11 2EE, t (020) 7229 5260, *www.travelbookshop.co.uk*.

In the USA

Book Passage, 51 Tamal Vista Bd, Corte Madre, CA 94925, t (415) 927 0960, t 1 800 999 7909.

The Complete Traveller, 199 Madison Av, New York, NY 10016, t (212) 685 9007, *www.completetravellerbooks.com*.

Rand McNally, 150 East 52nd St, New York, NY 10022, t (212) 758 7488.

Rand McNally Map Travel, 444 North Michigan Av, Chicago, IL 60611, t (312) 321 1751.

The Caribbean on the Internet

With so many visitors from the States, the Caribbean was generally quick to make its mark on the World Wide Web. Much is what you would expect, basically brochures on screen (without much critical opinion), but there are some useful sources, particularly for independent travellers. And hey, why not fix up a real-time screensaver from your favourite dive site in Bonaire (there really are some live underwater webcams in Bonaire).

All the **tourist boards** have websites and these contain plenty of practical information about hotels and restaurants, car hire and watersports companies. These are listed in the various practical-information boxes under the respective islands. A number of **commercial websites** (some of which are basically tour operators on line) also serve as variable sources of information. Here are a few:

www.definitivecaribbean.com
www.col.com
www.interknowledge.com
www.caribbeanmag.com
www.sunfinder.com
www.gocaribbean.com
www.onecaribbean.com

With the exception of the aptly named Definitive Caribbean website, most of these won't necessarily tell you enough to help you make that key decision over which hotel to choose, but they are a start. Ultimately you will probably need to talk to a tour operator or a travel agent anyway. Most tour operators in the metropolitan countries also have websites. You will also find a number of more commercial sites, which are offering deals on holidays to the islands.

Almost all Caribbean hotels now have home pages. These are really simply brochure screens, but they are useful in their accessibility and they will provide you with the basic facts and a sense of the place. If you want to know more, most have an email address attached via which you can send any queries. There is a screed of websites which collect together hotel and villa accommodation (for which the hotels tend to pay to be listed). However, as these do not generally allow you to contact the hotel direct, they are of limited use unless you want to make a booking. You can find a reasonable selection of hotels at *www.islandinns.com* and *www.wheretostay.com*. If you are specifically interested in all-inclusive hotels (Sandals, Club Med, etc.), then try *www.all-inclusive.com*. For

Calendar of Events

January

Most of the pre-Lenten *Carnivals* are just warming up, with weekend fêtes and the early stages of calypso and carnival king and queen competitions.

Aruba *New Year*. Singers and musicians known as *Dande* stroll from house to house as they chant.

Bahamas *Junkanoo*. Start of the pre-Lenten celebrations, with street parades quite similar to the carnival masquerades.

Barbados *Jazz festival*. Featuring performances from international musicians.
Windsurfing competitions.

Curaçao *Tumba*. New Year music festival.

Dominican Republic *Three Kings' Day*. Celebrates the end of Christmas.
Windsurfing competitions.

Grenada *Fishing tournament*.
Sailing Regatta.

Jamaica *Maroon festival*. Held early in the month, commemorates events dating back to the 18th century.
Sprint-triathlon. Thoroughly modern, held in Negril.

Martinique *La Fête des Rois*. With gastronomic flair.

Puerto Rico *End of Christmas*. Traditionally celebrated on 6 January.

St Barts *Music Festival*.

St Croix *Crucian Christmas Festival*. Culminates in early January with carnival-like parades.
Rhythm and Blues Festival. Held later on in the month.

St Lucia *Heineken Regatta*. Held annually.

St Kitts *Carnival*. Reaches its culmination.

February

Aruba, Bonaire, Carriacou, Curaçao, Dominica, Dominican Republic (on the weekend closest to the start of Lent), **Guadeloupe, Haiti, Martinique, St Barthélemy, St Lucia, St Martin, Tobago** and, of course, **Trinidad** *Carnival*. Reaches its height in February, in a three-day jump-up, with calypso and steel band competitions, and masked parades in the streets on Shrove Tuesday (*Mardi Gras*) or Ash Wednesday.

Barbados *Holetown Festival*. Commemorates the first settlement of the island in 1627.

Cuba *Jazz Festival*. Staged in Havana in February or March.

Dominican Republic *Independence Day*. Held on 27 February; national parades take place, interspersed among days of carnival activity.

Grenada *Independence Day*. Celebrations on 7 February, with jump-ups.

St Lucia *Independence Day*. Celebrated on 22 February.

March

For Easter see 'April'.

Montserrat *St Patrick's Day* on 17 March.

impartial write-ups of hotels and resorts across the Caribbean, have a look at *www.definitivecaribbean.com*.

It is the small hotels and inns that have the greatest potential with the web. Traditionally these hotels have never been able to get the word out (they never had the money they needed to spend on publicity), which is sad because some of them really represent the most charming side of the Caribbean. Now they are accessible as never before and, as the majority are owner-operated, you can expect them to respond to your enquiries. Some websites collect together listings of hotels in this category, but they can also be located through the search engines. The same also goes for individual villas. One website specifically devoted to **villas** is found at

www.caribvillas.com, but you can try any of the villa operators mentioned in the 'Where to Stay' section at the end of this chapter.

Many Caribbean **businesses** – car hire companies, island tour operators, watersports companies, yachts for day sails, even shops and tourist 'sights' – have websites now, which will help with specialist requirements. Among the best are those run by the **scuba diving** companies, nearly all of which have them. An increasing number of **restaurants** have homepages too, so you can check out the menu and the view in advance.

All of this is fine, but it tends to be posted by an organization which has something to gain from publicity so it is unlikely to be unbiased. Critical opinion is hard to come by. However, there are some sights which post **reviews**. Try

---

Sint Maarten *Heineken Regatta*.
St Thomas *Yachting competition*. Held late in the month.
Trinidad *Phagwah*. Street parades in which people spray each other with bright-red dye.
USVI *Anniversary*. Commemoration of the islands' transfer to American ownership on 30 March.

April

Easter sees *kite-flying* across the Caribbean, and many *sailing competitions* get under way.
Antigua *Classic Yacht Regatta*.
International Sailing Week or *Race Week*. Famous regatta.
Barbados *Easter Opera Season*. For three days.
Fish Festival. Easter festivities, Oistins Town.
BVI *Spring Regatta*.
Cayman Islands *Regatta*.
Batanabo. Carnival (sometimes late March).
Exumas and **Bahamas** *Family Islands Regatta*.
Grenadines *Bequia Regatta*. May be in March.
Jamaica *Carnival*.
Jamaican National Theatre Dance Company. Performances from their programme.
Martinique *Food Festival*. Formal Easter event.
Netherlands Antilles *Queen Beatrix's official birthday*. Parties are held on 30 April.
St Barts *Food Festival*. Celebrating Easter.
St Thomas *Carnival*.
Tobago *Easter goat and crab races* (yes, men and women with goats on leads).

May

Antigua *Sport-fishing tournament*.
Aruba Annual *Culinary exhibition* and *competition*.
French islands *Abolition Day*. Remembered with picnics and fêtes on 27 May.
St Croix *Triathlon*. A gruelling event, held early in the month.
St Lucia *Jazz Festival*. Held for three days early in the month.
St Martin *Food Festival*. Staged with lively jump-ups as well as all the classic cooking you'd expect.

June

Abacos and the **Bahamas** *Regatta*. Sailing events.
Aruba *Hi-Winds*. Amateur world champions windsurfing competition.
Triathlon.
Jazz and Latin Music Festival.
Bahamas *Goombay Festival*. Kicks off with street parades and reviews.
Puerto Rico *Bombay Plena*. Festival of African music and dance held in Ponce, at the beginning of the month.
St Vincent and the **Grenadines** *Vincie Mas*. Usually takes place towards the end of the month.
Tobago *Regatta*. A week's sailing.
Turks and Caicos Islands *Billfishing Tournament*.

www.gobeach.com, which covers reports of restaurants and other things. If you are going to the Dominican Republic, you can find good information and reviews at www.debbies dominicantravel.com.

The sites above deal mainly with tourism. There are of course many other websites of a more political nature and ones which help expatriate West Indians keep in touch with news of their islands. A website with books and other Caribbeanabilia for sale can be found at www.caribbeanavenue.com.

Children

Despite its reputation as a honeymooners' and couples' destination, travelling with children in the Caribbean is perfectly possible and you will find that in most islands the locals are indulgent and friendly towards them (they might be invited to join the screaming little-persons' posses that chase around the beaches and countryside). The majority of hotels will accept children, though they will provide only limited facilities for them. Children are sometimes allowed to stay for free in the same room as their parents and baby-sitters are usually on call in any hotel.

A few hotels at the top of the range have a policy of not accepting any children below a certain age, usually 12, and often not in the winter season; others have built special play-grounds for them (notably Malliouhana in Anguilla, Sandy Lane in Barbados, the Half Moon Hotel in Jamaica and Caneel Bay in St John) and provide nannies so that you can

July

Late in the month a number of other islands get their carnivals moving, **Sint Eustatius**, **Antigua**, the **Turks and Caicos** (*Provo Summer Festival*) and **Barbados** (*Cropover*), so that they culminate in the first few days of August. There are also plenty of *regattas*.

Bahamas *Independence*. Celebrated on 10 July.
  Bimini Blue Marlin Tournament. Takes place towards the end of the month.
Cuba *Moncada Garrison*. Anniversary celebrations of the garrison attack.
  Carnaval.
  Both held around 26 July.
Dominica *Domfesta*. Stages Caribbean cultural activities in July or August.
Dominican Republic *Merengue Festival*.
Martinique *Cultural Week*. With performances of classical art.
Nevis *Culturama*. A Caribbean cultural event – carnival parades and island-wide festivities.
Saba *Summer Festival*. Runs for a week with carnival events.
USVI *4 July*. Celebrated with fireworks and their own carnival.

August

Most of the former **British** islands have festivities on 1 August, the date of *Emancipation*.

Anguilla *Carnival*. Staged over a week.
  Regatta. At the start of the month.

BVI and the **Turks and Caicos** *Sailing race*. Held late in the month in Anegada.
Carriacou *Regatta*.
Curaçao *Salsa Festival*.
Grenada *Carnival*. Masqueraders drag the carnival floats over the hills of St George's.
Grenadines *Sailing races*. Held in Canouan.
Guadeloupe *Fête des Cuisinières*. Extraordinary and colourful festival which takes place on 11 August, St Laurent's day (the patron saint of cooks), with parades of dishes and blow-outs.
Jamaica *Independence Day*. Celebrations on the first Monday in August.
  Reggae Sumfest. An extravaganza of local and international reggae artists.
Martinique *Yoles rondes*. Sailing races.
St Barts *St Barthélemy's day*. Celebrated on the 24th.
  Pitea Day. Commemorates their connection with Sweden.
St Lucia *Rose Festival*. Held on 30 August, with a mock court, ball and music.
St Thomas *Game fishing tournament*. Fishing for blue marlin.
Tobago *Tobago Heritage Festival*.
Trinidad *Independence*. Celebrated on 31 August.

September

BVI *Foxy's Wooden Boat Regatta*. Held early in the month in tiny Jost van Dyke.

sun yourself in peace. A small clutch of hotels actually specialize in looking after children, providing an all-day diet of entertainment (finger-painting lessons, Nintendo, local dancing and mini-watersports) to keep them off your hands. One that is worth looking into is Boscobel Beach as well as the FDR Resorts in Jamaica.

If you have a large family it might be easiest to opt for a two- or three-room villa in a hotel complex or a flat in an apartment complex. Here there will usually be hotel facilities including watersports concessions and a restaurant. If you are happy to look after yourself, then you might take an independent villa. Children are accepted happily in most restaurants, and the tendency towards American food means you can always find a

burger and chips to keep them quiet. The Caribbean islands have few museums or daytime activities designed with children in mind, but of course their stock in trade, beaches, are good for keeping them happy.

Climate

Colonists once knew the Bahamas as the 'isles of perpetual June' because of their fair and clement weather. Generally speaking the climate over the whole Caribbean area is impeccable. As islands, their temperature is kept constant by the sea, so the climate is gentler than that in the continent that surrounds them. Frost is unknown and it is rarely even cold. The sun is hot year-round, of course, but you will find that, in 'winter', the

---

St Kitts and **Nevis** *Independence*. Celebrated on 19 September.
USVI *St John's Carnival*. Held near the beginning of the month.

October
Barbados *Music Festival*. Held in the St Lawrence area.
Bonaire and the **Bahamas** *Regattas*. Held in Bonaire mid-month, and in North Eleuthera.
Cayman Islands *Pirates' Week*. Staged with all sorts of festivities towards the end of the month.
Dominican Republic *Creole Week*. *Heritage Day*. Both celebrate local island culture. *Merengue Festival*. Staged in Puerto Plata in the second week of the month.
St Lucia *Bill-fishing tournament*. *Festival of the Marguerite*. On 17 October. *Jounen Kweyol*. On 28 October, a day of creole festivities.
Trinidad *Steel band competition*. Early in the month. *Diwali*. Very colourful Hindu festival of lights, held in October or November.

November
Barbados *Independence*. 30 November.
Dominica *Independence*. Celebrated on 3 November. Preceded by *Creole Week*.

St Martin/Sint Maarten *Concordia Day*. The two halves get together and hold joint festivities on 11 November.
Sint Eustatius *First salute to the American flag*. Commemorated on 16 November.
Trinidad *Pan Jazz Festival*.

December
All Caribbean islands celebrate *Christmas*; island gossip is played out in dance and song, as in **St Eustatius** on *Boxing Day*.
Bahamas *Junkanoo*. A carnival-like celebration which lasts into the New Year.
Martinique *Jazz and guitar festivals*. Held in alternate years.
Puerto Rico *Hatillo Festival of the Innocents*. A riot of excess, and well worth a visit. Held on 28 December.
Saba *Flag Day*. Celebrated on 7 December.
St Croix *Calypso and carnival jamboree*. Month-long Christmas festivities.
St Kitts *Carnival Week*. Starts about 20 December.
St Lucia *National Day*. 13 December. *ARC Rally*. Arrives in the island at about the same time, after an Atlantic crossing.
St Vincent *Nine Mornings*. A week of celebrations in the run-up to Christmas. *New Year*. Yet another good excuse for a jump-up.
Trinidad and a little in **Grenada** *Parang*. You may come across this, a special style of Christmas singing.

Average Temperatures in °C (°F)

	Nassau (Bahamas)	Kingston (Jamaica)	San Juan (Puerto Rico)	St John (USVI)	Port of Spain (Trinidad)	Willemstad (Curaçao)
winter	21 (69)	25 (76)	26 (78)	25 (76)	26 (78)	27 (80)
summer	27 (80)	28 (82)	28 (82)	28 (82)	27 (80)	28 (82)

edge is taken off the heat by a breeze. Conversely it can get quite hot, and humid, during the 'summer' months and it can be quite sticky into the evening. Air conditioning is not really necessary most of the year; if you are staying in a breezy, traditional style of building, fan ventilation is all you need.

The temperature varies just a few degrees across the year and across the geographical area, from Nassau, the capital of the Bahamas, in the north, to Port of Spain in Trinidad, which lies more than 1,000 miles farther south, just off the South American coast. In the larger islands it will occasionally reach 100°F. Temperatures drop at night; in summer there is no need to cover up, but you might need a sweater or jacket on a winter evening, particularly at high altitudes.

Caribbean seasons do not follow those in the temperate zones. There are two main seasons in the islands: wet, in which tropical showers pass by and offload thousands of gallons of water in seconds, before the sun comes out to dry it all up again; and the dry season, when it still rains, but less frequently or heavily. The seasons vary very slightly in timing between Nassau in the north and Port of Spain: the wet seasons are in May or June and October or November. A tropical shower will drench you (with warm rain) in a matter of seconds. You may consider taking a waterproof, but remember that the sun will dry you out almost as quickly as the rain wets you through. Of more concern are the cold fronts, which spin off the continental weather system up north any time from October to March, and put a blanket of cloud over the islands for three or four days at a time. They seem to have been a bit more frequent in recent years.

Hurricanes

Hurricanes are the most severe natural disaster in an area of otherwise benign weather. Turning anticlockwise in the northern hemisphere, hurricanes rise near the coast of Africa as evaporating and then falling seawater begins to spiral. Fed by warm winds over the ocean, they get a couple of thousand miles' run-up before they slam into the islands, blowing with sustained speeds of up to 200mph. At this speed the effect sounds more like explosions and massive percussions than winds. Hurricanes uproot telegraph poles, bend road signs horizontally, rip off tin roofs and hurl them around in the air at a couple of hundred miles an hour and disturb the sea up to 200ft below the surface (causing considerable damage to the corals). They also deliver massive deluges of rain, which cause yet more destruction, sweeping away roads and bridges: Hortense, which came through in 1996, was only designated a tropical storm, but it managed to drop 16 inches of rain on St Croix in about as many hours. After a hurricane, an island looks rather like a grey moonscape, with every leaf stripped from the trees in what is normally an overwhelmingly green area.

If you hear that a hurricane is on the way, find the strongest concrete bunker possible and shelter in it along with everybody else. If all goes quiet at the height of the storm, then you know you are in the eye (the very centre of the hurricane): make sure you batten down the hatches, because it will all start again within a few minutes. If you are unlucky enough to be in a sailing boat, the best place to head for is a mangrove swamp.

The most likely month for hurricanes is September: statistically the highest risk dates are between the 10th and the 20th. If in doubt, remember the traditional rhyme, which runs:

June too soon, July stand by,
September remember, October all over.

There has been a string of pretty bad hurricanes over the last fifteen years or so: Hurricane Gilbert swept through in 1988, wasting Jamaica and the Cayman Islands, and in 1989, Hurricane Hugo, the worst in a century, carved a swathe through Guadeloupe and then handsomely trashed Montserrat and St Croix. 1995 was also a bad year, with Hurricanes Luis and Marilyn arriving within a week of each other and flattening several islands in the northeastern Caribbean. Luis destroyed 1,200 yachts and ships in Sint Maarten and a whole lot of hotels besides; paint-stripped every building in Anguilla; and washed away Sandy Island. Hard on its heels came Marilyn, which caused most damage in the US Virgin Islands and dumped fearsome amounts of rain. St Croix got off lightly this time, but in St Thomas and St John a quarter of the houses were destroyed. In 1999 Hurricane Lenny caused a completely different sort of damage, sending out huge swells which trashed the beaches (literally emptying them of sand) from the Bahamas to Bonaire. Most recently, Hurricane Ivan (September 2004) laid waste to Grenada and the Cayman Islands, while Hurricane Dennis (July 2005) caused damage in Haiti and Cuba.

Eating Out

For information about the kind of local food and drink that is on offer throughout the Caribbean, *see* **Food and Drink**, pp.27–32.

It is not usually necessary to make a **reservation** in Caribbean restaurants, except at the most popular ones during the high season. Under the 'Eating Out' sections in this book, restaurants are divided into three **price categories** based on the usual price of a main course (*see* below). As some islands are generally more expensive than others, the pricing of these categories will vary a little according to the island. Steak, shrimp and lobster tend to be about 30% more expensive than the standard fish or chicken dishes and so they are not included within the categories cited here. Eating out in the Caribbean is not cheap, and you can expect service and government tax or recently VAT to be charged on top.

> ### Restaurant Price Categories
>
> | Category | Price Range (US$) |
> |---|---|
> | *Expensive* | 20 and above |
> | *Moderate* | 10–20 |
> | *Inexpensive* | under 10 |

Electricity

In most Caribbean islands the electrical supply is 110 or 120 volts at 60 cycles, and so American electrical appliances need no adaptor (British and French visitors will need to take one with them). The French islands work to 220 volts and the Dutch islands at 110. The British islands are mixed; those that have developed more recently tend to be on the American standard (BVI and Anguilla), but some of the British Caribbean islands have a 230 or 240 volt supply at 50 cycles per second. Even then, some individual hotels work on the American system, so it may be worth checking before you go. If the hotel rooms are not fitted with electrical appliances, ask at the front desk, as they may keep some stashed away.

Festivals

The biggest festivals in the Caribbean are the various carnivals. These are usually held just before Lent, on Dimanche, Lundi and Mardi Gras (and in some islands continuing onto Mercredi des Cendres or Ash Wednesday), but are sometimes staged in the summer at the end of the sugar harvest, usually in late July or early August (called *Cropover* in Barbados and the *zafra* in Cuba). The summer months are a popular time of year for festivities anyway (the West Indians think the weather is warmer then): there are many official celebrations and general blowouts in the British islands (around Emancipation Day, 1 August) and religious festivals in the Catholic islands (the *fiestas patronales* of Martinique and Guadeloupe, Puerto Rico, the Dominican Republic and Haiti). Many islands have slightly more formal events commemorating Independence days and National Memorials (even military parades in some islands).

As you would expect in the Caribbean there are many other less formal get-togethers (some them cannily staged at the low point in the season in order to increase numbers of tourists) and these are centred around music – calypso, steel pan, merengue, reggae and most recently jazz – and around sports, particularly based around the sea, with local and open sailing regattas and fishing competitions and latterly a few more conventional events: tennis and golf competitions sponsored by big international companies, and some triathlons and some cycling competitions. Finally, there are some island cultural events, from dance in Jamaica and story-telling in St Lucia and Dominica to Indian festivals in Trinidad and gastronomic blowouts in the French islands.

Whatever the official reason for the celebration, almost all Caribbean festivals are also an excuse for an organized party and so they invariably involve a jump-up (more Caribbean dancing) which will spontaneously appear in the streets or in a field or on the beach. It is often a bit like an oversized picnic, with cook-ups on the sidelines, where a half oil-barrel is turned on its side to make a brazier. Here chicken and fish are barbecued and then sprinkled with hot pepper sauce and soldier crabs are roasted in their shells.

The summer months are the best if you want to see the West Indians at play: there are a number of festivals in June, July and August. Things also get booked up around then. Generally speaking you will have no problem joining in the festivities in any Caribbean event: you will find that the islanders make you welcome. (*See* pp.47–50 for a full Calendar of Events throughout the year.)

Health

In the 18th century if you were caught in a cholera epidemic you could have looked forward to a tonic of diluted sulphuric acid and tincture of cardamom or ammoniated tincture of opium as treatment. There are references to 'this fatal climate' on gravestones and memorials throughout the Caribbean. Today, however, the Caribbean is basically a pretty healthy place.

You should check that your polio and tetanus inoculations are up to date and you may wish to have yourself immunized or take precautions against the following diseases. **Malaria** is sometimes a problem in Haiti and very occasionally in the backwoods of the Dominican Republic, so you are advised to take preventative medicines when visiting those countries – the course usually begins a week before you arrive and continues for four weeks after you leave the area. **Hepatitis**

occurs rarely: you can have an injection giving some cover against Hepatitis A, which is caught mainly from water and food. **Dengue fever** has occurred from time to time in the larger islands. There has been some incidence of **cholera** in South America over the last few years, but the threat to the islands seems to have receded. If you are travelling to the less-developed islands and wish to take sterile needles (and possibly plasma), make sure they are packed up to look official otherwise customs might begin to wonder.

There is quite a high incidence of venereal diseases around the Caribbean, including **HIV**, which according to some may have started in Haiti (there is little evidence that this is true, though it is prevalent there). The risks from casual sex are obvious.

Warnings

Sunburn can ruin your holiday in as little as a quarter of an hour, so it is worth being careful for the first few days. You are recommended to keep to short stints of about 15–20 minutes in the hottest part of the day (11am–3pm). Be particularly careful if you go snorkelling, because the sun and the cooling water together are lethal. Take care all day if you are sailing: the reflection off the sea and the white decks and sails are a fearsome combination. Take sunglasses, high-protection-factor sun cream or total block. Sunhats are easily found. Traditional West Indian methods of soothing sunburn include the application of juice of aloe, a fleshy cactus-like plant, which is used a lot in cosmetics anyway. Break a leaf and squeeze out the soothing juice. After-sunburn treatments include calamine lotion. Also, if you will be spending most of your time in and out of the water, you might take some talcum powder for your feet.

There are not many poisonous things around the Caribbean, but you may well come across the **manchineel tree**, which often grows on the beach. These are tall, bushy trees with a fruit like a small apple, known by Columbus's men as the apple of death (*manzana* means apple in Spanish). Do not eat them! Steer clear of the tree itself too, as the sap is poisonous. You should not even shelter under them in the rain because the sap will blister your skin. A palm tree may seem the ideal place to shade yourself in the height of the sun, but beware: people have been killed by falling **coconuts**.

Mosquitoes are a plague, though many tourist areas are treated to get rid of them. They can cause dengue fever (in the Greater Antilles) and malaria (in Hispaniola only). Most of all, they are irritating at night and if you're awake you'll hear them dive-bombing with a high-pitched squeak. Burn mosquito coils. Some hotels have mosquito nets for cosmetic reasons (they look pretty), but they may also help. Off the beaten track you might consider taking one. There are many insect repellents.

Less potentially harmful, but equally irritating, are the tiny invisible **sand-flies** which plague certain beaches after rain and towards the end of the afternoon. For a barely visible insect, they pack a big bite. There are one or two poisonous **centipedes** and only certain islands have poisonous **snakes** (or snakes at all for that matter).

Swimming holds very few dangers in the Caribbean, though among the reefs and rocks you should look out for **fire coral** and spiny **sea urchins** (little black balls with spines up to 6 inches long radiating in all directions). If you step on one, the spines break off, and give you a very unpleasant and possibly infected injury. **Sharks** are occasionally spotted in Caribbean waters by divers, but they have hardly ever been known to attack humans. Swimming is generally safe on most recognized beaches, but be careful on the Atlantic coasts where there is often an **undertow**.

Water

The water in most islands in the Caribbean is drinkable from the tap, but to be safe, particularly in the larger islands, you might want to drink the water served by the hotel to begin with. However, in Haiti and the Dominican Republic you should definitely only drink bottled water. Do not drink iced drinks off the street in these two countries, because the ice will not have been made with purified water. Get a soft drink or a coconut instead.

There is a shortage of water in many of the flatter islands, and so, even in expensive hotels, you may find that nothing comes out when you turn on the tap. You are always asked to conserve water where possible.

Insurance

You may find that insurance is included in your holiday package. If you are travelling independently, you should make sure that you're covered. Read the small print. A good policy should give full cover for your health: medical costs, hospital benefits, permanent disabilities and the flight home. There is usually a 24-hour contact number in the event of medical emergencies. The policy should also cover your possessions: in case of loss or theft, it should recompense you for lost luggage, money and valuables. Finally, most policies will cover you for travel delay and, most importantly, personal liability. You may find that certain sports, most notably scuba diving, are excluded from general policies, so you will have to arrange special cover on top.

If your own bank or insurance company doesn't have an adequate travel insurance scheme (they usually do), try the comprehensive schemes offered by **Trailfinders, t** (020) 7938 3939, or the 'Centurion Assistance' policy offered by **American Express, t** 0845 602 1108. Tour operators often include insurance in the cost of a luxury tour, but this does not always provide adequate cover.

Should anything be stolen, a copy of the police report should be retained. It will be required by your insurance company when making a claim.

Language

English is spoken in the tourist industry in most Caribbean countries, partly because many of the islands have a former colonial connection with Britain and partly because of the large number of American visitors. Most islands also have a local patois, an everyday language based on the original official colonial language (usually mixed with African words), but these are often incomprehensible to the foreign visitor.

English is the official language of all the British Commonwealth Caribbean countries and some others: Barbados, Trinidad and Tobago, the Windward Islands (Grenada, St Vincent and the Grenadines, St Lucia, Dominica), the Leeward Islands (Antigua, Montserrat, St Kitts and Nevis and Anguilla), the British and United States Virgin Islands, Jamaica, the Cayman Islands, the Turks and Caicos and the Bahamas. It is also widely spoken in Puerto Rico.

French is the official language of the French Antilles (Martinique, Guadeloupe, St Martin and St Barts), but English is often spoken in the hotels. French is also the official language of Haiti, though few people speak it outside the main towns because they talk *kreyol*. English is spoken in Haiti's bigger hotels.

Dutch is the official language of the Netherlands Antilles and Aruba, but you will find Papiamento is spoken in the Dutch Leeward Islands (ABC Islands), while English is traditionally the language of the Dutch Windward Islands.

Spanish is the language of Puerto Rico, the Dominican Republic and Cuba. English is widely spoken in Puerto Rico because of the American connection, but few people speak it outside the hotels in Cuba or the Dominican Republic. If you plan to go off the beaten track here, it is well worth learning some Spanish.

Living and Working in the Caribbean

Like sailing around the world, setting up in the Caribbean is a lifetime's dream for some. Beware! Things are not necessarily what they seem during a short visit. Battling with bureaucracy and local prejudices is a perennial problem, and island inertia can get people down, too. It may be best to rent for six months or so to learn the ropes and see if you like the way of life before you put money in.

Having said that, many people do adapt to the West Indies and certain islands do encourage investment. Buying rights vary from island to island, but most require that if you buy a plot of land you must build within a certain period, and often that you employ a local person. Details are available from the individual high commissions and embassies.

Working in the Caribbean is also not as easy as it might seem because most islands impose strict quotas of foreign workers on businesses, ensuring that the work remains for the islanders. Casual work is almost impossible to find. If you are lucky, you might find some work in the bars on islands where there is a large expatriate community or on islands with a large sailing contingent, where crews are sometimes needed. Americans have equal employment rights in Puerto Rico and the Virgin Islands, of course, and EU members can work (officially, at least) in the French islands, but the British have no special rights in the few remaining British Crown colonies.

Maps and Publications

There are just a few general Caribbean maps and they are available from any good bookstore or map store. Really detailed maps of individual islands are not generally available (either on the islands or at home). You might find them at a map specialist, but they are not really needed on the island unless you are going walking in remote areas. In most places it will be enough to get a photocopied map at the tourist offices. Some islands produce copies of ancient colonial maps and these can make nice souvenirs.

Most islands have their own newspaper; these tend to be published daily in the larger islands (islands such as Jamaica and Trinidad have a broadsheet and some tabloids) and perhaps two or three times a week in the smaller ones. Many American papers and magazines are on sale (usually a day or so late), but not so many papers make it over from Europe. There are only a couple of pan-Caribbean papers, including *Caribbean Week* and a sailing magazine for the Eastern Caribbean called *Compass*. The BWIA inflight magazine, *Caribbean Beat*, covers Caribbean-wide affairs.

Money

Generally speaking, the Caribbean is pretty expensive. To begin with, the flights are often expensive and if you stay on the tourist circuit you will find yourself paying prices not unlike those in Europe or the USA. However, if you get off the tourist track, stay in local West Indian guest houses in the towns and eat local food, it is possible to live more cheaply in most islands. All the same, do not expect to stay anywhere for much less than US$50.

A few Caribbean countries have their own currency, but many of the smaller islands share a denomination, often according to their colonial past. The US dollar, which is the official currency in some islands, is in universal demand throughout the Caribbean and at the moment it is permitted to circulate more or less freely in all the islands. Many countries have pegged their currency to it and so there is not much of a black market. Banking hours vary, but there are ATM machines available in nearly every island. Prices in the tourist industry almost throughout the Caribbean are quoted in or fixed to US dollars. However, if you go off the main tourist routes, it is a good idea to have local notes and change. It is also sensible to take small denominations.

From a Caribbean perspective, tourism is about getting money into the country, so you will have to contend with a plethora of taxes. In hotels there is usually a government room tax, which varies from 5% to 10% (along with service at 10% or even 15% this can mean that your bill is supplemented by a fifth or even a quarter when you come to pay, which is worth bearing in mind). In restaurants there is usually a government tax in addition. Service charges are an accepted system around most of the islands (except the French Caribbean, where, as in France, *service* is *inclus*). Usually it is charged at 10%, unless otherwise indicated. In the shops a sales tax is sometimes charged on top, but it is usually included in the price. Less visibly, many islands do not actually have a system of income tax and the burden is passed to the consumers in the form of sales taxes.

On a less formal scale, hustling is fairly widespread in the Caribbean. All visitors are presumed to have a few dollars that they would not mind releasing (they could afford the air fare after all) and some islands have a band of opportunists who will try to persuade you to do so in return for a variety of services. You are vulnerable particularly in the first 48 hours or until you have a bit of colour. The hustle factor varies from island to island. A firm and polite 'no' to whatever is offered is the easiest way to guarantee your peace.

Official Currencies

Before you set off, you will only need to check the exchange rates for those countries whose currencies float on the international exchange.

Barbados: Barbados dollar, fixed to US dollar (US$1 = BDs$1.98); US currency accepted in many places.

Trinidad and Tobago: Trinidad and Tobago dollar, fluctuates on the open exchange (presently US$1 = TT$6 approx.); US currency accepted.

Windward Islands and **Leeward Islands** (the former British islands of Grenada, St Vincent and the Grenadines, St Lucia, Dominica, Antigua and Barbuda, St Kitts and Nevis and the Crown Colonies of Montserrat and Anguilla): the Eastern Caribbean dollar, fixed to the US dollar (US$1 = EC$2.65); US currency accepted.

French Caribbean (French Antilles: Martinique, Guadeloupe, St Martin, St Barthélemy): euro (US$1 = €0.80 approx.); US dollar accepted in tourist areas.

Dutch Caribbean (Netherlands Antilles: Sint Maarten, Saba, Statia, Curaçao and Bonaire): Netherlands Antillean florin or guilder (US$1 = NAFl1.78); US dollar freely accepted.

Aruba: Aruban florin, fixed to the US dollar (US$1 = AFl1.77); US dollar freely accepted.

British and **US Virgin Islands**: Official currency is the US dollar.

Puerto Rico: US dollar.

Dominican Republic: Dominican peso (US$1 = RD$30 approx.), floats on the international exchange; US dollars are accepted in all tourist areas.

Haiti: Haitian dollar, officially made up of 5 gourdes and officially trades as US$1 = H$1, but in practice US$1 = 17–20 gourdes. US dollars are accepted by tourist hotels and under the counter by many businesses.

Cuba: Cuban peso, fixed artificially to the US dollar in tourist areas (US$1 = Cuban $1). There is a black market, with the US$ trading at Cuban $20 approx.

Jamaica: Jamaican dollar (US$1 = J$65 approx.), floats on the open market; US dollars are accepted in tourist areas.

Cayman Islands: Cayman Islands dollar, fixed to the US dollar (US$1 = 80 Cayman cents or CI$1 = US$1.25).

Bahamas: Bahamian dollar, fixed at par to US dollar, which is freely accepted.

Turks and Caicos Islands: US dollar is the official currency.

Exchange

The banks offer the best rate of exchange. At hotels you usually receive a lower rate. The exchanges in most islands will accept hard currency **traveller's cheques**: pound sterling, euro and Canadian dollar; but the US dollar is the most popular, particularly if you are going to a country where the dollar is an acceptable alternative currency. You will also get a better rate of exchange. Some banks charge for the exchange of traveller's cheques, however. Generally, banking is quite sophisticated in most islands, but service is often slow.

Credit cards are widely accepted for anything that is connected with the tourist industry: in hotels, restaurants and tourist shops. If you need to, you can draw cash on a credit card at the bank: there are Amex and Visa representatives on all the islands. **Personal cheques** are rarely accepted.

Packing

The pleasant weather and an informal air in the Caribbean means you can take a minimalist approach to packing. In the whole area, only a couple of restaurants require even a jacket and a tie for men (though most do like trousers and a shirt with a collar). For women, daytime wear is a skirt or shorts and a light shirt; evening wear is much the same, perhaps a longer skirt or trousers. Jeans are too hot in the summer. Also pack a sunhat, sunglasses, sun cream and a swimsuit (though they can be bought on arrival).

Photography

You will find that many West Indians either dive for cover or start remonstrating violently at the very sight of a camera. Some will talk about you stealing their soul and others about the money you will have to pay. If you see a good shot and go for it, you can usually talk your way out of trouble, but if you stop and chat first then most people will allow you to photograph them.

In the middle of the day, the brightness of the Caribbean sun bleaches all colour out of the landscape except the strongest tropical shades, but as the afternoon draws in you will find a stunning depth of colour in the reds, golds and greens. The plants of the Caribbean are colourful and particularly good after rain.

Film is generally expensive in the islands and the heat can be a problem too (you might want to keep it in the hotel fridge).

Post Offices

Post can take anything from 2 days to 3 months to get from the Caribbean to Europe or North America. Don't rely on it. You will probably have no need to go anywhere near a post office anyway because hotels usually have postcards and stamps and once you have written them they are happy to post them for you. Post office opening hours vary from island to island.

Shopping

Shopping is one of the Caribbean's biggest industries, but hardly any of the things that are sold here originate in the area. There are objects of cultural value to be found, particularly in the larger islands, but most of it is shipped in to satisfy the collector passions of long-distance shoppers (some of whom actually go on the same cruise year after year to take advantage of preferential customs allowances).

The islands follow roughly speaking the historical patterns of their nation, with the French the leaders in perfumes and designer clothes, and the Dutch, always great traders, with well-priced photographic equipment from the Far East. St Thomas, a traditional and particularly attractive port in the US Virgin Islands, where almost anything is on sale, is in danger of becoming one outsize emporium. The lure is, of course, the reduced prices (in comparison to the mainland) and every shop announces itself as 'duty-free' or 'in-bond'. The best duty-free shopping-centre islands in the Caribbean (some of which have been trading like this for hundreds of years) are Sint Maarten, St Thomas in the USVI, and Nassau and Freeport in the Bahamas. If you are after more elegant clothes and accessories, then St Barts is probably your best bet.

There is quite an active art scene now in many of the islands: galleries exhibiting work by local and expatriate artists are mentioned in the text. There are occasionally things of interest in the craft markets, but particularly on the bigger islands – Jamaica, Haiti and the Dominican Republic – you will find some highly original work. Best known is the *naïve* art from Haiti.

Sports and Activities

Deep-sea Fishing

A sport traditionally renowned in the Gulf Stream (between Key West and Havana, and between Florida and the Bahamas), but now possible throughout the Caribbean, is deep-sea or big-game fishing. Docked at the yachting marina, the deep-sea boats are huge, gleaming cruisers, slightly top-heavy because of their tall spotting towers, usually equipped with tackle and bait and 'fighting chair'. Beer in hand, you trawl the line behind the boat, waiting for a bite, and then watch the beast surface and fight as you cruise along, giving line and steadily hauling it in.

The magnificent creatures that you are out to kill are some of the largest fish in the world, including the blue marlin, which inhabits the deepest waters and can weigh up to 1100lb and measure 10ft in length. Giant or bluefin tuna can weigh up to 1000lb. Wahoo, around 100lb, is a racer and a fighter and the white marlin can weigh up to 150lb. Perhaps the most beautiful of all is the sailfish, with a spiny fan on its back, which will jump out of the water and 'tail' (literally stand upright on its tail) in its attempts to get free. Among the smaller fish you'll find blackfin and allison tuna, bonito, dorado and barracuda.

The best known areas are the ports off the Gulf Stream, on Bimini, and traditionally around Havana (though things are quieter there now), but you can easily charter a boat from the north coast of Jamaica and from Puerto Rico and the Virgin Islands (there are deep waters offshore). The most famous story about fishing is Ernest Hemingway's *The Old Man and The Sea*, which is set in a small fishing village east of Havana.

Bonefishing takes place in sandy-bottomed shallows not far from the shore, particularly in the Bahamas, but also in some other Caribbean areas. Pound for pound, bonefish are said to be the best fighters of all fish.

Sailing

For many people a **sailing trip** is the most memorable day of a Caribbean holiday. On most islands, there is a marina where you can find a crewed yacht. They are usually quite well publicized, but be careful as they can vary very much in style, from a day's full-on sailing on a racing yacht to a crowded, rum-soaked booze cruise. Lunch is usually included in the price and there may well be an open bar. They seek out coves and isolated beaches where you can have a picnic. The volcanic islands are particularly good for this, because as you sail along the coast, you see the vast and fertile landscape move gradually above you, but there are many popular sailing areas in the Caribbean and the Bahamas. Tried and trusted sites are the Grenadine Islands between St Vincent and Grenada, Antigua, the British Virgin Islands (centred around Sir Francis Drake Passage) and many of the Out Islands in the Bahamas. For sailing holidays *see* **Travel**, 'Tour Operators', pp.40–1, and sections under the Virgin Islands, the Grenadines, Sint Maarten and Guadeloupe.

Scuba Diving

The Caribbean and the Bahamas have some superb corals and fish, probably the best in the Western hemisphere. The variety is stunning, from the world's third-largest barrier reef just a few miles off the coast of Andros in the Bahamas, to the colourful seascapes of Bonaire and the Caymans, to warm water springs and bubble outlets under the sea off the volcanic islands.

The reefs are incredibly colourful. You will see yellow and pink tube sponges and purple trumpet sponges, sea feathers and sea fans (gorgonians) that stand against the current alongside a forest of staghorn, elkhorn and black coral and the more exotic species, such as the domes of startlingly white brain coral, star corals and yellow pencil coral. Near the surface the corals are multicoloured and tightly bunched as they compete for space; as you descend, the yellows and the reds and whites fade, leaving the purples and blues of the larger corals that catch the last of the sunlight at depth.

Many islands have laws to protect their reefs and their fish (there are hardly any places left in the Caribbean where you are allowed to use spear guns) and this is more or less successful. In certain islands you are asked not to buy coral jewellery because it will probably have been taken illegally from the reef. One of the few dangerous things on the reef are fire corals, which will give you a nasty sting if you touch one.

Other underwater life includes a stunning array of crustaceans and, of course, tropical fish. On the bottom you will find beautifully camouflaged crabs that stare at you, goggle-eyes out on stalks, starfish, lobsters, sea anemones and pretty, pink and white feather-duster worms. Around them swim angelfish, squirrelfish, surgeonfish, striped sergeant majors, grunts and soldierfish. Above them little shoals of wrasses and blue tang shimmy in the bubbles. If you get too close, puffer fish blow themselves up like a spiky football, smiling uncomfortably. And beware the poisonous stonefish. If you hear of lobsters migrating (as many as a hundred following one another in a line across the sea bed), then do make sure you go out and have a look.

At night a whole new seascape opens up as some corals close up for the night and others open up in an array of different colours. While some fish tuck themselves into a crevice in the reef to sleep (eyes kept open, or in a sort of sleeping-bag of mucus so that they cannot be detected by their scent), starfish, lobsters and sea urchins scuttle around the seabed on the hunt for food. Stop breathing for a moment, and you will hear the midnight parrotfish crunching on the coral polyps, spitting out the broken-down fragments of reef that eventually turn into sand.

The best islands for diving in the Caribbean are Bonaire off the coast of South America (for its slopes with excellent and colourful corals), the Cayman Islands (noted for their sheer walls), some of the remoter Bahamas and particularly the Turks and Caicos Islands. There are also a number of live-aboard dive boats based around the Bahamas and the Cayman Islands. Other islands with good reputations are Saba and Dominica. In the Bahamas shark diving has become a big thing in recent years.

Most dive-shops in the Caribbean are affiliated to PADI (many also to NAUI) and they will expect you to present a certificate of competence if you wish to go out on to the reefs straight away. All but the smallest dive-shops have lessons available in the resorts if you are a novice. An open-water qualifying course (which allows you to dive in a pair with another qualified open-water diver) takes about a week, but with a resort course you can usually get underwater in a morning. You will have a session in the swimming pool before you are allowed to dive with an instructor in the open sea. It is often possible to do 'referral' dives, in which you complete the open-water section of a diving course in the Caribbean after you have completed the classroom and swimming-pool parts of the course at home. For general information about scuba diving you can try www.3routes.com and www.scubasports.com.

The **snorkelling** is also good off many of the islands and most hotels have equipment. Take care if you go snorkelling on a sunny day soon after you arrive, as the water and the sun are a lethal combination on unprotected skin. In most places you can arrange glass-bottom boat tours and snorkelling trips. For those who would like to see the deeper corals, but who do not dive, there are submarines in Barbados, St Thomas in the USVI, Grand Cayman, the Bahamas, St Barts, St Martin, Montego Bay, Jamaica and Aruba.

Windsurfing and Kiteboarding

Because of the warmth and the constant winds off the Atlantic Ocean, the Caribbean offers superb **windsurfing**, particularly when the winds are at their highest in the early months of the year. The sport is well developed – several championship competitions have been held in the Caribbean – and you can hire a board on any island. Instruction is usually available. The best places to go are Aruba, the southern coast of Barbados, the north coast of the Dominican Republic (Cabarete) and the windward coasts of the French islands, where the sport is very popular.

Kiteboarding (surfboard plus kite, also known as 'kitesurfing') is hot in Antigua and is catching on fast elsewhere in the Caribbean.

Miscellaneous Watersports

On the smaller islands there is usually at least one beach where you will find all the watersports: anything from a windsurfer and a few minutes on waterskis to a parasail flight, a trip on a pedalo or a high-speed trip around the bay on an inflated sausage (it'll keep the kids quiet anyway). Glass-bottom boat tours are usually available and in most hotels you are able to hire small sailboats such as hobie cats and sunfish. Jetskis (standing up) and wetbikes (sitting) have made their mark in the West Indies and are available for hire at most major centres (though some islands have banned them) as are kayaks, which are fun on waves and good for reaching the more remote snorkelling areas around a rocky coastline. Prices vary considerably across the Caribbean. Most activities can be booked through the hotels or their beach concessionaires. There is not really that much beach culture in the Caribbean islands, but there are some beach bars where you can hang out. Rum cruises and sunset tours aboard a resurrected galleon complete with boozatorium and lots of walking the plank are available on the larger and more tourist-oriented islands.

The mountainous islands of the Caribbean literally create rain as the water-filled Atlantic winds race over them. Their rivers are worthy of continents and all over the islands you will find waterfalls and rock pools that make for excellent **river bathing**. Bilharzia is a problem on some islands (in lakes and slow-flowing rivers) so you are advised to take official advice before swimming there. In Jamaica, where there is good river bathing, you can also take a **rafting** trip on the larger rivers; quite expensive, but good fun (*see* pp.715–6).

Other Sports

Sports based on land include **tennis**, which is well served all over the Caribbean. There are courts in many of the hotels and island clubs. Occasional pro-am competitions are held. If there is no court at your hotel, arrange with another through the front desk, or wander in and ask. Hotels usually charge a small fee and generally have rackets and balls for hire.

Horse-riding is offered on the majority of the islands and this is a good way to see the rainforest and the sugar flats if you think that your calves might not be up to the hike. In Jamaica and the Dominican Republic you can even get a game of polo.

Golf courses are widespread in the Caribbean. They are usually open to visitors if they pay a green fee (which is often extremely steep: if it is important to you, do some research first because in some hotels the green fees are included in the package). If you decide to play, be flexible, as the courses will often give priority to hotel guests. Most courses have equipment for hire.

There is good **hiking** in the Caribbean islands, which are cut and crossed with traditional trails originally used by the likes of the *porteuses* (*see* **Martinique**) and the farmers of today. A walk in the rainforest is fascinating because the growth is so incredibly lush. Many of the Eastern Caribbean islands have an active volcano in whose crater you can climb; or you could make the walk to the boiling lake in Dominica's Valley of Desolation.

The heat will be most bearable between dawn (usually at around 6am) and 10am, before the sun gets too high, and then between 4pm and dusk. However, the higher you go, the cooler it gets, and the temperature in the forest is not bad in any case. It gets dark quickly in the Caribbean, so take care to be back by 6pm or you may find yourself stranded, at the mercy of such fearsome spirits of the Caribbean night as the *Soucouyant* and *La Diablesse* (*see* **Trinidad**, p.117). It often rains, of course, so take a waterproof coat; high up in the hills you will also need a jersey underneath because the winds can make it cold. Big, heavy boots are not necessary. Gym shoes or sneakers are usually enough, unless you are headed into very steep and slippery country, when you should have some ankle support: a pair of light, tropical boots would do. Increasingly, you will find guides who are well informed and can tell you all about the flora and fauna.

There are a number of islands with extensive **cave** systems which have been carved out of the limestone rock by the dripping of water. The best caves are in the Greater Antilles, though some have been overdeveloped (with electric buggies, hard hats and probably even piped music by now) and not all are open to the public. For hard-core speleologists, opportunities exist to explore uncharted potholes in the larger islands, where whole rivers disappear underground in the karst limestone. Puerto Rico and Jamaica hold the greatest appeal; both islands have active spelunker clubs that can provide the best information.

Telephones

Communications in the Caribbean are quite good, though they vary greatly from island to island and getting through in some of the less-developed countries can be a bit haphazard. Nowadays, in general, hotel rooms are fitted with direct-dial phones as standard and, if you need one outside, the public phones are quite dependable; there are usually booths at the marinas and in the towns. Many islands have a system of phonecards. The former British islands and remaining British Crown colonies have an extensive network run mainly by Cable and Wireless (with the advantage that a phonecard bought in any country using EC$ can be used all the way along the chain between Grenada and the BVI).

There are no coin phones on the French islands, where you will need a *télécarte*, which is also valid on all other French islands. If you are having trouble placing a call you can always wander into the nearest hotel, where they will help you out for a fee. Like everywhere else there has been a huge growth in mobile phones in recent years and on some islands you can hire one if you need to.

Time

Travelling to the Caribbean from Europe is particularly satisfying. You reach the island in the afternoon, usually in time to take an onward flight or skip down to the beach and watch the sunset and then, because of the extra hours and the long flight, you're fit to drop by the end of an early supper. Going to bed early in a strange bedroom with the sound of the sea outside is usually enough to wake you up early the next morning. Dawn is the best time of the day, being cool and calm. Be sure to get up and walk around so as to make the most of it.

Apart from Club Med enclaves (which have their own time schedule for some reason), the whole of the Eastern Caribbean (Barbados up to the Virgin Islands) and Puerto Rico and the Dominican Republic are 4 hours behind GMT. Haiti, Jamaica, Cuba, the Cayman Islands and the Bahamas work to Eastern Standard Time (5 hours behind GMT). There is no 'Summer Time' in the islands, so the difference will vary around the year according to whether European or North American Summer Time is in effect at the time.

'Caribbean Time', on the other hand, is an expression you will come across all over the islands. It refers to the West Indians' elastic and entirely unpredictable schedules. Businesses can be punctual, but in restaurants and shops they will have little sympathy with a slave to the second hand. The Jamaicans say 'soon come'; this can mean any time from now to tomorrow.

Tourist Information

The Caribbean tourist industry generates a huge volume of paper, from sleek, advertising-driven glossies found in hotel rooms down to humble leaflets left at strategic points for yachties and other passers-by. There is almost always a tourist information office at the airport, and they are happy to help out with accommodation, maps, directions and pertinent local advice and gossip. There is usually an information office in the main town and on larger islands there will also be tourist offices in the major tourist spots. For those who want more detail, there is usually an information department in the Department of Tourism itself. Opening hours vary across the islands; as a rule they follow the island's business hours, with respect for local traditions (such as a two-hour lunch break in some places). If you cannot find a tourist office, don't be reticent about asking for information or directions from a West Indian, as they will almost always go out of their way to help you.

All the Caribbean islands publish some sort of tourism magazine to help with orientation when you arrive on the island. These usually include lists of accommodation, restaurants and shops (generally listed even-handed without selection or recommendation) and some feature articles, as well as general advice about how not to get sunburned. Recommendations for watersports and tours tend to be advertising-driven in magazines such as these, so if you have a specific requirement (e.g. for a trained guide who can take you hiking in the rainforest) ring up and chat with the tourist board. Interpretation boards are sometimes in evidence at 'sights' of local interest and if you visit a local museum there is usually printed material on sale.

Where to Stay

The Caribbean has some of the finest and most luxurious hotels in the world. You can stay at island resorts so remote and quiet that you communicate by flag, on endless beaches which are deserted at dawn, in 18th-century plantation splendour with a view across the canefields, and in high-pastel luxury in the Caribbean's newest resorts. And then there are suites and cottages rather than rooms and even villas and villa resorts; there are specialist eco-resorts, scuba resorts and a few hotels that specialize in children. Many of the islands offer top-notch hotels, but try the Grenadines and the Virgin Islands for isolated island settings, Barbados for grand, long-established hotels set in magnificent gardens, St Kitts and Nevis for plantation-estate elegance, St Barts for chic and luxury, Anguilla for distinctive style and sumptuous, small-island charm, and Jamaica for reliable luxury.

When you reach the Caribbean, it is easy to imagine that you have arrived in some remote corner of paradise, but these hotels are businesses and they operate under quite difficult circumstances. To get an idea of what goes on behind the scenes, be sure to read Herman Wouk's *Don't Stop the Carnival!*, still killingly accurate despite being 40 years old. It is hard to look a hotelier in the eye after reading it.

The newest Caribbean hotels tend to be large, humming palaces with blocks of rooms decorated in a symphony of bright pastel colours set against white tile floors: the regimented dreams of international hotel corporations. However, there is a grand variety of places to stay in the Caribbean, and the classic Caribbean setting, a private beachfront cabin with a personal hammock hanging between two nearby palm trees, can be found all over the area.

Choosing Where to Stay

If you arrange your trip through a tour operator, you are likely to select your holiday on the basis of the hotel, perhaps because of its reputation, or because of a deal on offer through the tour operator. It is worth asking around and listening to what others say about it. Hotels are selected for this book on grounds of value (within their price category; *see* box, below), but also for other reasons such as their setting, quality of service, friendliness and general management. Many of the big names in Caribbean hotels are featured, but smaller, more offbeat places are included, too.

Note: Unless otherwise stated, all prices quoted in this book are for a double room in the peak winter season (without a meal plan). In almost every Caribbean island the hotels will add an obligatory government tax (usually between 7% and 10%) and a service charge, usually 10% but occasionally 15%.

Seasons

The Caribbean high season is traditionally mid-January until mid-April, with a small peak just before this at Christmas and New Year, when prices are at their highest. 'Off-season' travel will bring reductions of as much as 30% in some cases, making some of the idyllic places suddenly affordable. One problem with the Caribbean is that holidays invariably seem to revolve around the couple and so single travellers will often find themselves paying the same as a couple for a room. You can try bargaining, but it is unlikely to do any good.

All-inclusive Hotels

The all-inclusive hotel plan has become increasingly popular in recent years and has spread to most Caribbean islands now. As the name implies, once you have paid the initial bill you do not have to pull out your wallet again. It is easier to budget of course and to a large extent it is the solution for people who want nothing more than a beach and barely care what country they are in, but it has had the effect of discouraging people from leaving

Hotel Price Categories

Category	Price (US$) per room
Luxury	500 and above
Very Expensive	300–500
Expensive	150–300
Moderate	80–150
Inexpensive	under 80

Villa Operators

Many of the specialist tour operators have villa programmes, but there are also some villa specialists.

In the UK

Caribbean Chapters (via **Abercrombie & Kent**), St George's House, Ambrose Street, Cheltenham GL50 3LG, **t** 0845 070 0610, *www.akchapters.com*; USA **t** 1 866 493 8340, *www.villa-rentals.com*. Beautiful villas on the islands of St Barthélemy, St Martin, Anguilla, Nevis, the Virgin Islands of St Thomas, St John, St Croix, Tortola and Virgin Gorda, the Cayman Islands, Mustique, Bequia, Barbados, Jamaica, St Lucia, Grenada, Tobago, the Dominican Republic, the Turks and Caicos and Bahamas. At most properties maid service is included and at many the services of a cook.

The Owners' Syndicate, 6 Port House, Plantation Wharf, London SW11 3TY, **t** (020) 7801 9801, *caribbean@owners syndicate.com*, *www.ownerssyndicate.com*. Probably offers the largest selection of villas throughout the islands, at a range of different prices.

Villa Connections, 27 Park Lane, Poynton, Cheshire SK12 1RD, **t** (01625) 858 158, *info@villa-connect.com*, *www.villa connections.co.uk*. Offers villas in all the main Caribbean islands.

In the USA

French Caribbean International, 5662 Calle Real, Suite 333, Santa Barbara, CA 93117–2317, **t** (805) 967 9850, **t** 1 800 322 2223, *fci@frenchcaribbean.com*, *www.french caribbean.com*. Specialists in the French Caribbean islands, as the name suggests, who will arrange accommodation in hotels and villas, but not usually flights.

Wimco, 28 Pelham St, Newport, Rhode Island RI 02840, **t** (401) 849 8012, USA **t** 1 800 932 3222, *info@wimco.com*, *www.wimco.com*. At the top end of the range, with a selection of villas in St Barts, Barbados, Mustique, Anguilla, St Martin, Nevis, Saba, the Caymans, Turks and Caicos.

the hotel and exploring, and going out to try the restaurants for dinner (which in turn means that in some islands there are very few good restaurants left). There is now quite a wide variety of standards and prices within the all-inclusives and some are quite upmarket, offering on-tap champagne and à la carte dining. Jamaica, Antigua, St Lucia and increasingly Barbados have the most all-inclusive hotels, and the Sandals chain has many resorts throughout the Caribbean; there are also all-inclusives that specialize in looking after children. Originally the concept was a Caribbean version of Club Med, with an ongoing, permanent diet of sports and entertainment for those who wanted it. This has recently altered in some cases, with certain hotels offering a straight all-inclusive plan (all meals and drinks paid for) and fewer of the activities. It is worth checking which facilities are included in the package.

There is still a holiday-camp atmosphere about some all-inclusives, however, and their names often give a good indication of their theme: for example, Hedonism II or Couples (with the symbol of a pair of lions humping).

These high-pressure fun factories seem to encourage riotous behaviour, with as much alcohol as you can drink, dancing on the tables, mirrors on the bedroom ceiling and crash courses in marriage. They are well worth a look, if only for a day or two, after which you might feel like immersing yourself in a book.

Inns

Dotted sporadically around the Caribbean are some magnificent old gingerbread-style homes, often former plantation houses, that have been converted into inns. These are ideal for the independent traveller with a bit of cash, usually offering more personal service than the bigger hotels. Among the best are the *paradores* in Puerto Rico, often family-run, in charming old buildings hidden in the rainforest or the towns, or the inns tucked into the hillsides of Charlotte Amalie on St Thomas.

Some smaller hotels (too small to deal with the large tour operators) have banded together to form the **Carib Inns**, to help them with marketing. For information and bookings, contact: Unique Hotels, UK **t** 0800 373 742. Other, more general tour operators (*see* pp.38–41) often offer the same hotels at a slightly less expensive rate, but they do not usually give the same level of service either before travel (you may be on the phone for a while) or on the island.

Villas, Apartments and Condominiums

In addition to the many hotels there are also **villas** all over the islands, most of them relatively modern and well equipped. You can cater for yourself or arrange for a cook, and the smarter ones will have a pool.

Packages and prices vary according to the villa; some are elegant old plantation houses surrounded by canefields, others swanky new piles with trained chefs and butlers, and yachts to play with. The sky's the limit. Others are small and simple private homes without pretension. As a rule you can expect daily maid-service and for the house to be stocked with food and flowers for your arrival. Most companies offer car hire, but it is worth noting that often you will have to arrange your own flights (*see* pp.35–6). Some companies (BVI Club, Mustique Company and island-based villa operators) specialize in villas in particular islands (for details *see* under separate island sections). Contact them through the individual island villa-rentals organizations (*see* p.63) or the tourist boards.

The Caribbean now copes reasonably well with self-catering or efficiency holidays and so there are a large number of **apartments** on all the islands, some grouped together in one building like a hotel, others scattered in landscaped grounds. Some apartment complexes will have a restaurant or bar and some watersports facilities. Finally, **condominiums** are also springing up in many islands, answering to those who wish to invest in their vacation.

Guest Houses

These are the most economical option and they are more fun, cheaper, and often have far more character than bottom-of-the-range tourist hotels. They are usually presided over by an ample and generous mother figure (something of a West Indian institution, she has not changed much for about 200 years; *see* **Barbados**, 'Where to Stay', p.78) and staying in them can be a good way to be introduced to local West Indian life in just a few

days. You may notice a remarkable turnover of guests, as some guest houses rent rooms out by the hour as well as by the night.

In the major yachting centres you can sometimes persuade the yachties to give you a berth on the charter boats while they are in dock. Just go down to the marina and ask around; you may come up with something.

Camping

Rules vary throughout the islands and although it is generally not encouraged, particularly on the beaches, there are camp sites on the larger islands (the French Antilles and Cuba are quite well organized for camping). As a rule, permission should be obtained from the police before camping, but you will probably get away with it.

Women Travellers

West Indian men are quite macho by nature, so visiting women can expect a fair amount of public attention: matador poses in the Latin islands, or in the British islands the *soots* ('Soups, tss!'), a sort of sharp hiss between the teeth. Advances of this sort are usually laughed off or ignored by local women and visitors can do the same; they are often quite public and loud, but they are not usually persistent and are verbal rather than physical.

There is quite a big thing going on between the local lads and visiting women in the Caribbean. West Indians are quite forthright about sex in any case; even in some surprisingly smart hotels, male staff will make a pass at a single woman, or one whose man simply happens to be absent.

West Indian women are quite modest when it comes to exposing their bodies in public. It is almost unknown – except in the French islands – for a West Indian to go topless on the beach (though they often go naked when washing in the rivers, so be careful when you are out walking). They expect foreigners to observe the same rules. They also expect women to wear more than a swimsuit when out and about or in town, so you might take a cotton wrap.

Barbados

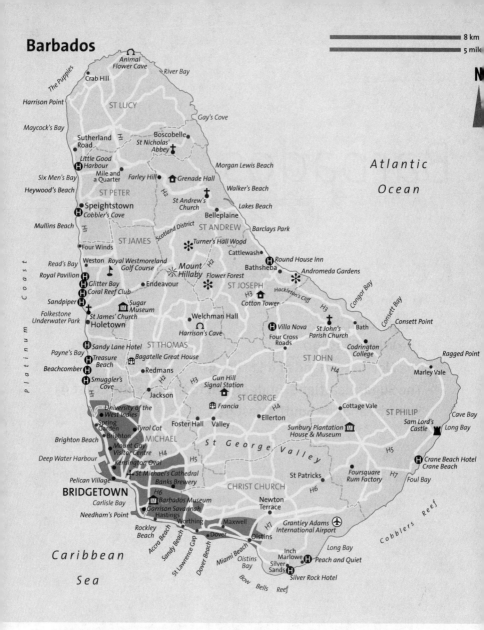

Barbados

8 km
5 mile

N

Highlights

1 Dine on the west-coast cliffs overlooking the moonlit Caribbean Sea
2 Intoxicate yourself on the aroma of fermenting sugar at the Mount Gay Rum
   Distillery in St Lucy
3 Get away from the crowds at the secluded coves cut into the southeast cliffs
4 Visit the acres of tropical plants at Andromeda Gardens on the Atlantic coast

Barbados stands alone, out in the Atlantic, about 100 miles beyond the rest of the Eastern Caribbean, a coral island with extremely fine golden-sand beaches and perhaps the most agreeable climate in the West Indies. The island is long established as a winter getaway and has had a trusty following of wealthy visitors over the last 50 years. Barbados is one of the Caribbean's most popular destinations.

'The whole place has an appearance of cleanliness, gentility and wealth which one does not find in any other island.' So thought Père Labat, a French Dominican monk and roving gastronome who visited Barbados at the height of its prosperity in 1700. The spirit of his opinion still stands in the graciousness and hospitality of the early 21st century. Education, literacy and health care, the social services in general, are the best in the English-speaking Caribbean (with the present exception of the Cayman Islands) and the poor are better off in Barbados than in most of the neighbouring islands. Barbados commands a position of influence out of proportion to its size within the Caribbean. This is the source of the renowned Bajan (native Barbadian) self-esteem, and quite a bit of mockery from other islanders. Altogether, the national motto, 'Pride and Industry', is quite appropriate for the Bajans.

Just 21 miles by 14, Barbados is occasionally dismissed as small, crowded and flat, but away from the built-up areas the cane-covered hinterland rises gently to 1,000ft heights at Hackleton's Cliff above the Atlantic. It is true that the island is populous, though: its 260,000 inhabitants make it the most densely inhabited island in the area. Most Bajans live along the sheltered west coast of the island and in the massive and ever-expanding suburb that runs from the capital, Bridgetown, all along the south coast. Just a few villages are tucked away inland. The Barbadians are over 90% of African descent, but there are small communities of white Bajans, including a visible and influential business community and the 'poor whites', descendants of indentured servants who have scraped a living from the land for centuries. There are not that many Bajans of mixed race and, if the island has a problem, it is the residue of a rigid system of colour prejudice.

Barbados's British heritage, which is stronger than in any other Caribbean island, once led the island to be called 'Little England' and even 'Bimshire'. The British influence is hardly strong now, but the 300-year connection has left a delightful and often old-fashioned charm in the manners, the buildings and even the language (you can hear distinct traces of a West Country accent in Bajan speech). Classically beautiful plantation houses stand in the swathes of sugar cane; cricketers in whites play beneath palm trees; and there is even an isolated area of rugged hills in the northeast familiarly known as Scotland. At times, though, it seems that Little England has managed to inherit some of the worst British foibles: pomposity and cliquish social attitudes. The island's colonial legacy is fading now (since Independence in 1966) as it thrusts on and modernizes. As elsewhere in the Caribbean, the strongest influence now is that of the United States.

With its charming islanders used to visitors and a long-established, broad-based tourism industry, Barbados is rightfully a top Caribbean destination, to which guests return year after year. It is fairly crowded, so if you are looking for beach-bound Caribbean seclusion this is hardly the place to come, but it is easy to have a good holiday here and it is ideal for a first visit to the islands – in whatever price category you choose: interspersed between some of the Caribbean's most expensive hotels there are many much cheaper places to stay. Things have sharpened up recently, with lively bars and a string of excellent restaurants, even gourmet delis with reliable supplies of foie gras and champagne. The famous west coast of Barbados, second home to a crowd of international sophisticates (in the past, people measured their status by whether they arrived on Concorde or by first class), has given it the nickname 'the millionaires' playground'.

History

The history of Barbados is bound inextricably with that of England and with the fortunes of West Indian sugar. In an area where islands changed hands with almost every war, colonial Barbados had 300 years of uninterrupted British rule. It was the first in the Caribbean to exploit sugar successfully, and even today many of the roads are lined each side with curtains of tall green cane.

Best Beaches

Payne's Bay: Popular west-coast beach with hotels, bars and some watersports.

Brighton Beach, Holetown Beach, Paradise Beach and **Treasure Beach**: Other stretches of west-coast sand. Brighton Beach is popular with Bajans at the weekend.

Folkstone: Marine Park area for snorkelling and swimming off Holetown, popular with the locals at the weekend; some facilities.

Mullins Bay: Active beach backed by casuarina pines, with a bistro and some sports.

Heywood's Beach: Just north of Speightstown.

Six Men's Bay and **Maycock's Bay**: Beyond the hotel strip you will find relative seclusion here. Bajans build fishing boats at Six Men's Bay.

Barclays Park, Gay's Cove and **River Bay**: Close to the northern tip of the island.

Bath: Atlantic-coast beach with safe swimming because of an offshore reef, popular with the Bajans on their weekend outings, which involve a cook-up on the beach and general fun and games. There are some simple facilities.

Crane Beach: Just beneath the surreal hotel of the same name, whose facilities you can use (*adm*), a superb stretch of sand, where there is good boogie boarding.

Foul Bay, Harrismith Beach and **Bottom Beach**: Three charming coves (the first named because of its reputation as an anchorage rather than its setting, which is charming) cut into the cliffs, secluded with excellent sand and quite large waves.

Silver Sands Beach: Just short of the airport, one of the liveliest beaches on the island at (windsurfing) competition time. Attracts a crowd of the Barbados body beautiful and a winter influx of nut-brown poseurs and straw-haired surf bums.

Miami Beach: Just beyond Maxwell, backed by casuarina pines.

Dover Beach: The culmination of the beaches at St Lawrence Gap. An active stretch, with some watersports.

Sandy Beach: At Worthing, a huge and gradually expanding stretch of sand, beach bars and hotels.

Accra Beach: Popular south-coast beach in hotel territory – crowds sizzling in lines.

The island was supposedly named by Portuguese visitors who passed by in the 1580s. They called the island Los Barbudos, or the 'bearded ones', after the long, matted and straggly shoots thrown off the upper branches of the banyan trees that grew near the coast. There had been native Amerindian settlements on Barbados – recent archaeological discoveries at the site of a marina development show that they were here as early as 1500 BC – but by the time the Europeans arrived none remained.

Barbados was claimed for England in 1625, and was settled two years later, in an expedition sent by Sir William Courteen. They found the island uninhabited except by some wild boars (left by early visitors as food for shipwrecked mariners). After wrangling and intrigue in the court of King Charles I, with the Earls of Pembroke and Carlisle in dispute over rights of colonization (and after a parallel armed battle on the island itself between the Windward and the Leeward men), the settlement flourished, assisted by a family of 40 Arawaks from Guiana who demonstrated how to cultivate tropical plants such as cotton, tobacco and cassava.

The colony exploded, and within 30 years Barbados was overcrowded. Fortune-hunters flooded in; indentured servants put themselves in servitude for years with a promise of land at the end of their term. Refugees came from the Civil War in England; others were deported by the notorious Judge Jeffreys for their part in the Monmouth Rebellion and sold into slavery. To be 'Barbadosed' was a recognized punishment in 17th-century England.

In an early piece of industrial espionage, the Dutch brought sugar cane to Barbados from Brazil. They taught the Barbadians how yield could be increased by ratooning, in which the cane was planted not sticking out of the ground but laid flat and buried, and they introduced boiling techniques. At first the crop was used only for producing rum, but it soon became clear how profitable sugar was for export to Europe. By the 1650s the whole of Barbados was planted with cane, even to the exclusion of growing provisions – cultivating sugar was so profitable that the Barbadians were happy to pay the price of imported food. Good merchantable muscovado sugar was used as currency for barter, even for the governor's salary. Willoughby Fort in Bridgetown was constructed as a defence against pirates in 1656 at a price of 80,000 pounds of sugar.

Whistler, a soldier, visited Barbados in the 1650s and described the population like this:

The island is inhabited with all sortes, with English, French, Dutch, Scotes, Irish, Spaniards, they being Jues, with ingones [Indians] and Miserabell Negors borne to perpetual slavery thay and theyer seed... This Iland is the dunghill whar our England dost cast forth its rubidg. Rodgs [rogues] and Hors and such like peopel are those that are generally broght heare.

The whores and rogues were sent out to provide manpower for the cultivation of sugar. Many of them moved on, leaving the 'Miserabell Negors', the African slaves who were already being brought over in their thousands from the west coast of Africa and whose descendants make up the majority of the Bajan population today.

The empire builders were so successful with their sugar that Barbados came to be called 'the brightest jewel in the English Crown' at the end of the 17th century. The

Cricket and the Constitution

The two most hallowed institutions to be adopted during 300 years' association with Britain are cricket and Parliament. As with so many other things, Barbados exerts an influence in cricket out of proportion to its small size. The island has won the regional championship, the Red Stripe Cup, more times than all the other islands combined. It has also provided a string of extremely gifted players to the West Indies side, including men such as Sir Frank Worrell (the first black captain of the West Indies team), Sir Clyde Walcott, Sir Everton Weekes ('the three Ws'), Sir Gary Sobers and more recently Joel Garner and Gordon Greenidge. Current and recent players include Desmond Haynes, Sherwin Campbell, Roland Holder, Courtney Brown, Corey Collmore and Ryan Hinds. If a Test Match is being played while you are visiting, be sure to go along (you will find that most of Barbados life stops for it anyway).

Although the first inter-island cricket matches were played here in 1865, Barbados has an even longer-standing association with Parliament. Founded in 1637, the Barbados Assembly is the third-oldest parliamentary body in the British Commonwealth, after Bermuda and Westminster itself. The destruction of its official building, the State House, in a fire in 1668, meant that the Legislative Assembly spent 60 years conducting its business in taverns, but it has become more sober since then. For centuries the institution was dominated by white Bajans, but in 1843 the first non-white member was elected. The late 19th century turned out to be a time of political crisis throughout the West Indies because Britain was keen to impose direct rule from London, bypassing the islands' assemblies. However, Barbados was the only Caribbean colony to keep its legislative powers intact.

Barbados has a bicameral parliamentary system, with elections held every five years to the 28-seat House of Assembly. Senate members, of which there are 21, are appointed by the Governor General (currently Sir Clifford Husbands) on the advice of senior politicians. The restored parliamentary buildings in Bridgetown can be visited by members of the public.

monopoly did not last, despite Barbadian efforts to protect their markets, as other islands started to cultivate the crop. Expensive equipment forced out the small-holders, and the plantations became fewer, larger and more profitable. Their fortunes waxed and waned with war and peace in the 18th century, as Britain, France and Spain vied for Caribbean supremacy. Fortunes were handsomely augmented by the usual Caribbean trade of smuggling, avoiding port taxes. Père Labat wrote that the captain of his barque worked hard unloading during the day, but far harder at night.

Barbados's unconquered history was due mainly to its position out in the Atlantic. From the Caribbean side, ships had to beat upwind towards it and could be seen for miles from a string of formidable fortresses along the west coast. The island was the headquarters of the British forces in the Caribbean for many years. But it was not only from outside that the island was threatened. The plantation slaves plotted rebellion from the beginning and they were ruthlessly treated when found out. The most famous revolt was Bussa's Rebellion, in 1816, caused by the slaves having incorrectly thought that the abolition of the slave trade in 1807 had granted them their freedom and that the plantation owners were illegally denying them this freedom. The revolt was initiated by torching the canefields and was put down with the loss of nearly 300 lives. Many more rebel slaves were deported to Honduras.

In 1838 the slaves were finally freed (after a four-year 'apprenticeship' period in which they were paid minimally but had to remain on their plantations) and the industry faltered. Many of the freed slaves emigrated because there was no land for them other than on the plantations. As sugar beet was developed in Europe, the sugar industry nearly collapsed, but, after 50 years in the doldrums, West Indian sugar was given preferential treatment and it was profitable again by 1910. Sugar and the rum produced from it are still very important to Barbados. The national coat of arms shows a fist grasping two canes, and the Bridgetown coat of arms has three rum puncheons.

The 20th century brought pressure for political change with the growth of trades unions in the 1920s and 30s. Eventually universal franchise came in 1951. Barbados was a member of the West Indian Federation but, when this failed in 1962, the island opted for Independence on 30 November 1966. Barbados remains within the British Commonwealth.

There is still a small sugar (and rum) industry as well as a manufacturing sector which produces garments, stainless steel and paper products. Amazingly, Barbados produces much of its oil requirements at the moment and has extensive natural gas. Offshore finance services are expanding and there is some data processing, but by far the biggest earner is tourism. The Bajans were severely affected by the recession in the early 1990s, but since the dawn of the millennium, life has begun to improve. Today the island is led by Prime Minister the Right Hon. Owen Arthur of the Barbados Labour Party, which was elected with 26 seats in January 2003, with the Democratic Labour Party (2 seats) in opposition. Elections are next due by January 2007.

Beaches

The beaches of Barbados are excellent and they offer something for every taste, from the fine golden sand and calm water of the protected west coast, round the southern point where the water is livelier and the sand becomes coral pink, to the windswept surfing beaches of the east coast, where the sea is positively rough and huge breakers bring in the full force of the Atlantic. There is a more or less continual stretch of sand on the west coast (despite a certain loss of sand over the years), running north from Bridgetown. It is an excellent place to walk. The whole 10-mile tourist stretch is redolent with the aroma of bodies gently sizzling in coconut oil, but it only gets crowded in clusters around the hotels and the public beaches. Here you will find general watersports operators (often attached to the hotels), offering anything from snorkelling gear to wetbikes and waterskiing trips. Be careful of the tall and bushy manchineel trees all along the coast. Their fruit was called the apple of death by Columbus, while the trees' poisonous sap causes a nasty rash and swelling.

South of Bridgetown the sand is fantastic too (if anything it seems to be increasing here) and there are plenty of active beaches with bars and watersports. Once you reach the southern tip the sports get more adventurous, with rougher water and the wind: windsurfing is best in the south, you can body-surf and boogie board in the southeast, and there is full-on surfing on the east coast (well, when the waves are up). For an out-of-the-way beach, go to the southeast, where there are some delightful coves cut into the cliffs with pink sand and fantastic aquamarine water – well worth the effort of a visit. Or go north, beyond hotel country. On the Atlantic side the surf comes pounding in and swimming is often dangerous, but the coast is spectacular to view, from Ragged Point in the southeast to Bathsheba, where crowds come to watch the surfers.

Hotels are usually happy for you to base yourself on their beach for the day if you want to use their facilities and have lunch there. All beaches in Barbados are public below the high-water mark anyway. There are lifeguards on some beaches and NCC rangers dressed in blue on most established beaches. There are only a few hucksters, who will offer the traditional array of services, including hair-braiding, tropical shirts and African carvings. They can be very persistent (and quite persuasive) when they get going, so if you do not want to buy you may have to do a bit of stonewalling. Barbadian modesty prevents nude and even topless bathing.

See also 'Best Beaches', p.68.

Flora and Fauna

When the Europeans first arrived in 1627, Barbados was entirely forested, but the trees were stripped within 20 years as the cultivation of sugar went ahead. **Turner's Hall Wood** in the centre of the island is the only place where the original forest remains. Around the island, however, you will see examples of the huge *Ficus citrifolia*, or 'bearded fig tree', a gnarly-trunked colossus with a curtain of aerial roots that resemble straggly beards, from which the island took its name.

Particular pleasures in Barbados are the hotel and private gardens, which are excellent (talk to any gardener for an introduction to tropical flora) and where you will find at least some plants in flower at all times of the year and particularly in the dry season, which neatly coincides with the winter holiday season (December to April). Besides the many palms, there are flowering trees, like flamboyant, which explodes into scarlet in the summer, and poinsettia, whose leaves turn scarlet in December, and of course limitless flowering bushes such as bougainvillea, ixora and heliconias, including lobster claw and bird of paradise. There are a number of public gardens and parks on view in the island: **Andromeda** in Bathsheba, **Grenade Hall Forest** in the north and the **Flower Forest** in St Joseph. The **Arbib Heritage and Nature Trail** (*t 426 2421*) offers a guided walk through the northerly parish of St Peter.

There are few wild animals in Barbados, though you will come across green monkeys (more brown with green patches), which were brought over from Africa 300 years ago. Other animals can be seen in the **Barbados Wildlife Reserve** in the north of the island. Birdlife is more varied. In the remote northern areas you can see three hummingbirds – the Antillean crested hummingbird, the purple-throated carib and the green-throated carib – as well as colourful tanagers and kingbirds. In the inland swamps you can see sandpipers, terns and warblers (the endangered yellow warbler is endemic to Barbados), and along the coast you will see solitary pelicans digesting their meal on an isolated rock.

Getting There

Barbados t (1 246–)

By Air

Barbados is geographically remote from the other islands in the Eastern Caribbean, but it is well served by air. As well as regular connections from Europe and North America, there are easy links to all the islands nearby, plus Guyana and Venezuela. All air tickets sold in Barbados are supplemented with a 20% government tax. Departure tax is Bds$25.

From Europe

British Airways, t 436 6413, flies almost daily from London Gatwick, as does Virgin Atlantic. BWIA, t 426 2111, has two or three direct flights each week from Heathrow and a new twice-weekly service from Manchester. There are numerous charter services on which you can buy seat-only tickets through UK travel agencies. From continental Europe, BWIA have services originating in Frankfurt, and a number of charter airlines operate out of Germany (LTU and Condor) and Holland (Martinair).

From North America

The best gateways on the American mainland are Miami and New York, from where there are a couple of scheduled flights each day, on American Airlines, t 428 4170; Air Jamaica, t 420 1956; or BWIA, t 426 2111. Connections are also possible through San Juan on Puerto Rico. Other US cities with scheduled flights include Boston and Philadelphia, from where there is a daily scheduled service on American Airlines. US Airways, t 800 428 4322, flies nonstop from Philadelphia and Charlotte. Air Canada, t 428 5077, has a daily flight from Toronto, and BWIA flies weekly. Canadian charter airlines include Royal and Canada 3000.

From Other Caribbean Islands

LIAT, t 434 5428, has the most services, flying to all the major islands between Trinidad and Antigua, and on to the Virgin Islands and Puerto Rico. Caribbean Star, t 436 1825, and its sister line, Caribbean Sun, offer similar destinations. Air Caraïbes/Air Martinique, t 431 0540, flies to the French island of Martinique, and BWIA makes the link to its home island of Trinidad. Air Jamaica links Barbados to Kingston and Montego Bay in Jamaica, another hub worth considering from the States. If you are flying on to the Grenadines, Mustique Airways, t 435 7009, and SVG Air, based in St Vincent, usually have daily share-charter flights, as does TIA (Trans-Island Air), t 418 1654.

By Sea

There are no scheduled ferry services to Barbados. If you want to head elsewhere by boat, find your way to the shallow draft harbour and talk to one of the captains who sail to the Windward Islands. They usually set off late in the week.

Getting Around

By Bus

Barbados has quite a good **bus** system, emanating mainly from Bridgetown and eventually reaching most parts of the island. It is a cheap way to get around and gives a good exposure to Bajan life. People say good morning when they board the bus and, if you are sitting, you may well be handed a package to hold. There is a mixture of public and private buses, most of them painted in Barbadian national colours, yellow and blue.

Then there are minibuses known as **ZRs**. These have something of a reputation with the Bajans because they will happily stop in the middle of the road and hold up all the traffic in order to pick up a passenger. Some ZRs still have massive on-board stereos and delight in playing the latest soca and Jamaican dub, which makes them fun to travel on (actually stereos were banned because schoolchildren used to play truant and spend their lunch money on a ride).

Private **minibus** terminals are next to the public terminals in Bridgetown, but out in the country all services use the same bus stops, with a red and white circle on a pole like an 8ft lollipop. Wave frantically.

For services south and east, the main public bus terminal is in Fairchild St, just across the bridge from National Heroes Square (formerly Trafalgar Square).

If you are travelling north, then you leave from near St Mary's Church, the Lower Green Station or the Pelican van stand. The public system runs to a vague schedule (West Indian time); private buses leave when they are full. All fares are Bds$1.50.

By Taxi

As a good tourist, you are really expected to travel by taxi. These can be arranged in any hotel foyer and at key points around the island: the airport, downtown Bridgetown and at certain taxi stands – Sunset Crest Taxi Service in Holetown, **t** 432 1006; the Maxwell Taxi Stand, **t** 420 6786; and St Lawrence, **t** 428 7292. Taxis are not metered in Barbados – fares are fixed instead. Most drivers are honest, but you may want to establish the price of a ride before you get in. Sample prices are: airport to St Lawrence Gap – Bds$25, airport to Bridgetown – Bds$35, airport to Holetown – Bds$45, airport to Speightstown – Bds$60; and from Bridgetown to St Lawrence Gap – Bds$25, Bridgetown to Holetown – Bds$25, Bridgetown to Speightstown – Bds$40, and Bridgetown to Bathsheba – Bds$45. A taxi driver would be only too pleased to give a tour of the island, for around Bds$35 per hour.

By Guided Tour

Most companies will pick you up at your hotel and include lunch on a full-day tour.
Island Tours, t 437 9389. Tours by bus and car, such as a day trip taking in some of the undeveloped north of the island and the wild and ragged east coast.
Island Safari, t 432 5337, *info@islandsafari.bb*, *www.barbadostraveler.com*. Offer **4WD** to remoter spots around the island.
Adventureland 4 x 4 Tours, t 429 3687, *fourby four@caribsurf.com*. As Island Safari.
Bajan Helicopters, t 431 0069. Helicopter tours that follow the coastline or cut across the dramatic centre of the island.

Car and Bike Hire

A good way to explore the countryside is by hire car, jeep or by the trusty favourite, a moke (formerly the Mini-moke, now a variety of Suzuki and Subaru). If you do set off, make sure to have a good road map because it is surprisingly easy to get lost in Barbados's endless fields of sugar cane. In the winter season there is often a waiting list for vehicles (up to three days), so consider arranging a car when you book your holiday. Firms give better deals for a three-day hire. Expect to leave a hefty deposit with the hire company unless you present a credit card. Most companies will deliver the car to your hotel. Car hire is pretty expensive in Barbados: rates start at US$50 per day for a mini-moke, plus taxes and CDW, and are marginally more for a large car. There are cheaper options, but you are advised to check the fine print very carefully. To drive in Barbados (this takes place on the left, as a rule) you need a special visitor's driving licence, which can be purchased on presentation of a valid driving licence at the car-hire companies, at the airport on arrival, or at any police station, costing Bds$10. Those over 70 must show a doctor's letter.

Corbin's Car Rentals, t 427 9531, *rentals@ corbinscars.com*, *www.corbinscars.com*.
Coconut Car Rentals, t 437 0297, *coconut@ caribsurf.com*.
Courtesy Rent-a-Car, t 431 4160, *courtesy@ goddent.com*.
Direct Car Rentals, t 420 6372, *www. barbadoscars.com*.
Drive-A-Matic, t 442 5017.
Sunny Isle Motors, Worthing, **t** 435 7979.
Sunset Crest Rent-A-Car, St James, **t** 432 1482, and on the south coast, **t** 426 1763.

Scooters can be hired through Fun Seekers, Christ Church, **t** 435 9171, and Caribbean Scooters, Worthing, **t** 432 8522, and on the Careenage in Bridgetown. You need a permit to ride a motor scooter (BDs$10). For **bicycles** try Fun Seekers, above, and Highland Adventure Centre, Canefield, St Thomas, **t** 431 8928, *neilhighland@hotmail.com*.

Tourist Information

Abroad

Information about Barbados can be found at *www.barbados.org*. Other websites include *www.caribnet.net* and *www.funbarbados.com*. The Tourism Authority has offices at:
Canada: 105 Adelaide St West, Suite 1010, Toronto, Ontario M5H 1P9, **t** (416) 214 9880, *canada@barbados.org*.

UK: 263 Tottenham Court Rd, London W1P 7LA,
t (020) 7636 9448, *btauk@barbados.org*.
USA: 800 Second Av, New York, NY 10017, t (212)
986 6516, *btany@worldnet.att.net*; 3440
Wilshire Bd, Suite 1215, Los Angeles, CA
90010, t (213) 380 2198, *btala@barbados.org*;
150 Alhambre Circle, 1000, Coral Gables,
Miami, FL 33134, t (305) 442 7471.

In Barbados

Once you are on the island you can get
tourist information and assistance with hotels
on the toll-free number, t 1 800 744 6244, and
at the main tourist offices:
Airport, t 428 0937.
Harbour Road, Bridgetown, t 427 2623.
Deep Water Harbour, t 426 1718, *btainfo@
barbados.org*, *www.barbados.org*.

Embassies and Consulates

British High Commission, Lower Collymore
Rock, St Michael, t 436 6694.
Canadian High Commission, Bishop Court, Hill
Pine Rd, t 429 3550.
US Consul General, Alico Building, Cheapside,
Bridgetown, t 431 0025.

Media

If you need further assistance on current
events and tips about where to find shopping
bargains, there is a plethora of advertising-led
magazines, maps and leaflets, including *Ins
and Outs of Barbados*, which is crammed full
of useful information, and broadsheets such
as the *Visitor* and the *Sunseeker*. The two main
Barbadian newspapers are the *Advocate* and
the *Nation*, which give good coverage of local
and international news and list forthcoming
events. Radio stations include the Voice of
Barbados (92.9 FM), which has a variety of
shows; CBC (900AM), which has lots of phone-
ins; and HOTT (95.3FM) and Liberty (98.1FM),
which both play Caribbean music.

Medical Emergencies

In a medical emergency, contact Queen
Elizabeth Hospital, on Martindales Rd in the
north of Bridgetown, t 436 6450, or dial t 115.

Money and Banks

The Barbados currency is the Barbados
dollar, which like many others is fixed to the
US dollar (rate US$1 = Bds$1.98), which gives
an easy approximate **exchange rate** of Bds$1
to US50c. All prices (except hotel rates) are
quoted in Barbados dollars and so it is worth
carrying them, though US dollars will be
accepted everywhere. Make sure to establish
which currency you are dealing in. **Credit cards**
are widely accepted by the hotels and restaurants and in tourist areas generally. **Banking
hours** are Mon–Thurs 8 or 9–3, Fri 8–5. You can
change money any time at the hotels (usually
for a marginally less favourable rate). There are
now a number of **ATMs** around Barbados
which accept credit and banker's cards.

National Trust

There is an active National Trust in Barbados,
t 426 2421. They organize a walk to a different
site of natural and historical interest each
Sunday, starting at 6am and 3.30pm and
lasting about 3hrs (details in the local
newspapers or phone the number above; adm
free but donations welcomed). They have a
programme of 'Open Houses' once a week
(usually Wed 2.30–5.30pm, winter season
only) which enables you to visit Barbadian
houses not normally open to the public –
locations published in advance in a leaflet.

Telephone Code

The IDD code for Barbados is t 1 246,
followed by a seven-digit island number. On
the island, dial all seven digits.

Maps and Books

In the Castle of my Skin, by George Lamming,
is about a black Barbadian boy growing up.
Christopher, by Geoffrey Drayton, narrates the
stifling life of a white Barbadian boy. Edward
Braithwaite's collections of poetry include
Rights of Passage. Good beach material is
Thomas Hoover's *Caribbee*, set in the time
when Barbados had a tavern for every 20
inhabitants. A publication set in modern times
in a mythical hotel on Barbados's west coast is
Platinum Coast, a steamy tale of international
people with unfeasibly large bank accounts
and egos to match. The bookshops are good,
stocked with plenty of things to read about
the Caribbean and most magazines. In

Bridgetown, try the Cloister Bookstore, Hincks St, or 'Pages', at Cave Shepherd on Broad St. In Holetown, head for the Sunset Crest Mall.

Festivals

Mid-January *Barbados Jazz Festival.* International players performing in different venues around the island.

January *Windsurfing and sailing competitions.*

February *Holetown Festival.* Commemorates the first settlement of the island in 1627 with a week's worth of exhibitions, tattoos and general jamboree.
Polo matches.

March *The Holder's Season.* A round of open-air opera performances and Shakespeare plays.

April *Oistins Fish Festival.* Celebrates the town's livelihood with blowouts.
Congaline Carnival. Begins a week of Easter street parades.

May *Mount Gay International Regatta.*
Gospelfest. Performances of church music.

First Monday in August *Cropover.* Culminates on Kadooment Day (the crop referred to is the sugar-cane harvest) and is the highlight of the Barbadian festival year. It is a major blowout along Carnival lines, with calypso-singing competitions, steel-band music and carnival 'bands' made up of hundreds of costumed players who strut through the streets to soca music.

October *Triathlon.*

November *National Independence Festival of the Creative Arts (NIFCA).* Exhibitions of the visual arts.
Surfing championship.

December *Road-running race.*

Occasionally *Pro-am golf and cricket tournaments.*

Throughout the year *Horse-racing.*

Shopping

Opening hours are generally Mon–Fri 8–6, Sat 8–noon.

Best of Barbados, with branches throughout the island. For Bajan or Bajan-designed products.

'Chattel villages', in St Lawrence, Hastings and Holetown. With local and imported products on sale.

Earthworks Pottery, Edghill Heights 2, St. Thomas, **t** 425 0223, *www.earthworks-pottery.com*. Open Mon–Fri 9–5, Sat 9–1.

Fairfield Greathouse Pottery, set in an old boiling house in St Michael. For Bajan products.

Foursquare Rum Factory. Here artists and craftmakers have workshops and galleries.

Gallery of Caribbean Art, Queen Street, Speightstown, **t** 419 0858, *artcaribbean@sunbeach.net, www.artgallerycaribbean.com*. Open Mon–Fri 9.30–4.30, Sat 9.30–2.

Heritage Park. For local crafts workshops.

Verandah Art Gallery, Bridgetown.

Watersports

On the main beaches on the west and south coasts you will find general watersports operators where you can fix up a kayak, a small sailing boat, a windsurfer, a jetski or arrange a ride on a bouncy banana, go parasailing or waterskiing.

Some shops are hotel concessionaires, but outsiders can usually use them.

Day Sails

For snorkelling and cruising up the west coast, or a sunset cruise, there are plenty of options available (with hotel transfers and a meal usually included):

Blackjack Charters, **t** 417 0691. Ask for Farmer Brown.

Secret Love, **t** 288 8142, *yachts@caribsurf.com, www.funbarbados.com/sailing*. A yacht.

Irish Mist, **t** 436 9201. A catamaran.

Cool Runnings, **t** 436 0911, *coolrunnings cruises@caribsurf.com*. A catamaran.

Small Cats, **t** 421 6419, *smallcats@sun beach.net*. They take a maximum of 12 passengers on their catamarans.

Jolly Roger, **t** 436 6424. For an afternoon of rum-soaked piracy and profligacy, with lots of shiver-me-timbers, dancing and walking the plank to loud music.

Deep-sea Fishing

Charters after swordfish or marlin can be arranged through the boats on the Careenage:

Blue Jay, **t** 429 2326, *burke's@caribsurf.com*.

Blue Marlin Charters, **t** 436 4322, *bluemrln@caribsurf.com*.

Scuba Diving

There are plenty of dive shops which will take you out and give instruction if you need it. Most of the dive sites are on the west coast, where the water is the calmest; a reef runs along the drop-off a mile or so offshore. There are some wrecks in Carlisle Bay and some reefs and wrecks not far from St Lawrence; sometimes there are drift dives down here. Some dive shops have photographic equipment; most will collect you from your hotel. Average prices are Bds$100 for a one-tank dive. Companies offering equipment and qualified instruction are:

Hightide Watersports, Coral Reef, St James, t 430 0391, toll free t 1 800 513 5763, *high tide@sunbeach.net*, *www.divehightide.com*.

West Side Scuba Centre, Holetown, t 432 2558, *peterg@sunbeach.net*, *www.barbados.org/ diving/westsidescuba*.

Coral Isle Divers, Bridgetown, t 434 8377, *barbados.org/diving/coralisle.htm*. A BSAC-accredited school.

ExploreSub Barbados, St Lawrence Gap, t 435 6542, *barbados.org/diving/explore/ explore.htm*. A PADI five-star centre.

Underwater Barbados, Hastings, t 426 0655, *www.underwaterbarbados.com*. A PADI five-star dive centre.

Snorkelling

Masks and fins are available at all the watersports shops and many hotels. You will find good reefs in Payne's Bay and at the Folkstone National Marine Park, near Holetown, and also off the Heywoods resort near Speightstown. Trips in a glass-bottomed boat on the west coast can be organized through most watersports shops. For a view of deeper Barbados corals without getting wet, contact Atlantis Adventure Submarine, t 436 8929; reserve a couple of days in advance in season.

Surfing

Popular on the island. There are big waves on the east coast at Bathsheba and there is a crowd there most days. It is also quite fun to sit in one of the bars, the Bonito Bar and Smokey Shop in Bathsheba, and watch the surf-gods at it in the Soup Bowl. Other surfing areas are Puppies and Crab Hill in the far north. For the merely mortal there are boogie boards for hire on the south-coast beaches, where the waves are gentler; try Accra Beach, Dover Beach or Crane Beach.

Windsurfing

A good option in Barbados. It is best along the south coast – experienced windsurfers should head for the southerly point, around Silver Sands, where the 1991 World Championships were hosted and where Mistral keeps an outfit at the Silver Sands Resort (Irie Man Action, t 428 2866) over the winter months (when the trade winds are at their strongest). There is a reef offshore so it is particularly good for waves (jump on the way out, surf back in). If you want to put down a 360, a table-top or a cheese roll, or watch them at it, or simply watch the crowds, this is the place to come. Slightly less extreme, and a good place to learn, is at Maxwell Beach, also Mistral, t 420 4452, which offers equipment hire and instruction, including kiteboarding tuition.

Other Sports

Golf

There are a number of courses on the island. They are well kept and have trolleys for hire; the wind is the main complication.

Royal Westmoreland, t 422 4653, *www.royal-westmoreland.com/golf*. Designed by Robert Trent Jones (two 18 holes), 6870 yards, par 72, access restricted to certain hotels (packages available), green fee astronomic.

Sandy Lane Course, t 444 2000, *www.sandy lane.com*. There are two neatly tended courses, with green fees around Bds$200 (free for hotel guests).

Barbados Golf Club, Durants, Christ Church, t 428 8463, *www.barbadosgolfclub.com*. A PGA-sanctioned course designed by Ron Kirby. Green fee around Bds$160 summer, Bds$230 winter.

Hiking

Walkers can find satisfying hikes in the hilly district of Scotland and along the rugged east coast. If you wish to set off alone, maps are easily available in town; otherwise, there are some excellent guided walks on the island. Try National Trust walks (*see* 'Tourist Information', above), which includes the Arbib Nature and Heritage Trail in Speightstown as well as the Sunday walks, and Hike Barbados, t 425 0073. Check out *www.barbados.org/hike.htm*.

Horse-riding

Brighton Stables, on the Spring Garden Highway, St Michael, t 425 9381. If you fancy a canter along the beach at dawn.

Caribbean International Riding Centre, t 422 7433. Tours of Scotland District.

Highland Adventure Tours, Cane Field, St Thomas, Barbados, t 431 8928, *neilhighland@hotmail.com*.

Mountain-biking

Flex Bicycle Rental, t 424 0321, and **Odyssey Tours**, t 228 0003, offer guided biking tours and walks.

Spectator Sports

Includes the **horse-racing** on alternate Saturdays in the season at the Garrison Savannah south of Bridgetown, and even **polo** (Barbados Polo Club, t 427 0022 for schedules) on the west coast. But **cricket** is the Barbadian national sport, and you will come across weekend matches all over the island and less formal games being played by children in the backstreets of the towns. Stop and watch – you may even be thrown the ball and told to bowl. Details of forthcoming League matches and international Tests, held in the Kensington Oval north of Bridgetown, can be found in the newspapers or by asking around.

Tennis

Most hotels have courts, usually for a fee of about US$6 per hour.

Where to Stay

Barbados t (1 246–)

As the nerve centre of the British presence in the Eastern Caribbean, Barbados has a tradition of hotels going back 200 years. The best known was the 19th-century 'Ice House', patronized because it brought the first cooled drinks to Barbados, but most were famous for a series of prodigious creole landladies who kept houses of varying states of disorder:

Sabina Brade, Hannah Lewis, who would complain of her lumbago, and Betsy Austin, a lady of massive size and earthy language who would become violent if her bill was questioned. For many of the tavern girls 'of erect figure and stately carriage...without shoes or stockings, in a short white jacket and thin short petticoat...a white turban on the head, neck and shoulders left bare', it was a business profitable enough to buy their freedom from slavery. But the most popular image of all is that of the gargantuan Rachel Pringle, an expansive matriarch, dressed in voluminous silk, of almost unmovable disposition, whose caricature by the cartoonist Rowlandson can be seen around the island.

Such seaminess belies Barbados's current clean-cut and efficient image. The island offers one of the best ranges of hotels in the Caribbean. Prices are very high in the smart hotels in season because of the island's reputation, but there is an excellent breadth of prices year round and it is possible to find a good deal in the summer months, particularly in hotel rooms and self-catering flats.

Some of the Caribbean's loveliest and most expensive villas are along the west coast of Barbados. Contact **Realtors Limited**, t 432 6930, *info@realtorslimited.com*, *www.realtorslimited.com*; **Alleyne Aguilar & Altmann Ltd**, t 432 0840, *villas@caribsurf.com*, *www.aaaltman.com*; and **Bajan Services Ltd**, Seascape Cottage, Gibbs, St Peter, Barbados, t 422 2618, *villas@bajanservices.com*, *www.bajanservices.com* – all with options between one and eight bedrooms. Operators abroad (who will put together a whole package for you) can be contacted through the tourist boards (*see* 'Tourist Information', above) and also *see* 'Tour Operators' in the Travel chapter, pp.38–41.

The smart set head for the Platinum Coast, which runs north along the west coast from Bridgetown up towards Speightstown. Some of the smartest and most expensive hotels in the Caribbean are situated here – some people actually wear their jewellery on the beach – set in gardens of tropical splendour and giving onto the gentle bays with golden strands, a fine place to see the Green Flash at sunset. The south coast is generally less luxurious and less expensive (most of the hotels work with high-volume package companies and there are also lots of guest houses) but it is more active and has a less exclusive feel. A good area to head for as an independent traveller is the southern tip of the island around Silver Sands, which has a lively feel for part of the year when the wind-surfers are around and otherwise is fairly quiet. There is public transport.

Bear in mind that all bills in Barbados will be supplemented with 7.5% VAT and, in almost all cases, a 10% service charge as well.

Luxury

Coral Reef Club, Holetown, **t** 422 2372, UK **t** 0800 964 470, US **t** 1 800 223 1108, *coral@caribsurf.com, www.coralreef barbados.com.* Guests return year after year to this family-run hotel with the stately grace of old-time Barbados. There are 85 large, individually decorated rooms and suites set in two- and three-storey villas scattered around luxuriant gardens and the large pool. Each has a balcony or patio with angled white louvres. The elegant coral-rock foyer, bar and dining room look out through the casuarina pines and mahogany trees to the beach, where there are watersports for the actively minded.

The Royal Pavilion, just north of Holetown, St James, **t** 422 4444, US **t** 1 800 866 5577, *royalpavilion@fairmont.com, www. fairmont.com.* Has a feel of manicured luxury in its pink-marble, Italianate central building with its pillars, arches and terra-cotta tiles. There is a certain formality (no children under 13, except July–Aug), but it is not overplayed. The two dining rooms are set on a veranda right above the waves and all 72 elegant rooms look onto the ocean and good beach from deep balconies. Guests have the use of the facilities at **Glitter Bay**, **t** 422 5555, same emails and website, the larger and less formal sister-hotel next door.

Sandy Lane Hotel, Payne's Bay, **t** 432 1311, UK **t** 0800 181 123, US **t** 1 800 233 3800, *reservations@sandylane.com, www.sandy lane.com.* Has long been renowned as one of the Caribbean's best-known and most luxurious hotels and has recently been given a massive, multi-million dollar refit so it is in splendid form. Limousine service will whisk you from the airport to this classical enclave

of sumptuousness with north and south wings either side of an amphitheatrical courtyard and set on 300 yards of delightful beach. Soft shades of pink and white run throughout the resort, in the coral-stone and pickled-oak fittings, and lend the resort an air of just-so elegance. All imaginable concessions to luxury – 24-hour room service by bellmen in cream suits, mock-antique cutlery in the dining room, afternoon tea – right down to the chilled towels at the beach. Also all the modern essentials – swimming pool, watersports, spa, golf, fitness centre and children's centres. A large and busy hotel, with dress codes at dinner, soigné, swanky and slightly self-important.

Very Expensive

Cobbler's Cove, just south of Speightstown, **t** 422 2291, UK **t** (020) 8367 5175, US **t** 1 800 890 6060, *reservations@cobblers cove.com, www.cobblerscove.com.* A charming, smaller resort that retains the calm and charm of the west coast as it once was. There are 40 suites, each decorated with wicker, rattan, Barbadian clay tiles and louvres, and each with a balcony or terrace looking out onto the hotel's charming gardens of golden palm, banana and trav-ellers' trees. Above the beach is the castellated main house with the dining room, central drawing room, which lends the hotel a congenial air, and the two most special suites, the Colleton Suite and the Camelot Suite. An excellent retreat, Cobbler's Cove is one of the Caribbean's few Relais et Châteaux (character, courtesy, calm, charm and, not least, particularly important in the Caribbean, cuisine). MAP in winter.

The Sandpiper, Holetown, **t** 422 2251, *coral@caribsurf.com, www.sandpiper barbados.com.* You might also consider the 45 slightly more casual suites and rooms of this place, the Coral Reef's friendly sister-hotel nearby, which are neatly situated in blocks in a charming garden, wrapped in pink, white and purple bougainvillea and palm trees of different sorts.

Villa Nova Country House Hotel, St John, **t** 433 1524, *villanova@sunbeach.net, www.villa novabarbados.com.* The legendary landmark, built in 1834, has been restored as a de luxe 27-room resort. The plantation house was the winter home of Sir Anthony Eden, British Prime Minister during the 1960s. Among his distinguished visitors were Queen Elizabeth II, Sir Winston Churchill, and Noel Coward. The coral stone mansion, bordered on three sides by a wide veranda, is set on fifteen tranquil hilltop acres and serves as the resort's centrepiece. It houses the reception, a bar, restaurant, boardroom, library, and card room. In the luxuriant tropical gardens, three new two-storey, colonial-style buildings contain the guest rooms and suites decorated by famous interior designer Nina Campbell, with hardwood floors, and 10-foot-high ceilings. They have air-con, CD player, DVD, and television; bathrooms with tubs, separate showers, double vanities, and bidets. The country resort has a swimming pool, two floodlit tennis courts, fitness facilities and large spa with ten treatment rooms.

Hilton Barbados, Needham's Point, t 426 0200, *www.hiltoncaribbean.com/barbados*. The 350-room Hilton Barbados enjoys a prime location on one of the most beautiful beaches in Barbados, about 10mins from Bridgetown and 20mins from the airport. One hundred rooms and suites are on the Executive Floor where the lounge provides guests with complimentary breakfast, hors d'oeuvres and refreshments throughout the day. The hotel's dining options include the Careenage Bar and Grille, the casual Lighthouse Terrace, and the Water's Edge beach bar. The hotel has a pool complex with whirlpool, a watersports centre, floodlit tennis courts, a fitness centre, and the Kidz Paradise Club.

Treasure Beach, Payne's Bay, t 432 1346, US t 1 800 223 6510, *reservations@treasurebeach hotel.com, www.treasurebeachhotel.com*. Has 25 very comfortable suites in staggered two-storey blocks running down to a fine stretch of the west coast beach. Each suite has a bedroom and a large sitting room with a view onto the pleasant gardens and pool. A quiet and friendly hotel.

Expensive–Moderate

Little Good Harbour, Shermans, St Peter, t 439 3000, *littlegoodharbour@sunbeach.net*,

www.littlegoodharbourbarbados.com. A delightful collection of one- and two-bedroom cottages in traditional West Indian style, with tin roofs, wooden louvres and balconies, and four-posters with muslin nets. Inside they are well appointed, with full kitchens, and decorated with Oriental carvings and Caribbean painting. Thirteen of the cottages are set in the small garden overflowing with greenery, and, on the other side of the road (it's not busy, though the occasional bus roars by) in the old restored fort, you will find two more rooms, the excellent restaurant, the Fish Pot, and the beach. It is quiet and friendly and has a sense of community that other hotels lack.

The Crane Beach Hotel, Crane Beach, St Philip, t 423 6220, *reservations@thecrane.com, www.thecrane.com*. Stands on the southeast coast of the island, in a truly dramatic setting on the clifftops, where the pool sits, its surreal classical columns and balustrades stamped against the turquoise of the Atlantic Ocean. There are 15 very comfortable rooms and suites, some set in a miniature coral-stone castle with hardwood floors and four-posters, in keeping with the colonial atmosphere of 1887, when the hotel was opened. There is a big development of luxurious apartments next door, but they lend the place a feel of activity that it lacked until recently.

Moderate

Beachcomber Suites, Payne's Bay, near Holetown, t 432 0489, *hassell@caribsurf.com, www.beachcombersuites.com*. If you are happy to cater for yourself, you can try this place, where there are huge studios and two-bedroom apartments, each well furnished and with a large balcony looking onto an excellent section of the beach. There is no restaurant, but each apartment has a full kitchen.

Smuggler's Cove, Payne's Bay, t 432 1741, *smugglerscovehotel@barbados.org*. There are 20 comfortable studios and one-bedroom apartments in a not terribly attractive block above the pool, but right on Payne's Bay (though the rooms don't look onto the beach). All have kitchenettes, but there is also a restaurant.

Sea Foam Haciendas, Worthing, t 435 7380, *seafoam@caribsurf.com*, *www.seafoam haciendas.com*. Offers 12 two-bedroom suites in a building with colonial Spanish touches, as the name implies, right on the beach. Very much self-contained and private, with full kitchens. Rates include maid service, and cooks and baby-sitters can be arranged.

Moderate–Inexpensive

Round House Inn, on the clifftops above Bathsheba, t 433 9678, *roundhouse@ sunbeach.net*. Has a magnificent setting on the wild east coast. There are four rooms in an old restored building: they are quite simple but have some style, with louvred doors and windows made of Caribbean woods, and straw matting on the concrete floors. It's quite busy because of the restaurant (*see* 'Eating Out', below), but the rooms are private and they make for an excellent retreat from the swank of the west coast.

Sea-U Guest House, in Tent Bay above Bathsheba, t 433 9450, *sea-u@caribsurf.com*, *www.funbarbados.com/lodgings/seau.cfm*. Here there are five rooms (perfectly pleasant, with muslin nets over the beds, four with kitchenettes) set in a modern wooden building in traditional Caribbean style, with a large veranda where you can while away your time in a hammock. A bar will fix meals for you.

Peach and Quiet, Inch Marlow, Christ Church, t 428 5682, *www.peachandquiet.com*. Offers 22 suites in stark white stucco and shingle-tile buildings in a windy beachfront setting of palms and casuarina pines. Very relaxed and peaceful.

Silver Rock Resort, Silver Sands, Christ Church, t 428 2866, *silver@gemsbarbados.com*, *www.gemsbarbados.com*. The windsurfers themselves tend to gather here, where comfortable studios and apartments are moderately priced. It has a bar and restaurant with a view of all the waterborne activity offshore.

Point View Apartments, Inch Marlow, Christ Church, t 428 8629, *pointview@caribsurf. com*, *www.barbados.org/apt/a65.htm*. Quite simple but comfortable and with a pool.

Inexpensive

Bajan Surf Bungalow, Powell Spring, Bathsheba, t 433 9920, *bsb@jorgen.com*, *www.jorgen.com/surf*. If you want to be among surfers there are just a few cheap rooms here: shared baths, central sitting/TV area and a decent platform to watch the activity on the waves.

Villa Marie, Fitts Village, Payne's Bay, t 432 1745, *villamarie@sunbeach.net*, *www.barbados. org/villas/villamarie*. A guest house offering bed and breakfast.

Claridge's Inn, near Mullins Beach, t 422 2403, *claridgesinn@aol.com*. A guest house with some kitchenettes.

Windsurf Beach Hotel, Maxwell Main Rd, t 420 5862, *reservations@butterflybeach.com*. Windsurfers gravitate here. Simple rooms with pretty floral décor in a purpose-built block, though they do not really overlook the sea. Really a quiet stopover but the wind-surfing crowd can make it quite lively.

Butterfly Beach Hotel, Maxwell, t 428 9095, *www.butterflybeach.com*. Sister-hotel to the Windsurf Beach Hotel, similar in style and marginally cheaper.

Maraval Guest House, Worthing, t 435 7437, *www.maravalbarbados.com*. Has six rooms (private baths) in a pretty green and white local house behind a white picket fence.

Shells Guest House, Worthing, t 435 7253, *guest@sunbeach.net*. Has seven simple rooms, some with shared bathroom.

Rio Guest House, St Lawrence Gap, t 428 1546, *rioguesthouse@hotmail.com*, *www.rioguest house.net*. Within a shout of St Lawrence Gap: three very simple rooms, some with shared bath, some private, with a small dining and kitchen area.

Eating Out

As in many of the Caribbean islands, some Bajan traditional dishes have a slave heritage. Thus cou-cou, a dish made from cornmeal and okra, is served with saltfish, once a hardship food. 'Peas 'n' rice' is a staple and is often flavoured with coconut. Besides the traditional pepperpot stew, a four-day boil-up, there is also plenty of seafood, including crab and sea-egg, the roe of the white sea-urchin, which is supposely an aphrodisiac.

The best-loved fish in Barbados is the flying fish, which you may well see if you go out sailing. It is a winged fish that flits and glides over the waves, sometimes for distances up to 100 yards. As well as being a national symbol, it is also something of a national dish, and you can see the daily catch brought into the Careenage in the late afternoon, in season between December and June.

Barbados has a steadily growing tradition of fine food, which makes a pleasant change in the British Caribbean, which is not renowned for its cuisine. High-quality ingredients are now readily available (both to restaurants and to gourmet delicatessens), literally flown in fresh from Europe and the States, and, despite a running debate about how many foreigners should be allowed in, there are an increasing number of chefs on the island with international experience. It is well organized generally, with fishermen phoning back their catch on mobile phones so that menus can be made up on time. Menus tend to be international, but there has always been a strong Asian influence too.

Generally the Bajans handle service well, which can be a problem elsewhere. The result is some excellent restaurants, offering superb food in charming locations: terraces on the waterfront just above the waves, garden settings, and verandas threatened by explosive tropical flora.

There are elegant restaurants dotted along the coastal cliffs of the west, a clutch of lively restaurants in Holetown, and plenty of easy eateries in St Lawrence Gap and along the south coast. Many of the hotels also have fine kitchens and, if you are staying at one of the Elegant Resorts of Barbados, you may try the others out. You can even dine out in old-time plantation splendour at **Sunbury** (**t** 423 6270). No restaurants require a dinner jacket any more, though there may be a dress code of trousers and a sleeved shirt. There is an encrustation of pizza huts, Chefettes and Barbecue Barns, but you can of course also eat fast food Bajan style, taking away a 'cutter' (a hefty sandwich) or rice 'n' peas in a polystyrene box from a 'Lunch Box' (a wagon), or picking up some roast corn, chicken legs

cooked on braziers, or a *roti* (*see* 'Eating Out' in the **Trinidad** chapter, p.113), at the roadside in the early evening.

Eating out in a restaurant in Barbados is not cheap. You are advised to reserve a table in the winter season: the most popular restaurants can be booked weeks in advance because people fax their reservations from home long before they arrive. The huge 15% VAT is now generally included in the prices, but you can expect a 10% service charge on top. Charges are made in Barbados dollars, but credit cards are widely accepted.

Categories are arranged according to the price of a main course: expensive = Bds$40 and above, moderate = Bds$20–40, cheap = under Bds$20.

The West Coast

Expensive

The Cliff, Derricks, St James, **t** 432 1922, *cliff@caribsurf.com*. Has maintained its spot among the island's best for a number of years now, in its superb setting on the west coast, literally cut into the face of the cliff on a tiny cove with waves floodlit. Tables are arranged in amphitheatrical tiers above an open-air floor with trees and flaming torches of slender metalwork, and on a large terrace above the sea itself. The menu garners tastes from around the world, particularly from Asia, to complement Caribbean and international ingredients – try the snow crab cake with coriander cream, coriander vinaigrette and red curry oil followed by Cajun-style barracuda on Asian noodles with pesto cream, all neatly presented on huge white china plates. Long list of daily specials and a strong wine list; also Cuban cigars.

La Mer, Port St Charles Lagoon, St Peter, **t** 419 2000. Mixes Asian flavours with the Caribbean. With tables looking out through arches onto the calm waters of the lagoon, it has a nice nautical edge, but the service and the cuisine are more formal. Try the Vietnamese rice paper rolls with marinated vegetables and follow with anything from a *filet du jour* of Barbadian fish in a Chablis *beurre blanc* to a river salmon steak smoked in sugar-cane tea with Périgord truffle

Béarnaise sauce, or a lemongrass and curry chicken supreme served with lentil dhal.

La Terra, Royal Westmoreland, Holetown, **t** 432 1099, *olives@caribsurf.com*. In an open-sided dining room, the setting is highly stylized Mediterranean. The excellent cuisine mixes Mediterranean, particularly Italian, with the Caribbean. There's an excellent wine list too. Brisk and efficient, but personable.

The Lone Star, between Holetown and Speightstown, **t** 419 0599, *lonestargarage@caribsurf.com*. Also set on a deck, this with a minimalist nautical feel – canvas overhead and wire stays as a balustrade. Lots of oysters, mussels and bruschetta to start (there is a seafood bar, or salad bar at lunch), then a long menu of pastas, risottos and grilled meats nicely done (the seared tuna comes with a caper *beurre noisette*), even some baltis. A little pretentious.

The Tides, **t** 432 8356, *info@tidesbarbados.com*, *www.tidesbarbados.com*. Here you also dine to the rhythm of the waves, with tables stretched along the front between casuarina tree trunks. The fare is Caribbean with an Asian touch – *millefeuille* of sun-dried tomato, Paris mushrooms and chargrilled local asparagus followed by a duet of chicken and shrimp braised in a home-made Thai curry paste, in coconut milk and fresh cream.

Olive's Bar and Bistro, Holetown, **t** 432 2938, *olive@caribsurf.com*. Set in an old Barbadian town house, the menu is mainly Mediterranean with a spicy Caribbean influence. Start with an excellent rum punch upstairs in the bar, a drawing room with wicker armchairs and palms and a small terrace, and then move down to the air-conditioned dining room indoors with its bare coral walls, or outside into the quiet garden under the shelter of a palm tree or a gazebo. Warm shrimps in a creamy garlic dressing over a mixed leaf salad followed by chicken breast in a pecan cracker-crumb served on dhal *roti* with split-pea rice.

The Mews, Holetown, **t** 432 1122. Also has a pretty setting in a house. You dine in the garden under trellises or in the small rooms upstairs. There is a long fish menu – seared yellowfin tuna with capers and coriander

cream – and international fare such as rack of lamb with a fresh spearmint jus.

Sassafras, St James, **t** 432 6386, *sassafras@sunbeach.net*. Caribbean-Asian fusion in a restored plantation house, set in a lovely garden. Air-conditioned bistro bar. *Open weekdays for lunch, dinner daily.*

Daphne's, Payne's Bay, St James, **t** 432 2731. Sister to the famous London eatery, the Bajan version offers contemporary Italian cuisine in an elegant setting: at the water's edge on the heart of the island's Caribbean coast. Extensive wine list. Cocktail hour 5–7pm with drinks at half-price.

Moderate

The Fish Pot, isolated a little to the north of Speightstown, in the village of Shermans (at Little Good Harbour Hotel), **t** 439 2604. Well worth the trip because it is quiet and charming. The tables are set on a very pretty deck right above the sand, and indoors in an old restored fort with louvred windows looking out onto a fantastic blue sea by day. Strong on fish as the name would suggest, simply but delicately prepared. Try the seafood crêpe, bound in a tarragon cream sauce and follow with fresh grilled kingfish steaks served with capers in brown butter.

Ragamuffins, Holetown, **t** 432 1295. This fun place is set in a brightly painted Caribbean clapboard house with louvres and decorated with fish-nets, brightly painted parrots, flowers and fish scenes. A lively bar, but good Caribbean fare too: fish cakes with aïoli dip followed by jerk chicken escalope and Caribbean stir-fries or West Indian shrimp curry. Cherry cheesecake for dessert. *Closed Sat.*

Angry Annie's, Holetown, **t** 432 2119. The name gives a hint of the riotous and lively air of this great place. Hard to miss, it is bright blue with luscious pinks, outrageous orange and electric green. A mix of Caribbean and international cuisine – Soufrière fish sizzled in citrus and Limer's lobster in garlic and chives, plus lots of pastas and curries.

Cocomos, Holetown, **t** 432 0134. Doubles as beach bar and gathering place for Bajans at lunch and after work. There is a long menu of international fare – hamburgers, smoked chicken salad and penne pasta – served on a deck right above the sand.

Inexpensive

You shouldn't expect to find very much that's cheap on the west coast unless you're happy with a bar snack at one of the beach bars or a takeaway. You might also be able to fix a meal through the many rum shops along the main road.

Fisherman's Pub, Speightstown. A red and white bar on the road with covered bar and a terrace on the waterfront surrounded by a picket fence. Breadfruit cou-cou, fried chicken or fried flying fish on a revolving menu. It is especially known for its fish, which is fresh daily except Sundays.

Pizzaz, Holetown, t 432 0227. Twenty pizza toppings, spare ribs, *rotis* and submarines to take away; also not a bad place to eat in, on a nice red and green deck.

The South Coast

Expensive

Josef's, St Lawrence Gap, t 435 6541, *joe.s@ caribsurf.com*. The finest restaurant on the south coast, in a former private home (and currently the Austrian Consulate), made of pink and white coral rock. You dine just above the waves in the garden, on levels among all the tropical trees, and in the breezy, open-sided house. The menu is varied: a sushi/sashimi plate and flash-seared tuna carpaccio with a thyme *salmoriglio* are among the starters, followed by perhaps a breast of duckling with a port wine sauce.

Pisces, St Lawrence Gap, t 435 6564. Has an excellent waterfront setting, in a white wicker dining room wrapped in greenery. As the name suggests, they have a long fish menu, including red snapper in turmeric and coconut cream, and a delicious seafood fettucine, with occasional exotic offerings like chub and sennet, or surf and turf. High pressure, fast turnover, but reliably good.

David's Place, St Lawrence Gap, t 435 9755. Looks over the sea and fishing boats from a pretty veranda setting. Some international dishes such as *escargots*, and some vegetarian dishes, but also Barbadian specialities such as flying-fish melts, deep fried and served with a pepper jelly dip, and an Arawak-style pepper pot.

Champers Wine Bar, Hastings, t 435 6644. A charming breezy setting on the waterfront, with upstairs and water-level verandas, where you drink chilled wine to the sound of chatter one side and the breaking waves on the other. A blackboard menu offers a shrimp and mango salad followed by grilled billfish in a tomato and sweet pepper salsa, and a volley of excellent puddings. Also bar snacks if a full meal is too much.

39 Steps, Hastings, t 427 0715. A nice setting upstairs in a modern version of the traditional wooden-style Caribbean house. Deep-fried camembert followed by blackened fish.

Moderate

Bellini's Trattoria, St Lawrence Gap, just away from the main strip, t 435 7246. Has a nice veranda setting, with tables ranged along the balustrade looking out over the sea and fishing boats. Pastas and pizzas but also some more sophisticated dishes such as the shrimp Bellini, sautéed in garlic and brandy in a light tomato cream sauce.

Café Sol, St Lawrence Gap, t 432 9531. A fun place to head for at the start of an evening out (and then remain there possibly for the whole evening, drinking at the barrel chairs looking out onto the road). It's a Mexican grill and, more importantly, a margarita bar. The inside is hung with Mexicalia – sombreros, flags, even chilli-pepper fairy-lights – and of course there is loud Latin music. Nachos and pitchers of sangria to start, and if it makes you peckish then there are macho burgers, burritos and *taquitos* to fill the pit in your stomach.

Carib Beach Bar, Worthing, t 435 8540. Here you can find a lively crowd and enjoy some fritters over a Carib beer.

Inexpensive

Roti Hut, Worthing, t 435 7363. *Rotis* and more regular Caribbean fare, plus ice creams to take away or eat in.

Baxter's Road, on the northern road out of Bridgetown. The old favourite late-night eating stop has lost its popularity a little.

Fish Market, Oistins. If you are peckish in the early evening here you can find a number of stalls that will sell you a fish meal. Pat's Place, Miss Anne's, Miss June's and Crazy Eddie offer a plate of fried fish with rice and peas or macaroni pie and a beer until late into the evening.

Chefette, t 435 6000, *www.chefette.com*. Barbados' largest fast-food chain with 13 restaurants, many with playgrounds. Chicken, burgers, pizza, ice cream.

The East Coast

Round House, near Bathsheba, t 433 9678 (*moderate*). Has a dramatic setting on a cliff. Superb salt-bread to go with home-made soups and breadfruit chips. Follow with salads and pasta or a more substantial platter such as a fish fillet with rice and peas.

Atlantis Hotel, Bathsheba, t 423 1526 (*inexpensive*). Sunday-morning buffet.

Edgewater Hotel, Bathsheba, t 433 9900 (*inexpensive*). Sunday-morning buffet.

Bridgetown

Waterfront Café, right on the Careenage, t 427 0093 (*moderate*). Offers coffee and quick bites – smoked flying-fish salad, or larger meals such as jerked pork in tomato salsa. Jazz Tues and Thurs nights.

Careenage, in old restored building with veranda on the Careenage in Bridgetown, serves Bajan buffet lunch weekdays and dinner at weekends. Jazz on Sundays.

Bars and Nightlife

Bajan Drink

The chiefe fudling they make in the iland is Rumbullion, alias Kill Divill and this is made of suggar canes distilled, a hot hellish and terrible liquor.

Barbados produces some of the finest rum in the world. Distilled from molasses, the thick liquid left over from the sugar-boiling process, many rums are left to mature in oak, taking on a darker colour with age. Mountgay is the best known: try their special five-year-old. Others worth trying are Cockspur Old Gold and VSOR. Local white rums include ESAF, once jokingly called 'Erskine Sandiford and Friends' in reference to a former Prime Minister, or otherwise 'Every Sunday Afternoon Free'. There are hundreds of rum shops on the island, mostly small clapboard shacks, where you will find the Barbadians 'liming', passing the time of day. If you would like to see the distillation process, there are tours of distilleries in Bridgetown (*see* pp.88–9).

Besides their good line in rum punches, the restaurants in Barbados serve superb fruit punches, fresh fruit and juices crushed with ice, and usually free of the pints of sticky grenadine syrup that elsewhere obliterate the taste. More traditional drinks include mauby juice, a bitter drink made by boiling bark and spices – 100 years ago 'mauby ladies' would ply the streets of Bridgetown with urns on their heads, offering drinks to quench a midday thirst. Nowadays you are mainly dependent on canned and bottled drinks, but you may be able to get a snow-cone in a plastic cup at the streetside. You will also find delicious home-brewed ginger beer, boiled up from grated root ginger, and sorrel, a sweet concoction made from the red flowers of the sorrel plant, known as the Christmas drink all over the Caribbean. The Bajan beer is the award-winning Banks brew.

Bars and Clubs

A French priest who came to Barbados in the 1650s claimed that there were 100 taverns for a population of 2,000. The ratio of 1 for every 20 people may have gone down a bit since the 17th century, when even the Barbados Assembly used to meet in the pub, but evenings in Barbados can be very lively. Generally speaking, the best areas are Bridgetown and the south coast, particularly around St Lawrence Gap and most recently at Holetown, where there is a cluster of lively bars and restaurants. There are some excellent bands in Barbados and they play live in the many clubs: Krosfyah are worth looking out for and you might also come across Second Avenue, Square One and IV Play.

Bajan entertainment for Bajans tends to be in rum shops, usually local wooden houses with their shutters pinned open, and there are scores around the island. It is worth stopping at one. Many bars in Barbados are a little more chichi and, oddly for the Caribbean, there are actually wine bars, where the Bajan *bons bourgeois* congregate over a chilled glass of Chablis. Then there are restaurant bars as well, where drinkers gather for a drink in the evening, before or after dinner.

Clubs usually charge an entry fee. For other raw and wholesome Bajan entertainment, you might go to a weekend dance or Bram – details in the paper (location, admission price and a picture of the host) – for boozing and a bit of wining and grinding to the latest soca and Jamaican dub.

John Moore, Weston, St James. A rum shop where you can catch a game of dominoes.

Buffy's Bar, Silver Sands. Drop into this rum shop for a local experience.

Champer's, Hastings. Another good wine bar.

39 Steps, Hastings. Worthwhile wine bar.

Crocodile's Den (known mostly as Croc's), Payne's Bay, St James. Sits in a large tin-roofed clapboard house hidden behind a line of wriggly tin at the time of writing. Concrete floor, bench seats, sports on TV, pool tables and plenty of riotous behaviour from the young crowd.

Coach House, near Croc's, Payne's Bay. Has live music most days and collects a lively crowd, some to watch the sport on telly.

McBrides, St Lawrence Gap. Also a great place to start a night out.

Café Sol, St Lawrence Gap. Loud salsa in the early evening. From here you can spill straight into the clubs.

After Dark, St Lawrence Gap. Air-conditioned, with five bars, one of them 75ft long. It offers live music, sports on the television and mixed Caribbean and international sounds.

Ship Inn, St Lawrence Gap. Also very popular, with live music, to which young Bajans dance or pulsate, depending on the available room.

The Reggae Lounge, St Lawrence Gap. An open-air club strong on reggae as well as local calypso; it can get quite lively.

The Boatyard, Bay St, Carlisle Bay, on the outskirts of Bridgetown. Popular with tourists and locals alike, it has a beachfront setting with an open-air bar with barrel seats, and a brick and concrete dance floor. A mix of live bands and live music (best nights Fri, Sat, Sun).

Harbour Lights, Carlisle Bay. Also very lively on its days (Fri, Sat, Sun), it is lit with flaming torches and sees plenty of live bands.

Beach Bars

If you don't want to base a beach visit around a hotel, there are a number of excellent beach bars, some easy-going, others a little smarter where you can expect to eat well.

Mullins Beach Bar, near Speightstown. A popular gathering point by day and evening. It has a very pretty setting with a white gingerbread terrace facing onto the sunset. After a major face lift, it is now a bistro, with a restaurant at night.

Cocomos, Holetown. A friendly spot with a deck on the sand, popular in the early evening with Bajans on their way home from work.

Nineteenth Hole, Hastings, Christ Church, next door to Amaryllis Beach Resort. A popular new watering spot.

The Boatyard, Carlisle Bay. A nightclub at night but by day has a bar and restaurant beneath the sea almond tree right on the sand at the head of the bay.

Sugar Reef, Accra Beach. All dressed up in white wood and parasols and can get lively.

Carib Beach Bar, Worthing. You will find a mixed crowd of Bajans and visitors under the parasols and palm trees here: snacks by day and often lively after dark.

Silver Sands Beach Bar. At its most active when the windsurfers are around in the winter.

De Kitchen, next to Boatyard. Friday night is the big night to mix with Bajan yuppies. Fabulous soups.

Shows and Theatre

Bajan Roots and Rhythms, The Plantation Restaurant, in the old boiling house of the Balls Estate in St Lawrence, **t** 428 5048, *www.theplantation.bb*. A show every Wed and Fri with fire-eating and flaming limbo, drinks and dinner.

Harbour Lights Beach Extravaganza, Marina Villa, Bay Street, **t** 436 7225, *www.harbourlightsbarbados.com*. Dinner show, music and dancing; different features each night. Check locally.

Frank Collymore Hall, Bridgetown. More formal entertainment: concerts and plays.

Bridgetown

Set on the broad sweep of Carlisle Bay on the southwest coast of Barbados, Bridgetown is a thriving Caribbean capital with a population of over 100,000. It is a typical Caribbean mix: grand old colonial structures with filigree metal balconies jostle with purposeful, modern pastel-coloured offices and glass-fronted shops, while out in the street markets hucksters tout their wares from trays to passers-by.

The heart of Bridgetown has always been the old harbour at the **Careenage**, an inlet that takes its name from the process of careening, in which a weight would be tied to a ship's mast to upturn it, exposing the hull so that it could be cleaned and painted. The lighters that once loaded the ships at anchor in the bay are now gone because Barbados has a deep-water harbour, but the jetties of the Careenage have some café life in the old warehouses and there are still local fishing craft and pleasure boats at dock. It is all quite picturesque nowadays, but about 300 years ago it was an offence worthy of prosecution to disturb the waters of the Careenage because the smell was so bad.

Presiding over the scene from **National Heroes Square** (formerly Trafalgar Square) on the northern shore of the Careenage is a **statue of Lord Nelson** in full uniform, erected in 1813 following his death at the Battle of Trafalgar. Nelson had been based in the West Indies for several years, and the Barbadians were grateful to him as the 'preserver of the West Indies'. The Barbadian tribute to him preceded the statue in London by 27 years. Traditionally he faces any danger that threatens Barbados and so in the past he has always faced the sea. In a recent redevelopment, however, he was inexplicably turned round. Bajan wags quip that he now faces the twin threats of the government buildings and the Central Bank.

The Square was originally known as The Green in English fashion and was once home to the pillory and the ducking stool (quite some punishment, evidently, considering the foul waters of the Careenage). Now there is a **waterfall** supported by the tails of dolphins. On the north side of the square are the **Public Buildings**, home of the Barbados Parliament, which were recently cleaned up to reveal bright Barbadian coral rock. Opened in 1874, the two long rounded Italianate buildings have been adapted to the tropics with green-louvred shutters and red tin shades. In the House of Assembly there is a stained-glass window commemorating the monarchs of England, from James I to Victoria, including a portrait of Cromwell, interesting in itself because of Barbados's Royalist sympathies during the Civil War.

Two minutes' walk east of National Heroes Square is **St Michael's Cathedral**, rebuilt with money raised in a lottery in 1789 after the early wooden structure was destroyed in the hurricane of 1780. It became a cathedral when William Hart Coleridge arrived in 1825 as the first Bishop of Barbados. Among the sculpted memorials and tablets is a font that dates from 1680 and is decorated with a Greek palindrome: ΝΙΦΟΝ ΑΝΟΜΗ ΜΑΜΗ ΜΟΝΑ ΝΟΦΙΝ, meaning, 'Wash the sin, not just the skin'.

On Magazine Lane, leading up to the functional buildings of the **Law Courts** and the **Public Library**, presented to Barbados by Andrew Carnegie in 1906, is the recently restored 19th-century **Synagogue** (*t 432 0840; adm*). It occupies the site of the original

17th-century building constructed by Jews who had escaped from Brazil and obtained permission to settle in Barbados on hearing that Cromwell had granted freedom of worship. Just inside the graveyard can be seen the bemusing headstone commemorating a certain Benjamin Massiah, no doubt a local celebrity, who 'performed the office of circumciser with great Applause and Dexterity'.

Now behind Nelson is **Broad St**, Bridgetown's main thoroughfare and business street, where elaborate colonial edifices with metalwork balconies that might belong in an English south coastal town are interspersed with modern shopping centres and banks. Parallel to Broad Street is **Swan St**, a popular local market, and on the other side is the seafront road, which leads to the deep-water harbour and cruise ship terminal. Opposite the fish market is the **Rasta Mall**, with rastaman stalls painted in red, gold and green, with anything from the speeches of Haile Selassie to sandals and herbal medicines on sale. Close by is the **Pelican Village**, an artisan's mall selling paintings, crafts, wickerwork and clothes.

Headed south from National Heroes Square you cross the **Chamberlain Bridge** (on which is a plaque with the Barbadian National Anthem) and join Bay St, which heads southeast, skirting **Carlisle Bay**, where yachts lie at anchor off the beach and the esplanade. A hundred years ago this area was a poor quarter renowned for smuggling, until the government bought it out and built the esplanade. Bay St itself is still a tatty area of old wooden buildings, nightclubs and poky bars that works by night as Bridgetown's red-light district, but there are also some very elaborate town houses with gingerbread pointings as intricate as lace.

The Barbadian flag was first raised in place of the Union Jack on the **Garrison Savannah** (t 426 0840), a 50-acre park surrounded by trees a couple of miles from central Bridgetown. It takes its name from its original use as a military training ground, and barracks in varying states of repair still surround the Savannah – today's military, the Barbados Defence Force, occupies the 18th-century St Anne's Fort across the road on the south side. The original **Guard House**, with its green-domed clock tower, is occupied by the Savannah Club. Nowadays, as well as the parades, the Savannah hosts sports such as racing, rugby and cricket.

In the handsome setting of the former garrison jail is the **Barbados Museum** (t 427 0201; www.barbmuse.org.bb; open Mon–Sat 9–5, Sun 2–6; adm), which gives an enlightening view of Barbadian history from its start as a coral-encrusted shelf, inhabited by various Amerindian tribes, to the archetypal sugar island, and on to 'Bimshire' and Independence. There are some particularly good displays in the Aall maps and prints gallery, and some peep-in views of old-time Barbados. Naturally there is an exhibit of a prisoner's cell. The exhibition gallery has revolving exhibits of local contemporary artists and there is a hands-on children's gallery.

Just north of the deep-water port and cruise ship terminal you can see the story of Barbados rum in a number of different places. At the **Mount Gay Visitor Centre** (t 425 9066; open Mon–Fri 9–4; adm; video presentation and guided tour of 45mins), a tin-roofed Bajan house, you will see the processes of ageing, blending and bottling (the rum is actually distilled in the north of the island), and, most interesting, barrel manufacture. You can have lunch if you want it, and of course you can have tastings. At the

Bridgetown

Barbados Tourism Authority

YMCA

ROEBUCK ST (HIGHWAY 3)

CRUMPTON ST

Central Bank & Frank Collymore Hall

St Michael's Cathedral

ST MICHAEL'S ROW

Fairchild Market

Bus Terminus

BRIDGE ST (HIGHWAY 6/7)

Plaza Cinema

PROBYN ST

Empire Cinema

Harbour Police Station

POL

Treasury Building

FAIRCHILD ST

BAY ST (HIGHWAY 7)

INDEPENDENCE SQUARE

MAGAZINE LANE

COLERIDGE ST (HIGHWAY 2)

Synagogue

Olympic Cinema

Parliament Buildings

HIGH ST

Dolphin Fountain

NATIONAL HEROES SQUARE

Statue of Lord Nelson

CHAMBERLAIN BRIDGE

Public Library

Law Courts

Central Police Station

POL

JAMES ST

James Street Methodist Church

BROAD ST

PRINCE WILLIAM-HENRY ST

SWAN ST

WHARF (HIGHWAY 1)

Careenage

Carlisle Bay

TUDOR ST

MILK MARKET

HINCKS ST

CAT'S CASTLE

ST MARY'S ROW

St Mary's Church

LOWER BROAD ST

PRINCE ALFRED ST

Bus Terminus

Bus Terminus

Fishing Harbour

Caribbean Sea

LAKES FOLLY

Bus Terminus

Rasta Mall

CHEAPSIDE

PRINCESS ALICE HIGHWAY

Fish Market

CHEAPSIDE

Bus Terminus

Pelican Village

N

200 metres

200 yards

West Indies Rum Distillery, the **Malibu Visitor Centre** (*t 425 9393, malibubeach@ sunbeach.net; open Mon–Fri 9–11 and 12–4; adm*) takes you through the same produc-tion of Barbados's famous coconut-flavoured rum, with a video presentation and then a guided tour through the different processes. The centre is set on Brighton Beach and there is a beach bar, so you can make a day of it, among all the cruise ship passen-gers, if you want. There's a lunch tour available and of course rum-tasting. Headed out of town on the Spring Garden Highway, where the Parade of Bands is held at Cropover, you will find the **Kensington Oval** (the island's main stadium and home of the cricket internationals) and then the **Cave Hill Campus**, one of three that make up the University of the West Indies. The other two are in Jamaica and Trinidad.

In the outskirts of the town a little inland you will find an excellent example of a private Barbadian home at **Tyrol Cot** (*t 424 2074; open Mon–Fri 9–5; adm*), built with stone and ballast brick, painted white and orange with green louvred windows. It is a little bigger than the cottage that 'cot' implies and it has a very attractive interior with antique furniture and personal collections of porcelain and statuettes. Built in 1854, the house belonged to Sir Grantley Adams, first Premier of Barbados and Prime Minister of the ill-fated West Indies Federation, and was the boyhood home of Tom Adams, who later became the second Prime Minister of independent Barbados. Tyrol Cot is surrounded by a small assembly of Bajan **chattel houses**, painted in traditional island colours (more subdued red and yellow or cream and brown than the bright turquoise, sky blue and lurid green that you see nowadays). Each one is the workshop of a traditional Barbadian artisan – pottery, leatherwork and sweets – with products on sale of course. There is also a **rum shop** with island rum and local fare.

The West Coast

Highway 1 leads out of Bridgetown to the north, along the west coast of the island, to Speightstown, Barbados's second town. Winter home to transient millionaires, the west coast is all hotels and expensive villas muscling in for frontage on the 10-mile strip of extremely fine beaches. Interspersed you will find local clapboard houses, rum shops, restaurants and the best sunset beach bars. It is odd to think that until the Second World War people would avoid this area and make the journey north by boat. It was considered unhealthy because of the coastal swamps and, anyway, the road was awful. But since the 1950s, people have flocked here from all over the world. In tourist jargon it is referred to as the Gold Coast, recently updated to the Platinum Coast.

Following the west coast road, which runs behind the seafront stretch of houses and hotels, winding over the small headlands and occasionally opening up onto a 'widow on the sea', you come to **Holetown**, 7 miles north of the capital. This is where the first European settlers made their home. It is apparently called so because it reminded sailors of 'the Hole' on the River Thames. It was here that Captain John Powell claimed the island for England, nailing a sign, 'James K. of E. and of this island', on a fustic tree in 1625. The proclamation has disappeared of course, but the event is recalled by a memorial in the town. Originally the town was called Jamestown, a name which still remains in the parish and in the Holetown church, **St James's**, the oldest on the island, 'erected here, on God's Acre, in the Olde Towne, 1629'. The church has recently been restored, revealing the bright coral rock.

Inland, above Holetown you will find the **Sugar Museum** (*t 432 0100; open Mon–Sat 9–5; adm*) at Portvale. In the restored boiling house of the old estate the story of sugar is told in old prints, models, signboards and artefacts from across the ages – boilers, crushers, steam engines. The museum stands in the grounds of the Portvale Sugar Factory, which is well worth a visit during the cane-cutting season between February and May.

Speightstown (pronounced rather like 'spoikestong') is about 12 miles north of the capital. Very early on, the town was a thriving port, used to land goods for the northern part of Barbados, before good roads were built. The town was known as Little Bristol because it had links with Bristol, then England's second-largest port. Its name even derives from that of a Bristol man, William Speight, a member of the Barbados Parliament in 1639. The town is developing fast at the moment, but there are still some charming old buildings and a certain easy-going air.

The North: Scotland and St Lucy

The imposed sophistication of the west coast evaporates with the last hotel just north of Speightstown, giving way to fishing villages in the bays and unfortunately an industrial plant amidst the simple attractive parish of St Lucy. Among the dramatic, limestone cliffs of the northern tip of the island is **Animal Flower Cave** (*adm*), a series of caverns thrashed out by the force of the waves. There are some blow holes and you might see an 'animal flower', a flower-like sea anemone which snaps back into its sheath when disturbed. It's a point to aim for if nothing else. In the nearby Pirate's Tavern, you can get a drink and escape the heat. It is well worth the visit to the **Mount Gay Rum Distillery** (*Spring Garden Highway, t 425 8757, www.mountgay.com*), where you will see huge vats of fermenting molasses and water, and the stills of the distillation process. You can see the ageing and blending at the Mount Gay and Malibu Visitor Centres outside Bridgetown, but a visit here is infinitely preferable because it shows the process from the beginning and is anyway less crowded and more personal.

Inland from Speightsown and St James the land rises quickly up a cliff onto a less developed plateau covered in sweeping plains of sugar cane; it breaks and folds into the rugged and mountainous **Scotland District** in the centre of the island. Here there are beautiful gulleys filled with mahogany trees and grand and steep hilltops that tower above the sparsely grassed east-coast slopes. It was to Scotland that the Catholics, 'barbadosed' by Cromwell, were sent to keep them out of the way. Their descendants lived here for centuries, in communities of 'poor whites' as they were known, but not many are left now. Escaped slaves would come to lie up here in the hope of casting off for St Vincent, 100 miles directly downwind and just visible on the clearest days from Mount Hillaby. Finally, the area also found favour with the planters, who built some of the finest plantation houses here. The roads are rough in the remoter areas of Scotland District, but it is worth making the effort to go there just for the views.

There is a magnificent view in all directions from the **Grenade Hall Forest and Signal Station**, but then it was a lookout and a link in the semaphore communication chain that could signal around the island in minutes. The original building has been excavated and restored. There is a short historical audio tape and descriptions of how the signalling functioned. Beneath is a small forest where there is a series of trails with signs which illustrate the complexities of the ecosystem and indicate plants used in local medicine: spiritweed and broomweed were used as diuretics, and briny roots against scurvy and as a purgative. Close by is the **Barbados Wildlife Reserve** (*t 422 8826; open daily 10–5; adm*), a small zoo with animals free to roam around a small wood, including native Barbadian tortoises, agoutis and spectacled caiman, an alligator, raccoons and armadillos.

Close by, **Farley Hill** (*t 422 3555; gardens open daily until dusk; adm*) is a park and garden set around the shell of a 19th-century mansion that was renowned as the smartest in Barbados in the late 1880s. It is a little sad since it was gutted by fire in the 1960s, but the gardens, with their magnificent royal palms and other labelled trees and plants, are peaceful and pleasant.

A couple of miles away is **St Nicholas Abbey** (*t 422 8725; open Mon–Fri 10–3.30; adm to house and gardens*), one of the two oldest mansions on the island and among only three Jacobean houses surviving in the whole of the Americas (along with Drax Hall, also in Barbados, and Bacon's Castle in Virginia, USA). Built around 1650 by a Colonel Berringer, it is not really an abbey but a fine stone building with an arched façade topped with curved gables (a reminder of the Dutch influence in the early days of settlement). Inside, the private house has some antique furniture and you will notice a curiosity in that the house has fireplaces, as though the inhabitants feared cold nights in the hills of Scotland. It is still a working plantation. Do not miss the film, shown twice daily (*11.30am and 2.30pm*), of Barbados in the 1930s, which includes footage of the Bridgetown Careenage, loading rum puncheons, mauby ladies pouring drinks from barrels on their heads, and shots of Barbados's windmills turning in the wind.

One of the finest views of Scotland District is from **Cherry Tree Hill**, from where one can look north to St Lucy and south over the island as far as Hackleton's Cliff in the parish of St Joseph. At one time about 500 windmills were employed in crushing cane on Barbados, and, as you descend the steep hill towards the coast, you come to the only one that survives intact, the **Morgan Lewis Mill** (*t 422 7429, natrust@sunbeach. net; open Mon–Sat 9–5; adm*). Its original crushing gear is on view.

Back on the main road you pass **St Andrew's Parish Church**. The parish is the least populous in Barbados and boasts the highest point on the island, **Mount Hillaby**, 1,160ft above sea level. It also has Barbados's only untouched forestland, **Turner's Hall Wood**, on a ridge leading from Mount Hillaby, the last remnant of the forest that once covered the whole of the island. The wood has a variety of trees, including the sandbox, the buttressed locust tree, which has a pod with foul-smelling but reasonably tasty flesh, and the jack-in-a-box tree that takes its name from its seed, which stands erect in a pod. You might also see a grey kingbird or a carib grackle. Not far off is the **Flower Forest** (*t 433 8152; open daily 9–5; adm*), with paths through magnificent tropical floral splendour and excellent views of Scotland in the distance. Trees and other plants include breadfruit, golden apple and mango, as well as spices and citrus.

If you continue along Highway 2 towards Bridgetown, you come to **Welchman Hall Gulley** (*t 438 6671; open daily 9–5; adm*), a cleft in Barbados's limestone cap that drips with tropical greenery, a canopy that nearly blocks out the sun and drops lianas down onto the array of shrubs and trees (about 200 species in all). On the short walk through the gulley you might think that you have descended to the depths of the island, but when you come out into the open you are presented with a fantastic view over northern Barbados and the Atlantic. The gulley and the caves were used by runaways and escapees of all sorts.

Further along Highway 2 is **Harrison's Cave** (*t 438 6640, harrisonscave@sunbeach. net; open daily 9–4; adm exp*), a series of underground rivers and limestone caverns hung with stalactite shark teeth that drip onto glutinous stalagmites, due to join up in a couple of million years. It is all a bit overplayed, with hard hats, strict guides, fat-wheeled buggies, and yet another handicraft shop, but the 500,000-year-old caverns are genuinely a stimulating sight.

The Sugar Heartland: Bridgetown to the Atlantic Coast

Highways 3 and 4 leave Bridgetown to the northeast, struggling through the ever-expanding suburbs before they pass into Barbados's sugar-cane heartland, where they disappear between curtains of the 12ft grass-like crop. Following the track of the old railway (now defunct), the land rises steadily from west to east, culminating in a cliff that gives broad and sweeping views of the east coast and Atlantic Ocean, and then descends to the old stations on the coastline and the railway terminus at Belleplaine, where the Bajans liked to escape for their picnics early in the 20th century. In the uplands, the roads are a maze linking small villages of colourful clap-board houses, chattel houses to the islanders, though these are gradually disappearing now as the Bajans move into larger and more comfortable concrete housing. You will also come across some of the island's finest plantation houses.

The first important landmark on Highway 4 out of Bridgetown is the **Banks Brewery** (*t 429 0474; open Mon–Fri 10–4; adm*), where you can see the award-winning beer created with malt, hops, local water, local yeast and a touch of local cane juice, through brewing, boiling, fermentation and lagering. **Francia Plantation House** (*t 429 0474, francia@caribsurf.com; open Mon–Fri 10–4; adm*), set in open tropical gardens with a panoramic view of the west coast, is a Bajan family home with echoes of Brazil in some architectural features and in the imported hardwood. There are West Indian prints and maps as well as a three-way seat for a pair of lovers (the third seat is for the girl's chaperone) and a dripstone, which provided clean and filtered water.

Gun Hill Signal Station (*St George, t 429 1358, natrust@sunbeach.net; open Mon–Fri 9–4; adm*) is one of the string of semaphore stations that could link the whole of Barbados within minutes. Set up in 1818, it was designed to warn of impending trouble from the sea, and able to advise that ships had arrived safely in port with merchandise or even pass the message quickly of an uprising among the slaves, by using flags by day and coloured lanterns at night. The communication tower at Gun Hill has been restored and provides a fine view of the island all around, as well as a map of the other stations in the network and some military memorabilia. Gun Hill was also used for convalescence for troops suffering from malaria and yellow fever. They tended to recover because the climate was fresher away from the sea and there are no mosquitoes at this altitude. On approach to the signal station you will see an odd-looking white lion, sculpted by a Colonel Wilkinson during his convalescence (hardly a masterpiece). **Orchid House** (*t 433 0306*), hidden among the cane fields, grows hundreds of orchids in its many gullies, ponds and rocky gardens as well as covered areas.

Hackleton's Cliff runs parallel to the coastline and commands another of Barbados's fine panoramas, with views both north and south along the Atlantic coastline from about 1,000ft above the sea. Just inside the parish of St Joseph is a former signal station, the **Cotton Tower**, a link in the semaphore chain from Gun Hill. It stands above a gully, the Devil's Bowling Alley, and has cracking views over Scotland to the north.

The windward coast of Barbados is lined with reefs sometimes up to 3 miles offshore, making it impossible for all but the smallest ships to put in here. But the reefs have little effect on the Atlantic breakers that barrel in and crash on the poised rocks the size of houses on the coastline, eroding it at the rate of 1ft a year. A typical windward-coast settlement is **Bathsheba**, a slightly ragged fishing village dotted with houses and windblown palm trees. There is a good mix of locals and tourists – fishermen still make their way out to sea through the reefs, but it is also popular with surfers because it offers the best waves on the island.

Andromeda Gardens (*t 433 9384, abg@caribsurf.com; open daily 9–5, special tour Wed 10.30am, otherwise self-guided; adm*), above the village, are well worth a visit. They are full to bursting with plants from all over the tropical world, ranging from tiny orchids to the tree that gave Barbados its name, the banyan, or bearded fig tree. Started in 1954, the gardens have grassy walkways through a valley alive with the smells and colours of a tropical explosion (the plants are labelled), and bowers where birds flit. You will see the native frangipani, with bright red and yellow petals; a wonderful variety of palm trees; heliconias by the hundred, including *Heliconia hirsuta*, or 'Twiggy'; orchids that look like five-winged purple and white butterflies; and *Ravenala madagascariensis*, the travellers' tree, which has a fan of broad leaves similar to a banana tree.

To the south of here, there is an extremely fine view from **St John's Parish Church**, which stands on the cliff 800ft above the Atlantic coast. The original church was constructed at a cost of 100,000 pounds of sugar in 1667 and was rebuilt in 1836 after the 1831 hurricane. St John's also has a strange history concerning its early vestryman Ferdinando Paleologus, who came to Barbados as a refugee after fighting on the side of the Royalists in the Civil War. His ancestors had been the Christian Emperors of Constantinople until they were driven out by the Turks in the 15th century. His remains were discovered in the destruction caused by the 1831 hurricane, head pointing west according to the Greek custom, and they were moved and reinterred in a vault with Greek columns.

To the southeast, on a shelf in the descending cliff, is **Codrington College** (*t 423 1140; adm*), a magnificent coral-stone seminary with an arched portico and views down to Consett Bay. Approached through an avenue of mighty cabbage palms, living columns up to 100ft in height, it is set in a garden of tropical plants with a lake. It was built in the early 18th century with money from a bequest from Christopher Codrington, a Governor General of the Leeward Islands whose grandfather was one of the earliest settlers of Barbados. A story is attached to two of the cabbage palms in the avenue, planted in 1879 by Prince Albert and Prince George, who were on a visit to the island. One palm flourished, but the other did not. When the news came that Prince Albert had died, the local Bajans showed no surprise and said, 'We knew he die soon. His cabbage die!' It is still a working theological college, but the grounds are accessible and there is a nature trail.

Suburbs and the South Coast

Like the west coast, the south coast of Barbados is gilded with beaches, mounds of golden sand on which the waves clap and rush. Just behind them are apartment blocks and hotels jostling for space in the extended suburb that contains the homes of the Bajan *bons bourgeois*. **Highway 7** runs from central Bridgetown to Oistins Town (about 5 miles), throwing off lanes that seek out the gaps and the coves, like **St Lawrence Gap**, the hub of south-coast nightlife. The suburbs have names like **Hastings**, **Worthing** and **Dover**, perhaps a reminder of home for nostalgic colonists in centuries past, but certainly less demure than their British counterparts. The hotels and restaurants of the south coast do not have the sophistication of the west coast, but there is a lively, relaxed atmosphere and good nightlife. Eventually the road passes into country, past the airport, though this itself is now prime development land and is steadily being gobbled up by the endless sprawl of concrete suburbs.

Oistins, where the sea flashes with colourful Barbadian fishing boats, is a fishing centre and Barbados's third-largest town. The market at the roadside comes alive each day in the late afternoon when the catch is brought in and sold, continuing into the evening (recently this has become something of an institution for islanders and tourists alike, who come to wash down grilled fish with a beer). According to Ligon, a visitor in the 1650s, it was called 'Austins Bay, not in commemoration of any Saint, but of a wilde mad drunken fellow, whose lewd and extravagant carriage made him infamous in the Iland'. It was in Oistins Town in 1652, at Ye Mermaid's Inn, that the 'Magna Carta of Barbados', the articles of capitulation, were signed by the Royalists, surrendering Barbados after a long siege to the Commonwealth Commissioners sent by Cromwell.

Past the southern point of the island and the airport you come to the **Foursquare Rum Factory** (*t 423 6669; open Mon–Fri 9–5, Sat–Sun 10–6; video presentation and tour*), a modern installation on the site of an old sugar estate that produces white and dark rums. The tour includes the old sugar factory (it closed in 1988 and the molasses for distillation is now brought from elsewhere), with its grinding mills, vacuum boilers and centrifuge, and then the distillery itself. Here you will see the process of rum, from mash, a mix of molasses, local water and yeast, through fermentation to alcohol and then to distillation in the mash column and the rectifier, and the resulting white rum. You'll also hear about the ageing in barrels made of American white oak, which are scorched on the inside to encourage colouring. You will even learn about the fusel oils and alcohol esters which cause hangovers. In the old coral-stone still house is the Art Foundry, where there are exhibition rooms, some working artists' studios and a print shop where they produce the labels for the rum bottles.

Farther along the coast is a notorious house in Long Bay, the crenellated **Sam Lord's Castle** (*open during the day; adm; occasional tour or day passes available for the hotel complex*), solidly built in 1820 (it was undamaged in the 1831 hurricane but scaffolding on the walls ended up 3 miles away). It is now surrounded by a hotel complex, but it is famous for the legend that surrounds its first owner, Sam Lord, a story that becomes more embellished with each telling. Lord was a greedy man, who was suspected of murder to gain inheritance and who was found out mistreating his wife cruelly, but he is also credited with causing shipwrecks on the reefs below his house, luring ships in to land by hanging lanterns in his windows, his palm trees, the horns of his cattle, or the antlers of his deer (delete as applicable). Then, so the story goes, he would offload the booty and bring it to his castle by way of an underground passage (conspicuously absent today).

He became an extremely rich man, favoured by a series of sudden deaths, but he was busily chasing yet another inheritance when he was uncovered. He had locked up his wife before a journey to England to talk her family into giving him some of her money, but she escaped and managed to get there before him and so he was arrested. However, a case brought against him was inconclusive. He is remembered in a book by a Lieutenant Colonel Drury, *The Regency Rascal*: whatever the legend that surrounds him, he was undoubtedly an extravagant rogue whose only bequests were debts, an impressive £18,000 in 1845, to go with his magnificent castle. It is suitably and lavishly decorated according to the period, with plasterwork ceilings and mahogany trimmings, Regency furniture and an extremely fine staircase. (It is often crowded because it works as the hotel lobby as well.) **Ragged Point** is the most easterly point on the island, a limestone cliff thrashed by the Atlantic.

Off **Highway 5**, the direct route back towards Bridgetown, is the **Sunbury Plantation House and Museum** (*t 423 6270, sunbury@caribsurf.com; adm*), where the pleasant lawned garden is set with coaches and iron farm machinery. The house, originally constructed in the 1660s, is restored in Georgian style to the state of a plantation house at the height of the island's sugar prosperity. There is a café in the grounds, operated by the Barbados National Trust.

Trinidad and Tobago

07

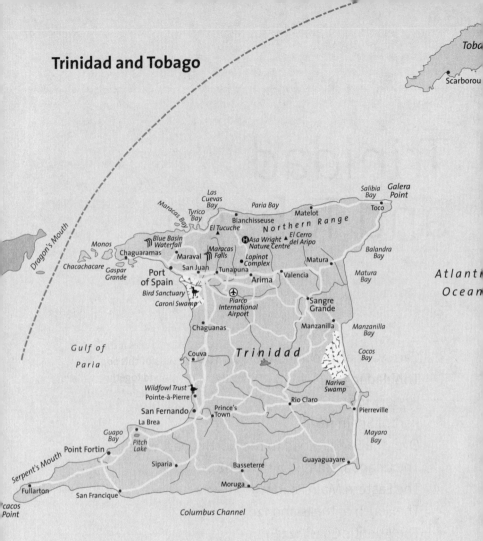

Trinidad and Tobago

Map labels:

Toba
Scarborou

Dragon's Mouth
Monos
Chacachacare
Gaspar Grande
Chaguaramas
Maracas Bay
Tyrico Bay
Blue Basin Waterfall
Maraval
San Juan
Port of Spain
Bird Sanctuary
Caroni Swamp
Las Cuevas Bay
Paria Bay
Blanchisseuse
El Tucuche
Maracas Falls
Tunapuna
Lopinot Complex
Arima
Piarco International Airport
Northern Range
Asa Wright Nature Centre
El Cerro del Aripo
Matura
Valencia
Sangre Grande
Matelot
Salibia Bay
Galera Point
Toco
Balandra Bay
Matura Bay
Atlanti
Ocean
Gulf of Paria
Chaguanas
Couva
Trinidad
Manzanilla
Manzanilla Bay
Cocos Bay
Nariva Swamp
Wildfowl Trust
Pointe-à-Pierre
San Fernando
La Brea
Guapo Bay
Point Fortin
Pitch Lake
Siparia
Prince's Town
Basseterre
Moruga
Rio Claro
Guayaguayare
Pierreville
Mayaro Bay
Serpent's Mouth
Fullarton
San Francique
cacos Point
Columbus Channel

Highlights

1 'Play Mas' – buy a costume and join in the Carnival street parade – or wear your oldest clothes and shuffle to steel pan at Jouvert

2 Take a boat trip into the Caroni Swamp on Trinidad to witness the evening flight of the scarlet ibis

3 Watch turtles nesting at night on the beaches of both islands

4 See 30 species of tropical birds before breakfast on the veranda of the Asa Wright Nature Centre on Trinidad

5 Scuba dive on the edge of the Atlantic, where rays play at one of the largest brain corals in the world

The twin-island state of Trinidad and Tobago is an unusual mix of two completely different Caribbean strains. Trinidad has the excitable bustle of a large and busy island, where at times like carnival, with its calypso singing and street masquerades, West Indian exuberance reaches its highest pitch. Equally colourful is the birdlife, unparalleled in the Caribbean. Just a few miles away, Tobago is a classic retreat in the Caribbean mould, a beach-bound idyll of white-sand beaches, hidden coves and easy island life. Together they make an unlikely but satisfying combination.

Trinidad and Tobago may be truly Caribbean in spirit, but geologically they are closer to South America. The northern range of mountains in Trinidad, just 7 miles off the continent, was separated from the mainland by rising water levels about 10,000 years ago. Trinidad is the largest of the Lesser Antilles (1,864 square miles, about 50 miles by 50). Unlike the other Antilles to the north, it is not volcanic and its heartlands are low agricultural plains. So close to South America, it is home to a surprisingly dense distribution of continental species, particularly birds. Tobago is a cumulus of forested peaks with some small coral-encrusted flatlands in the southwest that broke off from South America millions of years ago. It lies 22 miles off the northeastern tip of Trinidad and has an area of 116 square miles. Tobago's birdlife is also wonderfully varied.

There are about 1.3 million people on the two islands, which makes it the most populous country in the Lesser Antilles (Tobago has just 50,000 of this population). The islands were unwilling partners when they were first lumped together by the British Government in 1898, but they have grown closer, even if there is occasional dissent. Tobagonians complain that they are politically neglected and joke that Port of Spain is a den of thieves where you need eyes in the back of your head just to survive. In Trinidad, where there is a radically different population, nearly half composed of Indians, they laughingly claim that Tobago is backward, though they then admit that they like it that way because they can go on holiday there.

In fact, Tobago is developing fast at the moment. The tourism industry has expanded considerably in recent times and there is much more development scheduled for the future. Trinidad, which traditionally depended more on oil revenues than on tourism (it is an untypical Caribbean island because it does not have many of the palm-backed strands), has also begun to develop a little more and there are guest houses and hotels opening up in the remote coastal villages and the rainforest.

Trinidad and Tobago has long been a political leader in the Caribbean and, until the failure of the West Indian Federation in 1962, Chaguaramas outside Port of Spain was to have been the seat of the Caribbean Parliament. The leader of the country for many years was the charismatic historian and politician Eric Williams of the People's National Movement (PNM), who took Trinidad and Tobago to independence from Britain on 31 August 1962 and remained in power until his death in 1981. In 1976 the country became a republic, recognizing a President as Chief of State (presently George Maxwell Richards) rather than the Queen, though it has remained within the British Commonwealth.

There are two Houses of Parliament, a 31-seat Upper House and a 36-seat House of Representatives. The country is led by Prime Minister Patrick Manning of the People's

National Movement (PNM), who replaced Basdeo Banday of the United National Congress (UNC) after elections in late 2001. George Maxwell Richards, a university dean, was selected president by Parliament in March 2003.

Carnival, Calypso and Steel Pan

The country is also a Caribbean cultural leader. Steel pan and the calypso, a relentless song of stinging social comment, both of which are heard all over the Caribbean, were born here. Carnival, or Mas, is one of the three biggest in the world and is the model for most others held in the area. The 'Trinbagonians' must also take the credit and/or the responsibility for inventing the limbo dance.

Carnival

On Shrove Tuesday the streets of Port of Spain seethe with the bacchanal – fluorescent satin flashes by as a frenzied army of imps advances, each brandishing a trident. At their head is a massive devil with glowing eyes, a vast black mannequin with a demonic smile held aloft, sparkling with sequins. The Savannah and the length of Frederick St reverberate to a killing beat – vast articulated lorries stacked 30ft high with speakers, followed by a sea of costumed revellers dancing and shuffle-stepping in waves. It is the Parade of Carnival Bands and, at Trinidad Carnival, each band can contain as many as 3,000 'players' dressed to a common theme.

The build-up starts right after Christmas. The Trinidadians stage spectacles of calypso, steel bands, costume competitions and 'fêtes' all over the country – all culminating in a weekend of festivities and then a two day 'jump-up' in Port of Spain in which hundreds of thousands of people take part.

Mas (short for masquerade) was introduced by the French settlers who came to Trinidad at the end of the 18th century. At first it was the preserve of the plantocracy and the wealthy traders, who would move in masked processions from one open house to the next; but with emancipation in 1838, the slaves made the event their own. They danced in the streets with lighted torches, celebrating Canboulay (from *cannes brûlées*), the burning of the canefields. Drums led the processions and any instrument was used to make a tune: tin kettles, shack-shacks, even bottles and biscuit tins. In Victorian times the celebrations were frowned upon by the government and many official attempts were made to curb them, but these often ended in rioting (another meaning of the word bacchanal) as bands of revellers and groups of police armed with sticks took each other on.

Early in the 20th century the tradition of dressing up was revived and the drum-driven masquerade once again became the centrepiece of the Carnival. You will still see some of the figures of Ole Mas, *moko jumbies* (stilt men), *djab-djabs* (from French *diable*) and the elaborately dressed characters of the sailor bands. Steel bands led the processions in the years after the Second World War but now alongside them you will hear the relentless sounds of soca music as the engine-house of the pageant.

Mention Rio or New Orleans to a Trinidadian and they will laugh and assure you that Carnival in those cities is just a fashion show. Carnival is more accessible to outsiders here – you do not have to be a member of a club to 'play Mas'. People leave their jobs to get back to Mas, and without exception they get into the Trinidadian spirit of taking it all to glorious excess. If you want, it is possible to dance for four days and nights at a stretch.

The best moments to see are the calypso tents, the calypso competition finals, the steel band preliminaries and steel band finals. The street-dancing itself begins at 2am on Carnival Monday morning, as party-goers spill out onto the streets for Jouvert (pronounced *jouvay*). Players smear themselves with mud, oil and even chocolate sauce (beware if you wander by in smart clothes). After a couple of hours' rest they join the main Parade of Bands on Monday afternoon until late (when you can join a night band if you want) and then everyone comes out again on Tuesday. It is a crush and it is deafening, but there is nothing like it. The carnival road-march tunes of any particular year become ingrained in your memory as you hear them played over and over again; they will bring back the feeling of Carnival for years. The players continue to dance on Las'(t) Lap until midnight on Tuesday, when it all abruptly comes to an end, until next year of course. Some Calypso tents to look out for are Spektakula, Kitchener Calypso Review, Kaiso House, Kaiso Showkase and, most popular recently, Yangatang, which travels to different venues around the island and has lots of comedy as well as calypso. Also try Under the Trees at the Normandie Hotel, which has comedy and calypso.

If you wish to 'play Mas', you can turn up at a Mas Camp 10 days ahead of time and buy a costume in which to play for between US$100 and US$200. A few bands to consider are Harts (*www.hartscarnival.com*), which is quite 'bouge' (upper middle class and lighter in colour); Barbarossa (*www.barbarossaintl.com*); Legends (*www.legendscarnival.com*), which is full of the body-beautiful (they work out to get ready for Mas); and Minshell (*www.callaloo.co.tt*), which sees a more artistic and also a blacker crowd.

Calypso

The sounds that accompany Carnival – the relentless beat on the road march as the masqueraders dance through the streets and in the lively sparring in the concert halls – are calypsos. They are Trinidadian-born songs of life, love and lust – witty, lyrical, melodic, full of gossip and often political, but above all entertaining (in their comment or as dance tunes) and with as many styles as there are calypsonians (also known as *kaisonians*).

The roots of the calypso are obscure, but the songs were first sung in French creole in Trinidad during the 19th century. Early in the 20th century they became a source of popular entertainment and, as they started to reach a larger audience, they were sung in English. Since they have become popular in Trinidad, other islands in the area have adopted the form. They are a verbal newspaper of sorts and they deal with contemporary issues, commenting on politics, satirizing life's institutions (anything from love to the IMF) and occasionally descending into plain rudeness (smut, as it is known, has been causing controversy recently because it is an easy way of making a mark in a fiercely competitive arena). The songs are often irreverent and satirical, they have a fearsome cutting edge when it comes to ridicule, and they have been known to have a direct effect on politics. Most recently, though, they have come under threat from politicians, who were planning to outlaw certain name-calling in song and in the press.

But the calypsonian is also a performer, daring and outspoken, as seen in the annual calypso competition in the run-up to Carnival. The big calypsonians will spar with each other in song, ridiculing their opponents in their lyrics (there is a special word for personal insult in calypso, *picong*). Singers belong to a calypso tent (no longer a tent but a commercial group a bit like a recording label; names include Spektakula Forum, Calypso Revue and Kisskidee) where they perform the songs. Judges select a number of calypsonians from each tent to go on to the National Calypso Monarch Competition.

The finals are something like a variety show as the performers act out their theme. Calypsos must be timely and witty; the style can range from that of a raconteur to a pantomime artist. The repertoire is endless, but they are divided fundamentally into two main categories, both destined for different prizes: the slower and more melodic tunes with more thoughtful lyrics that compete for the calypso monarch title, and the faster, simpler dance tunes that vie for the road-march title (won by the song played the most as the bands cross the judging stages in the parade of bands). Very occasionally a single song can win both categories. A third prize is awarded in the Extempo competition (from 'extemporization'), in which singers ad-lib, verse by verse, in competition with one another (lots of *picong* here), on subjects handed to them seconds before.

After the Second World War, the calypsos were often backed by steel pan, but since the late 1970s this has been replaced by soca music (from soul-calypso), a much faster beat played on more conventional modern instruments. Above the definite African drumbeat can be heard the strains of European rock and often odd blends of Indian or Chinese sounds.

The names of the calypsonians are colourful in themselves: early singers included Attila the Hun, Lord Executor and the Roaring Lion. Another self-appointed lord is Lord Melody, who stands alongside Calypso Rose, the Mighty Chalkdust (a schoolteacher),

Carnival Calendar of Events

A typical Carnival stages calypso tents and Panorama (steel band) and King and Queen of the Band (the most elaborate and largest costumes) competition heats on the weekends before the beginning of Lent.

Friday before Lent: 'Ole Time Mas' Characters Festival, Piccadilly Green, Arima; King and Queen of the Bands semifinals; Extempo Calypso Competition finals.

Saturday: Junior Carnival Parade and Competition; Panorama final.

Sunday: Dimanche Gras, a day of fêtes; Calypso finals; King and Queen of the Bands finals.

Monday: Jouvert (a jump-up, 2–10am); Procession of Carnival Bands, starting at 1pm; Night Mas (mostly steel pan) in St James's.

Tuesday: Mardi Gras, Parade of Carnival Bands from 9am until late; Las' Lap.

Saturday night: Carnival Champions in concert.

Black Stalin, Crazy and Watchman (a policeman). The two mightiest (another popular prefix) calypsonians of all were Lord Kitchener, who died in early 2000 and who was famed for his orchestration and steel-pan compositions, and the Mighty Sparrow. They were on the scene for 40 years – Sparrow was first crowned monarch in 1956 and won again as recently as 1992. Current leading calypsonians to look out for are David Rudder and Machel Montano.

Steel Pan

As you walk along the street in Port of Spain, you might hear a rising, tremulous thunder of plinks and clangs. Suddenly you will hear a beat and the rhythm emerges: energetic, compulsive. It is an impressive sight to see a steel band. It is entirely a percussion orchestra and can have have as many as a hundred players all moving in time. At times the music can be raucous and rough; at other times it can sound like notes on velvet.

Steel pan, played on the stretched and tempered lids of oil drums (literally the discarded drums of the oil industry), was invented in Trinidad and was first heard at the end of the Second World War. It was backstreet music that came from the poorest sections of Port of Spain and initially it was frowned upon by the authorities. The pan-yards gave themselves names such as Desperadoes, Renegades and Invaders and they fought regularly amongst themselves and with the police.

But the movement picked up in popularity and then became more respectable. It soon replaced tamboo-bamboo as the music for the Carnival road march, initially as 'pan-around-the-neck' on the streets and later in larger lorry-borne bands. Steel pan has been superseded by soca only in the last 20 years. Many pan-yards are still active in Trinidad and it is definitely worth going along (just walk straight in) if you hear them playing. Pan competitions are held annually at Carnival (which is well worth attending) and every other year at the Pan is Beautiful Festival in October (it alternates with the School Steelband Music Festival). Pan Jazz is a also yearly festival held in November in which steel bands play alongside world-famous jazz musicians. Pan Ramajay (the word 'ramajay' means a combination of display, flair, virtuoso and plain showing off) is held in May and features pan players showing their finest skills in competition.

Trinidad

In the faces of Trinidad you will see echoes from around the globe: African, (East) Indian, European, Middle Eastern (called Syrian), Chinese and South American. It is an extraordinary mixture, and it has been made yet more complex and exotic as the races have intermingled. You will hear names such as Harris Mohammed and Winston Chang and see people wearing saris and African-style suits. On the skyline, Hindu prayer flags and the domes of minarets stand among the classically English parish-church towers. Even the musical rhythms (soca in this area) will be blended. In chutney-soca you can hear distinctly (East) Indian-sounding strains.

The two largest sectors of the population are African and Indian, each of which is about 40%. Other races include a few Chinese, though many have left in the last two generations, and Europeans, some British, but particularly the descendants of the French settlers of two centuries ago (French creole has become a catch-all term for white Trinidadians). Around 15% of the islanders are of mixed descent. There are the same unspoken rules of colour in Trinidad that exist throughout the Caribbean, and here they are further complicated by race (there are terms for the different mixes, such as Dougla for an Indian-African combination), but generally speaking it is a benevolent mix.

Nearly half of the population lives in the urban east–west corridor that runs between the capital, Port of Spain, and the town of Arima, in the lee of the northern range of mountains, which at the moment is mainly inaccessible and undeveloped (once it was patched with coffee and cocoa plantations). South of here, ranges of hills rise periodically out of much flatter land, which is given over to industrial and agricultural concerns, including oilfields and vast tracts of sugar cane. Because of the nature of the island you are likely to spend quite a bit of time in Port of Spain. However, it is well worth making the effort to get out into the country.

The island is highly industrial for the Caribbean. Oil and gas are the main earners, with significantly increased revenues in recent years due to the rise in energy prices. Other industries include asphalt and the export of manufactured goods, including cigarettes, foods and clothing. Despite the fertile soil, the agricultural sector is small. The intention is for tourism to increase.

For all their mixed heritage, the Trinidadians have a typically expansive and vital Caribbean attitude to life. They have never done anything by halves and so you can expect a lively time, especially if you attend an event like Carnival. But there are also some classic quiet spots where you can see the best birdlife in the Caribbean. Trinidad is not a typical tourist island, but with such a variety of cultural and natural assets it offers far more than a typical Caribbean beach to the traveller who wants to get off the beaten track.

History

In its early history Trinidad was called Iere, or 'island', as it was referred to by Arawak Indians from mainland South America. Unlike their cousins farther north, the Iere Arawaks managed to resist the cannibalizing Caribs who came by in waves around AD 1000, so escaping the *boucan* (on which meat was smoked).

The island was christened by Columbus himself in 1498. As he arrived in the New World on his third voyage he sighted three peaks in the southeast of the island and so he called the island Trinidad as a special devotion to the Holy Trinity. The Indians continued to resist any attempts at settling and they kept the Spaniards off the island for a hundred years until 1592. At the beginning of the 17th century, explorers began to use the island as a base for expeditions into the South American jungle in search of El Dorado, the Golden King.

Trinidad was officially a defensive Spanish outpost, but it was usually ignored in favour of the islands in the Greater Antilles and so it did not attract many settlers to

Best Beaches

Maracas Bay: A huge sweeping strand enclosed by vast headlands, which funnel the waves onto the shelved sand and enormous palm trees. Red flags mean a strong current. At Maracas Bay the thing to have is a 'shark and bake' – a fish sandwich – with a Solo soft drink or a Carib. Try Richard's, which has made a name for itself as the place to go and has a string of excellent chutneys and dips.

Tyrico Bay: Sand OK, waves often big enough to surf.

Las Cuevas Bay: Popular with Trinidadian weekend trippers, named after the underwater caves (changing rooms available).

Blanchisseuse Bay: Remote escape with good sand.

Paria Bay: A couple of miles beyond Blanchisseuse, usually deserted.

Balandra Bay, **Grande Rivière** and **Salibia Bay**: Near the northeastern tip of the island, these see the full force of the Atlantic, but there is protected swimming.

Manzanilla Bay, Cocos Bay and **Mayaro Bay**: Miles and miles of palm-backed sand, on the east coast running down to the southeastern corner of the island. The beaches face the Atlantic and so the waves can be big. Island lore explains that a boatload of coconuts from Brazil was washed up here: hence the palm trees.

Chaguaramas: The beaches are not that nice, but it's an easy run from Port of Spain, so people often swim here.

develop the fertile lands. There was just a small and beleaguered garrison, and the governing *cabildo*, which officially seems to have been called 'Illustrious', could not even afford the ceremonial clothes. A yearly Mass was said when a priest visited, but usually the only visitors to the island were on raiding parties. Insult was added to injury when the island's small trade in tobacco was banned (at one stage the word 'Trinidado' was used to refer to tobacco in the same way that the word 'Virginia' is used nowadays).

In 1783 efforts were made to develop the vast areas of untouched and fertile land in Trinidad and the Spanish king issued a *cedula* (decree) to encourage immigration. Grants of land were given to the 'subjects of powers and nations in alliance with Spain'. Catholics came from French colonies, some of them fleeing the revolutionaries and the slave uprisings in St Domingue (now Haiti), and set up cocoa and sugar plantations. Though the language has nearly died out, it is still just possible to hear French creole spoken in the mountains east of Port of Spain.

However, on 18 February 1797, the British fleet sailed into Port of Spain harbour and the governor, Chacon, had no choice but to scuttle his five ships and hand over the island. After 200 years as a Spanish island, Trinidad now became a British colony – a mainly French population administered by the British according to Spanish laws. The new British governor, Picton, tried to develop it into another sugar island, despite the growing lobby against slavery and revolts all over the Caribbean. Next door, South America was in turmoil and he had his hands full controlling the lawless population. His solution was to erect on the Government House lawn a set of gallows which he used liberally.

Emancipation came in 1834 and the freed men and women moved away from the cocoa walks and canefields, preferring to live in town or to farm a small plot of land. Large stretches of land were left unworked and so the government encouraged immigration again. In 1845 the first East Indians arrived on indentureships – their return passage paid in return for five years' work on a plantation. In all, by 1917, when indentureship was stopped by the Indian government, 145,000 Indians had come to Trinidad. Some went home when their time was up, but many took up the alternative offer of five acres of land and settled in the remote country areas, where their descendants still live today. The Indian workers were treated far better than their African counterparts had been a hundred years before, and their families were allowed to remain intact.

Adding further to the racial mix, Chinese workers came, renowned for their work in the canefields of Java and the Philippines and conspicuous in their pigtails, blue smocks and broad conical hats. In the 20th century the mix was completed by the arrival of settlers from the Middle East, many of them Syrians and Lebanese.

The energy which expresses itself so visibly at Carnival has a trickier side and Trinidad has suffered sporadic outbursts of political violence throughout the 20th century. Trade unions rallied the workers to confront the colonial authorities over the minimum wage in the 1930s, and this culminated in political unrest which eventually led to self-determination. Trinidad and Tobago gained independence from Britain on 31 August 1962. In 1970 the capital was brought to a standstill by Black Power protests and bands of guerrillas took to the hills. A short-lived but widely publicized coup attempt in 1990 foundered when the insurgents discovered that they did not have the anti-government following they expected.

Beaches

Trinidad's beaches do not have the precious picture-postcard feel of other Caribbean islands – try Tobago for that. Here there are fewer beaches to begin with and they are rugged and more spectacular. If you are staying in Port of Spain, you will have to travel quite a few miles to get to one. Some beaches have changing facilities and you can buy a drink and a snack on all except the most remote. The closest beaches to Port of Spain are on the north coast, a short ride over the Saddle. Buses run as far as Las Cuevas (depart George St, downtown), but only occasionally to Blanchisseuse. Further afield you will need a hire car, but it can be very rewarding because of the scenery and the secluded strands. See 'Best Beaches', p.105.

River Bathing

The rivers and rock pools in Trinidad's northern range provide some excellent river bathing if you want a change. Perhaps the easiest to reach is the **Blue Basin Waterfall** in Petit Valley off the Diego Martin Valley, west of Port of Spain. At 300ft high, **Maracas Falls** are worth a visit and can be found one mile off the road that runs north out of St Joseph. The **Paria Waterfall**, off the Arima to Blanchisseuse road, can be reached along a track that follows the river into the rainforest for an hour. There is a waterfall and a pool at the **Asa Wright Nature Centre** and there is good swimming in the **Caura River** at Eldorado Village and in the **Oropouche River** at the eastern end of the range.

Flora and Fauna

The flora and fauna of Trinidad is related to that of nearby South America and is consequently richer and more varied than on other islands. The vegetation looks Neolithic after the explosive lushness of the Windwards – vines and lianas grow to an immense thickness and the trees grow up to 200ft high clinging to the steep land. The rainforest flits and squawks all day long with incredibly colourful butterflies and birdlife and there are equally abundant mangrove and freshwater inland swamps.

Among the yellow and pink pouis, and 100ft bamboo sprouts (which look particularly pretty over remote rivers), you will find heliconia and chaconia (the crab-claw-shaped Trinidadian national flower) and a honeydew, which traps animals similarly to a Venus fly trap. There are 2,200 species of flowering plants and trees.

By comparison, mammals are relatively limited, though the 108 species is an abundance for a Caribbean island. They all originate in South America, so you might see an agouti, an opossum, an ocelot and even an armadillo. There are also a number of insects, including over 600 species of butterfly, and reptiles including snakes (47), lizards and the endless tree frogs that sing their shrill tune on the night air.

But the birdlife on Trinidad is the most spectacular – there are about 425 species that make an appearance during the year. The island is on a migratory route and like tourists they fly down here to escape the cold weather. You will often see parrots flying near the botanical gardens near dusk. Among the kiskidees (called so because of their call, which sounds a bit like 'qu'est-ce qu'il dit' in French) and bananaquits, motmots and macaws, there are 27 herons and 18 hummingbirds, which flash with fluorescence as they come to suck at a flower on the veranda, and species such as nocturnal oilbirds and white-bearded or golden-headed manikins (which true to their name spend a large proportion of their time displaying).

The swamps have an enormous variety of birdlife and water-borne life (from groupers to spectacled caymans and tree crabs). In among the mangroves, which grow with a complex network of roots like flying buttresses run riot, you will find tree oysters and the small silky anteater, locally called a sloth. And in the last rays of the sun, the trees in the Caroni Swamp light up with egrets and the colourful scarlet ibis, Trinidad's national bird (*see* p.120).

Trinidad has six Wildlife and Nature Reserves: three swamps (Caroni, Nariva in the east, and Point-à-Pierre) and three forests (El Tucuche, Valencia and the Asa Wright Nature Centre). Two of the most accessible are the **Asa Wright Nature Centre** in the northern range, where you can see toucans, honeycreepers and bellbirds, and, if a swamp does not sound too outlandish (it is fascinating), the **Caroni Swamp Bird Sanctuary**. Tours to the Caroni Swamp can be arranged through Nanan Tours, 38 Bamboo Grove Settlement No.1, Butler Highway, Valsayn, **t** 645 1305, *nantour@tstt.net.tt*, at about US$10 per person. Birding tours with a knowledgeable guide can be arranged through Geoffrey Gomes' Neotropical Nature Company, **t** 624 2223, *www.skybusiness.com/birdtourtrinidad*. Geoffrey takes tours in all types of

Getting There

Trinidad t (1 868–)

By Air

Trinidad has some of the best air links in the Caribbean, and Piarco Airport has recently been upgraded. It has its own airline – BWIA, often referred to as Bee-wee – and is served by numerous others. As well as good links to Europe and the USA, flights are easily arranged to places in South America, such as Guyana and Venezuela. A departure tax of TT$100 is payable.

From the UK

BWIA, t 627 2942, t 669 3000, has a number of weekly services each week direct from London Heathrow.

From North America

BWIA, t 627 2942, t 669 3000, flies daily to Miami and weekly to New York. American Airlines, t 669 4661, flies daily from New York via Miami. Continental Airlines, t 1 800 231 0856, flies from Houston. Air Canada, t 664 4065, and BWIA fly from Toronto.

From Other Caribbean Islands

Between Trinidad and Tobago there are about eight services a day on BWIA (see above). Further afield, BWIA stops off at other Caribbean islands en route for Trinidad, but LIAT, t 1 888 844 5428, is the major inter-island carrier and it links the island to all the major destinations in the Eastern Caribbean. Caribbean Star, toll free t 1 800 744 7827, has almost as many flights. Airlines linking to the South American continent include Surinam Airways, t 627 4747, and Aeropostal, which flies to Caracas – all handled by Piarco Air Services, t 623 7289.

By Sea

The ferry to and from Tobago leaves from the cruise-ship dock every day except Saturday, t 625 4906, in Tobago t 639 2417. The trip takes five hours and costs TT$50 economy, TT$60 tourist class. You might even try your luck at catching a schooner to Grenada in the Windward Islands.

Getting Around

From the Airport

Once you are past the Piarco Airport taxi touts, who are among the Caribbean's most persistent, travel in Trinidad is easy. If you do go by taxi, the trip to Port of Spain will cost around TT$120, but it is possible to do it for TT$3 on the public transport bus which leaves every hour. Piarco is 17 miles from Port of Spain and it takes about 45mins to cover the distance by car.

By Bus

There are two bus systems on the island: the government-run PTSC and the hundreds of private minibuses, or maxi-taxis as the contrary Trinidadians prefer to call them. Both systems start running at dawn and continue until late evening. PTSC is extremely cheap and links all the major towns for less than TT$6. As the government transport network, the buses have no plush seats or stereo systems like the private buses and tickets are only on sale during certain hours (they must be bought in the terminal office or in some shops). There is a regular, if infrequent, schedule, leaving Port of Spain from the former railway station on South Quay.

Maxi-taxis, which once were more akin to mobile discos than a system of transport, have been quietened down by law recently. Drivers caused so much controversy by playing Jamaican dub music (an insult to Trinidadian self-esteem to begin with) at such high volume, and supposedly by being irresponsible, smutty and generally corrupting of Trinidadian youth, that music was legislated against. Maxis are crowded and noisy, but still a good exposure to Trinidad life. They will take you to most towns and they are colour-coded according to the route they run. When you reach your destination, shout 'Driver! Stop!' (you will have to shout to be heard above the stereo system).

Faster, more comfortable and a little more expensive are share-taxis, private cars that follow (mostly the same) fixed routes. Most leave from the same point as the maxi-taxis: Independence Square for the east and west, and Woodford Square for St Ann's and St James. Jeeps for the north coast leave from

George St. There are no specific stops, so, when you want to get out, just tell the driver and for a little extra he will drop you at your door. Drivers leave when the vehicle is full.

By Taxi

Normal taxis are in plentiful supply and can be fixed up in the main squares and at all hotels. Some approximate prices are: airport to central Port of Spain – TT$120, airport to Asa Wright Centre – TT$150, downtown Port of Spain to Maracas – TT$80, downtown Port of Spain to Caroni Bird Sanctuary – TT$70, downtown Port of Spain to Asa Wright Centre – TT$120. To call a taxi you can phone:
Trump Luxury Taxi Service, t 634 2189.
Airport Taxi Co-operative, Piarco, t 669 1689.

By Guided Tour

Tours around Port of Spain and the island can be fixed through **A's Travel and Twin Island Tours**, 177 Tragarete Rd, Port of Spain, t 622 7664, or **Caribbean Discovery Tours**, 9B Fondes Amandes Road, St. Ann's, t 624 7281, *caribdis@wow.net*, *www.caribbeandiscovery tours.com*. A 2hr city tour costs about TT$300 (up to four people), a tour over to Maracas costs TT$450, a tour to the Caroni Bird Sanctuary costs TT$400, and to the Pitch Lake around TT$600 (6 hrs). Or try **Kalloo's**, Piarco Airport, t 669 5673, *www.kalloo.com*.

Car Hire

Trinidad is a big place and is worth exploring. There are plenty of vehicles for hire. The roads are adequate, though if you plan to go off the beaten track it might be worth investing in a 4WD. Licences from the UK, France, Germany, USA and Canada are valid in Trinidad and Tobago; driving is, generally, on the left; and you should wear your seat belt. When driving, carry your licence with you at all times along with your passport. Do not drive in downtown Port of Spain except for sport.

Expect to pay from US$60 per day, tax included, for the smallest car. Rental companies include:
Auto Rentals, at Morvant just outside Port of Spain, t 675 7368, *mail@autorentals.co.tt*, and at Piarco Airport, t 669 2277.
Econo-Car Rentals, at the airport and town, t 669 8072, *econocar@trinidad.net*.

Kalloo's, at the airport and Woodbrook, t 628 2934, *kallocar@tstt.net.tt*.
Singh's, at the airport, t 623 0150, *singhs@ trinidad.net*.
Thrifty Car Rental, at the airport, t 660 0602.

Tourist Information

Abroad

The Tourism and Industrial Development Corporation of Trinidad and Tobago (TIDCO) has a website at *www.visitTNT.com* and there is an email postbox at *tourism-info@ tidco.co.tt*. You might also find some interesting information at *www.tntisland.com*.

In Trinidad

In Trinidad, TIDCO can be contacted at:
Level I Maritime Centre, 29 Tenth Ave, Baratavia, t 675 7039, *www.sensational tours.com*. They give advice about accommodation and help with arranging trips.
Piarco Airport, t 639 0509.

Crime

The Trinidadians are occasionally known by other Caribbean islanders as 'Trickidadians' and they have a reputation for being a little rough and cheeky at times (they will always bargain when doing business). You are advised to be careful with regard to personal security, particularly in the eastern areas of Port of Spain and around the city at night.

Embassies and Consulates

British High Comission, 19 St Clair Ave, St Clair, t 622 2748, *csbhc@opus.co.tt*.
US Embassy, 15 Queen's Park West, Port of Spain, t 622 6371.
Canadian High Commission, PO Box 1246, Maple House, Tatil Centre, 3–3A Sweet Briar Road, St Clair, Port of Spain, t 622 6232.

Media

You can find details of current activities in the free tourist newspaper *Island Information*. You will also find useful information in the small annual magazine *Discover Trinidad and Tobago*, and both of the islands have their own small newspapers designed specifically for visitors. Local newspapers include the three dailies, the *Trinidad Guardian*, the *Trinidad Express* and *Newsday*.

Medical Emergencies

The Port of Spain General Hospital is on Charlotte St in the centre of town, **t** 625 2951.

Money and Banks

The currency is the Trinidad and Tobago dollar (TT$), which floats on the international exchange, presently at around US$1=TT$6. The US dollar is accepted in tourist areas. There is not much of a black market, but you should retain a (recent) receipt if you wish to change TT$ back when you leave the country. **Banking hours** are Mon–Thurs 8–3, Fri 8–12 and 3–5.

Shopping

Shops are open Mon–Fri 8–4.30 (often later), Sat 8–noon.

Telephone Code

The IDD code for both islands is **t** 1 868, followed by the seven-digit local number. If you are phoning between the islands, dial just the seven figures.

Maps and Books

The most eloquent form of expression in Trinidad life is probably the calypso, but there is a flourishing literature that first grew in the 1930s. **Eric Williams**, for a long time Trinidad and Tobago's Prime Minister, was also an accomplished historian and the author of *Capitalism and Slavery*, *From Columbus to Castro* and *A History of the Peoples of Trinidad and Tobago*, written at the time of Independence. Together with C. L. R. James (who died in 1989 in London) he changed the perspective of West Indians towards their history and culture, heralding the birth of West Indian Independence.

C. L. R. James wrote *Beyond a Boundary*, a charming autobiographical book about cricket and Trinidadian life in the 1920s. In *The Wine of Astonishment*, **Earl Lovelace** tells of the changes in town life during the Second World War. *Ways of Sunlight* by **Samuel Selvon** is a collection of short stories about rural life in Trinidad and 'hard times' in London.

Novelist **V. S. Naipaul** was born in Trinidad of a Brahmin family. His works set in Trinidad include *The Mystic Masseur* and *The Suffrage of Elvira*, two satires of the elections in the 1940s and 50s, and *A House for Mr Biswas*, which portrays the dissolution of traditional Trinidadian life. *Miguel Street* uses the perspective of a young boy to paint a charming picture of the characters in a Port of Spain street.

Festivals

See also 'Carnival, Calypso and Steel Pan', pp.100–103.

January/February *Carnival*.

March *Phagwa*. The Hindu New Year celebration. It has taken on the Carnival style of floats in the street with dancing and is celebrated by Trinis of all racial origin now. If you see a band of dancers covered in red food dye, they are out celebrating Phagwa.

October *Divali* (pronounced 'deewali'). The most colourful festival outside Carnival is the festival of lights, which was brought to Trinidad by Hindus in honour of Lakshmi, the goddess of light. Hundreds of thousands of *deyas*, little clay bowls with coconut-oil candles (and increasingly electric lights), are kept alight all night to show her the way. People throw open their houses and entertain guests with sitars and dancing and huge vegetarian meals.

December *Parang*. Another high moment in the Christian calendar. This is a special sort of singing that takes place in the run-up to Christmas, when *paranderos* sing their Annunciation songs in outlying villages. Originally from the Spanish *parranda*, parang has absorbed influences from Venezuela and is set to a typically Trinidadian rhythm. Instruments include the guitar, cuatro, maracas, violin and box base.

Variable *Hosay* (Hussein). A Muslim festival that remembers the martyrdom of Hussein (it brings in the Muslim New Year, but the date varies in the Christian calendar). Processions of tassa drummers follow models of Hussein's tomb through the streets and you will occasionally still see fire-eating and jugglers throwing sticks of fire.

Eid ul Fitr. Trinidadian Muslim festival to mark the end of Ramadan. Dates vary according to the Islamic calendar.

Watersports

There is not much in the way of watersports on offer in Trinidad. **Kayak** trips (more exploration than sport) can be arranged through the Kayak Centre in Chaguaramas, **t** 633 7871, *kayak@wow.net*, and in the south Kayak Adventures, **t** 681 7987, *kayakadventures@ hotmail.com*, will take tours into the swamps and rivers. There isn't much on offer in the way of **sailing** either, but you can go down to the marina at Chaguaramas and try your luck.

Other Sports

Trinidad is not as well organized as its sister island in catering for the traditional Caribbean watersports, so most of the popular Trinidadian sports are land-based.

Golf

There are three courses on the island, of which the closest to Port of Spain is the 18-hole St Andrew's course at Moka just beyond Maraval, **t** 629 2314. There are 9-hole courses at Chaguaramas, and Brighton near La Brea in the south.

Hiking

Wildways, **t** 623 7332, *wildways@trinidad.net*, *www.wildways.org*, will arrange hikes and cycle trips through the mountains and rainforest, plus kayaking to isolated coves.

Tennis

Can be arranged through the Trinidad Country Club, **t** 622 3470, in Maraval, or the Tranquillity Square Lawn Tennis Club, **t** 625 4182.

Spectator Sports

On Saturdays and Sundays the Savannah in central Port of Spain will be crowded with **football** and **hockey** matches. **Cricket** is also played on the Savannah, some games more formal than others. If you go to watch a match at the main Queen's Park Oval stadium, you might try to get into the 'rude-boy stand', where the banter is liveliest. **Horse-racing**, which used to be held on the Savannah, is now centred in Arima.

Where to Stay

Trinidad **t** (1 868–)

Trinidad does not have many resort hotels in the typical Caribbean mould. Most hotels are in Port of Spain itself, but there are some notable exceptions in the mountains around the town and increasingly along the north coast. A hotel room tax is charged on all rooms at 10%, and most places charge 10% extra for service (guest houses usually factor the taxes into their prices). Untypically for the Caribbean, many hotels in Port of Spain keep their rates the same year-round, except at Carnival, when you can expect room prices to rise by anything from 30% to 70%.

Though there are few beach hotels, some Trinidadians have built villas for themselves on the beaches, particularly in the northeast of the island, and it is possible to rent these at the weekend, or during the week when they are more likely to be available. Contact **Eckel and Quesnel Ltd**, **t** 622 4945, *homeseq@ wow.net*. Also check in the newspapers.

Expensive

Hilton Trinidad, Lady Young Rd, PO Box 442, Port of Spain, **t** 624 3211, UK **t** 0800 856 8000, US **t** 1 800 445 8667, *hiltonpos@wow. net, www.hilton.com/poshitw*. Worth a visit for the views alone. It is set on a hill in uptown Port of Spain and many of the rooms look out over the city, over the Savannah and the 'Magnificent Seven' to the hills in the west. It is known as the upside-down Hilton because the reception is at the top and the floors are numbered heading down the hill. International standards of comfort, with 'executive floors' for business travellers, but also facilities for holidaymakers. Two restaurants.

Moderate

Chancellor Hotel, 5 St Ann's Ave, St Ann's, **t** 623 0883, *info@thechancellorhotel.com, www.thechancellorhotel.com*. Its 30 rooms are equipped with data ports providing

Internet access and a comfortable, roomy workspace. Other facilities include a swimming pool, conference room, bistro and bar.

Courtyard by Marriott, Audrey Jeffers Highway, Invaders Bay, Port of Spain, **t** 627 5555, *courtyardbymarriott@tstt.net.tt*, *www.marriott.com*. Ten minutes from the centre (adjacent the National Stadium), this 119-room hotel offers free high-speed Internet access, a 24-hour food outlet, an exercise room, self-service laundry and dry cleaning services, car rental and transportation services desk.

Crowne Plaza, Port of Spain, **t** 625 3366, *eoffice@crowneplaza.co.tt, www.ichotels group.com*. Suitable for business travellers headed for downtown Port of Spain.

Hotel Normandie, 10 Nook Av, off St Ann's Rd, Port of Spain, PO Box 851, **t** 624 1181, *reservations@normandiett.com, www. normandiett.com*. Close to the Botanical Gardens to the north of the Savannah. A cosy setting around a courtyard, where a riot of banana and golden palm surrounds the swimming pool. One or two rooms are a little dark (there is a range of suites and rooms), but the loft apartments are very comfortable and it is a good place to base yourself in town. There is a busy shopping centre next door.

Kapok Hotel, 16–18 Cotton Hill, St Clair, Port of Spain, **t** 622 5765, *stay@kapokhotel.com, www.kapokhotel.com*. Set in a modern building at the northwest corner of the Savannah. Within easy reach of the city centre, it takes its name from a silk cotton tree that grows outside. Rooms are decorated with prints of the West Indies, and there is a pool in a palm courtyard.

Asa Wright Nature Centre, Spring Hill Estate, PO Box 4710, Arima, **t** 667 4655, *asawright@ caligo.com, www.asawright.org*. Set in a charming colonial estate house lost in the rainforest of the northern range. It is famous for its bird-watching and thus many people pass by during the day, but the 24 rooms are very comfortable. There is a swimming pool. Take afternoon tea on the magnificent veranda, amidst the sound of toucans, tufted coquettes (hummingbirds) and butterfly wings.

Mt Plaisir Estate Hotel, Hosang St, Grande Rivière, **t** 670 8381, *info@mtplaisir.com, www. mtplaisir.com*. Just 12 rooms on the beach in the delightful calm bay at Grande Rivière in the northeast. Particularly popular in the leatherback nesting season between March and August. Nice restaurant with Italian and creole fare on a veranda right on the sand and waves.

Inexpensive

An inexpensive way to stay, with the distinct advantage of seeing the Trinis in their homes, is in B&Bs, which you will find all over the northern part of the island. Houses are vetted by the Tourism Development Authority and prices start at about US$25 per night for a single and US$15 each in a double. A list can be found at the Tourist Board and at **Accommodations Unlimited**, Ariapita Ave, Port of Spain, **t** 628 3731, *owl@opus-networx.com*.

Pax Guest House, Mt St Benedict, Tunapuna, **t** 662 4084, *pax-g-h@trinidad.net, www.paxguesthouse.com*. 'In peace awhile here rest most welcome Guest.' Set beside a monastery in the hills above the Eastern Main Rd. There are 18 simple rooms, some with shared bathroom and veranda with a magnificent view of the valley and hills beyond. There is a dining room for meals, including afternoon tea, and walking trails on the 600-acre estate, even laboratory facilities if you want them.

Monique's, 114 Saddle Rd, Maraval, **t** 628 3334, *info@moniquestrinidad.com, www.moniques trinidad.com*. Set in a modern West Indian house, the 19 rooms all have private bath, air conditioning, cable TV and phone; some rooms have kitchenette.

Carnetta's House, Scotland Terrace, Maraval, **t** 628 2732, *carnetta@trinidad.net, www. carnettas.com*. Close to Monique's, just six rooms with private bath and kitchenette on request; with a pleasant homely feel.

The Pelican Inn, 2–4 Coblentz Av, Cascade, Port of Spain, **t** 627 6271, *theinn@pelican.co.tt*. Right above the bar of the same name (a popular gathering point for young Trinidadian drinkers). Twenty-four simple but adequate rooms with private bath in an old wooden setting. There's also a restaurant.

Mi Casita, 17 Carlos St, on Adam Smith Square in Woodbrook, **t** 627 4796, *micas@wow.net*. A family atmosphere with just six rooms.

La Calypso, 46 French St, off Tragarete Rd, **t** 622 4077, *aliciashouse@tstt.net.tt, www.alicias houstrinidad.com*. Eighteen very simple rooms, fairly clean, breakfast available.

Second Spring, 13 Damier Village, Blanchisseuse, **t** 623 8837, *secondspring@ trinidad.net, www.secondspringtnt.com*. If you would like to spend a few days over in Blanchisseuse, a number of suites and a cottage stand here in a garden on a dramatic rocky waterfront. Private and self-contained with a charming wooden deck, beaches nearby.

Surf's Country Inn, Lower Village, Blanchisseuse, **t** 669 2475, *mahernz80@ yahoo.co.uk*. Has a number of small rooms and apartments.

Whispering Palms, Mayaro, **t** 630 3336. In the far southeast of the island. A simple but comfortable stopover resort.

Eating Out

You can live in Trinidad without ever sitting down to a formal meal – snacks are available all day, everywhere. You can start right outside the airport when you arrive, perhaps with a *pow!* (the Chinese word for bread), a little white fluffball of dough, colour-coded with a spot for salt or sweet, or with one of Trinidad's most popular snacks, a *roti*, an envelope of unleavened bread with a filling of anything from curried shrimp to lentils. Spices are optional, but when you are asked if you want hot pepper sauce be wary. *Doubles* are similar: they are folded *bara* (more unleavened bread) with *channa* (split peas). *Aripa* is a cornflour pattie with mince stuffing, and *pastel* is a mix of peppers, raisins and beef wrapped in a dasheen leaf. *Aloo pie* (from the Indian for potato) is a doughy potato mix. Batter snacks include *phulori*, split peas in batter balls and *sahina*, made with dasheen, which you can dip into mango chutney, sweet or hot, or into pepper sauce, firebrand style. The stalls are invariably run by a charming and chattering clutch of ladies, who do their frying on outdoor ovens.

So much for the first course. You can follow the savoury mouthfuls with a whole volley of sweet snacks. Perhaps go for a *pamie* (pronounced 'pay-me'), sweet coconut in a pattie or wrapped in a banana leaf, or try *pone*, a creation of cassava flour, sugar and coconut. Then there are *bene balls*, crisp lumps of sesame snap in molasses, and for the very brave there are *tamarind balls*, sluggish sugary lumps with unverifiable specific gravity, and *salt prunes*, a child's sweet, both of them a torture of bitter and sweet.

If you do decide to sit down to a meal, you will find that Trinidad has a grand variety of styles, in keeping with its mixed heritage – Italian, Chinese, Indian, Thai, even Arab, and of course creole. Trinidad's restaurants tend to be active and noisy, full of friendly crowds, but there are one or two quieter places where couples can retreat. In general, prices in Trinidad are lower than in most tourist restaurants around the Caribbean. **Categories** are arranged according to the price of a main course: expensive = TT$90 and above, moderate = TT$60–90, inexpensive = less than TT$60. Bills are supplemented with a charge of 15% for VAT and usually a service charge of 10%.

Port of Spain

Ariapita Ave has recently emerged as Port of Spain's dining strip, and there are now about 15 restaurants and streetfront cafés, many of them set in restored traditional buildings.

Expensive

Plantation House, Ariapita Ave, **t** 628 5551. Creole fare in a fine creole setting. Here you will find the pink, white and green verandas and interior of a charming creole wooden house, where the eaves are festooned with greenery and gingerbread woodwork. There is a long menu of seafood and fish on offer, including crab meat amandine, and, in keeping with Trinidad's variety, creole, Spanish, gumbo and tandoori sauces.

Melange, Ariapita Ave, **t** 628 8687. Set in a distinctive colonial house in two shades of blue, this restaurant offers nouvelle creole cuisine. Perhaps start with red snapper stuffed with crab meat and then follow with the seafood *fettucine* – medallions of lobster, grouper and snapper folded in a thick béchamel, topped with pesto and Parmesan. Great salads.

Solimar, Nook Av, St Ann's, **t** 624 6267, *reservations@solimarcuisine.com, www. solimarcuisine.com*. A charming Caribbean setting, on a covered terrace hung with greenery just north of the Savannah. The fare is international with good fish dishes: start with the Solimar salad, 'from the market that day', and lamb loin *en croute* or grouper in a green Thai curry.

Il Colosseo, 16 Rust St, **t** 622 9018, *tamnakthai@tstt.net.tt, www.tamnak thai.co.tt*. Has a subdued air, with an air-conditioned dining room of Italianate columns, arches and gathered curtains. Dishes from around Italy, including a pasta speciality with plenty of seafood: *gamberoni del ré*, shrimp wrapped in bacon and a honey-mustard sauce.

Tamnak Thai Restaurant, 13 Queen's Park East, **t** 625 0647. On the Queen's Park Savannah in the heart of town, set in a beautifully restored colonial house. You dine either inside surrounded by Thai dancers or out on the patio among tropical gardens and a lily pond. A Thai menu, as you would expect, with favourites such as *tom yung gung* (hot and sour shrimp soup) or shrimp in curry paste, herbs and coconut milk.

Apsara, in the same building as Tamnak Thai, **t** 623 7659, *apsara@tstt.net.tt, www.apsara. co.tt*. Come here for an 'authentic Indian' meal (rather than Trinidadian Indian, which is different). Apsara is redolent with burning spices and has tent roofs, mock Indian furniture, puppets and elephants. Real tandoori ovens produce nan breads and tandoori lobster tails, or you might go for a *paneer tikka*, with cubes of cottage cheese made from buffalo milk, or a *naw rattan kurma*.

Rafters, 6A Warner St, **t** 628 9258, *rafters@carib-link.net, www.6Awarnerst. com*. A hip spot around town, frequented by a mainly white crowd. It is set in an old dry-goods store, its shutters and windows still intact, but now modernized inside with glass and fluorescent strip lights. Simple snacks one side, with dinner à la carte next door – dishes include Rafters ribs, chicken teriyaki and tiramisu.

Moderate

Jenny's on the Boulevard, Cipriani Bd, which runs up towards the Savannah, **t** 625 1807. Set in a lovely creole building, Jenny's offers, upstairs and downstairs, fine dining in a funky, faux-antique setting with striking décor including an angel and a bison's head, and a bar that resembles a British club. There are international and some Chinese dishes. They are known in particular for their excellent island lobster served in a garlic butter and lemon sauce and famous for their steaks.

Veni Mangé, 67A Ariapita Ave, **t** 624 4597, *veni@wow.net*. An excellent spot to stop by for weekday lunch. Here two Trinidadian sisters, Allyson Hennessy and Rosemary Hezekiah, have a lively restaurant in an old wooden-floored town house now painted bright orange, with elegantly wobbly tables. Excellent soups and other exotic Trinidadian creations – superb fish grilled in capers and spices or a daily vegetarian dish, followed by soursop ice cream. *Open for lunch; evenings Wed and Fri only, for drinks with informal snacks.*

Verandah, 13 Rust St, St Clair, **t** 622 6287. Slightly quieter, here the dining tables sit above the garden on a town house veranda. The fare is home Caribbean cooking – favourites include spiced beef-stuffed dumplings and fish dishes served in their own tomato-based sauces, followed by excellent ice creams. *Open Mon–Fri 11.30–2, Thurs and Sat 7–10pm.*

Woodford Café, 62 Tragarete Rd, **t** 622 2233. Excellent creole meals at lunch and dinner, and served with good Trini hospitality in an old Woodbrook house. Sees a good mix of locals and visitors alike, with a fun atmosphere. Everything's fresh from the kitchen, from fresh-baked breads, soups and salads to local curries.

The Lighthouse Restaurant, Pointe Gourd Rd, Crews Inn, Chaguaramas, **t** 634 4384, *inquiries@crewsinn.com*. Sits on an open deck raised above the harbour, looking out onto the forest of yacht masts. International fare – coconut shrimp and spag bol along with striploins.

Anchorage, Pointe Gourd Rd, The Hart's Cut, Chaguaramas, **t** 634 4334. You dine right above the water on a breezy covered deck. Good West Indian fare – start with a drunken mermaid (squid in batter and white wine) and follow with fish or seafood, perhaps a *run dem soucouyant*, sautéed shrimp in white wine. Watch out for the bats late on. The Anchorage gets particularly lively at the weekend, when the Trinis flood out of town. Some dancing.

Hong Kong City, Tragarete Rd, t 622 3949. A Chinese meal is a popular evening out in Trinidad. This place is brightly dressed up in Chinese décor of red velvet and golden dragons. The food is straight Chinese, plus a few dishes with West Indian ingredients – dasheen pork, beef with corilie and sweet and sour *lambi*.

Inexpensive

Breakfast Shed, on the waterfront, not far from the Holiday Inn Hotel. For a distinctly local Trinidadian feel, offering home-style rice 'n' peas with fried plantain at very good prices. It caters for local workers, who come in from the wharf nearby, so opening hours are 5am–3pm, although it's best to get there before 2pm.

Stall, Western Main Rd, opposite the Smokey and Bunty rum shop. You can get an excellent night-time *roti* here.

Low's, near the above stall. You can take away a Chinese meal.

Snack-wagons, t 657 5050, the eastern side of the Savannah. Here you can pick up a fried chicken or a burger for a few dollars.

Beyond Port of Spain

Surf's Country Inn, Blanchisseuse, t 669 2475 (*moderate*). Wholesome Caribbean fare – chicken and fish served with a volley of ground provisions – served in their hillside gazebos.

Soongs Great Wall, on the Circular Rd, San Fernando (*moderate*). A popular Chinese.

Bars and Nightlife

Like the restaurants, Trinidadian bars (often called pubs here) are lively, particularly at the weekend, when Port of Spain drops everything for a drink. You will find cocktail bars, where Trinidad-produced Angostura bitters add zing to the traditional Caribbean rum punch, a profusion of rum shops, fired by VAT 19, and the two local brews, light Carib and the darker, malty Stag beers.

Poleska, in the Country Club, Maraval. Has a slightly rarified air: manicured grounds, spacious lawns and saman trees. Lots of cocktails, including the Watermelon Martini and the Poleska Rum Punch. The bar is known too as a wine club and tends to draw an older crowd.

The Pelican, just beneath the Hilton, Port of Spain. An ever popular bar which sees a mixed and lively (younger) crowd who roll in after work for a drink or pack in later on for the live bands. You can leave your car numberplate as a memento of your visit if that's your style.

Rafters, Warner St, Port of Spain. Big after work on a Friday, with a video bar. Mainly a white crowd.

Bois Cano, Kapok Hotel, Port of Spain. A wine and cocktail bar, and a favourite 'cool-down' spot around town. Snacks, desserts, wines and coffees, to the strains of jazz.

Parrot, Grand Bazaar Mall, Port of Spain. This sees a lively crowd after work and on Saturdays.

Smokey and Bunty, Western Main Rd, St James's, Port of Spain. An approachable choice among the many rum shops.

The Anchorage, Pointe Gourde Rd, Chaguaramas. A trusty favourite. Has a huge area for live music and dancing on the waterfront.

Pier 1, Chaguaramas. Sees a busy trade at the weekend.

Club Coconuts, Cascadia Hotel, St Ann's, Port of Spain. Busiest Thurs–Sat.

Mas Camp Pub, on the corner of French St and Ariapita Ave, Woodbrook. Something of an institution. Here you will find anything from ballroom dancing to calypso singing. Each night is different and it's well worth checking out, if only to get a taste for the best in local entertainment.

62ND & 3RD, 62 Tragarete Rd, Woodbrook, Port of Spain. Popular with the capital's young professionals on Friday and Saturday nights for dancing and drinks. Dress code enforced: no shorts or beach sandals; admTT$6.

forest, including wetlands and rainforest, to cocoa estates, caves and coasts, and also covers turtle and dolphin watching. Ring a couple of days in advance. Other general tours include Pax Nature Tours, **t** 662 4084, *stay@paxguesthouse.com*, *www.paxguest house.com*, and Caribbean Discovery Tours, **t** 624 7281, *caribdis@wow.net*, *tradepoint. tidco.co.tt/cdt*.

There is little coral on Trinidad's shores because of the freshwater outflow from the Orinoco (go to the eastern end of Tobago for coral), but one of the world's largest species of turtle, the leatherback (it can weigh up to 1,200lb and is about 7ft long) comes to nest on both islands between March and August – on **Matura Beach** on the east coast of Trinidad and on Turtle Beach on Tobago.

Trinidad has large reserves of oil beneath its surface and these find odd ways of coming to the surface. The gases seep up through bubbling mud flues and the island has one of the Caribbean's oddest underworld phenomena in the **Pitch Lake** in the south of the island near La Brea (*see* p.121).

To help you orientate yourself, there are a number of good field guide pamphlets.

Port of Spain

Like so many Caribbean capitals, Port of Spain (population about 500,000) is set on the sea and framed by hills. It lies in the northwest of the island on the Gulf of Paria, in the crook of the Chaguaramas peninsula. The downtown area, which is set back from the docks and wharves of the waterfront (much of which has been reclaimed), is a gridiron of tight streets with concrete buildings. The city has an upbeat air at the moment and is looking better than it has for a while as new buildings go up and others are restored. Just north of here is the Savannah, a huge area of parkland in the centre of the city; scattered around it, the residential suburbs have some of the Caribbean's most elaborate and beautiful gingerbread houses. Beyond here the hills rise steeply in a green backdrop, too steep in places to have houses, but settlements creep along the valleys' floors behind the city.

Downtown the streets are mayhem, with share-taxis stopping at will and buses nosing for position among them; hucksters line the pavements of Frederick St, their trestle tables stacked with cassettes and mirror-shades or yards of T-shirts and under-pants. Everywhere there is the smell of batter snacks frying and the cry of peanut vendors. As in any large city, you are advised to be careful after dark. For every thousand charming Trinidadians, there is one tricky one. However, you'll need your wits about you to enjoy the city anyway, because it is extremely lively.

The original capital of the island was positioned inland at St Joseph as a defensive measure, but it was moved to the coast in 1757 when the new governor found his residence uninhabitable. The new town expanded rapidly as the island population soared at the end of the 18th century and trade picked up. The town was almost completely destroyed by a fire in 1808 and then laid out anew by Governor Woodford in 1813. Echoes of the British influence remain in the hefty colonial architecture and the spiked metal railings in the squares.

The business centre of the town is just above the waterfront, around **Independence Square**. Known as Marine Square until Trinidad's independence in 1962, it is not really a square at all, but a long wide street: the pedestrian island in the middle was recently redeveloped and renamed the Brian Lara Promenade, after the island's record-breaking cricketing hero. The city's two other main thoroughfares, Charlotte St and Frederick St, run north from here, the latter touching **Woodford Square**, the heart of Trinidadian politics, where you will see groups of people involved in political and no doubt less committed discussion. Demonstrations have occurred here, but its most important moments were as the 'University of Woodford Square', birthplace of Independence politics in the 1950s. On the western side of the square, the **Red House** is the seat of the Trinidad and Tobago Parliament, flights of grand columns, arches and classical pediments all topped by mansard roofs and a cupola. It was first painted red in 1897 for Queen Victoria's Diamond Jubilee and has been repainted and called so ever since. The chamber can be visited during session (*adm free*) and there is a spectacular bright-blue ceiling. On the south side of the square is the yellow stone Anglican Cathedral.

At the very top of Frederick St you will find the **National Museum and Art Gallery** (*t 623 5941; open Tues–Sat 10–6; adm free*), which exhibits Trinidadian life throughout the ages, from the Arawaks and early Spaniards to angostura, asphalt and oil. It also has a display of Carnival costumes and some of the excellent paintings of the Trinidad countryside by Michel Cazabon. Upstairs are more modern Trinbagonian paintings and a display of characters from island folklore, including Papa Bois, a friendly spirit who saves animals from hunters with the blow of a horn, the Soucouyant, an old hag who turns herself into a ball of fire and will suck your blood, and La Diablesse, who leads intoxicated men astray after a party and with a shriek of laughter dumps them in a thorn bush.

The Trinidadian claim that the **Savannah** is the biggest roundabout in the world is probably true – it has a 2½-mile circumference. At any rate, it has a special place in the heart of every Trini and it is a very attractive park, circled with huge trees. Once it was used to graze cattle that would terrorize the inhabitants, but now it is used more as a sports ground. According to C. L. R. James (*Beyond a Boundary*), it is big enough to contain 30 full-size cricket pitches, but at least some of them are now given over to hockey and football. The culmination of Carnival takes place here too. There is always a crowd of vendors at the roadside selling fresh fruit – sliced pineapple, oranges and particularly coconuts, which they slice in the usual manner. At night there are fast-food caravans serving burgers and hot dogs.

On the western side of the Savannah are the **Magnificent Seven**, a row of elaborate and imposing colonial mansions. Built early in the 20th century, they are a hotch-potch of styles, and include a mock Rhineland castle, a Moorish creation called Whitehall, and a mansion in the style of the French Second Empire known as the Gingerbread House.

On the northern side of the park are the **Royal Botanical Gardens** (*open during daylight hours; adm free*), 70 acres of garden where you can retreat from the bustle of Port of Spain in Banyan Lane, Raw Beef Walk (after a famous tree which seeps red sap like a joint of meat when cut) and Bougainvillea Dell. The gardens were laid out by Governor Woodford in 1820 and he moved his residence up here because they were so pleasant. Among the pink and yellow pouis is a cannonball tree (with fruit like a wooden cannonball but the most ephemeral flowers that drop to earth at dusk) and the oddly shaped chaconia, the national flower of Trinidad and Tobago. The official residences of the President and Prime Minister are in the gardens.

Nearby is the **Emperor Valley Zoo** (*open daily 9.30–6; adm*), named after a butterfly that once lived here, which exhibits Trinidad's deer and other South American animals, such as caymans (alligators), which lie frozen still with their mouths open, monkeys, tropical snakes, indigenous agouti and ocelots (a wild cat). Other cats include cougar, jaguar, lions and tigers. Toucans and macaws are on display.

The western suburbs of the town are a good place to visit because of the many restaurants and bars and the pretty gingerbread houses (particularly in **Woodbrook**). Beyond here, the district of **St James's**, on Tragarete Rd, is called the 'City that never sleeps' and is very lively. Traditionally it has a strong Indian population and you will know that you have arrived when you see a pink and green arch built in Indian style with minarets. Close by is a monument to the leading Calypsonian, Lord Kitchener.

The heights above Port of Spain are dominated by the usual series of forts; **Fort Picton** and **Fort Chacon** both stand in the east, above the crowded suburb of Laventille. Just beneath Laventille on Beetham Highway (on the road to the airport), the main Port of Spain **market** is one of the liveliest places in town and worth a visit. Dominating St James's on the other side of town, **Fort George** is half an hour's drive into the hills and has cannon and ramparts but is now mainly visited by lovers on a day out.

Over the Saddle Road to the North Coast

The Saddle Road runs north out of Port of Spain, from the northwest corner of the Savannah, through the wealthy suburb of **Maraval**, and then winds into the hills of the northern range. The scenery is majestic and makes the drive worthwhile even before you descend to the rural north coast. **Maracas Bay**, with its palm trees 100ft high, is a popular picnic place at the weekends. It is possible to reach the **Maracas Falls** and Trinidad's second peak, **El Tucuche** (from the Amerindian word for humming-bird), from here, but it is quite a hike. The villages of **Las Cuevas** and **Blanchisseuse** overlook the sea and their beaches are usually less crowded than Maracas Bay (*see* 'Best Beaches', p.105).

The Chaguaramas Peninsula

The route west out of Port of Spain follows the coast through the western suburbs and then beneath scrubby hills, passing the vast transshipment terminal (formerly used for bauxite) before coming to Chaguaramas, a popular area for day trips and evening entertainment. There are a number of good bars and nightclubs and the marinas are always full of visiting yachts. Chaguaramas is one of the areas that was leased to the Americans during the Second World War. The American presence on the island had a considerable effect on the Trinidadians because they paid so highly and spawned a large entertainment industry. 'Working for the Yankee Dollar' was the catch phrase of a calypso that spoke about the Trini girls deserting their menfolk for the rich American sailors.

Set in its concrete yard, the **Chaguaramas Military History and Aviation Museum** (*open daily 9–6; adm*) has displays of military hardware and planes. Inside there are boards on subjects such as the Spanish in Trinidad, the history of flight on the island, the U-boat war in the Caribbean (Port of Spain was attacked), Trinidadians who served in the Second World War, general military history and even the coup in 1990. Worth a quick look if that's your interest.

Off the peninsula are five islands in the **Bocas del Dragon** (the Dragon's Mouth), named by Columbus in 1498, where rich Trinidadians have built villas for themselves. On **Gaspar Grande** are some caves (*adm*) with stalactites and stalagmites and the remains of a fortress. **Chacachacare** is the biggest of the islands and has some strange red-brick buildings that once were a leper colony.

The Eastern Main Road

Running out of Port of Spain to the east as far as Arima, the corridor along the Eastern Main Road is the most populous area of the island outside the capital. Just out of the city is the **Angostura factory** (*tours Tues and Thurs, t 623 1841*), where the famous bitters are produced. An unrevealed number of spices and barks are selected by just four people and then percolated in alcohol to produce the bitters. The road skirts the southern side of the lush Northern Range of mountains on the left and, as you approach St Joseph, site of the original capital of the island, the St Augustine campus of the University of the West Indies is on the right. Overlooking the plain from 800ft up in the foothills is the **Mount St Benedict Monastery**. There is now also a school and a Catholic seminary there, and you can stay in the small guest house.

The **Lopinot Complex** (*open daily until about 5; adm free*), a restored 19th-century estate, is off the road from Arouca. In 1800, the Comte de Lopinot fled the troubles in St Domingue (now Haiti) and he settled the plantation he cut out of the jungle in the Arouca Valley, where he planted cocoa, cashew and coffee. Early in the year the immortelle trees flame bright orange in the valley. Visits to **caves** on the estate are also possible. **Arima** has a strong Amerindian influence deriving from a community of Arawaks that lived here 200 years ago. There is a small **museum** devoted to the Indians in Cleaver Woods Park, just west of the town.

One of the island's most appealing spots is the **Asa Wright Nature Centre** (*t 667 4655; open to outsiders daily 9–5; adm US$6 adults, $4 children, accompanied walks*), 1,200ft up in the hills above Arima, about an hour and a half from Port of Spain. Built in 1908, the estate house is very popular with naturalists and has some accommodation (*see p.112*), where you can witness the amazing colour and variety of the squawking, screeching rainforest. The veranda at the Nature Centre is one of the most charming places in the whole Caribbean, and you can realistically expect to see 25 species of birds before breakfast.

Five trails (varying between a few minutes and 3hrs) have been cut into the forest around the main house, and you will possibly see species such as the white-bearded or the golden-headed manikin, toucans and honey creepers, as well as some of Trinidad's 18 fluorescent hummingbirds and its 600 or so butterflies. The most famous inhabitant is the nocturnal oilbird, which comes out only at night and feeds on fruit that it picks from the trees while in flight. They were once hunted by the Arawaks for their oil, but now are protected and live in remote regions in caves.

Not far off is Trinidad's highest peak, **El Cerro del Aripo** (3,083ft), its sides mantled with rainforest and home to Trindad's rare piping guan. The **Aripo Caves** are extensive, with a forest of monstrous stalactites and stalagmites, and a colony of oilbirds' nests. You can also reach the **Cumaca Caves**, which have the largest population of oilbirds on the island, and the **Tamana Caves**, where there is a large colony of bats. Contact the guides listed in 'Flora and Fauna', p.107.

Beyond Aripo the main road turns south, but if you take a left you come to the east coast at Salibia, close to **Matura Beach**, where the leatherback turtle nests by crawling up onto the sand and digging a hole with her flippers before laying about 150 eggs. From here, the road leads to the northeastern point of the island and the rugged Toco coast. The area of **Grande Rivière** is also very popular for viewing turtles during the nesting season.

The South of the Island

The southern plains of Trinidad contain the agricultural lands, covered in green swathes of sugar cane, and the industrial and oil heartland that has made Trinidad rich in the past (you will see the drill heads pecking at the ground like huge metal chickens). You will also find a gentle, laid-back calm more typical of smaller islands around the Caribbean.

Take the Eastern Main Road out of Port of Spain and then turn south on the Uriah Butler Highway towards Chaguanas and San Fernando. The road skirts the **Caroni Swamp**, a wildlife reserve and bird sanctuary, which contains an enormous abundance of birdlife, with around 75 species. One of the island's most spectacular sights takes place here every evening, when the **scarlet ibis**, Trinidad's national bird, flies in to roost. You can take a leisurely tour at dusk (*starts around 4.30pm; TT$50 per person, depending on numbers; restless children not recommended*) as they arrive: for a moment whole trees will seem to be on fire with the scarlet of the ibis in flight. The knowledgeable guides will give you all sorts of anecdotes about swamp life – among the mangroves you might see a spectacled cayman (an alligator) or *Cyclopes didactylus* (a silky anteater) or perhaps a greater ani or a pootoo, whose eyes glow in the dark.

The highway continues to the town of **Chaguanas**, which has mushroomed in recent years. The population is mostly of East Indian descent and in the main street you will find the **Lion House**, once the home of V. S. Naipaul (it is private, so you cannot go in). From here the road passes sugar mills and the factories of heavy industry at Point Lisas and the tangle of silver pipes at Point-à-Pierre, the island's main oil refinery. It was bought by the Trinidad and Tobago government from Texaco in 1984, when the oil company withdrew. On the lakes within the refinery compound, the **Point-à-Pierre Wildfowl Trust** (*t 637 5145; open Mon–Fri 10–5, Sat–Sun 12–4; call in advance*) breeds wildfowl, mainly ducks, and encourages their reintroduction into the wild. It has trails and an education centre.

San Fernando, an urban sprawl with a population of 60,000, is Trinidad's second, slightly calmer city. The San Fernando Hill gives a good view of the city and the surrounding countryside. The **fish market** down by the bus station is worth a visit in the late afternoon.

The Pitch Lake

Open any time in daylight (remember that the round trip is about 6–8 hours by bus from Port of Spain) for a look at the small museum and a guided tour of the lake itself, on which you will learn more fantastic stories from the guide (adm free officially, but it is worth taking a guide, a bargain at TT$30 or so).

In the 'deep south', as it is jokingly known, is one of the Caribbean's most extraordinary phenomena, the Pitch Lake. As you approach the Pitch Lake through the town of La Brea, the side of the road is covered with splodges of black goo and an infestation of weeds. The lake itself is 100 acres of tar, slightly springy underfoot, with folds like a cake mix that move very, very slowly. When you step on it you leave an imprint and then very gradually you sink. Stay there for an hour or two and you will be stirred into the mix.

According to a legend of Iere, a chief once killed a sacred hummingbird, which so angered the gods that they punished him by engulfing his village in pitch. Although the 'lake' often turns up old artefacts in its continual stirring – from prehistoric tree trunks to biscuit tins – it has not yet produced a whole village to verify the legend.

More recent history has Sir Walter Raleigh caulking his ships with it – 'most excellent good and melteth not with the sun as the pitch of Norway'. However, when he brought it back to England and asphalted Westminster Bridge for the opening of Parliament, it did melt, clogging the carriage wheels and the horses' hoofs. Since then, Trinidad pitch has been used with more success on roads all over the world. Towns as far flung as Cairo, Bombay, Singapore and London were laid with it, as well as Port of Spain. Once it was tried as fuel for street lighting, but the smoke and the stench were so overpowering that it had to be stopped (though it was used to fumigate the town after a smallpox epidemic in 1920). It was even applied as a covering to prevent weeds growing, but it turned out to be such a potent fertilizer that the streets were infested in no time.

Old prints show the 19th-century mining methods. A pickaxe was used, and then a shovel to load up the carts with stringy black goo. Today it is more like a vehicle ballet, with JCBs scooping up the bitumen and dumping it in railway carriages. The railway is run as near to the mining site as possible, but with the lake constantly in motion it is difficult to get close.

The cake mix itself has seeped from the oil sands that lie beneath Trinidad and is apparently 'uniform in composition – made up of celloidal clay (30%), bitumen (54%), saltwater (3%) and ash (36%)'. As Quentin Crewe points out in *Touch the Happy Isles*, any composition that adds up to 123% has to arouse some doubts.

It is the largest lake of its kind in the world, but stories that this monstrous cauldron is of unfathomable depth and constantly self-replenishing are not true. A hole dug one day may be gone the next as the lake settles, but the level is steadily dropping. The Pitch Lake's main attraction is really in its history and mystery – visiting it is quite like wandering around on a bouncy car park. Take a flat pair of shoes, because high heels might get you swallowed up.

From La Brea, the southern main road continues along the peninsula to **Icacos Point**, from where you can see Venezuela about 10 miles away. Columbus was supposed to have dropped anchor at Los Gallos when he arrived in Trinidad in 1498. At **Siparia** there is a statue of a black Virgin which has become a focus of pilgrimage for Trinidadians of all religions, not just Christians. Her festival is on the Sunday after Easter, when she is carried around the town.

The Atlantic Coast

At Valencia, the Eastern Main Road turns south to Sangre Grande and reaches the Atlantic coast at Manzanilla (the Spanish word for the poisonous manchineel tree which grows here). But this coast is more noted for its coconuts – in all there are nearly 50 miles of palm trees that stand in a tangled network of trunks behind the coastline, which is a fantastic sight as you drive through them. In the season, the beaches towards **Guayaguayare** are covered in chip-chip shells, which make a favoured local dish, and off the southeastern tip of the island are the oil rigs which brought Trinidad its wealth in the 1970s. From the sea you can supposedly see the three peaks which inspired Columbus to call the island Trinidad.

As you drive back inland towards San Fernando through the canefields, you might pass the villages of Third Company and Sixth Company, named after black American regiments who were brought to Trinidad in the middle of the 19th century when the island was crying out for settlers. There is no mention of the Second Company because they were lost at sea.

Tobago

Tobago is completely unlike its sister island Trinidad. It has none of the press of Port of Spain, the varied racial heritage, or the glaring flamboyance of Carnival. In Tobago you will find laid-back life in classic Caribbean style. It is more typical of the rest of the Caribbean in its history and also in its tourism, which is more established than in

Trinidad. The industry has developed considerably in the last few years and it dominates the western end of the island. Beyond here, however – in the secluded coves of the north coast and the fishing villages of the east – you will still find some charming, undeveloped spots with slow-time Caribbean life.

Geographically, Tobago is related to Trinidad and South America, but in appearance it is more similar to the Windward Islands. A single spine of thickly forested mountains (up to 1,890ft) runs along its length, casting off spurs that reach out as headlands into the sea. Inland, rivers tumble and cascade in waterfalls, and on the coast there are huge crescent bays. Some of this land is the Tobago Forest Reserve, which has been protected for over 200 years. At the flatter, coral-based and more accessible western end of the island, the huge Buccoo Reef throws up white sand (this is why the hotels have gathered here, of course). The island offers superb natural life to visitors and this has spawned a good ecotourism sector. You can expect excellent scuba diving, and other natural highlights including turtle-watching and spectacular birdlife (unparalleled except, of course, by Trinidad).

Historically, Tobago has been more closely associated with the Windwards as well. Like them it was a plantation island and in its 18th-century heyday it was so successful that people would use the phrase 'as rich as a Tobago planter'. As you travel around the remoter parts of the island, you will see the waterwheels and stone buildings of the plantation age poking out of the undergrowth. The island's 50,000 population, unlike Trinidad's, is mostly African, descended from slaves who worked the plantations. Like the Windwards too, Tobago was also battled over incessantly in the race for Empire. By the late 19th century, however, when the sugar and cocoa plantations failed, the island was declared bankrupt and it was simply appended to Trinidad for political convenience.

Tobago is developing fast and there is a positive air about the island at the moment. The last few years have seen a large influx of people and investment. Scarborough, Tobago's capital on the southern shore, where about 10,000 people live, even sees traffic jams nowadays. You will still see the roadside 'parlours' (actually dry-goods stores) and farmers who live a simple life returning home from their plantation carrying their tools and produce; but, particularly at the western end of the island, Tobago is becoming steadily more built up, with large local homes and the villas of international holidaymakers (plenty also from Trinidad). Still, the island is holding it well. Tobago's glorious and turbulent past may be gone – the cannons at Fort King George point only at windsurfers and yachts now – but the island's charm lies in her calm and still unaffected manner, just as so much of the Caribbean used to be.

History

Some claim that Columbus sighted Tobago as he emerged through the Dragon's Mouth to the west of Trinidad from the Gulf of Paria on his third voyage in 1498, and called it Bellaforma. Whatever the case, he did not stop there, but continued west along the South American coastline. Tobago never became a Spanish island and until the late 18th century was not really a 'possession' at all. It saw so many settlements and sieges that it changed hands more often than any other island in the area.

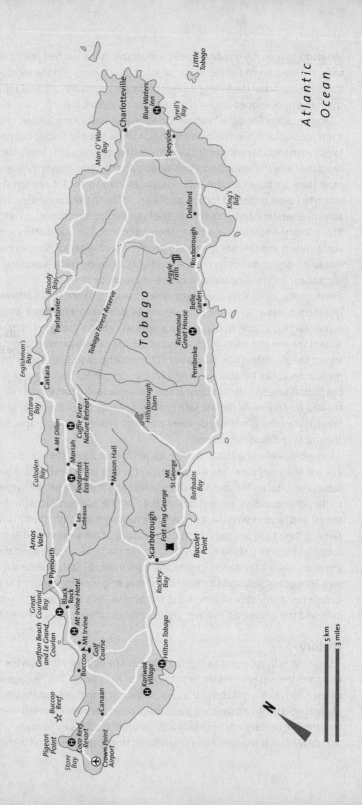

Tobago

Caribbean Sea

Atlantic Ocean

Little Tobago

Charlotteville

Man O' War Bay

Blue Waters Inn

Tyrell's Bay

Speyside

Delaford

King's Bay

Roxborough

Argyle Falls

Belle Garden

Richmond Great House

Pembroke

Bloody Bay

Parlatuvier

Tobago Forest Reserve

T o b a g o

Englishman's Bay

Castara

Castara Bay

▲ Mt Dillon

Cuffie River Nature Retreat

Moriah

Footprints Eco Resort

Mason Hall

Hillsborough Dam

Culloden Bay

Les Coteaux

Arnos Vale

Plymouth

Mt St George

Barbados Bay

Scarborough

Fort King George

Bacolet Point

Rockley Bay

Great Courland Bay

Black Rock

Grafton Beach and Le Grand Courlan

Mt Irvine Hotel

Mt Irvine

Buccoo

Golf Course

Hilton Tobago

Kariwak Village

Canaan

Pigeon Point

Store Bay

Buccoo Reef

Coco Reef Resort

Crown Point Airport

N

5 km

3 miles

Best Beaches

Along the north shore, east from Pigeon Point, there are many undeveloped beaches that are difficult to reach (best get yourself dropped off by a fisherman from Buccoo).

Mount Irvine Bay: Lively in season, with watersports and changing facilities.

Stone Haven Bay and **Great Courland Bay**: Hotel beaches, with some activity.

Turtle Beach: Some activity from the hotel, named after the turtles that come here to lay their eggs.

Arnos Vale: A small beach within the arms of massive headlands, and a good snorkelling reef. In hotel grounds.

Castara: Just a few shacks under the palm trees and you can get a snack and a drink.

Englishman's Bay: Probably the most beautiful of them all, a classic West Indian beach in a crescent curve, where the royal-blue water stands out against the green forestland and the palms. Very secluded; you will find the path down to it on the straight piece of road half a mile beyond Castara. Take a picnic.

Man O' War Bay: A charming corner of thick, granular sand (with some simple facilities) beneath the headlands along from Charlotteville. From here you can walk over to Pirate's Bay, a very private cove, with no watersports. Vendors often set up stalls during the day to sell soft drinks and simple meals. There are lots of steps.

Speyside: Passable, with some facilities (also a lovely strip of sand at the Blue Waters Inn on Batteaux Bay just beyond here).

King's Bay: Quite far east on the southern shore, with palm-backed grey sand and some facilities.

Canoe Bay: On the south shore, a less crowded alternative with shallow water and grey sand, thatched picnic tables and a snack bar and washing facilities (*adm TT$12*).

Store Bay: In the west, smaller but also lively, with changing rooms and breakfast sheds (local Tobagonian fast-food stores, which will provide food and drink) across the road. Also craft stalls. Trips can be arranged out to Buccoo Reef from here, departing late morning.

Pigeon Point: Tobago's liveliest beach. Plenty of soft sand, with shallow water and backed by palms for shade. Some watersports on offer – windsurfing, waterskiing (wetbikes at the entrance) – as well as lots of snack bars, craft and T-shirt shops, sitting areas and changing rooms, and an excellent view of the sunset. The beach is a business concern so you are asked to pay an entry fee of TT$12.

The Dutch were the first to claim it, in 1628, but all their expeditions were harried by canoes full of Caribs and Spaniards from Trinidad. King James I of England then granted the island to his godson Jacobus, Duke of Courland (a principality in modern-day Latvia), but each one of the six Courlander settlements failed too. Working on the same claim, that the English flag had been planted on the island in 1580 by some passing sailors, James's successor, Charles I, decided to grant the island to the Earl of Montgomery. To complete the picture, the French made similar claims, grants and settlements – Louis XIV made the leader of a French-backed expedition, Dutchman Adraien Lampsius, Baron of Tobago.

The settlements were intended to cultivate plantations of tropical produce for Europe and, to begin with, their main crop was tobacco. Tobago's name derives from the same Carib word as tobacco, though this was not what the Caribs called the plant. (To them a 'tobacco' was a yard-long, double-pronged tube that they used to blast their powdered drugs up each other's nose.) Still, smoking was popular in Europe by the late 1500s and 'freighting smoke' was a profitable occupation, even though the shippers had to run the gauntlet of the Spanish navy, who had instructions to root out the trade.

Towards the end of the 17th century, in an attempt to stop the fighting over the island, Tobago was declared neutral. The Treaty of Aix-la-Chapelle in 1684 allowed the island no defences and it was supposedly free for all nations to come and go. Within years the treaty was nicknamed the 'Pirates' Charter' because along with settlers came pirates who were being chased out of their traditional hunting grounds around Jamaica and the Bahamas. Man O' War Bay in the northeast was renowned for its 'safe retreat and commanding situation for cruize and plunder'.

Tobago was an attractive prize and, while some fought for her, others tried to gain the island by legal means. At one stage it was the cause of a touching Caribbean love story, set in the court of Marie Antoinette in France. A Swedish diplomat named Staël was wooing a Mademoiselle Necker, a courtesan, and she told him that she would only consent to marry him if he were an ambassador. He turned for support to the Queen, who wrote to King Gustavus requesting that he be made one. The King wrote back saying that he would consent, but that in return Staël must get him an island in the Caribbean, preferably Tobago. Staël bargained at the court, but the best he could do was St-Barthélemy in the Leeward Islands, in return for a warehouse in Gothenburg, because the French government would not relinquish Tobago. However, the Queen intervened once again with King Gustavus and secured the ambassadorship. Staël won the hand of Mlle Necker.

The 19th century saw the spiralling decline of the sugar industry, as a result of the emancipation of the slaves in 1834 and the cultivation of sugar beet in Europe. All the estates on the island became dependent on a single British firm, Messrs A. M. Gillespie and Co, and when that went bankrupt in 1884, Tobago was left ruined. The land was sold off at 10 shillings an acre and so the former slaves were able to buy themselves plots of land on which to grow their crops. Tobago became a very poor agricultural island.

For many years Tobago looked north in political matters. When under British rule in the 19th century, it had been one of the Windward Islands and, unlike Trinidad, which had remained under direct rule from London, it had always had some elected representation on its Governing Council. Now that it was in debt, it was simply attached to Trinidad, first as an economic arrangement, but then just placed under its control, as a 'ward', uninvited and largely unwanted. With this heritage, many of the Tobagonians feel that their island has suffered a continual neglect. There was no regular link with Trinidad until a steamer started to make the trip in 1910 – before that the mail was rowed the 22 miles over from Toco. Electricity did not reach the island until the 1950s, and the Prime Minister Eric Williams himself admitted in 1957 that the problem was

Getting There

Tobago t (1 868–)

By Air

Crown Point Airport in Tobago is served by some direct international flights from Europe and the USA, but most flights stop in Port of Spain, from where you can connect with regular Tobago Express services (the flight across takes 20mins). There is a departure tax from Trinidad and Tobago of $TT100.

From the UK

British Airways, t 639 0588, flies three times a week from London Gatwick. BWIA, t 639 3291, flies daily to Trinidad (usually via Barbados, Antigua or St Lucia). Virgin Atlantic flies on Mondays from Gatwick. Charter operators jmc fly direct to Tobago twice weekly.

From the USA

BWIA and American Airlines fly from New York and Miami to Trinidad, with onward connections. Otherwise, you can connect in Puerto Rico for American Eagle, t 669 4661.

From Other Caribbean Islands

The best scheduled flights to the rest of the Caribbean are on LIAT, t 639 0276. Charter operator TIA, t 639 8918, flies in occasionally from Barbados.

By Sea

A ferry, the *Panorama*, runs a daily service (except Sat) between Port of Spain and Scarborough in Tobago, approximately 6hrs. Return prices range from TT$50 for a seat to TT$160 for a cabin. Tickets are on sale Mon–Fri until 8.30pm; for information call t 639 2417.

Getting Around

By Bus

The government-run **bus** system (PTSC) runs all the major routes from Scarborough. It is extremely cheap and runs to a schedule, every half-hour to Crown Point, but only once an hour or two elsewhere. Tickets must be bought in advance at the main office in Scarborough and at offices around the island.

A good alternative are the **route taxis** (private cars) that work the same roads, usually with more frequency. These pause for the few seconds it takes to fill with passengers at their various departure points in town. Ask around for your destination: from Scarborough to Crown Point – TT$7, Plymouth – TT$4, Buccoo – TT$4, departing from Carrington St on the waterfront; and to Speyside and Charlotteville – TT$11, departing from James Park on Burnett St. Out in the country, flag them down with a frantic wave.

By Taxi

Plenty of regular taxis are available at the airport, the taxi-stand in Scarborough and through all the hotels. They are quite expensive. Some sample prices are: Crown Point Airport to Pigeon Point – TT$35, Scarborough – TT$50, Plymouth – TT$65, and Charlotteville – around TT$250. A tour by taxi costs around US$25 per hour, or TT$250 for a half-day's excursion. Companies include:
Airport Taxi, at the airport, t 639 0950.
Downtown Taxis, in town, t 639 2659.

By Guided Tour

Banwari Experience, Bourg Malatresse, Lower Santa Cruz, t 675 1619/624 8687, *banwari@tstt.net.tt*.
Good Time Tours, t 639 6816, *www.goodtimetourstt.com*.
Sun Fun Tours, t 639 7461.
Hummingbird Helicopter Services, t 639 7159, *hummingbird@trinidad.net, www.hummingbirdhelicopters.com*. Helicopter tours: 'round d island', 'Sunset Soirée' or 'Crusoe Cruise'.

Hitch-hiking

Hitching works quite well in Tobago, but check whether the driver will expect you to pay before you get in.

Car and Bike Hire

For maximum flexibility – to explore the bays at the eastern end of the island and to see Tobago in its variety, and then go out to dinner in the evening – you need to get hold of a **hire car**. Four-wheel-drive is useful if you intend to explore along remoter roads, which sometimes turn into muddy tracks. Driving is on the left, generally, and there is an unfeasibly low official speed limit of 30mph. A licence from the UK, France, Germany, USA and Canada is valid in Trinidad and Tobago, and, when driving, you are supposed to carry it with you at all times, along with your passport. Also, wear your seat belt.

Expect to pay US$40–45 per day for a car, plus insurance. Car-hire firms, many of which are based at the airport but who deliver to your hotel anyway, include:

Auto Rentals, t 639 0644.

Econo-Car Rentals, Crown Point, opposite airport, **t** 660 8728, *sales@econocarrentals ltd.com, www.econocarrentalsltd.com.*

Peter Gremli, t 639 8271.

Spence Rentals Services, Crown Point, **t** 639 8082.

Sherman's Auto Rentals, t 639 2292, *shermans@trinidad.net, www.shermans rental.com.*

Singh's Auto Rentals, Grafton Beach Resort, **t** 639 0191

Thrifty Car Rental, Rex Turtle Beach, **t** 639 8507.

Baird's Rentals, **t** 639 2528, rents **motorbikes**, as does Modern Bikes, **t** 639 3275. You can find **bicycles** at Glorious Ride Cycle Rental, **t** 639 7124. Bicycles are about US$15 per day.

Tourist Information

Abroad

TIDCO have a website at *www.visitTNT.com*, which has some useful information. There is also some interesting stuff at *www.tntisland. com*, a personal website. There is an email postbox for information on Tobago at *tourto-bago@tstt.net.tt.*

In Tobago

For information call **t** 639 INFO 6436. Offices include:

NIB Mall, Carrington St, Scarborough, **t** 639 2125.

Crown Point Airport, **t** 639 0509.

Speyside, **t** 660 6012.

Cruise ship complex, Scarborough. *Open when there is a ship in harbour.*

Embassies and Consulates

See 'Tourist Information' under 'Trinidad', p.109.

Media

You will also find useful information in the small annual magazine *Discover Trinidad and Tobago*, and Tobago has a newspaper called *Tobago Today* for visitors.

Medical Emergencies

Tobago County Hospital is on Fort St in Scarborough, **t** 639 2551.

Money and Banks

The currency is the Trinidad and Tobago dollar (TT$), which floats on the international exchange and stands at about US$1=TT$6. Hotels will accept US dollars and most accept credit cards, but it is a good idea to have some TT$ while you are out on the island. There is a bureau de change at Crown Point Airport. A (recent) receipt must be presented if you wish to change money back when you leave. Banking hours are Mon–Thurs 9–2, Fri 9–1 and 3–5.

Shopping

Open Mon–Fri 8–4.30, Sat 8–noon.

Telephone Code

The IDD code for Tobago is **t** 1 868 followed by a seven-digit number. For local calls, dial the seven digits.

Maps and Books

Possibly the earliest book set on Tobago (and one of the earliest English novels) is *Robinson Crusoe* by Daniel Defoe (published in 1719), which tells the story of a shipwrecked sailor who lives on the island for nearly 30 years.

Festivals

January–mid/end of February *Carnival.* Like its counterpart in Trinidad, the Tobago Carnival is a major blow-out which starts soon after New Year and culminates with Mardi Gras at the beginning of Lent (usually mid–end February). You can catch a calypso tent for a month beforehand.

Easter Goat and crab races and a general jump-up in Buccoo on Easter weekend (at Mount Pleasant and then Buccoo).

April *Carib International Fishing Tournament.*

May *Angostura Regatta*. Four days of sailing.

July and August *Tobago Heritage Festival*. An old-time wedding at Moriah are among the celebrations of Tobago traditions.

September *The Great Race*. A powerboat race from Trinidad to Store Bay.

Watersports

If watersports – snorkelling, kayaking, windsurfing, outings on small sailboats and scuba diving – cannot be arranged through your hotel, you will probably find them at Pigeon Point and Mt Irvine Bay Watersports, **t** 639 9389.

Day Sails

For a day's sailing up the Caribbean coast to secluded bays with good snorkelling, try:

Chlöe, **t** 639 2851. An attractive yacht.

Kalina Cats, **t** 639 6304.

Natural Mystic, **t** 639 SAIL, *mystic@tstt.net.tt*.

Deep-sea Fishing

Dillon Tours and Charters, aboard *Super Cool*, **t** 639 8765, *dillons@tstt.net.tt*, or through 'Frothy' De Silva on *Hard Play*, **t** 639 7108, at US$500 for a full day.

Scuba Diving

Diving is good all round Tobago, though the best reefs are at the eastern end of the island, in the currents that run from the Atlantic up the Caribbean islands. Many are drift dives – more rewarding if you have an appropriate level of experience, but you can expect to see large fish (they grow well on the nutrients on the currents), including barracudas and often manta rays, as well as an absolutely vast brain coral (24ft across). Popular dive sites include the Sisters, London Bridge and Black Jack Hole.

Aquamarine Dive, Scarborough, **t** 639 4416, *amdtobago@trinidad.net*, *www.aqua marinedive.com*.

Man Friday Diving, Charlotteville, **t** 660 4676, *dive_tobago@hotmail.com*.

Tobago Dive Experience, Speyside, **t** 639 7034, *info@tobagodiveexperience.com*, *www.tobagodiveexperience.com*.

Adventure Eco-Divers, Black Rock, **t** 639 8729, *info@adventureecodivers.com*, *www. adventureecodivers.com*.

Scuba Adventure Safari, Pigeon Point, **t** 660 7767, *info@divetobago.com*, *www.dive tobago.com*.

Wild Turtle Dive Tobago, Pigeon Point, Bon Accord, Tobago **t** 639 7936, *kevin@wildturtle dive.com*, *www.wildturtledive.com*.

Equipment and instruction are available through all operators and it is worth remembering that some hotels include diving packages in their rates. A single-tank dive costs around US$35–40.

Snorkelling

Many boats take swimming and snorkelling tours to Buccoo Reef, with departures from Store Bay and Pigeon Point (about US$15). Most stop on the way back at the Nylon Pool. Take a swimming costume and make sure that the boat has a mask your size. There are also good reefs at Arnos Vale, and at the eastern end of the island at the Blue Waters Inn and at Charlotteville.

Surfing

Popular in the winter when the waves are at their biggest; alternatively, boogie boards are available most of the year. If you are travelling independently, there is a general watersports shop at Mt Irvine Bay Watersports, **t** 639 9389.

Other Sports

Golf

There is an 18-hole course at the Mt Irvine Hotel, **t** 639 8871, and a PGA-listed 18-hole course at the Tobago Plantations Lowlands Estate Golf and Country Club, **t** 639 8000, *sales@tobagoplantations.com*, *www.tobago plantations.com*. The green fee is US$95.

Hiking

Tobago has excellent walking and there are now a number of guides who take excellent, personalized tours in which you discover all sorts of wonderful historical and natural information (about the ongoing processes of life in the forest and how leaf-cutting ants fit into it, for instance) as well as the simple sights, such as the waterfalls. The birdlife in Tobago is also specatacular. Trinidad may have over 400 species, but Tobago herself has over 200, including the red-billed tropicbird, the admirably named rufous-vented chachalaca, the blue-crowned motmot and the red-footed booby. Many of these can be see in the Tobago Forest Reserve in the centre of the island, which also has a number of marked trails, including the six-mile Gilpin Trace. Contact:

David Rooks, Scarborough, t 756 8594, *rooks tobago@yahoo.com, www.rookstobago.com*. Arranges bird-watching and plant-watching hikes into the rainforest between Roxborough and Parlatuvier and on Little Tobago.

Newton George Nature Tours, t 660 5463, *ngeorge@tstt.net.tt*.

Pat Turpin, Man O'War Bay Cottages, Charlotteville, t 660 4327, *pturpin@tstt.net.tt*.

Renson Jack, t 660 5175.

All these people will also arrange turtle-watching trips in season (March–July) if requested. See also the excellent *Eco-Adventure* magazine.

Horse-riding

Try Palm Tree Village, t 639 4347, for a gallop along the sand at Rockley Beach or a walk into the fertile inland areas.

Tennis

Many hotels have courts. If yours doesn't, tennis can still be arranged at reception.

Where to Stay

Tobago t (1 868–)

With better beaches, Tobago offers more in the way of typical Caribbean beach hotels than Trinidad – recent building in Tobago has brought a number of new resort complexes. However, Tobago is actually untypical of the rest of the Caribbean because the island has so many delightful West Indian hideaways tucked into coves and up in the hills, including a number of good guest houses.

Tobago also has some good villas, both in villa 'estates' (*see* below) and individual villas dotted around the island. If you wish to hire one, contact **Tobago Villas Agency**, PO Box 301, t 639 8737, **Abraham Tobago Realty**, t 639 3325, *abreal@trinidad.net, www.abrahamrealty.com*, or the **Sea Horse Inn** (*see* below).

Unlike in Trinidad, hotels in Tobago tend to stick to the Caribbean's traditional high (Christmas to April) and low seasons. You can also expect bills in all hotels to be supplemented by 10% for government tax (like restaurants, hotel dining rooms have to charge 15% VAT) and usually 10% for service (guest houses factor this into their prices).

Very Expensive

Stonehaven Villas, Stone Haven Bay, t 639 0361, *stonehav@tstt.et.tt, www.stone havenvillas.com*. The most elegant and comfortable place to stay in Tobago, offering a collection of villas ranged on the hillside above the bay. Architecturally they ring with echoes of the French colonial Caribbean of the 18th century, with grey-tiled mansard roofs, louvred shutters pinned out at an angle, hefty interior walls and faux-antique furniture, but they also have all the comforts you could need for modern living, including a full kitchen, air conditioning and an infinity pool on the large balcony. There is a 'clubhouse' with a dining room, but there are live-in maids who will shop and cook for you. *Expensive for three couples sharing*.

Blue Haven Hotel, Bacolet Bay, just outside Scarborough, t 660 7400, *reservations@ bluehavenhotel, www.bluehavenhotel.com*. More typical of modern Caribbean comfort and style, this hotel was famous in the 1950s and has recently been reopened. It stands on 15 acres of verdant land just above the shoreline, with a pretty, brown-sand beach just down below, and has 55 quite small but very stylish rooms looking out to sea. There is a good dining room.

Coco Reef Resort, near Pigeon Point, PO Box 434, t 639 8571, UK t (01753) 684 810, US toll free t 1 800 221 1294, *cocoreef-tobago@ trinidad.net, www.cocoreef.com*. Offers high-grade comfort and service in 125 sumptuous rooms. It's a bit overplayed with all the statuary, classical pillars and arches in the foyer, but is popular and a good hotel. There's a rustic beach-style restaurant down on the sand of a quite disappointing beach, but Pigeon Point is not far off.

Mount Irvine Bay Hotel and Golf Club, PO Box 222, t 639 8871, UK t (01753) 684 810, US t 1 800 537 8483, *mtirvine@tstt.net.tt*, *www.mtirvine.com*. With echoes of a country club, laid out in the expansive setting of its own golf course and lawned gardens. Calm, very quiet and quite large, with 105 rooms which have all the standard international comforts. Rooms stand in blocks overlooking the dining room in the restored sugar mill, or the garden festooned with tropical plants, and onto the sea.

Expensive

The Palms Villa Resort, Signal Hill Old Road, **t** 635 1010, *info@thepalmstobago.com*, *www.thepalmstobago.com*. Five, three-bedroom villas set in 10 acres of landscaped gardens. Each has air-con, living room, kitchen, cable television, swimming pool, veranda, and housekeeper.

Hilton Tobago, Lowlands, **t** 660 8500, *www.hilton.com*. On Tobago's windward southwest coast, three miles from Scarborough. The hotel occupies 20 beach-front acres that are part of Tobago Plantations with a 90-acre natural lagoon and protected mangroves. The three-storey hotel is designed to suggest the plantation setting of its surroundings. In one direction is an 18-hole championship golf course and in another, a huge free-form pool with swim-up bar overlooking a white sand beach. Five dining venues, two tennis courts, health club, and watersports.

Plantation Beach Villas, Stone Haven Bay, **t** 639 9377, *plantationbeach@tstt.net.tt*, *www.plantationbeachvillas.com*. Just beneath Stonehaven Villas, these three-bedroomed villas stand above one another among the tropical greenery of the bay, where there is a nice beach. Built in colonial style, in wood, with steeply pitched roofs, balustrades and gingerbread trimmings. Each villa has a huge wooden veranda with high-backed wooden chairs. Inside there are large rooms with ceiling fans (bedrooms air-conditioned) and full kitchens. There is a pool and a bar down below; no restaurant, but cooking can be arranged on request. *Moderate for three couples sharing.*

Old Donkey Cart House, Bacolet, just outside Scarborough, **t** 639 3551, *olddonk@opus.co.tt*, *www.carthouse.com*. A hip and friendly welcome, set around a delightful old

wooden West Indian house which nestles in tropical fairy-lit gardens. There are 12 secluded suites and apartments, two in the old house and 10 behind, in two modern buildings standing either side of a pool – these are very attractive, with wooden floors and louvred doors, windows and balconies. Some have four-posters, made with Trinidadian wood and draped with mosquito nets, and a sea view. All have TV, fridge and phone. There's an excellent penthouse. The beach is not far away.

Arnos Vale Hotel, **t** 639 2881, *reservations@ arnosvalehotel.com*, *www.arnosvalehotel.com*. Plenty of old-time West Indian charm and fading elegance awaits you on a 400-acre estate hidden away on the north coast. It is dominated by an old plantation house, site of the bar and dining room, down from which you walk through a tight, luxuriant valley to the pool, and beyond to a pretty and very private beach. The 29 rooms, some breezy, others air-conditioned, stand on the verdant hillside around the old estate house, in a block down by the pool, or overlooking the beach itself. Magnificent birdlife to entertain you at breakfast.

Moderate

Kariwak Village, Store Bay local road, at Crown Point, PO Box 27, **t** 639 8442, *kariwak@tstt. net.tt*, *www.kariwak.co.tt*. You will find a very pleasant and friendly atmosphere at this 'holistic haven and hotel'. The 24 air-conditioned rooms, furnished with locally made furniture, are set in shingle-wood and thatch-roofed cabanas that stand around a pool and in a lovely tropical garden. There is a TV room, but the resort hopes to take you away from all that, with programmes of yoga, t'ai chi, shiatsu and Ayurvedic massage. Kariwak is not actually on the beach, but there is a shuttle to Pigeon Point. It has a library and bar with some entertainment.

Footprints Eco Resort, Culloden Bay, **t** 660 0118, US toll free **t** 1 800 814 1396, *info@footprints eco-resort.com*, *www.footprintseco-resort. com*. You are similarly cocooned from the outside world here, tucked away in a narrow valley, down a steep and rickety road. There is a permanent backdrop of breaking waves in the resort, which has just a few rooms overlooking the sea and some villas (and a small museum) dotted around the valley. As the name suggests, they have an environmentally friendly policy, concentrating on preservation and protection of the environment as well as local purchasing of furnishings and food.

Manta Lodge, Windward Road, Speyside, **t** 660 5268, *dive-manta@trinidad.net*. Overlooking Goat Island on the northeast corner of the island, Manta Lodge was designed to be a family-style tropical hideaway for divers, bird-watchers, artists and nature-lovers. The lodge has 22 ocean-view bedrooms, each with private bathroom and balcony, with a choice of ceiling fan or air-con, but no phone or television. The restaurant serves local and international cuisine with fresh seafood. There's a jogging track, fresh water swimming pool, and full dive facilities.

The Sea Horse Inn, Stone Haven Bay, PO Box 488, **t** 639 0686, *seahorse@trinidad.net*. Really a restaurant (*see* opposite) with four rooms attached, set just above the beach at Stone Haven Bay. The rooms overlook a small courtyard festooned with brightly coloured tropical blooms. They are neat and modern in good Caribbean style, with a wooden interior and a balcony. Very quiet during the day, but quite busy at night because of the restaurant. Turtle-watching can be arranged from here.

Toucan Inn, Crown Point, **t** 639 7173, *bonkers@trinidad.net*, *www.toucan-inn.com*. Another small enclave, where eight hexagonal cabanas (each with two rooms), tropical greenery and a wooden dining room with a pointed roof are clustered around a swimming pool. Rooms are quite simple but pretty, with teak furnishings and stark white walls. The atmosphere here is fun.

Cuffie River Nature Retreat, Runnemede, PO Box 461, **t** 660 0505, US **t** 508 823 1190, *info@cuffie-river.com*, for US bookings *nature@cuffie-river.com*, *www.cuffie-river. com*. A lovely forest retreat, situated above a bend in the Runnemede River, everywhere overhanging with bamboo and other tropical plants. The building itself is a bit of a disappointment, but the setting and the reception are excellent and the rooms are large and nicely decorated, with balconies to

enjoy the peace after one of many walks in the surrounding area.

Blue Waters Inn, just beyond Speyside, **t** 660 4341, *bwi@bluewatersinn.com*, *www.blue watersinn.com*. Thirty-eight rooms are ranged here on the shores of the charming Batteaux Bay, with wonderful views through the craggy old sea grape trees to the sea and the islands. There is a variety of rooms, self-catering 'efficiencies' and one- and two-bedroom bungalows (some kitchen facilities). There are lots of watersports and onshore activities.

The Speyside Inn, Speyside, **t** 660 4852, *speysideinn@trinidad.net*, *www.caribinfo. com/speysideinn*. A very friendly spot across the road from the waterfront in Speyside, a short walk from the (relative) activity of the town. The nine rooms and cabins are built around the shell of an old colonial house with an open-fronted dining room (serving well-prepared local food) where you can expect to meet the other guests. Quiet, no phones or TVs, but very personable and picturesque.

Inexpensive

For bed and breakfast in private homes, a good way to see Tobagonian life, contact the Tourist Office in Scarborough about the **Bed and Breakfast Association**, c/o Federal Villa, 1–3 Crook's River, Scarborough, **t** 639 3926, *maredwards@hotmail.com*. The cost is generally about US$25 per person. In the towns of the eastern end of the island (e.g. Speyside and Charlotteville), you can find very cheap rooms by asking around.

Man O' War Bay Cottages, Man O' War Bay, **t** 660 4327, *mowbc@tstt.net.tt*, *www. man-o-warbaycottages.com*. Overlooking the waves just along from 'downtown' Charlotteville are these six cottages scattered around a pretty garden in the shade of huge sea almond trees. The cottages (1–4 bedrooms) are relatively simple and quite old in style, but they offer the ultimate in West Indian seclusion.

Cholson Chalets, Charlotteville, **t** 639 8553. A little cheaper, this has 12 rooms with kitchenettes right on the waterfront in Charlotteville overlooking the fishing boats. Simple but clean and neat.

Atlantic View Guest House, Speyside, t 639 2267. You can stay very cheaply at this big blue house.

Country Haven Guest House, Top Hill St, Speyside, t 660 5901. A bargain guest house with two rooms.

Sea-Side Garden Guest House, Buccoo, t 639 0682. Across from the waterfront (where you can get a trip to the beach), a nicely decorated, modern house with four rooms, an apartment and a friendly reception.

Cocrico Inn, Plymouth, t 639 2961, *cocrico@tstt. net.tt, www.hews-tours.com*. Comfortable rooms, set in a modern block with a pool and restaurant.

Jetway, Crown Point, t 639 8504. Very simple, with functional but clean rooms. Right opposite the airport.

Eating Out

There are some good restaurants outside the hotels in Tobago. In general, dining out in the island is not as expensive as elsewhere in the Caribbean. **Categories** are arranged according to the price of a main course: expensive = TT$70 and above, moderate = TT$30–70, inexpensive = less than TT$30. Restaurants must add VAT at 15% and they will usually add service at 10%.

Expensive

Rouselle's, Hilton Tobago, t 639 4738. Stylish and pleasant ambience. Artwork on the walls and, as it turns out, on the plate too – vegetables arrive neatly arranged, often in a smile. There's a set menu of gourmet local cuisine, using the best of Tobago's local produce in creative adaptations of traditional recipes. Playful, personable and hip.

Sea Horse Inn, Stone Haven Bay, t 639 0686. A lovely tropical setting, where you dine on a terrace beneath palms and cascades of bougainvillea, just across from the waves of Stone Haven Bay. There's a long cocktail list to choose from before a meal of innovative creole and international cuisine. Strong on seafood, particularly lobster, using the area's five unique species, and also tropical fruit sauces to complement island produce. Start with gingered shrimps, served on a base of fresh pear, followed by catch of the day grilled in island herbs and served on pak-choi with an orange pepper sauce. Good wine list, cigars and lots of fresh coffee.

Old Donkey Cart House, Bacolet, Scarborough, t 639 3551. An alluring and romantic setting on a deck set in a fairy-lit tropical garden. You sit in outsize wicker chairs in view of the working kitchen, dining on creole and Indian fare. Steaks and salads, Calcutta shrimp (with mushrooms) or kingfish sautéed in wine and garlic. Good wine list.

Shirvan Watermill, Shirvan Rd, in the west, t 639 0000. Offers international and creole fare on a large covered patio attached to a former windmill, looking onto a garden lit at night (with a waterfall as the name suggests). Hot fish salad with tomato vinaigrette followed by Shirvan honey-style duck or a chicken breast in lime and ginger sauce.

La Tartaruga, Buccoo, t 639 0940. A fine Italian restaurant where you sit inside or on a charming deck sheltered by banana plants. There's excellent freshly caught fish and homemade pastas with sauces made from herbs grown in the garden. Friendly and efficient.

Patino's Courtyard Café, Buccoo, t 639 9481. Has tables looking over a courtyard, pool and a waterfall. International fare with a speciality in seafood – their *mahi-mahi* is served in a coconut cream sauce, and Island Shrimp is sautéed with pineapples and served in a light curry sauce.

Papillon Restaurant, at the Old Grange Inn, Mount Irvine, t 639 9941. You will eat reliably well here, on the tropical garden terrace or in the air-conditioned interior. A long seafood menu: local conch (seasonal) cooked in coconut, or a seafood casserole in ginger wine, with generous servings of plantain and ground provisions, followed by *Tobago pone* for pudding.

Arnos Vale Water Wheel Restaurant, Arnos Vale Rd, north of Plymouth, t 660 0815. The restaurant is set in a jungle of greenery, in and around the ruins of a 19th-century sugar plantation and waterwheel whose original machinery is still in place. The dining room is in the former wheelhouse along side the Franklin River. A variety of local and international dishes are served with a emphasis on chicken and seafood.

Live music and dance on alternate nights. It's a bit touristy but worth it for the setting.

Black Rock Café, Black Rock, t 639 7625. A chi-chi pink and white veranda setting. Plenty of steaks, seafood and fish, but also some local dishes. Perhaps start with a beef *pastel* and follow with shrimp in curry sauce.

Moderate

Blue Crab, corner of Robinson and Main Sts, Scarborough, t 639 2737. You will be welcomed into a classic West Indian setting, on a veranda with trellises and flowers, and get the best of local food here. There is a set menu: pumpkin soup or fish chowder, followed by the daily catch grilled, curried or creole, or coal-pot chicken. Lots of juices and breads, mangoes, bananas and avocados from the garden, and all the local vegetables. *Reservations only. Closed Thurs.*

Taj Terrace, Pigeon Point, t 639 9020. For East Indian fare in the West Indies (remember Trinidad's Indian population).

Inexpensive

Jemma's Sea View Kitchen, Speyside, t 660 4066. It's worth stopping at this series of 'tree house' decks – suspended wooden houses with curtains and floral tablecloths – right on the waterfront in Speyside. Jemma is a Seventh Day Adventist, so she is closed on Friday night and Saturday and will sell you no alcohol (though you can take your own if you want). *Set menus.*

Redmans Restaurant, Speyside. Right next door to Jemma's, this place has a simple setting and offers similar fare – 'a wide variety of dishes at affordable prices'. Basically chicken, fish and some more exotic food.

Sharon and Pheb's, Charlotteville, t 660 5717. There are a number of local snack stalls for a *roti*, but this one offers fine chicken or fish on a pretty red and white veranda above the street and the banana trees.

Gail's, Charlotteville. Come here for a wholesome platter of chicken or fish with a small tonnage of ground provisions.

Original House of Pancakes, Milford Road. All-day breakfast and Internet access – waffles, omelettes and of course pancakes for breakfast, and then more adventurous fare by day such as Cajun-style fish and salads.

Stalls, Store Bay. A clutch of vendors in newly spruced-up stalls, who sell the famous Tobago crab and dumpling on a polystyrene plate, *callaloo* and a *coocoo*, or curry goat and 'buss up shut' (paratha bread, or 'bust-up shirt') – Miss Esmie, Sylvia, Alma, Miss Joicie's, Miss Trim and Miss Jean, all in a row. *Open until about 10pm.*

Bars and Nightlife

Bars and Clubs

On top of the following, you can always wander into any hotel or restaurant bar.

Bonkers, Toucan Inn, Crown Point. A popular bar.

Golden Star, Crown Point. This club is the place to go, particularly on Wednesday, when there is a 'Scouting for Talent' night in summer (apparently it is your talent at karaoke that is at issue). Variety show at weekends during the winter.

The Copratray, Bon Accord. A busy club.

Hendrix's Bar, Buccoo. On Sunday night you should try 'Sunday School', a jump-up that kicks off late (10pm) and spills across the street to the beach bar.

Beach Bars

In remoter parts of the island, most bays have a waterfront rum shop.

Beach Bar, Pigeon Point. The best-known beach bar, and it is a good place to come for a day out – you can take a cocktail onto the jetty to watch the sunset.

Taxi Co-op Pub, Store Bay. Here the drivers take a bit of time off alongside the beach-goers.

Mount Irvine Bay Hotel, Mount Irvine Bay.

Surfers Restaurant and Bar, Mount Irvine Bay. A public beach facility where you can lime with the Tobagonians and grab a bite to eat.

Cecilia's, Turtle Beach. A small shed where you can get a burger or a cooked fish with fries.

Jemma's, Speyside. For a fruit juice.

Diver's Den Grill and Bar, Crown Point, t 639 8533, www.diversdentobago.com. The latest hang-out for a late night lime. Entertainment daily except Sunday.

Robinson Crusoe, Hilton Tobago, t 660 8500. Friday night lime in Carnival atmosphere. Happy hour, entertainment.

'one of stark poverty'. Many Tobagonians have left the island to look for a better life in Trinidad and elsewhere.

The Tobagonians have occasionally talked of secession, but nothing has come of it – yet they do have a generally independent outlook. Unlike the Trinidadians, many people here own the land they live on (and where traditionally they cultivated their crops). As well as sending two politicians to the national Parliament in Trinidad, the Tobagonians elect representatives to the 12-member Tobago House of Assembly. Presently the People's National Movement is in power, with eight seats, and the National Alliance for Reconstruction are in opposition with four.

Beaches

At the western end of Tobago you will find typical Caribbean picture-postcard beaches: white sand and palm trees with windsurfers cutting a fluorescent dash across the surreal blue of the sea. They can get quite busy but are not usually too crowded. Go along the north shore to the east, though, and there are secluded coves with curves of golden sand where you will find nobody but a few fishermen. The beaches on the south coast are not as nice, but there are a few steep-sided bays where the waves chase one another into the sand. *See* 'Best Beaches', p.125.

Scarborough

Scarborough, Tobago's main town, clambers over the side of a hill above Rockley Bay, on the south coast not far from the western tip of the island. It has a population of 10,000 and is a little ramshackle, with just a few nice old wooden buildings among the tatty overlay of concrete ones and brighter recent development, a fairly typical Caribbean mix of banks and local stores. It used to be that Tobagonians only ever came to town when they had something to collect off the ferry and it can still be pretty sleepy nowadays, though Carrington St can get lively when all the rum shops and *roti*-sellers are open.

Fort King George stands sentinel 400ft above the town and has commanding views east along the coastline and west as far as Trinidad. The stone and brick barracks, which share the hilltop with the nice wooden creole buildings that are now used by the Tobago hospital, were abandoned in 1854 (after destruction in a hurricane in 1847), but they have been restored and it is quite peaceful now to sit among the cannons and trees. There is an excellent **museum** (*open Mon–Fri 9–5; adm*) in the old guardhouse in the former citadel, where you can see Tobago history and cultural life revealed in a series of displays: Amerindian patterned pottery with animal faces (supposedly the animals that barred the way in the afterlife); a mock-up of an Amerindian burial site; the colonial plantation era, including militaria and some cartoons in the priceless series of *Johnny Newcome* (to the Caribbean) about his troubles with creole love and life; musket balls; buttons; a BOAC cocktail pourer; and even a bird of paradise (*see* p.138). There is also a fine art gallery nearby with changing exhibitions.

Walking down the hill you pass among the old stone colonial buildings and homes, including the Tobago **House of Assembly**, on its small tree-shaded square, which was completed in 1825. On **Gun Bridge**, the railings are made from rifle barrels, flanked by cannon. From here, steep streets and alleys lined with local houses lead down to the waterfront area, which has steadily expanded inland over the past decades with modern concrete official buildings. Behind the Scarborough Mall are the bus station and the new **market square**, which is quite lively in the mornings with vendors and limers. Modern development has continued along the waterfront, but Carrington St, where the ferry from Trinidad docks, is still the heart of the town, where the taxis tout for business and the breakfast sheds do their daily trade, opening up at 7am and serving snacks all day.

In a valley behind the town are the Scarborough **Botanic Gardens** (*open during daylight hours; adm free*), a green and pleasant retreat after the (relative) hustle and bustle of the metropolis. There are some marked plants and many, many palms. If you are interested in batik you might visit the **Cotton House** factory, shop and café in Bacolet, on the road east out of town, beneath the fort.

The West End

The west end of Tobago is the heartland of the island's tourism industry. Here you will find the hotels concentrated around Crown Point and along the northwestern coastline, where the beaches are. But a considerable population of Tobagonians also lives in this area, in the many 'traces' (like the 'gaps' of Barbados), side roads which seek out the intricacies of the shoreside and interior country. Near Crown Point you may hear elaborate stories about Robinson Crusoe's life (his 'cave' is just below the airport). A fellow claimed he saw him there not long ago.

On an island that was at war so often, there are also remains of many forts. Not far from Store Bay and the beach and small pedestrianized zone of vendors' stalls (and food stalls), you can see **Fort Milford**, a former fortress with impressively thick walls and a few French and British cannon (both nations used it, though it was actually built by the Dutch in 1777), which now acts as a small park with sea almond trees and flowerbeds in the fortifications.

Offshore from Pigeon Point, a palm, and swamp-backed promontory that was once called Flying Fish Point, is **Buccoo Reef**, Tobago's best-known underwater sight. It attracts scuba divers, snorkellers and boat-borne non-swimmers alike. In the vast area of coral heads just a few feet below the surface – forests of seafan and staghorn coral and lobes of white brain coral – you will find black and yellow rock beauties, stoplight parrotfish and angelfish loitering, and trumpetfish hanging around (vertically). Considerable damage has been done to Buccoo Reef over the years by careless visitors and souvenir hunters, and although there has been legislation for some time it is not properly enforced. However, there are some surprisingly large fish on the reef and it is a fun day out. Organized tours depart from Store Bay and Pigeon Point, some in glass-bottom boats, but times vary, so check beforehand. The **Nylon Pool**, on the way out to the reef, is an offshore sand bar where the pale turquoise water is waist- to thigh-deep and the warm sand caresses your toes. Visible from the Point, beyond the long stretches of beach that are best accessed by boat, is the town of **Buccoo** (from where you can get a fisherman to drop you off), a fishing village with a couple of guest houses.

Plymouth, Tobago's second town, developed as a fortification and dwelling on the point covering Great Courland Bay, is an excellent natural harbour where yachts still ride at anchor. It's a village really, with a few shops and a petrol station. The defence, **Fort James** (named after Jacobus of Courland, who sent settlements to this area of the island in the 17th century), is little more than massive walls and cannon, and a few goats, next to the sports ground.

From Plymouth you can return to Scarborough, or continue along the north coast road, which passes into deep forest before emerging periodically onto the coastline. At the fishing villages of **Castara** and **Parlatuvier** you will see the fishing boats with their double rods sticking out either side in the bay and the fishermen drying their nets waiting for the tide to turn. Returning via **Moriah** or **Les Coteaux**, you will find Tobago at its most rural and traditional, though even here houses are now built in concrete rather than wood. This is the rich plantation land of 200 years ago and you will still see the sugar and cocoa estate buildings and crushing gear poking out of the undergrowth.

Windwardside

The south coast of Tobago is known as Windwardside because of the Atlantic trades that blow for most of the year. As you head east from Scarborough, the country becomes steadily more rugged and overgrown and the road switchbacks and chicanes as it clambers onto the hillsides and drops down into the bays. The settlements get steadily more scarce and you will see just a few houses in a plot of beaten earth with a massive breadfruit tree for shade. In plantation days, workers from each estate would carry its produce down to the nearest bay, from where it would be picked up by ship. The distance to Charlotteville in the northeast of the island is about 15 miles, but it can take well over an hour to get there.

At Studley Park (site of the Prime Minister's residence in the island, Blenheim, and of the island's one-time capital in the 1760s, Georgetown) you can take a left turn onto a winding road that disappears into the rainforest, passing the Hillsborough Dam and then descending to Mason Hall. A mile after you leave the coast, you can walk to the **Green Hill Waterfall** just off the road. Farther along the coast, **Carapuse Bay** takes its name from the turtle shell or carapace, a legacy from the 17th century, when turtlers would come to the island. Turtles were a valuable source of meat, particularly as they could be kept alive on their backs for weeks until their meat was needed. Outside Roxborough is the turning to the **Falls of Argyle Natural Park** (*adm; guides compulsory*), a cascade that tumbles in three falls over a rockface into two swim-mable pools. It is a 20-minute walk.

At the eastern tip of the island there are two delightful towns, Speyside and Charlotteville. Once the end of the line, they are both 'discovered' now (small cruise ships even put into Charlotteville), but they are still well worth a visit, particularly for their diving. **Speyside** looks out into Tyrell's Bay and towards the island of **Little Tobago**. This is also known as Bird of Paradise Island, because in 1909 Mr Ingram, the owner of the island, brought a colony of the birds from New Guinea, where they were becoming extinct. The mating dance was a spectacular sight, with wings held aloft to reveal a golden plumage that was kept constantly shimmering by strutting and side-stepping. No birds are left there now, but there is one on view in the museum in Scarborough.

The road labours up over the point into the rainforest, where wisps of cloud hang in the bamboo and immortelle trees, and then drops steeply into a charming, almost amphitheatrical bay. **Charlotteville** is a classic West Indian fishing village, where the red-roofed houses are stacked top to toe above one another. The sea birds clamour offshore in flocks and high above them frigatebirds cruise on the winds while the islanders sit waiting for transport and chatting in the shade of the sea almond trees that line the waterfront. Once, the most important moment in the day, the arrival of the fish catch, would be announced with the blow of a conch shell, but now much of the fish is put on ice and exported. The north coast road leads beyond Cambleton to Parlatuvier, but it is not surfaced and is passable only in the dry season.

The Windward Islands

The Windward Islands

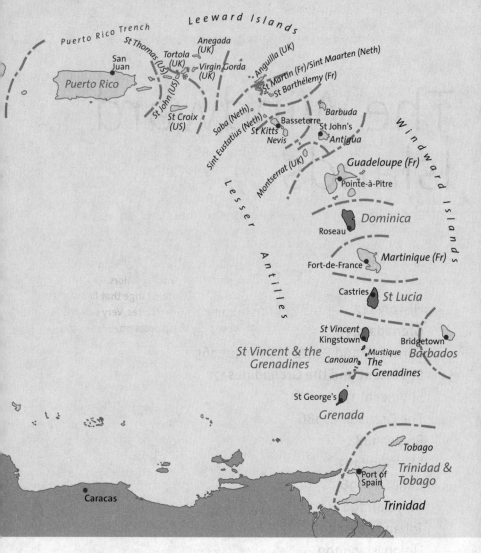

Highlights

1 Take a water taxi across the bay in St George's, Grenada's capital and one of the prettiest towns in the Caribbean

2 Sail the Grenadines, by yacht or by ferry, and put into tiny, comatose islands such as Bequia, Carriacou and the Tobago Cays

3 Buy a box of tropical fruits in season at the market in any of the islands

4 Hike the interior, particularly in Dominica, which has some of the thickest rainforest in the Caribbean

The four independent nations of the Windward Isles stand like a line of Titans in the Southeastern Caribbean. Each one in sight of the next, these massive fertile peaks soar thousands of feet from the water, separating the Atlantic Ocean from the Caribbean Sea.

The Windward Islands are all similar in appearance and are among the most beautiful and fertile in the Caribbean. They rise sheer from the water to serrated volcanic peaks, usually stacked with rain clouds formed by Atlantic winds that are forced up the islands' slopes. Their altitude gives them their own micro-climates. Rainfall here is measured in feet, and it crashes down the hills in torrents and waterfalls. It also feeds the dripping, sweltering forest: a monstrous tangle of trees, creepers, bushes and ferns clambering over one another in botanical pandemonium. The islands are so fertile that clumps of bamboo will grow to over 60ft in height, creaking even when there is no wind. The gardener's most useful tool is the machete.

The name Windwards began as a geographical term, describing the islands to the windward of the usual arrival point for ships in the Caribbean, around Martinique or Dominica, but during the 19th century it became a British political designation. Since then the islands have gone their own way politically but the term still remains in use as a description of their geographical position, particularly among sailors.

In fact the islands are a series of volcanic peaks on a mountain range that lies along a fault line on the sea bed between the Atlantic and Caribbean plates. Very slowly the Atlantic crust is forcing its way under the Caribbean plate and occasionally the magma throws up lava through the volcanoes. Though the eruptions are thought to have calmed down somewhat over the last few million years, these volcanoes are still active, and each of the main *soufrières* blows about once a century, causing earthquakes that reverberate along the whole chain of the Lesser Antilles. On one day in 1867, weird happenings on Grenada in the far south of the chain, where the harbour water swelled and contracted as though the underworld were breathing, were echoed by seismic activity as far north as the Virgin Island of St Thomas.

Each one of the Windwards has its *soufrière*, a sulphurous volcanic vent. The St Vincent volcano and those on nearby Martinique and Guadeloupe in the French Caribbean are the most violent, tending to blast out volumes of lava and superheated gases that collapse mountains and destroy anything in their path, as well as a plume of gas and a shower of pumice stones. In the last few years it has been Montserrat, one of the Leewards to the north, which has shown the most activity, spewing forth lava and pyroclastic flow and showering the islands with ash. In other islands things are usually less extreme: fumaroles constantly let off steam through vents above the water line and below (which makes for interesting dive sites). In Dominica there is even a volcanic steam bath, the Boiling Lake, that lets off sulphurous fumes so disgusting as to kill off all the plant life. In the Grenadines there is an underwater volcano (Kick 'em Jenny), now quite close to the surface, whose activity has been spotted by pilots flying over the area. Eventually they expect it to break the surface, creating another island in the Grenadines.

The Windwards are also on the fringes of the hurricane belt. Usually the impact area is the Leeward Islands to the north of here, but occasionally the Windwards are visited by these outsize whirlwinds, the first landfall after a 2,000-mile run-up across the Atlantic. Hurricanes, which can be hundreds of miles across, are indescribably destructive. Not only do winds damage the crops and houses (literally sandblasting them in some cases, stripping off every square inch of paint), but the torrential rains that accompany them sweep away roads and collapse bridges. In addition, Hurricane Lennie, which carved through the Caribbean in 1999, caused terrible damage up and down the island chain because of its 'swells', very heavy seas that caused immense coastal damage. In 2004 Hurricane Ivan levelled Grenada, damaging 90% of all buildings. Despite such destruction, hurricanes are a part of life here and recovery is fast.

In sharp contrast to the nearby French islands of Martinique and Guadeloupe, which seem almost like mainland France, the Windwards are pretty undeveloped. There is still agriculture. Small cultivators still provide the daily markets with produce, but the banana and other small-scale agricultural industries (nutmeg in Grenada and arrowroot in St Vincent) have had a tough time over the past few years. Steadily the islands are developing a Western style of life. There has been quite a lot of building over the last few years, with shopping centres, island infrastructure and larger family homes, and of course most new building is in concrete rather than the traditional wood.

Expectations are changing too. Whereas the older generation had a tough farmer's existence attached to the land, most of the youth of today are unwilling to live like this. Many would prefer to take their chances in town. On an island such as St Lucia, a large proportion of the population lives in the capital, Castries. The largest industry now is tourism, which contributes most of the foreign exchange needed to buy medicines and essentials and then the luxuries that the islanders would like. For all of this change, there is one thing that doesn't change – the friendly welcome you will get from the islanders themselves. If you ever want to talk, you simply stop anyone you come across in the street.

History

Human history in the Windwards is split-second in comparison with the volcanoes and plate tectonics and is reckoned to have started about 4,000 years ago, when the early waves of Indians touched the islands on their migration north from the South American mainland. For 3,000 years these Arawaks led what is supposed to be a peaceful existence centred on agriculture and fishing. Pieces of their pottery are still to be found in the islands today, as are their rock carvings.

Around AD 1000, their peace was disturbed by the Caribs, another, more belligerent South American Indian tribe, who followed them along the island chain. The newcomers were reportedly cannibals (though there is little evidence of anything more than ceremonial killing) and they made short work of the gentle Arawaks as they bludgeoned their way north, murdering the men and adopting the women as family as they moved. At the time of Columbus's arrival 500 years later, the Caribs had island-hopped as far as the Virgin Islands and were beginning to raid Borinquen, now Puerto Rico. On the earliest maps of the Americas, the Windward Islands are marked as the 'Cannibal Isles', such was the terror they conjured up in the minds of sailors.

Bananas

A familiar sight in the Windward Islands is the messy swathes of banana trees covering a whole valley floor, their leaves tousled and arched in irregular directions. Look closely and you may see them lashed together for support by a network of string, their dark green fruits, or 'hands', protected by blue plastic bags.

The banana is native to China and Malaysia and had made its way to the Canary Islands by 1510. Its botanical name is *Musa sapientum*, or 'muse of wise men', and, according to Indian legend, sages would sit under their huge leaves for shade and savour the fruit. Bananas had lost their popularity with Caribbean colonists by the start of the 19th century, when they were regarded as a suspect fruit because of their colour and shape: they were thought 'to excite urine and to provoke venery'.

There are over a hundred different varieties of banana, the most widely known in Europe being the cavendish, locally known as the *gros michel*, which is large and yellow when ripe. Less known is the smaller and sweeter canary banana or rock fig (considered *l'amie de la poitrine* by Père Labat), which is about 4 inches long. But the most exotic and sweetest of them all is the secret fig, which grows no longer than about 2 inches. There are also many unsweet varieties to be seen in the Caribbean, such as plantain, tasty when fried, and other starchy vegetables, the green fig and the bluggo. Names vary from island to island.

In fact bananas do not grow on trees at all, but on a stem of unripe leaves packed closely like a cigar, growing out of a rhizome underground. As each new leaf forces its way up, it stands erect like a bright green scroll and gently unfurls, bending gracefully as it is superseded by another. The leaves, sometimes 10ft long by 2ft, start off with a beautiful green sheen that makes rainwater dance like mercury, and as they age they become shredded and look like an untidy head of hair.

When a plant bears fruit, it throws out a long trunk with a purple heart at the tip, which opens to reveal little black teeth in rows. These teeth are the end of the fruit, which swell until the bunches appear like so many fingers sticking up. A trunk produces one 'bunch' of bananas, which may have as many as ten 'hands' or 'finger rolls'. Each plant produces fruit only once, after which it dies and another shoot takes its place in the same spot.

The blue plastic bags protect the maturing bananas from the scratches of lizard claws, insects and birds. The 'Banana Boat Song', with its 'Day Oh!' chorus made famous in the 1950s by Harry Belafonte, was originally sung by banana packers as they loaded the United Fruit Company ships in Jamaica at night: 'Come Mr Tallyman, come tally me banana, Daylight come and me waan go home'.

The banana is a very important export crop in the Windwards. The packing stations can be seen all over the islands and farmers carry the fruit down the hill in time for the weekly visit of the Geest ships that make the three-week round trip from Europe. The trade was protected by agreements, mainly with Britain, from the 1950s to the 1990s and brought in lots of foreign exchange, but in the last few years these agreements have broken down in the face of the free market and competition with the 'dollar banana', which is grown more economically in Central America. The market has contracted considerably.

The Spaniards gave them a wide berth and headed for the bigger and less hostile islands of the Greater Antilles.

But as the race for Empire began, in the early 1600s, so the Europeans encroached on the Lesser Antilles, settling, colonizing and planting and at the same time conducting a war that would eventually lead to the genocide of the Caribs. The mountainous Windwards became the heartland of Carib resistance to the invaders. A treaty of 1660 supposedly ensured that the Indians would be left alone on St Vincent and Dominica on condition that they kept the peace elsewhere, but the governments connived with the colonists' campaign of extermination because the land was proving to be so valuable. The Caribs from Dominica and the 'Black Caribs' from St Vincent (a mixed race of Caribs and escaped African slaves) conducted a desperate campaign to defend themselves right up to the beginning of the 19th century.

The 18th century was also the height of French and British rivalry. Every war in Europe sent shock waves to the Caribbean, and the Windwards were invaded and snatched, then repeatedly taken back. Fleets from the two nations would tear up and down the island chain, ransacking the colonies and annexing them, only to see them given back at the next treaty. Despite blockades, the islands were extremely valuable to the colonial powers as they brought in a vast wealth in sugar. (For the islanders themselves, wars and the colonial armies prevented them from getting on with the business of planting.) The importance of the Caribbean can be seen in the Treaty of Paris in 1763, when the French traded their rights in the whole of Canada in order to retain a foothold in the islands by keeping Martinique, the most prosperous of their islands. By the early years of the 19th century, the final pattern was fixed – Martinique was French and the Windward Islands were in British hands. You will still see the residue of French influence in the Windwards. Many of the place names are French, as are the *anses* (bays) and *mornes* (hills), and in Dominica and St Lucia (and to a lesser extent Grenada) you will still hear French creole, which survives as the first language of the people even though the official language has been English for nearly 200 years.

If the 18th century was a turbulent and prosperous one, the 19th saw a steady decline to obscurity and poverty in the Windwards. Their major industry, sugar, became uncompetitive as sugar beet was grown more economically in Europe, and attempts at cultivating other crops met with limited success. A highlight was emancipation in 1834. Unlike in Barbados, where there was no unowned land and the former slaves were effectively forced to continue working on the plantations to make a living, the freed slaves on the Windwards voted with their feet, preferring to take a plot of land in the hills where they could be their own masters. The islands became backwaters, declining to the point where Dominica had only a fortnightly postal service.

The Windwards (except Dominica, which did not join the Windwards until 1939) were grouped under a governor in St George's, Grenada, and in 1874 Crown Colony status was enforced and direct rule was transferred to London. As the political scene changed after the Second World War, universal franchise came in 1951 and internal self-government in 1967. The Windward Islands ceased to exist as a political unit in 1960, as the islands were on the path to Independence. All four nations remain within the British Commonwealth and the Queen is represented by a Governor General. The highest court of appeal is the Privy Council in London. Attempts to link the islands in a federation had failed as early as 1763 and again in 1885. The Windwards were a part of the short-lived West Indian Federation in 1958 and since 1981 they have been part of the Organization of Eastern Caribbean States, which promotes economic integration between the smaller Commonwealth countries in the area.

Grenada

Grenada and its Grenadines are strung out over 50 miles or so in the far south of the Caribbean, at the foot of the Windward Islands chain, about 90 miles north of Trinidad and the South American coast. The island of Grenada itself is typical of the Windwards in its tropical beauty, with towering mountains mantled in explosive rainforest, and coastal inlets and bays furred with palms and white-sand beaches. To its north, Grenada (pronounced 'gre-nay-dah') is linked to the island of St Vincent by the Grenadines, a 60-mile string of coral islands and cays, towering peaks that soar out of the water and sand bars that barely make it to the surface. Two of the inhabited Grenadines, Carriacou and Petit Martinique, belong to Grenada, and together the three islands are home to a population of about 100,000.

Grenada's capital, St George's, is the prettiest harbour town in the whole Caribbean. It is set in a massive volcanic bowl, and its slopes are lined with red-tiled roofs that descend to the edge of the bay, where yachts and old-fashioned schooners have long lined the waterfront and now cruise ships dwarf the daily activity. Beyond the capital, the island is wonderfully fertile and green. Measuring just 12 miles by 21, Grenada calls itself the Spice Isle because its fertile soil produces spices for markets all over the world. In the valleys of the mountainous interior you will see the fruit and spice plantations and the cocoa walks, where orange immortelle trees stand aflame above the cocoa trees early in the year. Nutmeg, from which come the spices nutmeg and mace, is Grenada's most famous spice and it is important enough to the island to appear on the national flag. People lay their drives with nutmeg shells in Grenada, which gives off a wonderful aroma, and if you walk through the cocoa plantations you will occasionally get a whiff of bitter chocolate.

Grenada is quiet and easy-going in true Caribbean style, but it is remembered for an event not so long ago, in October 1983, when it was thrust into the international news. Following a revolution it became the site of an invasion that set the might of the United States onto a tiny Caribbean island. The customary Caribbean quiet did not take long to return, though the event remains a contentious issue to this day in the minds of many Grenadians.

Like the other islands in the area, Grenada is seeing considerable development at the moment as the islanders build homes for themselves and the government and developers work on the infrastructure. The island is less developed than St Lucia, but it sees a steady stream of tourists to its broad range of hotels. Grenada is also well positioned for exploring the Grenadines, by yacht, by ferry and by island-hopping plane.

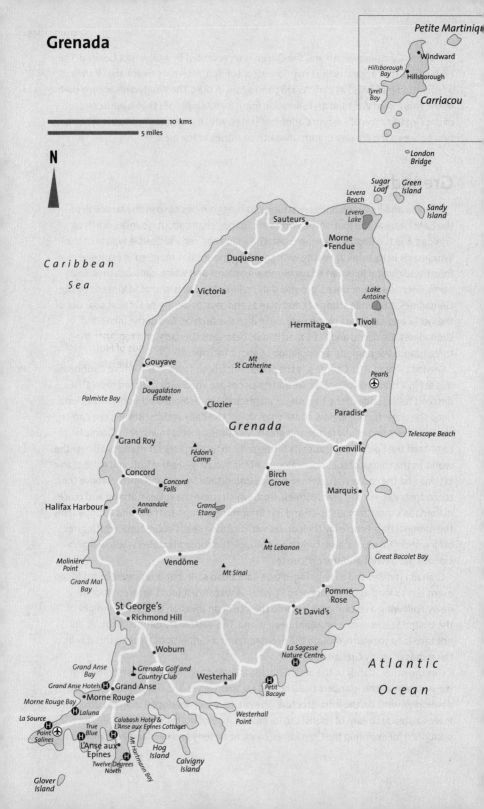

Best Beaches

Grand Anse: Two miles of pristine sand south of St George's, where many hotels are located, with plenty of watersports and a couple of beach bars.

Morne Rouge Bay: Sometimes known as BBC Beach after a defunct discotheque, an attractive stretch of sand in a deep bay with a perfect sunset view most of the year, with two delightful coves, Dr Groom and Magazine Beach, beyond it.

L'Anse aux Epines: Another popular south-coast beach (when spoken, it sounds something more like 'lansapeen') to the south of Grand Anse. Quite a thin stretch of sand at the head of the bay, with some restaurants for snacks.

Westerhall Point, La Sagesse, Bacolet Bay and **Telescope Beach:** These are some of the underdeveloped beaches to be found among the finger-like protrusions of the southeastern coast. Lovely, quiet and mostly undeveloped.

Bathway Beach: At the northeastern tip of the island, looking out into the Atlantic. Safe for swimming because of an offshore reef. The water at nearby Levera Beach is rougher. Take a picnic to this area.

Palmiste Bay and **Grand Mal Bay:** The Grenadians' favourite stretches, on the west coast.

Visitors should take note that Grenada suffered terribly at the hands of Hurricane Ivan, which passed by in September 2004. Despite the destruction of the island's nutmeg industry, and damage to 90% of buildings, the resilience and spirit of the Grenadian people enabled them to move forward with recovery, even when much of the island remained without water, electricity and basic services. The airport resumed normal operations in time for the winter season, as did many of the hotels and restaurants. Carriacou and Petit Martinique were spared. By the winter season of 2005–6, almost all hotels expect to be fully restored.

History

From the earliest sightings, travellers have spoken of Grenada's physical beauty and fertility. To 16th-century Spanish sailors coasting the Windwards it was supposedly a reminder of home, the hills above the city of Granada. However, early attempts to settle 'Camerhogne', as the island was known before their arrival, failed due to the presence of the Caribs. Englishmen came in 1609 in the ships *Diana*, *Penelope* and *Endeavour*, but they were chased off, as were later settlers sponsored by the Frenchman de Poincy.

In 1650, the Caribs actually invited the Frenchman Du Parquet, from Martinique, to settle the island. He came with 'two hundred men of good stamina', arriving to a salute of guns, and promptly erected a cross and a fort. He bought the island from the Caribs for 'cloth, axes, bill-hooks, knives, glass beads, mirrors and two large bottles of eau-de-vie (brandy) for the chief himself'. It was not long before the Caribs decided the deal was not a good one after all and by 1654 they were locked in a duel with the French for possession of the island. Reinforcements came for the French from Martinique by ship and for the Caribs from St Vincent and Dominica by canoe.

It was a brutal time. The Caribs roamed the island killing French hunters and then attacked the French settlement. But, armed only with bows and arrows against the guns of the French, the Caribs were eventually forced up to the north of the island where, rather than be captured and killed, they are supposed to have thrown themselves off a cliff to their deaths (the region is called 'Sauteurs' in memory of the event). The settlers didn't have it all their own way, though. A new owner of the island, the Comte du Cerillac, sent a brutal governor who so abused his power that the islanders tried him and sentenced him to be hanged. At this he pleaded noble birth, which gave him the right to be beheaded. There was no executioner on Grenada, so the islanders eventually had him shot.

In the early 1700s the island became an important French colony, as a plantation island and as a refitting station on the route from Martinique, the French headquarters in the Caribbean, to South America. But in the endless rounds of 18th-century wars, Grenada was blockaded and captured again and again as the navies whittled through the island chain. As the island changed hands, the names were changed from French to English and back again: Fort Royal became St George's and Gouyave on the west coast became Charlotte Town. Some of the names stuck, but many of the original French names still remain in Grenada even today, as does the creole language to a lesser extent. Despite the difficulties brought by the wars, the island remained prosperous and was thought of as 'the second of the English Islands' (after Barbados).

It was not long before the French were back. Grenada was taken almost by mistake because an attack on Barbados was made impossible by bad weather. Admiral d'Estaing entered St George's harbour, and the Irish troops of his ally Count Arthur Dillon attacked by land. The island surrendered. Hard on his heels came the British Admiral, 'Foulweather Jack' Byron, but even though some of his ships made it into the harbour, he could not draw the 'mere gasconade of a vapouring Frenchman' into battle and so the French won Grenada again. The British Governor and the island's colours were shipped off to France. The latter were strung up above the High Altar in Notre Dame and the former was eventually returned to Britain.

Once the British were back in control, the British Grenadians were vengeful over their treatment at French hands. They confiscated church lands and made the French Grenadians submit to the 'Test', an oath demanding a rejection of transubstantiation, impossible for a Catholic. Many chose to emigrate to Trinidad, where the Spaniards were crying out for settlers and where the Grenadian refugees made up a part of what is still today an important element of Trinidad's population, the 'French Creoles'. On the island itself the grievances increased, fired by the harsher treatment of the slaves under the British and by the French Revolution, which was being spread from Guadeloupe by Victor Hugues. Eventually it erupted into open rebellion in 1795.

Fédon's Rebellion and Onwards

The revolt was led by Julien Fédon, a mixed-race planter. From Guadeloupe the revolutionaries brought 'arms and ammunition, caps of liberty, national cockades and a flag on which was inscribed in large characters, 'Liberté, Egalité ou la Mort'. The rebels overran the whole island, killing prisoners along with suspected collaborators. Their first strike was on the east coast, at La Baye, near modern Grenville, where British settlers were taken from their beds and shot, and at Charlotte Town, where the Governor himself, Sir Ninian Home, was captured trying to return to St George's. He was one of 51 hostages taken to the rebel mountain stronghold, eventually to be slaughtered on Fédon's personal instructions as the rebels came under threat from the advancing British troops.

St George's never fell to the rebels but it took a year before reinforcements under Sir Ralph Abercromby defeated the guerrillas. Their leaders were captured and executed immediately or exiled to Honduras, but Fédon himself was never taken. Some think he drowned in an attempt to escape to Trinidad, but others said that he made it to Cuba. His estate at Belvidere, from where he ran the insurrection, is just below one of Grenada's mountain peaks, now known as Fédon's Camp. By the end of the conflict, Grenada was in ruins.

When the slaves were freed in 1838 they took over small plots of Grenada's fertile land. Unlike the other Windwards, Grenada remained reasonably prosperous during the decline of the 19th century. Agriculture was the economic mainstay: bananas and cocoa were grown, along with spices such as cinnamon, bay leaf, allspice and ginger.

With the failure of the Federation, when attempts to unite all the British Caribbean islands into one country foundered in 1962, and after a later failure to unite with Trinidad and Tobago, Grenada became an Associated State of Britain in 1967. They were not long in deciding on Independence and Grenada became an independent nation within the British Commonwealth on 7 February 1974. Grenada's first leader was Eric Gairy, a volatile and charismatic man whose political heritage was in the oil-fields of the Caribbean island of Aruba. Elected as early as 1951, he was fondly thought of by many Grenadians as the champion of workers' rights against the colonial government. After Independence his leadership became steadily more corrupt, wasteful and bullying, and he used a secret army called the Mongoose Gang to impose his will unofficially.

In the early 1970s the socialist New Jewel Movement was formed. Initially clandestine, to avoid harassment from the overbearing government, the NJM steadily gained ground, allying itself with the disillusioned opposition to Gairy, including the influential and traditionally conservative business class. They also armed themselves in preparation for revolution.

Revolution and Invasion

On 13 March 1979, with Gairy out of the country, 38 armed members of the NJM stormed the army barracks at True Blue on the south coast of the island and attained power in a bloodless coup. With popular support, they began a social experiment unprecedented in the Commonwealth Caribbean. Considerable improvements were made in health care and in education, and general economic growth came over the next four years. However, the repressive nature of the People's Revolutionary Government's programmes gradually became clearer: the press was stifled, political detainees were held untried, and then, when Grenada forged closer ties with Cuba and the Eastern bloc, the Grenadian Revolution began to excite international disapproval.

The Spice Island of the Caribbean

Grenada is known as the Isle of Spice – the source of the island's prosperity at the start of the 20th century. Even though Grenada's one-third share of the world market in nutmeg is now lost and market prices are at a low ebb, spices are still a profitable business and you are bound to be offered them for sale in the streets. Two good places to visit are the Minor Spices Society, next to the Market in St George's, and Arawak Islands Ltd, which is set in a pretty creole house just outside Belmont.

Nutmeg is the island's principal spice. In the past it has been used as a charm to ward off illness and today it is used in remedies against colds by the islanders as well as in Vicks Vapour Rub. In the Second World War, oil of nutmeg was in demand for aircraft engine oil because it does not freeze at high altitudes. Nutmeg was introduced into Grenada in 1843, supposedly at a party, where it was added as a mystery ingredient to the top of the regular planter's punch – the party was no doubt a success, and Grenadians have never drunk a rum punch without nutmeg since.

The tree (which has the botanical name *Myristica fragrans*) is evergreen and grows up to 60ft in height. Its fruit looks like a yellow apricot and the Grenadians will tell you that no part of it goes to waste. When it ripens, the flesh splits open, revealing a brown nut covered with a red wax netting, and it drops to the ground. The fruit must be collected at once to prevent it from rotting and then the parts are separated.

The outer flesh goes into making jams or preserves, while the nut is processed to make the spice nutmeg. Finally, the red netting is used for a second spice, mace, which is stored for six months and then graded as the spice itself, or used as a preservative in food or cosmetics, to be exported in tea chests. The 'nut' is put through a crusher which removes the shell and then the kernels are graded by throwing them into water. Those that float are used in pharmaceuticals, but the good ones sink and they make the spice that ends up floating on a rum punch.

It is not commonly known that mace and nutmeg come from the same plant. A London bureaucrat caused great hilarity among estate workers when he sent notice that the international market price of mace was on the increase and that of nutmeg

Under this pressure from outside and facing straitened economic circumstances on the island, the PRG foundered in an internal split. The leader, Maurice Bishop, was placed under house arrest by the other members of the Central Committee, but eventually his supporters brought him to St George's, where they congregated at Fort George. Bernard Coard and others of the opposing faction of the PRG sent down troops who fired on the crowd to disperse it, killing about 60 people, then shooting Bishop and five of his close associates inside the fort. The whole island was placed under a 24-hour curfew for four days. Then, on 25 October 1983, the US 82nd Airborne Division invaded and took the island over.

Massive aid and assistance came in the first couple of years and US President Reagan himself made a visit in February 1986, but it tailed off once Grenada was seen to acquiesce. Many Grenadians do think of the invasion as the 'rescue mission' and are grateful to Reagan for sending troops. Others will never forgive the USA for what seemed to them an unwarranted show of force against a small country by a big

decreasing and so cultivators would be advised to grow more of the first and hold on the latter. The two biggest nutmeg factories are in Gouyave and Grenville and they are well worth a visit (*open weekdays; see* p.163).

Another tree seen all over the island is the cocoa tree, *theobroma* or 'Food of the Gods', with hand-sized, purple pods sprouting indiscriminately from trunk and branches. They grow in cocoa 'walks', as the valley plantations were called, alternate male and female trees up to 30ft high, which go on producing for up to a hundred years, usually in the shade of the much larger immortelle tree, famed for its orange blooms. The pods are collected and broken open to reveal a (delicious) white sticky-sweet gel and up to 30 cocoa beans. The beans are fermented, piled into a wooden sweating box with a little water and turned regularly, and the white pulp degrades. Next the brown beans are laid out onto huge trays, or *boucans*, where they are dried in the sun, again constantly being turned, or 'danced', by the workers, who shuffle through them in lines. At this stage they begin to smell of bitter unsweetened cocoa. From here they are exported, as Grenada has no large processing plant. For local consumption though, some beans are processed and the oily product is rolled into sticks, which can be grated into boiling water to make cocoa for breakfast.

Other spices cultivated in Grenada are cinnamon bark, bundles of which can be bought in the markets rolled up in pink ribbon; cloves and pimento or allspice, so-called because it tastes like cinnamon, clove and nutmeg (Jamaica and Grenada are the only islands in the Caribbean in which the latter grows). Ginger, bay leaves and vanilla are also grown. Many are used in confectionery and the flavouring of food or as a preservative. Apart from local use for their alternative medicinal properties (bay rum and lemongrass are used to quell fevers; corilie for hypertension; oil of ginger is said to reduce pain), many are exported for use in the pharmaceutical industry.

Following the terrible impact on Grenada's agriculture of **Hurricane Ivan** (September 2004), it is difficult to say what the future holds for the island's spice industry; it will take considerable investment and many years before new trees and plants bear fruit once again.

power in whose backyard Grenada happened to be. There is still considerable support for Maurice Bishop, if not for his deputies.

Grenada remains within the British Commonwealth and has two Houses of Parliament, a 13-member Senate and a 15-member House of Representatives elected for five-year terms. The country is led by Prime Minister Dr Keith Mitchell of the NNP, the New National Party (jokingly called the No Nonsense Party), which was elected in 1999 with a full complement of 15 seats, then re-elected in 2004, but with only 8 seats. Elections are next due in 2009.

Flora and Fauna

Like the other Windward Islands, much of the interior of Grenada is too wild and remote to be inhabited and so there are large tracts of rainforest that are untouched, but which you can explore by a series of trails (many start out from the **Grand Etang** in the National Park). You will see huge gommier and mahogany trees, grappled by

Getting There

Grenada t (1 473–)

By Air

Grenada has reasonable international air links, with some direct flights from Europe and from North America, arriving at Point Salines Airport in the southwestern tip of the island. The airport has certainly opened the island up for visitors, whatever its military applications might have been – it was one of the stated reasons for the American invasion. If there is no direct flight, it is always possible to make a connection, the same day, via Barbados, Trinidad or Antigua. Departure tax is EC$50; children aged 5–10 years pay half as much; under-5s are exempt.

From the UK

There are two flights a week on British Airways, t 440 1664, from Gatwick, and a twice-weekly service on jmc, t 440 2796. There are no direct scheduled flights from Europe.

From North America

BWIA, t 444 1221, has flights from Miami and New York via its Trinidad hub; Air Jamaica flies Tues, Fri and Sun nonstop from JFK/New York, as well as providing flights from several major US cities via its Montego Bay hub. American Eagle, t 444 2222, flies daily from American Airlines' hub at San Juan in Puerto Rico.

From Other Caribbean Islands

There are plenty of options for travelling to the nearby islands, Barbados, Tobago, Trinidad, St Vincent and, further up the island chain, to Antigua, with LIAT, t 440 2796; Caribbean Star, t 439 0681; and Air Jamaica, t 444 5975. SVG Air, t 444 3549, com, www.svgair.com, hops through the Grenadines as far as St Vincent. Rutaca fly from Margarita off the Venezuelan coast.

By Sea

There are many ferry services each week between Grenada and its major Grenadine island, Carriacou, often continuing on to Petite Martinique. The Osprey, t 440 8126, osprey@caribsurf.com, www.ospreylines.com, makes the trip twice a day on weekdays, once at the weekend, in 2hrs. Cheaper and slower boats also make the run most days. There's a flexible schedule: check at the Carenage in St George's or the Tourist Board. There are occasional (cargo) boats to Trinidad which may allow you to travel as a paying passenger.

Getting Around

By Bus

Buses run all the main routes in Grenada and can be flagged down from the roadside with a frantic downward-pointing finger. Rap on the metalwork when you want to get off. On board they are quite crowded and often they give you a good introduction to Caribbean music (currently there is an excellent selection of reggae doing the rounds). They leave from the main Market Square on the Esplanade side of town (ask around for your destination), starting at dawn and running until about 7 in the evening and infrequently into the night. After the run to church on Sundays, services are less frequent.

Some prices are: St George's to Gouyave – EC$3, to Sauteurs – EC$5 and to Grenville – EC$4.50. To the Grand Anse area and to the top of the L'Anse aux Epines road, the ride costs EC$1.50 and buses run frequently.

By Taxi

The alternative is to go by taxi, which is very expensive but easily arranged at a hotel, in town or at the major beaches. Often the drivers are a mine of information and are happy to give an impromptu tour. Sample rates, set by the Grenada Board of Tourism, are: from St George's to Grand Anse – US$8, to L'Anse aux Epines – US$14, to Point Salines Airport – US$15, to the Grand Etang – US$33 return, and to Gouyave and Dougaldston – US$45 return. To hire a taxi by the hour costs US$20 and drivers are available for a day's outing. The Grenada Hotels Taxi Drivers Association can be contacted on t 444 4882 and Grencab on t 444 4444.

Car and Bike Hire

Car hire is another possibility and a good way to see the island if you are prepared to brave the vagaries of the Grenadian road and can remember to keep to the left. You will need a visitor's licence, which can be bought (EC$30) from the police at the fire station on the Carenage, or from the rental companies, on presentation of a valid licence from home. Rental cars, from about US$45 per day with taxes on top, are available from:

David's Car Rentals, **t** 444 3399, *www. davidscars.com*.

Maitland's Motor Rentals, **t** 444 4022. Also rents out motorbikes.

MCR Car Rental, **t** 440 5398, *royston@ caribsurf.com*.

Sanvics 4x4, **t** 444 5227. Cars and Jeeps.

Spice Isle Rentals, the Avis rental in St George's, **t** 440 3936. Also Jeeps.

Y&R Car Rentals, **t** 444 4448, *y&r@caribsurf. com*, *www.y-r.com*.

Tourist Information

Abroad

Grenada's home page is at *www.grenada grenadines.com* and there is also information at the Grenada Hotel Association Web site: *www.grenadahotelsinfo.com*.

Canada: 439 University Ave, Suite 920, Toronto, Ontario M5G 1Y8, **t** (416) 595 1339, *grenadator@sympatico.ca*.

UK: Grenada Tourist Office, CIB Communications, 1 Battersea Church Rd, London SW11 3LY, **t** (020) 7771 7016, *grenada@ cibgroup.co.uk*.

USA: Grenada Tourist Office, Richartz, Fliss, Clark & Pope, 305 Madison Av, New York, NY 10165, **t** (212) 687 9554, *noel@rfcp.com*.

In Grenada

Board of Tourism, Burns Point (cruise ship terminal area on the Carenage), St George's, **t** 440 2001, *gbt@caribsurf.com*. *Open daily 8–4*.

Point Salines airport, **t** 444 4140. *Open daily 7am–9pm*. Accommodation and advice.

Embassies and Consulates

British High Commission: 14 Church St, St George's, **t** 440 3222, *bhcgrenada@ caribsurf.com*.

Canadian High Commission: in Barbados (*see* **Barbados**, p.75).

US Embassy, Lance Aux Epines Stretch, St George's, **t** 444 1173, *usembtgd@ caribsurf.com*.

Media

The *Grenadian Voice* and the *Grenada Informer* are the island's weekly newspapers, listing local events as well as covering Caribbean news. The Grenada Board of Tourism puts out a number of complimentary publications: *Greeting*, a glossy magazine with tourist information, general articles and a list of options if you are struck with a shopping crisis; and the pocket-sized *Discover Grenada*.

Medical Emergencies

Contact St George's Hospital, **t** 440 2051/2/3.

Money and Banks

The Grenadian currency is the Eastern Caribbean dollar (shared with a number of other British Commonwealth Caribbean countries), which is fixed to the US dollar at a rate of EC$2.65 = US$1. It is advisable to be sure which currency you are dealing in, as a bargain may suddenly turn out to be nearly three times better or a taxi fare considerably more expensive.

Life in Grenada is pretty expensive at the moment, though good prices can still be found for accommodation. **Banking hours** are Mon–Fri 8–1, some until 2; Fri also 3–5.

Telephone Code

The IDD code for Grenada is **t** 1 473, followed by a seven-digit number.

Festivals

It is also always worth looking to see if there are any celebrations taking place in Carriacou (*see* p.166) and making your way up there.

January/February *Grenada Sailing Festival*. This major four-day regatta (**t** 440 4809, *www.grenadasailingfestival.com*) hosts competitive and less competitive yachting races around the island, starting as far away as Barbados and Trinidad.

7 February *Independence Day*. A jump-up (general dancing in the streets).

Easter *Kite flying*.

June *Grenada Spice Jazz Festival.*

August *Carnival.* In Grenada this is celebrated in August rather than at the beginning of Lent, but it is still three days of dancing in the streets of St George's with Carnival parades, steel bands and calypso singing. If you'd like to 'play Mas' (i.e. buy a costume and jump up with the parades), contact the Tourist Board for the name of a band. *Carriacou Regatta.*

November *Extempo.* Singers ad-lib on subjects given to them moments before, or spar with one another in song.

November/December *'End of Hurricane Season' Regatta.*

Mid-December *Parang Festival.* Parang, a special sort of Christmas music, has its own festival.

Throughout the year *Saints' days.* Grenadian towns celebrate their saints' days with plenty of drinking and dancing as well as cultural displays.
Sailing races.
Deep-sea fishing tournaments.

Shopping and Galleries

Shops are open Mon–Fri 8–4, Sat 8–noon. Look out for the work of Grenadian artists Michael Paryag and Elinus Cato, and Carriacouans Canute Caliste and Frankie Francis. The following are worthwhile galleries:

Art Grenada, t 444 2317. Based in the large Grand Anse Shopping Centre.

Yellow Poui Art Gallery, Cross St, St George's, **t** 440 3001. Named after a Caribbean tree, it features West Indian art and is particularly impressive for its Primitivist paintings and West Indian scenes by foreign painters and sculptors.

Watersports

For jet-skiing or water-skiing, etc, it is best to go to Grand Anse, where you can fix up a jetski. Try World Wide Watersports, **t** 444 1339, for a flight under a parasail or being dragged around the bay on a bouncy banana, or Sky Ride, **t** 440 1568. Water-skiing, kayaks, small

sailing craft and windsurfers are available through the hotel concessionaires.

Day Sails

If you want to go to a secluded bay or to chase whales or dolphins, then contact:

Footloose Yacht Charters, t 440 7949, *footloose@caribsurf.com.* They arrange day sails and sunset cruises.

First Impressions, t 440 3678, *starwindsailing@ caribsurf.com, www.catamaranchartering.com.*

Rhum Runner Tour, t 440 4386. For an afternoon of fun with the cruise ship passengers or a rum-and-reggae-soaked sunset cruise.

Deep-sea Fishing

Try one of the following companies, all costing about US$500 a full day, or $300 for half a day:

Reel Affair II, t 440 3669, *ral@caribsurf.com.* Offers day trips trawling the depths to the west of Grenada.

Bezo Charters, t 443 5021, *westrum@carib surf.com.*

Sailing

See also 'Festivals', above.

Grenada is one of the setting-off points for a sail through the Eastern Caribbean and particularly, of course, the Grenadines (there are other companies in the Grenadines themselves and also in St Lucia).

Grenada itself has endless coves along its ragged southern coastline (though inexperienced sailors are requested not to sail here). The bases are found here, around L'Anse aux Epines and in St George's, from where you can run the leeward coast of the island north, beneath Grenada's towering, rainforested mountains, to the spectacular, open water of the Grenadines, where the sea, sand and snorkelling are superb and there are islands with just a few palm trees and swim-up bars.

Scuba Diving

Grenada is surrounded by reefs on all sides. Some of the better known are Boss Reef and Whibble Reef in the southeast, Shark Reef to the south of the airport, and Molinière Point just north of St George's. You can also dive the *Bianca C,* a 600ft liner which was scuttled after a famous fire in the Carenage and is now thought to be the largest wreck sitting upright in the world. Dive the upper decks and then take a turn around the swimming pool. Single tank dives cost from about US$45; packages and certification available. Try one of the following companies:

Aquanauts Grenada, True Blue Bay Resort, St George's, **t** 444 1126, *aquanauts@caribsurf. com*, *www.aquanautgrenada.com*.

Dive Grenada, Flamboyant Hotel, Grand Anse, **t** 444 1092, *divegda@caribsurf.com*, *www. divegrenada.com*.

Snorkelling

There are good shallow seascapes in L'Anse aux Epines and at Molinière Point north of St George's.

Other Sports

Golf

Play a nine-hole course near Grand Anse, at the Grenada Golf and Country Club, **t** 444 4128, with a green fee of EC$50.

Hiking

Walking in Grenada has developed in recent years and there are some good tours which will reveal to you the wonders of the rainforest. It is well worth taking a walk through the tropical rainforests, perhaps to one of the waterfalls. Contact:

Henry's Tours, **t** 444 5313. Well-organized walks, reaching parts of the island that are off the beaten track.

La Sagesse Nature Centre, **t** 444 6458, *lsnature@caribsurf.com*, *www.lasagesse.com*. For a day out and a walk.

Sunsation Tours, **t** 444 1594.

Telfor Hiking Tours, **t** 442 6200.

Horse-riding

It is possible to tour the rainforest in the dry season, and beaches and canefields during the wet – contact The Horseman, **t** 440 5368.

Mountain Biking

Try Ride Grenada, **t** 444 1157, and Trailblazers, **t** 444 5337, *adventure@caribsurf.com*, *www.grenadajeeptours.com*, who offer some

guided tours. Expect to pay a daily rate of around US$15.

Tennis

There are courts at many of the hotels and in the Grand Anse area.

Where to Stay

Grenada t (1 473–)

Most of Grenada's hotels are to be found in the southwestern corner of the island between St George's and the airport. The island has a good range of accommodation, with large, brisk and humming resorts typical of Caribbean tourism at the moment, all air conditioning, Jacuzzis and satellite televisions, but also some small places, with a little more personal character. If general life in Grenada is quite expensive, the island offers a good range of places to stay at the lower end of the market. All hotels have to charge an 8% government tax on the bill and most will also add 10% service as well.

There are a number of villas for rent on Grenada, many of them to be found in the southwestern corner of the island. Contact **Villas of Grenada**, PO Box 218, **t** 444 1896, *gpm&vog@caribsurf.com*; **Grenada Realtors**, PO Box 534, St George's, **t** 444 4255; or **Spice Isle Villas**, PO Box 1234, **t** 444 5166, *spiceisle villas@caribsurf.com*, *www.spiceislevillas.com*.

Luxury–Very Expensive

Calabash Hotel, at the head of Prickly Bay, L'Anse aux Epines, PO Box 382, **t** 444 4334, UK **t** (01603) 700 800, US **t** 1 800 528 5835, *calabash@caribsurf.com*, *www.calabash hotel.com*. The most comfortable, elegant and calm hotel in Grenada. There are 30 breezy suites, each with a private pool or a whirlpool, set in an arc of two-storey cottages (with pretty trellis woodwork) that surround an expanse of lawn with palms and calabash trees, looking towards the beach. Inside, the rooms are bright in modern Caribbean style, with wicker furniture. Breakfast is served on your balcony but the dining room, Rhodes Restaurant, which is hung with very pretty thunbergia vines, is one of the best and prettiest on the island.

Spice Island Beach Resort, Grand Anse Beach, PO Box 6, St George's, **t** 444 4258, US **t** 1 800 223 9815, *spiceisl@caribsurf.com*, *www.spice beachresort.com*. This used to be the island's leading resort, but it was badly damaged by Hurricane Ivan in September 2004. The hotel was being rebuilt at the time of writing and is scheduled to reopen in late 2005 after a $10 million investment. The new hotel will provide the full complement of modern facilities, with all-inclusive packages.

Laluna, Morne Rouge Bay, **t** 439 0001, US **t** 1 800 628 8929, *res@crownintmark.com*, *www.laluna.com*. Has a great deal of style. It sits, in a swatch of delightful jangling colours, stacked on the steep green hillside of the bay – washed blues, purples, russet and burnished gold (drawn from the Italian island of Pantelleria). The 16 one- and two-bedroomed cottages are furnished in tropical minimal, with bold-coloured curtains, four-posters and showers with a peephole on the horizon, and each has a nice bamboo-covered veranda with a plunge pool. Modern style and comfort – air-con, TV, VCR, stereo, Indonesian furnishings – but it is the hip atmosphere that makes Laluna different from anything else in Grenada.

Bel Air Plantation, St David's Point, **t** 444 6305, *belair@caribsurf.com*, *www.belairplantation. com*. A delightful collection of 11 brightly coloured, traditional cottages in their own cove in the south of Grenada. The cottages are ranged on a hillside and run down to a very pretty waterfront. A quiet getaway. Self-catering, with a good dining room too.

Expensive

La Source, Point Salines, PO Box 852, **t** 444 2556, *lasource@caribsurf.com*, *www. lasourcegrenada.com*. An all-inclusive resort with an all-over-body-holiday agenda (a never-ending diet of spa treatments, light cuisine and watersports). Damage from Hurricane Ivan closed the hotel for more than a year. The resort expects to reopen sometime in early 2006 with 12 more rooms, a renovated spa and an additional swimming pool and beach bar.

Coyaba Beach Resort, Grand Anse Bay, PO Box 336, **t** 444 4129. Has 70 rooms in blocks that run down to the beach. The hotel was destroyed by Hurricane Ivan and is being rebuilt to a higher degree of luxury. It plans to reopen by March 2006 as a four-star resort with 70 de-luxe rooms and 10 new suites. Tennis, squash, gym and a pool.

Moderate

Lance aux Epines Cottages, L'Anse aux Epines, **t** 444 4565, *cottages@caribsurf.com*, *www.laecottages.com*. Eleven comfortable, older-style Caribbean apartments offer an excellent deal and reasonable comfort. One- and two-bedroom self-catering units and cottages, with ceiling fans and tile floors (air-con in the bedrooms, all of which have been renovated since Hurricane Ivan), are set in a sandy garden above the beach. It's a low-key hotel with no dining room or pool, but with several restaurants nearby.

Twelve Degrees North, L'Anse aux Epines Bay, PO Box 241, **t** 444 4580, *12degrsn@caribsurf. com*, *www.twelvedegreesnorth.com*. Another good retreat, a collection of eight apartments on the clifftops with fully equipped kitchens, each with its own cook/housekeeper who is yours alone for your stay. So named because it lies exactly 12 degrees north of the equator, it takes a maximum of 20 people, children not allowed. There is a pool and palm-thatch bar on the beach.

The Flamboyant Hotel, Grand Anse Bay, PO Box 214, **t** 444 4247, *flambo@caribsurf. com*, *www.flamboyant.com*. Sixty-three standard rooms (*moderate*), suites and apartments, which sit on the rising ground behind Grand Anse at the far end of the beach. Has a fair bit of style. The nicest apartments are set in the older villas (which come with fans and wooden floors) rather than the newer air-conditioned blocks. All have balconies with views of St George's.

True Blue Bay Resort, True Blue Bay, PO Box 1414, **t** 443 8783, *mail@trubluebay.com*, *www.truebluebay.com*. A small and personable retreat tucked away in the southwestern peninsula, no longer simply blue, but bright yellow, purple and lilac with red tin roofs as well. There are 15 rooms in a variety of waterfront apartments, bay-view rooms and two-bedroom cottages, and Tree Top Suites, all comfortable, festooned with bougainvillea and with private balconies and hammocks. There is a good view from the pool and a terrace restaurant right on the waterfront. A passable beach nearby, plus scuba on the premises.

La Sagesse Nature Centre, St David's, PO Box 44, **t** 444 6458, *lsnature@caribsurf.com*, *www.lasagesse.com*. Set in the miniature grandeur of an estate house with an arched façade and a curious staircase hidden away in tropical greenery just behind the beach. There are 12 fan-ventilated rooms in all (one with air-con), four of which are in the estate house. There is also a charming bar and a new restaurant set among the trees and giving onto a nice beach in a classic bay enclosed by headlands. Well worth considering if you want the best in island charm and isolation.

Petit Bacaye, Petit Bacaye Bay, PO Box 655, **t** 443 2902, UK **t** (01794) 323227, *hideaways@wellowmead.u-net.com*, *www.petitbacaye.com*. A collection of palm-thatched cottages scattered around a sandy garden of crotons, oleander and bougainvillea. Set in its own bay just beneath a small village, Petit Bacaye is small, with just seven one- and two-bedroom cottages (small verandas, walk-in mosquito nets over the beds, fine showers and kitchenettes in the bigger cottages) and it has a lovely low-key atmosphere. There is a small bar and restaurant, where you can get the chef to cook up the fresh fish landed each day by the fishermen who work in the bay.

Cabier Ocean-Lodge, Crochu, St Andrew's, **t** 444 6013, *info@cabier-vision.com*, *www.cabier-vision.com*. Even more remote, down a long and rickety lane through a charming local village, this hotel sits at the tip of a promontory with superb sea views either side. There are a variety of rooms in the main villa, with sitting decks around the pretty garden, and outlying cottages, which look down onto a delightful and natural, palm-backed beach. An Austrian couple has managed Cabier since May 2004, and there are now a range of wellness treatments on offer to guests.

Morne Fendue Plantation House, Morne Fendue, **t** 442 9330, *caribbean@caribsurf.com*, *www.mornefendue.com*. Has a commanding position in fantastically green Grenadian scenery. The building itself is an old West Indian plantation estate house and has a slightly antique air. There are five rooms, most sharing a bathroom, and a two-storey annexe with eight double rooms. There are always plenty of people passing by for lunch (*see* 'Eating Out', below).

Grand View Inn, Grand Anse Bay, PO Box 614, **t** 444 4984, *gvinn@caribsurf.com*, *www.travelgrenada.com/grand.htm*. A small hotel which retains a certain older Caribbean charm and style in some of its rooms. It is set in the former Soviet Embassy compound, complete with guard post at the entrance, and has a magnificent view, as the name suggests, to St George's and the mountains beyond. A mix of large and breezy older rooms and more modern air-conditioned ones, all with kitchenette and cable TV. There is a great view from the terrace of the restaurant, Pirate's Cove.

Monmot Hotel, L'Anse aux Epines, **t** 439 3408, *monmothotel@caribsurf.com*, *www.monmothotel.com*. This 20-suite hotel opened in mid-2004 and is situated just 10 minutes from airport. It has a pool, restaurant and a contemporary, fresh look.

Blue Horizons Garden Resort, Grand Anse, **t** 444 4316, *blue@caribsurf.com*, *www.grenadabluehorizons.com*. After Hurricane Ivan, the hotel closed for a major US$1.2 million renovation and upgrading. It was scheduled to re-open in July 2005. Located across the road from the beach, it caters to divers, nature enthusiasts, and travellers seeking a tropical destination at affordable prices. All 32 air-conditioned rooms are to be completely refurbished with new bathrooms and kitchen appliances including refrigerator, stove, coffee maker and toaster. Amenities include cable TV, radio, safe, ironing board and iron. Attached is La Belle Creole, widely acknowledged as one of Grenada's best restaurants.

Inexpensive

South Winds Holiday Cottages and Apartments, Grand Anse Bay, PO Box 118, **t** 444 4310, US and Canada **t** 1 800 223 9815, *chands@caribsurf.com*. There are 19 rooms all of which come at good prices. The Brown

Sugar restaurant (*see* below) is on the premises too.

Roydon's Guest House, Grand Anse Bay, **t** 444 4476. A comfortable and simple place within a shout of the beach. Just six rooms.

Mitchell's Guest House, Tyrell St, St George's, **t** 440 2803. Has 11 rooms sharing bathrooms.

Homestead Guest House, Gouyave, **t** 444 8526. A simple stopover.

Grenada Rainbow Inn, Grenville, PO Box 923, **t** 442 7714, *www.grenadarainbowinn.com*. Fifteen self-contained units with a local restaurant.

Eating Out

It might be that the Grenadians have retained their interest in and a flair for cooking from the days when the island was French. At any rate, the abundance of island produce makes Grenada a good place for classic West Indian fare: callaloo, breadfruit, christophene and green fig, as well as the more exotic *tatou* (armadillo) and *manicou* (opossum). There is 'international fare' on offer too, often in hotels, for those who feel too far from home in the West Indies, but Grenada has plenty of charming restaurants, often taking advantage of good settings.

Eating out in Grenada is pretty expensive at the moment, and then you can expect a service charge of 10% plus 8% VAT to be added to your bill.

Categories are arranged according to the price of a main course: expensive = EC$50 and above, moderate = EC$20–50, inexpensive = less than EC$20.

Expensive

Rhodes, Calabash Hotel, L'Anse aux Epines, **t** 444 4334. Celebrity chef Gary Rhodes makes the best use of local ingredients to offer an innovative Caribbean and international menu – jerk chicken fillet, Grenadian honey duck and Caribbean peppered steak are some of his specialties. One of the best places to eat in Grenada.

The Beach House Restaurant and Bar, Ball's Beach, **t** 444 4455. Offers 'New Caribbean' cuisine, a mix of local and international ingredients and techniques. Set on a very pretty double wooden deck with pegged louvres and surrounded by the trill of tree frogs and the wash of the waves, you dine on Fisherman's Soup (a broth of spiced fish, shrimp and lobster), followed by blackened or Cajun fish and finish with Grand Etang Mud Pie or a coconut cheesecake.

Coconut Beach Restaurant, Grand Anse Bay, **t** 444 4644. Has a very nice setting in a purple wooden house at the head of the bay, with tables out on the sand under palm-thatch parasols or inside in full view of the working kitchen. The fare is Caribbean and French creole – chicken breast *à la sauce féroce* or catch of the day in lemon butter, Nantais butter or mango chutney. Simpler food is available during the day.

Brown Sugar, Grand Anse Bay, **t** 444 4310. High on the hill above the road leading south out of Grand Anse, there are just a few tables in a brightly coloured dining room. The dishes are named after Grenadian expressions and characters: La Ja Blesse (a shrimp starter) is a Caribbean she-devil, Wash Yuh Foot an' Come (conch in a creole sauce) means 'come however you are dressed', and the striploin steak, from the States, is called Ba' John, aka the village bully, no doubt a political reference to events past.

Moderate

Mt Rodney Estate House, near Sauteurs, **t** 442 9420. A former plantation estate house built in the 1870s. A set menu is served on the bright orange and green terrace – soup, pumpkin or pawpaw, followed by a choice of fish or chicken with wholesome Caribbean ground provisions and home-made ice creams. Coffee is served on the veranda, where there is a lovely view. *Lunch Mon–Fri; reservations only.*

Morne Fendue Plantation House, **t** 442 9330. Old stone plantation house which offers lunch. Nutmeg shells laid out on the drive give off a heady smell of spice as you drive up. Traditional Caribbean callaloo and island specialities (the pepper pot has been on the go for 14 years, since the much older one was interrupted by the 1983 troubles), taken on the veranda with fine views of the Grenadian landscape. *Reservations essential.*

Aquarium, Point Salines Beach, **t** 444 1410. A beach bar by day but looks good at night too. You dine in an open-air gallery supported by telegraph poles just above the waves: try the Aquarium medley – shrimp, scallop and fish or callaloo cannelloni and *spanakopita*. There's a guest villa next door.

Boatyard, L'Anse aux Epines, **t** 444 4662. An eatery with international fare and a passing foreign trade, set on an open veranda overlooking the yachts at anchor. Steak and fish, salads and burgers.

The Red Crab, L'Anse aux Epines, **t** 444 4424. With pub-style décor inside, tropical garden outside, and international food.

La Belle Creole, Blue Horizons Garden Resort, Grand Anse, **t** 444 4316, *blue@caribsurf.com*, *www.grenadabluehorizons.com*. The resort's gourmet restaurant is considered by some to be the best in Grenada. Owner Arnold Hopkin was one of the first to create a Caribbean cuisine using international dishes with a Caribbean twist, such as callaloo quiche. After the 2004 hurricane the restaurant was rebuilt in a new design.

Tout Bagai, St George's, **t** 440 1500. The name is creole for 'everything is possible'. It sits upstairs in a modern block at the end of the dock in town, with bright blue sea murals and hung with fish nets. Simple fare by day – *rotis* and batter-fried *lambi* strips with fries – and some more sophisticated dishes in the evening, such as flying fish in a lemon caper sauce or scampi *provençal*. Watch the dress code: 'No Hats, No Sleeveless Tops, No Untidy Attire, Dress Elegantly Casual...'

Tropicana, Lagoon Road, St George's, **t** 440 1586. On a veranda right on the road into town, opposite the cinema, serving trusty Chinese and international fare, from fried rice to shrimp and *lambi* specials, *rotis* to hamburgers. The restaurant is attached to a 20-room inn.

Inexpensive

Nutmeg, Carenage, St George's, **t** 440 2539. Well worth a stop for a juice and a commanding view of the harbour from upstairs. Simple platters followed by nutmeg ice cream if you actually want a meal.

Rudolf's, Carenage, St George's, **t** 440 2241. Attracts a lively crowd, with pub-style benches and an egg-box ceiling; steaks, seafood and omelettes.

The Carenage Café, Carenage, St George's. A nice stop for a juice and a croissant, a salad or a sandwich, right on the waterfront road.

Bars and Nightlife

Bars

There are plenty of bars in St George's where you can join the locals in a game of dominoes and a white rum (Clarke's Court of varying percentage proof). Most of the restaurants also have bars which are worth investigating.

Sur la Mer Bar, BBC Beach, beyond Grand Anse. It's hard to beat for a sunset drink.

Aboo's, on the waterfront, St George's. Gets quite busy.

Ye Olde Farm House, Cross St, opposite the Yellow Poui Gallery, St George's. A busy spot.

Clubs

Fantazia 2001, Morne Rouge Beach. Can be lively at the weekend.

Cotbam, Grand Anse. Pulls a crowd.

Le Sucrier, at the Sugar Mill, south of Grand Anse. Can get pretty wild (Wed–Sat) and is a good way to meet the locals.

Island View, Woburn. Popular with locals.

Beach Bars

There are some good seaside haunts with secluded bars.

Aquarium, Point Salines Beach, **t** 444 1410. A neat and pretty dining deck supported by telegraph poles and lost in greenery. Open for lunch and dinner (*see* under 'Eating Out'). Some limited watersports.

The Beach House, Ball's Beach. On a superb strip of sand, set on a pretty gingerbread deck beneath enormous trees.

La Sagasse Bar and Restaurant, La Sagesse Bay, **t** 444 6458. A quiet and delightful place tucked away in the trees. Ideal for a day. Transfers, lunch and a guided walk through the local woodlands for about US$30.

Bar, Petit Bacaye Bay. Set in a charming cove.

Sur la Mer Bar, BBC Beach, beyond Grand Anse. An ideal liming spot with a cracking view of the sunset, if you can see through the fishing nets and shutters.

creeping vines and lianas that threaten to throttle the path, and if you go higher, beyond the montane forest into the elfin woodland, there are stunted trees and ferns. Living in the forest are a few animals, including mona monkeys, opossum, a species of nine-banded armadillo and many birds, including tanagers and the odd hawk. The Grenadian national bird is the endemic and endangered Grenada dove, of which fewer than 100 are thought to exist. There are a number of mangrove areas in Grenada, including **Levera** in the northeast and **La Sagesse** estuary in the southeast, which have an entirely different birdlife. Here you may see coots and flycatchers and the more traditional seabirds such as pelicans and boobies. The national flower of Grenada is the bougainvillea, which you will see around hotels all over the island.

If you wish to go on a walking tour of island wildlife, you can find knowledgeable guides by calling in advance the **Tourist Board**, t 440 2001, or the **Grand Etang National Forest Office**, t 440 6160. Also see 'Hiking' under 'Other Sports', p.155.

St George's

Named after King George III, the capital of Grenada is the prettiest harbour town in the Caribbean. Stacked on an amphitheatrical hillside are lines of warehouses, homes and churches with ochre-tiled and red tin roofs that glow in the evening light against the rich tropical green of Grenada's slopes. St George's is still very much a working port and many ships put into the harbour – cargo vessels, cruise ships, fishing boats, water taxis and, of course, the brightly painted schooners from the Grenadines which you will see tied up on the wharves of the Carenage.

The old parts of town date from the late 18th century, when the original buildings were destroyed in fires. It is sprinkled with fine old creole houses, built of brick in soft shades of rose, yellow and beige and embellished with elaborate ironwork balconies and the occasional porch that was used to keep sedan chair passengers from getting wet in the rain. St George's is built over the backbone of a hill and is split into two main halves: the Carenage, on the inner harbour, and the Esplanade, which fronts onto the Caribbean Sea. The two sides are linked by a network of steep cobbled streets and stepped alleys. At Carnival, when the costumed masqueraders wind through the streets of St George's, the steel band floats have to be winched up the cobbled streets and then held back from running away down the other side.

Once, St George's Harbour was an inland lake, but now it can take ocean-going vessels. It was the crater of a volcano, from which the sides have crumbled. It is extinct, but not entirely dormant, as was shown by a curious and alarming incident in 1867, when volcanic activity was felt throughout the Caribbean. At five in the afternoon the level of the water in the Carenage suddenly dropped by 5ft and the Green Hole started to bubble and steam, letting off sulphurous gases. Moments later, the level of the sea rose to about 4ft above the normal, only to be sucked down and rise again a number of times, as though the underworld were breathing.

The **Carenage** is the centrepiece of the town, the very attractive curved waterfront lined with old mercantile buildings which are still used by businesses today. The statue on the waterfront, by Wharf Rd, is a repesentation of **Christ of the Deep**, dedicated to the people of Grenada after their efforts to save the passengers of a cruise liner, the *Bianca C*, which burned in Grenada harbour in 1961. Nearby, the island's British heritage is retained in the **red telephone boxes**. There are plenty of cafés and bars around the waterfront where you can catch a drink and a rest when your feet overheat from walking around the town. One of the best views of the town can be had from a water-taxi trip across the harbour (*price US$2*).

One of the finest and oldest creole houses is the former French military barracks on Young St, now home to the **Grenada National Museum** (*open Mon–Fri 9–4.30, Sat 10–1; small adm*). Here Arawak petroglyphs are on view, alongside Empress Josephine's marble bathtub (she spent her childhood on the nearby island of Martinique), copper kettles, a rum still from the days of sugar, old island maps and pictures of St George's, and some descriptions of the flora and fauna. Worth a quick visit.

Forts and churches dominate the heights of St George's and many of them stand on Church St, the ridge road that gives on to both sides of the town. Close to Fort George, which overlooks the harbour mouth, is the **Scots Kirk**, a Presbyterian church erected in 1831. A little farther up is the **St George's Parish Anglican Church**, rebuilt in 1825 on the site of an original 1763 French Roman Catholic church. It contains plaques commemorating the victims of the Brigand's War, or Fédon's Rebellion, and the 51 hostages, including the Governor, Ninian Home, who were murdered by the 'execrable banditti'. Still on Church St is **York House**, the Grenadian House of Parliament. But the best position of all is commanded by the **Roman Catholic Cathedral** (many Grenadians are still Catholic from French days), built in 1818.

The other half of St George's is the **Esplanade**, or Bay Town, which looks onto the Caribbean Sea. It was hard work getting over the ridge to the market from the Carenage and so at the end of the 19th century a tunnel was constructed, linking the two. The **Sendall Tunnel**, named after the Governor, is over 100 yards long and still used now for heavy traffic.

The Esplanade has lines of old warehouses overlooking the sea, and on the waterfront itself is the **fish market**, alive when the catch is brought in at the end of the day. The main **St George's market** is a couple of blocks inland from the Esplanade, on open ground between Granby and Hillsborough Sts. There is a typical Caribbean ironwork-covered market building, but most of the activity takes place out on the square, where colourful golf umbrellas shelter the vendors and their produce – root vegetables and tropical fruits (and of course Grenadian spices) – from the sun and from passing rainstorms. The best day to visit is Saturday, in the morning, but it is lively on any weekday morning (it is quiet on Sundays). If you have not been waylaid already by the spice women who ply the streets of St George's, at the back of the square on Grenville St you can visit the **Minor Spices Society**, which smells of the cinnamon, cloves and allspice on sale there.

Only two forts remain of what was once a protective ring of defences on the heights above St George's. **Fort George** dominates the harbour mouth, with a fine view of the Carenage and the open sea, and it is now the main St George's police station. Constructed in 1706, it spent a spell more recently as Fort Rupert (named after the father of Maurice Bishop who was killed in a riot in 1974). It was here that Maurice Bishop himself and his colleagues were shot on 19 October 1983. Cannon still poke over the battlements and underground there is a warren of tunnels and caverns, supposedly leading to a series of underground passageways from one fort to the next (now blocked off). Tours are possible.

On the rising ground that forms the backdrop of St George's harbour, among the homes of prosperous Grenadians, is **Marryshow House**, a creole building that was once the home of the Grenadian political leader and architect of the West Indies Federation, Theophilus A. Marryshow. Now part of the University of the West Indies, it does not have much for visitors to see inside, but it is a pretty creole house with gingerbread trimmings and slanted louvres. Higher still is **Government House**, with a fine view over the harbour and town. Built in 1802 of brick with arches and dormer windows, it is the official residence of the Governor General and it cannot actually be visited. The most spectacular view of the town can be seen after a stiff climb up **Richmond Hill**, which commands the harbour and the coast as far as Point Salines in the southwest. Once there were four forts in all, started by the French after they captured the island in 1779 and completed by the British. Fort Frederick is in reasonable repair and there is a campaign to restore Fort Matthew.

In the suburbs behind Richmond Hill you will find the **Bay Gardens** (*open daylight hours; adm*), a botanical garden set in the grounds of a former sugar mill. Here you will see a huge range of Caribbean flora – vivid blooms of purple, pink and scarlet among the endless shades of green. It is well worth finding a guide to tell you about the many species on display.

The West Coast

The Grenadian coastline is a series of headlands and bays, spurs of land thrown off from the volcanic peaks, interspersed with valleys carved out by rivers where you'll find some of Grenada's spice plantations. The road, initially laid out by the French in the 18th century, follows the coastline, all hairpins, switchbacks and overhung by cliffs – and with fantastic views. You will see the Grenadians doing their laundry in the rivers. The names recount the island's mixed history – Happy Hill, Molinière, Beauséjour Bay and Halifax Harbour.

From St George's the Esplanade road leads up the west coast, passing the ruin of the old communal lavatory on the bayfront and on to **Queen's Park** on the outskirts of the town, site of the new National Stadium and general sports ground. Inland from Concord, following the Black Bay River upstream among the nutmeg and cocoa plantations, are the **Concord Falls**, a series of three waterfalls lost in the forested mountains. It is possible to drive to the lowest one, but the other two must be reached on foot: the first takes 25 minutes, and the next is 1.5 hours' walk. However, each fall has a pool in which you can swim after the climb. In high season you will probably not be alone, but it is a pleasant walk. It is even possible to walk up to Grand

Etang (about 5 hours' climb; *see* p.165). Back on the coast, **Black Bay** is named after its appearance, which is black volcanic rather than white coral sand.

Just outside Gouyave is the **Dougaldston Estate**, a charming old plantation of clapboard and tin-roofed buildings and dilapidated farm machinery, where cocoa and nutmeg are grown among allspice, tonka beans and coffee. In years past, the estate would ring to the sound of violins as the workers 'danced' the cocoa beans to dry them evenly in the *boucans*, shuffling in lines and turning the cocoa beans with their feet. The *boucans*, vast trays that are pulled out from beneath the building to catch the sun, are on wheels so that they can be rushed underneath in case of rain. In the main building, heavy with the smells of cinnamon, cloves and nutmeg, the old processes can be seen, worked by the Grenadian women. It is possible to buy the spices on display.

Gouyave (French for 'guava') is a little farther along the coast. Set on a promontory, the town's old creole houses of faced stone and yellow St George's brick are past their best now, but the place is alluring in its faded prosperity. Travelling in the 1940s, Patrick Leigh Fermor came across a sweepstake here, in which the first prize was a free funeral for the ticket holder or for any friend or relation. The biggest building in Gouyave is the **Grenada Nutmeg Cooperative Association** (*adm*), with floors full of sacks, tea chests and machinery, the air redolent with the sweet-spice smell of nutmeg.

Set on a sweeping bay on the north coast is the village of **Sauteurs**, the island's third-largest town and the scene of one of the saddest moments in Grenada's history, when the retreating Caribs were surrounded by French troops and reputedly threw themselves to their death in the sea rather than be killed. And so, in French, the place became known as La Morne des Sauteurs, 'Leapers' Hill'. Following the coast road west out of the town (past the stadium) you reach the turning up to the **Mt Rodney Estate House** (by reservation only, *see* 'Eating Out', p.158), a former plantation estate house built in the 1870s. It's a great place to visit for lunch. Alternatively you might try **Morne Fendue Plantation House** (by reservation only, *see* 'Eating Out', p.158), another old stone plantation house with wrought-iron balconies which also offers lunch and a great view of the surrounding country.

Towards the northeastern point of the island is **Levera Bay**, a strip of golden sand with fine views of the offshore islands. Nearby is **Levera Lake**, an extinct volcanic crater like Lake Antoine to the south, and at **Bedford Point** itself are the ruins of an old fort.

The South Coast

With its white sand beaches so close to St George's, the southwestern tip of Grenada is the hotel heartland. The countryside is flatter and drier than the island interior so most of Grenada's sugar was grown here. The southern coastline is a long succession of deep bays and promontories, where many wealthy Grenadians build their homes and where cruising yachts put in for shelter. Farther east the coast becomes more remote, but judging by the names it has a romantic history – Morne Délice, Mamma Cannes, Perdmontemps, and Après Tout.

A couple of miles south of St George's, **Grand Anse** is the most popular beach on the island, with about 2 miles of blinding-white, satin-soft sand. A number of hotels front onto the sand, but the beach does not usually become too crowded. The area has seen considerable building in the last few years, both hotels and private houses. Farther round the point are a number of small bays, pleasant and secluded, though the peace will occasionally be interrupted by planes passing overhead as they come in to Point Salines Airport at the island's southwestern tip. On the airport road, which has become increasingly developed with factories now, you will see a **monument to the American veterans** killed during the Grenada invasion in 1983. Just along the southern coast is another popular bay, once called Prickly Bay by the English, but now usually known by its French equivalent, **L'Anse aux Epines** (often rendered 'Lance aux Epines'). It has some fine hotels and apartments, spread out on the thin strip of sand at the head of the bay and on the clifftops. Visible out to sea south of Grenada is Glover Island, operated as a whaling station in 1925 by the Norwegians.

Calvigny Point was the site of the main camp of the People's Revolutionary Army in the time of Maurice Bishop, and the area saw considerable military activity during the American invasion. Beyond the charming fishing village of Woburn, **Fort Jeudy**, now an expensive housing estate, speaks of earlier conflicts, when a fort used to guard the entrance to Egmont Harbour. A little farther on is the **Westerhall Rum Distillery** (*tours possible*), the producer of light and dark rums, including jack-iron, an almost mystical drink in which ice sinks.

The coast road winds through the former plantations and past secluded beaches such as **La Sagesse Bay** and **Bacolet Bay** until it reaches **Marquis**, just south of Grenville. This settlement was the first target in Fédon's rebellion, where the English inhabitants were dragged from their beds and killed. **Laura Gardens**, another spice garden in the rich and fertile interior above here, are worth a quick look, to see the plantations and then the collection of Grenada's many spices.

Over the Grand Etang to the East Coast

To a Grenadian, 'over the Grand Etang' means going over the mountains and through the centre of the island, on roads that wind and switchback as they climb steadily into Grenada's staggeringly lush interior of mountains dressed in ferns, grasses and elfin woodland. The best road to take from St George's goes along the St John's River, past the stadium in Queen's Park, but it is also possible to go via Government House and left at the roundabout. From here you climb to the oddly named Snug Corner and eventually to the Grand Etang itself. Remember to look behind as you climb for some of the island's most spectacular views, as far as Point Salines in the southwest. Just off the road are **Annandale Falls**, a 30ft cascade (only really impressive in the rainy season) that races into a bathing pool, surrounded by tropical greenery. The valley was the scene of considerable fighting in the 1983 invasion.

At the summit of the range is the **Grand Etang** (Great Pond), another extinct volcano crater. Set in a Government Reserve, its water is cold and metallic blue (estimates of its depth vary from 14ft to fathomless). The **Grand Etang Forest Centre** (*open Mon–Sat 8–4; adm free;* see *also p.160*) has illustrations of local flora and fauna and a description of the Caribbean's geological past: two chains of volcanic islands created by the shifting of the Atlantic and Caribbean tectonic plates. There are also short walking tours around the Grand Etang and into the rainforest in the mountains, where you will see explosions of bamboo, tree-top ferns and creeping vines. You might also see birds such as Grenada's hummingbirds, tanagers and the occasional cuckoo, as well as armadillos and opossums.

Some way off is **Morne Fédon**, also called Mt Qua Qua. Much of the fighting in the 1795 rebellion led by Fédon, who owned the estate at Belvidere just below the mountain, took place in this area. The mountain stronghold was situated on the three spurs of the peak, each named after one of their slogans, Champ La Liberté, Champ L'Egalité and Champ La Mort. It is a couple of hours' hike to get there. Also in this area are the two **Mt Carmel Falls**, cascades which drop 70ft into icy rock pools.

Descending to the windward side of Grenada the road passes among tiny villages clinging to the hillsides down to the cocoa-receiving station at **Carlton**, where the beans are processed and prepared for shipment. After an hour's walk off the road in St Margaret's you will find the **Seven Sisters Falls**, worth a detour for a swim, though you should ask permission to walk over the private land. Eventually you arrive at the coast at **Grenville**, set on a large bay sheltered by reefs. It is still referred to as La Baye, as it is known in French creole. There are a few solid stone structures that speak of its former position of importance, the 'second city' to St George's. The countryside here is known as Grenada's lifeblood, the island's breadbasket, and it is dotted with plantation houses. In the town itself, the **covered market** and **fish market** are the centres of activity. Graceful Grenadian sloops can often be seen at the waterfront, calling in on their trips between the Grenadines and Trinidad. There is also a nutmeg factory, the **Nutmeg Cooperative Processing Station** (*adm*) that is worth a visit.

North of here is the **River Antoine Rum Distillery**, which functions using old-time Caribbean machinery, its crushing gear still driven by a waterwheel. You can sample the fearsome rum they produce. **Lake Antoine** is the crater of a volcano reckoned to be extinct, though underground forces are still at work just beyond here, at the **mineral springs**, which emit wisps of sulphurous gas. Further on, the **Levera National Park** is used as a picnic area by the Grenadians at the weekend. You may well see doves in the woods and oystercatchers along the shore.

Carriacou and Petite Martinique

Carriacou and Petite Martinique, the only two other inhabited islands in the country, lie about 15 miles north of Grenada, at the northern limits of Grenadian territory. Strictly speaking, the border with St Vincent slices the north end off the two islands, but they have not come to blows over it recently. In fact, a lack of getting worked up over anything is a key feature of these two islands, which are delightfully laid-back and fun to visit.

Among the smaller uninhabited Grenadian islands are Les Tantes and the Sisters and one that even calls itself London Bridge. The underwater volcano by the name of Kick 'em Jenny, perhaps a corruption of the French '*Cay qui me gêne*', is so called because the water around it is renowned for being very rough (seasickness pills advised if you go anywhere near it). LIAT pilots who fly over here have reported seeing movement under the water, and the seismic instruments in Trinidad regularly detect it. Many reckon that it is growing slowly as it belches and that eventually another Grenadine might appear.

Carriacou

Carriacou is gentle and quiet (just 8 miles by 5), with a population of about 7,000, who are known as 'kayaks'. It is mountainous, though not high enough to have the tropical lushness of Grenada itself, and is bordered with the supreme white-sand beaches of the Grenadines. Tiny islets lie off its shores, nothing more than sand and a few palm trees.

The first settlers of Carriacou (from the Indian *Kayryouacou*) were French turtlers fishing in the sea or taking the turtles on the island's fine sand beaches as they came to lay their eggs. Eventually it was settled as a plantation island, growing mainly cotton, but also supporting two sugar estates that provided the island with rum.

The island is well known for its tradition of boat-building and you will still occasionally see these graceful boats being built here. And it is also known for smuggling, something of a Caribbean tradition. It is so endemic that calls have been made by the islanders to make the island duty-free. Shippers, legal or otherwise, are called 'traffickers' hereabouts: they take produce from Grenada down to Trinidad or Barbados, returning with tinned food, snacks and manufactured goods. Cargoes from Sint Maarten and the other duty-free islands and the odd consignment of whisky and foreign-brand cigarettes do occasionally go astray in a cove en route. The mainstay of the declared economy is agriculture, vegetables sent to market in Grenada, and sheep and goats, looking confused, tied up in bags so that only their heads protrude, on their way to market in the other islands. The island used to be cultivated all over and carefully husbanded, but the cattle and goats get everywhere now. The agricultural concerns are dying steadily as young Carriacouans (as elsewhere in the Caribbean) are not keen to work the land. There has been considerable development in island infrastructure over the past few years, in roads and guest houses for visitors who come up from Grenada, but life is pretty much as it has always been.

It is fascinating to see the skeletal hulls of cedar steadily take shape on the shoreline in Windward, and more recently Tyrell Bay, as the Carriacouan shipwrights create their boats. Not so many big ships are built any more, but many smaller boats are. Much of the wood is white cedar from Carriacou, but the main keel piece is greenheart imported from Guyana. The work is done by hand, following a tradition supposedly bequeathed by a Scots ancestry. The launching ceremony is a major festivity and well worth a visit if you hear of one. The blood of a goat is sprinkled on

Getting There

Carriacou/Petite Martinique t (1 473–)
To get to Petite Martinique you will first have to take a boat or plane to Carriacou.

By Air
If you go by air you'll experience Lauriston on Carriacou, one of the Grenadines' gentler airstrips (no mountains to negotiate), though you might be surprised to find that the island's main road runs diagonally across the middle of it. Local airlines include SVG Air, t 443 7362, *cayak@caribsurf.com, www.svgair. com*, and Airlines of Carriacou, t 443 7362, both with scheduled flights to Grenada and St Vincent. Departure tax from Carriacou is EC$10.

By Sea
Getting to Carriacou is part of the fun – coasting Grenada's leeward (western) side from St George's gives spectacular views of the fertile slopes that tumble from Mt St Catherine, and then there is a horizon dotted with the Grenadines. It is possible to go by yacht or by the hydrofoil or ferries that leave from the Carenage in Grenada, best of all on one of Carriacou's own graceful schooners. If you are travelling on through the Grenadines, the MV *Jasper* heads for Union Island on Monday and Thursday, about midday (EC$20).

There is a fairly regular crossing (not quite daily) from Hillsborough in Carriacou to Petite Martinique on the *Osprey*. Alternatively, hire a boat in Windward on Carriacou.

Getting Around

On Carriacou a rudimentary **bus** service runs out from Hillsborough to Tyrrel Bay and the other way to Windward.

Taxis are available through Lincoln (pager 441 7014), who, along with other taxi drivers, will fix an island tour. **Cars** can be hired (for regulations *see* Grenada, p.153) through Martin Bullen, t 443 7204, and John Gabriel, t 443 7454. **Bicycles** are available through Wild Track Cycles, t 443 6472, *wildtrackcycles@ grenadines.net*.

There's no need for transport on Petite Martinique.

Tourist Information

Tourist Office: Patterson St, Hillsborough, Carriacou, t 443 7948, *carrgbt@caribsurf.com*.
Web site: There is some selective information at *www.grenadagrenadines.com*.
For everything else, *see* Grenada, p.153.

Festivals

7 February *Independence Day*.
Start of Lent *Carnival*. Held at the traditional Caribbean time, unlike in Grenada.
April/June *Maroon Jazz Festival*.
Early August *Regatta*. The liveliest and most spectacular moment in the Carriacouan calendar. Yachts come from all over.
December *Parang Festival (see* Trinidad, p.110).

Watersports

Sunset trips and deep-sea fishing are also available from the scuba diving companies listed below.

Scuba Diving
Single tank dives cost around US$50. Novice instruction is available. There are three scuba shops on Carriacou:
Arawak Divers, Tyr ell Bay, t 443 6906.

the boat as it is blessed and then it is launched to the sound of drums, while everybody looks on dressed in their Sunday best.

You will find almost every conceivable alcohol in Carriacou, but the island's special drink is jack-iron, or the jack, which, quite apart from being extremely strong, has the peculiar and disarming quality of making ice sink in it. Not much is distilled here any more – most of it comes from Trinidad.

Carriacou Silver Diving, just outside Hillsborough, t 443 7882, *scubamax@carib surf.com, www.scubamax.com*.

Tanki's Watersports Paradise, L'Esterre Bay, t 443 8406. Tanki will take you to Pagoda City, to the caves at Kick 'em Jenny or to loiter among a various large schools of barracuda.

Snorkelling

There is excellent snorkelling around the little islands in Hillsborough Bay on Carriacou (*see* 'Beaches', below). Onshore on Carriacou, go beyond the rock of Anse la Roche.

Where to Stay

Carriacou t (1 473–)

There has been plenty of building in Carriacou recently, unfortunately without much concern for style. If you are happy to look after yourself, **Down Island Ltd**, t 443 8182, *islander@caribsurf.com, www.island villas.com*, has around 20 self-catering villas on their books.

Expensive

Caribbee Country House and Nature Preserve, at Prospect towards the northern end of Carriacou, t 443 7380, *caribbee@ caribsurf.com, www.caribbeeinn.com*. This is one of the Caribbean's gems and the nicest place to stay in Carriacou by a long way. It has the grace and charm of the old West Indies – four-poster beds, muslin nets, ceiling fans that whip the sea breezes through louvred windows. It has just 10 rooms and suites, the newest of which have a magnificent setting on a ridge pointing out to sea and balconies or terraces. Perfect for lazing around in privacy. Their bistro serves French creole dishes, including fresh

fish in herbs and spices, with entrées from EC$35. Easy atmosphere – you leave your shoes at the door. Anse la Roche is a short walk away.

Moderate

Green Roof Inn, on the coast just north of Hillsborough, t 443 6399, *greenroof@carib surf.com, www.greenroofinn.com*. This looks west over the sea and to the sunset. Family run, the inn has just five individually furnished rooms and is within walking distance of some nice beaches. A friendly, Swedish reception and a great view from the balconies.

The Silver Beach Hotel, Hillsborough Bay, t 443 7337, *silverbeach@caribsurf.com, www. silverbeachhotel.com*. Has a passable setting in a modern building right on the sand. The 16 simple air-conditioned rooms are in garden cottages and a block on the beach-front. With some watersports and some self-catering rooms.

Inexpensive

Paradise Inn, L'Esterre Bay, t 443 8406, *paradiseinn@caribsurf.com, www.paradise.cacounet.com*. There are seven comfortable rooms (one single), all fan-ventilated with tiled floors, wicker furniture and private baths. Popular with the diving crowd. There are meals available at the beach bar.

Ade's Dream House Guest House, Main St, Hillsborough, t 443 7317, *adesdea@caribsurf. com, www.grenadines.net/carriacou/ ade.htm*. A three-storey cream, grey and red-brick giant with 23 rooms (some with bath, some with shared), some self-catering, some air-conditioned.

John's Unique Resort, just north of Hillsborough, t 443 8345, *junique@carib surf.com, www.grenadines.net/carriacou/*

Beaches

Carriacou is rimmed with fine white beaches, most of which will be deserted. Look normally to the west coast, or on a still day try the windward (east) coast. Beyond the airport is a fine strip called **Paradise Beach**. On the western side of the island there is a good harbour at **Tyrrel Bay** and strips of sand which make for good sunbathing and sunset viewing. There is even passable sand right off **Hillsborough**. The best find of all, though, is **Anse la Roche**, in the northwest. Getting there is half the fun and is some-

johnresort.html. An equally massive place, concrete and soulless, but can see a good young crowd.

Patty's Villa, Main St, Hillsborough, **t** 443 8412. Set in a pretty garden, this restored home has a certain West Indian style. The dining room's right on the waterfront.

Hope's Inn, L'Esterre Bay, **t** 443 7457. Very simple and right on the beach.

Carriacou Yacht and Beach Club, Tyrell Bay, **t** 443 6123, *cyc@grenadines.net*. Easy-going, with just four rooms on the south side of the bay on the waterfront.

Alexi's Luxury Apartment Hotel, Tyrell Bay, **t** 443 7179. One of a number of guest houses on the main strip. Ten suites with kitchenettes and three single rooms with private bathrooms.

Constant Spring Guest House, Tyrell Bay, **t** 443 7396. Very simple, with three rooms and shared kitchen and bathroom.

Petite Martinique **t** (1 473–)

Seaside View Holiday Cottages, **t** 443 9007, (*inexpensive*). Just four rooms with a bar and cooking facilities. A fine view of the island of Petit St Vincent and other Grenadines. Simple and low-key.

Melodies Guest House, **t** 443 9052 (*inexpensive*). A budget option.

Eating Out

Carriacou

There are quite a number of restaurants outside the hotels in Carriacou, but Carriacou's truly laid-back style extends to most kitchens, so eating out is a little haphazard. You often find yourself waiting for an eternity for literally anything to eat (much of it is defrosted only when you place your order).

Moderate

Callaloo, Main St, Hillsborough, **t** 443 8004. A charming spot where you sit at tables on the waterfront with a fantastic view. There is a long list of cocktails to start, followed by callaloo soup, of course, and then honey-ginger chicken breast or local catch in garlic butter. There are sailing scenes painted on calabashes on the walls. Lunch-time salads and sandwiches.

The Seawave Restaurant, Hillsborough, **t** 443 7337. Wholesome West Indian fare: local soup followed by chicken or fish with a tonnage of ground provisions, then tropical fruit ice cream.

Poivre et Sel, Tyrell Bay, **t** 443 8390. Serves French fare on a balcony upstairs: fish *en papillote* followed by crêpes Suzette.

Le Petit Conch Shell, Tyrell Bay. Sits back from the beachfront. Soups to start, then chops, burgers, chicken or fish. On a small veranda setting, or air-con inside.

Inexpensive

Scraper's, Tyrell Bay. For a spicy barbecue chicken.

Twilight Bar, Tyrell Bay. For chicken or fish.

Petite Martinique

Palm Beach Restaurant, **t** 443 9103 (*moderate*). For reliable local fare.

Bars and Nightlife

Carriacou

There are a number of waterfront bars here, palm-thatch lean-tos where you can sit with a rum punch and watch for the Green Flash.

Alexi's Bar, Tyrell Bay. With a palm-thatch shelter and a cannon to sit on.

The Anchor Bar, Hillsborough. Where you can stop and catch up on island gossip.

---

thing like a treasure hunt. On the track north from Bogles look for a gnarled tree leaning over the road; turn left by the boulders down on to a track through the bush to a clearing with a dried pond and a ruin; then right and down the hill at a black rock which you recognize because it usually has a conch shell perched on the top. Anse la Roche is an idyllic cove. Round the northern point beyond here is another superb beach in Windward Bay, called **Petit Carenage**. Be careful with personal security on isolated beaches in Carriacou as there have been thefts and worse.

It is also fun to take a trip to one of the sand bars in Hillsborough Bay, tiny islets with just a few palms: **Mabouya** (from the Indian for 'evil spirits'), **Jack Adam**, whose name is a mystery, and **Sandy Island**, sometimes indistinguishable in the haze, which is supposedly silting away at the moment. A number of boats operate out of Hillsborough, serving day-trippers from Grenada. Ask around for spaces, or contact Snagg's Water Taxi, **t** 443 8293, or Carriacou Silver Diving, **t** 443 7782.

Around the Island

Stretched along the seafront, **Hillsborough** is the only settlement that constitutes a town. The centre of activity is the jetty, which comes alive when the boats bring mail and provisions. The two streets contain all the island's official buildings (including Immigration if you come by boat), banks and telephone company. There is a **museum** (*small adm*) in a restored cotton ginnery building, with a display of Amerindian history including zemies and pottery figurines, patterned body stamps and a well casing, a series of bottomless pots placed over a spring; of European heritage are weapons, lime juicers (with spikes like a bed of nails), oil storage urns and even a bed pan. The small **botanical garden** is now in extreme disrepair, with just a couple of benches beneath the palm trees.

Above the town is the great house of **Belair**, with its windmill tower, from where the view stretches both ways along the chain of the Grenadines, south to Grenada and as far as St Vincent in the north. The area was used by the PRG as their principal army base during their tenure in the early 1980s. Heading south from Hillsborough, you pass the airport, which has recently installed electronic gates to hold up the traffic when a plane is coming in, and then **L'Esterre**, where you can visit the art shop of **Mr Canute Caliste**, whose naïve paintings are now world-famous. Beyond here is the area of **Tyrell Bay**, a popular anchorage for yachts heading up and down the island chain.

Petite Martinique

The inhabitants of this tiny island, which lies about 3 miles east of Carriacou, are also fishermen and boat-builders, reputedly even more closely involved in smuggling than their neighbours. Perhaps as a result, they are supposed to have one of the highest per capita incomes in the Caribbean. In an effort to clamp down on smuggling there has been a joint operation between the Grenadian government and the Americans to build a coastguard dock (officially to help in preventing the drugs trade). They got no help from the Petite Martinicans, who promptly burned it down (they have a history of throwing customs officers off the island during previous attempts). However, it looks as though it is there to stay now.

The Petite Martinicans are fiercely independent. There is a small and close-knit community of about 1,000 islanders. The atmosphere on the island is slightly listless, the main activity being at the dock when a ship puts in, and at festival time – there is a regatta in April. The island's name (which for grammatical correctness is spelled Petite, but which is pronounced more like 'Petty') is thought to come from the fact that, like the island of Martinique, it has snakes. It is said that rival colonies would introduce snakes on to islands to make life more difficult for the settlers.

St Vincent and the Grenadines

St Vincent and the Grenadines offer a classic Caribbean combination, of local island life and luxurious small-island seclusion. Side by side stand the staggering lushness and friendly way of the Windward Islands, and the slow-time, easy life of the tiny Grenadines, 30 islands strung out over 60 miles of strikingly blue sea, each a short hop from the next. Once the heartland of Indian resistance against the European colonists, where Caribs would ply the waters in their war canoes, St Vincent and the Grenadines are now cruised by more peaceful craft. The islands have become a sailor's paradise and home to some of the smartest hotels and villas in the world.

St Vincent stands in the north, set between the Atlantic and the Caribbean Sea, like a massive cut emerald with facets of lush forested slopes stacked irregularly, rising to the central mountain range of Morne Garu. At 18 miles by 11, this fertile island is the smallest link in the Windward Islands. It is so rough and mountainous that even now no roads cross the body of the island. They run instead up the coasts. In the north, St Vincent is dominated by the mighty Soufrière, a distinctly active volcano, which last blew in 1979, showering the island with ash and adding yet more fertilizer to the extraordinarily rich land. You could almost expect a pencil to take root in the deep brown earth of the Mesopotamia Valley. In Kingstown are the oldest botanical gardens in the Americas, 20 acres of spectacular tropical abundance of scarlet, yellow and purple blooms.

Many of the 111,000 islanders live a simple life dependent on the land or the sea. With little industry, there is high unemployment and, despite severe problems with the banana trade, agriculture is still the economic mainstay. The principal exports are bananas, coconut products and arrowroot, a starch once used by the Indians as an antidote to poisoned arrows and now used in biscuits, computer paper and baby food. Fruit and vegetables are sent to nearby Barbados, and as far afield as the Virgin Islands. St Vincent itself is still relatively undeveloped, increasingly so in comparison with its neighbours Grenada and St Lucia: there are not too many tourists and it is unscarred by the high-rise concrete monstrosities of mass development. It doesn't really have the beaches anyway. The Grenadines depend much more heavily on tourism, though, and an hour's sail will take you from simple island life to the most expensive island luxury. In centuries past, the Grenadines would be leased out for a hundred years on West Indian charters and turned into plantations. Nowadays, developers lease them to create some of the most exclusive resorts in the world.

The tropical island idyll is perfected here, isolation with a view over dazzling white sand to islands that fade to grey on the sea horizon. You can be so secluded that you communicate by flag. Two hundred years ago the message might have been 'Bear to leeward, danger, reefs'. Now, with room service just at hand to pamper you, you are

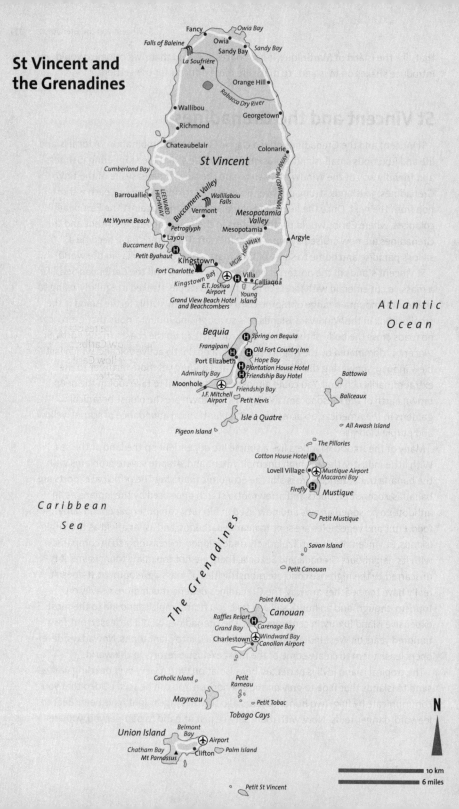

St Vincent and
the Grenadines

St Vincent

Fancy

Falls of Baleine

Owia Bay

Owia

Sandy Bay

Sandy Bay

La Soufrière

Orange Hill

Rabacca Dry River

Wallibou

Georgetown

Richmond

Chateaubelair

Colonarie

Cumberland Bay

LEEWARD HIGHWAY

Barrouallie

Wallilabou Falls

Mt Wynne Beach

Vermont

Buccament Valley

Mesopotamia Valley

WINDWARD HIGHWAY

Petroglyph

Mesopotamia

Layou

Argyle

Buccament Bay

Petit Byahaut

VIGIE HIGHWAY

Kingstown

Fort Charlotte

Villa

Kingstown Bay

E.T. Joshua Airport

Calliaqua

Young Island

Grand View Beach Hotel
and Beachcombers

*Atlantic
Ocean*

Bequia

Spring on Bequia

Frangipani

Old Fort Country Inn

Port Elizabeth

Hope Bay

Plantation House Hotel

Admiralty Bay

Friendship Bay Hotel

Moonhole

Friendship Bay

J.F. Mitchell
Airport

Petit Nevis

Battowia

Baliceaux

Isle à Quatre

Pigeon Island

All Awash Island

The Pillories

Cotton House Hotel

Mustique Airport

Lovell Village

Macaroni Bay

Firefly

Mustique

*Caribbean
Sea*

Petit Mustique

Savan Island

Petit Canouan

Point Moody

Raffles Resort

Canouan

Grand Bay

Carenage Bay

Charlestown

Windward Bay

Canollan Airport

Catholic Island

Petit
Rameau

Petit Tobac

Mayreau

Tobago Cays

Union Island

Belmont
Bay

Airport

Chatham Bay

Clifton

Palm Island

Mt Parnassus

Petit St Vincent

The Grenadines

N

10 km

6 miles

more likely to string up: 'Orange juice, coffee and croissants' or 'We do not want to be disturbed'.

History

With little strategic value, inhospitable St Vincent was given a wide berth by the early European visitors. Hairoun was wild even among the 'Cannibal Isles'. It was a Carib stronghold, and the newcomers would all too often be confronted by a shower of arrows and the barbecue spit. As the Europeans picked off the other islands in their quest for empire, St Vincent was bypassed and gradually it became a sanctuary for the Caribs, left as a European no-man's-land as late as 1750, a place where the Carib race could live out the last of their days.

St Vincent also became a refuge for slaves, who first arrived in 1675, when a slave ship was wrecked off Bequia. As word got out, escaping Africans made their way from the islands around, St Lucia and Grenada, to join them. From Barbados, slaves would cast off on rafts and drift a hundred miles with the wind in a desperate bid for freedom.

The Africans mixed with the local Indians, the Yellow Caribs, to create a 'tall and stout' race known as the Black Caribs. This fierce new tribe took over the resistance to the European colonizers and eventually dominated the original Yellow Caribs, taking their land. Faced with extinction at the hands of their cousins, the Yellow Caribs promptly invited the French to settle St Vincent in 1719. The French settlers brought African slaves to work plantations. Fearing for their freedom, the Black Caribs retreated to the hills, where they distinguished themselves from the newcomers by wearing bands around their calves and upper arms and by deforming their babies' skulls in old Carib style with tightly bound slats of wood, giving them foreheads that sloped upwards to a point.

The Black Caribs kept the colonizers at bay for another 50 years. In the Treaty of Aix-la-Chapelle in 1748, St Vincent was too hot to handle and so officially it was left neutral, with an unwritten clause that the European powers would fight over it later. By 1763 it was British. The new owners wanted the Black Carib land for their plantations and so they went in and took it in the First Carib War.

But soon afterwards the French were in control. They came in three sloops of war in 1779, unchallenged by the merchants of St Vincent, who were wide-eyed at the opportunity of trade. The soldiers were all at work on the Governor's plantation up north and the key to the battery was apparently lost in any case, so the invaders just landed and took the place over. In moments the island had surrendered.

Four years later the British were back, and they were faced with another Black Carib uprising in the 1790s in the Second Carib War, or Brigands' War, whipped up by Victor Hugues in Guadeloupe, who was spreading revolutionary fervour around the islands. Duvallé, a violent leader, swept down the east coast, burning the plantations and killing the British planters by passing them through the crushing gear in the sugar mills. On the west coast the overall chief, Chatoyer (also Chattawar), spared them such destruction, save for a single sideboard which he sliced with his cutlass to show his intentions. Their armies came together like pincers in the south and they fortified themselves on the hills above Kingstown.

Chatoyer was killed in combat with the Militia Colonel Alexander Leith as Dorsetshire Hill was stormed. On his body was found a silver gorget, a present from Prince William, later King William IV, who had met him on a visit to the West Indies in the ship *Pegasus*. Chatoyer had dreamed of forging an island home for the Black Caribs, but his dreams died with him.

For a year the Black Caribs held on, attacking the British from the heights and slinking back into the jungle, but eventually, in 1797, General Abercromby gained the upper hand, razing their settlements and destroying their crops. He threatened them with surrender or extinction and 5,000 gave themselves up. They were deported to Roatán Island in the Bay of Honduras (their descendants can still be found there, a thriving community). The Caribs living in the north of the island today are descended mainly from the few Yellow Caribs to survive the wars, forced to the north coast as the settlers took their fertile land. With the cannon silenced and the colonial map fixed in the early 1800s, St Vincent ended up in British hands and became another quiet agricultural island, growing sugar, Sea Island cotton and arrowroot, of which they held a large share of the world market.

Governed as part of the colony of the Windward Islands, St Vincent and the Grenadines became an Associated State of Britain in 1969 and then took their Independence on 27 October 1979, remaining within the Commonwealth. The present Governor General is Sir Frederick Ballantyne and the country is led by Ralph E. Gonsalves of the Unity Labour Party, which was elected in March 2001. The opposition is the New Democrat Party, led by Arnhim Eustace. Elections are next due in 2006.

St Vincent

Beaches

Steep-sided and volcanic, St Vincent has mainly black-sand beaches, except in the south, where the coast slopes more gently out towards the Grenadine Islands and where the wave action on the coral reefs pushes up whiter sand. The east coast, with the big breakers coming in from the Atlantic, is quite rough – for seclusion and the afternoon sun it is best to go to the leeward coast with its sheltered bays with black sand and fishing villages. The only busy beaches on St Vincent are in the south, the thin strips of sand around Kingstown and Villa.

Flora and Fauna

St Vincent is extraordinarily fertile and if you visit the upper valleys you will find a whole new world of explosive tropical vegetation. Vast areas of the island are unsettled, crossed only by farmers' tracks. Close to Kingstown is the fertile **Mesopotamia (Marriaqua) Valley**, where a great deal of the produce grows that later makes its way to market. There are also hummingbirds and tropical mockingbirds to be found among the heliconias and anthuriums in the **Montreal Gardens**, situated at the top of the valley.

Another fertile area is **Buccament Valley**, inland from Layou on the west coast, where vast forests of bamboo rise to 60ft and the rainforest begins, an infestation of creeping vines and lianas that clamber over gommier and mahogany trees. There are trails in the Vermont area and it is here that you have the best chance of spotting the endangered St Vincent parrot (*Amazona guildingii*) around dawn. Unique to the island, it has a white, blue and yellow head, a tawny brown body with blue wing tips and a tail of green, blue and yellow. The female is more colourful than the male and usually lays two eggs. There are thought to be only about 450 to 500 of these protected birds left. Another endemic species seen in the same area is the whistling warbler. It can also be seen in its reserve in the **St Vincent Botanical Gardens**. In the north of the island is the **Soufrière Volcano**, where the vegetation is different again, as rainforest gives way on the heights to elfin woodland, home to the rufous-throated solitaire.

Kingstown

The capital of St Vincent is set on the mile-wide sweep of Kingstown Bay at the southwest corner of the island. A town of about 16,000, it is surrounded by a ring of steep ridges spiked with palm trees, running from Cane Garden Point in the south to Berkshire Hill, where Fort Charlotte commands a magnificent view of the 60-mile string of the Grenadines. Downtown in quaint cobbled streets, modern glass-fronted shops stand out against the faded grandeur of old stone warehouses in the business centre near the waterfront. Vaulted walkways keep off the rain, the arches supporting the wooden upper storeys of the houses and sloping tin roofs, all strung together by a profusion of telephone wires.

On the higher ground of Kingstown stand the old colonial houses, once majestic in their open tropical gardens. Now they are jostled for space as the Kingstown suburbs

Getting There

St Vincent t (1 784–)

For information on how to get to the Grenadines, *see* p.187.

By Air

There are no direct flights to St Vincent from outside the Caribbean, so most visitors travel via Barbados, St Lucia or Grenada. *See* 'Getting There' under those islands.

LIAT, t 457 1821, flies from St Lucia, Grenada and Barbados. Caribbean Star, t 456 5555, flies from St Lucia and Grenada. Grenadines Air, t 456 6793, Mustique Airways, t 458 4380 and SVG Air, t 456 5610 operate shared charters between Barbados and St Vincent & the Grenadines. These carriers also operate numerous flights from Antigua, St Kitts, Tortola, Dominica, St Lucia, Grenada, and Trinidad and Tobago to St Vincent.

There is a departure tax of EC$40.

Getting Around

By Bus

The south coast of St Vincent and the major valleys are well served by dollar-buses, always a lively part of Vincentian life. The buses are cheap and you'll get to know your passengers pretty well, and the current popular tunes. As elsewhere in the Caribbean, many have a name on their bonnet: Hot Wax, Squealer, KRAP, Road Rash and, more enigmatically, Chemist and Polite. Buses leave from the new terminal on the Kingstown waterfront. Out on the road they can be waved down with a downward-pointing finger and an expectant face. To be dropped off, you must shout, 'Driver! Stop!'

Services on the coastal roads are sporadic so leave plenty of time to get there and back, but they run to Villa until as late as 11pm. Some fares are: Kingstown to Villa (Aquatic Club) – EC$1.50, to Mesopotamia – EC$2.50, to Georgetown – EC$4, to Layou – EC$2, and to Wallilabou – EC$3.

By Taxi

Taxis are readily available, at a rate fixed by the St Vincent Government or at EC$40 per hour. They can be arranged from hotels or found in the Market Square. Sample prices are: Kingstown to the airport – EC$20, to Villa – EC$25, to Fort Charlotte – EC$25, and to Layou – EC$50. From Arnos Vale Airport to the Villa/Young Island area costs EC$25.

By Guided Tour

Trips to the Grenadines and island tours, anything from a city tour to trips to remote villages and plantations or the volcano, can be arranged through one of the following:

Baleine Tours, t 457 4089, *prosec@carib surf.com*.

Fantasea Tours, t 457 4477, *fantasea@carib surf.com*.

HazECO, t 457 8634, *hazeco@caribsurf.com*, *www.begos.com/hazecotour*.

Sailor's Wilderness Tours, t 457 1712, *sailors tours@hotmail.com*.

Sam's Taxi & Tours, t 456 4338, *sam-taxi-tours@caribsurf.com*.

Sea Breeze Nature Tours, t 458 4969, *seabreezetours@vincysurf.com*.

Treasure Tours, t 456 6432, *treasuretours@ vincysurf.com*.

Car and Bike Hire

To drive a **hire car** in St Vincent you need to purchase a local driver's licence (EC$75; on presentation of a valid licence from home) at the airport or from the Licensing Authority on Halifax St in Kingstown (unfortunately you cannot do this with the car-hire companies). Driving is on the left and if you get lost do not hesitate to stop a Vincentian and ask for directions. Cars can be hired at a daily rate of about US$45 with deposit and insurance on top, from the following Kingstown companies:

Avis, t 456 2929.

Ben's Auto Rental, t 456 2907, *bensauto@ caribsurf.com*.

Greg's Rental Services, t 457 9814, *gregg@caribsurf.com*.

Rent & Drive, t 457 5601, *rentanddrive@ vincysurf.com*.

Motorbikes are available through Trotman's Depot, t 482 9498. **Bicycles**, or a cycling tour, are available through Sailors Cycle Centre, t 457 1712, *modernp@caribsurf.com*, *www.vincy.com/sailor*.

Tourist Information

Abroad

The official St Vincent and the Grenadines website is at *www.svgtourism.com*. The Hotel and Tourism Association is at *ww.svghotels.com*.

The St Vincent and the Grenadines tourist offices abroad are:

Canada: 333 Wilson Ave, Suite 601, Toronto M3H 1T2, **t** 416 457 1502, *svgtourismtoronto@ rogers.com*.

UK: 10 Kensington Court, London W8 5DL, **t** (020) 7937 6570, *svgtourismeurope@ aol.com*.

USA: 801 Second Ave, 21st Floor, New York, NY 10017, **t** (212) 687 4981, **t** 1 800 729 1726, *svgtony@aol.com*.

In St Vincent

Financial Complex, Cruise Ship Terminal, Bay St, Kingstown, **t** 457 1502, *tourism@ caribsurf.com. Open Mon–Fri 8–4.15*.

E.T. Joshua Airport, Arnos Vale, **t** 458 4685.

For those making connecting flights via Barbados, there is the St Vincent and the Grenadines desk at Barbados International Airport, **t** 428 0961 *(operates daily 1–8pm)*.

Embassies and Consulates

US/Canadian citizens are recommended to contact their embassy/high commission in Barbados *(see p.76)*.

British High Commission: Box 132, Granby St, Kingstown, **t** 457 1701, *bhcsvg@caribsurf.com*.

Media

The Hotel & Tourism Association produces *The Inns & Outs of St. Vincent and the Grenadines* (formerly *Escape Tourist Guide*). The Ministry of Tourism & Culture produces *Life In St Vincent and the Grenadines* (formerly *Discover*). Both publications have a wealth of useful tourist information.

Medical Emergencies

Contact the Milton Cato Memorial Hospital in Kingstown, **t** 456 1185.

Money and Banks

The **currency** of St Vincent and the Grenadines is the Eastern Caribbean dollar (EC$2.65 = US$1), but the **US dollar** and **traveller's cheques** are widely used too. Major **credit cards** are also accepted in the tourist centres. Be sure which currency you are dealing in, for example in taxis.

Banking hours are Mon–Thurs 8–1 or 3pm, Fri 8–5. For those passing through the island on their way to the Grenadines, there is a Bureau de Change at E. T. Joshua Airport, open Mon–Friday 8.30–12.30 and 3.30–5.30.

Shopping

Shops are open Mon–Fri 8–4, Sat 8–noon.

Telephone Code

The IDD code for St Vincent is **t** 1 784, followed by a seven-digit local number. On the island, and between the Grenadines, dial the full seven digits.

Festivals

January *Blues Fest*.

March *National Heroes Month* and *Heritage Month*.

April *Fisherman's Month*.

End June/early July *Carnival* (called Vincy Mas). The main event in the Vincentian calendar. A month of calypso competitions culminates in a jump-up in the streets of Kingstown, with steel bands and wild pageants of dancers all fired by rum and Hairoun, the Vincentian beer.

From 14 December *Nine Mornings Festival*. Christmas gets an early start. Vincentians stage nightly dances and parades through the streets, with carol singers and steel bands.

Watersports

St Vincent is not that developed and you will be dependent on the larger hotels and the dive shops for equipment. *See* below.

Day Sails

There are a lot of companies who arrange day sails through the Grenadine Islands and to the Falls of Baleine. Some of the hotels also have yachts on call for their guests. Contact: **Baleine Tours**, **t** 457 4089, *prosec@ caribsurf.com*.

Calypso Tours, t 456 1746, *calypso@caribsurf.com*, *www.vincy.com/calypso*. Offering a lively sun, fun and rum cruise.

Caribbean Fun Tours, t 456 5600, *info@ caribbeanfuntours.com*.

Fantasea Tours, t 457 4477, *fantasea@ caribsurf.com*, *www.fantaseatours.com*.

Sea Breeze Nature Tours, t 458 4969, *www.vincy.com/seabreeze*.

Princess Ria Tours, t 528 8989, *rogeradams@vincysurf.com*.

Sailing

The Grenadines are among the world's top sailing destinations. The islands are extremely beautiful, dramatic yellow and grey-green colossi that stand out against a bright blue sky and an aquamarine sea. As you cruise, dolphins play at the prow of your yacht and schools of gar fish jump up ahead, 20 silver flashes sewing their way through the water. But the big attraction is to moor in a secluded bay where the water is crystal clear and the beach is pristine white, and the Grenadines can provide this too. As a general rule, the Grenadines are less developed than the British Virgin Islands and the sailing is more exposed. Many people charter yachts out of Grenada and St Lucia and then make their way to the Grenadines, but in St Vincent you can arrange to charter through:

Barefoot Yacht Charters, Blue Lagoon, beyond Calliaqua on the south coast, t 456 9526, *barebum@caribsurf.com*, *www.barefoot yachts.com*. They have a fleet of bare boats and a sailing school.

Sunsail, Blue Lagoon, t 458 4308, *sunsailsvg@ caribsurf.com*, *www.sunsail.com*, *www. lagoonmarina.com*.

TMM, t 456 9608, US t 1800 633 0155, *sailtmm@caribsurf.com*. With bare boats and crewed yachts.

Scuba Diving

There is a general website at *www.scubasvg. com*. The fish life of the Grenadines is good and there are some excellent coral reefs on the leeward shore of St Vincent, where you will find caves and a wall from 20ft. Contact:

Dive St Vincent, Villa, t 457 4928, *bill2s@ divestvincent.com*, *www.divestvincent.com*.

An excellent option, if you are travelling down the islands, is to buy a 10-dive 'rollover' package, which can be spread between Dive St Vincent, Dive Bequia and Grenadines Dive (in Union Island).

Dive Fantasea, Villa, t 457 4477, *divefantasea@ vincysurf.com*, *www.divefantasea.com*.

Snorkelling

There is very attractive coral off Young Island and equipment is available in Villa. Snorkelling tours and Grenadine Island tours are offered by Baleine Tours, Villa, t 457 4089, *prosec@ caribsurf.com*.

Other Sports

Hiking

Walking in St Vincent's fertile country is a pleasure that has been enjoyed by visitors for more than 200 years. It is an adventurous 3hr hike up through seasonal forest, rainforest, and elfin and montane woodland to the lip of the Soufrière, from where there is a cracking view of the steaming crater and across the island. If a 4,000ft climb seems daunting, follow instead the Vermont Nature Trails in the Buccament Valley off the Leeward Highway, where there is a chance of seeing the St Vincent parrot in the evergreen forest and the rainforest.

The lush mountainsides of St Vincent are cut by waterfalls, perfect for a walk through the forest and a dip. The most spectacular are the Falls of Baleine in the north of the island (these must be approached by sea and there are plenty of operators who will take you there; *see* 'Day Sails', above), but others can be found at Trinity, up from Wallilabou, and inland from there at Hermitage. On the windward coast there is good walking around Colonarie and there are rock pools which make for good swimming in the South Rivers Valley, unless of course somebody has got there before you to do their washing or to take a bath.

Guides are available through the Tourist Board, the Forestry Department or through the tour companies listed under 'Getting Around', above. Or contact:

Sailor's Wilderness Tours, t 457 1712, *sailors tours@hotmail.com*.

Where to Stay

St Vincent **t** (1 784–)

St Vincent remains relatively undeveloped, untouched by international hotel corporations and their concrete plant. Most of the hotels are small (the largest has just 30-odd rooms) and many have the friendly atmosphere of West Indian inns and are set in attractive old-fashioned houses, family homes or the old buildings of Kingstown. Apart from the few in Kingstown, the hotels are mainly on the white sand beaches of the south coast, particularly around Villa, which is about 10 minutes' ride from the capital. There is never a problem finding a room in St Vincent (but you are advised to book ahead for the more exclusive retreats) and there are very good prices available, too. However, a 7% government tax will be added to all hotel bills and most hotels charge a 10% service charge.

Very Expensive

Young Island, PO Box 211, **t** 458 4826, US **t** 1 800 223 1108, *youngisland@caribsurf.com*, *www.youngisland.com*. Lying 200 yards off the south coast of St Vincent and reached by a wonderful old African Queen-style tub, this resort offers hospitality in true Vincentian style. There are 30 cottages of local stone scattered on the slopes of the tiny island and lost in a profuse and charming tropical garden. Each room has its own terrace and is screened, with huge louvred windows and ceiling fans to chop the cool sea breeze. You dine under small palm-thatched huts lost in the greenery, looking onto the beach and across to St Vincent. There is a tennis court on the island and some watersports are laid on. You can vary nights in the hotel with nights aboard one of the yachts. Don't miss the hammocks on the beach, slung under a palm-thatch roof, big enough for two.

Petit Byahaut, **t** 457 7008, *info@petitbyahaut.com*, *www.petitbyahaut.com*. Off the beaten track in style and location, hidden in a cove on the leeward coast where the emerald water is enclosed by huge headlands. It is accessible only by boat. The 'rooms' are permanent tents with tin roofs, each lost in hillside greenery and invisible from the next, with hammocks and showers, ranged on the hillside above the bay. Bathroom walls are usually palm trees and you may have a loo with a view. Plenty of peace and seclusion. It's a nature-lover's resort and environmentally friendly (solar power) with low-fat, healthy eating on the dining terrace. All meals and watersports (except scuba) are included in the daily rate.

Expensive

Grand View Beach Hotel, Villa Point, **t** 458 4811, *grandview@caribsurf.com*, *www.grandviewhotel.com*. A 19th-century, cotton plantation, great house set in eight acres of tropical gardens on the south tip of St Vincent, with a view of the Grenadines. There are 19 rooms, two restaurants (Wilkie's and Grand View Grill), a fitness centre, sauna, pool, tennis and squash courts.

Moderate

Roy's Inn, Kingstown, **t** 456 2100, *roysinn@vincysurf.com*, *www.roysinn.com*. Set high on the hill overlooking the town, on the site of the former Governor's residence. Classical features run riot, with white pillars and balustrades around the pool and a mock antique air in the drawing and dining room (which is good). Beauty salon and gym. Quiet and private.

Beachcombers, Indian Bay, near Villa, PO Box 126, **t** 458 4283, *beachcombers@caribsurf.com*, *www.beachcombershotel.com*. A charming small inn set in the sloping gardens of a former private house, where gazebos and cottages sit among mango trees and tropical shrubs running down to a small stretch of beach. Very quiet and friendly, with 13 comfortable rooms in bright tropical colours (all with phone, fans, terrace, and some with air-con). There's a nice open-sided beach bar and good pool deck, even a health spa in the new block.

The Cobblestone Inn, Kingstown, PO Box 867, **t** 456 1937, *cobblestone@caribsurf.com*, *www.cobblestoneinn.com*. Set on multiple levels around a courtyard in a fine old warehouse with a wooden interior. Bright, floral furnishings in the 19 air-conditioned rooms with phones, TVs and private baths, and a rooftop restaurant.

Adam's Apartments, Arnos Vale, t 458 4656, *abel@caribsurf.com*. Six self-contained apartments with cooking facilities.

Inexpensive

Bella Vista Inn, Kingstown Park, above Kingstown, t 457 2757. There is an odd and friendly charm here. Simple rooms, some with private bath, all with hot and cold water and fans; breakfast and dinner available.

Eating Out

By and large, Vincentian food is solidly West Indian. Some restaurants will take credit cards, but ask beforehand. There is a 7% government tax to add to all bills, and most restaurants will charge 10% for service. **Categories** are arranged according to the price of a main course: expensive = EC$50 and above, moderate = EC$20–50, inexpensive = less than EC$20.

Expensive

Young Island, t 458 4826, *youngisland@caribsurf.com, www.youngisland.com*. One of the best restaurants in St Vincent, offering one of the most romantic settings in the Caribbean. The menu is eclectic but you can count on seafood and a choice of six delicious breads.

Lime Restaurant and Pub, Villa, t 458 4227. There is a lively atmosphere here, with two dining rooms: a formal one on a raised veranda festooned with greenery; or, for snacks, on a covered terrace hung with fish-abilia. Long international menu with seafood – devilled crab back or fillet of fish – with pub specials including fish and chips and cottage pie. Pizzas to take away, some entertainment and a long list of dubious-sounding cocktails – try a Lime Orgasm or Slippery Nipple.

Basil's Bar and Restaurant, Kingstown, t 457 2713. Set in old-time Kingstown. Popular at lunch for the buffet. Dinner is grilled seafood crêpe followed by steamed fish or shrimp in ginger sauce.

Moderate

Beachcombers, Indian Bay, near Villa, t 458 4283. On a pleasant deck looking onto the garden and the beach: daytime sandwiches, burgers and *rotis*; in the evening stir-fried fish or a fillet of fish in herb butter.

Vee Jay's Rooftop Diner, Upper Bay St, Kingstown, t 457 2845. Lunch and dinner, with a live band on Fridays. Good West Indian and international fare.

Aggie's, Kingstown Hill, t 456 2110. You will find a variety of seafood such as whelks and conch, or a grilled fish in a creole sauce, always accompanied by local fruit juices.

The Bounty, Halifax St, Kingstown, t 456 1776. You can grab a *roti* or a sandwich at lunch time.

Club Calabash, Bentick Square, Kingstown. The speciality is West Indian fare.

Paradise Restaurant, Villa. West Indian and international selections.

Sunshine Restaurant & Bar, Grenville Street, Kingstown. Mostly West Indian dishes.

There are any number of pizza shops and Kentucky Fried Chicken shops in Kingstown and environs.

Bars and Nightlife

Nightlife is pretty quiet in St Vincent and is centred mainly on the hotels, which stage steel bands occasionally. Villa is a natural gathering place where you will find visitors and passing sailors ashore for a beer and a game of darts and then discos at the weekend. In Kingstown there are any number of bars in which to sit and have a Hairoun or an award-winning EKU beer, both of which are brewed in St Vincent. In addition to St Vincent's powerful rums, you might also try a sea-moss (made with seaweed, milk and spices) or a linseed (as in linseed oil), both slightly sick-sweet drinks that are supposed to be aphrodisiacs.

Lime Restaurant and Pub, Villa. *See* 'Eating Out', above.

Aggie's, Kingstown Hill. Collects an amusing crowd of locals.

Marcomay, Villa. Draws a young crowd.

Extreme, Kingstown. Draws an even younger crowd.

Vee Jay's, Upper Bay St, Kingstown. Ever popular, with calypsonians and bands.

The Attic, corner of Melville and Grenville Sts, Kingstown. Big-screen TVs and pictures of jazz musicians.

encroach. Overlooking the town from their perches on the heights are the modern houses of today's wealthy Vincentians, some of whom have returned to their island and built homes after working abroad for years.

Down on the **waterfront**, Kingstown is always busy: cargoes of tinned food and timber are hauled aboard and stacked under tarpaulin at the Deep Water Pier, where the massive hulks of cruise ships seem to hover above the town, and at the Grenadines Wharf, where the boats depart for the journey south to the Grenadines. Along the waterfront are the Financial Complex and the **National Bank**, a modern colossus towering above the town. Beyond here are the bus terminal and the new **fish market**, where men in stained working coats pour out boxes of sprats and slap brightly coloured snappers on the marble slabs. Close by is the now candy-coloured **Central Market** building, from which the bustle spills out onto the pavements of Bay St and Bedford St. In the hustle, trays of sweets are thrust under your nose and the market ladies, their skirts rolled up over their knees, remonstrate with buyers, selling their fruits and vegetables from the piles on tables and blankets spread out before them.

Officialdom keeps its distance from all this activity on the other side of Halifax St, opposite a small grass square with a war memorial, behind the iron railings of the **Law Courts**. The building, with its small but imposing stone façade, green tin roof and louvred windows with white surrounds, is where the 15-member St Vincent Parliament and six senators meet.

The Kingstown skyline of steep sloping roofs is broken by church towers. The large Methodist church stands nearly opposite **St George's Anglican Cathedral**, a brightly painted Georgian structure with a castellated clock tower, which was built in 1820 as the cathedral of the Anglican diocese of the Windward Islands, partly from government money that came from the sale of Carib lands. The stained-glass window with the red angel was supposedly commissioned by Queen Victoria for St Paul's Cathedral, in honour of her first great-grandson (later King Edward VIII), but she rejected it on the grounds that in the Bible the angels were dressed in white. It was given to Bishop Jackson by Dean Inge of St Paul's and he brought it to St Vincent. Inside, a tablet commemorates Major Alexander Leith, a hero of the Brigands' War of 1795, who killed the Carib leader Chatoyer. The most surprising architectural feature of Kingstown is the **Roman Catholic church**, presbytery and school. Built in 1823 and enlarged in 1877 and 1891, it is a riot of styles in dark brick, a hodgepodge of Romanesque arches and Gothic pointings that would be more at home in a medieval European fantasyland.

The St Vincent Museum (*open Wed 9–12 and Sat 2–6, plus when there is a cruise ship in town and for pre-arranged groups; adm*), which was in the grounds of the Botanical Gardens, has moved. At the time of writing it was still looking for a home, though it was possibly going to one of Kingstown's lovely old stone buildings (formerly the Public Library), complete with arched portico on the corner of Halifax St and South River Rd. Wherever they end up, the exhibits are the same, fierce and sublime faces in stone and pottery left by the Arawaks and Carib Indians and later artefacts from the Black Carib wars of the 18th century.

The St Vincent Botanical Gardens

Open dawn–dusk; adm free, but depending on the number of people you might give a guide EC$15 for an hour's tour.

Behind the town, on the steep slopes facing into Kingstown Valley, just off the road north to Layou, are the Botanical Gardens, the oldest in the Americas and one of the delights of the Caribbean. The walkways and lawns are bordered by an overwhelming abundance of tropical splendour: bushes bursting with the brightest flowers, trees with heavy aromas, and palms that soar and sway overhead.

Founded in 1765, the gardens were run commercially in order to propagate useful species from all over the world in the Caribbean, and were connected to the Botanical Gardens at Kew in London. Interestingly it was to the West Indies that Captain Bligh was heading on his fateful voyage in the *Bounty* in 1787. He was on a commission for the Society of West Indian Merchants to bring the breadfruit tree from the South Seas to St Vincent, where it could be used as food for the slaves on the plantations. Cast adrift with 18 loyal officers by his mutinous crew, he sailed 4,000 miles to Timor without the loss of a life.

Six years later, this time in the ship *Providence*, he succeeded in bringing over 400 specimens of the breadfruit tree to St Vincent intact, and offshoots of them still grow in the gardens today. Ironically, the slaves would not touch the new food when it first arrived, but nowadays the huge perennial tree, with its lustrous dark green leaves shaped like medieval flames, can be seen all over the Caribbean. The starchy fruit starts life as a small green lollipop and then turns over with the weight, swelling to the size of a cannonball and dropping to the ground with a thud. Boiled or steamed, it is a popular supplement to the 21st-century Caribbean diet.

The guides are helpful (basically you will not escape without one). In their jargon they offer an 'educational tour', which is probably worth taking because, even if their botanical knowledge is often a little shaky, they do know all the amusing plants to show off, telling stories and crushing leaves for the aroma – cinnamon, citronella, camphor and clove. There is a small trail at the bottom of the garden with signboards to illuminate the wet tropics, with descriptions of epiphytes, cycads and coconuts.

The gardens are well worth a visit, a fascinating hour even for botanical novices. They are full of gems like the sandpaper tree, with leaves as rough as emery paper, and the velcro tree, *flambago*, related to flax, to which material sticks. And there is the waterproof lotus lily, on which water rolls in beads like mercury (put them underwater and the waterproof pink leaves take on a silver sheen and then come out dry). There is the tree of life, or *Lignum vitae*, whose wood is so hard that it was used to replace iron as bearings for propellor shafts; the sealing-wax or lipstick palm that seeps bright red; and the mahogany tree, whose pods explode, releasing a shower of whirling seeds like a sycamore. At sundown, when the white-painted trunks of the palms loom in the obscurity, the flowers of the cannonball tree that open in the day fall to the ground, and the air is heavy with the aroma of jasmine.

Above the Botanical Gardens to the north is the house of the Governor General, and to the eastern side, where you might hear chattering and squawking, is an **aviary** with the endangered blue-brown St Vincent parrot – some of which are in a captive breeding programme after recovery from illegal hunters. There are a few other animals on show, including an agouti and a Barbados green monkey.

Fort Charlotte

Open during office hours (roughly speaking); adm.

This lumbering giant on the Berkshire Hill promontory is worth a visit if only for the fantastic view north along the leeward coast, on to Kingstown and over the Grenadine Islands scattered to the south. It is a pleasant half-hour walk from town, through local communities and mostly uphill. Constructed at the beginning of the 19th century and taking its name from George III's queen, Fort Charlotte was once the island's main defence, with barracks for 600 men and 34 cannon. For all this hardware and manpower, the fort saw action only once, an argument between two men just outside the gates, in which a Private Ballasty killed Major Champion in 1824. The perpetrator was tried and hanged on the same spot.

The fort stands 630ft above the sea and is approached by way of a steep causeway and through an arch. Only a few of the cannon remain (and interestingly they point inland) and the barracks now house a museum of the Carib Wars. It is illustrated with a series of paintings by Lindsay Prescott, picturing important moments such as the death of the Carib Chief Chatoyer and the deportation of the Black Caribs in 1797.

Around the Island

The South

Leaving Kingstown Valley to the east, you come to the airport at Arnos Vale. From here the road (the Vigie Highway) leads inland to **Marriaqua**, often known as **Mesopotamia** after a town that is spread along the sides of this extraordinarily lush valley. The steep ground is terraced and the rivers come together at the spectacular **Yambou Gorge**. Kids play cricket in the road by the pastel-coloured houses perched on the hillsides among a profusion of greens: banana, breadfruit and coconut.

The ridge at **Vigie** (French for 'look out') gives spectacular views of Kingstown. The Carib camp was situated here in the war of 1795–6 and it was fortified with earth-filled sugar hogsheads (cone-shaped moulds through which molasses was dripped after boiling). Higher up, lost in the mountains, are the **Montreal Gardens**, with walkways through the tropical foliage, nutmegs and citrus. The gardens specialize in anthuriums, grown here commercially and seen all over the West Indies, with a heart-shaped leaf like a vividly coloured plate and a long thin protrusion.

Following the coastline from E. T. Joshua Airport, the Windward Highway leads past the expensive houses of St Vincent's prime residential area to **Villa Point**, a charming line of former family holiday homes built in the early 20th century. They are all similar in style, with tall, gently sloping corrugated tin roofs. They have been converted into restaurants and small hotels, which has given the area a friendly seaside feel.

Opposite Villa, a little way out to sea is **Young Island**, one of the Caribbean's most charming settings for a hotel (*see* 'Where to Stay', p.179). Young Island takes its name from a Governor Young who brought a black stallion with him to St Vincent in the 18th century. The horse was admired by a chief of the Black Caribs, whereupon the gallant Sir William Young said, 'It is yours!' The chief took him at his word and rode off on it. Some time later, the Governor was with the Carib chief again, on the balcony of Government House in Calliaqua, and he admired the island off the coast. Not to be outdone, the Carib, who owned the island, said at once, 'Do you like it? It is yours!' It has remained Young Island ever since. The island is private, but visitors are allowed when the hotel is not full – you might go over in the evening for a cocktail. There is a telephone on the dock at Villa Point to call the ferry.

Fort Duvernette, behind Young Island, is an outcrop of rock that rises a sheer 200ft out of the water and is covered in dark green vegetation, marked on old maps as Young's Sugar Loaf. There are two batteries, still with some mortars and cannon from the reigns of George II and George III, covering the southern approaches to St Vincent, though it is now favoured more for its beauty than for any strategic significance. A staircase to the heights is cut out of the rock, and is worth the climb for the view across to the Grenadines. Visits can be arranged through the Young Island Hotel.

A little farther along the coast is the quiet town of **Calliaqua**, once St Vincent's capital and the residence of the Governor in Sir William Young's day.

The Windward Highway

The Windward Highway cuts in from the south coast beyond Calliaqua and emerges on the Atlantic at **Argyle**. Immediately the sea is rougher, with huge ocean breakers. This fertile sloping land originally belonged to the Carib Indians but the European planters steadily ate into it. As the road twists along the coastline, the skeletons of the old plantation prosperity are just visible, overwhelmed by the tropical under-growth. New plantations, acres of bananas and coconuts, can also be seen at every turn. Inland from Argyle, a short walk off the road to Mesopotamia that passes through the Yambou Gorge, are some **rock carvings**, squiggles and ghostly faces carved by the Arawak Indians, who lived on the island until about AD 1000.

Georgetown, 22 miles and a good hour's drive from Kingstown, was once a pros-perous centre, servicing the plantations of the windward coast. Now it is an empty town, its buildings run down. Beyond Georgetown, in the shadow of the Soufrière Volcano, the road crosses the **Rabacca Dry River**, a river course in a rainstorm and the path for lava after a volcanic explosion, and passes into the former Orange Hill Estate, once one of the largest coconut plantations in the world. In the villages of **Sandy Bay** and **Fancy** live the descendants of the Yellow Caribs. Even though they have now mixed and have considerable African blood, their Indian heritage of lighter skin and almond eyes is still clearly visible.

At **Owia** on the isolated northeastern tip of the island, about an hour beyond Georgetown on the rough roads, is a large pond fed by the sea, but protected from it by a barrier of rocks, a good place to stop for a swim. There is an **arrowroot factory** (*call in advance, t 458 6172; adm free*) in the town which may be visited.

The Soufrière Volcano

Dominating the whole of the northern end of the island is the St Vincent Soufrière Volcano, 3,000ft high and definitely still active, blowing occasionally in a pall of smoke, thunder and flame. Farmers in St Vincent speak of extraordinary abundance following the eruptions – outsize fruits that come out of season because the ash acts as a fertilizer.

The Soufrière spat fire in 1718 and then blew properly in 1812, spewing into the air ashes and sand that floated down on the island, leaving a white covering inches thick like snow. The pall of smoke was illuminated by darting electric flashes and accompanied by violent thunder, an earthquake and a stream of lava overflowing from the boiling crater. The cloud even plunged Barbados, 100 miles away, into darkness. Then it was quiet for another 90 years until 1902, when it blew again (in tandem with the cataclysmic explosion at St Pierre on Martinique), killing 2,000 people, mostly the descendants of the Caribs living on St Vincent's northern shore. On this occasion it rained stones for miles downwind, bombarding the fleeing Vincentians. The streams ran thick with ash and the noise was so terrible that people thought the island was sinking.

It was quiet until 1971, when a minor eruption created an island of lava in the crater lake, but on Good Friday, 13 April 1979, the Soufrière blew once more. A vast cloud of ash rose 20,000ft into the sky, and explosive gases boiled over the crater lip and raced down the mountainside, destroying any crops and houses in the way.

For all the activity, the Soufrière is quiet most of the time and it is a popular tour to explore the area and to climb it. The best places to approach it from are the Rabacca Dry River on the east coast, just north of Georgetown, and Richmond, north of Chateaubelair on the leeward coast, which is a gentler climb. It is about three hours' climb to the summit (from where you can descend 750ft into the crater, which steams from time to time). You are advised to arrange a guide and to take some food.

The Leeward Highway

The Leeward Highway winds along the west coast of the island, climbing over massive ridges and promontories and dropping into deep coves, some of them good shelters for passing yachtsmen, where small fishing villages of pretty clapboard houses sit on black, volcanic-sand beaches. Inland the valleys are steep-sided and draped in greenery.

About 3 miles from Kingstown the road passes the majestic Peniston or **Buccament Valley**. At the head of the valley there are nature trails that lead up into the depths of the rainforest in the hills. The road rejoins the coast at Layou, where there is a **petroglyph**, Arawak impressions scratched on a 20ft rock. It can be reached on foot by a 10-minute walk, though visitors should ask permission because it is over private land (ask at the Ministry of Tourism and they will arrange a guide). The road then passes on to the fishing village of **Barrouallie**, and just off the road not far up-river from **Wallilabou** you will find a fall that pours into a small rock pool, ideal for a midday dip. Ask around for directions. The road continues through the town of Chateaubelair and eventually comes to an end at **Richmond**, where there is an attractive bay and beach with just a few houses. A 15-minute hike inland from here you will find **Trinity Falls**, a stunning area surrounded by lush greenery where you can walk behind the cascade. Take a swimming costume for a dip in the two pools and the hot springs up above.

In the far north of the island are the **Falls of Baleine**. Here the river, which rises on the Soufrière, races down through the tropical forest and drops into a rock pool in a 60ft spray of warm water. They are inaccessible by road, so visits are made by boat – a great day out from Kingstown, coasting the leeward side of St Vincent, past all the fishing villages and landing on the northern tip of the island. From there it is a short walk in the river bed to the rock pool and the falls themselves, where you can swim. Outings can be arranged through one of the tour operators listed above (*see* 'Day Sails' under 'Watersports', p.177).

The Grenadines

Scattered over the 80 miles between the volcanic peaks of St Vincent and Grenada are the Grenadines, 30 tiny islands and cays that rise dramatically out of the Caribbean Sea and many more reefs and sand bars that barely cut the surface into surf. Here you will find some superb, deserted strips of sand, glaringly white against an aquamarine sea, protected by a rim of offshore reefs, where lines of silver breakers glint in the haze.

The Grenadines are some of the finest sailing grounds in the world – the white triangles of yachts ply from island to island, from the pretty waterfronts to isolated beaches and swim-up bars. An occasional clipper ship will cruise by with a full rig of sails. Each one an hour's sail from the next, the Grenadine Islands are an island-hopper's paradise.

Life for the locals is a much tougher prospect. Many of the islanders are poor, earning as little as US$5 for a day's work when they can get it, with expensive imported food to buy. Unemployment is high and very occasionally the inhabitants of the Grenadine Islands do feel neglected. (In 1979, just after Independence, there was an uprising on Union Island and 40 of the islanders staged an armed revolt.) Things have been changing steadily over the past few years. Tourism has provided considerable development and employment and it is generally accepted as a good thing by the islanders. Most of the time you can expect to be welcomed with customary Caribbean charm.

There is a traditional connection with the sea. Some islanders are fishermen and on the smaller islands there is something of a 'when the boat comes in' mentality, with life revolving around the dock when the mail boat makes its thrice-weekly visit, bringing the mail, as well as the weekly supply of soft drinks, beer, gas bottles and sheets of galvanized tin and sacks of cement for building.

There are some wonderful places to stay, many of them exclusive island resorts, just a few rooms on an isolated cove, or cottages ranged around the coastline of a secluded island. And then there are developed islands like Mustique, with luxury villas, and Bequia, with its pretty waterfront with bars and small hotels and robust local community. The Grenadines are not as developed as the Virgin Islands and they

Getting There

The Grenadines t (1 784–)

In the Grenadines you can register in Bequia, Mustique, Canouan and Union Island.

By Air

There are no direct flights to St Vincent or the Grenadines from outside the Caribbean, so most people travel via Barbados, St Lucia or Grenada.

From St Vincent

Small airlines link St Vincent (for getting to St Vincent, *see* p.176) to the Grenadines (Bequia, Mustique, Canouan, Union and Carriacou). Mayreau, the Tobago Cays, Palm Island and Petit St Vincent have no airstrip at all. SVG Air, **t** 457 5124, *svgair@caribsurf.com*, *www.svgair.com*, will stop on an island if there are more than two people who want to get off on their run down the islands, linking St Vincent to Bequia, Canouan, Union Island and Carriacou (Grenada). Air Caraïbes, **t** 458 4528, touches Union only and heads north to Martinique.

From Barbados

For those arriving at Barbados, the most reliable way to get to the Grenadines is to take one of the regular 'shared charter' flights. (In fact these flights are regular enough to be scheduled, but they are not listed on airline computer networks because they are officially charter airlines.) Contact Mustique Airways, **t** 458 4830, UK **t** (01242) 604 030, US **t** 1 800 526 4789, *info@mustique.com*, *www.mustique.com*; SVG Air, **t** 457 5124, *svgair@caribsurf.com*, *www.svgair.com*.

By Sea

The Grenadines are really about the sea and it is fun to travel by the local mail boat and the many smaller craft that make the island run. The mail boat, the MV *Barracuda*, **t** 456 5180, makes three sailings a week each way between Kingstown on St Vincent and Union Island, touching Bequia (1hr), Canouan (2hrs), Mayreau (1hr) and on to Union Island (30mins). It travels south on Mondays and Thursdays, north on Tuesdays and Fridays, and both ways on Saturdays. Fares are good: from St Vincent to Bequia – EC$15, to Canouan – EC$20, to Mayreau – EC$25, and to Union Island – EC$30.

Getting Around

By Air

Island-hopping by plane is the quickest and easiest way of getting around the Grenadines. You will also get some cracking views along the way. There are one or two slightly hairy airstrips – you can enjoy watching the next plane approach once you are safely on the ground.

Canouan and Bequia often have cross-winds, there is a steep descent and sometimes a bouncy landing on Mustique, and even with Union's new strip you still nearly touch the tree tops with the right wing tip as you turn in to land. The islands are typically low-key and you may come across nonchalant signs like:

CAUTION – AIRCRAFT
LOOK LEFT

See 'From St Vincent' under 'Getting There', above, for details of flights linking the islands and beyond.

By Sea

See 'Getting There', above, for details of the mail boat linking the islands. Once in the Grenadines you can visit other islands on day trips, with picnic and snorkelling gear included. You might also be able to persuade a fisherman to drop you on the next island, or luckier still, hitch a ride on a yacht.

Tourist Information

See 'St Vincent', pp.176–7, for general information. *See* individual islands for details of local tourist offices.

Festivals

Many of the Grenadine Islands stage regattas (Bequia at Easter and Canouan in May or June), after which there are always jump-ups.

have a rawer, more natural Caribbean air. Whether you are ensconced in luxurious seclusion in a private island resort or island-hopping by fishing boat and ferry, the Grenadines offer some of the best in easy island living.

Bequia

Bequia (pronounced Beck-way) is one of the Caribbean's neatest and prettiest island hideaways. Largest of the St Vincent Grenadines (an irregular splash, 5 miles by 2), it lies 9 miles, or an hour's sail, south of Kingstown. The sea approach to the main town of Port Elizabeth is glorious, as the rocky headlands glide by on both sides, towering above you.

The island is quite developed – Port Elizabeth caters well to the tourists, with T-shirts strung up at the waterfront like washing – but it holds it well. There is a picture-postcard perfection about Bequia and it is easy to be captivated by the island's charm. The 7,000 Bequians themselves are quiet and independent, still claiming to be a bit wary of 'Vincentians', who might almost come from a world away. A small community of white Bequians have lived isolated up on the hill above for years, though the younger generation has moved down now and are more visible in the community. There is a long tradition of boat-building on the island (and recently model boats for sale in the shops).

Around the Island

It is fun to explore Bequia, though 'sights' are limited. As you enter the harbour, Admiralty Bay (chosen by the British Navy as a port, but never occupied because of a lack of fresh water), you will see some dwellings built into the cliffside. Called **Moonhole** after a natural arch in the rock, they are private residences, perched right above the waves. Tours can be arranged (*t 458 3277*). The residents do not take kindly to people poking around uninvited. There is a small **fort** on the other side, on the point at Hamilton, where five cannon cover the approaches to Admiralty Bay. It is delightful to stroll from Port Elizabeth along the waterfront in the **Belmont** area, a

> ## Best Beaches
> **Lower Bay**: On the south side of Admiralty Bay (on which Port Elizabeth sits). The sumptuous golden sand is easily reached by sea taxi (just loiter on the Frangipani Hotel jetty, EC$15) or land taxi.
>
> **Princess Margaret Beach** (once **Tony Gibbons Bay**): A more secluded inlet, a little walk over the headland from Lower Bay, through the scrub.
>
> **Friendship Bay**: On the south coast is this huge half-moon of passable sand, with a view to Petit Nevis (an island still occasionally used by whalers from Bequia to section their catch).
>
> **Industry Bay** (also called **Crescent Bay**), **Spring Bay** and **Hope Bay**: East-coast coves worth a visit. Though it is officially against the rules, people have been known to skinny-dip at Hope Bay.

Getting There

Bequia t (1 784–)

By Air

Bequia is quite easy to get to. You fly into J.F. Mitchell Airport in the southwest of the island (taxi fare into Port Elizabeth EC$30). *See* 'Getting There', p.187, for details of flights from St Vincent and Barbados.

By Sea

Often there will be four or five sailings a day from St Vincent. The mail boat MV *Barracuda* stops there five times a week too (on its runs through the Genadines), though you may not want to depend on this because it has been known to sail straight past the harbour mouth, leaving potential passengers stranded.

Getting Around

Irregular **dollar-buses** (costing EC$2.60) ride up the steep slope from Port Elizabeth and over to Paget Farm.

Taxis are available through Challenger Taxi Service, t 458 3811.

Cars can be hired through Handy Andy Rental, t 458 3722, *mitchell@vincysurf.com*; B&G Jeep Rental, t 458 3760, *gideontaxi@vincysurf.com*; Olive's Rentals, t 457 3640, *olive@vincysurf.com*; Phil's Car Rental, t 458 3304, *julies@caribsurf.com*; Parnell's Moke Rental, t 457 3066.

Tourist Information

By the pier, Port Elizabeth, t 458 3286, *bequiatourism@caribsurf.com*, *www.bequiatourism.com*. Open Mon–Fri 8.30–6, Sat 8.30–2, Sun 8.30–12.

Maps and Books

There is an excellent bookshop, the Bequia Bookshop, on the waterfront in Port Elizabeth, with books and maps from around the Caribbean. Look out for *Bequia Sweet Sweet*, a book about the island.

Festivals

The liveliest times of year in Bequia are Christmas, when Admiralty Bay has barely a square foot of spare mooring space, and during the Easter Regatta.

January *Bequia Music Festival.*
March *Bequia Game Fishing Tournament* and *Bequia Easter Regatta* (sometimes April).
July *Bequia Fisherman's Day.*

Watersports

Watersports are best arranged through the hotels.

Day Sails

Though there are no major yacht charter operators in Bequia, there are plenty of yachts available for the day. Trips to the nearby offshore islets, to Mustique and along the coast of St Vincent to the Falls of Baleine, can be arranged on the following boats:

Friendship Rose, t 458 3661. An old Bequian schooner.

Michael Tours, Paget Farm, t 458 3801.

Passion, t 458 3884, *passion@caribsurf.com*. A catamaran. Also offers sport fishing.

Pelangi, Frangipani Hotel, t 458 3255, *frangi@caribsurf.com*. A yacht.

Quest, t 458 3917. A yacht offering overnight trips down through the Grenadines.

The Achiever II, Grenadines Adventure Sailing Co., t 458 3817, *quest@bequiasvg.com*.

Scuba Diving

You will find good reefs around Bequia and the smaller islands nearby. A wall drops from 30ft to 100ft and there are wrecks at the Devil's Table and Moonhole. The west coast of the island has been designated a national park: black-tipped sharks, rays and seahorses have been seen at the wall at West Cay. A one-tank dive costs about US$45.

Contact:

Bequia Dive Adventures, Belmont, t 458 3247, *adventures@caribsurf.com*.

Dive Bequia, Gingerbread Complex, Admiralty Bay, t 458 3504, *bobsax@caribsurf.com*, *www.divebequia.com*.

Dive Paradise, Friendship Bay, **t** 458 3563, *info@paradisebequia.com*, *www.paradise bequia.com*.

Snorkelling

Most of the dive companies listed above will also fix snorkelling tours.

Windsurfing

Windsurfers can hire equipment at the Gingerbread Complex on Admiralty Bay.

Where to Stay

Bequia t (1 784–)

Many of Bequia's small hotels (only one hotel has as many as 30 rooms) are set in fine buildings, restored forts or old family holiday homes. They have charm and character, lost in tropical gardens on the heights or down on the seafront in Belmont overlooking Admiralty Bay and the yachts at anchor.

As the island becomes more accessible, it is worth reserving a room on Bequia, particularly in the winter season.

Villas are available, through **Bequia Villa Rentals, t** 458 3393, *beqvilla@caribsurf.com*.

Very Expensive–Expensive

The Friendship Bay Resort Hotel, Friendship Bay, PO Box 9, **t** 458 3222, *friendshipbay@ caribcominc.com*, *www.caribcominc.com*. A charming hideaway on the south side of the island. Twenty-seven rooms and a honeymoon suite stand just above the beach and in blocks scattered around the main house (dining room and bar) on the steep hillside and tropical gardens; all are brightly coloured and very comfortable, some with gingerbread fretwork and many with a porch and a fantastic view. There is a charming bar and restaurant down on the beach (*see* under 'Eating Out'). Family-run and friendly, quite quiet and low-key (no TVs or even telephones in the rooms, but some watersports and yachts for sailaway packages).

Old Fort Country Inn, Mt Pleasant, east coast, PO Box 14, **t** 458 3440, *info@oldfortbequia.*

com, *www.oldfortbequia.com*. Small and private, set in an old stone house isolated high on the hilltop, from where there is a fort's eye view of the Grenadines, occasionally as far as Grenada. There are just five apartments in the house, each with its own individual charm, with wooden floors and big windows – rush mats and muslin nets on the beds – set in a garden with copper boilers, hammocks and a pool. With stone floor, arches and even a fireplace, the openfronted dining room is charming. It serves French, Italian and creole fare and looks out onto a pretty garden where peacocks, dogs and donkeys roam.

Spring on Bequia, Spring Bay, east coast, **t** 458 3414, US **t** (612) 823 1202, *springonbequia@ caribsurf.com*. Very quiet and isolated, with a dramatic setting looking over the palms on Bequia's isolated east coast. Just 10 rooms ranged in cottages of local stone on a steep hillside: rooms are louvred all around with hefty wood and have a large stone porch. Studiedly spartan, but ideal if you're happy to be utterly quiet and selfcontained, with minimal services and correspondingly lower prices. Freshwater pool and tennis court, plus all meals available. *Closed in summer.*

Moderate

Frangipani Hotel, Admiralty Bay, PO Box 1, **t** 458 3255, *frangi@caribsurf.com*, *www.frangi pani.net*. A delightful West Indian inn right on the waterfront. It has retained an air of the family house that it once was (it is the house of former Prime Minister Sir James Mitchell). There are 16 rooms in all, some simple ones in the charming wooden main house and then more comfortable units scattered around the gardens behind, where copper sugar boilers are shaded by mango trees and red and white frangipani. Prices vary considerably.

The Gingerbread Hotel, Belmont, **t** 458 3800, *ginger@caribsurf.com*, *www.begos.com/ gingerbread*. Not quite the authenticity of the Frangipani, but a modern West Indian building with many of the nice old traditional Caribbean features – louvred French doors onto balconies, ceiling fans, four-posters with muslin netting and, of course, the gingerbread woodwork of the name. Lively restaurant with entertainment a couple of times a week.

Inexpensive

L'Auberge des Grenadines, Belmont, **t** 458 3201, *auberge@caribrestaurant.com, www.carib restaurant.com*. A small setup with just five simple but comfortable rooms with cable TV, and a nice restaurant out front.

The Creole Garden Hotel, Lower Bay, **t** 458 3154, *dcreole@caribsurf.com, www.creolegarden. com*. High up on the hillside but still within a shout of the beach. Recently built in modern Caribbean style with concrete walls and tin roofs and smothered in greenery. There are five quite simple rooms and two one-room apartments with nice views. Some self-catering, but a good local restaurant and a friendly atmosphere.

Keegan's Beach Resort Ltd, Lower Bay, **t** 458 3530, *keegansbequia@yahoo.com*. A simpler stopover, now with a brightly painted deck. Fan-ventilated apartments and 11 rooms, one on the beach. *Rates include breakfast and dinner.*

The Lower Bay Guest House, Lower Bay, **t** 458 3675. Simple West Indian guest house lost in a tropical garden. Eight double rooms (some with shared bath), central TV room and veranda to sit on. Meals available.

Julie and Isola's Guest House, Back St just behind the jetty, Port Elizabeth, **t** 458 3304. Twenty simple rooms with private bathrooms. All meals available.

Eating Out

There is a surprising variety of dining on offer around Bequia, with Italian, French and French creole, as well as international and, of course, local fare.

The settings are more reliable than the food – as in so many islands, the standard and the service are a little haphazard – but with luck you'll have a good evening out. Generally,

eating out is quite expensive. Expect a 7% government charge at hotel restaurants and 10% for service to be added to your bill no matter where you eat.

Categories are arranged according to the price of a main course: expensive = EC$50 and above, moderate = EC$20–50, inexpensive = less than EC$20.

Expensive

L'Auberge des Grenadines, Belmont, **t** 458 3201. On the waterfront, French and Caribbean cuisine with plenty of seafood, including a lobster *vivier* from which you can pick your own and have it cooked flamed in rum or in lime butter.

Le Petit Jardin, Back St, Port Elizabeth, **t** 458 3318. Sophisticated French cuisine served in the subdued surroundings of a wooden dining room. A daily changing menu with lots of lobster, fish and seafood, including conch (the menu reads 'this known aphrodisiac is cooked in a very special way to enhance its power'). Other dishes include a *magret* of duck in a pink pepper sauce followed by a *méli-mélo de goyave* or a marble cheesecake.

The Gingerbread House, Belmont, **t** 458 3800. This restaurant provides an upstairs view of the yachts in harbour from an open veranda on the waterfront, looking through a filigree of gingerbread fretwork. Salads and burgers are served by day, with fancier fare at night – fish chowder or West Indian pumpkin and split-pea soup, speciality curries, spicy or mellow in coconut, and a long list of puddings.

Old Fort Country Inn and Restaurant, Mount Pleasant, **t** 458 3222, *info@oldfortbequia. com, www.oldfortbequia.com*. The setting and ambiance are as enjoyable as the creole, French and Italian cuisine.

Friendship Bay Restaurant, Friendship Bay, **t** 458 3222, *friendshipbay@caribcominc.com, www.caribcominc.com*. This hotel bar and restaurant, Spicy 'N' Herby, is set down on the beach with a wooden floor, bamboo rusticity and excellent food.

Dawn's Creole Garden, Lower Bay, **t** 458 3154. In another typical West Indian setting on the hillside at the end of the bay. Serves excellent creole food, with plenty of varieties of fresh fish in Dawn's creole sauce (clove, ginger and nutmeg), accompanied by a volley of side dishes including breadfruit, sweet potato and plantain. Set menus.

Moderate

Fernando's Hideaway, Lower Bay, t 458 3758. Dependably good and a lovely local experience on a simple veranda tucked up in the hillside greenery, with conch-shell flowerpots and candles in Easybake flour packets. Offers fixed menus only, starting with soup and continuing mostly with fish, caught by Nando himself, filleted and baked with spices, accompanied by good West Indian vegetables (christophene and cheese or plantain fritters), finishing off with a fudge pie or cake. Goat water on Saturdays. *Reservations only.*

The Frangipani Hotel Restaurant, Admiralty Bay, t 458 3255. The most popular restaurant and bar in Bequia is something of an institution where locals, tourists, and old salts all hang out together.

The Salty Dog, Port Elizabeth, t 457 3443. The newest addition to Bequia's restaurant/bar scene, where the lively atmosphere keeps patrons going until the wee hours. There's a pool table, cable television and an excellent, reasonably-priced buffet lunch served daily. *Happy Hour 5–7pm; Saturday is Ladies Night with free cocktails 9–11pm.*

Sugar Hill Restaurant, Mt Pleasant Rd, t 458 3773. High on the ridge on the Mt Pleasant Rd, a pink and purple deck looking both north and south. Hearty West Indian fare – callaloo, pumpkin soup or fish chowder to start; fish, *lambi*, lamb, chicken, pork or lobster to follow.

Mac's Pizzeria, Belmont, t 458 3474. Set on a wooden veranda above a luxurious tropical garden along the waterfront, this pizzeria is ever popular and busy. As you'd expect from the name, Mac's serves a host of different pizzas, but also other dishes such as salads, quiches, lasagnes and Macnuggets (tasty codfish balls).

De Reef, Lower Bay, t 458 3958. Beach bar and restaurant on this popular but uncrowded beach. Informal dining for lunch and dinner. Specializing in seafood and curried conch. Three-course dinner by reservation only; seafood buffet dinner with band every other Saturday, in season. Sunday afternoon jam sessions have become an institution at De Reef.

Inexpensive

Green Boley, Belmont, t 457 3625. Right on the waterfront. Set in a bamboo-fronted shed, very easy-going, with simple local fare and tropical fruit juices to a Caribbean musical accompaniment.

Bars and Nightlife

Bars

Many of the restaurants in Bequia also double as bars. The Belmont waterfront (better known as Admiralty Bay) is a good place to head to as it is usually quite lively.

Some of the hotels listed above have an occasional jump-up – ask around.

De Reef, Lower Bay, t 458 3958. *See* under 'Eating Out'.

Frangipani Hotel, Belmont. Try the bar.

Whaleboner Bar and Restaurant, next to the Frangipani Hotel, Belmont. There is a barbecue and steel band jump-up on Thursdays in season.

The Gingerbread Bar and Restaurant, Belmont. Has live music, a string band, a couple of times a week.

Beach Bars

There are beach bars on nearly all Bequia's beaches, pleasant spots to take time out from sizzling and snorkelling.

Dawn's Creole Beach Café, Lower Bay. For soups, sandwiches and cigars.

Spicy 'n' Herby, Friendship Bay. A waterfront bar with chairs swinging from the ceiling to help your balance after a few too many rum punches.

The Crescent Beach Inn, Industry Bay. A lovely, isolated spot for a day out.

narrow walkway that passes between the sea and the pretty bars and restaurants that line the seashore. The east of the island is much more remote and undeveloped, though villas are gradually being built there too: you may come across tropicbirds and the scissor-tailed frigatebird. On Park Beach in the northeast of the island is the **Old-Hegg Turtle Sanctuary**, where you will see endangered hawksbill turtles of various ages tended by islander Orton King.

Mustique

The island of Mustique has a lore all of its own. Its image is one of almost absurd exclusivity, an enclave reserved for the very rich – famous, notorious or anonymous. Personages as incongruous as Princess Margaret and Mick Jagger have made this place their Caribbean retreat.

The island is run as a company, the Mustique Company, which over the last 35 years has turned an undeveloped scrubby outcrop infested with the mosquitoes of the name into a paragon of 21st-century luxury. Shareholders invest in the company by buying a villa or by buying one of the 120 or so plots of land and then building on it – a not inconsiderable investment as the going rate is about US$800,000 for the plot, and then there are the costs of building your dream house. Through a series of committees (made up of interested shareholders), the company takes care of the infrastructure and development of the island (the environmental committee have arranged for the burying of all cables and paving of steep stretches of road to prevent erosion, for instance), including health care and the education of the local children. The Mustique Company is the biggest employer in St Vincent after the Government, and they turn in about 10% of the country's GDP.

The direction of the island has changed a little in recent years, since some of the leading lights of the island, including Colin Tennant (now Lord Glenconner), have moved on. It is still extremely expensive nonetheless. Incredibly neat, Mustique has a sedate air, pricked by the occasional character who washes up at Basil's Bar. It is possible to come across the transient millionaires around the island, if you can spot them among the roving sailing bums.

Best Beaches

Lagoon Bay: In the southwest, a gently curving strip of sand with a palm fringe and shallow water. Some picnic areas and shelters.

Gelliceaux Bay: You can walk round to this charming and secluded cove from Lagoon Bay.

Endeavour Bay: In the northwest. Generally the busiest beach because of the nearby Cotton House Hotel, which has a general watersports shop which includes Dive Mustique.

L'Ansecoy Bay: In the north, pleasant but often windswept.

Macaroni Bay: On the east coast, which feels the brunt of the Atlantic waves, but it has mounds of bright white sand and one or two umbrella shades.

There are some excellent beaches scattered on Mustique and walkways have been built to provide access to some of them. The most protected are in the southwest.

Around the Island

Just 3 miles by 1.5, the island is small enough to walk around in a couple of hours (look out for the iguanas, which are pretty big, and for the mysterious wild cattle, which leave their prints when they come to drink at the pools by night, though they haven't been seen recently). You are quite likely to arrive by air at the pint-sized, bamboo-clad terminal building. From here roads encircle the island, linking all the

Getting There

Mustique t (1 784–)

Flights to Mustique come mainly from Barbados (on Mustique Airways and others) and St Vincent (scheduled flights are by Mustique Airways, SVG Air and Grenadines Air) – see 'Getting There', p.187. There are no boat services to Mustique.

Getting Around

If walking seems too energetic, it is possible to hire a 'mule' (like mini-mokes). Enquire at the main office near the airport.

Sports

If you fancy **scuba diving**, contact Dive Mustique, Cotton House Hotel, Endeavour Bay, **t** 456 3486. There are **tennis** courts and there is a stable with horses for **riding** out on the beaches and around the island.

Where to Stay

Mustique t (1 784–)

Visitors to Mustique generally take a villa: about 50 of the 90-odd luxurious piles dotted around the island are up for short-term rent. These vary in style from an Etruscan palace to chi chi gingerbread cottages, with between two and seven rooms. All come with maid service, gardeners and cooks – in fact all that is needed to ensure the ultimate rest-cure. With names like Nirvana and Serendipity you get the idea that this might be as near to heaven

as the developed world of the 21st century can manage. Villas are not cheap, to say the least. Prices for a two-bedroom villa start at US$6,500 per week in winter and US$3,500 in summer. Three bedrooms start at US$6,500 in winter and at US$4,000 in the summer. Four-bedroom villas range between US$6,000 and US$18,500 for a week in winter and start at US$4,000 in summer. Five bedrooms are $10,000 or more in the winter. Then you add 5% government tax and an 8% administration charge.

Contact **Mustique Villa Rentals**, PO Box 349, St Vincent, **t** 488 8000, *villarentals@ mustique-island.com, www.mustique-island.com*. In the UK they can be contacted at Chartham House, 16A College Ave, Maidenhead, Berks SL6 6AX, **t** (01628) 583 517, *mustique@euro-contacts.co.uk*; and in the USA and Canada, Resorts Management Inc, 456 Glenbrook Rd, Stamford, CT 06906, **t** 203 602 0300, *rmiresorts@juno.com*.

The other places to stay on Mustique are a single hotel and a very upmarket bed and breakfast:

Luxury

The Cotton House Hotel, t 456 4777, UK reservations through Leading Hotels of the World **t** 0800 181 123, US and Canada reservations **t** 1 877 249 9945, *cottonhouse@caribsurf. com, www.cottonhouse.net (outrageous luxury)*. Set on rolling lawns and gardens in the northwest of the island, around the old windmill of the sugar estate. The 20 rooms and suites are landscaped in small blocks and are furnished with four-posters with muslin netting. Each has a balcony or terrace overlooking nearby islands, or west for the villas and the beaches. Past the library and school, **Lovell Village** is the recognizably West Indian part of Mustique, with the island church and the police station, and it is here that many of the people employed by the Mustique Company live.

Heading down the hill you pass an **aviary** with some endangered St Vincent parrots and you come to **Britannia Bay**, really the only busy part of the island. The 75 or so fishermen, some of whom have worked out of the island for generations before the company arrived, have their huts here. There is a small fish market where you can sometimes buy fresh fish. The main jetty for the supply boat from St Vincent is here and Basil's Bar sticks out into the water. Close by there is a foodstore, bakery and

incomparable sunsets. On one side is Endeavour Bay (Caribbean), and on the other, L'Ansecoy Bay (Atlantic). The pool is on the hilltop surrounded by the restored walls of an old plantation structure, and there is a beach bar on the nearby beach. The heart of the hotel, though, is the main house, a breezy, single-storey stone building with a huge drawing room and bar inside: guests gather for drinks before moving out to the candle-lit tables of the dining room ranged around the veranda. The new spa is staffed by a team of professional therapists.

The Firefly, t 488 8414, *fireflymus@caribsurf. com, www.mustiquefirefly.com*. In case you might feel a little extravagant staying at the Cotton House, you can stay here for just a snip (by comparison, anyway, as it's a shade under US$500 a night for two). Perched on a steep hillside overlooking Britannia Bay and the Grenadines to the southwest, the Firefly has just four rooms and a great deal of style and charm. The bar, with dining room and general sitting area, is a gathering place for visitors and islanders who come to drink from the long list of cocktails and listen to whoever's around and entertaining at the time (it has been Phil Collins and Nigel Kennedy before now). From here you descend by spiral staircase to the rooms, with four-posters, mosquito nets and huge windows for the breeze and the view (some showers with a view too). Rooms are very comfortable, fan-ventilated rather than air-conditioned. Stone steps descend through the steep garden to the double-level pool and bar (for snacks by day; they also do picnics if you are going off exploring). The cry goes that you do not have to be a

millionaire to stay on Mustique because you can come here, but, if you do, be sure to come with plenty of loot even so. Rates include breakfast in your room. The dining room is popular so you need to reserve.

Eating Out

Eating out in Mustique is a little limited.

The Cotton House, t 456 4777 (*expensive*). Elegant dining: 'international fare with a Caribbean twist'.

The Firefly, t 456 3414 (*expensive*). You dine in candlelight to a fantastic view of the bay. The menu, which offers fresh local food, changes each day: calamari sautéed in garlic and lime butter with a spicy kuchela chutney, followed by grilled swordfish with plantain creole hash and fresh local vegetables, or a seafood crêpe with garlic mash.

Basil's Bar, t 488 8350 (*expensive*). A restaurant, despite the name, which has a setting from paradise: an open-sided construction of bamboo slats with a rush-work roof that juts out into the water on stilts. Tables and bench seats surround the dancing area and bar, so you can admire the sunset and the views of the Grenadines over the gin palaces that bob in the bay. The fare is international: Basil's creole shrimps followed by a vegetable lasagna or grilled daily catch. Basil's is particularly popular on Wednesdays in season (*adm US$10*), when the yachts bring their passengers ashore and the millionaires venture out from their villas for the jump-up. Drinks, including a Mustique Grin, a Mule (after the car) or a Basil's Highball, will set you back about US$5.

coffee shop and Mustique's pretty gingerbread boutiques, Treasure Fashion and Treasure Boutique. There is even an antique shop. Britannia Bay is also the best anchorage for yachts.

Canouan

Crescent-shaped Canouan lies 25 miles from St Vincent in the middle of the Grenadines, a scrubby island measuring 3 miles by 1.5. It has a population of about 850, most of whom live on the protected leeward coast of the island. Until recently, the island was almost completely undeveloped, with just a couple of very low-key places to stay and not so much as a bank or supermarket. For years Canouan was neglected – people expected to 'get their feet wet' when arriving here because there wasn't even a jetty.

Over the last few years, though, Canouan has seen a change. A hotel development company has built a hotel in most of the north of the island, bringing the trappings of the modern world – ranges of hotel rooms have been constructed; pools, restaurants, tennis courts and beach bars have been built; a golf course has been laid; and roads

Getting There

Canouan t (1 784–)

By Air

Canouan is now served by American Eagle direct from San Juan, in Puerto Rico. Grenadines Air and SVG Air fly from St Vincent. From Barbados you will need to consider the shared charters; otherwise, you will have to charter a private plane (*see* 'Getting There', p.187).

By Sea

A very good way to get to the island is from St Vincent or the other Grenadines on the five weekly visits by the mail boat, the MV *Barracuda* (*see* 'Getting There', p.187).

Getting Around

Hire cars are available through most of the hotels.

Festivals

The island is at its liveliest during the regatta season in May, when the different districts compete against one another in sailing races.

Watersports

The **snorkelling** is particularly good in Windward Bay (east) and Glossy Bay (southwest). For watersports, use the hotels:
Blueway Diving International, Tamarind Beach Hotel, t 458 8044, *blueway@carenage.com*. Offers instruction as well as snorkelling trips and day sails to other islands.
For yacht charters, try:
Moorings Yacht Charters, Raffles Beach Club, t 458 8044,*yacht@moorings.com*, *www. moorings.com*. One of the major sailing and bare boat chartering companies.

Where to Stay and Eat

Canouan t (1 784–)

Raffles Beach Club, t 458 8000, *info@raffles-canouanisland.com*, *www.raffles-canouan island.com* (*luxury*). The Raffles Beach may seem incongruous in the Caribbean – a Mediterranean-style resort, with a Mexican colour scheme in burnt orange, red, yellow ochre and pastel pink, and pointy Thai-inspired roofs like kitten ears. There's certainly nothing else like it in the islands. Guests don't just dress up for the evening: they wear their jewellery to the beach. For all of the external oddity, though, the rooms

have been cut around the north of the island, leading to plots for more villas. As usual it has all been received with mixed feelings by the islanders. On the one hand it brings opportunities, but on the other they see outsiders coming in and restricting access to their beaches and taking the employment. This includes the Vincentians, who once jokingly thought of Canouan as 'some people on a rock, somewhere' but have been quick to come in and claim the jobs. It has been a difficult experience. There has been some friction with 'the Roman Empire' (the resort is built and managed by Italians) but the development is at least in the north of the island, out of sight most of the time.

The centre of island life is **Grand Bay** in the southwest, which is divided into districts – Retreat, Balance, Batchelor's Hall Bay (site of the island electricity plant) and St Ann's Point. There are a few small shops to stock up at if you are passing by on a boat. Before the hurricane of 1921, most of the population lived in the 'Village', in the north of the island. Their old abandoned church has been swallowed up in the hotel development.

The island has a few hidden coves and beaches to explore. **Grand Bay** itself has magnificent sand, as does **Friendship Bay** in the south.

are exquisite inside, huge, minimal, with Bulgari in the vast bathrooms and a fantastic view down to the sea. There is an air of a country club about the place – golf course, casino, plenty of tennis courts and excellent levels of service. There are four restaurants – La Piazza for Italian cuisine; the open-air Gondahl Beach Bar & Grill for casual dining; the Beach Club Restaurant for grilled meat; and La Varenne for gourmet French cuisine, where you can eat caviar and select from 34 champagnes.

Canouan Beach Hotel, PO Box 530, **t** 458 8888, *joenadal@caribsurf.com*, *www.canouan-beach-hotel.com* (*very expensive*). Isolated in the south of the island beyond the airstrip. The 32 simple rooms are ranged in blocks looking south from a sandy garden on a spit of land with beach on either side. Full board, watersports and catamaran excursions. The Anchor Inn serves West Indian seafood.

The Tamarind Beach Hotel, Grand Bay, **t** 458 8044, *info@tamarind.us*, *www.tamarind.us* (*expensive–moderate*). The hotel sits tucked into the top end of the huge Grand Bay on a superb strip of sand. The 42 rooms are in three modern and rather disappointing turquoise-roofed blocks (make sure to get a room upstairs, where the ceilings are higher), but they are very comfortable, with stained-wood interiors, louvres and nice balconies. There are two restaurants: the smarter Palapa restaurant for Caribbean cuisine, and mock rustic Pirate Cove beach bar. Plenty of watersports. The hotel is mainly used by staff at the Carenage, but officially it is open.

Crystal Apartments, Grand Bay, **t** 458 8356 (*moderate*). Apartments in some charming old wooden Caribbean houses with full kitchens. Individual rooms are sometimes on offer, too. Otherwise, it is a good place to eat, for a chicken or fish dinner off a bright red tablecloth.

Anchor Inn Guest House, Grand Bay, **t** 458 8568 (*moderate–inexpensive*). Set back from the beach a little way, in a modern concrete house. There is a friendly atmosphere; guests in the four fan-ventilated rooms (private baths) have the use of a sitting room. Good home Caribbean cooking is available in the dining room. *Price includes breakfast and dinner.*

Silver Lining Restaurant and Sports Bar, **t** 482 0348 (*moderate*). International cuisine.

Villa Le Bijou, **t** 458 8025 (*moderate–inexpensive*). Creole and seafood.

There are also a few local bars on the high ground above Grand Bay where you can get a meal or a drink.

Mayreau

With just 180 inhabitants and no airstrip, this island blip of 1.5 square miles is almost the most secluded of them all (the Tobago Cays nearby win that claim). There are no roads or cars, though there is new jetty. Cows making a journey from Mayreau are winched up onto deck, and if alighting here they are simply herded off into the bay and left to swim for it.

The islanders lead a very simple life, living in the small cluster of houses on the side of Station Hill above **Saline Bay**. But things are moving on and some money is coming into the island: the rum shops are becoming restaurants and the islanders have

Getting There

Mayreau t (1 784–)

Getting to Mayreau presents a few practical problems, but it is visited five times a week by the mail boat, which originates in Union Island and St Vincent. Alternatively, you might persuade a fisherman to take you (they often visit to sell their catch) or pay a water taxi to carry you over from Union. You might even get a lift on a yacht. *See* 'Getting There', p.187.

Sports

Snorkelling is recommended at the northern point and on the windward beaches, where the sand is framed with sea grape bushes. Or you could go **walking** and take advantage of the island's views from the high ground, north to Canouan, east to the Tobago Cays and south to the majestic peaks of Union Island.

Where to Stay

Mayreau t (1 784–)

The Salt Whistle Bay Club, t 458 8444, USA and Canada t 1 800 561 7258, VHF channel 16 and 68, *swwwbreserve@gmx.net*, *www.salt whistlebay.com* (*luxury*). Set on a stunning, crescent-moon bay in the north of Mayreau, the Salt Whistle Bay Club is about as remote as you can get, with 10 very comfortable rooms around a neatly raked sandy garden of palms, sea grape and cedar trees (hammocks slung everywhere between them). The central area has a bar (and a small library) and a series of circular stone gazebos where you can sit out to eat and take in the evening air. The rooms are quite simple but very comfortable, with tiled floors, polished stone walls, king-size beds, rattan furniture, ceiling fans, dark-stained wooden louvres and window-screens. Bathrooms are open-plan and have a large stone shower. There's no need for locks on the doors; phones are available, but nobody bothers to have one. The club is very quiet and low-key, but there are often yachts in the bay and so there is sometimes a lively crowd at the bar. Some watersports.

Dennis's Hideaway, t 458 8594, *denhide@ caribsurf.com*, *www.dennis-hideaway.com*. VHF Channel 68 (*inexpensive*). This is the only other place to stay on the island, but it has a certain modern West Indian style – five plush rooms set in two modern concrete houses in the centre of Mayreau's town, each with a balcony with a view. There is a small veranda dining room and bar below, which collects a crowd of passing yachtsmen in the evenings and where Dennis himself plays guitar (otherwise there's a steel band sometimes).

Eating Out and Bars

On Mayreau, entertainment consists of an occasional discotheque or a film screening in the restaurants and rum shops.

Island Paradise Bar, Restaurant & Disco, t 458 8941, VHF Channel 68 (*moderate–inexpensive*). It is worth going a little way up the hill from town to this place, which is set on an attractive veranda. Wholesome West Indian food, and an occasional string band.

Best Beaches

Saline Bay: Just south of the town.

Salt Whistle Bay: In the north, also a particularly good anchorage. It is reached on a path through the bush from the top of town (ask).

Twazam: Just north of town (pronounced Twazane, perhaps from Trois Anes, French for Three Donkeys).

rebuilt their houses in concrete rather than in wood. Mayreau has received electricity and telephones relatively recently (in January 1995 the island had the most modern phone system in the world). Above the town you will find the tiny **Catholic church** (most of the islanders are Catholic, because the island was owned, as much of it still is, by a single Catholic family). It is made of stone and painted bright blue, with a small series of calvary paintings and helpful signs such as 'Responsibility and Good Behaviour Always Win'. Beyond here, small **trails** lead through the scrub down to pastures and cultivations and to the bays from which the local fishermen work.

Tobago Cays

The Tobago Cays (pronounced 'keys') are five uninhabited islets set in the circle of Horseshoe Reef, an underwater world as spectacular as the island views above the surface. The islands – Petit Rameau, Petit Bateau, Barabel, Jamesby and, out on its own, Petit Tobac – are furred with scrub and sand, and the water is crystal clear all around, out to the limit of the reef, which is marked by a circle of silver breakers. You will cruise in between the reefs and drop anchor in the shallows of a pristine white-sand beach. Devotees of the Tobago Cays talk of them as the closest thing to heaven – and somehow it is true. Or was, because the Tobago Cays are so well known that they have actually become quite crowded, particularly in high season (December until April and especially at Christmas). Day sails come over from Union Island (people fly in from as far away as Barbados). However, if you are yachting through the islands, it is well worth a look to see if it's not too crowded. The islands have recently been granted National Park status, and there are ongoing discussions with UNESCO to make it a World Heritage Site, so there is no building on the cays and no spear-fishing. Hopefully this will protect the reefs and fish because the **snorkelling** is still superb – head out towards the Atlantic side. You are asked not to leave any litter (which has also been a problem recently) and it is better not to pay anyone to take it away because it is often dumped just round the corner.

Union Island

Midway down the Grenadines stands the spectacular-looking Union Island, with parched yellow slopes draped down from the sharp peaks of the oddly named Mount Parnassus and Mount Olympus, also known as the Pinnacle. Just over 3 miles square,

Getting There

Union Island t (1 784–)

By Air

Union Island is well served by air: contact SVG Air, t 458 8882; Air Caraïbes, t 485 8305; and the share charters from Barbados, including Grenadines Air and Mustique Airways, t 458 8770.

By Sea

It is also possible to sail from here to Carriacou (twice weekly ferry) for about EC$25 (plus departure tax EC$30), and of course to St Vincent on the mail boat.

Getting Around

Inexpensive mini-buses serve Union Island. Fares start at EC$2 (tour rates US$30 for one to five people and US$8 for each extra person). The Anchorage Yacht Club rents bicycles.

Tourist Information

There is a small tourist office in Clifton, t 458 8350. Union Island is a Port of Entry to St Vincent and the Grenadines.

Watersports

Day Sails

Capt Yannis, t 458 8513. About US$60.
Chantours, t 432 5591, *chan@caribsurf.com*.
Scaramouche, t 458 8418. A catamaran.
Wind and Sea, t 458 8569.

Sailing

VPM Du Four Antilles, t 458 8894. A yacht-chartering company based at Bougainvilla.

Snorkelling and Scuba Diving

Snorkelling on reefs around the island and scuba diving off Union Island and Mayreau (where there is the 1918 wreck of the British gunship *Purina*) can be arranged. A single-tank dive costs US$50. Contact:
Grenadines Dive, t 458 8138, VHF Channels 16 and 68, *gdive@caribsurf.com*.
Dive Anchorage, Anchorage Hotel, t 458 8221.

Where to Stay

Union Island t (1 784–)
The Anchorage Yacht Club Hotel, north of Clifton, t 458 8221, *aycunion@caribsurf.com*, *www.ayc-hotel-grenadines.com* (*expensive–moderate*). A small and busy resort with a

Union Island has a population of 2,600 and it has quite a positive buzz at the moment. It has been cleaned up and there is money coming in from the large numbers of tourists who pass through. Some stay, but Union Island is mainly the gateway to the other southern Grenadines nearby: the Tobago Cays, Palm Island, Petit St Vincent and Mayreau. On the island itself, an absurdly large development (with a 150-room hotel, a golf course and a 300-slip marina) which never got off the ground lies mouldering in the south. Union Island is a sailing centre and yachts crowd in the bay off the main town of Clifton.

The island has two main centres: **Clifton**, close to the airport (you'll see the planes sweep overhead as they come in to land), which stretches along the waterfront, a

Best Beaches

Big Sand Beach: In Belmont Bay, north of Clifton, this beach has shallow water and fine sand screened by bushes.

Chatham Bay: In the west of the island. Perhaps the best place to go for a secluded day at the beach, with miles of (as yet) undisturbed strand. There are no facilities, so be sure to take water and a picnic.

constant bustle and turnover, Grenadine style, of yacht crews and passengers, many of them French-speaking from the islands to the north. There are 12 rooms in a garden of palms looking out over a passable beach towards Palm Island, some with air-con, some fan-ventilated, but otherwise all mod cons. The restaurant, on an open terrace, serves French and Italian food.

The Clifton Beach Hotel, t 458 8235 (*moderate*), and the nearby **Guest House** (*inexpensive*). Provide simple and clean air-conditioned and fan-ventilated rooms with bathrooms.

The Sunny Grenadines Hotel, south of Clifton, t 458 8327 (*inexpensive*). Eighteen rooms in small units with ceiling fans. Set among the palm trees with a sometimes lively bar that gives on to a rickety wooden jetty, perfect for lounging in the evening light. Local fare in the dining room, including curry conch and steamed snapper.

Eating Out and Bars

See also the hotel-restaurants, above.

The West Indies, just north of Clifton, near the Anchorage, t 458 8311 (*moderate*). A pretty terrace in the lively waterfront area, with an aquarium. French and creole fare.

T & N Bar, Variety Store and Bike Rentals, Clifton (*moderate*). No bikes any more, but a shoe shop for your shopping delectation. Dining room upstairs, for local dishes of chicken and fish creole.

Janti's Café and Bar, Ashton, t 458 8343, VHF Channel 16 and 60 (*moderate*). A hip spot with a distinct nautical theme: sand on the floor, aquarium and the stern of a boat as the bar.

Big Sand Restaurant & Bar, t 485 8447, info@bigsandhotel.com, www.bigsandhotel.com. Local and French cuisine and weekly Sunday barbecue on the beach. Fresh bread, and lobster in season.

Seaquarium Restaurant, Bougainvilla, t 458 8678, bougainvilla@caribsurf.com. French and creole dishes, and lobster. Bakery, marina and furnished apartments.

Lambi's Restaurant, Clifton, t 458 8549. West Indian buffets of up to 50 different dishes. Steel-band jump-up and dancing nightly. Free dinghy pick-up from Palm Island.

The Secret Garden and Art Gallery, Clifton. Approached by a corridor of crazy paving overblown with tropical blooms and fencing. A nice veranda with bench seats for a beer and a chat.

The Eagle's Nest, Clifton. A general local bar and club.

cluster of docks, hotels, bars and the occasional strange-looking municipal building; and **Ashton**, on the southern side, a quieter and more local town.

Palm Island

With a population of just two cows until recently, Palm Island (130 acres), or Prune Island as it used to be known, has been transformed over the last 30 years into a delightful **island resort** (t 458 8824, US t 1 800 345 0356, palm@eliteislandresorts.com, www.eliteislandresorts.com; all inclusive plan; luxury) with 40 hotel rooms that face out to sea over the magnificent Casuarina beach that runs the length of the sheltered west coast.

There is an elegant air of retreat here, with no telephones or televisions to disturb the peace in the rooms, which are set in stone cottages, each with a small terrace behind a low wall and a view over the raked sand to Union Island, about 20 minutes off by boat. Inside, rooms are furnished with rattan and have wide vertical Vincentian louvres to encourage a breeze (or you can close the room off and air-condition it).

There is a delightful restaurant on a wooden deck beneath palm thatch. The island has a forest of palm trees standing over the sandy garden, and some watersports.

Petit St Vincent (PSV)

Petit St Vincent, a self-contained **island resort** (*t 458 8801, US t 1 800 654 9326, psv@fuse.net, www.psvresort.com; luxury*), is the most southerly of the St Vincent Grenadines; from here it is possible to see people walking about on Petit Martinique, part of Grenada. But this is about as close to the crowds as you will get on PSV (as habitués know it), because this island resort specializes in luxurious seclusion. If you like, you can even order room service from your beach hammock. You get peace at a price at PSV.

Exertion is a walk to the beach and, since the island is completely surrounded by them, even that will not be too far. The cottages are spread out for maximum seclusion, each one isolated from the next. They are extremely comfortable, but they conform to an older Caribbean style of comfort, with no phones, no TVs and no air conditioning. The island's idea is that you should be allowed to shut out incessant modern communication for a while and do nothing but read, walk and swim – in fact, you communicate with room service by flag, simply by placing an order in the post box, raising the flag and retiring to further inactivity. If you do wish to stretch some muscles, there is a tennis court, and watersports are laid on (windsurfers, hobie cats and kayaks). The central bar and restaurant stands on rising ground in the south of the island, with boutique, library and a sandpit for the owner's many labradors: guests who want to venture out of their cottages gather there before dinner (outsiders will find that the service is pretty unforthcoming). Finally, day sails are on offer, to the Tobago Cays and to tiny Mopion, the original sand bar with absolutely nothing but a palm-thatch umbrella.

If prices are a concern, PSV might not be for you, as such luxury comes at about US$915 per couple per night (FAP with meals and the facilities of the resort) in the winter season, and US$585 or so in the summer months.

St Lucia

Hold St Lucia, and the rest may perish!

The call to arms on behalf of St Lucia was raised so often that she become known as the Fair Helen of the West Indies. Desire to possess her moved whole armies and led to her changing hands 14 times. She is a charmed isle, not so much for her strategic value nowadays, but for her people, among the friendliest in the Caribbean, and for her natural beauty: hidden coves, tropical abundance and the Pitons, twin volcanic pyramids from the south seas.

Lying between Martinique and St Vincent, St Lucia (pronounced 'St Loosha') is another island peak in the Windward chain, with slopes that soar from the sea to a central mountain spine crested by Morne Gimie (3,117ft) and then fall away in forest-

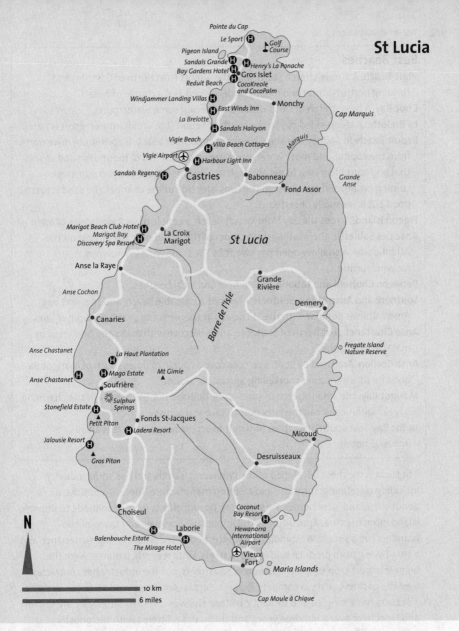

St Lucia

Pointe du Cap
Le Sport
Golf Course
Pigeon Island
Sandals Grande
Bay Gardens Hotel
Henry's La Panache
Gros Islet
Reduit Beach
CocoKreole and CocoPalm
Windjammer Landing Villas
East Winds Inn
Monchy
Cap Marquis
La Brelotte
Sandals Halcyon
Vigie Beach
Villa Beach Cottages
Vigie Airport
Harbour Light Inn
Marquis
Sandals Regency
Castries
Babonneau
Grande Anse
Fond Assor
St Lucia
Marigot Beach Club Hotel
Marigot Bay
Discovery Spa Resort
La Croix Marigot
Anse la Raye
Grande Rivière
Anse Cochon
Dennery
Barre de l'Isle
Canaries
Anse Chastanet
Fregate Island Nature Reserve
La Haut Plantation
Anse Chastanet
Mago Estate
Mt Gimie
Soufrière
Stonefield Estate
Sulphur Springs
Fonds St-Jacques
Petit Piton
Ladera Resort
Micoud
Jalousie Resort
Gros Piton
Desruisseaux
Choiseul
Coconut Bay Resort
Laborie
Hewanorra International Airport
Balenbouche Estate
The Mirage Hotel
Vieux Fort
Maria Islands
N

10 km
6 miles

Cap Moule à Chique

clad hills to lush valleys of bananas, tropical overgrowth and beaches mounded with golden sand. Some 27 miles by 14, St Lucia has a volcanic vent, a fumarole called La Soufrière, a bubbling and stinking morass which claims the dubious distinction of being the only 'drive-in' volcano in the world.

The 153,000 St Lucians are mostly descended from Africans who were brought to the island as slaves in the sugar heyday of the 18th century. More than one-third live in the extended outskirts of the capital, Castries, which shambles over hills above a sheltered harbour in the northwest.

Best Beaches

Vigie Beach: A 2-mile stretch starting at the airport (just north of Castries) and running north. Natural and mostly undeveloped, but a couple of hotels.

Choc Bay: A nice stretch of sand with a bar offering some watersports.

La Brelotte: A steep-sided bay to the south of Reduit (the Windjammer resort is here).

Reduit Beach: In Rodney Bay, the island's most popular beach, a 20-minute drive north from the capital, and most watersports are on offer. Miles of mounded sand so soft that you stumble trying to get through it. Also bars in case you feel sunstroke coming on. Beyond the town on the Gros Islet side of the channel, the sand is just as good but it is usually deserted

Pigeon Island: Across the bay from Reduit Beach, a couple of secluded strips of sand.

Anse des Sables: In the southeastern corner of the island near the airport on the Atlantic side. A shallow, open bay swept by the trade winds, renowned for windsurfing.

Between Choiseul and Laborie: Very simple and local beaches.

Soufrière and **Anse Mitan**: Soufrière itself has a passable beach, and the next bay, Anse Mitan, is popular with the St Lucians at the weekends, with a couple of bars.

Anse Chastanet: Just north of Soufrière, an idyllic cove with dark sand, sheltered by massive headlands.

Anse Cochon: Accessed by boat, a remote cove a couple of miles south of Marigot Bay, good for an afternoon's snorkelling and lazing around.

Marigot Bay: The small stretch of sand is not brilliant, but the setting in the charming bay is magnificent: call the ferry over to take you across.

La Toc Bay: Just south of Castries (difficult to access because there is an all-inclusive hotel).

St Lucia is the most developed of the Windward Islands and has some industry, including oil refining, furniture and clothing manufacture. There is a positive air about the island: new homes are springing up and efforts have been made to improve island infrastructure. Agriculture is still important, however, and many of the islanders live a simple West Indian existence, tied to the land, earning sustenance and a small living from produce sold in the markets. Until recently, bananas were the biggest export crop, employing 2,000 or so farmers, but the industry has contracted over the past few years in competition with Central American producers.

St Lucia has a tangled and romantic history: she was disputed bitterly by the British and French for over a hundred years, and the island is littered with the ghostly fortresses of forgotten wars, still visible among the encrustation of modern hotels. The influence of the French remains in the *mornes* (mountain peaks), *anses* (the sheltered bays), the culture – the population is mostly Catholic and there are distinct flashes of French style in the way they act and dress – and in, of course, the language. Every visitor will hear the strains of the local French-based patois spoken in the streets, tantalizingly like French for a moment and yet impossible to pin down. English is the official language of St Lucia and so parents will bring up their children in that language to help them 'get on', even though they always talk in patois between themselves.

St Lucia is one of the Caribbean's most popular destinations at the moment – the 18th-century war cry 'To St Lucia! To St Lucia!' has been raised once again. Now the air- and seaborne invaders have come in their droves, overrunning the beaches, swamping Castries and storming the heights of Morne Fortune. The island has opted particularly for the all-inclusive format, in which people pay up front and don't pull out their wallet again, some hardly venturing forth from the resort compound. This is a pity because the island is good to explore and there are many small and charming spots (hotels, bars and restaurants) hidden away in coves and bays where the calm and beauty of Fair Helen still remains.

History

Santa Lucia first appears on a royal *cedula* of 1511 marking out the Spanish domain in the New World, and then on a Vatican globe of 1520. It is not known who discovered it, or why it was named after the virgin martyr of Syracuse, but the St Lucians celebrate St Lucy's day, 13 December, as their national day.

Hewanorra, as the Caribs called St Lucia, was a favoured hide-out for the pirates and privateers of the 16th century. They came to scourge the Spaniards in the Indies, and men like Frenchman François le Clerc (better known to the Spaniards as Pie de Palo because of his wooden leg) would lie up at Pigeon Island in the north of the island, on the lookout for shipping to plunder, just as the admirals of the European navies would 200 years later. In 1553 de Clerc left for a grand tour in which he sacked the major towns in Santo Domingo, Puerto Rico and Cuba. Attempts to settle St Lucia began at the turn of the 17th century. The first, in 1605, really happened by accident, when the *Olive Blossom* limped to St Lucia after being blown off course on the Atlantic crossing. She was headed for the Guianas in South America, but, short of supplies, 67 of her passengers took their chances in St Lucia and bought huts and food from seemingly friendly Carib Indians. The Caribs soon changed their tune, though, and after five weeks of hostilities just 19 of the settlers were still alive, so they made a final purchase of a canoe and paddled off to South America. Another English attempt in 1639 survived for 18 months unmolested before the Caribs attacked. The Indians winkled them out of their fort by burning red pepper in the wind, a trick they used to catch sleeping parrots. Almost all the British were killed.

Just as Charles I of England granted St Lucia and other islands officially in the Spanish domain to the Earl of Carlisle in 1627, so Cardinal Richelieu felt free to offer islands 'not possessed by any Christian prince' to the French West India Company in 1642 and soon the French settlements in the West Indies began to appear. The scene was set for the next 200 years: settlements, battles and treaties, a rivalry that would see St Lucia change hands a ridiculous 14 times. Once the Caribs were wiped out, the island steadily turned from a rabble of deserters, loggers and turtlers to a pros- perous colony, cultivating sugar. With Louis XVI guillotined in January 1793 in Europe, Britain and the Republic of France were at war again in the Caribbean and the revolutionaries raised the *tricolore* in St Lucia. With its revolutionary sympathies and a guillotine erected in the capital, the island became known as Ste Lucie la Fidèle. The British fought their way back into Castries in 1796, but the Armée Française dans les Bois (a guerrilla force) held the rest of the islanders to ransom for another year. The subsequent war and treaty left St Lucia in British hands and the planters promptly got back to the business of cultivating sugar. The slaves were emancipated in 1834.

In 1885 Castries became one of the two principal coaling stations in the British West Indies, along with Kingston, Jamaica, filling a thousand steamships a year and gaining yet more importance when the Panama Canal was opened in 1914. Women would be seen climbing the gangways with 110lb baskets of coal on their heads, smoking pipes or singing shanties. After the Second World War, as the West Indian islands moved towards political self-determination, St Lucia became self-governing in 1967 and then took Independence on 22 February 1979.

The country is still a member of the British Commonwealth, with an elected parliament after the Westminster model and headed by a Governor General, presently Dame Pearlette Louisy. The island is governed by the St Lucia Labour Party under Dr Kenny Anthony, who hold 14 of the 17 seats in Parliament. The other seats are held by the United Workers' Party, who were in power for thirty years until 1997. The next elections are due in 2006. St Lucia's economy depends mainly on tourism, but bananas also contribute to foreign exchange earnings. Most are sold in Britain. The industry has been in serious decline recently as the preferential arrangements with Britain and the European Community have collapsed and their market has been undercut by Central American 'dollar bananas'.

Beaches

St Lucia's best white-sand beaches lie on the protected leeward coast at the northern end of the island, between Castries and the northern tip. Here you will find the most active beaches, with hotels and watersports. To the south of Castries most of the beaches have dark volcanic sand, often in secluded coves where the mountains fall steeply down to the coast. You will find that although officially there is public access to every beach, some of them are effectively closed to visitors because the hotels operate an all-inclusive policy (and would demand a full day's fee to use their facilities). However, Reduit Beach offers most things. *See* 'Best Beaches', p.204.

Flora and Fauna

Like all the Windwards, St Lucia has exuberant flora. There are coastal mangrove swamps (near Savannes on the southeast coast) where you can see the mangrove cuckoo and the tropical mockingbird and warblers, and plains flown over by hawks and herons. The white bird that keeps a silent vigil by the grazing cows is the cattle egret, which found its way over from Africa early in the 20th century. In the higher reaches of rainforest you will find the Antillean crested and the purple-throated hummingbird. The upper rainforest is also home to the endangered St Lucia parrot. Over the coast and the offshore islands, you will come across tropicbirds and magnificent frigatebirds.

Getting There

St Lucia t (1 758–)

By Air

Flights from outside the Caribbean fly into Hewanorra International Airport near the southern tip and 40 miles south of Castries. If you are flying within the Caribbean, it is better to aim for the George F. L. Charles Airport (also known as Vigie) just outside the capital. There is a departure tax of EC$54 (US$21).

From the UK and Europe

BWIA, t 454 5075, and British Airways, t 454 6172, have twice-weekly flights. On days without direct flights, the best connections are via Barbados. Charter operators also fly from the UK (Britannia and jmc, both t 454 8186) and France (Air Liberté, same phone). Also consider flying via Paris and Martinique.

From North America

BWIA, t 454 5075, flies from New York via Trinidad and Barbados. Air Canada, t 454 8186, flies weekly from Montreal and Toronto. US Airways fly from Boston and Philadelphia.

From Other Caribbean Islands

There are links to most major islands nearby. LIAT, t 452 3051, flies to Barbados, north to Antigua and south to Trinidad and also to Caracas. Air Jamaica flies to Jamaica, from where there are onward connections. Air Caraïbes, t 452 2463, originates in Martinique and flies south to the Grenadines. Caribbean Star flies from Puerto Rico. To charter a plane, try Eagle Air Services, t 452 9683.

By Sea

A hydrocat, *L'Express des Isles*, t 452 2211, *www.express-des-iles.com*, runs connections to the island of Martinique and then beyond to Dominica and to Guadeloupe.

Getting Around

By Bus

Private minibuses run all the main routes around the island. Gros Islet and the north are served frequently and buses continue until as late as 10pm (later on a Friday), leaving from Darling Rd in Castries. Buses heading south leave from Bridge St, departing until the late afternoon. For a day trip to Soufrière you must be quite careful because the last bus back to Castries leaves by mid-afternoon, after which time you will have to take the longer route via Vieux Fort. Some sample prices are: Castries to Gros Islet – EC$2, to Dennery – EC$3 and to Soufrière or Vieux Fort – EC$7.

By Taxi

By the hour a taxi costs about EC$55, and a day tour in a taxi can be shared for about EC$350 between four people. Sample one-way fares are: Castries to Vigie Airport – EC$15, to Hewanorra Airport – EC$120, to Rodney Bay – EC$40, and to the Cap Estate – EC$50.

Taxis can be arranged at hotels. Or try:
Courtesy Taxi Service, Castries, t 452 3555.
Gablewoods Mall Taxi Stand, t 451 7521.
Marigot Bay Taxi, t 453 4406.
Rodney Bay Taxis, t 452 0379.
St Lucia Taxi Service, in the south, t 452 2493.

Car and Bike Hire

Car hire provides the opportunity to explore inland byways like the rainforest road out of Soufrière and the route to Grand Anse northeast of Castries. A temporary driving licence is required, costing EC$30 on presentation of a valid licence from home to the police at either airport or in Castries. Driving is on the left.

Many hire companies have desks at the airports and typically they will require a deposit or a credit-card imprint. Cars cost from US$55 per day, from:
Avis, t 452 2202.
Cool Breeze Jeep Rental, t 458 2031. Jeeps only.
CTL Rent-A-Car, t 452 0732.
H&B Car Rental, t 452 0872.
National, t 450 8721.

You can hire **motorbikes** through **Wayne's Motorcycle Centre**, Vide Bouteille, t 452 2059, with motorbikes from US$35 a day and scooters from US$30.

By Guided Tour

Heritage Tours, t 451 6220, *sluheritage@ candw.lc*. An excellent series of tours of historical and cultural interest.
Jungle Tours, t 450 0434. General island tours.

St Lucia Helicopters, t 453 6950, *sunsea@ candw.lc*, *www.stluciahelicopters.com*. Helicopter tours – in half an hour you can fly between the Pitons, hover in rainforested valleys and zoom yachts. North and south island tours at about US$200 for 10mins.

Solar Tours, Choc Bay, t 451 9041. General island tours.

St Lucia Reps/Sunlink Tours, Reduit Beach Avenue, t 456 9100. One of the island's long-established tour companies offers a wide range of standard tours.

Tourist Information

Abroad

There is a website devoted to St Lucia at *www.stlucia.org*. There are tourist offices in the following places:

Canada: 8 King St East, Suite 700, Toronto, Ontario M5C 1B5, t (416) 362 4242, toll free t 1 800 456 3984, *stlb-canada@aol.com*.

UK: Collingham Garden, London SW5 0HW, t 0870 900 7697, *www.stlucia.org*.

USA: 9th Floor, 800 Second Ave, New York, NY 10017, t (212) 867 2950, toll free t 1 800 456 3984, *info@st-lucia.com*.

In St Lucia

In St Lucia itself you can write to the main tourist office at PO Box 221, Sureline Bldg, Vide Bouteille Highway, t 452 5968, *slutour@ candw.lc*. There are also information desks:

Point Seraphine Shopping Complex, across the harbour from downtown Castries, t 452 7577. *Open when cruise ships are in dock.*

Jeremie St, Castries, t 452 2479.

Vigie Airport, t 452 2596. *Closed 1–3pm.*

Hewanorra Airport, t 454 6644.

Soufrière, t 459 7419.

Embassies and Consulates

US/Canadian citizens should contact their embassy/high commission in Barbados.

British High Commission: NIS Waterfront Building, 2nd Floor, Castries, t 452 2484, *britishhc@candw.lc*.

Media

The Tourist Board puts out two publications – *Visions of St Lucia*, a glossy magazine with practical details and feature articles; and the monthly broadsheet, the *Tropical Traveller*, for a more topical view. The *Voice* newspaper is published in Castries three times a week, with local news and events. Other local papers include the *Mirror*, published on Thursday, and the *Star*, *One Caribbean* and the *Crusader*, which are published at the weekend.

Money and Banks

The official **currency** of St Lucia is the Eastern Caribbean dollar, which is fixed to the US dollar at EC$2.65 = US$1. US dollars are widely accepted in tourist areas, but generally the word 'dollar' refers to the Eastern Caribbean dollar. It is worth establishing which currency you are dealing in. **Banking hours** are Mon–Thurs 8–3, Fri 8–5.

Shopping

Shops are open Mon–Fri 8.30–12.30 and 1.30–4, Sat 8–noon.

Maps and Books

One of the English-speaking Caribbean's most celebrated authors is St Lucian poet and playwright Derek Walcott, who won the Nobel Prize for Literature in 1992. His works, which often adapt worldwide themes to a Caribbean setting, include *Omeros*. Another St Lucian author is Garth St Omer, whose works include *The Lights on the Hill*. If you can track down a copy of *St Lucia, Tours and Tales*, by Harriet Durham and Florence Lewisohn, do so, because it gives a well-presented and amusing background to the island. And you might even find a copy of the *St Lucia Diary* of Lt J. H. Caddy, a military man who served time in the West Indies in the 1830s – a revealing description of his life riding out and dining out with occasional military manoeuvres.

The Sunshine Bookshop in Gablewoods Mall has a good selection of foreign newspapers and books about the Caribbean and St Lucia.

Festivals

22 February *Independence Day*. Official activities.

Just before Lent *Carnival*. A blow-out of costumed street parades led by bandwagons stacked with speakers. Calypsonians and Kings and Queens of the Bands play to the crowds in the Marchand Stadium before they spill onto the streets, where the beat is so strong that even the buildings seem to rock in time with the dancers (in fact, parts of Castries are built on reclaimed land and they really do move).

May *Jazz Festival*. An excellent festival, with a broad selection of heavyweight jazz musicians and easy-listening artists. *Festival of Comedy*.

30 August *Rose and the Marguerite*. Musical celebration, set around an imaginary court and its retinue, complete with finery, ceremonial garb and flower cockades. They stage a ball, and are led by a chanterelle and a band (banjo, cuatro, boom boom and drum). Well worth attending.

September/early October *Billfishing competition*.

17 October *Rose and the Marguerite* (*see* Aug).

28 October (weekend nearest) *Jounen Kweyol*. The creole language (spoken by most St Lucians) is remembered during this festival. Culinary and musical blow-outs are staged.

22 November *St Cecilia's Day*. The patron saint of music is remembered by island calypsonians and panmen. During the day musicians from outlying villages ride the roads playing from vans, and then in the evening they collect for competitions.

13 December *National Day*. A round of sailing races, fêtes and jump-ups.

Watersports

Watersports are on offer in many of the hotels. Otherwise you can fix almost anything at Reduit Beach, including glass-bottom boat rides, water-skiing and parasailing, or a trip on a sunfish or a hobie cat.

Day Sails

Endless Summer I and *II*, **t** 450 8651. For a day cruise of yo-ho-ho down to the Pitons, you can try these ever popular catamarans.
Unicorn, **t** 452 6811. A 140ft square-rigged brigantine. Trips to the Pitons.

Deep-sea Fishing

There is a billfishing tournament in St Lucia each September/early October. Half-day trips can be arranged from US$400, a full day from US$800. Contact:

Captain Mike's Watersports, Vigie Cove, **t** 452 7044, *capt.mikes@candw.lc*.
Mako Watersports, Vigie Cove, **t** 452 0412.

Sailing

All down its west coast, St Lucia is indented with coves that make protected harbours for yachts. There are three marinas on the island, each with its own historical and romantic lore. In the north, Rodney Bay marina lies behind Reduit Beach. In Vigie Cove behind Point Seraphine is a smaller marina convenient for Castries, and a few miles south of here is Marigot Bay.

If you are crossing the Atlantic, the Atlantic Rally for Cruisers takes place annually in November/December each year and culminates in St Lucia. Contact **World Cruising Club**, 120 High St, Cowes, Isle of Wight, UK, PO31 7AX, **t** (01983) 296060, *mail@worldcruising.com*, *www.worldcruising.com/arc*.

St Lucia is also a great place to start a sailing holiday in the region. Many people charter a yacht here and then head down to the Grenadines. Contact:

DSL Yachting, Gros Islet, **t** 452 8531, *info@ dsl-yachting.com*, *www.dsl-yachting.com*.
Sail Loft, Rodney Bay, **t** 452 8648.
The Moorings, Marigot Bay, **t** 451 4357, *moorings@candw.lc*, *www.moorings.com*. Has a large fleet of bare boats and some crewed yachts, too.

Scuba Diving

There is a general website on scuba diving in St Lucia at *www.stluciascuba.com*. Diving here is excellent and well organized, with visibility up to 100ft and colourful coastal marine life. Instruction and equipment (including underwater cameras) are available through the large operators. Most of the diving takes place on the west coast; two popular areas are Anse Cochon and Anse Chastanet near Soufrière, where the reefs start at 15ft below the surface. A single-tank dive costs around US$45. Most hotels will provide snorkelling gear for a minimal fee, if you wish to chase after angelfish. Contact:

Buddies Scuba, Rodney Bay, **t** 452 9086, *www.rodneybaymarina.com/buddies*.

Dive Fair Helen, Vigie Marina, t 451 7716.
Scuba St Lucia, Anse Chastanet, t 459 7755, *www.scubastlucia.com*.

Windsurfing

Windsurfing is available at the main beaches through hotel watersports shops, but for experts the best winds are on the Atlantic Coast: in the north in Cas en Bas (take the right turn just before Gros Islet town); and in the south of the island, near Hewanorra Airport, you will find operators on Anse des Sables. Contact:

Island Windsurfing, t 454 7400, *windsurf@ slucia.com*. A Mistral Centre with bases in Reef Beach Café and Anse des Sables.
Zimmi Surf Centre, Vieux Fort, t 454 7579.
Club Mistral St Lucia, t 454 3418; *www. slucia.com/windsurf; www.stluciakite boarding.com*.

Other Sports

Golf

St Lucia Golf and Country Club, Cap Estate, near the northern tip of the island, t 450 8523. Has one 18-hole course and an additional nine holes. Clubs, carts and caddies are available for hire.
Sandals La Toc, t 452 3081. Nine holes.
Mini-golf, Gros Islet.

Hiking

A number of trails have been developed in the rainforest; walks can be arranged through the Forestry and Lands Dept, t 450 2231, or the St Lucia National Trust, Vigie, t 452 5005.

Horse-riding

Hire of horses and riding instruction are available. Rides cost about US$40 per hour and will take you for a canter along the beach and a picnic in a secluded cove on the Atlantic Coast. Contact:
International Pony Club, Cas en Bas, t 452 8139.
North Point Riding Stables, Cap Estate, t 452 8273.

Tennis

It's available at all the big hotels and most will let you play on their courts.

Where to Stay

St Lucia t (1 758–)

St Lucia has an excellent variety of hotels. Many are on the beaches of the northern leeward coast, facing the calm Caribbean Sea and the sunset, some of them humming hives of high-pressure luxury in the typical Caribbean beach-resort mould. But St Lucia also has some charming smaller hotels offering classic Caribbean seclusion in fantastically dramatic settings, tucked away in the island's coves or in view of the Pitons.

Many hotels follow an all-inclusive plan, including a number of more luxurious resorts, but there is still a good range of properties for the independent traveller. In recent years a number of small and individual hotels and guest houses have opened up (in all price brackets), and so it is worth trying out more than one in the course of a week.

Hotel bills (unless you are in an all-inclusive resort) are supplemented by a government tax of 8%, and most hotels also levy a 10% service charge.

There are plenty of villas on the island and accommodation in them can be arranged through outside operators or by the local company **Tropical Villas**, t 450 8240, *tropvil@candw.lc, www.tropicalvillas.net*.

Very Expensive

Ladera Resort, near Soufrière, PO Box 255, t 459 7323, US t 1 800 738 4752, *ladera@candw.lc, www.ladera-stlucia.com*. In its striking setting 1,000ft above the sea, perched on the shoulder of the Petit Piton and surrounded by greenery, Ladera is the ultimate in peace and tropical tranquillity and has one of the finest settings in the Caribbean. There is a variety of rooms, suites and one- to four-bedroom villas in stone structures that perch on a ridge-top. All of them are open-fronted to take best advantage of the view and with a delightful intimacy with the tropical night, the breeze and the peep of the tree frogs. Inside they have dark-stained wood and some antique furniture, a plunge pool with a view and delightful touches like mosaics and conch-shell taps in the bathrooms. Very quiet and elegant ambience. Beach shuttle to Anse

Chastanet and Jalousie Beach. Dining with a view at the Dasheene Restaurant, for excellent modern Caribbean cuisine.

Anse Chastanet, PO Box 7000, t 459 7000, UK t 0800 894 057, USA/Canada t 1 800 223 1108, *ansechastanet@candw.lc, www.anse chastanet.com*. In a fantastic and dramatic setting, tucked into its own remote cove at the end of a steep and rickety road out of the town. There are 49 rooms in the resort, ranged on the steeply rising ground from the very pretty dark-sand beach (12 rooms), up past the main dining room and bar, where the rondavels and huge suites (some of them open-sided – showers with a view) have magnificent views, with some overlooking the Pitons. All rooms are furnished in colourful French Caribbean 'madras' material and are fan-ventilated rather than air-conditioned. Friendly atmosphere and busy down on the beach, where there is a bar and watersports (particularly scuba), but of course very peaceful in the privacy of the rooms. Higher up the hill, a new group of suites – each with a pool – is nearing completion. These will be the most de luxe and expensive units with a separate reception area, restaurant and concierge services. In addition to watersports, the resort offers hiking and biking excursions and boat transfers to its adjoining beach where there are the 18th century ruins of the sugar estate.

East Winds Inn, La Brelotte Bay, PO Box 193, t 452 8212, UK t (01242) 604 030, US t (212) 545 8437, *eastwinds@candw.lc, www.east winds.com*. A low-key and extremely comfortable smaller hotel set in a very attractive lawned garden of bamboo and mango trees running down to a beach with a good stretch of sand. There are 30 rooms in two main styles: stone and wooden cottages with gingerbread pointings, a small porch and screened windows, very comfortable inside with bamboo and rattan furniture and sunken showers made of stone; and breezy octagonal rondavels with large porches, louvred windows and tall cane-backed chairs. Four rooms are set in a block that looks through the trees to the beach. There is a pool with a swim-up bar and a nice palm-thatch dining area close to the beach. Elegant and quiet. All-inclusive plan,

with some nice house wines to go with the excellent fare in the dining room, and some dine-around options. No children in season.

Windjammer Landing Villas Beach Resort, La Brelotte Bay, PO Box 1504, t 452 0913, US t 1 800 743 9609, Canada t 800 267 7600, *windjammer@candw.lc, www.windjammer-landing.com*. The white arches and orange roof tiles stand out starkly against the shades of green on the bay. There are 168 extremely comfortable rooms in varieties of one- to four-bedroom apartments and villas – all with maid service and some with their own plunge pool and sunning area. From the breezy central area laid with terracotta tiles you descend through the tropical gardens to a long and pretty curve of beach. There are also four restaurants and four swimming pools. Plenty of activity – tennis and watersports – by day, and some entertainment in the evenings.

Le Sport, Cap Estate, PO Box 437, t 450 8551, US and Canada t 1 800 544 2883, UK t 0870 220 2344, *lesport@candw.lc, www.lesport.com.lc*. Devotes itself to a scheduled body-holiday for office-weary executives. As the name suggests, there are plenty of sports, both land and waterborne – golf practice, stretch classes, archery, and pool volleyball when it rains. And for less energetic rejuvenation, you can try the Moorish relaxation palace (chandra head, neck and shoulder massage, remineralizing body wraps, salt loofah body buff, Swiss needle showers and full-on Swedish massage). Calorized cuisine or plain old chocolate indulgence, including the delightful restaurant Tao. All-inclusive plan.

Sandals Grand St Lucian Spa resort, Gros Islet, t 455 2000, *sglmail@sgl.sandals.com, www.sandals.com*. The most comfortable of the large beach hotels, stretched along the waterfront. 284 rooms, some of them 'swim-up' in two- and three-storey blocks. Watersports, spa, grills and smart restaurants. One of three Sandals resorts on St Lucia. Guests of one have access to all.

Jalousie Hilton Resort and Spa, Soufrière, PO Box 251, t 459 7666, US t 1 800 445 8667, *www.hilton.com*. More than a hundred rooms ranged over the steeply rising ground between the Pitons, some with views of the sea, others with a backdrop of tropical greenery. A shuttle carries you around the resort, to the main house (built around the old sugar plantation estate building), the spa up above (for a massage with a view), the pool terrace on the waterfront, the restaurants and the helicopter pad, in case you need it. The hotel was recently acquired by the Le Sport group, and will be converted into a 'Body Holiday'-style resort in 2006.

Expensive

Mago Estate Hotel, Soufrière, PO Box 247, t 459 5880, *monica@candw.lc, www.mago.hotel. com*. A small and individual hotel with just a few rooms lost in greenery and perched on a steep hillside high above the town and beach. The lounge, dining room and bar are built into the rock face itself, and the rooms (with some four-poster beds) and pool are ranged beneath them, all with excellent views. Quiet, quite hip and a delightful secluded hideaway.

Stonefield Estate, just south of Soufrière, t 459 7037, *brown@candw.lc, www.stonefield villas.com*. Has 11 one- to three-bedroom villas scattered around the charming gardens of an old plantation estate, in full view of the Petit Piton and a short walk from Malgretoute Beach. Painted in bright Caribbean colours outside and furnished in the best West Indian traditions, with antiques, four-posters and mosquito nets, and they have louvred doors and windows, with fans to encourage the breeze. Utterly calm and charming, with a very low-key atmosphere. Pool with a view (of the Petit Piton). Each cottage has a fully equipped kitchen, but there is also a restaurant.

Marigot Beach Club Hotel, Marigot Bay, t 451 4974, *mbc@candw.lc, www.marigotdive resort.com*. Down on the waterfront, behind the screen of tall palm trees on the spit of land. The series of studios and villas (24 in all, comfortable with bright white décor, a kitchenette and porch, plus fan ventilation) are ranged on the steep valley side amid the tropical bushes and trees. The central area is on the shoreline itself: a passable beach, watersports shop, pool and a brightly painted restaurant and bar. An easy air, with yachtsmen and a passing crowd. Stay-and-sail packages available.

Oasis Marigot, Marigot Bay, t 451 4719/4185, UK t 0800 965 015, US and Canada t 1 800 263 4202, *info@oasismarigot.com, www.oasis marigot.com*. Seventeen large and comfortable one- and three-bedroom villas high on the hill above the Marigot Beach Club and elsewhere around the bay.

Discovery at Marigot Bay, t 458 0790, *www.marigotbay.com*. A large resort and villa development due to open in late 2005. In addition to 57 one- and two-bedroom luxury apartments, it will have several restaurants, a spa, a 60-berth marina and a marina village with shops and watersports.

Moderate

Bay Gardens Hotel, PO Box 1892, Castries, t 452 8060, *baygardens@candw.lc, www.bay gardenshotel.com*. On the south side of Rodney Bay, close to the shops, restaurants and bars of Reduit Beach. The hotel has 71 air-conditioned rooms, each with terrace or balcony, refrigerator, bathroom, cable TV, phone and radio. In addition to a restaurant and bar, there are two swimming pools, a Jacuzzi, library, three conference rooms and a new fully-equipped business centre.

Bay Gardens Inn, Rodney Bay, PO Box 1892, Castries, t 452 0255, *baygardensinn@ candw.lc, www.baygardensinn.com*. Sister to Bay Gardens Hotel, with 32 modest air-conditioned rooms with clock-radio, cable television and phone. Superior rooms come with tea/coffee maker. There is a restaurant, bar, and pool with separate swim-up bar. A third member of the group, Bay Gardens Beach Resort & Spa, is under construction directly on Reduit Beach and is scheduled to open in November 2006. It will have 80 de luxe rooms and 40 one- and two- bedroom suites in four plantation-style buildings. Rooms will be equipped with flat-screen television, high-speed Internet access, and Wi-Fi in public areas.

Sea Horse Inn, Marigot Bay, PO Box 1825, t 451 4436, *seahorse@candw.lc, www.seahorse-inn.com*. An excellent place to stay – small, intimate and impeccably clean and neat. Set in a former private house, made of stone with windows and balustrades picked out in yellow and green. Now an upmarket bed and breakfast, it has a large central sitting area and dining room upstairs, and five comfortable rooms each with their own sitting area. Nice and breezy and very private (no air-con nor phones). There's a pool on a deck in the garden and a lovely view over the lagoon. Breakfast only; no kitchenettes.

The Inn on the Bay, Marigot Bay, PO Box 387, t 451 4260, *info@saint-lucia.com*, *www.saint-lucia.com*. Just five rooms in a very modern villa looking back onto the bay from the southern headland. Quiet and personable (the owners live upsatirs), with a nice pool and sun deck with a view, plus books and games to keep you busy. No children.

Villa Beach Cottages, Choc Bay, PO Box 129, t 452 2691, *huntec@hotmail.com*, *www.villabeachcottages.com*. Not the best position, just off the main road, but the 14 self-contained rooms stand shoulder to shoulder in their own compound right on the sand. They are dressed up with gingerbread woodwork outside and nicely presented inside, with local architectural touches. There are also exchange possibilities with La Dauphine Estate House, a very pretty plantation house lost in the jungle above Soufrière in the south of the island.

Coco Kreole Resort, Rodney Bay Village, t 452 0712/0774, *reservations@coco-resorts.com*, *www.coco-resorts.com*. Offers an 'authentic' Caribbean experience: Caribbean décor and paintings by different Caribbean artists. All 20 rooms include Wi-Fi, cable television, DVD, CD player, cordless phone and mini-fridge. 'Hosts' are trained and dedicated to specific rooms to give personal service.

Coco Palm Resort, Rodney Bay Village, t 452 0712/0774, *reservations@coco-resorts.com*, *www.coco-resorts.com*. A new hotel in French Caribbean plantation style with 72 rooms and 12 suites – all with air-con, ceiling fans, CD players, cable television, DVD, Wi-Fi and minibars. Ground floor rooms have patios or direct access to the pool; suites have spacious bathrooms, walk-in closets, Jacuzzi tub and separate shower and a sitting area with its own bath and shower.

The Still Plantation and Beach Resort, Soufrière, t 459 7261, *duboulayd@candw.lc*, *www.thestillresort.com*. Studios in the plantation or rooms on the beach, plus pool, restaurant and good view.

Inexpensive

Henry's La Panache Guest House, Cas en Bas Road, near Gros Islet, t 450 0765, *augustinh@candw.lc*. A small spot with a lot of style. Just eight comfortable rooms scattered on a hillside around a couple of charming and rustic Caribbean decks (tin roofs on wooden poles) in a garden where stone walkways meander through tropical profusion. Friendly and easy-going air, with lots of information, particularly on natural history. Hot water and showers in private bathrooms, plus fan ventilation. Kitchens and fridges in rooms, but breakfast and snacks available by day, and creole dinners sometimes.

Balenbouche Estate, between Laborie and Choiseul, PO Box 489, t 455 1244, *balenbouche@candw.lc*. A restored 200-year-old plantation house in the far south of the island in a charming garden setting with the atmosphere of the old West Indies. Eight rooms in total, set in a bungalow and in the old main house, which has antique furniture and creaking floorboards (quite thin walls). Some shared baths. Friendly atmosphere with lots of good advice on things to do in the area and of course endless speculation on the origin of the name.

The Mirage Hotel, Laborie, t 455 9763, *www.cavip.com/en/hotels/mirage*. A lovely hotel set in a local community, hidden in palms and sea almonds right behind a white-sand beach. Just five rooms, quite simple but spacious (both fan-ventilated and air-conditioned), in villas. A friendly reception and a nice dining room that serves local creole food.

La Haut Plantation, above Soufrière, t 454 6026, *allainj@candw.lc*, *www.candw.lc/lahaut*. The name literally means 'up there' and it gives an idea of the setting, way up above the town. Six large apartments with rattan furniture and a balcony or terrace, kitchenettes, plus restaurant with a view.

Camp Site, Anse la Liberté, near Canaries. With cabins, cooking and washing facilities, as well as trails and an interpretation centre.

Harbour Light Inn, just out of Castries, t 452 3506. Handy for the airport, set in a modern structure without much charm. Simple rooms with a choice of standing fans or air-con, private baths, and restaurant.

Eating Out

St Lucia's French heritage extends to the food, and the West Indian ingredients take on new life here in such creole dishes as *soupe germou* (pumpkin and garlic soup) and *poule dudon* (treacle and coconut chicken stew). As in any other of the islands, it is worth getting a spread of vegetables, cooked in all the different ways – plantain boiled and fried, breadfruit, yam and christophene.

A surfeit of all-inclusive hotels in an island tends to spell the death knell for eating out and it seems that the restaurateurs in St Lucia have had quite a tough time as so many of the hotels have gone that way. However, some good restaurants remain and so it is worth eating out. There are also some good restaurants in the hotels themselves.

When it comes to cheap or takeaway food, you will find endless snacks and pastries on offer, some of them fried on braziers in front of you. A float is a deep-fried dough cake and you will find variations such as codfish or corned-beef fritters. Finish off with a coconut pattie or a delicious St Lucian fruit cake.

Most large or hotel restaurants will accept credit cards; local ones will accept EC (Eastern Caribbean) dollars willingly and US dollars at a pinch. All bills are supplemented with an 8% government tax and most add 10% or sometimes 15% for service as well. **Categories** are based on the price of a main course: expensive = EC$50 and above, moderate = EC$20–50; inexpensive = less than EC$20.

Castries and the North

Expensive

The Coal Pot Restaurant, Vigie Marina, **t** 457 5566, *xavier@candw.lc, www.coalpot restaurant.com*. Has a delightful setting on a wooden deck on the waterfront overlooking the slightly industrial Vigie Cove on the outskirts of Castries (signs off the airport road). You dine on excellently prepared and presented French and creole cuisine in an open-sided, shingle-roofed deck, with artwork on the walls. There is a blackboard menu with a long selection of fish, for which there is a choice of sauces - creole, ginger, lemon or coconut – and lamb fillets and good salads. Intimate air, with good service and a nice reception.

Froggie Jacques, Vigie Cove, **t** 458 1900, *riouxj@candw.lc, www.froggiejacques.com*. Opposite The Coal Pot on the other side of Vigie Cove, named after a Frenchman called Jacques. You sit in a nice deck above the water or in the garden festooned with greenery: pan-seared king scallops followed by oven-baked chicken breast stuffed with smoked fish served in a lemon sauce. Long cocktail list if you want to linger on the waterfront. Easy-going and friendly.

The Green Parrot, Red Tape Lane, Morne Fortune, **t** 452 3399, *greenparrot@candw.lc*. Set in the dining room of the hotel, French and creole food (including some Caribbean curries): *Les Potages et Oeufs*, *Les Poissons* (the *bonne femme* is glazed in mushrooms and white wine), *Les Plats du Jour* (including beef thunderballs *à la flambée*), *Les Grillades* and *Les Entremets*. Set four-course menu with six or seven choices. Island luminary Chef Harry will sometimes entertain the guests himself by singing and dancing.

Great House Restaurant, Cap Estate, **t** 450 0450, *greathouse@clubsaintlucia.com*. It occupies the site of an old plantation house and has been rebuilt with some of the old West Indian charm. You enter through louvred doors and dine in the gracious mock-antique Caribbean interior or out on the veranda where vases overflow with greenery. Try snails in *millefeuille* with shiitake mushrooms followed by roast dorado in champagne *beurre blanc*. Finish up with soursop ice cream. Set menu or à la carte. *Closed Mon*.

Tao, at Le Sport, Cap Estate, **t** 450 8551. From the time this sophisticated restaurant opened in 1999, it has garnered rave reviews and set a new standard of cuisine in St Lucia. The extraordinary creations by young and talented Filipino chef Juan Agad, are best described as East-West fusion. Like the cuisine, the décor of Tao is a handsome blend of Asia and the New World.

Charthouse, Rodney Bay, **t** 450 8115. Set on the waterfront in a timber-frame house hung with ferns and palms. You dine on house specialities of seafood and prime rib steaks or some hickory-smoked ribs. *Closed Sun*.

Capone's, Rodney Bay, t 450 0284. If you think you might like an air-conditioned speakeasy with a feeling of mock-gangsterism, then try this place, where the menu is Italian. Start with a Prohibition Punch, followed by chicken with spinach, cheese and red peppers. The bill comes in a violin case. If you cannot remember the code word ('Al sent me'), there is a pizzeria next door.

Buzz Seafood & Grill, Rodney Bay, t 458 0450, *www.buzzstlucia.com*. Run by a well-know St Lucian restaurateur and local chef, specialities at this popular place include Moroccan spiced lamb shanks, chicken wellington and West Indian pepperpot. Steaks and lobster are also on the menu. Reservations necessary. *Open Dec–Mar daily 5.30, closed Mon April–Nov.*

Scuttlebutts Waterside Bar & Grill, Rodney Bay Marina, t 452 0351. On the waterfront, with breakfast, lunch and dinner served inside or on deck. Good wines and speciality drinks including a wide choice of Caribbean rums and beer. Ample mooring facilities for dinghies, Internet access, daily weather-watch, crew-news, swimming pool, shower facilities and delivery service from restaurant to boat.

Moderate

The Lime, Rodney Bay, t 452 0761. Another ever-popular place for simple fare daytime and evening. Caribbean and international menu: a fisherman's platter (fish, shrimp and *lambi* in lemon butter) or omelettes and burgers. *Closed Tues.*

Spinnakers Beach Bar and Carvery, Rodney Bay, t 452 8491. On the beach and very popular. Good fresh food and great atmosphere with quite a buzz at lunch time.

Oceana Seafood Restaurant, Castries, t 456 0300. An inexpensive local favourite.

Inexpensive

Kimlan's, Derek Walcott Square, Castries, t 452 1136. A trusty favourite with the locals. Simple St Lucian fare, including excellent tropical juices, with bench seats on a balcony which give an excellent view of the square. *Rotis*; chicken, fish or beef stew; or curry with a volley of ground provisions. *Closed Sun.*

Laurel's Creole Restaurant, on the road to La Brelotte Bay, t 452 8457. An excellent place for local food. It has a modern terrace hung with greenery and set with green plastic tables, where you will eat *accras* (fish batterballs) and hefty portions of local green fig and saltfish or creole fish.

Takeaway vans, Castries. You can get a juice and a local meal in a polystyrene box in the daytime.

Local restaurants and burger bars, Gros Islet.

South of Castries

If you are travelling around the island, there are some wonderful stopovers. On the route south make sure to stop in at Marigot Bay, the idyllic cove on the west coast where small bars and restaurants sit on the waterfront surrounded by greenery and the steep slopes of the valley walls.

Expensive

Mago Estate Hotel, Soufrière, t 459 5880. Has a wonderful position, tables laid out beneath a huge rock in a cliff face, overlooking the town and bay (at the end of a very rickety drive off the main road out of town). Very well prepared and presented French and creole food.

Dasheene Restaurant, Ladera Resort, near Soufrière, t 459 7323. Dining with a view (if you get the right table). Excellent modern Caribbean cuisine. *Book the best table or arrive early.*

Bang Between the Pitons. Sits on the waterfront between St Lucia's twin peaks. The setting is like a West Indian village and there are pretty clapboard houses and palm trees set around a yard where the tables sit under shelters. The menu is Caribbean, with sunshine soup (from pumpkin), followed by jerk (from Jamaica) and escoveitched fish. Access easiest by boat.

Moderate

The Shack Bar and Grill, Marigot Bay, t 451 4145. The nicest place to eat in the bay, set on a deck with a red-painted floor and white trellising around the side. Shack pumpkin soup or a seafood crêpe followed by a rasta pasta or a grilled chicken breast with tropical salsa, then a banana or pineapple flambé.

Doolittle's, Marigot Bay, t 451 4974. Just along from the spit with all the palm trees, on a bright yellow and blue deck. Here you can get international fare with a Caribbean accent: local fish and lobster with some Caribbean vegetables.

Château Mygo, Marigot Bay, t 451 4772. Named because of the local pronunciation of Marigot. On the waterfront next to customs, a colourful deck with a menu from around the world. Burritos, burgers, local fish and chips.

La Haut Plantation, just north of Soufrière. Offers a nice mix of local and international fare: creole fish or *lambi* with local vegetables, followed by banana, poppy seed or coconut cake. Fantastic view across the valley.

La Marie's Restaurant, Soufrière, t 459 5002. Sits in a charming old building on the waterfront near the main dock. A worldwide menu, with calamari provençal, chicken tikka and Thai-style curry king prawns.

Seafood Friday, Anse la Raie. With lobster and octopus cooked on braziers on the street.

Inexpensive

J-J's Paradise, Marigot Bay, t 451 4076. At the head of the bay. Trusty local fare here, particularly popular on a Wednesday, when it's crab night (they cook up crabs in a pot).

Bars and Nightlife

Most of the big hotels offer some entertainment, so you may see a few thighs singed under the limbo pole and hear Caribbean classics such as 'Yellowbird' and 'Scandal in the Family', but there are some more local entertainments too, in which everyone makes the best of Bounty Crystal, a local white rum; Old Fort; or the award-winning 'Piton – La Bière Sent Lisi', also recently called the 'Mystic Brew'.

Bars

Kimlan's, Derek Walcott Square, Castries. *Closed Sun*.

Spinnaker's, Reduit Beach. Has music on Saturday evenings and also offers food and jazz.

The Wharf, Choc Bay. Sees a lively crowd.

The Lime, Rodney Bay. A popular gathering point at the weekends before the crowd moves on to a club.

Clubs and Dancing

The Indies Nightclub, Gros Islet, t 452 0727. The 'in' place at the time of writing. Wednesday is ladies' night and Friday is also popular.

Jump-up on Friday nights, Gros Islet. The best-known party in the island is this weekly event, when four or five clubs spill out on to the street, speakers turned into the road pumping out soca, reggae and the latest zouk from Martinique, visible just a few miles to the north. It has become a bit of a tourist event, but it is still quite fun. You can pick up grilled fish and chicken legs, cooked in braziers on the street and served with hot pepper sauce.

J-J's Paradise, head of Marigot Bay. Like the jump-up in Gros Islet but less crowded – all sorts of streetside activity on a Wednesday. J-J's offers a free round-trip water-taxi service from your hotel; reservations can be made online at *www.oasismarigot.com*.

Beach Bars

Spinnakers, Reduit Beach. Set on a palm-thatch and wooden deck right on the sand, so that you can admire the view, and there's a TV in case you're missing the sport.

The Wharf, Choc Bay, t 450 4844. Burgers, *rotis* and salads to go with the daytime diet of watersports, plus evening sunset view.

Doolittle's, Marigot Bay. An excellent setting beneath some tall palms.

Bar, Anse Chastanet. With a superb view over the dark sand to the sunset.

Harmony's, Malgretoute Beach, south of Soufrière, t 459 5050. Quite a stony beach, but popular with St Lucians at the weekend.

Sandy Beach, Anse des Sables. Brightly coloured and good for snacks.

The Reef, Anse des Sables, t 454 9249. Hidden in the sea grapes.

Rumours Restaurant and Cocktail Bar, Rodney Bay, t 452 9249. The 'in' place. Opens late, dance floor, great place to meet friends.

Charlie's Piano Bar and Night Club, Rodney Bay, t 458 0565, *www.nightlifestlucia.com*.

Café Claude Restaurant, Rodney Bay, t 458 0847.

The Jerk Pit, Old Shamrocks Yard, Rodney Bay. In a little trailer. Serves great jerk with great service. Reasonable too.

There are far fewer mammals, but there are many reptiles, from frogs to iguanas. One you will certainly hear is the tree frog, who peeps rhythmically at night, particularly after a rainstorm. Turtles also come to lay their eggs on St Lucian beaches between March and August. The St Lucia National Trust, **t** 452 5005, *natrust@ candw.lc*, manages a number of St Lucia's Nature Reserves, which include the **Maria and Fregate Islands** on the east coast and the **Pigeon Island National Landmark** (as the name indicates, this is really a site of historical interest, but some of the plants are marked). There is a **Marine Park** in the Soufrière area which has been zoned into marine reserves and recreational areas, helping to protect the environment (preserving it for scuba divers among other things). Yachts need to buy a permit to anchor here. A campsite has been opened in **Anse la Liberté** near Canaries, with a local plant nursery and a nature interpretation centre as well as trails through the local area. Those with a particular interest in the natural life can contact the Forestry and Lands Department, **t** 450 2231, **t** 453 2287, who can arrange knowledgeable guides for birders and plant or animal watchers.

Castries

If history were to be replayed as you cruised into Castries harbour, the hills around you would swarm with troops, the air hang heavy with the smell of gunpowder, and the ground and the harbour be stained scarlet with blood. Castries was one of the most bitterly contested places in the whole of the Caribbean.

The town lies on the protected leeward coast of the island, at the head of an irregular and almost landlocked bay, framed by forested hills that rise in folds into the distance. The harbour mouth is guarded by Vigie Point (French for 'lookout'), covered in yellow-brick barrack buildings and the graveyards of Empire – you get a good view of them as you come in for the final wobbly descent into Vigie Airport. The French have actually returned. They keep their embassy in one of these buildings.

Castries takes its name from the Maréchal de Castries, a French colonial minister who was governor of the island in 1784. The name stuck, despite being rejected at the time of the French Revolution, when the town was known as Félicité-ville. Set out on a gridiron pattern, the centre of the town is mostly modern, concrete and functional. Near the market on Jeremie St, there is even an area of neo-brutalist housing estate imported from 1960s Britain. But despite Castries's rather unfortunate habit of burning down (1796, 1812, 1927 and 1948), it has a few pockets of old creole architecture, mostly in the southeast corner of the town at the top end of **Chaussee Rd**. The creole balconies overhang the pavement on sturdy wooden stilts, and the gingerbread patterns on the eaves here are more intricate than on any island in the Eastern Caribbean besides Trinidad. In all, the town supports about 60,000 people.

The centre of the town is **Derek Walcott Square**, so named after he won the Nobel Prize for Literature in 1992 (its previous name, Columbus Square, had long been controversial). In its centre is a magnificent saman tree which provides shade from the tropical sun. On the east side of the square, Laborie St, is the **Roman Catholic**

Cathedral, which has an ironwork and wooden interior with yellow stained glass; a brightly painted, patterned roof; and colourful murals in which many of the figures are depicted as Africans. Opposite the cathedral stands the **library**, an imposing colonial structure. Farther along Laborie St you come to the small **Constitution Park** and the **Court and Parliament buildings** (both modern). This area, with William Peter Boulevard running off it, is the business and gravitational centre for limers and shoppers.

Another lively area of town is the **market** on Jeremie St, a magnificent old red iron market erected at the start of the 20th century. Recently renovated, it is now flanked by newer concrete buildings containing more markets and craft markets. The whole area is jumbled full of furniture, straw bags and sweetmeats and resounds to the chatter of buyers and the market ladies from the country, who sit watching over piles of eddoe, tannia, christophene and yam. Beyond here you will find the old **Botanical Gardens**, now more of a park, but a small patch of green in a seething city.

Morne Fortune (pronounced 'Fortunay' and supposedly meaning the Hill of Good Luck) looms above the town. Now this area is partially bypassed because of a new road – and quieter and nicer for it – but it is here that the fiercest battles took place in the 18th century. Nowadays the soldiers would be fighting their way through the scarlet and purple blooms of the bougainvillea in the private gardens as the road winds its way back and forth to the summit. The old imposing military hulks, barracks, stables and gun emplacements have been taken over by the modern-day establishment as official buildings. The **La Toc Battery** has been opened: a low 19th-century battery made of concrete with a couple of old cannon that point at the trees now that they have grown to obscure the view. There is also a **walking trail**.

Close to the summit stands the tatty **Fort Charlotte**, which dates from the late 18th century, but not far off most of the old colonial buildings now contain schools and a department of the University of the West Indies. There is a monument to the bravery of the 27th Inniskilling Regiment, who actually made it all the way to the top in 1796, and also a monument to Sir Arthur Lewis, the first St Lucian Nobel Prize winner and first Chancellor of the UWI. Nearby is **Government House**, the official residence of the Governor General, built of grey stones with white trimmings in the 1890s.

From the top of the Morne you get one of the finest views in the West Indies. To the north it commands Vigie Airport and then along the coast to Pigeon Point. On clear days it is quite possible to see Martinique. The view is also spectacular to the south, where the Pitons are visible in the distance.

North of Castries

As you head north out of town, you run along the harbour, passing the new office blocks on the right and the **fish market** with its colourful boats on the left. A side road leads left to the Institut Franco-St Lucien, a curious white pyramid, and then on to the Point Seraphine cruise ship dock and shopping complex.

Time was, not so long ago, when the cars had to be cleared off the road to allow planes to land at Vigie Airport, which handles short-haul island-hopper flights. Now the airstrip runs alongside **Vigie Beach**, so, if you want some last minutes of sun and sand before leaving, there are 2 miles of protected bay here. It is the site of many a forgotten invasion and the fortifications that opposed them, 18th-century strong- holds that now lie buried under the bastions of the 20th-century Caribbean tourist hotels. The island opposite the Sandals Halcyon Hotel is called **Rat Island**, a former nunnery, now deserted. From the top end of **Choc Bay** a side road branches through the hills to the other side of the island, where you will find the attractive half-moon bay of **Grand Anse** on the Atlantic coast. The family of the Empress Josephine had a sugar estate at Paix Bouche on the windward side of the island. Despite Martinican insistence to the contrary, the St Lucians claim that Josephine was born in St Lucia. At the **Marquis Estate** (*t* 452 3762) you will see a working plantation producing bananas and copra (dried coconut) and hear descriptions of old-time crops such as cocoa and coffee, and of course sugar. After the estate visit you can take a trip down the Marquis River to an Atlantic coast bay for a swim.

The main road north from Castries, which is being steadily developed with houses and shopping centres, emerges from the rolling hills onto **Rodney Bay**, named after the British admiral who made St Lucia his headquarters in the late 18th century. This is the location of Reduit Beach and many of St Lucia's hotels, restaurants and, most recently, private homes on every slope. In the bay the yachts and gin palaces lie at anchor in formation, just as Rodney's warships did over 200 years ago.

Across the marina entrance stands the village of **Gros Islet**, famed for its parties on Friday nights when the few streets of simple, brightly painted clapboard houses seethe with dancers until the early hours. The town was proudly called Révolution when St Lucia was holding out at the time of the French Revolution.

The 'islet' (called **Pigeon Island**; a ferry runs across from Rodney Bay Marina several times a day) from which the town takes its name is in fact no longer an island. It was joined to the mainland in the early 1970s by an artificial causeway, part of a vastly expensive tourist development programme that foundered, leaving just a few aban- doned foundations and a perfectly protected and stunning bay. Despite now being a promontory, Pigeon Island continues to be called Pigeon Island. It lies 1 mile across the bay, a barren outcrop with two peaks that the British fortified as soon as they took the island from the French in 1778. The stone ramparts and defences are still visible: 18th-century gun batteries, gun slides and the sunken 'musket redoubt' (a last-ditch defence); 19th-century barracks and cookhouses. The most recent buildings are from an American Second World War listening station. Since the earliest visitors came to St Lucia, Pigeon Island has been used as a vantage point to watch over Martinique, visible 20 miles away. Now the area is a National Park and there is a shop and a small **Interpretation Centre** (*adm*) in the recently restored officers' mess. Among the Amerindian artefacts, models of soldiers and pictorial descriptions of barrack life, there is a visual display of the Battle of the Saints in 1782.

At the northern tip of the island is the **Cap Estate**, an expensive residential area with a couple of hotels, some very smart villas and a golf course. The Landings, meanwhile, is set to become a multi-million dollar villa and marina when it is completed in 2007.

Castries to Soufrière

The route to Soufrière from Castries follows a tortuous path above the leeward coast of the island, a series of switchbacks struggling up over the headlands and cruising down into the river valleys where fishing villages nestle among the palms. Alternatively, take a yacht and coast along the island for two hours and you will see the road straggle south against the backdrop of the St Lucian mountains, so often shrouded by passing rainstorms. Whichever route you take, the journey culminates in one of the most exciting views in the whole of the Caribbean, the twin peaks of the Pitons that soar from the sea's edge like vast tropical pyramids.

On land you can either wind up over the summit of Morne Fortune or take the coastal road, both of which bring you into **Cul de Sac**, a wide valley once riffling with sugar cane and now carpeted with banana trees, past the wire and security lights of the huge Hess oil bunkering facility. From here the road climbs a ridge and drops into another huge valley, at **Roseau**, also filled with bright green banana leaves that splay gracefully in an arch until their tips reach the ground. As you reach the valley floor you come to a side road which leads to **Marigot Bay**, one of the most charming natural features in the Caribbean, a steep-sided harbour festooned with palm trees. For now, it is now an idyllic hideaway with a cluster of low-key hotels and villas on the hillsides and bars around the waterfront. Yachts sit serenely on the calm of Hurricane Hole, an extremely safe anchorage. Construction of a new resort and villa community is under way. So the tranquillity may be about to change for good. In 1778, Admiral Barrington is supposed to have eluded d'Estaing by bringing his fleet into the bay and camou-flaging the ships with palm fronds. More recently, *Dr Doolittle* with Rex Harrison was filmed here. A small boat-taxi links one side to the other.

Farther down, just off the main road, you pass the **Barbay Distillery** (*t 451 4258, www.sludistillers.com/tour; open Mon–Fri; adm*), which can be visited on their Rhythm of Rum Tour. Set in a modern building, it shows the processes of fermentation and distillation that produce the local Bounty Rum, in its various white and red forms, and Titasse, a coffee rum. There are tastings of course. The best view of the Roseau Valley is from the heights just as you leave it to drive farther south.

The two fishing towns of **Anse la Raye**, where you will see a fine church, and **Canaries** lie on river mouths at the sea's edge. From here the road cuts deeper inland and then climbs into the rainforest, a profusion of majestic ferns, bamboos and grasses that sprout from the deep-brown earth, and ancient-looking lianas that hang from trees high above. Finally the road clears another summit and, emerging from the dank rainforest, you are faced with the twin points of the Pitons, which stand out in the glare of the sun. The word '*piton*' means 'spike' and they are thought to be the sides of an eroded volcanic crater. They have long been a sailor's landmark and are spectacular when viewed from the sea, but the best view is from the leeward coast road – they have an identical shape and slide dramatically into place beside one another as you descend towards Soufrière.

The town of **Soufrière** itself lies in a valley beneath the Petit Piton (2,461ft). It is one of the oldest settlements in St Lucia, a thriving port in the mid-18th century, and takes its name from the volcanic vent nearby that emits sulphurous clouds. For a while in the 1790s it held the honoured republican name of La Convention, after the revolutionary tribunal in Paris. The town has been cleaned up and has an upbeat air at the moment, but it maintains some of its antique atmosphere around the central **Elizabeth Square** with its attractive old stone façades and wooden creole homes that survive from French times, their eaves a gingerbread filigree beneath corrugated-iron roofs. Some of the traditional life persists. On Saturday morning there is a market on the seafront and you may see cocoa beans drying in the sun on the pavement. The bay is extremely deep, dropping straight away as steeply as the Pitons rise above the surface. For those brave enough to swim in a fathomless place like this, the water has warm and cold patches, created by the volcano beneath the surface.

Inland from Soufrière, the road comes to the **Diamond Falls and Botanical Gardens** (*adm*), on the Soufrière Estate, where a path leads through tropical gardens into a cleft with a waterfall gushing into a small rock pool. The water descends 1,000ft from the volcano above, where it leaves the ground at 106° Fahrenheit, and has coloured the river bed orange and gold with the volcanic mud. The water supposedly has similar properties to the water of Aix-les-Bains in France and is reputed to have considerable curative powers, 'efficacious in cases of rheumatism and kindred ills'. If you are happy to risk carbonate of magnesia and phosphate of lime then you can take the waters (brought down from higher up the mountain). Alternatively you can take a steamy bath in it. The gardens are pleasant to visit and you can expect to see typical Caribbean plants such as lobster claw and ginger lily, but also less usual ones such as breadnut (a relative of the breadfruit) and a gri-gri palm with a hairy trunk. The old waterwheel was used to crush sugar cane and limes.

The road to Diamond continues inland, climbing steadily into the St Lucia rainforest and losing itself in **Fonds St Jacques**, now a nature reserve where, among the wild orchids and the montane woodland on the lower slopes of Morne Gimie, you might catch a glimpse of the endangered St Lucia parrot.

Travelling south from Soufrière back on the coast road, the road climbs for a couple of miles to **Morne Coubaril Estate** (*t 459 7340; adm, half-hour guided tour*), a restored and working plantation high in the mountains. Here you will see a glimpse of traditional life in 18th-century St Lucia, including a plantation village with 'voltivier' roofs made of bamboo-like shingles on wattle and daub walls, and methods of processing tropical products, such as coconuts (used for oil, margarine and suntan lotion), cocoa (which is processed and dried here) and the local flour, from the manioc (better known as cassava). There's a bar and restaurant for local food and juices.

Not far off are the **Sulphur Springs**, St Lucia's well-behaved solfatara. In the collapsed crater is a bubbling and steaming morass, 7 acres in size, devoid of plant-life, with grey mud pools that hiss and smell gently of stink bomb. There was a vapour explosion at the soufrière in 1766, but nothing too violent has happened since then. It is not expected to erupt because it constantly lets off steam (which you can smell on the air in the region). Paths are clearly marked and you are no longer allowed to wander around on it because the mud pools have been known to move suddenly (one person was swallowed to the waist and ended up with third-degree burns). You may see a couple of rusty pipes sticking out of the ground, an attempt to tap the heat for power generation. As the tourist brochures say, the soufrière is a 'drive-in' volcano. For the tourists who dare venture forth from the protection of their car, there are guides who will ply them with more soufrière lore for a small fee.

From the mountain heights of the Pitons, the road descends steadily through the southern plains that once blew with sugar cane, to Vieux Fort at the most southerly tip of the island. It passes through the fishing villages of **Choiseul**, with its black and white cemetery, and **Laborie**. Both are quiet and unaffected West Indian towns, full of clapboard houses on blocks, standing in neat yards in the shadow of breadfruit trees. Perhaps you will arrive on the day when the open-air butcher is at work, boiling up black puddings for passers-by. At Choiseul, the **Arts and Crafts Development Centre** displays and sells local handiwork including rocking chairs and carvings. There is a small restaurant if you want to stop for lunch.

Vieux Fort is named after a fortress, mentioned already by the island-hopping monk Abbé Raynal when he travelled the islands in the mid-17th century. St Lucia's second town, it is windswept and stands on an open bay, looking south towards St Vincent. It was here that the sugar industry was first set up in 1765, but now the town is quiet and the few streets seem empty. **Hewanorra International Airport** (then called Beanfield) nearby was first built by the Americans during the Second World War as a refuelling point on their routes between the United States and Europe; now it receives long-haul flights from both directions.

Protruding into the rough water between the Atlantic and the Caribbean by Vieux Fort is the **Moule à Chique Peninsula**, offering fine views towards St Vincent, a grey-green stain about 25 miles away to the south. The **Maria Islands** nature reserve, meanwhile, lies off the Atlantic coast just out of Vieux Fort. Those interested in discovering the delights of the *kouwès* snake (this is the only place on the globe where this grass snake lives), a lizard called *zandoli te* and the wheeling world of frigatebirds and brown noddies should contact the National Trust (*t 452 5005*).

Vieux Fort to Castries: the Windward Coast

The Windward Road winds along the rough Atlantic coast, over the spurs and the valleys thrown off by the central spine of mountains, and passes through the planta-tions that provide St Lucia's food and export fruit. You can see the tropical abundance at first hand in a number of places, including a couple of plantations that are over 200 years old. The estate at **Mamiku** (*t 455 3729, www.mamiku.com*) dates from the 18th century and there are forest trails through the old plantation grounds, where you will learn about the old crops and the uses of other plants in traditional island medi-cine. At the **Fregate Island Nature Reserve** there is an observation trail where you can hope to see St Lucian orioles and tremblers and where frigatebirds nest in the summer months. At **Dennery** is one of the island's largest banana plantations, with acres of huge and bright green leaves unscrolling and getting steadily shredded by the wind. The **Errard Plantation Tour** also passes through old plantations, of coffee bushes, bananas and nutmeg and cocoa trees that grow around the old estate house. You will see the process of getting mace from the nutmeg fruit and the 'sweating' and drying of cocoa beans (*see* 'The Spice Island of the Caribbean', pp.150–1). From here the main road cuts inland, over the **Barre de l'Isle** ridge, among the lianas and bushy ferns high up in the rainforest, and then descends into Cul de Sac Valley, from where you can make your way back into Castries.

Dominica

Dominica is practically all mountains and rainforest, a jumble of peaks and spurs so rugged and dramatic that the island has its own microclimate. Of all the islands that Columbus is supposed to have described to Ferdinand and Isabella of Spain by crumpling a piece of parchment and throwing it onto the table with a 'Like this, your Majesties', Dominica is the one he would be most likely to recognize today. Wags claim that it has hardly changed since he was here 500 years ago.

In its 29 miles by 16, Dominica has mountains over 4,500ft, higher than anything on the British Isles. The water-laden winds of the Atlantic Ocean clamber up its slopes and then stack in huge clouds on the mountain tops, poised immobile before they ditch their load. The rainfall here is measured in tens of feet and romantics will tell you there is always a rainbow somewhere in the mist-veiled peaks of the island. The natural life is unparalleled and vegetation is explosive. A plot untended for 10 years will be 5ft under with trees as thick as your leg and a gardener's most useful tool is a machete. Dominica is overwhelmingly green.

Dominica (pronounced 'Domin-eek-a') is the least developed of the Windward Islands and, for all the fertility, it is hard for the islanders to make a living. Many parts of the island are very poor and you will see more subsistence farmers working small plots cut out of the hillside here than on the other islands. For years it was difficult enough to get to the island and only relatively recently new roads have opened up parts that before could be reached just on horseback. Vans travel between the villages selling anything from tinned milk to Sunday dresses.

Apart from its wildlife, Dominica's most remarkable heritage is that it is home to the last surviving traces of the Carib race. To the Caribs, the island was *Waitukubuli* or 'Tall is her body', and the wild terrain meant that it was the last island to be settled by Europeans. Once proud and warlike, the Caribs were left in peace on Dominica for a while, but ultimately they could not defend their homeland from the newcomers. There are no native Carib-speakers left, but their descendants are easily recognized in Dominica by their Amerindian features.

A quarter of Dominica's 71,000 or so population live in the capital, Roseau, on the protected Caribbean coast. The island lies between two French islands, Guadeloupe to the north and Martinique to the south. Dominica was settled initially by the French, but then it went through the usual political confusion, ending up in British hands. The official language in Dominica has been English for nearly 200 years, but French patois can be heard all over the island and most of the population is Catholic.

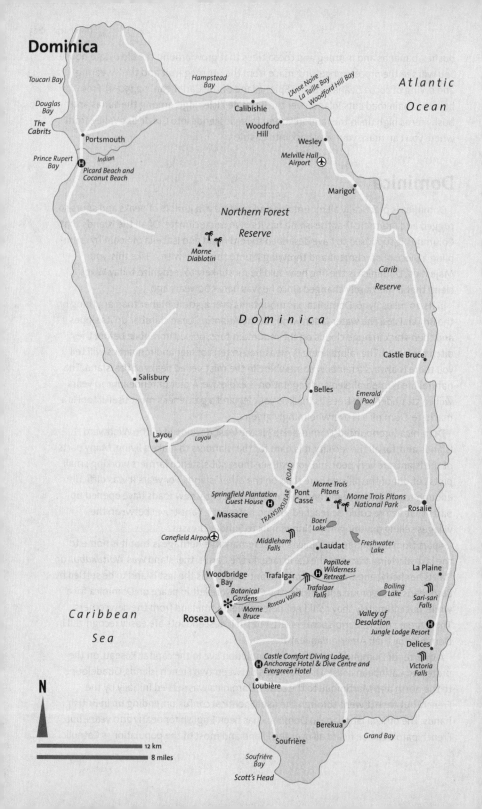

Best Beaches

Hampstead Bay, Calibishie (Pointe Baptiste) and **Woodford Hill Bay**: Dominica's best sand, quite remote in the northeast but dramatic and overhung by cliffs, and often with large waves (but also reefs offshore). Take a map, or good advice about how to get there, and all you need in the way of food and drink. Do not leave any valuables unattended in these areas. Other secluded coves to look out for are Hampstead I and Billy Boo.

Prince Rupert Bay: Near Portsmouth. The sand is black but passable in this area and there are good stretches of beach with some watersports and hotel bars to which to retreat.

Mero: A good stretch of dark sand facing the sunset with a beach bar at the Castaways Hotel, plus some watersports.

In a part of the world renowned for its palm-fringed and dazzling white-sand beaches, Dominica is an odd man out. There is not a lot of tourism and most of the visitors who come are there for the diving and the natural life. The few beach resorts are set on dark sand and there are few restaurants and bars in the typical Caribbean mould. Visitors are expected to join in local life. Dominica is unpretentious and its beauty lies rather in its spectacular interior and its coral-clad underwater slopes. It rightfully calls itself the Nature Island of the Caribbean. Five hundred years after Columbus crumpled his parchment, patches of Dominica are still 'unexplored jungle'.

History

Waitukubuli was christened on 3 November 1493, as Columbus made land after five weeks at sea on his second voyage to the New World. The day of the week was a Sunday, and to give thanks for the safe passage of his fleet the explorer called his new discovery Dominica.

As the heartland of the 'Cannibal Isles', Dominica was given a wide berth by the Spaniards, and only pirates, fishermen and foresters braved its coasts. In the very early years, the Spaniards considered creating a harbour on the island (in the protected area around Portsmouth) where their ships could refit and take on water after the Atlantic crossing, but they did not reckon on the opposition of the resident Indians.

The Caribs kept the Europeans at bay for 200 years. Dominica was officially neutral as late as 1748, left 'to the undisturbed possession of the native Indians' (Treaty of Aix-la-Chapelle), and a retreat for the Caribs squeezed out of the neighbouring islands. But Dominica's position between the two French colonies of Martinique and Guadeloupe meant that it was too important to be disregarded for long, and in the 1750s the French moved in. The campaign against the Caribs was so ruthless and thorough that there were just 400 survivors, who retreated to the windward coast where they would be left alone.

Then, like the other Windwards, Dominica was caught in the crossfire of the European conflicts, blockaded each time war was declared and encouraged to plant madly in times of peace. Traditionally, the French settlers planted coffee and the

British sugar. The island was also a free port and for a while did a brisk trade as a slave market. In 1763, after the Treaty of Paris granted the island to Britain, the French lands were promptly sold to English planters.

Dominica's mountainous and fertile interior offered easy sanctuary for runaway plantation slaves, or 'maroons', who hid out in small communities in the hills. Initially they were happy with just their freedom, but, rallied by leaders with names such as Congo Ray, Jacko, Zombie and Jupiter, they soon began to steal cattle and torch estate buildings, encouraging other slaves to join them. The island militia was first sent out against them in 1785, flushing them out in the network of tracks in the hinterland.

As the French Revolution took effect in the Caribbean, French Royalists fled to Dominica from Martinique and Guadeloupe. Republican revolutionaries followed them clandestinely, offering freedom to the island slaves if they rose up against the planters (slaves on the French islands had been freed in 1794). They smuggled arms to the maroons and there was an invasion from Guadeloupe in June 1795, but the hills were cleaned out again and the invasion was repulsed.

With the French in the ascendancy again in Europe in the early 19th century, Dominica was threatened once more, along with the other British Caribbean islands. In 1805, armed ships appeared in Roseau Bay, flying the Union Jack. At the last moment they tore it down and ran up the *tricolore* instead. Admiral La Grange was besieging the island for France and he blockaded Roseau. After chasing up and down the island, La Grange ransomed the town for £12,000, took all the slaves he could lay his hands on and sailed off to St Kitts. Maroons were still hiding out in the hills and they rose up again in a guerrilla war between 1812 and 1815. Eventually crushed by Rangers, the leaders were hanged, but they are remembered in the name of the peak near the town of Belles, Morne Nègres Marrons. With Emancipation in 1834, Dominica became a refuge for French slaves from the neighbouring islands, where slavery had been reintroduced in 1802. Until 1848, when the French banned it once again, the slaves would make the perilous journey on home-made rafts at night in their bid for freedom. Dominica's own freed slaves moved away from the plantations, preferring to cut a plot of land out of the fertile interior, growing the produce they needed and selling the surplus at market. The new Dominicans were self-reliant and independent, with a spirit that would erupt at times – there were riots when the government demanded taxes for roads or even called a census.

Dominica is large and fertile, but the island was particularly poor. Some industries flourished, however, the most notable being Rose's, now part of the Cadbury Schweppes Group, which provided lime juice for British ships. The drink became popular beyond the requirements for naval rations and in 1875 a factory was set up in Roseau to extract lime juice from the thousands of acres that were planted with the fruit. For a while, Dominica was by far the world's largest producer of limes. After the Second World War this trade declined and bananas took their place.

Despite spending most of its colonial life in the Leeward Isles, in federation with Antigua and Montserrat and islands further north, Dominica is much more similar to the Windward Islands and it became one of them in 1939. In 1951 the vote was given to all Dominicans over the age of 21 and the island became self-governing in 1967. In

Dominican Writers and Artists

The writer Jean Rhys (1890–1979) came from Dominica. Her family owned an estate in Grand Bay and she was born in Roseau, but she left the island when she was 16 and moved to Europe. Many of her books include nostalgic memories of the Dominica of her childhood. Fame came with *Wide Sargasso Sea* (1966), some of which is set in the oppressive atmosphere of colonial Dominican society at the turn of the 19th century. Another Dominican authoress and politician, Phyllis Shand Allfrey, wrote the novel *The Orchid House*, also set on the island and screened by the BBC. The story of a private soldier's life is recorded in *Redcoats in the Caribbean* by James Aytoun, published by Blackburn Recreation Services Dept for the Cambridgeshire Regiment.

Dominica was very fortunate in the visit of the Italian painter Agostino Brunias, who stayed on the island for many years in the late 18th century, recording the Dominican way of life and events. His paintings are extremely lively, giving a fascinating view of the lives of the free creoles, the plantations, vendors' stalls, dances and women washing clothes in the streams, much of which can still be seen in different forms today.

the ground-swell of the new political freedom, the Dominica Labour Party, led by Edward Le Blanc, rallied the voters and was thrust to power. The 1970s saw social unrest as demonstrations, racist attacks and strikes held the island to ransom and a state of emergency was declared more than once. The Dreads, so-called because they wore their hair in dreadlocks, took to the hills. On 3 November 1978, 485 years to the day after the island was discovered by Columbus, Dominica took its independence from Britain. Then a few months later Hurricane David arrived – Roseau was literally flattened, there were 37 deaths and 80% of the population were left homeless. The political unrest continued: an emergency government had to be installed, followed by two coup attempts and an invasion party which was arrested before it left the States. Today Dominica is led by the Hon. Roosevelt Skerrit of the Dominica Labour Party in a coalition government with the Dominica Freedom Party, with a total of 12 of the 21 seats in the Dominica Parliament. The United Workers Party is in opposition with nine seats. Next elections are scheduled for August 2010.

Beaches

Dominica has no white coral-sand beaches in the typical Caribbean mould and most beaches tend to be dark volcanic grey or jet black except in the far northeast, where there are some golden-sand beaches in the high-sided coves. Beach-bound tourists tend to head for Portsmouth, where there are some nice beach bars and some limited watersports, or to the northeast. Around Roseau, the waterfront is made up of fist-sized rocks that clatter as they race and recede with the waves.

See also 'Best Beaches', p.225.

Flora and Fauna

Much of Dominica is 100ft deep in tropical rainforest, undergrowth, overgrowth and canopy so thick that it is dark at midday. Trees vie with each other to grow tallest, stretching up to reach the sunlight, while lianas and creeping vines take an easier route, grappling the tree trunks and using them to climb. In the branches sit orchids and ferns that explode in graceful curves. The forest gushes with water; it squawks and chirrups and is a botanist's utopia. With so many species in such good condition, Dominica has been called a living museum.

The Dominican forest has different zones, depending on elevation. At the lowest altitudes you will find cultivated patches, or the thick secondary forest that occurs when cultivated land is left fallow. Vines, ferns and many flowering trees and plants are found here. Above this, typical rainforest has a canopy at 100ft – huge tree trunks, some with buttressed roots, soar out of the forest floor, which is often relatively clear. Trees such as the gommier and the chataigner have bromeliads and orchids residing in their branches. Next, the montane forest is smaller and many of the trees have aerial roots. The sunlight does penetrate to the forest floor and so there is more ground growth including grasses and ferns. Finally, at the highest altitudes you will find elfin forest, stunted trees covered with mosses and lichens, plants that prefer the clouds and almost constant rain.

The **Morne Trois Pitons National Park**, a 17,000-acre reserve of rainforest in the centre of the island, is the Caribbean's oldest nature reserve and it contains many of the island's natural attractions (*see* 'Morne Trois Pitons National park', p.239). On the northern edge of the park, off the Transinsular Road, are the **Middleham Trails** (*see* p.242), leading to waterfalls lost in greenery – look out for, or keep you nose open for, the Stinking Hole, where colonies of bats live. On the western slopes of the park is the **Dominican Rainforest Aerial Tram** (*t 704 3350, www.rainforestaerialtrams.com*), a modified ski lift which provides the opportunity to witness Dominica's fabulous scenery from the tree tops. Just outside the park is the **Emerald Pool** (*see* p.242), a tame but popular cascade falling into a rock pool. Other visits to falls in the south include a walk up the **Sari-sari River** from La Plaine, and the **Victoria Falls** above Delices. The **Northern Forest Reserve** is far larger and contains the island's highest peak, Morne Diablotin, and the parrot habitat, where you are most likely to see the island's two endangered parrots.

There are many **marked walking trails** in Dominica's parks. On paths the best footwear is a light pair of walking boots, but if you are walking up rivers you might opt for the local red, gold and green plastic sandals, nicknamed toyotas (because they hold the road well). Also remember a waterproof coat, a picnic and, if you are out for a long day, take a jersey, too. As anywhere else, you are advised to take little money and jewellery with you when you go off the beaten track in Dominica. *See* also 'Hiking' under 'Other Sports', p.231.

Some 166 species of bird live in Dominica or migrate here with the tourists for the better weather during the winter season. Among the common bananaquits and bullfinches, the exotic flycatchers and fluorescent hummingbirds, Dominica has two endemic parrots. Both are endangered, and the *sisserou* is portrayed on the national flag. The *sisserou*, or imperial parrot, is one of the largest parrots in the world and has a purple breast and green wings. The smaller red-necked amazon or jacko is a little less scarce and might be seen racing by in a flash of scarlet. To have a hope of seeing

Getting There

Dominica t (1 767–)

By Air

There are no direct flights to Dominica from outside the Caribbean. LIAT, t 448 2421, has several daily flights heading up or down the island chain from Antigua or Barbados, as does Caribbean Star, t 445 2181. Air Caraïbes, t 448 2181, flies between Guadeloupe and Martinique, stopping off in Dominica. American Eagle, t 445 7204, fly from the USA via San Juan in Puerto Rico.

There are two airports on Dominica: Melville Hall and Canefield. Melville Hall is inconveniently located 35 miles northeast of Roseau, so it is probably best to aim for Canefield if you can, which is just north of the capital. There is a departure tax of US$30.

By Sea

A ferry touches Dominica en route between Martinique and Guadeloupe: the *Express des Iles* (t 448 2181, *www.express-des-iles.com*) stops by at least once a day except Thursday, docking at the ferry terminal on the Bayfront in Roseau. A departure tax of US$18 applies.

Getting Around

By Bus

Public transport is mostly by Japanese van (with teenage minders leaning out of them to shout for passengers) and by unwieldy government bus. The major routes are all served, but remote towns have only infrequent services (it is possible to get stranded in outlying areas). Hitching works quite well.

Buses travelling south from Roseau go from the bottom end of King George V St near the Old Market Square; for the Roseau Valley from the top end opposite the Police Headquarters. If you are heading north, buses leave from near the new market building, next to the West Bridge. Fares from EC$1.50 to EC$10.25.

By Taxi

Taxis have fixed rates: Roseau to Canefield Airport – EC$21, to the southern hotels – EC$15, to Papillote – EC$40; and Canefield Airport to southern hotels – EC$40, to Castaways – EC$40, and to the Portsmouth area – EC$110. The trip to Melville Hall Airport from Roseau is EC$140 per person, with usually a minimum of two people (you will find that people hitch a ride on any car or minibus going). For an island tour, taxis can be hired for about US$18/hour.

Car Hire

Car hire costs around US$45 per day, jeeps US$55, and most companies will deliver to your hotel. You will need a local driver's licence, which can be obtained from the Traffic Department in Roseau, at the airport and at the car-hire companies (price US$12).

Budget Rent A Car, Canefield, t 449 2080, *budgetdominica@cwdom.dm*.

Bonus Car Rental, t 448 2650, *cphillip@ cwdom.dm*.

Garrawaye Rent-A-Car, t 448 2891, *garrawaye@cwdom.dm*, *www.delphis.com*.

Island Car Rental, Goodwill Road, Roseau, t 255 6844.

Eddie Savarin Tours & Taxis, t 245 2242, *eddie tours2001@yahoo.com*.

Melville Hall Airport, t 445 8789, *www.auto tradeltd.com*.

Valley Rent a Car, Goodwill Rd, t 448 3233, *valley@cwdom.dm*, *www.valley dominica.com*.

Tourist Information

Abroad

There is a decent website at *www.dominica. dm*. You might also try *www.visit-dominica. com*, *www.delphis.dm* and *www.cakafete.com*.

UK: MKI, Mitre House, 66 Abbey Rd, Bush Hill Park, Enfield, Middlesex EN1 2QE, t (020) 8350 1000, *mki@ttg.co.uk*.

USA: Dominica Tourist Office, 110-64 Queens Blvd. Box 427, Forest Hills, NY 11375, t (718) 261 9615, *dominicany@msn.com*, *www. dominica.dm*.

In Dominica

Dominica National Development Corporation, PO Box 293, Valley Rd, Roseau, Dominica, t 448 2351, *ndctourism@cwdom.dm*. There is a tourist information kiosk at the Old Post Office on the waterfront in Roseau, at the nearby cruise ship berth and at each of the airports: Canefield, **t** 449 1242, and Melville Hall, **t** 445 0751.

Crime

You are advised to be careful about personal security when in Dominica, particularly when on isolated beaches and remote roads in the countryside. Do not leave valuables unattended on the beach at any time.

Embassies and Consulates

US/Canadian citizens should contact their embassy in Barbados (*see* p.76).
British Consulate (the local High Commission is in Barbados): PO Box 2269, c/o Courts Roseau, **t** 448 7655.

Media

Local newspapers include the *Chronicle*, which is published on Fridays, and the *Independent* and *Tropical Star*, which are published on Wednesday and Friday.

Medical Emergencies

The main hospital in Roseau is the Princess Margaret Hospital, **t** 448 2231. For emergency services, dial **t** 999.

Money and Banks

The currency is the Eastern Caribbean Dollar, which is fixed to the US dollar at EC$2.65 = US$1. Prices are often published in both dollar currencies, so it is worth knowing which currency you are dealing in. **Banks** are open Mon–Thurs 8–2, Fri 8–4.

Post

It is best to address letters to the Commonwealth of Dominica, because otherwise they often end up in the Dominican Republic.

Shopping

Shops are open Mon–Fri 8–4, often with a stop for lunch, and Sat 8–1.

Telephone Code

The IDD code for Dominica is **t** 1 767 and this is followed by a seven-digit island number (these all begin with 44 and so are often only written with five digits). When you are on the island, dial the full seven digits.

Festivals

Lent *Masquerade*. Dominica's traditional Carnival, with feasting, fantastic costumes and general revelling in the streets.
July/August *The Emancipation Celebrations* (formerly Domfesta). Festival of local arts, crafts and performing arts.
Last Friday in October *Jounen Kweyol*. A celebration of the creole language and customs, with cooking events and national costume.
Weekend after Jounen Kweyol *World Creole Music Festival*.
3 November *Independence Day*. Centering on folk arts, as well as the traditional Caribbean jump-up. Raconteurs compete with one another in telling humorous anecdotes.
Throughout the year *Saints' days*. As in many Catholic Caribbean countries, some villages in Dominica celebrate their saints' days with a Mass and then a party.

Watersports

With the exception of excellent scuba diving facilities, watersports are only now being developed in Dominica and you will be dependent on the hotels for the most part. General watersports operators include:
Castaways Hotel, Mero, **t** 449 6245, *enquirys@castaways-dominica.com*, *www.castaways-dominica.com*.
Dominica Tours, Anchorage Hotel, **t** 448 2638.
KHATT's, PO Box 1652, Roseau, **t** 448 4850, *khatts@cwdom.dm*, *www.kenshinterland tours.com*.
Nature Island Dive, **t** 449 8181, *natureidive@cwdom.dm*, *www.natureislanddive.com*. Offers kayaking and snorkelling around the southern area.

Day Sails

Sailing trips can be booked through the above watersports operators and through **Carib Cruises**, which has a 70ft catamaran.
Cobra Tours, **t** 445 3333, *info@cobratours.dm*, *www.cobratours.dm*.

Deep-sea Fishing

Half-day and full-day charters are available. Costs range from US$400–800. Contact the Dominica Watersport Association, **t** 488 2188,

info@dominicawatersports.com, www.
dominicawatersports.com.
Game Fishing Dominica, t 449 6638,
saphy@cwdom.dm, www.gamefishing
dominica.com.

River-bathing

Perhaps preferable to sea-bathing is swimming in Dominica's rivers. There is plenty of flowing water on the island. So much, in fact, that they sell it to drier islands such as Antigua and Sint Maarten to the north. Some good places to swim are at the Trafalgar and Middleham Falls, the Rosalie River on the east coast and the White River in La Plaine, whose source is the Boiling Lake. For a full day's outing you can float and clamber down the Layou River, starting at Belles in the rainforest on the transinsular road and working your way down through the Layou flats towards the west coast. You can also swim at the Gingerette Nature Sanctuary, t 440 3412, rastours@cwdom.dm.

River Kayaking

Guided kayaking trips are available for half- and full-day excursions. Kayaks can also be rented by the hour. Ask your hotel or contact the Dominica Watersports Association, t 488 2188, info@dominicawatersports.com, www.dominicawatersports.com.
Cobra Tours, Portsmouth, t 445 3333, info@cobratours.dm, www.cobratours.dm.
Nature Island Dive, PO Box 2354, Soufrière, t 449 8181, natureidive@cwdom.dm, www.natureislanddive.com.
Wacky Rollers, t 449 8276, wackyrollers@ yahoo.com, www.wackyrollers.com.

Scuba Diving and Snorkelling

The island has an established reputation for its corals and fish, which are plentiful and in good condition for the Caribbean. Dives take place on the reefs along the leeward coast, mainly in the south near Scott's Head in Soufrière Bay, and also in the Marine Park in Douglas Bay just north of the Cabrits. Brain corals, black corals and sponges are all on view on the walls and boulder-strewn drop-offs. There's also excellent fish life, snake eels, seahorses and squids with larger schools and a greater variety than elsewhere. Dominican oddities include hot- and cold-water springs under the surface (at Champagne in Soufrière Bay you will see and and feel the warm bubbling water, discoloured with sulphur and iron) and clear water beneath cloudy river outflows. There are also some wrecks.
Anchorage Dive Centre, Anchorage Hotel, just south of Roseau, t 448 2638, www. anchoragehotel.dm.
Cabrits Dive Centre, Portsmouth, t 445 3010, cabritsdive@cwdom.dm, www.cabritsdive. com. Has easy access to sites in the Marine Park to the north of the Cabrits.
Dive Castaways, Mero, t 448 7812, dive castaways@cwdom.dm, www.castaways dominica.com.
Dive Dominica, Castle Comfort Dive Lodge, just south of Roseau, t 448 2188, dive@cwdom. dm, www.divedominica.com.
East Carib Dive, Mero, t 449 6575, www.east caribdive.dm.
Nature Island Dive, t 449 8181, natureidive@ cwdom.dm, www.natureislanddive.com.

Other Sports

Sports on land are relatively limited, though there are **tennis** courts at some of the hotels and there is even a **squash** court at the Anchorage Hotel.

Hiking

Hiking in Dominica's unspoiled rainforest is the principle attraction for many visitors. See 'Flora and Fauna', p.228, for information on where to walk. Information and help with trained guides can be found through:
Antours, 29 Great Marlborough St, t 448 5634, antours@yahoo.com, www.antoursdm.com.
Division of Forestry, Botanical Gardens, Roseau, t 448 2401, ext 3417.
Dominica Tours, t 448 2638.
Otherwise, you can arrange a walk with:
Ken's Hinterland Adventure Tours, t 448 4850, khatts@cwdom.dm.
Wacky Rollers, Roseau, t 449 8276, wacky rollers@yahoo.com, www.wackyrollers.com.

Horse-riding
Highride Nature Adventures, New Florida Estate, Roseau, t 448 6296, highriders@

cwdom.dm. One of the last remaining estates in Dominica to maintain a family tradition of horsemanship.

Wacky Rollers, Roseau, **t** 449 8276, *wacky rollers@yahoo.com, www.wackyrollers.com*.

Mountain Biking

Becoming increasingly popular in the island's spectacular back country. Contact:
Nature Island Dive, t 449 8181, *idive@cwdom.dm, www.natureislanddive.dm*.

Whale-Watching

Twenty-two species of whales and dolphins have been identified in Dominica's waters. During winter months visitors are more likely to see sperm whales; summer is better for pilot whales. Rare sightings of beaked whales, Brydes whales and Fraser dolphins have been recorded. Most boats are equipped with hydrophones for locating pods. Tours cost around US$45–50 per person. Contact:

Anchorage Hotel Dive Centre, t 448 2638, *anchorage@cwdom.dm, www.anchorage hotel.dm*.

Dive Dominica, t 448 2188, *dive@cwdom.dm, www.divedominica.com*.

Where to Stay

Dominica t (1 767–)

Dominica's hotels are mainly small, often family-run affairs, some of them set in the old-time buildings around the coast or hidden among the island's exuberant foliage (as you sit on the veranda you can practically see it grow). Few except the dive hotels have a resort feel, and there is usually no difficulty in finding a room.

Dominica has some extremely fine rain-forest retreats, with magnificent settings in the mountains that take the best advantage of the island's scenery, but which are a little untypical for the Caribbean. The rooms are often quite basic, though they usually have hot and cold water, and they are quite remote.

If you wish to hire a villa, contact the Tourist Board, but one is mentioned below. The government levies a tax of 5% and most hotels charge service of another 10%.

Expensive

Evergreen Hotel, south of Roseau, PO Box 309, **t** 448 3288, *evergreen@cwdom.dm, www. avirtualdominica.com/evergreen.htm*. Low-key with small blocks of rooms around a courtyard, and a pool and sundeck set on the seafront. The rooms in the waterfront building are very comfortable, but the orig-inal house has charm too. There is a chic glass-fronted dining room. There is no beach here really, but smooth fist-size rocks that clatter and jangle as the waves move over them. Just 16 rooms, with air-conditioning, phone and cable TV.

Castle Comfort Diving Lodge, south of Roseau, **t** 448 2188, *dive@cwdom.dom, www.dive dominica.com*. If you are coming to Dominica specifically to dive, you might choose this place, where there is an active atmosphere as the daily dives go out followed by quiet and chat as divers relax after their exertions. Fifteen rooms altogether, four very comfort-able ones in the block on the waterfront (wicker furniture and bright blue décor, with a balcony looking onto the sea). Friendly air, plus good diving packages.

Picard Beach Cottage Resort, south of Portsmouth, PO Box 34, **t** 445 5131, *picard beach@cwdom.dm, www.avirtualdominica. com/picard.htm*. A collection of eight wooden cottages set in a pleasant tropical garden right on the beach. Each one has a small veranda. Very quiet and low-key.

The Fort Young Hotel, Roseau, PO Box 519, **t** 448 5000, *fortyoung@cwdom.dm, www. fortyounghotel.com*. Stands above the waterfront in town, its 73 rooms set among the old battlements of the fort that guarded the town approaches for a couple of centuries. The attractive courtyard is still laid with flagstones and the pool and bar are lost in foliage within. Facilities include inter-active TV and high-speed Internet access.

Moderate

The Anchorage Hotel and Dive Centre, south of Roseau, PO Box 34, **t** 448 2638, *anchorage mail@cwdom.dm, www.anchoragehotel.dm*. Has 32 rooms looking out to sea (go for the ones upstairs) and a block of standard rooms above the swimming pool. There is also a large and often lively terrace bar and dining room. Rooms have air-con, phone and cable TV.

Sutton Place Hotel, 25 Old St, Roseau, PO Box 2333, **t** 449 8713, *sutton2@cwdom.dm, www.avirtualdominica/sutton.htm*. The most charming hotel, where there are nine suites and rooms in an old three-storey stone town house which has been beautifully restored and refitted inside. It is small and intimate, with some four-posters and lacquered furniture. A pretty dining room in yellow and red with chandeliers, and a basement bar that you leave through the barrel hatch. Some rooms have kitchenette; all have balcony, TV, phone, air-con and fan.

Garraway Hotel, 1 Dame Eugenia Charles Blvd, Roseau, **t** 449 8800, *garraway@cwdom.dm, www.garrawayhotel.com*. Conveniently sited a short distance from the town centre, the hotel's 20 doubles and 11 suites offer a choice of ocean or mountain view. All rooms have Internet connection; wireless access is available in some rooms.

Castaways, Mero, PO Box 5, **t** 449 6245, US **t** 1 888 227 8292, *enquirys@castaways-dominica.com, www.castaways-dominica.com*. Dominica's best beach hotel, set on black sand. There is a large and attractive terrace with the bar and the Almond Tree Restaurant, from which the wings run on either side, containing 24 rooms in all. There is a fantastic view of the sunset through the flamboyant trees and palms and from the palm-thatch beach bar. There's also a dive shop, though no pool. Rooms are in an older Caribbean style, with rattan mats and tiles, all with balcony, air-con, fan, phone and TV.

Coconut Beach Hotel, Portsmouth, PO Box 37, **t** 445 5393, *cbh89ck.netscape.net, www.coconutbeachhotel.com*. Set on the brown-sand beach and has a pleasant, quiet air. There are 22 units, apartments and bungalows, each with air-con or a ceiling fan; all have kitchenette. Very nice waterfront bar and restaurant (seafood a speciality).

Papillote Wilderness Retreat, near Trafalgar, Roseau Valley, PO Box 67, **t** 448 2287, *papillote@cwdom.dm, www.papillote.dm*. Practically throttled by its 12 acres of tropical garden. There are six rooms and two units in a cottage which are quite private despite the daily turnover of visitors. The restaurant is on the garden terrace and serves local food.

Jungle Bay Resort & Spa, Point Mulatre, **t** 446 1789, *junglebay@cwdom.dm, www.junglebaydominica.com*. This new wellness resort is surrounded by 55 acres of tropical forest near Dominica's World Heritage Park. The ecologically designed resort was built with volcanic stones and tropical hardwoods, blending a rustic feel with comfort. Twenty-one of the 50 cottages, perched on wooden posts in the forest, are ready for use. The resort has two restaurants, yoga studios, a mini-conference centre, gift shop, and spa. Hikes to waterfalls and scenic vistas nearby.

Tamarind Tree Hotel, Macoucherie, Salisbury, **t** 449 7395, *peyers@cwdom.dm, www.tamarindtreedominica.com*. In the centre of Dominica's west coast on top of a 100-foot cliff, offering great views of Morne Diablotin, Dominica's tallest mountain. A small hotel of nine rooms, all with bath, ceiling fan, phone, fridge and wheelchair access. Restaurant and swimming pool too.

Inexpensive

Springfield Plantation Guest House, PO Box 456, **t** 449 1401, *springfield2@cwdom.dm, www.cwdom.dm/springfield2* (*some rooms moderate*). Somewhat remote, high up on the Transinsular Road. It is set in an old timber-frame estate house on 200 acres of former plantation grounds; all wooden floors, exposed beams and a fantastic view down the valley. Two apartments and eight rooms, some with an antique air with louvres and four-poster beds. Generally quiet, though there are students in residence sometimes because Springfield is also an educational centre.

The Layou Valley Plaza, PO Box 192, **t** 449 6895, *lrh@cwdom.dm*. Hidden in the hills of the Dominican heartland with a superb view over the uninterrupted greenery of the rainforest in the Upper Layou Valley looking towards Morne Trois Pitons. It is set in a modern villa with white walls, dark-stained wood and hanging greenery. Just six rooms, stylishly simple, and good home cooking (or you can cook for yourself).

Pointe Baptiste, c/o Mrs G. Edwards, Calibishie, **t** 445 7322, *manager@pointebaptiste.com*,

www.avirtualdominica.com/pointeb/htm.
If you fancy staying in a classic West Indian villa and catering for yourself, this has one of the loveliest settings in the Caribbean. Set on the cliff tops of the north coast, the main house has a huge balcony with views of the islands of Marie Galante and Guadeloupe. There is a golden-sand beach just below. The house, with its creaky wooden floors, drawing room and library, has an old-fashioned aura rarely found elsewhere. Housekeeper service. Villa rates for six people in season divide down to a very good cheap rate.

D'Auchamps Cottages, Laudat Valley, PO Box 1889, t 448 3346, *honychurchs@cwdom.dm*, *www.avirtualdominica.com/dauchamps.* Two small and pretty stone cottages with nice, wood-laid interiors, muslin nets over the beds and louvres that peg out on stilts, set in the profusion of the tropical greenery in Laudat Valley above Roseau. Full kitchens.

Roxy's Mountain Lodge, Laudat, Roseau Valley, PO Box 265, t 448 4845, *roxys@cwdom.dm.* Seven rooms in the original house and a new chalet. A good starting point for hiking in the National Park and a friendly, quiet air.

Sister's Sea Lodge, Prince Rupert's Bay, near Portsmouth, t 445 5211, *sangow@cwdom.dm.* Six simple rooms in concrete and stone cottages, open plan with fans. No phone or TV. Hot showers in a stone partition.

Mango Beach Resort, Prince Rupert's Bay, t 445 3099. Set in a modern block on the beach, fan-ventilated with TV and phone.

Vena's, 48 Cork St, Roseau, t 448 3286, *venas@cwdom.dm.* The birthplace of the Dominican novelist Jean Rhys, offering simple rooms off a creaky corridor.

Kent Anthony Guest House, 3 Marlborough St, Roseau, t 448 2730, *islandman89@hotmail. com.* A friendly and dependable haunt with chat and cheap rooms.

Ma Bass Central Guest House, 44 Field's Lane, Roseau, t 448 2999. Some rooms with private bathroom.

Douglas's Guest House, Bay St, Portsmouth, t 445 5639. Very simple.

Veranda View Guest House, Calibishie, t 445 8900, *lawrencet@cwdom.dm.* Just two very simple bedrooms with private bathroom and mosquito nets on the beds, in a wooden house right on the beach.

Eating Out

Dominica is quiet and you will not find a great many places to eat at night outside the hotels. You will find good traditional Caribbean food, however: callaloo or pumpkin soup followed by fish or a curry goat sitting among prodigious quantities of local vegetables such as plantain, green fig and breadfruit. Dominica also has one or two specialities such as mountain chicken or *cwapaud* (in fact, breaded frogs' legs); crayfish; crab-backs stuffed with land-crab meat; and tiny fish in cakes called tee-tee-ree, fish-fry which are caught at the river mouth in a sheet. There is a government tax of 5% added to all bills and most restaurants add a service charge of 10%. **Categories** are arranged according to the price of a main course: expensive = EC$50 and above, moderate = EC$20–50, inexpensive = less than EC$20.

Expensive

La Robe Creole, Fort St, Roseau, t 448 2896, *www.larobecreole.com.* For an evening out in old-Roseau elegance, set in a lovely stone town house. It is decorated with red and yellow chequered madras tablecloths and cushions on tall-backed wooden chairs – the waitresses also wear traditional madras costumes, from which the restaurant takes its name. Start with accras or crab-back and follow with steamed shrimp with creole sauce or mountain chicken in beer batter and coconut flakes (in season), followed by banana flambéed at your table. Their *callaloo* is the best in the Caribbean. A mixed creole and international menu, with an often lively atmosphere. *Closed Sun.*

Moderate

Torrino, Kennedy Ave, Roseau, t 449 8907. The only Italian restaurant in town, with an Italian flag to mark it on the street. The fare is Northern Italian and nicely presented: pastas, steaks, local fish. Quite simple but a lively atmosphere some evenings. *Closed Sun.*

Pearl's Cuisine, Castle St, Roseau, t 448 8707. Set in a nice old creole town house with its tables set out on a balcony above the street. Good traditional Dominican food.

Callaloo, King George V St, Roseau, t 448 3386. Award-winning restaurant serving *calalloo* soup and other specials including lobster, crayfish and mountain chicken.

Paiho, 10 Church St, Roseau, **t** 448 8999. One of the Chinese restaurants (with Dominican adaptions) in town: shark fin soup on an old Dominican balcony above the street. *Closed Sun lunch.*

World of Food, Cork St, Roseau, **t** 448 3286. At Vena's guest house, where the open tin-roofed dining room gives onto a paved courtyard with a mango tree (you dine to the occasional thud and bump, bump, bump in season). Full suppers of soup followed by chicken and fish and a volley of local vegetables and then ice cream.

Guiyave, Cork St, Roseau, **t** 448 2930. Good for lunch. Has a very attractive setting with a green and white balcony upstairs hung with plants. A long menu with baked chicken with glazed spinach followed by local ice cream.

The Cartwheel Café, Bay St, Roseau, **t** 448 5353. Another lunch spot, popular with island businesspeople. It is set in a stone and wooden building with a few tables set among plants: sandwiches and salads or more substantial plates of chicken and pork.

Evergreen Hotel, south of Roseau, **t** 448 3288. The food is served in a chic glass-fronted dining room.

The Anchorage Hotel and Dive Centre, south of Roseau, **t** 448 2638. There is a large and often lively terrace bar and dining room.

Purple Turtle, just north of Portsmouth on the beach, **t** 445 5296. An easy setting where yachties gather for a meal of international/local fare over a beer and sailing stories.

Sister's Sea Lodge, Prince Rupert's Bay, **t** 445 5211. The building itself is modern, but everything else is rustic. You sit at bench seats, sharing a whole meal presented on a banana leaf alongside rice and huge plantain chips organically grown in the garden: freshly caught grilled fish (the owner is a fisherman) sold by weight, or salad of squid.

Inexpensive

Mousehole Snackette, Roseau. Usually teeming with schoolkids at lunch time. You can get a pattie and a fruit juice – sorrel, soursop, lime and tamarind according to the season – followed by a coconut. Specialities are Cornish pastie or fish pie.

Bars and Nightlife

Bars

Many restaurants double as bars, and some of the hotels have happy hours, BBQs and a band in season – the Anchorage Hotel (*see* above) has an occasional steel band – but otherwise you will rely on Dominican entertainment: rum shops, discos and local fêtes, which are at their liveliest at the weekend. There are limitless rum shops on the island, where you will be welcome to try out a few of the Dominican rums: Red Cap, Soca Rum, D Special and, if you can find it, Mountain Dew. Bois Bandé (pronounced 'bawbandy'), a local concoction made from tree bark, has an interesting story which you might enjoy investigating. Recently the island has begun to brew its own beer, called Kubuli.

Cornerhouse Café, Old Market Square, Roseau, **t** 449 9000. An internet café, bar and restaurant, popular with a young professional crowd.

Wykie's, Old Street, Roseau. A favourite with island-execs and passers-through, a cosy creole town house lined with bamboo.

Cellars, downstairs in the Sutton Place Hotel, Old St, Roseau. Karaoke, jazz and a wide-screen television for major sporting events. Live bands every Wed. Evenings heat up about 11pm.

O'Byrne Pub & Grub, Castle St, Roseau, **t** 440 4337. Lively Irish-themed pub. *Open Mon–Thurs 5–11pm, Fri–Sat 5pm–1am.*

Clubs

The Warehouse, Canefield. The island's main dance club, packed on Saturday. Recorded disco, reggae, and other music is played 11pm–5am in this 200-year-old stone building, once used to store rum.

Magic, Loubière. There is a mix of music: Jamaican reggae, soca from down south and French Caribbean zouk.

The Zone Health Club and Sports Bar, Canefield, **t** 449 3601.

Beach Bars

Beach bars, Portsmouth.

East Carib Dive, Salisbury Beach at the river mouth. A nice, lazy spot under a palm-thatch roof.

the parrots (a trip can be arranged through one of the operators listed under 'Hiking', p.231) you may have to get up extremely early and hike into the hills to a special hide. Another bird almost unique to Dominica is the *siffleur montagne* or mountain whistler, which whistles its single melancholy note in the rainforest.

As all over the Caribbean, fauna is much more limited. Agouti and a rare 3ft iguana scurry around the heights, and manicou creep quietly. All around there is the constant susurration of island insects: you may see cockroaches wiggle antennae four inches long and there is a stick insect called *chouval bwa*. Out at night you may come across luminous flickering points that are fireflies and hear the blacksmith beetle, so large and monstrous that it clanks. There are five species of snake, none of them poisonous. One of the rarest but most surprising is the shy boa constrictor, known as *tête chien* because of the shape of its head. Outside the Amazon basin it is found only in Dominica. It has been known to grow to 20ft long and as thick as a man's leg.

It might be possible (depending on the season) to arrange to catch crayfish and frogs, later served as mountain chicken. Hunting for frogs takes place at night, with the aid of burning torches that have a fatal attraction for the animals.

Whale watching is possible from Dominica in the season (November to March), when the whales come from up north to mate and calve in the calm, deep waters on the leeward coast. Humpbacks, pilot whales, dolphins and particularly sperm whales, accompanied by their 20ft calves, have been known in the area. Tours are long and of course a sighting is not guaranteed, but they can be arranged through the Anchorage Dive Centre, just south of Roseau, **t** 448 2638, *anchoragemail@ cwdom.dm*, *www.anchoragehotel.dm*, and Dive Dominica, Castle Comfort Dive Lodge, also south of Roseau, **t** 448 2188, *dive@cwdom.dm*, *www.divedominica.com*.

Roseau

Roseau, Dominica's capital, has 20,000 inhabitants, about a quarter of the population, and is the only sizeable town on the island. Framed by towering mountains on one side and looking out to an uninterrupted sea horizon on the other, the town stands at the mouth of the Roseau River and takes its name from the French word for the reeds that grew here, which the Caribs would use to poison the tips of their arrows. Lacking a proper harbour (that is in the Canefield area further north, where the drop-off is less severe), it was never supposed to be the island's capital, but the intended site of Portsmouth was found to be unhealthy and so the administrators moved here in the late 18th century.

Roseau keeps many features of a traditional West Indian waterfront town. It was extensively rebuilt after Hurricane David in 1979, but it has not been redeveloped out of character and there are still many old creole houses. Most modern building is now of concrete, but there have been plans to zone parts of the old town and so the colonial character remains. Only the occasional satellite dish stands out among the shanties and the streets of traditional warehouses near the waterfront. With strong stone foundations and shuttered doorways that let through the breeze, the old storehouses and shops are topped with wooden upper storeys and steep roofs, many of them embellished with gingerbread fretwork. Some have balconies over the pavement, supported by sturdy wooden columns and giving welcome shelter in Roseau's regular tropical rainstorms. Although the town looks a little neglected, its roofs rusted and the buildings a bit run-down, these attractive houses give Roseau a charming atmosphere. Wherever you go in Dominica people seem to greet you, usually in French patois, but the liveliest spot in Roseau is the **market**, which can be found next to the river mouth. There is a large covered area of tables, but the Dominicans mostly prefer to spread out their produce – guava, grapefruit, golden apple and ground provisions – on the ground in the open, with golf umbrellas to protect them from the sun and plastic sheeting at the ready for when it rains.

At the southern end of the **Bayfront**, which is gradually being redeveloped and is looking quite good at the moment, is the **Dominica Museum** (*open Mon–Fri 9–4, Sat 9–12; adm*), a very well-laid-out display of Dominican natural life – geological subduction zones, petrified wood and fossilised leaves – and then a look at the island's human heritage in displays of pre-Columbian axe heads, pottery, a *coulevre* (for squeezing the poisonous juice from cassava) and a canoe. Plantation times are revealed in maps (showing just how developed the island once was), prints by Agostino Brunias, and lime *equelles* for rinding the fruit; and town and country life in displays about Roseau's mixed-race ascendancy and in household utensils used by subsistence farmers. Just behind the museum is the **Old Market Plaza**, a cobbled square which was formerly the market and once the site of Roseau's slave-trading and public executions. There is a small tourist information desk on the square and a curious telephone-box-like structure that was supposedly used in auctions.

Walking northwest from Old Market Plaza on Castle St and Virgin Lane, you come to the Catholic **Cathedral of the Assumption**, built in dark stone with Romanesque arches and completed in 1841. Even though the majority of Dominica's population was Catholic, the official Anglican government would grant no money for the building of the cathedral. Summoned by a bell, the faithful would come out at night and carry stones from the Roseau River to the site. On the waterfront south of Old Market Plaza, **Fort Young**, once Roseau's main defence, is now a hotel. It was erected in 1775 and visitors to the hotel will still see a few slim and elegant-looking cannons hanging around the foyer and courtyard.

Behind the town, at the foot of Morne Bruce, are the **Botanical Gardens**, which date from 1891. Landscaped with open lawns, they must be the only place of their kind that appears less fertile than the country surrounding them. There are 150 species, including traditional Caribbean plants such as allamanda and bougainvillea and some less well known: *pompon rouge*, or powder puff. Trees include cannonball, teak and pink poui, and a giant baobab tree that came down in 1979, when Hurricane David uprooted over half the garden's species, still lying on top of the yellow school bus that it crushed. It has even begun to flower again. A few of the plants are named, but it is really more of a park now: serious botanical visitors should go to the various gardens around the island. However, it is worth going to the **aviary** in the corner of the gardens, where you can see some of Dominica's endangered parrots.

A path climbs **Morne Bruce** from the gardens, 500ft up through the creaking bamboo, to the crown-like Catholic memorial. The *morne* takes its name from the 18th-century engineer who fortified it and it gives an excellent view across the town, covering the bay. Most of the buildings have fallen down now. Early in the 20th century the *morne* was thought to be haunted: troops would be heard marching and supposedly a bugle sounded on dark nights.

The Roseau Valley

The extension of King George V St leads out of the town and across a clattering wooden suspension bridge into the Roseau River valley (the bridge may seem high, but the Roseau River has been known to rise 20ft in as many hours), straight into the Dominican heartland. It is a fantastic area, a massive, steep-sided valley where the air hangs chill in the shaded corners and the road winds up though a tunnel of amazing vegetation which opens out periodically to reveal magnificent views. Some of Roseau's more prosperous citizens have retreated into the cooler heights of the valley, side by side with farmers who manage to terrace the absurdly steep valley walls.

For a first-hand view of Dominica's extremes of vegetation you can go to the charming **D'Auchamps Gardens** (*t 448 3346; adm*) about halfway up the valley, where tropical flora (wild, domestic and medicinal) is revealed in all its rampant grandeur. A path leads through areas filled with plants from a traditional village garden, herb gardens, orchards and the rainforest, plus indigenous Dominican plants. You will learn about *mibi*, aerial roots and vines used for local weaving; the local thatch called *z'ailes mouche* or flies' wings; how oil comes from coconuts and flour from cassava. You can take a self-guided tour following a plant list for a small charge, but, as always with botanical gardens, it is much more interesting if you can get a guided tour.

At the head of the valley, 5 miles upriver from Roseau, just beyond the village of Trafalgar, are the **Trafalgar Falls**, two spectacular cascades that tumble 90ft from the lip of a gorge, the water whipped into a maelstrom by upward winds, spattering down among titanic black boulders and orange iron-discoloured rocks. The vegetation is prodigious and provides pockets of quiet as you climb, before you emerge into the blanket of fine spray and white noise that fills the gorge, a deafening hiss and roar that drops into the pools of hot and cold water. The falls are smaller now that some of the water has been harnessed for hydroelectricity. The falls are easy to reach on a short outing from Roseau and you can drive to within 10 minutes of them. Take a swimming costume and gym shoes if you like clambering over rocks, and consider getting a guide (for perhaps EC$15–20). You might need a jersey for your return because it can also get a bit cold and wet in the wind.

Twin pipes lead down from the falls, unfortunately giving it a bit of an industrial feel, carrying water to a hydroelectric generating station. They pass **Papillote Wilderness Retreat** (*t 448 2287; see* 'Where to Stay', p.233), where a small hotel is set in a charming 12-acre garden of truly Dominican profusion, with streams of rushing water spewed out by ornamental fish and iguanas. There are forests of white-leafed hibiscus, bromeliads and aroids, and orchids like butterflies, all sheltered by vast sprays of bamboo overhead (some plants are named). There is also a naturally heated mineral bath, for which the water comes from the springs higher up the mountain. This is a good place to stop for lunch on the veranda, and a swim in warm or cool water.

Morne Trois Pitons National Park

At the head of a side valley is the village of **Laudat**, the best dropping-off point for the 17,000-acre reserve. You can reach the **Freshwater Lake** by vehicle, a couple of miles beyond Laudat. The lake is at 2,500ft and its history and mystery is really more attractive than its actual physical presence. In the early days of colonization, the lake was haunted variously by a vindictive mermaid who would lure travellers to drown them, and, according to a writer called Oldmixon in 1708, by 'a vast monstrous Serpent, that had its Abode in the before-mentioned Bottom (an inaccessible Bottom in the high mountains)'. A 40-minute walk beyond the Freshwater Lake, towards the Morne Trois Pitons, the island's second-highest peak, you come to the **Boeri Lake**, in the crater of an extinct volcano. The path climbs to 2,800ft, passing over streams and through the thickest jungle. On days when the rain clouds are not obscuring them, the views carry down to the Atlantic coast, over whole hillsides of green with barely a human structure in sight. Again the walk is really more interesting than the lake.

Dominica's volcanic heartland is the **Valley of Desolation**, appropriately named because very little will grow there – even Dominican vegetation is killed off by sulphur emissions. This fetid area, among the jumble of (almost) extinct volcanoes, four hours' walk away and over two mountains, is laid with titanic boulders and sulphurous cesspools of diabolic colours. The volcano beneath it all erupted last in 1880, showering Roseau with volcanic ash.

At its centre is the **Boiling Lake**, a seething and bubbling morass like an angry Jacuzzi, constantly steaming at between 180 and 200°F, and fed by (occasionally poisonous) gases from underneath that make the whole lake rise by several feet. It has been known to measure about 70 yards across, but the level rises and falls. It has also been known to disappear down the plughole, re-emerging with a geyser spout.

Around the Island

South from Roseau

The road south from Roseau leads along the coast through the suburbs of Charlotteville and Castle Comfort, past a clutch of the island's hotels. In the 18th century a string of forts and batteries ran along the coast to the southern tip at Scott's Head. From Loubière, an impossibly steep road branches inland, climbing to the oddly named Snug Corner and over the summit, descending beneath the cliffs to the citrus orchards and banana plantations at **Berekua** on Grand Bay, where fort ruins stand beneath the vast cliffs of the windward coast.

On the coast road, eventually you come to the valley of **Soufrière**, one of the earliest areas of the island to be settled by the French. The town takes its name from the sulphur outlets farther up the valley, which flow into the river and provide heated water for bathing or washing clothes. It is a pleasant walk up the river among the

6oft bamboo trees that creak constantly and over to Grand Bay on the Atlantic side of the island, but if you feel like refreshing yourself with a drink, be careful: you might scald your hand.

The southern point of the island is dominated by **Scott's Head**, a spit of land jutting into the Caribbean Sea. There is little left of Fort Cacharou, which once dominated it and was attacked many times in the past. On one occasion Dominicans sympathetic to the French got the British soldiers drunk and spiked their guns with sand, enabling the French to overrun the fort with ease. The view from Scott's Head to Martinique, 20 miles south, and back along the leeward coast of Dominica, is stunning.

North from Roseau up the Leeward Coast

Despite being proposed in the 18th century, the road link from Roseau to Portsmouth, Dominica's second town in the north of the island, was one of the last to be completed, with some cuttings into the cliff face over 5oft deep. The journey had to be made via the other side of the island or by boat until well into the 20th century. The leeward coast is supposedly in the 'rain-shadow' of Dominica's central mountain range, meaning that it is dry. However, this should be judged by Dominican standards: it can still drench you without a moment's notice. The road follows the coast, passing Woodbridge Bay, the cruise-ship dock and the deep-water port, where goods for the capital are unloaded. Just before the airport at Canefield is the **Old Mill Cultural Centre**, in the grounds of an old plantation estate. The gardens contain an aqueduct and waterwheel as well as less ancient steam-driven cane-crushing gear.

Just beyond Canefield you come to the settlement of **Massacre** (pronounced more as in French than as in English), the site of a sad episode that took place between two half-brothers, one half-Carib, the other European, in the early 1600s. Indian Warner was born in St Kitts, son of Governor Warner by a Carib woman, but had to flee when his father died and so he went to Dominica, becoming a Carib chief. The massacre took place when his brother Phillip was sent by the Governor of the Leeward Islands on a campaign to 'put down' the Caribs in 1674. Phillip and his troops are supposed to have feasted with the Caribs and then he initiated the massacre by stabbing his brother. Beyond here you cross the **Layou River**, the island's longest. It flows broad and slow by the time it reaches the coast, but a road follows its tumultous course inland for a while, where you will see spectacular scenery including cliffs.

Soon the leeward road passes beneath Dominica's highest peak, **Morne Diablotin** (4,747ft), which takes its name from the black-capped petrel, supposedly a diabolically ugly bird that once lived on its slopes, prized by hunters in the 18th century. With webbed feet and black and white plumage, the diablotin was about the size of a duck and nested in the ground, flying down to the sea to fish at night. The *morne* itself can be climbed (guide recommended) in about three hours and the view is superb, though more often than not it is obscured by the clouds.

The coastal road continues to Dominica's second town of Portsmouth, crossing the **Indian River** just before the town. It is possible to arrange canoe trips up the river, where the banks are tangled with mangrove roots and the canopy is festooned with flying tropical overgrowth.

Portsmouth, another tired-looking town of 3,000 inhabitants with dilapidated wooden buildings, stands at the head of **Prince Rupert's Bay**, sheltered in the north by a promontory. The bay itself takes its name from the royalist prince who arrived in the West Indies in 1652 to find that Barbados and the Leeward Islands were in the hands of the Commonwealth. Two centuries ago the huge bay would see as many as 400 navy ships at anchor if a campaign was brewing. On the northern side of the bay is a promontory called the Cabrits (the name Cabrits derives from the Spanish word for goat – animals left here as fresh meat for future arrivals low on stocks after the Atlantic crossing), where you will find the **Cabrits National Park**, two forested hills scattered with the fortifications of **Fort Shirley** and other batteries and military buildings. The fort, dating from the 1770s, has been restored to its fearsome brimstone glory after more than a hundred years of decay since it was abandoned in 1854 by the British. For an idea of the fort's former glory, take a look at the commandant's house with its cut-stone classical façade which is now being overtaken by massive tangled tree roots. The restoration received an award from American Express. Marked trails cover the promontory and there is a small **museum** (*adm free*).

From Portsmouth a side road leads north past the anchorages at **Douglas Bay** and **Toucari Bay**. It was from an estate just north of Toucari that John Mair and friends watched the Battle of the Saints in April 1782. They were breakfasting in the portico as the battle began (*see* **Guadeloupe**, p.304).

The main road around the island leads inland from Portsmouth, winding into the hills, through violent Dominican fertility alternately soaked and shone upon at half-hourly intervals, and rejoining the north coast after 5 miles. In this area Dominica's best **beaches** can be found in the coves that look out towards the French islands of Marie Galante and the Saints. Beneath bright orange and muddy cliffs are beaches of large-grained golden sand, sometimes flecked with jet-black magnetic particles (*see* 'Best Beaches', p.225). The road continues to the villages of **Wesley** and **Marigot**, where unlike in most Dominican villages English is spoken as the first tongue rather than French creole. They were settled by Antiguans and other Leeward Islanders who came as construction labourers and stayed when their work was finished.

The Transinsular Road to the East Coast

The grandly named Transinsular Road, formerly known by the even grander name of the Imperial Road, winds its laborious way into the Dominican highlands from Canefield Airport. For years, journeys to the Atlantic coast had to be made by boat or on horseback along paths throttled by vegetation, but the Imperial Road commenced its journey to windward in 1909, setting off into the jungle, switchbacking gradually up thousands of feet and only emerging on the Atlantic coast in the late 1950s.

It always seems to be raining somewhere up in Dominica's hinterland and you will certainly see a few rainbows among the peaks. The road also provides an excellent way to see some of Dominica's extraordinary fertility (you cut through the northern part of the Morne Trois Pitons National Park). Road signs are grappled with growth, lines of plants sit on telegraph wires, whole slopes are covered with elephant ears and creeping vines, there are fluorescent green ferns so large that they might fly away, and waterfalls that descend from heights invisible from below in the spray.

The **Middleham Trails** lead off the main road and cross over the hills to the Roseau Valley at Laudat, via the **Middleham Falls**, stunning waterfalls 500ft in height. At Pont Cassé there is a roundabout where the road splits three ways: left to the Layou Valley and back down to the leeward coast; right to Castle Bruce and the southeast corner of the island; and the Transinsular Road continues straight on to the Atlantic coast just short of Marigot and Melville Hall Airport. At **Belles** it is possible to join the higher reaches of the Layou River for a day-long hike and swim through flats and gulleys that emerge on the Layou road a couple of miles short of the west coast. Arrange a guide and take a pair of gym shoes and a swimming costume.

Back on the Castle Bruce road, a tamer walk through the jungle can be made at the **Emerald Pool**. Walkways are carefully marked out and lead down to the small pool, where a tiny cascade races into the warm and dank recess; roots like knotted fingers grapple rocks furred with moss. However, do not expect it to be isolated enough to go skinny-dipping. The road passes beneath Dominica's second peak, Morne Trois Pitons, and then throws off another branch that leads to Rosalie and La Plaine. Atlantic breakers pound the windward shore, where there are cliffs hundreds of feet high. Before the road was built, stores had to be winched up from the bays below. In Dominican creole, the Atlantic coast is known as *au vent*, literally 'in the wind'.

Carib Territory

The Caribs retreated to the Atlantic coast of Dominica in the 18th century when Europeans took over the island. In the hundred years to 1750 their numbers had reduced from about 5,000 to 400 and they knew their struggle was lost, so they took up a peaceful life as far as possible from the invaders.

The Carib Territory itself (then called the Carib Reserve) was not created until 1903, when Governor Hesketh Bell allotted some 3,700 acres to the few hundred remaining Caribs. A hereditary chief was presented with a mace and an official sash and was referred to as 'King'. However, he was implicated in a smuggling racket in the 1930s and the position went into abeyance until 1952, when the 'Chief' was reintroduced as an elected post within the local government system. The Caribs have adopted a West Indian lifestyle, living in clapboard houses on stilts rather than their original *carbets* (pointed thatch huts), and they make a living in a similar way to other Dominicans. They do maintain some Carib traditions, such as building canoes, dug out from trees that they fell high up in the forest, and skilful weaving of rushes and reeds. They sell woven baskets (which fit inside one another like Russian dolls), mats and ornaments. One curious object is known as the wife-leader. It is a mesh of interwoven reeds that tightens when you put it over your finger and pull it, trapping you.

There are said to be no purebred Caribs left in the Territory, but the Carib features, which are like those of South American Indians, are immediately recognizable. Carib hair, dark and sleek and once the pride of their ancestors, is still much admired by Dominicans today (many of whom have tight African curls).

The French Caribbean

09

The French Caribbean

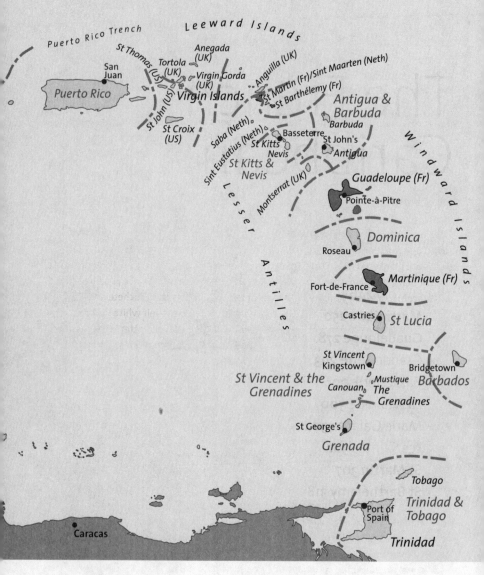

Highlights

1. Discover the story of St-Pierre, once the Paris of the Lesser Antilles, and its nemesis, Mont Pelé, on the island of Martinique

2. Sail Guadeloupe's offshore islands – cruise Les Saints or wash up in Marie Galante

3. Dine on the finest French food in a Caribbean setting on the swanky island of St Barthélemy, or on creole delights in nearby St Martin

Midway down the chain of the Lesser Antilles are the islands of Martinique and Guadeloupe, the two large French outposts in the Caribbean. Together with the islands of St Barts and the French half of St Martin, which lie 150 miles to the north in the Leeward Islands, these two make up the French West Indies.

The familiar verve of the French is ever-present in these islands. Chic customers glide by shops filled with Christian Lacroix and Yves St Laurent, and lovers linger over a meal under coloured awnings while citizens play *boules* on the dusty town squares. There is a certain *coquetterie* in the dress and manner – on the autoroutes you will find yourself competing with Peugeots and Citroëns driven with a nonchalance both French and Caribbean (a fearsome combination). In Fort de France, the capital of Martinique, there is even a Parisian haste, a *je-m'en-foutisme* untypical of the laid-back Caribbean. The illusion of being in France – all the pleasure on the one hand and the frustrations on the other, of their style and infuriating obstructiveness – is only spiked by the unfamiliar bristle of coconut palms and the variety of skin tones among the faces.

But familiar Caribbean strains run through French islands too. The air pulses to the sound of the relentless French Caribbean rhythm, *zouk*. Away from the towns, the slopes are blanketed in typical Caribbean rainforest and the flatlands with sugar cane or bananas sewn up in blue plastic bags. There the islanders walk at a relaxed and graceful pace, carrying the twin tools of the West Indies, the machete and the umbrella. You will sometimes still see *blanchisseuses* at work, their white washing spread all over the rocks at the river side, keeping up a constant chatter of creole, the mix of French and African that has developed in the islands. The markets, under red corrugated-iron roofs, are typical Caribbean mayhem.

Although the smaller, more northerly islands of St Martin and St Barts are politically attached to Guadeloupe, it is really Martinique and Guadeloupe that are cultural sisters. These two have a stronger creole history and tradition; St Martin and St Barts have developed much more recently and in atmosphere they are really more like France in the tropics than French West Indian.

Politically, France has taken a radically different approach to its colonies from that of Britain. Instead of encouraging a gradual move to independence, France has embraced her Caribbean islands, taking them into the *République* and giving them the status of overseas *départements*, equal to that of Savoie or Lot-et-Garonne. Martinique and Guadeloupe are *régions* in their own right, with the extra powers and responsibilities brought by decentralization in 1985. They are administered by a *préfet* appointed by the French government. Their people vote in French elections and they each send three deputies and two senators to the National Assembly in Paris.

In standard of living alone, the contrast with neighbouring islands is striking, and it could never be maintained without direct support from Paris. Most French Antilleans appreciate the benefits and would not change their situation, except to gain the maximum self-government while under the French umbrella, but there are some who envy the other islands their autonomy. Independence movements have expressed themselves in graffiti campaigns and have occasionally erupted into violence, with bomb attacks.

But the official line is that life should be French, with all the benefits that brings. Milk costs the same as it does in the *métropole*, as continental France is called, and so does a car. There is National Service. Rumour has it that they even fly in croissants. To some Frenchmen the islands seem like an expensive burden, but then they are also a bridgehead in the Americas. Besides, most of the money sent here is used to buy French goods.

Due to the many American visitors, English is quite widely spoken in the French Antilles. However, it is much better if you can understand French if you are to deal with officialdom or if you want to go off the beaten track. In the villages on Martinique and Guadeloupe, and the islands off Guadeloupe, like Marie Galante and Les Saintes, you will hear creole or French and little else. Also, museums (and menus) are in French. The islands of St Martin and St Barts have a stronger French-speaking heritage and you will hear very little creole there.

History

The earliest French involvement in the Caribbean was as pirates and privateers in the 16th century. In fact it was a French pirate who had revealed to the whole of Europe what wealth the Spaniards were gaining in the New World. Off the Azores in 1523, Jean Fleury captured two Spanish ships which contained the riches of Montezuma's palace in Mexico, a prize worth millions.

Life 'beyond the line' was dangerous, because capture by the Spaniards meant certain death, but men like François le Clerc (known to the Spaniards as *pie de palo* because of his wooden leg) ran a fleet of 10 ships and scoured the Caribbean Sea and the Bahamas for plunder. In 1553 he sacked nearly every major town, ransoming hundreds of thousands of pounds. Many of the buccaneers, who centred on the island of Tortuga off Hispaniola in the 17th century, were Frenchmen, and eventually this led to the establishment of France's most successful colony in St Domingue, now Haiti.

It was on a privateering expedition in 1624 that the first French colony accidentally came into being. Pierre d'Esnambuc, after a fight with a Spanish galleon off the Cayman Islands, was forced to put in for repair at St Christopher, where the British had just established a colony. He made friends with the Governor, Sir Thomas Warner, and helped to protect him from the Caribs. Two years later he was back, and they settled the island together. From this 'Mother Colony of the West Indies' both nations looked farther afield. De Poincy, a Grand Cross and Bailiff of the Order of the Knights of Malta, whose name is remembered in the poinciana tree all over the Caribbean, directed the expeditions in the name of the Compagnie des Iles d'Amerique. Despite the opposition of the Caribs, the French boldly set out for the large Windward Islands of Martinique and Guadeloupe, planting settlements there in 1635.

In 1647, the age of *l'or blanc* began, and sugar cane, introduced by Dutch Protestants fleeing the Inquisition in Pernambuco, soon blanketed the islands. With a sharp eye for new technology, the French soon developed into the leading exporters of refined sugar to the voracious European markets. The industry required labour so slaves were brought over in their hundreds from Africa. Development went forward apace and, in

1669, the seat of government was moved from St Kitts to Martinique, a shift that was to guarantee the island's predominance over the other French colonies into the 20th century. Most of the trade with mainland France was conducted through St-Pierre on Martinique.

The 17th century was a time of expanding empires, and land was so valuable that they would snatch whatever they could get. Gradually, the French expanded their domain southwards, settling the swathe of islands from Guadeloupe to Grenada. French buccaneers settled on St Barts and the Virgin Islands, and from Tortuga they moved into the western area of Hispaniola, which eventually became St Domingue (now Haiti).

By the 18th century, the French and British were at loggerheads in the Eastern Caribbean and they harried one another's colonies mercilessly. During the Seven Years' War, the British ripped through the islands and captured Martinique and Guadeloupe. It was considered so vital to retain a foothold in the Caribbean that, at the Treaty of Paris in 1763, the French were prepared to relinquish all their claims to land in India, Louisiana and Canada (which simply had to be written off as *quelques arpents de neige* – a few tracts of snow). But with the British overstretched in the American War of Independence a few years later, the French in their turn whittled through the islands, reclaiming all their old colonies.

The French Revolution had profound effects in the islands. The traditions of *Egalité* and the Rights of Man had particular significance in the Caribbean because they could hardly tolerate slavery. The planters and officials shuddered at the ideas emanating from their capital, but each colony turned out differently. In Martinique the planters and royalists remained in the ascendancy: rather than lose everything they actually preferred to call in their old enemies, the English, to bolster the prosperous old regime. In Guadeloupe, however, the revolutionaries gained the upper hand. There was a reign of terror: the slaves were liberated, the planters put to death or exiled, and the plantations, symbols of the *ancien régime*, were destroyed (there are no pre-revolutionary estate houses left in Guadeloupe). And the humanitarian ideas emanating from Paris proved to be the death of France's most prosperous colony, St Domingue. In 1794 it erupted in an armed rebellion by the slaves, a war of liberation that led to the founding of the world's first black republic, Haiti. Following the Napoleonic Wars, the other islands were returned to France and they have remained in her hands ever since.

Schoelcher and the Abolition of Slavery

The reintroduction of slavery in 1802 caused terrible disruption in Guadeloupe, where many of the former slaves preferred to die rather than lose their freedom. By 1834 slavery was abolished in the British colonies. Nearby St Lucia and Dominica were free, and so slaves on the French islands put out on rafts in a break for freedom.

Victor Schoelcher, the Father of Emancipation in the French Caribbean, was born in Paris in 1804 and entered the family firm of porcelain-makers. In 1829 he undertook a journey on behalf of the firm to Mexico, Cuba and the southern States. His business was not particularly successful, but having witnessed the depredations of slavery his

Language and Culture

French colonization was always a more thorough-going affair than that of the British, and French culture can be seen to have penetrated all parts of French Caribbean life. The French Antilles have a deep pride in both French culture and their own creole version of it; there are understandable objections to the occasional accusations of being 'black Frenchmen' with no culture of their own.

It is often said how beautiful the people of Martinique and Guadeloupe are. The faces show a greater variety of colour than the British and Dutch Caribbean islands. Though the French islands always had a slightly higher proportion of whites, the old settlers were clearly also less prudish about taking an African mistress. The mix of racial strains is more thorough (though still not as thorough as in the Spanish islands) and it has created some striking faces.

And a hundred years ago the *doudous* (from *douce chérie*) of Martinique and Guadeloupe were as chic as their metropolitan counterparts. They presented themselves with characteristic Gallic flair (as they still do), bedecked in reams of brightly coloured cotton and yards of lace petticoat, with a *foulard* thrown over the shoulder. You can still see the chequered madras material in the two large islands. But the focal point of the impression was the construction of the hat. This too was fashioned of bright silk material, often yellow and checked, and there was supposedly a code in its design:

Tête à un bout (one point): my heart is for the taking.

Tête à deux bouts: my heart is taken.

Tête à trois bouts: my heart is spoken for, but you can try your luck.

The French Antilles were one of the leading centres of *Négritude*, a French literary and philosophical movement of black consciousness that was born in the 1930s. Martiniquans Etienne Lero and Aimé Césaire, together with Léopold Senghor of Senegal, re-examined the position of the black man, formerly the slave, and his relation to the white man, the colonial master. Aimé Césaire became famous with his *Cahier d'un Retour au Pays Natal* in 1939 and a later play *La Tragédie du Roi Christophe*. He was also a leading light in Martiniquan politics, holding the office of mayor of Fort de France for nearly 50 years.

Creole is the mixed language that has developed in many parts of the French colonial world, and the Caribbean islands which have seen a French presence each have a version of their own. You will hear it spoken in Dominica, St Lucia and occasionally

life was changed for good. On his return to France he embarked on a career as a polemicist and pamphleteer, mobilizing the public imagination through his works. He continued for 15 years, but powerful lobbies opposed him, and it became clear that only a political reversal in France could affect the situation in the Caribbean colonies.

As it had been 60 years before, it was a revolution that overturned the law, and in 1848 Schoelcher, the committed Republican, had his chance. On 27 April the law was passed abolishing slavery in the French colonies once and for all. Schoelcher was put in charge of dismantling slavery and he went to the Antilles. He was elected deputy of Guadeloupe.

Grenada, which the French have owned at one time or other, and even as far away as Trinidad, taken there by French Royalists fleeing the *patriotes* in revolutionary times. The Eastern Caribbean creoles are not, however, mutually comprehensible with the kweyol of the Haitians, once also French subjects. There are creoles in French Guyana in South America and in Réunion, the two other French overseas *départements*, and also in Mauritius. Curiously, the two smaller French islands, St Martin and St Barthélemy, have traditionally spoken English and latterly pure French. The creole language is a classic Caribbean melting pot, a pidgin formed by early settlers from different countries in order to communicate with each other, and then steadily changed by the influx of African slaves, none of whom spoke a common language because they were purposely split up to destroy their traditions. French is clearly audible in creole and for tantalizing moments the stream will let you hold on to words and even phrases, but suddenly it will whiplash and escape your grasp, chasing off in a flurry of unaccustomed vowels and peculiar utterances. In the same way, in the rhythm and intonation, and in the sharp un-Gallic sounds, are distinct echoes and resonances of African languages. Sensibly, they seem to have got rid of the impossible-to-pronounce letters of French, 'u' and 'r', substituting 'oo' and 'w' instead.

But French is the official language of the islands, used in the schools and by the authorities, as well as on the menus, of course. It is mainly the country people who speak creole and, as you must speak the official language to 'get on', people will actually bring up their children without using the language at all, speaking to them only in French. There is little written in creole because it has always had an oral tradition, particularly in song.

Most French Caribbean authors write in French and they have won plenty of French literary prizes over the years. Some to look out for are, from Martinique, Patrick Chamoiseau, winner of the Prix Goncourt with *Texaco* (also *Solibo Magnifique*, which is set in Fort de France), Aimé Césaire, Edouard Glissant, Joseph Zobel (*Rue Cases-Nègres*), Rafaël Confiant (*Eau de Café*, winner of the 1991 Prix Novembre), Daniel Boukman, Xavier Orville and Ina Césaire (*Island Memories*). Guadeloupean writers include Maryse Condé, whose finest book is probably *La Vie Scélérate*, Simone Schwarz-Bart (known for her *Ti Jean l'Horizon, Pluie et Vent sur Telumé Miracle* and *Un Plat de Porc aux Bananes Vertes*, with husband André), Max Jeanne, Daniel Maximin, Ernest Pépin and Gisèle Pineau, author of *La Grande Drive des Esprits*.

After Emancipation, the French Antilles, like the British islands, were short of labour for the canefields as the freed slaves left the plantations to form their own villages. By 1870, some 80,000 East Indians, or *Z'indiens*, as they are known in creole, came to the islands as indentured labourers. Their faces are less visible nowadays, but you will still see Hindu temples dotted around the islands.

The French colonies in the Caribbean followed the vagaries of the various *empires* and *républiques* of French politics until 1946, when Martinique and Guadeloupe were elevated to the status of *départements* and later into *régions*. They are governed by an elected island assembly, the Conseil Régional, and a governor appointed in France.

Martinique

Martinique has traditionally been the flagship of French culture in the Caribbean. It was the richest of the colonies and in the 19th century its social hub, St-Pierre, the 'Paris of the Lesser Antilles', was renowned all over the Americas. Fashion followed Paris to the letter, and the great plays of the age were staged in the St-Pierre Theatre.

Though the spirit of St-Pierre died in 1902, when the city was destroyed in a cataclysmic volcanic explosion, Martinique is still that little bit more chic. The island is more developed than its *confrères*, and with 430,000 citizens, about a third of whom live in the capital Fort de France on the southeast coast, it is the most populous island in the Lesser Antilles after Trinidad. Martinique is a central link in the Eastern Caribbean island chain, lying between the Windward Islands of Dominica and St Lucia. It measures 48 miles by 19 at its widest point (75 by 30km) and, with its curious skiing-glove shape, it has an area of 416 square miles (1,080sq km). It seems larger because it is so highly developed. The north is dominated by the steep volcanic mountain of Mont Pelé (4,656ft) and from there the land steadily falls away south to the central sugar plains of Lamentin and Fort de France, before rising again into the *mornes* (hills) of the southern peninsula. The island is of volcanic origin, except in the south, where age-old coral limestone formations have been pushed up out of the sea.

The French heritage constantly bombards the eyes, from the billboards to *boules* on the town square. The Martinicans have a surprisingly faithful attachment to France, stronger than that of their compatriots in Guadeloupe, whom they consider a little wild and unpredictable. Despite subsidies from France that amount to a total of about 70% of the island's GDP, Martinique receives a lot from tourism, which brings in approximately as much as the rest of Martinique's exports combined. In 2004, the island received a total of 630,000 stay-over and cruise-ship tourists. The next principal earner is agriculture: one-third of the land is under cultivation and you will see banana plantations everywhere, and sugar cane, used for sugar and rum.

Most of the tourism in Martinique is concentrated around a few towns in the south of the island, and you can certainly have a good time there enjoying the best of the island's beaches and the good restaurants. But Martinique gives an excellent exposure to French Caribbean life, and its towns, rainforests and the remote east coast can be stimulating and satisfying to explore.

History

Martinique was discovered at the turn of the 15th century, on Columbus's first, second or fourth voyage, depending whose history you believe (it was actually his first landfall on his fourth voyage). Columbus apparently thought the island was inhabited by a tribe of Amazons because he was greeted only by women shouting '*Madinina*'. The Carib men must have been away raiding another island. Similarly, the origins of the name Martinique have been obscured by zealous historians. It may have been named for St Martin, but most think that the name derives from the Carib word '*madinina*', thought to mean 'the island of flowers'.

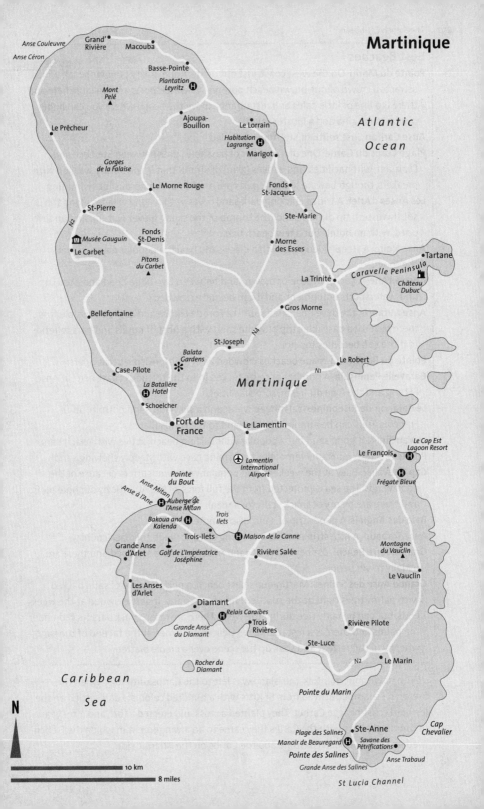

Best Beaches

Pointe du Marin: On the west coast, just out of Ste-Anne, a very popular beach which attracts a crowd of nut-brown beach poseurs. All watersports are available here and there is a line of little cafés and restaurants above the beach where you can linger over an Orangina and a lobster salad.

Anse Caritan: Just south of Ste-Anne, secluded.

Plage Corps du Garde: One of a number of passable spots between Ste-Luce and Diamant, with facilities, and 2 miles (3km) of strand that is constantly washed with breakers, though beware because parts are marked as dangerous for swimming.

Les Anses d'Arlet: A trio of cracking dark-sand coves with fishing villages along the southwestern tip of the island (the thumb of the skiing glove). Natural and undeveloped, with no hotels but a few beach bars.

Anse Noire: A steep-sided cove with a black-sand beach, a popular day out from the town.

Anse à l'Ane: A 500-yard strip of brown sand between two huge headlands. You can find watersports equipment and it can be quite crowded.

Anse Mitan: In the developed area south of Fort de France and easily accessible from there by ferry, a passable strip of white sand with a host of hotels and bars to retire to if the sun becomes too hot.

Pointe du Bout: Man-made beaches crowded with high-pressure vacationers.

Caravelle Peninsula: A number of coves tucked in to the tortuous coast here, at Anse l'Etang and the Baie du Trésor; some facilities.

Le Baignoir de Joséphine: Waist-deep water and a silky-soft sand bottom, off Le François. Trips can be arranged to here and to the Fonds Blancs.

Le Vauclin: Not good sand but a popular windsurfing beach, active with beach bars.

Pointe Macré: A quiet and remote but charming cove with steeply shelving sand.

Cap Chevalier: Busy at the weekend and popular with windsurfers because of the good winds. The sea is protected from the full force of the Atlantic by offshore reefs and there are plenty of snack stalls for a meal.

Baie des Anglais: A good strip of sand, also remote (*adm*).

Anse Trabaud: A nice strip of sand, but a long drive through the back-country.

Grande Terre Beach: Just beyond the Grand Anse, it is more secluded and there are usually fewer people.

Grande Anse des Salines: Martinique's best beach, a perfect curve of sand backed with palms trees right at the southern tip of the island. It gets crowded at the weekends, but can be fairly free during the week. There are often snack bars tucked under the palms and there is a restaurant, Les Délices de la Mer, at the far end of the sand, where you can retreat and soak up the scene over a creole platter.

With or without menfolk, the island was left to the Caribs until 1635, when the Breton d'Esnambuc arrived from St Kitts with a hundred colonists and settled on the leeward coast near Le Carbet. They planted a cross and erected a fort, and after years of running battles with the Caribs they came to an arrangement in which the French lived on the Caribbean coastline and the Caribs on the Atlantic side.

Just as Barbados became the leading British island, so Martinique became the leading French colony in the 1650s. The islanders became fantastically rich growing sugar and shipping it out to Europe. They had an uneasy relationship with the French Crown: in 1717 the Governor tried to enforce the *exclusif* (a law stipulating that trade from Martinique must be made exclusively with France) and promptly found himself taken prisoner with his Intendant and simply sent back to France as an unwanted nuisance. A more conciliatory governor was sent out to replace him, one who was prepared to turn a blind eye to unofficial trading.

In the 18th century Martinique changed hands a number of times, like all the islands in the area, snatched by roving navies and swapped for other prizes at the end of each successive war. A new storm rose on the horizon as the ideas of the Revolution reverberated in the Caribbean. Martinique was divided along traditional lines: the townspeople, or *patriotes*, adopted the cockade and allied themselves with the revolutionaries, and the planters struck for the royalists. Initially the *patriotes* took the island, rallied by the Revolutionary Lacrosse from St Lucia. General de Rochambeau and the Revolution came to the island in triumph; Fort Royal became République-ville. But within a year the planters had turned the tables and had contrived to get the British in, in order to restore the *ancien régime* and their prosperity. Martinique was relatively stable for the next 20 years under British rule and did not see the troubles that occurred in the other colonies of Guadeloupe and St Domingue.

In the first half of the 19th century, forces were mobilized against slavery in France, initially by Cyrille Bissette, a Martinican, and then by Victor Schoelcher (*see* pp.247–8). Slave riots took place in Le Carbet, St-Pierre and in Grande Anse. With the coming of the Second Republic, the abolition of slavery in the French islands was proclaimed on 27 April 1848.

1902 was a momentous date for the colony because of the eruption of Mont Pelé, which completely destroyed St-Pierre, then the commercial and cultural centre of the island. Fort de France took its place. In 1946, Martinique became a *département* with the same status and responsibilities as any other in *le métropole*, and in 1985 it became a *région*.

Beaches

Martinique has beaches to suit every taste – busy strips with hotels and water-sports and more isolated palm-fringed coves with fishing villages. Most lie on the protected Caribbean coast, but there are also quite a few hidden in the nooks and crannies of the Atlantic shore. The sand is best in the south; in the north it becomes dark and volcanic. Beaches are public in Martinique (though you may have to pay in some cases for access over private land) and, although most hotels do not mind outsiders, one or two discourage them for the benefit of their guests. Most charge for the use of their facilities. The area south of Fort de France is very popular and many of the hotels are located on the beaches there (easily reached by ferry from the city). If you are in the north, your nearest beaches are likely to be in the lee of the Caravelle Peninsula, but only go on a calm and sunny day because otherwise the sea will be rough.

Flora and Fauna

Martinique has the best of both worlds, the verdant profusion in the mountainous rainforests and the open plains that now blow with sugar cane and bananas, where cattle once were allowed to run wild in buccaneer-style farming. The rainforest is fantastic and well worth seeing, by walking (*see* 'Hiking', p.258) or even simply by driving through it. There is an excellent road through the **Pitons du Carbet** and **Fonds St-Denis** where the ferns explode at the roadside. Just above Fort de France there is a display of tropical plants and trees at **Balata Gardens**. You will see tropical plants from around the world.

Island fauna is fairly typical for the Eastern Caribbean (including the *colibri* or hummingbird; the manicou, an opossum-like creature; and the *mygale* or trap-door

Three Crowned Heads

In the 17th century, a Françoise d'Aubigné, the daughter of a colonial functionary, spent her childhood at the northern parish of Le Prêcheur, just as the colony was becoming prosperous. When she returned to Europe, she embarked on a course that would take her to the royal court of France. She became Madame de Maintenon and in 1684 she secretly married Louis XIV.

Martinican legend also relates a story of two young cousins, Yéyette and Aimée, who were walking one evening when they came across an old woman known in the area as a fortune-teller. They gave their palms to be examined and eventually she made her pronouncement: 'You,' she said to the first, 'will be an Empress, and you –' talking to Aimée '– will be more than an Empress.' She walked off, refusing to respond to their pleas for more detail. Aimée Dubuc de Rivery was soon sent to a convent in France to complete her education and the incident was forgotten. But on her return journey to Martinique she was caught in a storm off the European coast and was taken captive by Barbary pirates. The Bey of Algiers sold the passengers of the ship as slaves, but kept Aimée because he was captivated by her beauty. Eventually he made a present of her to the Grand Turk in Constantinople. There, she penetrated the deepest secrets of the seraglio, to become the favourite of the Sultan, lover of his successor and finally the Sultana Validé, adoptive mother of Emperor Mahmoud II.

Her cousin Yéyette was born Marie-Rose Joséphine Tascher de la Pagerie, in Trois-Ilets in 1763. Her family had fallen on hard times, but when offered an advantageous match her parents married her off to the son of a former governor, Alexandre Vicomte de Beauharnais, and she too went to France. At one stage Joséphine was condemned to death as a noble, but she was set free when Robespierre fell. Within a few years she married Napoleon Bonaparte, General of the French army in Italy. On 2 December 1804 she became his Empress. Many consider Joséphine a shallow woman, and it is somewhat surprising that the Martinicans should be so proud of her, particularly as she was behind the reintroduction of slavery in the French islands in 1802. There was a curious incident in 1992, in which a statue of Joséphine on the Savanne in Fort de France had its head knocked off in an ironic political statement. The head has never been returned.

Getting There

Martinique t (596–)

By Air

An airport security tax of €13 is payable by all passengers leaving Martinique (this is usually included in the price of the ticket).

From Europe

Air France, t 55 33 00, has daily flights from Paris and weekly connections from other French cities, including Lyon, Toulouse, Bordeaux and Nantes. These are supplemented by charters operated by Nouvelles Frontières, t 70 59 70; AOM, t 70 09 16; and Air Liberté, t 42 18 34.

There are no direct flights from other European countries; travellers can connect in Paris, or fly via Barbados, St Lucia or in some instances Antigua.

From the USA

American Airlines, t 42 19 19, and Air Caraïbes have regular services through the airport hub at San Juan, Puerto Rico. Air France also routes via Miami.

From Other Caribbean Islands

Air Caraïbes, t 42 16 10, has hopper flights to Union Island, Mustique, St Vincent, Barbados and St Lucia, and north along the island chain, via Dominica, Guadeloupe and Antigua to St Martin. Air Calypso, t 42 12 72, flies north to Guadeloupe and St Martin. Air France flies to San Juan, Puerto Rico, and Port-au-Prince in Haiti. LIAT, t 42 16 02, serves islands to the north and south of Martinique, originating in Antigua and Trinidad. Cubana, t 42 17 30, flies to Cuba.

Charter planes are available through Antilles Aero Service, t 51 66 88, *www.airantilles.com*.

By Sea

Hydrofoils run between Martinique and Guadeloupe, touching Dominica en route: Express des Iles, Terminal Inter Iles Bassin Radoub, 97200 Fort de France, t 63 12 15, *www.express-des-iles.com*; Brudey Frères, t 70 08 50; Caribbean Ferries Cie, t 63 68 68.

There are also occasional sailings south to St Lucia.

Getting Around

By Bus

Public buses are a cheap way of travelling around the island and they depart from the Parking, on the waterfront at Fort de France, or from the main square in other towns. You will find both **public buses**, which follow a vague time schedule, and *taxis collectifs* (TCs), share-taxis (they can be a mini-bus or a car) that run a fixed route and depart when they are full. At the terminus, ask around and you will be directed to the first one headed in your direction. If you wish to get a bus from the airport into Fort de France (no buses run the route directly), you must cross the main road, beyond the car park in front of the terminal building, and flag down a *taxi collectif* on the other side.

Public buses are only allowed to stop at official stops, but you might be able to flag down a TC on the roadside if you are lucky. *Arrêt!*, shouted loud enough to be heard above the noise of the stereo system, is the word used to indicate that you want to get off. The buses run from 5am until about 7pm and the TCs a little longer. On Sundays and on public holidays the public transport system packs up in mid-afternoon and you can quite easily be left isolated. Some approximate prices are: Fort de France to airport – €2, to Trois-Ilets – €3, to St-Pierre – €3, to Ste-Anne – €7.

By Ferry

The tourist areas on the south side of Fort de France bay (Pointe du Bout, Anse Mitan, Anse à l'Ane) are best served by ferry (*vedette*). These leave from the waterfront next to the Savane, close to Fort St-Louis, with a regular schedule to Pointe du Bout from 6am–midnight; 20-minute crossing; round trip €6.

By Taxi

Taxis are readily available at the Parking downtown or at the airport and can be ordered at any hotel. There is a stand in Le Marin, t 74 62 78. Some examples of fares are: from Lamentin Airport to: city centre – €16, Pointe du Bout – €40. Taxi-drivers are willing to take **day tours** (many of them speak English). If divided between four people, the price for a day's drive is reasonable value, but be sure to fix the price beforehand. Taxi companies include:

Martinique Taxis, t 63 63 62.
Taxis Savane, t 60 62 73.
Radio Taxis Service, t 63 10 10.
Radio Telephone Taxi, t 63 63 62.

By Guided Tour

Island tours are easy to organize in full- and half-day tours (usually taking in a meal as well).

ACF Aviation, t 51 07 17, *acf-aviation@ wanadoo.fr*, *perso.wanadoo.fr/acf-aviation*. Sightseeing tours by plane.
Alizes Air Services, t 62 24 25. Plane tours.
Banana Tours, t 63 66 77, *banana.tours@ wanadoo.fr*.
Heliblue, t 66 10 80, *www.heliblue.com*.
Madinina Tours, 89 rue Blénac, t 70 65 25, *madinina.tours@wanadoo.fr*; airport t 42 17 07.
STT Voyages, 23 rue Blénac, Fort de France, t 71 68 12.

Car and Bike Hire

For maximum mobility, plenty of hire cars are available. In comparison with other islands nearby, Martinique's roads are good, though the islanders tend to drive with an abandon both French and Caribbean. Driving is on the right and your own licence is valid for the first 20 days, after which time an international driving licence is required. Maps are usually handed out by the hire companies. Found at the airport, in Fort de France and in the tourist centres, the hire companies offer cars from about €40–50 per day with taxes on top. Major credit cards are accepted as deposit. Companies (most of which have offices in town as well as at the airport) include:

Avis, t 42 11 00, *www.avis.com*.
Budget, t 42 16 97, *www.budget-antilles.com*.
Discount, in Trois-Ilets and around the south, t 66 54 37.
Europcar, in Fort de France, t 42 42 42, *info@ autolocation*, *www.europcar.mq*.
Funny Rent Motorcycles, t 63 33 05. You can rent scooters through them, with outlets all over the island.
Hertz, t 42 16 90.
Jumbo Car, t 42 22 26, *www.jumbocar.com*.
Pop's Car, t 42 16 84, *www.popscar.mq*.

Tourist Information

Abroad

In other countries you should be able to get information through the various Maisons de la France. There is a Martinique website: *www.touristmartinique.com*. You can also find detailed information at *www.martinique.org* and *www.frenchcaribbean.com*.

Canada: 1981 McGill College, Suite 490, Montreal, H3A 2W9, t 514 288 1904.
France: 2 rue des Moulins, 75001 Paris, t 44 77 86 00, *preinadelaide@aol.com*.
USA: 444 Madison Av, 16th Floor, New York, NY 10022, t (212) 838 7800, t 1 800 391 4909, *martinique@nyo.com*.

In Martinique

The main tourist office on the island is on the waterfront in Fort de France. Around the island you will find some information offices in the various town halls, and of course you can also find plenty of information in the hotel foyers.

You'll find the tourist offices at:
Immeuble Beaupré, Pointe de Jaham, t 61 61 77, *infos.cmt@martiniquetourism.com*, *www.touristmartinique.com*. *Open Mon–Fri 7.30–12.30 and 2.30–5.30, Sat 8–noon*.
Le Lamentin Airport, t 51 28 55.
Fort de France, 76 rue Lazare Carnot, t 60 27 73.

Embassies and Consulates

The American Consulate in Martinique is at 14 rue Blénac, Fort de France, t 63 13 03.

Media

With its suitably sexy slogan, 'Les Sens du Plaisir', the Martinique Tourist Board puts out several publications, including *Choubouloute*, providing useful information such as watersports companies and ferry times, and there is also a restaurant guide, *Ti Gourmet*, to help you get to grips with the all-important island dining experience.

Medical Emergencies

In the case of a medical emergency, contact the Hôpital Pierre Zobda Quitman, 97232 Lamentin, t 75 15 15, or SOS Medecins, t 63 33 33, and if you need to contact the police, call t 17.

Money and Banks

The currency of Martinique is the euro, which exchanges roughly at US$1 = €0.80, though of course it floats on the open market. US dollars are accepted in the larger hotels, but it is more convenient to carry euros for shops and restaurants. Major credit cards are also accepted in tourist areas and in Fort de France. Traveller's cheques in dollars or euros are accepted in many shops in town. Sometimes payment by credit card or by traveller's cheque will mean a discount on prices. Service is included (*compris*) in restaurant bills on the island.

Banks are open for exchange Mon–Fri 7.30–noon and 2.30–4. There is a bank in all the main towns.

Shopping

Shops open Mon–Fri 8.30–6, with a long break for lunch in the heat of the day (usually 12–2.30).

Telephone Code

The IDD code for Martinique is t 596, followed by a six-digit local number.

Festivals

January/February *Carnival*. The major festival in the year, which starts on the day after New Year's Day and continues with weekend processions until the beginning of Lent, when there are five solid days of dancing and street parades. On *Lundi Gras* they stage 'burlesque weddings' in transvestite costumes, *Mardi Gras* is the day of the red devils and Ash Wednesday sees black and white costumes and culminates in the burning of *Momo*, the Carnival spirit.

May *Emancipation*. Another key date in the calendar is on the 22nd, the date of the Emancipation of the slaves in the French West Indies, remembered with general blow-outs.

July *Bastille Day*. Held on the 14th, it is celebrated in the Antilles as in France. Fort de France stages a series of concerts and theatrical events at its Cultural Festival.

November. The annual sailing race to bring over the first case of Beaujolais Nouveau from the *métropole*.

December *International Jazz Festival* or *World Crossroads of the Guitar*. Martinique clubs and venues come alive with these festivals, held in alternate years.

Various dates *Fête Patronale*. Many towns celebrate their saint's day, with a round of races, competitions, outdoor dances and barbecued chicken legs. They take place mostly between July and January, and it is well worth checking the newspaper or Tourist Board to find out if one is going on. *Cultural festivals*. Also held in the towns, with shows, parades and sailing races: Le Robert (April), St-Pierre (May), Le Marin and Ste-Marie (both August).

The *Yoles Rondes*

The *yoles rondes* are distinctive Martinican yawls with square sails and it has become popular to race them. They have huge square sails on a bamboo mast and are sailed by a crew of 11 or 12 men who clamber about on poles a good 6ft out above the water to make the best of the winds. They are often raced at the traditional Martinican *fêtes patronales*, but there is also a special eight-day **regatta** held around the island each July. There are many other regattas, with more regular yachts, centred on the sailing clubs at Le Marin (early June) and Fort de France (late June).

Watersports

Day Sails

Coasting the Caribbean shore of Martinique in a yacht can be a fun day out. There are excursions from the tourist areas on the Caribbean coast and off the Atlantic side as well; some go as far as St Lucia for a weekend. Go through the hotels for a yacht in your area, or try:

Aquabulle, Port de Plaisance du Marin, t 74 69 69.

Aquascope Seadom Explorer, Pointe du Bout, t 68 36 09, www.aquascope.martinique.com. A semi-submersible boat for a dry view of the corals.

Aquascope Zemis, Ste-Anne, t 76 83 71. Semi-submersible; reserve in advance.

L'Ile Bleue, Pointe du Bout, t 66 10 13.

A particularly popular excursion is the trip to the Baignoir de Joséphine and the Fonds Blancs, sand bars that rise to just below the surface near Le François (though it can be a bit crowded).

It is also fun to take the day out to La Maison de l'Ilet Oscar, t 47 75 40, where there is a charming restaurant and some facilities. You can go on an organized tour:

Albert Mongin, t 54 70 23.
La Cygne, Hotel la Riviera, Le François, t 54 68 54.

Deep-sea Fishing

Diamond Rock Hotel, Le Diamant, t 76 46 00.
Little Queeny, t 76 24 20.
Maverick Too, Le Diamant, t 76 24 20.

Kayaking

Aventures Tropicales, Cap Chevalier, t 64 58 49.
Caraïbes Coast Kayak, Ste-Anne, t 76 76 02.
Club Nautique, t 74 92 48.
Fun Kayak, t 56 00 60.
Les Kayaks du Robert, t 65 70 68.
Rod Evasions, t 48 49 98.

Sailing

Martinique is a popular starting point for yachting holidays, many of which head down the island chain towards the Grenadines. There are marinas in Fort de France, Pointe du Bout and Le Marin and many of the big charter firms work from here offering skippered or bare boats. Contact:

The Moorings Antilles, t 74 75 39, *costserv@moorings.mq*.
Star Voyage, Pointe du Bout, t 66 00 72.
Stardust, Le Marin, t 74 98 17.
Sun Sail, Le Marin, t 66 09 14.

Scuba Diving

Scuba diving is popular in Martinique, well-organized and available in all the resorts. The best dive sites for corals are around the southern edge of the island, off Ste-Anne, around Diamond Rock and on the southwest coast around Les Anses d'Arlet (excellent for **snorkelling**), where you will find forests of sea fans and sponges. There are many other reefs along the Caribbean coast, as well as some wrecks off St-Pierre, sent to the bottom in 1902. Many of the big hotels have diving and teaching facilities (a medical certificate and insurance is necessary). A single-tank dive coasts around €35.

Planète Bleue, Pointe du Bout marina, t 66 08 79, *planbleue@ais.mq*, *www.planete-bleue.mq*.
Ste-Luce Plongée, t 62 40 06, *mail@sainteluceplongee.com*, *www.sainteluceplongee.com*.
Sub Diamond Rock, on the south coast, t 76 10 65.
Tropicasub, in the north, t 78 38 03, *tropicasub@hotmail.com*, *www.multimania.com/tropicasub*.

Windsurfing

A popular sport on Martinique, so you can hire equipment on all the major beaches, usually through the hotels. Cost ranges from €10–15 per hour. Advanced sailors should head for the Atlantic coast, around Le Vauclin, for waves, and Tartane on the Caravelle Peninsula for surf. You can hire boards at:

Club Nautique du Marin, Le Marin, t 74 92 48, *clubnautique-du-marin@wanadoo.fr*.
Le Club Nautique du Vauclin, Pointe Faula outside Le François, t 74 50 83, *cn-vauclin@wanadoo.fr*, *www.cnv.fr.fm*.
Alizes Fun Dillon, Cap Chevalier, t 74 71 58, *alizefun@wanadoo.fr*, *www.alizefun.com*. On the busy Anse Michel beach.

Other Sports

Golf

There is just one golf course on Martinique, though it's well-known:

Golf de l'Impératrice Joséphine, just south of Trois-Ilets, t 68 32 81, *info@golfmartinique.com*, *www.golfmartinique.com*. An 18-hole Robert Trent Jones course, par 71. It gets booked up, but it is worth a try. *Green fee €43*.

Hiking

Organized trips into the rainforest are arranged by:

Aventures Tropicales Antilles, t 75 24 24, *aventures-tropicales@wanadoo.fr*, *www.aventures-tropicales.com*. Canyoning excursions.

Bureau de la Randonnée, t 78 30 77.
Couleurs Locales, Morne Vert, **t** 55 59 12.

Horse-riding

If you would like to see the rolling *mornes* or the beaches of southern Martinique on horseback, then there are several stables on the island:
Black Horse Ranch, La Pagerie, Trois Ilets, **t** 68 37 80.
La Gourmette, outside Fort de France, **t** 64 20 16.
L'Hippocampe, Le Lamentin, **t** 57 06 71.
Ranch Jack, above Anse à l'Ane, **t** 68 37 69, *ranchjack@wanadoo.fr*.
Ranch des Trois Caps, near Le Marin, **t** 74 70 65.

Mountain-biking

If you would like to explore the island by bike, contact:
Aventures Tropicales, t 75 24 24.
V. T. Tilt, Anse Mitan, Trois-Ilets, **t** 66 01 01.
Blue Monday, Diamant, **t** 76 18 80.
Localbikes, Fort de France, **t** 63 33 05.
Sud Loisirs, Ste-Anne, **t** 76 81 82.

Spectator Sports

Cockfighting can be seen in many islands across the French- and Spanish-speaking Caribbean. It is quite a spectacle, and though it may well appear cruel to a visitor, cock fighting is a sport followed avidly by the Martinicans.

The pit is a circular ring banked steeply with seats, which on Sunday becomes a melee of gamesmen with fistfuls of bank notes, shouting to place their bets. All goes silent when the cocks are brought in by their owners, carefully prepared for months with alcohol to make their skin hard, and groomed especially for the fight. The owners posture about in the ring for a while, showing off their beasts to the crowd, testing the sharpness of the knives attached to their claws.

Eventually the two cocks are released in the ring and all hell breaks loose: in the fury of the pit where the cocks lunge and lash, and in the stands, where men are standing and yelling, brandishing their fists. There are cockpits in Le Morne Rouge, Ducos, Le Lamentin and Rivière Pilote.

The **mongoose** was originally introduced to Martinique to reduce the snake population. Ironically, the animals promptly struck up a mutually beneficial arrangement in which the mongoose would avoid the snake by sleeping during the night and have a free run at the chickens (and other birds, some of which have become extinct as a result) in the daytime. As if in revenge, the islanders now wheel the two out against one another for sport.

Where to Stay

Martinique t (596–)

Martinique is a surprise as regards its hotels. You might expect that there would be a string of luxurious and stylish enclaves of quiet and luxury in the island, but in fact there are only a couple (you have to go to St Barts for real luxury). The majority of hotels in the island are in the mid-range. You will, however, find the full range of settings, from the modern Caribbean dream on the beach to tiny *auberges* set in old gingerbread houses, hidden in the rainforest. Many of the best hotels are quite isolated, particularly from Fort de France, and with an island this size it is a good idea to have a car to get around (check with your hotel when making a booking because many of them have arrangements with the car-hire companies). It is worth doing a bit of exploring and you may want to move from place to place. Rates quoted are for a double room, breakfast often included.

Very Expensive

Hotel Cap Est Lagoon Resort & Spa, Le François, **t** 54 80 80, *info@capest.com*, *www.capest.com*. This new 50-room resort on the east coast is considered the best on the island. The rooms are finely furnished in modern décor and have coffee maker, hairdryer, mini-bar, dataport, room service, and free newspaper. Facilities include restaurant, bar, swimming pool, spa, tennis, free parking and baby-sitting. Beach nearby; small pets allowed.
Habitation Lagrange, 97225 Le Marigot, **t** 53 60 60, *habitation.lagrange@habitation.lagrange. com*, *www.habitation-lagrange.com*. One of

the most original hotels in Martinique. It is a little remote and isolated in the northeast, but that is part of its charm; if you are happy to be off the beaten track (at the end of a rather rickety riverside drive), it is a pleasant place to stay. It is set in a beautifully restored sugar plantation house, turreted and wrapped around with a cast-iron balcony, dating from the end of the 17th century and restored in 1990 after being left derelict for many years. Downstairs the tall doorways are panelled with dark wood and the walls are painted with murals and hung with prints of the old West Indies. There are just 16 rooms in all, fitted with bright furnishings and creole antiques, wicker-back and rocking chairs, murals and curious sculptures. The floors creak because they are wooden and the bathroms are old-style with enamel and gold-lined taps. Very personable style and service, the only four-star hotel with French Caribbean chic.

Kalenda Resort, Trois-Ilets, t 66 00 00, US t 1 800 543 4300, *ventesfdf@kalendaresort-hotels.com, www.kalendaresort-hotels.com*. International standards of comfort and service.

Sofitel Bakoua Martinique, Trois-Ilets, t 66 02 02, *www.sofitel.com*. If the beach is the most important feature, this is a reliable choice, with infinity pool and beach bar on stilts. Set across from the Fort-de-France Bay.

Expensive–Moderate

Manoir de Beauregard, 97227 Ste-Anne, t 76 73 40, *manoirdebeauregard@cgit.com*. In the south of the island you will find this very pleasant small hotel, set around a charming and vaguely ecclesiastical-looking estate house which dates from the early years of the 18th century and has recently been restored after being gutted in a fire. The main house has black and white tiles and a grille metalwork entrance with heavy wooden furniture. The three rooms upstairs are decorated with antique furniture and four-poster beds. The others, making just 11 in all, are in a separate block across the garden, and are more modern. Quiet and pleasant atmosphere, swimming pool, air

conditioning in the rooms, beach not far off. *Open December–May.*

Relais Caraïbes, La Cherry, 97233 Le Diamant, t 76 44 65, *relais.caraibes@wanadoo.fr*. Here you will find a charming retreat, where 15 rooms (air conditioning, no fans) are set in neat and pretty cottages in a profuse tropical garden. The main house is excellent, with its creole furniture and eastern rugs, set around a sunken garden; also the bar area and the open-sided dining room, which looks over the pool to a fantastic view of the sea down below. Each room is air-conditioned and has a terrace with a hammock, and also TV and fridge. The Relais Caraïbes is quite isolated, but you can hire a car there and guests can use the facilities of the Novotel Diamant on the beach a walk away down below.

Frégate Bleue, 97240 Le François, t 54 54 66. An even smaller stopover, with just seven rooms in a private house. It is a Relais du Silence and it lives up to its quiet and peaceful name. A good feel with antique furniture and Persian carpets but also modern comforts (air conditioning, television and telephones, pool, and kitchenettes in the rooms, though there is now a dining room too). There is a distinctly international air about the place, and the owners, who live on the property, speak English. Again quite remote above the Atlantic coast, but within a shout of all the activity offshore.

Hotel Karibea La Plantation Leyritz, 97218 Basse-Pointe, t 78 53 92, *hleyritz@cgit.com, www.alizea.com/leyritz*. Has an isolated setting, in handsome gardens on a cane- and banana-covered hillside in the north-east. The 18th-century plantation house has been rebuilt as a hotel and the slave quarters turned into the 50 hotel rooms (considerably improved since 200 years ago). The hotel can get a bit busy during the day, as a lot of visitors come by for lunch, but the early evening restores the planta-tion idyll.

Moderate

Auberge de L'Anse Mitan, at the end of the beach at Anse Mitan, t 66 01 12, US t 1 800 468 0023, *www.fwinet.com/aubans*. Slightly isolated from the hurly-burly of the tourist resort, a retiring enclave of faded elegance. Built in the 1930s as a family home, it has an elegant foyer with wicker furniture set among the greenery and white tiles and a fine view over the bay to Fort de France. The 20 rooms and 6 studios are hung with prints, showing an older Martinique, but they have all the essentials of modern comfort, phones, air conditioning and showers.

La Bonne Auberge, Anse Mitan, 97229 Trois-Ilets, t 66 01 55. Another option in the middle of Anse Mitan is this friendly hotel and its restaurant, Chez André, both festooned in greenery with 30 comfortable and simple air-conditioned rooms in blocks. No pool, but the sea is a minute's walk away.

Hotel Valmeniere Karibea, Fort de France, t 75 75 75, *reservation@hotelvalmeniere.com*, *www.karibea.com*. A three-star hotel close to the main highway that connects Lamentin International Airport. An ideal place to stay for business trips (it's in the heart of the business district).

Hotel Diamant les Bains, 97223 Le Diamant, t 76 40 14, US t 1 800 223 9815. Rooms in the hotel building and cabins scattered around the garden of palms and ginger lily that run down to the sea. The rooms are pretty with white décor and bright colours (television, air conditioning, fridge and telephone). The hotel is friendly and serves good local food on the terrace above the garden. Miles of brown sand beach to walk, and a pool.

Hotel Palm Beach, 97223 Le Diamant, t 76 47 84, *palmbeach@wanadoo.fr*, *www.hotel palmbeach.com*. Sits right on the sand at the entrance to Diamant town. There are just nine rooms in a modern house, where guests gather in the central salon and outside on the restaurant terrace under the trees. Some nice furniture in the rooms, some with air-conditioning, plus fans. Friendly reception and atmosphere.

Le Manguier, Tartane, 97220 La Trinité, t 58 48 95. Stands on the hillside looking north over offshore islands. There are 16 studios, very comfortable though not huge, set in four modern buildings that take a little from the old Caribbean style (louvres, balconies and tin roofs), in a steep garden of rampant greenery, with a pool with a view. Quiet and

charming. There is no restaurant but rooms have kitchenettes and there are places to eat within walking distance.

La Caravelle, above Anse l'Etang, 97220 Tartane, t 58 07 32. Sits on the side of a hill above a nice beach. Up above you will find the main reception room, the pretty dining room and a terrace with a view; the 15 rooms are in a modern block below, quite simple, without TVs and air conditioning, but perfectly acceptable.

Le Madras, 97220 Tartane, t 58 33 95. In the town of Tartane itself, '*les pieds dans l'eau*' (literally 'feet in the water', meaning right on the beach). It has 13 neat, modern rooms on the first floor, each with fan, TV and phone. Downstairs the large dining room has a good view of all the activity of the pier and the offshore island.

Inexpensive

Auberge du Marin, 21 rue Osman Duquesnay, Le Marin, t 74 83 88. A cheaper option, this is a friendly haunt on the spine of the hill. A young crowd filters through the simple rooms and central sitting area and dining room in a covered courtyard. Five rooms only, with shared baths.

Auberge La Sikri, 97214 Le Lorrain, t 53 81 00. Set high on the hillside of agricultural land above the town of Le Lorrain. There are eight rooms upstairs with private baths and hot and cold water (not air-con because there is no need) and a pleasant gathering point in the dining room, serving creole cuisine, and salon downstairs. Lots of advice about walking in the area.

Abri Auberge Verte, 97216 Ajoupa Bouillon, t 53 33 94. Twelve rooms in hillside cottages with louvres and terraces; a pool and an overlarge dining room with creole food. The management can arrange anything from hikes to cockfighting evenings.

Le Christophe Colomb, 97221 Le Carbet, t 78 05 38. Stands in a modern block just behind the black-sand beach and its screen of palm trees. Four studios with kitchenettes and six rooms, but some share bathrooms and showers. Quite simple, but passable and clean; dining room; very calm and easy-going area.

Le Grain d'Or, at the roadside on the way into St-Pierre, on Anse Turin, t 78 06 91. A nice setting. The attractive old wooden house has a pool and a terraced restaurant (*myriade d'accras, lambi citron*). Eight rooms.

La Nouvelle Vague, 97290 St-Pierre, t 74 83 88. In St-Pierre itself, with a waterfront restaurant on the terrace.

There are not many very cheap places to stay on the island, but Martinique is linked to the **Association des Gîtes Ruraux**: their office is at 9 bd Général de Gaulle in Fort de France, t 73 74 74, *www.gites-de-france.fr*; or by post at Relais des Gîtes de France BP 1122, Maison du Tourisme Vert, Boulevard du Général de Gaulle, 97248 Fort de France Cédex. They have some 300 gîtes around the island, including flats and houses for rent by the week and by the month. The other budget alternative is **camping**:

Courbaril Camping, Anse à l'Ane, t 68 32 31. For around US$5 per night with chalets too.

Le Nid Tropical, Ste-Anne, t 68 31 30. Spaces and facilities just off the beach.

Eating Out

Martinican food has a traditional French flair and is considered by many to be the best in the Caribbean. Here, you can make your holiday almost entirely gastronomic, as there are cafés and open-air restaurants to linger in at every turn. You will find traditional *cuisine gastronomique*, but also its Caribbean or creole equivalent. Lovingly prepared, the dishes are often spiced and, of course, it is all in the sauces.

Some creole dishes, many of them slightly more luxurious versions of usual Caribbean dishes, are: *crabe farci*, a very spicy stuffing of crabmeat in a crab-shell, traditionally served on Easter Monday; the avocado *féroce*, with a spicy fish filling; *blaff*, a way of cooking fish (the name is supposed to imitate the noise it makes when thrown into the water) with thyme, peppers, clove, parsley and onion; *accra*, seasoned cod or greens fried in batter; *écrevisses, soudons, oursins* and even *chatrous* (shrimps, clams, sea urchins and octopus). *Colombo* is the delicate French Caribbean version of curry goat or chicken, and *z'habi-*

tants is a local preparation of crayfish. *Touffé* is a method of cooking in a casserole, as is *fricassée*, another popular dish. *Boudins* are local spiced sausages. *Blanc manger* is a traditional pudding, a sort of coconut custard, made with milk, coconut, cinnamon, vanilla and nutmeg. Of course every good meal starts with an apéritif (*see* 'Bars and Nightlife', p.265) and it may be finished with a rum *digestif* too. Despite the local association with rum, there is certainly something of the traditional French homage for wine and it is imported in large quantities.

Many of the hotels have fine kitchens, but it would be a pity to miss out on one of the island's best-loved pastimes by not dining out as well. Fort de France has its share of restaurants, some in the heart of town, others overlooking the melee from verandas on high. France's other colonial interests are also represented in Martinique in Vietnamese and African restaurants. There are small restaurants to be found all over the island, so if you wish to join the Martinicans in an afternoon's gastronomy, ask them when you come to a new town. Wandering and finding a restaurant is part of the fun, of course. Restaurants in Fort de France tend to be closed on Sundays, but in the tourist towns it may be another day of the week. A recent addition is pizzerias, which have appeared in all the main tourist towns.

The booklet *Ti Gourmet* lists many of Martinique's restaurants, with translations of the menus into English, recipes and useful facts including which are open on Sundays. **Price categories** are based on a main course (excluding shrimp and lobster), divided as follows: expensive = above €20; moderate = €10–20; inexpensive = less than €10. Lunch is usually a little less expensive, but not much. Service, however, is *compris*.

Fort de France and Around

Expensive

La Canne à Sucre, Patio de Cluny, t 63 33 95. For years, owner Gérard Virginius had the best restaurant in Pointe-à-Pitre, where he pioneered creole nouvelle cuisine. At this restaurant on the north side of Fort de France, his creativity continues.

La Belle Epoque, 2.5 km rte de Didier, t 64 01 09. Nine tables on the spacious terrace of a pretty turn-of-the-19th-century house. Enjoy light, creative dishes by young Martinican chef Yves Coyac. Elegant and excellent. *Open Tues–Sat.*

Le Foulard, Schoelcher, t 61 15 72. By the sea north of the capital, this long-established favourite serves excellent seafood and French and creole specialities.

Moderate

Le Mareyeur, 183 Bd de la Point des Nègres, t 61 74 70. A seafood restaurant just off the main road to Schoelcher, heading north out of town. Quite a simple dining room with red and white chequered tablecloths, but the fish are exotic – *assiette des fruits de mer* (shrimps, cockles, mussels, crayfish and bigornes), *beignets de requin* (shark fritters) and fish fricasséed, blaffed and paellaed. Some entertainment. *Closed Sat lunch and Sun.*

Marie Sainte, 160 Rue Victor Hugo, t 63 82 24. An excellent creole restaurant. *Accras, beignets, fricassée de coq, morue case nègre* (from the novel) in a simple dining room. *Open for lunch and some evenings in the week; closed Sun.*

La Cave à Vins, t 70 33 02. Set in a small pink dining room behind the wine shop of the name. It serves regional specialities from the *métropole: la véritable andouillette à la moutarde de Meaux* and a *filet de sole tropicale à la vanille Bourbon.*

Inexpensive

Vegetable market, rue St-Louis. An excellent option at lunch time. There are a number of stalls and snackettes, good for a sandwich or a platter.

Caravans, parked between the Savane and Fort St-Louis. Great for dinner. Communal tables are set out under large awnings, where you will sit among Martinican families on an evening out, everyone shouting above the sound of *zouk* music and the roar of rebellious gas stoves and generators. It stays open late, and you can get a *brochette* or a platter loaded with meat and veg.

Lina's Café, rue Victor Hugo, t 71 91 92. Stays open all day and specializes in sandwiches.

North of Fort-de-France

Moderate

L'Auberge de la Montagne Pelée, Route de l'Alleron, Le Morne Rouge, t 52 32 09. Evening service by booking only. The unusual location at the base of the volcano makes it special along with its creole specialities, particularly freshwater crayfish in a variety of dishes. *Open daily from noon–5pm.*

La Vague de St-Pierre, St-Pierre, t 78 19 54. Another waterfront view from the terrace. Here you will be served with traditional French creole fare – *fricassée* and *colombo* and *blaff*, on a deck above the sea.

Le Fromager, St-Pierre, t 78 19 07. There is a fine view over the whole town and bay from here. Pickled flying fish and *canard à l'ananas* – but watch out for bus tours.

Le Trou Crabe, Le Carbet, t 78 04 34. A pretty setting right on the sand: *chatrou bonne femme* (octopus in a local sauce) and *poulet au coco* (chicken in coconut).

Inexpensive

La Factorerie, Quartier du Fort, St-Pierre, t 78 12 53. Set in a hillside garden next to the ruins of the Eglise du Fort, the alfresco restaurant belongs to an agricultural training school whose three-part programme teaches students to serve, sew, and raise crops. Two daily three-course menus plus a variety of à la carte selections are available. *Closed Sat and Sun evenings. No credit cards.*

Le Relais Prechotain, Le Prêcheur, t 52 92 98. Try this place, set in a colourful building on the waterfront. A cool spot to linger, overlooking the sea.

Le Coin les Pêcheurs, Le Carbet. A rustic cabin and bar, where you can get an elementary platter.

Anse Mitan and Pointe du Bout

Moderate

La Villa Créole, Anse Mitan, t 66 05 53. Has a candlelit gingerbread veranda looking on to a profuse garden. Creative creole and French cuisine is accompanied by dancing and the serenading of the patron and others. Try *filet d'agneau Bergerie* or *aiguillettes de lambi à la Provencale. Closed Sun and Mon lunch.*

Chez André, under the awnings at the Bonne Auberge Hotel, **t** 66 01 55. Another friendly restaurant, with a veranda setting draped in flowers. Known for its *velouté de lambi* (cream of conch soup) and *accras de crevettes* (shrimp fritters).

Au Poisson d'Or, on the road to Pointe du Bout, **t** 66 01 80. A very nice dining room with a bamboo ceiling and plenty of greenery. Creole fare – *soupe z'habitants* followed by *oursin frit* (in season) or a *côte de porc* with *christophines au gratin* – or simple veal chop with *frites. Closed Mon.*

La Langouste, by the ferry jetty, Plage de L'Anse Mitan, **t** 66 04 99. You can dine here on a veranda with a view. It has a fixed menu or *z'habitants* and *colombo de poulet* à la carte.

Le Nid Tropical, over the headland in Anse à l'Ane, **t** 68 31 30. Situated in a pretty yard fenced off from the beach. Creole fare – *daube de lambis* (conch) *à la crème de champignons*, or *filet de boeuf au ti-vieux. Closed Sun eve and Mon.*

Chez Jojo, close to Le Nid, Anse à l'Ane, **t** 68 47 92. Has a simple beach setting and serves local food – *boudin de lambi* and *ananas* (pineapple) *flambé.*

Les Anses d'Arlet

It is well worth heading over to the Anses d'Arlet on the Caribbean coast, where you will find some fantastic settings along the waterfront in the dozy settlements. In the Grande Anse d'Arlet you will find a clutch of good places to retreat to from the overhead sun.

Expensive

Ti Sable, Grand Anse d'Arlet, **t** 68 62 44. Serves grilled food and fresh fish landed by the local fishermen and a speciality creole and lobster buffet. Under palm-thatch parasols and a huge sea grape tree, in the yard of an old Caribbean beach house.

Moderate

Quai Sud, next to Ti Sable, 27 Allée des Raisiniers Sud, Grand Anse d'Arlet, **t** 68 66 90. Here you can get a deep-fried camembert to go with seafood and fish.

Les Anses d'Arlet, on the black-sand beach of the same name, **t** 68 62 82. A lovely setting under palm trees and behind bamboo fences, an old tin roof held up by old wooden spars. Local food – fish, chicken and salads, *accras, brochettes.*

The Southern Coast

Expensive

Poï et Virginie, Ste-Anne, **t** 76 72 22. A charming dining room right on the waterfront (the best seats are just above the sea), set with wooden and wicker furniture, the walls lined with bamboo and hung with Haitian paintings. You might try the *plateau de fruits de mer* for two (*araignées, tourteaux, cigales, gambas, soudons, huîtres, langouste* and *palourdes*). Phone 24 hours in advance for this. Otherwise try the delicious lobster-tail with mayonnaise. *Closed Tues, Wed lunch.*

Les Filets Bleus, Ste-Anne beach, **t** 76 73 42. Has a palm garden with statues looking down onto the beach. Fine local fare – *court bouillon* or *civet de chatrou.*

Moderate

Chez Lucie, Le Diamant, **t** 76 40 10. Here you can start with *beignets de crevettes* and follow with a *fricassée*, a *blaff* or a speciality seafood dish.

Chez Christiane, Le Diamant, **t** 76 49 55. Serves creole fare in a nice old building in town.

Le Diam's, Le Diamant, **t** 76 44 46. A pleasant stop on the square, for simpler lunches or dinners.

Kaï Armande, Ste-Luce, **t** 62 52 67. Serves local food and seafood as well as some African specialities.

La Paillote, Rue Bouille St Pierre, **t** 78 04 01. Near the marina, with chairs and parasols under huge coconut palms.

La Dunette, Ste-Anne, **t** 76 73 90. Another smaller restaurant in a hotel just along the seafront, where you will find chicken *pipiri* (grilled and served with rice cooked in cinnamon and coconut) and a house speciality of *friture de volaille aux lambi envoûtée de passion*, conch and chicken in a passionfruit sauce.

Les Tamariniers, Ste-Anne, **t** 76 75 62. A pretty dining room hung with greenery next to the church, for novel creole cuisine including *blaffs* and *banane flambée.*

Le Touloulou, Ste-Anne, **t** 76 73 27. There is a lobster *vivier* here, where you can select your choice and you can follow with an *ananas flambé* or an ice cream from an endless choice of flavours.

Les Délices de la Mer, at the end of Grande Anse des Salines, **t** 76 71 34. Has a fantastic view of the bay and the hills beyond from its terrace. *Fricassée d'écrevisses* and *avocat aux crevettes*.

Inexpensive

There are many crêperies and snackette wagons in Ste-Anne, both down on the beach and in the town.

The Atlantic Coast

Moderate

Kai Nono, Route de Club Nautique, Le François, **t** 54 32 76. A fun spot.

Aux Fruits de la Mer Chez Fofor, St-Joseph, **t** 65 10 33. Upstairs above all the waterfront activity. Seafood specialities, as the name suggests.

Le Don de la Mer, La Trinité, **t** 58 26 85. Set on a pretty terrace above the sea: shrimp broth followed by fresh fish and by *banane flambée*.

L'Oasis, St Luce, La Trinité, **t** 62 32 22. A good place for a plateful of fricasseed crayfish and *christophine au gratin*.

Le Colibri, Morne des Esses, **t** 61 91 95. One of the most renowned kitchens on the island. Clothilde Paladino has won prizes for her original variations on local recipes, including *tourte aux lambis* (conch pie), *écrevisses buisson* and *bisque, soufflé de christophene* and *flan au coco*. Family-run with a West Indian welcome; good value too.

Bars and Nightlife

The traditional Martinican apéritif is the *ti punch*, which is prepared with the same ceremony as the local food. The sugar (or cane juice) is heaped in the glass and the lime is squeezed quickly and dropped in before the white rum is poured and stirred vigorously. In times past only the cane juice would have to be paid for in bars because the rum was so plentiful. Many restaurants also have fruit punches, made from fruits which have been steeped in rum, which are delicious. The local beer in Martinique is Lorraine, a passable brew. There is an infinity of local bistros, rum shops and supermarkets in Martinique.

There are many nightclubs and discos. Any town staging a *fête patronale* will have public dances where you will be welcome to join in. For local discotheques, of which there are many out in the sticks, you can ask around. Some of the hotels have discotheques and they also stage folklore shows.

There are plenty of bars in Fort de France and the busiest area is the Parking on the waterfront. The boulevard Allègre has a number of billiard halls, bars and slot-machine arcades among the crêperies.

Le Terminal, Fort de France. Overlooks the Parking from a balcony. A hip place where a mix of local executives and visitors loiter over absinthe cocktails or one of about 50 beers and rums until 2am.

Le Cheyenne, on the Parking, Fort de France. Worth a try.

Mayflower, rue Ernest Déproge, Fort de France. Gets quite lively.

Ti Sable, Grande Anse d'Arlet. A more formal beach bar.

Méridien, Trois-Ilets, **t** 66 00 30. A casino; *adm exp*.

Casino de la Batalière Plaza, Schoelcher, **t** 61 73 23. *Open daily Mon–Fri 8pm–3am, Sat–Sun 8pm–4am*.

Clubs

Manhattan Club, 18 rue François Arago, Fort de France. A good place to hear *zouk* music.

Le Negresco, 109 rue Ernest Déproge.

New Hippo, bd Allègre.

Le Zipp Club, Dumaine, Le François.

Top 50, La Trinité.

Entertainment

L'Atrium Cultural Center, Fort de France, **t** 60 78 78. The premier venue for the performing arts, offering a yearlong schedule of international artists.

CMAC (Centre Martiniquais d'Actions Culturelles), bd du Général de Gaulle, Fort de France, **t** 61 76 76. Cultural events.

SERMAC, Parc Floral, Fort de France, **t** 73 60 25. Cultural events.

spider) but Martinique is unfortunate in suffering from a scourge that most of the Windwards lack – the *fer-de-lance* snake. Called *trigonocephalus* because of its triangular head, it grows up to 6ft long and has a pair of eyes that are supposed to glow orange in the night. It is curious that it came to be here in the first place, as its nearest relatives are somewhere in South America. In the times of fierce competition during the sugar years, snakes were sometimes surreptitiously introduced into the islands to make other planters' jobs more difficult, but the *fer-de-lance* has been here since before the Europeans arrived. Though the snake is extremely poisonous to humans, it poses little danger to visitors because it steers well clear of any inhabited locations. However, if you are rootling around in the undergrowth or stealing a stem of bananas, watch out.

There is a system of National Parks in Martinique. At the far tip of the Caravelle Peninsula is the **Réserve Naturelle de la Caravelle**, where there are a number of habitats, including dry forestland, savanna, cliffs and mangrove swamps. There are walking trails to explore them (*t* 47 18 00).

Fort de France

The capital of Martinique is set on a huge bay on the leeward side of the island, looking out on to the Caribbean Sea. Framed with hills of dark-green rainforest, it was chosen, like all Caribbean capitals, for its harbour and strategic value. Now, transatlantic yachts lie in the bay, attracted more to the waterfront cafés than the protective walls of Fort St-Louis.

Though it has been the administrative centre of Martinique since 1681, Fort de France was a dozy and unhealthy backwater until the beginning of the 20th century, when the eruption of Mont Pelé destroyed the social and commercial capital of the island, the illustrious town of St-Pierre, farther north. From just 10,000 inhabitants living in the gridiron streets between the Rivière Madame and the Rivière Monsieur, it has exploded to a city of over 100,000 people, spilling into suburbs along the coast and creeping steadily farther up into the surrounding hills. The people of Fort de France are known as the *Foyalais*, from a corruption of the town's 17th-century name, Fort Royal.

If you would like Fort de France's secrets to be revealed in a guided tour, contact **Azimut** (*t* 60 16 59), who offer historical, shopping and night-time tours.

The original settlement grew up around the looming battlements of **Fort St-Louis** (*guided tours Tues–Sat; adm exp*) on the promontory, which was first established in 1639. The fort is still in the hands of the Navy and, though it is quiet now, it has been assaulted any number of times. In 1674, 160 men were faced by the Dutch Admiral de Ruyter, who arrived at the head of 48 ships and 3,000 men. The French evacuated the fort pretty quickly and so the Dutchmen, lulled into a false sense of security, paused over some kegs of rum, only to find themselves harried by sober and determined Frenchmen. The Admiral cut his losses when a thousand of his men were killed and let the town be. There are guided tours of the fort, through the network of caverns, dungeons and ramparts, to hear the story of the invasion. The fort juts into the sea, enclosing on one side the old Carenage, where ships would be 'careened'. Weights were tied to their masts and they were tipped up so that their hulls could be cleaned. Now it is the other side, the Baie des Flamands (flamingos), which is busier, where hundreds of yachts ride at anchor.

Across the road (the former moat) from Fort St-Louis is the **Savane**, the large central park of Fort de France, which is towered over by lines of vast royal palms. Their solid grey trunks stand like marble columns, soaring to 100ft before they burst into curved fronds. In an alley on the northern side you will find a statue of Joséphine, the Martinican who became an Empress. Before she was 'beheaded' (as a form of protest someone made off with her head), her face was turned towards her home in Trois-Ilets, across Fort de France bay to the south. Two other memorials are dedicated to the war dead and to Belain d'Esnambuc, the explorer and founder of the colony, who stands scouring the horizon for land. The Savane, where the Martinicans come in the evenings to 'promenade', is bordered by cafés and by the boulevard Alfassa water-front, the site of all major events such as carnival and military parades.

Facing the Savane on the rue de la Liberté is the **Musée d'Archéologie** (*t* 71 57 05; *open Mon–Fri 9–1 and 2–5, Sat 9–noon; adm*), which deals with the Amerindian history of the island. The life of the Arawaks and Caribs, from their first arrival at the time of Christ to AD 1500, when the Spaniards appeared, is portrayed in a rich display of pottery and pictures.

At the northwestern corner of the Savane is the **Bibliothèque Schoelcher**, a baroque iron agglomeration of arches, domes, fretwork and rivets, touched with russet and turquoise. The building was constructed by Henri Picq for the Exhibition of 1889 in Paris, at which the Eiffel Tower was the centrepiece, and then was dismantled and shipped out here to accommodate the library of Victor Schoelcher (*see* 'History', pp.272–5). It is a working library with over 200,000 documents, and houses occasional exhibitions.

Within the confines of the ring road, the streets of Fort de France are narrower and the buildings taller than in most Caribbean towns, its pavements cluttered with Peugeots and Citroëns and the shop windows decked out with chic-looking mannequins. In true French form, the street names commemorate many of France's political and literary heroes.

The classical building to one side of the Bibliothèque is the **Préfecture**, the seat of the Administrator, who is appointed by the Interior Minister in Paris. Other attractive buildings in the town include the **Palais de Justice**, which overlooks a small square with a statue of Schoelcher, and the old **Hôtel de Ville**, now a theatre. On the place du Père Labat is the **Cathédrale St-Louis**, the sixth to be built on the site. This one dates from 1878, its predecessors having been destroyed by fire, hurricane and earthquake. It has beautiful stained-glass windows, an impressive organ and metalwork balustrades. Close by are the meat market, set in an old building, and the vegetable and flower market, where you can get an excellent lunch and stock up on spices.

On the banks of the Rivière Madame is the **Parc Floral**, a former exhibition ground with trees and modern sculptures (now unfortunately used as a car park as well).

There are artists' galleries and cafés in the former military barracks at the rear, where there is a **museum** (*open Tues–Fri 9–12.30 and 2–5.30, Sat 9–1 and 3–5*) devoted to island geology. Outside is a series of **markets** dotted among the streets, with ranges of tables sheltering under huge gaudy parasols, selling anything from locks of straight black hair (to be plaited into tight African curls) to avocados. Worth a visit is the fish market on the western bank of the Rivière Madame, where women sell the fish caught and landed by the fishermen, from dawn until about 5pm.

The hills surrounding the capital are covered with houses, high-rise blocks and the '*instituts*' of a developed French *département*. As in the other islands, the Martinican *bons bourgeois* build their homes high on the hills for the fresher air and the commanding view. Across the Rivière Madame, the suburbs clamber up into the hills both inland and west along the coast, to Schoelcher.

South of Fort de France

The many coves and white-sand beaches make Martinique's southwest coastline the magnet for tourists. They centre around two areas, **Pointe du Bout**, near **Trois-Ilets**, within sight of Fort de France across the bay, and at **Ste-Anne** at the southern tip of the island.

If you do not cross Fort de France bay by ferry, the main road skirts the bay, past the airport, and the D7 turns right at Rivière Salée. **La Maison de la Canne** (*t 68 32 04; open Tues–Sun 9–5; adm*) is devoted to the history of sugar and rum and is set in a restored rum distillery. It has impressive models and sugar hardware on display.

Just before the town of Trois-Ilets another central piece of Martinican history is on view in **Le Musée de la Pagerie** (*t 68 34 55; open Tues–Sun 9–5; adm*), the childhood home of the Empress Joséphine. Some of the sugar estate buildings have been restored and filled with the Empress's belongings, including portraits and some letters written to her by Napoleon. The setting, in a small valley of typical Martinican profusion, is idyllic. The **Parc des Floralies** nearby (*open Tues–Fri 8.30–5, Sat and Sun 9.30–1pm; adm*) is a working horticultural garden which can be visited to see Caribbean flora in all its extreme fertility.

Trois-Ilets is a small town set around a square above the sea which takes its name from the three small islands in the bay. It was in the 18th-century church that the future Empress was christened Marie-Rose Joséphine Tascher de la Pagerie in July 1763. Her mother, Rose-Claire du Verger de Sannois, is buried in the church. Just north of here is the tourist resort of **Pointe du Bout**, a conglomeration of hotels, cafés, restaurants and boutiques, and a marina which has grown up on the point and on the white-sand beach of Anse Mitan.

The coastal road rises into cliffs as it turns south: the tourism evaporates and the land becomes drier and more windswept, where the shoreline is pitted with tiny coves with a profusion of coconut palms and small strips of sand. It is still quite natural and undeveloped and you will see fishermen's orange and green boats on the shoreline and their blue nets slung in the trees to dry. The road winds up over the

Two Dominican Monks

Two Dominican monks, Père du Tertre and Père Labat, visited Martinique in the 17th century and wrote memoirs of their trips. Their stories and observations about life make fascinating reading.

Père Dutertre was a soldier and romantic who turned to the Church late in life and came to the Caribbean in the 1650s. He was fascinated by the novelties of the New World and on his return he wrote his *Histoire Générale des Antilles Habitées par les Français*. The work is full of observations about the natural life of the islands and of the Carib Indians, whom he makes into naturally egalitarian and melancholic dreamers, probably one of Rousseau's sources for his idea of the noble savage 100 years later.

Père Labat spent 10 years in the Caribbean until 1705, living mainly in Martinique, but undertaking missions all over the area, which he relates in his *Nouveau Voyage aux Iles de l'Amérique*. In his book you will find him tending souls by spiritual means or defending them with a cannon instead, celebrating Mass for buccaneers and chatting with enemy admirals. He details the system of compensation among the buccaneers for the loss of a limb, he invents a new system for distilling sugar into rum, and, being a confirmed gastronome, his writing is sprinkled with descriptions of meals of sumptuous proportions. His interest is inexhaustible; he is unfailingly humorous, earthy, adventurous and an incorrigible busybody. Strangely, he is wrongly accused by folk tradition in Martinique of introducing slavery into the island. A hundred years ago, his name was used as a threat against naughty children – *Moin ké fai Pè Labatt vini pouend ou!* (I'll make Père Labat come and take you away!) – and his ghost would apparently be seen walking the *mornes* above St-Pierre at night because his soul could find no rest. Certainly he was sanguine about the treatment of slaves – he ordered one man to be given 300 lashes – but it was a cruel age.

He had a number of close shaves too. At one point his ship was captured by Spanish pirates after he had refused to fire the only cannonball because he said it was needed to crush the garlic. He was about to be put to death, but a moment later he found all his captors on their knees around him. While rootling through his luggage they had found a cross of the Holy Inquisition. Of course it was there completely by chance, he claims, but it was enough to set him free.

There is an abridged English translation of his work, *The Memoirs of Père Labat*, by John Eaden, published in 1931.

cliffs and down into **Grande Anse d'Arlet**. It is a charming bay, less known than the beaches at Pointe du Bout, but popular with yachtsmen. Two miles (3km) farther on is another cove with the picturesque village of **Les Anses d'Arlet** between the headlands and then a third cove called the Petite Anse d'Arlet.

The best route to take from here follows the vagaries of the coastline and descends from the heights of Morne Larcher, past a brightly painted miniature wooden house at the roadside, once a monk's retreat, and along the flat into the town of **Le Diamant**, which is set on the magnificent sweep of the Grande Anse du Diamant and its 2-mile beach with brown sand and crashing breakers.

Off the Point, a mile from the shore, is the **Rocher du Diamant**, a pitted outcrop that rises sheer from the water to over 500ft. This rock, sometimes referred to as HMS *Diamond Rock*, witnessed one of the most curious of all episodes in the eternal struggles for empire between the French and British at the turn of the 18th century. The two nations were facing each other across the St Lucia Channel. From his lookout at Pigeon Island on St Lucia, Commodore Hood was stuck. All he could do was watch as the French ships dodged behind the Rock within the cover of their own guns, and sailed away unharmed. Hood decided to fortify the Rock.

For 18 months it stood as a British enclave within cannon-range of Martinique, denying the channel to French shipping. It was garrisoned by 120 men, who hoisted five cannon up on a rope from a ship, the HMS *Centaur*, 'like mice, hauling a little sausage', and built fortifications and outhouses. It became quite a community, with goats and rabbits and the captain's dog and cat. Rope ladders were fixed to get from the upper battery to the shore, and the mail and food were delivered in a communication bucket from the supply ship.

In May 1805 the French decided that they had had enough and they descended on the Rock in force. The two sides slugged it out for three days and two nights, until the British capitulated. When he eventually got back to Barbados the commander, Captain Maurice, was court-martialled for surrender, but then congratulated by Nelson for putting up such a good show. Ruins remain dating from the time the French sacked the Rock, but they are rarely visited and the crossing is often rough.

Heading further east, you will come to the **Trois Rivières Rum Distillery** (*open Mon–Fri 9–noon and 2.30–5; guided visits every 30 mins; free*), a working sugar and rum factory, where between February and July you can see the cane fed into the machines, cut to length, moved along a conveyor through three-stage crushers and the juice run down into a collecting vat while the bagasse is returned to fire the 100-year-old steam engine. Hot and noisy, but interesting, and then you test the vintages. Two miles beyond the town of Rivière Pilote you will come to the modern sugar works and rum distillery at **La Mauny** (*guided tours at 10, 11, 12.30, 2 and 4*). The huge works were built in 1984 and the whole process is explained on the tours, after which there is a free rum sampling and plenty to buy. Back on the coast road at Anse Figuier is the **Martinique Eco-Museum** (*open Tues–Sun 9–5; adm*), which shows island life for the Caribs and Arawaks and then European and African colonists, up to 1950, with mock-ups of their houses and mannequins at work and play. Quite complicated and detailed, but lots of information (in French), including all the words derived from the Carib language: *alligator, avocat*...

On the dry Ste-Anne peninsula you return to Martinique's tourist heartland. The town of **Le Marin**, where there is an attractive coral-rock church, is the centre of the sailing industry, as is demonstrated by all the yachts in the marinas, and farther around the bay is **Ste-Anne**, a small but friendly town. Five miles (8km) farther on you come to the southern tip of the island at the **Pointe des Salines**, where the land is covered in cactus scrub. From the point, St Lucia is clearly visible on a fine day, beyond the lighthouse on the Ilet Cabrits. It is named for its salt flats (or salt ponds depending on the season).

From Le Marin the road cuts across to the Atlantic coast through steadily expanding villages where the islanders are building their villas. **Le Vauclin** is the first major town, a cluster of nice old buildings around a church that sits on a hillside running down to the sea. There is an active fish market. Inland is the **Montagne du Vauclin**, at 1,640ft the highest in the south of Martinique. From the top, the panorama is fantastic, stretching as far as the Caravelle Peninsula in the north and to the southern tip of the island.

Headed north you come to **Le François**, where there are some more attractive old wooden houses, now steadily being swamped by new concrete suburbs. There is a classic French West Indian cemetery, with mausolea covered in black and white tiles, but the church looks as though it might be about to undergo a space-age transfiguration.

Habitation Clément (*open daily 9–6; adm*) is one of the finest colonial plantation houses in the whole Caribbean. On a hilltop sheltered by huge and ancient trees stands a house with a wooden interior and a tiled and louvred gallery, furnished with superb colonial antiques and old prints of French Caribbean life. There is a display of the process of rum, with exhibitions and films of coopering and the distillery which worked until 1978. Ageing and bottling still continue here, so the sweet smell of rum hangs in the exquisite gardens, where there are 300 tropical species on view.

The road back to Fort de France passes through the Lamentin plains, the agricultural heartland of the island, which blow in green waves of bananas and sugar cane.

Fort de France to St-Pierre

The road (N2) from today's capital to its spiritual ancestor, the once-august city of St-Pierre, runs along the Caribbean coast, clinging to the headlands that cast out into the sea and sweeping down into the bays. The land is steep and rugged, with a covering of scrub that makes it look a bit like Corsica. North of Case-Pilote the dry cliffs at sea level give way to tropical rainforest in the foothills of the Pitons du Carbet, Martinique's second-highest peak.

Schoelcher, 3 miles (5km) from the centre of Fort de France, was a fishing village by the name of Case-Navire until 1899, when it was renamed in honour of the abolitionist shortly after his death. Now the *commune* of Schoelcher, creeping ever higher into the hills, takes the overspill from Fort de France. It has one of the colleges of the University of the French Antilles.

A number of small towns, each laid out in typical French Antillean style, with a town hall and church facing one another across the square, lie in the mouths of the valleys. Fishermen work from the black-sand beaches and you will see their blue nets spread out to be repaired. Their boats are painted bright colours to make them visible at sea and given lyrical evocative names such as *Regret de Mon Père* and *On Revient Toujours*.

Case-Pilote is named after a Carib chief who lived in this area and who welcomed the French when they settled, allowing Père du Tertre and the other Dominican missionaries to work among his people. Towards the end of his life he moved to Rivière Pilote in the south of Martinique. **Le Carbet** takes its name from the rectangular thatched houses in which the Caribs lived. The town, which has a number of pretty wooden houses, fronts onto a coconut-lined beach on which Columbus is supposed to have landed during his visit. Not far inland is the small **Plantation Lajus** (*open Mon–Fri 8–5, Sat shop only 9–12; adm*), home of Rhum J. Bally. The rum is not distilled here, but you will see it aged in vats and oak barrels, turning the fiery white '*rhum agricole*' into a mellow gold. The old creole house was built in 1776, and the garden can also be visited.

In the hills above Anse Turin, signposted from the main road, is the **Musée Gauguin** (*t 77 22 66; open daily 9–5.30; adm*), commemorating the French artist, who lived on Martinique in 1887 before he moved on to Tahiti in the Pacific. There is a permanent exhibition of Gauguin's letters and sketches, and some of his paintings (in reproduction). Other traditional Martinican topics are covered as well, including the description of the checked madras headdress and its codified intricacies by Lafcadio Hearn. Occasionally there is also an exhibition of work by local artists.

St-Pierre

Until 1902, St-Pierre was the cultural and commercial heart of Martinique and one of the prettiest towns in the Caribbean, considered the Paris of the Lesser Antilles. The red-roofed warehouses were stacked in lines on the hillside, overlooking the magnificent bay, where 30 ships might sit, delivering luxuries to the *Pierrotins* and loading the sugar loaves and rum puncheons that were the town's stock in trade.

The oldest town on the island, it grew up around the fine harbour, protected from the Atlantic tradewinds by Mont Pelé. Although the administrative centre soon moved to Fort Royal because of its superior strategic setting, the town thrived immediately from its beginnings in the 17th century.

The cobbled streets and the seafront promenade of 'Little Paris' were walked by the smartest Antillean ladies of the day, creole beauties with brown skin dressed in voluminous and brightly coloured skirts, parasols over their shoulders to keep off the sun. Cafés and cabarets did a grand trade on Saturdays, as did the cathedral on Sunday. In 1902, the illustrious town of 26,000 inhabitants was the most modern in the area, with electricity and telephones, and connected from one end to the other by tram.

But for all the human endeavour, St-Pierre was living beneath one of the Caribbean's most violent volcanos, the Mont Pelé (the bald mountain). It had stayed silent for the first 200 years of the town's existence, until 1851 when it grumbled, blanketing the town with volcanic ash and creating a lake in its crater.

Towards the end of April 1902 the rumblings started again, this time accompanied by plumes of smoke that flashed with lightning. Four people from St-Pierre climbed to the lip of the crater and found that the lake had disappeared and that it was now a cauldron of boiling mud, with an icing of ash racing over the surface in the wind. The rivers fed by it were poisoned by sulphur emissions and ran with dead fish.

On 5 May, the crater split open and an avalanche of mud and lava slid down the mountain to the north of the town, engulfing a factory and killing 25 workers. Despite the ever-increasing plumes of smoke, still lit by lightning, the Governor came from Fort de France to urge the *Pierrotins* not to leave (there was an election at the time). News came that the Soufrière volcano on the island of St Vincent had blown and it was thought that this would relieve the pressure on Mont Pelé. Though about 1,000 did choose to leave for Fort de France at dawn the next morning, the majority stayed put.

At a couple of minutes before eight on 8 May, Ascension Day, the mountainside itself split and gaped open as the eruption began. A shock wave hit the town at a speed of MACH 3 and this was followed by a pyroclastic flow; a cloud of poisonous gases burst out of the crater, thrown to a height of 300ft along with flames and molten lava which then swept down the mountainside at 250 miles an hour and engulfed the town. Only the north and south walls of houses remained standing as their interiors were swept out. With a temperature of 400°C, the cloud vaporized the town and then poured on down to the sea, turning it into a seething cauldron and setting the ships ablaze or capsizing them with a tidal wave.

Within two minutes, 30,000 people were killed. They were knocked to the ground by the force of the *nuée ardente* and carbonized where they lay. Glasses wilted and pots and pans drooped in the heat. The city passed into complete darkness, pierced only by the light of burning houses. There was one survivor in the city itself. Auguste Cybaris had been thrown into a police cell the night before for being drunk. No doubt he woke with a start at eight the next morning, but the thick stone walls of his cell protected him from the heat and the grilled window kept out the fumes. He lived out his days until his death in 1955 with the Barnum Circus, appearing in a replica of his cell.

One ship also survived, the HMS *Roddam*, which was cut from its mooring by the tidal wave. Several of the crew were burned alive on deck by showers of molten lava and others died jumping overboard. The ghostly shell, heaped with grey volcanic ash, crawled into the harbour at Castries, St Lucia, later that day, its captain severely burned but still at the wheel.

Lafcadio Hearn

The traveller Lafcadio Hearn lived near St-Pierre for two years in the late 1880s and he painted a series of tender pictures of Martinicans and their lives: the *blanchisseuses* (launderesses) who rise at 4.30am when the local alarm clock, the *cabritt bois* (a cricket), stops chirruping, covering the rocks on the River Roxelane with the washing that they beat and scrub; the *porteuses* who carry supplies weighing up to 120lb on their heads, singing as they cross the mountain range in the heat of the day; a man infatuated by the *guiablesse* (a zombie), who leads him to his death when he tries to kiss her.

It may all be a bit romanticized, but his *Two Years in the West Indies* is a charming book and gives an unforgettable picture of Martinique before St-Pierre was destroyed by Mont Pelé.

The volcano continued to spit fire and lava over the next few months, but gradually calmed down. At the same time, there arose one of the most curious phenomena in the whole history of the Caribbean. In November of 1902, a glowing needle of solidified lava began to protrude from the crater. The plug steadily pushed upwards, until it reached a height of 800ft. After nine months it eventually collapsed.

After so many stories about the cataclysm at St-Pierre and the talk of the ruins, it comes as a bit of a surprise to discover that people actually still live there. It is a busy country town. No doubt the inhabitants have faith in the team of boffins who live on the slopes of the mountain listening out for future rumbles. The cobbles of the old town can be seen protruding through the tarmac, and the blackened walls and stairways still run down to the palm-lined promenade on the waterfront. The skeleton of the old theatre and the stone shells of the 18th-century warehouses have a slightly forbidding air, but the market and shops bustle happily around them. However, they still stand in the shadow of Mont Pelé, a monstrous and brooding colossus.

The **theatre**, with its double staircase, is a copy of the one in Bordeaux. Just nearby is the cell in which Cybaris spent the night after his drinking spree. Down on the waterfront there has been some restoration recently and you will see the newly repaired **Maison de la Bourse**, the old exchange, a tall and pretty creole building with overhanging balconies which are louvred and closed off. A traditional iron **market** building has also been put up and there is some trade in there; otherwise there are plenty of cafés along the waterfront. There is all the activity of the modern-day market farther along the waterfront. Across the Roxelane River to the north is the **Quartier du Fort**, the site of the first settlement on Martinique. The ruined fort near the seafront was erected by d'Esnambuc in 1635 when he arrived, planted a cross and claimed the island for France.

The **Musée Volcanique** (*t 78 15 16; open daily 9–5; adm*), established in 1932 by the American volcanologist Franck Perret, has an explanation of the volcanic eruption and exhibits including clocks that stopped at 8am precisely and nails fused together in the heat of the *nuée ardente*. Guided tours do a circuit and release you to admire the view of the bay from the balcony. **Le Musée Historique de St-Pierre**, on the rue Victor Hugo (*t 79 74 32; open daily 9.30–5; adm*), contains pictorial exhibits of life in St-Pierre before the disaster in 1902. A little trolley train runs around the town with a commentary, if you can bear the embarrassment, four times daily during the week (*t 55 50 92*).

North of St-Pierre

As the road follows the coast north, skirting the slopes of Mont Pelé, you come to a less developed side of Martinique. **Le Prêcheur**, one of the first areas to be settled in the 17th century, was the childhood home of Françoise d'Aubigné, who would later become the Marquise de Maintenon. There are hot volcanic springs on the route up Mont Pelé. There is an excellent distillery to visit just outside the town, the **Distillerie Depaz**. Sign boards guide you through the process: cane cutters, huge aluminium vats for fermentation, still pots for distillation and warehouses which store the barrels. The estate house is stunning, but cannot be visited. Farther north along the coast you come to **Habitation Céron** (*adm*), a distillery which dates from 1658, a charming series of buildings which follow a narrow valley engulfed in rainforest. As well as the old sugar estate buildings there is a '*gragerie*', or cassava mill, and a walk through the gardens where the plants are named. Now it also works as a crayfish farm, for which it is famed. Over the years, Habitation Céron has added activities, such as horse-riding and swimming. The restaurant specializes in crayfish and creole cuisine.

Anse Céron itself is a black-sand beach of unmanicured beauty. The coastal road does not run all around the island, but stops just beyond here. However, it is possible to walk from here through the forest to the village of Grand' Rivière. The 12-mile (20km) walk over the cliffs of St Martin takes about 6 hours, though you should allow longer in the rainy season when the going is harder.

St-Pierre to the Atlantic Coast

A commanding view of St-Pierre Bay can be had from the road that climbs past the cemetery. From here it continues into the rainforest in the foothills of the Morne des Cadets in les Pitons du Carbet and to **Fonds St-Denis**, an agricultural village perched on the mountainside over hairpin bends. This road was one of the early approaches from Fort de France to St-Pierre through the plantations lands; called La Trace, it was cut out of the hills by the Jesuits in the 17th century. In the village of **Le Morne Rouge** you will find a third museum dedicated to the volcano and its disastrous effects on the town below, **La Maison du Volcan** (*t 52 45 45; opening times limited, so phone before visiting; adm*). You need to speak French to get the best of it. There are films and pictures of the town before the event and of the lava flow glowing as it flowed down the mountainside. The destructive power of the volcano was equivalent to a 100-megaton bomb.

A hundred years ago this route was walked by the *porteuses*, with huge trays on their heads, laden with anything that needed to be carried to the Atlantic coast. It is a route steep enough to make a car strain, but these young women would carry up to 100lb for 15 hours a day with nothing but a drop of rum and some cake to keep them going. Just beyond Le Morne Rouge is the dropping-off point for hikers headed to the summit of **Mont Pelé**. If you attempt this, it is advisable to take a guide. Also, as there are often clouds parked on the summit, take a waterproof jacket to keep off the wind and wet. There has been only one rumble from Mont Pelé since 1902, but if it starts to rain pumice stones, clear out quick.

The route continues over to the Atlantic coast, descending through the forest, where the road is overhung by vast sprouts of bamboo and 10ft tree ferns. **Ajoupa-Bouillon** is a pretty town laid out either side of the main road, which is lined with flowers and a red plant called *roseau*. From here, two natural sites are worth visiting: the Saut Babin, a 40ft waterfall half an hour's walk southeast of the town, and the **Gorges de la Falaise** (*adm*). For the latter, you cut in from the road just above the town, going north on a path into the forest (about half an hour's walk, essential to ask for directions) and you will come to the river, which has carved a narrow bed for itself out of the volcanic rock. Take a swimming costume; it can be crowded. At **Les Ombrages Botanical Gardens** (*open 9–5; adm*) there is a botanic path through the rainforest, shaded by 100ft bamboo trees. The plants, from the rainforest and domestic gardens, are marked – *calathea ornata* (musical paper) and *culotte du diable* (devil's trousers).

As the mountainside descends and turns into plains, so the rainforest gives way to cultivation: pineapples, bananas and fields of sugar cane. In the 18th century, this area was completely covered with plantations, cane as far as the eye could see, broken periodically by a cluster of buildings: the estate house, outbuildings and a windmill.

Basse-Pointe, on the coast, is the birthplace of the retired mayor of Fort de France, Aimé Césaire, and it has had a strong East Indian influence since the Indians came to Martinique in the 19th century as indentured labourers. There is a Hindu temple just outside the town. Inland is the **Plantation Leyritz** (*t 78 53 92; open 8–6; adm to the plantation gardens*), an old plantation house which has been restored as a hotel (with rooms in the slave quarters) and gardens. Machinery is scattered around the grounds and the old outhouses are fitted out as a restaurant. There is an odd exhibition of intricate dolls made from dried flowers.

The village of **Macouba**, named after the Carib word for fish, stands on cliffs at the northern tip of the island, looking out over the channel to Dominica. It was a prosperous settlement in the 17th century, when it derived its wealth from the cultivation of tobacco. The final stretch of road continues through wild country to **Grand' Rivière**, an isolated fishing village.

Fort de France to the Pitons du Carbet

In the 17th century, the Jesuits cut a road through the mountainous interior of Martinique, linking the new administrative centre of Fort de France with the social and commercial hub at St-Pierre overland. 'La Trace' was initially just a track cut into the rainforest, used by horses and pedestrians, but in the 19th century it was enlarged by the army and then in the 20th century it was made into a major road. Today it makes a spectacular drive through some of the island's best scenery.

Across the Madame River, La Trace climbs through the prosperous suburb of **Didier**, favoured by the creole ascendancy for its commanding panorama, where spectacular villas perch above Fort de France in gardens of tropical flowers. As the town thins, the road winds into primeval rainforest, clinging to the hillside.

Suddenly a mirage arises before you, the **Sacré Cœur** from Montmartre, transported to Martinique… Erected in 1923 to give thanks for the lives of those who died in the First World War, it is not an exact replica, but its dome and spires stand brilliant white against the sparkling green of tropical rainforest and inside there is a warm glow from the stained-glass windows. There is a good view of Fort de France and the south of Martinique from the car park.

Soon La Trace becomes buried in the rainforest and the mountains loom either side. Six miles out of the capital, at the **Balata Gardens** (*t 64 48 73; open daily 9–5; adm*), the botanical pandemonium is momentarily set into order. Two hundred species have been brought from tropical regions all over the world and cultivated in the garden, numbered so that you can put names to them: bananas, bamboos, orchids and endless palms. As you walk the paths you will see ferns like velvet, shrubs with flowers like little plastic animals or shaped like a fisherman's hat, and all around a plethora of palm trees. After a tropical shower the whole garden glints in the sunlight and the view opens out again as far as St Lucia. The gardens, an enjoyable tour even for uncommitted gardeners, give an idea of the absurd abundance of the Caribbean islands. The N3 then moves into the peaks and valleys of the **Pitons du Carbet**, running a contorted route as far as Deux Choux, where the old road descends into St-Pierre and on to Morne Rouge.

La Trinité and Around

La Trinité is the second-largest town on the island and an administrative centre for the northern Atlantic coast. The town is set on a sheltered bay and has an esplanade that teems with activity when the day's catch is brought in. In the hills above, the town of **Morne des Esses** is known for its weaving, techniques supposedly developed from its Carib heritage. The **Atelier de Vannerie** (*open Mon–Sat 8.30–5.30*), the basket-weaving workshop, is devoted to the art.

Beneath La Trinité on the coast is the **Caravelle Peninsula**, a windswept outcrop that juts 7 miles into the Atlantic Ocean. It has recently been developed and has become something of a centre for tourism in Martinique. A number of hotels have been built there in recent years. The peninsula is hilly, with a shoreline of cliffs and small coves and rich orange earth. The last few square miles are a National Reserve and there is a small network of paths for walkers who wish to see the varied flora. You will also find the ruins of the **Château Dubuc** (*open Mon–Fri 8.30–noon and 2.30–5.30, Sun 8.30–noon; adm to the museum*), the remaining walls of a 17th-century castle with a magnificent view. There is a small museum and an assortment of sugar coppers, from which the estate derived some of its wealth – the rest was made in smuggling. The N4 leads from La Trinité back to Fort de France, cutting through the hills via Gros Morne, the seat of government during the patriots' rebellion in 1790.

Continuing north along the coast, the N1 comes to **Ste-Marie**, with an attractive church built in Jesuit style. Just beyond the town is the **Musée du Rhum** at the St James distillery (*t 75 30 02; open Mon–Fri 9–1 and 2–4.30, Sat and Sun 9–noon*). The old creole plantation house and the modern factory stand near one another, looking onto a garden full of sugar relics of all ages – crushing gear and steam engines. Inside the creole estate house is more sugar paraphernalia: rum barrels and boiling coppers, alongside a history of the sugar industry in Martinique. The informative tour is free and it culminates in a tasting room, stacked to the ceiling with bottles of rum, which are available for purchase.

It is worth taking the detour a few miles inland to the **Musée de la Banane** (*t 69 45 52; open Mon–Sat 9–5; adm*), which is set on a working banana plantation. There is an exhibition giving details of the history and culture (and agriculture) of the banana. There are botanical prints from 200 years ago and adverts from early in the 20th century, and you will learn odd facts (such as: in Indian legend it is a banana not an apple that 'Eve' gives to 'Adam'). A path leads you through the plantation, where you will see species such as *yamgambi*, *ice cream* and *bendetta*. During the week you can visit the packing house, where the banana 'bunches' are brought in, divided into 'hands', cleaned and then boxed.

L'Habitation Fonds St-Jacques was once a thriving Dominican community and sugar plantation. It was run by Père Labat, who resided here in the 1690s, taking over a run-down plantation and turning it into the most prosperous on the island within two years. Some buildings have been restored and there is a small museum on the subject of sugar in the 18th century. The coastal road continues to wind through the planta-tions and along the shoreline to the town of Le Lorrain.

Guadeloupe

The *région* of Guadeloupe is made up of a number of islands scattered over 150 miles (240km) of the Lesser Antilles. Altogether they have an area of 658 square miles (1,705sq km) and a population of around 410,000. Of the smaller islands, Les Saintes, La Désirade and Marie Galante lie close to Guadeloupe itself; St Martin (which shares an island with the Dutch Crown colony of Sint Maarten) and St Barts (St Barthélemy) lie to the north, amongst the Leeward Islands. Guadeloupe is by far the largest of the group and is shaped like a huge butterfly. Guadeloupe is in fact two islands, pushed together by geological movement, and each wing shows a different side of the Caribbean: in the west, Basse-Terre is mountainous and has the explosive luxuriance of the volcanic islands, its slopes covered with banana plantations and rainforest; the softer contours of Grande-Terre to the east have the coral reefs and white-sand beaches. Besides the exotic combination of French and West Indian elements, the large size of the island and the variety of countryside make Guadeloupe one of the most rewarding islands to visit.

The small town of Basse-Terre on the west coast of the island is the capital of Guadeloupe, but Pointe-à-Pitre on Grande-Terre has long been the commercial centre. Grande-Terre is more populous and industrialized, and its gently sloping *mornes* are covered in 12ft curtains of sugar cane.

The island's economy has always been agricultural. Coffee gave way to sugar (and rum) and most recently to tropical fruits such as bananas. But as with so many Caribbean islands, tourism has grown here and become the primary industry most recently. Unemployment runs at around 30 per cent, but the standard of living is kept at a roughly similar level to that of mainland France and so Guadeloupe appears far more prosperous than other islands nearby.

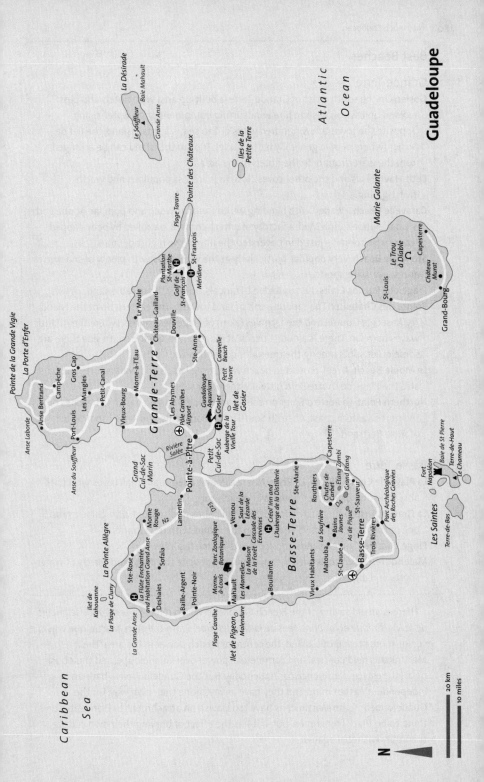

Guadeloupe

Best Beaches

Grande-Terre

Gosier: On the south coast of Grande-Terre, a built-up area with hotels and best avoided unless you wish to hire windsurfing equipment or go water-skiing. Opposite the town, a few hundred yards out to sea, is a small island, the Ilet de Gosier (where people generally bathe nude). Trips to the island can be arranged from the waterfront or in the hotels in the area.

Petit Havre: This and the other coves close to it are less populous and worth investigating.

Caravelle Beach: Heaped with blinding white sand, crowded and popular. At one end is Guadeloupe's Club Med, a factory of entertainment, patrolled by peak-capped security personnel – just don't overstep the line of the high-tide mark.

Ste-Anne Beach: Very popular, particularly at the weekends, with plenty of snackettes and some watersports.

Plage des Raisins Clairs: Just outside St-François, busy, with passable sand.

Pointe des Châteaux: The tapering spit of land towards the eastern tip of the island. Try Anse à la Gourde and the 1.5 miles (2km) of Plage des Salines, where the Atlantic waves barrel in. There is a nudist beach at Plage Tarare. On the south side there are some quiet spots among the trees along the roadside.

Le Moule Beach: A reef-protected beach with some hotels and watersports and bars; also the Plage de l'Autre Bord (literally 'the other side').

Northern Point: La Porte d'Enfer on the Atlantic side, and two passable beaches on the northwestern coast, Anse du Souffleur at Port-Louis, and Anse Laborde just out of Anse Bertrand.

Basse-Terre

La Plage de Cluny, Tillette, La Perle: Near La Pointe Allègre, all small coves with passable sand and palm trees, some with beach bars.

La Grande Anse: A huge bay backed with tall palms and stacked with golden sand, one of the most attractive beaches on the island, with restaurants.

Plage Caraïbe: Golden sands and rocks, with some facilities.

Malendure: Opposite Ilet de Pigeon, very lively, despite the dark sand. Plenty of watersports and day trips.

There is an old saying of the French Caribbean which refers to '*Les grands seigneurs de la Martinique et les bons gens de la Guadeloupe*'. From the start Martinique was the senior, more prosperous island, the centre of French power in the area. The Martinicans held political and commercial power over Guadeloupe, and their business interests and influence continue today. But the Guadeloupeans have an independent cast of mind and they have always gone their own way. For the Guadeloupeans, the Martinicans have too slavish an attachment to France. It is one thing to be 'Black Frenchmen' but, if it has the effect of burying their own culture, then they will rebel against it.

Politically Guadeloupe has benefited from more autonomy in recent years, but it has also become more answerable for budget expenditure. France grants a huge amount of cash each year and the material benefits are clear to see, but there are some Guadeloupeans who would rather go it alone, without the protection of the Republic. The issue is an emotive one which erupts occasionally in violent campaigns, as it did in the late 1970s. Things have gone a little quieter of late because France basically rebuilt the island after the terrible destruction of Hurricane Hugo in 1989.

History

To the Caribs, Guadeloupe was Karukera, thought to mean 'the island of beautiful waters'. Columbus was struck by the beauty of the waterfalls on the heights when he passed by on his second voyage in November 1493. He christened the island Santa Maria de Guadalupe de Extremadura but soon moved on. The 'Cannibal Isles' were dangerous country and, apart from one attempt by the Spaniards in 1525 to settle Guadeloupe so that their ships could take on water and refit here after the Atlantic crossing, the island was left well alone.

It was another hundred years before the next Europeans arrived in force. Led by de l'Olive and Duplessis, 600 French settlers disembarked in June 1635. They attacked the Caribs, driving them off the island within a few years to refuges in Dominica and St Vincent.

Guadeloupe was administered from Martinique. Not only did the Martinican Governor General have the ultimate say on affairs in Guadeloupe, but Martinique maintained a commercial hold. Trade to France had to be conducted through St-Pierre, where the merchants would inevitably give a low price for Guadeloupean sugar, even after the extra costs of transportation. Revenge was sweet when four years under British rule (1759–63) turned out to be very prosperous ones for Guadeloupe because vast markets opened up to them in Britain and America.

During the French Revolution the Guadeloupean *patriotes* gained the upper hand, ousting the planters. They welcomed the revolutionary Victor Hugues and the new regime was installed. A guillotine was erected and 300 were beheaded. From his base on Guadeloupe, Victor Hugues rallied the slaves and liberal Frenchmen on all the Windward Islands with the promise of freedom, but within two years the rebellions were crushed and Hugues' position in Guadeloupe was unsure.

A momentous event took place on 16 Pluviôse of Year 2 (4 February 1794). Following the declaration of the Revolutionary Convention in Paris, the slaves in Guadeloupe were set free. However, a reactionary regime was installed at the beginning of the 19th century and slavery was re-established in July 1802. There were bloody riots, and many Africans preferred to commit suicide rather than submit to slavery once again. Finally, in 1848 the slaves were freed once more, largely due to the efforts of Victor Schoelcher (*see* 'History', p.247), who was subsequently elected deputy for Guadeloupe.

Guadeloupe was blockaded in the Second World War because it sided with the Vichy Government, but soon after the war, like Martinique and French Guyana on the South American coast, it became a French Overseas *département*, with the same status as the mainland *départements*.

Beaches

For soft white sand brushed by palm trees and susurrating waves, go to the southern side of Grande-Terre. Some beaches become quite crowded because the area is fairly built up with hotels, but you can usually find a spot to yourself at the eastern end towards Pointe des Châteaux. Take a picnic with you because there are fewer beach bars there. Alternatively, there are the less typical beaches on the north-western coast of Basse-Terre. The spurs and shoulders thrown off the mountains produce small protected coves between steep headlands. This area is much less populous, but has some excellent beaches with golden-brown sand which have a wilder charm about them. Bathing topless is quite normal in Guadeloupe (though the West Indians themselves do not usually do it) and bathing nude is permitted in some places. All beaches are public and most hotels will allow you to use their facilities. *See* 'Best Beaches', p.280.

Flora and Fauna

Guadeloupe is a geographical oddity because the butterfly's two wings are islands of completely different geological origin, separated by a small stretch of sea, the Rivière Salée. It is the meeting point of the two island chains that make up the Lesser Antilles – an inner chain of tall volcanic peaks that runs from Grenada up to Saba and the outer ring of coral islands from Marie Galante through Grande-Terre to St Martin and Anguilla.

Still odder are the names of the two islands: Basse-Terre and Grande-Terre. You might think that Grande-Terre would be the taller mountainous island, smothered in tropical rainforest, and that Basse-Terre would be lower. It is the other way around. There is a logical explanation, originating in now obscure sailing terminology. Basse-Terre is simply the 'lower ground' with regard to the prevailing wind. The pattern is repeated in the islands of Les Saintes, where Terre-de-Bas is downwind of Terre-de-Haut.

Guadeloupe can offer the best of Caribbean flora in its two halves. Grande-Terre's coast is lined with mangrove bushes and the white coral beaches for which the Caribbean is famous. And in Basse-Terre there is the spectacular beauty of the rainforest as well as the fascinating, if smelly, attraction of the **Soufrière** volcano.

The **Parc National** covers some 12,000 acres of the Basse-Terre mountains and they are as fertile as any in the Windwards. In the upper branches of the rainforest is another forest of hanging plants and explosive greenery – orchids and cycads, lianas grappling upwards to reach the sunlight and dropping aerial roots. Here you will see Guadeloupe's three hummingbirds and the woodpecker, a *tapeur* in French, with a black stomach and back and a blue tinge to its wings, and perhaps a tiny *gobe-mouche* or Lesser Antillean peewee with an ochre-coloured breast. You might even see a Hercules beetle, a 6-inch monster that makes a metallic clanking noise. The stunted elfin woodland in the cloudy and windswept heights of the mountains has a whole new flora of dwarf palms and creepers. The headquarters of the Parc National is in St-Claude above Basse-Terre (*Habitation Beausoleil, 97120 St Claude, t 80 24 25, www.parcsnationaux-fr.com/guadeloupe*).

Getting There

Guadeloupe t (590–)

By Air

The main airline of Guadeloupe is Air France, t 82 61 61. Air Caraïbes, t 21 13 34, runs inter-island services from the airport at Pôle Caraïbes, a couple of miles from Pointe-à-Pitre.

From Europe

There are daily flights on Air France from Paris and depending on the season a weekly service from Marseille, Toulouse and Lyon. There are also charter flights on AOM, t 21 14 84; Air Liberté, t 21 14 68, www.antilles-info-tourisme.com/air-liberte; and Nouvelles Frontières, t 21 14 41.

From North America

Air France serves Martinique from Miami. Connections from the USA can also be made via San Juan in Puerto Rico, served by American Eagle, t 21 13 66. There are flights from Montreal on Air Canada, t 21 12 77.

From Other Caribbean Islands

Guadeloupe is linked south to Martinique and north to the smaller French islands of St Martin and St Barts on Air Caraïbes and Air France. If you are flying to the English-speaking Caribbean, LIAT, t 21 13 93, has flights north to Antigua and beyond, and south to Dominica. Charter aircraft tend to leave from Le Raizet, the old terminal.

By Sea

Two companies run ferries between Guadeloupe and Martinique, touching Dominica, with occasional sailings as far as St Lucia: Express des Iles, Quai Gatine, Pointe-à-Pitre, t 83 12 45; and Brudey Frères, La Darse, in central Pointe-à-Pitre, t 91 60 87.

Getting Around

By Bus

The public bus system is a good way to get around Guadeloupe and it reaches all major towns, eventually. The buses can often be heard before they are seen, as they are all equipped with extensive stereo systems. If you want to get on one, simply wave it down and if there is space the driver will stop. You will get to know the music of Guadeloupe, and your fellow passengers, quite well. There are bus stops, but it is not necessary to use them unless you want to escape from the sun; to get off, you must either yell *Arrêt!*, or press the buzzer, which usually sounds like an air-raid siren. Buses leave when they have enough passengers and run from dawn until about 6pm. On Sundays and on public holidays the public transport system packs up in mid-afternoon and you can quite easily be stranded.

If you are catching a bus from Pointe-à-Pitre, your departure point will depend on the destination. The route along the south coast of Grande-Terre (Gosier – €1.10, Ste-Anne – €1.50, St-François – €2) is served from near the place de la Victoire, on the eastern edge of La Darse, next to the ferries. To the northern part of Grande-Terre, buses depart from the Mortenol Station, across the dual carriageway from the Centre des Arts. Buses to the airport leave from the centre of town, on rue Peynier.

If you are headed for Basse-Terre (island), all buses leave from the Bergeverin Station on bd Chanzy. Ask around for the correct bus: some go just to Lamentin or around the northern coast to Deshaies; others turn south and run down the eastern coast and on to Basse-Terre, the island capital. The trip to Basse-Terre takes around two hours and costs €5. The last bus in both directions between the two major towns departs at around 6pm. Miss it and you are stranded.

By Taxi

Guadeloupean taxis work on a fixed-rate basis and can be picked up in Pointe-à-Pitre (place de la Victoire, bd Chanzy and others), at the airport and at all the major hotels. Some taxi drivers speak some English and will give an impromptu tour. They are also happy to take a party out for the day at around €70 for a half-day and €120 for a full day (four people). Some numbers for taxis are:

Radio-taxis CDL, t 20 74 74.

SOS Taxis, general, **t** 35 42 18; at place de la Victoire, Pointe-à-Pitre, **t** 83 99 99; and Cours Nolivos, Basse-Terre, **t** 81 79 70.

By Guided Tour

Sightseeing trips, taking in the principal sights on one or other island and usually with a lazy lunch-stop scheduled, can be arranged through the travel agents in town, or through any hotel lobby.

Air Tropical, St-François, **t** 35 05 15, *aviateur@ais.gp, www.air-tropical.com*. Flights by light plane can be booked here.

Georges Marie Gabrielle Voyages, **t** 82 05 38.

Héli-Inter Caraïbes, **t** 91 22 83. Sightseeing by helicopter: zooming the Chutes de Carbet, the mountains of Basse-Terre and the Pointe des Châteaux on Grande-Terre.

Jet Tours, Abymes, **t** 82 26 44.

Car and Bike Hire

Guadeloupe is a large island and, to get the best of its great variety, you really need a car for at least some of the time. With the benefits of the EU, the roads in Guadeloupe are (usually) quite good, and Guadeloupean drivers push them to the limit. A foreign driving licence is valid for 20 days (a year's driving experience is necessary) and after that an international driving licence is needed. Avoid driving in central Pointe-à-Pitre if humanly possible. Deposit is around €300, unless you pay by credit card. Rates start at about €45 per day. Some firms with offices at the airport are:

Avis, **t** 21 13 54.

Budget, **t** 21 13 49.

Europcar, **t** 38 73 88, *www.europcar.gp*.

Karib Rent, **t** 26 90 33. Motorbike rental too.

Pop's Car, **t** 21 13 56, *www.popscar.gp*.

Tropic Car, **t** 91 84 37.

Tourist Information

Abroad

The main website for Guadeloupe is at *www.antilles-info-tourisme.com/guadeloupe*. There is also plenty of information at *www.webcaraibes.com/guadeloupe, www. voile-en-guadeloupe.com, www.guadeloupe-info.com* and *www.lesilesdeguadeloupe.com*.

France: 2 rue des Moulins, 75001 Paris, **t** 01 44 77 86 00. Elsewhere in Europe you are advised to go through the various Maisons de France.

USA: French Government Tourist Office, 444 Madison Ave, New York, NY 10022, **t** 1 800 391 4909.

In Guadeloupe

On island, there are tourist information offices (*open Mon–Fri 8–5 and Sat 8–noon*) in the following places:

Pointe-à-Pitre: Office Départementale, 5 square de la Banque, BP 422, 97110 Pointe-à-Pitre, **t** 82 09 30.

St-François: just off the place de la Victoire, opposite La Darse on the avenue de l'Europe, **t** 88 48 74.

Basse-Terre: Maison du Port, **t** 80 56 40.

Bouillante: opposite Pigeon Island, **t** 98 73 48.

Media

The Tourist Board produces a booklet called *Bonjour Guadeloupe*, full of useful facts like where to get your hair cut as well as advice on beaches and nightclubs. If you're on a gastronomic steeplechase, the pocket-sized *Ti Gourmet* has restaurant and other information, and *Sentiers Gourmands* lists the finest creole restaurants on the archipelago.

Medical Emergencies

In a medical emergency, there is a casualty room at the main Pointe-à-Pitre Hospital at Abymes, **t** 89 10 10. The police can be reached on **t** 17.

Money and Banks

The legal currency of Guadeloupe is of course the euro, which exchanges at US$1 = €0.80 approx. US dollars and traveller's cheques are accepted in payment for hotel bills and generally on the tourist circuit. Credit cards are also widely accepted. However, if you go off the beaten track be sure to take euros. Hotels will change money, at a slightly inferior rate to the banks. In restaurants **service** is *compris*.

Banks are open Mon–Fri 8–noon and 2–4. Some banks open on Saturdays: try Crédit Agricole and Banque Nationale de Paris.

Shopping

Shops open Mon–Fri 8–noon and 2–6. They usually take 2 hours for lunch.

Telephone Code

To dial directly to Guadeloupe, the IDD code is **t** 590, followed by six digits. On the island, the six digits suffice.

General Information

Guadeloupe is generally lower-key than Martinique, but you may find that the Guadeloupeans are quite private. This is not to be confused with unfriendliness – ask for assistance, even in faltering French, and they will usually go out of their way to help you. There is an almost complete absence of hustlers, too, which makes a refreshing change. Petty theft against tourists, however, is certainly not unheard-of.

Festivals

January–February *Carnival*. Gets going at the very beginning of the year and there are parades and competitions all over the island each weekend as Lent approaches. It all culminates in a three-day street party on *Lundi Gras*, *Mardi Gras* and *Mercredi des Cendres* (Ash Wednesday), when the spirit of *vaval* is burned for another year. The whole thing is taken very seriously and it is fun to follow on with the streams of dancers as they parade around, dressed as imps and buccaneers, shuffling and dancing to the relentless beat of drum-driven French Caribbean music.

May *Schoelcher Day*. Held in commemoration of the abolition of slavery (21st).

July *Bastille Day*. Formal celebrations, held on the 14th as in France.

Festag. A festival of the Arts, mid-month.

August *Fête des Cuisinières*. One of the Caribbean's most enjoyable spectacles is the cooks' festival, which takes place in Pointe-à-Pitre. Island delicacies are dedicated and gastronomic parades take place before the customary over-indulgence in eating and dancing.

November *All Saints' Day*. Cemeteries are lit up with candles to the dead and people stay up all night in their honour.

Saint Cecilia's day. Musical festival (22nd).

Various dates *Fête Patronale*. Each individual town's saint's day.

Watersports

The best place to pursue watersports is on the sheltered southern coastline of Grande-Terre (where most of the hotels happen to be). Hotel watersports shops often have small sailing dinghies and snorkelling gear for hire to non-guests. Basse-Terre has grown recently in popularity and the liveliest area there is Malendure, opposite Ilet de Pigeon.

Day Sails

Leisurely tours, rum punch in hand on a yacht or a glass-bottomed boat, are plentiful. Many go to the the islands in the Cul de Sac Marin and to the offshore islands, Marie Galante and Les Saints, or to the remote and undeveloped island of Petite Terre.

Awak, 31 les Lataniers, **t** 88 53 53, *awak2004@wanadoo.fr*. Offers a day trip to the Petite Terre nature reserve, including lunch.

Clarisma Tour, 3 Chemin Gros Cap, Le Port, **t** 22 51 15, *www.clarisma-gp.com*. Cultural and educational boat trips in the mangroves.

King Papyrus, Bas du Fort, **t** 90 92 98. Daytime jaunts of tee-ree-ree and walking the plank, and night-time sails where the mountains of Basse-Terre loom like Titans in the moonlight.

Le Nautilus, Plage de Malendure, **t** 98 89 08, *www.nautilus97.com*. Takes day cruises to the Ilet de Pigeon.

Paradoxe Croisières, 24 Perinet, 97190 Gosier, **t** 20 90 05, *reservations@paradoxe.fr*, *www.paradoxe.fr*.

Privilege Croisières, Pointe-à-Pitre, Marina, **t** 84 66 36, *tiptopcruise@wanadoo.fr*. Catamaran day trips to Petite Terre, Marie Galante, Les Saints, Dominica.

Sun Evasion, 24 Perinet, Gosier, **t** 20 90 05, *reservations@sunevasion.fr*, *www.sunevasion.fr*. Sailing day trips.

Deep-sea Fishing

Day and half-day tours in search of tuna and kingfish in the Caribbean Sea. Most popular on the west coast.

Caraïbe Pêche, Bas du Fort marina, Grande-Terre, **t** 90 97 51.

Corail Bleu, Village Viva, Gosier, **t** 90 70 85, *info@corailbleu.com*, *www.corailbleu.com*.

Fishing Club Antilles, Bouillante, **t** 98 70 10.

Les Hauts de Deshaies, Deshaies, la Haut Matouba 97126, t 28 52 06, *les-hauts-de-deshaies@wanadoo.fr*. Big-game fishing and excursions to Caret and the Saintes.
Le Rocher de Malendure, t 98 70 84.

Kayaking

Tam Tam Pagaie, Ste Rose, Port de Pêche, Morne Rouge 97115, t 28 13 85, *tamtam-pagaie@wanadoo.fr*. Kayak trips.
Ti Evasion, La Colline au Moulin, Châteaubrun, Ste Anne, t 24 89 56, *ti-evasion@wanadoo.fr*.

Sailing

If you want a proper sailing holiday, yachts can be chartered, bare-boat or crewed, for a day, a week or more (for sailing trips to Marie Galante, Les Saints and Dominica), from the companies in the Port de Plaisance marina in Bas du Fort, just outside Pointe-à-Pitre:
Moorings Guadeloupe, Gosier, t 90 81 81.
Star Dust, Gosier, t 90 92 02, US t 1 800 772 3500.
Star Voyages Antilles, Gosier, t 90 86 26.
Other marinas are at St-François, Deshaies and Rivière Sens near Basse-Terre.

Scuba Diving

At its best on the west coast of Basse-Terre off Bouillante, where there is a marine reserve established by Jacques Cousteau around the Ilet de Pigeon. Single-tank dives cost around €50–60. Contact:
Aux Aquanautes Antillais, Plage de Malendure, t 98 87 30.
Les Heures Saines, Malendure, t 98 86 63, *heusaine@outremer.com, www.heures-saines.gp*. They dive under PADI and NAUI as well as CMAS, the French system.
Plaisir Plongée Karukera, t 98 82 43.
UCPA, Chemin de l'Anse à Sable, Bouillante 97125, t 98 89 00, *ucpa.bouillante@wanadoo.fr*. Diving and hiking excursions. Full-board accommodation.

Windsurfing

Very popular in Guadeloupe. Equipment can be hired all along the southern coast of Grande-Terre, particularly in St-François, where advanced sailors collect on the Plage du Lagon, where you will see the sailboards beating back and forth on the sideshore winds. Over on the north side in Le Moule, an offshore reef causes waves. Hire boards through:
La Base Nautique Regionale, Ecole de Voile, St Anne, t 88 12 32.
Karukera Surf Club, Le Moule, t 23 10 93.
UCPA, St-François, t 88 64 80.

Other Sports

Golf

On the edge of St-François is the 18-hole Robert Trent Jones course, t 88 41 87, *saint-françois.golf@wanadoo.fr*.

Hiking

On land, exploration of the National Park is best done on foot and there are two main drop-off points: La Traversée, the D23 road across the middle of the island, and the foothills of La Soufrière. Contact:
Emeraude Guadeloupe, 97120 St-Claude, t 81 98 28. For personal treatment.
Jacky Action Sport, Baie Mahault, 14 rés Louverture, La Jaille, t 26 02 34, *jacky.noc@wanadoo.fr*. Mountain guides, canopy tours, equestrian sports, hiking, river-hiking and canyoning.
Jungle Safari Adventure, t 56 17 03, *jungle safariadventure@wanadoo.fr*. Explore off the beaten track in daylong 4x4 tours.
Nature Experience, Résidence Bois Joly-BP 351, Abymes, t 20 75 78.
Organisation des Guides de Montagne de la Caraïbe, Maison Forestière, Matouba, t 80 05 79.
Sports d'Aventure, rue Courbail, Gosier, t 35 04 28, *sportdav@wanadoo.fr*. Excursions in 4x4 vehicles, sea-kayaking, hiking, river-hiking and canyoning.

Horse-riding

On the beaches of Grande-Terre or for a day's picnic. Contact:
Le Attelages du Comté, Comté de Loéhad, Ste Rose, t 56 61 12. Horse-driven wagon rides.
La Belle en Croupe, Marie Galante, St-Louis, t 97 18 69, *la.belleencroupe@wanadoo.fr*.
La Domaine de Belle Plaine, Ste Rose, t 28 71 70, *cheval-guadeloupe.com*.

Ranch des 2 Ilets, Deshaies, Métuvier Base Vent, t 28 51 93. Equestrian farm, horse-riding, restaurant.

Mountain biking

The companies listed under 'Hiking', above, also arrange tours by mountain bike, called VTT in French. Otherwise, contact:

Espace VTT, t 88 79 91.

Odacy Moto Tour, Petit Paris, t 80 34 08, *celise@odacy.com*, *www.odacy.com*. Quad-bike and motorbike excursions.

Vert Intense, Basse-Terre, Marine Rivière Sens, t 99 34 73, *info@vert-intense.com*, *www. vert-intense.com*. Canyoning, mountain biking, hiking La Soufrière and rivers in the heart of the national park.

Canyoning and Canopy Tours

Canopée, Plage de Malendure, Bouillante, t 26 95 59, *canopeeguadeloupe@wanadoo.fr*, *www.canopeeguadeloupe.com*. Canyoning.

Mangofil, St-Claude, La Bonifierie, Morin, t 81 10 43, *mangofih@wanadoo.fr*. Sequence of 50 crossings from tree to tree: Tyrolean traverses, rope bridges.

Where to Stay

Guadeloupe t (590–)

Guadeloupe caters for most tastes, with a few havens of discerning grandeur at the top of the range, through the big beach hotels to smaller haunts that attract a crowd of independent travellers exploring the island. If you are moving around, two very useful lists are those for the *relais créoles*, or inns, and the slightly cheaper *gîtes*, which can be contacted through: **AVMT**, 12 Faubourg Alexandre Isaac, 97110 Point-à-Pitre, t 82 02 62, and **Gîtes de France**, t 91 28 44. Otherwise go through the **Office du Tourisme**, 5 square de la Banque, 97110 Pointe-à-Pitre, t 82 09 30. Some of the nicer ones are mentioned below, but the list is not complete.

Bas du Fort and Gosier on Grande-Terre are the island's principal resort areas and they have lines of hotels along the seafront. Elsewhere on the southern coast, Ste-Anne and St-François each have a few beach resorts. After a week on the beach you might like to move to easy-going Basse-Terre, which has some fun *relais* and *gîtes* dotted around the countryside, lost in gardens of tropical luxuriance. In larger hotels they will probably speak English, but you will need some French if you step beyond the main tourist areas. Breakfast is usually included in the room rate. A service charge of 10% or 15% will be added to your hotel bill.

Grande-Terre

Very Expensive

Méridien Hotel, PO Box 37, La Cocoteraie, St-François 97118, t 88 79 81, *reservations. centreuk@lemeridien.com*, *www.guadeloupe. lemeridien.com*. If you like a more active resort-style hotel on the beach with all the usual luxury amenities, then this could be for you. The 50 suites are in very modern-looking blocks ranged tightly around a huge pool, with dining room and pool bar on islands in the middle, decorated with huge Chinese vases. The rooms are extremely comfortable, decorated in strong colours: pink, blue and green. All have balconies. Watersports are available on the private beach and many other facilities in its sister-hotel next door.

Plantation Ste-Marthe, 97118 St-François, t 93 11 11, US t (212) 673 3660, *psm@netguacom.fr*, *www.sainte-marthe.gp*. A large but comfortable hotel just outside St-François. It stands out a mile because of its distinctive Louisiana style, with the metalwork balustrades on the huge balconies. Inside, the 96 rooms are extremely comfortable, with all conveniences. Large pool, plenty of sports facilities, shuttle to the beach and some entertainment.

Sofitel Auberge de la Vieille Tour, Gosier, t 84 23 23, *h1345@accor.com*, *www.accorhotels. com*. Sits on a headland above the sea and now has 150 rooms and 32 suites. This makes it large but the setting is still good, over-looking attractive grounds that slope towards the hotel's own beach. It retains something of an old colonial air, in the plantation house and the subdued atmosphere of the two restaurants and bar, spiked only by the windsurfers down below and the boutique in the old windmill.

Expensive

La Toubana, PO Box 63, 97180 Ste-Anne, **t** 88 25 78, *toubana@leaderhotels.gp, www.leader-hotels.gp*. One of the most *sympathique* hotels on the island. It stands high above a sandy cove, centred on a very attractive dining room with elegant metal furniture and a hilltop sitting area from where the view stretches out over the pool and to the islands and on to Dominica (or Club Med the other way) beyond. The rooms are scattered in 32 bungalows on the descending hillside, very comfortable with kitchenettes and surrounded by gardens. Some bungalows for four people, air-conditioned, TVs, tennis court. Easy-going local crowd and some entertainment in the evenings.

Moderate

Cap Sud Caraïbes, Petit Havre, 97190 Gosier, **t** 88 96 02, *pthavre@softel.fr*. A pleasantly unassuming *relais créole* on the hill in a residential area halfway between Gosier and Ste-Anne. The 12 rooms are in a simply designed modern block which stands above a pool on the hillside close to the Petit Havre beach. Private and friendly.

Le Petit Havre, 97190 Gosier, **t** 85 20 83. A similar feel to the Cap Sud, with 11 quiet and simple rooms.

Auberge Le Grand Large, Ste-Anne, **t** 85 48 28, *info@aubergelegrandlarge.com, www.aubergelegrandlarge.com*. A slightly less comfortable but equally well-positioned retreat just along from the Mini Beach, where there are simple rooms in the main house and in colourful bungalows (some kitchenettes) set in profuse tropical gardens.

Village Caraïbes Carmelita's, St-Félix, 97190 Gosier, **t** 84 28 28, *auberge.carmelita@wanadoo.fr, www.villagecaraibes.com*. Another passable option close to the beach, with 14 air-conditioned bungalows, some with kitchenettes, in a lawned garden with a swimming pool.

Inexpensive

Les Flamboyants, 97190 Gosier, **t** 84 14 11. An excellent retreat set high on the hill in Gosier, with a pool and open gardens out front, which overlook the Ilet de Gosier and Basse-Terre beyond – a moment of calm in the holiday hustle of the tourist town. The main house is an old villa, with an aquarium and fishing trophies, sharks and turtle shells on the wall. There are 20 studios and rooms, quite simple with air conditioning; breakfast only served in the dining room.

La Formule Economique, Montauban, Gosier, **t** 84 54 91. Goes by an odd name but it has a lively atmosphere, in a villa tucked away at the back of the town. It is centred on a lively dining room on a balcony decorated with clocks, model ships and plenty of bottles of rum. There are just eight simple rooms.

Sodex Vacances Guest House, on the main road, Gosier, **t** 84 10 25. Some very simple rooms and studios in a block overlooking a garden of Guadeloupean profusion.

Hotel St-John, Pointe-à-Pitre, **t** 82 51 57. If you need to be in the town, you might try this space-age hotel, in which the 44 rooms lurk in a profusion of arches and overhanging eaves.

Karukera, Pointe-à-Pitre, **t** 91 75 55, *www.village-karukera.gp/us*. Four rooms with private baths.

Victoria Palace, Pointe-à-Pitre, **t** 83 12 15. Fifteen rooms, some with shared baths.

Basse-Terre

On the island of Basse-Terre the hotels are a little bit more spread out – this half of Guadeloupe does not have so many of the picture-postcard beaches, but some of the hotels and inns have excellent settings above the water or hidden in the rainforest. Some hotels will have a car ready for you at the airport if you request it.

Expensive

Le Jardin Malanga, 97114 Trois Rivières, **t** 92 67 57, *malanga@leaderhotels.gp, www.leader-hotels.gp*. At the southern tip of the island, in Trois Rivières, where you will find a charming setting. An old wooden estate house restored in colonial style sits on the hillside among the banana fields, overlooking the islands of Les Saints to the south. There are 12 rooms with modern comforts (king-size beds, video, mini-bar, phone, air-con) in the main house and three Guadeloupean *cases*, or wooden cottages.

Excellent old-time atmosphere, with creole cuisine.

Tainos Village, Deshaies, t 28 44 42. An Indonesian-style de luxe hotel composed of seven authentic Javanese homes. Its restaurant features salads for lunch, while dinner is a more elaborate menu of French and creole cuisine.

Moderate

L'Auberge de la Distillerie, 97170 Petit Bourg, t 94 27 68. Just off La Traversée (D23), a good stopover, which is set on a hillside looking back towards Grande-Terre. Next to the main house stands a large covered terrace with the dining room and salon for occasional entertainment. It is friendly and low-key. Named after tropical flowers, the 14 rooms are quite simple but comfortable, and they have an air of old-time Guadeloupe, each with a balcony and a hammock giving onto a profuse garden, where there is a small pool.

Créol' Inn, Bel'Air Desrozières, 97170 Petit Bourg, t 94 22 56. Just down the hill, in the quiet, there is a small cluster of Guadeloupean *cases* or wooden cottages (built in the style of the old-time Caribbean) with louvred doors and gingerbread trimmings in a profuse tropical garden. The *cases* are self-contained, with telephone, TV and fan; each also has a veranda and a well-equipped kitchenette. Restaurant and shop with food.

La Flûte Enchantée, 97126 Deshaies, t 28 41 71, *flutench@wanadoo.fr, www. flute-enchantee.com*. One of the most charming hotels on the island, hidden away in a tropical garden as thick as jungle. At the top of the garden stands the central house with its open sitting area where guests linger in the early evening before moving to the dining room, which gives on to the lit pool. Beyond, the garden has paths (and a small railway) which lead down to the 12 fan-ventilated rooms situated in cottages; each has a terrace and a small kitchenette downstairs and bedroom upstairs. There is a charmed air about the place, which lives up to its romantic name.

Habitation Grande Anse, 97126 Deshaies, t 28 45 36, *info@grande-anse.com, www.grande-anse.com*. Another easy-going spot with 26 rooms. They come in a variety: studios with kitchenettes and some apartments. The dining room, set on a creole veranda looking out onto a lawned garden, and the pool are down below, and the rooms run in a tight stagger up the hill behind.

Inexpensive

Chez Dampierre, 97114 Trois Rivières, t 92 98 69. Nine wooden and tin-roofed bungalows are set on a small area of hillside. They are quite small, but are passably comfortable and self-contained with kitchenettes.

Gîtes Checheti, 97114 Trois Rivières, t 92 96 40. Three bungalows with rooms and studios set in nice gardens high above the town; a quiet stopover.

La Paillotte du Pêcheur, near Grand Anse, t 92 94 98. If you would prefer to be down on the seafront, within a couple of kilometres of Grand Anse beach, then you can stay here, where there are just a few apartments and a dining room.

Hotel Relais Houëlment, 34 rue de la République, Basse-Terre, t 81 44 72. Right at the foot of town.

La Casa du Père Labat, outside Basse-Terre, t 81 98 79. Three very simple rooms, air conditioning or fan, with a fine creole dining room. *Lunch only*.

Gîte de Vanibel, 97119 Vieux Habitants, t 98 40 79. A charming spot among the restored remains of a plantation high up in the hills. Self-catering apartments, made modern but retaining the stained wood, the louvres and the verandas of times past. Classic Caribbean gardens and some of the coffee plantation machinery still on view.

Le Rocher de Malendure, 97125 Bouillante, t 98 86 63. Nine bungalows of which three sit on the *rocher* itself.

La Grange Bel ô, on the Chemin Poirier, t 98 71 42. A charming creole house standing in a garden above the coast.

Le Duc'Ery, 97170 Petit-Bourg, t 95 73 95. En route to Grande-Terre you will find an excellent stopover here, a modern house with old creole overtones which stands high above an agricultural valley. Friendly reception, assistance with tours in the area, and good prices.

Eating Out

With its French roots, Guadeloupean cooking is excellent and the island will not disappoint those who wish to take part in a gastronomic steeplechase or just take some time out from the rigours of sitting on a beach. And many of the settings are excellent too, small cafés on the waterfront (Ste-Anne and St-François each have a string of them) and verandas on a hillside grappled by alla-manda and slender fingers of bougainvillea, with the tremulous thunder of the rain on an iron roof.

The Guadeloupeans cook a full range of French food, but of course the island has a long tradition of creole food: fish and island meats like goat, spiced sauces, tropical vegeta-bles and fruits. There are Guadeloupean versions of many dishes you will find in Martinique (their point of origin is usually contested) and they will be stamped with the island flavour. Snapper, *lambi* (conch) and *langouste* (lobster) are favourites, in a *blaff* (a way of boiling fish), or goat in a *colombo* (a French West Indian curry), served with flavoured rice and peas or local vegetables such as plantain or christophene and spiked with creole sauces. French wine is often drunk with a meal but, like their *confrères* in Martinique, the Guadeloupeans are slaves to the *petit ponch*, a rum-based apéritif that is small only in name, and the *ponch à fruits*, in which fruits are steeped in rum and sugar, giving it a sweet flavour.

There are literally hundreds of restaurants and cafés in Guadeloupe (at the last official count about 700), so the choice is limitless. There are Vietnamese and even Lebanese restaurants here. Most are fairly relaxed, but in the smarter ones men are sometimes required to wear a jacket. Eating out is not exactly cheap, but surprisingly the smartest restaurants are not drastically more expensive than the less smart ones.

Price categories are based on the price of a main course: expensive = €15 and above; moderate = €8–€15; and inexpensive = less than €8. Obviously many restaurants offer a menu of the day. You will find them at €10 to €20. Service is *compris*.

Grande-Terre

Expensive

Côté Jardin, Bas du Fort marina, t 90 91 28. An excellent French restaurant in a comfortable setting, tucked away behind the waterfront. Meats are imported from mainland France but the fish is local of course. You sit inside in an air-conditioned dining room, at elegant white-laid tables in wicker chairs, some with huge peacock backs, with all the activity of the kitchen in view. Try *gambas flambés du planteur passion* or *cuisse de canard confite* served with *pommes sautées paysanne* or, if you want to be extravagant, lobster, *émincé de langouste, sauce saffron*. Popular with business and political people for lunch, cool and elegant for dinner; excel-lent wine list. *Closed Sun.*

Le Dampierre, just off the main road at the eastern end of Gosier, t 84 53 19. Set in a modern villa and popular with local businessmen and families for its inventive creole fare.

Le Flibustier, just off the main road at the eastern end of Gosier, t 88 23 36. Has a certain style – set on a hill like a pirate's look-out and decorated inside with the beams of a galleon. It's quite rumbustious: wine by the pitcher, chef with his hair tied back, who barbecues your meal and then presents it to you on a huge wooden platter. Naval battles and portraits of pirates on the walls. *Closed Mon, Sun eve.*

Lalapalooza, Gosier, t 84 58 58. Part Latin bar with live DJ, part restaurant, it has intro-duced a new concept to Guadeloupe's dining and dancing scene and become a meeting place for locals and French expatri-ates. The European menu features grilled lobster, seafood and meats flavoured with hints of local produce and spices.

Kotésit, rue de la République, St-François, t 88 40 84. Has a pretty setup, with blue and white awnings on a wooden deck right on the small waves. French and creole fare: *vivaneau* (snapper) *et sa sauce, panaché de poissons poêlés* or lobster straight from the live tank.

Le Zagaya, St-François. Stretching out over the water on a green and white deck, this is found behind the streetfront façade of a pretty old creole house. Again lobster is a speciality, or start with a *salade de chèvre aux raisins* and then try *ouassous flambés* or *à la provençale*, followed by a *clafoutis aux fruits* to finish.

Le Château de Feuilles, near Campêche (well signposted), **t** 22 30 30. A sedate day out lingering over a long lunch time can be enjoyed here, in a charming creole villa and garden miles from anywhere. French and creole fare – *choucroute de poisson de papaye verte, charlotte au corossol* (mousse and cream) and a between-course swim if you feel like it, just beside the tables, followed up with one of 20 different varieties of fruit-flavoured rums. *Open Tue–Sun, 11.30–4. A meal (cocktail, starter, main dish, dessert and wine) costs about €50.*

Moderate

La Sirène, Bas du Fort marina. Does a good crêpe.

Les Pieds dans l'Eau, St-François. A popular spot.

Le Mareyeur, St-François, **t** 88 44 24. Another good choice.

La Paillotte de Pêcheur, Grande Anse, Trois-Rivières, **t** 94 98 92. The 'fisherman's hut' specializes in seafood, notably fresh lobster. A fish dinner with appetizer and main dish costs about €14, lobster is priced according to weight. The family-run business also rents out three bungalows. *Open daily for lunch 12.30pm and dinner except Sun 7pm.*

Inexpensive

Recently a number of roadside pizzerias and *roulottes* (snack wagons) have put in an appearance all over Guadeloupe and they make a fast alternative to the traditional sit-down blow-out. You will find *grillades* in Ste-Anne and St-François. If you are feeling peckish late at night in Pointe-à-Pitre, there are snackwagons on the place de la Victoire. Afterwards you might like to grab an ice cream from the vendors with wooden buckets (they will explain how they work too).

Express Grill, on the main road outside Gosier. An excellent place for a simple plate of chicken and chips. *Open daily until 1 or 2am.*

Basse-Terre

Basse-Terre has a number of good places to eat, dotted around the whole island, but particularly on the free and easy west coast around Malendure.

Expensive

Chez Clara, on the waterfront road, Ste-Rose, **t** 28 72 99. The dining room is on a very comfortable deck with a tin roof and you sit at wicker chairs. Clara herself presides, talking you through the menu on a chalkboard – fish and shellfish landed on the pier right across the road, a *feuilleté* or a *ragout de lambi* (conch) with a *gratin de fruit à pain* (breadfruit). Superb creole fare, popular with the locals. *Closed Wed, Sun eve.*

Chez Franko or **Les Flamboyants**, Ste-Rose, **t** 28 86 61. You could try either of these, both of which offer *blaffs* and *courts-bouillons*.

Domaine de Séverin, **t** 28 34 54. An old plantation house on the northern slopes of the island on a sugar plantation. *Ecrevisses* (crayfish, from the pond on the estate) *en civet au vin rouge* or *feuilleté de lambi. Lunch Tues–Sun, dinner Thurs–Sat.*

La Nova, Deshaies, near La Perle beach, **t** 28 40 74. Set on a breezy, split-level terrace outside a modern local house. Serves creole cuisine and local dishes made with regional ingredients. Prix fixe and à la carte menus. *Open for lunch and dinner daily except Tues.*

Le Karacoli, Grand Anse, Deshaies, **t** 28 41 17. You may find yourself dodging the twice-weekly tour buses. You can catch a good lunch on the tropical terrace here. Creole food – *assiette belle négresse*, with all the fish and seafood you might want to try (*boudin, accras* and tropical crudités) followed by a *tartane du thon* or a *croustillant de lambi.*

Le Coin des Gourmets, Bord de mer-l'Embarcadère, Trois-Rivières, **t** 92 75 08. Next to the landing stages of the inter-island ferries and only a few steps from the Archaeological Gardens, this seaside eatery specializes in seafood and creole cuisine.

Le Mouillage, Deshaies, **t** 28 41 12. Popular for creole cuisine; their speciality is *ouassous en sauce*, but you can get a *blaff de poisson et légumes* followed by *banane flambée*.

Le Rocher de Malendure, Malendure, t 98 70 84. You dine on any one of a multitude of different decks, looking through profuse tropical greenery to Ilet de Pigeon. It is a fish restaurant – *escalope de marlin pané* or *ouassous en sauce*, even a fondue, but if you've been diving you might have the *assiette du plongeur* (sushi, Tahitian fish, smoked fish); some meat dishes.

La Touna, Bouillante, on the waterfront, t 98 70 10. Serves fish and lobster landed nearby. The cuisine is creole and French, seafood and fish, on a neat and pretty veranda. Some bar-trade with deep-sea fishermen dropping in to tell their war stories.

Caprice des Iles, Baillif, next to the castle at the corner, just before Basse-Terre, t 81 74 97. Right next to the road but with a terrace on the waves. Offers a fine welcome and good French and creole cuisine. *Accras, boudin* and *vivaneau à la crème d'avocat*, followed by a *feuilleté de banane caramelisée*.

Le Tamarinier, St-Claude, t 80 06 67. A fun restaurant where you will get the best in '*cuisine familiale et creole*'.

Moderate

Le Madras, Deshaies, t 28 40 87. Very local and offers creole fare inside a small, dark dining room set with madras tablecloths. *Boudin lambi* and stuffed crab backs. Lunch and dinner, set on a nice terrace.

Chez Paul, Matouba, Rivière Rouge, t 80 01 77. A nice lunch-time stopover. *Accras* followed by *féroce* with hot pepper or a *fricassée* with a spicy sauce and of course a volley of local vegetables.

Le Houëlment, Basse-Terre. Local fare.

Bars and Nightlife

Zouk is the current musical beat of the French Caribbean, another bustling rhythm with a double beat, often with echoes of West Africa. It can be heard on the buses and in the clubs, each as crowded as the other, along with just about all the other Caribbean beats. You get to know the songs as they are played over and over again: hear them again when you get home and you will start to twitch. Most clubs have a door charge of around US$10, which usually includes the price of a drink. Outside the hundreds of bistros and bars you will find a few spots where hip chicks and lover-boys gather for an early-evening drink. They are centred around the tourist areas.

Zoo Rock Café, t 90 77 77. Bas du Fort marina. A loud and lively bar, which is all dressed up like a ship with square portholes and rigging; inside there is a black and white décor like zebra patterning.

Barrio Calente, Bas du Fort, t 90 80 96. Meet and mix in a Latin-Spanish-Moroccan atmosphere at the bar with music. *Open Tues–Sun 7pm–dawn*. Restaurant, too.

Caribbean Café, 30 rue de Docteur Cabre, Basse Terre, t 95 45 64. Colourful courtyard setting; DJ in the evening; snacks, fish and vegetarian dishes.

La Cascade, just off the main road to Ste-Anne. For dancing. *Open Tues–Sat*.

New Land, just off the main road to Ste-Anne. A disco. *Open weekends*.

La Toubana Hotel, outside Ste-Anne. A good place to enjoy a hilltop view and a cocktail.

Caraïbe Club, Gosier. Casino.

Beach Bars

In Grande-Terre you will find bars and bistros along the popular beachfronts, to which you can retreat when the sun is at its height. Ste-Anne and St-François have a string of cafés along the waterfront where you can cast a critical eye at the windsurfers' technique over a beer or two. There are also snack bars along the road to the eastern tip at Pointe des Châteaux. You can have a good day out at the Plage de l'Autre Bord outside Le Moule, where there are beach bars and small huts for a local meal. In easy-going Basse-Terre you will find beach bars spread out in the isolated bays. On the Plage de Malendure and on the mile-long strip of Grand Anse near Deshaies there are lots of sheds and snack wagons under the palms.

Chez Francine, t 28 80 03, Plage de Cluny, Basse-Terre. Francine has a wooden house and a covered terrace swallowed in banana and bougainvillea underneath the palms. There are deckchairs on the sand and soursop or coconut milk to accompany *accras* (codfish batterballs). The best of all, and well worth stopping for.

Racing among the jumbled mountains are endless waterfalls that tumble into rock pools – ideal spots for a dip. There are lakes, hot springs, and, in the south, the curiosity of the volcanic peak itself, where the ground steams day and night. The mountains here are also crossed by a series of tracks, many of which can be combined to make a good day's walk. Some leave from and return to **La Maison de la Forêt** on road D23; others are more adventurous and cross from one side of the island to the other (*see* 'Basse-Terre', p.299). Guided tours can be arranged through the Organisation des Guides de Montagne de la Caraïbe (*t 80 05 79*) and Les Amis du Parc National (*t 81 45 53*).

There is little wildlife on Guadeloupe, but what there is can be seen in the **Parc Zoologique Botanique** on La Route de la Traversée (D23) that cuts across the middle of the park. In the hills you might be lucky enough to see the *raton laveur*, the racoon, or an *agouti*, a little mammal like a guinea pig introduced by man into many of the islands.

On the lower land of Grande-Terre the flora and fauna are completely different and you will see egrets and endless doves in the rolling *mornes*, and sandpipers, snipe and yellowlegs (greater and lesser) around the mangrove swamps. On the coast there are pelicans and tropicbirds. You can find these, alongside a host of crabs and other crustaceans, in the **Réserve Naturelle de Grand Cul de Sac Marin**, 650 acres of mangrove and swamp and 850 acres of marine park. There is also a marine reserve in the area of Ilet de Pigeon on the west coast of Basse-Terre.

Grande-Terre

Pointe-à-Pitre

The town of Pointe-à-Pitre, the commercial capital of the island and major port, lies on the southern side of Grande-Terre, in the Petit Cul-de-Sac, the inlet formed as the two parts of the island have been pushed together. It has a population of 26,000 concentrated in the centre of the town, but 100,000 altogether including the suburbs along the coastline. The town first began to grow in the 1760s, during the British occupation of Guadeloupe, and supposedly takes its name from a Dutchman named Pieter, who had lived on the point near La Darse a century earlier.

Pointe-à-Pitre is hardly an attractive town, though some two-storey wooden buildings do give an inkling of its former mercantile pride. It has developed haphazardly, upset by earthquakes (1843), fires and hurricanes, the latest of which, Hurricane Hugo, cut through in 1989. In the centre the old Pointe-à-Pitre has a similar charm to that of a French provincial town, with buildings with louvred windows and balconies abutting on one another, and the smells of coffee and pâtisseries exuding onto the street below. With its tall buildings and narrow streets, Pointe-à-Pitre becomes very crowded during the day, with cars parked up on every inch of pavement.

Beyond the boulevard Chanzy, the newest *quartiers* have sprung up in a crop of ferro-concrete monstrosities from the 1950s, proof against earthquake perhaps, but incredibly ugly. They have forced the traditional West Indian shacks farther out along the coast.

A **guided tour** of Pointe-à-Pitre can be made, with explanations of the town's history and traditions, through Pointe-à-Pitre Tour (*t* 90 04 71), though there may have to be a minimum of four people.

La Darse (meaning 'harbour') is still the heart of town life. Markets appear on the wharves at dawn, as the ferries and the buses come and go, dropping people off for the day's work. Just above La Darse is the main square, **place de la Victoire**, whose name commemorates victory over the British by Victor Hugues and the revolutionary army in 1794. In his reign of terror, Victor Hugues erected the guillotine here, but now the square (partly given over to a car park, unfortunately) is more peaceful. It is planted with royal palms and mango trees (some sadly torn out by Hurricane Hugo), and is lined with cafés and a few nice old buildings, where the *Pointus* (the inhabitants of Pointe-à-Pitre) like to sit during the day and take the evening air under the busts of famous Guadeloupeans. Behind the square, on the rue Alexandre Isaac, is the **Cathedral of St Peter and St Paul**, constructed in Empire style in 1807.

The main street, **rue Frébault**, with shops full of goods from mainland France, leads through the commercial heart of the town, down to the **Marché de St-Antoine**, an iron market with a red corrugated-iron roof. Guadeloupe may be one of the most developed islands in the area, but this is a truly Caribbean institution. It pulses from early morning, with the smell of fruits and spices, and offers anything from avocados to earrings for sale. Even for French speakers, the joking and haggling in creole is impossible to keep up with.

The **Musée Schoelcher** (*open Mon–Fri 8.30–noon and 2–5.30, Sat 8.30–noon; adm*) is set in an impressive stone and stucco town house with a double staircase and metal-work balustrades (built in 1887) on the rue Peynier, outside which is a small *sans-culottes* statue of Victor Hugues the revolutionary. The museum contains some of the personal collections of the abolitionist, assembled in his 15-year struggle to outlaw slavery in the French colonies: pamphlets against the slave trade and a copy of the proclamation outlawing slavery, some prints comparing facial appearances (with some particularly unpleasant ones comparing black people to animals) and some death masks, reflecting Schoelcher's interest in phrenology (with which he disagreed).

Another leading light in Guadeloupe is celebrated in the **Musée St-John Perse** (*open Mon–Fri 9–5, Sat 9–noon; adm*), set in an elaborate late 19th-century creole house on the rue Nozières. The poet and diplomat Alexis St-Léger was born on the island of a long-standing family and was awarded the Nobel Prize for Literature in 1960. The story of his life is told upstairs, and downstairs there are revolving exhibitions. The house itself looks a little odd, surrounded on all sides by louvres: it was supposed to have been shipped, in kit form, from Louisiana.

The South Coast

Protected from the Atlantic weather by the rolling limestone 'Grands Fonds', the southern coast of Grande-Terre has the mildest climate on the island and has become the centre for the tourist industry. The action of the waves on the coral shores has pushed up white-sand beaches, and on them the hotels have mushroomed. The main areas are Bas du Fort, just out of Pointe-à-Pitre to the southeast, and the towns of Gosier, Ste-Anne and St-François.

Leaving Pointe-à-Pitre on the road to Gosier (N4), you pass the buildings of the university and come to **Bas du Fort**, a busy area where there are a number of tourist apartment blocks and hotels around a marina, with restaurants and bars. Round the point is the **Guadeloupe Aquarium** (*open daily 9–7; adm exp*), which exhibits tropical fish from all over the world in the 20 or so tanks. You will see lionfish with fancy-dress tail and fins, fish that shine as though lit by ultraviolet in a discotheque, and a trapezoidal character called *lactophrys triqueter*, who will spit poison at you. It culminates in the walk-through shark tunnel. Commanding the Grande Baie, a little farther round and covering the approaches to Pointe-à-Pitre, is the **Fort Fleur d'Epée** (*open daily 9–6; adm free*). These coral-rock ramparts cut into the hillside were stormed and gallantly defended in the days of Empire but now it is really just a park within fortress walls and it is visited mainly by picnickers and lovers.

The town of **Gosier**, a centre of tourism on the island, spreads along the shore for several miles, and the hotels have encrusted the old town, cluttering the hillside down to the beaches and bringing with them a plethora of restaurants, bars and discotheques. The name Gosier derives from the *grand gosier*, or pelican, which can be seen all over the Lesser Antilles and occasionally fishes off the Ilet de Gosier, a couple of hundred yards off shore.

Ste-Anne and **St-François** are two other towns whose incomes have switched from fishing to sport fishing, though among the motorboats with huge fishing rods sticking into the air you will still see *gommiers*, the brightly painted local fishing boats. Both towns still have a promenade, where fishermen's houses and restaurants mingle, looking across the sea towards Dominica.

Inland from the coast you come immediately into the **Grands Fonds**, a landscape of limestone that has eroded into many tightly clustered hillocks (it looks very regular from the air), which are tussocked with growth on top. For centuries they were carpeted with 10ft of sugar cane. In the early years of the 18th century, Ste-Anne was the commercial centre that catered for them, but by the end of the century it was already in decline, its prosperity destroyed by Guadeloupe's internal turmoil. On the dock at St-François, where the yachts are moored, you will see flashes of local West Indian life as the ferry from the island of La Désirade puts in. Its inhabitants are mainly farmers and they bring their sheep, stuffed into sacks with just their heads sticking out, to sell in Guadeloupe.

Beyond St-François, Grande-Terre tapers to a spike pointing out into the Atlantic Ocean and culminates in the cliffs of **Pointe des Châteaux**. The wind is strong off the ocean here and the waves have carved eerie shapes out of the rocks, including a blowhole that answers moments after a wave has disappeared under the lip of the rock. The landscape looks a little like Brittany, as though Guadeloupe had simply broken off the west coast of France and been transported 4,000 miles west. From the cross on the point, high above the waves, it is possible to see La Désirade, a table mountain with sweeping sides which emerges gracefully from the sea 6 miles (10km) away, and the uninhabited islands of Petite Terre. On the northern side of the peninsula is the **Plage Tarare**, a nudist beach.

The N5 leads north from St-François through the canefields and now residential land to **Le Moule**, on the Atlantic coast, where the waves come relentlessly barrelling in – suffering continuously from the Atlantic winds, the houses in the town were built with no doors facing east. Le Moule knew some prosperity as the principal port on Guadeloupe's eastern coast in the sugar years, and ships would edge in on the waves to the anchor ports still visible, but now it is poor and broken down. The town was wasted by Hurricane Hugo in 1989 and many of the buildings were destroyed. The **Musée Edgar Clerc** (*open Thurs–Tues 9–12.30 and 2–5.30, Wed 9–12.30; adm*) is devoted to pre-Columbian history with Arawak archaeological remains displayed. There is also a distillery just outside the town, the **Distillerie Bellevue** (*open daily 9–5*), manufacturers of Damoiseau rums. The various processes of rum distillation are on view and of course the visit culminates in a free tasting.

Northern Grande-Terre

In the northern areas of Grande-Terre, the land lies lower and in places is covered with mangrove swamp. It is fertile land, and everywhere you will see the cone-shaped shells of abandoned windmills, some still with their crushing gear discarded inside. In **Morne-à-l'Eau** is one of the best examples of the French West Indian chequerboard cemetery, with acres of black and white tiles on the mausolea. On the Festival of All Saints' there is a ceremony in which the whole graveyard is lit with candles. At **Port-Louis**, there is a view over the Grand Cul-de-Sac Marin enclosed between the two halves of the island. Basse-Terre rises spectacularly, grey-green in the distance, topped with vast clouds.

On the northwestern coast of the island is **Anse Bertrand**, another town that saw its most prosperous times in the sugar heyday of the 18th century. The most northerly point on the island is **Pointe de la Grande Vigie**, where the cliffs stand 250ft above sea level. On a clear day Antigua, 35 miles (56km) north, is visible from the point. Close by is **La Porte d'Enfer** (Hell's Gate), a massive fissure in the cliffs.

Basse-Terre

A coastal road circles Guadeloupe's mountainous volcanic wing and, through the middle of the island, La Traversée cuts a path up and over the rainforest to the Caribbean coast.

Leaving Pointe-à-Pitre, the N1 crosses to Basse-Terre over the **Rivière Salée**. Before the two parts of Guadeloupe were linked by bridge in 1906, the crossing was made by ferry. On one occasion, a party of Guadeloupeans were making for a ball in Pointe-à-Pitre when they were swept out to sea. Garbed in evening dress, they drifted for five days before washing up on St Thomas in the Virgin Islands.

The East Coast

The main road (N1) to the town of Basse-Terre takes a left turn and travels down the eastern coast, beneath the towering mountainsides, before crossing over to the

Caribbean coast near the southern tip. **Ste-Marie** is thought to be the place where Columbus landed on his second voyage in 1493, meeting his first Caribs.

   Capesterre takes its name from its position (*capesterre* means windward in French, and the village is upwind of *Basse-Terre*). Outside the town, the **Plantation Grand Café** (*open Mon–Fri 9–5, plus Sat and Sun 9–12 in winter season; adm*), a working banana plantation, is worth a visit. The tour includes an explanation of the process of cultivation, gathering and washing, sorting and boxing on a conveyor of hooks, a visit to the plantation house and, not to be missed, an alley with about 20 different species of banana and plantain from the world over: *velutina* (from Assam), *beccarii* (Borneo), *basjoo* (Japan). It is also worth making a visit to the **Distillerie Longueteau** just below here (*open Mon–Sat 9–12; adm*), particularly during the harvest, which lasts about six months from the end of January or early February. It is a distillery of *rhum agricole*, made from pure sugar-cane juice rather than molasses and you can see the whole process, from crushing in the vast and vicious-looking machines to fermentation and distillation in vats and the eventual products – a white rum and a gold rum. As you leave the town of Capesterre you pass along the **Allée Dumanoir**, a tunnel of magnificent royal palms. They stand like living grey columns (the telegraph wires were once simply nailed into them), soaring to 100ft, bursting with spiked fronds and tapering in a single 10ft spine.

   Inland and uphill from St-Sauveur, at the end of the **D4** road that winds up through the banana plantations into the rainforest, are the three **Chutes de Carbet**. Two of the falls cascade into rock pools from over 300ft. The middle one falls 350ft and can be reached on a well-marked path, and the lowest tumbles 65ft into a pool where you can take a dip after the short walk. It is these falls that Columbus mentions in his diary when he talks of 'a waterfall of considerable breadth, which fell from so high that it seemed to come from the sky'. From here the path leads on up into the rainforest, towards the summit of the **Soufrière**, a three-hour walk. Back down the hill, there are several lakes just off the road: the **Etang Zombi** and the **Grand Etang**. The **As de Pique**, a lake in the shape of an ace of spades, is beyond the serene Grand Etang.

   The N1 coastal road continues to the village of **Trois Rivières**. Down the hill and close to the harbour (where boats leave for the islands of Les Saintes) is the **Parc Archéologique des Roches Gravées** (*open daily 8.30–5; adm*), where the main exhibit is a series of maniacal squiggles and outlandish faces on a rockface. They were carved by Arawak Indians before the Caribs bludgeoned their way onto the island in about AD 1000. The rock is set in a small botanical garden, in which plants are marked, including those used by the Arawaks. Another few miles brings you through a ravine to the Caribbean coast and down into Basse-Terre.

Basse-Terre Town and Around

   The town of Basse-Terre (14,000 inhabitants), the administrative capital of Guadeloupe, lies on the coast in the shadow of towering volcanic mountains. It is just 20 miles (33km) from Pointe-à-Pitre as the crow flies, but the journey takes about two hours by road because it twists and turns so laboriously over its 44-mile (70km) length.

Some of the route is impossibly steep and windy, but take heart: lines painted on the road show that the Guadeloupeans actually compete in cycling races along here.

Founded by Houël in 1643, Basse-Terre is built on a hill and is much more attractive than the commercial city of Pointe-à-Pitre. It retains an antique feel that the other town has lost. Just above the port, stone houses with upper storeys of shingle-wood tiles and clapboard crowd over the narrow streets. The imposing official buildings, churches and town houses with wrought-iron balconies give it a gentrified air.

Behind the activity of the main streets, on the few areas of flat ground, there are two main squares: the **Jardin Pichon** and the **place du Champ d'Arbaud**, surrounded by the old buildings of Basse-Terre. Covering the harbour from the southern edge of town, **Fort Delgrès** is another lumbering colossus of a fortress with huge embrasures that now stand unemployed. It expanded steadily from its beginnings in about 1650, when Houël erected the first battlements, and has also seen plenty of action. There are acres of ramparts and it is easy to imagine the roar of the cannon and the smell of cordite. There is a small **museum** in the fort (*open daily 9–5; adm free*), giving a good rundown of its history and of Basse-Terre.

Like any prosperous Caribbean port, the town has spread up the hill, where the wealthier inhabitants take a cooler and loftier view of the proceedings in the city centre. The district of **St-Claude**, strung out over the bends of a sinuous mountain road, contains some the most attractive houses on the island. A side road leads to the town of **Matouba**, which has a large East Indian population (who came here as indentured labourers in the 19th century). Just above the town is the Guadeloupe **Parc National**, where there are a number of walking trails or '*traces*'. The Trace Victor Hugues leads from Matouba up into the mountains and down towards Petit Bourg on the other coast. Other *traces* lead to La Maison de la Forêt or down to Petit Bourg. These are long and demanding walks, so you should be well equipped before setting out.

High in the rainforest is the **Maison du Volcan** (*open daily 10–6; adm free*), a museum. It is set in a garden festooned with greenery and tells of vulcanism in general, and La Soufrière, which lurks just above it, in particular (including its eruption in 1976). Also close by are the **Bains Jaunes**, hot-water springs, and the **Chutes du Galion**, more waterfalls. The road leads farther up onto the slopes of the volcano itself, an extremely steep path, wide enough for one car, that stops 1,000ft below the craters, at **Savane à Mulets**.

La Soufrière lives up to its name, as the summit is a morass of sulphurous fumaroles and solidified lava flows where plants are poisoned before they take root. It is still quite active, constantly letting off steam and occasionally rumbling and showering the neighbourhood with flakes of volcanic dust. It erupted in 1695 and in 1797. In 1837 the whole of Basse-Terre quaked but this was followed by 120 years of silence until 1956 and then considerable activity in the 1970s. There were dust and gas explosions, geysers appeared in lakes, and the rivers turned into mud and lava flows. At one point there were a thousand tremors a day and 70,000 people were evacuated from the southern end of Basse-Terre.

From Savane à Mulets, you can make the summit in under three hours, on a path that passes between boulders tossed out by the eruptions. At 4,813ft (1,467m), La

Soufrière is the highest point in the Eastern Caribbean. When the clouds are not in attendance (though they make the whole climb that much more eerie), the view from the top is a cracker.

La Traversée

La Traversée (D23) cuts across the middle of the island of Basse-Terre, climbing to the twin pyramids of the Mamelles (at 2,500ft) through whole roadsides of ferns and banana plants and then descending in switchbacks to emerge on the Caribbean coast at Mahault. The road gives an excellent view of the rainforest in all its luxuriance, with occasional panoramic flashes between the trees.

At Vernou, a retreat where the wealthy have built their villas and set them in tropical gardens, is the **Saut de la Lézarde** (the lizard's leap), a waterfall and rock pool in a gulley at the foot of an impressive slope covered in banana trees. Higher in the rainforest, where it becomes dark because the canopy is so thick and grotesque mosses creep on the floor, is the **Cascade des Ecrevisses**, a tame fall where the Guadeloupeans like to go for a day out at the weekend.

La Maison de la Forêt (*open daily 10–5; adm free*) is a museum that describes Guadeloupe's natural life, from the *pâte calcaire* of Grande-Terre and early volcanic rumblings 15 million years ago to the flying cycads and bromeliads of today's tropical rainforest. It is well set out and explains the forest ecosystem, especially the effects of rain. It is a little technical and unfortunately only in French. There are a number of marked walks through the forest that start and finish at the museum.

The Traversée reaches its summit at the **Mamelles**, from where there is a spectacular view, and then begins to descend in hairpins to the coast. From the heights a number of paths lead off into the forest, some of them the old *traces* that were walked by the *porteuses* with huge loads on their heads. The Trace des Crêtes leads down to the Caribbean coast near Marigot and the Route Forestière de Grosse Montagne leads back towards Pointe-à-Pitre. **Morne-à-Louis**, unfortunately scarred by its television transmitter, offers more views over the cumulus of peaks in mountainous Basse-Terre. Just down the hill from here is the **Parc Zoologique Botanique** (*open daily 9–5; café; adm*), where a lacklustre series of cages among the creeping vines exhibits Guadeloupe's limited fauna (raccoon, mongoose, terrapins and iguanas) and unlimited flora, some of which is marked. La Traversée joins the N2 on the Côte-sous-le-Vent (the rain shadow), the Caribbean coast, at Mahault.

Around the Northern Tip

From the Rivière Salée the N2 runs to the northern tip of the island and then down the length of the western coast. To begin with, the land is blanketed with sugar cane, but this changes as the road passes into the shadow of the mountains.

The **Domaine de Valombreuse** (*open daily 9–5; adm*) is a working garden laid out over 10 acres where you can see an overwhelming variety of tropical flora: spice gardens, orchids, exotic shrubs and flowering trees, and a humid river ravine with tall trees and creepers. At the **Domaine de Séverin** you will see a working sugar-cane crusher, with a conveyor about 2ft wide driven by a water wheel (it gives an idea of the labour intensity of this old industry). There is a small museum and shop next door, where you can buy the eventual product, rum. The **Musée du Rhum** (*open daily 9–5*), close by in Bellevue above Ste-Rose, continues the story. It gives a history of cane – sweet bamboo – from Persian times to its use in Europe in the sweet drinks of the 17th century and of course in rum. Plenty of rum paraphernalia – machetes, carts and copper boilers. Rum is on sale.

La Pointe Allègre is the northernmost tip of Basse-Terre and it was the spot chosen by the first settlers of Guadeloupe in June 1635. It was a shaky start, as they were constantly battling the Caribs. Eventually they decamped and headed for the south-western coast at Basse-Terre.

Deshaies is an attractive fishing village that lies in a small bay, from which the road winds up and over to **Pointe-Noire**, a town dating from the 17th century. The **Maison du Bois** (*open daily 9.30–4.30; adm*) is a small museum just south of the town, with exhibits of traditional machinery, tools and furniture from the French Antilles, all in tropical woods. The secrets of boat-building, straining the poisonous juice from manioc to make cassava meal, and the styles of gingerbread woodwork on the eaves of Caribbean houses are displayed. It is worth a visit. The **Trace des Contrabandiers** (smugglers' route) leads across the mountain range in the centre of the island from the Maison du Bois. A three-hour walk through the forest passes beneath Morne Jeanneton and will bring you into the hills above Lamentin.

Another story of a natural product can be followed at the **Maison du Cacao** (*open daily 9–5; adm*) not far down the road. A series of boards in the main house and around the garden (where there are cocoa trees and other tropical crops) explains the history, culture and harvesting of cocoa and some of its beneficial properties: serotonin, which occurs naturally in the bean, is an anti-stress agent and there is an indecipherable anti-depressant in there too. At the end of the visit there is a tasting, of course, and plenty to buy, including locally processed cocoa in blocks.

At **Mahault**, La Traversée (D23) cuts across the island on the quickest route back to Pointe-à-Pitre. Alternatively, the N2 continues down the coast to Malendure, the popular beach and dropping-off point for the Pigeon marine reserve. Founded in 1636, **Vieux Habitants** was supposedly named by its early inhabitants, who moved here after serving out their indenture (a three-year contract in exchange for their passage to the island), to avoid confusion with those who still had time to serve. From here the road continues to Basse-Terre.

La Désirade

'Quand bleuira sur l'horizon la Désirade'
Apollinaire

La Désirade takes its romantic name from the Spanish *deseata* (the desired one). In the 16th century the standard Atlantic crossing arrived at Guadeloupe and after four

Getting There

La Désirade t (590–)

You can reach La Désirade with Air Guadeloupe, t 82 47 00, on **scheduled flights** twice daily, or by **ferry**, leaving daily from the marina at St-François. **Yachts** also take day trips from the marina.

Tourist Information

There is no tourist office, so you are advised to contact the Mairie, t 20 01 76.

Getting Around

When on the island, you can reach a **taxi** on t 20 00 62 and **hire a car** or a **bicycle** through Loca Sun, t 20 07 84, who will also take you on an island tour. Alternatively you could **walk** the length of the island in a day. Look out for the ruined buildings of the leper colony near Baie Mahault and iguanas and agoutis. Island **tours** and **scuba diving** can be arranged through Tony Dinane, t 20 02 93.

Where to Stay and Eat

La Désirade t (590–)

As well as the following, people let out rooms in their houses. Full meal plans are available at the hotels.

Hotel l'Oasis, t 20 02 12 (*inexpensive*). Eight air-conditioned rooms in the Quartier du Désert.

Le Mirage, t 20 01 08 (*inexpensive*). On the beach, where there are seven rooms with fan ventilation and TVs.

Camping, Baie Mahault.

L'Esplanade, Baie Mahault, t 20 06 05 (*inexpensive*). A decent restaurant.

La Payotte, t 20 01 94 (*inexpensive*). A fish and creole restaurant.

or five weeks at sea the sailors would be longing for land. La Désirade was often the island they saw first. Some feel that the real origin of the name is the word *descada*, meaning dry, which would be equally appropriate.

La Désirade lies about 6 miles (10km) off the Pointe des Châteaux, the easternmost tip of Grande-Terre. It is a table mountain, 8 miles by 1 (13 by 2km), with gracefully rising slopes topping 900ft above sea level. It is windswept and covered in cactus scrub. The northern coast is a line of rugged cliff faces, cut into strange shapes. The south of the island is protected from the wind and it is here that the 1,600 inhabitants and most of the thousands of iguanas have chosen to live, spread along the coast from the main settlement of Grande-Anse. There is a track up to the highest point, the Grande Montagne, from the village of Grande-Anse.

La Désirade is dry and was settled only by a few poor white settlers at the beginning of the 20th century. For many years it was a leper colony. Without the plantations there were no slaves and so the population of La Désirade remains predominantly white (also true on Terre-de-Haut in Les Saintes, but not so in Marie Galante). Today life is extremely simple and the economy of the island is mainly agricultural (sheep and small plots), or connected with the sea (fishing and boat-building). It is one of the least developed islands of the Caribbean – a reliable water supply was only intro-duced in 1991, by pipe from Guadeloupe. If you would like an utterly secluded escape, you can find it in La Désirade.

Reef-protected, golden-sand beaches are at Grande-Anse, Le Souffleur and at Baie Mahault.

Marie Galante

In contrast to La Désirade, Marie Galante has a more typical history for the Caribbean. The land was fertile enough to bear sugar and so, during the 18th century, it was covered with it down to the last square inch. Sweeps of cane blew in the breezes and every few hundred yards were the cone and sails of a sugar mill. The cane still grows, but Marie Galante's hundred mills, which once stood proudly at nearly two for every square mile, are run-down and are steadily being devoured by tropical undergrowth.

Shaped like a football, Marie Galante is a flat 59 square miles (158sq km) and looks similar to Grande-Terre, just 20 miles (32km) to the north.

The 20,000 inhabitants live on the protected areas of the coast, around the main settlement of Grand-Bourg. Sugar is still important to the economy (there are three remaining distilleries and Marie Galante rum is renowned) and there is some agriculture. The rum is the principal ingredient in the celebrations on Marie Galante, which are so popular with the people from Dominica that on public holidays they come streaming over in small boats to join the fête.

The island takes its name from Columbus's flagship, the caravelle *Santa Maria de Galante*, in which he led his second expedition to the New World in 1493. After coasting Dominica and failing to find a harbour, he saw Marie Galante and cruised north. For a while the island became a refuge for the Caribs fleeing the larger islands but in the age of Empire it quickly became a strategic base, the first stop on an invasion attempt on Guadeloupe. The Dutch stripped the island systematically in 1676 and the British occupied it a number of times before it finally settled to France in 1815.

There are some very attractive beaches on the western coast of the island, to which the Guadeloupeans come for the weekend. The best are the palm-backed strand at **Vieux Fort** in the northwest and the beautifully calm **Petite Anse** near Capesterre in the southeast and, close by, **Plage de la Feuillère**.

Inland there are canefields and sugar mills (*moulins*) on view – the **Moulin de Basse** and one at the **Château Murat**. In the château, which has been restored to its 18th-century splendour, is the **Eco-Musée de Marie Galante** (*open Mon–Fri 7.30–12.30 and 2.30–5.30, Sat and Sun 7.30–12.30; adm free*), dedicated to island traditions and of course the history of sugar. There are a number of sugar factories and rum distilleries: **Distillerie Poisson** in the west and **Distillerie Bielle**, inland at Rabi. North of here is a cave that goes by the name of **Le Trou à Diable** (the Devil's Hole), which descends quite deep underground. You should take a torch and the right footwear if you venture down it.

Les Saintes

Les Saintes are a collection of small islands that lie 7 miles (11km) south of Basse-Terre. They are volcanic, and rise sharply out of the water to nearly 1,000ft, but they look tiny between the colossi of Basse-Terre and Dominica, the next Windward Island

Getting There

Marie Galante t (590–)

There are regular **flights** (usually three a day) from Guadeloupe on Air Guadeloupe, t 82 47 00, and also on Marie Galante Aviation, t 97 77 02, who also charter out small planes as **air-taxis**, to Basses Airport, t 97 82 21, in the south.

Ferries link Marie Galante to Pointe-à-Pitre several times a day: it's an hour's sail from La Darse in place de la Victoire. Contact L'Express des Iles, t 83 12 45, or Brudey Frères, t 90 04 48. The journey brings you to Grand-Bourg or St-Louis. A tour to the island can be arranged from Pointe-à-Pitre; ferries and yachts also make the crossing from St-François.

Getting Around

Taxis can be contacted on t 97 81 97 and there are **cars and scooters for hire** (best booked in advance) through Auto Grande Savane, t 97 76 58; Magauto in Grand-Bourg, t 97 98 75; or Locsol, t 97 76 78. It is quite possible to make a **tour** of the island in a day; contact Max Savonnier, t 97 41 75, or El Rancho, t 97 81 60. There is a marina at St-Louis.

Tourist Information

There is a **tourist office** on island, t 97 56 51, info@ot-mariegalante.com, with a website at www.ot-mariegalante.com.

Sports

A general **watersports** operator is Man Ballaou, t 97 75 24, in Grand-Bourg, who will arrange windsurfing and kayaks as well as scuba diving. The company will also set up excursions inland, including **hiking** and **mountain biking**.

Where to Stay

Marie Galante t (590–)

There are quite a few places to stay on Marie Galante, some of them family-run and fairly simple. There are about 15 *gîtes* on the island (*see* p.313): call t 97 64 33, or the Maison de Marie Galante in the main tourist office in Guadeloupe, t 97 10 41.

Inexpensive

Auberge de l'Arbre à Pain, rue Dr Etzol, Grand-Bourg, t 97 73 69. Seven air-conditioned rooms in a modern house.

Le Touloulou, near Capesterre, on Petite Anse beach, t 97 32 63. The bungalows here are set around a very pretty waterfront terrace restaurant.

Le Soleil Levant, t 97 31 55. Not far off Petit Anse beach, with rooms and apartments.

Le Salut, St-Louis, t 20 01 94. Has 15 rooms with fans or air conditioning.

Gîte Le Refuge, t 97 02 95. Friendly, with a nice view from above the coast.

Au Village de Ménard, near St-Louis, t 20 09 45. Seven modern and simple bungalows set around a pool on a clifftop, for those who are happy to look after themselves.

Eating Out

Each of the hotels has a dining room (Le Touloulou is good), but there are also plenty of places to eat out in Marie Galante.

Moderate

Maria Galanda, Grand-Bourg, t 97 50 56. Good creole and some Italian fare.

Espace Poirier, Grand-Bourg, t 97 77 05. Lies in the middle of the town, in a wooden house with tin roof and balcony surrounded by tropical plants. An excellent creole restaurant – fish soup and seafood.

Bambou Club, Capesterre, t 97 36 98. A charming spot, where you dine at chequered table-cloths in a tin-roofed dining room with bamboo walls and windows, just off Petite Anse beach. Creole fare: *bébélé* soup and spiny lobster *à la bambou*.

La Braise Marine, Capesterre, t 97 42 57. Try this charming place for a creole menu.

La Rose du Brésil, t 97 47 39. Another attractive place with creole fare.

A-Ka Pat, St-Louis, t 97 05 74. A very rustic affair right on the waterfront with a wooden terrace under a breadfruit tree. Fish and seafood specialities.

Getting There

Les Saintes t (590–)

Getting to Les Saintes is pretty easy. The islands are linked by many **ferries** from Pointe-à-Pitre (1 hour's sail) and from Trois Rivières (20mins) on the southern coast of Basse-Terre. Terre-de-Haut has a magnificent harbour and it is a pleasure to see the peaks glide by as you arrive.

There are airstrips on both islands and two daily **flights** from Pointe-à-Pitre to Terre-de-Haut, t 99 51 23, but if you don't like flying, beware, because the landing can be a bit hair-raising.

Getting Around

There are several daily **sailings** from Bourg, on Terre-de-Haut, to Terre-de-Bas, often touching Bois-Joli. Terre-de-Bas has an **airstrip** suspended on a spit of land 100ft above the sea.

There are no cars for rent (part of the charm of the islands), but on Terre-de-Haut you can **hire a scooter**:
ARS, t 99 52 63.
Dabriou, t 99 53 32.

Tourist Information

There is a small tourist office, t 99 58 60.

Sports

Day sails are available through Sea Lab, t 99 56 10, and a general **watersports** operator is UCPA in Marigot, Terre-de-Haut, t 99 54 94. **Scuba diving** is available through Espace Plongée, t 99 51 84, and the Centre Nautique des Saintes, t 99 54 94.

Where to Stay

Les Saintes t (590–)

As well as the options below, there are rooms for rent in Terre-de-Haut at good prices, t 99 53 83 (*moderate*). There are also some rooms in Terre-de-Bas.

Moderate

Bois Joli Hotel, Anse à Cointre, Terre-de-Haut, t 99 50 38, *bois.joli@wanadoo.fr*. At the Bois Joli Hotel there are 21 rooms and eight bungalows scattered around a central house where there is a pool and pleasant deck above the sea.

Kanaoa, main bay, beneath Fort Napoléon and beyond the house built like a boat that juts out into the water from a cliff, Terre-de-Haut, t 99 51 36. Set in a series of attractive creole-style buildings with a waterfront dining terrace.

Le Village Créole, near Kanaoa, t 99 53 83. Twenty-two duplexes in a garden of croton and bougainvillea.

Le Poisson Volant, Terre-de-Bas, t 99 50 99. Just simple rooms.

Eating Out

The hotels have some decent dining rooms and are good places to track down dinner, but there is also a clutch of bistros and salad bars set on the waterfront in Bourg.

Moderate

El Dorado, Bourg, Terre-de-Haut, t 99 54 31. Set in a wooden house on the main square, you dine on French and creole fare: home-smoked fish and grilled steak, or they also serve pizza.

L'Anse Mouillage, Bourg, Terre-de-Haut, t 99 50 57. Close to the wharf as you arrive, and serves creole specialities including *boudin de poisson* (blood sausage from fish) or a conch *fricassée*.

La Paillotte chez Nadia, Marigot Bay, Terre-de-Haut, t 99 50 77. A very pretty setting under palm trees around a small gingerbread house. *Lunch only, plus Wed eve for dinner and dancing.*

Inexpensive

Chez Eugènette, Plage de Grande Anse, Terre-de-Bas, t 99 81 83. Set on a blue and white deck right on the sand.

A la Belle Etoile, Plage de Grande Anse, Terre-de-Bas, t 99 83 69. Creole food served up in a pretty setting.

down the line. Stand on Le Chameau, the highest point on Terre-de-Haut, and you will feel as though you are on the lip of a swamped volcano crater; the islands make an almost perfectly round bowl.

Two of the islands are inhabited (3,000 people in all) and their populations are curiously different. Terre-de-Bas was a plantation island and the people are mostly descended from the Africans taken there as slaves. Terre-de-Haut, on the other hand, was never planted and so there were never many slaves. Instead the islanders were descended mostly from white Frenchmen, originating from Brittany and Normandy – you can still see their blonde hair and blue eyes. Their skin does not tan in the sun and it is clear that many of them are inbred. They are renowned fishermen, though, and before the age of baseball caps they would wear strange-looking *salako* hats to protect themselves from the sun – white material stretched over a bamboo frame that sits close on the head like a small parasol. These 'coolie hats' are thought to have been brought by a Chinaman in the 19th century.

Les Saintes were supposedly named by Columbus in honour of All Saints' Day. They were settled and fortified in 1648 in order to defend the island of Guadeloupe. The ramparts can still be seen on the heights. Nowadays the islands are very peaceful and they have a charming, seductive atmosphere, so much so that there are more than 350,000 visitors each year.

The Battle of the Saints

To British historians, Les Saintes' most famous moment came in 1782, when the islands had a ringside view of the most decisive naval battle of the period, one which established British dominance in the Caribbean for the next 30 years.

The Battle of the Saints (*La Bataille de la Dominique* to the French) was fought on 12 April 1782. The British were beleaguered at the time, having recently lost the American War of Independence. De Grasse had successfully cut the British supply lines, and now he was turning to the British Caribbean colonies. His target was Jamaica, the richest British colony, and he was on his way to join the Spanish navy at Santo Domingo to attack it.

Leaving Martinique, de Grasse headed north. He was sighted by Rodney and the chase was on. For three days Rodney shadowed de Grasse without being able to commit him to a fight. Eventually they met off Les Saintes and the two lines, each of 30 ships, bore down on each other in slow motion in parallel and opposite directions, the French coming from the north. At eight in the morning the first broadside was fired. The fleets filed past one another, cannonading, until 11 o'clock, when Sir Charles Douglas, with Rodney on the bridge of the *Formidable*, saw a gap in the French line, just a few ships behind de Grasse's flagship, the *Ville de Paris*. He steered for it and broke through the French line. The ships to his rear followed him through and in the manoeuvre they separated the French flagship from the bulk of the fleet. The French ships, so close together they made 'one object to fire at', were decimated. De Grasse stayed on his flagship, with 110 guns and 1,300 sailors, throughout the conflict and, when finally she was taken, he was one of only three men left uninjured. The whole scene had been clearly visible from Dominica and Les Saintes, and as darkness fell ships were seen burning into the night. Five of the French ships were taken and one sunk, and the rest of the tattered fleet headed for Cap Français under Admiral Bougainville and for Curaçao off the coast of South America. When the two admirals met, de Grasse is supposed to have said, 'You have fought me handsomely,' and Rodney to have replied, 'I was glad of the opportunity.'

In the Second World War the islands saw no action. Fort Napoléon was used as a prison for those Guadeloupeans who disagreed with the decision to side with the Vichy regime.

The Islands

There is one main settlement on **Terre-de-Haut**, called **Bourg**, otherwise known as *Le Village*, which is set on a superb harbour. It has a silent, magical air. There are just four or five very attractive streets of creole houses, almost all of them with red tin roofs. Between the cafés on the waterfront you will see the fishermen who sit and chat over a game of dominoes. Terre-de-Haut is pretty touristy (it sees quite a lot of day-trippers from the mainland), but it handles it well and the island has a charming feel. The best beach is in **Baie de Pont Pierre**, but there is also good sand at **Marigot Bay**. On the south coast you will find seclusion at **Anse du Figuier**, named for the tree rather than the leaf, though even fig leafs are discarded at **Anse Crawen**. On land, all the 'sights' are within walking distance (eventually). The lumbering fortress on the hilltop, **Fort Napoléon** (*open daily 9–noon; adm*), is the island's principal sight. Completed in 1867, it commands the bay and has a magnificent view to Guadeloupe and down to Dominica. The fort has exhibitions of modern art and a museum of local history (including pictures of the Battle of the Saints) set in the vast, cool stone ramparts. Outside, among the cannon runners in the grass on the once formidable battlements, there is a botanical garden. There are a number of walks around the island. One peak worth climbing is **La Bosse du Chameau** (camel's hump) at the other end of the island, where the *tour modèle* dwarfs Fort Napoléon and gives a fine view from nearly 1,000ft over the whole area.

You can visit **Ilet à Cabri** (Goat Island) where there is another fort, called Fort Joséphine. **Grand Ilet** is a protected sea-bird reserve and can be visited by prior arrangement. **Terre-de-Bas** has a number of ruined estate buildings inland and a couple of good beaches, including Grande Anse, the site of one of the island's two settlements, and the Anse à Dos on the leeward coast.

The least known of all Les Saintes is the island of **St-Jacques**. Christened Santiago de los Vientos Alicios, it was jokingly known as 'Jack of all Trades' to the English filibusters who plied their trade of 'cruize and plunder' from its shores. The only historian to mention it is a certain Father Jerome Zancarol, who wrote that the food was good, the girls were beautiful and that the islanders' morals were the worst he had come across anywhere in the world. Apparently, sailors have heard the sound of violins on the 61st meridian, but the only record of the island's illustrious story is in *The Violins of St Jacques*, by Patrick Leigh Fermor.

St Martin

French St Martin shares an island with Sint Maarten, a member of the Netherlands Antilles (*see* p.411) and it is the smallest island in the world to be shared by two nations. The French half in the north is divided from the Dutch side by an imaginary line, marked only by an obelisk and a *Bienvenue/Welkom* sign.

Situated at the north of the Eastern Caribbean chain, St Martin looks across to British Anguilla and is about 21 square miles (54sq km) in area (the Dutch half is around 16 square miles/43sq km). From afar the island is attractive; its beaches glint yellow against the blue of the sea and inland the yellow-green scrubland rises majestically to hills of 1,200ft. About 13 miles (21km) southeast is the other French island *commune* of St Barthélemy.

When you arrive, you will find that St Martin is crowded and built up. Everything is right here, though, for a trusty French break in the tropics, with windsurfers whistling across the bay and waterfront bistros ideal for lingering and watching a lunchtime fashion show – and even Paris-trained hairstylists who will come to your hotel room. And in the gourmet restaurants, of which there are plenty, the food is served with customary French flair: a jaunty coquetry and at times a certain infuriating nonchalance.

Beyond the seaside screen of beach chairs and palm trees, you will still find a few pockets of real French West Indian life, with French Caribbean markets and manners. *Zouk*, the music of the French islands of Martinique and Guadeloupe, is heard most in the local clubs.

If anything, over the past few years, St Martin has become more French than it was, as large numbers of investors and immigrants from France have come to the island. They expect the place to be as French as possible, and so the *supermarchés* are full of French food and the cars are French. You will even see people playing games of *pétanque*. The population has rocketed with the tourist industry, now by far the largest income generator. There is a certain French exclusivity in the language, but it is possible to get by in English.

The other major contributor is the French government. St Martin is a *commune* in the *région* of Guadeloupe and it is administered by a *sous-préfet* appointed from Paris. The islanders vote members on to the *conseil général* that sits in Basse-Terre, Guadeloupe, and directly in the French elections.

History

Although the two communities on either side of St Martin avoided each other for most of their history (a road between the two was not built until some way through the 20th century), it was not always possible: their pasts were occasionally linked and anyway quite similar. St Martin's history is included under Sint Maarten (*see* p.413).

Beaches

There are excellent beaches on both sides of the island (*see* also 'Sint Maarten', p.413). Those nearest the hotels are usually active and lively, but there are some more secluded ones too. Topless bathing is perfectly acceptable here and there are a few

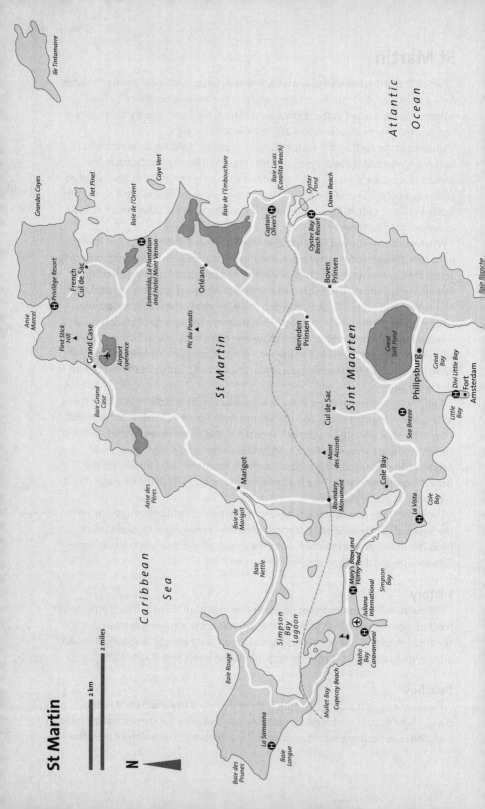

nude beaches (Baie de l'Orient is the only official one, but it has been known to happen at Baie Rouge and Baie Longue). On the larger beaches there are often concessionaires who will hire out snorkelling and windsurfing equipment (some beaches also have changing facilities). Some of the island's best beaches are on the eastern Atlantic coast, even though the sea is a little rougher there. You may see the word *'anse'* on the French side – it means cove and there are one or two delightful ones to visit. There has been some theft on beaches all over the island and so you are advised not to leave belongings unattended. *See also* 'Best Beaches', p.310.

Marigot

Like its Dutch counterpart Philipsburg, Marigot has just a few streets, clustered between the sea and a salt pond, but, whereas the Dutch town looks inwards to its shops, Marigot looks out across the water. It is quite a nice small town, with active areas on two sides where you can sit and linger with just a few distractions between meals.

The old warehouses of the esplanade, **bd de France**, are now fitted out with bistros, streetfront awnings and parasols, and there is a new central area on the waterfront with some snack bars, a car park and the local market (*best Wed and Sat mornings*), where there are tourist stalls but also local produce (much of it shipped in from other islands) on sale. Behind, the few streets have recently been restored and you will see the old wrought-iron balustrades of the few town houses and municipal buildings among the pastel-fronted shopping arcades. The marina **Port la Royale** is another lively area, lined on all sides with restaurants and bars. Some new roads have been built recently in an attempt to alleviate the inevitable problems of traffic.

The town, which takes its name from the swampy area of land that once existed in the corner of the bay (reclaimed long ago), first grew up in the 1680s, when the danger of raids that had forced the islanders inland to Orléans was passed. In the 1760s the fear revived; this time it was navies on the rampage rather than marauding boatloads of pirates, and so **Fort Louis** was constructed on the heights above the town, its outer walls using the contours and rock formations already there and its inner citadel a separate building. It is neat and well kept and has a few cannon that command a fine view of Anguilla, from where the old adversaries would nip over at the first sniff of war. The path to the fort leads past the church, with its fresco of a black Virgin in a Caribbean scene, the hospital and the Sous-préfecture, the residence of the island administrator.

Around the Island

The road west from the town leads from Baie Marigot and the Simpson Lagoon to Sandy Ground and is lined with hotels and local residences. On the left you will come to the excellent **St Martin Museum** (*t 29 22 84; open Mon–Sat 9–1 and 3–6, English*

Best Beaches

Baie Longue (Long Bay): A cracking mile of soft golden sand on the west of the French side, probably the best beach on the island. The best swimming is at the bottom end (near the Samanna Hotel). Take food and drinks.

Baie des Prunes (Plum Bay): Just round the corner, an afternoon suntrap, but with palms for shade and good snorkelling (but watch out for the rocks when swimming).

Baie Rouge: A fantastic stretch of golden sand with crystalline water that looks north toward Anguilla, liveliest at its eastern end. Huts have parasols, beach chairs and snorkelling gear for hire and drinks for sale. From the eastern end you can swim round to an idyllic smaller cove, Crique Lune de Miel (Honeymoon Cove).

Baie Nettle: The built-up strip to the north of Simpson Lagoon that runs into Marigot. The sand is all right and most watersports can be arranged here.

Anse des Pères (Friars' Bay) and **Happy Bay**: Two small isolated coves between Marigot and Grand Case. Some watersports and a couple of beach bars on Anse des Pères.

Baie Grand Case: Even the towns are on passable beaches in St Martin; a string of restaurants and bars sit above the water on this stretch of superb sand: sports equipment is available and there are plenty of places to retreat to at the height of the sun.

Anse Marcel: This has been built up and so the valley is dominated by an infestation of mock-classical gingerbread, but the beach has brilliant white sand enclosed by enormous headlands. A short walk round the western point takes you to the tiny and secluded Duck Beach.

Baie de l'Orient: On the east coast as the name suggests, a stunning mile of fine white sand and clear blue water. It is very active at the northern end, with lines of beach chairs and sports on offer (even massage on the beach). There are some swimming areas and some areas reserved for motorized sports, which are available here (even trips on a little seaplane). Officially the southern end is a naturalist beach and so the odd nudie might wander by.

Islands: St Martin also has some offshore islands in the northeast, where you can go for a day's excursion: the Ilet Pinel, not far offshore at French Cul de Sac (from where you can get a ferry) and Ile Tintamarre.

and French; *adm exp*), with very detailed, if quite technical descriptions of the archaeological history of the island: the Archaic or Ciboney Indians, who left shaped shells and stone tools, the Huecoid Arawaks, who are remembered in their pottery and amulets, the Saladoid Arawaks, with more intricate pottery with ghostly faces, and lastly the Caribs, who left their *zemis*, stone interpretations of their gods. There are also colonial artefacts: swords, musket balls and bottles; indigo, cotton and sugar. Finally the early 20th century is remembered in a series of old-time photographs of the island.

Leaving Marigot in the other direction you pass beneath the **Pic du Paradis**, the island's highest point, from where on a clear day there are fantastic views of islands as far away as Nevis (about 60 miles).

Getting There

St Martin t (590–)

By Air

Most flights arrive at Juliana International Airport on the Dutch side of the island (code SXM), which has excellent services and is the hub for the area. *See* p.415 for details of flights into Juliana Airport from Paris (Air France, **t** 51 02 02), Amsterdam (KLM), Miami and New York (American Airlines, Continental and US Airways), and San Juan in Puerto Rico (American Eagle), and connections to other Caribbean islands. Air Antilles Express, **t** 87 35 03, *www.airantilles.com*, offers inter-island flights. There is a departure tax of €20/US$20.

On the French side, Espérance Airport (code SFG) near Grand Case cannot take jet aircraft, but some hopper flights do put in here on Air Caraïbes, **t** 87 10 36, *info@aircaraibes.com*.

By Sea

There are daily ferry links to St Barthélemy, on the new high-speed catamaran *Rapid Explorer*, **t** 542 9762, *www.rapidexplorer.com*. *Voyager*, **t** 87 10 68, *www.yoyager-st-barths.com*, departs twice daily from St Martin, for a 75min trip. *Voyager* also does a weekly run to Saba. There is a ferry from Blowing Point, Anguilla, to Marigot if you wish to go across for the day (20 min; about US$24 return); departures about every half-hour.

Getting Around

By Bus

If you arrive at the airport on the Dutch side, the easiest way up to the French half is by taxi as hardly any buses run past the airport. Buses do run from Marigot down to Philipsburg and up to Grand Case, with the occasional link on to Orléans. They leave from the rue de Hollande behind Marigot (fare to Philipsburg about US$1.50) from early in the morning for the workers and they run until about midnight (not so late to outlying areas).

By Taxi

Taxis come two a penny (except in price) and are easily available at both airports and at the hotels. A taxi rank also works from the Marigot waterfront, **t** 87 56 54, and from Quartier d'Orléans, **t** 87 31 44. For a taxi boat call **t** 87 91 74.

Sample prices are: Marigot to Grand Case – US$10, east coast – US$15, Baie Longue – US$15, Juliana Airport – US$12, Philipsburg – US$12.

By Guided Tour

A morning's tour of the island is easily arranged, though there is not much to see except views across St Martin to the surrounding islands. Shopping stops and time to pause in the bistros are built in to the tour. Hotel desks will fix one for you or you can go through:

St Martin Evasion, DNC, BP 1144, Marigot 97062, **t** 87 13 60, *sxmevasion@power antilles.com*.

Car and Bike Hire

For maximum mobility, to hunt down a few duty-free bargains in Philipsburg or go out to dinner in the evenings, hire a car. There are plenty available at around US$45 per day with taxes, jeeps from about US$55. Any foreign licence is valid and driving is on the right side of the road. Hotels will arrange for cars to be delivered. The island's three towns do get congested, so leave plenty of time to get to the airport.

Some local firms as well as big international rental companies work from the Dutch side (*see* 'Sint Maarten', p.416). If you are fond of scams and are prepared to spend a couple of hours being given the hard sell about 'investment in vacationing' in a condominium complex, you can sometimes score a '$50 off your rental bill' voucher.

Avis, t 87 50 60. Has an outlet on the French side.

Europcar, t 77 10 46.

Flamboyant, Grand Case, **t** 87 50 99.

Hertz, t 87 40 68. Also on the Dutch side.

Island Transportation, Marigot, **t** 87 91 32.

Location 2 Roues, Galerie Commerciale, Baie Nettle, **t** 87 20 59. Contact this place to hire a scooter or bicycle.

Rent-A-Scooter, t 87 20 59. Motorcycles as well as scooters.

Sandyg, Sandy Ground, **t** 87 88 25.

Tourist Information

Abroad

The official website is at *www.st-martin.org*. You might also try *www.sxmhotels.com*, which has information and deals. Of course you can also find plenty of information on the Dutch side's website, at *www.st-maarten.com*.

France: 30 rue Saint-Marc, 75002 Paris, t 01 53 29 99 99, *otsxmparis@aol.com*, *www. st-martin.org*.

Canada: Maison de la France, 1981 Ave MacGill College, Suite 490, Montreal, Quebec H3A 2W9, t (514) 876 9881.

USA: St Martin Tourist Board, 675 3rd Ave, Suite 1807, New York, NY 10017, t 1877 956 1234, t (212) 475 8970, *sxmtony@msm.com*.

In St Martin

Route de Sandy Ground, Marigot, 97150 St Martin, t 87 57 21, *sxmto@aol.com*, *www. st-martin.org*. Sits on the waterfront in Marigot. *Open Mon–Fri 8.30–1 and 2.30–5.30, Sat 8–noon*.

Media

If you think you might be spending time on the beach, remember to make a selection from the superabundance of tourist literature that litters the airport when you arrive. Of all the magazines, the most revealing and best informed is the publication *Discover*, which has some features alongside the normal tourist advice. *Reflets* is the official Tourist Board publication and there are a number of dining guides. *Saint-Martin Week* magazine is another. Radio St Martin on FM 101.5 plays a good variety of Caribbean music.

Medical Emergencies

In a medical emergency, there is a hospital in Marigot, t 87 87 67.

Money and Banks

The official **currency** of St Martin is the euro (US$1 = €0.80 approx). However, with so many visitors from America, the greenback is accepted everywhere; in local shops and eateries you may receive your change in euros and cents. **Credit cards** are widely accepted all over the island.

There are three **banks** in Marigot and they keep different hours, so you can usually find somewhere to change money during the day. Hotels are always willing to change money, but the rate will not be so good.

Shopping

Shop hours as in France: Mon–Fri 9–1 and 3–7. In Marigot you might try Oro de Sol for watches and Cartier for jewellery.

Telephone Code

To telephone St Martin from abroad, the IDD code is t 590 followed by the six-digit local number. Within St Martin, dial just the six digits. Phoning from the French to the Dutch side, dial t 00 599 and then the seven-digit number, and from the Dutch to the French side dial t 00 590 followed by the six digits. There are no coin boxes on the French side and so you will need to buy a *télécarte* from the post office or the few newsagents that stock them.

Festivals

February–March *Carnival*. Celebrated at the beginning of Lent (usually end February or early March) with street parades in Marigot and Grand Case on *Mardi Gras* and *Mercredi des Cendres* (on the Dutch side, Carnival is at Easter).
Heineken Regatta. Held annually in March in both parts of the island.

July *Bastille Day*. Sees fireworks (14th).
Schoelcher Day. Celebrated on 21 July with sailing races in traditional island vessels.
Grand Case. Holds a general blowout at the end of July.

November *St Martin's Day*. Joint celebrations with the Dutch side.

Various dates A number of deep-sea fishing tournaments are held during the year.

Watersports

St Martin caters quite well for watersports around its beaches, around the hotels and particularly on Baie de l'Orient, the liveliest on the island, where you can fix anything from beach volleyball and parasailing to a round-island guided tour by jet-ski, t 27 49 94. Most hotels have sailing dinghies for hire and they are usually available to allcomers. General watersports operators include:

Blue Ocean International, Baie Nettle, t 87 89 73, *contact@blueocean.ws, www. blueocean.ws.*

Kontiki Watersports, Baie de l'Orient, t 87 46 89, *www.sxm-game.com.*

Kali's, Anse des Pères, t 51 07 42. Kayaks.

Day Sails

Lots of possibilities in St Martin, arranged through the hotel concessionaires or watersports shops. Some day cruises go to other islands like Anguilla. Contact:

Marine Times, Marigot, t 52 02 53, *marine times@wanadoo.fr.* Also offers cruises to Anguilla.

MV *Voyager*, t 87 10 68, *voyager.sxm@ wanadoo.fr.* Sails to St Barts.

Orient Bay Catamarans, t 87 78 04, *obernaz@yahoo.fr.* Another option for a cruise to St Barts.

Sea Hawk, t 87 59 49. Day cruises to Anguilla.

Deep-sea Fishing

Trips can be arranged (about US$700 for a full day) at the marinas. There are good fishing grounds off the Anguillan islands, where you can cast for bonito and spiked-back wahoo. Contact:

CSB, Port la Royale Marina, on the lagoon in Marigot, t 87 89 38.

Deep Sea Fishing, t 87 86 83.

Major Fishing, t 87 96 76.

Sailing

There are three marinas where yachts can be hired for a day, a week or a month, perhaps for a trip to a neighbouring island. The biggest is Port de Lonvilliers in Anse Marcel.

The Moorings, at Captain Oliver's Marina on the east coast, t 87 32 55, *www.moorings.com.*

Nautor's Swan Charter, Port de Lonvilliers, t 87 35 48, US t 1 800 356 7926, *nautor.swan@ wanadoo.fr, www.nautor-swan.com.*

Stardust Marine, Port de Lonvilliers, t 29 50 50. Yachts and pleasure craft for hire.

Sunsail, Port Royale Marina, located on the lagoon in Marigot, t 29 50 50, *maritime@ wanadoo.fr.*

VPM, Anse Marcel, t 29 41 35, *vpmsaint-martin@cgit.com.*

Scuba Diving

You will see the reefs patrolled by sergeant-major fish and grunts off the bay of Grandes Cayes on the shoreline and offshore around the islands in the northeast. A single-tank dive costs around US$45. Dives and instruction (PADI and NAUI) are available through:

Blue Ocean Dive Centre, Baie Nettle, t 87 89 73.

Octoplus, Grand Case, t 87 20 62, *octoplus@smea.fr.*

Scuba Fun Dive Centre, Anse Marcel, t 87 36 13, *contact@scubafun.com, www.scubafun.com.*

Snorkelling

There are excellent corals (do not pick any or use a spear gun against the fish, as they are protected) in places off St Martin, particularly off the northeast of the island where there is a marine reserve.

The best beaches are Baie Rouge near the western point of the island and Caye Vert opposite Baie de l'Orient on the Atlantic side (also Ilet Pinel and Tintamarre). There are many glass-bottom boats and a large semi-submersible:

Seaworld Explorer, departs from Grand Case, contact on the Dutch side, t 52 40 78, *www.atlantisadventures.com/stmartin.*

Windsurfing and Kiteboarding

Windsurfing is very popular on the French side of the island. You can get a board in Baie Nettle or Grand Case, but the winds are best on the east coast, where Baie de l'Embouchure is a good place to learn because of the gentler sea and onshore winds, and Baie de l'Orient is the one to head for if you like speed sailing. Contact:

Club Nathalie Simon, t 21 41 57, *info@ wind-adventures.com, www.wind-adventures.com.* For all standards of windsurfers; kiteboarding lessons.

Club Orient Watersports, t 87 33 85.

Kitesurfing School, t 29 41 57, *www. go-kitsurfing.com.*

Other Sports

Golf

There is a course on the Dutch side:

Mullet Bay Resort, t 00 599 545 3069, ext 1850. Green fees are very high, US$110 for the 18 holes, and residents of the hotel have preference in teeing off.

Hiking

A number of trails have been cut into the St Martin scrub, taking in the Mont des Accords and the Pic du Paradis, which give cracking views of the islands and lowlands. The island's limited flora and fauna ranges from soldier crabs in their conical shells to the mournful white cattle egret on land and the yellowlegs who scurry around the mangrove swamps. **Action Nature, t** 29 22 84.

Horse-riding

An early-morning dip on horseback can be arranged through:

Bayside Riding Club, near Baie de l'Orient, **t** 87 36 64, *bayside20@hotmail.com*.
OK Corral, Oyster Pond, **t** 87 40 72.

Mountain biking

This has recently grown up on the island and there are now trails cut all over the place. Contact:

Bike Power Cycle, t 87 13 74.
Frog Legs, t 87 05 11, *frog.legs@wanadoo.fr*.

Tennis

There are about 50 courts on the island, many of them lit for night-play. Contact any of the larger hotels.

Where to Stay

St Martin **t** (590–)

Until recently it was the Dutch side that had the block resort hotels, thrown up by speculators as an investment, but they have now arrived in St Martin too. However, there are also a few more stylish places to stay dotted around the island, such as the French West Indian inns. Except in guest houses, the rates quoted usually include breakfast. A small government tax of 5% is added to your bill, and service is 10% or 15%.

Luxury

La Samanna, Baie Longue, PO Box 4077, 97064 St Martin Cedex, **t** 87 64 00, US **t** 1 800 854 2252, *lasamanna.orient-express.com*. An enclave of super-luxury, set above the magnificent sweep of Baie Longue in the west of the island. The main house, with its palm-thatched dining room with wicker chairs, stands on a bluff above the pool and sea, and the 80 extremely elegant and comfortable rooms, suites and villas are ranged right behind the sand, set in pretty tropical gardens. A theme of stark white and royal blue, the colour of the sea on a bright day, runs through the resort. Top-notch service and comfort and a simply superb sunset. Every comfort to give you the ultimate rest-cure (weights room, massage and beauty treatments, 24-hour room service). Certainly the most elegant place on the island to stay as well as the most expensive.
Privilège Resort and Spa, Anse Marcel, 97150, **t** 87 38 38, US **t** 1 800 874 8541, *privilege@wanadoo.fr, www.privilege-spa.com*. Has a rarefied position high on the side of the hill in Anse Marcel, in the north of the island. There are 37 rooms, some perched with a cracking view towards Anguilla, pleasant and comfortable, with bright Caribbean décor and all the necessities for a luxurious life (TV, VCR, radio, minibars). The hotel specializes in spa treatment with massages, shiatsu, lymphatic drainage, tonic cure, hydrojet, seaweed body mask, algotherapy, water-jet steam room... and there is a sports centre: weights room, tennis, golf practice, squash, racketball and shuttles down to the beach below. If you need a body-holiday there's plenty on offer here, and the atmosphere is quite brisk and efficient.

Expensive

Marquis Hotel Resort & Spa, Anse Marcel 91750, **t** 29 42 30, US **t** 800 742 4276, *hotel-marquis@wanadoo.fr, www.hotel-marquis.com*. Fourteen spacious rooms and suites in a creole style – all with king bed, satellite television, minibar, sofa bed, phone and a large terrace looking out over a panoramic view of the bay. Spa, fitness centre, four tennis courts and swimming pool.

Esmeralda Resort, Baie de l'Orient, PO Box 5141, 97071 St Martin, **t** 87 36 36, *esmeralda@ wanadoo.fr, www.esmeralda-resort.com*. Lies in the cluster of hotels at the top of Baie de l'Orient, and is probably the most comfortable. Sixty-five units set in pretty terraced villas that echo the best of old Caribbean style with louvres, verandas and gently sloping roofs. The rooms, which look onto their own pool, have all you need in the way of 21st-century comfort, with wicker furnishings, king-sized beds, TVs, phones, safes and kitchenettes. Sports on offer right on the sand, but a fine place to sit and relax on an old-time veranda.

Captain Oliver's Hotel, Oyster Pond, 97150 St Martin, **t** 87 40 26, *infoweb@captainolivers. com, www.captainolivers.com*. Surrounded by all the activity of the marina with an easy, nautical feel. There are 35 rooms, all brightly decorated with white tiles and pastel colours, with balconies overlooking the marina or the offshore islands towards St Barts. Kitchenettes in the rooms. Covered bar of dark wood with a pool one side and the harbour the other, where the boats dock. The hotel is not on the beach, but there is a large pool on the point and a boat taxi will take you across to Dawn Beach. Watersports and sailing.

Hotel Mont Vernon, Baie de l'Orient, BP 1174 Baie Orientale, 97062 St Martin, **t** 87 62 00, US **t** (212) 673 3660, *www.mont-vernon.com*. An active resort-style hotel which sits on a hillside above the beach. Lots of watersports and evening entertainment.

Hotel La Plantation, Baie de l'Orient, **t** 29 58 00, *hotel@la-plantation.com, www. la-plantation.com*. Another nice spot, with the advantage of being just above Baie de l'Orient. Forty-nine rooms (16 suites and 33 studios) in styles that reflect old Caribbean architecture: wood-tiled roofs that reach over verandas with carved wooden balustrades and louvres (they can be closed off and air-conditioned or opened up to the breeze). Inside they are comfortable and modern, with cable TV and phone. There are two restaurants.

Moderate

Grand Case has a number of smaller mid-range hotels and guest houses. Most do not have pools, but they are right above the waves.

Pavillon Beach Hotel, Grand Case, PO Box 5133, **t** 87 96 46, *pavillon.beach@wanadoo.fr*. Stands high above the sand in a modern building on the waterfront and has 17 compact studios and suites with kitchenettes, and a pretty terrace with balustrade from which to admire the sea.

Hévéa Hotel, 163 bd de Grand Case, **t** 87 56 85, *hevea@outremer.com, www.hotel-hevea. com*. A stylish spot, set in and around a restored colonial house across the road from the beach and in more modern buildings behind. Some rooms have been redone in old West Indian style, with muslin bednetting and dark wooden furniture. There is a nice dining area and a sitting area where the guests gather and read the books scattered around or chat in the early evening.

Chez Martine, PO Box 637, Grand Case, **t** 87 51 59, *chezmartine@powerantilles.com, www. chezmartine.com*. Just five large and comfortable air-conditioned rooms and one suite giving on to a large terrace in a house in Antillean style, carpeted and with some king-sized beds with wicker headboards. Quite private and quiet, and a nice restaurant on a terrace right above the waves.

Grand Case Beach Club, 21 rue du Petite Plage, **t** 87 51 87, US **t** 1 800 537 8483, *www.grand casebeachclub.com*. Seventy-five newly renovated ocean-front rooms and apartments in five two- and three-storey buildings separated from the beach by a colourful garden. Excellent beachfront restaurant and bar. Facilities include watersports, tennis and swimming pool.

Inexpensive

There are also some cheapish places to stay on the Dutch side (*see* pp.419–20).

Cigalon, in the backstreets of Marigot beneath Fort Louis, **t** 87 08 19, *www.cigalon.hotel.com*. The guesthouse rooms are a little enclosed but there is a nice terrace with vines growing over it from where you can watch town life go by.

Eating Out

Eating out is something of a pastime in St Martin and there are some excellent restaurants on the island – offering both classical French cuisine and its creole counterpart. In fact, between them, the two sides of the island have about 500 places to eat so, if you are one for a gastronomic steeplechase, there is plenty to occupy you here. Most of the restaurants serve basically French food which has often been adapted to fit the climate: 'cuisine française aux parfums des îles' as one restaurant expressed it neatly. Pretty well anything you would want to eat will be served here – duck, oysters, some venison – some of which don't really belong to the Caribbean. It is all imported daily from France and Miami. There is not really any need to dress up anywhere in the island except in the smartest hotels, but most restaurants would prefer you not to go in shorts during the evening.

Prices are not cheap, but on the French side service is compris. **Categories** are arranged according to the price of a main course: expensive = US$20 and above; moderate = US$10–20; inexpensive = under US$10. For restaurants on the Dutch side, see pp.420–1.

Expensive

Grand Case calls itself the 'gourmet capital of St Martin' and has a string of excellent restaurants. They all make the best of their settings on the waterfront – at night their lights shine out into the bay like a bar code – and so you will find yourself sitting at the edge of a terrace right above the waves. Most of them offer fundamentally French fare with a concession to the Caribbean in the lighter sauces and the mix of fruits and other spices.

Fish Pot, 83 bd de Grand Case, t 87 50 88. Perhaps the finest, set on a very elegant veranda with dark-stained wood and blue and white furnishings above the beach, where birds twitter along in their own search for food. Start with sea scallop kebab in a coconut mango sauce or soupe des poissons des Caraïbes followed by a filet de daurade coriphène in a lemon and Jamaican pimento sauce or a magret de canard.

L'Auberge Gourmande, 89 bd de Grand Case, t 87 73 37. Charmingly set in a stone town house with louvred windows and doors opening on to the street. Friendly and intimate dining room for Caribbean and French fare: millefeuille de mahi-mahi au beurre de citron et orange (pastry-caked mahi mahi with orange and lemon butter sauce) or poulet poche aux pommes et au cidre (chicken breast in apples and cider).

Le Tastevin, 86 bd de Grand Case, t 87 55 45. Has an air of well-ordered calm; you sit in a charming waterfront dining room among palm-tree trunks and tropical foliage, with some alcoves reaching out towards the waves. Again French cuisine and some creative concessions to Caribbean flavours – rosaie de St-Jacques aux fruits de la passion (scallops in a passion-fruit sauce) and médaillons de thon (tuna) sur un lit d'aubergine.

Le Gaïac, Front de Mer, t 51 97 66, www.le-west-indies.com. On the terrace of the West Indies Shopping Mall, overlooking Marigot Bay, the gourmet restaurant is one of the best in St Martin. The menu offers French cuisine with Caribbean flavours. Dinner only.

Le Rainbow, 176 bd de Grand Case, t 87 55 80. A third excellent option in the town. A little more casual in style, and the food is studiedly simple but is equally good. Here too you can also sit right above the water. You can start with a compendium of tastes in the noix de St-Jacques, terrine de saumon et crevettes, au beurre Nantais followed by a filet de vivaneau (snapper) au croustillant de parmesan d'oignons.

La Vie en Rose, bd de France, Marigot, t 87 54 42. An ever-popular dining room, which has a commanding view over the waterfront square from the first-floor balcony with white and candy-pink awnings. Innovative French cuisine is what they boast – try les tournedos d'espadon et de thon aux cinq poivres (sword-fish and tuna in five peppers) or filet de vivaneau en croûte et sa crème de safran et caviar. A rose for the lady at the end of dinner and an impressively large bill.

Moderate

Sunset Café, Grand Case Beach Club, Grand Case, t 87 51 87. Set on pilings like a dock at the water's edge, the casual restaurant serves for the best seafood in St Martin at affordable prices. Menu also has continental food, American favourites and snacks.

L'Escapade, 94 bd de Grand Case, **t** 87 75 04. A charming, family-run restaurant where you dine on the waterfront veranda attached to an old creole house. There are two cocktail rooms in the older part of the house and then you move above the water to dine on French and creole cuisine. Start with a lobster bisque and then try mahi mahi in a vanilla sauce or a *tartare de thon et sa mousseline de raifort* (raw tuna tartare with horseradish), followed by one of the many fruit ice creams.

Le Bistrot Nu, allée de l'Ancienne Géôle, Marigot, **t** 87 97 09. Hidden in an alley in the backstreets of Marigot (on the left as you leave Marigot to the north, opposite the school). This is one of the liveliest creole restaurants and has the very original setting of an old wooden creole house. *Paysanne* salad and Provençale scallops, even a *boudin*, a creole blood sausage. It is fun, but it is small, so you have to be quite flexible about when you eat. *Open Mon–Sat 6.30–midnight.*

Case Creole, Sandy Ground, **t** 87 28 45. In a pretty French Caribbean *case* with wooden walls and gingerbread pointing. The cuisine is French creole, so you can expect *boudins* and *colombos* to go with fresh fish.

Yvette's Restaurant, hidden away in the Quartier d'Orléans, **t** 87 32 03. Serves excellent West Indian cuisine; lobster or conch stew or a seafood platter. *Closed Wed.*

Paradise View, Hope Hill, **t** 77 15 12. A dead cool setting above Orient Beach with a lovely view out to sea through large windows.

Le Poulet d'Orléans, Orléans, **t** 87 48 24. Set in a traditional island house with a brightly decorated domestic veranda out front. Cosy atmosphere for great French Caribbean fish and (of course) chicken dishes.

Inexpensive

In Marigot you can eat quite cheaply in the café bars along the waterfront, where there are often evening grills. Grand Case has some pleasant places to eat for a cheaper meal.

Calmos Café, Grand Case, **t** 29 01 85. A cool beach-side setting, where you eat under parasols and palm trees.

Les Lolos, Grand Case. One of the best places to eat, where the food is cooked in front of you on flaming grills in the neat new building at the roadside: Jimbo Lolo, Chez Germaine, Cool Out Bar, Starzie's Place, Chez Cheryl and Talk of the Town. Grilled chicken, ribs, lobster, shrimp, stuffed crab, johnny cake, macaroni, plantain and rice and peas, take away or sit in at the easy-going waterfront bars.

Bars and Nightlife

There are no casinos on the French side, but if you feel in need of a flutter there are plenty on the Dutch side of the island.

La Belle Epoque, Terrace des Naufrages, Port Royale Marina, **t** 87 87 70. A pleasant café.

L'Arawak, opposite the Bar de la Mer, Marigot, **t** 87 99 67. Always popular, with live music.

Tatoo, Baie Nettle Bay, **t** 87 78 64. Can get lively – pizzas and beer, rock music.

Surf Club South, Cul de Sac, between Grand Case and the Baie de l'Orient, **t** 29 50 40. Also gets quite lively.

Chez Raymond, Terres Basses, **t** 0690 27 44 97. Antillean specialities. Live music on Sundays.

Beach Bars

There are a number of free and easy haunts above the waves in St Martin where you can linger over a beer after a dip.

Coco Beach, **Waikiki Beach**, **Bikini Beach**, **Kakao Beach** and **Kontiki Beach**, Baie de l'Orient. Each with a range of coloured beach chairs out front and most with a covered terrace and tables scattered around a sandy garden; salads, grills and some creole dishes.

Calmos Café, Grand Case, **t** 29 01 85. Cable-barrels under parasols, and golden palms on the sand.

Kali's Beach Bar, Friar's Bay, **t** 49 06 81, *kali-beach-bar@wanadoo.fr*, *www.kali-beach-bar.com*. A hip spot where you might spend hours admiring the colours of the sea to the tune of reggae and dub or just the susurration of the waves. Standard West Indian chicken and fish is served on the wooden deck above the sand. Full-moon party.

Friar's Bay Beach Café, near to Kali's, **t** 49 16 87. Stages live music on Sun evenings in season.

Grand Case is really a single shoreside street lined with old and new houses and festooned in tropical greenery, set on the wide sweep of the magnificent Baie Grand Case. There is a friendly feel to the place and it regularly draws crowds of tourists to its excellent restaurants and bars. But there is also something of a local West Indian life here and you might even see a cockfight in a pit at the western end of the village. Other spectator sports include watching the planes come in over the rooftops to land at the airstrip just behind the town. On Sundays there is often a jump-up on the beach, with a disco on the pier and braziers cooking chicken and soldier crabs in their shells.

Beyond here you come to the **Butterfly Farm** (*t 87 31 21; open daily 9–4.30; adm exp*), which is worth a quick visit. There are 30 or so tropical species from around the world. To a background of suitable music you will see them through their two-week lifespan: from caterpillar and then chrysalis, like jade and electric blue earrings, through emergence, flight, feeding (on the over-ripe fruits left lying around), more tipsy flight, mating and then death. Species include the owl butterfly, the zebra, the postman and huge monarchs.

Orléans, or the 'French Quarter', is a collection of villas and one or two shops, which used to be the capital of the French half of the island in the early days.

St Barthélemy

St Barthélemy is one of the most chic, civilized and least-known parts of France. Here bronzed beauties cruise by on the beaches in just a nuance of a bathing costume, and out in the bay the water whistles with windsurfers in red, white and blue. Dior, Chanel, Lacroix, mobiles and *mobylettes*, jazz, restaurants to linger in, *haute cuisine* and Veuve Cliquot champagne. The island's even got its own brand of perfume. It's a chichi playground, as only the French could conceive. Even tourist brochures are stylish and sexy in St Barts.

Lying 15 miles (24km) southeast of St Martin in the north of the Lesser Antilles, St Barts is a crooked six miles by three (10km by 5km) – folds of volcanic lava and rubble that have been pushed up from beneath the ocean and sprouted a mantle of scrub. The fragmented coastline has some lovely coves, many of them culminating in perfect strands. There is an admirable neatness about the place and it is very attractive, as well as surprisingly rugged for an island of its size. St Barthélemy (pronounced 'San Bar-tailer-mee' in French) is the island's formal name, but it is hardly ever used. It is usually known as St Barth in French and St Barts in English. There are about 6,000 islanders.

Strangely, for much of the 19th century, St Barts belonged to Sweden. It was a successful trading outpost. But they wave baguettes happily in the streets nowadays. Despite their interlude as Swedes, the St Barthéleminois are mostly descended from French settlers and you might see a traditional bonnet or hear a snatch of a strange French dialect in the shops in the original villages. The population has always been predominantly white because there were never many slaves.

As the tourist industry has steadily grown in the last 30 years, St Barts has taken on an overlay of the *République* – there is practically no recognizable West Indian culture outside the cultivated prettiness of the tropical gardens – and has turned from one of the quietest Caribbean islands in the area into a trusted home-from-home for a star-studded cast of expatriate French and Americans. Like many Caribbean islands it was raffish and eccentric in the early years and there was no telling whom you might rub shoulders with in the bars. Nowadays it has less of the raw edge and a more professional, thoroughgoing attitude to tourism.

They do it with gusto and aplomb, though, and it is easy to have an excellent holiday in St Barts. There are some superb restaurants with huge wine cellars (some restaurateurs actually ship wine young in St Barts because it travels better); there are art galleries in the hotel foyers and fashion shows in the beach bars to amuse you over lunch. The island is a little snobby at times, but people are on holiday, so it is generally friendly and easy-going. It is the favoured haunt of a crowd of transient millionaires on their crusade against winter.

History

St Barts was not visited by Columbus, but later travellers called the island after his brother, Bartolomeo, who went with him to the New World. Like the rest of the Leewards it was given a wide berth by the Spanish colonists for their first

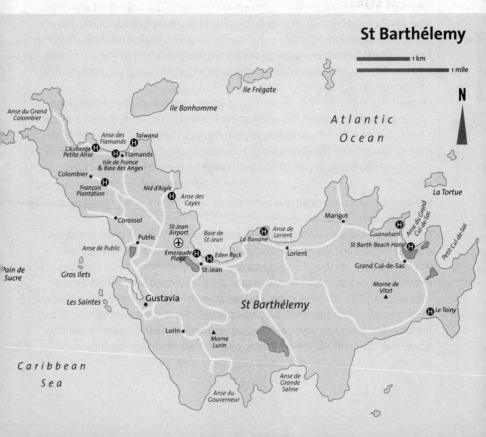

St Barthélemy

Best Beaches

Anse du Gouverneur and Anse de Grande Saline: Both have stacks of bright white sand that shelve steeply into the sea in their own deep bays, with views of the volcanic peaks of Saba, St Eustatius and St Kitts. Both are popular, as you will see by the hundred-yard line of mini-mokes and jeeplets, but as yet there are no beach bars. Take all you need in the way of water and food, and shade as well because there are not even parasols for hire. Anse du Gouverneur is best approached via Lurin (south out of Gustavia) and Anse de Grande Saline from St Jean. Bathers at Anse de Grande Saline tend to shed more and more clothes the further west you head.

Petit Cul-de-Sac: A small secluded cove bordered by mangrove.

Anse du Grand Cul-de-Sac: A shallow bay protected by a reef; good for swimming and windsurfing (receives winds straight off the Atlantic). There are a couple of hotels here, where you can get a drink and a meal or find watersports equipment. If you are feeling chic and wealthy, you might take lunch at the unfeasibly stylish Lafayette Club.

Lorient: In the east of the island as the name suggests, a nice curve of white sand. It is quiet, and good for families with children.

St-Jean: A calm double curve of perfect sand where the tanned scooter-brigade congregate, exercising their windsurfers or taking an occasional dip. The beach restaurant at Eden Rock has a pretty veranda retreat for real beachfront *dégustation*.

Anse des Flamands: 600 yards of quite big waves (watch the undertow) which wash large scallop patterns into the sand; a stunning view of the deserted Ile Bonhomme.

Anse du Grand Colombier: A walk off the beaten track from Petit Morne, palm-shaded and usually very secluded (take water and a picnic). West facing, so a cracking view of the sunset.

Corossol: Beyond the town to the north is another suntrap beneath the hills, in the fishing village of Corossol. Just down from the nets and the boats there is a strip of beige sand so soft that you sink up to your shins, and there's a cracking sunset view.

Anse de Grand Galet: The closest beach to Gustavia (about 10 minutes' walk), where shells are washed up in piles of pink and orange on the soft light-brown sand.

hundred years because Ouanalao, as the Caribs knew the island, was dangerous cannibal country.

Settlers came in 1659, eking a living out of the scrubby, difficult ground with such crops as tobacco and indigo, but the main source of income for the next hundred years really lay in the island's position and in its well-protected coves. Smugglers and pirates, en route from South America to the Bahamas, would use the bays to repair their ships, and the islanders made a tidy profit by selling them the provisions they needed to refit. The original St Barthéleminois were Frenchmen from Normandy and Brittany. They had a few slaves, domestic ones only because there were no plantations. Even late in the 18th century there were still less than 1,000 inhabitants on St Barts.

Then, on 1 July 1784, the St Barthéleminois woke to find that their island was no longer owned by France, but that they were on lease to Sweden. The King of France had simply swapped it for a warehouse in Gothenburg and trading rights in the Baltic, without even consulting them. St Barts was Sweden's only colony in the Caribbean and little remains of their influence except the old stone warehouses on the waterfront and a few street names in Gustavia, the capital. The Swedish reign benefited the islanders, however. King Gustav promptly declared the island a free port and before long St Barts was using the advantage of its position on the trade routes from Europe to the burgeoning United States and prospering as a market. While the other islands were held to ransom in the wars at the turn of the 18th century, St Barts continued to rake in the loot.

As soon as peace came to the Caribbean in the early 19th century and the seaborne trade waned, the island fell into a decline and the Swedish venture failed. The population, which had reached 5,000, began to tail off, particularly after the Swedish king emancipated the island's slaves in 1847. There was no land for the freed slaves to settle so they emigrated, mostly to the then Danish Virgin Islands (nowadays they are the USVI, to which there was another emigration from St Barts in the 1950s). In the end, King Oscar II put sovereignty to a referendum, and the islanders voted 351 to 1 to return to French rule. On 16 March 1878 St Barts was handed back to France.

Appended to Guadeloupe once again, the island's decline continued. When Guadeloupe was made an overseas *département* of France in 1946, St Barts became one of its *communes*, under its financial control. St Barts has retained its duty-free status since Swedish days.

Today it is administered, along with nearby St Martin, by a *sous-préfet* appointed from Paris. The islanders vote members on to the Conseil Général and the Conseil Régional, which sit in Basse-Terre, Guadeloupe, and directly in the French elections. Like St Martin, St Barts receives some assistance from the French government via Guadeloupe for roads and large municipal projects. Tourism is the big earner at the moment and the island maintains an exclusive and luxurious style.

Beaches

St Barts has magnificent beaches, mounds of golden sand tucked away in coves cut into the coastline, protected on both sides by mountainous headlands. Topless bathing is accepted and happens everywhere, but, surprisingly on a French island, nudity is against the rules. All beaches are public, though you may have to get permission to cross somebody's land (ask if they stop you). *Anse* means cove. The island's two best beaches are on the south coast: Anse du Gouverneur and Anse de Grande Saline.

Gustavia

Only hints of a Swedish heritage remain in St Barts' capital after a hundred years and the recent tourist redevelopment. Almost all of the original Swedish town was

Getting There

St Barthélemy t (590–)

By Air

St Barts cannot take international flights but it is well served from islands nearby, of which the most accessible is Sint Maarten (good connections); depending on your point of origin you might also head for Guadeloupe, Antigua or San Juan in Puerto Rico.

St Barth Commuter, t 27 54 54/27 54 58, *st-barth.commuter@wanadoo.fr*, *www.st-barths. com/stbarth-commuter*, has many flights each day to Juliana Airport in Sint Maarten, as does Winair, St Barts t 27 61 01, Sint Maarten t 00 599 55 4210, US t 1 800 634 4907, *www.fly-winair.com*. Air Caraïbes, t 27 61 90, *info@ aircaraibes.com*, *www.aircaraibes.com*, flies from St Martin (Grand Case), Guadeloupe, Puerto Rico and as far as Santo Domingo in the Dominican Republic. Air St Thomas, t 27 71 76, *air.st.thomas@worldnet.att.net*, *www. airstthomas.com*, flies from Puerto Rico and St Thomas.

From Antigua there are regular 'share-charter' flights on Carib Aviation, t 1 264 497 2719. You can charter a plane from these latter airlines, or through Air Culebra, Puerto Rico, t 787 268 6951, *airculebra@sprynet.com*, *www.airculebra.com*.

The airstrip on St Barts, t 27 65 41, situated on the improbably named Plaine de la Tourmente, is one of the most 'sporting' in the Caribbean. The main problem is that, whichever end you make your approach, there is a hill just where you should be lining up. And so from one end passengers get a close inspection of some hillside forest and the roof of a hotel, and from the other they drop close enough to the road to read car-drivers' T-shirts. If you look over the pilot's shoulder, it may seem that he is going to miss the runway, but the small planes are so manoeuvrable that they can turn on a sixpence. The runway in St Barts closes at dusk, but you can usually make connections the same day from Europe and the USA. There is a delightfully low airport tax of €6.

There are also helicopters available through St Martin (*see* p.311).

By Sea

If this all sounds a bit much, there are seaborne links to St Barts from St Martin (both Marigot and Philipsburg) on the new high-speed catamaran, *Rapid Explorer*, Pointe Blanche, St Maarten, t (599) 542 9762, *www.rapidexplorer*. Two others are *Voyager*, t 27 10 68, *voyager.sxm@wanadoo.fr*, *www.yoyager-st-barths.com*, which departs twice daily from St Martin, and the high-speed ferry, *The Edge*, t 544 2640, which leaves once daily, Tues–Sat, from Pelican Marina, St Maarten. To charter a high-speed boat to come and pick you up in St Maarten, contact Marine Service, t 27 70 34.

Getting Around

Taxis are usually available at the airport during the day and on the main quay in Gustavia, though it is occasionally difficult to get one after dinner in the evening. You can also order them through a hotel or through the central number in Gustavia, t 27 66 31, and at the airport, t 27 75 81. From the airport to Gustavia will set you back US$8–10 and to Grand Cul de Sac about US$17–20. There is no bus service on St Barts, but **hitching** is a reasonably dependable way to get around the island.

Car and Bike Hire

Recommended. It is fairly expensive, but of course it gives you much more flexibility. The island favourites are the Smart Car (with colour-changeable panels in case it doesn't go with your outfit) and the Suzuki jeep – it used to be the mini-moke and its Volkswagen equivalent, the Gurgel, but they have mostly disappeared now. These can just about cope with St Barts' many steep hills.

Some of the big international names operate out of the airport and many hotels keep cars for their guests. If you will want one during the high season, you should order it in advance. A foreign driving licence is valid, credit cards are accepted, driving is mostly on the right, and most companies will deliver to your hotel. The minimum price in season is about US$35 a day plus taxes. **Budget**, t 27 66 30, *budget@wanadoo.fr*.

Hertz, t 27 71 14.

Island Car Rental, t 27 70 01, *islandcr@saint-barths.com, www.islandcarrental.com.*

Smart of St Barth, t 29 71 31, *smart.of.st.barth@wanadoo.fr, www.car-rent.fr.*

Tropic' All Rent a Car, t 27 64 76, *tropic.all.rent@wanadoo.fr.*

Turbe Car Rental, t 27 60 70, *sbbh@saint-barths.com.*

Scooters are also easily available for hire, though they are less likely to get you up the steep hills:

Chez Béranger, t 27 89 00.

Rent Some Fun, t 27 70 59. The exclusive Harley Davidson dealer (if there are any on island), for scooters and bigger bikes.

Tourist Information

Abroad

Internationally, publicity for St Barts is handled by Guadeloupe (*see* p.284) and the Maisons de France around the world. The island has a website at *www.st-barths.com.* You can also find information on *www.sb-wm.com.*

In St Barts

Quai Général de Gaulle, Gustavia, t 27 87 27, *odtsb@wanadoo.fr. Open Mon–Fri 8.30–12.30 and 2–5, Sat 9–12.*

Information bureau, St Jean Airport. *Keeps the same hours.*

Media

There is an annual glossy magazine, *Tropical St Barth*, with features about the island and some advice on sports, shopping and restaurants, and the annual *Ti Gourmet* gives hints about restaurants.

Medical Emergencies

In a medical emergency, the Gustavia Hospital is on the seaward arm of the town, on the rue Jean Bart, t 27 60 00.

Money and Banks

Generally speaking, St Barts is very expensive. Though the official **currency** is the euro, the US dollar is accepted universally (US$1 = €0.80 approx). If you are one to watch

exchange rates, then you might find that you can get a marginally better deal in euros than in dollars. Credit cards are accepted by all shops, restaurants and hotels. In restaurants, service is *compris* (remember this when paying your bill). Hotels add a service charge of 10–15% to your bill.

Banks open on weekdays until mid-afternoon. BFC opposite the airport is open on Saturday mornings and Crédit Agricole in town has an ATM.

Shopping

Shops are open Mon–Fri 8.30–noon and 2–5. St Barts has been allowed to keep its tax-free status from Swedish days and so you may find some (relative) bargains.

Telephone Code

The IDD code for St Barts is t 590 followed by a six-digit number. If you are calling within the island, dial just the six digits. There are no coin boxes on the island and to use a public phone you need a *télécarte*, bought in advance at the post office. If you do need to make a call, any hotel front desk will help out, for a price.

Festivals

St Barts stages a number of traditional French and Caribbean events as well as get-togethers for interested sportsmen and wine drinkers.

January *St Barts' Music Festival.* Held mid-month with performances of chamber music, dance music and jazz by top international musicians.

February/March *Carnaval.* Takes place around Mardi Gras, with dances at the weekend culminating on Ash Wednesday with the black and white parades and the burning of Vaval, the spirit of the French Caribbean carnival.

April *Film Festival.* Celebrating Caribbean films, held late in the month.

Festival Gastronomique. Some years the island holds the St Barts Food Festival, in which restaurateurs and wine merchants from the major vineyards in France collaborate to create 10 days of menus from around the regions of France (it is a French food festival, though some restaurant owners do produce creole dishes too), culminating in a party in Gustavia.

May *Yacht festival.* Held mid-month in alternate years, there are celebrations around the arrival of yachts from Lorient in France.

August *Saints' Days.* Gustavia (17th), St-Louis (25th) and the eastern towns (27th and 28th) come alive in trusted Caribbean style – jump-ups in the street.

Feast day of St Bartholomew. St Bart himself is commemorated with fireworks and a regatta (24th).

Watersports

St Barts offers plenty in the way of watersports; the main centres are St-Jean beach and the Anse du Grand Cul-de-Sac, but the hotels do have some equipment for hire, including snorkelling gear, windsurfing boards and small sailing boats. The main watersports companies are:

Marine Service, Quai du Yacht Club, Gustavia, **t** 27 70 34.

Nautica FWI, **t** 27 56 50.

Océan Must, La Pointe, Gustavia, **t** 27 62 25.

Day Sails

Yachts are available through the above watersports companies and include the catamaran *Ne Me Quitte Pas* at Marine Service or *Jamaica Bay* through Nautica. **Motorboats** are available through them, or alternatively try **St Barth Caraïbes Yachting**, **t** 27 52 48.

Deep-sea Fishing

Casting for marlin and kingfish. Six people for a half-day costs about US$400. Contact **Marine Service**, above. Or Patrick Laplace, a professional deep-sea fishing guide, **t** 27 61 76.

Scuba Diving

Also easily arranged on the offshore reefs and islands, where there are marine reserves. Expect to see striped sergeant-major fish gliding by followed by grunts, and long-spined urchins lurking in among the sea fans and staghorn coral. Reefs include the offshore

rocks of Les Saints, Gros Ilets and Pain de Sucre. A one-tank dive costs from US$45.

La Bulle, at Océan Must, **t** 27 68 93.

Mermaid Scuba, Grand Cul-de-Sac, **t** 58 79 29. Led by an environmental biologist.

Plongée Caraïbes, **t** 27 55 94, *www.plongee-caraibes.com*.

St Barth Plongée, **t** 27 54 44. Certification courses available.

West Indies Dive, at Marine Service, **t** 27 70 34. PADI certified.

Snorkelling

Try the reefs at Petite Anse beyond Anse des Flamands, Anse Maréchal and the Grand or Petit Cul-de-Sac.

Windsurfing and Small Sailing Boats

Carib Waterplay, St Jean Beach, **t** 27 71 22.

Eden Rock Sea Sports Club, Baie de St-Jean, **t** 27 74 77.

Reefer's Surf Club, found in the east, **t** 27 67 63. Surfing arranged.

St Barth Water Play, Baie de St-Jean, **t** 61 38 40. A BIC centre.

Wind Wave Power, Anse du Grand Cul-de-Sac, **t** 27 82 57. A Mistral-affiliated shop. It is a good place to learn because it is protected inshore, but there are waves farther out.

Other Sports

Horse-riding

Ranch des Flamands, **t** 27 13 87.

St-Barth Equitation, **t** 62 99 30.

Tennis and Squash

There are courts at many of the hotels – **Guanahani** and the **St Barth Beach Hotel** – as well as the **Sports Club of Colombier**, **t** 27 61 07. There is even a squash court at the **Isle de France** hotel on Flamands beach.

Where to Stay

St Barthélemy t (590–)

St Barts has some extremely expensive and sumptuous hotels (none larger than about 60 rooms) in keeping with its exclusive image. You will find everything laid on to make sure that you have the most luxurious time, including life's essentials like art exhibitions in the foyers and on-call hairdressers. More seriously, they are run to a very high standard and many are set in delightful tropical gardens. Most hotels have arrangements with car-hire companies and will arrange a vehicle for you on request. Some hotels offer considerable reductions in summer packages. Service is usually charged at 10%.

There are also many villas to rent on the island. Contact:

Sibarth, Maison Suédoise, rue du Centenaire, Gustavia, **t** 27 88 90, *villas@sibarth.com*, *www.sibarth.com*; UK **t** 0800 898 318 (US working hours); France **t** 05 90 16 20; Germany, **t** 01 30 81 57 30.

Ici et Là, Quai de la République, Gustavia, **t** 27 78 78, *infosvilla@icilastbart.com, www.icilastbart.com*.

St Barth Immobilier, rue Auguste Nyman, Gustavia, **t** 27 82 94.

Luxury

Eden Rock Hotel, Baie de St-Jean, **t** 27 79 99, *info@edenrockhotel.com, www.edenrock hotel.com*. A delightful atmosphere and a charming setting, clustered around the Eden Rock of its name, a lump that rises out of St-Jean beach on the airport flight path. A theme of rich tropical red and green (reflecting the red tin roofs and Caribbean foliage perhaps) runs through the small resort, from the terrace dining room on the hilltop which is decorated with antiques, down to the Sand Bar, a popular daytime bistro, below on the beach (where there are watersports). There are six rooms on the Rock itself, perched right above the water's edge, and ten ranged either side on the beach, all neatly decorated and extremely comfortable, with all modern comforts. There are three restaurants, a tapas bar and a spa. Eden Rock is close to all the action of St-Jean, and has a friendly and intimate air.

Le Toiny, Anse de Toiny, **t** 27 88 88, UK **t** 0800 960 239, France **t** 1 45 72 96 50, US **t** 1 800 278 6469, *letoiny@saint-barths.com, www. letoiny.com*. Just 12 one-bedroom villas and one three-bedroom villa stand on the hillside, looking over the Anse de Toiny to St Kitts (there is no beach there, but each villa has a pool with a view to infinity). The villas are enclosed for maximum privacy and are decorated in old colonial style – wooden parquet floors, mahogany furniture and four-poster beds, replicas from Martinique – but have all the luxuries too, down to the two TVs hidden away in cupboards, video recorder, CD player, exercise bike and a shower in the open air. There are kitchenettes, but also room service and an excellent restaurant (the hotel is a member of the Relais et Châteaux chain). Car necessary.

Hotel Isle de France, Baie des Flamands, BP 612, **t** 27 61 81, *isledefr@saint-barths.com, www.isle-de-france.com*. Offers beachfront sumptuousness on the north coast. The mock-classical main house stands majestically above the sand, with 12 marble-floored suites with antique furniture and some private Jacuzzis in outsize bathrooms, and views over the pool to the sea beyond. Across the road behind, there are 17 very comfortable rooms and suites in bungalows scattered around a garden with tall latanier palms. Quiet and elegant.

Taïwana, Baie des Flamands, **t** 27 65 01, *taiwana@wanadoo.fr*. Next door at the end of the beach is this 'well hip' and idiosyncratic hotel. It's difficult to recommend personally because guidebook writers (along with anyone else they do not like the look of) are unceremoniously booted out, but the place seems to have an easy exclusivity about it. If you stump up the loot, there's pretty well anything you might want, from helicopter transfer from Sint Maarten and champagne breakfasts to famous acquaintances in the next-door room (which are apparently magnificent and come in a serried rank of ochre, vermilion and royal blue stucco cottages), and of course privacy (from riffraff).

Guanahani Hotel, Anse de Grand Cul-de-Sac, BP 609, 97098 St Barthélemy Cédex, **t** 27 66 60, UK **t** 0800 181 123, US **t** 1 800 223 6800, *guanahani@wanadoo.fr, www.leguana hani.com*. Very much a resort hotel, set in gently descending gardens that culminate on secluded beaches. There are 75 rooms in cottages, brightly painted and furnished with stylish lamps and fittings, each with their own terrace (some with sea view) and 16 of them with private pools. There is a restaurant and bar on the beach, for a break from the endless diet of watersports, and an à la carte dining room. Quite large, so it can be active (there is some entertainment at night), but the cottages are private so you can also shut yourself away.

Very Expensive

François Plantation, Colombier, t 27 80 22, US t 1 800 207 8071, *info@francois-plantation. com, www.francois-plantation.com*. Stands high on the hillside above Colombier, from where some of the 12 rooms have a magnificent view of the north coast from their private terrace. The estate house has an old-time Caribbean elegance, with an antique drawing room and dining room with hefty antique furniture, where you will find classical French cuisine. The rooms stand in brightly painted hillside cottages, old Caribbean *case* style built anew and set in superb tropical gardens, and they are furnished in dark-stained tropical wood. Quiet and reserved.

La Banane, Quartier Lorient, t 52 03 00, *info@labanane.com, www.labanane.com*. A hip spot, beautifully set in a garden of outrageous tropical profusion. Just nine rooms, set in old creole wooden *cases* gathered around a couple of pools with imitation rock waterfalls. Inside the rooms are studiedly eclectic in style, with antique furniture, colourful tiles and louvres on the windows. The bathrooms are excellent, part outdoor and overgrown with tropical flora. Share a shower with a banana plant.

Expensive

Hotel Emeraude Plage, St-Jean, 97133 St Barts, t 27 64 78, *emeraudeplage@wanadoo.fr, www.emeraudeplage.com*. Sits on the beach in the middle of St-Jean, 30 rooms in quite tightly clustered bungalows running back from the sand itself in a garden of hibiscus. All rooms have air-con but can be opened up to get the breeze and they have TVs and a full kitchen. You can be self-contained if you want, but it is a friendly place: there is a central area with a library where guests meet, and it's a good option for families.

St Barth Beach Hotel, Anse de Grand Cul-de-Sac, t 27 60 70, *sbbh@saint-barths.com, www.stbarthbeachhotel.com*. Sits right on the beach, with 36 comfortable rooms in a modern two-storey block. Rooms are comfortable, air-conditioned with bright pastel fittings, and there are plenty of watersports right outside.

Hotel Baie des Anges, Anse des Flamands, PO Box 162, t 27 63 61, *annie.ange@wanadoo.fr*. Just ten rooms with kitchenettes on the superb sand of the Anse des Flamands. All modern comforts: air-con, fans, cable TV and video, with an excellent seafood restaurant.

Moderate

L'Auberge de la Petite Anse, Anse des Flamands, PO Box 117, t 27 64 89, *apa@ wanadoo.fr*. Stands on the clifftop at the top end of the Anse des Flamands, with rooms in the 16 bungalows.

Le P'tit Morne, PO Box 14, Colombier, t 27 62 64, *leptitmorne@yahoo.fr*. Fourteen apartments in villas that stand high on a hillside overlooking the offshore islands to the north of St Barts. It is in a remote corner of the island and is quiet, but the rooms are fine and there is a pool.

Inexpensive

Sunset Hotel, Gustavia, t 27 77 21, *sunset-hotel@wanadoo.fr*. Rooms with air-con, fridge, TV and phones and a very bright colour scheme.

Le Manoir de St Barth, Lorient, t 27 79 27, *studiooceane@wanadoo.fr*. A small resort (seven rooms) built in mock Norman style – cottages with exposed wooden beams and plasterwork – around a pretty garden behind the village. Comfortable and secluded, with breakfast by the waterfall.

Hotel Normandie, Lorient, t 27 61 66, *studiooceane@wanadoo.fr*. Set back from the seafront in Lorient on a minor road. Seven rooms with air-con, TV and fridges and small restaurant, a small sitting room and pool.

Nid d'Aigle, Anse des Cayes, t 27 75 20, *lenidaigle@wanadoo.fr*. Way up on the hillside on a extremely steep drive, just three rooms with a pool.

Eating Out

There are some excellent restaurants in St Barts. Some of the best are in the hotel dining rooms – try the gourmet restaurant at Eden Rock in St-Jean, Le Gaïac at Le Toiny, the Ile de France hotel and La Route des Epices at François Plantation. With ingredients imported daily from France, the cuisine is sometimes heavyweight classical French, but you will usually find concessions to the climate – meats come in a *jus* rather than a sauce and there are exotic ingredients – and even *nouvelle cuisine créole*. The settings are delightful, some on the waterfront, others in converted hilltop homes or in the old buildings of Gustavia. Just as in *le métropole*, eating and restaurants are a way of life – you will find restaurateurs and a few randomly chosen guests and friends lingering over a bottle of wine long after the kitchen has closed. Tapas and sushi are on offer and on this island you can even get a ready-made gourmet picnic to take to the beach, from La Rôtisserie in St-Jean. Dining out in St Barts is quite expensive, but it is worth remembering that service is *compris*. Some restaurants offer set menus as well.

Categories are arranged according to the price of a main course: expensive = €20 and above; moderate = €10–20; inexpensive = under €10.

Expensive

Le Sapotillier, Gustavia, t 27 60 28. A very pretty setting in an old stone house in the heart of town, with top-notch fare of course. You dine inside or in a vine-covered garden (the original *sapotillier*, or soursop tree, is gone, but there is another one close by). The menu and the products are almost entirely French – *ravioli de foie gras* or a *fricassée de grenouilles*, *concassée de tomates*, *jus persillé* (frogs' legs fricassee with tomato and parsley sauce) or a *poulet de Bresse* (organically raised in France) *en cocotte*. Stylish, with attentive service.

Maya's, Public, t 27 75 73. On the waterfront just out of town, you dine on a deck with colourful deckchairs. There is a short but daily changing menu in 'global' style – Caribbean creole, Asian and Italian. Chicken

comes served in a coconut sauce or in *sauce chien*. Ever-popular, breezy and chic.

L'Esprit de Saline, on the road to Anse Saline, t 52 46 10. Rave reviews are consistent for this casual place in a rustic setting surrounded by gardens. French fusion food, beautifully presented. Menu changes daily.

Le Boubou's, Grand Cul-de-Sac, t 29 83 01. It's a little unexpected to find a Moroccan restaurant in St Barts, but it's a popular haunt. Some Moroccan tents, carpets and lamps, but the view is open to the turquoise of the bay. Tagines, plus Moroccan salads such as carrots in cumin and aubergine in honey.

Le Gommier, Grande Saline, t 27 70 57. Quite isolated in the south of the island, close to the excellent beach at Grande Saline (from which it is a great lunch-stop). An excellent setting in an open-sided building and the most delicately prepared creole cuisine – codfish fritters followed by delectable fresh fish or more exotic *colombo* or conch – by one of the island's most successful chefs.

Le Lafayette Club, Anse du Grand Cul-de-Sac, t 27 62 51. If you are feeling extravagant, you might want to spend a few luxurious hours here at a beachfront restaurant, charmingly set on a deck overlooking Grand Cul-de-Sac. Grilled fish or marinated raw salmon or a beef fillet with Roquefort sauce. Valet parking and fashion shows to keep you amused while you dine. *Winter season only, lunch only*.

Moderate

Le Ti St Barth, Pointe Milou, t 27 97 71. A well-hip spot with a DJ, slim and sleek waitresses and full-moon parties, all in a very pretty setting high on the hillside in the east of the island. Some tables sit outside under wriggly tin and vines, others in the meandering series of rooms inside. Creole specialities including *accras* (fish fritters) and *boudin* (blood sausage) but also *brochettes* and more adventurous dishes such as local fish cooked in tropical fruits.

La Gloriette, Grand Cul-de-Sac, t 27 75 66. A simple setting on a pretty blue and white deck looking out onto the bay. There is a mix of fare, some French dishes and then some

Caribbean creole specialities: a *salade de chèvre* or a *ragoût de lambi*.

New Born, t 27 67 07. A local fish restaurant where the waiters are the fishermen themselves and the walls hung with fish-abilia such as nets and floats. Conch *gratinée* and then grilled lobster (taken from the *vivier*) is served in a coconut curry sauce or *requin fumé* (slowly smoked shark). After dinner you can taste one of many rums flavoured with passion fruit, guava or lime.

Paradisio, Gustavia, **t** 27 80 78. Set in a pretty house with blue and yellow trelliswork and a terrace outside. French and creole: *bisques* and *bavarois*, *fricassée* and fresh fish with daily specials. A funny and friendly atmosphere.

La Mandala, on the hill in Gustavia, **t** 27 96 96. Worth a visit, at the very least for its fantastic view over the town, and its comfortable, low-slung Oriental furniture. It also offers interesting fare: start the evening with tapas Caribbean style and then pick from the menu, which mixes French and Asian cuisine (mainly Thai).

Eddy's Restaurant, downtown Gustavia, **t** 27 54 17. Set in a courtyard garden of original Swedish walls, there are tables outside among the greenery and others under cover, where the solid teak table and chairs are lit by hanging bamboo lamps. A mix of Caribbean and Thai flavours, reggae and *zouk* and a hip air.

L'Escale, across the harbour, Gustavia, **t** 27 81 06. Ever-popular and offers simple fare presented by waiters who dance for you: pizzas and pastas in comfortable brown cane armchairs on a wooden deck on the bay, good for sitting and watching the activity of the bay.

Wall House Restaurant, Quai du Wall House, **t** 27 71 83, *www.wall-house-stbarth.com*. French and creole cuisine. In a quiet corner overlooking Gustavia harbour, with a light lunch menu and an elegant one for dinner.

Inexpensive

La Crêperie, Kungsgatan, Gustavia.
Entre'Acte, Gustavia.
La Créole, St-Jean.
Le Repaire (its unlikely subtitle is *des rebelles et des émigrés*), on the waterfront at the

entrance to Gustavia, **t** 27 72 48. A good spot for lingering over breakfast or light lunch.

Bars and Nightlife

St Barts has a low-key attitude to entertainment (one tourism publication even warns that people looking for 'heavy action, glitter and gambling should be sent elsewhere'), but it is there in a few bars and piano lounges around Gustavia and the St-Jean area. St Barts' famous names have been known to put in an appearance. Some of the restaurants strung around the waterfront of Gustavia double as bars before and after dining time.

Le Bête à Z'ailes (aka Baz), next to the Post Office, Gustavia. A good setting at the head of the bay, this place has the suitable air of a very comfortable yacht with a stripped wooden interior. Tapas with a view in the early evening (and then fish or salad later on; *inexpensive*).

Eden Rock, Baie de St-Jean. Has an excellent early-evening tapas bar, with a lovely view over the bay.

La Mandala, above Eden Rock. A great place for a cocktail, on a terrace with Far Eastern furniture and huge cushions, sipping a sunset cocktail to the tune of jazz, rock and reggae.

Carl Gustaf Hotel, above La Mandala. A superb view from its terrace for a champagne cocktail.

L'Iguane, Quai de la République (in a small shopping arcade), Gustavia. You can try here if you would prefer sushi to tapas. *Maki*, *tenerkil*, *idako*, *tataki*. (There is another Iguane in Grand Cul-de-Sac.)

Le Select, Gustavia town centre. Set in an old mock-brick house, with a garden where hip chicks and tanned windsurfers collect. Lively, often live music.

Bar de l'Oubli (the bar of forgetting), Gustavia town centre. If you prefer to watch than be watched, then you might retreat across the road to the balcony of this auspiciously named bar.

Le Petit Club, Gustavia, next to Coté Jardin, **t** 27 66 33. One of a few nightclubs.

La Licorne, Lorient. Local disco.

Feelings, Lurin, **t** 27 88 67. Nightclub.

destroyed by hurricane and a fire in 1850, and only a couple of houses remain in use (on the rue Sadi Carnot and the rue Jeanne d'Arc). But the street names – Vikingagatan, Hwarfsgatan, and Ostra- and Westra-Strandgatan on the waterfront – give an unusual impression for the Caribbean. The name Gustavia is taken from the enlightened despot King Gustav III who leased St Barts from France and gave the island the free-port status that enabled it to prosper.

Today the population of Gustavia is just a few hundred, a fraction of what it was 200 years ago when the harbour was filled with merchants and the warehouses were overflowing. Sailing craft are filling the harbour once again, though – the waterfront is given over almost entirely to marina space in season – as they cruise between the Virgin Islands and Antigua. And the port still maintains its mercantile tradition with chic-looking mannequins displaying Armani and Hermès clothes at duty-free prices. But it is no longer Swedish in atmosphere: nowadays, with endless bistros, art galleries and police wearing *képis*, the ambience is distinctly French.

At the four points around the harbour stand the tired old fortresses that once guarded Gustavia. It is possible to visit **Fort Gustave** on the road out of town, from where there is a magnificent view of the harbour. Another remaining Swedish feature of Gustavia is the distinctive triangular-roofed **clock tower** known as the Swedish belfry. It stands high above the town next to the *sous-préfecture* (formerly the island prison) and was originally built as a church tower. The **English anchor** at the head of the harbour is about 200 years old, but it has only been in St Barts since 1981, when it was dragged here by mistake from St Thomas in the Virgin Islands. It was left on the quay and has just become part of the furniture.

The **Municipal Museum** (*open Mon–Thurs 8–noon and 1.30–5.30, Fri 1.30–5, Sat 8–noon; adm*) can be found near the point of the bay, in the Wall House, an old Swedish warehouse that has been restored. On display you will see prints and pictures of old-time St Barts, alongside mock-ups of the traditional cottages and artefacts from island life (including a sling for lifting cows onto boats and a fishing boat). There are also displays on the Swedish lineage of the island and some rushwork articles made of the *latanier* palm. The large building beyond here is the *Mairie*.

Around the Island

For an island with no peak over 1,000ft, St Barts is surprisingly hilly and rough. There is little rain, not much cultivation, and the hills are infested with scrub, tall torch cactus and the distinctive St Barts palm tree, the *latanier*. For centuries the villagers were completely isolated from one another and would meet only in church after walking for hours along tortuous paths hacked out of the undergrowth. Nowadays the island is cut and crossed with impossibly steep and windy roads and the furthest reaches are occupied by holiday villas. In the narrow valleys you will see mournful white cattle egrets waiting for food while their companions graze.

You might catch snatches of a strange language in the country, the old speech of the islanders' Norman ancestors (the communities were so isolated that people living just 5 miles from one another spoke with a different accent). And you may just still see the womenfolk wearing their traditional frilled bonnets, or *calèches* – starched and prim white hats that keep the islanders' Norman skin protected from the sun. They are nicknamed *quichenottes*, supposedly a corruption of 'kiss-me-not', because it is rather difficult to get another face underneath them.

North of Gustavia the sea road cuts inland to St Barts' small industrial estate at Public and then emerges on the coast again at **Corossol**, a fishing village, where the houses clutter the slopes of a valley that opens onto the beach. In Corossol they wear the *calèche à platine*, with multiple hems, a frilly border and little chance of scoring a kiss. Farther up the coast in **Colombier** and in **Flamands** they traditionally wear the *calèche à batons*, strengthened with wooden slats. There is a private sea-shell collection on view in Flamands at the **Inter Oceans Museum** (*t* 27 62 97; *open daily 9–5; adm*), where you can see giant clams with wavy lips and some miniature creations of incredible intricacy.

All over this northern area you will see the *latanier* with its trunk tangled with a confusion of stubs and then a series of fronds that grow like scratchy fans. When dried these leaves are very skilfully woven by the local women into hats, bags and table mats. Corossol is probably the best place to buy them.

Northeast of Gustavia, **St-Jean**, the site of the earliest settlement on the island, has become the centre of the tourist industry in St Barts – the old town has been swallowed by recent development and so when you arrive at the airport you are greeted by a neat collection of bistros and chichi boutiques.

As you go east the villas thin out on the hills and old St Barts begins to appear – drystone walls and distinctive houses with red roofs and sloping plastered walls. A few fishermen still work out of **Anse de Lorient**. Boobies nest on the clifftops, and in the mangroves you may see a pelican digesting a meal in the sun. The road rings the eastern end of the island, around St Barts' highest peak, **Morne de Vitet** (about 930ft), emerging on the southern coast, where there are magnificent views as far as Statia and St Kitts, and then returning to the north coast at St Jean.

The Leeward Islands

10

The Leeward Islands

Highlights

1 Soak up the historic, nautical atmosphere of Nelson's Dockyard in Antigua
2 Take a day trip to Barbuda from Antigua for the phenomenal beaches and the extraordinary frigatebird colony in the mangroves
3 Stay in one of the delightful plantation-house hotels in St Kitts and Nevis
4 Sample the superb restaurants and bars of Anguilla, often in beachfront settings

The Leeward Islands lie in the north of the Lesser Antilles, a link of smaller islands in the arc between the mountainous Windwards in the south and the Virgin Islands in the Greater Antilles. They stretch over 150 miles, scattered around the Dutch Windward Islands and the French islands of St Barthélemy and St Martin. This is an attractive area of the Caribbean. As you look from one island to the next, the sea horizon is studded periodically with islands that rise grey and majestic in the haze.

The Leewards stand in two lines. In the west are Montserrat and the twin islands of St Kitts and Nevis, invariably capped in cloud, soaring from the water in a chain, the northern extension of the chain of the Windward Islands (*see* p.141). They have many of the features of the Windwards – high rainfall, stunning, luxuriant vegetation and the same massive, majestic beauty. They are the peaks of a submarine mountain range, still volcanically active. Until recently they were thought to have quietened down, but the recent activity on Montserrat showed that belief to be unfounded.

Antigua, Barbuda and Anguilla, on the other hand, are coral-based, and lie on the eastern lip of the Caribbean crust, pushed up as the Atlantic plate forces its way west underneath. The remnants of much older volcanoes that are definitely dormant, these islands lie lower in the sea than their westerly counterparts and their climates are milder. This is an advantage in the rainy season, when the other islands are often shrouded in cloud. Physically they are not as impressive, with a mantle of sparse and scrubby vegetation, but between them these three islands boast some of the Caribbean's finest sand.

The Leeward Islands lie in the middle of the hurricane belt, and, from time to time in the season (which lasts from July to October, with the occasional hiccup like Lennie in November 1999), they are visited by these outsize whirlwinds, their first point of contact with land after a 2,000-mile run-up across the Atlantic. Hurricanes are indescribably destructive – Hurricane Luis in 1995 destroyed 1,200 yachts in the lagoon in St Martin and Hurricane Hugo in 1999 caused major damage to over 90% of the houses in Montserrat. Not only do the winds damage crops and houses (literally sand-blasting them in some cases, stripping off every square inch of paint), but the torrential rains that accompany them sweep away roads and collapse bridges. And as Lennie showed, the swell created by them can whittle down the islands, destroying docks and emptying beaches of their sand.

The six islands were British colonies and a hundred years ago they were lumped together for administrative convenience as the Presidency of the Leeward Islands. Today, Anguilla and Montserrat remain Overseas Territories of Britain, but since the early 1980s Antigua and Barbuda and then St Kitts and Nevis have gone their own way.

Antigua

The graceful and welcoming contours of Antigua inspired Columbus to name the island in honour of a statue of the Virgin in Seville Cathedral, Santa Maria de la Antigua. Its rolling yellow-green hills and the sweeping curves of its bays are soft on the eye after the towering volcanic violence of the Windwards. Barbuda, Antigua's smaller sister island 30 miles to the north, is even gentler and more laid-back, nowhere reaching above 210ft.

Antigua (pronounced more as in 'beleaguer' than in 'ambiguou(s)') has a population of 66,000 and is the largest of the Leeward Islands (108 square miles). For years it was the linchpin of British influence in the area – St John's was the seat of government, and the principal military and naval fortifications were here. The island became fully independent from Britain in 1981, but it still maintains an important position in the British Caribbean with an influence out of proportion to its size. It is the hub for inter-island transport and, crucially for the Caribbean, it has an international test cricket ground.

Antigua's shape has something of a confused amoeba about it, with pseudopodia heading off in every direction. These headlands enclose superb bays – used so successfully by navies and by smugglers over the centuries and now more peaceably by sailors. Except for one corner of ancient volcanic outflow in the southwest, the island is made entirely of limestone coral. The Atlantic coast, beaten by the waves over the millennia, looks pitted and scarred like a neolithic cake mix, but on the protected shores of the Caribbean side the gentler wave action on the reefs has pushed up miles of blinding white sand.

Antigua has an excellent climate, drier and gentler than that of its southerly neighbours. The same northeast trade winds blow in from the Atlantic, but Antigua does not collect the rain clouds that linger above the Windwards. The early settlements were plagued by a lack of water and in 1731 a bucketful of it was reputed to have been sold for three shillings. This is not to say that Antigua does not experience tropical rainstorms, however: they can definitely catch you unawares and the proverbial bucketful will soak you in seconds.

For much of its history, Antigua's coastline bristled with forts and ships of the line, and the land was covered to the last inch with canefields, dotted occasionally with a windmill and estate house. But now the 160 plantations have gone and their fields have turned into rolling scrubland, where the dilapidated conical shells of the windmills stand silent without their sails.

Today the land has a new regime; the coast is lined with the 20th-century bastions of the hotel industry, and inland Antigua is dotted with communications aerials. The former naval presence is still reflected today in the huge numbers of yachts that base themselves in the southeast, around English Harbour. A high proportion of the island's income is derived from tourists and these are split roughly half and half between hotel guests and cruise passengers. Just as the colonial masters in their dockyards and barracks were an ambivalent presence in the 18th and 19th centuries, forcing the Antiguans to toe the British line when really they would have been happy trading with any passing ship, so the tourists are something of a mixed blessing. They bring the much-needed money for development, but they are a burden on island resources. The Antiguans are pretty cool, however, and they are mostly prepared to overlook the problems for the advantages. Antigua has experienced a period of considerable growth recently. There has been lots of building on the island,

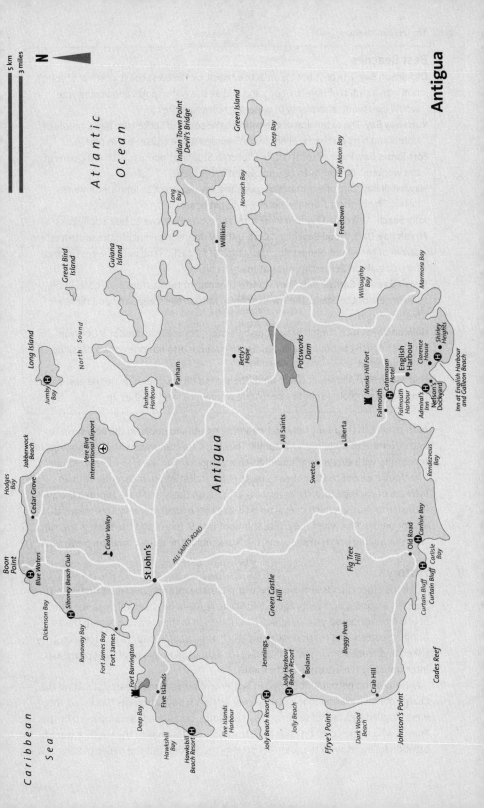

Best Beaches

Dickenson Bay: The best bet for an active beach, on the west coast, north of St John's, home to a clutch of hotels. Good sand and all the watersports and posing you would ever want; also plenty of watering holes to retire to.

Runaway Bay: The extension of the coast to the south of Dickenson Bay, a couple of hotels and bars on the excellent sand. Crowded when cruise ship in port.

Fort James Bay: Further south again (closer to St John's), popular with Antiguans at the weekend, but tends to be uncrowded in the week.

Hawksbill Bay: One of a number of coves and bays south of St John's, many with hotels. The farthest from the hotel is a nudist beach.

Jolly Beach: Also called *Lignum Vitae* after the wood. You have to buy a daily pass.

Ffrye's Bay, **Dark Wood Beach** and **Crab Hill Bay** (Johnson's Point): In the southwestern corner of the island, almost deserted strips of fantastic sand with the best chance for being alone. Some bars but not many facilities.

Morris Bay and **Carlisle Bay**: They stand either side of the Curtain Bluff hotel in the southwest of the island; the waves splay in fans on the steep sand and there are reefs to explore.

Galleon Bay: A nice stretch of sand, just a water-taxi ride from Nelson's Dockyard, inside English Harbour. Nearby Falmouth Harbour also has one or two passable strips of sand.

Half Moon Bay: A lovely curve of sand. The sea is a bit rougher here on the east coast.

Long Bay: A protected spot in a deep cove where nice sand washes up.

both private, in the many new houses springing up, and public in the new hospital and government buildings in St John's. The shops are crammed with the trappings of modernity, with everything from high-tech computer hardware to Tommy Hilfiger.

Antigua is one of the Caribbean's more popular destinations. Recently, with an increase of package tourists, many of the hotels on the island have adopted the all-inclusive format, in which guests tend to stay in the hotel property. This means that, except on the days when the cruise ships put into St John's and the town is overrun with marauding bands of shoppers, the island holds the tourist invasion pretty well.

History

Like the other islands in the northeastern Caribbean, Antigua saw its first island-hoppers around 4,000 years ago, when Stone Age Ciboneys arrived by canoe from South America. 2,000 years later Arawaks followed in their island-hopping tracks, bringing pottery and continental plants such as pineapple, papaya and tobacco. They fished and tended small plots of cassava for a thousand years until their peace was interrupted by the intrusion of the Caribs.

Antigua's first permanent European settlement arrived from nearby St Kitts in the charge of Philip Warner in 1632. Like earlier settlers whose attempts had failed, they were plagued by a lack of water and by the Caribs, occasionally accompanied by the French, who nipped over on raids from the Windward Islands to the south. A war of attrition followed, with the colonists determined to force out the native Indians. Law

No.88 in the old Antiguan Statute Book for 1693 reads 'An Act to encourage the destroying of the Indians and Taking their Periagoes (canoes)'. It took its course. By 1805, the law was simply marked down as 'Obsolete'.

Antigua became the archetypal West Indian sugar factory. The technology was introduced by Christopher Codrington from Barbados in 1674, and within a few years every available inch of land was covered with sugar cane. The cultivation of sugar involved large workforces of slaves and this gave Antigua its present population of those of mainly African descent. As the Caribbean empires flourished in the 18th century and the wars for territory heated up, the British chose Antigua as their main military and naval base in the Leeward Islands, creating a link between their other defences in Barbados to the south and in Jamaica in the Greater Antilles. The fortifications at Shirley Heights above English Harbour on the south coast proved so formidable that the French and Spanish navies simply avoided them.

In the 19th century the wars came to an end and the empires crystallized. The abolition movement managed to outlaw slavery in 1834, but the freed slaves had no choice but to continue working the plantations. There was no other source of employment. The slaves were free, but their situation hardly improved. As sugar declined in the late 19th century (the price of West Indian cane sugar could not compete with subsidized European beet sugar), Antigua waned and the island became another poor, neglected outcrop in the Caribbean backwater. It was not until the 20th century that things began to pick up again. The latest empire to make itself felt is of course tourism, which Antigua has developed for the past 40 years. A wartime agreement granting the United States bases on the island brought a large influx of Americans during the Second World War, and this put the island on the map. The agreements are still retained and the US Air Force and Navy still have bases in Antigua.

Sailing

Antigua stages one of the major regattas in the Caribbean sailing year, **Antigua Sailing Week**, or Race Week, which is held at the end of the winter season before all the yachts take off across the Atlantic to spend the summer in the Mediterranean. It attracts sailors from everywhere, and so for two weeks around the actual event the Antiguan waters are busy with craft of all sorts. There are five major races, each with a number of different classes, and each followed by another fleet of sails along for the ride. Many of the races skirt the island and so Antigua's hills offer a fantastic view of the proceedings if you would prefer a land-based vantage point. The races are of course a good enough excuse for what the Caribbean does best, which is to mix a rum punch and get everyone to 'jump up' afterwards. There are plenty of silly races and wet-T-shirt competitions for non-sailors, and the week winds up with the Lord Nelson's Ball, a formal affair (for the Caribbean anyway), and prize-giving. For information, contact PO Box 406, St John's, **t** 462 0374, *www.sailingweek.com*.

Held just before Sailing Week is the **Classic Yacht Regatta** which brings together yachts passed by the committee as 'of classic design', many of them fantastically beautiful with long-forgotten configurations of sails (three races). Contact the Classic Yacht Regatta, **t** 460 1707, *www.antiguaclassic.com*.

Antiguan politics have a similar heritage to those of other British islands. Trade unions sprang up all over the Caribbean in the thirties and the islanders rallied to them, first as a way to organize political power in the face of colonial rule and later to develop into the movement for self-determination and eventually Independence. Vere Bird, a President of the Antigua Trades and Labour Union in the 1940s, became the leading light in Antiguan politics, becoming Chief Minister, and in 1967 Prime Minister under 'Associated Statehood'. He became the first leader of independent Antigua and Barbuda on 1 November 1981 and continued as Prime Minister until 1994, when his Antigua Labour Party was taken over by his son, the Hon. Lester Bird. In March 2004, the Bird political dynasty came to an end when the United Progressive Party, led by Labour activist the Hon. Baldwin Spencer, defeated Lester Bird. The Governor of Antigua is Sir James Carlisle.

Beaches

Between them, Antigua and Barbuda have some of the loveliest beaches in the Caribbean. Time was, not so long ago, that Antiguan families would simply move on if anyone was already on their favourite beach when they arrived for their Sunday picnic. Now they can be crowded, relatively – perhaps ten people scattered over a mile of isolated sand. In between the main beaches (*see* 'Best Beaches') are any number of small coves where you can be alone. Ask an Antiguan.

There is something for every taste on the island, and for once the tourist brochures' claims are correct: you can walk alone on a bay of silken sand, where coconut palms bend and brush the beach and the waves fizz around your toes, carving scallop shapes in the sand; or you can cut a windsurfing dash on crowded strands where the body-beautiful roam. In some places, though, mosquitoes dive-bomb you as you doze and the sandflies do bite, so you might have to evacuate in late afternoon. Take repellent if you go off the beaten track. All beaches are public in Antigua, but the land behind them is sometimes owned by a hotel which may therefore restrict access. All-inclusive hotels may charge a day's fee for using the beach (which would include use of the sports equipment and facilities of the hotel). *See* 'Best Beaches', p.336.

Flora and Fauna

Set in the yellow-green expanses of scrub, Antiguan gardens are splendid with the bright pinks and purples of hibiscus and bougainvillea. There is one pocket of lusher vegetation in a mainly dry island, Fig Tree Hill in the southwest, where you will see slopes covered in elephant ears and of course fig trees (the local name for the banana). Flitting in its foliage you can find Antigua's two hummingbirds and several doves. On the plains you are bound to see the ever-present mournful cattle egret, standing sentinel and sometimes on the back of the cattle that give it its name.

In the coastal ponds (there are many, behind the hotels on Dickenson Bay, in the creeks on the east coast and by Jolly Beach) you will see boobies, terns and sandpipers as well as the ubiquitous pelican. You can also visit the offshore islands, including Great Bird Island, which is particularly known as home to the red-billed tropicbird.

Getting There

Antigua t (1 268–)

By Air

Antigua's Vere Cornwall Bird International Airport has excellent connections around the Caribbean and from Europe (about 8 hours) and North America (3 hours from Miami). It is a hub for the northeastern Caribbean. A departure tax of EC$50 (about US$20) is payable except by those who have spent less than 24 hours in the country.

From Europe

There are frequent flights from Britain: British Airways, **t** 462 0879, flies three times a week; Virgin, **t** 462 0876, once a week and BWIA, **t** 462 1260, twice a week. A number of charter airlines (handled at the airport by Port Services, **t** 462 2522) also fly from the UK.

From North America

BWIA, **t** 462 1260, and American Airlines, **t** 462 0950, have direct flights from JFK New York and easy connections via Miami and San Juan in Puerto Rico. Continental fly from Newark, New Jersey, and BWIA fly from Toronto, as does Air Canada, **t** 462 1147. Air Jamaica and US Airways fly via Montego Bay.

From Other Caribbean Islands

Antigua is the headquarters of LIAT, **t** 462 0700, so the airline has more flights to and from this island than anywhere else. On LIAT, Caribbean Star, **t** 461 7827, *www.flycaribbean star.com*, and other carriers there are daily direct flights to all the islands between San Juan in the north and Trinidad and Barbados in the south. Another option is Carib Aviation, **t** 462 3147, who offer three flights a day from Barbuda and a daily service across from Nevis and other islands like Anguilla and the BVI. Carib Aviation will charter aircraft as well, as do Norman Aviation, **t** 462 2445 and Fly BVI, *www.fly-bvi.com*. Helicopters can be chartered from Caribbean Helicopters, **t** 460 5900, *helicopters@candw.ag*.

By Sea

There are no scheduled boat services to or from Antigua. You might persuade a freighter captain to let you aboard, but your best bet is to get a passage on a yacht, of which there are many based in English Harbour.

Getting Around

By Bus

The bus service in Antigua has improved in recent years and it is now possible to reach all except the remotest parts of the island seven days a week. There is a fairly regular service between St John's and English Harbour in the southeast of the island. Other roads are run less frequently. The airport now runs a bus route called 'Coolidge' to and from St John's. A number of the hotels run buses for their workers, so you might be lucky enough to catch a ride with them. There are marked bus stops at the roadside which, unlikely as it may seem for the Caribbean, are generally used.

The East Bus Station, on Independence Avenue in the outskirts of St John's, serves the north and east of the island. Within its own new compound opposite the St John's market is the West Bus Station, from which buses leave for villages in the southern part of the island. Travelling on the buses is cheap, and the longest fare across the island costs around EC$3.

By Taxi

Good tourists, of course, go by taxi, and there is a superabundance of them in St John's and at the airport, who charge official rates. They can also be ordered through all the hotels. The government fixes taxi rates and it is worth establishing the price (and currency) before setting off. The ride from the airport into St John's costs US$15, to Dickenson Bay US$15 and from St John's or the airport to Nelson's Dockyard about US$25. There are taxi stands: the 24-hour taxi service, **t** 462 5190, at the West Bus Station and the Reliable Taxi Service, **t** 462 1510. Many of the taxi drivers are knowledgeable about Antiguan lore and so you will often get an impromptu tour if you wish, but any taxi driver would be happy to take you on a more formal tour of the island, which will cover many of the island sights. A day's tour costs around US$80–100 and is easily fixed through any hotel, or through the United Taxi Association, **t** 562 0262.

Hitch-hiking

Hitch-hiking around the island works adequately. To signal to both car and bus drivers, the traditional Caribbean sign is to point rapidly and repeatedly at the ground. For safety, it is best not to hitch-hike alone.

By Guided Tour

The following companies offer a range of tours to less-explored island sights:

Bo Tours, t 462 6632, *www.botours.com*.

Caribbean Helicopters, t 460 5901, *helicopters@candw.ag*, *www.caribbean helicopters.net*. Offers tours of Antigua, Barbuda and Montserrat Volcano.

Island Safari Tours, t 562 5337. Tours of outlying villages and Fig Tree Hill.

Tradewind Tours, t 573 5501, *sales@tradewind tours.com*, *www.tradewindtours.com*.

Tropical Adventures, Redcliffe Quay, St John's, t 480 1225, *tropad@candw.ag*, *www.tropicalad.com*. Excursions including snorkelling, kayaking and off-road Jeep tour.

Tropikelly Trails, t 461 0383, *www.tropikelly trails.com*. Offers popular off-road Jeep tour.

Wadadli Travel and Tours, t 462 2227.

Car and Bike Hire

Hiring a car is probably the best way to get around the island. Drivers must obtain a temporary permit, available from the rental company or the police on presentation of a valid driving licence and payment of US$20. If you are driving out into the country, take a reasonable map because there are few road-signs. There is supposedly a 40mph speed limit and driving is mainly on the left, though there are recognized chicanes around the potholes. If you wish to go off the main roads it is advisable to get hold of a four-wheel-drive car, of which there are plenty for hire. The price of a day's hire starts at US$45 for a car and $60 for a Jeep. Rental companies, in St John's, English Harbour and the airport, include:

Avis, t 462 2840.

Biggs Car Rental, t 562 4901.

Cheke's Scooter & Car Rental, t 562 4646.

Coleds Brokerage Services, t 462 0464.

Dollar Rent-a-Car, St John's, t 462 0362.

Hertz Car Rental, t 481 4440.

Lion Car Rental, English Harbour, t 460 1400.

Thrifty Car Rental, St John's, t 462 1776.

Bike rental is available from:

Paradise Rentals & Charters, Jolly Harbour Marina, t 460 7125, *paradise@candw.ag*, *www.paradiseboats.com*. Mountain bikes, kids' bikes and scooters.

Sun Cycles, t 461 0324. Hire bicycles from here – they deliver to your hotel.

Tourist Information

Abroad

A website with general information is at *www.antigua-barbuda.org*. You can also try *www.antiguanice.com*.

Canada: 60 St Clair Ave East, Suite 304, Toronto, Ontario M4T 1N5, t (416) 961 3085.

UK: 15 Thayer St, London W1M 5LD, t (020) 7486 7073, *antbar@msn.com*.

USA: 610 Fifth Ave, Suite 311, New York, NY 10020, t (212) 541 4117; 25 SE 2nd Ave, Suite 300, Miami, Florida, t (305) 381 6762.

In Antigua

The tourist board puts out a number of magazines with articles of general interest about the island and lists of restaurants and boutiques. There is a tourist information desk at the airport, but the main tourist office is found at:

Ministry of Tourism, PO Box 363, Queen Elizabeth Highway, t 462 0480, *deptourism@candw.ag*.

Embassies and Consulates

British High Commission, PO Box 483, Price Waterhouse Centre, Old Parham Rd, St John's, t 462 0008, *britishh@candw.ag*.

US Consul, Bluff House, Pigeon Point, English Harbour, t 463 6531, *ryderj@candw.ag*.

Media

A number of newspapers are published on the island, including the *Antigua Sun*, the weekly *Outlet* and the daily *Observer*, with suitably dozy headlines such as 'Driver Slams into Parked Car'...

Medical Emergencies

In a medical emergency, there is a 24-hour casualty room at the St John's hospital, just off Hospital Road, t 462 0251.

Money and Banks

Antigua and Barbuda share their **currency**, the Eastern Caribbean dollar, with the other countries in the OECS (Organization of Eastern Caribbean States), from Anguilla in the north down to Grenada in the south. The EC$ is fixed to the US$, at a rate of about US$1 = EC$2.65. US dollars are accepted everywhere on the island, though change will sometimes be given in EC$. Credit cards are also widely accepted by hotels, restaurants and shops and as security for car hire. Though confusion rarely arises, it is a good rule to establish which currency you are dealing in. **Banking hours** are Mon–Thurs 8–2, Fri 8–4. Exchange can always be made at the larger hotels, but the rate will not be as good.

Because most necessities have to be imported, Antigua can be quite expensive.

Telephone Code

The IDD code for Antigua is **t** 1 268 followed by a seven-figure local number. On-island, dial the seven digits.

Maps and Books

Antigua was lucky in that the English wife of a planter, a Mrs Lanaghan, wrote of the island, her life, and the customs of its people in *Antigua and the Antiguans* in 1844 (recently reprinted in two volumes). You may also find a copy of *To Shoot Hard Labour*, in which an Antiguan, Samuel Smith (1877–1982), tells stories going back to Emancipation (his grandmother was a slave) and his working life. There are also one or two informative booklets that describe the historic sights of the island. *The Romance of English Harbour* deals with Nelson's Dockyard, and *Shirley Heights* by Charles Jane tells the story of Shirley Heights and its defence of the island.

A modern Antiguan writer who now lives in the States is Jamaica Kincaid, author of *Annie John*, a disturbing book about a childhood on the island, and also *A Small Island*.

First Editions, in the Woods Centre Mall behind St John's. Has a good selection of Caribbean books.

Lord Jim's Locker, Falmouth Harbour. Excellent choice of nautical books, guides and novels.

Map Shop, St Mary's St, St John's, **t** 462 3993.

Shopping

Antigua has a number of galleries in which you will see the works of Caribbean painters as well as arts and crafts. Shops are usually open Mon–Sat 8.30–4 or 5pm, with an hour off between noon and 1pm. They will often stay open later when a cruise ship is in dock.

Coates Cottage, Lower Nevis St, Redcliffe Quay. Here you will also find the works of Antiguan painters.

Elvie's Pottery. Authentic Antiguan terra-cotta-coloured clay pottery.

Fine Art Framing, Redcliffe Quay, **t** 562 1019. Carries an interesting range of local art.

Harmony Hall, difficult to find, on the east coast at Brown's Bay, **t** 460 4120, *harmony@ candw.ag*. Arts and craft from all over the Caribbean – colourful work with calabashes and baskets. There is a great outdoor restaurant and a bar in the old windmill. It's a long drive from town but worth it. *Open Nov–May*.

Hide Out Restaurant & Art Gallery, Piccadilly Mamora Bay, **t** 460 3666.

Seahorse Studios, Redcliffe Quay. Original paintings, prints and jewellery.

The Rhythm of Blue, **t** 727 8844. Combination of Nancy Nicholson's pottery and local scrimshaw works.

Festivals

The sailing **regattas** mentioned earlier in the chapter (*see* 'Sailing', p.337) are very lively occasions. There are other smaller events throughout the year which can be fun to attend, so it is worth asking around when you are on the island.

January *Hot-Air Balloon Festival*. Usually held this month, and has become quite a popular occasion, with balloons filling the sky above the island, 'nightglow' shows after dark and fantastic views if you are in a balloon.

April *Sailing Week*

May *Sports fishing tournament*.

July *Carnival competitions*. For 10 days or so late in the month, winding up to the finals.

August *Carnival competition finals*. Held early in the month: Calypso King (listen out for commentary on Antiguan politics) and Carnival Queen (brings contestants from all over the area), steel bands (if you hear them practising, then wander in) and junior competitions. The traditional *j'ouvert* (pronounced 'jouvay') takes place on the morning of the first Monday in August, and the streets will then pulse to the carnival parades until Tuesday evening.

October *Performing Arts Festival.* Held over three days.

Watersports

Antigua is particularly good for sailing, but like the other coral islands it has some fine reefs, so snorkelling and diving are a pleasure. The best beach for general watersports is Dickenson Bay.

Day Sails

Day sails often go to the offshore islands – Prickly Pear, Green Island and Bird Island – and take in a picnic and some snorkelling. They are available through:

Kokomo, t 462 7245, *www.kokomocat.com.* Catamaran trips.

Sentio, out of English Harbour, **t** 464 7127, *www.sailing-antigua.com.*

Wadadli Cats, t 462 4792, *www.wadadlicats. com.* Catamarans.

Jabberwocky Yacht Charters, t 773 3115, *paulandkatesmith@yahoo.co.uk.* Fifty-foot yacht with crew.

Ivy Yacht Charter, Falmouth Harbour. Sail to a private beach. Including lunch and drinks.

Capt. Nash Sailing Cruises, t 560 0014, *nash@caribbean-marketing.net.*

Deep-sea Fishing

Trips, casting for marlin and tuna, can be fixed up through some of the large hotels, or try the following operators:

Antigua & Barbuda Sports Fishing Club, t 460 7400, *basicblue@candw.ag, www.antigua barbudasportfishing.com.* Holding its 40th Annual Sport Fishing Tournament in 2006.

Overdraft, t 464 4954, *nunesb@candw.ag, www.antiguafishing.com.*

Sailing

Yachting is a big activity on the island, with marinas around the traditional naval harbour sites of English Harbour and Falmouth

Harbour on the south coast, and at the Jolly Beach resort on the west coast. Yachts of all sizes can be hired, crewed or bareboats, for days, a week, or longer. Charter companies include:

Antigua Yacht Charters, t 463 7101, *liz@antiguayachtcharters.com, www.antiguayachtcharters.com.*

Nicholson's Yacht Charters, English Harbour, **t** 462 6066.

Scuba Diving

Some good dive sites are: Cades Reef, a 2-mile protected reef off the south coast, nearby Farley Bay and Rendezvous Bay, and Boon Point, the northernmost tip of Antigua. The reefs have claimed quite a few ships over the years and so there are plenty of wrecks to dive. Diving and instruction (a one-tank dive costs around US$45) can be arranged through Antigua Dive Operators Association, *http://divetravel.netfirms.com,* or any of its following members:

Deep Bay Divers, t 463 8000, *www.deepbay divers.com.* They have a number of locations.

Dive Antigua, Halcyon Cove, Dickenson Bay, **t** 462 3483, *birkj@candw.ag, www. diveantigua.com.*

Dockyard Divers, Nelson's Dockyard, **t** 464 8591, *www.dockyard-divers.com.*

Jolly Dive, Jolly Beach Resort, **t** 462 8305, *www.jollydive.com.*

Octopus Divers, Nelson's Dockyard, **t** 460 6286, *www.octopusdivers.com.* Both Dockyard Divers and this outfit cover reefs and wrecks on the southern coast.

Snorkelling

There are reefs on all sides of Antigua, which offer excellent marine life, including sergeant-majors, parrot fish and larger, fish-like rays and the occasional dolphin. Equipment can be borrowed from most hotels.

Windsurfing, Kiteboarding & Kayaking

Many hotels have equipment, but intermediate and advanced windsurfers should go to Windsurfing Antigua, **t** 462 3094, in the northeast, where the winds are stronger. Other spots include Dutchman's Bay, Jabberwock Beach and Hodges Bay around the corner to the north.

Antigua

343

KiteAntigua Kitesurfing Centre, Jabberwock
Beach, St John's, t 460 3414, nik@kiteantigua.
com, www.kiteantigua.com. Closed Sept–Nov.

Antigua Adventures, t 562 7297,
www.antiguaadventures.com. Quad-biking,
kiteboarding, visit to Stingray City Antigua.

Antigua Paddles Kayak Eco Trips, t 463 1944,
labarrielc@candw.ag, www.antiguapaddles.
com. Tours include kayaking, swimming,
snorkelling, uninhabited island nature walk.

Other Sports

Golf

There is one 18-hole course at the Cedar
Valley Golf Club, t 462 0161, to the northeast of
St John's, and another at Jolly Harbour, t 462
7771 ext. 608.

Horse-riding

A ride through Antigua's rolling dry hills or
along the beaches can be arranged with the
Spring Hill Riding Club near Falmouth, t 460
1333, www.springhillridingclub.com.

Where to Stay

Antigua t (1 268–)

Antigua has a few fine resort hotels tucked
away in their own coves along its tortuous
coastline. Many of them are extremely expensive retreats, ideal for the luxurious seclusion
that the Caribbean does so well, and one or
two sit in splendour in the historical setting of
English Harbour. In general Antigua has gone
for the 'all-inclusive' plan in a big way recently,
in which everything (meals, watersports and
often drinks) is paid for in advance and you do
not need to use any money. A number of villas
are available through **Caribrep Villas, t 463**
2070, caribrep@caribrepvillas.com, www.
caribrepvillas.com. Otherwise try **Very Intimate
Places (VIP)**, www.antigua-vip.com, which
represents owner-operated guest houses and
hotels (none larger than 50 rooms), all of
which provide personalized services.

Hotel rooms in Antigua are by no means
cheap and the bill is then supplemented by a
8.5% government tax and usually by a 10%
service charge (except in the all-inclusives).

Very cheap rooms, sometimes clean, can only
be found in the south of St John's, beyond the
market. There are some guest houses that can
be contacted through the Tourist Board.

Luxury

Curtain Bluff, PO Box 288, t 462 8400, US
t (212) 289 9888, www.curtainbluff.com.
Antigua's finest and most elegant hotel, and
one of the Caribbean's most long-established, Curtain Bluff lies isolated on the
south coast, above a good double beach
where the mounded sand is carved into
scallop patterns by the waves. Set in magnificent gardens, the hotel is stately and quiet,
with 66 huge suites and smaller rooms
ranged on the rising flank of the headland
that overlooks the beach. There are many
activities on offer within the all-inclusive
price: fitness room, watersports, tennis and
squash, and, after this, drinks in the bar at
7pm. There is a fine dining room with an
extremely long wine list; a jacket and tie are
required for dinner during the high winter
season. Closed during the summer months.

Jumby Bay, Long Island, PO Box 243, St John's,
t 462 6000, jumbyres@candw.ag, www.
jumby-bay.com. Another enclave of rarified
luxury, this time isolated on its own island
off the northern shore of Antigua. The 50
rooms, suites and villas, some in rondavels,
others in a small block, are scattered around
vast and gently sloping parkland that
descends to the superb main beach. Each
has a view and is spacious and comfortable,
decorated with dark-stained wood. There is
an elegant, quiet and rarified air about
Jumby Bay, with evening dining up at the
Great House, a former sugar estate house.
Watersports, tennis and croquet.

Carlisle Bay, Old Road, St Mary's, Antigua,
t 484 0000, info@carlisle-bay.com, www.
carlisle-bay.com. The look here is minimalist
urban chic. This is the first Caribbean
venture of British hotelier Gordon Campbell
Gray, best known for One Aldwych. Set on a
secluded beach on Antigua's south coast,
facilities include free-form pool, tennis
courts, gym, spa, a gourmet restaurant
serving Asian fusion cuisine, and a separate
beachside bar-restaurant. Rooms are set
either directly on the beach or just back

from the beach in three-storey terraced villas. Inside, the minimalist tone is set by a subdued colour scheme, dark-wood furniture and costly fabrics (Thai silk curtains and Frette bed linen). There is nothing minimal about the in-room facilities, which include espresso machines, wireless Internet access, satellite TV and DVD/CD players.

Expensive

Blue Waters, PO Box 256, St John's, t 462 0290, UK t (01327) 831 007, US and Canada t 1 800 557 6536, res@bluewaters.net, www.blue waters.net. Set in its own protected cove on the northwestern tip of the island, with lovely tropical greenery and paths winding among gazebos and pools. The main buildings have a colonial theme, with classical arches, gingerbread woodwork, picket fences, and breezy central areas with market-style 'hurricane roofs', but the atmosphere is studiedly modern and relaxed. There are 77 rooms and suites in a variety of configurations (including the delightful Rock Cottage, which sits on its own promontory) and most of them overlook the beach. All-inclusive.

Galley Bay, t 462 0302, US t 1 800 345 0356, reservations@antigua-resorts.com, www.eliteislandresorts.com. Stands between a perfect beach and a lagoon on Antigua's west coast. Some of the 76 rooms and large, split-level suites are ranged along the beachfront, decorated with bright and colourful Caribbean fittings, but there are also the distinctive and slightly strange-looking Gauguin cottages, which have exposed wattle and white stucco walls with palm-thatch roofs. Quaint. All have air-con, fans, phones and TVs. In among the landscaped gardens of tropical crotons and golden palms are a spa and beauty salon, the Gauguin restaurant, tennis court, watersports desk, juice bar and a large pool with unlikely-looking waterfalls. All-inclusive.

Cocobay, t 562 2400, US t 1 800 816 7587, cocobay@candw.ag, www.cocobayresort. com. Situated on a headland in the southwest of the island, with distinctive, wooden West Indian design in its architecture. The 41 rooms are in cottages on a hillside, mock-rustic with 'tongue and groove' wooden walls, louvred windows, shingle roofs, planter's chairs on the small balconies and a shower with a view over the protected cove to the north. The central area right on the point continues the West Indian theme, with bar, dining room and pool with a view. The atmosphere is also studiedly simple, with no TVs or phones. Quiet and peaceful.

Inn at English Harbour, PO Box 187, English Harbour, t 460 1014, info@theinn.ag, www.theinn.ag. The main house stands on the hillside above the sailing activity of the harbour. There is a quiet and intimate air about the hotel, helped by the antique-looking stone buildings up top and their setting among charming tropical gardens. Nine rooms are ranged across the hillside and down below on the beach there are 24 delightful suites alongside the pool and beach bar. All mod cons and comforts. Also watersports. In the evening a shuttle runs up to the main house where you take cocktails and then dinner on the dining terrace, sheltered with date palms.

Copper and Lumber Store, PO Box 184, Nelson's Dockyard, t 460 1058, www.copperlumber antigua.com, clhotel@candw.ag. This has authentic historic charm. It has been historically reappointed in the old brick magnificence of one of the dockyard's finest buildings. Huge wooden supporting beams and slender balustrades run through the building and there is a Georgian dining room and quaint dungeon-like bar; rum puncheons in the courtyard, and 14 rooms and suites named after Nelson's ships... Dreadnought, Victory. It is well restored and attractive. There is no pool, but the beach is a short boat-ride away.

Moderate

Galleon Beach, English Harbour, t 460 1024, UK t (01242) 604030, US t 1 847 699 7570, galleonbeach@candw.ag, www.galleon beach.com. This has a lovely setting just across from the Dockyard. It is a series of cottages and villas scattered across a sweep of open gardens that rise from the seafront in Freeman's Bay to the lumbering slopes of Shirley Heights. There are 28 one- and two-bedroom cottages, a beachfront and a garden. Quite simple but comfortable.

Siboney Beach Club, Dickenson Bay, PO Box 222, t 462 0806, *siboney@candw.ag*, *www.siboneybeachclub.com*. If you would prefer to be on the beach, then this is the best bet, on Dickenson Bay. There are 12 very comfortable suites set in a three-storey block, each with a balcony looking out onto a tropical garden and pool. It has a lively thatch-roofed restaurant looking over the beach through the palm trees, just a short walk down the sand from all the noise and activity of the beach bars and watersports.

Hawksbill Beach Resort, about 4 miles from St John's, PO Box 108, t 462 0301, *hawksbill@candw.ag*, *www.hawksbill.com*. An active beachfront-style hotel, this takes its name from the oddly-shaped rock that lies off one of its four (one clothes-optional) beaches. From an old plantation house and windmill on a promontory, the 111 rooms are strung out along the waterfront in blocks and cottages. Quite large and lively, pool, most watersports available, tennis, comfortable rooms and some evening entertainment. All-inclusive.

Coco's Antigua, PO Box 2024, Jolly Bay, t 460 2626, *cocos@candw.ag*. This series of cottages decorated in traditional Caribbean style is set on the rising ground of a promontory on the tortuous western coastline of the island. It is small and friendly with just twenty rooms, which overlook the shallow waters of Jolly Bay. At the upper end of this price category.

The Admiral's Inn, PO Box 713, Nelson's Dockyard, t 460 1027, UK t (020) 8940 3399, US t 1 800 223 5695, *admirals@candw.ag*. A magnificent setting right on the harbour in Nelson's Dockyard, in the former engineers' office and storerooms, with beautiful worn bricks that were shipped out as ballast and dark wooden beams and floorboards. Fourteen rooms in all: some large ones on the first floor, others tucked away in the sail loft. Dining room on a deck out front among guinep and casuarina trees. No pool or beach, but a short boat ride from Freeman's Bay – and anyway, the charming, historic atmosphere more than makes up for it.

Falmouth Harbour Beach Apartments, near the Admiral's Inn (*see* above), Nelson's Dockyard, PO Box 713, t 460 1027/1094, *www.dockyard-divers.com/falmouth.htm*. Twenty-two studio apartments with kitchens set on the harbourfront and on the hillside. Modern and well fitted, they each have balconies and verandas, some sports facilities and all the nautical activity and restaurants nearby.

Jolly Beach Resort, PO Box 2009, St Johns, t 462 0061, UK t (01372) 469 818, US t (954) 919 0191, *info@jollybeachresort.com*, *www.jollybeachresort.com*. Located on Antigua's west coast and set in 40 acres of tropical gardens bordering a mile-long beach. A lively all-inclusive resort for all ages. Facilities include two swimming pools (one with waterfall and Jacuzzi), five bars, five restaurants, water sports, Internet room and wedding gazebo. Widely used in tour operator packages.

Jolly Harbour Beach Resort, Marina and Golf Club, PO Box 1793, St Mary's Parish, t 462 3085, *www.jollyharbourantigua.com*. One of the largest marina, golf and beach resorts in the Caribbean, spread over 350 acres. A complex of two-bedroom, self-catering waterfront villas with kitchens. Amenities include 18-hole golf course, massive sports centre, shopping centre, supermarket, pharmacy, bank, two beaches, two helicopters, casino, 105-berth marina, five restaurants and bars. Widely used by tour operators.

Catamaran Hotel, PO Box 958, Falmouth Harbour, t 460 1036, US t 1 800 223 6510, Canada t 1 800 424 5500, *catclub@candw.ag*, *www.catamaranantigua.com*. On the northern shore of Falmouth Harbour you will find very good value at the Catamaran, set in a couple of modern blocks with mock-classical pillars and balustrades. There are 16 comfortable, fan-ventilated rooms in blocks on the waterfront, some kitchenettes, and a restaurant on the dock at the Catamaran marina nearby. The beach is passable, with a few watersports on offer.

Inexpensive

Murphy's Apartments, All Saints' Road, St John's, t 461 1183. Less expensive rooms can be found here on a hill above town, where there are thirteen reasonably comfortable apartments with kitchens and a hearty Antiguan welcome.

Eating Out

The food in Antigua is quite similar to that of other British West Indian islands: hotels tend to offer studiously 'international' fare and local food has a good mix of fresh local fish and traditional Caribbean ground provisions. There are some exceptions, though, where you get good food in the best Caribbean settings. There is also surprising variety in the restaurants, with French and Italian fare as well as West Indian. Most of the good restaurants are in St John's or in the southeastern area of the island around English Harbour, which is quite lively because of the yachting fraternity. Restaurants add a service charge of 10% and there is a 7% sales tax on top. **Categories** are arranged according to the price of a main course: expensive = EC$50 and above; moderate = EC$20–50; inexpensive = under EC$20.

Around St John's and the North

Expensive

Julian's Alfresco, Runaway Beach, **t** 562 1545, *julian@candw.ag*. The most elegant evening out, in the charming dining room of an old St John's house, with exposed beams and wooden interior dressed in a theme of light and dark green. You can start with a cocktail in the courtyard or bar upstairs, then repair to the candlelit, linen-covered tables, where waiters are poised to bring you an *amuse-bouche* and dishes under silver cloches. The cuisine is a modern adaption of classical French techniques and touches of Caribbean and Cajun. Try the *ceviche* followed by cumin-roasted fresh fish. *Closed Mon.*

Chez Pascal, Galley Bay, **t** 462 3232. The service and the cuisine here are traditionally French in style, though Pascal, the chef, also uses the best of Caribbean ingredients: *crevette au safran* (saffron shrimps) followed by a *magret de canard* or a *filet de vivaneau gré bloise* (snapper in capers and lime with a touch of cream). The restaurant, on a terrace with classical arches and balustrades around a lit pool, is quite remote out on Galley Bay Hill. The road is bumpy and then very steep, but it is well worth the effort.

Le Bistro, in the north of the island, **t** 462 3881. Set in a modern villa with tables on a veranda lost in greenery. The menu is French but there are Caribbean touches: start with a light crab soup with snow crab meat and *cilantro*, and follow with roasted *mahi mahi* in a red wine Chambertin orange sauce or a crispy Long Island duck glazed in honey and a sweet and spicy orange sauce.

The Home Restaurant, Gambel's Terrace, off Fort Rd, St John's, **t** 461 7651. Tucked away in the northern suburbs, you will find a friendly reception in an old Antiguan home from the sixties. They serve 'Caribbean Haute Cuisine' (adapting international recipes to Caribbean ingredients and using locally available fruits) from a menu and a long list of daily-changing specials on the blackboard. After fishcakes in a papaya-pimento sauce there is Arawak duck served in a pineapple rum or mango sauce (or sorrel-papaya sauce at Christmas), or chicken shrimp coconut St Lucia served in a coconut shell.

Hemingway's Caribbean Café, St Mary's St, St John's, **t** 462 2763. Set in one of St John's most charming wooden houses, white and green with a red tin roof, Hemingway's is lively and ever-popular: sit at the bench seats on the gingerbread veranda if you can. The specialities are creole food and seafood – start with a local pumpkin soup and follow with a Bajan flying fish. Lunches are simpler – burgers and salads. *Closed Sun.*

The Pavilion, 7 Pavilion Drive, Coolidge, **t** 480 6800, *www.thepavilionantigua.com*. Fine dining that comes highly recommended by savvy Antiguans. One-of-a-kind wine cellar. Jacket for men mandatory.

The Beach Restaurant (formerly Spinakers), Dickenson Bay, **t** 480 6940, *thebeach@candw.ag, www.bigbanana-antigua.com*. Great international cuisine by the beach; becomes Antigua's hotspot on Fri evenings.

Papa Zouk, opposite Princess Margaret School, St John's, **t** 464 7576. Best fish and rum restaurant in Antigua.

Sticky Wicket, 20 Pavilion Drive, Coolidge, **t** 481 7000, *www.thestickywicket.com*. For cricket fans, with Hall of Fame and memorabilia.

Moderate

The Commissioner Grill, Redcliffe St, St John's, **t** 461 1883. Excellent local food in a converted warehouse. A good welcome to go with trusty international and West Indian fare – spicy shrimp creole and marinated conch.

The Redcliffe Tavern, Redcliffe Quay, St John's, t 461 4557. Set in an old 'skirt and shirt' building on Redcliffe Quay – an old brick-built sugar warehouse, complete with winding gear and other machinery. International menu, some West Indian.

Pizzas in Paradise, Redcliffe Quay, St John's, t 462 2621. Ever-popular and lively, with solidly international fare, pizzas particularly of course, and often a musical accompaniment to your meal.

Inexpensive

There are a number of smaller, local restaurants in St John's, good places to stop for lunch and to gather for a drink at the end of the day. If you want to eat more cheaply in town, there are a number of snack joints in the market area where you can grab a chicken or a pattie.

Mamalolly's, Redcliffe Quay, St John's, t 562 1552. A vegetarian café, with a daily changing menu and good local fruit drinks.

The Roti King, on the corner of St Mary's St and Corn Alley, t 462 2328. Serves local West Indian dishes and *rotis*, envelopes of dough with a cooked filling which originate in Trinidad, further south in the island chain.

Pari's Pizzas and Steakhouse, Dickenson Bay, up the hill and round the corner. You can take out or eat in, seated in deckchairs on a covered yellow and green veranda with trelliswork and hanging plants.

Around English Harbour

Many places in the English Harbour area are open only seasonally, from Nov–April.

Moderate

HQ2 Restaurant and Bar, Nelson's Dockyard, t 562 2563, *hqantigua@hotmail.com*. Top-notch Asian-fusion cuisine in the delightful setting upstairs at the former Head Quarters building in Nelson's Dockyard – you sit inside in view of the working kitchens (across the lobster *vivier*) or outside on the veranda looking out towards the harbour mouth. Thai squid salad in a lime chilli dressing followed by a sweet chilli marinated lamb with fresh basil pesto or a hot and sweet fresh fish in cajun spices and

fresh yogurt. Fine wine list and a selection of aged Caribbean rums as *digestifs*.

Southern Cross, Falmouth Harbour, t 460 1797, *southcrossrest@candw.ag*. Sit on a breezy deck high above the water on padded safari chairs, looking out over the ink-black harbour and the lights of all the yachts. The fare is fine Italian and international: veal *mignon* with a gorgonzola sauce and home-made pastas.

Colombo's, Galleon Bay (the other side of English Harbour from Nelson's Dockyard), t 460 1452. Italian seems to be the flavour of the decade in this corner of the island: this is one of two excellent spots in the southeast. Here you dine on an open-sided terrace with wicker lamp shades. International and Italian fare, lots of home-made pastas. Some entertainment, particularly Fridays.

Alberto's, Willoughby Bay, t 460 3007, *albertos@candw.ag*. Tucked away on its own in Willoughby Bay and definitely worth making the detour for. It is set on a wooden deck with sloping tin roofs, trellis and lots of greenery. Steaks and some Italian dishes: veal *pizzaioli* or a ravioli of salmon and asparagus. Can get quite lively when people play the piano for fun. Popular at weekends.

Moderate

There is a clutch of simpler but fun places to eat scattered around English and Falmouth Harbours, patronized by a lively crowd of itinerant yachtspeople.

Le Cap Horn, between English and Falmouth Harbours, t 460 1194. Set on a pretty veranda, with a mantle of greenery around the trellis, this offers French fare in suitably culinary language – the *pétoncles* (scallops) come in a *rosace à l'Anis* and the pork as a *piccata de porc*. There is a pizzeria next door, where your order is cooked on a wood fire.

Eden Café, just outside Nelson's Dockyard, t 460 2701. This is perhaps the nicest spot by day; set in a garden behind an oversize yellow and green picket fence. Smoothies, focaccia, salads and sandwiches. In the evening (from 7pm) it becomes **Abracadabra**, t 460 1732. A lively Italian restaurant with a popular bar outside.

Catherine's Café, at the Slipway across from Nelson's Dockyard, t 460 5050. You sit at wicker tables on a deck right on the waterfront of English Harbour; there are baguettes and more sophisticated fare.

Mad Mongoose, between English and Falmouth Harbours, t 463 7900. A fun, lively spot: it's a bar and eatery, with some tables in a yard out front and others in an indoor dining room and bar (next to the pool table). Thoroughly international style: roast pork or pan-fried dolphin. *Closed Mon.*

Grace before Meals, between English and Falmouth Harbours. A shed selling burgers, *rotis* and hot-dogs.

Cloggy's, t 463 8083. English Harbour (next to Abracadabra). Serves Dutch cuisine with a Caribbean twist.

Bars and Nightlife

There are plenty of lively bars offering all-day drinking and then happy hours in the evening, particularly along Dickenson Bay, in town and around English Harbour. In St John's, there are also lively haunts in the nice old buildings of the streets around Redcliffe Quay.

You might even want to try Antigua's own island-brewed beer, Wadadli. Once this was so horrible as to be nearly undrinkable (even when the importation of other beers was banned as an encouragement, still nobody drank it), but now it is lighter and passable. It is even sold in Germany as one of the world's only beers made from (desalinated) sea water.

Galley Bar (and Boutique), Nelson's Dockyard. Day-long drinking to be had.

Main Brace, at the Copper and Lumber Store. In season you might try 'twofers' (two for one) here on a Tuesday or a Friday.

Last Lemming, downstairs at the Antigua Yacht Club, Falmouth Harbour. A popular place to move on to, it's quite busy on any night.

Shirley Heights Lookout, above English Harbour. Something of an island institution. A good spot for a sunset drink, but particularly on a Sunday afternoon when a band plays in the sunset (starting at 3pm). It attracts a riotous crowd by the early evening.

Lashings, Sandhaven Beach, Runaway Bay, t 462 4438, *www.lashings.com*. A nice spot on the beach. Entertainment three nights a week and takeaway pizza till late.

C & C Wine Bar, Redcliffe Quay, St John's. A casual but sophisticated wine bar, especially good for South African wines.

Steely Bar & Restaurant, Jolly Harbour Sports Centre, t 462 6260. Lively, friendly bar and eatery with good Caribbean cuisine; open-air or covered dining overlooking the marina. Live music on Friday.

Casinos

King's Casino, the second you step off the cruise ship into Heritage Quay.

Departure lounge, airport.

Casino Riviera, Runaway Bay. An alarmingly lit place.

Coral Reef Casino, Jolly Harbour.

Beach Bars

The bars in Dickenson Bay and Runaway Bay often continue into the evening.

The Beach Restaurant, Dickenson Bay, t 480 6940, *www.bigbanana-antigua.com*. A popular independent bar among the scattering of hotel bars on this bay; you can get a pleasant meal after sizzling in the sun.

Lashings, Runaway Bay, t 462 4491, *www.lashings.com*. Top of the crop at the moment. They occasionally play beach cricket (watch out, you may come up against Antiguan Richie Richardson, who is part-owner). There is a pretty deck at one end where you can take advantage of the massive menu and a busier drinkers' area at the other.

Miller's by the Sea, Runaway Bay. This is a neat series of parasols ranged behind a conch-shell-topped wall. It is quite large, so, for something a little more secluded, you can head further down the beach to Fort James, where there are a couple of bars.

Darkwood Beach Bar. One of a number of great sunset-watching bars on the endless strands of the southwest: a few parasols stand in front of a stretch of white trellis-work.

Creole Beach Bar, Crab Hill Beach. You'll find this small, tin-roofed shed in the south-western corner, where you can get a beer and a good, simple meal.

Turner's Beach Restaurant, at Johnson's Point, t 462 9133. A bar and grill with palm-thatched parasols and plastic chairs.

The Nelson's Dockyard National Park, which consists of about 15 square miles of the south of the island, is not a park in the sense of an area reserved for wildlife. In fact it is a centre for tourism, taking in bus tours and considerable yachting activity. It claims to be 'an ever-evolving environment which preserves our history, culture and nature alongside today's needs'. There are some important natural areas in this part of the island, however, including a wilderness area in Rendezvous Bay. On the east coast, Half Moon Bay is also a Wildlife Reserve and can be toured. Tropikelly Trails (*t 461 0383*) can provide guides who are well informed about the natural life of the island.

Fortress-foraging

In the 18th century, Antigua's coastline bristled with forts and fortlets, many of which still exist, though many are also buried 15ft deep in scrub. Aficionados and fort boffins will enjoy rootling around the ruins, and of course they still have the fantastic views for which they were built in the first place.

Fort James (early 18th century) and **Fort Barrington** guard the entrance to St John's harbour. Fort Barrington, on the south side, has a plaque commemorating William Burt, the Governor in whose tenure it was built. On it he signs himself *Imperator et Gubernator insularum Carib* (Emperor and Governor of the Leeward Islands). This Governor had some difficulties with the islanders, especially after drawing his sword at dinner and attacking some imaginary intruders who were supposedly lurking behind his chair.

Johnson Point Fort is at the southwestern corner of the island. Farther east, as you pass through Falmouth, **Monks Hill Fort** (as it is known to most Antiguans, though its name was officially Great George Fort) looms up on the hill. Built in the 17th century, it was a refuge for the women, children, slaves and cattle in case of attack by the French and their Carib allies. The track to the fort turns off the main road at the village of Liberta, and is only passable by four-wheel-drive vehicles. **Fort Berkeley**, a short walk beyond Nelson's Dockyard, was built in 1744 to guard the entrance to English Harbour. It is connected to Fort Charlotte on the other side of the channel: its soldiers would haul up a chain boom if a seaborne invasion was threatened. Above Fort Berkeley the ground is crawling with earthworks and gun emplacements and on the other side of the harbour are the major fortifications of **Shirley Heights**. *The Old Forts of Antigua* by T. R. St Johnston gives a rundown of the strongholds which made the island, for its size, the most fortified place in the world.

St John's

Antigua's capital, St John's, stands on gently rising ground above a large bay, its streets laid out on a gridiron plan. There has been considerable building recently and although many of the older wood and stone buildings with overhanging balconies still remain, the town is taking on an increasing overlay of universal modernity as larger, functional concrete buildings muscle in.

More than a third of Antiguans live in or around the ever-expanding St John's. The town centre is showing the fruits of the island's prosperity with shops full of computers and clothes from all over the world, but a more traditional West Indian life can be seen just a few minutes' walk out of the centre of the town. Here you will still see the chaos of the market or fishermen making lobster pots and mending nets.

In centuries past most visitors arrived in Antigua via the harbour, passing beneath the two defensive outposts at Fort Barrington and Fort James at the mouth of the bay. Many still do, in the cruise ships that Antigua invites in. First steps ashore will lead into the vast ersatz, air-conditioned environment of **Heritage Quay**, with all its duty-free shopping and slot machine arcades. If you are not on a cruise ship or scouring for bargains, then you may want to avoid this. Instead, go to **Redcliffe Quay**, an area of old St John's that has been restored, a short walk along the boardwalk. It too is a shopping complex (though altogether a more pleasant experience), with galleries, craft and clothes shops. It is worth a detour for its cafés and restaurants even if you're not on the hunt for a bargain. There are old town houses and warehouses with stone foundations and clapboard uppers, with brightly painted shutters and louvres. There's even a red British phone box to make you feel at home.

The life of St John's is not far beyond. Towering above the town's activity from its stately position at the top of the rising ground are the twin grey towers of the **Cathedral of St John the Divine**. The octagonal structure was erected in 1845 after one of Antigua's relatively frequent earthquakes, and to prevent similar damage the interior has been completely lined with pine. The two life-size statues that stand at the gates of the cathedral, St John the Baptist and St John the Evangelist, were destined for French Dominica in the 18th century, but they were captured by a British warship and brought to Antigua.

The **Old Court House**, on the corner of Long Street and Market Street, dates from 1747, though it has been rebuilt a number of times, most recently after the earthquake in 1974. Now it is home to the **Museum of Antigua and Barbuda** (*t 462 1469; open Mon–Fri 8.30–4, Sat 10–2; adm free, EC$2 suggested*), and it houses an exhibition of Amerindian Antigua (known to them as *Wadadli*), with *zemies* from the 100 archaeological sites on the island, as well as colonial and more modern Antiguan memorabilia, including Viv Richards' (an Antiguan) cricket bat, used when he broke the world record for the fastest Test century.

Since Antigua began to host West Indian cricket Test Matches in 1981, the venue has been the stadium up above the cathedral. In 1736 this area was used as an execution ground following a slave rebellion. The ringleader Prince Klaas and four others were broken on the wheel (a punishment in which the victim was strapped to a cartwheel and his bones broken one by one), six were 'put out to dry' (hung in chains and starved) and 58 were burned at the stake. The Antiguans now enjoy watching the similar roastings meted out to visiting cricket teams. If there is a game on while you are in town, go to it. On Independence Avenue running south from here, there has been a lot of building around Dredger's cricket field, where you will see the House of Parliament, a white modern building where the Antigua Parliament conducts its business, the government complex and the new St John's Hospital on the hill.

A walk back through downtown St John's will take you to the new market building, the Fisheries Complex and the new West bus station, all enclaves of traditional West Indian mayhem, where the banter seems as much a part of the game as buying the local produce or catching a bus.

The Northern Coastline

The area north of St John's is the most developed in the island, both by the tourist industry, which has built hotels all around the coastline north of Runaway Bay and Dickenson Bay, and by prosperous Antiguans who have moved out of town to live in large villas set in hibiscus and bougainvillea gardens. At the eastern side of the northern coast, beyond the airport, is **Long Island**, a low island a few hundred yards offshore, once used for grazing cattle and sugar cultivation. Now home to an expensive hotel and villa complex, Jumby Bay, it was traditionally famed for exporting far more sugar than it could possibly produce, all illegally shipped in from Guadeloupe. Having sworn in seven hogsheads for export before the magistrate, the owner would promptly add the letters 'ty' and ship out that amount to eager British markets.

The main road passes the Vere Bird International Airport and beneath hills littered with windmill shells and modern communications aerials before returning to St John's.

East of St John's

Travelling due east from the capital on the Old Parham Road, you pass through lowlands that once were covered with canefields. A turn left leads to the old town of **Parham**, one of the first settlements and oldest harbours on the island. The few remaining old buildings are now surrounded by small clapboard houses set among the palm trees and more recent tourist development around the boatyard.

One of the oldest sugar plantations on the island, **Betty's Hope**, is off the main road to Indian Town Point on the east coast. The estate house is just foundations on the highest point now, but the twin cones of the sugar works and several outhouses have survived. One windmill has been restored with all its machinery and you can walk around the ruins of the boiling and curing house. In the visitor centre itself (*open Tues–Sat 10–4*) there is a small model of it as a working plantation and there are tools and descriptions of sugar planting, harvesting, crushing, boiling and curing and rum distilling and shipping.

The main road continues to the east coast, limestone brittle that has been buffeted and smashed over the millennia by the Atlantic's wave action. The coastline gives some cracking views of the jade and royal blue sea flecked with whitecaps. The much vaunted **Devil's Bridge** is a natural span cut out of the rock at Indian Town Point. On a rough day the area is spectacular as the full force of the ocean thrashes against the coral coastline, compressed and hissing as it bursts up through blowholes. Antigua's coastline has many indentations here, creating deep and well-protected bays, and just around the corner from all the spray are beaches tucked in the coves, as at Long Bay.

Just farther south, the village of **Freetown** was settled soon after Emancipation in 1834. The liberated slaves formed their own villages away from the plantations, often in remote areas such as this where they could settle on unused land.

St John's to English Harbour

If St John's was the administrative centre of the Leeward Islands, the British Navy maintained its rule of the Caribbean waves (often successfully) from the southeast of the island, at what is now English Harbour. The All Saints road leads south out of St John's past the market through the centre of the island, rolling scrubland dotted occasionally with the cone of a windmill. The development, now concrete houses which have replaced the pretty wooden shacks that once were standard Antiguan homes, has stretched to this area of the island and so there are houses either side of the road through the villages of **All Saints** and **Liberta**, another town created by the freed slaves. Eventually you run down to the south coast, and skirting the edge of the huge Falmouth Harbour, you come to **English Harbour**. The secluded inlet is now one of the prettiest and most picturesque spots in the Caribbean, but 200 years ago the West Indies was a hardship posting, and one visitor considered Antigua 'one of the most infernal places on the face of the globe'. On his first visit, the future Admiral Nelson thought of Antigua as a 'barbarous island' and the dockyard now bearing his name as a 'vile spot'.

Nelson's Dockyard

Set on a point deep in the tortuous recesses of English Harbour, Nelson's Dockyard (*adm, for which a tour is available*) is a conglomeration of restored stone warehouses, workshops and quarters that once made up an 18th-century naval station. Were it not for the flowery tropical shirts on the tourists and the gleaming white of the yacht hulls, you might imagine you could hear the whistles and drum rolls of an active barracks. The waters are still plied by sailing craft, and you can watch the yachts manoeuvring between the headlands and making for open water much as they did 200 years ago.

At the entrance to the dockyard, once guarded to deter intruders, you will be waylaid by the inevitable T-shirt sentry at the small shopping arcade. Once inside, the charm of the place takes over. The quarters, with gently sloping roofs that reach out and shade balconies, have all been repaired, as have the old sail loft and workshops. Cannon, capstans and the odd anchor stand proud in mock menace and the boat-house pillars and sprays of tropical flowers give an air of groomed antiquity.

The dockyard was abandoned by the Navy in 1889 and fell into disrepair, but was restored by the Society of the Friends of English Harbour and reopened in 1951 as Nelson's Dockyard. Even if it has his name, Nelson himself certainly had no love for the place. He was based here for three years, as the young captain of HMS *Boreas*, between 1784 and 1787. He cruised the Leewards for much of the time, but during the hurricane season, when the French fleet was absent from the Caribbean, he spent time in the dockyard, jokingly threatening to hang himself.

He fell out with the islanders by enforcing the Navigation Act, which declared their profitable trade with American ships illegal (he had to stay on board his ship for eight weeks to avoid arrest when they took him to court). It was a pretty miserable time, though he found some solace in his marriage to Fanny Nesbit, a young widow from the nearby island of Nevis. He was happy to leave the Caribbean and did not return except briefly in 1805, hot on the tail of Villeneuve and the French fleet, in a chase of thousands of miles that culminated in the Battle of Trafalgar.

Nelson's Dockyard is a bit of tourist trap, with hotels, bars and restaurants, and you can expect to see a few blisteringly red package-holiday conscripts press-ganged on to tour-bus lunches. However, with all the yachts and working chandleries and repair shops, the place also retains a nautical air. Also there are always a few latter-day sailors loitering on shore for a few days, looking for grog and a brawl like their predecessors in centuries past. There are excellent signs illuminating the different buildings and how they were used.

In the attractive wooden building that was once the naval officers' house you will find the **Nelson's Dockyard Museum**. It covers the whole story of English Harbour, including the natural environment (from earthquakes to termites), the Arawaks and Caribs (with displays of their tools and pottery), the early Europeans (navigation instruments), and the people who lived in the dockyard (graffiti and tools such as blacksmiths' bellows and caulkers' tools). There are some small interactive models (e.g. to show how the capstans outside were used for careening), 'Nelson's bedroom' and a gift shop. There is a children's section in which they can learn to climb a rope.

On the opposite shore from the dockyard, **Clarence House** stands on the hill. This handsome Georgian Caribbean house, constructed of coral rock and with a large louvred veranda, was built in 1787 for Prince William Henry, later to be King William IV, who was in command of HMS *Pegasus* stationed at Antigua. He was a friend of Nelson and gave away Fanny Nesbit at their marriage. Clarence House is the official country residence of the Antiguan Governor General and was under restoration at the time of writing.

Scattered all over the steep hillsides above English Harbour is the garrison of **Shirley Heights**, another extended family of barracks with arched walkways, batteries, cisterns and magazines. It was fortified in the 1780s by General Shirley, the Governor of the Leeward Islands from 1781 to 1791, in order to defend the harbour below. The fortifications had an uninterrupted view across to Guadeloupe, giving advanced warning of any impending French invasion, which means that the view is exhilarating. Once the fortress was constructed, the French never considered invading again, of course. The site was abandoned in 1856 and fell into ruin, but some buildings have been repaired. At the top of the hill you will find the **Dow's Hill Interpretation Centre** (*open daily 9–5; adm*) where a multimedia show takes you through a fairly simple display of Antigua's history, through American Indians, Columbus, European explorers and settlers, the plantation era and merchants, the triangle of trade and then naval years to modern Antigua and its carnival and Sailing Week. There is also a gift shop and a café with a view.

The Southwest

Many of Antigua's fine beaches are on the west coast south of St John's and these include Deep Bay, Hawksbill Beach and Dark Wood Bay. Inland, among the shaggy green hillocks, is **Green Castle Hill**, where there are some odd rock formations that have come to be known in tourist lore as the megaliths, imaginatively thought by some to have been used by the Caribs as a sort of shrine. The view is particularly good from the top of the hill.

The road emerges on the sea and skirts the coastline for several miles, in the lee of the Shekerley mountains, Antigua's biggest hills. The tallest among them is the 1,319ft **Boggy Peak**, from which the view extends to Guadeloupe in the south and as far as St Kitts to the north on a clear day. It is also possible to see Barbuda, Antigua's sister island. To reach the peak you must take the steep road inland from Cades Bay on the south coast. The coastal road is a pleasant drive, where you can see fields of black pineapple, a small and succulent variety that Antigua exports.

At Carlisle Bay and the town of **Old Road** (from the old word 'roadstead' meaning harbour), the coastal road cuts inland up Fig Tree Hill, the island's lushest and most attractive area. At the village of Swetes, it forks south towards English Harbour or north back towards St John's.

Barbuda

Barbuda's great attractions are its marine life and its beaches. Virtually undisturbed and visible very close to the surface, the reefs are forested with corals that move gently with the water and teem with fluorescent fish. And the beaches are magnificent: the sand on Barbuda is supreme, the beaches are measured in miles and it is difficult not to be alone. There is so much sand that they even export it.

The island is 62 square miles of scrubland that barely clears the water, lying about 30 miles north of Antigua. It is made entirely of limestone coral deposits that have encrusted an outcrop on the same geological bank as Antigua. The Highlands, in the north of the island, struggle to top 211ft. The contours of Dulcina, as the island was known to the Spaniards, are even gentler than Antigua's and the pace of life considerably slower.

Caribs prevented early settlement of the island, but when they were wiped out, a Christopher Codrington leased the whole island as a private estate. The Codrington name is left everywhere on the island: in the only settlement, just a few streets of concrete or clapboard houses, in the name of the airstrip, in the lagoon on which it sits. The island stayed within his family from 1674 until about 1870, at a rent to the Crown of 'one fat sheep, if demanded'. Because the soil was not fertile enough to

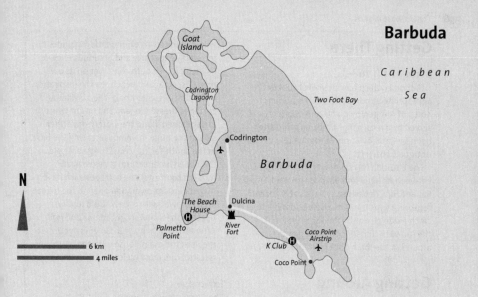

Barbuda

Caribbean Sea

support sugar cane, it was used as a ranch for stock and work animals, a farm for provisions, a deer-park and eventually a cotton plantation. Many of the animals are still seen wandering about much as they always have, and the ubiquitous Caribbean goat gets everywhere. There are even rumours that Barbuda was used as a slave farm, where the tallest and strongest slaves were encouraged to breed. Amateur anthropologists maintain that this is the reason for Barbuda's abnormally tall population.

In 1976 the 11-person Barbuda Council was set up and the island was granted elected government (nine members are elected and two are appointed). It has a strange political arrangement, with land owned in trust by the Council. Barbudians simply get the permission from the Council to build on it and then do so. They are currently galvanizing and looking to develop the island. But, as in so many island partnerships, the island has an uncomfortable relationship with Antigua, by whom they feel neglected. Certainly the Antiguans would like to get hold of the land to develop it and in 2000 they challenged the communal ownership in the courts. There are occasional words about the advantages of being independent of Antigua.

With about 1,500 inhabitants, Barbuda is extremely quiet, and it is still surprisingly undeveloped as Caribbean islands go. The main activities are fishing and traditional

Best Beaches

South-coast beach: Runs between Coco Point and River (the port area).

Lewis Beach, **Palm Beach** or **Quinnell Beach**: Between Palmetto Point (which has mounds of pink-tinted sand) and Cedar Tree Point. Perhaps ask to be dropped here after a trip to the frigatebird sanctuary. Seventeen miles of magnificent, completely deserted sand.

Two Foot Bay and **North Beach**: On the northern coastline.

Getting There

Barbuda t (1 268–)

Barbuda (which has an unlikely but entirely appropriate airport code, BBQ) is 20mins north of Antigua by plane, and Codrington is served by a return flight morning and afternoon by Carib Aviation, Barbuda t 460 0004, Antigua t 462 3147.

The Barbuda Ferry, a power catamaran, runs between Antigua and Barbuda on Wed, Thurs, Sat and Sun, departing St John's at 8.30am, returning 5pm. It might also be possible to catch a ride on one of the ships that makes the run with tinned food and essentials; ask around at the main dock in St John's, Antigua.

Getting Around

There are a few **cars** available for hire, through individuals: ask at the airport. **Taxis** are available through the hotels, or contact Eric Burton, t 460 0078. Alternatively, try to **hitch** a ride. Most drivers that pass will offer you a ride anyway, but, with few cars headed anywhere you might want to go, it can be a long wait. If you would like a **tour** of the island, contact George Burton, t 460 0103, or Paradise Tours Barbuda, t 460 0081.

Tourist Information

The **tourist office** can be found at the Council Building, t 460 0077.

Because most goods are imported, Barbuda tends to be quite expensive. Bring things that you cannot live without. EC dollars are preferred, but US greenbacks are accepted.

Where to Stay and Eat

Barbuda t (1 268–)

There are just a couple of places to eat outside the hotels, set in modern concrete buildings. The food is solidly West Indian with the occasional dish cooked in white wine.

Luxury

The K Club, t 460 0300, US t 1 800 648 4097, UK t (01453) 835 801, *kclub@candw.ag*. The island's limited accommodation includes an incredibly expensive and luxurious enclave located on the south coast. Set on its own 2-mile of spectacular beach, it's the inspiration of fashion designer Krizia. The 20 villas and cottages, dressed in jade and bright white, are stretched along the waterfront either side of the huge main house, taking the best of the south-facing view. Using some old Caribbean architectural style (with all modern comforts), the cottages each have a huge bedroom, a veranda open to the breeze and a shower with a view. It is a luxury beach club – watersports, tennis and golf. After all the activity, you can enjoy gourmet meals in the main house with the few other guests. Stars most welcome.

Expensive

The Beach House, Palmetto Point, Barbuda, t 537 1352, *info@thebeachhousebarbuda. com*, *www.thebeachhousebarbuda.com*. Set on a spectacular stretch of pink sand, 20mins drive from the airport, this new 'barefoot luxury' hideaway is for travellers who really want to get away from it all. Guests have their own 'personal service ambassador' (a sort of combined butler and concierge) who meet them upon arrival, unpack their bags, draw a bath, arrange outings, and make sure guests have all they need. The 21 suites, all facing the ocean, are elegantly furnished in cool, minimalist style with the four-poster bed positioned in front of sliding glass doors. Sea-water swimming pool, lagoon and beach.

Moderate–Inexpensive

Nedd's Guest House, Codrington, t 460 0059. Cheaper accommodation.

Bus Stop Bed and Breakfast, Codrington, t 460 0081. (Not that there are any bus stops on the island, of course.) A cheaper option.

Palm Tree and Park Terrace, near the airstrip, t 460 0517. Local restaurant and bakery.

Lime Bar, overlooking Codrington Lagoon. This lime-green, yellow and purple bar is a typical Caribbean liming spot, a tin-roofed bar and disco overlooking the lagoon with a special thatched DJ box for Friday and Saturday nights.

West Indian subsistence agriculture with some building. 'Wrecking' was another source of income, as the reefs around Barbuda have been known to claim many ships in their time. There are reckoned to be around 200 shipwrecks off the island. The islanders don't smuggle from other islands much any more, but Spanish Point is well known as a dropping point for airborne drugs deliveries. Tourism amounts to two extremely expensive hotels, a small resort and local guest houses.

The few hundred Barbudians left on-island (many have emigrated but revisit their families often) have a tight-knit community, nearly all of them living in the only town (really a village), Codrington. The most common names (most people are called one of them) are Beazer, Thomas, Harris and Nedd. The islanders show a welcoming interest in visitors. One person claimed that on arrival at the airport not so long ago, he was greeted with the words: 'But nobody said you were coming...'

Around the Island

The only town, **Codrington**, is a little tatty and extremely dozy. Its centre is around the now dilapidated Warden's House, the cricket ground and the old pond. It touches **Codrington Lagoon**, where you can take a boat out into the mangroves to see the colony of frigatebirds, which circle, distinctive dark arrow shapes with scissor tails, overhead to thousands of feet. The best time to go is between October and February – the mating and later the hatching season. You will see the males display, with their impossibly large gullets puffed up like vast red footballs so that their heads are forced skyward and their throats resonate with a clacking noise. The females cruise around and make their choice. From December their ungainly chicks start to hatch. To arrange the trip, ask around in town (try to find Pat Richardson).

The island's main sight is in marginally better condition. **River Fort** is a Martello tower with a skirting of walls that stands on the south coast, its gun turrets without cannon now, but still guarding the approach to the original island dock and harbour. It is a favourite picnic area with the islanders. For many years the island was a deer-park for the Codringtons and people do still hunt them and shoot duck. At the southeastern point **Palister Reef**, just south of Coco Point, has been made an Underwater National Reserve. **Spanish Point** is quite spectacular. The slabs of coral rock are battered by the Atlantic waves.

Highland House is the Codrington estate house that was built in 1750, but was never really occupied. Its ruins, just walls, outhouses and a cistern steadily being reclaimed by the scrub, are visible a few miles north of the village. There are caves to be explored in the northern part of the island, including Dark Cave, where a passage with fresh water leads 100 yards underground. Coral reefs grow off nearly all Barbuda's coasts, waving forests of staghorn and elkhorn where angelfish, trumpetfish and wrasses flit, and they make extremely good snorkelling. The corals are so close to the surface that it is hardly necessary to dive, so divers have to look after themselves.

Redonda

The chain of Caribbean volcanoes passes by about 30 miles west of Antigua and among its peaks rises the tiny pimple of Redonda, so named because of its nearly round shape. It stands between Montserrat and Nevis, a circle of cliffs sparse on top, uninhabited except by birds. In its 1 mile by one-third of a mile, it reaches an impressive 970 feet.

For nearly 400 years after its discovery by Columbus it was ignored, but eventually in the 1860s somebody realized that centuries' worth of bird droppings could be put to good use. Guano mining began, and at the height of production 30 years later the island produced 3–4,000 tons of phosphate annually.

That the island should be worth something to somebody was enough to bring claims of sovereignty from all the powers in the area, and so before long Redonda was annexed by the British and attached to Antigua, capital of the Leeward Islands.

However, a rival royal bid was made by an Irishman who happened to sail past in 1865. One Matthew Shiel, himself of regal stock, maintained he was descended from the ancient Irish Kings of Tara, claimed the island and appointed himself king. He may in fact have had right on his side: despite the presence of the superpowers of the age in the Caribbean for nigh on four centuries, none of them had apparently made a formal claim to the island. The fact that the British 'annexed' Redonda gives this added credibility. In 1880 Matthew Dowdy Shiel abdicated in favour of his son, another Matthew Shiel, born in nearby Montserrat, when the boy reached the age of 15. At his coronation, Matthew Phipps Shiel took the title King Felipe I. Later he left for England, intending to train as a doctor but actually embarking on a literary career and eventually becoming a successful novelist. Thus the court of King Felipe was established in England. It was a literary assembly, with courtiers such as J. B. Priestley and Rebecca West.

Subsequently the line passed to the poet John Gawsworth, self-styled King Juan I. With the kingdom's continuing prosperity in the middle of the 20th century, an 'Intellectual Aristocracy' was established in commemoration of M.P. Shiel's literary achievements. Peers of the Redondan realm included such other literary and not so literary luminaries as Dorothy L. Sayers, the publisher Victor Gollancz, Arthur Ransome, Lawrence and Gerald Durrell, Diana Dors, Dirk Bogarde and Dylan Thomas. The Kingdom of Redonda was fêted and well known in its day. Matthew Phipps Schiel (1865–1947) himself was known for an overly florid and luxuriant prose style. A few of his books are still in print because there were revivals of interest in him in the 1920s and 1960s. His most famous work was *The Purple Cloud* (1901), an allegory in which the world is threatened with destruction. John Gawsworth's work has also been largely forgotten since his death in 1970.

This most illustrious of Caribbean lineages was thought to have gone into decline, but over the years it has reappeared in a number of places. As 'incorporeal property', the title can be bequeathed or given away like an English manorial title, or for that matter sold, whatever the current incumbent decides (and there are rumours of John

Gawsworth selling it for a bottle of red wine in his favourite hostelry, the Alma in South London). Unbelievably, it has become the source of some controversy and dispute, pricking the fancy of quite a number of otherwise mature people. There are a number of claimants to the throne.

One line has been traced to the county of Norfolk in England and it now apparently resides with the fifth King of Redonda, King Leo. He regards his reign as 'a trusteeship, to perpetuate and develop for posterity a charming and unique quirk of history... The realm is pledged to keep the memory and literary achievements of M.P. Shiel and John Gawsworth 'green' through its Intellectual Aristocracy...'

Another putative King of Redonda actually visited the island in 1979. Jon Wynne-Tyson (a literary executor of both M.P. Shiel and John Gawsworth as it happens) made a visit with a court historian and reaffirmed his suzerainty over the domain by planting his flag, blue, brown and green in colour and 'made from pairs of old royal pyjamas by Her Royal Highness, Jennifer Wynne-Tyson'. In a spirit of European cooperation, he passed on the literary executorships to the leading Spanish author Xavier Marías (author of *A Heart So White*, *Tomorrow in the Battle Think on Me* and short stories *When I Was Mortal*). But not the title of King, which went to King Bob the Bald, a writer and yachtie based in Antigua.

Though Redonda is uninhabited now, there was once a post office there and it is possible to find Redonda stamps. There are some websites dedicated to Redonda. Try *www.redonda.org* and *www.antiguanice.com/redonda*.

Montserrat

Montserrat, the most southerly of the Leewards, has a jumbled interior of rain-forested mountains worthy of one of the Windward Isles to the south, but at 39 square miles (it is 11 miles by 7 miles at its widest point) its serried peaks are smaller, its slopes are gentler and island life is even slower. Like the Windwards, it also has a *soufrière*, a volcanic vent, which until recently was reckoned to be one of the Caribbean's less active volcanoes. But then in July 1995 it started to erupt, and it has held the island to ransom ever since. The capital, Plymouth, had to be abandoned and islanders who did not leave altogether were evacuated to the northern half of the island. Once, Montserrat had 12,000 inhabitants. Now there are reckoned to be about 5,000.

Volcanic problems aside, Montserrat has always been an attractive place. Without the typical white Caribbean beaches (its volcanic geology already saw to that, giving it dark sand instead), it never suffered a large beach-bound invasion, which meant that it retained a tranquillity now mostly lost to the rest of the West Indies. Instead it attracted a more stately visitor. It could be relied upon. People actually retired there. Now it has all changed, of course. Understandably the islanders have taken a while to come to terms with living in the shadow of the threatening colossus in the south. Most accept that it will affect their lives for the forseeable future. And they are still remarkably welcoming to outsiders.

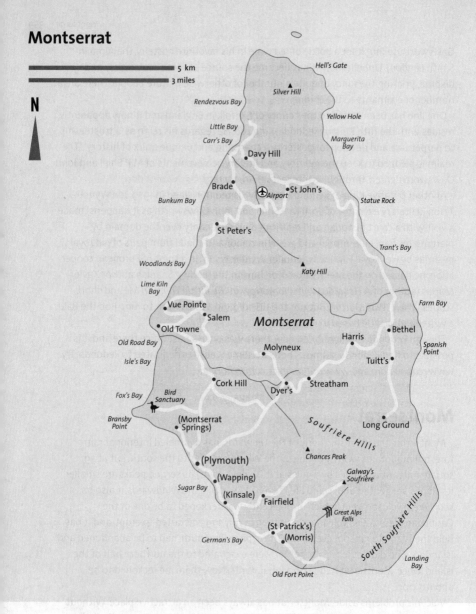

Montserrat

5 km

3 miles

N

Hell's Gate

Silver Hill

Rendezvous Bay

Yellow Hole

Little Bay

Carr's Bay

Marguerita Bay

Davy Hill

Brade

Airport

St John's

Bunkum Bay

Statue Rock

St Peter's

Trant's Bay

Woodlands Bay

Katy Hill

Lime Kiln Bay

Vue Pointe

Salem

Montserrat

Old Towne

Bethel

Old Road Bay

Harris

Spanish Point

Isle's Bay

Molyneux

Tuitt's

Fox's Bay

Bird Sanctuary

Cork Hill

Dyer's

Streatham

Bransby Point

(Montserrat Springs)

Soufrière Hills

Long Ground

(Plymouth)

Chances Peak

(Wapping)

Galway's Soufrière

Sugar Bay

(Kinsale)

Fairfield

Great Alps Falls

South Soufrière Hills

(St Patrick's)

(Morris)

German's Bay

Landing Bay

Old Fort Point

Montserrat has a considerable, if distant, Irish heritage which, along with its luxuriant appearance, has led to its being called the 'Emerald Isle' of the Caribbean. Many of the place names are clearly Irish, and although the islanders are obviously of African descent, at times it seems that you can hear an Irish lilt in their speech, momentary strains of brogue in the stream of West Indian. Whether this is imagined or not, Montserratian speech is one of the softest and most attractive of all variations in the English-speaking Caribbean. For all the Irish heritage (there used to be a shamrock on one of the eaves of Government House), the island has been a British colony for most of its history. It is one of just five British Overseas Territories remaining in the Caribbean, administered by a Governor appointed from London in partnership with the island legislature.

Poor Montserrat. It is such a charming island and it deserves better than its run of terrible luck. It was roundly trashed by Hurricane Hugo in 1989 – there were 10 deaths, an estimated 95 per cent of houses were damaged and not a single electricity pole was left standing – and then, when it was recovering and picking up again, the volcano started to rumble. Now the southern half of the island has been declared a no-go zone – Plymouth was pretty much destroyed. There was a time when total evacuation of the island was considered (this was eventually rejected because the northern part of the island is safe). Worst of all, though, it is impossible to know how long the problems will continue. The hope of the people, who have shown remarkable resilience, is that the worst of the volcanic activity is behind them. The new airport will be completed sometime in late 2005.

A few years ago it was hard honestly to recommend going to Montserrat, but the picture is definitely looking up. There's certainly nothing to stop anyone going – a few faithful regulars keep returning as they always have – and a few others have visited out of curiosity. It is not a typical Caribbean holiday, but if you do go, you will be met with customary good cheer and courtesy because, for all its troubles, Montserrat is still a delightful island.

History

Alliouagana (thought to mean 'land of the prickly bush') was deserted when Columbus passed on his second voyage. The Caribs were off raiding elsewhere. He paused long enough to name the island Santa Maria de Montserrate after the abbey near Barcelona in Spain and sailed for Hispaniola. Only pirates braved the Caribs' attention over the next 140 years.

Montserrat was settled in about 1632 as a separate colony for the Catholics from mainly Protestant St Kitts, the then English island about 40 miles to the northwest. Many of the settlers were Irishmen, as was the first governor, and the island soon gained a reputation as a place where Catholics and the Irish were welcome. They came from Protestant Virginia, and the population was also swelled after the Battle of Drogheda in 1649, when Cromwell deported many of the Irish prisoners of war. Irish indentured labourers from the other islands would make their way here once their term was served on another island.

As with so many islands, the first half-century of colonization was a litany of hurricanes, earthquakes and seaborne attacks. The raiders were French, Dutch and Spanish and, of course, the Caribs, who arrived in their hundreds, burning and looting, killing the men and carrying off women and slaves. The Irish colonists had an understanding with their French coreligionists and often when the raids took place their property would be left alone. But relations between the Montserratian settlers themselves were hardly any more peaceful. Laws had to be passed to prevent them from hurling insults at each other in the street, such as 'English Dog, Scots Dog, Cavalier, Roundhead and many other opprobrious, scandalous and disgraceful terms'.

By the late 17th century the land was covered with sugar cane well up into the hills. Because of the steep terrain, the cured sugar was loaded on to mules and casked only on the shore before shipping. Sugar meant slaves and a large number of Africans were brought in to work the canefields, giving Montserrat its mainly black population today. The occasional rebellions were put down ruthlessly. One was arranged for St Patrick's Day in 1768 when the slaves intended to take over Government House, but the plans were overheard by a slave woman who told the planters and the rebels were captured and executed.

As sugar failed and Emancipation came, other crops were grown and Montserrat became famous for limes. It was the second Caribbean exporter of the fruit after Dominica and much of the crop, 180,000 gallons one year, went to Crosse and Blackwell in Britain. Cotton became an export crop at the end of the 19th century and formed the basis of the Montserratian economy well into the 20th century. Like other Caribbean islanders, the Montserratians had moved onto small plots of land and were leading a simple agricultural existence. At the time of Emancipation in 1834 they worked for sixpence a day, the lowest wage in the Caribbean and, a hundred years later, their situation was still the worst in the Leewards.

This pitiful state led to considerable emigration from the island when a better life seemed possible elsewhere, and so most Montserratians have a relative who left for the canefields in the Dominican Republic or to work in oil in Curaçao. The exodus culminated in the 1950s, when 5,000 left for Britain. Subsequently, an influx of 'resident tourists', as they were known, many of them retired Americans and Canadians, brought the population back to about 12,000. Most recently there was a wave of incoming Dominicans and Guyanese, who came to work in the construction industry in the aftermath of Hurricane Hugo. Recently of course the movement has been the other way as the Montserratians left for Antigua and Britain and some of them to Canada and the United States.

Montserrat had a late start on the political scene. Robert Griffith and William Bramble led the Montserratians in their efforts to obtain a fair wage and in their political aspirations. The Montserrat Labour Party took all five seats in the first elections in 1951 and again in 1955. Internal affairs on the island are governed by a nine-seat Legislative Council which is elected every five years. Since April 2001 the island has been led by Dr John Osborne of the New People's Liberation Movement with seven of the nine seats (with the two members of the National Progressive Party in opposition). With what's left of the population living in the northern third of the island, the traditional constituencies were not used in the April 2001 election. Instead there was a single constituency and each voter had up to nine votes. Elections are next due by April 2006. As a British Overseas Territory, ultimate executive power rests with the Governor, representative of Queen Elizabeth II.

The Anatomy of a Volcano

Until recently Montserrat's *soufrière* was considered one of the less active in the Caribbean. Like the others it rumbled occasionally and let out the occasional gas emissions, but Montserrat was thought not to have erupted seriously for about 4,000

Getting There

Montserrat t (1 664–)

In the aftermath of the volcanic eruption, a new airport has been built at Geralds (between Sweeneys and St John's). Winair has been awarded a two-year contract to operate scheduled flights between Montserrat and Antigua on 19-seater Twin Otter aircraft.

The ferry *Opale Express*, t 491 2362, Antigua t 480 2980, departs from Heritage Quay in St John's (Antigua) twice a day and takes about 1hr 20mins to make the crossing to Port Little Bay in Montserrat. There is a departure tax of EC$45 or US$16.

Getting Around

By Taxi

The taxi drivers in Montserrat are known by name. Try Thomas 'Fombo' Lee, t 491 2347.

By Guided Tour

An island tour can be arranged through the taxi drivers, or through:
Carib World Travel, Woods Centre, Antigua, t 268 480 299, *arthurtonp@candw.ag*.
Runaway Tours, t 491 2776.

Car and Bike Hire

Cars or motorbikes can be rented through:
Ethelyne's Car Rental, t 491 2855, *www.winlyn.com*.
Montserrat Enterprises, t 491 2431.
Tropical Mansion Suites, t 491 8767.
Imagine Peace Bicycle Rental, t 491 8809.

Tourist Information

There are no tourist offices abroad, so to get information you will need to contact the Montserrat Tourist Office in the island itself: Box 7, Montserrat, t 491 2230, *mrattourist board@candw.ag*, *www.visitmontserrat.com*.

Embassies and Consulates

UK citizens are referred to the British High Commission in Antigua; American and Canadian citizens should refer to their consulates in Barbados.

Media

The island newspaper is *The Montserrat Reporter*, published weekly.

Money and Banks

The currency of Montserrat is the Eastern Caribbean dollar (fixed to the US dollar at EC$2.65 = US$1). The US greenback is also widely accepted, though expect your change in EC dollars.

Telephone Code

If you are calling Montserrat, the IDD code is t 1 664 followed by a seven-digit island number which begins 491. When on-island dial the full seven figures.

Watersports

Sports and activities can probably still be organized. General watersports including **scuba diving** can be arranged through:
Sea Wolf Diving, t 491 6859, *bryncunning ham@yahoo.com*, *www.seawolfdiving school.com*.

Day Sails and Deep-sea Fishing

Boat trips to isolated coves around the island and offshore at Plymouth can be arranged. Contact:
Danny Sweeney, t 491 5645. He also offers deep-sea fishing trips.

Where to Stay

Montserrat t (1 664–)

Just a few of hotels have remained open on the island. There are also rooms in private

years and the islanders (if not the vulcanologists) hoped it to be on its way to extinction. It came back to life with a vengeance in July 1995.

There are three sorts of eruption in Montserrat: phreatic, in which steam and ash or sometimes gravel emerge in a grey cloud; and pyroclastic, when slides of superheated ash, gases and rubble make it over the lip of the crater walls and head off down the

houses which can be contacted through the Tourist Board, the *visitmontserrat.com* website. Also try Tradewinds Real Estate, t 491 2004, *tradewinds@candw.ag*, *www.trade windsmontserrat.com*; and West Indies Real Estate, t 491 8666, *wirerealest@candw.ag*, *www.wirerealest.com*.

There is a 10% government tax on hotel rooms and villas and sometimes a 10% service charge will be added to your hotel bill.

Moderate

The Vue Pointe Hotel, Old Road Bay, t 491 5210, *vuepointe@candw.ag*, *www.vuepointe.com*. This hotel has ultimate easy old-time Caribbean grace and an attentive and welcoming air. The rooms are arranged around the sloping, lawned garden in three small blocks and a few comfortable octagonal rondavels, with balconies, huge beds, and louvres and fans to coax the island breezes and keep you cool. The main house, with library and pool, stands high above the Caribbean coast. Vue Pointe is family run, and a friendly crowd of regulars often gathers at the bar and restaurant. A beach bar is down below and there are watersports on the bay. There are two tennis courts and 14 cottages, 12 of which have kitchenettes.

Tropical Mansion Suites, close to Little Bay Beach, Sweeneys, PO Box 404, t 491 8767, *hotel@candw.ag*, *www.tropicalmansion.com*. Set in a modern Caribbean palace, three storeys of arches, balustrades and balconies, completed in 1999 in the north of the island. There are 18 rooms with all mod cons, cable TVs and fans, some rooms with kitchenettes. Restaurant, bar and pool.

Inexpensive

Erindell Villa Guest House, Woodland, t 491 3655, *erindell@candw.ag*, *switchboard. com/erindell*. A modern house in a pretty tropical garden with a swimming pool and a

fine view of the sea. Rooms have cable TV and kitchenettes.

Montserrat Moments Inn, Manjack Heights, t 491 7707, *flogriff@candw.ag*. Just four rooms with cable TV, fridge and air-con.

Eating Out

Montserrat's culinary tradition is mainly West Indian, based on the tropical vegetables and fruits that you will find on sale at the market, and the fish and animals that can be caught here. The island's Irish heritage is reckoned to reach as far as the food in goat water, a stew of goat meat with herbs, often served at festivities. Another local delicacy, only served on Dominica and Montserrat, is mountain chicken, which hops wild in the hills before it reaches your plate. In fact, it is not a chicken at all, but an outsize frog. Most of the restaurants have either closed or relocated to the north of the island in the present troubles.

Vue Pointe Hotel, t 491 5210, *vuepointe@ candw.ag*. The dining room here is probably the best place to eat.

Ziggy's, Mahogany Loop, t 491 8282. A great place offering excellent West Indian and international fare including lobster quadrille and Jamaican-style 'jerk' pork. Finish off with a sublime chocolate sludge.

The Good Life, Little Bay, t 491 4576. Caribbean dishes served in a modern, blue-roofed building overlooking Little Bay from the top of the hill.

Tina's Restaurant, Brade's Main Rd, t 491 3538. Hearty West Indian fare – chicken and fish with a tonnage of ground provisions.

Roots Man Beach Bar, Carr's Bay, t 491 5957. Vegetarian and Caribbean creole meals.

Jumping Jack, Vue Pointe Hotel. serves pub grub: fish and chips, burgers, chicken and mushroom pie. Fisherman Danny Sweeney catches the fish and his partner, Margaret, does the home cooking. *Open Wed–Sun for lunch and drinks. Dinner served Friday night.*

hillside. They run on a cushion of air at amazing speed, almost soundlessly, incinerating anything in their path. When they reach the sea they skitter and glide on the surface, steaming and fizzing. The third is a lava explosion, of which there have been a handful, exploding magma. Rain brings further problems because it causes mudflows: ash, rocks and general debris compound into sludge, which slides down the island's *ghauts* (river ravines) without warning.

Ash, which is like fine concrete dust, is actually the pulverized residue of rock from inside the volcanic crater. On Montserrat, it fell to depths of several feet, smothering the south of the island completely, giving the houses a ghostly grey roof-cladding and turning the landscape into a moonscape, suffocating and killing the vegetation. (Strangely, in smaller quantities, it has exactly the opposite effect, bringing incredible fertility; it made the grass on the Belham Valley golf course grow frantically, before it was covered by mudflows, that is.) Like Saharan dust, volcanic ash gets absolutely everywhere, leaving a grey film on everything, even inside sealable containers in the kitchen. As you walk on it, it crumps and crunches with each pad of your feet and rises in little clouds, hanging in the air and getting into your hair and nose. And, like concrete, when it mixes with water it becomes hard. Ash has been known to blow as far away as St Martin and St Vincent.

The recent activity began in 1992, when increased earth tremors began to be felt. On 18 July 1995 the islanders heard a long low rumbling, apparently like a distant jet, accompanied by smells of sulphur and some falls of ash. The volcano was very much alive again. This continued for a couple of months until 21 August, which is remembered as 'Ash Monday' because of a major ash-fall that put Plymouth, the capital, in darkness in the middle of the day. A few days later the situation was regarded as serious enough to merit evacuating the people living in the south of the island. To add insult to injury, Hurricane Iris came along, ripping out the temporary

Blarney

Of all the echoes you hear in West Indian English, the strongest in the speech of Montserrat is Irish. Some visitors have even claimed that the Montserratians have the gift of the gab and a truly Irish wit. The West Indians have a pretty mean sense of humour anyway (just nip down to the market and catch the banter), but particularly after a few rum punches, you might just think that you are in Galway.

In the 17th century, there were about 1,000 Irish families on the island, but since then, most of the original white settlers have left. However, their names certainly live on in black Montserratian families, such as Farrel, Daly and Ryan, as a quick look at the Montserrat telephone directory will show. The Irish harp is a national symbol and appears on the Montserratian stamps.

There is a nice story from the 19th century about an Irishman who arrived from Connaught to find himself addressed by a black man in Connaught brogue. He asked how long the man had been in Montserrat. 'Shure, yer honour, and three years it is that I've been here.' Flabbergasted, the Irishman replied, 'Glory be to God. And do ye turrn black in thot toime?' and got on the first ship back home (*The Pocket Guide to the West Indies*, Sir Algernon Aspinall, 1938).

Fans of Caribbean *soca* music will immediately recognize the name of (the Mighty) Arrow, who comes from Montserrat and whose calypso '*Hot Hot Hot!*' made it to the top all over the world a few years ago.

accommodation. Montserrat was lucky, though, that Hurricanes Luis and Marilyn did not hit the island full-on, but passed by farther north.

In November 1995 a 'dome' appeared next to Castle Peak, a large extruding area of superheated material that was constantly changing, building up and then collapsing, pushing up 'spikes' (*see* 'Martinique', pp.298–9), which then fell over. At night it glowed in places where rocks had rolled down and left the incandescent interior exposed for a while. In December 1995 the people were evacuated again for a couple of months. In April 1996 there was a third evacuation, north of the exclusion zone, which cuts the island between Richmond Hill on the west coast and Spanish Point on the east. Everyone crowded into the villages of the northwest. Businesses were run out of lorry-containers, the library became the prison, schools worked in morning and afternoon shifts; the main room at the Vue Pointe Hotel became chapel, courtroom and weekly disco.

Plymouth had to be abandoned. Lying on an open bay on the southwest coast, it was a classic small West Indian town, with old Georgian 'skirt and shirt' buildings – stone lower storeys with columns and arches and wooden upper storeys, topped with shaded balconies and red tin roofs. Once it had a population of 3,500. Now it is entirely deserted and largely destroyed – burned by the pyroclastic flows and then covered by ash-falls and mudflow. For a while, people would return to clear the ash off their roofs from time to time and to keep their houses and fields in order (in June 1997, 20 people were killed when an eruption occurred suddenly and they were caught working their fields in the exclusion zone).

The south of Montserrat is still too dangerous to be repopulated and so the island infrastructure has been re-centred in the north. A port was built in Little Bay and schools and housing throughout the north of the island. The islanders were given the option of relocating to Britain or Antigua, reducing the viability of the remaining community on Montserrat.

The volcano is still active, roaring and rumbling from time to time. The dome has continued to grow (after a short break between March 1998 and November 1999) and it is now more than a kilometre across in places. Rocks still tumble off the summit and there are occasional explosions and pyroclastic flows. But the dome is spectacularly beautiful to look when it is not obscured (which it often is because of the steam it emits and the inevitable Caribbean clouds). For those who do go and want to view the volcano, Garibaldi Hill, above the Vue Pointe Hotel, has a good view of Plymouth and the volcano itself. The latest updates about the volcano can be found at *www.mvomrat.com*.

Flora and Fauna

The confusion of soufrières or secondary craters and the mingling of mountains and hills make it like an enlarged picture of the moon.

Montserrat has the same botanic exuberance as the Windward Isles to the south – the thick dark earth cultivates a luxuriant flora: explosions of bamboo, mosses on the march, creepers grappling down below, and above, orchids and airborne ferns. The national flower is the yellow *Heliconia caribaea*, known locally as lobster claw because of its odd shape, and the island tree is the hairy mango.

The national bird, the Montserrat oriole, is indigenous to the island. Its plumage is black and yellow and it can be found up in the mountains along with the purple-throated carib, one of Montserrat's three hummingbirds. Thrashers and bananaquits abound in the hibiscus and bougainvillea of the lower slopes and you might be lucky and see a chicken hawk hovering, spying out a meal. On the shoreline you can see waders such as the common gallinule and some species of heron, alongside cattle egrets, kingfishers and the odd booby or a tropicbird with its long tail feathers.

Montserrat's landborne wildlife is limited to agouti (very shy, guinea-pig-like rodents), lizards, 'mountain chickens' (frogs) and tree frogs, which make their shrill night-time call all over the Caribbean. You have a good chance of seeing iguana, a prehistoric-looking, tank-like lizard, at the cliffs at the Vue Pointe Hotel.

St Kitts and Nevis

St Kitts and Nevis stand side by side in the arc of diminishing volcanic peaks in the Leeward Islands. Their concave slopes rise gracefully through shoreside flatlands to rainforested and often cloud-capped summits, fertile greens offset against the blues of the tropical sea and sky. They have strikingly beautiful views of one another, across the Narrows, a channel just two miles wide.

There is a strong and vibrant West Indian culture to these two islands, unlike on some others nearby, where life has been swamped by the international tourist industry. Unless you hide out in the tourist ghetto or lock yourself away in plantation splendour (St Kitts and Nevis have a stunning collection of plantation house hotels), you cannot help but notice the local life around you. Expect to be accosted in the street. You may be asked for money or given a slug of rum. Either way, the Kittitians (pronounced as in 'petition') and Nevisians (as in 'revision') will let you know their thoughts on life. Between them the islands have a population of 45,000, of whom about 10,000 live on Nevis (more Nevisians also live in St Kitts). Even with a steadily developing (if small) tourist industry, St Kitts and Nevis have faced difficult economic times and they are quite poor. Visit, though, and you will find two quite different Caribbean islands, both welcoming and laid-back in classic old-Caribbean style.

For all the differences between them, St Kitts and Nevis lived fairly amicably together in their political unity, which was established when they took their Independence together from Britain in 1983, until fairly recently. Internal rivalry is of course very strong – every Kittitian has a relative on Nevis and vice versa – and the annual inter-island cricket match is a fiercely contested event. There have been occasional political rumblings on the smaller island – it seems that the Nevisians really are revisionist after all – but the movements towards Independence from St Kitts in the late 1990s came to naught.

St Kitts and Nevis

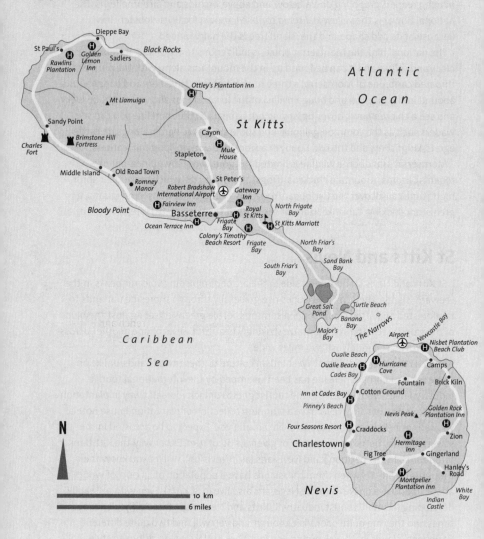

History

St Kitts was once known as the 'Mother Colony of the West Indies', because it was the first island in the Lesser Antilles to be settled permanently. *Liamuiga*, the Carib name for St Kitts, supposedly means 'fertile land' and it was the commercial possibilities of this fertility, and a distance from the Spaniards in the Greater Antilles that attracted European colonists in the early 17th century. They came to plant tobacco.

The first settler was the Englishman Thomas Warner, who arrived in 1623. Next year he was joined by a French privateer, Pierre Belain d'Esnambuc, who called in to repair his ship after a fight with the Spaniards near the Cayman Islands. Welcomed by

Warner, the Frenchman stayed for a while and then went to France to persuade settlers to return with him to St Kitts. The two men arranged to share the island and in 1627 divided it into three, with the French in the north and around Basseterre, and the English in the middle.

One of the main reasons that the French and English were happy to team up was that they needed to protect themselves against the Caribs, who were none too pleased about this intrusion into their islands. The battles began even in 1626, with the Caribs rallying in their canoes from other islands including Dominica and Guadeloupe, but the Europeans held their own. Steadily the Caribs were forced out and Liamuiga became St Kitts. The Spaniards were no more pleased at this intrusion into their backyard in the New World and in 1629 their fleet attacked the settlement. During the skirmish the colony was destroyed, but, as was to be the routine all over the islands, as soon as the invaders were gone the settlers filtered back and got on with their planting. The new settlers also started to look farther afield. Competition for empire was hotting up and English expeditions were sent to settle nearby islands. Nevis was one of the many 'Charibby Islands' made over arbitrarily to the Earl of Carlisle by Charles I in 1627 and the next year Oualie, as the Caribs called it, was promptly taken by the British. Montserrat and Antigua were settled in 1632. The French boldly took on the larger and more hostile Windwards to the south, heading for Martinique and Guadeloupe.

On St Kitts itself, the scene was set for the next 200 years – the French and British would be constantly at each other's throats. At one stage they managed to fall out on the basis that a tree had grown. A banyan marking the border in the north of the island had enlarged by putting out a few years' worth of aerial roots and the land enclosed by the 'change' in the border just happened to include 250 French houses. War was just averted on that occasion, but St Kitts passed from one power to the other like a shuttlecock. Brimstone Hill was built and besieged. And as the navies whittled through the islands Nevis took a fair beating too. In 1706 the French swooped in, destroyed what they could (about £1 million's worth), and left with around 3,000 slaves.

At the beginning of the 19th century, the British finally gained the upper hand in the endless series of wars and so both islands found themselves in the hands of the British, with whom they remained until Independence. Only a few hints of French influence remain in St Kitts today: a fleur-de-lys on the national coat of arms and, most notably, the name of the capital – Basseterre.

When the islanders were not being besieged, they were planting sugar cane furiously. Nevis stuttered on its route to prosperity, but prosperous it became, eventually being dubbed the 'Queen of the Caribbees'. At one stage a fleet of 20 ocean-going ships was devoted entirely to serving the island, sailing out with luxuries and manufactured goods such as tools and returning loaded with sugar loaves. The sugar industry also needed slaves and in the late 17th century Nevis had a slave market. Vast numbers of Africans were brought over. When the ships arrived in port, these frightened men and women would be oiled up before being made to parade through the streets singing, prior to being taken to auction.

With the 19th century, the West Indian sugar industry went into decline and the mansions into decay, though the planters kept up their balls and finery as long as they could. And after Emancipation in 1834, the 'apprenticeship' system soon broke down in 1838 and the slaves were finally freed. On such small islands, slaves were effectively forced to remain on the plantations, but eventually independent villages like Challengers on the leeward coast of St Kitts grew up.

The late 19th century was a lean period for all the Caribbean islands and St Kitts and Nevis slipped into obscurity. The sugar industry had more and more difficulty competing in the world market as Cuba and Santo Domingo gained the ascendancy. Today, apart from a small income from sugar, St Kitts–Nevis is dependent on a slowly expanding tourist industry.

Politics

St Kitts and Nevis are united in a constitutional Federation, in place since Independence from Britain in 1983. The two islands were originally shunted together in 1882, as the colonial authorities in London made one of their many political rationalizations, and they formed a part of the Presidency of the Leeward Islands. The island of Anguilla was also appended to the Basseterre administration in 1871. The three islands followed much the same course as the other British colonies in the 20th century, led by the clamour for political change in Jamaica, Trinidad and Barbados in the 1930s. In 1951, the islanders were given the vote and the St Kitts and Nevis Labour Party, rallying the voices of people who had been given no political say before, swept the board. 'Associated Statehood' in 1967 brought more internal self-government, but at this point Anguilla, which had felt neglected by the government in St Kitts, staged one of the world's lesser-known revolutions and made its claims for secession heard (see p.395). After a 15-year row, Anguilla left the State of St Kitts–Nevis in 1982.

At Independence in September 1983, the Nevisians wanted to make sure they would not end up in the same position as Anguilla and so they renegotiated the settlement, inserting an 'escape clause' that allows them to secede from Federation with St Kitts if two-thirds of the Nevisians choose to do so. Nevis has its own five-member elected assembly to govern its own affairs. In the 11-member House of Assembly of St Kitts–Nevis, three of the seats are allotted to constituencies on Nevis and these can easily hold the balance of power. St Kitts–Nevis remains within the British Commonwealth. At the moment the country is headed by Prime Minister Denzil Douglas of the St Kitts and Nevis Labour Party which was elected in March 2000 with seven seats in the House. The opposition are the three members of the Concerned Citizens Movement from Nevis. The next elections are due to be held in 2009.

Flora and Fauna

The lower slopes of St Kitts are bright green with sugar cane (at least for the next few years, though the industry may well be brought to an end soon), but both islands have thick and fertile growth, starting as scrub and grassland at the shoreside and rising to rainforest, where you will find swathes of elephant ears, and gommier and

Spanish oak trees whose upper branches dangle with lianas and explode with orchids and cycads. Close to the summits of the mountains the rainforest gives way to stunted elfin woodland.

Around the bright red flamboyant tree, poinciana (named after the first French Captain General on St Kitts, de Poincy), and bougainvillea, you will see typical island birds such as the purple-throated carib and other hummingbirds, daring bananaquits and bullfinches. Offshore, you can see pelicans and the occasional frigatebird, and in the lowland thickets you may spot a warbler or a pearly-eyed thrasher. St Kitts' few deer have been forced to the north now that the road on the southeast peninsula has disturbed their peace, but they are shy.

You are more likely to come across the green vervet monkey, introduced in the 17th century, which lives on both islands. About a foot high, it lives in the hills and travels in packs, making a nuisance of itself and eating crops (the only crops it doesn't eat are pepper and ginger). You can tell when one is angry by the white line above its eyebrow which it wiggles at you furiously.

St Kitts

The familiar name St Kitts (from St Christopher) has been used by the Kittitians since the 18th century. It is not known how the island took the name of the travellers' saint (Christopher Columbus, who passed the island on his second voyage, did not call it this), but perhaps later explorers named it in his honour.

St Kitts is the larger of the two islands (68 square miles) and is shaped a bit like a paddle, set in the water so that the handle points southeast. The blade is covered in a ridge of volcanic mountains, tumbling steeply from the summits and then flattening out gracefully towards the sea. The slopes are traced with *ghauts*, or ravines, which look a bit like huge volcanic stretchmarks and give an idea of the upheaval that the mountains once underwent.

Like many islands in the Caribbean, St Kitts became immensely wealthy as a sugar factory in the 17th and 18th centuries (it was worth building the massive Brimstone Hill to defend it), but unlike most other islands, the flatlands of St Kitts are still covered with canefields – for the moment at least. The industry hardly pays its way, and it is due to be wound down over the next few years.

In contrast to Nevis's quiet and almost comatose nature, there is a slightly raw air about St Kitts, which is more typical of larger Caribbean islands. The majority of the Kittitians are charming, though, and will happily engage you in conversation. It is worth getting out to explore the northern areas of the island.

Basseterre

Basseterre, the small capital of St Kitts, has plenty of charm. It stands on the mile-wide sweep of a south-facing bay; a grid of streets lined with stone and wooden 'skirt and shirt' houses and sheltered by the magnificent green slopes of Monkey Hill and the South Range. It is home to about 13,000 Kittitians (about half the population).

Best Beaches

In the mountainous northern areas of St Kitts the beaches are mostly of black sand – there are not actually that many because of the rocky coastline – but in the southern peninsula, which has been opened up by the peninsular road, the sand is golden brown. Here you will find a number of good beaches which, more often than not, are deserted.

Frigate Bay (on the Caribbean side): Still the island's most popular beach, where you will find facilities for watersports, a bar and a restaurant where you can get a meal. Its opposite number on the Atlantic side, North Frigate Bay, is pounded by ocean waves.

Friar's Bay: Over the headland going south from Frigate Bay, this is the nicest on the island and usually quiet and empty enough to feel secluded (though it has often been slated for development). On public holidays and when a cruise ship is in the bay there will be a cook-up and drinks on sale. Palm- and scrub-backed with a lagoon inland, it has magnificent views and superb mounded golden sand.

Sand Bank Bay: On the Atlantic side, with shallow water that rushes with wind and waves between huge headlands: no facilities and quite difficult to find, along a rickety sandy track leading left off the main road.

Major's Bay: Easier to find but not so nice, a thin strip of sand backed by a salt pond.

Banana Bay and **Cockleshell Bay**: Have development, now defunct, on their passable sand, and no shade or facilities.

Turtle Beach: One of the most popular beaches with watersports facilities, bar, and frequent steel bands. You are also likely to see monkeys.

The name 'Basseterre' and its protected site have come down from the French, who first settled the area, but apart from this and the (not quite) gridiron layout of the town, very little else French survives. The town was adopted by the British in 1727, in preference to their capital at Old Road. Today, the church towers, stone Georgian buildings and even the pointed iron railings speak of the island's 350-year association with Britain. Life itself is changing as the colonial memory recedes, but echoes remain in the uniforms of the police, Bedford trucks and distinctly British clock-chimes. Recent construction has given the town a little more of an upbeat air, but just behind the modern waterfront you will find traditional tatty Caribbean streets of delightful, fading buildings from two centuries ago.

Visitors in the 19th century entered Basseterre through the arch of the **Treasury Building**, the domed colonial structure on the waterfront that housed the customs. Nowadays this is marooned inland by a huge new development, Port Zante, which includes shops and cafés, cruise-ship terminal, and marina. The old town still sits in gracious state, stone buildings with timber-frame upper storeys and not far from the waterfront is the old heart of the town, the Circus, where an elaborate green Victorian clock tower stands beneath a ring of royal palms.

In the business streets behind the Circus, the government buildings can be found on Church Street and **St George's Anglican Church** on Cayon Street, built and rebuilt on the site of a French church of 1670. The formal centre of colonial Basseterre was Pall

Getting There

St Kitts t (1 869–)

By Air

Robert Llewelyn Bradshaw Airport, 2 miles from Basseterre on St Kitts has no direct scheduled services from Europe or the USA (though there are charter flights). Newcastle Airport on Nevis can only take short hopper flights, but there are easy links both from Antigua and from St Kitts itself (*see* below for connections between the two). There is a departure tax of US$22 (St Kitts), US$20 (Nevis), and an environmental levy of US$1.50.

From the UK and Europe

The easiest connections are via Antigua (*see* p.339), from where hopper flights (theoretically) link up with British Airways, Virgin and BWIA services from London. BWIA, British Airways and Virgin Atlantic have daily services from Heathrow, Gatwick or Manchester via Antigua or Barbados. KLM and Air France fly to St Maarten.

From the USA and Canada

The easiest connections from the USA are made via the American Airlines hub in San Juan, Puerto Rico, from where there are regular flights on American Eagle, t 465 2273. US Airways fly nonstop from Philadelphia and Charlotte. BWIA fly from New York to Antigua; Continental and USAir from New York to St Maarten and San Juan.

From Other Caribbean Islands

St Kitts is easily accessible by the hopper flights that pass up and down the island chain touching most of the islands between Antigua and San Juan, Puerto Rico. Try: American Eagle, t 465 2273; LIAT, St Kitts t 465 2286, Nevis t 469 9333; Caribbean Star, t 465 5929; WinAir, St Kitts t 465 8010, Nevis t 469 9333; Carib Aviation, St Kitts t 465 3055, Nevis t 469 9295.

By Sea

There are three inter-island ferries, which run between St Kitts and Nevis: the MV *Carib Queen*, the MV *Sea Hustler* and the MV *Caribe Breeze* (there are usually six or seven sailings a day each way, about 45 minutes; EC$20 return).

The views are magnificent as the mountains shift slowly above you. Kenneth's Dive Centre runs a **water-taxi** service for a minimum of four passengers, t 466 5320, and you can also contact Blue Water Safaris, t 465 9838.

Getting Around

The ride from the airport into town is little more than a mile. If you do not want to go by cab (EC$18), it is a short walk over the sugar railway to the main road, where a minibus will pick you up in a matter of minutes and take you to Basseterre for EC$1.

By Train

The St Kitts Scenic Railway National Tour, t 465 7263, is a wonderful way to get a feel for the island. The 30-mile route passes small villages, farms and old sugar estates, providing passengers with great views of the sea and countryside. Two daily tours. Tickets can be purchased at the Needsmust station or the Scenic Railway office in Bassettere.

By Bus

Buses, 'Rude Boy' and 'Who Loves you Baby?', run the roads of St Kitts intermittently from 6.30am until about 8pm. Headed to the main part of the island (there are no buses to the southeast peninsula), they depart from the waterfront next to the Nevis Ferry Terminal in Basseterre, leaving when they are full. They do not generally circle the island, but run along either one coast road or the other, which means that you can be stranded in the northern canefields. Getting on to a bus is as easy as flagging it down on the roadside; to get off you must shout 'Driver, Stop!' EC$4 will get you to the north of the island.

By Taxi

Taxis are readily available. In Basseterre you will find them at the Circus and they can also be arranged through hotels. Fares are fixed by the government. Some prices are: airport to Basseterre – EC$18, to Frigate Bay area – EC$11, to Rawlins Plantation or Golden Lemon at the northern end of the island – EC$25; and from Basseterre to Frigate Bay – EC$20, to Brimstone Hill – EC$40, to Rawlins Plantation or Golden Lemon – EC$55.

Most taxi drivers will also be willing to take you on an island tour, which costs around US$60 for three hours. Taxis can be ordered through the St Kitts Taxi Association, t 465 4253, and the Circus Taxi stand, t 465 3006.

Hitch-hiking

If you get stranded in the canefields of the north, then hitch. It's a good alternative to other forms of transport anyway.

By Guided Tour

Organized island tours can be arranged through taxi drivers or travel agents in town. They take about 3½ hours, and can include lunch at one of the plantation houses. **Greg's Safaris**, t 465 4121, *g-safari@caribsurf. com, www.skbee.com/safaris*. Offers an interesting drive around the island, visiting areas otherwise inaccessible because they are on private land (*see also* 'Other Sports', p.376). **Kantours**, t 465 3054, *kantours@caribsurf.com*.

Car and Bike Hire

Car hire gives the most mobility, particularly if you are staying in the north of the island, and a small car can be hired from about US$40 per day, or a Jeep for slightly more. Before driving in St Kitts, you must purchase a local driving licence, obtainable on production of your own licence and EC$62.50/US$23 at the fire station in Cayon Street, Basseterre. Companies will collect you and smooth the process. Driving is on the left. Some hire firms are:
Avis Car Rental, t 565 6507, *www.avis.com*.
Caines, Prince's Street, Basseterre, t 465 2366, *cainrent@caribsurf.com, www.cainrent.com*.
Delisle Walwyn and Co, just off the Circus, Basseterre, t 465 8449, *delwal@caribsurf. com, www.delisleco.com*.
TDC Rentals/Thrifty, t 465 2991, *tdcrent@ caribsurf.com, www.tdcltd.com*.
Fun Bikes, Cayon St, t 662 2088, *www.stkitts leisure.biz*. Quad bike tours.

Tourist Information

Abroad

The official island website is at *www.stkitts-nevis.com* but you can also find information at *www.skbee.com*.

Canada: 133 Richmond St West, Suite 311, Toronto, Ontario M5H 2L3, t (416) 368 6707, *canada.office@stkittstourism.com*.
UK: 10 Kensington Court, London W8 5DL, t (020) 7376 0881, *uk-europe.office@ stkittstourism.com*.
USA: 414 East 75th St, New York, NY 10021, t (212) 535 1234, *info@stkittstourism.kn*.

In St Kitts

Tourist information desk, Robert Llewelyn Bradshaw Airport.

Department of Tourism, Pelican Mall, Bay Rd, PO Box 132, Basseterre, t 465 4040, *mint c&e@caribsurf.com, www.stkitts-nevis.com*.

The Tourist Board puts out a glossy magazine, *St Kitts and Nevis Visitor*, with essential information on restaurants and shopping.

Embassies and Consulates

British citizens are referred to the High Commission in Antigua; American and Canadian citizens are referred to their consulates in Barbados.

Media

The *Observer*, published weekly in Nevis, is the islands' unaffiliated newspaper. The others are the *Labour Spokesman*, which is published twice weekly by the ruling Labour Party, and the *Democrat*, the voice of the People's Action Movement. Radio stations include the inimitable Radio ZIZ, Radio Paradise, a religious station with gospel music, and VON or the Voice of Nevis.

Money and Banks

The **currency** of St Kitts and Nevis is the Eastern Caribbean dollar, as with other former British colonies in the area. It is fixed to the US dollar at a rate of US$1 = EC$2.65. US dollars are accepted all over the island. Major credit cards are accepted in the tourist areas.
Banking hours are Mon–Fri 8–2 (many remain open on Fridays until 5pm). Some also open on Saturday mornings, 8.30–11.30.

Telephone Code

The IDD code for St Kitts and Nevis is t 1 869 followed by a seven-digit local number, beginning with 465 or 466 in St Kitts. Between the islands and on-island, dial the seven digits.

Art Galleries

Spencer Cameron Gallery, Independence Square, Basseterre, **t** 465 1617. *Open Mon–Fri 9–4, Sat 9–2.30.* Set in a pretty colonial building. It exhibits some African but mostly Caribbean paintings, maps and limited edition prints of island scenes.

Kate Design, Bank St, Basseterre. Paintings and silks by Kate Spencer. Its sister gallery at Rawlins Plantation can be visited on a lunch stop during a tour of the island.

Festivals

January *New Year's parades.*
March/April *Easter-Community Festival.*
May *International Triathlon.*
June *Music Festival.* Held each year over the last weekend of the month, and featuring four days of local calypso music, reggae, soul, *soca*, Latin and gospel music.
July/August *Culturama.*
September *Independence Day.* Held on the 19th, is celebrated with traditional Caribbean feasting and festivities.
October *Tourism Week.* Includes a food fair and seaborne activities like sailing races.
December *Carnival.* The main event in the Kittitian calendar, taking place just before Christmas and lasting into New Year. It is a week of jump-ups, calypso, beauty-queen shows and masquerades. Not many tourists attend, though plenty of Kittitians return to the island for the festivities and it is fun to watch the events in the stadium at Warner Park and around the streets of Basseterre. *J'Ouvert* is held in the streets of Basseterre in the small hours on Boxing Day. Grab a chicken leg and a Carib lager from one of the ladies fanning braziers at the edge of the park and join the crowd. For more formal information about the bands, **t** 465 4151.

Watersports

The best place for watersports is Frigate Bay, in the hotel area south of Basseterre. Otherwise the beaches are fairly remote, except at the Turtle Beach Bar in the far south, where there are some facilities. There are regattas during Tourism Week in November and occasional races to other islands.

For windsurfing, sailing and general watersports, try:
Kenneth's Dive Centre, **t** 465 2670. Jet skis are available to hire from here.
Mr X Watersports, **t** 465 0673.
Turtle Beach Bar, **t** 465 9086, *www.skbee.com/travel/turtlebeach*.

Day Sails

Scheduled catamaran cruises (trips to Nevis, sunset or daytime picnic and snorkelling extravaganzas) and charters can be fixed through:
Blue Water Safaris, **t** 466 4933, *waterfun@caribsurf.com.*
Leeward Islands Charters, **t** 465 7474.

Deep-sea Fishing

Trips for steely-eyed shark fishermen or women can be arranged by day-sail companies, or on *Panda*, **t** 465 4438.

Scuba Diving

A fair bit to offer, with submarine volcanic vents for explorations as well as the usual reefs, where if you are lucky you can see stingrays and even dolphins and whales. Much of the diving takes place off Nevis (a 10-minute run across the channel if you are in the south). Companies will provide instruction and referral training from courses back home. A single-tank dive costs around US$40 and operators have underwater photographic equipment.
Blue Water Safaris, Basseterre, **t** 466 4933, *waterfun@caribsurf.com.*
Dive St Kitts, **t** 465 1189, *brbh@caribsurf.com.*
Kenneth's Dive Centre, Newtown Bay Rd, Basseterre, **t** 465 2670.
Pro Divers, Horizon Villas, Frigate Bay, **t** 465 3223, and at Turtle Beach, **t** 465 9086.

Snorkelling

The best is in White House Bay off the south peninsular road, where there is a reef in 12ft of water, and in the nearby areas of Ballast Bay and the delightfully named Shitten Bay, though these two can only be reached by boat. If you are driving around the north of the island, there is good snorkelling off Old Road on the leeward side of the island and Dieppe Bay on the northern coast.

Other Sports

Golf

Four Seasons, t 469 9494. On Nevis.

Golden Rock, t 465 8103. Nine-hole course.

Royal St Kitts, in the Frigate Bay area, **t** 465 8339. A challenging and unforgiving 18-hole championship course.

Hiking

On land there are well-organized tours around St Kitts, that make a close and informative inspection of plantation ruins (the conical windmills and tall square steam chimneys that you see from the road), and follow rivers up through the ever-encroaching undergrowth to hidden rock pools and waterfalls, high into the rainforest.

Greg's Safaris, t 465 4121, *g-safari@caribsurf. com, www.skbee.com/safaris*. Excellent walks are available. You will be told about island flora, fauna, folklore and medicinal plants as you climb through the St Kitts back-country, on walks that follow the old trails that once networked the island: one follows the route of the old English military road that linked the two sides of the island, another takes you up 3,792ft to the top of St Kitts's highest peak, Mount Liamuiga, and into its crater.

Kriss Tours, t 465 4042. There are full-day and half-day hikes.

Horse-riding

A more leisurely look at St Kitts' plantation history may be had on horseback, riding around the island or simply cantering along the beach. This can be arranged through Trinity Stables, **t** 465 9603, *www.islandimage. com/trinity/trinity*. It is planned (as it is every year) to make it possible to ride on the sugarcane train that circles the island through the canefields.

Where to Stay

St Kitts **t** (1 869–)

St Kitts (and Nevis) has far and away the finest collection of plantation-house hotels in the Caribbean. Many are still surrounded by sugar cane as they were 200 years ago and they still retain the grace and hospitality of the era – they are small and are run in the style of a private house, with guests meeting informally for drinks before dinner. As former estate houses, most of these hotels are not on the beach, and so you might like to hire a car for mobility. Children are sometimes not encouraged. There are no really good beach hotels on St Kitts as yet, but the Frigate Bay area has some purpose-built shoreside condominium complexes. Hotels are supposed to be under construction on the southeast peninsula, but all seem to have fallen foul of Caribbean inertia somehow. St Kitts also has a number of villas for hire all over the island: details can be obtained from the Tourist Board, or *see* 'Where to Stay', pp.62–4. A government tax of 9% is added to hotel bills and most also add a 10% addition for service.

Very Expensive

Rawlins Plantation, PO Box 340, St Kitts, **t** 465 6221, US **t** 1 800 346 5358, *rawplant@ caribsurf.com, www.rawlinsplantation.com*. One of the Caribbean's supreme settings in the reworked buildings of a sugar estate on the slopes of Mount Liamuiga. There are just 10 very comfortable rooms scattered in wooden cottages and stone outbuildings (one in the windmill) among the tropical trees and hedges of the lawned estate gardens, each of them very private. When you feel like company you repair to the main house itself, with library and dining room, where among the stone walls, louvred shutters and antique furniture you take cocktails and then dinner on the veranda overlooking the pool and grounds. A bewildering variety of tropical fruits for breakfast, followed by a buffet lunch (worth attending if you are not staying there, for the saltfish and *funchi* and the candied sweet potato) and then dinner of chicken and mango or lobster in puff pastry with a tarragon cream sauce. If this sounds over-indulgent then you can walk in the forests above the estate or knock a ball about on the grass tennis court. Rawlins has a reliably elegant atmosphere and there are few places like it anywhere in the Caribbean.

Golden Lemon Inn, Dieppe Bay, **t** 465 7260, US **t** 1 800 633 7411, *info@goldenlemon.com, www.goldenlemon.com*. Set in a 17th-century trading warehouse on the waterfront in Dieppe Bay. It is now meticulously restored and the old stone walls are more likely to echo with piano and singing accompaniment after dinner than the rumbling of rum barrels. There are 16 rooms, with wooden floorboards and louvred windows, gracefully furnished with antiques and with huge beds. But most charming are the 10 suites, which have been exquisitely decorated, each in a different style; tropical, oriental, Egyptian, and more.

Ottley's Plantation Inn, PO Box 345, t 465 7234, US t 1 800 772 3039, *ottleys@caribsurf.com*, *www.ottleys.com*. A magnificent setting in lawned gardens that descend gently from the steep slopes of the mountains down towards the coast, with views to the Atlantic Ocean. The Great House has original stone foundations with restored timber upper stories, and has nine of the 24 rooms (they are huge and share the vast balcony) retaining its old colonial grandeur with antiques and reproduction furniture. The other rooms stand in restored estate outbuildings and newer cottages (built in traditional West Indian style) beyond the pool and restaurant, and have private pools. Again there is a private house atmosphere.

Expensive

St Kitts Marriott Resort, t 466 1200, *www.st kittsmarriott.com*. Set on the Atlantic coast, the 648-room Marriott is one of the largest hotels in the Eastern Caribbean. It has six restaurants, three pools, a spa and health club, tennis courts, casino, children's programme, and an 18-hole golf course.

Turtle Beach Apartments, t 469 9086, *gary@caribsurf.com*. Two-bedroom apartments on the beach, with full kitchen facilities, two bathrooms, maid service, phone, television and DVD, hammock, snorkelling and fishing equipment.

Sugar Bay Club, t 465 8037, *sugarbayclub@ caribsurf.com*, *www.eliteislandresorts.com*. An all-inclusive resort reflecting the natural informality of St Kitts. Hidden between the beach and an 18-hole golf course. Family and adult-only pools, kids' club, tennis, fitness room, two restaurants and bars.

The Ocean Terrace Inn, close to town among the villas of Fortlands, PO Box 65, t 465 2754, US t 1 800 524 0512, UK t (020) 8350 1000, *otistkitts@caribsurf.com*, *www.ocean terraceinn.net*. Isolated from the relative hurly-burly elsewhere in a walled garden that rambles across the hillside. The 76 rooms (air-conditioned with satellite television) make it sound large, but they are scattered around the main house and garden pool, where you can swim or take a Jacuzzi and drink at the pool bar before dinner with a view of Nevis.

Frigate Bay Beach Resort, PO Box 137, t 465 8935, *frigbay@caribsurf.com*, *www. frigatebay.com*. Not actually on the beach but a short walk away (also near the golf course), a regular Caribbean hotel setup with three-storey blocks overlooking a pool. They are brightly painted, in a theme of strong yellow and blue, and have a little atmosphere. The 64 rooms are a good size and some have kitchenettes.

Timothy Beach Resort, Frigate Bay, PO Box 81, t 465 8597, US t 1 800 288 7991, *tbr-stkitts@ usa.net*, *www.timothybeach.com*. At the southern end of Frigate Bay just above the beach on the Caribbean side. There are 60 plush and comfortable rooms and suites in blocks and a walkway of *crotons* and bougainvillea down to the pool and restaurant with a sunset view. There are kitchenettes in some rooms.

Moderate

Gateway Inn, Frigate Bay, PO Box 64, t 465 7155, *gateway@caribsurf.com*. Within walking distance of the beach (oddly positioned at the top of the ridge), it has simple air-conditioned rooms with cable TV, a little past their best, but a good price.

Mule House, t 466 8086, *www.holiday-rentals. co.uk/mulehouse*. If you are happy to be out of the way on the eastern Atlantic coast, then you might try this quiet and low-key place. Four self-catering apartments in a modern house, with balconies and comfortable furnishings. Weekly rates.

Palms All-suite Hotel, Basseterre, PO Box 64, t 465 0800, *palmshotel@caribsurf.com*, *www.palmshotel.com*. A pleasant stopover in the very centre of town, right on the Circus with all the comforts. It is air-conditioned and carpeted, with cable TV and video.

Inexpensive

Glimbaro Guest House, Cayon St, Basseterre, t 465 2935. Ten rooms, simple, functional, pink, some shared and some private baths, restaurant downstairs.

Sea View Guest House, Basseterre, t 466 6759. Right on the waterfront in town. Probably the cheapest place in town at the moment: it is purely functional, air-conditioned, modern and central.

Fairview Inn, PO Box 212, t 465 2472, US t 1 800 223 9815, *wall@caribsurf.com*, *www.best-caribbean.com/fairviewinn*. Set in a pretty Kittitian estate house overlooking the Caribbean coast, with wooden floors and ceilings. It hasn't the style of the other inns of St Kitts, but prices itself accordingly. There are 30 rooms in stone cottages behind the great house, which has a busy and friendly bar. In need of renovation.

Eating Out

The food in St Kitts is fairly typical of the British Caribbean: chicken, fish or goat, fried or in a stew, served with a ton of Caribbean vegetables. The more adventurous dining rooms will serve not only these, but also more exotic ingredients in tropical fruit sauces and some traditional European recipes. There is of course the rather less traditional burger to be found in the resort hotels, but it is well worth getting out to find a more Caribbean meal, either in the plantation houses, which serve excellent buffet lunches and set dinners, or in the side streets of Basseterre. Most places accept credit cards. There is a government tax of 7% added to all bills and usually a 10% service charge as well. **Categories** are arranged according to the price of a main course: expensive = EC$40 and above; moderate = EC$20–40; inexpensive = under EC$20.

Expensive

Marshalls, Horizons Villas, Frigate Bay, t 466 8245. A slightly more rarified ambience than the pool-side setting would imply: you sit under a pretty white awning with curtains gathered at the poles, some tables looking south and east along the coast. The cuisine is Caribbean and international, prepared by a chef from Jamaica, which is where the

ackee and saltfish starter originates. Follow with a pan-roasted sea bass in a cilantro-lime sauce or duck breast in port and raspberry.

Fisherman's Wharf, Basseterre, t 465 2754. With a waterside setting, on a wooden deck with bench seats. Seafood and grilled fare (cooked in view of the tables) including barbecue shrimp, seafood kebabs and shark steak. Quite a lively atmosphere, on special nights and at weekends.

Rawlins Plantation Inn, t 465 6221, *rawplant@ caribsurf.com*, *www.rawlinsplantation.com*. The inn is well known for its excellent cuisine created with great care by a chef who combines French discipline with her West Indian heritage. Features produce from the garden, with a bewildering variety of tropical fruits for breakfast, followed by a buffet lunch which draws guests from across the island. Fine wines are stored in the old, cool cellar. Reservations only.

The Royal Palm, Ottley's Plantation Inn, t 465 7234, *ottleys@caribsurf.com*, *www.ottleys. com*. The setting is beautiful and the menu full of creative dishes. The Sunday brunch is a particular favourite with Kittitians as much as hotel guests.

Golden Lemon, t 465 7260. Open for breakfast, lunch and dinner. Famous, all-inclusive Sunday Brunch. Evening dinner in the candlelit antique-filled dining room is particularly pleasant.

Moderate

Doo Wop Days Italian Café, Frigate Bay, north side, t 465 1960. Right in hotel heartland in Frigate Bay, a lively restaurant with a theme of fifties, sixties and seventies music with records all over the walls, pictures of happy punters and an original Rock-Ola jukebox. Enclosed and air-conditioned, but a pretty terrace outside for drinking. A short menu with steaks, sandwiches and pastas.

Circus Grill Bar and Restaurant, Basseterre, t 465 0143. On a breezy wooden terrace overlooking the Circus. An international menu with lots of grilled food and Caribbean dishes such as creole lobster.

Ballahoo, on the Circus, Basseterre, t 465 4197. A popular spot for a daytime drink or a cocktail at dusk, and light or fuller meals all day long. Sit on a veranda right in the centre of town. Quite a few tourists, but some locals too – chilli shrimps or Italian chicken breast. Very full menu all day and always a vegetarian dish. *Closed Sun.*

Stone Walls Tropical Bar and Eating Place, Princes St, Basseterre, t 465 5248. A charming Kittitian courtyard (of stone walls as the name suggests), with conch shell paths and profuse greenery. Grilled dishes with Cajun and Caribbean flavours, early evening bar.

Bayembi, Bank St, Basseterre, t 466 5280. The haunt of the students, which makes it lively in the early evening. Daytime burgers and in the evening more substantial West Indian meals such as rice 'n' peas.

Manhattan Gardens, Old Road, t 465 9121. Set in an old stone and timber house: serves simple burgers and West Indian dishes for lunch and mainly seafood for dinner.

The Sprat Net, Old Road. A Kittitian gem, directly across the road from Manhattan Gardens on the waterfront, next to the stone walls of an old fort. A classic West Indian bar; easy atmosphere. Grilled chicken, fish, rib or lobster, corn on the cob, johnny cakes. *Open from sunset, Wed–Sun.*

Bobsy's, t 466 6133, *bobsy@caribsurf.com.* Caribbean atmosphere with local and international dishes and featuring fresh lobster. Karaoke, dancing and entertainment. *Open daily for lunch and dinner.*

Dolce Cabana, Frigate Bay, t 465 1569, *www.dolcecabanaclub.com.* A traditional Italian restaurant serving authentic dishes. Relax at the beach bar and enjoy the Caribbean view or sunbathe on the beach. Live music, dancing, tourists and Kittitians.

Mr. X's Shiggidy Shack Bar & Grill, t 663 3983. Open nightly for dinner. Grilled fish, lobster, chicken in traditional Kittitian style. Open bar, live music, bonfire on Thursdays.

Oasis Sports Bar, Frigate Bay, t 466 6029. With eight large TV screens where you can watch major American sports telecasts while enjoying burgers, salads and sandwiches. *Open Wed–Mon until the wee hours.*

Inexpensive

On Fridays and Saturdays you'll find that the Kittitians cook up chicken and fish on braziers at the streetside.

Chef's Place, Church St, Basseterre, t 465 6167. Serves West Indian food mainly to a local crowd. Delicious pumpkin or carrot soup, followed by turtle, saltfish and local fish. *Open for lunch and dinner.*

Victor's, New Town, Basseterre, t 465 2518. One of several local hide-outs in Basseterre where you can get traditional chicken or fish and tropical juice. Here you will dine on Kittitian fare – plates of curry goat heaped with green fig and sweet potato.

Pizza Place, Central St, Basseterre. You can get an excellent takeaway pizza or a *roti* here.

Gilly's, Sandown Rd, Basseterre. Fry chicken takeaway.

Wendy's, Cayon St, Basseterre. Good if you want some fry chicken to go.

Bars and Nightlife

Much of the entertainment in St Kitts is centred around the hotels or beach bars.

StoneWalls, Basseterre. If you fancy a drink (perhaps a Carib, brewed under licence from Trinidad) with some Kittitians after work, this place gathers a crowd of professionals in its pretty courtyard. *See above too.*

Tiffin, off Pond Road (turn at Uncle Jerry's corner), Basseterre. There are plenty of rum shops like this one around the town.

Fisherman's Wharf. Live music at the weekend.

Beach Bars

Turtle Beach Bar, t 469 9086. An excellent spot for chilling out on the beach in the far south of the island, overlooking Nevis. There is good sand, and seats and hammocks among the seagrape trees, with food on the covered deck of the bar itself. Good snorkelling just offshore and other watersports such as kayaking, windsurfing and scuba diving. Follow the south peninsular road past Great Salt Pond and then take a left.

Monkey Beach Bar, Frigate Bay. Ever-popular; an octagonal wooden hut at the bottom of the beach where you can get a daytime drink between stints on the windsurfer or a sundowner. It is busiest on Fridays, when the crowds stay late.

Sunset Café, Frigate Bay. Just above the Monkey, on a deck overlooking the beach.

Mall Square, known since 1983 as **Independence Square**, which is bordered by the imposing grandeur of the Georgian houses and the **Roman Catholic Co-Cathedral of the Immaculate Conception** with its impressive rose window and breezy interior with arched windows. Further east on the waterfront, you come quickly to the boats and drying nets in the fishermen's district. In the yards of beaten earth, small clapboard houses are shaded beneath a breadfruit tree or a palm. Just north of Port Zante is the main bus station and ferry terminal, from which the ferries leave for Nevis.

The old buildings of 19th-century Basseterre, warehouses with dark stone foundations and bright white upper storeys, stretch out along Bay Road parallel to the sea. As you walk along the waterfront you will cross over St Kitts's notorious *ghauts* (pronounced guts), or river ravines, which are channelled down the middle of the streets (when in flood they are fearsome and have been known to wash parked cars out to sea). Travelling further west you come to the large villas in the gentrified district of Fortlands, locally referred to as 'the old aristocratic area'. The Governor General's residence can be seen from the road in Greenlands, but it is not open to the public.

Clockwise around the Island

A coastal road circles the island beneath the central mountain ranges, winding in and out of the *ghauts*, everywhere surrounded by canefields. Today the cane is crushed in one central factory, fed by a circular railway line around the island, but there were once 156 separate estates and the ruins of the old windmills and steam chimneys still stand proud behind curtains of bright green cane. Now that most of them are dilapidated, it is hard to imagine the atmosphere of a functioning plantation, but the rusting copper vats and the crushing gear still give a menacing air of industry and ceaseless human activity.

A couple of miles west of Basseterre, **Bloody Point** was the scene of an early massacre of the Caribs in 1626 when, in spite of their differences, the English and French teamed up. They were tipped off by a Carib woman that the Indians were preparing to attack and so the Europeans ambushed them, supposedly killing 2,000. Strangely, the infant son of the Indian chief, Tegreman, was allowed to live and was brought up in the family of Ralph Merrifield in England. At **Old Road Town**, capital of the English part of the island in the 17th century, you can see one of the Indians' artistic memorials, their rock carvings: lozenge-bodied and antennaed cartoon characters waving at you from the face of black volcanic rock. Just above the town is **Romney Manor** (*open Mon–Fri 8.30–4*), an old plantation house that is the home of Caribelle Batik (*t 465 6253, www.caribellebatik.com*). The Indonesian process has been turned to West Indian colour and style – fluorescent fish-life and pastel nightlife.

A mile farther on is the town of **Middle Island,** where you will find the tomb of Sir Thomas Warner in a small green and white gazebo in the churchyard of St Thomas Parish Church, approached by an alley of palms. Warner was the pioneer British settler, who was knighted at Hampton Court by Charles I for his efforts. He first arrived in 1623 and died here in 1648, a 'noble and much lamented gent'. From St Kitts, he had settled Nevis, Antigua and Montserrat.

Beyond Middle Island, an 800ft peak rises next to the coast, on the flank of Mount Liamuiga itself. Its contours appear square because a massive fortress sits on the summit – a 38-acre stronghold with a citadel presiding over bastions, miles of ramparts, parade grounds, barracks, powder magazines and an amphitheatrical cistern. Brimstone Hill, named because of the sulphur which you can still smell nearby, is a fitting name for this monster – the whole edifice is built of burnt black stone. The hill was first fortified in the 1690s and was attacked unsuccessfully many times. Eventually it was considered impregnable, but then in 1782 it was stormed by the French. They shelled the fortress for weeks until there were breaches in the ramparts 40ft wide and not a building was left standing. When they eventually surrendered, the occupants were permitted to march out of the fortress with colours flying in recognition of their bravery. The fortifications were rebuilt and Brimstone Hill became known as the Gibraltar of the West Indies. It was never attacked again.

Today much of Brimstone Hill has been restored and it bristles with cannon once more. But despite the odd whiff of sulphur the hellish aspect of Brimstone Hill has gone: the ramparts are overgrown with bougainvillea, and the Kittitians picnic in the grounds. The view from the summit is magnificent and ranges from Montserrat and Nevis in the south to Statia, Saba, St Martin and St Barthélemy in the north. There is an orientation centre downstairs with a short video presentation and in the citadel at the very summit is the **Fort George Museum** (*open Mon–Wed and Fri–Sat 9.30–5.30, Thurs and Sun 2.30–5.30; adm*), displaying uniforms, maps and weapons alongside the history of St Kitts.

Sandy Point, a typical West Indian town where clapboard rum shops and the odd old stone building jostle new concrete structures, is the second-largest town on the island (population 7,500). In the 17th century the Dutch were the great traders in the Caribbean and they kept a trading post at Sandy Point. A fire in 1663 cost them 65 warehouses full of tobacco. The island which lies 5 miles off the coast is Dutch St Eustatius. **Charles Fort**, another impressive military structure built in 1672, later became the island's leper asylum. From here, the road runs through the canefields around the northern point of St Kitts, in the shadow of Mount Liamuiga.

Mount Liamuiga (pronounced 'Liar-mweagre') is the highest point on the island at 3,792ft, and there is a crater lake just below the lip. The volcano, which was known for most of its history as Mount Misery, is (almost) inactive; it has been known to rumble very slightly once in a while. Dieppe Bay takes its name from the island's French heritage, which lasted until the early 18th century. The dilapidated stone and wooden buildings give an idea of the town's former prosperity as a sugar port. Returning down the Atlantic coast to Basseterre, the road passes the Black Rocks, volcanic extrusions that have blackened into weird black shapes since their eruption millions of years ago.

At Cayon a road cuts inland to Basseterre, running through the villages of Stapleton and St Peter's. Just beyond Stapleton is the **Fountain Estate House,** built on the site of La Fontaine, the residence of illustrious French Governor de Poincy in the 1640s. Not only was he Captain General, he was also Knight of Malta. He arrived with due pomp and circumstance and promptly erected himself a four-storey château in keeping with his station. The magnificent building was destroyed by an earthquake in 1689 and only the chapel and the steps remain.

The inland road rejoins the coast road as it approaches Basseterre, just by the central **Sugar Factory**. This monster is a proper factory, with conveyor-belts feeding vast metal maws, banks of crushers that squeeze the very last drop of juice from the cane, and disgorge just a white pulp known as *bagasse*. All St Kitts' cane is brought in on the narrow-gauge railway track that runs around the northern part of the island. Among the modern equipment, vast brightly coloured baskets full of cane, you can see the discarded coal-fired engines of seasons past. It also has a **distillery** that makes the Kittitian rum, CSR. There are no regular tours, but it is usually possible to visit it during the cane-crushing season, between February and June, by asking at the gate.

South of Basseterre

Passing through the last of the canefields, and some of St Kitts' small industry (including the Headquarters of the Organization of Eastern Caribbean States's central bank), the road south from Basseterre climbs a ridge out of town and then descends into the tourist enclave of **Frigate Bay**, which is isolated from the local heart of St Kitts. In times past, Frigate Bay itself was the scene of early morning duels between slighted members of the St Kitts nobility, but now it tends to be clubs at dawn on the golf course and a bit of jousting on jet skis.

In 1989 a road was constructed that opened up the south of the island beyond Frigate Bay. Plots of land have been sold, and large international hotel companies have begun to muscle in on the beaches. From Frigate Bay, the road leads past the old salt ponds, common property in the days when the island was shared by the French and English, and comes to Cockleshell Bay and Banana Bay, where there are magnificent views of Nevis.

Nevis

At times it is the only cloud in the sky, but there is almost always a cloud on the summit of Nevis. Like all the tall volcanic Caribbean islands, Nevis blocks the path of the racing Atlantic winds and, as they rise and condense, they stack in huge immobile cumulus clouds. This permanent white wreath supposedly reminded the Spanish travellers of the snow-capped peaks of home and so the island came to be called *Nuestra Señora de las Nieves*, Our Lady of the Snows. Gradually, the name has been shortened to Nevis (pronounced 'Nee-viss').

Nevis is almost circular (6 by 8 miles) and from the sea can look like a regular cone; deep green slopes rise in sweeping curves to the central Nevis Peak at 3,232ft. About 10,000 Nevisians live in settlements dotted all around the island.

For all its size, Nevis was the capital island in the Leewards for a time and the island was so illustrious that it was known as the 'Queen of the Caribbees'. Then, it had a population of 45,000, of whom 15,000 are said to have been white. Island society was so august and the estate houses so grand that ladies could walk down the stairs

Best Beaches

Pinney's Beach: Nevis's stunning 3½-mile strand, which starts just north of Charlestown and is backed along almost its entire length by a confusion of palm trees, a cat's cradle of trunks and then a starburst of fronds. The golden-brown sand shelves steeply into the sea and the scene is perfected by some cracking views of St Kitts. It is a good long walk and there is the occasional beach bar where you can stop to fortify yourself or linger over a sunset view.

Oualie Beach: Farther round the coast to the north, more golden-brown sand and a superb view across to St Kitts over the Narrows. A lively beach, with watersports, shops and a bar at the hotel, and it sees a nice crowd.

Lovers' Lane Beach: Excellent steeply shelved sand, no facilities and not much shade, but you are quite likely to be alone. It is quite difficult to find, along a rickety trail just after the hill.

Newcastle Bay: More steep-sloping sand and quite big waves.

Indian Castle: Below Gingerland, with excellent sand and somewhat rough water; no shelter or facilities.

three abreast, panniered skirts and all. The 'old-time' architectural elegance of the West Indies, which has been swallowed up by development almost everywhere else in the Caribbean over the last 30 years, is still just about visible in Nevis, in the finely crafted bridges and dark stone walls that poke out of the ever-encroaching jungle. The plantation-house hotels also retain the old grace and finery of centuries past and are some of the most exquisite hotels in the Caribbean.

Nevis is the smaller and quieter partner in the Federation with St Kitts, and although a century of association across the Narrows has forged close relations with St Kitts, it has not diminished Nevis's own traditions. The islanders have their own, five-person elected assembly (which meets just three or four times a year). When the Deputy Governor General of St Kitts and Nevis is in residence you will always see two flags flying: one is for the Federation of St Kitts with Nevis and the other Nevis's own flag.

In the late 1990s the issue of secession came to a head after simmering for years and the Nevisians considered severing links from the Federation of St Kitts–Nevis. It's a traditional Caribbean problem: the smaller partners in what were generally convenient colonial administrative organizations have always felt put upon as the larger partner keeps the political power, usually by weight of population, and therefore the political mandate, and generally it treats its own islanders better. It was a hot political potato for a few years but eventually secession was sidelined. It is not mentioned much on the island any more.

The Nevisians go more placidly than their fellow countrymen. In school, the children learn that there were no slave rebellions in the island's history which, if it were true, would probably make Nevis stand alone throughout the whole Caribbean. Certainly the Nevisians are extremely polite and they all have time to stop and talk to a stranger. But like everywhere in the Caribbean, Nevis is changing as its tourist industry winds into gear. Jobs in the tourist industry have prevented the traditional

Getting There

Nevis t (1 869–)

By Air

The newly upgraded Vance W. Amory Airport receives a daily American Eagle flight from the San Juan hub in Puerto Rico. There are also easy links both from Antigua and from St Kitts itself, which has an international-length runway (but has no direct scheduled services from Europe or from the USA). There is a departure tax of EC$53 (US$20) and an environmental levy of US$1.50.

From the UK and Europe

The easiest connections are via Antigua (*see* p.339), from where hopper flights (theoretically) link up with British Airways, Virgin and BWIA services from London. It is also possible to make same-day connections via Sint Maarten from Paris (Air France) and from Amsterdam (KLM). There are direct charter services from the UK and Germany in season.

From the USA and Canada

The easiest connections from the USA are made via the American Airlines hub in San Juan, Puerto Rico, from where there is a daily flight on American Eagle, t 465 2273. Or you can make your way to Sint Maarten or Antigua and take a hopper flight from there. It is even possible via the Virgin Islands. A number of charter airlines also fly into St Kitts.

From Other Caribbean Islands

St Kitts is easily accessible by the hopper flights that pass up and down the island chain between Antigua and San Juan, Puerto Rico. Most of them stop in Nevis too. Airlines with scheduled flights include LIAT, St Kitts t 465 2286, Nevis t 469 9333; and Caribbean Star, t 465 5929. Winair, St Kitts t 465 8010, Nevis t 469 9333, flies in from Sint Maarten; and Carib Aviation, t 465 3055, Nevis t 469 9295, Antigua t 462 3147, has nine-seater and five-seater planes on 'share charter' from Antigua.

From St Kitts

The local inter-island 'bus' service is really the ferry, of which there are three, with six or seven sailings a day each way (about 45mins; EC$4–9 one-way, depending on which service is used). The views are magnificent as the mountains shift slowly above you. Kenneth's Dive Centre runs a **water-taxi** service, t 466 5320, and you can also contact Blue Water Safaris, t 465 9838. Alternatively you can transfer by **helicopter**: Island Helicopters, t 465 1325, *helico@caribsurf.com*.

Getting Around

By Bus

There is an unscheduled but fairly regular bus service that sets off from Charlestown in both clockwise and anticlockwise directions (though not all the way round the island in one direction). Buses – 'Roots', 'Rumours' and the admirably logical 'Busman' – leave from the town centre and run until 10pm (later on Saturdays); the fare is about EC$3.

By Taxi

Taxis are available near the pier in Charlestown, at the airport, through the hotels or through the Nevis Taxi Drivers Association, t 469 1483, or the City Taxi Stand, t 469 5631. Some sample prices are: Charlestown to Pinney's Beach – US$8, to Oualie Beach – US$13, to Newcastle Airport –

haemorrhage of islanders, who left to find a better life elsewhere. The island has an unaccustomed buzz about it at the moment. There is building everywhere – new houses are creeping higher and higher up the hillsides, there are yet more hotel plans afoot, the number of cars has rocketed and there is even congestion in Charlestown. People actually seem to be in a hurry on what traditionally was a comatose island. In just a few years Nevis has lost its innocence.

For all of this, Nevis is still much less developed than most other Caribbean islands and it has oodles more charm than many other islands that pretend to be undiscovered.

US$15, to the Golden Rock Hotel – US$16. Taxis can also be hired for a three-hour island tour for around US$60.

Hitch-hiking
Hitch-hiking works quite well in Nevis.

By Guided Tour
Tours of the island (by vehicle) last 3–4hrs and they can take in lunch at a plantation house if you make a prior arrangement. You can contact a taxi driver direct (*see* above), or go through a travel agency:

TDC Airlines, **t** 469 5238.
Marlon Brando, **t** 663 2013, **pager** 467 9976.
TC's, **t** 469 2911.
Teach, **t** 469 1140.
Tropical Tours, 22 Canyon St West, Basseterre, *kisco@caribsurf.com*.

Car and Bike Hire
You need a local licence to drive in Nevis, obtained on presentation of your own licence and EC$24 to the police in Charlestown, Gingerland or Newcastle. There is basically one road, about 20 miles long, that runs around the island, with one or two branches leading off it. Watch out for the goats, who seem to find the tastiest grass at the roadside. Cars get very booked up at Christmas, so you might want to arrange one in advance.

Car rental starts at around US$50 per day, and a Jeep costs slightly more. Hire firms include:

Avis, **t** 469 5199.
Nevis Car Rental, at the airport, **t** 469 9837.
Striker's Car Rental, **t** 469 2654.
TDC Rentals, **t** 469 5430, *tdcrent@ caribsurf.com*.
Windsurfing 'n' Mountain Biking Nevis, Oualie Beach, **t** 469 9682. Hires out bicycles.

Tourist Information

Abroad
For tourist information offices abroad *see* 'St Kitts', p.374.

In Nevis
Bureau of Tourism, Main St, Charlestown, **t** 469 7550, *info@nevisisland.com*, *www. nevisisland.com*. They are very helpful.

There are information desks on the waterfront in Charlestown and at the airport.

The Tourist Board puts out brochures and a glossy magazine, *St Kitts and Nevis Visitor*, with essential information on restaurants and shopping. *See* also 'St Kitts', p.374.

Telephone Code
The IDD code for St Kitts and Nevis is **t** 1 869 followed by a seven-digit local number, beginning with 469 in Nevis. Between the islands and on-island, dial the seven digits.

Art Galleries

Café des Arts, Charlestown, **t** 469 7098. Set in a pretty white wooden house on the road heading east. On sale there are hand-painted silks and prints and some tropical table mats by Kate Spencer from St Kitts.

Eva Wilkin Gallery, Gingerland, **t** 469 2673. *Open Mon–Fri 10–3, or call in advance*. Set in the shell of an old windmill to the east of Charlestown. Eva Wilkin lived and painted for many years in Nevis and some of her work is on view, alongside exhibitions of other painters. There is a shop downstairs.

Gallery of Nevis Art, on the road towards Pinney's Beach. Bright and colourful tropical work by Caribbean artists and expatriates.

Charlestown

The island's capital and only town is Charlestown, a few streets of pretty old stone buildings with wooden balconies and gingerbread trimmings ranged along the Caribbean coast of the island. The town gravitates around the two small squares – Memorial or Independence Square and Walwyn Square – though they are actually more like triangles of grass because of the lie of the land. Here hucksters sell sweets and drinks, bus drivers wait for passengers and a small crowd of limers passes the time of day. Named in 1671 after King Charles II, the town is home to 1,500 Nevisians,

Festivals

Most special days are also celebrated with horse-racing.

February *Tourism Week*. Horse racing, treasure hunt, music, and arts and crafts displays.

Easter *Good Friday*. Kite-flying competitions.

May/June *Sailing regatta*. Races between local fishing craft, making a colourful sight.

July *Culturama*. The main island festival in Nevis, held in memory of Emancipation late in the month, with its climax on the first Monday in August. There are regular Caribbean Carnival activities, so you can expect to see calypso and string band competitions, and costumed masqueraders strutting through the streets of Charlestown.

September *Independence Day* on the 19th. Parades and horse races.

October *Sport-fishing competition*.

Watersports

There are just a few places where you can take part in watersports, on Pinney's Beach and at Oualie Beach. For water-skiing and small-boat sailing, the calm waters of the west coast are ideal. General watersports equipment can be hired through the Four Seasons Hotel (*see* 'Scuba Diving', below), where there are concessionaires, but a better bet is probably Oualie Beach, where you can arrange water-skiing or a sunfish or small boat through:

Nevis Water Sports, **t** 469 9060, *seabrat@ caribsurf.com, www.windsurfingnevis.com*.

Turtle Tours, **t** 469 8503, *www.beach-works. com/turtletours*. Kayaking and snorkelling.

Windsurfing Nevis, **t** 469 9682, *windsurf@ caribsurf.com*. For kayaks and hobie cats.

Under the Sea, Sealife Education Centre, Tamarind Bay, **t** 469 1291, *www.underthe seanevis.com*. A first-hand experience with sea creatures, followed by a snorkelling trip.

Day Sails

Caona, at the Four Seasons Hotel, **t** 469 9494. Day trips at sea on a catamaran, with snorkelling and a barbecue picnic.

Sea Nevis, **t** 469 9239. Arrange day sails, whale-watching trips (when the whales are passing) and water taxis.

Scuba Diving and Snorkelling

The best area for snorkelling is around Newcastle and Nisbet Plantation. Scuba rental and instruction is available through:

Scuba Safaris, Oualie Beach, **t** 469 9518, *scubanevis@caribsurf.com, www. divenevis.com*.

Four Seasons Resort, Pinney's Beach, **t** 469 1111. If you wish to go further and deeper, to explore caves and hot springs coming off Nevis's now dormant volcano.

Windsurfing

Oualie Beach is a good spot because inshore it is relatively protected, but further out, where the winds are concentrated by the Narrows, there are bumps and jumps. Further around the coast at Newcastle, the Atlantic winds make for more extreme sailboarding.

Windsurfing Nevis, **t** 469 9682, *windsurf@ caribsurf.com*. Offers instruction, 'guaranteed success', BIC and Mistral boards and Up and Tushingham sails.

Other Sports

Golf

There is a very neat and well-kept 18-hole course designed by Robert Trent Jones II

who live mainly in a suburb of modern buildings that has grown up behind the original town.

Next to the ferry dock the waterfront is a string of gazebos and a small tourist market, with shops in the restored cotton ginnery. Close by is the main **Charlestown Market**, where the fruits and spices are heaped on the tables and lightning banter fills the air from soon after dawn. Back on the waterfront, the old stone warehouses that muscle in shoulder to shoulder have been redeveloped and now house cafés and restaurants among the modern businesses.

attached to the Four Seasons Hotel, t 469 9494. People fly in from the islands around to play it, though it is extremely expensive and hotel guests have preference in teeing-off times.

Fishing

Deep Venture, t 469 5110, *mattlloyd@caribsurf. com*. Half- and full-day charters.

Eurika Deep Sea Fishing Charter, t 469 8317.

Nevis Water Sports, Oualie Bay, t 469 9060. Full- and half-day charters with tackle and drinks.

Venture II, t 469 9837. Half- and full-day trips on a 28ft sport-fishing boat, with bar.

Hiking

There are some worthwhile hikes into the Nevisian jungle, which take a look at the island's more exotic flora and visit the old plantation estates. There are endless ruins on the island, and they make excellent foraging grounds for the walker or historian – the skeletons of mansions and boiling houses gape in their decay, cane-crushing rollers and boiling coppers are littered around long-overgrown gardens. Some old estates worth seeking out are **Montravers House**, inland from Pinneys Beach, which was the finest on the island when Nevis was the Queen of the Caribbees (it even had a moat); and on the windward Atlantic coast, the **Coconut Walk Estate** ruins and the **Eden Brown Estate House**, famous for its ghost, the tortured bride who lost her husband in a duel with his best man on the very night of her wedding.

You are advised to take a guide when walking off into the country:

Eco-Tours, t 469 2091. Offers leisurely walks through the plantations.

Heb's Nature Tours, Zetlands Village, Gingerland, t 469 3512, *hebnature@hotmail. com*. Wide range of tours, from hiking up

Nevis Peak, to bush medicine tours, village tours and monkey walks.

Sunrise Tours, t 469 2758. Guides for a variety of hikes from leisurely village walks to climbing Nevis Peak.

Top to Bottom, t 469 9080. Rainforest walks, bush medicine tours, and tours up Nevis Peak or to the old plantation estates.

The **Nevis Historical and Conservation Society**, which is based at Alexander Hamilton House (the museum in Charlestown), organizes a monthly hike and other events. For a calendar of events, call them on t 469 5786.

Horse-riding

There is a Jockey Club in Nevis, with race meetings 10 times a year, mainly on public holidays. A ride in the foothills of Nevis Peak or a canter through the surf can be arranged by:

Hermitage Stables, t 469 3477.

Nevis Equestrian Centre, t 469 8118, *guilbert@caribsurf.com*.

Mountain biking

Contact Windsurfing Nevis (*see* above), which has good bikes for hire and three levels of tour, from a gentle and general historical ride through to technical single track with amazing views.

Where to Stay

Nevis t (1 869–)

Like St Kitts, Nevis has some extremely fine plantation hotels, where you can bask in gracious splendour just as the planters did 200 years ago. They are quiet and low-key and although most are not on the beach, the hotels usually run shuttle buses. If being right on the sand is the most important thing, then

At the northern end of town, set in a grassy garden on a lane called Low Street, is **Alexander Hamilton House**, an attractive replica of a famous stone building that dates from the 1680s. It was the birthplace and home for five years of the architect of the American Constitution, Alexander Hamilton, whose face you will see on the US$10 bill. Hamilton was born in the house in 1757 of a Nevisian mother and a Scots father and lived there until he was five, when they moved to St Croix in the Virgin Islands. From there Alexander eventually left to complete his legal education in the States. Later, as a patriot during the American Revolution, he was George

there are also some nice beach hotels. Nevis is building steadily, some stylish hotels and some in modern concrete. An 8% government charge is added to all bills and most hotels also add 10% to your bill for service.

There are also a number of villas and cottages dotted around the island, for those who would prefer to be independent. Contact the Tourist Board, or:

Hart of Nevis, t 469 2328, *hartofnevis@ caribsurf.com*. A number of houses and villas for rent, most of them with pools.

Sea Shell Properties, Main St, Charlestown, t 469 1675, US t 1 800 457 0444, *www.nevisvillas.com*. As Hart.

Luxury

Four Seasons Resort, PO Box 565, Pinney's Beach, t 469 1111, US t 1 800 332 3442, Canada t 1 800 268 6282, *reservations@fourseasons. com*, *www.fourseasons.com*. Sits on a superb stretch of Pinney's Beach. It is large, sumptuous, swish, brisk and without much character, but does a reliable beach-bound body-holiday – great spa in garden setting, watersports and day cruises, tennis and golf, low-calorie meals and king-sized beds.

Very Expensive

Montpelier Plantation Inn, PO Box 474, t 469 3462, *montpinn@caribsurf.com*, *www. montpeliernevis.com*. A tropical island idyll of centuries past, where you will find a gracious old West Indian ambience with a certain English style. There are 17 large rooms in cottages scattered around the grounds of a magnificent estate house, all linked by paths that wind among flamboyant trees, frangipani, palms and mango trees. The plantation is lost in the southern hills of Nevis, but there are shuttles to the

beach and the hotel has a tennis court and a pool. The dining room, on a veranda off the Great Hall, overlooks the lit gardens.

Nisbet Plantation Beach Club, near Camps, t 469 9325, US t 1 800 742 6008, *nisbetbc@ caribsurf.com*, *www.nisbetplantation.com*, . This has the advantage among the plantation hotels of being set in 30 acres of lawned estate that run down to the beach. There is a magnificent view from the great house to the seafront down an alley of tall palms where the 38 excellent rooms and suites are scattered in bungalows. During the day you can pass the time at the beach (which has passable sand, though it is a little windy sometimes), pool and beach restaurant. In the evening you retreat to the great house, an exquisite setting for dinner.

Expensive

The Hermitage, St John's Parish, t 469 3477, US t 1 800 682 4025, *nevherm@caribsurf.com*, *www.hermitagenevis.com*. This has a supreme setting on the southern-facing slopes of Nevis. The great house, a classic West Indian timber-frame building from the 1740s with louvred windows on stilts, is surrounded by mango trees and other tropical greenery. The 15 rooms are set in pretty Caribbean cottages with traditional shingle walls and tin roofs, wrapped in gingerbread woodwork and bougainvillea. The rooms have wooden interiors with four-poster beds and antiques and all have hammocks on their balconies from where you can savour the view. Some cottages have kitchens.

Moderate

Golden Rock Plantation Inn, PO Box 493, t 469 3346, *goldenrockhotel@caribsurf.com*, *www.golden-rock.com*. A slightly simpler

Washington's aide-de-camp and was known as the 'Little Lion' because he was 5ft 7in tall and his blue eyes were said to turn black when he was angry. It was he who, having trained as a lawyer, first suggested the Federation of the American States in the form that was eventually adopted, and with its founding he became First Secretary to the American Treasury. He died in a duel with a political opponent, Aaron Burr, in 1804.

The building houses the **Museum of Nevis History** (*open weekdays 8–4, Saturday 10–1; small adm*) where there is an excellent chronological display of the island from

plantation hotel set 1,000ft up the mountainside and threatened with being swallowed up by its 96 acres of garden. You approach on a rickety, stone-lined drive up a steep hill to a small complex of old estate buildings converted into the hotel. Just 14 rooms, which stand in modern blocks behind the main house, some of them furnished with antiques or bamboo four-posters. The shell of the old windmill has been converted into a honeymooners' suite.

Oualie Beach, Oualie Beach, t 469 9735, *oualie@oualie.com*, *www.oualie.com*. This has plenty of casual Caribbean style: a small, laid-back beach hotel just above the golden sand of Oualie Beach, which sees a fun crowd during the day. There are 34 bright and breezy rooms in cottages with gingerbread trimmings and superb views of St Kitts, which you can gaze at from the screened verandas. Some rooms have mahogany four-poster beds with canopies. There is a lively bar and restaurant serving West Indian meals and plenty of watersports are available right outside.

Hurricane Cove Bungalows, Oualie Beach, t 469 9462, *hcove@caribsurf.com*, *www.hurricanecove.com*. These eleven bungalows are perched above Oualie Beach and are ranged around the headland with magnificent views out to sea. They are built simply of carefully finished wood, with muslin nets over the simple wooden beds, window shutters on stilts and a sitting area with huge windows. One-, two- and three-bedroom units with full kitchens, some with private pools, but no restaurant.

Inn at Cades Bay, Pinney's Beach, t 469 8139, *cadesbay@caribsurf.com*, *www.cadesbayinn.com*. Standing at the very top of Pinney's Beach, these 16 studios are set in staggered single-storey blocks just above the sea. They are furnished with mahogany beds with muslin nets and decorated with Mexican tiles. They are fan-ventilated and air-conditioned, with TV, and each has a patio from which to watch the sunset.

Mount Nevis Hotel & Beach Club, Shaws Road, Newcastle, t 469 9373, US t 800 75 NEVIS, *mountnevis@aol.com*, *www.mountnevishotel.com*. Set on a north-facing mountain slope, the hotel commands great panoramic views of Nevis and the sea. Its 28 rooms have a good range of facilities, including cable TV; suites have kitchens. There is a fitness centre, pool, and tennis court. The nearby beach club has a restaurant and beach pavilion. Diving, snorkelling, water-skiing, horse-riding, golf, and deep-sea fishing can be arranged. Family friendly.

Meadville Apartments, Charlestown, PO Box 66, t 469 5235, UK t (020) 8289 9685, *mgmeade@caribsurf.com*. Simple self-catering apartments in town: clean and quite comfortable, with balconies.

Inexpensive

Seaspawn Guest House, Charlestown, PO Box 233, t 469 5239, *seaspawn.nevis@caribsurf.com*. Out on the edge of Charlestown with 18 clean and simple rooms each with a private bath. It is a good place from which to explore Nevis if your hotel is not the main point of the holiday.

Daniel's Deck, Charlestown, t 469 5765. Close to the town centre, no-nonsense rooms with private bathrooms at very cheap prices.

Philsha's Guest House, Pinney's Road, Charlestown, t 469 5253, *philshasnevis@hotmail.com*. Newly-built one- and two-bedroom self-contained units with air-con, phone and cable television.

Amerindian times to the present, with ghostly Arawak faces in pottery, pictures of 'old-time' Nevis with explanations of old island architecture, porcelain from the Bath Hotel, home crafts, and documents from the life of Alexander Hamilton himself. Upstairs, approached by a stairway from the grassy and tree-shaded courtyard, is the Nevis House of Assembly, where the five-man Nevis Parliament holds its parliamentary sessions every four years.

Headed in the other direction (east) out of town you will see the old **Bath Hotel**, a huge block of a building above the road to the right. It was constructed in 1778 in

Eating Out

The finest food and the best settings are found on the verandas of the plantation house hotels (the Thursday night fish barbecue at Nisbet is well known and both Montpelier and the Hermitage have elegant dining rooms). There are an increasing number of good restaurants outside the hotels in Nevis. Most restaurants add a 10% service charge to your bill. **Categories** are arranged according to the price of a main course: expensive = EC$40 and above; moderate = EC$20–40; inexpensive = under EC$20.

Expensive

The Hermitage, St John's Parish, **t** 469 3477. For some of the finest cuisine in Nevis, reserve for dinner and join the owners' guests for cocktails in the parlour and food in the antique-filled dining room. On Wednesday nights, there's a traditional West Indian BBQ with roast pig and music by the Sugar Mill String Band.

The Mill, Montpelier Plantation Inn, **t** 469 3462. The 18th-century mill has been turned into a speciality restaurant where three nights a week up to 14 guests dine on a four-course fixed menu in a romantic, candlelit setting. Very expensive.

Miss June's Cuisine, Cades Bay, **t** 469 5330, *www.missjunes.com*. For an excellent and thoroughly original night out, Miss June's serves a compendium of dishes in a villa in the Jones Estate (unmarked, just off the main road, next to the two-hole Nevis Golf Club). Begin with cocktails in the drawing room and move next door for a set menu of six or seven courses: soup, fish, a multiplicity of main dishes and vegetables on a buffet and then puddings, which Miss June talks you through (it can be as many as 30 dishes in all). Coming from Trinidad, she cooks plenty of spicy, Indian-inspired food, but also expect Asian, gourmet Caribbean and international fare. The menu varies nightly. She doesn't open every night and you must make up a minimum party of eight – by reservation only, but well worth making the effort to get there.

Eddy's Restaurant, Independence Square, Charlestown, **t** 469 5958, *cadesbay@carib surf.com*. This is the best restaurant in town, despite its unlikely name. It is set in a very attractive old town house, where you dine in the wooden interior on creaking floorboards or on the veranda looking out on to the square. Daytime fritters and salads, *rotis*, night-time specials of soup followed by catch of the day, and dishes such as voodoo pasta. Some entertainment, bar attached.

Bananas Bistro, Cotton Ground, **t** 469 1891. A delightful setting on a rocky outcrop just above the main road behind Pinney's Beach, where you dine on a rickety pink and green terrace under a tin roof. An international menu with dishes as varied as French onion soup, moussaka and Thai roast pork salad. There's a bar in the old creole house, with the funkiest loos on the island.

Unella's By the Sea, Waterfront, Charlestown, **t** 469 5574. Overlooking the yachts and the lights of St Kitts from the waterfront in town, this quiet haunt is set upstairs on a stone-walled balcony and deck. Dishes include grilled fish served with capers and lemon or shrimp scampi sautéed in garlic.

Moderate

Le Bistro, Chapel St, **t** 469 5110. Set in a pretty old wooden house in the back streets of town, where you dine among profuse

grand Nevisian style, complete with ballroom, balconies and accommodation for 50 guests. In Nevis's heyday people would come and stay here in order to take the spa waters, which come out of the ground at temperatures as high as 108°F. Supposedly they resemble those of Baden-Württemburg and were renowned for the treatment of rheumatism and gout. The waters were first mentioned by some visitors before Nevis was even settled. A captain John Smith, leader of the Jamestown settlers of Virginia, called here first in 1607. Some of his fellow travellers had been scalded by manchineel sap when they sheltered under the tree in the rain, but here they found 'a great poole,

tropical greenery. International fare with Caribbean touches – deep-fried Brie to start then salad and a crispy coconut chicken.

Tequila Sheila's, Cades Bay, t 469 8139. Overlooking the beach at the top end of Pinney's Beach (and a yacht which washed ashore during Hurricane Marilyn). Flaming torches stand outside the open-sided pink and lime-green gazebo where you can linger over grilled seafood or Mexican fare.

Café des Arts, Main St, Charlestown, t 469 7098. Makes the best of its setting in a courtyard behind Main St in town, with tables under a tree and umbrellas. Coffee and cakes, or salads and sandwiches while you ruminate over what to purchase from the art gallery in the same building.

Inexpensive

Most villages have a 'chicken and ribs cookout' on Friday and Saturday nights, starting about 5pm. There's music, cold beer, fresh-cooked chicken and ribs, and dominoes.

Muriel's Cuisine, Happy Hill Drive, t 469 5920. For the best in local food, a classic West Indian restaurant set in a modern house, with flowery plastic tablecloths and a daily varying menu of curries and stews and *rotis*, served with excellent johnny cakes.

Cla Cha Del Restaurant, Cotton Ground, t 469 1841. From Claudia, Charles and Delroy, a slightly cavernous dining room just above Pinney's Beach. Classic West Indian setting and fare – chicken, fish and spare ribs served at plastic tables and chairs with a red rose.

Bars and Nightlife

If you want to catch a sunset drink you can wander along to any of the bars along Pinney's Beach, or try the bars in town. There is something of a circuit of bars during the week. Some of the hotels lay on entertainment, perhaps a piano player or a steel band.

Eddy's, Charlestown. Often has a lively crowd in the early evening.

Nisbet Plantation Hotel, St James Parish, t 469 9325. On Thursday people gravitate to the fish cookout here.

Matt's Long Bar (it is very long), at Le Bistro, Charlestown. Crowded on Friday.

Four Seasons Resort, t 469 1111. Live calypso music nightly by the Caribbean Roots or steel pan music. Call for schedules.

Golden Rock Plantation Inn, t 469 3346. West Indian buffet on Saturday nights with The Honey Bees, oldest of Nevis' string bands.

Beach Bars

Pinney's Beach has a number of shoreside stopovers, ideal for lunch time and a lazy afternoon on the beach. A clutch of them has gravitated around the Four Seasons:

Sunshine's, just outside the Four Seasons compound, Pinney's Beach, t 662 8383. A dead cool hang-out dressed up in red, gold and green, where you can grab a beer and listen to reggae all afternoon.

Beachcomber, Pinney's Beach, t 469 1192. Set in a converted villa: daytime snacks and seafood dishes, then drinks in the early evening followed by slightly finer fare.

Sanddollar, Pinney's Beach, t 469 5319. It is set back from the sand, but gathers a crowd from time to time.

Tequila Sheila's, Cades Bay. An open-sided gazebo on the sand at the very top of the beach. Jazz on Sundays.

Oualie Beach Restaurant, Oualie Beach, t 469 9735. An excellent place to spend the day, farther around the coast where there is often a lively crowd.

where in bathing themselves they found much ease...they were well cured in two or three days'. The hotel was dilapidated for many years, although it has survived the earthquakes and hurricanes well. The bathhouse is no longer fully functioning either, though if you are scalded by a manchineel tree, you can still rush around here and take the waters from the stream.

Just behind here you will find **Government House**, built in 1909, the official Residence of the Deputy Governor General of St Kitts and Nevis, which sits in lawned gardens on a hilltop that overlooks the town. Next door is the **Horatio Nelson**

Museum, where the exhibit 'Nevis in the Time of Nelson' details Nelson's life and times in the West Indies. Nelson was based at English Harbour in Antigua on HMS *Boreas* in the 1780s, soon after American Independence and was unpopular with the West Indians because his job was to enforce the Navigation Laws (which banned their very profitable trade with countries other than Britain – they even sued him once and he had to stay on board his ship for eight weeks to avoid being locked up). However, eventually he found solace with the young widow Fanny Nisbet, whom he first met at Montpelier House. The bride was given away by Prince William Henry (later to become King William IV), who was based in Antigua at the time. There is an impressive collection of Nelson memorabilia: letters, maquettes of ships and pottery from toby jugs made in his image to the porcelain used at his marriage feast.

Anticlockwise on the Island Road

Back on the main road, the town gradually thins into countryside with new concrete houses sitting behind their fences and old wooden homes on small plots of beaten earth scattered at the roadside. As you drive, you will come across age-old stand-pipes, delivering water as they have for the last hundred years, and impromptu roadside markets which switch sides at midday to take advantage of the shade.

The Nelson story continues briefly at **Fig Tree Church**, a small stone sanctuary in a tropical garden, which is where the marriage between the future admiral and Fanny Nisbet took place. His signature can be seen in the register (a photocopy). The couple soon returned to England, but the marriage did not last and Nelson became involved with Lady Hamilton. The marriage took place on the Montpelier Estate, off the road to the right (you can see a commemorative plaque on the stone gatepost). Here you will also find the **Nevis Botanical Garden** (*t 469 3399, www.botanicalgardensnevis.com; open Nov–Mar Mon–Sat 10–4; varied schedule May–Oct*), which tames the island's rampant growth into manicured lawns and areas devoted to different species from around the world including cacti, orchids, palms, lily ponds (with sculptures of dolphins and mermaids), a rose and vine garden and a special conservatory devoted to rainforest, in which there is a slightly curious Mayan temple. At the centre is a nice West Indian house, all balconies and balustrades, with a fine view of the sea, a café and gift shop.

The main road continues to circle the island, passing wonderful old stone walls, bridges and the ruins of plantations poking out of the greenery up to the northern shore. At **Camps** on the northern side of the island, you can follow the coast road to Oualie or take a road that leads into the forest and through the hills and emerges on the Caribbean coast at Cades Bay at the **Soufrière**. This is an active volcanic vent that first appeared with a hiss and a sulphurous stench when an earthquake struck in 1950. It is a bit lukewarm now, with just the odd trace of stink bomb and some heated and barren patches of earth, but is a reminder that the underworld is not so far away in the Caribbean.

The main road returns to Charlestown along the Caribbean coast, skirting behind Pinney's Beach. You will pass close to the site of **Jamestown**, the first capital of Nevis, which slid into the sea during an earthquake in 1680. It is said that one man escaped the quake when the jail collapsed around him: 'Redlegs' Greaves, a Scots gentleman pirate who retired to an estate on Nevis after a lifetime of freebooting, had been recognized by a former comrade in revelry and had been thrown in jail. Having been spared by the earthquake, he was eventually pardoned. From here the road winds through the manicured gardens and golf course of the Four Seasons Hotel and into town.

Anguilla

Anguilla is a flat and barren island, 16 miles by 3 and largely 15ft deep in scrub. Inland, the 'eel' (its name supposedly derives from eel in Spanish) is hardly an attractive place, but along its writhing coastline Anguilla has some of the Caribbean's most spectacular beaches – mounded with sumptuously soft and blinding white sand, set in an electric blue sea. On a coast 45 miles long, there are about 30 of them.

Anguilla is the most northerly of the British Leeward Islands and it lies about 5 miles from the French part of St Martin, pointing north and east into the Atlantic. Sombrero Rock, its dependency, is the northernmost point in the chain of the Lesser Antilles. The 10,000 or so Anguillans are ice cool – for a small Caribbean island there is a remarkable air of independence and self-assurance. The island is quiet to the point of sedation and it seems that nothing could ruffle Anguilla's calm. But it is worth remembering that 20 years ago, when they wanted to secede from St Kitts and Nevis, they took to the scrub and staged a (small) revolution. As so often in the Caribbean, the Anguillans you meet on-island are only half the story, as there are probably more abroad than there are on Anguilla itself. Historically the island was never able to offer its people a living and so they have always travelled. Now, mainly through tourism, Anguilla is more prosperous than ever and some Anguillans are actually coming back.

The island has recently moved into the Caribbean big league and there has been a huge amount of building, some of it extremely smart and stylish, albeit in some unexpected architectural styles, including Moroccan, space-age and Greek. Besides the hotels there are also plenty of villas and private homes. Among all the modern development, however, you will still just see a few people who lead fairly simple West Indian lives, in shingle and clapboard houses set in a small plot of beaten earth.

Anguilla specializes in a brand of reliable low-key high luxury and has a string of extremely smart hotels, among the best in the Caribbean, though there are also some less expensive places to stay. There is also good variety in the restaurants – again unexpectedly for a British Caribbean island peopled mainly by Americans it has become a place where you can expect to eat seriously – and a string of lively beach bars. For the moment the island has an easy air because it is not too crowded.

Apart from the impeccable beaches, it is the Anguillan people that make this barren islet a special place. As they greet you with the slightest wave and a soothing 'all right, all right', it is hard to imagine that there was ever a raised temper here, let alone a revolution.

Anguilla

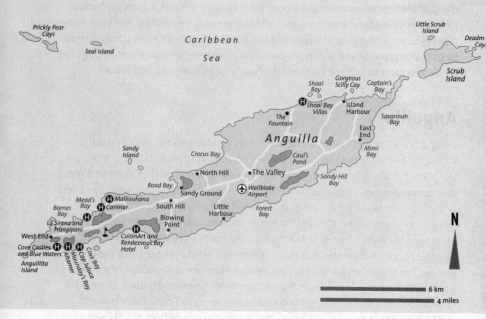

History

In Amerindian times, Anguilla went by the name of *Malliouhana* and although it was probably christened Anguilla by a Spaniard, Spain herself ignored the island because it offered no quick returns. The Spaniards' only fleeting interest in the island was in 1633 when the Dutch moved in. They promptly attacked it.

Around 1650 some Englishmen, an assorted bunch of rovers and misfits, had a go at settling the island. They arrived to find that Anguilla was 'filled with alligators and other noxious animals, but the soil was good for raising tobacco and corn, and the cattle imported multiplied very fast'. Salt could also be harvested and this continued until quite recently.

Anguilla did not really turn out that well as a plantation island, perhaps because the settlers were more interested in other things; soon it was a 'nest of pirates and smugglers and outlaws, dangerous to every neighbouring island and a disgrace to the British name'. But the Anguillan settlers were themselves vulnerable to the usual raids and ransackings of the Caribs and other Europeans. The French defeated them and occupied the island and the Irish attacked a number of times, leaving settlers behind in their turn (you can just hear echoes of Irish in Anguillan English, attributable to this and to a 19th-century shipwreck). The defenders had more success in the 18th century, though. In 1744 they repelled a large French force that landed at Rendezvous Bay. The story goes that when the Anguillans ran out of ammunition, they loaded up the weights from their fishing nets in order to keep up their fire.

The early settlers rented the island from the Crown for the price of 'a fat capon, a kid, or one ear of Indian corn on every feast day of St Michael the Angel' and made of it what they could. Slaves were brought to the island, but the estates could not support them, so they were left to grow their own food or fish for four days a week. They were even encouraged to go abroad, using their skills as coopers or carpenters to earn a living. Venturing as far afield as Trinidad and the Dominican Republic, they dealt in merchandise and practised a bit of smuggling. A tradition of boat-building grew up on the island. At one stage even the Governor was an 'honest old sloop man'. As they sailed, they would send home contributions from the money they earned abroad, 'remittances' that were the backbone of the economy until quite recently.

Initially Anguilla had no governor and was administered by a notable on the island such as the doctor, who also acted as magistrate, but in 1825 the island was attached to St Kitts for administrative convenience. The Anguillans had very little in common with the people of this successful sugar colony founded on slave labour, which in any case was about 60 miles away to the south, beyond the French island of St Martin. Occasionally they protested to the British Government, but without success. With little representation in the St Kitts House of Assembly, the Anguillans were treated as poor relations and they had to fight hard even to get their name added to the title of the country of St Kitts and Nevis in 1951.

The Revolution

In 1967, when all the British Caribbean colonies were given internal self-rule as 'Associated States' with Great Britain, with the option of Independence not far off, Anguilla suddenly found itself faced with the possibility of Independence in union with St Kitts and Nevis. The islanders promptly staged a revolution. On 30 May 1967, they rounded up the Kittitian policemen and shipped them out, refusing to recognize the authority of the Basseterre Government.

From the beginning the situation bemused outsiders, who wrote it up as 'the mouse that roared' and 'the eel that squealed', but they did not reckon with the determination of the Anguillans, who went as far as staging a tiny invasion (unsuccessful) of St Kitts to pre-empt attempts to take Anguilla by force. They held referenda and wrote their own constitution.

Disbelieving colonial officials were dispatched to persuade the Anguillans to rejoin St Kitts–Nevis, but the islanders were adamant. With political tension mounting in 1969, British troops were sent to occupy the island in an operation which was later dubbed Britain's 'Bay of Piglets' after the invasion of Cuba a few years before. Not a shot was fired, and now disbelieving soldiers arrived to find themselves cheered and welcomed by people singing 'God Save the Queen'. When the troops were withdrawn, the London Metropolitan Police took over. All around them Caribbean countries were shaking off the colonial yoke, but Anguilla decided that it did not want Independence at all. It preferred to remain a Crown Colony of Britain. The whole episode is hilariously retold in Donald Westlake's *Under an English Heaven*, republished not long ago, available in Anguilla and complete with priceless photographs.

The political solution was long in coming, but eventually in 1982 Anguilla was granted its own constitution, with ministerial government headed by a Governor and ministers chosen from a seven-member House of Assembly. The Government is led by

Best Beaches

Shoal Bay: On the northern shore. The island's most popular beach and also one of its finest, with mounds of sand that are carved into scallop shapes by the meandering waves; you can walk for miles. There are one or two hotels and beach bars to retire to if the heat of the sun gets too much and there are reefs offshore for snorkelling. 'Elegant' floating rafts, 'fluffy' beach towels and 'reliable' snorkelling gear are for hire at Skyline Beach Rentals.

Sandy Ground: A busy half-moon bay with a line of bars and restaurants right on the sand. It is a working bay, with ships unloading at the jetty and yachts at anchor, but the bars give it a good atmosphere.

Mead's Bay and **Barnes Bay**: Further west along the north shore, with more blinding white sand with hotels standing on the clifftops above them and fantastic sunset views. Both have bars to retreat to in the hotels, and watersports equipment for hire. Dolphin Discovery, t 497 7946, *www.dolphindiscovery.com*, is a programme to enable people to swim with dolphins on Mead's Bay.

Honeymoon Beach: At the far western end of the island you will find a couple of tiny inlets with golden sand, enclosed by cliffs, which are perfect secluded suntraps, including this bay.

Maunday's Bay: Another magnificent curved strip of sand on a protected cove, home to Cap Juluca, whose Moorish domes stick out of the tropical greenery.

Cove Bay, leading into **Rendezvous Bay**: A 2-mile stretch of superb sand; some hotels, but good for walking morning or evening; it's always easy to find an isolated spot with the hills of St Martin in view.

Little Bay: A tiny cove just to the east of town, cut out of the cliffs and so secluded that you must go by boat (unless you are prepared to clamber down the rock face, in which case there are ropes to assist you). No facilities; quite often day tours from St Martin.

Mimi Bay and the wilder **Savannah Bay**: At the eastern end of the island, both quite windy and isolated, also walking beaches.

Captain's Bay: In the far northeast, a perfect and isolated cove, the ultimate secluded retreat.

Offshore islands: Anguilla's uninhabited cays – Deadman's Cay, Sombrero, Scrub and Little Scrub, Dog, Seal, Gorgeous Scilly Cay and Prickly Pear Cay – may sound like a surreal shopping list, but there are some excellent stretches of sand on them and you can arrange to visit on a day trip. Visible from Road Bay is Sandy Island, the archetypal paradise island, just a bar of sand with excellent snorkelling. Perhaps this is where the Lamb's Navy Rum girl lives. (Sandy Island was actually washed away during Hurricane Luis in 1995, but it has silted back again.) Day trips are arranged easily through Sandy Island Enterprises, t 497 6395.

Chief Minister Osbourne Fleming of the AUF (Anguilla United Front), who was reelected in March 2005. The current Governor of the island is Alan Huckle.

Today some Anguillans depend on fishing for their livelihood, sailing to catch lobsters and the indigenous local speciality, Anguillan crayfish, which sell for a very

Getting There

Anguilla t (1 264–)

By Air

The modest Wallblake Airport in the centre of the island cannot take long-haul flights and so you must make a connection in the Caribbean, though it is usually possible to reach the island in the same day. Transit points are Antigua, Sint Maarten and San Juan in Puerto Rico.

The journey by sea from Marigot, St Martin, is a more charming way to arrive. There is a departure tax of US$20 (EC$53).

From Europe

The easiest connections are made in Antigua, where a number of local scheduled and 'shared charter' airlines link up with the regular British Airways, Virgin and BWIA flights to ensure a relatively trouble-free onward journey. LIAT, t 497 5000, has a couple of flights a day, and Carib Aviation, Antigua t 462 3147, *carib@candoo.com, www.candoo. com/carib*, operates a 'share charter' with regular services: they quote a seat-only price. Air France, KLM and Lufthansa fly to Sint Maarten, from where it is an easy hop by plane or boat.

From the USA

The main gateways for Anguilla are San Juan, from where American Eagle, t 497 3131, has two flights a day, and Sint Maarten, which is also well served from the States (*see* p.441).

From Other Caribbean Islands

Winair (Windward Island Airways), t 497 2238, provides an air link from St Thomas and Sint Maarten. LIAT, t 497 5000, serves Anguilla from Antigua, San Juan and the Virgin Islands. Trans Anguilla Airways, t 497 8690, is the only charter line.

By Sea

Ferries link the port of Marigot in the French territory of St Martin with Blowing Point on the south of Anguilla. Services leave roughly every 30 minutes during the day and the crossing is 20 minutes. You will have to pay a departure tax from St Martin of US$10. There is a departure tax of US$3 (EC$8) when you're leaving Anguilla by sea.

Getting Around

By Taxi

Taxis can be arranged at the airport, t 497 5054, or at Blowing Point, t 497 6089, and at any of the hotels. Drivers are happy to drop you for the day on a remote beach and then return to collect you. Most will give impromptu tours of the island, but organized tours cost US$50 for a couple of hours for two people. Contact: Frank Webster, **pager** 724 0256, or Harry's Taxi, t 497 4336. Prices for journeys are fixed (quite expensively) by the Government. Some examples are: the airport to Shoal Bay – US$12 (and from Blowing Point – US$16), The Valley – US$6 (US$12), Sandy Ground – US$10 (US$10), Cove Castles and the southwestern end of the island – US$22 (US$20).

Hitch-hiking

With no bus service in Anguilla, hitch-hiking is workable and may introduce you to some amusing islanders.

Car and Bike Hire

Car hire gives the most mobility and cars are readily available, from about US$40 plus taxes. A local licence must be obtained, but this is easily done on presentation of a valid licence from home to the company at the time of hire, or to the police in The Valley, price US$20. Driving is on the left and the speed limit is 30mph. Traffic usually does proceed at a stately pace, but watch out for the couple of roundabouts and the single hanging traffic light. Some of the many companies also hire out Jeeps (at about US$50 plus taxes):

Apex/Avis, t 497 2642, *avisxa@ anguillanet.com*.

Connor's Car Rental, t 497 6433, *lucy@ sintmaarten.net*.

Island Car Rentals, Airport Rd, t 497 2723, *islandcar@anguillanet.com*.

Triple K, t 497 2934, *www.hertztriplek.com*.

For scooters and bikes, try:

Boo's Cycle, just above Sandy Ground, t 497 8523. Scooters for hire.

A&S Cycle Rentals, in Lower South Hill, **t** 497 8803. Scooters and also bicycles.

Tourist Information

Abroad

There are plenty of websites with information about Anguilla. Try *www.anguilla-vacation.com*, and *www.mycaribbean.com* for general island information. There is also lots of practical and general information at the various incarnations of *www.web.ai*. and *www.news.ai*.

Canada: 116C Hazelton Ave, Toronto, Ontario, **t** 416 944 8105, *xbermedia@aol.com*.
UK: 7a Crealock St, London, SW18 2BS.
USA: 246 Central Ave, White Plains, NY, 10606, **t** 914 287 2400, *mwturnstyle@aol.com*.

In Anguilla

On the island, information and assistance can be obtained from the helpful office: Anguilla Tourist Board, PO Box 1388, The Valley, **t** 497 2759, *atbtour@anguillanet.com*, *www.anguilla-vacation.com. Open Mon–Fri 8–5.*
Information booth, airport.

Embassies and Consulates

UK citizens are referred to the British High Commission in Antigua; American and Canadian citizens should refer to their consulates in Barbados.

Medical Emergencies

There is an emergency room and ambulance service at the Cottage Hospital in The Valley, **t** 497 2551 (or dial **t** 911).

Money and Banks

The **currency** of Anguilla is the Eastern Caribbean dollar (fixed to the US dollar at a rate of about US$1 = EC$2.65). The US dollar, best carried in the smaller denominations, is perfectly acceptable, though you will occasionally receive your change in EC$. If you are on a tight budget, it is better to use EC$. Credit cards are accepted at all hotels and in some shops. **Banking hours** are Mon–Thurs 8–3, Fri 8–5.

Shopping

Shops keep variable opening hours, with one thing in common – a respectable lunch break.

Telephone Code

If telephoning from outside the island, the IDD code for Anguilla is **t** 1 264, followed by 497 or 498 and then a four-figure number.
If calling within the island, just dial the seven digit number.

Festivals

February *Annual Moonsplash.*
  ABC Flower Show.
March *Annual Jazz Festival.*
May *Anguilla Day.* Celebrated with a round-island boat race.
June *Official birthday of the British Queen.* Festivities with a fair and boat races.
August *Summer Festival.* The main event in the Anguillan calendar. The centrepiece Carnival, which borrows a lot from other Caribbean Carnivals, with floats and dancers 'jumping up' as they cruise around town in troupes, all wearing themed costumes, and calypso competitions, where the Anguillans sing of island life and love.
  Race Week. Held at the same time, and unique to Anguilla, the nation of seafarers and boat-builders. Traditional fishing boats are pitted against one another in races from bay to bay around the island.
November *Tranquillity Jazz Festival.*

Watersports

There are plenty of possibilities for an active beach and water-borne life in Anguilla's electric-blue sea. You are really dependent on the hotels, most of which have simple equipment (**snorkelling** gear, **windsurfers** and small **sailboats**); otherwise head down to Sandy Ground, where you can arrange watersports trips, though this is still pretty low-key by most island standards.

Day Sails

Chocolat, **t** 497 3394, *ruan@anguillanet.com*. Catamaran for charter.

Sandy Island Enterprises, t 497 6395, *www.net.ai.sandyisland.com*. You may want to make a special trip to Sandy Island.

Gotcha, t 497 2956, *gotcha@caribcable.com*. Cruises around the coastline, snorkelling trips, day trips to St Martin or St Bart's, airport transfers and more.

Deep-sea Fishing

For wahoo and tuna and sailfish, trips can be arranged with **No Mercy**, t 497 6383, through Sandy Island Enterprises. A half-day's sail with full tackle costs from US$450.

Snorkelling and Scuba Diving

There are some good coral reefs right offshore, including Little Bay (*see* 'Best Beaches', above) and Shoal (another name for reef) Bay – there is a marked snorkelling trail in Shoal Bay. Dive sites are to be found all around the island, particularly towards the western end, where reefs flash with butterfly-fish and angelfish or a shimmering cloud of fry, and also on the offshore cays. There are also wrecks (some deliberately sunk), where you might see a jackfish or an octopus. A single-tank dive costs US$60, with equipment on top. Complete instruction and equipment hire are available through:

Anguillan Divers, Mead's Bay, t 497 4750, *axadiver@anguillanet.com*.

Shoal Bay Scuba and Watersports, in the eastern end of the island, t 497 4371.

Other Sports

Golf

A Greg Norman 18-hole championship golf course – Anguilla's first – is scheduled to open in late 2005.

Hiking

The Anguilla National Trust organizes some visits to places of interest (including turtle watches) around the island from time to time. It is worth checking if anything is happening while you are on the island, t 497 5297.

Horse-riding

If you want to gallop along the beach and through the scrubland you can contact:

El Rancho del Blues, t 497 6164.

Seaside Stables, The Cove, t 235 3667, *seahorses@caribcalble.com*.

Tennis

There are courts at a number of the bigger hotels. Try also:

Anguilla Tennis Academy, Blowing Point, t 540 454 0285, *anguilla70@aol.com*, *www.tennis.ai*. Opening winter 2006.

Where to Stay

Anguilla t (1 264–)

Although the island is best known for its luxury hotels and villas (some of them are among the Caribbean's best), there is a good range of accommodation in Anguilla, including some less expensive hotels, apartments and guest houses, so the island can suit almost anybody's tastes.

You can locate some of the mid-range accommodation through **Inns of Anguilla** (*www.inns.ai*), which has hotel rooms at around US$100 a night in season. There are also many apartment complexes, with self-catering accommodation in all price ranges. Most of the hotels are set on Anguilla's pristine beaches. There is also a good range of self-catering accommodation in Anguilla. Rooms and apartments tend to be set in a central building or clustered around a central garden; some will have a restaurant but all have kitchens.

The Government levies a room tax of 10% and most hotels charge service at 10%.

A good alternative in Anguilla is to stay in a **villa**, of which there have been some truly spectacular examples built recently. The first two below must be rented privately, but villa rental companies, listed below them, will arrange for you to stay at the many other villas on the island. Perhaps check them out while you are there in preparation for a return visit.

Altamer, t 498 4000, US t 1 888 652 6888, *info@altamer.com*, *www.altamer.com*. Situated next to Cove Castles and built in a similar architectural style, this luxurious three-villa complex is also available for private rent.

Cerulean, t 497 8840, US t 1 888 72 VILLA, www.ceruleanvilla.com. Privately rentable villa.

Keene Enterprises Ltd, PO Box 28, t 497 2544, keene-ent@anguillanet.com, www.keenevillas.com. Villa rentals.

Island Dream Properties, t 498 3200, jacklep@anguillanet.com, www.islanddreamproperties.com.

Professional Realty Services, t 497 3575, prorealty@profgroup.com, www.profgroup.com/provillas.

Sunset Homes, t 497 3666, edwards@anguillanet.com, www.sunsethomesonline.com.

Temenos, Long Bay, t 222 9000, www.temenosvillas.com. Three very expensive, luxurious villas on the beach, with pool, tennis courts, phone, air-con, ceiling fans, private chef and watersports.

Luxury

The Malliouhana Hotel, PO Box 173, Mead's Bay, t 497 6111, US t 1 800 835 0796, malliouhana@anguillanet.com, www.malliouhana.com. One of the Caribbean's finest, it stands on the cliffs above the mile-long stretch of Mead's Bay Beach on Anguilla's northwestern coastline. Tall and slender arches and terracotta tiles on floor and roofs give a slightly Mediterranean impression, but the name Malliouhana is distinctly Caribbean, taken from the Amerindian word for the island. The 56 rooms, which include a few vast and spectacular suites, are luxuriously decorated with paintings by Haitians Jasmin Joseph and Henri Brésil and carvings from Indonesia. All rooms have balconies, many overlooking the bay and the sunset. Watersports include windsurfers, skiing and sunfish; there are tennis courts, a spa, two swimming pools, a children's centre and a gym. There is also a superb restaurant on the clifftops, with French cuisine touched by the Caribbean and a wine cellar of around 20,000 bottles, as well as a bistro for lighter meals on the beach. Dependably well run, with a well-deserved reputation.

Covecastles, PO Box 248, Shoal Bay West, t 497 6801, US t 1 800 223 1108, covecastlas@anguillanet.com, www.covecastles.com. A haven of understated super-luxury, set on the magnificent curve of Shoal Bay West. But Covecastles is also done in high architectural style, standing strikingly white and geometrical against the blue of the sea, its strange windswept façade staring at a superb vista of St Martin. The 36 rooms, each of which has a view, stand in the 14 two-, three- and four-bedroom villas and they are spacious and elegant, with huge curved white walls, cantilevered staircases, terracotta tiles and rattan furniture. Villas come with housekeepers and villa (room) service – they can personalize the menu if you want – and some watersports. There is also a fine dining room.

Cap Juluca, PO Box 240, Maundray's Bay, t 497 6666, US t 1 888 858 5822, capjuluca@anguillanet.com, ww.capjuluca.com. Also has its own inimitable style – a line of white Moorish domes that rise in a line out of Anguilla's superb southwestern sands (on Maunday's Bay) – they give a surreal impression after a day in the Anguillan sun. The 98 rooms are palatial, with private balconies, and the bathrooms are no less than luxurious, glass-sided and looking out onto a small private patio. Plenty of watersports, a fitness centre, tennis courts and even croquet. Another extremely fine hotel, with a restaurant, Pimms, set in the slender arches on the waterfront, and a pool terrace restaurant for lunch.

CuisinArt Resort and Spa, PO Box 2000, Rendezvous Bay, t 498 2000, US t 1 800 937 9356, reservations@cuisinart.ai, www.cuisinartresort.com. Another striking resort which lines the delightful sand of Rendezvous Bay, this time in 10 villas with Greek architectural inspiration – white stucco and rich blues. Inside, the 93 huge rooms (60 of which are junior suites) have a theme of bright, floral yellows and blues. The central area of the resort – where the dining rooms, bars and boutiques are situated – is set behind in a large main building overlooking the swimming pool and so there is a busy, active feeling about the hotel. The cuisine is contemporary Caribbean in all three restaurants, including the Santorini, with ingredients from their own hydroponic garden.

Very Expensive–Expensive

La Sirena, PO Box 200, Mead's Bay, **t** 497 6827, US **t** 1 800 331 9358, *lasirena@anguillanet. com*, *www.la-sirena.co*. A fine setting – white stucco buildings with Spanish tiles and woodwork balconies clustered around a swimming pool and an explosive bougainvillea garden at the western end of Mead's Bay. Twenty-five comfortable rooms, a number of two- and three-bedroom villas and an upbeat atmosphere with entertainment sometimes around the dining room and bar.

Carimar Beach Club on the Beach, PO Box 327, **t** 497 6881, US **t** 1 800 235 8667, *carimar@ anguillanet.com*, *www.carimar.com*. Apartments (24 in all) in modern blocks, with arched balconies and topped with Tuscan-style roof tiles, either side of a pretty tropical garden, everywhere exploding with tropical growth, leading down to the superb sand of Mead's Bay. Bright white and modern decor with wicker furniture in large living rooms and patios, all modern comforts.

Frangipani Beach Club, Mead's Bay, PO Box 1378, **t** 497 6442, US **t** 1 800 892 4564, *info@frangipani.ai*, *www.frangipani.ai*. The comfortable and spacious rooms and suites are set in a mock Spanish palace, bright pink with curved red roof tiles and balconies with classical balustrades. There are one- to three-bedroom apartments.

Shoal Bay Villas, PO Box 81, Shoal Bay West, **t** 497 2051, US **t** 1 800 722 7045, *sbvillas@ anguillanet.com*, *www.sbvillas.ai*. This has an excellent setting lost in the palms of Shoal Bay. There are 15 units (studios, one- and two-bedroom apartments) standing around a pool, or looking out onto the fantastic sand and activity of the bay itself right outside. There is a dining room, the palm-thatched Le Beach Restaurant, which stands beneath the palms on the sand.

Blue Waters Beach Apartments, PO Box 69, Shoal Bay West, **t** 497 6292, *www.news.ai/ ref/bluewaters.html*. On the other Shoal Bay, at the eastern end of the island. Just seven one-bedroom and two two-bedroom apartments. They stand in stark white buildings with stained-wood louvres, fan ventilation; a quiet resort with no watersports or central area, very private.

Moderate–Inexpensive

Rendezvous Bay Hotel, PO Box 31, Rendezvous Bay, **t** 497 6549, US **t** 1 800 274 4893, *rbhaxa1@aol.com*, *www.rendezvousbay. com*. A quiet resort in an older Caribbean beach-club style. There is a simple central main house with dining room, games room and library where guests gather and mingle at meals. The rooms stand in two areas: an older block in a rocky garden and newer villas on the fantastic sand of Rendezvous Bay itself, each decorated with white tiles and wicker furniture. Very quiet and very low-key.

Sydans Apartments, Sandy Ground, **t** 497 3180, *sydans@hotmail.com*, *www.inns.ai/sydans*. A good choice if you want to be close to the action of Sandy Ground.

Lloyd's Guest House, Crocus Hill, **t** 497 2351. Simple, spotless rooms, all of which have been renovated.

Harbour Lights, PO Box 181, Island Harbour, **t** 497 4435, US **t** 1 800 759 9870, *news.ai/ ref/harbourlights*. Just four rooms above the waves of Island Harbour. Quiet and simple, but friendly.

Arawak Beach Inn, Island Harbour, **t** 497 4888, *relax@arawakbeach.com*, *www.arawak beach.com*. Varied rooms, some with four-poster beds, vaulted ceilings, views across the bay, kitchens, air-con and television, and all with ceiling fans. The casual restaurant overlooks the pool and it's a short walk to two secluded coves.

Caribbean Seaview, Long Path, **t** 497 4662, *d-3ent@anguillanet.com*, *www.seaview.ai*. Modern one- and two-bedroom suites and a spacious studio overlooking a large pool with an extended view of the sea and neighboring island. Units are equipped with compact kitchens, appliances, cable television and telephones.

Ferryboat Inn, Blowing Point, **t** 497 6613, *ferryb@anguillanet.com*, *www.ai/ ferryboatinn.com*. Private beach house with seven apartments, this family-run property is set on a quite beach facing St Martin and just 3mins walk to the ferry dock. The restaurant serves a varied selection of cuisine with a West Indian flair.

Madeariman, Shoal Bay East, t 497 3833, *info@madeariman.com, www.madeariman. com*. Four attractively furnished, comfortable suites and one studio with shaded verandas overlooking a garden, a few steps from the sea. The suites are well equipped with air-con, cable television, mini-fridge, microwave and coffee maker. There is a small open-air restaurant.

Lloyd's Guest House 1959, Crocus Hill, The Valley, t 497 2351, *lloyds@anguillanet.com, www.lloyds.ai*. A quaint, warm house offering nine cosy rooms, all with ceiling fans. West Indian hospitality is especially enjoyable when dining at the family-style dinner table.

Eating Out

There is a string of excellent restaurants dotted around Anguilla, many of them in charming shoreside settings. This might be quite unexpected on a barren Caribbean island which is formerly British and has mainly American visitors, but with such wealthy travellers who like to eat out, and a lucky proximity to St Martin (through which there is daily imported food from both Miami and France), a tradition of serious restaurants has grown up. Some of the best food is to be found in the hotel dining rooms (try **Malliouhana**, **Covecastles**, **Cuisinart**, **Cap Juluca** (all *expensive*), but it is definitely worth looking around. There are places where you can have a quiet and intimate evening for two, but then of course there are livelier restaurants as well. There are a number of restaurants down in Sandy Ground, where you can grab a meal and then join the activity of the bars. Obviously there is plenty of fish and seafood and it is definitely worth tasting crayfish and spiny lobster, caught in Anguillan waters. You will of course find local West Indian haunts where you can pick up a pattie or a chicken leg for lunch and trusted local fare for dinner.

Eating out is not cheap in Anguilla, but credit cards are accepted in the major restaurants if you don't want to think about it at the time. **Categories** are arranged according to the price of a main course: expensive = US$30 and above; moderate = US$15–30; inexpensive = under US$15.

Very Expensive–Expensive

Altamer Restaurant, Shoal Bay West, t 498 4040. Set on the beachfront in the inimitable architectural style of Covecastles and Altamer, all cantilevered white stucco and distinctive geometrical shapes. The menu is French with some Caribbean ingredients. Try the *boudin blanc de homard truffé et sa crudité de celeriac* (a home-made lobster, chicken and truffle sausage with celeriac salad laced with truffle oil) to start and follow with a *filet* of local fish served with a *noisette* of garlic and lemon butter or even a quail *aux calvados*, marinaded in grapes and apples. Gracious, hip and elegant.

Blanchards, Mead's Bay, t 497 6100. Considered by some to be the top spot on the island. Set in a pretty, floodlit garden in Mead's Bay within earshot of the breaking waves, where you dine in a delightful room looking through large windows or outside under the eaves. The cuisine gathers influences from around the world to make an eclectic and thoroughly satisfying mix: Cajun and American southwest, Thai and other Asian tastes, as well as some Caribbean flavours, on a daily menu (with fresh food imported daily from Miami via St Maarten), all beautifully presented and delicious. Very elegant. Reserve in advance (people actually fax their reservations down to the island ahead of time). Excellent wine list.

Hibernia, Island Harbour, t 497 4290. A small and intimate restaurant in the northeast, well worth making the journey to get there. Here you dine on a prettily decorated terrace with a view onto a lit garden, with meticulously prepared dishes presented by the owners themselves. The owners travel around the world during the off season, so their cuisine, mainly French with Caribbean ingredients, is touched with a taste of India and the Far East. Start with a combination of house-smoked fish (wahoo, kingfish, tuna and dolphin) or a *terrine de foie gras* with tropical fruits on toast, and follow with a basil and coconut-milk Thai casserole of Anguillan crayfish with steamed noodles or a *blanc de poulet farci aux cèpes et aux noix* (chicken breast stuffed with mushrooms and nuts in a spinach sauce). *Closed Mon.*

Koal Keel, The Valley, t 497 2930. Set around a delightful old Anguillan house, the Koal Keel offers an eclectic menu – part French, part Caribbean, part Indian. The new tandoori oven specialities are very popular, particularly the North Indian-style butter chicken with basmati rice, grilled asparagus and crispy sweet peppers. At lunch the lobster sandwich is a big hit, while dinner choices include seared foie gras on a bed of country greens in a spicy caramel sauce, and rack of veal in tarragon juice with truffle potatoes.

Deon's Overlook, South Hill, t 497 4488. High on the hillside above Sandy Ground, where you sit on a veranda with a view of the lights below. The restaurant is strong on fish and Italian specialities, as well as crispy duck, Black Angus steak and the all-time favourites, garlic-crusted snapper or wood-grilled triggerfish.

Zen, South Hill Plaza, t 497 6502. Features a small, select menu with sushi, sashimi and maki. Three tasty miso soup combos are offered along with salads and very special chef's creations like sushi with caviar and foie gras.

Mango's, Barnes Bay, t 497 6479. A very pleasant setting on a terrace right on the sand, open to the evening breeze beneath a huge white awning. 'New American' cuisine that gives exotic variations on Caribbean food – seafood angel-hair pasta and the house speciality of grilled crayfish tails, served in a curry of lime and coconut milk. Brisk and breezy. *Dinner Wed–Mon.*

Moderate

Cedar Grove Café, Rendezvous Bay Hotel, t 497 6549. A menu of innovative Caribbean cuisine with an Old World touch. Lunch is light: salads, burgers, pizza and pastas. Original dinner dishes include teriyaki-marinated ginger tuna, rosemary pumpkin soup with blackened shrimp, and scallion-crusted rock grouper with curried oil. West

Indian barbecue buffet with live music on Sunday evenings.

Flavours, Back Street, South Hill, t 497 0629. Part steakhouse – all certified Angus beef, standing rib roast, porterhouse, tenderloin, braised short ribs; part Caribbean – sugar-cane juice marinated duck breast, mojito chicken, jerked double pork chop; and lots of dishes rarely seen on menus. Entrées are accompanied by fresh bakes, ratatouille relish and Caribbean tuber 'lasagna.'

Barrel Stay on the Beach, Sandy Ground, t 497 2831. Gastronomic treats include home-made foie gras, dark chocolate truffles, home-baked breads and vegetarian delicacies. Portions are generous, the service quick and friendly.

Roy's Bayside Grill, Sandy Ground, t 497 0154. The big bar makes a great hang-out and the blender is in a soundproof cabinet so as not to disturb the gentle lapping of the waves at the door. There's an outdoor gas-flame broiler with its own chef to tend the grilled mahi-mahi, swordfish or Scottish salmon steak, lobster and Black Angus steaks.

Oliver's Seafood Grill, Long Bay, t 497 8780. Set on a double deck on the sand of Long Bay, with a bar downstairs and the dining room up above. Refined West Indian fare – Anguillan pumpkin soup followed by cray-fish creole. Lots of fish and seafood, or some simpler pastas.

Smokey's, Cove Bay, t 497 6582. A lovely setting in the southwest of the island. Beach barbecue to Caribbean gourmet, served at candlelit tables with white tablecloths: fish chowder of bullfoot soup followed by stewed chicken or grilled snapper with fresh lemon.

Ripples, Sandy Ground, t 497 3380. On the road just behind the beach itself, a shuttered dining room, brightly decorated in shades of pale purple and peach. Bench seats and tables, a lively buzz in the air most nights. Local and some English dishes: conch fritters, fish and chips and themed evenings including curry nights.

Inexpensive

There are sometimes roadside fry-ups and vans selling chicken and fish.

Roti Hut, parallel to the airstrip (with its accompanying drive-in ice-cream stop). Pick yourself up a *roti* or a fry chicken.

Bars and Nightlife

The best bars are really the beach bars (*see* below) – there is a regular Sunday afternoon crowd at Shoal Bay – and the hotel bars. Anguillan nightlife is quiet (the locals sometimes take the ferry over to St Martin for the nightclubs there, and there are casinos in Dutch Sint Maarten if that's your thing) and so you are best advised to keep your ear to the ground to find out where the crowds are going. There is sometimes a barbecue or a band at one of the hotels.

Roy's, on the beach in Crocus Bay, t 497 2470. If you are feeling homesick for British beer, then you will find Newcastle Brown (and Guinness) at this pub-style bar, with darts, happy hour and a riotous atmosphere. Also serves fish and chips. Roy's has a second restaurant with a good bar on Sandy Ground beach.

Ripples Bar, Sandy Ground, t 497 3380. Has a happy hour on Saturdays.

Rafé's, on the clifftop above Sandy Ground, right at the corner in the road. A nice spot. This wooden and tin-roofed lean-to is built with planks and driftwood, with a few standing plants on the gravel floor. Chicken, ribs and kebabs with garlic bread, but also popular as a bar late on.

Dune Preserve, western end of Rendezvous Bay (reached along a well-signed but very rough road). How do you decorate a sand-dune and turn it into a bar? By building a galleon on it. Bankie Banx, Anguilla's best-known singer-songwriter, has collected boats and driftwood from around the island and turned them into this bar atop a sand-dune. Multiple decks, barrels as tables, boats as bars, as roofs, emerging from the walls... Occasional concerts from Bankie Banx himself are hosted here. This is very simply one of the coolest spots anywhere in the Caribbean.

La Sirena, Mead's Bay, t 497 6827. Has a weekly show by a troupe of dancers called Mayoumba.

Johnno's, Sandy Ground. It is definitely worth joining in the 'jump-ups' (usually Wed and Fri), which can get crowded and pretty wild.

Pump House, in the old salt factory building, t 497 5154. Good pizza, light meals and live entertainment Wed–Sat.

Beach Bars

There are some cool and easy beach bars around the island where you can find a fruit punch or a beer and a salad, or a full-blown meal to fill a gap during the day's beach activity.

Agatha's Place, Prickly Pear Cay.

Johnno's, Prickly Pear Cay.

Johnno's, Sandy Ground. A lively bar stuck between the (relatively) more formal restaurants; you will find light meals in the daytime, though really it comes alive when there is a crowd after dark.

Uncle Ernie's, Shoal Bay. A popular haunt, this wooden lean-to is festooned with photos of satisfied customers and has a grill permanently on the go.

Madeariman Reef, Shoal Bay. An open-sided bar looking over the sand from the trees.

Gorgeous Scilly Cay, offshore from Island Harbour, t 497 5123. Eudoxie Wallace, Gorgeous to his friends, has landscaped the Cay with parasols, conch-shell walls and thatch shelters. Wave from the pier and they will come and pick you up for a day's 'liming' and snorkelling and a lobster lunch. Music three times a week in season, even a helipad to make it easier for you. *Closed Mon.*

Palm Grove, at Junks Hole on the windswept Savannah Bay, t 497 4224. This is way out at the eastern limit of the (sandy) road on the south side of the island, but very popular. A wooden lean-to settled under the palms on the bright white sand. Some watersports and excellent grilled crayfish for lunch (which can be quite slow), popular on Sundays.

Trattoria Tramonte, Shoal Bay West, near the Blue Waters Apartments, t 497 8819. This has a perfect setting: safari chairs on a nice deck looking out over the superb sandy bay and across to St Martin. Northern Italian food, salads and Caribbean fish *carpaccios* and more complex dishes for dinner (*moderate*).

good price. But most work is in the construction industry or in tourism, which has taken off since the early eighties. On an island where life has been precarious for so long, Anguilla is more prosperous now than it ever has been.

Beaches

Anguilla's superb sand makes her beaches some of the best in the Caribbean. There are miles and miles of it, glaringly white and so thick and soft that it makes you stumble as you walk. Breakers clap and hiss as they race in a flurry of surf towards the palms and the sea grape. You will not find any crowded beaches on the island, though you can find watersports equipment at the hotels if you want action. There are miles of strand to walk in the cool of the early morning, and you can sizzle to your heart's content in the heat of the day. If beaches are your thing, Anguilla is close to paradise.

Anguilla lies at an angle close to the prevailing winds off the Atlantic and this means that with just a slight variation beaches can vary from one day to the next with regard to calmness, particularly at the eastern end of the island. Before setting out to somewhere remote, it is worth checking if the beach is calm. Two words of warning: beware of manchineel trees, which bear a poisonous apple and will blister you if you sit under them in the rain, and skinny-dipping, officially not allowed.

See 'Best Beaches', p.396.

Around the Island

The Valley (population about 600) is Anguilla's capital, though you should not think that this makes it a town; the density of houses is just slightly greater than elsewhere. Some official buildings, malls and a few shops are bunched around a triangle of roads and a set of hanging traffic lights.

Headed west from The Valley, the road moves into more open country very quickly, passing the airport and making towards the developed southwestern tip of the island. Anguilla's plantations were never very successful, but **Wallblake House** (*www.wallblake.ai; open Mon, Wed and Fri for tours 10–2*) is an attractive great house with a stone foundation, a wooden 'upper' and a shingle roof. Built in the late 18th century, it is set behind a white picket fence and has a cistern similar to those on the islands of Saba and Statia (Sint Eustatius) farther south. The house is private, but tours can be arranged through the Archaeological and Historical Society. Driving west you come to a couple of roundabouts; at the second there is a side road down to **Sandy Ground,** a small village with some traditional Anguillan houses set on a thin spit of land between the sea and the last of the working saltpans. The pans are disused now, but as the sun and wind continue to do their work the water still becomes curiously discoloured, lavender and grey. The top road continues to snake further west, throwing off side roads. The **Anguilla Heritage Collection**, which recently moved to East End, has artefacts taken from Anguilla's past: cooking pots, bottle and hurricane lamps, photos and old shoe lasts, even an old .303 that was left behind in a hurry by a Kittitian policeman. A turning left heads down to **Blowing**

Point, the departure point for boats to St Martin, but the main road continues to the hotels and isolated settlements at the island's western end.

Heading north and east from The Valley, you pass quickly into open country once again, which is dotted periodically with Anguilla's attractive old wooden houses and the half-built newer concrete ones. There are a couple of local settlements in this less-developed area, one at **Island Harbour** on the north coast, from which many of Anguilla's fishermen set off. On the beach you will see the fishing boats, brightly painted so that they are more visible at sea, and built to a unique Anguillan design. In the main house of the Arawak Beach Resort there is a small display of Amerindian artefacts (plus some reproductions and some exhibits from modern-day Arawaks in Guyana) – *metape* strainers to get the poison juice out of cassava, pottery, cotton spindles and jewellery made of shells.

Anguilla's only historical sites can be found in this area. Just off the road close to Lower Shoal Bay, the **Fountain** (*closed, under renovation*) is contained within a National Park and has a number of Amerindian rock carvings around the island's only reliable source of water, cartoon faces which are each struck by the sun's rays in the course of the year. At **Sandy Hill Bay** are the remains of a 17th-century fort, now site of a police substation.

The Dutch Caribbean

11

The Dutch Caribbean

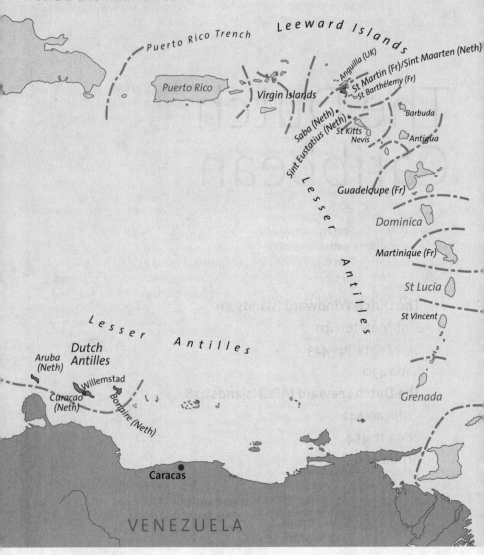

Highlights

1 Dive the undersea slopes of Bonaire to see their phenomenal colours

2 Shop duty free on Front St in Philipsburg, Sint Maarten

3 Whistle across the bay on a windsurfer at the northwestern tip of Aruba

4 Enjoy the old-time ambience of Saba, where nearly every roof is red

5 Try walking in a straight line across the swaying Koningin Emmabrug in colourful Willemstad, Curaçao

The Dutch Caribbean (Netherlands Antilles and Aruba) is made up of two groups of three islands, separated by about 500 miles of the Caribbean Sea. The Dutch Windward Islands, Sint Maarten, Sint Eustatius and Saba (or the three S's in tourist jargon), are in the northeastern Caribbean, between the Virgin Islands and Antigua. Five hundred miles to their lee, off the coast of South America, are the trio of the Dutch Leeward Islands, Aruba (now autonomous), Bonaire and Curaçao (the ABC islands).

The Netherlands Antilles may be within the Dutch kingdom, but they are by no means a tropical version of Holland. The Dutch were never great colonizers and what influence they had has been creolized. In Curaçao, curly gables will take you momentarily back to Amsterdam; road signs are in Dutch everywhere; postboxes are painted Royal Dutch red; money is guilders and florins; the tastes and sounds of Holland percolate through.

But the reminders are fleeting: the gables may be there, but the *landhuizen* (Dutch country homes) look odd painted orange and surrounded by miles of cactus; drivers here are much more akin to their fellow West Indians than the good burghers of the Netherlands; and the guttural sounds of Dutch have a curious ring when thoroughly mixed with Spanish as in Papiamento (*see* p.440). Neither group of islands actually uses Dutch as a mother tongue. The Dutch Windwards have been strongly influenced by the English-speaking islands around them, and the Leewards are an enigmatic and exuberant mix of strains from all over the area – but they are distinctly West Indian.

Dutch Caribbean History

The Dutch first came to the Caribbean as traders in the early 17th century. Of the European nationalities beginning to protrude into the Spanish domain in the New World, only they had the fleets and so they acted as middlemen for the new colonies that were springing up in the area. In an early piece of industrial espionage, they took the techniques of sugar cultivation from Brazil and introduced them to the islands of the Lesser Antilles. Then they provided the funding and the machinery, and shipped the produce back to eager markets in Europe.

Rather than colonize in the New World the Dutch chose to occupy certain strategic ports and from there they carried on their trading and attacked the Spaniards. In the 1620s the Dutch West India Company took Sint Maarten because it was en route from Europe to their possessions in Brazil, and later moved in on the nearby islands of Saba and Sint Eustatius as well. At the other end of the Caribbean they chose the ABC islands because there was salt there (on Bonaire), which they needed for their herring industry, and because Curaçao has one of the largest harbours in the world. At the beginning of the 18th century, the Dutch ports of Curaçao and Sint Eustatius were two of the three richest in the Caribbean (with Port Royal in Jamaica). Their warehouses were filled to bursting with goods; hundreds of ocean-going vessels would put in each year and offload silks, slaves and gunpowder. Strictly speaking, trade with other colonies was illegal because they were under monopoly trading laws, but their goods were in demand and so they made a tidy profit smuggling, too.

Prizes so rich inevitably became targets and in the endless run of 18th-century wars the islands were at the mercy of the navies that chased each other around the

Caribbean Sea. Sint Eustatius changed hands 22 times in all, its fortunes pilfered handsomely each time. But the wharves would fill up again almost as quickly, as trade with Venezuela and the North American colonies picked up.

The six islands eventually landed in Dutch hands for good in 1816 and then gradually, like the rest of the Caribbean, they were forgotten. The ports failed as world trading patterns changed and the islanders turned to planting: crops like cotton and cochineal cactus, sisal (for rope) and aloe. Even these died with emancipation, which was declared by the Dutch in 1863.

It was not until the early 20th century that prosperity returned to some of the islands when oil was discovered in South America. Royal Dutch Shell and EXXON built refineries in Curaçao and Aruba in the 1920s and these two islands boomed, experiencing a wave of prosperity that waned only in the 1980s.

Since the 60s the Netherlands Antilles have joined the tourism race, particularly in Sint Maarten and Aruba, where hotels have sprung up on any available beach space. The islands have also resurrected the Dutch tradition of entrepôts (like the free ports of Curaçao and Sint Eustatius two hundred years ago) to encourage modern traders. These seaborne shoppers arrive in port just as they always did, with a fistful of dollars to spend, only nowadays they are offloaded by the thousand from cruise ships.

Politics

For years the name Curaçao was used to refer to all the Dutch possessions in the Caribbean and it is only really since the Second World War that the different islands have become known in their own right. In 1936 the Netherlands Antilles *Staten* (Parliament) was created and the colonies were made an integral part of the Kingdom of the Netherlands.

After the war (when Holland was occupied by Germany and the islands had to look after themselves), self-determination gradually moved into the political foreground. Autonomy, internal self-government, was granted in 1954, but unlike many Caribbean islands, the Dutch Caribbean has not actually taken the further steps towards Independence. With the exception of Surinam, which became independent in 1975, they have preferred to remain a part of the Kingdom of the Netherlands.

The administration was centred in Willemstad and, as the Curaçaoans automatically had a majority in the *Staten* due to the size of their population, they tended to dominate the other islands. The Arubans particularly, with political aspirations of their own born of their oil wealth, resented the fact that decisions concerning their own internal affairs had to be passed in Curaçao. Eventually they struck out for their own self-government (*see* 'Status Aparte', p.468) and they were granted a separate status (still within the Kingdom of the Netherlands), with a view to later independence, which they have still not taken.

More recently, Sint Maarten, also on a wave of prosperity because of its tourist industry, voiced similar requests, but these have been turned down by the Dutch government. Now that Aruba has left the Netherlands Antilles, Curaçao returns 14 senators to the 22-member *Staten*, Bonaire 3, Sint Maarten 3 and Saba and Sint Eustatius 1 each. The governor of each island is appointed by Queen Beatrix of the

Netherlands on the advice of Parliament. Since 1986, each island has been responsible for its own decisions and its budget, once it has been allocated by the central
government in Curaçao. The Netherlands Antilles are led by Prime Minister Etienne YS
of the PAR, the Restructured Antilles Party. Elections are to be held in 2006.

The Dutch Windward Islands

Sint Maarten

Sint Maarten/St Martin is the smallest island in the world to be shared by two
nations. The southern half is one of the Netherlands Antilles, a part of the Kingdom of
Holland, and the northern part is a *commune* of France (*see* 'St Martin', p.307). The
distinct personalities of the two sides of the island are still just recognizable, though
with the building mania of the last 25 years it has taken on a universal wash of
concrete, and the feel of the island has changed irreparably.

Of Sint Maarten's 17 square miles, between 4 and 5 of them are under water in
lagoons and salt ponds. Above the waterline, Sint Maarten is covered in yellow-green
scrub, with startlingly steep and attractive hills that rise to around 1,200ft. From the
heights there are excellent views – Sint Maarten is surrounded by islands. It is rather
like a modern-day Babel – overdeveloped and confused. It has excellent beaches,
dependable Caribbean sunshine and loose development laws. Together these are
enough to have brought development corporations swooping in. They have built with
abandon, throwing up resorts on any strip of sand they can find. Sint Maarten bulges
with glittering casinos, shopping malls and fast-food joints; there are timeshare sales
and latterly a market in timeshare re-sales. Hotels come in complexes here, and
tourists by the jumbo-load.

Interestingly, all the languages of Babel are there, too. You will hear the gutteral
vowels of Dutchmen alongside the drawl of Texans; Dutch, French and Spanish fill the
air. English-speaking West Indians have flooded in from down-island; Dominican girls
sit and chat in upbeat Spanish; you will hear Haitian Kreyol and the babble of
Papiamento (*see* p.440), the extraordinary language from the Dutch Leeward Islands.
The island has a thoroughly international, and inter-Caribbean atmosphere, with lots
of Latin music and other sounds from around the islands.

Sint Maarten has also adopted Sint Eustatius's traditional role as the Dutch
entrepôt in the Windwards. The streets of the capital, Philipsburg, are lined with air-
conditioned boutiques, brimful with duty-free bargains. And cruise liners disgorge
still more tourists on one-day shopping extravaganzas. It is mercantile mayhem. The
confusion is complete. But after centuries in the doldrums, the island is more prosperous now than it has ever been. So many tourists arriving each year cannot but
have an effect on island life. If you style yourself a traveller, then Sint Maarten is really
a place of curiosity, although the people who live there and on the islands nearby
swear by it. You might take a look en route to another, more peaceful island. But if you
like a well-oiled vacation (often an impeccable package deal), with beaches,

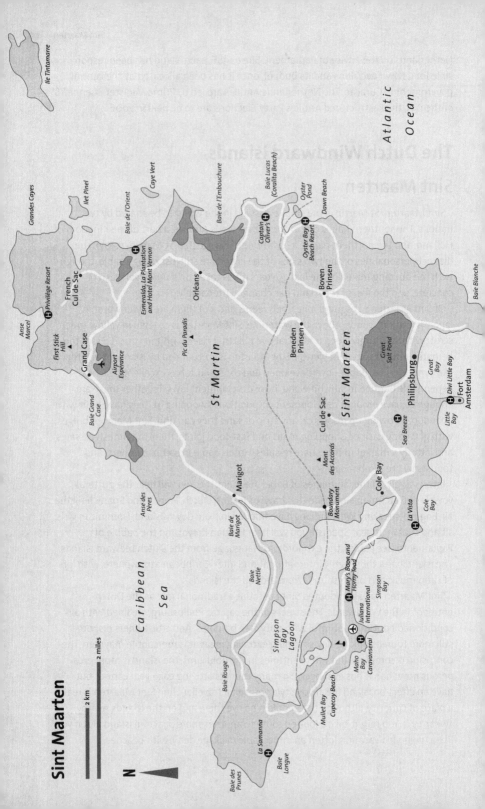

watersports, entertainment and a truly amazing variety of restaurants just a buggy-ride away, then Sint Maarten might be your place.

History

Though the PR moguls may swear otherwise, it is unclear whether Columbus ever saw Sint Maarten. He might have seen it on his second voyage, on 12 November 1493, as he sailed past Statia (Sint Eustatius) and Saba. He did name an island after the saint (St Martin's Day is 11 November), but this was probably Nevis. As other sailors came by, the name was fixed as Sint Maarten.

The Caribs and Arawaks continued to live here on and off for 140 years after his arrival. Settlement was difficult as there was no permanent water supply, but the Spaniards were not initially interested in the island anyway, and only made occasional raids to take people to work in their gold mines. To the Indians, Sint Maarten was *Sualouiga*, supposed to mean 'land of salt'. And it was the saltpans that

Best Beaches

Mullet Bay Beach: A classic stretch of Caribbean sand in the mile-long sweep of a gently curving bay; also Sint Maarten's busiest, with the thousands of guests of the nearby hotels, transported here by the buggy-load from the cruise ships. All watersports are available and there are plenty of shaded retreats, with palm-thatch umbrellas, where you can replace the fluids lost steaming in the sun.

Cupecoy Beach: A series of suntraps close to the border with the French side at the western end of the island, all with a cracking view of the sunset. Coves with golden sand slope gently into the sea beneath 50ft cliffs. At the northern end of the beach nude bathing is permitted. For Sint Maarten, Cupecoy is relatively secluded, though you are hardly likely to be alone.

Maho Bay: There is a sign here warning you that low-flying jumbos can ruin your bathing. Don't stand up when one's going over – they literally come that low. Hotels also hover above most of its length, making it another busy beach, buzzing with windsurfers and wetbikers. If the going gets too hot, you can always retreat to the terrace and watch the approach path of the incoming aeroplanes.

Simpson Bay: A fantastic, mile-long half-moon sweep just south of the airport, literally overrun with sand in places – one of the island's best. It's quiet for Sint Maarten, but popular with windsurfers. It's also home to one or two of Sint Maarten's smaller easy-going hotels and guest houses, so you can get a drink or lunch in the unpressurized environment of a beach club.

Great Bay: Even Philipsburg itself has a reasonable strip of sand, with a magnificent view onto Saba from just behind Front St. Perhaps spare a moment to take a walk here before getting back into the shopping fray and exercising your credit card in another bout of impulse-buying.

Dawn Beach: A fine strip of sand on the Atlantic coast of the island. There are a couple of hotels here, but the crowds do not usually penetrate this far and so it is relatively quiet. The beach has a view of the dawn sun and of St Barts, but on a windy day the sea will be too rough for comfort.

eventually attracted the Europeans to Sint Maarten, as they ventured out from the original settlement in St Kitts. Some Frenchmen arrived in 1629, and in 1631 they were followed by the Dutch West India Company.

The Spaniards were spurred into action by the interest these countries were showing in Sint Maarten, and in 1633 they arrived with a fleet of 50 ships and expelled the settlers. But whatever they tried, the settlers kept creeping back and so the Spaniards eventually decided to put a garrison here. They fortified the point at the entrance to what is now Great Bay. By all accounts it was a miserable outpost, where the soldiers had rats for company and food.

The Dutch soon occupied Curaçao off the coast of Venezuela, but they were still looking for a port in the northern Caribbean, en route from their colonies in Brazil back to Europe. In 1644, Peter Stuyvesant, a director of the Dutch West India Company, led an attack on Sint Maarten to take the island back. It was in this engagement that Stuyvesant (later Governor of New York, then called Nieuw Amsterdam) was hit by a cannonball and lost his leg. In 1648 the Spaniards abandoned the garrison in Sint Maarten and the Dutch and French soon made their way back on to the island.

The agreement on sharing the island dates from 1648, and the traditional story tells of a Dutchman and a Frenchman setting off in opposite directions, with a bottle of liquor apiece to keep them going, walking around the coast until they met, where-upon a line was to be drawn between the two points. How the French got the bigger share is explained variously: the Dutchman's gin made him sluggish/he dozed off under a tree/the wily, wine-drinking Frenchman sent a girl to waylay him (delete as applicable). The sad drab truth of the matter is that the two sides decided that they would do well to stop skirmishing, and so they signed a treaty on a hill that came to be called Mount Concordia. The saltpans remained common property and the two sides arranged that they would not fight each other even if their mother countries went to war. This happened many times and the treaty was broken with the same regularity. The island changed hands 16 times, often with British involvement. The communities had little to do with each other except to march over and skirmish on the other side, and so it was not until the 20th century that a road was built to link the two halves of the island.

Sint Maarten saw some small prosperity as a plantation island, cultivating tobacco and growing provisions for nearby Sint Eustatius in the boom years of the 18th century. Sugar and cotton were also grown. Another industry that continued into the 20th century was the harvesting of salt from the inland ponds. At its height, Sint Maarten produced four million kilograms.

In 1848 the French emancipated their slaves in St Martin. Many of the Dutch slaves fled across the border, staying there until the Dutch declared emancipation in 1863. Gradually Sint Maarten's fortunes waned and it became poor and forgotten. Many of the islanders left in search of work elsewhere. And so it remained until about 35 years ago, when the tourist industry started to grow. In the 1950s, the population of the Dutch side dropped as low as 1,500 but it has increased out of all proportion since then. The offical population is 41,000 on the Dutch side, with another 36,000 on the French side.

Getting There

Sint Maarten t (599–)

By Air

Most flights arrive at Princess Juliana International Airport, which is something of an air crossroads for this area of the Caribbean. It is particularly busy on Sunday afternoons, when many organized tours change over. A departure tax of US$20 is payable, except for destinations within the Dutch Caribbean (US$6).

From Europe

The French connections are the best. Air France, t 800 237 2747, operates three times a week from Paris, and there are charter airlines from Paris and other French cities. There is also a weekly flight from Amsterdam on KLM, t 800 374 7747.

From the USA

American Airlines, t 800 624 6262, flies in direct from Miami and New York, and there are plenty of connections from other American cities through their Caribbean hub in San Juan, Puerto Rico. Other airlines tend to fly during the winter season: Continental, t 800 231 0856, fly from New York, as does Delta and US Airways, t 800 622 1015, from Philadelphia and Charlotte. BWIA, t 800 538 2942, touches the island as it breaks its journeys from further south in the Caribbean (e.g. Trinidad, St Lucia and Barbados). Charter airlines include GWV, t 800 225 5498; and Air Transat, t (905) 405 8585, from Canada.

From Other Caribbean Islands

Sint Maarten is well served from around the Caribbean. Winair, t 800 634 4907, t 544 2230, reservations@fly-winair.com, www.fly-winair.com, is based in Sint Maarten and flies to all the nearby islands. The other Dutch Windward Islands are reached a couple of times a day from Juliana Airport (return about US$60). LIAT, t 800 468 0482, flies hopper schedules north and south along the island chain and touches most of the islands from Santo Domingo in the Dominican Republic down to Antigua and on further south. BonairExpress, t 542 1564 flies from Curaçao, Aruba and Bonaire, plus Caracas, with occasional flights to San Juan, Santo Domingo and Port of Spain. Air Caraïbes, t 545 4136, fly from the main French islands of Martinique and Guadeloupe to the south. Air St Barth, t 545 3150, has plenty of flights each day from St Barts (see also 'Getting There', p.322). Caribbean Star flies from Antigua; Caribbean Sun from San Juan.

By Sea

Anguilla is just a 20-minute ferry ride out of Marigot, or you can go on *Santino*, 'the snorkelling luncheon party boat', and *Lambada*, both t 544 2640. St Barts, perhaps the most chic piece of France anywhere, is 12 miles southeast of Sint Maarten, reached aboard *Voyager*, t 542 4096, and the new *Rapid Explorer*, t 542 9762, www.rapidexplorer.com, which depart from Bobby's Marina in Philipsburg, or Marigot on the French side. Saba, where pretty gingerbread villages are clustered on sheer volcanic slopes, is an hour's sail away in the motorboat *The Edge*, t 544 2640, and on *Voyager*.

Getting Around

By Bus

A stream of buses links Philipsburg to Marigot and Grand Case. Only the occasional bus strays onto the airport road. The fares are US$1–2 depending on your destination. Buses are quite frequent until 10 or 11pm between Marigot and Philipsburg. They leave from Back St in Philipsburg.

By Taxi

Taxis are the government-approved, quite expensive, tourist-recommended method of travel and they wait in superabundance at Juliana Airport and in town. They are not metered, but rates are fixed by the Tourist Board. Some sample prices are: Juliana Airport to Philipsburg – US$12, to Marigot – US$15, to Grand Case – US$20. From Philipsburg to Marigot – US$12, to Grand Case – US$18. In the unlikely case that you cannot flag one down, there is a taxi stand just behind the court house in Philipsburg, and you can also arrange them through any hotel. There are despatch offices at the Taxi Association in town, t 542 2359, and at the Airport Taxi Stand, t 545 4317.

Hitch-hiking

Hitch-hikers will find that a large proportion of the thousands of cars on Sint Maarten pass without stopping. If you are patient, it works.

By Guided Tour

Tours of Sint Maarten are available, though there is not much to see apart from the views of the island and other islands. You will ride from shop to hilltop to restaurant in a little safari buggy. Tours can be arranged through any hotel desk (they will pick you up) or through:

Calypso Tours, t 544 2858.

Island Reps Tours, t 545 2392. US$15 for about 3½ hours.

Sint Maarten Sightseeing Tours, t 545 2115.

Car and Bike Hire

If you want to test out the different beaches in the day and restaurants on the French side at night, it is worth hiring a rental car, of which plenty are available from around US$30 per day or US$45 for a jeep, plus insurance. Foreign driving licences are valid in Sint Maarten and driving is on the right-hand side of the road. Many hire companies are based just outside the airport, but companies will also deliver to the hotels. There are far too many cars on both sides of the island, even with the new roads that have been built, so expect traffic jams in the three small towns.

If you are prepared to spend a couple of hours being given the hard sell about 'investment in vacationing' in a condominium complex, then you can sometimes score a '$50 off your rental bill' voucher in one of the many promotional rags.

Adventure Car Rental, Airport Rd, Simpson Bay, t 544 3688, *barre@megatropic.com*.

Alamo Car Rental, t 542 5552.

Alpha Car Rental, Airport Rd, t 545 2885, *alphacar@sinmaarten.net*.

American Scooter, t 545 2811.

Avis, Cole Bay, t 544 2316, US t 1 800 228 0668.

Excellent Limousine Service, t 545 3983, US t 1 800 599 9408, *excellim@sintmaarten.net*. You can hire a limousine, if that's your style.

Fortuno, Sea Breeze Hotel, t 542 3420, *fortuno@sintmaarten.net*, *www.sea breezehotel.com*.

Harley Davidson, t 544 2704, *www.h-dst martin.com*. Harley Davidson motorbikes

and scooters are available at this rental shop, in case you like the idea of cruising the Caribbean on a dream machine.

Hertz, t 545 4541.

Tri Sports, t 545 4384, *www.trisportsxm.com*. Mountain bikes.

Tourist Information

Abroad

There is no tourist office dealing specifically with the Dutch Caribbean in Britain – it is best to write to New York or to the islands themselves. There is a website at *www.st-maarten. com*. Also try *www.sxmtravelguide.com*, and, of course, you can get information about the French side of the island on their website at *www.st-martin.org*.

Canada: 703 Evans Ave, Suite 106, Toronto, Ontario, M9C 5E9, t (416) 622 4300.

Netherlands: Cabinet of the Minister Plenipotentiary of the Netherlands Antilles, Badhuisweg 175, NL 2597 JP, 's-Gravenhage, The Hague, t 070 306 6111.

USA: 675 Third Ave, Suite 1807, New York, NY 10017, t (212) 953 2084, t 1 800 786 2278.

In Sint Maarten

As well as the following, there are also quite a few strategically placed information offices which encourage you to visit the time-share complexes as well as giving tourist information.

The Vineyard Office Park, 33 WG Buncamper Rd, Philipsburg, t 542 2337, *info@st-maarten. com*. *Open Mon–Fri 8–noon and 1–5*.

Information desk on the waterfront, where the launches drop the cruise-ship passengers. *Open Mon–Fri 8–noon and 1–5*.

Information booth, Juliana Airport. *Open Mon–Fri 8–noon and 1–5*.

Information office, harbour in Marigot. *Open Mon–Fri 9–12.30 and 2–5*.

Media

The Sint Maarten tourist industry is well organized; you will be bombarded with brochures and magazines. If you can find a copy, the magazine most worth reading goes by the name of *Discover*, and is produced in tandem by the tourist offices from both sides of the island. *The Daily Herald* is the local rag.

Medical Emergencies

In case of an emergency, the Sint Maarten Medical Centre is on Cay Hill, t 543 1127.

Money and Banks

The official currency on the Dutch side is the Netherlands Antilles florin/guilder, which is fixed to the US dollar (US$1 = NAFl 1.78). However, you will only see this money if you are in a local supermarket or on a bus, as all transactions in tourist hotels and restaurants on both sides of the island can be carried out in US dollars as well. Where there might be confusion, make sure which currency you are dealing in. And remember, NA florins are not accepted on the French side. **Credit cards** are widely accepted on the Dutch side, as are traveller's cheques. Personal cheques are not accepted. You can change money at any of the hotel receptions, but the rate will not be as good as at a bank, of which there are five or six in Philipsburg.

Banking hours are Mon–Fri 8.30–3 or 3.30, sometimes with an extra hour on Friday afternoons, 4–5.

Shopping

All visitors are encouraged to go shopping as part of their vacation, and maps are even provided to ease your passage through the jungle of Philipsburg's four streets.

Sint Maarten is a free port and so there is no duty – clearly there are plenty of good bargains for professional and casual shoppers, though the island hardly has the status that Sint Eustatius had 200 years ago.

For fashion you might try Ralph Lauren and Tommy Hilfiger, and for jewellery Carat. Little Switzerland has good crystal and porcelain, Delft Blue has Dutch chinaware and you can find souvenirs at the Shipwreck Shop.

Shop opening hours are Mon–Sat 8–noon and 2–6, with hours extended to Sunday morning if there is a cruise ship in town.

Telephone Code

To telephone Sint Maarten from abroad, dial IDD code t 599 followed by a seven-digit local land-line number (beginning 54 or 55). Within Sint Maarten dial just the seven digits. Phoning from the Dutch to the French side, dial 00 590 and then the six-digit number;

from the French to the Dutch side dial 00 599 followed by the seven digits. There are no coin boxes on the French side and so you will need to buy a *télécarte* from the post office or the few newsagents that stock them.

Festivals

March *Heineken Regatta.*
April *Carnival.* Celebrations are along traditional Caribbean Carnival lines, including calypso singing and costumed parades through the streets of Philipsburg. *Queen Juliana's birthday* (30th).
June/July *June Fest.* Shared by both sides of the island – cultural events and blow-outs. *Bastille Day.* You can always nip over to the French side on the 14th (July).
November *Concordia Day* (actually St Maarten's day, on the 11th). Shared by both halves of the island.
Various dates *Bike races and triathlons.*

Watersports

Sint Maarten's well-oiled tourist machine offers the full range of watersports. Most large hotels have snorkelling gear, windsurfers and small sailing craft on offer to their guests; more exotic sports like parasailing and jet skis are easily found on the busier beaches. If you are travelling independently and wish to hire sports equipment, you can use the hotels' rental companies.

The main centres on the Dutch side are:
Aquamania Watersports, Pelican Resort, Simpson Bay, t 545 2640, *www.sxmtravel guide.com/aquamania.*
Aqua World Boat Rental, t 545 4533, *www.stmaartenaquaworld.com.*
Kayak Tour, t 557 0112, *sxmkayaktour@ wanadoo.fr.*
Trisports, Airport Rd, Simpson Bay, t 545 4384, *trisport@stmartinstmaarten.com, www.trisportsxm.com.* Kayak tours.

Day Sails

Excursions, anything from a snorkelling and picnic trip to an offshore island to sunset booze cruises, are available all over Sint Maarten, in a variety of different styles of boats.

Bay Island Yachts, Simpson Bay, **t** 544 2798.
Blue Beard, **t** 577 5935, *www.sailbluebeard.com*.
A catamaran that departs daily for Anguilla.
Bubba Charters, **t** 557 4747. Fishing.
Golden Eagle, **t** 543 0068.
Lambada, **t** 544 2640.
Random Wind Sailing Charters, **t** 547 5742,
www.randomwind.com. Includes day
snorkels and Green Flash sunset tours.
Santino, **t** 544 2640. Motorboat to Anguilla.

Deep-sea Fishing

Trips can be arranged through the following,
or the major watersports operators above.
Blue Water Sport Fishing, Simpson Bay,
t 545 3230.
Lee's Deep Sea Fishing, **t** 544 4233.

Kayaking

Tri Sports, **t** 545 4384, *www.trisportsxm.com*.
Mountain bikes, kayaking, hiking.

Sailing

If you wish to hire your own boat for a day or
a week or more, a number of the Caribbean's
big charter operators have bases in St Martin
(*see* p.313).

Scuba Diving and Snorkelling

If you would prefer to admire the marine life
in more peaceable circumstances, Sint
Maarten has some good offshore reefs for
snorkelling. Try the rocks at the end of Little
Bay and Simpson Bay, where you will see
shoals of pink and yellow fish dip and dart. On
the rockier east coast the reefs at Dawn Beach
are good, but best of all are the small islands
off the French side, Ilet Pinel and Ile
Tintamarre (also called Flat Island). Deeper
underwater off the east coast there are forests
of coral, plied by angelfish and squirrelfish,
and off the south coast is the wreck of the
HMS *Proselyte*, cannons and anchor encrusted.
A single-tank dive costs around US$45.
Contact the main concessionaires or:
Dive Safaris, Bobby's Marina, Philipsburg, **t** 542
9001, *www.divestmaarten.com*.
Ocean Explorers Dive Centre, Simpson Bay,
t 544 5252, *divesm@megatropic.com*,
www.stmaartendiving.com.
Seaworld Explorer Semi-Submarine,
t 542 4078.

The Scuba Shop, Simpson Bay, **t** 545 3213,
www.scubashop.net.
Tradewinds Divers, Great Bay Marina,
Philipsburg, **t** 542 3910.

Windsurfing and Kiteboarding

You can get gear at the general watersports
places above, but advanced sailors will find
the best winds on the French side, at Baie de
l'Orient and Baie de l'Embouchure on the
northeast coast.
Little Bay Watersports & Dive Centre,
t 552 7749.

Other Sports

Golf

Mullet Bay Resort, **t** 545 2801. An 18-hole
course backing onto the lagoon. All equipment can be rented and there are pros to
improve your game. Green fees outrageous
at around US$110 in season for the 18 holes
(includes cart). Residents of the hotel pay
half-price and have preference in teeing off.

Hiking

Authentic French Tours, **t** 87 05 11.
Dutch Hiking Club, **t** 542 4917.
Olivier Borensztejn, **t** 62 79 07.

Horse-riding

Bayside Riding Club, near Orient Beach,
t 87 36 64.
Crazy Acres Riding Centre, **t** 544 5255. Go for an
early-morning dip on horseback.
Horse N Around Riding Stables, Cole Bay, **t** 595
600, *hgcourt@yahoo.com*.
Lucky Stables, Cape Bay, **t** 544 5255, *www.lucky
stable.com*.
OK Corral, Oyster Pond, **t** 87 40 72.

Mountain biking

There are trails all over the island. For a
guide, contact:
Tri Sport, **t** 545 4384, *trisport@stmartin
stmaarten.com*.

Tennis

There are about 50 courts on the island,
many of them lit for night play. Contact any of
the larger hotels.

Where to Stay

Sint Maarten t (599–)

Pretty much every available area of beach space in Sint Maarten is developed and so the coastline has an encrustation of resort-style hotels and condominium complexes. Among them, however, you will find one or two small hotels with some character and charm, particularly in the Simpson Bay area. Many offer 'efficiencies' (self-catering apartments). There are plenty of villa rental companies, so if you are looking for a villa out on its own they might be able to find one for you. Try **Leslie's Vacation Villas**, t 544 3107, *leslies@sintmaarten. net*, *www.lesliesvacationvillas.com*.

It is worth remembering that hotels usually add the statutory government tax of 5% and 5% hotel tax, and then a handsome 15% charge for service (sometimes less).

Expensive

Oyster Bay Beach Resort, PO Box 239, Oyster Bay, t 543 6040, US t 866 978 0213, *oyster@ sintmaarten.net*. If you want to stay in a resort hotel, you might try here. The 200 rooms stand in a range of mock castles made of white stucco with views out towards St Barts (some also look over the main building, where there is a courtyard with white parasols). All the rooms are air-conditioned and have TV and fans, and some have fridges. They are furnished with white wicker on terracotta tiles. It has been enlarged recently, but retains its slightly rarefied atmosphere. There are watersports available, and tennis courts.

Divi Little Bay Beach Resort, PO Box 61, just outside Philipsburg on the western arm of Great Bay, t 542 2333, US t 1 800 367 3484, *info@diviresorts.com*, *www.diviresorts.com*. The rooms stand in lines above the pool and in imitation-Spanish blocks on the point, where you will find attractive suites with balconies and Jacuzzis. Facilities include watersports and diving, tennis and enter-tainment around the pool or in the discotheque.

La Vista, PO Box 2086, 53 Billy Folly Rd, Pelican Cay, t 544 3005, *lavista@megatropic.com*, *www.lavistaresort.com*. Beyond the concrete infestation of Pelican Cay is this small and pleasant resort. It is not on the beach and is quite a way from town, but it is self-contained and has a pool and terraces which look over the Caribbean Sea. There is a good atmosphere of seclusion from Sint Maarten's humdrum. There are 32 junior and penthouse suites decorated in high Caribbean pastel in very comfortable cottages, with kitchenettes and all other 21st-century conveniences.

Mary's Boon Beach Plantation, 117 Simpson Bay, t 545 7000, *info@marysboon.com*, *www.marysboon.com* (US address PO Box 523882 Miami FL 33125). A very low-key retreat with an old-time Caribbean ambi-ence. Guests gather in the main house, where there is a small library and a charming bar and dining room on a balcony open to the waves. There are 15 large studios and some one- and two-bedroom units, brightly decorated with Italian tiles and Balinese furniture, dressed outside with wraparound verandas and gingerbread trim, and set in a very pretty tropical garden of hibiscus and coconut palms. All are air-conditioned with cable TV and phones, but have traditional West Indian fans as well. Makes an ideal retreat from the humdrum. Some watersports, exercise room and pool.

Caravanserai Beach Resort, Beacon Hill Rd, Burgeaux Bay, t 545 4000, *caravanserai@ sintmaarten.net*, *www.caravanseraibeach resort.com*. Seventy-five ocean- and garden-view rooms and one-bedroom suites with kitchen. All rooms have private balcony or patio, cable TV and VCR.

The Inn at Cupecoy, 130 Lowlands, t 545 4333, *theinnatcupecoy@yahoo.com*, *www.theinn atcupecoy.com*. The five de-luxe rooms are available as hotel rooms or as a five-bedroom villa on a weekly basis. Each room has a king-size bed, cable television and a CD/DVD player. Bathrooms feature marble showers with rain-shower heads and Rolex fixtures atop marble vanities.

Moderate–Inexpensive

Horny Toad Guest House and Apartments, PO Box 3029, 2 Vlaun Dr, Simpson Bay, t 545 4323, US t 1 800 417 9361, *info@thtgh.com*, *www.thehornytoadguesthouse.com*. An excellent retreat, which has a variety of one-bedroom apartments in a building right on the beach and set in a pretty garden. Eight units, all with fully equipped kitchens (no hotel dining room) and private balconies with a view of Saba; very personable and friendly atmosphere from owner-operators.

Pasanggrahan Royal Guest House, PO Box 151, Front St, Philipsburg, **t** 542 3588, US and Canada **t** 1 800 223 9815, *tini@megatropic. com*. Almost invisible in the recent concrete explosion in town, there is a hotel which retains a certain old-time Caribbean style. The reception area and restaurant are set in a charming green and white town house (formerly the government rest house) with gingerbread woodwork and louvred shutters, overlooking an overgrown palm garden. There is an old-fashioned air, with high-backed wicker chairs and portraits, and afternoon tea served in the garden. It is also right on the sand. Some of the 30 units are in the main house with one particularly fine suite above it, but a new modern block has been built to take the rest; no televisions or phones in rooms.

Inexpensive

Sea Breeze Hotel, just off the main road to Cole Bay outside Philipsburg, Cay Hill, **t** 542 6054, US **t** 1 800 223 9815, *seabreeze@sint maarten.net*, *www.seabreezehotel.com*. If you don't mind being off the beach, then you can get a good deal and a perfectly comfortable room here. It's set in a modern block, with 30 rooms with phones, TVs, aircon and kitchenettes. It might be an idea if you have a car.

Jose's Guesthouse, Back St, Philipsburg, **t** 542 2231. Simple rooms.

Marcus Guesthouse, Front St, Philipsburg, **t** 542 2419. Here there are 11 rooms with private baths and fan ventilation.

Eating Out

Sint Maarten is as cosmopolitan in cuisine as it is in languages and so you will find a bewildering selection of restaurants – anything from Mexican to Vietnamese, supported by an endless range of burger and pizza joints. Dutch food is not widely available, although Dutch East Indian is (Javanese).

There's even a sushi bar. Obviously the island is strongly influenced by the States (there are daily flights delivering fresh food) and you will find some cheery American-style eateries and some decks on the waterfront a bit reminiscent of Florida. The more upmarket restaurants are usually French or Italian. It is not necessary to cross to the French side of the island for good French cooking, though you should consider heading over there because there are some excellent restaurants (*see* pp.316–7).

Reservations are advisable in season. All but the smallest restaurants accept credit cards. Generally speaking, eating out in Sint Maarten is expensive and you can expect a 10–15% service charge to be added to your bill. **Categories** are arranged according to the price of a main course: expensive = US$20 and above; moderate = US$10–20; inexpensive = under US$10.

Expensive

Le Bec Fin, Billy Folly 25, Simpson Bay, **t** 544 3930. Classical French cuisine and some French creole dishes in a lovely setting, with louvred windows on stilts to give you the best of the view. Soufflés and crêpes, racks of lamb and beautifully presented local fish.

Le Perroquet, Airport Rd, **t** 545 4339. A calm and stylish dining room – you sit among tropical greenery, with a view through louvred windows onto the lagoon. The menu is French with some concessions to the Caribbean: *canard croquant* in Grand Marnier sauce; and some oddities such as wild boar and alligator. Follow up with *fraise flambée*, a 13th-century recipe which uses green peppercorns. Service brisk but friendly. *Closed Mon*.

Saratoga, Simpson Bay Yacht Club, **t** 544 2421. Contemporary international cuisine in a good waterfront setting. It's quiet and elegant in style and has a good selection of wines to go with crab and lobster cakes and more substantial fare.

Da Livio, Philipsburg waterfront, **t** 542 2690. A very popular Italian restaurant, near the foot of town, with a mural announcing its European heritage. You dine on a terrace right above the water. *Aragosta fra diavolo* (lobster in spicy red sauce) or the *manicotti della casa* (with ricotta cheese, spinach and tomato). Wines from the Venice area. *Closed Sun*.

Antoine's, Philipsburg, **t** 542 2964. A French restaurant, with a very pretty terrace setting with blue awnings above the waves. *Canard montmorency* in a brandy sauce or grouper in almonds, followed by profiteroles.

Wajang Doll, Philipsburg, **t** 542 2687. A taste of the Dutch East Indies in the Dutch West Indies. The dining room is on a veranda behind a pretty wooden creole house, close to Antoine's. You'll discover it by the smells as you walk by – lemongrass and galanka root. Distinctive Indonesian fare in *nasi goreng* and dragon-mouthed *sambals* and the *rijstafel*, which is made up of 14–19 separate dishes.

Moderate

The Greenhouse, near Great Bay Marina, **t** 542 2941. For views over the yachts and of the sunset with pool tables on a breezy deck. Offers standard international fare: burgers, salads and steaks. Some drinks specials, plus music and dancing in the evenings.

Seafood Galley, near Great Bay Marina. With a pub-style interior and a seafood restaurant at the side. Start with the raw bar – oysters, clams and rock-crab claws – followed by creole shrimp or soft-shelled crabs in creole butter.

Bananas, Simpson Bay, **t** 544 3500. Fun and friendly place with good fare. Start with calamari and peppers and continue with stuffed *mahi-mahi* and garlic mashed potato. Bananas come as a starter or a pudding.

Turtle Pier, quite close to the terminal on Airport Rd, Simpson Bay, **t** 545 2230. A place well worth pulling over for, its deck sticking out onto the lagoon. Collects a good crowd of yachties around the bar (with some rusting hulks left by Hurricane Luis to admire). Daytime salads and burgers, plus a long seafood menu for the evenings, when there are specials: all-you-can-eat BBQ-ribs, or lobster nights. Happy Hour is between 5 and 7. Music several times a week.

Chéri's Café, Maho Plaza, **t** 545 3361. At the entrance to the Maho Bay complex – ever lively, usually crammed with tourists all trying to be heard above the calypso music. Cheap drinks.

Inexpensive

Ric's Place, Simpson Bay. An American-style sports bar where you can keep up with the stateside sports while enjoying unlimited refills of iced tea, or the 'largest selection of beers on the island…' They also serve simple burgers and some Mexican fare.

Bars and Nightlife

Some of the restaurants above double as café-bars – *see* Ric's Place, Chéri's Cafe, The Greenhouse and Turtle Pier. You will also find some excellent bars and places to dance on the French side (*see* 'Bars and Nightlife', p.317). There are 12 casinos in Dutch Sint Maarten, in the big hotels and along Front St in town. Some hotels have shows over dinner a couple of times a week.

The Boathouse, Simpson Bay, **t** 544 5409. Hung with rigging, with regular live music. You can't miss it because there's a boat outside.

Soggy Dollar, Simpson Bay. Tucked away among all the others is this smaller, easier spot which offers a good beer with a quiet crowd (and a laundry if you need it).

Bliss, Beacon Hill Rd, **t** 545 3996, *www.thebliss experience.com*.

Q Club, Maho Village, *www.qclubdisco.com*. Two bars, two dance floors, and an elevated VIP lounge.

Beach Bars

The busiest and best beach bars are really on the French side, on Baie de l'Orient, but there are a couple of beach bars in Simpson Bay, on the strip near the bridge where all the watersports take place.

Indiana Beach. Develops St Maarten's habit of theme parks with a pseudo-Indiana Jones creation, where wooden elephants appear to be wandering through the profuse tropical greenery, stalked by pith-helmeted waiters serving solidly international food: daytime soups, salads and sandwiches followed by ribs, steaks and racks of lamb.

Bamboo Bernies, Caravanserai Resort, Beacon Hill Rd, **t** 545 3622, *www.bamboobernies-stmaarten.com*. Tiki bar, sushi bar, beach club, music.

Everyt'ing Cool, Great Bay, Philipsburg.

Mr Busby, Dawn Beach, **t** 543 6088. On the more remote east coast, where there is a fearsome-sounding list of cocktails to keep you oiled in the sun.

Beaches

The beaches all over the island are excellent (*see* 'St Martin' in the **French Caribbean** chapter for the beaches on the French side, pp.307 and 310). Along the irregular, indented coastline, wave action has ground down the coral and pushed up the grains in blinding-white mounds of sand on the shore. And with so many resorts and complexes, every conceivable activity is available on Sint Maarten. Modern-day knights joust on their jet skis, dipping and darting on the waves, inspected from above by parasailors and by scuba divers from below. Screaming children can be stunned into rapt silence by being dragged around the bay on a high-speed sausage. Senior citizens ply the water sedately in pedalos. If you go over to the French side there are also one or two nude beaches, and topless bathing is perfectly acceptable (it is also becoming more common on the Dutch side). You will find facilities of some sort on all the beaches in Dutch Sint Maarten – some hotels have a shower room, for which they make a charge. A word of warning: there has been a certain amount of theft on the beaches; don't leave belongings unattended. *See* 'Best Beaches', p.413.

Philipsburg

Downtown Philipsburg has just four streets, stretched out along the full length of a sand bar that separates the Great Salt Pond from Great Bay. The Head of Town lies in the east and the Foot of Town in the west. Philipsburg is being rebuilt in concrete, but among the air-conditioned malls and modern office blocks you will see a few old traditional gingerbread homes. At the tip of the Great Bay's eastern arm is the new cruise port, developed in attractive West Indian style.

Pedestrianized **Front St** (Voor Straat) sells itself as the 'Shopping Centre of the Leewards', and the arcades and alleys (*steegjes*) manage successfully to delay most of the cruise-ship arrivals that come in safari boats (the marine equivalent of the tourist bus), to Wathey Square, the little central square known locally as **de Ruyterplein**. Along almost its entire length Front St is full of little arcades of theme-Caribbean architecture, everywhere hung with signs like 'Caution: Falling Prices!', warbling and occasionally clunking as you pass the slot arcades, or ringing with bells like the shop Little Switzerland. Of course there are some bargains to be had and there are one or two galleries with art that is probably worth seeking out. To round the experience off, you can go and taste guavaberry liqueur, in all its frighteningly bright concoctions in an aggressively brightly painted (but quite nice and old) wooden house. **Back St** (Achter Straat), where the harvested salt was once stored in vast white stacks, has the administrative buildings and churches.

There is a **museum** (*open Mon–Fri 10–4, Sat 10–12; adm*) at the Head of Town in the arcade nearest the pier, set upstairs in an old town house, where island archaeology and history are revealed in pottery shards, Spanish buttons and pipes, colonial maps, china plates and recent marine recoveries.

Behind Philipsburg is the **Great Salt Pond**, its stone dividers still in place like little dykes, which was common to both nations in the 17th century, when salt was important for preserving meats that could not be frozen. Since the industry folded in 1949, land has been reclaimed to expand Philipsburg and part of it is used as the island rubbish tip. Much of the local life has been squeezed out of Philipsburg, but you can still hear a lively medley of music and languages – the unaccustomed stream of not-quite Spanish is Papiamento. Now people tend to live in the suburbs behind the salt pond, where you get an idea of Caribbean life in the raffle-ticket booths and the limers hanging around the superettes and rum shops.

On the back side of the Salt Pond are the small **Zoological and Botanical Gardens** (*t 543 2030; open Mon–Fri 9–5, Sat and Sun 10–6; adm*), housing Caribbean and South American animals. The town continues up over the hill and down into the French side. There are some more remote areas down towards the coast.

Around the Island

The Sint Maarten countryside has little to offer. Much of it is as overgrown as the beaches, with houses rather than hotels. But the coast has superb views looking south to the other islands, grey stains on the horizon on a hazy day, but magnified and green if tropical rains have washed the sky. You can often see St Kitts about 45 miles away and Nevis is very occasionally visible from Cole Bay Hill. Beyond the immediate area of Philipsburg, the island has a fairly 'international' lifestyle which devotes itself to tourism, with hotels and condominium complexes and everywhere roadside restaurants and bars.

At the point on the western arm of Great Bay are the ruins of a fort built by the Spaniards in the 1630s. They demolished it when they abandoned the island and the remains were rebuilt by the Dutch and named **Fort Amsterdam**. The route to the French side of the island leads from Cole Bay. The border is marked by a small **obelisk**, but there are no formalities and unless you are looking out for it you will probably enter France without knowing.

Sint Eustatius

Sint Eustatius is a tiny island with a glorious and glittering past. In the 18th century it was so rich that it was known as the Golden Rock; its warehouses were brim-filled with silks, silver and guns from all over the world. At that time it was one of the most important places in the Caribbean, actually the first country in the world to recognize the United States, when Governor de Graaff saluted the merchant ship *Andrew Doria* in 1776. But Sint Eustatius's glory has gone. The warehouses have decayed and its fortune has waned.

Statia to her friends, Sint Eustatius has an area of just 8 square miles and is situated close to St Kitts, about 30 miles south of Sint Maarten. The island is of volcanic origin: hills in the north descend to a central plain, where the capital and only town, Oranjestad, stands on the leeward coast, and then rise again in the south to the Quill (1,890ft), a perfectly shaped volcano, now extinct.

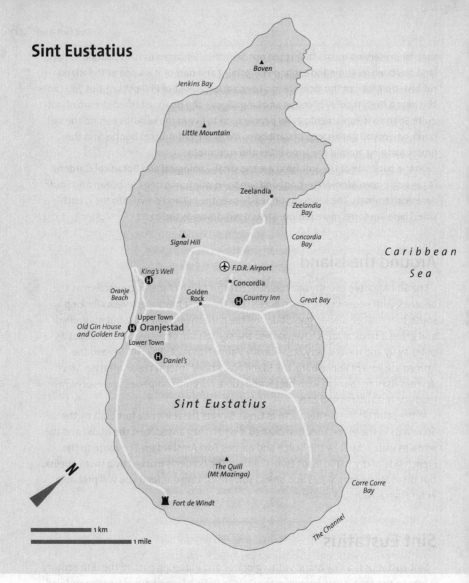

Sint Eustatius

Boven ▲

Jenkins Bay

Little Mountain ▲

Zeelandia •

Zeelandia
Bay

Concordia
Bay

*C a r i b b e a n
S e a*

Signal Hill ▲

✈ F.D.R. Airport

King's Well Ⓗ

• Concordia

Oranje
Beach

Golden
Rock

Ⓗ Country Inn

Great Bay

Upper Town
Old Gin House
and Golden Era

Ⓗ Oranjestad

Lower Town

Ⓗ Daniel's

Sint Eustatius

The Quill ▲
(Mt Mazinga)

Corre Corre
Bay

▲ Fort de Windt

N

⊢———⊣ 1 km

⊢————⊣ 1 mile

The Channel

The population of Statia (pronounced stay-shah) is now about 2,000, a fraction of
the numbers who lived and traded here in the 18th century. It is extremely quiet. If you
go, remember that the glittering tradition remains in only a few dilapidated red and
yellow brick and stone walls. There is a small and limited amount of tourism. For now,
Statia is the least developed island in the area, and she can only wait until the waves
of Caribbean fortune favour her again.

History

Settled by the Dutch West India Company in 1636 after a failed attempt on St Croix
in the Virgin Islands, Statia's beginnings were modest – small cultivations of tobacco
and sugar. But the company had its eyes on trade. Only they had fleets large enough

Best Beaches

Smoke Alley Beach or **Oranje Beach**: Off the road down to Lower Town on the calm Caribbean side, with an excellent view of the sunset: popular among the Statians at the weekends. There is a beach bar, decorated with fishing nets and coloured lights, which sticks out into the sea.

Crooks Castle: Beyond Lower Town, another passable sunning and snorkelling spot.

Corre Corre Bay: On the Atlantic side of the island, a secluded cove. Skirt round the Quill to the southeast on Mountain Rd and the path down to the bay is marked.

Concordia and **Zeelandia Bays**: Two miles of good walking and beachcombing for flotsam cast ashore by the Atlantic.

to supply the burgeoning West Indian colonies in the 17th century, and over the next hundred years Oranjestad in Sint Eustatius, along with Willemstad in Dutch Curaçao, became the most important market in the New World.

It started with slaves, for whom there was ceaseless demand in the sugar islands nearby. The Statian merchants were often paid in kind (hogsheads of sugar and puncheons of rum were accepted currency), so the warehouses filled up and Sint Eustatius became a massive entrepôt, presided over by merchants from Europe and the Americas. By 1750 the warehouses stretched all along the waterfront in Lower Town and as space ran out the merchants constructed dykes to reclaim land from the sea, so that they could build a second line of warehouses. Over the next forty years, these became so full that the doorways were blocked up and the goods were hauled in and out through holes in the roof.

Strictly speaking, almost all of the trade was illegal because of monopoly trading laws imposed by the other European nations (which demanded that the colonies should trade only with their mother country). This did not endear the Statians to local colonial authorities. But the Dutch in Sint Eustatius recognized no trading laws and the sugar manufacturers in the West Indies knew that they would get a better price and immediate payment if they sold their goods to the merchants in Sint Eustatius (rather than shipping them all the way home). Thus they were prepared to smuggle them there. In 1779 Statia grew around 500,000 pounds of sugar, but according to official records it managed to ship about 25 million pounds.

So prosperous an island was a valuable prize and altogether Statia changed hands a ridiculous 22 times, taken by roving navies as they vied for supremacy in the Caribbean. Despite a ring of about 15 forts, Statia was never properly defended.

Oranjestad was a free port (an early version of duty-free) and any ship that cared to come into harbour to trade was welcome. At the height of the island's prosperity there could be a hundred ships offshore at any time. Statia became famous as an arms depot, with rifles and ammunition passing through in vast amounts. Gunpowder turned in a profit of over 100%. American blockade runners would dodge the British Navy and smuggle arms to the colonists in sugar barrels.

It was with this trade in mind that Governor de Graaff saluted an unknown flag on a ship that arrived in harbour on 16 November 1776: the American colonist merchant ship, the *Andrew Doria*. Even if the gesture was not deliberate, it was certainly a momentous event, as it was the first time that a foreign power had recognized the sovereignty of the United States. The British were furious and the Dutch apologized, recalling de Graaff.

Maverick Statia was attacked again soon after de Graaff's action when Admiral Rodney sailed into harbour with 15 warships on 3 February 1781, seeking revenge. For the next few months he systematically plundered the island, confiscating all the goods in the warehouses and the personal fortunes of the Statian merchants. He even kept the Dutch flag flying above the port and lured in another 150 unsuspecting ships. When he auctioned off all the goods, the profits exceeded £3 million, of which he kept a sizeable proportion for himself. Understandably, the merchants did what they could to save their riches and stories tell of an unusually high number of deaths and funerals. The coffins were loaded with gold. As soon as he discovered the trickery, Rodney promptly had them all dug up again. When he had had enough, the British abandoned the island.

Statia never really recovered, and since then the island has suffered an ever-declining spiral. As trading foundered, the plantations were started up again, but they failed quickly when slavery was abolished by the Dutch in 1863. The warehouses on the waterfront were dismantled so that their bricks could be sold on to other islands. The population dropped as the prosperity waned. Those that were left became subsistence farmers, or depended on remittances sent by relatives working abroad.

Today Statia is very quiet and has only a small tourist industry (around a hundred hotel rooms), attracting mainly divers and hikers. The government is the largest employer and the only other major industry is an oil storage facility and refinery. The island has a listless and slightly tatty air, but a Dutch government and EU project has helped to restore some of the buildings from Statia's heyday. The present Lieutenant Governor of Sint Eustatius is Mr Eugene R. Abdul. The island has two commissioners and one senator, Mr Clyde I. van Putten, who sits in the Senate in Curaçao.

Beaches

There are only a couple of beaches in Statia and they do not have the white sand for which the Caribbean is known. Generally, the Atlantic side is unsafe for swimming because of the undertow. See p.425 for best beaches.

Oranjestad

Statia's only settlement, tiny Oranjestad, has two parts, Upper and Lower Town, which are separated by a 100ft cliff. During Statia's supremacy as a trading port, goods were kept in the warehouses down below, between the cobbled street and the waterfront, and many of the traders would live up above in Upper Town. Today the Statians still live up above, in new 'gingerbread' houses that have forced aside the dark-stone 18th-century foundations and barrel-vaulted graves, and in more modern concrete houses. The two halves are linked by an old stone walkway built in 1803 (and by a longer road). Down below, Lower Town has now fallen into almost complete

Getting There

Sint Eustatius **t** (599–)

By Air

Sint Eustatius is best reached via Sint Maarten (*see* p.415) and is served several times a day by Winair, **t** 318 2362, *www.fly-winair. com*. There are occasional flights to the island from St Kitts. On approach, the plane often circles the volcano. There is a departure tax of US$5.65 within the Dutch Caribbean and US$12 elsewhere. A couple of charter planes work in and out of the island: José Dormoy, **t** 318 2646; and Alvin Courtar, **t** 318 2218.

Getting Around

By Taxi

Getting around Sint Eustatius is easy enough on foot, but there are taxis if you do not want to walk up the hill. A **guided tour** of the island can be made, and if you spin it out to two hours it will cost around US$35. They can be ordered at any hotel desk, or through:
Rosie Lopes, **t** 318 2811.
Josse Daniel, **t** 318 2358.

Car and Bike Hire

There are a few cars for hire, at around US$35 per day (driving is on the right):
ARC Car Rental, **t** 318 2595.
Brown's Car Rental, **t** 318 2266.
Lady Ama's Services, Fort Orange St, **t** 318 2451.
Mansion Scooter and Car Rental, **t** 318 2626.
Rainbow Car Rental, **t** 318 2811.
Richardson Jeep Rental, **t** 318 2149.

Tourist Information

Abroad

There is no tourist office for Sint Eustatius in the UK or USA, so you should contact the island directly (the island website is at *www.statiatourism.com*) or contact:
Netherlands: Antillen Huis, Badhuisweg 173–5, 2597 SP 's-Gravenhagen, **t** (070) 30 66111.

In Sint Eustatius

Sint Eustatius Tourism Development Foundation, in Upper Town, **t** 318 2433. *Open Mon–Fri 8–12 and 1–5.*
Desk at the airport.
St Eustatius National Parks Foundation, Gallows Bay, **t** 318 2884, *senp@goldenrock net.com*. *Open Mon–Thur 7am–5pm, Fri 7am–4pm, Sat–Sun 9am-12pm.*

Medical Emergencies

In a medical emergency, contact the Queen Beatrix Hospital, **t** 318 2211, in Oranjestad.

Money and Banks

The island currency is the Netherlands Antilles florin (US$1 = NAFl1.78), but US dollars are accepted everywhere alongside it. Credit cards can be used in hotels but at small stores and restaurants you will need to pay in cash. Banking hours are Mon–Fri 8.30–3.30.

Telephone Code

To telephone the island from abroad, dial IDD code **t** 599 followed by a seven-digit island number beginning 318, except from the other Dutch Antilles, from where you dial a zero before the seven-figure number. On the island, dial just the seven digits.

Maps and Books

One or two books deal with Statia's famous past, including a good (if a little academic) history, *Sint Eustatius: A Short History of the Island and its Monuments* by Ypie Attema.

Festivals

July–August *Carnival*. The main event in the year over 10 days from late July to early

---

dilapidation. Just a few buildings have been restored from the old ruins of red and yellow brick, and some stone foundation walls are visible on the shoreline leading out into the water. The outer rim of houses has completely disappeared since the dyke was broken by a hurricane and the sea swept back in, but on a calm day it is just

August. Similar to other Caribbean carnivals, with a pyjama jump-up in the early morning at *jouvert*, a Carnival Queen and a calypso competition, culminating in the burning of Momo, the spirit of the Carnival.

November *Statia Day*. Remembers the day in 1776 when Statia saluted the young United States of America (the 16th).

Coronation Day. In memory of the crowning of Queen Beatrix of the Netherlands.

Watersports

Watersports are limited in Statia (no small sailing boats for hire and no water-skiing). For snorkelling, try Jenkins Bay in the north.

Scuba Diving

Seems to be on the up at the moment. Advocates claim that there are the same pristine corals and fish as there are off nearby Saba and reefs that are clean and barely explored. There are some walls and pinnacles and some archaeological sites. About 200 vessels are thought to have sunk off Statia, but the old wrecks themselves do not offer that much because the wood has invariably rotted away, leaving just a pile of ballast stones. After a storm, however, the sea still turns up the occasional 18th-century bottle, blue trading beads or a rare ducat.

The water, between 30m in depth and high water in a number of sections of coastline (Gallows Bay to White Wall, Jenkins Bay to North Point, Oranjebaai), is designated a marine park and there is a US$3 fee per dive.

There are three operators on the island:

Dive Statia, Lower Town, Oranjestad, t 318 2435, *info@divestatia.com*, *www.divestatia.com*.

Golden Rock Dive Centre, t 318 2964, US t 1 800 311 6658, *grdivers@goldenrock.net*, *www.goldenrockdive.com*.

Scubaqua, Lower Town, Oranjestad, t 318 2345, *dive@scubaqua.com*, *www.scubaqua.com*.

Other Sports

Hiking

The National Parks authority has marked about 12 trails around the island, of which the most popular are those up the slopes of the extinct volcano, the Quill, and then down into its crater. The Statians have a tradition of **land-crab hunting** by torchlight in the crater at night, which is a fun way to spend an evening. A guide can be provided by the Tourist Board for an outing to the crater; if you go at night, you are advised to take one. North of Oranjestad you might see coastal tropicbirds, distinctive with their long twin tail-feathers. A guide can be found through the **museum**, t 318 2288.

Tennis

There is a floodlit court at the Community Centre, in the southern area of town.

Where to Stay

Sint Eustatius t (599–)

There are just a few hotels on the island, plus one or two guest houses, and it is possible to rent cottages through the Tourist Board. There is a 7% government tax on rooms. You can also expect a service charge of 10% to be added to your bill.

Old Gin House, Lower Town, t 318 2319, *reservations@oldginhouse.com*, *www.oldginhouse.com* (*expensive–moderate*). There is a delightful air of old-time grace about the Old Gin House. Its restaurant and bar, the Mooshay Publick House, is built of the ballast bricks from which the old Statian warehouses were built two centuries ago (brought from Holland by the trading ships in the days of the Golden Rock). The rooms, set in more modern blocks around the pool, are dressed up in bright Caribbean colours and are very comfortable and elegant.

possible to see the base of the walls which run between Crooks Castle and Betty Bay, below the surface of the water.

The town takes its name from **Fort Oranje**, a fortress which rides high on the clifftop above the Lower Town. It was built by the Dutch in 1636 on the site of an earlier

The Golden Era Hotel, PO Box 109, Lower Town, **t** 318 2345, US **t** 1 800 223 9815, *goldera@goldenrock.net* (*moderate*). On the waterfront, a modern construction that has none of the atmosphere of old-time Statia. There is a pool and bar down on the waterfront and a dining room which serves West Indian and international fare; rooms simple and passable, with cable TV and fridge.

Country Inn, **t** 318 2484, *countryinn@statiatourism.com* (*inexpensive*). Just six secluded and well-priced apartments, set in a garden far away from the hustle of Oranjestad in Concordia. Rooms have cable TV.

King's Well Hotel, on the main road down to the Lower Town, **t** 318 2538, US **t** 1 800 692 4106 (*inexpensive*). Simple rooms and good company here. Eleven rooms in a modern villa; there's a fantastic view if you get one looking out to sea. The owners are friendly and so their terrace dining room attracts a crowd from all around.

Daniel's, Rose Mary Laan, **t** 318 2358 (*inexpensive*). Guest house.

The Stone Oven, Faeschweg, Upper Town, **t** 318 2489. Creole cuisine. A trusty West Indian setting, with wooden tables and bright tablecloths; serves fish and chicken.

Ocean View Terrace, near the tourist office, **t** 318 2934. There is a nice café inside the stone courtyard of the government guest house: satay chicken, shrimp and steak dishes. Pleasant atmosphere as professionals drop by for a bite for lunch or a drink on the way home.

Sonny's Place, Fort Oranje Straat, **t** 318 2609. Head here if you feel like a Chinese meal or a *roti*. A garden bar with trellises and a pool table inside.

Blue Bead, Gallows Bay, Lower Town, **t** 318 2873. Right on the waterfront, a nice spot where you will be served steaks, chicken and fish platters and Indonesian dishes (from the Dutch East Indies in Indonesia) as well as simpler salads. Two centuries ago blue beads were a currency in Statia and they still wash up occasionally on the beaches.

Eating Out

Statian food is generally international and West Indian and it tends to be quite simple. It is worth adding the hotel dining rooms into the equation (*see* above). Credit cards are often not accepted and, though there's rarely pressure on space, you may want to reserve to let them know that you're coming. Most restaurants also double as bars.

Price categories below are arranged according to the price of a main course: expensive = US$15 and above; moderate = US$8–15; inexpensive = under US$8.

Moderate–Inexpensive

L'Etoile, up the hill on Heilgerweg, **t** 318 2299. Best of the independent restaurants. Serves local fare – start with a callaloo soup and follow with creole catch of the day.

Bars and Nightlife

Nightlife in Statia is limited to the hotels and the local bars:

Cool Corner, opposite the museum, **t** 318 2523. Probably the coolest bar in town (right in the middle), where the Statians can be found limin' at all hours of day and night: a wooden shed with coloured lights visible from outside and TV playing permanently. Chinese fare on offer.

Franky's, de Ruyterweg. A bar where you can slug a beer with the Statians and the occasional band that plays here.

Largo Heights. A disco at Chapel Piece.

Smoke Alley Bar & Grill, Lower Town, Gallows Bay, **t** 318 2002, *titanic@goldenrock.net*. Open-air beach bar and restaurant serving home-made food cooked to order. Live music and DJ every Friday night. *Open Mon–Sat 11.30–2 and 6–10. Happy hour Fri 6–9.*

French fort. Even though the island was attacked so often, the fort saw little action. Some reports state that it is poised so precariously that it dared not fire its guns in case the whole structure slipped and fell off the cliff into the Lower Town. Fort Oranje has settled comfortably into its modern unwarlike role: of sitting and looking pretty. If you dare go close to the edge, it has an attractive view across Lower Town. Among its monuments, the most significant commemorates the firing of the salute to the *Andrew Doria* on 16 November 1776.

The **Sint Eustatius Museum** (*open Mon–Fri 9–5, Sat and Sun 9–12; adm*) is located in Simon Doncker House just off the Wilheminaweg and central square. Admiral Rodney made it his headquarters when he ransacked the island in 1781. The exhibition has an Amerindian section with old Indian pottery and artefacts from the extensive archaeological programmes that have taken place in Statia; there are two very attractive period rooms, restored to the time of Statia's prosperity, with impressive antique furniture and a planter's tea service, and a more recent room, 'Granny Statia', exhibiting life on Statia within the last hundred years. Also on view are some small china pieces from the Nanking cargo (which was on order to the Dutch West India Company in Sint Eustatius when the Dutch East India Company ship that was carrying it sank in the South China Sea); they arrived two hundred years late, but they made it.

The **Upper Town** has some pretty and well-kept old houses made of stone and wood, but mostly it is a little tatty and goats, chickens and donkeys tend to have the run of the place. Statia's sizeable Jewish community, who suffered most of all during Rodney's ravages in 1781 (not only was all their money taken but they were deported as well), is remembered in the ruins of the **Honen Dalim Synagogue**, on the little alley, Synagoogpad. On the Kerkweg, the **Dutch Reformed Church** tower, with a cemetery full of barrel-vaulted graves, has been restored and gives a fine view of the harbour.

Around the Island

South of Oranjestad is Statia's volcano, the **Quill**. It is perfectly shaped, with concave slopes rising to nearly 2,000ft and a circular crater, from which it takes its name (*kuil* in Dutch means pit). Inside the crater, which is 900ft across and 550ft deep, is a moist and tangled rainforest, where the trees grow tall in their efforts to reach the sun and mosses infest their trunks. Some cultivation takes place in here. Its highest point is Mt Mazinga.

There are thought to have been about 19 forts dotted around Statia's barren coastline; a few are lost without trace. At **Fort de Windt** on the southern tip of the island, a couple of cannon look south over the superb view of St Kitts.

Saba

Saba is impossibly steep, an impressive mountain outcrop just 5 square miles in area, a central cone surrounded by little lieutenants. Standing about 30 miles to the south of Sint Maarten, the volcanic island of Saba is the final peak in the chain of volcanic islands that runs in an arc from Grenada in the far south. Near the summit, Saba can seem like a tropical Gormenghast – clouds swirl through the dripping greenery and the gnarled branches of ancient trees are clad in creeping diabolic green

mosses. Curiously, Mt Scenery (2,885ft), the island peak, is the highest point in the Kingdom of the Netherlands.

Besides the capital, The Bottom, there are three main villages on the island's slopes (Windwardside, St John's and Hell's Gate). They appear almost alpine with their stepped alleys, switchbacks and steep retaining walls (the base of one house perched on the roof of the one below) and their spectacular views: you are so high up that you can often see the curve in the horizon. There is a delightful, almost pastoral calm about the place as well.

Saba (pronounced say-bah) is incredibly neat. Tidy gardens tamed from the tropical jungle nestle behind white wooden picket fences; fluorescent blooms stand out against the whitewashed clapboard walls of the houses with their horseshoe-shaped chimney pots. Curiously, every single roof in Saba is painted red.

You have a good chance of getting a person's name right in Saba if you call them Mr or Mrs Hassell (about a quarter of the population are called Hassell). However, beware, because you might just come across a member of the two rival Saban dynasties, a Johnson or a Simmons. The population is just 1,200 (mostly of British descent) and it is untypical in the Caribbean for being roughly half white and half black. With few plantations, most slaves on Saba were domestic servants and their numbers never exceeded those of the white population. Though the islanders all know each other, there are unspoken rules concerning skin colour (as there are in many Caribbean islands) and, even today, there is little intermarriage between the races. And as with many small islands, much of the youth has left in search of work and adventure. Sometimes the population appears to be mainly grandparents and infant grandchildren.

Relatively speaking, there is a large population of expatriates, about 250, many of whom are students or teachers at the Saba Medical School. About three-quarters of

'The Road that Could Not Be Built'

The Sabans decided in the 1930s that they needed a road, since anything from a bean to a grand piano had to be painfully carried around on the network of pathways that crisscrossed the island. Initially, upon seeking expert advice, they were simply told that they shouldn't bother to try. But the Hassells and the Johnsons were made of sterner stuff than that: islander and future architect of The Road Josephus Lambert Hassell decided to take a correspondence course in civil engineering. In 1938 work began at Fort Bay, slowly winding its way uphill for the next five years to The Bottom. In 1947 the first car arrived on Saba, and by 1951 it could be driven to Windwardside.

The completed 19-mile stretch of The Road clings to the mountainside and climbs to 1,800ft as it winds from village to village. As you drive, there are some unexpected but stunning views. To the builders' credit, The Road was repaired for the first time in the late 1980s.

the tourists who visit the island come for scuba diving, for which Saba has a justifiably good reputation.

Saba is quiet, calm, sedate and very stable. It is certainly not a place for a wild time, or for a beach-bound resort holiday (again it is untypical for the Caribbean in that there simply are no beaches here). However, if you are looking for a quiet Caribbean retreat with a gentle, old-time air, then Saba is a satisfying and very pleasant place to stay.

History

A stream of famous visitors passed by the island in the 16th century, among them Sir Walter Raleigh and Piet Heyn, the Dutch privateer, but most thought better of trying to land. Somebody must have done so, however, because in 1632 a shipwrecked crew of Englishmen found a plentiful supply of fruit on the trees but no inhabitants (it was a tradition that sailors would plant food-bearing trees for just this sort of occasion). The first permanent settlement of Saba was made by Dutchmen from nearby Sint Eustatius in about 1640, and they were joined by a succession of misfits, many of them English-speakers. In 1665 an English pirate named Morgan paused to capture the island and he promptly deported everyone who wasn't English.

Saba was almost impregnable. There were few easy landing sites and the terrain was so precipitous that storming the island presented quite a problem. For their part, the Sabans are supposed to have defended themselves by man-made avalanches. They constructed platforms at the top of the ravines and loaded them with boulders. At the approach of an enemy, they simply knocked out the supports. In 1689 the French had a go, after successfully capturing Sint Eustatius, but decided in the end to leave the island alone. From then on, most changes of allegiance were by political arrangement. In 1816 the island was handed back to the Dutch for the last time.

The great Caribbean rover, Père Labat, dropped by in about 1700 and found that the islanders' principal trade was in boots and shoes – even the parson was a cobbler. Labat bought six pairs. Since then, the Sabans have been in many trades. They had some success growing sugar in the fertile parts of the island, and for this they brought in African slaves, whose descendants are still on the island. Slavery is reckoned to have been benign here compared with elsewhere in the Caribbean.

In the 19th century the Saban men took to the sea and became renowned sailors. They were much in demand by the shipping lines and they captained ships sailing all over the Americas. (Give them a bit of encouragement and old Sabans will gladly tell you of the days when 'the boats were made of wood and the men were made of iron'.) The economy of the island was supported by the contributions that they sent back to their families. At home, with no men around, the Saban women adopted lacemaking, or drawn-thread work, an industry that continues today.

As shipping waned in the 1930s, the oil industry boomed in Curaçao and Aruba, the Dutch Leeward Islands off the coast of Venezuela, and the menfolk rushed away to get work there. All these departures have reduced the population of Saba from around 2,500 to its present level. Today the 'remittance money' sent home by Sabans abroad has dwindled, but returns from tourism have increased. Other industries include the export of lobsters from local waters. Recently a University Medical School has been created and so there are quite a number of students during term time. Saba also receives grants from the Central Government of the Netherlands Antilles in Curaçao, to which they send one elected senator and two commissioners. The island has an appointed Lieutenant Governor, presently Mr Antoine Solagnier.

Beaches

Saba has no 'beaches' as beaches are generally thought of in the Caribbean. However, a patch of migratory grey volcanic sand returns annually to the north coast of the island in the spring, staying over the summer until about November. This is at **Well's Bay**, at the end of the road from The Bottom. On a calm day, it makes a good picnic spot. The other place occasionally referred to as the 'beach' is the concrete ramp down into the water at **Fort Bay**, but you may not want to sunbathe there when the quarry is working.

The Bottom, and On From There

The Bottom is the capital of Saba and, despite its name, sits at an altitude of 850ft. It is a jumble of white walls, red roofs and green shutters set in neat little gardens, sitting in the bottom of a bowl (the word *botte* means 'bowl' in Dutch) thought to be the crater of Saba's extinct volcano. There are still some cobbled streets, laid with large stones. The evening shade comes early to The Bottom as it is towered over by vast forested escarpments. The Dutch, Antillean and Saban flags fly alongside one another in front of the **Lieutenant Governor's residence** at the southern end of the town, a gingerbread house defended by a couple of fearsome cannon (at least four-ouncers).

Close by, down the hill and through the 'chicane', you come to **Fort Bay**. This is the island's main port and it has quite an industrial quality about it, with a quarry, the

Getting There

Saba t (599–)

By Air

Flying into Saba is something of an experience. Juancho E. Yrausquin airport is on Flat Point – named so because it is one of the only flat places on the island (even if there is a 130ft cliff at either end). At 1,312ft, this strip is one of the shortest in the world (this includes most aircraft carriers) and, as you look at it from the air, it seems impossible that anything could land on it. But be reassured: the STOL Twin Otters can land on a sixpence and usually they only use half the runway. There are a number of photographs on the walls of the airport illustrating some past events, including a 'spectacular prang' in 1971.

The only scheduled flights that go to Saba are the five or so each day on Winair, t 318 2362, US t 1 800 634 4907, reservations@fly-winair.com. They originate in Sint Maarten and sometimes touch down at Sint Eustatius.

There is a departure tax of US$5 if you are travelling to Sint Eustatius or to Sint Maarten and US$20 for elsewhere.

By Sea

You can also get to Saba by the power-yacht The Edge, t 544 2640, aquamania@sint maarten.net, departing Wed–Sun from Pelican Marina on Simpson Bay. The return from Saba departs Fort Bay at 3.45 pm, arriving in St Maarten at 5pm. Cost is $60 return for adults, $30 for children. One-way $40 adults and $20 children. There are a number of organized day trips on offer from Sint Maarten.

Getting Around

By Taxi

With no buses, getting around Saba is really limited to taxis. The taxi fare from one end of the island to the other is around US$15. Taxi drivers are willing to give a **tour** of the island, taking in the historical sights and views and a stop for lunch. They know about catching the last plane out, though it would probably not go without you anyway. A day's tour for two will cost around US$50, with a small charge for extra people. For a taxi, call t 416 2281.

Hitch-hiking

Hitching works very well and will introduce you to the Sabans. It is usually enough to sit on the wall at the edge of town for someone to pick you up.

Car Hire

A few hire cars are available and they can be rented for about US$60 per day. Remember to drive on the right, and that Saba's only petrol station is in Fort Bay, t 416 3272, on the coast below The Bottom. Cars can be hired from: **Caja's Car Rental**, The Bottom, t 416 2388, takijah77@hotmail.com.

Tourist Information

Abroad

The Saba website: www.sabatourism.com. **Netherlands/Germany**: Dutch Caribbean Travel Center, Karlstrasse 12, D 60329 Frankfurt, t (069) 240 0183.

In Saba

Saba Tourist Office, on the road down to The Bottom, Windwardside, t 416 2231, iluvsaba@unspoiledqueen.com. The staff are helpful and will also send information abroad. Open Mon–Fri 8–5.

Medical Emergencies

In case of a medical emergency, contact the M. A. Edwards Medical Centre, t 416 3288, in The Bottom.

Money and Banks

The currency of Saba is the Netherlands Antilles florin (US$1 = NAFl 1.78), but US dollars are accepted everywhere. Banks are generally open on weekday mornings. Places accustomed to tourists, for instance hotels and dive shops, will accept credit cards. Others will not.

Telephone Code

Not so many years ago, isolated Saba had only a weekly mail service, but now communications are rather easier. To telephone the island from abroad, dial t 599 and then the seven-digit Saban number beginning 416. If phoning within the island, dial all seven digits.

Festivals

July Saba's *Summer Festival*. Held in the last week of July, with calypso shows, a festival parade in the streets and the usual jump-ups in the evenings.

Watersports

There is not much in the way of watersports other than diving, but kayaks and sunset cruises around the island can be arranged through the three dive shops.

Scuba Diving

Saba rightfully has a name as a diving destination. The island's slopes descend as steeply beneath the water as above and the coral growth there is as lush as the flora on land. There are caves, pinnacles and lava flows, and good visibility, often as much as 100ft. The fish life is abundant, big and not too shy, and the small marine life is excellent. Expect patrols of sergeant majors (striped and very aggressive) and soldierfish to dart around the coral forests and sponges; you might also see a turtle or a migrating humpback whale or a formation of flying gurnards.

The **Saba Marine Park** was established in 1987 to protect the marine life, and has placed mooring sites in the seabed (the coastline is so rough that all dives are made from boats). They can be contacted on **t** 416 3295, *www.sabapark.com*.

Saba has a four-person decompression chamber. A one-tank dive costs around US$45. There are three dive operators on the island:

Saba Deep Diving Centre, Fort Bay, **t** 416 3347, US **t** 1 888 DIVE SABA, *diving@sabadeep.com*, *www.sabadeep.com*.

Saba Divers, Scout's Place Dive Hotel, **t** 416 2740, *sabadivers@unspoiledqueen.com*, *www.sabadivers.com*.

Sea Saba, Windwardside, **t** 416 2246, *seasaba@aol.com*, *www.seasaba.com*. Useful website.

Other Sports

Hiking

All over the island you will see the stone walls of old-time Saba, when the villages of the island were linked in a network of stepped pathways (before the arrival of cars in 1947). People would walk or ride a donkey to get around. Any older Saban will tell you about the morning rush hour (a crowded ¾hr walk) over the hills from Windwardside to The Bottom, and how the islanders used to arrive at parties in their walking boots. A few of the ingenious old paths remain and they make good walking trails. A favourite walk is up to Saba's summit, Mt Scenery, best when the peak is not engulfed in cloud. It is hot work and a good 1½-hour hike, though you can miss the first bit out by taking the upper road.

The flora is fairly typical of the steep volcanic islands, with whole hillsides of elephant ears on the lower slopes and an ever-thickening rainforest with its profuse growth that eventually gives way to elfin woodland. Perhaps you will see a trembler or a garnet-throated hummingbird in the woodland.

There are a number of trails in the northern part of the island, between Well's Bay and Hell's Gate, where there are a couple of abandoned villages. In these remoter areas you will see sea birds rising on the updraught as the winds rise on the island slopes. You may come across terns and brown noddies as well as tropicbirds and Saba's national bird (it appears on the island crest), Audubon's shearwater, locally known as a *wedrego*. Further details of walks on the island are available from the tourist office in Windwardside or through James Johnson at the Trail Shop, **t** 416 2630, home **t** 416 3307, who will talk you through the nature and history of the island as you go.

Where to Stay

Saba t (599–)

There are a surprising number of places to stay on Saba. As well as a red roof, each has the cosy and friendly atmosphere for which the island is known. There are also about 20 villas and cottages for hire, some of them the charming wooden Saban cottages dotted around the island – more details on these can be obtained from the Tourist Board or through Saba Real Estate, **t** 416 2209. Many of the hotels offer diving packages in conjunction with the dive shops. There is a government hotel tax of 5% to be added to rooms and hotels also add a service charge of 10% or 15%.

Very Expensive–Expensive

Willard's of Saba, PO Box 515, **t** 416 2498, *willard@sintmaarten.net*, *www.willards ofsaba.com*. Perhaps the most luxurious resort on the island, isolated above Booby Hill with a truly amazing setting looking south. There are just three rooms in the main house and two two-room bungalows perched on the hillside above the (heated) pool and hot tub with a view. Very modern and plush – bright white with bright pastel fittings. Excellent restaurant; tennis court.

Queen's Garden Resort, PO Box 2, Troy Hill, **t** 416 3494, US **t** 1 800 599 9407, *info@queen saba.com*, *www.queensaba.com*. Also set in modern buildings that stand high above The Bottom, on a hillside smothered in rainforest, with views to the sea. There are 12 apartments and 3 villas around the pool; all modern and comfortable with cable TV, full kitchens and some have private Jacuzzis. There is a restaurant in the hotel as well.

The Gate House, Hell's Gate, **t** 416 2416, US/Canada **t** 1 866 709 8058, *info@saba gatehouse.com*, *www.sabagatehouse.com*. Set on a mountainside with spectacular views. Comprises three small buildings housing a villa, a cottage, and a hotel with wraparound balconies or patios. Furnished in Caribbean style, each room has hardwood or Mexican tiled floors and paintings by local artists. The cottage has a private terrace, living/dining room, kitchenette, bedroom and bath. The hotel and cottage share the pool, located on top of the property. The villa, spacious enough for eight, has four bedrooms, three baths, large dining room, living room, fully equipped kitchen, and a secluded pool.

Moderate

Cottage Club, **t** 416 2386, *cottageclub@ unspoiledqueen.com*, *www.cottage-club.com*. Sits on sloping ground in Windwardside, with a small assembly of cottages in island style – white shingle walls, gingerbread trimmings, green window frames and a red tin roof – standing beneath the stone main house. Good interiors, large rooms with full kitchens and modern fittings (cable TV, fans, phones), each with a balcony from where you can watch the planes belly-flopping on to the runway 1,500ft below.

Scout's Place, looking southwest from the top of the ridge in Windwardside, **t** 416 2740, *sabadivers@unspoiledqueen.com*, *www. sabadivers.com*. Fifteen simple rooms overlooking the attractive roofs and jungle-like greenery. There is a lively open-air bar, where the Sabans stop off on their way home from work, and the dining room is presided over by Diana Medero.

Juliana's, Windwardside, **t** 416 2988, *www. julianas-hotel.com*. Eleven private rooms, some with kitchenettes and some with their own balconies facing the Caribbean Sea. There is a dining room, Tropics Café, and a pool, all surrounded by white picket fences and gingerbread woodwork.

Ecolodge Rendez-Vous, Windwardside, **t** 416 5507, *info@ecolodge-saba.com*, *www. ecolodge-saba.com*. Built to attract naturelovers, hikers and divers, the resort has 12 solar-powered terraced cottages at the edge of the rainforest. Each cottage has a different Saban nature theme, and sleeps up to four people. Some cottages have a kitchenette; none have phone or television. You make do with birds and stars for entertainment. The restaurant serves breakfast, lunch and dinner, using vegetables from the garden. After hiking you can recharge in the new sweat lodge and hot and cold tub.

Inexpensive

Caribe Guest House, The Bottom, **t** 416 3259. Six rooms with private baths; although there is no restaurant, the kitchen is for the use of the guests.

El Momo Cottages, PO Box 519, Booby Hill, **t** 416 2265, *info@elmomo.com*, *www. elmomo.com*. The cheapest but by no means the least attractive place to stay on the island clings to a steep hillside. There is a small central area, a charming pool and a nice deck for sitting or lying in the hammock. The five rooms are very simple (it's close to camping, this), outdoor basins with views and a communal bathroom with sun-heated hot water for your shower. Breakfast and packed lunches available.

Saba's Treasure Guest House, Windwardside, t 416 2244, sabastreasure@hotmail.com. Conveniently located on Main Street, the inn offers three guest rooms, shared bathroom, use of a fully equipped kitchen and living/dining area. Its restaurant serves steaks, seafood and local dishes and pizza.

Eating Out

You are likely to eat in the hotel dining rooms. Most serve a combination of local dishes – callaloo followed by fry chicken – alongside standard American fare. Many dining rooms and restaurants also double as bars. It is worth making a reservation at the hotel dining rooms in season.

Price categories are arranged according to the price of a main course: expensive = US$15 and above; moderate = US$8–15; inexpensive = under US$8.

Moderate–Inexpensive

Brigadoon, Windwardside, t 416 2380. Outside the hotels, you'll find good seafood and creole fare here, sitting on a small terrace with fairy lights and trellis. International dishes and seafood: fresh fish daily, creole shrimp, even a breast of duck.

Saba Chinese Restaurant, Windwardside, t 416 2268. Try here if you feel like a Chinese meal, in a modern Saban house, where there is a huge selection of traditional dishes.

Guido's Pizzeria, Windwardside, t 416 2230. There is also an Italian restaurant, with pizzas and pastas, ravioli, even veal parmigiani, but also burgers.

My Kitchen, Windwardside, t 416 2539, caru@unspoiledqueen.com. Well located for hikers who want to carry a lunch with them. Or, they can relax on the open deck for lunch or dinner and enjoy the paintings by local artists on sale. The menu offers steaks, seafood, European–Caribbean fusion dishes.

Lollipops, between St John's and The Bottom, t 416 3330. Classic local cuisine: try fish or chicken with local vegetables – breadfruit, sweet potato and yam.

Kaffiehuis, The Bottom. For mid-morning refreshment you could try this coffee house.

In Two Deep, by the harbour in Fort Bay, t 416 3438. Swap a few scuba war stories at a lacquered wood bar with stained-glass-effect scenes of underwater life. Sandwiches and salads in air-conditioned comfort.

Family Deli and Bakery, The Bottom, t 416 3858. On the main road to Fort Bay, with local seafood, creole and Latin cuisine, steaks, burgers, sandwiches, salads, pizzas and vegetarian dishes. Serves breakfast too.

Rainforest Restaurant, t 416 3888, info@ecolodge-saba.com. Daily menu depends on what's available from the garden and the sea. It includes fresh salads and such favourites as coconut shrimp red curry, mahi-mahi with a creole sauce, or rib-eye steak, vegetarian dishes, home-made ice cream, and freshly baked pie.

Midway Bar & Restaurant, St John's, t 416 3271. Specializes in local cuisine, including goat, chicken, and barbecues. Enjoy a panoramic view of The Bottom, surrounding hills and the sea along with good music.

Bars and Nightlife

When Père Labat visited in 1701, he wrote: 'The settlers live as it were in a large club and frequently entertain each other.' It is pretty much the same today, except that they congregate in the bars dotted around the island, many of which are in the hotels and the restaurants. You might try out Saba's own rum-based liqueur, which is steeped in cinnamon, cloves, brown sugar and fennel seeds: quite a smooth and tasty concoction.

Hypnotic, The Bottom. Disco and snack bar.

Galaxy, at Guido's Pizzeria, Windwardside. If you want to go dancing, this place is open at the weekend.

Pop's Place, t 416 3408, Fort Bay. Rum shop.

Swinging Doors, Windwardside, t 416 2506. The owner has captured the neighbourhood watering hole formula with a well-stocked inventory – simple fare (hamburgers, hot dogs, fries), and a wealth of unsolicited opinions. It's fun and lively.

Tropics Café, Windwardside, t 416 2469, info@julianas-hotel.com. A great ocean view; regular theme nights and happy hours; movies by the pool on Fri night; live Steel Pan music on Mon, with BBQ Surf & Turf. Full cocktail menu available from the well-stocked bar.

electricity plant, the petrol station and the arm of the dock, which has stretched out into the sea since 1972. Before that, landing was a skilled technique which involved beaching the row boat on one wave and scrambling out before the next one broke over you. At the other end of The Bottom, 520 steps lead down to **Ladder Bay**, the other main port, off the new road to Well's Bay. These steps have seen everything from shoes to the kitchen sink transported up and down them in their time. You might see a charcoal-burner's pit on the way down.

The Road passes by way of St John's to **Windwardside**, Saba's second settlement, which is scattered over the mountainside at around 2,000ft and, because of this, occasionally disappears in the clouds. You'll see more white picket fences, barrel graves or cisterns, and steep alleys. In one of the many neat houses, you will find the **Saba Museum** (*open Mon–Fri 10–12 and 1–4; adm US$2*), dressed up as it was in its prime 150 years ago. It exhibits Saban memorabilia from Indian axe heads to a Victorian mahogany four-poster bed with pineapple motifs. Outside the museum is a bust of 'El Libertador', Simon Bolivar, who recruited men here in 1816 for his struggle against the Spanish authorities in South America. There is a fantastic view across to Statia from the **Lookout**, just up the hill from Windwardside.

From Windwardside, The Road switchbacks its way through terraced cultivation to the alpine village of **Hell's Gate** (a curious adaptation of the original name of Zion's Hill), where each house seems to be held in place and prevented from tumbling down the hill by the one above. The church was only constructed in 1962. From here The Road makes its 19 curves to get down to Flat Point, where the airstrip is situated.

The Dutch Leeward (ABC) Islands

Each of the ABC Islands is long and thin, poised irregularly a few miles off the coast of South America. You can see the mountains of Venezuela from them on a clear day and yet the islands are not geologically connected to the continent. They are made up of packed lava and ashes pushed up from the sea floor over the millennia. As the sea has risen and receded around them, generations of coral have left reefs on their slopes, lining their coastlines with a stone like a sort of limestone brittle, locally called *klips*.

Because they are low-lying, the Caribbean winds race over them, hardly pausing to form clouds and rain as they do elsewhere, and so these islands have none of the lushness and exuberant fertility of other West Indian islands (rainfall here is just 20 inches annually as opposed to 300-odd inches in the Windwards). Instead they are semi-arid and look something like Arizona – parched flatlands covered with about 10ft of thorny scrub and the occasional candelabra cactus standing around in an exclamatory pose. The rolling scrubland of all three islands is known in Papiamento as *cunucu*. The average temperature is 82°F, but the Passatwinden (Dutch for the trade winds) take the edge off the heat. Sucked inevitably towards the equator, they are sometimes almost strong enough to lean against standing up, particularly in the early months of the year when they are at their height. Like the Sirocco and the Föhn, they actually send people a bit dotty, so you will know what's up when drivers seem psychotic in February. Another curious effect they have is on a native tree called the divi-divi; its branches become a gnarled and knotted brush pointing southwest, resembling a woman bent at the waist in a gale, her shawl and thigh-length hair swept away on the wind.

One of the most striking things about the ABC Islands is the colours. The buildings here do not have the pastel wash of most Caribbean islands, nor the primary glare of Haiti, but a strong and distinctive colour scheme all of their own – ochre, orange and russet brown, with the occasional dark green and even vermilion. It was in 1817 that the Governor, Vice-Admiral Kikkert, whose eyes were supposedly suffering from the combination of the white-washed walls and the Caribbean sun, decreed that no building should be painted white. The orange *dakpannen* (Dutch roof tiles) and the curious colours of the walls soak up the sunshine. You will see Portakabins and mausolea imitating the colour scheme, and even the Curaçao national bird, the *trupial*, is conveniently a shade of gold and orange.

With South America so close, Latin life runs strong through the islands. You will hear salsa and merengue on the buses, and some Latin features are visible in the Dutch and African faces. Spanish is clearly audible in the language and hinted at in the islanders' dress – they often hold themselves with Latin poise. There is some competition between the islands. When Aruba took its Independence in 1986, the Curaçaoans threatened to take a shotgun to the Aruban bird on the Autonomy Monument in Willemstad. In return, the Arubians will tell you Curaçaoan waters are shark-infested. They both dismiss the Bonaireans, who apparently sing their Papiamento.

History

A succession of Indian tribes lived on the three islands before Columbus discovered the New World. For the last three hundred years, it was the Caiquetios, who came under a *cacique*, or chieftain, from the mainland. They had a peaceful enough life, fishing and trading in their *piraguas*, hollowed-out canoes, and chewing chicle leaves (from the tree that provides the substance for chewing gum), which they kept in bowls slung around their necks.

But things were to change with the arrival of the Europeans. The first came in 1498 as they explored the coast of South America – Alonso de Ojeda, one of Columbus's lieutenants, and Amerigo Vespucci, the Florentine explorer whose name was later mistakenly given to the whole continent of America. Vespucci called Curaçao the 'Land of the Giants' because the Indians were so tall. Old prints show diminutive conquistadors clad in helmets and clutching pikes staring up at vast Indians with clubs and bows and arrows.

The islands offered nothing to the Spaniards in their search for El Dorado and the Fountain of Youth, so all three were marked down as *islas inutile* (useless) and passed over. Indieros, red slave traders who dealt in Indians from the South American continent, used the islands as a base and they shipped off those who lived there to work in the goldmines in Hispaniola. Those they left behind were encouraged to chase off any other Europeans showing an interest in the island.

Papiamento

Of all the creole languages that have developed in the Caribbean, the most enigmatic is Papiamento, spoken only in the Dutch Leewards. Its heritage is thought of as almost mystical: a blend of strains from Spain, Portugal, Holland, England and France, from Africa and even from local Indian languages.

The language developed as a pidgin in the 17th century as the port of Curaçao grew. Into the mix of Dutch traders and African slaves came Portuguese-speaking Jews from Brazil and other South Americans who spoke Spanish. In the 18th century, Papiamento (the word means 'babble' and is supposedly closely related to the word 'parliament') crystallized as the language of the three islands. It took on a life of its own, with expressions to reflect local existence: '*Pampuna no sa pari calbas*', 'the pumpkin plant bears no calabash' (a Caribbean way of saying 'like father like son'), and '*Un macacu ta subi palu di sumpinja un biahe so*', 'a monkey climbs a cactus only once' ('once bitten, twice shy'). From Curaçao, the language spread to Aruba and Bonaire, where it has now developed different accents.

Unlike on other Caribbean islands, where the creoles are usually treated with a certain ambivalence, Papiamento is spoken by islanders across the social spectrum. It is used in the home, in church and in newspapers. Dutch may be the official language, but Papiamento is now also used in schools.

Listening to Papiamento can give the impression that you are hearing a stream of Spanish; words will seem to offer meaning, but then the impression will dissolve as the unlikely guttural sounds of Portuguese and pursed Dutch noises jump out at you. Papiamento is a good language to get worked up in and no doubt you will hear the islanders do just that.

In 1527 the Spaniards did make a settlement of Curaçao and bred cattle there. Jack Hawkins, the English pirate, visited the island in 1565 and described it as 'one great cattle ranch'. He saw a hundred oxen butchered in one day. The hides were stripped for curing and their tongues cut out to be eaten. The rest of the carcass was thrown into the sea.

Isla inutil or not, Curaçao proved a perfect base from which the Dutch could harry the Spaniards in the Indies in the early 17th century. The Dutch West India Company descended on it in 1634 and, in a fairly typical invasion for the time, they chased the 20 Spanish settlers around the island for three weeks until, exhausted, they surrendered. To protect the rear approaches of Curaçao, they put garrisons on Bonaire and Aruba in 1636. The Spaniards, intent on keeping other Europeans out of their empire in the New World, decided to sack Bonaire in 1642, but they arrived to find that, as usual, the Dutch had fled. They pillaged and burned the settlement for a week and then left, so before long the Dutch came back at their leisure.

In 1638 the governor of Curaçao was Peter Stuyvesant, perhaps best known now for being on the front of a cigarette packet. Later he would become the Director General of all the Dutch possessions in the New World, which he administered from Nieuw Amsterdam, now New York. He set the island on course for its great prosperity, and by the 1650s it was flourishing. Merchants flooded in and the Dutch fleets fed the trade.

The driving force behind the success of Curaçao was traffic in humans to work the burgeoning Caribbean sugar plantations. Native Americans were replaced by black Africans, and the infamous slave trade was under way. On arrival after four to six weeks on the horrific 'Middle Passage', the slaves would be rubbed down with oil and paraded through the streets singing before being auctioned. Buyers came to Curaçao from all over the Caribbean, and at its height in the 18th century about two-fifths of all slaves brought to the Americas came via Curaçao.

Meanwhile, Aruba and Bonaire were kept as farms to supply the senior colony of Curaçao. They were left unsettled, except by ranchers and a few government farmers who scratched the infertile soil together to grow maize. Aruba was particularly known for its horses, which were sold on plantations in the Caribbean and in South America. Paardenbaai (Horses' Bay), the original harbour off Oranjestad, is where they were traditionally loaded and landed. Bonaire was more of a cattle ranch. Boca Slaagbaai in the northwest is where the animals were slaughtered just before being shipped to Curaçao. Its main commodity, though, was salt (in the days before refrigeration it was essential for Dutch trading ventures between Europe and the New World). The harvesting took place in the shallow ponds in the south of the island and the industry has continued on and off until today.

Curaçao became a valuable prize and its fortunes waxed and waned on the winds blowing from Europe – wars put the island under blockade, but brought untold riches in the supply of arms and gunpowder. The British invaded twice during the Napoleonic Wars, once capturing Curaçao while everybody was out celebrating the New Year, but by 1816 the islands were back in Dutch hands.

Connections with South America were strong and the islands, particularly Aruba, just 15 miles from the mainland, were often a political refuge. 'El Libertador', Simon Bolivar, came here after the collapse of the First Republic in 1812. As late as 1927 the Curaçaoans found themselves invaded by the Venezuelan rebel leader Rafael Simon Urbina, who stormed Fort Amsterdam and stole all the weapons before departing with the Governor as a hostage. Two Curaçaoans buried in the Panteon Nacional in Caracas for their part in the Venezuelan War of Independence are Luis Brion and Manuel Carlos Piar.

Then decline began and even trade failed. Successive governors tried different schemes to keep the islands afloat financially, including the cultivation of aloe, now used in cosmetics, cochineal dye and sisal for rope. The salt industry was continued in Bonaire, and in 1825 gold was discovered in Aruba. Bonaire was so poor after the slaves were emancipated in 1863 that, in their despair, the government put it up for sale. The islanders reached their lowest point at the end of the 19th century and many went abroad to look for work, sending money back to keep their families at home. They went off to the (then) Dutch colony of Surinam or joined the streams of West Indians who dug the Panama Canal.

'The Ditch', as the canal was known, immediately reaffirmed Curaçao's status as a port, but it was the discovery of oil in Venezuela that would change Curaçao and Aruba so dramatically and secure the two islands' prosperity for the 20th century. Their Dutch heritage meant a stable political climate and their steep shores allowed the approach of ocean-going tankers which could not get to the South American coast. Crude oil was shipped in shallow-bottomed boats from Venezuela, refined and then shipped on in ocean-going tankers. Royal Dutch Shell moved into Curaçao in 1915 and built a refinery, and in 1924 the Lago Oil and Transport Company, a subsidiary of Standard Oil of New Jersey (EXXON), came to Aruba. Workers flooded into the islands to join the boom, from the Dutch Windwards and Surinam and from the English colonies. The populations rocketed, each multiplying by five times. The refineries directly employed as much as 15% of the population of both islands.

The islanders talk in apocalyptic terms about 'Automation', which slashed the workforce in the 1950s and 60s. The ageing plants were dealt another blow in the early 1980s when OPEC agreements forced up the price of crude oil and the industry foundered. The two giant oil companies have sold up and moved out, and now the refineries work at massively reduced capacity. The islands depend now mainly on tourism.

Curaçao

Traditionally Curaçao has always been the heart of Dutch influence in the Caribbean, the powerhouse of their trading ventures and the administrative centre of the Dutch Caribbean. Even its name is fancifully thought to come from the Portuguese word for heart, *corazon*.

Curaçao is oddly shaped, a bit like a rebellious bow tie, and, at 38 miles by 9, it is the largest of the Netherlands Antilles. It is hardly an attractive island. Like its neighbours it is low and scrubby, covered in *cunucu*, with cacti that strike theatrical poses. Its shores are cut with inlets that make perfect harbours.

With 145,000 islanders, Curaçao is heavily populated. Centuries of business as a trading port have brought racial strains from all over the world, giving it a very mixed population. Like Aruba, it experienced boom years in the 20th century when Shell built a vast refinery and bunkering station on the island. The money poured in and the population rocketed, from 33,000 in 1915 to 145,000 in 1975. Jokers claimed that the Curaçaoans liked to change their clothes twice a day and their car every three months in those days, but it all changed when 'Automation' cut the refinery workforce from 18,500 to 4,000.

In the early 1980s things got even worse with the oil crash and the world economic recession. The price of oil plummeted and sales decreased, and eventually Shell sold the refinery and left in 1985. The volume of trade passing through the port (still one of the largest in the world) has rallied after the problems in Panama, as did offshore finance, another important sector. The government of Curaçao is trying to increase tourism and this is now the island's second industry.

Curaçao's economy may be depressed, but that does not mean that the island itself is, for that would be to underestimate the Curaçaoans. A few may have left the island to find a better life elsewhere, but most have an irrepressible Caribbean spirit and a conviction that the future will see them right.

For details on Curaçao's history, *see* 'Dutch Leeward History', pp.439–41.

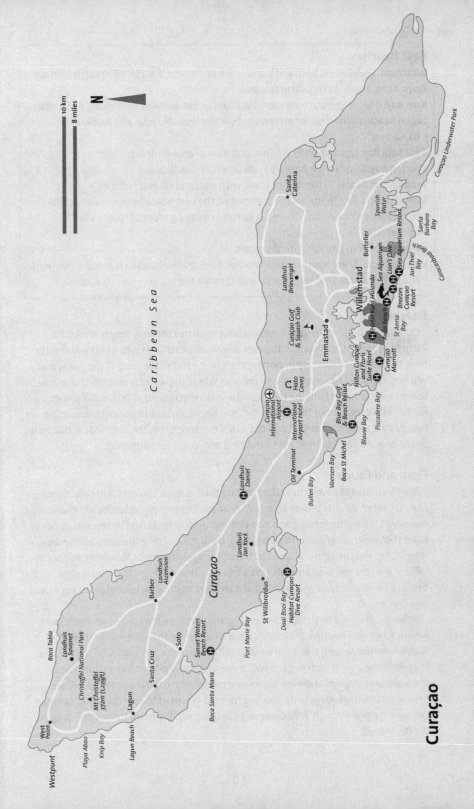

Best Beaches

Westpunt: The water is fresh and translucent. In the heat, you can retire to the clifftops.

Playa Abao: The water is jade in colour.

Knip Bay: A beach popular with the Curaçaoans at the weekend, with changing facilities.

Lagun Beach: With a few fishermen's huts, a tiny secluded cove just below the Bahia Inn.

Daai Booi Bay: Down from St Willibrordus, a small cove enclosed in cliffs.

Vaersen Bay: Close to the Bullen Bay oil terminal – secluded.

Seaquarium Beach: To the east of town, with watersports and facilities.

Santa Barbara Bay: To the east of Willemstad, the best beach, very popular with the Curaçaoans at weekends. There is a bar and changing rooms. There is a fee for car parking.

Caracasbaai: Also popular with the locals.

Klein Curaçao: There are also some beaches here, an uninhabited outcrop off the east end of the island. Trips can be arranged through the big watersports shops.

Beaches

Curaçao's coastline does not have any long stretches of sandy beach like Aruba. Rather the coast is scalloped with coves and small beaches. Hotels like the Marriott have skirted the problem by importing their own sand. In the west of the island you will find secluded sun traps cut into the *klips* where the water is warm and shallow. Some beaches have changing rooms and a small shop selling drinks, but if you go farther afield remember to take a picnic. You might also take a parasol because the beaches are usually shadeless and the sun is extremely hot. The north coast, battered by the onward swell of the Caribbean Sea, is too rough for swimming.

Flora and Fauna

The three islands have similar flora among their outsize boulders and sand dunes. The blanket of scrub is broken by prickly pear and organ pipe cactus, locally known as *kadushi* (it is used for fencing and also ends up in soup here), and by several species of plant that were cultivated on a commercial basis, for instance the spiky and fleshy-leaved aloe and the agave, also called the century plant, with its flowering 30ft stem.

There are very few land animals, just a few lizards and the iguana, who is shy because he also ends up in a traditional dish. You might be lucky enough to see a deer on Curaçao.

However, there is a large variety of birds, partly because they stray over from South America, but also because the islands are a stopover for the winter migration from North America. Among the usual bananaquits (which you will no doubt see because they will have a go at your sugar bowl), there are yellow orioles, hawks and doves, the odd hummingbird and even burrowing owls. In the coastal ponds you will see herons and other wading birds trawling for food. A tour of the natural life of Curaçao can be arranged through **Wild Curaçao**, t 561 0027, and **Dornasol Tours**, t 868 2735, *dorli@cura.net*.

Getting There

Curaçao t (599 9–)

Curaçao has extremely good air connections, from Europe, the USA, South America and points around the Caribbean, to its airport at Hato, 7 miles (11km) north of Willemstad. An airport tax of US$20 is payable upon leaving Curaçao, NAFl 10 to the Dutch Caribbean.

By Air

From Europe

There are services from Amsterdam on the Dutch airline KLM, **t** 465 2747. An alternative is to travel via Miami (*see* below).

From North America

American Airlines, **t** 869 5707, fly a daily service direct from Miami. They also fly to their hub in San Juan, Puerto Rico, which is served on American Eagle.

From Latin America

Curaçao is well connected to the South American mainland. There are regular services from Caracas, Bogotà and Baranquilla. There are also links with Paramaribo in Surinam and Georgetown, Guyana.

From Other Caribbean Islands

There are numerous flights linking Curaçao with Aruba and Bonaire on BonaireExpress; there are more services at weekends, but these tend to be the most heavily booked. The Dutch Windwards are served by twice-daily flights from Sint Maarten. For the rest of the Caribbean, the options are Port of Spain in Trinidad (twice weekly), Montego Bay in Jamaica (four a week), and Santo Domingo in the Dominican Republic (four a week).

Getting Around

By Bus

There is a **public bus** system in Curaçao and the important routes are run roughly every half an hour to an hour. NAFl 1.50 will get you around town and NAFl 2.50 will take you up to Westpunt, as far as you can go. Use the bus stops. There are two terminals in Willemstad, one serving the east end of the island and the harbour area, the other serving the hotel area, the airport and the west. Private **minibuses** also run to any destination on the island.

You will also see **share taxis**, like South American *colectivos*, running the town routes. Again, it is best to wait at a bus stop, but sometimes they will stop if you flag them down. NAFl 1.50 for a ride (US90c).

By Taxi

Taxis are not metered so it is worth fixing the price before setting out. They can be found at any of the hotels and through the main despatch office, **t** 869 0752. Some sample prices are: Punda to the airport – US$20, to Hilton Curaçao Piscadera area – US$18, to Underwater Park area – US$18; airport to Otrobanda – US$20, to Hilton Curaçao – US$18.

By Guided Tour

The going rate for an island tour by **taxi** is about US$30 per hour. For **bus tours** try:
Casper Tours, t 465 3010.
Taber Tours, t 737 6637, *tabertours@ curacao.com, www.curacao.com/tabertours*.

A walking tour of Willemstad can be arranged through:
Island Style Tours, t 747 7777, *www.tourism-curacao.com*.
Old City Tours, t 461 3554, *ibmcur@ibm.net*.

Willemstad

Willemstad has been a trading port for centuries. **Punda** at the harbour mouth, a Dutch port transported to the tropics, dates from the 18th century, and in the recesses of the harbour is the Schottegat, Punda's 21st-century equivalent, all factories and container wharves. Willemstad is still one of the busiest harbours in the world – so many ships use the channel that the hotel at the harbour entrance has had to take out marine insurance just in case.

Car Hire

Plenty of rental cars are available. Foreign and international licences are valid, and prices start at around US$35 per day. Driving is on the right.

Avis, t 868 1163, *avis@curacao.com*, *www.curacao.com/avis*.

Budget Rent-A-Car, t 868 3466, *budgetna@cura.net*, *www.curacao-budgetcar.com*.

National, t 869 4433, *natcur@cura.net*, *www.nationalcuracao.com*.

Star Rent-A-Car, t 462 7444, *reservation@star-curacao.com*, *www.star-curacao.com*.

Thrifty Car Rental, t 461 3089, *thriftycuracao@morenogroup.com*, *www.thrifty.com*.

Tourist Information

Abroad

The official website devoted to Curaçao is at *www.curacao-tourism.com*, but you can also find information at *www.curacao.com*. Gay travellers can try *www.gaycuracao.com*.

Netherlands: Curaçao Tourist Bureau Europe, Vasteland 82–4, 3011 BP Rotterdam, **t** 414 2639, *info@ctbe.nl*.

USA: 7951 SW 6th St, 216, Plantation, FL 33324, **t** 800 328 7222, *jbgrossman@aol.com*.

In Curaçao

The Tourism Bureau issues a yellow pamphlet called *Curaçao Holiday*. Tourist Office, 19 Pietermaai, PO Box 3266 Willemstad, **t** 434 8200, *info@ctdb.net*. Information desk, airport.

Emergencies

In a **medical** emergency, there is a 24-hour room at St Elizabeth's Hospital, **t** 462 4900. The **police** can be reached on **t** 114.

Money and Banks

The currency of Curaçao is the Netherlands Antilles florin or guilder (NAFl), which is fixed to the US dollar at a rate of US$1 = NAFl1.78. However, the US greenback is widely accepted all over the island. Major credit cards are accepted in all the hotels and any but the most offbeat restaurants and guest houses.

Banks are open Mon–Fri 8.30–noon and 1.30–3.30.

Telephone Code

The IDD code to call Curaçao is **t** 599 9, followed by a seven-figure island number. On the island just dial the seven digits.

Festivals

January–February *Carnival*. The big event of the Curaçaoan calendar. Weekends see *tumba* street parades and the main festivities are held in the last few days in the run-up to Lent, including more costume masquerades, all-night jump-ups and the burning of Rey Momo, the spirit of carnival.

March *Blue Marlin Tournament*.

May *Curaçao Sailing Regatta*. Based at Zanzibar on Jan Theil Bay.
Jazz Festival

September *Curaçao Salsa Festival*.

Shopping

Hours are 8–12 and 2–6. Just as they did 200 years ago, traders will stay open longer if a large ship has come into town. Most shops will close for a couple of hours at lunch.

If you are looking to score a few duty-free purchases, then Curaçao is a good bet because it has some of the Caribbean's best shops –

The **Handelskade**, overlooking St Anna Bay, is one of the Caribbean's most impressive and unlikely sights – an apparition of Amsterdam in the Caribbean sun, a line of tall pastel-coloured buildings with curly gables and orange roof tiles. Two hundred years ago, the waterfront at Punda (which takes its name from the point on which it sits) buzzed with ocean-going ships, offloading their cargoes for storage in these warehouses. Walled against a land attack and built unusually tall because of the confined space, Punda's narrow alleys gathered around Fort Amsterdam at the beginning of the 18th century, as the big Dutch trading houses sent their agents to Curaçao.

some visits may even be billed as a 'shopping experience'. A large proportion of the wares are unfortunately mass-produced tourist rubbish (twee clogs and windmills made in Dutch Delft Blue china), but, because Curaçao is such a massive trading port, it is surprising what can turn up. US residents returning home can take in up to $600 of duty free goods.

Watersports

Watersports centre around the seafront hotels. Otherwise try:
Seaquarium Beach, t 461 7343.

Day Sails

Bounty, t 560 1887, *www.bounty adventures.com*.
Insulinde, t 560 1340. Stops at the Tugboat and Spanish water for snorkelling.
Sail Curaçao, t 767 6003. Has sailing yachts.
Mermaid Boat Trips, t 560 1530, *www. mermaidboattrips.com*. Sails three times weekly with up to 60 people to Klein Curaçao for the day.

Deep-sea Fishing

The Curaçao Yacht Club, Brakkeput Ariba, t 767 4627, *www.caribseek.com/yachtclub*, arranges the 'Blue Marlin Tournament', a yearly event in early March, and they will also fix up deep-sea fishing trips. Also try:
Let's Fish, Caracasbayweg 407N, t 561 1812, *captain@letsfish.net, www.letsfish.net*.
Miss Ann Boat, Jan Sofat 232-A, t 767 1579, *missannboattrips@interneeds.net, www. missannboattrips.com*. Fishing trips for wahoo, tuna, marlin, sailfish and dorado.
Pro Marine Yacht, *jarojaro@cura.net*. Deep-sea fishing expert with seven boats.

Scuba Diving

Curaçao's underwater world is excellent, with 12 miles of reef on the southeastern shore of the island set aside as the protected Curaçao Underwater Park. Visibility is often up to 100ft. Wreck dives include the SS *Oranje Nassau* and the 'car wreck' – an artificial reef made from old cars dating back to the 1940s.
All West Diving, Westpunt, t 864 0102.
Atlantis Diving, 6 Drielstraat, Willemstad, t 465 8288, *diving@cura.net*.
Diving School Wederfoort, St Michielweg, t 888 4414.
Duke's Diving, Caracas Bay, t 747 0444.
Ocean Encounters, Lion's Dive Hotel, t 461 8131, *info@lionsdive.com, www.lionsdive.com*.
Safe Diving, Lagun Beach, t 864 1652.
Scuba Do, Jan Thiel Beach, t 767 9300.
Tucan Diving, Kontiki Beach, t 465 3796, *tucan diving@cura.net*.

Snorkelling

You will find excellent corals within a breath of the surface in many of the bays along the south coast.

In the Underwater Park, a snorkelling trail has been created, between the Seaquarium and Jan Thiel Bay, but you must go by boat to reach it. Most dive operators and beachfront hotels can provide snorkelling gear.
The Sea Aquarium, t 461 6666, *www.cuaracao-sea-aquarium.com*. Now has an underwater observatory and sea lion section.

Other Sports

Golf

Curaçao Golf and Squash Club, Emmastad behind the harbour, t 737 3590. Nine-hole golf course with unusual sand greens.

Willemstad's mercantile tradition is continued today and picturesquely precious Punda is still bulging with goods on sale, now displayed in air-conditioned comfort for the benefit of the less hardy seagoers who arrive by cruise ship rather than by clipper.

Another amusing and surprising feature of Punda is the **Koningin Emmabrug** (the Queen Emma Bridge), which links it to Otrobanda. It stands on 15 or so pontoons, which buck and sway with the swell of the sea, making it impossible to walk in a straight line (people jerk in unison as they cross, like a crowd of choreographed drunkards).

The first pontoon bridge was erected in 1888 by Leonard B. Smith, and was free to people without shoes. It is free to everybody today and so there is no need to take off

Blue Bay Curaçao Golf and Beach Resort, Landhuis Blauw, t 868 1755, *www.bluebay golf.com*. An 18-hole championship course.

Hiking

Hiking trails run throughout the 4,500-acre Christoffel National Park, and the two-mile Rif Recreation Area has a surfaced track for jogging. See *www.hikingcuracao.com*.

Horse-riding

For a day out riding in the *cunucu*, contact: **Rancho Alfin**, Christoffel National Park, t 864 0535.
Rancho Ashari, Groot Piscadera, t 869 0315.
Rancho Allegre, Gr. St Michiel, t 868 1181.

Windsurfing and Kayaking

Windsurfing and kayaking are as popular here as in Aruba and Bonaire, particularly among the Curacaoans. For novices, there are facilities at beachside resorts, but for advanced and professional windsurfers, it's the north coast where the wind pounds the rocky coast. For kayaking, it's Spanish Waters.

Where to Stay

Curaçao t (599 9–)

Curaçao has an abundance of new hotels in all price ranges. There are some major resort complexes set on the coastline, with international standards, but you will also find smaller, lower-key spots inland. Curaçao gets pretty hot in summer and so it is worth paying extra for a fan or air-conditioning. There are many apartments for hire, starting at about US$200 for a week's rent; contact the Tourist Board. There is a 5% government tax on all rooms and most hotels charge 12% for service.

Expensive

Avila Beach Hotel, Penstraat, Willemstad, t 461 4377, *info@avilahotel.com*, *www.avila hotel.com*. Still the most charming hotel in Curaçao. It has 90 rooms in all, some in a plush block, others in the original antique building (the British Governor's residence in 1812), but it retains its rarefied and sophisticated air. A mixed crowd, some younger and some seasoned travellers, congregates on the two beaches and at bar.
Breezes Curaçao and Casino, east of Willemstad, t 736 7888, *sales@breezes curacao.net*, *www.breezescuracao.com*. Perhaps the most sympathetic of Curaçao's large and humming all-inclusive hotels. This family-oriented resort is located on the beach in front of the National Underwater Park. It has a wide range of sports, including a 5-star PADI Peter Hughes Dive Centre. There are three restaurants, five bars, three pools and a children's playground.
Curaçao Marriott Beach Resort, Piscadera Bay, t 736 8800, *reservations@marriottcuracao. com*, *www.marriotthotels.com*. The 247-room resort is one of Curaçao's most attractive hotels, designed in the spirit of the island's historic architecture. Set on the beach, it has three outstanding restaurants, a large pool in a tropical setting, tennis courts, dive facilities and watersports. There is a casino, too, and a children's programme.
Floris Suite Hotel, Piscadera Bay z/n, t 462 6111, 800 781 1011, *info@florissuitehotel.com*, *www.florissuitehotel.com*. This new all-suite hotel has many echoes of Curaçao's past in its design. The facilities include a pool, beach bar, two restaurant, floodlit tennis court, fitness room, diving and snorkelling.
Hilton Curacao, J.F. Kennedy Blvd, Piscadera Bay, t 462 5000, *reservations.curacao@*

your shoes as the toll-dodgers used to. But you may arrive at the shore to find that it has disappeared (there is an engine attached to the end pontoon). This is because the bridge has to open to let in the ships arriving in Willemstad harbour. While the Queen Emma Bridge is closed, a ferry (free to people with or without shoes) makes the crossing from about halfway down the Handelskade. It announces its departure with a siren.

On Sha Caprileskade, round the corner from the ferry terminal, is the **floating market**, where a line of Venezuelan sloops berth against the quay, shaded by vast awnings attached to their masts. Snapper and flying fish, stacks of melon and finger rolls of miniature bananas are piled on monumental slab tables on the wharf. The

hilton.com, www.hiltoncaribbean.com. Just 10mins from the airport, with restaurants, bars, casino, pool, tennis court, dive and watersports centre, miniature golf, spa and fitness centre.

Hotel Kurá Hulanda, Langestraat 8, t 434 7700, reservations@kurahulanda.com, www. kurahulanda.com. This hotel is the centre-piece of Dutch millionaire Jacob Gelt Dekker's Project Kura Hulanda, which took 65 historic buildings in Otrabanda and meticulously restored them to house his charming hotel, a world-class African museum, four restaurants, two pools, a spa and fitness centre, and conference space.

Moderate

Habitat Dive Resort Curaçao, Rif St Marie-Willibrordus, PO Box 304, t 864 8800, curacao@habitat-diveresort.com, www. habitatdiveresort.com. Sister to the famous Captain Don's Habitat in Bonaire. Located on the coast 30mins west of Willemstad. There is a beach, restaurant, pool and extensive dive facilities with unlimited shore diving. Rooms are set in colourful chalets with air-con, kitchenettes and balconies.

Hotel Holland, 524 F. D. Rooseveltweg, t 868 8044, www.hotelholland.com. Near the airport, with 40 very comfortable rooms and a dive shop. A bit isolated from town, but a friendly hotel with a casino.

Lion's Dive Hotel and Marina, just above the Seaquarium, t 461 8100, info@lionsdive.com, www.lionsdive.com. A statement in pastel pink and lime green, bananas, bougainvillea and balconies. Rooms are quite small, but comfortable. The hotel is home to Rumours, one of Curaçao's best bars, and it attracts a young and lively crowd, who dive by day and booze by night.

Sunset Waters Beach Resort, on the coast west of Willemstad, t 864 1233, US t 1 866 5 SUNSET, info@sunsetwaters.com, www. sunsetwaters.com. A smaller hotel with just 35 rooms. The rooms are modern and air-conditioned with cable television and they stand on the hillside above the sea, relaxed and isolated from the bustle of the town hotels. Watersports and scuba. All inclusive.

Inexpensive

Landhuis Daniel, on the road to West Point, t 864 8400. A small hotel set in an old country house. Just 10 rooms, with pool and watersports, small and friendly.

Jaanchie's Apartments, Westpunt, t 864 0126. Within easy reach of the island's best beaches. It is small and has a popular open-air restaurant which will serve you island delicacies like cactus soup and iguana stew. The 17 or so rooms are simple, but the asking price is good and you can bargain from there.

Eating Out

There are a surprising number of good restaurants in Curaçao, both in regard to their cuisine and atmosphere. With its tangled heritage, the island has food from all over the world. Most restaurants add a service charge of 10% to their bills. **Price categories** are arranged according to the charge for a main dish: expensive = US$18 and above; moderate = US$10–18; inexpensive = US$10 and below.

Expensive

Larousse, Penstraat 5, Willemstad, t 465 5418, larousse@interneeds.net. Set in a lovely listed Curacaoan house that dates from 1742. With just nine tables (reservations are essential), it has an intimate and elegant ambience.

produce is mostly grown in Venezuela and is shipped to Curaçao overnight in time for the early morning market. The supply seems never-ending and if you ask for something not on display, the trader will rootle around on board ship and find it. Prices are very good here, though bargaining may secure you an extra tangerine or two.

The original centre of the town is **Fort Amsterdam**, built by the Dutch immediately after they arrived in 1634. It is now the seat of the Government of the Netherlands Antilles and also houses the Governor's Residence. There is a small **museum** (adm) of religious artefacts in Fort Church, which still has a British cannonball buried in its outside wall from an attack in 1804.

The cuisine is classical French – *les asperges, les viandes, les poissons*. An excellent evening out.

Wine Cellar, Concordiastraat, Willemstad, **t** 461 2178, *nicocornelisse@yahoo.com*, *www.wine cellar.an*. Opposite the cathedral, a rarified and elegant atmosphere with just 10 tables, white linen on mock-antique furniture. The cuisine is contemporary French and international, and they are renowned for their lobster. Excellent wine list.

Fort Nassau, **t** 461 3086, *fortnassau@curacao. com*, *www.curacao.com/fortnassau*. An excellent setting and nice cuisine to go with it. You take your cocktails on the battery, where there is a cannon's-eye view of Willemstad, and then move through for New World cuisine – seared shrimp in pepper vodka or the day's catch in tropical fruit chutney on a bed of beans and pancake – surrounded by the old battlements.

Le Clochard, in the Riffort at the mouth of the St Anna Bay, **t** 462 5666, *clochard@ attglobal.net*, *www.bistroleclochard.an*. Cocktails are accompanied by the hull of an occasional passing freighter. French and Swiss cuisine by candlelight in the fort's cavernous jail and the old barrel-vaulted cistern – shrimp Provençal and *rösti* in white wine and mushrooms. Take a constitutional on the battlements. *Closed Sun.*

Fort Waakzamhied, **t** 462 1044. Has a cracking position, around the battlements of another fort, where you sit on a breezy terrace and watch the lights of Otrobanda. All meals are grilled on the barbecue and accompanied by salads and chips. A nice informal atmosphere and often a crowd of Curaçaoans.

Avalon, Caracasbaaiweg 8 Salina, **t** 465 6375. With its edgy, Art Deco design, this is Curaçao's place of the moment. The relaxed, lounge-like atmosphere draws locals and tourists with its imaginative menu and speciality drinks. Signature dishes include crispy red devil snapper, adobo-crusted hanger steak and vegetarian dishes, including Thai red curry bowl and grilled marinated Portobello steak. There's a martini menu and long wine list, Cuban cigars and cognacs.

Angelica's Kitchen, Hoogstraat 49, **t** 562 3699, *www.angelicas-kitchen.com*. Diners here can play both chef and gourmand. A minimum of 10 participants dress up as chefs and read over the recipe that will serve as dinner. The dishes are mostly based on French or Italian cuisine with local influences, but can include Caribbean fare. Trained chef Angelique Schoop created her Kitchen in her century-old landmark childhood home, which she restored. Reservations are necessary.

Astrolab Observatory Restaurant, Langestraat 8, Willemstad, **t** 434 7700, *hotel@kura hulanda.com*, *www.kurahulanda.com*. On the grounds of the Hotel Kurá Hulanda complex, adjacent to the garden, the restaurant is named for the world-class collection of scientific instruments on display nearby. It serves contemporary cuisine indoors and out; specialities include fresh fish, lobster and beef dishes. Good wine cellar.

Moderate

Zambezi, at the Ostrich Farm, Groot St Joris West z/n, **t** 747 2777, *malan@cura.net*. A most unusual restaurant where most dishes are based on the locally produced ostrich meat of the farm. A large selection of South African wines, brandy and Zambezi beer. Enjoy the nightly campfire.

Golden Star, 2 Socratesstraat, Willemstad, **t** 465 4795. A classic West Indian restaurant,

On Columbusstraat is the **Mikve Israel Synagogue**, the oldest in the Americas. Modelled on the synagogue in Amsterdam, it was built in 1732 by the large community of Jews that had taken refuge in Curaçao a century earlier. The floor around the mahogany altar is sprinkled with white sand in memory of the journey through the desert and two of the four chandeliers date from 1707 and 1709. In the courtyard is the **Jewish Historical Museum** (*open Mon–Fri 9–11.45 and 2.30–5; adm*), where a 250-year-old *mikvah* (a ceremonial bath) and circumcision instruments are on display. The **Beth Haim Cemetery** (House of the Living), also the oldest in the Americas, dates from 1659 and is on the inner harbour, just outside Willemstad to the northwest.

air-conditioned with plastic tablecloths, fake roses and excellent local food. Try *carni stoba* (meat stew) or *stoba de carco* (conch and vegetable in a strong creole sauce).

Playa Forti, Westpunt. You might also try here, on the clifftops at the western tip of the island, with a cracking sunset view.

Inexpensive

If you are still feeling peckish after a night out on the town, you can grab a snack at a *truck di pan* (literally a 'bread truck'), found all over the island. You choose between a *pan galina* (chicken), *pan steak* or *porchop*, hacked in half, doused in hot pepper sauce and served up in a bread roll.

Marshe, just next to the circular market in Punda. One of the best places to eat on the island, a lively local spot for lunch Curaçao-style. You eat at communal slabtop tables alongside bus drivers and local business people, while the food is cooked over charcoal stoves around the edge of the building. Exotic *sopi* (soups) of local fish and traditional *juwana* (iguana) are available and to follow you can try a good Caribbean 'rice and peas' dish or another Curaçaoan favourite like *stoba*, meat stew made with papaya, or *komkomber* (cucumber) or even *snijboonchi* (if you dare). *Lunch Mon–Fri.*

Choices Mongolian Grill, Van Eyck van Voorthuyzenweg 5, t 462 8082, *sawasdee@curinfo.an*. Your choice of chicken, beef, pork, fresh seafood, vegetables and sauces are weighed and given to a chef to grill and serve on a sizzling hot shield. A meal fit for Genghis Khan himself.

Kurá Hulanda Museum Restaurant, Langestraat 8, Otrobanda, t 434 77 00, *hotel@kurahulanda.com*, *www.kurahulanda. com*. An open-air restaurant at the entrance to the anthropological Kurá Hulanda Museum, serving light lunches and full dinners in a unique historical setting.

TuTu Tango, Plasa Mundo Merced, Punda (Behind The Movies), t 465 4633, *www. tutu-tango.com*. A hip and happening spot with an Indonesian buffet on Wed and Sat. Famous appetizers, known locally as 'tutu's', are offered all week.

Bars and Nightlife

Most of the regular nightclubs are in the area of the Lindberghweg, and there are 10 casinos in Curaçao, all of them located within the hotels (most open from 2pm until 5am).

Nemo, at the Lion's Dive Hotel. Set on a terrace above the sea, a very popular bar.

Banana's, Schottegatweg Oost 193. Serves food early, with a young, hip crowd hanging out and dancing until late at night.

Zen, Salinja 124. A laidback lounge that fits its name perfectly.

Fort Waakzamheid, Otrobanda. For a cocktail and a view try their terrace.

Playa Canoa, a fishing bay on the north coast. Another good weekend venue, popular with the locals, where they dance on Sunday afternoons.

Beach Bars

K-Oz, Salinja 124. Located above Zen, it offers an outdoor patio leading into a hip club with a retro feel. Red walls, a DJ booth and a large dance floor are inside with a bar in the back serving up red hot cocktails.

Wet & Wild Beach Club, Sea Aquarium Beach Bapor Kibra, t 561 2477. The dancefloor meets the sand at this pumping night spot. Loud beats and cold drinks make it a popular local hangout.

As Punda expanded (the town walls were demolished in 1861), the wealthy Curaçaoan traders built their Dutch colonial town houses away from the trading centre, in areas like Scharloo and Pietermaai along the coast. The **Bolivar Museum** (*open Mon–Fri irregular hours*), on Penstraat, has antiques and some memorabilia from the South American Wars of Independence led by Bolivar in the early part of the 19th century; it is set in an odd octagonal building, where his family took refuge in one of his two stays in exile on the island.

The traders also crossed over St Anna Bay to **Otrobanda** (literally 'the other side'). The area was rundown and ramshackle until renovations over the last decade saved

Curaçao Liqueur

On a still day, the tangy smell of orange peel drying in the sun used to hang on the Curaçao air. It was the skins of the laraha orange, which were being made into Senior Curaçao of Curaçao liqueur, original namesake of the more famous Bols. These green Valencia oranges, which grow normally elsewhere, grow small and bitter in the barren earth of Curaçao (the tree features on the national coat of arms) and you can see the distilling process at the **Curaçao Liqueur Distillery** (*t 461 3526; open Mon–Fri 8–noon and 1–5; adm free; samples on offer, with plenty of opportunity to buy*) in the hall of the Landhuis Chobolobo on the outskirts of Willemstad. It is a small operation, just four or five vats. Distinctive round bottles with slim tall necks are corked and labelled by hand. The original orange liqueur is best, but there are three other flavours on offer. If you catch a whiff of something pungently sweet, then it is Curaçao's current smell, the refining crude, that hangs on the air around the oil refinery.

much of its 18th-century Dutch Rococo architecture. Project Kurá Hulanda was undertaken by Dutch millionaire Jacob Gelt Dekker, who restored 65 rundown 18th- and 19th-century buildings in Otrabanda. The buildings now house, among other things, a charming hotel and a world-class African anthropological museum.

A classic Curaçaoan building with raised balconies and twin pointed roofs, the old sailors' hospital on Van Leeuwenhoekstraat has been converted into the **Curaçao Museum** (*open Mon–Fri 9–noon and 2–5, Sun 10–4; adm*). Inside there are artefacts from the chicle-chewing Caiquetios, early Delft Blue china, a merchant's tablet advertising a tobacco shop, a revolving exhibition of island painters and a typical Curaçaoan kitchen, painted with red and white spots (supposedly it makes flies dizzy, but more likely it is superstition).

On the sea as you leave Otrobanda is the Curaçao **desalination plant**, which produces around 1.6 billion gallons of water from seawater annually. Time was when the oil tankers used to bring water as ballast and the Curaçaoans complained that it tasted of oil, but now the desalinated water is pure enough to brew Curaçao's Amstel beer. On the waterfront here, leading past the fishing huts, the Curaçaoans take the air in the early evening.

Fort Nassau, on the hill behind Punda, is no longer a fort, but still has the commanding view over the harbour and its approaches for which it was originally built. Behind, it looks over **Emmastad**, the most modern extension of the capital, where you will find the container wharves and dry docks. Around the edge are the suburbs, with supermarkets, cinemas and fast-food joints, where the majority of Curaçao's 145,000 population live, with neat fenced gardens, a satellite dish and two cars. The fort also has one of the best views of the **refinery** and, on a still day, you will recognize the pungent smell that hangs on the water (a cross between pitch and petrol). This monolithic assembly of silver chimneys and silos was once the largest refinery in the world, but has been rundown since Shell sold the plant to the Curaçaoan Government in 1985. Recently it has been reactivated by Isla NV, owned by Petroleos de Venezuela.

On Fokker Weg, you will see the futuristic **Autonomy Monument**, a sculpture of six birds commemorating the self-determination of the Netherlands Antilles in 1954. Aruba's bird remains despite its political separation in 'status aparte' in 1986 (*see* p.466). And on Rijkseenheid Bd is the **Amstel Brewery**, the only one in the world that uses distilled seawater. Amstel, whose familiar red and white bottle tops you will see all over the Caribbean, started to brew under licence here in 1960 and today they produce 3 million gallons of lager annually. In a walk among the copper vats you will see the malt, germinated barley sent out from Holland, mixed with Curaçao water, fermented to make 'wort', and matured. You can follow this with a visit to the bar.

Around the Island

Curaçao's 15ft-high *cunucu* is dotted occasionally with the orange roofs and white gables of the *landhuizen*, Dutch colonial plantation houses. Driving through the scrub, you will also see the original slave houses, with angled walls and shaggy maize-thatch roofs surrounded by cactus fences. Unlike other islands, where many slaves moved to the towns after emancipation, many more remained on the land in Curaçao, scratching a living from the earth. Hummingbirds and mockingbirds live in the scrub and along the northern coast you might be lucky enough to see an osprey.

A number of the *landhuizen* can be visited. Perhaps the best is the **Landhuis Brievengat** (*t 767 8344; open Mon–Fri 9–noon and 3–5; adm*), once an aloe and cochineal plantation that has been restored to show life in the early 18th century when the house was built. Brievengat is just north of Willemstad, close to the sports stadium. Every Wednesday and Friday evening there is a public dance (*admission NAFl10*) and one Sunday each month there is a day jamboree with music and folk dancing.

Other *landhuizen* worth visiting include **Jan Kock** (*t 884 8087; irregular opening times, telephone beforehand*), and **Ascension**, restored and still used by the Dutch Navy (*open first Sunday of each month from 10am onwards*). The 17th-century **Chobolobo Landhuis** on the outskirts of Willemstad is the home of the Curaçao Liqueur Distillery, well worth a visit (*see* 'Curaçao Liqueur', opposite).

Driving west from Otrobanda, the coast road passes the main hotel strip and Bullenbaai oil terminal, where the storage tanks rise and fall as they are filled or emptied into the ocean-going tankers. On the road to the airport you will find the **Hato Caves** (*open daily 10–5, tours on the hour; adm*), where there are hourly tours that guide you through the geology of the island and explain the life and religion of the Indians, whose petroglyphs you will see on the rock faces. Near Ascension you will find the **Country House Museum** (*open daily 9–4; adm*), a mud-and-thatch house of the type built by the former slaves when they were freed in the 19th century.

At the northwestern tip of the island is the **Christoffel National Park**, 4,500 acres of nature reserve on the slopes of Curaçao's highest hill, Mt Christoffel (1,239ft). The park is laced with trails, for walkers and for vehicles, clearly marked and with displays of the semi-arid flora of the Dutch Leeward Islands, including the divi-divi and agave. Iguanas, like Neolithic lizards, scuttle about and you might even see a Curaçao deer, a flitting orange troupial or an inquisitive-looking barn owl with a heart-shaped face peering at you. Some paths lead to the summit of Mt Christoffel, from where it is possible to see the mountains of Venezuela on a clear day. The entrance to the park is at the Savonet Landhuis (*itself not open to the public*), where there is a **museum** (*t 464 0363; open Mon–Sat 8–4, Sun 6–3; adm*) of Curaçaoan geology and natural history, with exhibits of Caiquetio Indian life.

Passing **Boca Tabla**, a cave which reverberates and echoes each time a wave crashes into the cave mouth, the road leads to the sedate village of West Point and the *kadushi* cliffs at the western tip of the island.

East of Willemstad is the **Curaçao Seaquarium** (*open Sun–Thurs 10–10, Fri and Sat 10am–midnight; adm*), where you can spy the underwater world indigenous to Curaçao – anything from an anemone or a panting shark with a beady eye to corals like a hundred pink molar teeth. You can take a glass-bottom boat out to the reef from the Seaquarium or don scuba gear and dive with sea lions. In the shop you might pick up a Dutch onion skin or a continental squat (types of bottle).

In the northeast of Curaçao is an **Ostrich Farm** (*t 747 2777, www.ostrichfarm.net*), one of the largest ostrich farms outside Africa, with visitor centre and restaurant.

Bonaire

The underwater life of Bonaire is supreme. Miles of spectacular corals line its shores and the warm water flits with tropical fish – flashes of pastel and fluorescent colours amid the wonderful shapes of the seascape. It is a Diver's Paradise. So says every car number plate on the island, anyway. Shameless PR perhaps, but the island has managed its reefs well and it has a justified reputation as one of the world's top diving destinations. It is also a quiet but trusty Caribbean escape.

Bonaire is the second largest of the Netherlands Antilles (a crooked 24 miles long by 5) and it lies 30 miles east of Curaçao, 40 miles from South America. It is mostly low and parched scrubland, with salt ponds in the south and rolling land that rises to the 784ft peak of Mt Brandaris in the northwest. The name Bonaire is supposedly derived from the local Indian *bo-nay* meaning 'low country' – the Netherlanders would have felt at home when they arrived in 1626.

Bonaire has a population of about 11,000. There are just two small settlements, Kralendijk, the capital on the leeward coast, and Rincon in the north, with sporadic development elsewhere. The Bonaireans are fairly quiet. They joke that their neighbours, the Curaçaoans, are wild and spendthrift, whereas they consider themselves more measured and careful. Before the days of bank loans, the Bonaireans had a system called the *samm* in which they would club together, pooling a sum of money every month, which they would each receive in rotation, enabling them to buy an animal or building materials for a house (the practice still continues in some cases). Generally, the Bonaireans are extremely gracious and welcoming.

Bonaire has never seen the extreme wealth of Curaçao and Aruba, but in the early 21st century this lack of development is one of the things that makes it attractive,

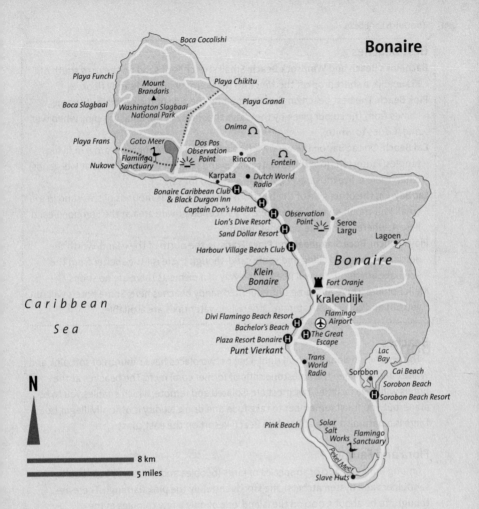

Bonaire

Boca Cocolishi

Playa Funchi

Playa Chikitu

Mount
Brandaris

Playa Grandi

Boca Slagbaai

Washington Slagbaai
National Park

Onima

Playa Frans

Goto Meer

Dos Pos
Observation
Point

Rincon

Fontein

Flamingo
Sanctuary

Nukove

Karpata

Dutch World
Radio

Bonaire Caribbean Club
& Black Durgon Inn

Captain Don's Habitat

Observation
Point

Seroe
Largu

Lion's Dive Resort

Lagoen

Sand Dollar Resort

Harbour Village Beach Club

Bonaire

Klein
Bonaire

Fort Oranje

Caribbean

Kralendijk

Sea

Divi Flamingo Beach Resort

Flamingo
Airport

Bachelor's Beach

The Great
Escape

Plaza Resort Bonaire

Punt Vierkant

Lac
Bay

Trans
World
Radio

Cai Beach

Sorobon

Sorobon Beach

N

Sorobon Beach Resort

Pink Beach

Solar
Salt
Works

Flamingo
Sanctuary

Pekel Meer

8 km

5 miles

Slave Huts

particularly to divers, who make up about half of the island's trusty crowd of around 60,000 visitors. Besides tourism, the island earns some money from the salt industry, which has been revived, automated now to bring it into the 21st century; from oil storage; and from radio transmitting stations, Radio Nederland Wereldomroep (the Dutch World Service), and the religious broadcasting station, Trans World Radio. At the moment Bonaire is more prosperous than it has ever been.

The island has changed considerably over the past few years, though it has been carefully steered along 'sustainable' lines. The investment that was once so hard to come by is now clearly visible. Hotels have sprung up and the islanders are building houses for themselves too. The old feeling that time forgot Bonaire has pretty well evaporated, but it is still possible to escape here for a rest cure. It is still relatively quiet after dark. Most visitors are in bed by about 10pm, building up their strength for another day underwater. For details on Bonaire's history, *see* 'Dutch Leeward History', pp.439–41.

Best Beaches

Bachelor's Beach and **Windsock Beach**: Small stretches of sand on the road south of Kralendijk, a short drop off the *klips* into the warm water and sandy floor.

Pink Beach: The best beach on the island, along the side of the salt flats. Its name comes from the colour given by the corals that grow in the area (it is pink when wet and it dries to white).

Cai Beach: On Lac Bay on the windward coast, where the mangroves grow in flying tangles. Protected from the Atlantic waves and popular with the locals at weekends, when there is live music every Sunday and food for sale.

Lac Bay: On the other side of the bay from Cai Beach, it has mounds of soft sand in a small half-moon-shaped cove. There is a screened private area at the Sorobon Beach Resort, where clothes are 'optional' (*adm*).

Playa Funchi, **Boca Slaagbaai** and **Playa Frans**: In the north of the island, worth the detour for the snorkelling and some sand, though there is little shelter from the sun. Take anything you will need in the way of a picnic as there are no shops.

Klein Bonaire: There are some unfrequented sandy beaches here. Some hotels will run you out and collect you later on. Otherwise, water taxis are available.

Beaches

The beaches in Bonaire are all right. One or two places have mounds of soft pink and white sand between the limestone cliffs of former coral reefs. The beaches at the hotels will have facilities, but most are isolated and remote, which enables you to be alone, but you must remember to take food and drink. Nudity is officially illegal, but there is a naturalist area at Sorobon Beach Resort on the east coast.

Flora and Fauna

Among Bonaire's 200 or so species of birds (boobies and pelicans, bananaquits, sandpipers and oystercatchers), the king is certainly the pink flamingo. There are thought to be about 5,000 on the island, one of only a few colonies in the western hemisphere. Flamingos are shy birds and quite easily disturbed (by humans at least, though they seem to have got used to aeroplanes), so the Bonaireans are understandably reticent about revealing the exact location of the two nesting sites on the island. However, you can fix up a guided visit through **Bonaire Tours** (*t* 717 8778, *info@bonairetours.com, www.bonairetours.com*) to the northern colony by Goto Meer in the afternoon (it is not permitted to visit the southern colony in the salt pans). If you have binoculars or a telephoto lens, take them because you will not be allowed too near, particularly while they are breeding in the early part of the year.

Flamingos nest on little round mounds of mud about a foot high, on which is poised a single large egg. When either parent is not occupied with incubation, you will see them standing around in groups, legs bent forward at the knee, passing the time of day. To feed they have to visit the salt-water lakes dotted around the island, where they advance in ranks, heads moving left and right underwater as they trawl for food. It is a little water shrimp that they find there that gives them their striking pink colour.

Scuba Diving and Snorkelling

Bonaire, often ranked among the top few scuba-diving destinations in the world, is famous particularly for its range of incomparably colourful coral and its sloping drop-offs (not vertical walls, but slopes of between 45° and 60°) that start anything from 20 to 100 yards offshore. Visibility is often over 60ft and can be as much as 100ft.

Brain corals with jigsawed hemispheres, sheet coral and star coral jostle for space on the reef with gorgonians and the forests of elkhorn and staghorn. Close to the surface, the corals tend to grow bunched together, reaching up for the sunlight, but as you descend and the reds, oranges and yellows fade, you find flat and bulky corals of blue, purple and brown. (Until you put a light on, that is, when their true colours are revealed in all their glory.) Fish life glides by beneath the surface, dipping and darting in little shoals; peacock flounders change colour at you, a little school of needlefish will come and poke at you. Angelfish coloured a deep rich blue or bright yellow and black purse their lips and the four-eyed butterflyfish wink. Look out for seahorses and Christmas tree worms, and you might even see a green turtle or a shovel-nosed lobster. While some fish grunt and swim away, crabs witness you with a fixed look of shock, eyes out on stalks and upturned in quizzical amazement. At night the whole seascape changes: some fish wrap themselves in a sleeping bag of mucous and some corals close down for bed, but orange tube corals wake up and transform into orange tubes. Nocturnal brittlestars light up if touched, and tarpons attracted by your flashlight will swim up and nose at you.

The reefs on Bonaire are managed by the **Bonaire Marine Park**, which has jurisdiction over nearly the whole of the coastline to a depth of 200ft and imposes strict laws against the removal or killing of any marine life within the area. It has placed mooring sites in the reefs to protect them. The park charges an admission fee valid for one year: US$25 for scuba divers; US$10 for others. All first dives in Bonaire must be shore dives, to help you remember your buoyancy skills. Most of the 80-odd dive sites are on the protected leeward coast of the island and around the islet of Klein Bonaire, none more than a few minutes' boat ride away from Kralendijk. The hulk of the *Hilma Hooker*, a ganja-runner that went down after its load of 25,000lbs of resin was confiscated, makes a good wreck dive.

Many of Bonaire's reefs are close enough to the shoreline to be reached with a mask and snorkel and you will see crowds of tropical fish loitering close in, too. As with diving, watch for fire corals – many colours, but always white fringes – which will give you a nasty sting. Equipment can be hired for the day from the dive shops. The sites in Bonaire are all named. As you head north from Kralendijk, try the Cliff, where there is fine elkhorn coral, and 1,000 Steps, where you will find blue tang and parrotfish loitering in the underhangs of the coral foreshore. At Karpata you will find a good diversity of fish and occasional turtles. South of Kralendijk you can cast off the waterfront and be right among the reefs. Try Windsock at the end of the runway, where there are plenty of fish and occasional rays. There are also plenty of sites on Klein Bonaire, where you can find gorgonians, star and brain corals at Captain Don's Reef and Rock Pile.

Getting There

Bonaire t (599–)

By Air

Bonaire has quite good air connections for so small an island. You can also fly via Aruba or Curaçao, which are both well-served and have endless connections to Bonaire. There are also flights from Caracas in Venezuela. The Flamingo Airport Bonaire is located at Plaza Medardo Thielman, t 717 5600.

There is a departure tax of US$20 (international and Aruba), or US$5.75 (within Netherlands Antilles).

From Europe

KLM, t 9465 2747, has numerous flights direct from Amsterdam, and also via Curaçao and Caracas.

From the USA and Canada

The two primary carriers from the USA are: Air Jamaica, which flies four times a week to Bonaire via Montego Bay; and American Airlines/ American Eagle, which serves Bonaire three times per week via the San Juan hub in Puerto Rico. GWV also charters planes weekly from Boston.

In Canada: Canada 3000 flies a weekly charter from Toronto.

From Other Caribbean Islands

BonairExpress, t 717 0707, www.bonairexel.com, flies several times a day between Bonaire, Aruba and Curaçao. It also flies between Sint Maarten and Bonaire via Curaçao.

Divi Divi Air, t 5999 888 1050, www.flydivi.com, has regular flights between Bonaire and Curaçao on a seven-passenger Cessna 402 and a nine-passenger BN2-Islander. Current fairs are US$40 one-way.

Getting Around

By Bus

There is a sort of bus service in Bonaire – minibuses known as 'autobuses' run sporadically from the centre of Kralendijk up to Rincon. No buses run south past the airport.

By Taxi

Taxis meet the flights and can be ordered through hotels or from the central depot, t 717 8100. They are unmetered, with fixed prices for each run.

Prices increase by 25% in the hours between 8pm and midnight, and by 50% from midnight until 6am. Some sample prices include: airport to Kralendijk – US$8; to Captain Don's Habitat – $11. If you wish to take a tour of the island, any taxi driver will oblige; the rate is around US$25 per hour (about 3 hours is all you will need).

Hitch-hiking

Hitch-hiking around the island is relatively dependable.

Car and Bike Hire

You will be most mobile in your own vehicle and there are plenty available for hire on the island. A licence from an EU country, the States or Canada is valid in Bonaire and prices range from around US$40 a day for a small car, plus insurance.

Driving is on the right. A number of hotels also provide cars for hire, so check at the front desk.

AB Car Rental, t 717 8980, info@abcarrental.com, www.sunrentals.an/abcarrental. Jeeps are available, too.

Avis, t 717 5795, avis@bonairelive.com, www.avisbonaire.com.

Everts Car Rental, t 717 8719, evertesscar@curinfo.an, www.evertscarrental.com.

Hertz, t 717 7221, renatacar@bonairelive.com, www.bonairenet.com/hertz.

Island Rentals, t 717 2100, info@islandcarrental bonaire.com, islandrentalsbonaire.com. Jeeps are available.

Total Carrental Bonaire, t 717 7372, info@totalbonaire.com, www.totalcarrental bonaire.com.

Scooters and bicycles can be hired from:
Cycle Bonaire, part of Total Carrental Bonaire (see above).
Hot Shot Scooter and Cycle Rental, 4 Kaya Bonaire, t 717 7166, info@rentofunbonaire.com, www.rent ofunbonaire.com.

Tourist Information

Abroad

There is no tourist office specific to Bonaire in Britain, but you can get information through the Dutch office and from the excellent Bonaire website, *www.infobonaire. com*. You can also find information at *www.yellowpagesbonaire.com* and *www.Bonairenet.com*.

Canada: t 1 800 BONAIRE.

Netherlands: Basic Communicaie BV, Mariettahof 25–9, PO Box 462, NL 2000, AL Haarlem, The Netherlands, t (023) 543 0704, *europe@tourismbonaire.com*.

USA: Bonaire Tourism Corporation, Adams Unlimited, Rockefeller Plaza, Suite 900, New York, NY 10020, t (212) 956 5912, t 1800 BONAIRE, *usa@tourismbonaire.com*.

In Bonaire

Tourism Corporation of Bonaire Information Office, 2 Kaya Grandi, a little inland in Kralendijk, t 717 8322, *info@tourism bonaire.com*.

Emergencies

In a **medical** emergency, there is a hospital in Kralendijk, t 717 8900. Good news for divers: the island has its own decompression chamber.

For **police**, call t 717 8000, t 113, or go to 4 Kaya L. Simon Bolivar.

Money and Banks

Officially, Bonaire's **currency** is the Netherlands Antilles florin or guilder (NAFl), which is fixed to the US dollar at a rate of US$1 = NAFl1.78. However, you may not even see this currency because the greenback is perfectly acceptable for all transactions.

In local shops you may receive change in florins. Restaurants and hire shops in Bonaire are prepared to accept most credit cards and the hotels take traveller's cheques. **Banks** open Mon–Fri 8.30–noon and 2–4, sometimes without a break for lunch.

Shopping

Shops open Mon–Fri 8–noon and 2–6.

Telephone Code

To telephone Bonaire from abroad, the IDD code is t 599 followed by a seven-digit island number beginning with 717 or a mobile number which follows no pattern. If phoning within the island, dial the whole seven digits.

Festivals

February *Mardi Gras*. The Bonaireans get out into the streets in costume at Carnival time.

April *Harvest Festival*. Into costume again.

24th and 29th June *Local festivities*.

September *National Day*. A general jump-up around the island on the 6th, particularly in Rincon.
Sailing competition.

October *Annual Sailing Regatta*. Held over five days in the second week of October.

Throughout the year *Fishing tournaments*.

Watersports

Deep-sea Fishing

Trips are easily arranged at the Harbour Village Marina or through your hotel. A tournament is held each spring.

Big Game Sportfishing, t 717 6500, *biggame@ bonairefishing.com*, *www.bonairefishing. com/biggame*.

Fishing Bonaire, t 790 1228, *www.bonaire fishing.com/siri*.

Multifish Charters, t 717 3648, *info@multifish. com*, *www.multifish.com*.

Piscatur, t 717 8774, *piscatur@bonairetours. com*, *www.bonairetours.com/piscatur/about*. Will take out four fishermen in a 30ft diesel boat, for US$550 per day. This includes tackle and bait; catch cooked on board.

Kayaking

Kayaks can be hired by the hour from a number of hotels, or try:

Bonaire Dive & Adventure, t 717 5252, *info@bonairediveandadventure.com*, *www.bonairediveandadventure.com*.

Jibe City, Lac Bay, t 717 5233, *info@jibecity.com*, *www.jibecity.com*. They offer guided trips in the mangroves around Cai Beach.

Mangrove Info and Kayak Center, t 790 5353, *info@bonairekayaking.com, www.info bonaire.com/kayaking.*

Outdoor Bonaire, t 785 6272, *hans@ outdoorbonaire.com, www. outdoorbonaire.com.*

Also try Buddy Dive Resort, Captain Don's Habitat and Plaza Resort Bonaire.

Sailing and Day Sails

A sailing regatta is held annually in October, five days of racing around the island.

Aquaspace, **t** 717 2568, *info@aquaspace bonaire.com, www.aquaspacebonaire.com.* If you are not prepared to get wet, you can still enjoy the marine life of the island in a glass-bottomed boat.

Oscarina, **t** 790 7674, *www.bonairesailing.com/ oscarina.* A 42ft cutter available for charter.

Pirate Cruise of Bonaire, **t** 790 8330, *turtlesnorkel@hotmail.com, www. remarkable.com/bonaire/pirates.html*

Seawitch, **t** 0560 7449, *seawitch@infobonaire. com.* A 56ft ketch available for a day's picnic or a sunset cruise.

Samur, **t** 717 5592, *info@samursailing.com, www.infobonaire.com/samur.* Contact them should you feel the urge to ride on a real Thai junk.

Woodwind, **t** 786 7055, *woodwind@telbonet. an, www.woodwindbonaire.com.*

Scuba Diving and Snorkelling

Bonaire is extremely well-organized to cater to divers and many of the hotels have special dive packages. Nearly all of them offer introductory courses for those who want to learn. Once you have arranged your equipment, it is quite possible to take off in a car and choose your own shoreline to dive off.

A number of dive centres also cater to underwater photography and you can hire the cameras and vast lighting equipment from the centres listed below. If you are not a diver, it is still possible to see the reefs with a mask and snorkel. Many of the hotels stage slide shows of the coral reefs as well. And if you are missing the reefs when you are at home, you can check out the Bonaire reefcam at *www.bonairewebcams.com/ BonaireReefCam.*

Bonaire Dive and Adventure, t 717 2227, *info@bonairediveandadventure.com, www.bonairediveandadventure.com.*

Captain Don's Habitat, t 717 8290, *bonaire@habitatdiveresorts.com, www.habitatdiveresorts.com.*

Dive Inn Bonaire, t 717 8761, **t** 717 8513, *info@diveinnbonaire.com, www.dive innbonaire.com.* An independent operator with good rates for equipment hire and instruction.

Divi Flamingo Beach Hotel, t 717 8285, *dividive@waterhousetours.com, www.divebonaire.com.*

Great Adventures Bonaire, Harbour Village, **t** 717 7500, *reservations@ harbourvillage.com.*

Windsurfing

Bonaire Windsurf Place, t 717 2288, *info@bonairewindsurfplace.com, www.bonairewindsurfplace.com.*

Jibe City, Lac Bay, **t** 717 5233, *info@jibecity.com, www.jibecity.com.* Waist-deep water and constant onshore winds can be found at Lac Bay.

Other Sports

Gyms

A Place for You, t 717 2727.

BonFysiotherapie, t 717 7030, *bonfysio@infobonaire.com, www.infobonaire.com/bonfysio.*

Fit 4 Life, Plaza Resort Mini Mall, **t** 717 2500, ext. 8210, *info@aplaceforyoubonaire.com, www.infobonaire.com/aplaceforyou.*

Joe's Fitness Centre, Les Galleries Shopping Mall, **t** 717 2842.

Horse-riding

Kunuku Waharama, t 717 2500, *marion bonaire@bonairelive.com.* Offers half-hour and hourly rides, as well as carriage rides for the more sedate.

Mountain-biking

Bonaire Dive and Adventure, t 717 2227, *info@bonairediveandadventure.com, www.bonairediveandadventure.com.*

Hot Shot Scooter and Cycle Rental, 4 Kaya Bonaire, t 717 7166, info@rentofunbonaire.com, www.rentafunbonaire.com.

Outdoor Bonaire, t 785 6272, hans@outdoorbonaire.com, www.outdoorbonaire.com.

Tennis

There are a number of tennis courts in town (*free*) and at the following hotels (*adm* for non-guests). Many of them are equipped with floodlights for night games.

Professional instruction is also available:

Harbour Village, Kaya Gobernador N. Debrot 72, Playa Lechi, t 717 7500, www.harbourvillage.com.

Plaza Resort Bonaire, 80 J.A. Abraham Bd, t 717 2500, info@plazaresortbonaire.com.

Sand Dollar Beach Club, 79 Kaya Gobernador N. Debrot, t 717 8738. *Open daily 9–9.*

Where to Stay

Bonaire t (599–)

Bonaire's hotels are mostly ranged along the protected leeward coast of the island, many of them in a cluster along the shoreline north of Kralendijk. They are all new and few have much natural charm, but the Bonaireans make the place very pleasant because they are so welcoming. When diving is at issue, the atmosphere tends to be brisk and businesslike, but with regard to anything else it is typically Caribbean and very low-key.

There are not many inexpensive places to stay in Bonaire. On top of this there is a room tax of US$5.50 (sometimes $6.50) per person per night and most hotels will charge 10–15% for service.

Bonaire also has a number of villas for rent (though of course many of the hotel 'rooms' are actually self-contained apartments):

Sun Rentals, 65 Kaya Grandi, Kralendijk, t 717 6130, info@sunrentals.an, www.sunrentals.an.

Tourism Corporation of Bonaire, 2 Kaya Grandi, Kralendijk, t 717 8322. Will provide a list.

Expensive

Harbour Village Beach Club, 72 Kaya Gobernador N. Debrot, Playa Lechi, t 717 7500, US t 1 800 424 0004, reservationsusa@harbourvillage.com, www.harbourvillage.com. Modern Caribbean luxury in clustered two-storey villas that do have the feel of a village, centred on the pool and bar, or overlooking the lagoon. There are 29 very comfortable rooms and suites, each with a view of the marina or the hotel's fine beach. Watersports, spa on offer, even a restaurant on a mock pirate yacht.

Plaza Resort Bonaire, 80 J. A. Abraham Bd, t 717 2500, US t 1 800 766 6016, info@plazaresortbonaire.com, www.plazaresortbonaire.com. Has 198 huge ocean- and lagoonside suites and villas (one- and two-bedroom) set in 12 acres of pretty tropical gardens. There are three restaurants, one with top French fare.

Moderate

Sand Dollar Condominium Resort, 79 Kaya Gobernador N. Debrot, Playa Lechi, t 717 8738, US t 1 800 288 4773, info@sanddollarbonaire.com, www.sanddollarbonaire.com. Situated a mile or so north of Kralendijk, this zigzag of two-storey blocks sits on the waterfront opposite Klein Bonaire, with a feel of cool modernity. Fully furnished self-catering apartments and studios and one- to three-bedroom condos.

Captain Don's Habitat, 85 Kaya Gobernador N. Debrot, t 717 8290, US t 1 800 327 6709, bonaire@habitatdiveresorts.com, www.habitatdiveresorts.com. Attractive suites, villas and cottages, and a pool. There are now 93 rooms in the sandy garden of cactus, palm and aloe, but the Habitat has kept the friendly feel of a diving inn. There is a small beach, but the gravitational pull is of course towards the diving pier. Some other watersports and entertainment a couple of nights in the week. Most stays are sold as diving packages.

Lion's Dive Hotel Bonaire, 91 Kaya Gobernador N. Debrot, t 717 5580, info@lionsdivebonaire.com, www.lionsdivebonaire.com. A resort with 31 self-contained apartments north of Kralendijk. Comfortable with bright Caribbean pastel colours and all mod cons. Friendly atmosphere.

Buddy Dive Resort, on the coast north of Kralendijk, PO Box 231, **t** 717 5080, *info@buddydive.com*, *www.buddydive.com*. An active resort feel to this hotel, which stands in blocks above a central swimming pool and beach bar. Rooms and self-contained apartments decorated in white with bright Caribbean colours.

Divi Flamingo Beach Resort and Casino, 40 J.A. Abraham Bd, astride the promenade at the southern limits of Kralendijk, **t** 717 8285, US **t** 1 800 367 3483, *www.diviflamingo.com*. A resort feel. It is a hive of activity, relatively speaking, with a dive-shop, a casino, a couple of pools, 129 rooms and the Chibi Chibi restaurant, which has a charming setting on stilts above the floodlit sea (reserve early if you want a waterfront table). It is one of Bonaire's first hotels and the regime has softened a bit since it was used as the island internment camp for Germans living around the Caribbean in the Second World War.

Sorobon Beach Resort, Sorobon 10, **t** 717 8080, *info@sorobonbeachresort.com*, *www.sorobonbeachresort.com*. Bonaire's 'naturist' resort. In a traditional Caribbean beach-club style, 30 quite simple but perfectly comfortable rooms in wooden chalets stretched along the beach in a sandy garden with palm sunshades. Self-catering facilities, but no air-conditioning. There is a screened, clothes-optional beach and a small, family-style restaurant and bar. 'Unspoiled, Unhurried, Unclothed, Unforgettable...' Daily shuttle service into Kralendijk.

Bruce Bowker's Carib Inn, 46 J.A. Abraham Bd, on the waterfront in the south of Kralendijk, **t** 717 8819, *info@caribinn.com*, *www.caribinn.com*. An original dive inn, still with the atmosphere that Caribbean inns once had. Ten rooms, very low-key, no restaurant or bar, but most rooms and suites have kitchenettes.

Inexpensive

Great Escape, 97 E. E. G. Bd, to the south of the airport, **t** 717 7488, *greatescape@bonairelive.com*. A delightful setting in a modern Spanish-style villa with swimming pool and palapa sunshades out back in the pleasant tropical gardens. Just 10 rooms with a low-key feel and friendly service; ideal for independent travellers.

Bonaire Caribbean Club, Playa Lechi, PO Box 323, **t** 717 7901, *info@caribbeanclubbonaire.com*, *www.caribbeanclubbonaire.com*. If you want to get away from the main strip, this place is lost in the Bonaire *kunuku*. Just 15 rooms, some with kitchenettes, scattered around a garden.

Black Durgon Inn, 145 Kaya Gobernador N. Debrot, **t** 717 5736, *bkdurgon@bonairelive.com*. Situated at the north end of Playa Lechi, this is an eight-bedroom inn, with one-bed apartments and a two/three-bed villa. All rooms have air-conditioning and cable TV, in a relaxed setting with views of Klein Bonaire.

Hotel Rochaline, 7 Kaya Grandi, Kralendijk, **t** 717 8286, *info@mainstreetbonaire.com*, *www.mainstreetbonaire.com*. Twenty-one simple but air-conditioned rooms on the seafront in the downtown area of Kralendijk.

Rose Inn Bed and Breakfast, 4 Kaya Guayaba, Rincon, **t** 717 6420, *instyle@bonairelive.com*. Six rooms with air-conditioning, close to the National Park.

Eating Out

There is a clutch of surprising restaurants on tiny Bonaire and you can expect to eat well (the chefs have been successful in Caribbean competitions lately). Generally, the menus are international, particularly in the hotels, but you will find some good local restaurants. None is particularly cheap.

Categories are arranged according to the price of a main dish: expensive = US$20 and above; moderate = between US$10 and $20; inexpensive = US$10 and below. Service is charged at 10%. For more information, check *www.bonairerestaurants.com*.

Expensive

Rendez-vous, 3 Kaya L. D. Gerharts, Kralendijk, **t** 717 8454. Situated in the middle of town, with an easy atmosphere. You can eat on a streetfront veranda or just inside in an air-conditioned dining room. International fare, with exotic mixes of Caribbean ingredients in traditional dishes. Start with their shrimp bisque or a seafood *seviche* and follow with an ensemble of fresh salmon and shrimp with a sauce of passion fruit. Leave your lighter as a memento of your visit if you like. *Closed Thurs.*

It Rains Fishes, Bayside, 24 Kaya Jan Kraane, Kralendijk, **t** 717 8780. Set on a deck right on the waterfront in town. There are tapas available, or start with *patatas bravas* topped with a spicy 'mojo rojo' sauce, or a *carpaccio di Napoli* (beef with a pesto sauce and parmesan) and follow with a salad speciality or a baby sole with lemon and capers.

Capriccio Ristorante, 1 Kaya Isla Riba, **t** 717 7230. Top-knotch Italian fare is sereved here – fresh pastas and pizzas but more adventurous food, too, in a modern house with an intimate setting. Tables inside, some in alcoves, or outside on a terrace, underneath a tree. There's a great view of the sea and setting sun.

Richard's Waterfront, 60 Abraham Bd, Kralendijk, **t** 717 5263. Dine on a breezy Bonaire terrace overlooking the waterfront in the south of town. Tasty home-made soups and specialities in seafood and local fish. The bar attracts a crowd of locals. *Closed lunchtime.*

Bistro de Paris, Kaya Gobernor 46, **t** 717 7070. A new French-owned and operated restaurant situated in a small white house with a terrace serving French cuisine. *Open Mon–Sat for lunch and dinner.*

Lion's Den, Lion's Dive Hotel, **t** 717 5880. Sits on the waterfront with the waves lapping the cliffs below. Innovative takes on Caribbean ingredients, with fruit sauces to go with fish and a coconut flavour to go with shrimp.

Moderate

Kon Tiki, Lac Bay, **t** 717 5369, *info@kontiki bonaire.com*, *www.kontikibonaire.com*. Ten minutes' drive out of the (relative) bustle of town, Kon Tiki is set on Lac Bay with tables looking over the sandy garden to the sea. Popular dishes include catch with

pasta, pan-fried fish served in a pesto sauce and baby shrimps, or an Argentinean steak wrapped in bacon with an olive sauce. Friendly service in a bright and breezy dining room.

Mona Lisa Bar and Restaurant, 15 Kaya Grandi, Kralendijk, **t** 717 8718. A colourful, lively place with a mix of Dutch, French and Indonesian cuisine; bar snacks are available until late. *Closed Sat and Sun.*

Le Flamboyant, Kaya Gobernor 12, **t** 717 3919. A charming, new restaurant with patio dining and varied international fare. *Open daily for dinner only.*

Inexpensive

There are snack bars in town for simple grilled chicken and there is a *refreskeria* on Kaya Simon Bolivar. For some of the best local fare, stop at any sign that says '*Aki se ta bende kuminda kriyoyo*' (local food for sale) and get a *kabritu stobe* (goat stew) or a *piska hasa* (grilled fish).

De Islander, Kaya Caracas, Kralendijk, **t** 717 3420. Grills and hearty West Indian fare, including steaks and burgers, rice and peas with fish.

Cozzoli's Pizza, Harbourside Shopping Mall, Kralendijk, **t** 717 5195. Pizza and fast food, plus excellent pastries. Also found in Rincon.

Bars and Nightlife

Karel's, perched over the sea in the centre of Kralendijk. The hippest bar on the island has seats tightly packed around the cocktail counter with the waves washing back and forth beneath you, with live music and dancing (*Fri and Sat*).

Movieland Cinema, Kaya Prinses Marie, **t** 717 2400, **t** 0960 7371, *www.InfoBonaire.com/ cinema*. If you'd rather not exert yourself, head for here. *Closed Mon and Tues.*

Divi Flamingo Beach Resort & Casino, **t** 717 8285. Try here if you fancy a flutter – it's the only barefoot casino in the Caribbean. *Closed Sun.*

Jibe City, Lac Bay. Here you can get drinks and simple food (*open daytime only*) on the beach.

Bonaire has little in the way of landborne animals, apart from wild donkeys and goats, who nibble at everything in sight, but you will see plenty of lizards and the occasional prehistoric-looking iguana. A guided tour with a naturalist as guide is available through **Nature Tours, t** 717 7714.

Kralendijk

Bonaire's small capital, Kralendijk (pronounced as in 'marlinspike'), lies on the protected inner coastline of the island, looking across to the uninhabited coral outcrop, Klein Bonaire. It has a few neat streets of brightly painted buildings among the traditional Dutch Antillean russet and ochre colours, gardens filled with banana and palm trees, and is patrolled by lazy dogs and lizards. To the island inhabitants, the town is known familiarly as 'Playa' (Papiamentu for beach), really a bit of an exaggeration because there is only a measly strip of hard sand here. Kralendijk (meaning coral dike) is a rather more appropriate name because the shoreline is mostly a coral limestone wall.

The town has always been a backwater and there was not even a pier until the 20th century. Before that, ships would tie up to a cannon sticking out of the ground. Today the waterfront comes alive when the boats from Curaçao put in, but the main centre is on Kaya Grandi, which has recently come out in a profusion of stores and a shopping mall. The Tourism Corporation will give you a walking map of the town.

Fort Oranje surveys the scene as it has since the middle of the 19th century, its cannon covering the bay. Close by is the **fish market**, a mock-classical temple dressed in pink, which looks slightly out of place for the Caribbean, though it is well used as the local market, selling imported vegetables, fruits and occasionally fish. Behind here in the centre of town is a **bust of Simon Bolivar**, who visited the island during his campaign to liberate the peoples of the South American mainland from Spanish colonial rule.

The **Museo Boneriano** (*Kaya J. C. v/d Ree, t* 717 8868; *open Mon–Fri 8–noon and 1–5; adm*) is set in a lovely traditional building with an orange-tile roof and typical mustard-coloured walls picked out in white. It's an excellent museum which gives a wide-ranging look at the island's history and natural life, with exhibits of island shells, dyewoods, salt, the mythology of Bonaire, agricultural artefacts, local building techniques and domestic dripstones, furniture from the 1940s and 50s and musical traditions. There are also paintings by local artists.

Around the Island

Headed south out of Kralendijk the road skirts a lagoon and rejoins the coast at the airport, passing Trans World Radio. The countryside is flat, desolate and wet. The southern toe is just a rim of land separating Bonaire's **salt pans** from the sea.

Continuing around the coastline, you will see two small communities of **slave huts**, built in about 1850 in traditional Leeward Islands style, with square-topped gables and palm thatch. These two-man shelters were constructed in accordance with the slaves' wishes in preference to a single dormitory. There are also a number of obelisks, originally painted blue, white and red (the colours of Holland), which were used to guide ships to the correct part of the coast. The road leads round the southern tip of the island and up the east coast, past Sorobon and back to Kralendijk.

Two roads lead north out of Kralendijk, one following the leeward coast past the hotels (northwards only, past the BOPEC oil storage bunkers, the Radio Nederland antennae and the desalination plant), and the second cutting inland through the *kunuku* to the opposite coast, on which you come back to town. As the settlers crept into the island in the early 1800s, they settled the area north of Kralendijk, and you will see human order imposed on the scrub – tall cacti trained to make hedges around the simple old Dutch Antillean houses of baked mud and maize thatch.

East of the village of Rincon, a lane leads out towards the coast and to the cavern at **Onima**, where there are Caiquetio inscriptions on the roofs of the caverns. Using the red dye for which the island was known early on by the Europeans, the Indians scrawled their diabolic squiggles and cartoon faces on the dark orange rock. **Rincon** was settled early, its inland site giving the inhabitants a chance to escape marauding raiders, and it is now a sleepy Bonairean village dressed in Dutch Antillean orange.

The **Washington Slagbaai National Park** (*open daily 8–5, but no entry after 3pm; adm, also changing fee for the beach*) preserves 22 square miles of northwestern Bonaire, home to some of the island's 200 or so species of bird (you have a chance of seeing parrots, parrakeets and white-tailed hawks) and the occasional iguana, though these are shy because they fear the cooking pot. Traditional Bonairean crop plants are also there: aloe, divi-divi, sisal and agave, a small explosion of cactus leaves at

Salt

The salt ponds in Bonaire, dammed off with low mud walls, are an unexpected delight. As the water progresses through its course from seawater to salt, it runs through a series of surprisingly delicate colours – the faintest green, then grey, lavender and finally pink, before eventually turning into the bright white of the mature salt. You will see the harvested crop in huge blinding-white mountains, stacked by a conveyor belt and a vast double-armed crane.

Seawater, the sun and constant winds are the essential ingredients for the salt industry. In Bonaire the process takes about 18 months from the moment the seawater is introduced into the *pekelmeer* (pickle lake). By opening and closing locks, it is passed through condensers, gradually evaporating more and more, until it becomes brine, and then on to crystallizers. Here the salt forms over the course of a year in depths of about 8 inches. It is washed and stacked before export.

Slaves were brought in to work the salt pans. It was gruelling work and their existence was miserable. Their families lived 15 miles away in the north of the island and they were allowed home for one day a week. The industry collapsed soon after emancipation in 1863 because it was unviable without forced labour. It was precarious at the best of times (too much rain would ruin the crop) and the industry lay dormant for a hundred years before being revived in the 1960s by the Antilles International Salt Company NV. It is now owned by Cargill. Unfortunately, tours are not available. The salt produced on Bonaire's 9,000-acre 'farm' is used for industrial purposes.

ground level with a stalk up to 30ft in height, and the West Indian cherry. A number of trails are marked around the park, for drivers and for walkers, including a path to the summit of Mt Brandaris. Slagbaai, a cove on the western tip of the island, means 'slaughter bay', and was where animals were killed before being shipped out to Curaçao. (Bonaire was used by the Curaçaoans as a ranch for a couple of centuries.) Near the entry there is a small **museum**, where you will see plantation artefacts and descriptions of cactus fence-building.

Aruba

Aruba lies within sight of South America, just 15 miles north of the Paraguana Peninsula in Venezuela. It is 20 miles long by 6 wide; with a rainfall of about 17 inches a year (less even than Bonaire and Curaçao), its low-lying land and few hillocks are parched and scrubby with cactus, dotted only occasionally by diabolic boulders and divi-divi trees. The island's name is supposed to derive from the native Indian words for shell, 'ora', and island, 'oubao'.

Like Curaçao, Aruba saw an explosion of prosperity in the 20th century with the arrival of the oil industry. EXXON built the then largest refinery in the world on the island in 1929, and the population exploded from 8,700 to 60,000 by 1972. For centuries a poor backwater, Aruba changed completely, and from nothing became very prosperous. Today the population is about 90,000.

But in recent years the oil industry has foundered and so the islanders have thrown themselves with gusto into the latest Caribbean industry, tourism. The island has a façade of overwhelming modernity, and has geared itself up to the arrival of over half a million tourists a year. It has opted for tourism on a grand scale – pristine and well packaged, in huge air-conditioned blocks, with glitzy floor-shows and in-house doctors. They do it pretty well. The new hotels in the high-rise strip are impressive and very comfortable. It is crowded and a little sanitized, but it is well organized and so you get a good body-holiday in Aruba. And the Arubians themselves are probably more gracious about the invasion of tourists than any other Caribbean islanders.

It is possible to spend a week on the island without meeting an Arubian, but this would be a pity because they are a spirited bunch. In 1986, after 50 years of political wrangling, they achieved something which most Caribbean islands only ever dream of: they defied the colonial administration and won consent to go it alone as an autonomous country, with 'Status Aparte'.

So close to Venezuela, Aruba has a strong South American heritage, displayed in the faces and the language. Aruban Papiamento is more Spanish than that of the other two islands. Aruba's tangled racial heritage is more South American Indian than African because there were never really any slaves on the island.

Every car that cruises by in Aruba proclaims 'One Happy Island' from its number-plate. So it may seem, now that the island has its freedom to guide its own affairs as an autonomous country, but the future is not without its difficulties: the island is overwhelmingly dependent on tourism. However, beyond the tourism superstructure

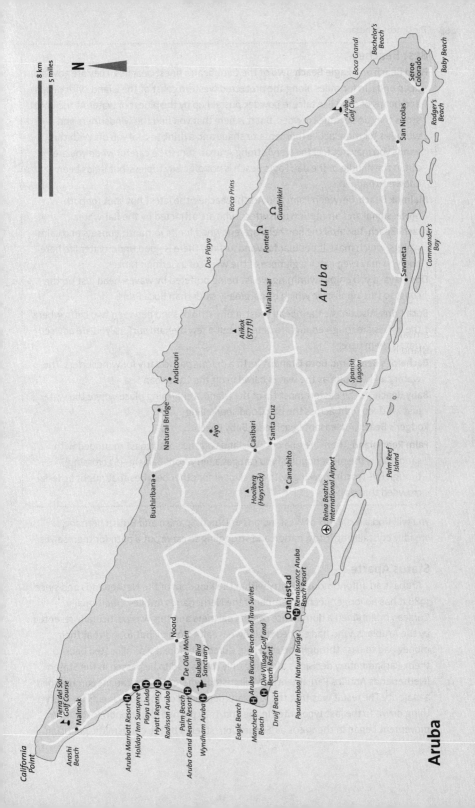

Aruba

California Point

Arashi Beach

Tierra del Sol Golf Course

Malmok

Aruba Marriott Resort
Holiday Inn Sunspree
Playa Linda
Hyatt Regency
Radisson Aruba
Palm Beach
Aruba Grand Beach Resort
Wyndham Aruba

Noord

De Olde Molen

Bubali Bird Sanctuary

Divi Village Golf and Beach Resort

Eagle Beach

Manchebo Beach

Aruba Bucuti Beach and Tara Suites

Druif Beach

Paardenbaai Natural Bridge

Oranjestad

Renaissance Aruba Beach Resort

Bushiribana

Natural Bridge

Ayo

Casibari

Santa Cruz

Canashito

Andicouri

Arikok
(577 ft)

Hooiberg
(Haystack)

Reina Beatrix
International Airport

Dos Playa

Boca Prins

Fontein

Guadirikiri

Miramar

Aruba

Savaneta

Spanish Lagoon

Palm Reef
Island

Commander's
Bay

Boca Grandi

Bachelor's
Beach

Seroe
Colorado

Baby Beach

San Nicolas

Rodger's
Beach

Aruba
Golf Club

N

8 km

5 miles

Best Beaches

Palm Beach and **Eagle Beach**: Two of the Caribbean's finest beaches. They are 30yds deep and run for miles along the protected western coast of the island, with heaps and heaps of sand like talcum powder, pushed up by the bluest of water. At the hotel strips they do become crowded, but it is here that you find the windsurfers and wetbikes for more active moments, or shade and a drink to cool you off. With the winds you may not feel the (very) strong Aruban sun, so be careful when you are out in the middle of the day. Eagle Beach is not officially topless, but it has been known to happen.

Malmok Beach: Between Palm and Arashi beaches, the latest hot spot for both professional and amateur windsurfers, who are attracted by the flat water.

Arashi Beach: Towards the northern tip, renowned for its romantic sunsets and calm waters, which make it popular for windsurfing. There is good underwater life here and you may even catch a glimpse of the wreck of a German tanker.

Dos Playa: If you enjoy swimming whilst being buffeted by waves, head just up the coast to this small cove which is marginally safer than Boca Prins.

Boca Prins: Also on the Caribbean coast, a tiny strip of sand between two cliffs, where the waves are rough enough to deter all but a few diehard surfers; you are advised not to swim here.

Bachelor's Beach and **Boca Grandi**: Worth a detour, particularly for windsurfers. The water can be rough as the waves barrel in off the Caribbean Sea.

Baby Beach: At the easternmost tip of the island, a charming place where the water is just 4ft deep right across the bay. Good snorkelling.

Rodger's Beach: A pleasant beach near Baby Beach.

Palm Reef Island: There are one or two islands off the south coast mounded with sand; this is the most popular (you can get a ferry from Balashi – $3 crossing), though it is worth checking with the skipper for other beaches that might be less crowded that day.

you will find a lively mix of West Indians of Dutch, Spanish and British heritage, steadily crystallizing into a nation and struggling to carve out a path for themselves.

Status Aparte

Aruba is an autonomous country within the Kingdom of the Netherlands and since 1986 it has no longer been a member of the Netherlands Antilles. Traditionally, Curaçao maintained a dominance over its partners and this was particularly resented by the Arubians, who had earned their own wealth from oil but found that their money had to pass through the coffers in Curaçao before it was allocated back to them. Parliamentary decisions affecting only Aruba had to be passed in the Staten (Netherlands Antilles Parliament) in Willemstad, where the Curaçaoans commanded a majority. The result was that the Arubians depended on the Curaçaoans for every-thing down to the last typewriter. In the end, they pushed for autonomy. The movement began in the 1940s as 'Separacion', steered by the charismatic politician

Getting There

Aruba t (297–)

By Air

Aruba is very well connected by air with many flights from the USA as well as from Europe and South America. Reina Beatrix Airport is a couple of miles from the main town of Oranjestad. Departure tax is generally included in the price of your air ticket.

From Europe

KLM, t 9465 2747, has several nonstop flights each week from Amsterdam, where there are easy connections from all over Europe. Or you can go via Curaçao, which has connections to other cities in Europe (*see* p.220).

From the USA

American Airlines, US t 1 800 433 7300, *www.aa.com*, has several daily flights from Miami and New York, as well as Boston, Los Angeles via San Juan and Miami. Other services include Continental from Houston and Newark; Delta from Atlanta and New York; ATA Leisure from Chicago; US Airways from Boston, Philadelphia, New York and Charlotte; and United from Chicago, Washington/Dulles.

From Other Caribbean Islands

There are links from nearby Curaçao and Bonaire on Bonaire Excel. American Airlines has links from San Juan and Santo Domingo in the Dominican Republic (Curaçao also has good connections in the Caribbean; *see* p.445).

From Latin America

There are flights to Maracaibo, Valencia and Caracas in Venezuela, Bogotá in Colombia, as well as San José in Costa Rica, Quito in Ecuador and Lima in Peru.

Getting Around

By Bus

There is quite an efficient **bus** service in Aruba, linking Oranjestad to the southeast of the island and also running west and then north along the hotel strip (fare US$1.50). Buses also run from the airport into town.

Buses run to an official schedule and the drivers almost stick to it. Roughly speaking, there is one an hour up until early evening, with a bus every 15mins on the 'hotel route'. **Minibuses** also run local routes (AFl2.70–3.60).

By Taxi

Taxis are available at the airport, in town and at all the hotels, or they can be fixed through Aruba Transfer Tour and Taxi at the Alhambra Bazaar, t 582 2116. They can be quite expensive and they are unmetered, so fix the price before you set off. US$20 will get you from the airport to the high-rise strip, and US$13 as far as downtown. Prices increase after midnight.

By Guided Tour

Taxi drivers, who all speak English, are quite well versed about island history and folklore and will happily give an island tour. The charge is around US$30 per cab for an hour on the road. Island tours by bus can also be fixed up through private tour bus companies:

De Palm Tours, L. G. Smith Bd, Oranjestad, t 582 4400, *www.depalm.com*.

Watapana Tours, 166 Bushiri, Oranjestad, t 583 5191.

Car and Bike Hire

If you want added flexibility, there are plenty of rental cars in Aruba and you can pick one up at the airport. Foreign driving licences are accepted and driving is on the right; roads are good. Daily rates start at around US$35, with insurance on top.

Avis, 14 Kolibristraat, Oranjestad, t 582 8787, *avis.aruba@setarnet.aw*.

Budget, 1 Kolibristraat, Oranjestad, t 582 8600, *budgetaruba@setnet.aw*, *www.budget aruba.com*.

Thrifty Car Rental, t 585 5300, *thriftyaruba@ setarnet.aw*, *www.thrifty.aruba.com*.

National, Oranjestad, t 582 5451, *national@ natcararuba.com*, *www.natcararuba.com*.

Ruba Rent-a-Car, Airport Booth 11, t 583 1020, *rubarent@setarnet.aw*, *www.rubarent-aruba.com*.

There's also bike hire available.

Pablito's Bike Rental, La Quinta Beach Resort, Eagle Beach, t 587 8655.

Tourist Information

Abroad

There is a website devoted to Aruba at www.arubatourism.com. The government site is at www.aruba.com, and you can also find information at www.visitaruba.com.

Canada: 5875 Highway 7, Suite 201, Woodbridge, Ontario, L4L 1T9, t 905 264 3434, 800 268 3042.

UK: The Saltmarsh Partnership, 25 Copperfield Street, London, SE1 0EN, t 020 7928 1600.

USA: 1000 Harbour Bd, Weehawken, NJ 07087, t (201) 330 0800, 800 862 7822; Greater Miami Office, 1 Financial Plaza, Suite 136, Fort Lauderdale, Florida 33394, t (954) 767 6477; Atlanta Office, PMB Box 355, 1750 Powder Springs Road, Suite 190, Marietta, GA 30064-4861, t (404) 892 7822.

There is a general freephone number, t 1 800 TO ARUBA.

In Aruba

Aruba Tourism Authority, PO Box 1019, 172 L.G. Smith Bd, Oranjestad, t 582 3777.

There is also a small but helpful office in the airport and one in the cruise-ship terminal.

Medical Emergencies

In a medical emergency, there is a casualty room at the Dr Horacio Oduber Hospital on L.G. Smith Bd, t 874 300. However, before phoning for an ambulance (t 911), check with the hotel front desk because there could be a house-doctor on call.

Money and Banks

With 'Status Aparte' in 1986, Aruba adopted a **currency** of its own, the Aruban florin (AFl), which, like many Caribbean islands, they fixed to the US dollar (at a rate of US$1 = AFl1.77). However, with their economy so closely geared to American visitors, they also accept US dollars in nearly all transactions. **Credit cards** are accepted in any but the smallest restaurants.

Service charges in Aruba are usually 15%. The Netherlands Antilles guilder (the currency of nearby Curaçao and Bonaire) is not accepted in Aruba. **Banks** are open Mon–Fri 8–12 and 1.30–4. You will get a slightly better exchange rate at the bank than at a hotel cash desk.

Shopping

Shops are open Mon–Fri 8–12 and 2–6, longer if there are cruise ships in. Shops at the Alhambra Bazaar stay open until midnight.

Telephone Code

The IDD code for Aruba is t 297, followed by a seven-digit Aruban number. From within the island, just dial the last seven digits.

Festivals

January *New Year.* The Arubians have a tradition of open house, in which choirs and troupes of singers go from home to home singing *dandes*, songs like a melodic version of medieval Gregorian chants. Fireworks at midnight highlight the celebration.

February *Carnival.* The major event in the Aruban calendar, held in the run-up to Lent. Starting with the Lighting Parade, there is a kiddies' romp, and then musicians' competitions, and it all culminates eventually in the Old Mask Parade on the Sunday before Lent along the waterfront in Oranjestad, to music so loud that the streets seem to vibrate.

May *Soul Beach Music Festival.*

June *International Hi-Winds Amateur World Challenge.*

October *Aruba Music Festival.* An annual festival with big-name performers.

Watersports

Aruba has the whole range of opportunities for watersports, from waterskiing to fleets of wetbikes. The principal centre is Palm Beach, but hotels usually have equipment available for their guests. Water-skiing, motorboat hire and parasailing are easily arranged on the high-rise hotel strip at Palm Beach. If you want to tame a jet ski, you will find a little daytime colony of them at the top of Eagle Beach. There are three large sporting outfits that operate from town and can be contacted through desks in the hotels:

De Palm Watersports, t 582 4400, *depalm watersports@setarnet.aw, www.depalm.com.*

Pelican Watersports, t 587 2302, *pelican-aruba@setarnet.aw, www.pelican-aruba.com.*

Red Sail Sports, Palm Beach, t 586 1603, *info@redsailaruba.com*, *www.redsailaruba.com*.

Day Sails

Most hotels have small sailing boats on hand, but if you would prefer to take a day's cruise on a larger yacht, this is also possible through the watersports companies above or through individual operators. Trips will vary from a sunset cruise on a trimaran with full boozatorium and on-board steel band to a full-blooded day's sail on the Trades.

Mi Dushi and *Tattoo*, t 586 2010, *www.aruba adventures.com*. 'Party cruises' on a huge motoryacht.

Tranquilo, t 585 7533, *tranquilo@ visitaruba.com*. Sailing yacht.

Wave Dancer, t 582 5520, *cruise@arubawavedancer.com*. Trimaran.

Deep-sea Fishing

Deep-sea fishermen can go out in search of sailfish, bonito and kingfish in the waters around Aruba. Six fishermen can hire a boat for around US$350 for a half-day, US$500 for a full day. The Deep Sea Fishing Tournament is held each year in October through the Aruba Nautical Club, t 585 3022. Contact:

De Palm Tours, t 582 4400.

Kenny's Toy, t 582 5088.

Rainbow Runner, t 586 4259.

Red Sail Sports, t 583 1603.

Scuba Diving

A reef runs all along the protected leeward coast of Aruba, giving miles of diving, often with 100ft visibility, for scuba-diving enthusiasts. The best marine life is on the south coast between Spanish Lagoon and Commander's Bay, where there are a number of offshore islands. Coral has also begun to encrust Aruba's two wrecks: the *Antilia*, a German freighter that was scuttled off Malmok, and the *Pedernales*, an oil transporter also sunk in the Second World War by a submarine.

Instruction is available through many of the hotels, starting in the swimming pool and venturing out onto the reefs. Dives cost around US$50 each for a one-tank dive, and can be arranged through the hotel or through the major sports shops.

Aruba Pro-Dive, t 582 5520, *www.aruba prodive.com*.

Dax Divers, t 585 1270, *dcarlos52@hotmail.com*.

Native Divers, t 864 763, *nativedivers@ setarnet.aw*, *www.arubaparadise. com/nativedivers*.

Pelican, t 582 7302, *pelican-aruba@ setarnet.aw*, *www.pelican-aruba.com*.

Red Sail Sports, t 586 1603, *info@redsailaruba.com*, *www. redsailaruba.com*.

Snorkelling and Glass-bottom Boats

There are reefs along the south coast at Arashi and Palm Beach and farther afield at Baby Beach at the southeastern end of the island. Trips can be arranged through the big operators. If you would prefer not to get wet, you can try a **glass-bottom boat** through the major watersports operators above. Try also:

Atlantis Submarine, Seaport Marketplace Marina in Oranjestad, t 588 6881, *aruba reservations@atlantissubmarine.com*, *www.atlantisaruba.com*.

Discovery, t 875 875. Glass-bottom boat.

Seaworld Explorer, t 836 090.

Windsurfing and Kayaking

The classic place to windsurf is off the upper end of the west coast, just beyond the high-rise strip, where the winds get a clean run across the island. Close in it is a good spot for beginners because the water is flat and shallow and farther out the winds build up. Instruction is easily available. A windsurfing tournament, the Hi-Winds Pro Am, is held each year in June.

Intermediate and advanced sailboarders can sail waves at Boca Grandi (easiest because it has a sandy bottom), at the northwest point, and along the southern coast, where there are sideshore winds. Some hire companies will allow you to take their boards to these places:

Aruba Kayak Adventures, t 582 5520.

Excursions at De Palm Island.

Roger's Windsurf Place, Malmok, t 586 1918, *rogerwindsurf@setarnet.aw*, *www.rogers windsurf.com*.

Sailboard Vacations, t 586 2527, *sbv@setarnet. aw*, *www.arubasailboardvacations.com*.

Velasurf, Pelican Watersports, t 587 2302, *www.pelican-aruba.com*.

Other Sports

Golf

Aruba Golf Club, t 584 2006. Course with nine holes on which you play off 18 tees.

Divi Golf and Beach Resort, J. E. Irausquin Blvd. 47, t 583 5000, *www.divigolf.com*. New course with driving range and golf school.

Tierra del Sol, t 586 7800, *www.tierradelsol. com*. A top eighteen-hole course.

Horse-riding

If you want to ride the cactus plains of the *cunucu*, horses are available through:

Desert Rose Equestrian Centre, t 594 7806, *www.arubadesertrose.com*.

Rancho El Paso, 44 Washington, t 587 3310, *ranchoelpaso@hotmail.com*, *www.rancho elpaso.bizland.com*. One-hour rides in the countryside or two-hour rides to the beach.

Rancho del Campo, 22E Sombre, t 535 0290, *www.ranchodelcampo.com*.

Rancho Notorious, Boroncana 8E, t 586 0508, *info@ranchonotorious*, *www.rancho notorious.com*. Offers trips to the beach and countryside.

Tennis

Tennis can be fixed up through any number of hotels. Otherwise try:

Aruba Racquet Club, Rooi Santo 21, Palm Beach, t 586 0215. World-class tennis centre.

Where to Stay

Aruba t (297–)

Aruba's hotels have gravitated to two main areas. The strip at Palm Beach is affectionately known as the 'high-rise hotels' and it is easy to see why. It looks a bit like Miami Beach, a mile's worth of skyscrapers humming above ant-like vacationers. Activity is intense – casinos, Vegas-style shows and serried ranks of jet skis. Slightly lower-key, but on an equally good beach (Eagle Beach), are the 'lower-rise hotels', where some less imposing structures lurk among the ferro-concrete monsters. For villas and apartments, of which there are plenty, you can contact the Tourist Board. All hotels charge a 11% government room tax and 10% service charge.

Very Expensive–Expensive

Hyatt Regency, Palm Beach, t 586 1234, US t 1 800 233 1234, *sdhyattaruba@setarnet.com*, *www.hyatt.com*. In the high-rise strip, stands tall with 360 luxurious rooms and suites. You glide up to an atrium set with pillars, dark-stained beams and wrought-iron chandeliers, passing into a palm garden with split-level pools, waterfalls, waterslide, a restaurant in mock ruins and, finally, to the beach. All the requisites for a body holiday – tennis, watersports, spa and aerobics, etc.

Divi Aruba Beach Resort, 45 J. E. Irausquin Bd, Druif Beach, t 582 3300, US t 1 800 554 2008, *info@diviaruba.com*, *www.diviaruba.com*. On Druif Beach around the southwestern point of the island, in the area of the 'low-rise hotels'. It has 200 rooms in blocks strung along the seafront and partially hidden in a tropical garden. There is a more relaxed air about this place, but it too offers all the sports, a couple of restaurants and a bar by the pool. *All-inclusive only.*

Aruba Marriott Resort and Stellaris Casino, L. G. Smith Bd 101, t 586 9000, US t 1 800 223 6388, *www.marriott.com*. A plush resort that opened in 1995, with more than 400 oversized oceanfront guestrooms, 100ft^2 balconies, casual and formal dining, casino, a free-form swimming pool with swim-up bar, health spa, meeting and banquet facilities, watersports and a spectacular beach.

Renaissance Aruba Beach Resort & Casino, L. G. Smith Bd 82, Oranjestad, t 583 6000, *sales@arubarenaissance.com*, *www. renaissancehotels.com*. More than 500 well-appointed rooms and suites, in a convenient spot at Seaport Village or in the Marina Tower, with casino, theatre, spa and shopping mall. From its unique waterway on the ground floor, a speedboat whisks you to the beach on Renaissance Island.

Moderate

Allegro Aruba Beach Resort, Palm Beach, t 586 4500, US and Canada t 1 800 858 2258, *www.occidentalhotels.com*. Dressed in the strong pastel shades of today's Caribbean. Again a good feel, with international standards of service. It has 420 rooms, three restaurants, watersports, swim-up bar, casino and a nightly show. *All-inclusive rate.*

Bucuti Beach Resort, Eagle Beach, **t** 583 1100, *bucuti@setarnet.aw*, *www.bucuti.com*. The new Tara Beach Suites and Spa, pastel and plush, are in their own wing. Each has a kitchen unit, desk and great view. The whole property is now wireless. The compact spa has all the fittings, including Vichy shower and relaxing lounge. A pirate ship restaurant, partially submerged in the sand, provides for casual evening entertainment.

Manchebo Beach Resort, 55 J. E. Irausquin Bd, **t** 582 3444, US **t** 1 800 528 1234, *info@manchebo.com*, *www.manchebo.com*. On the point of the vast Eagle Beach, with 72 rooms and a dive shop.

Inexpensive

Vistalmar, 28 Bucutiweg, Oranjestad, **t** 582 2200. A small hotel off the traditional Aruban tourist track, with rooms set in a villa on the seafront, with kitchens, maid-service and watersports.

Talk of the Town Beach Resort, PO Box 564, Oranjestad, **t** 582 3380, *tottbeachclub@setamet.aw*, *www.talkofthetownaruba.com*. In the outskirts of town on the road to the airport, a sympathetic businessman's stopover. The 63 rooms are set around the pool and palm courtyard. It is low-key and away from the main beach area (it has its own small strip across the road).

Coconut Inn, 31 Noord, **t** 586 6288, *coconutinn@setarnet.aw*, *www.coconutinn.com*. Reasonably priced rooms, usually with kitchens, near the high-rise strip.

Cactus Apartments, 5 Matadera, Noord, **t** 582 2903, *cactus.apts@setarnet.aw*. Not far from the downtown area.

Palm Beach Apartments, 39 Palm Beach, **t** 586 7786. Also near the downtown area.

Aruba Blue Village Suites, 37 Cunucu Abao, **t** 587 8618, *aru.blue.v@setarnet.aw*, *www.arubavillage.com*.

Eating Out

As befits the mix of Aruba's population, there are restaurants of almost any nationality in Aruba – Argentinian, Chinese, German, Japanese – as well as almost any style – grill, gourmet, seafood, bistros, pizza huts. And, of course, do not forget Aruban food itself, for dishes such as *sopito* (fish chowder with coconut), *calco stoba* (conch stew) and *keshi yena* (spiced chicken covered with Dutch cheese). Many restaurants are set in old Aruban town and country houses. Portions are usually large and most restaurants add a 15% service charge to your bill.

The Aruba Gastronomic Association, Salina Cerca 39-E, Noord, **t** 586 1266, *www.arubadining.com*, has a great dine-a-round programme. Buy tickets in a variety of combinations from a selection of 30 restaurants. Ask at your hotel for details. Also, the *Aruba Vacation Planner*, published by De Palm Tours, *www.depalm.com*, has sample menus with prices for many leading restaurants.

Categories are arranged according to the price of a main dish: expensive = US$25 and above; moderate = between US$15 and US$25; inexpensive = US$15 and below.

Expensive

Papiamento, 61 Washington, Noord, **t** 586 4544, *papiamento@setanet.aw*, *www.papiamentorestaurant.com*. Sit outside on the terrace for the best meal on the island. The plantation house is one of the oldest in Aruba and you can eat French and Caribbean specialities here, presented in clay pots (which you break with a hammer), or on a marble slab, which sizzles at your table. The seafood combination is superb (lobster, shrimp, crab, scallop and others on a bed of home-made noodles), or you can try local catch, home-smoked by the owner, Eduardo Ellis, a man with a compelling chuckle.

Chez Mathilde, 23 Havenstraat, Oranjestad, **t** 583 4968. Set in an Aruban town house. The menu is French, tournedos and thermidor served in candlelit intimacy, complemented by an extensive wine list.

Le Dome, J. E.Irausquin Blvd 224, **t** 587 2527, *ledome@setarnet.aw*, *www.ledome-aruba.com*. Clever décor in distinct sections gives the appearance of four different restaurants. Dine on the porch; inside in a garden atmosphere, in the Salvador Dalí room, or in a French bistro. Mussels are the speciality, flown in fresh from Belgium. But don't pass up the tasty breast of duck or those famous Belgian waffles. Lunch, dinner and outstanding Sunday brunch.

Moderate

Gasparito, 3 Gasparito, quite close to the high-rise strip, **t** 867 044. There are a number of restaurants serving Aruban food, of which this is the nicest. It is set in a pretty Aruban house – tiled floors, white-washed walls and *dakpannen*; all over the walls inside you will see Aruban paintings as the dining room doubles as a gallery. You might try the *combo* (fish cake, *kari kari* and chicken stew) or *shrimp en coco* (in coconut milk and brandy), followed by *banana na forno* (banana baked in cinnamon syrup). *Open for lunch and dinner*.

The Old Cunucu House, 150 Palm Beach, **t** 861 666. You can eat outside on the terrace or in another Aruban homestead. The menu is a bit more international, but you can have the house veal escalope in white wine cream sauce, or pan-fried, brandy-flamed conch.

Driftwood, 12 Klipstraat, Oranjestad, **t** 583 2515. For the best of Aruban seafood: *kreeft* (lobster), *carco* (conch) and *masbangoe* (sardines).

Brisas del Mar, 222A Savaneta, **t** 584 7718. A small seafood restaurant on the waterfront, with views of the departing freighters.

Inexpensive

At the *refresquerias*, a cross between a bar and a bakery, where you can sit out on the pavement with a beer, you can get *pan bati*, a sort of flat johnny cake, and *rotis*, pastry envelopes stuffed with meat that originate from Trinidad. If you are peckish, and see a vision of a white truck coming at you out of the night, then stop it – it will be a snack unit, the mobile equivalent of a *refresqueria*.

Nos Cunucu, Tanki Leendert 145K, **t** 582 7122, *noscunucu24@hotmail.com*. Local Aruba at its best. Try papaya stew and daily seafood specials, served in a casual indoor/outdoor setting by waitresses wearing traditional Aruban dress. Family picnics are held on Sundays, with grilled specialities and a dance show.

The Dutch Pancakehouse, Seaport Marketplace, Oranjestad, **t** 583 7180. Owners are from Holland and really know their pancakes, hand-made and baked from an old family recipe. Work your way through 75 varieties in this garden setting by the sea.

Bars and Nightlife

Aruba's well-oiled tourism machine has a whole smorgasbord of entertainment laid on, with Carnival shows and cabaret extravaganzas, or join-in limbo shows and congas to steel bands. There are even Country and Western evenings for the homesick. Details available through the hotels. There are now 11 casinos on the island, but the best has to be the **Alhambra Bazaar**, where, if your luck is out, at least you can be sure of getting something for your money in the all-night shopping arcade. Aruba has three **bar-hopping bus tours** guaranteed to quench your thirst: Kukoo Kunuku, **t** 586 2010, *www.aruba adventures.com*; Banana Bus, **t** 993 9757; and Fiesta Hopper, **t** 582 4400.

Bars include:

The Lounge, Renaissance Aruba Beach Resort, L.G. Boulevard 82, Oranjestad, **t** 583 6000. Super-sophisticated, with the utmost in minimalist décor, this popular retreat overlooks the casino floor. Open to 6am.

Jimmy's Place, Kruysweg 15, Oranjestad, **t** 582 2550. A popular pub a little further down the boulevard, with cold beers and great traditional Dutch melted-cheese sandwiches.

Bahia, Weststraat 7, **t** 588 9982. Set upstairs on an open balcony in the downtown area (if you want to dance then you can go inside).

Charlie's, Main Street, San Nicolas, **t** 584 5086. Something of an institution – for 50 years it was a drinking man's bar, but now women are welcomed too. The ceiling is festooned with anything from car number plates to favourite videos.

Kokoa Beach Bar, on the beach in front of the Aruba Grand Beach Resort. Try here for more typical island music, where you can enjoy a drink with a great view of the setting sun.

Black Hog Saloon, next to La Cabana Resort, **t** 587 6625, *www.blackhogsaloon.com*. Aruba's answer to the biker's bar, the place jumps until all hours with dancing and bar-stool races. Regular all-you-can-eat BBQ nights.

Carlos n' Charlie's, Weststraat 3A, **t** 582 0355. A branch of the famous Mexican restaurant and bar that's found its way to several Caribbean islands and is often a raucous scene with patrons dancing on the tables.

Gilberto François Croes, known as Betico, and after endless lobbying, the Dutch Government agreed to their wishes and granted Aruba 'Status Aparte'.

On 1 January 1986, Aruba raised its own flag and became autonomous, though still within the Kingdom of the Netherlands, with its own currency and elected Parliament, finally separate from Curaçao. They were due to take full Independence in 1996, but they have seen the difficulties that the other islands in the Caribbean have had and so these plans have been shelved indefinitely. The Kingdom of the Netherlands still has responsibility for defence and foreign affairs and is represented by Governor Fredis Regunjol. Aruba is led by Prime Minister Nelson Oduber of the MEP (Movimiento Electoral di Pueblo) Party. The next elections are due to be held in September 2005.

Oranjestad

Named in 1824 after the Dutch royal family, Oranjestad (pronounced *Oran-yeh-stat*; population around 17,000) sits on Aruba's principal harbour, Paardenbaai (Horses' Bay), in the southwestern corner of the island. Today, cruise ships arrive to deliver tourists in their thousands, but 200 years ago, when the island was really just a ranch, it was horses, which were driven off the side of the deck to swim for land.

The oldest building on the island, **Fort Zoutman**, stands sentinel above the bay and its fleet of glinting yachts. Built in 1796, Fort Zoutman saw action only once, when the British invaded in 1799, and now it houses the **Aruba Historical Museum** (*t 582 6099; open Mon–Fri 9–12 and 1–4; adm*), which houses Indian artefacts and scenes from Dutch colonial days. At J. E. Irausquinplein 2A, you will find the **Aruba Archaeological Museum** (*t 582 8979; open Mon–Fri 8–noon and 1.30–4.30; adm free*), which delves deeper into Aruban Indian life with displays of Caiquetio tools and a couple of 2,000-year-old skeletons, found buried in vast clay pots and under turtle shells.

Today, Oranjestad's front-line defences are glitzy duty-free shopping arcades in mock Dutch colonial buildings. Behind this pastel façade, plied by droves of tourists, is a more natural Oranjestad, much of it built in the boom period of the 1930s, where Aruban homes and bars open onto the street. The old town houses have angled tile roofs with dormer windows and tall louvred doors that encourage a breeze through the rooms.

The town has an impressive collection of coins from all over the world in the **Numismatic Museum**, behind the police station at 7 Zuidstraat (*t 582 8831; open Mon–Fri 7.30–noon and 1–4*), displaying 30,000 pieces of money from 400 countries across the world, from ancient Byzantium, through sunken treasure to Aruba's own currency, introduced in 1986. It is also possible to see a private collection of shells owned by the De Man family, **18 Morgenster St** (*t 582 4246; by appt only*) in the outskirts of the town.

Around the Island

As you fly in to land on Aruba, the island looks impossibly small, with just a few folds in the scrubland, but it can take a surprisingly long time to get around it. If you venture further than the beach, you will see farmsteads decorated with magical symbols – circus-like decorations of stars, kiss-curls and lozenges – surrounded by cactus fences. Just a few of these simple old Aruban dwellings remain, clay houses with roofs of cactus wood and dried grass, built after Emancipation in 1863.

Travelling west along the coast from Oranjestad town centre, you come to Aruba's commercial wharf and the industrial estates, and then you immediately emerge into hotel territory at Eagle Beach. As the road swings north, you will see an unexpected sight: a genuine scarlet Dutch windmill from Friesland. Built in 1804, **De Olde Molen** was transported and reassembled here as a tourist attraction in 1961. Unfortunately, the Aruban winds turned out to be so strong that they were forced to take off the sails. It is now a restaurant. The **Aruba Butterfly Farm** (*t 586 3656, www.the butterflyfarm.com; open daily 9–4.30; adm exp*) is worth a visit. You can see more than 30 species from around the world being nurtured from pupae to chrysalides and then emerging to full-blown and brightly coloured butterflies.

Close by is the **Bubali Pond**, once a salt pan, but now an official birdlife reserve protected from development by the government. It provides a refuge for the island's birds, many of whom fly in at sunset to roost there for the night. Apart from the usual pelicans and frigate birds who sit poised on rocks or in the bushes, you can see turnstones and sandpipers strutting around searching for food in the water.

East of the capital, heading towards the northern coastline, you pass through Ayo, where the *cunucu* is interrupted by an assembly of oddly shaped boulders, granite rocks the size of buildings. At **Balashi** and **Bushiribana**, you can see the ruins of the gold mines and the smelting works. Gold was discovered in Aruba in 1825 and the island experienced something of a gold rush, which lasted until 1913 (another explanation for Aruba's name is '*ora uba*', meaning 'gold was found here'). Many birds feed on the fruit of the organ cactus (they look like pipes) and hanging in the trees you may see the little bag nest of the oriole. Grassquits and orange troupials flit around the scrubby vegetation. At **Andicouri** the coastline has been carved into a **natural bridge**, a 30-yard span of coral wall, by the Caribbean waves.

Southeast of Oranjestad, the road passes the airport and beneath the **Hooiberg** (meaning 'haystack'), a local landmark (with steps in it which make its 541ft even easier to climb), on to **Frenchman's Pass**, an impressive gulley on an island so flat, and to Spanish Lagoon, and then to the island's industrial area and the site of the distillation plant.

San Nicolas, Aruba's second town, has a population of 15,000. It grew up around the gates of the Lago oil refinery that opened here in 1929, and quickly became bigger than Oranjestad itself. So many of the workers came from the British Caribbean islands that the streets of wooden shanties once looked like a town in Trinidad. You will hear English spoken in the streets.

North of San Nicolas, you will come across caves with Amerindian hieroglyphs on the roof at **Guadirikiri** and **Fontein**. Some of these exploding squiggles and schematic faces are thought to be genuine, but others were more likely drawn by a European film-crew that was here about ten years ago. Inscriptions (genuine) can also be found on rocks at **Arikok** on the route back to Oranjestad.

The Virgin Islands

12

The Virgin Islands

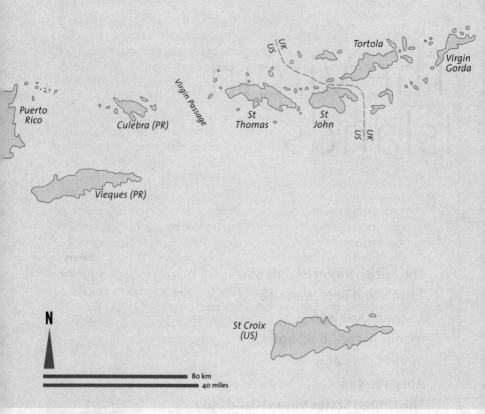

Highlights

1 Sail surrounded by islands in Sir Francis Drake Passage and wash up at one of the British Virgin Islands' many beach bars

2 Explore the giant's playground of semi-submerged volcanic rocks at the Baths, Virgin Gorda

3 Retreat to the secluded calm of tiny St John

The Virgin Islands must have been a nightmare for the early cartographer – more than a hundred islands scattered over 1,000 square miles; forested volcanic colossi that soar from the water and tiny cays that barely make it above the surf. One smudge and he would have been finished. To sail among them is a glorious sight, as stunning as it was 500 years ago when Columbus himself passed through. He was so awestruck by their beauty that he compared them to St Ursula and her 11,000 virgins – a name which has remained ever since.

The Virgin Islands lie at the eastern extremity of the Greater Antilles, 50 miles east of Puerto Rico. Eighty miles to their east, across the Anegada Passage, are the Leeward Islands, which run south from Anguilla and Sint Maarten. The Virgin Islands are nearly all of volcanic origin (now completely inactive) and so they rise steeply out of the water to as much as 1,000ft within a few hundred yards of the coastline. From their summits the views over the islands are superb. The island peaks run in two main lines, facing each other across Sir Francis Drake Passage.

Politically, the islands fall into two groups, both of them possessions: in the west are the United States Virgin Islands, an unincorporated Territory of the USA; and to their east lie the smaller British Virgin Islands, one of Britain's five Overseas Territories in the Caribbean. The USVI has a much larger population (about 120,000 compared with the BVI's 20,000). However, many BVIers have moved to the USVI to live and work. The population of both groups is mainly of African origin, descended from former slaves but, besides the Virgin Islanders themselves, there are large communities of Puerto Ricans and West Indians from down-island, as well as expatriate communities of mainland Americans and some British.

The United States Virgin Islands are more developed than their British counterparts. In St Thomas, life is upbeat and clearly American – you will see the big cruising cars, drive-through banks and fast-food joints, and 10-year-olds wearing outsize sneakers with an infestation of untied laces chatting about HBO TV. St Croix, the largest of the Virgin Islands, is not the most developed (St Thomas is) and because of its agricultural history it has a more pastoral air. St Thomas itself has been a very successful port for hundreds of years and is the mercantile centre of the islands. St John nearby is completely the opposite. It is almost entirely given over to the National Park and in places its slopes rise from shoreline to summit in uninterrupted green. There are two pockets of development, Cruz Bay in the west and Coral Bay around the tortuous coastline at the eastern end. St John has a quiet but undoubted charm.

Life in the BVI is generally gentler and slower still (the USVIers like to take a break there) but things have been moving on apace recently. Tourism is the principal industry, but because so much of it takes place on the water in the BVI, it is generally less visible there; however, Tortola particularly has seen rapid growth. In parts of the BVI, you can still just see some trace of an older West Indies – wooden houses, cows loose on their tethers and the occasional person riding a donkey – but as with the USVI this is steadily disappearing. Traces of the British, who have all but withdrawn from this tropical colony, remain only in the scarlet pillar boxes and telephone boxes and the peaked caps of the customs officials. The name is kept with a limited pride but with willingness when it comes to the effect it has on tourism and offshore business.

In the past, there was talk of the two groups of islands forging closer political links, with the BVI attaching themselves in some way to the USVI to gain from the investment that tourism was bringing to the economy. There were even rumours in the 1960s that the British Government had offered to sell the islands to the United States. Now that they have a highly successful tourist industry of their own, and have seen how recent development has turned out next door, most BVIers are glad they didn't. They did adopt the US dollar as their currency, however, and this has had undoubted benefits. Many BVIers, or 'Belongers' as they are known, do work in the USVI and they take their money back home to the BVI to build a home for their retirement.

Most people who come to the Virgin Islands will spend time on the water: on a ferry, belly-flopping onto the sea as their seaplane comes in to land, in snorkelling gear, or cruising in a yacht between secluded coves and waterfront beach bars. The cartographer's nightmare is a sailor's paradise.

The British Virgin Islands

The British Virgin Islands – 50 or so reefs, rocks and raging volcanic towers – are sprinkled across the sea to the northeast of the USVI. They run in two main lines about 3 miles apart, enclosing the Sir Francis Drake Channel. The bays make magnificent anchorages, as good now as when Columbus passed by, and later when pirates caroused and careened their ships here. The British Virgin Islands are some of the best sailing grounds in the world, and on land their coves hide some great places on which to be marooned (particularly in five-star luxury).

Tortola is changing as the tourism industry develops and there is an increasingly upbeat air in the island. Construction has recently broken the green continuity of the hillside scrub as the islanders build themselves larger homes and outsiders build vacation villas. Cruise ships arrive and spill yet more people onto the tiny island. Virgin Gorda, on the other hand, is only gradually being developed, and so life still moves at a dozier, more typical Caribbean pace. The other islands are developed only with hotels and private villas.

There are about 20,000 inhabitants in the BVI, most of whom live on Tortola. However, for generations they have been travelling to the US Virgin Islands and there are probably more than 20,000 living there. The BVIers benefit from their special status and from having the dollar as their currency, but they talk fearfully of how the USVI have been overdeveloped and of the crime level there. In the BVI the policemen carry truncheons rather than guns.

In times past, the BVI have looked east to the Leeward Islands and they still do in some matters such as sport, carnival and music, which is mostly calypso. However, most BVIers admit that American influence will inevitably increase and the old Caribbean and British ways recede. There is continual American investment and most consumer goods originate in the USA anyway. Basketball is a popular sport with the youth (as it is all over the Caribbean) and it is probably a matter of time before softball overtakes cricket in popularity.

The majority of visitors to the BVI come for the sailing and the islands have angled their tourism cleverly at the upper end of the market, setting themselves up as a sophisticated Caribbean playground. They do it pretty well. The BVI are fairly expensive, but they are mostly easygoing and there is a lower hustle factor than elsewhere in the islands, even if the Belongers can be a little unforthcoming sometimes. You can get a very good tropical break in the BVI and for a price you can get luxurious seclusion on a tropical island resort.

History

History and legend are closely intertwined in the Virgin Islands – the coves and bays that make such perfect quiet and secluded anchorages for yachts were also ideal as pirate hangouts, and so the two have become confused. As late as 1792, when the British had officially been in control for over a hundred years, Tortola was still described as a 'pirates' den'. Of course the islands' most important activity, smuggling, was never recorded anyway.

When Columbus first arrived here in the late 15th century, the Virgin Islands were seeing waves of the belligerent Carib Indians from down-island. They were stopping by on their inevitable progress through the islands, occasionally raiding Arawak Borinquen (now Puerto Rico). But the Spaniards on Puerto Rico turned out to be more of a match than the Arawaks, and in 1555 they turned the tables, bearing down on the Caribs in the Virgin Islands and wiping them out.

Soon after the Caribs were eliminated, another threat began appearing in the Virgin Islands – pirates. They used the bays to anchor and careen their ships and then climbed the heights to watch for a sail to appear on the horizon. Jack Hawkins and Sir Francis Drake passed through, the latter giving his name to the channel through which he escaped in 1585 after raiding the Spanish *flota* with the riches of Mexico aboard. There are endless legends of buried treasure in the BVI.

The first permanent settlers on the islands were Dutch buccaneers and cattle ranchers, who arrived on Tortola in 1648. They sold the smoked meat to passing ships. In 1672, they were ousted by English buccaneers and the eastern Virgin Islands were taken over by England. Despite the official status, the smuggling continued as the buccaneers became settled.

Although the islands are not particularly fertile, they were able to grow cotton and experienced some prosperity at the height of the sugar era during the 18th century. Slaves were brought here and the steep hillsides were terraced and planted with cotton and cane. Quakers who came to the islands had a hand in freeing some of the slaves (they thought slavery immoral and rallied against it) and the plantations folded quickly, even before Emancipation in 1838. As they failed, so the white population left. In 1805, the population was about 10,500 (9,000 slaves) and, a century later, there were 5,000, of whom two were white. The remaining islanders became subsistence farmers on the land abandoned by the planters. This has only changed in the last few decades with the advent of the tourist industry.

Early on, the British Virgin Islands were governed by an elected council, but in 1867 this was abolished and the islands were simply appended to the Leeward Island Federation as a 'Presidency'. The British Virgin Islands are still an Overseas Territory of Britain and are nominally administered by a Governor appointed in London, but since the Second World War they have steadily taken on internal self-government. There is a 12-member elected council with a ministerial system. The Chief Minister is the Hon. Ralph T. O'Neal of the Virgin Islands Party and the opposition leader is the Hon. Dr Orlando Smith of the National Democratic Party. Elections are next scheduled for 2007.

The biggest foreign exchange earner is tourism. Of the nearly 800,000 visitors each year, there are just over 450,000 cruise ship arrivals, and of the rest 60% come for the

Getting There

British Virgin Islands t (1 284–)

By Air

The BVI has no long runway (the biggest aircraft that can land on Beef Island, the islands' main airport, is a 49-seater) and so you will have to make a connection to get there. The main hub in the area is San Juan in Puerto Rico and plenty of airlines make the onward connections, though if travelling from Europe, you might consider changing in Antigua or Sint Maarten and joining the inter-island hoppers. Alternatively, you can charter a small plane. The main airfield is on Beef Island at the eastern end of Tortola, but there are also smaller strips in Virgin Gorda and Anegada. There is a departure tax of US$20 if you are leaving by air.

From the UK

There is a weekly charter with Air 2000 into St Thomas (see p.515), from where you can connect to the BVI on the same day. It may be preferable to fly via Antigua, from where LIAT, t 495 2577, or any of the smaller charter airlines will make the connection (see p.339).

From the USA

Connecting flights can be arranged via San Juan, Puerto Rico (e.g. American Airlines and Delta from Atlanta; see p.554), and through the USVI (see p.515).

From Other Caribbean Islands

There are flights to Tortola from Puerto Rico on American Eagle, t 495 2559, and LIAT, t 495 2577, who also fly to Antigua, St Kitts and Sint Maarten, to which Winair, t 494 2347, also makes the link. Local airlines include Clair Aero Services, t 495 2271; Continental Connection, t 495 1044; and Air St Thomas, t 495 5935, air.st.thomas@worldnet.att.net, www.air stthomas.com, which flies in from the USVI. Caribbean Star, t 494 2347, flies daily from Beef Island to Antigua, and onward to Anguilla, St Maarten, St Kitts, Dominica, St Lucia, Barbados, St Vincent, Grenada, Trinidad and Guyana. Cape Air, t 495 2100, www.flycapeair.com, have scheduled flights from the USVI and the smaller Puerto Rican islands of Vieques

and Culebra. Services to Virgin Gorda are more limited, though there are direct links from San Juan and St Thomas on Air St Thomas and on Air Sunshine, t 495 8900, US t 1 800 327 8900, www.airsunshine.com. Planes can be chartered through Fly BVI, t 495 1747, and Caribbean Wings, t 495 6000, US t 1 800 234 2213, carwings@yahoo.com. Island Helicopters International, Beef Island, t 499 2663, offer aerial sightseeing.

By Sea

There are plenty of ferries from St Thomas, USVI, to Tortola in the BVI. Many depart from the Charlotte Amalie waterfront, touching West End on Tortola and then continuing to Road Town. The crossing takes just over an hour with customs. Companies include Roadtown Fast Ferry, t 494 2323, to St Thomas; Native Son Inc, t 495 4617, and Smith's Ferry Services, t 494 4495. Speedy's, t 495 5240, runs a service three times a week from St Thomas to Virgin Gorda, a two-hour ride through Sir Francis Drake Channel. Or you can go with Inter-Island Boat Services, t 495 4166, which also link St John to West End on Tortola, usually four times a day. There is a departure tax of US$5 if you are departing by boat.

Getting Around

The British Virgin Islands are well served by ferries. The main terminals are at West End and Road Town on Tortola, Beef Island near the airport, and at The Valley and North Sound in Virgin Gorda.

There are seven or eight sailings each day between Road Town and The Valley, on Speedy's, t 495 5240, and Smith's, t 494 4495. There is also a link from the airport to Virgin Gorda (The Valley and the North Sound), on the North Sound Express, t 495 2138 (reservations recommended), making about four trips a day. North Sound Express boats are sleek and fun to ride as they skim across the water with a sonorous rumble. There are six daily sailings (fewer at the weekend) from West End to Jost van Dyke on the New Horizon Ferry Service, t 494 9278, has up to five departures daily. Peter Island is served by the Peter Island boat, t 495 2000, which departs from the CSY marina in Road Town, with about 10 crossings a day, and there are links to Marina Cay off Beef Island and around the North Sound Gun Creek, Saba Rock and Leverick Bay. There are no actual ferries to Anegada, so if you want to visit by sea, your best bet is to take one of the many day sailing cruises, or you can **fly** with Clair Aero Services, **t** 495 2271, which makes the trip to Anegada four times a week. Otherwise you'll have to charter.

Up-to-the-minute ferry schedules can be found in the BVI *Welcome* tourist magazine. An alternative way of travelling in the Virgin Islands is to go to the marinas and talk somebody into taking you on their yacht.

Tourist Information

Abroad

The Tourist Office's *Welcome* tourist guide has been put online and so you can access some information direct from the screen at *www.bviwelcome.com*. Their 'Electronic Beach Bar' is a general chat forum in which you can swap stories and opinions. You will find plenty of information at *www.b-v-i.com* and on *www.islandsonline.com*. If you are a sailor, you might want to check *www.destinationbvi.com*.

UK: Upper Grosvenor St, London W1K 7PJ, **t** (020) 7355 9585, *infouk@bvi.org.uk*.

USA: 1270 Broadway, Suite 705, New York, NY 10001, **t** (212) 696 0400, *ny@bvitouristboard.com*; 3450 Wilshire Bd, Suite 1202, Los Angeles 90010, **t** (213) 736 8931, *bvila@bvitouristboard.com*; 3400 Peachtree Rd, Suite 1735, Lenox Towers, Atlanta, Georgia, **t** (404) 467 4741, *bviatlanta@worldnet.att.net*.

There is a general toll-free number in the US, **t** 1 800 835 8530.

In the BVI

Road Town: AKARA building, De Castro St, Wickham's Cay, PO Box 134, **t** 494 3134, *bvitourb@surfbvi.com*.

Virgin Gorda: Virgin Gorda Yacht Harbour, **t** 495 5181.

Media

The Tourist Board puts out the quarterly *Welcome* tourist guide, in which you will find plenty of useful practical information, and the latest investment opportunities. There are two weekly newspapers published in the islands, the *Beacon* and the *Island Sun*. The tourist paper the *Limin' Times* gives an up-to-the-minute breakdown of boozing opportunities.

Medical Emergencies

In a medical emergency, dial **t** 999 or contact the Peebles Hospital in Road Town, Tortola, **t** 494 3497. On Virgin Gorda there are clinics in Spanish Town, **t** 495 5337, and at North Sound, **t** 495 7310.

Money and Banks

The currency of the BVI is the US dollar (adopted in 1967). You will find that major credit cards are very widely accepted in the hotels, restaurants and shops. **Banking hours** are Mon–Thurs 9–3, Fri 9–5.

Shopping

Shops generally keep hours of Mon–Sat 9–5.

Telephone Code

The IDD code for the BVI is **t** 1 284 followed by a seven-digit number. On-island, people always tend to say a number as five digits (as it used to be), but when you call you must dial seven figures.

Festivals

Many **regattas** are staged each year by the BVI Yacht Club, **t** 494 3286, the main event being the Spring Regatta in April.

April *Spring Regatta*. The main sailing event, held over three days in Sir Francis Drake Channel.

Easter Festival. Kite-flying competitions for the kids, held in Virgin Gorda.

May *Foxy's Wooden Boat Regatta*. Held at Foxy's, in Jost van Dyke (*see* p.497).

June/July HIHO (Hook in, Hold on) *Windsurfing Challenge*. Another fun event; call **t** 494 0339 for information.

July *Carnival*. The highlight of the BVI calendar, which builds towards the end of the month and culminates in early August. There are bands and calypso competitions at the Carnival Village in Road Town, Tortola, and then the carnival bands parade through the town. Go if you get the chance.

Christmas *Music festival*. Scratch and Funchi bands play – banjo, washboard, bathtub (bass) and sometimes ukelele and flute.

31 December *New Year Party*. This huge celebration at Foxy's, in Jost van Dyke, is definitely worth a look.

Watersports

There are plenty of opportunities for watersports fanatics around the BVI. In fact, not to spend some time on the water is really to miss the point. For general beach-bound watersports the best beach is probably Cane Garden Bay on Tortola.

Sailing

The only option for sailors without qualifications is to hire a **crewed yacht**, of which there are plenty available in the BVI. Many of these are owner-operated and so they can give a more personal touch. They can pick you up wherever you want and they provide local knowledge. Although bareboats can be ordered directly from the charter company, to book a crewed yacht you should contact a yachting broker in your own country; details are available through the tourist boards (*see also* **Travel**, p.44). For charter companies based in St Thomas, *see* pp.515–16. Another option to consider, particularly if you have children, is a **flotilla**, in which a number of yachts sail around the islands together.

There are about ten **marinas** in the BVI where you can take on all the provisions and services you will need. In Tortola, there are marinas in Road Town, Wickhams Cay I, which is closest to town, and Wickhams Cay II, Nanny Cay, Fat Hog's Bay and Soper's Hole Marina at West End. Other, smaller marinas are scattered along the southern shore towards the eastern end of the island. In Virgin Gorda, you can go to the Virgin Gorda Yacht Harbour, **t** 495 5555, and the Bitter End Yacht Club in the North Sound.

The two largest **bareboat** charter operators are The Moorings and Sunsail, both based in Tortola. For bareboat charters, companies give a briefing before you set out and they will provision your yacht on request. If you want one, most have skippers who will settle you in for a couple of days and then leave you to get on with it. The Moorings and Sunsail have other outlets elsewhere in the Eastern Caribbean and so you can sail to other islands down the chain if you wish.

BVI Yacht Charters, Inner Harbour Marina, Wickham's Cay I, Tortola, **t** 494 4289, *sailbvi@ surfbvi.com*, *www.bviyachtcharters.com*.

Footloose Sailing Charters, Wickham's Cay II, Road Town, Tortola, **t** 494 0528, *www.jolly monsailing.com/footloose*. This is a cheaper alternative, and takes on some boats once they have left the Moorings fleet.

The Moorings, Wickham's Cay II, Road Town, PO Box 139, **t** 494 2332, US **t** 1 800 368 9994, *yacht@moorings.com*, *www.moorings.com*.

Sunsail, Soper's Hole, West End, Tortola, **t** 495 4740, US **t** 1 800 327 2276, *sstortola@surfbvi. com*, *www.sunsail.com*.

Virgin Traders, PO Box 993, Nanny Cay Marina, Tortola, **t** 495 2526, US **t** 1 888 684 6486, *cruising@virgin-traders.com*, *www.virgin-traders.com*.

Scuba Diving

There are some good reefs in the BVI, where staghorn and elkhorn stand tall by sponges and seafans, and patrols of sergeant majors and triggerfish follow wrasses, grunts and groupers. Spiked sea urchins and spiny lobster lurk in the crevices and depths. For all the islands that soar to 1,000ft from the sandy bed there are also plenty of coral-clad pinnacles that do not quite make the surface, and these make good diving grounds. The most popular sites are the Indians near Norman Island, Cistern Rock near Salt Island, Blonde Rock and Painted Walls between Dead Chest and Salt Island, and Alice in Wonderland to the south of Ginger Island. Also the Dogs off Virgin Gorda.

There are also a number of wreck dives in the islands, among them the RMS *Rhone*, which is excellent. A Royal Mail ship that sank off Salt Island in a hurricane in 1867, the 310ft *Rhone* lies in depths from 30ft down to 90ft. Other wreck-dive sites include the *Chikuzen*, a ship in 70ft of water, 6 miles north of Beef Island. Further north of here, Anegada is the only coral-based island in the group and it has the richest marine life of all. There is a park fee of $1 to dive.

sailing. Other industries include construction (the scars of quarrying and building plots are visible in the hillsides), some light manufacturing and an expanding offshore finance sector.

Sailing and Charters

Cruising Sir Francis Drake Channel is one of the finest experiences the Caribbean can offer. The islands lie like sleeping animals around you, set between a fantastic blue sea and sky; close at hand, small cays move past you as you cruise, and on the horizon the volcanic colossi do not budge. You can moor in coves where headlands enclose a horseshoe of white sand and a few palms and where the water is so clear that the boat seems to be suspended in the air. When it gets too hot on board, swim to the beach and collapse there. At sunset there is nothing better to do than to head ashore for the easy activity of a beach bar.

The Virgin Islands offer some of the best fair-weather sailing in the world – the waters are safe and sheltered by the large islands, but there are constant breezes. Anchorages are good, the distances between them are short and the sailing itself is relatively easy (with the exception of Anegada, there are few reefs) and so the area is ideal for bareboat chartering. The industry is well developed and charter companies have chase boats and vehicles. The BVI also have an excellent string of beach bars and restaurants which make for a lively bar-hopping holiday if you prefer.

The charter companies have yachts of all sizes available for hire, from simple 30-footers for two to luxury motor-cruisers with on-board Renoirs, jetskis and clay-pigeon traps. Crewed yachts come with a skipper and a cook, but there are plenty of bareboats for those who would prefer to look after themselves. Yachts usually have snorkelling equipment, but as you go up the scale there will be video recorders, wind-surfers and often diving gear. Prices start at around US$150 per day per person and for extreme luxury expect to shell out around US$500 (though really the sky is the limit). Hire is a little cheaper in the summer months (as much as 30% off) and you will find the channel and coves a little less crowded then.

Tortola and Beef Island

Tortola (the Turtle Dove) is the largest of the British Virgins (21 square miles) and set in a huge bay on its south coast is the BVI capital, Road Town. The island is irregularly shaped, long and thin and 10 miles by 3, but the roads are so wiggly as they pass in and out of the coves that it takes 45 minutes to get from one end to the other, and it is so mountainous that you cannot cross over from one side to the other without ascending to about 1,200ft. Mount Sage, whose upper slopes are covered with such lush and explosive greenery that it is almost rainforest, is the highest point in all the Virgins (1,716ft). It is worth exploring the heights, if only for the magnificent views of the other islands. About 15,000 of the 20,000 BVI population live on Tortola.

Tortola has lost its innocence recently. There has been a massive building spree in the past few years and now the difference from the USVI is not so marked. With a

Tortola and Around

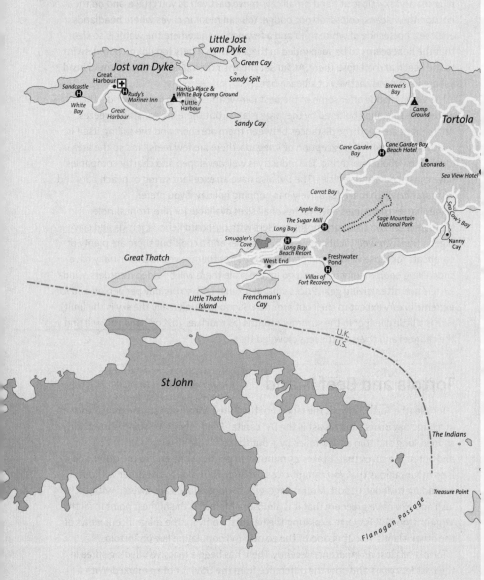

Little Jost
van Dyke

Jost van Dyke

Great
Harbour

Sandcastle
White
Bay
Great
Harbour

Rudy's
Mariner Inn

Green Cay

Sandy Spit

Harris's Place &
White Bay Camp Ground
Little
Harbour

Sandy Cay

Brewer's
Bay

Camp
Ground

Tortola

Cane Garden
Bay

Cane Garden Bay
Beach Hotel

Leonards

Sea View Hotel

Carrot Bay

Apple Bay

The Sugar Mill

Long Bay

Smuggler's
Cove

Long Bay
Beach Resort

Great Thatch

West End

Villas of
Fort Recovery

Freshwater
Pond

Sage Mountain
National Park

Sea Cow's Bay

Nanny Cay

Little Thatch
Island

Frenchman's
Cay

U.K.
U.S.

St John

The Indians

Treasure Point

Flanagan Passage

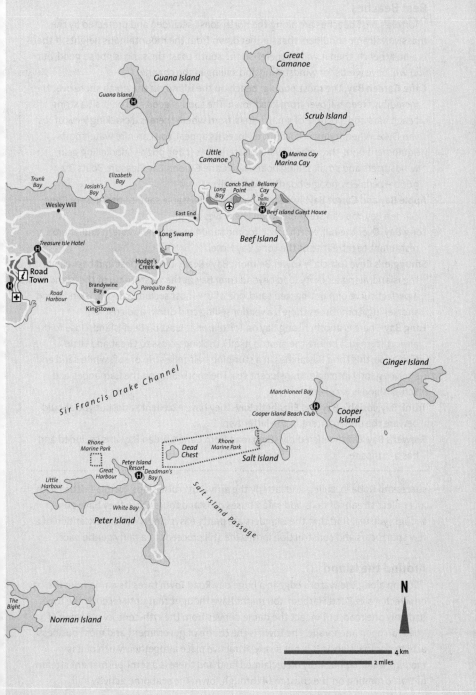

Best Beaches

Tortola's best beaches are along the north coast, secluded and protected by the massive volcanic shoulders that lumber down from the mountainous heights. If there is a busy beach, then it will be there. On the south coast the sand is not so good, but you will have winds for windsurfing and sailing in the channel.

Cane Garden Bay: The most popular beach on the island, on the north shore over the incredibly steep hill over from Road Town. The sand is good and on it sit a string of beach bars and a couple of small hotels, from where there is a cracking view of Jost van Dyke. When frying in coconut oil loses its appeal, you can hire watersports equipment here, through Baby Bull Watersports (*t* 495 9627 – snorkelling gear, windsurfers and small sailing boats) and Cane Garden Bay Pleasure Boats (*t* 495 9660 – pedaloes, boogie boards and surfbikes).

Apple Bay and **Carrot Bay**: Two small coves with passable sand to the west of Cane Garden Bay. You can surf here when the waves are up.

Long Bay: Over the hill, worth a visit for the sand towards the western end; there's a restaurant to retreat to at the Long Bay Hotel.

Smuggler's Cove (officially Lower Belmont Bay): Really the prettiest and best beach on the island, along a rickety road beyond Long Bay, at the western tip of the island. It is a perfect curve of palm-backed sand, one of the most secluded on the island; good snorkelling. Sometimes there's a vendor selling cold drinks and crisps.

Long Bay: There is another Long Bay on Tortola, or at least on Beef Island, close to the airport (turn just before the airstrip itself). Looking across to Great and Little Camanoe, this Long Bay arches in a stunning half-mile strip of soft white sand and shelves gently into calm translucent sea. The snorkelling on the Camanoes and Scrub Island is excellent.

Trunk Bay, **Josiah's Bay** and **Elizabeth Bay**: They have excellent sand, but you should beware the undercurrent in the latter two.

Brewer's Bay: Off the incredibly steep road from Cane Garden Bay; it is secluded and has a campsite.

successful trade in sailing and latterly the arrival of cruise ships, Tortola beetles with an endless stream of taxis and safari buses on island tours. Once they have gone, though, you will find that the islanders are pretty easygoing. With the exception of a few sports cars and construction lorries, life still proceeds at a fairly gentle pace.

Around the Island

Strung along the water's edge in a huge bay, **Road Town** takes its name from the bay on which it sits, Road Harbour. You might have thought that until recently the town had only one road, but in fact the name derives from the 17th-century meaning of 'road', an open anchorage. The town is the centre of government and most business activity for the islands. It is not a very attractive place altogether. Much of it is modern, built haphazardly on reclaimed land and there is a semi-permanent stream of traffic running on the coast road through town. The seaborne activity still

Getting There

Tortola t (1 284–)

See 'Getting There' under 'The British Virgin Islands', p.482.

Getting Around

By Bus

There is a rudimentary bus service that runs along the south coast of Tortola, emanating from Road Town (fares $1–3; timings unpredictable). Catch it if you can find it.

By Taxi

The most reliable method of travel is by taxi, readily found in town and the airport or ferry terminals. Prices are fixed, pretty steeply, by the government, so you may want to ensure the price beforehand. Road Town to West End, Cane Garden Bay or Beef Island costs around US$14. You can order one through:

BVI Taxi Association, t 494 2322.
Waterfront Taxi Stand, t 494 4959.
West End Taxi Association, t 495 4881.

An island tour by taxi costs around US$45 for up to four people; otherwise you can contact Travel Plan Tours, t 494 2872, *romasco@caribsurf.com*, or BVI Adventures, t 494 8500, *www.bviadventures.com*.

By Air

Sightsee by plane on a run down Tortola to Soper's Hole and then along the small island chain up to Necker Island:

Caribbean Wings, Beef Island, t 495 6000.
Clair Aero, Beef Island, t 495 2271.
Fly-BVI, Beef Island Airport, t 495 1747.
Island Birds, Beef Island, t 495 2002.
Island Helicopters International, Beef Island, t 499 2663.

Hitch-hiking

Hitch-hiking is possible, and about as haphazard as anywhere else.

Car and Bike Hire

Maximum flexibility comes with your own hire car, but at a price (from about $80 per day plus taxes in winter, less in summer). If you wish to drive, you must obtain a BVI temporary driving licence (from the car rental agency or Traffic Licensing Office on production of $10 and a valid licence from elsewhere). There is often a hefty deposit (credit cards OK). Driving is mostly on the left and the speed limit is supposedly 40mph in the country and 20mph in town. Watch out for speed bumps in the settlements and traffic jams in Road Town at the beginning and end of the working day (9am and 4.30pm). Rental firms include:

Avis, Road Town, t 494 3322.
Dollar Rent-A-Car, Road Town, t 494 6093, *www.dollar@surfbvi.com*.
Hertz Car Rental, West End, t 495 4405, *www.hertzbvi.com*.
International Car Rentals, Road Town, t 494 2516, *intercar@surfbvi.com*, *www.go2rsite.com/international*. Cars and jeeps.
Last Stop Sports Bike Rentals, Port Purcell, Wickham's Cay II, P.O. Box 993, Road Town, t 494 1120, *www.laststopsports.com*.
National Car Rental, Duffs Bottom and Long Bay, t 494 3197.
Tola Rentals, t 494 8652, *www.tolarentals.com*.
3P Scooter Rental, Valley, Virgin Gorda, t 495 6870, *3pscooter@surfbvi.com*.

Watersports

General watersports operators include:
Baby Bull Watersports, Cane Garden Bay, Tortola, t 495 9627.
Boardsailing BVI, Trellis Bay, Beef Island, t 495 2447, *www.windsurfing.vi*.
Cane Garden Bay Pleasure Boats, Tortola, t 495 9660. Kayaks.
Hi Ho, Prospect Reef Resort, Tortola, t 494 7694.
Last Stop Sports , Wickhams Cay II, Road Town, t 494 1120, *www.laststopsports.com*.
Splash Sports, West End, Tortola, t 495 4942.

Day Sails

If you're not sure you want to do the actual sailing bit, there are plenty of options for day sails: half-day or full-day trips and sunset extravaganzas. These include trips to an offshore island with picnic and snorkelling stops, usually across the channel to Norman Island or Virgin Gorda, but occasionally a full day out to Anegada. Contact:

Kuralu, t 495 4381, *kuralucharters@surfbvi.com*, *www.kuralu.com*. For a day on a catamaran.

Patouche Charters, t 4946300, *patouche@ surfbvi.com*, *www.patouche.com*. A 48ft catamaran.

Tikitas Yacht Charters, t 494 4179, *www.islands online.com/tikitas*. Single-hulled yachts.

White Squall, t 4942564, *www.whitequall2. com*. A traditional schooner.

Deep-sea Fishing

Good within a short distance of the BVI, the cost is around $700–900 for a full day, including tackle and bait. You must have a permit; contact Fisheries Division, t 494 3429. Contact:

Blue Ocean Adventures, t 499 2837, *blueocean@hotmail.com*.

Persistence Charters, at Soper's Hole, West End, t 495 4122.

Sailing Courses

See also 'Sailing', p.484. If you would like to test out the Virgin Islands' winds and waters, but would rather not take out a 50ft yacht, many of the hotels have small sailing boats. If you want to learn to sail a yacht contact:

Bitter End Yacht Club, Virgin Gorda, t 494 2745, *www.beyc.com*.

Full Sail, t 4940512, *fullsail@surfbvi.com*, *www.fullsailbvi.com*. Offer a six-day live-aboard course.

Nanny Cay Resort & Marina, just west of Road Harbour, Road Town, t 494 2512, *docks@ nanny.com*. Docks, water, fuel, ice, electricity, chandlery, showers, dive shop.

Offshore Sailing School, at the Prospect Reef Hotel, t 454 1700, US t 1 800 221 4326, *sail@offshore-sailing.com*, *www.offshore-sailing.com*. A five-day land-based course.

Sistership Sailing School, t 495 1002, *www.sailsistership.com*.

Scuba Diving

All dive companies will provide instruction and referral training if you have completed part of your training back at home. A single tank dive costs $55, two tanks $80, and there is a park fee of $1. Companies include:

Blue Water Divers, Nanny Cay Marina, t 494 2847, t 494 0198, *bwdbvi@surfbvi.com*, *www.bluewaterdiversbvi.com*.

Dive BVI, Virgin Gorda Yacht Harbour, t 495 5513, *www.divebvi.com*.

Dive Tortola, Road Town, t 494 9200, *dive tortola@surfbvi.com*, *www.divetortola.com*.

UBS Dive Center, East End, t 494 0024, *mail@scubabvi.com*, *www.scubabvi.com*.

Underwater Safaris, The Moorings, Road Town, t 494 2332, US toll free t 1 800 537 7032, *undsaf@caribsurf.com*, *www.cooper-island. com/scuba*.

Windsurfing

Equipment and lessons can be found at:

Boardsailing BVI, at Nanny Cay, t 494 0422, and Trellis Bay, t 495 2447, *jwright@surfbvi. com*, *www.windsurfing.vi*. At Trellis Bay in the northeast, the onshore winds are funnelled between the islands into the bay, which itself remains calm. They also have kayaks, and use BIC, Mistral and Fanatic equipment. Hire is $20 per hour, $55 per day.

Other Sports

Horse-riding

Shadows Stables, based in the Ridge Rd near Skyworld, t 494 2262. They will take you through the rainforest on Sage Mountain or down to Cane Garden Bay.

Mountain-biking

Last Stop Sports, Nanny Cay, t 494 0564, *lssbikes@caribsurf.com*, *www.laststop sports.com*. They have mountain bikes as well as watersports equipment for hire.

Tennis

There are courts in many of the hotels and at the Tortola Tennis Club in Road Town.

Where to Stay

Tortola t (1 284–)

Tortola has only a few nice hotels (the BVI's smartest hotels are mostly on Virgin Gorda or on their own island) and not all of them are on or even near beaches – many are quite functional stopovers which are used as a base by sailors. There are very few cheap places to stay anywhere in the BVI (with the exception of the many camp sites). For some reason, most of the hotel rooms in Tortola seem to have kitchenettes. It is worth enquiring about weekend and other packages. A government tax of 7% will be added to all bills.

With so little to choose from, it is definitely worth considering taking a **villa** on Tortola; there is a good variety.

Areana Villas, in Long Bay and Cane Garden Bay, **t** 494 5864, *areanavillas@candwbvi.net*, *www.areanavillas.com*. Villa complex.

BVI Club, *bvic@vch.co.uk, www.vch.co.uk/villas*. Villa rentals.

My Private Paradise, **t** 495 9814, US **t** 1 800 862 7863, *info@myprivateparadise.com*, *www.myprivateparadise.com*. You can find some individual villas (i.e. not part of a complex) through this company.

Very Expensive

Guana Island, PO Box 32, **t** 494 2354, US **t** 1 800 624 8262, *guana@guana.com, www.guana. com*. This offers some of the best in Virgin Islands luxury and seclusion, on a private island of 850 acres just north of Beef Island. Tennis, watersports (windsurfing, sailing, fishing trips and seven beaches) and even croquet are there, but the club is most special for its gracious atmosphere amid superb hillside settings. Each of the simple but elegant and comfortable rooms – almost Mediterranean in style it seems, with white stucco and coloured shutters – has a terrace and an expanse of view in its isolated setting. From solitude in the rooms, you can venture to the company of the main house (relative company, anyway, because there is a maximum of 30 guests), with dining room and, of course, library, or to the beach for the watersports. Afternoon tea, honour bar and a friendly dining room on a veranda with a view – pure luxury.

Expensive

The Sugar Mill, Little Apple Bay, PO Box 425, **t** 495 4355, US **t** 1 800 462 8834, Canada **t** 800 209 6874, *sugmill@surfbvi.com*, *www.sugarmillhotel.com*. Charming and intimate, set in restored stone estate buildings surrounded by luxurious tropical greenery. The 24 rooms are modern, white and bright and very comfortable, ranged on the hill behind, each with a wonderful view of Jost van Dyke from the balcony, over the pool, seaside beach deck and restaurant (for lighter, daytime meals). The hotel is renowned for its dining room: you take cocktails in the gazebo of tall arches and then move to the setting of antique stone walls in the old boiling house, to the tune of water falling into copper kettles (*see* 'Eating Out').

Long Bay Beach Resort, PO Box 433, **t** 495 4252, US **t** 1 800 729 9599, *res@longbay@idestin. com, www.longbay.com*. The 105 rooms (*cabañas*, studios and villas) are scattered around Long Bay, a picturesque cove in the west of the island. They stand in the seagrape just behind the excellent sandy beach and on the steep hillside behind, each very comfortable with bright décor and all mod cons (full kitchens in some cases). Breakfast terrace by the pool, dinner in the elegant Tropical Garden dining room in the main house on the hillside.

Villas of Fort Recovery, Towers, West End, PO Box 11156, St Thomas USVI 00801, **t** 495 4354, US **t** 1 800 367 8455, *ftrhotel@surfbvi.com*, *www.fortrecovery.com*. A small hotel with a friendly and attentive atmosphere built around an old fort on the water's edge near West End. There are 17 villas in a variety of configurations (one to four bedrooms), set in pretty pebbledash and shingle-sided cottages surrounded by tropical flowers, all with balconies or patios with a view over the passable beach (calm for swimming and good for snorkelling) out to sea and Frenchman's Cay and other islands. All have air-con, cable TV, videos, full kitchens (though continental breakfasts are included) and local artwork on the walls.

Marina Cay, PO Box 626, Road Town, **t** 494 2174, *marinacay@pussers.com*. A little more secluded, this hotel is set on a tiny blip (no more than 100 by 200 yards) offshore at the eastern end of Tortola. There is a quiet, intimate air most of the time because there are just four rooms and two two-bedroom villas tucked away around the island. However, you can expect some activity with passing yachts and other visitors who come to enjoy the beach and the few watersports (including scuba) by day, the bar at sunset – there is a fantastic view from the sunset bar on the heights – and the dining room in the evening.

Moderate

Treasure Isle Hotel, PO Box 68, Road Town, t 494 2501, US t 1 800 233 1108, *www.treasure islehotel.com*. A very comfortable spot which stands above the marinas on the hillside, with a pool and a restaurant, the Lime 'n' Mango, on a pretty deck. Just 40 rooms and three suites, with typical Caribbean comfort, TV and air-con.

Beef Island Guest House, PO Box 494, Trellis Bay, East End, t 495 2303, *mongoose@ surfbvi.com*. An excellent and friendly guest house with just four rooms set in a house, around a central living area that is open to guests (with video and paperback library). Right on the beach and calm waters of Trellis Bay, this is a fun spot with seclusion or activity (e.g. windsurfing) just a short walk away. Rate includes breakfast at the rustic beach bar, De Loose Mongoose, next door.

Moderate–Inexpensive

Cane Garden Bay Beach Hotel (better known as Rhymer's), PO Box 570, t 495 4639, *www. bviguide.com/rhymers*. Sits right on the beach, painted in faintly alarming shades of pink and lemon yellow. There are 21 rooms, all with air-con, TV and kitchen equipment, quite simple, in the centre of the action.

Inexpensive

Sea View Hotel, PO Box 59, t 494 2483, *seaview hotel@surfbvi.com*. On the road west out of Road Town just beyond Government House. Twenty-two simple rooms with kitchens, set in a modern block with a pool and bar – at the upper end of this price category.

Brewer's Bay Campground, t 494 3463. Set on the bay of the name on the north coast, with showers, loos, a concessionary shop and cooking facilities hidden among the seagrape and palms; fixed sites and bare sites, also very cheap.

Eating Out

Most restaurants and hotel dining rooms in Tortola are 'international' in style, though there are one or two other nationalities

(mostly Italian) represented besides West Indian fare, which features in some good local haunts. It is worth bearing in mind all the beach bars, some of which can be reached by land as well as by sea – many have charming settings on a waterfront deck. The waterfront restaurants can usually be contacted, and a dinner ordered, on the VHF radio, channel 16 or 68. Generally speaking, eating out in the BVI is expensive. Most restaurants charge service at 10%.

Categories are arranged according to the price of a main course: expensive = US$20 and above; moderate = US$10–20; inexpensive = US$10 and under.

Expensive

Brandywine Bay, t 495 2301. This is the most elegant restaurant in Tortola, and has an excellent setting in an open tropical house on a headland east of Road Town (about a 10min drive). Start with a cocktail on the plant-filled terrace and move to the stone-built dining room hanging with greenery. The menu is international with a taste of Florentine fare, often grilled and then served with artistic attention to detail: home-made mozzarella and *pomodori* or beef *carpaccio* flavoured with lemon, capers and olive oil dressing, *bistecca alla fiorentina* and nightly changing pasta specials; long wine list, including Italian. *Closed Aug–Oct.*

The Sugar Mill, PO Box 425, Little Apple Bay, t 495 4355. This is well worth a visit: the set Caribbean and international menu revolves fortnightly and combines classical ideas and techniques with Caribbean fruits and spices in an innovative and satisfying way: smoked conch terrine or Caribbean sweet potato soup with gingered shrimp to start, followed by fresh fish with sundried tomatoes and a herb vinaigrette or tropical game hen with orange-curry butter. The owners write cookbooks and are wine experts.

Captain's Table, on the waterfront by Village Cay Marina, Road Town, t 494 3885. The dining room overlooks the yachts of the Inner Harbour marina from a terrace festooned with greenery and with outhanging awnings. There is a daily French and international menu – sautéed scallops in mango vinaigrette or a rack of lamb in rosemary sauce, also a live lobster speciality, followed by *crêpes suzette*.

C & F Bar and Restaurant, Purcell Estate, **t** 494 4941. For the best in West Indian food. A classic setting on a tin-covered terrace with red concrete floor, plastic tablecloths, fake roses, fish-abilia on the walls and waiters watching the telly. Not much ambience and definitely not low-fat, but delicious shrimp in lemon butter and a ton of ground provisions, prepared by Chef Clarence the Grillmaster. Good fun for a large party. Go east from Road Town, left at the roundabout, left again and it's next on the right.

Moderate

Cala Maya, Hodge's Creek Marina, **t** 495 2126. 'Caribbean New Cuisine', which uses the best in local Caribbean ingredients and some Italian techniques, served on a brightly decorated (yellow and purple) deck right on the waterfront: conch lasagne, lobster black tagliatelle or West Indian roast pig.

Pusser's Outpost, Road Town, **t** 494 3897. The stylized old-time nautical décor – stained wood and wicker chairs with maquettes of sailing ships and figureheads – doesn't skimp on 21st-century comforts. The international menu includes tenderloin in flaky pastry and Pusser's Fisherman's Platter.

Jolly Roger, West End, **t** 495 4559. You will eat reliably well here. There are barbecues with live music quite a few nights, but also more sophisticated fare, lots of seafood and an international menu with some Asian Fusion.

Fat Hog Bob's, Maya Cove, **t** 495 1010. In case you're hankering after some American ribs, they serve the best on the island, besides local fish and huge steaks and burgers. Set in a wooden building right on the water's edge: horseshoe pits, big-screen TV, 'creative' bartenders, all in all 'a Caribbean Bob-B-Q'.

Mrs Scatliffe's restaurant, Carrot Bay, **t** 495 4556. For something truly West Indian, set on the tin-roofed veranda of her home in Carrot Bay on the north side. The menu offers fine West Indian fare: *callaloo* or breadfruit soup with home-made bread, pot-roast pork or chicken and coconut, and superb ice creams; sometimes a scratch-band, or just the cooks singing in the kitchen while they work; remember to reserve.

Palm's Delight, Carrot Bay, **t** 495 4863. A classic West Indian setting on the rocky shoreline of Carrot Bay, albeit in a lime green, pink and purple house. Classic West Indian fare: steam fish or fry fish in a creole sauce (they are particularly good for fresh fish), or chicken in ginger wine.

Last Resort, Bellamy Cay, just off Beef Island, **t** 495 2520. A great spot for a lively evening out, this has an open veranda with barrel chairs and a donkey that likes to stick her head through a doorway to be fed. Hot buffet dinner: pumpkin soup followed by chicken in curry and honey (or roast beef and Yorkshire pudding). Always has entertainment: it's particularly noted for a show in which the owner takes the mickey out of life, the universe and yachtsmen, but there's also music and comedy. Ring for the ferry.

Inexpensive

Capricio di Mare, opposite the ferry pier in Road Town. This café has true Italian style if you want to linger over a cappuccino. Daytime salads and sandwiches; evening pastas and pizzas.

The Virgin Queen, just near the roundabout in Road Town, **t** 494 2310. If you are feeling a little homesick for the NBA or for Guinness on tap, head out to this pub, where you'll find the television constantly going. English pub food and pizzas.

Midtown Restaurant, Main St, Road Town, **t** 494 2764. Has plastic tablecloths in an air-conditioned dining room setting with classic West Indian fare – curry goat and fry fish.

Roti Palace, Abbott Rd, Road Town, **t** 494 4196. The place to try a *roti* – a spicy envelope of bread with chicken or beef.

Bars and Nightlife

There is always a lively drinking crowd out in Tortola – yachties and newcomers alike. There are plenty of tourist bars, with the pretty mock-nautical setting of the Pusser's Pubs, but there are also classic West Indian rum shacks, too. The national drink of the BVI (for the tourists anyway) is the Painkiller, usually mixed with local Pusser's Rum (cream of coconut, orange juice, pineapple juice and rum, topped with nutmeg), but there are endless other exotic cocktails. And now there is a local beer (well quite local, in that it is brewed in St Croix in the US Virgin Islands), Foxy's Bitter, named after Foxy and his famous beach bar in Jost van Dyke.

Bomba's Shack, Capoon's Bay, **t** 495 4148. Known for its mushroom-based drinks additives. Don't miss Bomba's full-moon party if you are on island at the full moon.

Ceta's by the Sea, next door to Bomba's. Sees a *funchi* band in the season.

Sebastian's on the Beach, Apple Bay, **t** 495 4212. Another popular bar, this gets very busy on Sunday nights.

Pusser's Store and Pub, just across from the ferry terminal in Road Town, **t** 494 3897. At this ever-popular haunt, the nauticalia of model ships and shields and the dark-stained wood and brass give it the feel of a British naval-theme pub – you even get your drink in a glass pint mug.

Virgin Queen, an upstairs bar next to the roundabout in Road Town, **t** 494 2310. You can get American light beers here as well as Beamish and Boddingtons.

Paradise Pub, on the outskirts of Road Town, on the road to West End. A more traditional Caribbean waterfront bar set around a covered courtyard with a veranda looking out on the water; darts and rowdy drinking games, plus dancing at the weekends.

Pusser's Landing, Frenchman's Cay, **t** 495 4554. Ever-popular, with good food too.

Jolly Roger, West End, **t** 495 4559. Garish, but a good bar.

Quito's Gazebo, Cane Garden Bay, **t** 495 4837. Live music nightly; dancing at weekends.

Myett's, Cane Garden Bay. Has live music a couple of times a week.

Skyworld, on the Ridge Rd, **t** 494 3567. If you want a cocktail and a fantastic view, you can try here (also serves food).

Beach Bars

Cane Garden Bay is lined with bars standing almost shoulder-to-shoulder, with nice wooden decks right on the sand, where you can retreat for a beer and a salad, burger or grilled fish in the heat of the day and watch the yachts run over to Jost van Dyke. Some are also worth visiting at night, when there are often live bands and big crowds.

Bomba's Surfside Shack, Apple Bay. The best of Tortola's classic beach bars, Bomba's is at the west end on the north shore. True to its name, it is a shack made of driftwood (it's one of the few places which has benefited from the hurricanes of recent years). It's a great spot for chilling out, particularly at the monthly full-moon party, which is famous for its jars of unusual drinks additives. Who knows, perhaps you too will feel like decorating the walls with your knickers after a heavy evening's liming.

Nathan's Snackette, at the bottom end of Long Bay. Sit at plastic chairs on a simple deck looking out to the waves: the fare consists of sandwiches, burgers and jerked chicken legs.

Quito's Gazebo, Cane Garden Bay. This bar gets very busy on evenings late in the week, but they also offer a good spot for chilling out by day, with drinks and snacks.

Paradise Club, Cane Garden Bay. You can have a game of darts to go with your Red Stripe at this friendly bar.

Stanley's Welcome Bar, Cane Garden Bay. Follow more Caribbean pursuits (just the Red Stripe) here.

Rhymers, Cane Garden Bay, **t** 495 4639. They have nightly Caribbean jump-ups.

Myett's, Cane Garden Bay. This is a series of gazebos hiding among the palms where you eat upstairs with a fine view of the beach and a heavy reggae accompaniment.

De Wedding, Cane Garden Bay. 'Every day is like a wedding' at this quieter, isolated bright-blue bar, down at the far end of the beach.

Nicole's Brewer's Bay Beach Bar. A good stopover.

Bamboo Bar, Brewer's Bay. Hides in a forest of palms behind the curve of soft brown sand.

De Loose Mongoose, Trellis Bay, Beef Island, **t** 495 2303. Stop for a snack at an excellent and friendly bar on the beach. If you look offshore here you can see two island blips in the bay: the further one (sometimes quite difficult to spot as it merges into a bigger island behind) is Marina Cay.

Pusser's Bar, Marina Cay. Slake your thirst and get a meal and some watersports to keep you busy when you're tired of sizzling in the sun. A free ferry runs over from Beef Island – makes a nice day out with its small beach.

continues in the town, however, in the marinas and the ferry dock, and this gives the place a pleasant nautical air.

If you approach by sea, a grandiose building with a line of slender arches dominates the waterfront: the government offices or **Central Administration Complex**. Not far inland, beyond the traffic running on the original shoreline, you will find **Main St**, where there is a clutch of older BVI buildings, clapboard wooden houses (some brightly painted) with shingle tiles, most of which contain shops. The **BVI Folk Museum** (*open Mon–Fri 9.30–4.30*) is worth a quick look. It is set in a pretty blue and white timber-frame house with wooden shutters, and contains a small exhibition of natural life and human history in Amerindian pottery and plantation artefacts. There is also some crockery from the RMS *Rhone*, which sank off Salt Island in 1867. Continuing on Main St, you come to a string of island institutions to detain you: among the various bars stand the Episcopal Anglican and the Methodist churches. The island prison, which was wedged between them, is now out east.

Just off Main St farther inland, the small **J. R. O'Neal Botanic Gardens** (*open Mon–Sat 9.30–5.30, Sun noon–5*) give an excellent exposure to the diverse tropical flora of the Caribbean. Around a short alley of royal palms are laid-out cactus gardens, a lily pond and a fern house and, of course, endless tropical flowers. There are some medicinal plants, and occasional benches where you can rest your feet. Many of the plants are marked. A charming place to stop for a moment.

Roads lead out of the town in both directions along the wiggly coastline, passing Tortola's other small settlements in the many bays, West End and Long Look (in the east), where many Belongers have returned to build their homes. If you want to get to **Cane Garden Bay** (a popular north-coast beach), you must head inland and up. The ridge road runs along the backbone of Tortola and gives some superb views of the other islands.

Sage Mountain National Park, which contains the highest point in the Virgin Islands (1,780ft), is a small area of (almost) rainforest, where tall and slender trees soar and hanging vines drop to the ground, and where the ferns and philodendrons quiver on the breeze. Since the 1960s, the park has been allowed to grow naturally and the vegetation, which in places looks lush enough to belong to the bigger Windward Islands, is thought to be similar to the island's original growth before the land was cleared for planting. A number of trails have been cut through the forest, and there are some lookouts from which the views are superb. Above Brewer's Bay is the **Mount Healthy National Park**, where there is a fairly intact windmill which was used to crush sugar cane in plantation days. If you would like to see the continuation of the process, you can visit the **Callwood Rum Distillery** in Cane Garden Bay, where you can see rum being produced according to age-old methods.

Back down on the coast road, heading west from Road Town, you come to Sea Cow's Bay and Baugher's Bay, and the road eventually wiggles into **Frenchman's Cay** at the western end of the island. Once this was a favoured pirate hideout – it was easily defended and had good lookouts. Nowadays there is still a working boatyard, a very busy marina and a collection of pretty pastel boutiques and bars. Close by is the **West End**, the ferry terminal for the USVI and Jost van Dyke.

Heading east from town, you pass the large H. Lavity Stout Community College in Paraquita Bay and then come to the settlement at East End. Over on the north coast in **Josiah's Bay**, you will find an old plantation estate house and the ruined walls of other estate buildings, which saw prosperity as a sugar factory in the 18th century and then again as a rum distillery in the age of Prohibition in the States, when the rum would be smuggled to thirsty illicit drinkers. Josiah's Bay Plantation is now an art gallery. Back on the southern shore, the main road eventually reaches a toll bridge, which crosses to **Beef Island**, the site of the airport. The island takes its name from its former use as a cattle ranch by buccaneers, but now all there is to see are a few goats and guest houses, private villas and the occasional 48-seater plane pitching and reeling as it comes in to land – note the nonchalant sign at the roadside: '*Beware low-flying aircraft*'.

Great Camanoe and **Scrub Island** also lie off the northeast tip of the island and they have a few private homes. To visit them, take a boat from Beef Island. **Guana Island** is private and is devoted to a hotel, a classic island retreat (*see* 'Where to Stay', p.491). **Marina Cay**, however, also with a hotel out in Trellis Bay, can be visited for the day.

Jost van Dyke

The little island of Jost van Dyke lies about 4 miles off Tortola's West End. It is a perfect place to be marooned; there is a sleepy, very Caribbean air and it is less developed than the other islands (though ominously it is poised for development). Still, for the moment there is hardly anything there – just a couple of square miles of scrub, idyllic beaches and bars to retreat to, and about 120 inhabitants, who cluster around the two main settlements of Great Harbour and Little Harbour at opposite ends of the island. A dirt track leads between the two, but there are hardly any vehicles. Jost van Dyke received electricity and telephones only relatively recently and some traditional West Indian life remains – cattle and goats wander around dragging their tethers and you might see a charcoal bonfire smoking away. There is nothing to see above the waterline. Industry includes a little sand-mining and building. Surprisingly, Jost van Dyke, which is supposedly named after a Dutch pirate, used to be cultivated and terraced from shoreline to hilltops (1,070ft) to grow cotton and sugar cane. In those days, this barren outcrop was quite prosperous. It is also the birthplace of two famous men.

Dr John Lettsom was born to a Quaker planter family in 1744 and eventually became the founder of the London (later British) Medical Society and the Royal Humane Society. He is remembered for his efforts in the rhyme:

I, John Lettsom,
blisters, bleeds and sweats 'em
If, after that, they please to die
I, John Lettsom.

Getting There

Jost van Dyke **t** (1 284–)

There are six daily sailings (fewer at the weekend) from West End to Jost van Dyke on the Jost van Dyke Ferry Service, **t** 494 2997.

Watersports

Sandy Cay in the east is good for snorkelling, and there is a small watersports shop, Wendell's, in Great Bay.

Where to Stay

Jost van Dyke **t** (1 284–)

Sandcastle, White Bay, postal address Suite 201, 6501 Red Hook Plaza, St Thomas, USVI 00802, **t** 495 9888, *relax@sandcastle-bvi. com*, *www.sandcastle-bvi.com* (*very expensive–expensive*). This is a Caribbean dream, with six cottages (two of them air-conditioned) lost in a garden of palm trees on White Bay, a stunning white-sand cove with absurdly blue water. The rooms are simple, but there is hot water now. Very secluded and low-key – hammocks, some watersports if you want them, the Soggy Dollar bar, good dining room with a nightly-changing four-course dinner, and a library to keep you busy. The occasional crowd of yachtsmen drops in and sometimes the beach is crowded because of cruise yachts.

Rudy's Mariner's Rendezvous, Great Harbour, **t** 495 9282 (*moderate–inexpensive*). This has just five simple rooms with kitchenettes and a restaurant.

Harris's Place, Little Harbour, **t** 495 9295 (*inexpensive*). You can get a well-priced room at this friendly spot. There's a bar that offers snacks too.

White Bay Camp Ground, Little Harbour, **t** 495 9312, **t** 495 9358 (*inexpensive*). Tents or cabins at very reasonable prices.

Eating Out and Bars

All the restaurants in Jost van Dyke double as bars, and some of them have entertainment and a barbecue in the week. You can call up on the radio, channels 16 or 68.

Expensive

Sandcastle, White Bay, **t** 495 9888. You can have a candlelit dinner above the surf here – black bean soup followed by Cajun blackened fresh local fish in a pineapple and raisin chutney with vegetables done to a turn. Famous for their potent sundowners.

Moderate–Inexpensive

Gertrude's, White Bay. Hidden among the palm trees, now dressed in bright orange.

Jewel's Snack Shop, near Gertrude's, **t** 495 9286. Burgers and salads during the daytime.

Ali Baba's, Great Harbour, **t** 495 9280. This is a covered terrace on the sand with an attractive wooden bar. Local fare.

Foxy's, Great Harbour, **t** 495 9528 (or reserve on channel 16). At the eastern end of the bay, this is a riotous place with multiple decks under rush and tin roofing on the waterfront. Endless business cards, nautical flags, the odd hammock under the palms and now their very own beer, Foxy's Bitter. Foxy himself will occasionally sing to you (about you and where you come from) over the barbecue and in season he has live music a couple of times a week. The highlight of the year is the New Year's Eve party, which attracts as many as 2,500 people from 300 yachts. Also very popular is Foxy's Wooden Boat Regatta in August or September.

Foxy's Taboo, East End at Diamond Cay, **t** 495 4258. Foxy's newest place, serving seafood and light fare. Live music.

Abe's by the Sea, Little Harbour, **t** 495 9329. This covered terrace on the waterfront festooned with fishnets and fan coral has plenty of happy punters to judge by the photographs they leave. West Indian fare and fish, with some specials.

Sidney's Peace and Love, Little Harbour, **t** 495 9271. Decorated in a serious shade of yellow. The punters leave their T-shirts as a memento; local fare.

Harris's Place, Little Harbour, **t** 495 9295. Close to Sidney's and Abe's, this purple and pink bar has a sandy terrace for drinks and simple meals.

Best Beaches

Great Harbour and **White Bay**: Two fantastic bays on the south coast, with particularly good snorkelling.

Sandy Cay: A blip with a fine beach and good snorkelling.

Sandy Spit: Just off Green Cay, this is the archetypal sandy spit with nothing but a few palm trees and luscious, foot-deep sand.

His fellow Quaker, born on the island in 1759, was William Thornton, another medical doctor, who campaigned against slavery in the islands. He became a US citizen and won the competition to design the Capitol in Washington, later serving as the first superintendent of the US Patent Office.

Islands in the Chain

Heading southwest along the line of amoebic islets and cays on the southern side of Sir Francis Drake Channel, you pass **Fallen Jerusalem**, a national park made of similar boulders to those at the Baths on Virgin Gorda, and then **Round Rock**. Next in line, **Ginger Island** is uninhabited, but there is a popular bar and a small hotel set on the protected anchorage of Manchineel Bay in **Cooper Island**.

Next in the line (beyond the blip of Cistern Rock, where there is good snorkelling) is **Salt Island**, another 200 acres of scrubland that enclose a salt pond (which you may smell on the wind as you pass). Once the population of this island was as high as 100, mostly involved in the collection of salt, which they would sell to passing ships (the rent of the island is still set at one sack of salt a year payable to the Queen of England, but apparently it is not often demanded any more). Today the population is not usually more than about four or five, though building is just beginning on the sandy seafront at 'The Settlement'. Nowadays, most people come to Salt Island to visit one of the Caribbean's finest wrecks, the shell of the 310ft **RMS *Rhone***. She just missed reaching the open water in a violent storm in 1867, and now lies on her side in two bits in depths from 30 to 80ft, her ribs scattered higgledy-piggledy. Snorkellers can enjoy the shallower end, playing in the exhaled bubbles of the divers below, an eerie experience. The area around the wreck is a Marine National Park and so the usual rules apply.

Next in line, **Peter Island** lies about 5 miles across the channel from Road Town harbour and is almost entirely devoted to an extremely luxurious hotel. The only other inhabitant lives in a small wooden house across the bay. Just off Peter Island is a cay called **Dead Chest,** a small scrub-covered lump that calls to mind the pirates who used these anchorages before today's sailors arrived. Blackbeard is supposed to have left 15 of his more rebellious sidekicks here with just a cutlass and a cask of rum. The pirates did not survive long, but the island was immortalized in the sea shanty:

Fifteen men on a dead man's chest
Yo ho ho and a bottle of rum.
Drink and the Devil have done the rest
Yo ho ho and a bottle of rum.

Where to Stay and Eat

British Virgin Islands t (1 284–)

Peter Island Resort, PO Box 211, **t** 495 2000, US **t** 1 800 346 4451, *www.peterisland.com* (*luxury*). A luxury tropical island retreat – 52 rooms and three villas, plus two new villa estates, the beginning of a multi-million dollar residential development. The guest rooms are divided between the marina side (which has a nice, active, nautical feel), where you will find the reception, the pool and bar and the main dining room, and the beach side, with rooms in two-storey stone and wood cottages. The latter line the superb sands of Deadman's Bay along with the beach restaurant which sits surrounded by fantastic tropical greenery. Guest rooms on the beach side have received a recent upgrade, while at the far end of the beach, the resort has added an elaborate spa complex. The mood is a touch formal, but fairly low-key, and there is entertainment each night in season. Besides Deadman's Bay, where the waves break in scallop-shell shapes, White Bay Beach is secluded and isolated. There are some limited watersports, plus bicycles to get around on. If you would like to go over to Peter Island for dinner (reservations please), the ferry sails a couple of times during the evening from the Peter Island Marina on the eastern side of Road Town harbour, Tortola.

Cooper Island Beach Club, PO Box 512, **t** 495 9084, VHF Channel 16, US **t** 1 800 542 4624, *info@cooper-island.com*, *www.cooper-island.com* (*moderate*). Has 12 comfortable, fan-ventilated rooms set in pretty blocks, some in gingerbread buildings, and each with a nice view through the palm trees to the bay. There are just a few cottages, a boutique, a dive shop, Underwater Safaris, for guided dives and tank refills (the island also has quite good snorkelling), and, of course, the yellow and lilac beach bar itself, which offers daytime and evening meals – conch fritters and chicken *roti* and sautéed shrimp in butter and white wine, plus some barbecues. It depends on the crowd, but it can get very lively.

William Thornton Floating Bar and Restaurant, The Bight, Norman Island, **t** 494 0183, VHF Channel 16 (*moderate*). Offshore, in the protected anchorage of the Bight, you will find one of the Caribbean's most unlikely, but sometimes most lively bars, the 'Willy T' as it is familiarly known by the crowd of latterday pirates and tourists who turn up for the evening. Built for a timber trader, it now has a restaurant serving international and local fare and a bar famous for a variety of drinks, including body shots (a slightly sultry variation on the theme of a tequila shot) and a multiple-shot dispenser with the glasses positioned on a waterski. Well worth a look if there is a crowd in. Serves seafood.

The last BVI island in the chain, next to the US Virgin Island of St John, is **Norman Island**, which also features in pirate lore because treasure is supposed to have been found here and some think that the island was the inspiration for Robert Louis Stevenson's *Treasure Island*. Ruins remain from past settlement, but Norman Island is home only to a few goats, seabirds and a bar today. The snorkelling at the Indians and at Treasure Point caves, where there are caverns partly submerged in water, is excellent.

Virgin Gorda

Virgin Gorda lies within sight of Tortola across Sir Francis Drake Channel, and when you get there, Road Town seems almost like an uncaring metropolis. Life here proceeds at an even more sedate pace and you will find that the people all greet each other. Come to that, they may all know each other anyway, because there are only

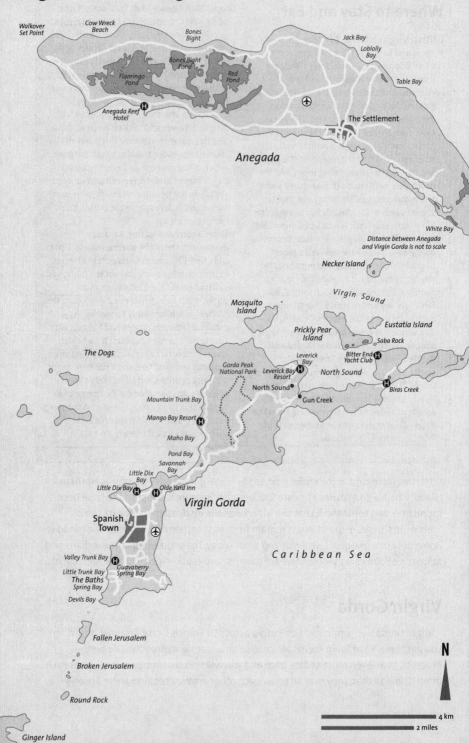

Virgin Gorda and Anegada

Walkover Set Point

Cow Wreck Beach

Bones Bight

Jack Bay

Loblolly Bay

Bones Bight Pond

Table Bay

Flamingo Pond

Red Pond

Anegada Reef Hotel

The Settlement

Anegada

White Bay

Distance between Anegada and Virgin Gorda is not to scale

Necker Island

Virgin Sound

Mosquito Island

Prickly Pear Island

Eustatia Island

Saba Rock

The Dogs

Gorda Peak National Park

Leverick Bay

Bitter End Yacht Club

Leverick Bay Resort

North Sound

North Sound

Mountain Trunk Bay

Gun Creek

Biras Creek

Mango Bay Resort

Maho Bay

Pond Bay

Savannah Bay

Little Dix Bay

Little Dix Bay

Olde Yard Inn

Virgin Gorda

Caribbean Sea

Spanish Town

Valley Trunk Bay

Little Trunk Bay

Guavaberry Spring Bay

The Baths

Spring Bay

Devils Bay

Fallen Jerusalem

Broken Jerusalem

Round Rock

Ginger Island

N

4 km
2 miles

Best Beaches

The Baths (in sequence heading south: **Valley Trunk Bay**, **Little Trunk Bay**, **The Baths**, **Spring Bay**, also known as the Crawl, and **Devils Bay**): These can be reached on marked paths through the scrub, leading off from Mad Dog Bar, a wooden house with a veranda on the hilltop, where you can get a hot dog or a sandwich. There is another more formal restaurant on the hilltop which tends to attract day trippers, Top of the Baths. Down on the beach itself, shaded by vast rocks is the Poor Man's Bar, a shack with some facilities where you can get a beer and a snack.

Savannah Bay, **Pond Bay** and **Maho Bay**: Isolated coves on the west coast as you head north out of town, under the broad sweeping arc of the towering volcanic hills. There are a few villas and places to get a drink and something to eat, but generally it's pretty quiet.

Leverick Bay: A lively spot with a bar (not much sand) and some watersports equipment – you can windsurf over to the beaches on Mosquito Island, where there are some good strips of sand to collapse onto. You will find a classic beach bar on Prickly Pear Island: the Sandbox is a long wooden shack with lots of watersports – jet skis and glass-bottom boat tours – and loungers for a bit of sizzling and time out from the snorkelling.

1,500 of them. There is a charming and slow West Indian life here, with some older wooden houses in among the newer encrustations of concrete. Most of the hotel rooms don't have locks on the doors on Virgin Gorda, for good reason.

Virgin Gorda was the 'fat Virgin', according to the Spaniards, because they thought its shape from the south was like a pregnant woman reclining. For a while, Virgin Gorda was the capital island among the British Virgins, but in 1741, Tortola took over. The island is 8 square miles in area and, like Tortola, it is long and irregularly shaped, rising from plains in the south to 1,370ft at Gorda Peak in the north. Generally speaking, the island is furred with scrub and cactus, inhabited by lizards and geckos. Supposedly there is also a very rare 5ft iguana that lives in the hills. Birds include warblers and the usual cattle egrets on the plains, and you may find that the odd cheeky bananaquit takes a fancy to your lunch.

Around the Island

The island splits quite neatly into two, with settlements at each end, barely connected through the hilly scrubland between. In the south is **Spanish Town**, or **The Valley** as it is known, the closest thing to a town; its few houses are clustered on the rising ground above the main port and marina. The few old wooden West Indian houses are now marginalized and dwarfed by modern Caribbean concrete, each fenced to keep out the grazing animals. In the north of Virgin Gorda is the **North Sound**, a huge bay almost enclosed by islands and reefs.

The south of the island is best known for the curious assembly of vast rocks called **the Baths**, a giant's playground of granite boulders along the western shore. These smooth rocks, which hardly seem to belong in the Caribbean, are buried to their necks in sand and jumbled on one another, creating caverns where the waves crash and

Getting There

Virgin Gorda t (1 284–)

By Air

You can fly in to Virgin Gorda on charters from San Juan or the USVI, on Air Sunshine, t 495 8900, *email@airsunshine.com*, *www.airsunshine.com*, and Air St Thomas, t 495 5935, *www.airstthomas.com*, or through charter airlines, *see* p.482.

By Sea

The main ferry terminals are situated at The Valley (Spanish Town) and North Sound. Speedy's, t 495 5240, runs a service three times a week from St Thomas to Virgin Gorda, a two-hour ride through Sir Francis Drake Channel, and makes seven or eight daily trips between Road Town, Tortola and The Valley. There is also a link from the airport to Virgin Gorda on the North Sound Express, t 495 2138 (reservations recommended), making about four trips a day.

Getting Around

By Taxi

Taxis will often let you hop in on someone else's fare and will ask for a few dollars for the ride – check how many before you get in. Taxis can be found at the car hire places below and through the hotels.

Hitch-hiking

You will have no problems hitch-hiking on Virgin Gorda.

Car Hire

There are cars and jeeps available (for regulations and prices *see* 'Getting Around' under 'Tortola', p.489). Hotels often have cars available for their guests too. Contact:

Andy's Taxi and Jeep Rental, The Valley, t 495 5252, *fischers@candwbvi.net*, *www.islandson line.com/fischerscove*.

L&S Jeep Rental, t 495 5297, *landscarrentals@ surfbvi.com*.

Mahogany Car Rentals, The Valley, t 495 5469, *mahoganycarrentals@surfbvi.com*, *www.mahoganycarrentalsbvi.com*.

Watersports

The island divides neatly into two halves: if you are staying around the North Sound all the sports are available through the various hotels. Leverick Bay has some sports, including parasailing and windsurfing (also a spa for the less physically active), and Prickly Pear Island has some motorized sports. In the south of the island there is slightly less on offer, but you can fix up some sports in the marina. Try also:

Bitter End Yacht Club, Biras Creek, North Sound, t 494 2745, *www.beyc.com*.

Leverick Bay Watersports, t 495 7376.

Day Sails

Hotels have equipment, including Boston whalers.

Bitter End Yacht Club, *see* above.

Leverick Bay Charter Services, t 494 7421, *leverick@surfbvi.com*.

Misty Isle, in the main marina, The Valley, t 495 5643.

Deep-sea Fishing

The best way to fix up a deep-sea fishing trips is through the hotels.

Scuba Diving

Diving is quite expensive in Virgin Gorda. However, there is plenty on offer within a short boat ride, including Dog Island, Ginger Island and the Invisibles, and some ships

race and you can clamber about. They are as impressive underneath the water's surface as above and make for good snorkelling. More granite boulders like those at the Baths make up Fallen Jerusalem off the south coast of the island. It has this name because it looks like a ruined town crumbling into the water. The island is a National Park and so fishing is prohibited, as is collecting the corals. You are asked to be careful when anchoring a yacht or swimming near the reef. Back on Virgin Gorda, the

which have sunk intentionally or unintentionally. Contact:

Dive BVI, Yacht Harbour, near Spanish Town, t 495 5513, and in Leverick Bay, t 4957328, US t 1 800 848 7078, *info@divebvi.com*, *www.divebvi.com*.

Kilbride's Sunchaser Scuba, North Sound, Virgin Gorda, t 495 9638, US t 1800 932 4286, *info@sunchaserscuba.com*, *www.sunchaserscuba.com*.

Kayaking

The warm, protected waters of the BVI are ideal for kayaking. Beachfront hotels and watersports operators provide equipment.

Windsurfing

This can be fixed up through the Bitter End Yacht Club on North Sound and at Leverick Bay (*see* p.502).

Other Sports

Hiking

There is a trail to the top of Gorda Peak, which is part of the BVI National Park System, t 494 2039, *www.bvinationalparkstrust.org*, which has park maps and hiking tours.

Tennis

There are courts in many of the hotels on Virgin Gorda.

Where to Stay

Virgin Gorda t (1 284–)

Luxury

Biras Creek, PO Box 54, t 494 3555, UK t 0800 894 057 (during Californian hours), US t 1 800 223 1108, *biras@biras.com*, *www.biras.com*. This is one of the Caribbean's finest hotels and has been offering high-grade, low-key luxury to returning guests for years. The 33 suites are strung out on the breezy Atlantic waterfront, where you are sent to sleep by the wash of the waves (it may seem loud on the first night, but they encourage you not to move for at least a couple of nights because most people come to love it), and in a sandy garden behind. The restaurant is set above in the main house on the heights – guests gather for drinks before dinner and then move to the dining-room terrace. There is a superb view across the North Sound and out to the Atlantic, the moon glinting on the sea's surface. One of the Caribbean's few Relais et Châteaux, Biras Creek has an elegant and rarefied air of well-manicured Caribbean luxury and will not let you down.

Little Dix Bay, PO Box 70, t 495 5555, t UK (020) 7259 5599, US t 1 888 767 3966, *ldbhotel@caribsurf.com*, *www.littledixbay.com*. A grand and luxurious resort set on a reef-enclosed, half-moon curve of sand backed with palms and seagrape, in the south of the island. It is quite large with 102 rooms in raised octagonal cottages, but they are spread out along the waterfront in beautifully kept tropical gardens. The main dining room is under the distinctive double-pointed shingle roofs and around the central sugar mill. Watersports and tennis accompany Caribbean island tranquillity.

Necker Island, t 494 2757, UK t 0800 716 919, US t 1 800 225 4255, *necker@surfbvi.com*, *www.neckerisland.com*. A stay on Necker Island might be the ultimate Caribbean dream for some. You get the island to yourself (there are prices for different multiples of guests), though there are 'celebration weeks', in which couples can join a mix. Necker island has beds for 26 guests in the main house and the three smaller Balinese cottages (Bali Hi, Bali Lo and Bali Cliffs). The open-sided main house, with its magnifi-

remains of a very early **copper mine** can be found close by on the arid southeastern tip among the plant life of cacti and succulents such as agave. There are a small number of hotels in the southern area of the island, but plenty of bars and restaurants which thrive off the yachting traffic.

A road leads past the airport, up over the high ground and down to the northern part of Virgin Gorda; from on top, you will have a magnificent view down the Sir

cent hilltop setting and views as far as Tortola, is the nerve-centre of the island. It has a snooker table and excellent sitting area with books, board games, video recorders and CD players, hammocks and an exercise room. Two pools (one on the beach, where there is a bar and lunch terrace), tennis courts and all meals included at the huge dining-room table. A statue waves you welcome and goodbye.

Expensive

Bitter End Yacht Club, North Sound, PO Box 46, t 494 2745, US t 1 800 872 2392, US t (312) 944 2860, binfo@beyc.com, www.beyc.com. Bitter End has a busier, more club-like atmosphere, and there is a nautical feel in the dark-stained wood and brass and pewter tableware in the dining room, as well as the constant waterborne activity. A sense of desert-island seclusion within a shout of civilization can be found in their luxurious, mock-rustic cabins on the hillside. A couple of restaurants and entertainment in season, with hammocks everywhere, but you should spend at least some time on the water. Lots of activity, sailboats, kayaks and some jet skis.

Moderate

Leverick Bay Resort, PO Box 63, t 495 7421, US t 1 800 848 7081, leverick@caribsurf.com, www.virgingordabvi.com. Offers the least expensive deal in the northern half of the island. The 18 rooms stand on the hillside above the bay, each alarmingly brightly decorated, with air-con, TV and full kitchen as well as a cracking view from the balcony. Very comfortable, though, and some activity around. They also handle a number of one- to five-bedroomed villas in the area.

Olde Yard Village, PO Box 26, t 495 5544, US t 1 800 653 9273, info@oldeyardvillage.com, www.oldeyardvillage.com. A charming, small

property in the style of a West Indian inn, where you are welcomed by the owners themselves. It is situated just off the road to the north of the island and has 14 fan-ventilated rooms (half of them air-conditioned if you want that) overlooking a charming garden of oleander, palms and seagrape, where there is a pool, Jacuzzi, hammocks hanging in the trees, a library and video room and an excellent restaurant. They have won awards for their environmental policy.

Ocean View Hotel, PO Box 66, The Valley, t 495 5230, butu@surfbvi.com, www.bviguide.com/wheelhouse. Right behind the marina in town, a modern block surrounded by trees, with simple but pleasant enough rooms.

Mango Bay Resort, Maho Bay, PO Box 1062, t 495 5672, mangobay@surfbvi.com, www.mangobayresort.com. Just a few one- and two-bedroom self-catering villas, quite spacious but a little past their best, lost in profuse greenery on a nice beach. Bordering on the inexpensive price category.

Guavaberry Spring Bay, PO Box 20, Valley Trunk Bay, t 495 5227, gsbhomes@surfbvi.com, www.guavaberryspringbay.com. A surprising and very pleasant retreat: hexagonal chalets on stilts, swallowed in explosions of tropical plants and the rocks of the Baths. There are 21 rooms in one- and two-bedroom chalets with full kitchens. All simply furnished, but with nice West Indian louvres and screens, and fans to whip up the breeze. Very peaceful and secluded, a short walk from the best of the beaches.

Eating Out

In the north of the island, there are really only hotel dining rooms for eating out in the evening, and elsewhere dining out can be a slightly haphazard business, though you can get a simple snack at the beach bars – try **Saba**

Francis Drake Passage and then the other way to the North Sound. Trails to **Gorda Peak** are marked off this road. The **North Sound** is a huge protected bay encircled by islands and reefs, with hotels and a settlement clustered along its edges. The road splits, leading left down to **Leverick Bay**, a tourist development of hotels and villas, and on to **Gun Creek**, a local town scattered over the hillside. Opposite Gun Creek are the Bitter End Yacht Club and Biras Creek, two more hotels. Enclosing the sound on

Rock and **Prickly Pear Island** – or a trusty West Indian meal in one of the local bars.

Categories are arranged according to the price of a main course: expensive = US$20 and above; moderate = US$10–20; inexpensive = less than US$10.

Expensive

Biras Creek Hotel, t 494 3555. Has a magnificent setting high on the hill; haute cuisine, a superb wine list and a five-course dinner for a fixed price.

Chez Bamboo, in the southern half of the island, t 495 5752. There is a large fairy-lit courtyard, surrounded by trellis, painted orange and blue and hung with tropical plants. The fare is international, with fish-grilled wahoo with fresh mango chutney and some French dishes, including *poulet au citron*. Follow up with a pumpkin pecan pie.

The Rock Café and Sam's Piano Bar, The Valley, t 495 5482. You can dine inside in the air-conditioned, alarmingly modern house or on small decks among the rocks and waterfalls. Burgers, Mexican and Italian dishes to go with a pool and sometimes live music.

Moderate

Lighthouse Restaurant and Beach Bar, Leverick Bay, t 495 7154. This looks like a brightly painted gingerbread house and has a mock-nautical ambience, plush armchairs and Painkiller cocktails; wings, ribs, pastas and lots of local fish.

Giorgio's Table, Maho Bay, t 495 5684. This is a charming Italian restaurant tucked away in the isolated recesses of Maho Bay (more easily reached by yacht than by car really), with a lovely view of the islands from a shorefront deck. Pizzas and pastas for lunch and more substantial fare at dinner from a short menu, including *filetto ai funghi*

porcini and daily specials. (At the expensive end of this category.)

Anything Goes, The Valley, t 495 5062, VHF Channel 16. Another simple spot in town, set on a concrete-floored and tin-roofed courtyard behind a fence: the mainstays include grilled kingfish and local vegetables, curries and burgers.

Thelma's Hideout, on the Little Dix Bay Rd, t 495 5646. Be sure not to miss this spot, a fairy-lit West Indian yard with plastic chairs behind a white picket fence, trees and hanging plants. Hearty local fare: doved pork, baked chicken and curry goat; ring to reserve a table, and a dish. (At the inexpensive end of this category.)

Inexpensive

The Bath and Turtle, Yacht Harbour, t 495 5239. Set in the shopping centre at the marina, this is a gathering point for yachties and can get quite lively. Pub food, patisserie and a lending library.

The Crab Hole, South Valley, t 495 5307. Another amusing local stopover, for a stew of chicken or fish, on a simple deck with ongoing pool and dominoes in the backstreets of The Valley.

Bars and Nightlife

Many of the restaurants in town double as bars, which hot up after dark. And don't forget the full-moon party, which is held each month on Savannah Bay.

Mine Shaft Café, past the zebras on Coppermine Rd, t 495 5260. The deck has an excellent view over the island from above the Atlantic shore. Salads, grills and seafood and a weird variety of cocktails, including the Cave In, for which the ingredients are lowered in a bucket.

the Atlantic side are **Prickly Pear Island** and the tiny **Saba Rock** and **Mosquito Island**. Slightly further out are **Eustatia Island**, which has just a couple of private houses, and **Necker Island**, a small green lump rimmed with sand set in the translucent blue. The latter is owned by entrepreneur Richard Branson, who has built a house there and a couple of villas in Balinese style. It is private (above the high-water mark), but can be hired (*see* p.503).

Anegada

Anegada lies out on its own about 15 miles north of the main group of the British Virgins, visible only from the mountaintops of Tortola and Virgin Gorda. It is unlike the other islands because it is not of volcanic origin. Rather it is a coral cap that just makes it above sea level (there is nothing over 28ft), rimmed with reefs and about 14 miles of beach. Anegada means 'the drowned one' in Spanish, a fitting name

Getting There

Anegada t (1 284–)

By Air

Anegada's airstrip is located northwest of The Settlement. Clair Aero, **t** 495 2271, makes the trip from Tortola four times a week. You could also charter a plane with Fly BVI, **t** 495 1747, *www.fly-bvi.com*, who also offer day trips to the island.

By Sea

Smiths Ferry Services, **t** 494 4454, operates between Roadtown, Tortola and Anegada, with two sailings on Thursdays and one on the last Sunday of the month. Fares: adults $50 return ($35 one-way); under-12s $35 return ($20 one-way).

Getting Around

There is no public transport on Anegada. Which leaves you no option but to hire a car or a bicycle:

Anegada Reef Hotel Setting Point, **t** 495 8002. Has a few jeeps and bicycles for hire, as well as diving and fishing equipment (*see* below).

DW Jeep Rentals, The Settlement, **t** 495 9677. Hires out jeeps and vans.

Watersports

Anegada is the only coral-based island in the BVIs and it has the richest marine life of them all. There is a park fee of $1 to dive. Contact:

Anegada Reef Hotel, Setting Point, **t** 495 8002. For scuba diving, bonefishing or deep-sea-fishing trips.

Where to Stay

Anegada t (1 284–)

Anegada Reef Hotel, Setting Point, **t** 495 8002, *aneghtl@surfbvi.com, www.anegadareef.com* (*expensive*). Small and low-key in the best lazy Caribbean style, with 20 rooms, some oceanfront, others in the garden among casuarina pines on the island's protected southwestern shore. The restaurant prepares excellent lobster, as well as other seafood and fish on the beach barbecue.

Neptune's Treasure, PO Box 2711, Blender's Bay, **t** 495 9439, *neptunetreasure@surfbvi.com* (*moderate*). Four rooms, each with private bath and a porch in a modern building, with an honour bar; some tents available.

Mac's Place Camping, central Loblolly Bay, **t** 495 8020, VHF Channel 16.

Anegada Beach Campground. Tents are cheap and a bare site costs less than US$10.

Eating Out

Big Bamboo, Loblolly Bay, **t** 495 2019, VHF Channel 16 (*moderate*). Beach bar with good food on offer.

Flash of Beauty, east end of Loblolly Bay, **t** 495 8014, VHF Channel 16 (*moderate*). A beach bar with tasty snacks.

Cow Wreck Beach Bar and Grill, on the north side, **t** 495 9461 (*moderate*). Try the fish and lobster while looking out at the waves.

Pomato Point, **t** 495 9466, VHF Channel 16 (*moderate*). South of the Cow Wreck, it serves international fare and barbecues. Reserve by 4pm.

Dotsy's Bakery and Sandwich Shop, The Settlement, **t** 495 9667 (*inexpensive*). This bakery also serves low-priced sandwiches and salads.

because it is full of lagoons and marshes and is occasionally further soaked by passing tidal waves.

At 15 square miles, Anegada is the second largest of the British islands. It is arid and scrubby and supports little life other than goats and donkeys. However, there is an ancient colony of about four hundred 20lb, 5ft iguanas. Once these animals lived all over the Virgin Islands, but they featured heavily in a local stew and so they are now endangered. Moves have been made to protect them by taking some to Guana Island, off Tortola. Only about 250 people live on Anegada, centred around **The Settlement,** and traditionally the islanders have depended on the sea for a living. When they were not away pirating or smuggling, they fished or looted the ships that were wrecked on the reefs. There are an estimated 300 sunken ships on **Horseshoe Reef**, which runs off the eastern end of the island. According to some estimates, there is a billion dollars of treasure on Anegada's reefs. Anegada's underwater life is superb. The coral reefs are endless forests of seafans, barrel sponges and gorgonians, abounding with fish – parrotfish, squirrelfish and thin trumpetfish hanging upright in the water.

The United States Virgin Islands

The US Virgin Islands consist of three main islands and around 70 cays, most of which are too small to be inhabited. The largest of all the Virgin Islands is St Croix (84 sq miles), which lies on its own, 40 miles south of the main group. St Thomas (33 sq miles) is the next largest, and the islands' capital, Charlotte Amalie, is situated in a magnificent bay on its southern shore. Four miles east of St Thomas, you will find the third main island in the group, St John (just 16 sq miles).

The islands were bought by the USA in 1917. For 250 years before that, they were Denmark's only colony in the Caribbean. Echoes of the Danes remain in the pretty waterfront towns with their warehouses and narrow stepped alleys (still with names like Raadet's Gade and Gamle Gade) and the now-ruined plantation windmills out in the country. Danish was never spoken much here so the language has gone, but it seems strange that in a part of America they should still drive on the left. In most other respects, the islands are emphatically American in style – everywhere there are yellow hanging traffic lights, drive-through burger joints and cheery waitresses in shorts. You can have a good time here, but the paradise façade hides most of the same problems that affect the other Caribbean islands. The tourist invasion is relentless. It is big business (the USVI receive nearly two and a half million visitors each year) and the islands are almost completely dependent on it.

The US Virgins (with the exception of St John, where building has been purposely restricted – it still has genuine small-island charm) are among the most developed islands in the Caribbean. Hotels and condominiums cover the hillsides and there can be as many as six or seven cruise ships in Charlotte Amalie harbour at one time. This is tourism at its most advanced – with stateside entertainment shipped in, carefully packaged 'vacationer's investment opportunities' and lots of reductions on car hire, restaurants, even watersports. The islands are too developed for some tastes, but they

Getting There

US Virgin Islands t (1 340-)

By Air

The two largest islands, St Thomas and St Croix have international airports, and these have excellent connections with the States.

From Europe

There are no direct scheduled services and so you will have to travel via Antigua (*see* p.339) or Sint Maarten (*see* p.415), though some charters fly out of Europe to St Thomas. There are many daily connections through Miami on American Airlines, *www.aa.com*, so this might be an option. Iberia, UK t 0870 609 0500, *www.iberiaairlines.co.uk*, has a daily flight to San Juan from Madrid. Condor, Germany t (810) 233 7130, *www.condor.de*, operates a weekly charter from Frankfurt.

From the USA

St Thomas and St Croix are served by numerous airlines.

American Airlines, t 1 800 474 4884, *www.aa. com*. From Miami, New York and Boston.

Continental, t 1800 231 0856. From Newark.

Delta, t 1 800 221 1212, t 776 1011. From Atlanta.

United Airlines, t 800-UNITED, *www.united.com*.

US Air, t 1 800 842 5374. From Philadelphia.

Many of these services stop first at St Thomas then continue to St Croix. From other points in the USA, passengers can fly to San Juan in Puerto Rico (*see* p.554), from where there are endless connections.

From Other Caribbean Islands

San Juan, which is a hub for the area, has numerous shuttle services to both St Thomas and St Croix with American Eagle, US t 1 800 474 4884; Air St Thomas, t 776 2722, US t 1 800 522 3084, *air.st.thomas@worldnet.att.net*, *www.airstthomas.com*; and Air Sunshine, t 1 888 879 8900, *www.airsunshine.com*. There are direct links to Anguilla, Sint Maarten, St Kitts and Antigua with LIAT, t 774 2313, and Caribbean Sun, t 866 864 6272, *www.flycsa. com*. Bohlke International Airways, t 777 9177, *www.bohlke.com*, and Clint Aero Charter, t 776 3958, are local charter services.

Getting Around

By Air

There are countless island hoppers that link St Thomas and St Croix, but the most original way to make the link is by seaplane. The service can be a little sporadic but it has been going strongly recently. These beasts (known as the '*Goose*' and the '*Mallard*' on-island) bounce over the waves as they struggle to get airborne and, once in the air, they thrum like an outsize tuning fork; they are fun to ride. The terminal in St Croix is in downtown Christiansted and in St Thomas it is next to the Havensight Mall in Charlotte Amalie. Contact Seaborne Airlines, t 773 6442, *www.seaborneairlines.com*. If you would prefer not to declare your body weight (needed for correct balancing of the seaplanes), then you might try Air St Thomas or Clint Aero Services (*see* 'From Other Caribbean Islands', above).

By Sea

For Cruz Bay in St John, ferries depart from Red Hook at the eastern end of St Thomas every hour on the hour, 8am–midnight daily, with sailings as early as 6.30am, Mon–Fri. Crossings the other way start earlier, running

remain very popular, mainly with American visitors. There is considerable variety within the islands and it is worth making the effort to visit another from your chosen one (consider the BVI as well). The setting is wonderful – the towns are as pretty as any in the West Indies and, of course, the sea, sand and sailing are impeccable.

History

At the time that Columbus arrived in the Caribbean in 1492, the Virgin Islands were seeing the first waves of attacks on the Greater Antilles by the Carib Indians. These

6am–11pm. The journey takes 20 mins. There is no reason to book as the ferries rarely reach their capacity. There is also a 30min ferry from Charlotte Amalie to Cruz Bay, departing six times a day, daily. Contact Transportation Services, t 776 6282.

If you would prefer to charter your own yacht around the USVI, contact:

Charter Yacht Owners' Association, Frenchtown, St Thomas, t 777 9690, US t 1 800 944 2962, info@cyoacharters.com, www.cyoacharters.com.

Virgin Islands Charteryacht League, 3801 Crown Bay, Suite 204, St Thomas, USVI 00802, t 774 3944, US t 1 800 524 0261, info@vicl.org, www.vicl.org.

For bareboats you can contact a number of companies, including:

Caribbean Yacht Owners' Association, in the lagoon at Compass Point, St Thomas, t 777 9690.

Island Yacht Charters, American Yacht Harbour, Red Hook, St Thomas, t 775 6666, US t 1 800 524 2019, sailing@iyc.vi, www.iyc.vi.

Virgin Islands Power Yachts, t 776 1510, www.vipyachts.com.

It is also worth talking to the tourist board or yacht-broking companies in your own country.

In St Thomas, there are **marinas** at Flagship (at the Yacht Haven), the Sub Base, Frenchtown, and there are three in the lagoon at Red Hook. In St John, there is a marina in Coral Bay, and in St Croix there are a number of them, including Green Cay, Gallows Bay and Salt River.

There are two annual **charterboat shows** in November and May each year in Charlotte Amalie harbour in St Thomas.

Tourist Information

Abroad

The tourist board has a website at www.usvitourism.vi and each island has its own website in the pattern of www.st-thomas.com. You can also find good information on www.vivisitorguide.com.

Canada: 703 Evans Av, Suite 106, Toronto, Ontario M9C 5E9, t (416) 622 7600.

UK: Power Road Station, 114 Power Road, Chadwick, London W4 5PY UK, t (020) 8994 0978, donm@destination-marketing.co.uk.

USA: 1270 Av of the Americas, Suite 2108, New York, NY 10020, t (212) 332 2222, usviny@aol.com; 3460 Wilshire Bd, Suite 412, Los Angeles, CA 90010, t (213) 739 0138; 2655 South Le Jeune Rd, Suite 907, Coral Gables, Miami, FL 33134, t (305) 442 7200, usvimia@aol.com; 444 North Capital St, Suite 305, Washington, DC 20001, t (202) 624 3590, usvidc@sso.org.

There is also a US freephone number: t 1 800 372 USVI.

In the USVI

Head Office of the USVI Department of Tourism: PO Box 6400, Charlotte Amalie, St Thomas 00804, t 774 8784.

US Virgin Islands Hotel & Tourism Association, www.virgin-islands-hotels.com.

Money and Banks

The currency of the US Virgin Islands (and the BVI for that matter) is the US dollar. Credit cards are accepted in hotels and all but the smallest shops and restaurants. Tipping is the same as in mainland USA, 10–15%. **Banking hours** are Mon–Thurs 9–2.30, Fri 9–2.30 and 3.30–5.

belligerent island hoppers, who decorated themselves with red warpaint and feathers, had come up all the way from South America over the previous centuries and had squeezed out the Arawaks as far as the Leewards. They would pass through the Virgin Islands in their vast war canoes on raids from down-island, make a lightning attack and steal a few women, and then paddle back again. The Spaniards battled successfully with them over the next century, trying to keep them away from Puerto Rico. But as the first scourge receded, another arrived. Pirates began to infest the islands, taking refuge there after their raids on Spanish shipping and settlements.

Shopping

St Thomas (particularly) and the other Virgin Islands offer some of the Caribbean's finest hunting grounds for shoppers. American citizens are encouraged to spend with special tax concessions when they return home – their duty-free limit is doubled from $400 worth of goods to $1,200, with yet more concessions on drink (USVI rum). Shops are open Mon–Sat 9–5, though they will often open up for the cruise ship trade.

Telephone Code

The IDD code for the USVI is t 1 340, followed by a seven-figure number. If you call within or between the islands, dial just the seven figures.

Maps and Books

One of the best books to come out of the Caribbean is Herman Wouk's *Don't Stop the Carnival*, which tells the story of a mainlander who comes down to the islands and buys a hotel. In an unending litany of comic woe, every conceivable disaster befalls him in a book that is excruciatingly funny and ruthlessly tense (very unlike later books by Wouk). Budding hotel managers would be advised to read this book; the hoteliers themselves swear by it. It is rather difficult to look them in the eye after reading it. **Dockside Bookshop**, Havensight Mall, St Thomas. Has an excellent selection of Caribbean books.

Festivals

Naturally the USVI has more than its share of regattas, mostly held in St Thomas, of which the following list is just a small selection.

During festivals and celebrations on St Croix, you'll see *mocko jumbie* stilt dancers along the streets.

January *Island Hopper Race*. Event held by St John Yacht Club.

February *Caribbean Ocean Racing Triangle*. Regatta held in St Thomas.

17 March *St Patrick's Day*. A grand parade in St Croix.

Rolex Cup Regatta. Annual sailing event at St Thomas Yacht Club, t 775 6320.

April *St Thomas's Carnival*. A huge and colourful party held in true Caribbean style. Carnival continues through the month with talent shows, calypso revues and a food fair, culminating in parades and a spectacular firework display.

May *Charter yacht show*. Held in Charlotte Amalie, St Thomas.

June *Optimist Regatta*. Held in St Thomas.

July *St John Cultural Celebration*. Festivities around the week of 4 July, and the two preceding weeks.

August *Atlantic Blue Marlin Tournament*, www.abmt.com.

September *Annual chilli cook-off*.

September/October *Pigs in Winter*. Autumn regatta with races held over two days, St Thomas.

November *Charterboat show*. Annual event, in Charlotte Amalie harbour, St Thomas.

Laser Regatta. Women's sailing regatta, St Thomas.

Thanksgiving Jump-Up. For information, call t 713 8012.

Thanksgiving Day Regatta. St John.

Mumm's Cup Regatta. Three days of racing, which starts and finishes off the east coast of St Croix, t 773 9531.

December *St Croix Festival*. Starts early in the month and continues until 6 January.

In the 1620s, adventurers started to arrive and to plant crops – the Dutch and English and French settled in St Croix – and buccaneers took over the smaller islands, letting cattle roam and then killing it and selling the cured meat to passing sailors (Beef Island in the British Virgin Islands takes its name from this). These islands became stopping-off points for ships travelling up and down the island chain and for those that had just crossed the Atlantic. The Virgin Islands became known as markets, and goods would be brought here for distribution all over the Caribbean. Pirates would also offload their loot here, and then spend time ashore, revelling and waiting for another expedition.

The Danes moved in to St Thomas in 1665 and allowed the trading to continue. Business was so successful that by the end of the 17th century, the British Admiral Benbow described St Thomas as 'a receptacle for thieves' (as seen from an English official perspective, at least). In 1724 the island was declared a free port and it was soon on its way to being the richest port of its day. The Danes claimed St John in 1684 (though they did not settle it until 1717) and they bought St Croix from the French in 1733 for 750,000 francs. Both these islands were soon covered with sugar cane. The Danish islands' neutral status sheltered them from the worst effects of the wars between Spain, France and Britain. In wartime, they were entrepôts and a haven against the marauding freebooters (hired by the warring nations to harry enemy and neutral shipping), and in peace they were the headquarters of the smuggling trade in the area. Slave auctions also brought in huge revenue. In the War of American Independence, they shipped arms to the colonists. British objections to the trade led to two occupations in the Napoleonic Wars (1801 and 1807), but the islands were handed back to Denmark in 1815.

The Danes were the first to abolish the slave trade, in 1792, but slavery itself was not abolished until much later. In 1848 the Danish King Frederik VIII issued an edict that all slaves would be emancipated in 1859, but on hearing this the slaves revolted. When the Governor-General Peter von Scholten, a man with a mixed-race mistress himself, faced the crowd on St Croix to make the announcement, he realized that he was unwilling to impose the law and simply announced that he was freeing them then and there. The slaves remained free and the Governor was tried for dereliction of duty, but was eventually acquitted. At about this time, the islands went into financial decline: sugar failed in St Croix and St John as it did in most of the West Indies, and trading in St Thomas fell off, too. Eventually, the islands became a burden to the Danish government, and so they began to look for a way of getting rid of them.

The United States first showed interest in the islands in 1866, but at that stage the Virgin Islanders themselves vetoed the transfer. The subject came up again when the Americans were concerned about German naval movements in the Caribbean in the First World War. This time, the islanders voted for secession to the United States and the Americans bought the islands for $25 million. Early on, the islands were administered purely as a naval base because of their strategic position, but in 1927, the islanders were granted citizenship of the USA, and in 1931 the islands were placed in civil jurisdiction.

Initially, the Governor was appointed by the President in consultation with the elected Senate of the USVI, but this was changed in 1970 and, since then, the Governor has been chosen by the Virgin Islanders themselves in elections held every four years. Since 1972, they have sent a delegate to the House of Representatives, though he has no vote and so has more of a lobbying role. Though the islanders are US citizens, they do not vote in national elections. Unlike Puerto Rico, which is part of the federal banking system, taxes paid in the USVI stay within the islands. The current Governor is Dr Charles Turnbull, and the next elections are scheduled for 2006.

In 1931 the American President, Herbert Hoover, described the US Virgin Islands as 'an orphanage, a poor house' and, soon after, the Virgin Islands Company was established to improve the infrastructure. The production of sugar was centralized and industry was stimulated through tax incentives. In 1966 a huge oil refinery was established on St Croix by the Hess Oil Company. Other industries in operation today include the production of rum, some light manufacture and the assembly of parts from outside the islands.

The USVI have one of the highest per capita incomes in the Caribbean. By far the largest income generator today is the tourism industry, which topped nearly two million visitors when Hurricane Marilyn struck in September 1995. Many long-term residents left the islands for good and for a while arrivals declined, but the islands have rebuilt their confidence once again and are now attracting more like two and a half million visitors per year.

St Thomas

The life of St Thomas has traditionally centred around the island's magnificent harbour, a steep-sided bowl partly closed by islands which has attracted shipping from the earliest days. The lines of 18th-century trading warehouses in Charlotte Amalie are just as busy today as they have ever been, and the harbour teems with yachts, motorboats and cruise ships.

St Thomas is one of the most developed islands in the whole Caribbean. About 50,000 people live on its 33 square miles, most of them in the extended suburb of Charlotte Amalie, the capital town in the USVI. Buildings have sprung up on all available land – villas, hotels and vacation condominiums – and there is even a rush hour. Only in the west end of the island, beyond the airport, is it less built up. It is a crowded place and there is some tension (much of it racial). But overdeveloped as it is, the island is attractive to many for its good hotels and upbeat tempo. Top entertainment acts come down to perform in the island hotels, maintaining St Thomas's tradition as the 'nightclub of the Virgin Islands' and, of course, if you want to join the fray, St Thomas has some of the best shopping in the Caribbean.

Charlotte Amalie

Charlotte Amalie is a classically pretty Caribbean town – red roofs and bursts of palm fronds that scatter the hillsides around a bay and steep alleys that lead down to the harbour. The warehouses on the waterfront are doing a roaring trade as they have on and off for over 300 years. Even in 1700, Père Labat, the roving Dominican monk and self-confessed gastronome from Martinique, found silks from India and gold-embroidered Arabian muslin cloth. It was all off-loaded by pirates who stopped in port to spend their loot before heading seawards again for more 'cruize and plunder'. The infamous Blackbeard, Edward Teach from Bristol, was known to have hidden out here when he was not on the high seas.

Encouraged by the Danes, the trade became a little more regularized and at its height the harbour would see as many as 1,300 vessels in a year. In the late 18th

St Thomas

Windward Passage

St John

Lovango Cay

Mingo Cay

Pillsbury Sound

Grass Cay

Great St James Island

Dog Island

Little St James Island

Point Pleasant Resort

Pavilions and Pools

Sapphire Beach

Coki Beach

Coral World

Thatch Cay

Ritz Carlton

Sea Horse Cottages

Cowpet Bay

Nazareth Bay

Secret Harbour Beach

Red Hook

Little Hans Lollik Island

Hans Lollik Island

Mandahl Bay

New East End

Tutu

Frenchman's Bay

Bolongo Bay Beach Club

Leeward Passage

Mahogany Run Golf Course

Magens Beach

Drake's Seat

Magens Bay

Charlotte Amalie

Fort Christian

St Thomas

Marriott's Morning Star Beach

Bolongo

Bolongo Beach

Buck Island

Outer Brass Island

Inner Brass Island

Brass Channel

Dorothea Hull Bay

St Peter

Hassel Is.

St Thomas Harbour

Frenchtown

Bolongo

Marriott's Frenchman's Reef

Morningstar Beach

Limetree Beach

Caribbean Sea

Water Island

Stumpy Bay Beach

Botany Bay

Fortuna

Brewers Bay Beach

Virgin Islands National Park

South Side

Contant

Cyril E King Airport

Lindbergh Beach

Crown Bay

Frenchcombe

Island Beachcomber

Flat Cays

Saba Island

Southwest Road

N

4 km

2 miles

Best Beaches

All beaches are public in the USVI and there are one or two places with changing facilities. Topless and nude bathing is frowned upon, but it's been known to happen in Little Magens. You are advised to keep an eye on belongings left on the beach while you swim.

Magens Bay: The island's best-known and most popular beach, a superb, mile-long strip of extremely fine sand and coconut palms protected by a huge arm thrusting out into the Atlantic Ocean. It is on the north coast of the island and to get there you have to go over the central mountain range, which gives a fantastic view. Gets crowded at weekends. There are changing facilities, beach bars and restaurants, for a slice of pizza or a pattie (*paté* in local language), and snorkelling equipment for hire (*adm $1, parking $1*). There are one or two tiny strips of sand along the arms of Magens Bay where you can sometimes be alone: Little Magens has a platform beach among the rocks of the northern arm, and there's Paradise Beach opposite here on the south side (approach by a side road off the Hull Bay road).

Hull Bay and **Dorothea Bay**: Isolated coves west of Magens Bay, a bit stony, with a local feel. Fishermen depart from here.

Brewers Beach and **Lindbergh Beach**: On the south side of the island either side of the airport and relatively free of crowds. There are snack stalls at the weekends and evenings.

Morningstar Beach: At the Frenchman's Reef Hotel, east of Charlotte Amalie.

Bolongo Beach, **Cowpet Bay**: On the southern shore; each has a hotel where you can hire watersports equipment.

Sapphire Beach: On the Atlantic-facing east side; good for the snorkelling.

Coki Beach: Next to Coral World and can get very busy. There is good snorkelling and diving, but it is mainly a people beach – sunbathing, hair-braiding, jet skis and loitering by the snackwagons. There are lockers in Coral World if you are there for the day.

Mandahl Bay: East of Magens Bay. Quite secluded with good snorkelling, though the surf can get up.

Offshore Islands: For real seclusion, it is worth considering a trip to one of the off-shore islands. Recommended are Hans Lollick to the north of St Thomas, Great St James to the east and Saba and Buck Island off the south coast. Trips can be arranged through the watersports operators.

century, the future architect of the American Constitution, Alexander Hamilton (on the reverse of the $10 bill), decided the town was so rich that 'gold moved through the streets in wheel-barrows'. The seaborne arrivals continue – marauding characters pour off the ships, with fists full of dollars to spend – but nowadays they race past the rum shops and load up into little safari buses instead, ready to go shopping in the network of alleys downtown. The wares still come from all over the world; they are just shipped in legally, that is all. It is fascinating mercantile mayhem and it gets quite frantic, so you are advised to avoid Charlotte Amalie on a busy day (when as many as ten cruise ships have been known to call in).

Getting Around

By Bus

There is a bus service around St Thomas, run by VITRAN and designed primarily for the islanders themselves, but there is nothing to stop you hopping on board if it's going where you want to. Services are reasonably frequent from the outskirts of Charlotte Amalie (along the waterfront and out through the suburbs) to Red Hook and then along the Smith Bay road and west out to Bordeaux, running until about 8pm. No standing, maximum fare $1, *'exact change only, please'*.

By Taxi

Taxis are everywhere and work to fixed rates (displayed in some hotels; the taxis themselves are unmetered). All the same, it's best to check the fare in advance. You might find that other passengers hop in along the way, which is accepted practice. There are single rates, but for two people the trip from Charlotte Amalie to the airport costs around $11, to Magens Bay – $14.50, to Coki Beach – $17 and to Red Hook – $18. If you don't see one on the street, taxi drivers can always be found through the hotel lobbies. Drivers will happily take you on a tour of the island – about $30 per hour for two people with extras paying $12. However, this can be arranged more cheaply if you are prepared to go by safari bus. Taxi phone numbers include:

VI Taxi Association, t 774 4550.
Virgin Islands Taxi Radio Dispatch, t 774 7457.

By Air

You can take an trip on a **seaplane** through Seaborne Airlines, **t** 714 3254, *www.seaborne airlines.com*: they take off and land in the harbour and then zoom the islands, running as far north as Necker Island in the chain of the BVIs. There's also sightseeing by **helicopter**, with Air Center Helicopters, **t** 775 7335, *www.aircenterhelicopters.com*.

Hitch-hiking

A very small percentage of cars will stop for a hitch-hiker on St Thomas, and on an island with thousands and thousands of them it can be a pretty depressing wait.

Car and Bike Hire

Car hire is the best way of getting about if you are travelling around the island a lot. Cars are easily available for upwards of $40 per day with insurance on top, but the roads become extremely congested in town, so leave plenty of time. A valid driving licence is enough. Remember that in the US Virgin Islands you must drive on the left.

The many car hire firms (at the airport and in town) include:

Amalie Car Rental, *www.amaliecar.com*.
Dependable Car Rental, t 775 2253, US **t** 1 800 522 3076, *www.dependablecar.com*.
Discount Car Rental, t 776 4858, US **t** 1877 478 2833, *www.discountcar.vi*.
E–Z Car Rentals, t 775 6255, US **t** 1 800 524 2027, *ezcar@viaccess.net*.

Tourist Information

While on the island, you can get tourist information at the airport, at Emancipation Square in Charlotte Amalie and at the West India Company dock, where the cruise ships let off their passengers. A general telephone number for information is **t** 774 8784. There is a plethora of tourist material and the island produces a bright yellow brochure, *St Thomas This Week*, with advice on beaches, watersports and other essentials like shopping and investment in real estate. Websites devoted to St Thomas include *www.st-thomas.com*.

Medical Emergencies

In a medical emergency, contact the St Thomas Hospital and Community Health Centre, **t** 776 8311. The bigger hotels sometimes have a doctor on call.

Crime

You are advised to be careful with regard to personal security after dark in Charlotte Amalie.

Shopping

There are two main shopping areas on St Thomas, the Havensight Mall, by the West India cruise-ship dock, where three lines of air-conditioned, glass-fronted boutiques jostle for business, and downtown Charlotte Amalie, which has been involved with trade for over 300 years and is really an outsize emporium. In this network of alleyways and streets, you will find everything on sale from Swiss watches and jewellery from the world over to Chanel perfumes and chic French modes. There is a small mall at Mountain Top, so you can shop with a view if you want. It is known for arts and crafts, as is Tillett Gardens.

The new mall at Paradise Point (just a cable-car ride above Havensight Mall) has an artisan's gallery. Try La Romana for Italian clothes. A. H. Riise and Little Switzerland sell jewellery and Tropicana perfumes. The Dockside Bookshop, Havensight Mall, St Thomas, has an excellent selection of Caribbean books.

Watersports

The hotels have windsurfers and small sailing craft available if you wish to sail around the bay in a hobie cat or a sunfish, and snorkelling gear for exploring underwater. If life is more fun on a wetbike, again try the big hotels, particularly around the eastern end of the island, where the liveliest beaches are Limetree Beach, Coki Beach and Sapphire Beach. You can even arrange parasailing in the comfort of a flying deck chair complete with stereo.

Day Sails

For snorkelling and a picnic on an offshore cay or an isolated bay, try contacting the following:

Daydreamer and *Coconut*, t 775 2584, gdavis@vipowernet.net, www.day dreamervi.com. Two catamarans offering day trips.

Fantasy, t 775 5652, info@daysailfantasy.com, www.daysailfantasy.com. Sloop taking small numbers.

Independence, t 775 1408, independence@ pocketmail.com, www.independence44.us. Small yacht.

True Love, t 779 1640, staff@caribbeandaysail. com, www.sailtruelove.com. For more old-time Caribbean authenticity, you can sail to an offshore cay on this schooner.

Deep-sea Fishing

For wahoo, skipjack, sailfish, tuna and white and blue marlin, contact:

Fish Hawk II, Red Hook, t 775 9058.

Marlin Prince, Red Hook, t 779 5939, www.marlinprince.com.

Nauti Nymph, t 775 5066, powerboats@nautinymph.us.

Prowler, t 779 2515, www.prowlersportfishing.com.

See and Ski, t 775 6265, www.seeski.com. Powerboats can be rented here.

Glass-bottomed Boats

If you would prefer not to get wet, you can try Atlantis Submarine, t 776 5650, www. atlantisadventures.com, which provides excursions under the waves for a close inspection of the submarine underworld. It leaves from the Havensight Mall, near the cruise-ship dock, price around $72.

Kayaking

Kayaks are available through many operators, but Virgin Islands Ecotours, t 779 2155, www.viecotours.com, run a kayak tour through the mangroves and lagoons, where you will learn about the importance of the mangrove swamp and may see rays and tarpon.

Homer's Scuba and Snorkel Tours and Berry Charters, 10-1 Hull Bay, t 774 7606, hcallow@attglobal.net.

Mangrove Adventures, Compass Point Marina, t 771 6689, www.mangroveasventures.com.

Scuba Diving

There's also plenty on offer to divers around St Thomas. The crystalline water often has visibility up to 100ft, and the Virgin Island outcrops, forested above the surface, are covered in coral below. Simple dive sites off the south coast include Cow and Calf and the shelves of St James Island, Water Island and Flat Cay near the airport, and more advanced sites are the tunnels at Thatch Cay and the spine of Sail Rock off the west coast. Divers from St Thomas also go to the RMS *Rhone* off Salt Cay in the BVI.

Once again, the hotels usually lay on equipment and often they can give instruction, but there are outside dive operators if you are travelling independently. Dives cost from about $50 for a single tank dive. There is a decompression chamber on the island, t 776 2686. Dive companies include:

Aqua Action, t 775 6285, *aquaaction@ islands.com*, *www.aadivers.com*.

Chris Sawyer Diving Centre, t 775 7320, t 1 800 882 2965, *sawyerdive@worldnet.att.net*, *www.sawyerdive.vi*.

Coki Beach Dive Club, t 775 4220, US t 1 800 474 COKI, *pete@cokidive.com*, *www.cokidive.com*.

Underwater Safaris, t 773 3737, *info@diveusvi. com*, *www.scubadivevi.com*.

Snorkelling

The Virgin Islands are surrounded by reefs, and St Thomas has some excellent ones, where you can hang around in a school of triggerfish or linger among the seafans. Coki Beach is often busy and other worthwhile spots include Sapphire Beach, Secret Harbour, Great Bay and Botany Bay. Offshore islands with good reefs include Hans Lollick to the north and Lovango Cay, Mingo Cay and Grass Cay off the east coast.

Windsurfing

Can be fixed up at the hotel beaches on the south shore and on the eastern side where the winds are the best, for example at Point Pleasant Resort, t 775 7200, and at Bluebeards Beach and Sapphire Beach. Also try West Indies Windsurfing, t 775 6530.

Other Sports

Golf

Mahogany Run Course, on the northern side of the island, east of Magens Bay, t 777 6006, US t 1 800 253 7103, *www.mahogany rungolf.com*. Eighteen holes. Green fees about $120. Watch out for the Devil's Triangle, holes 13, 14 and 15, the middle one of which has you driving over the sea.

Biking

Water Island Adventures, t 714 2186, *bike waterisland@att.biz*, *www.waterisland adventure.com*. Bike tour and swim on Water Island.

BOB Underwater Adventures, t 715 0348, *www.bobusvi.com*. Underwater motor scooter. True.

Tennis

There are limitless courts on the island and a game is best fixed through a hotel. Guests usually play for free but visitors will be charged a fee.

Where to Stay

St Thomas t (1 340–)

St Thomas has its share of large and expensive luxury beach resorts, mainly scattered along the south and east coasts of the island, but it also has a surprising collection of excellent small hotels in Charlotte Amalie, many of them set in charming antique townhouses on the hillside with a view of the town below. Many hotels offer packages if you contact them in advance, but it is made easy for you if you arrive without a booking because there is a hotel booking booth with direct phone lines at the airport. The government adds an 8% room tax to all bills and most places charge 10% for service.

Villas are also available all around the island, many of them on the slightly less developed north side:

Calypso Realty, PO Box 12178, VI 00801-5178, t 774 1620, US t 1 800 747 4858, *www.calypso realty.com*. A villa-booking agency.

Crystal Cove, t 779 1540, US t 1 800 524 2038, *www.paradisepropertiesvi.com*. Villa complex.

McLaughlin Anderson Luxury Villas, 100 Blackbeard's Hill, t 776 0635, US t 1 800 537 6246, *villas@worldnet.att.net*, *www. mclaughlinanderson.com*. Villa agency.

Sapphire Village, t.779 6910, US t 1 800 874 3535, *www.antillesresort.com*. Hotel with villas attached.

Luxury

Ritz Carlton, 6900 Great Bay, USVI 00802, t 775 3333, US t 1 800 241 3333, *www.ritzcarlton. com*. The most elegant and luxurious place to stay in St Thomas. The balustrades and pediments of a mock Italian Renaissance palace painted in tones of peach look a little odd amid the permanent blooms of bougainvillea and the luxuriant Caribbean sky, but the amphitheatrical setting of the rooms, standing in blocks above a superb bay, is magnificent. Watersports facilities around the pool and beach, with a rarefied atmosphere in the main house and dining rooms. Very plush throughout, with boutiques in case the beach palls.

Very Expensive

Marriott's Morning Star Beach Resort, PO Box 671, t 776 8500, US t 1 800 524 2000, *resorts@marriot.vi*, *www.marriot.vi*. This small section of the larger Marriott Frenchman's Reef has a secluded feel, set in its own cove outside Charlotte Amalie. There are 96 extremely comfortable rooms, set in large buttery yellow and bright blue villas that stand along the good Morningstar Beach. Inside they have all the modern facilities, such as cable and satellite TV and air-con, but also with some attractive older Caribbean features, such as balconies and louvred shutters. Pool, health club, spa and a couple of restaurants, including the Tavern on the Beach, which serves regional American and Asian fusion cuisine. EP or all-inclusive plan.

Expensive

Point Pleasant Resort, 6600 Estate Smith Bay, t 775 7200, t 1 800 777 1700. There are 95 extremely comfortable suites in villas ranged on a steep hillside with wonderful gardens and wooden decks that give a superb view of the islands to the east. Each has a large and breezy main room and fully equipped kitchen.

Pavilions and Pools, 6400 Estate Smith Bay, t 775 6110, US t 1 800 524 2001, *pavand pools@islands.vi*, *www.pavilionsand pools.com*. A smaller, very private retreat, with personal service, with 25 large and comfortable units on the forested hillside either side of a small central area. Each looks onto a private, enclosed deck with a personal pool and all are air-conditioned with kitchenettes, cable TV, VCR and phones and have showers with garden greenery. It's a friendly hotel, but you can shut yourself away with books from the small book

exchange. Trails run down to Lindquist Beach; all the activity of Sapphire Beach nearby. It's a good idea to have a car.

Hotel 1829, PO Box 1567, Government Hill, Charlotte Amalie, t 776 1829, US t 1 800 524 2002, *info@hotel1829.com*, *www.hotel1829. com*. Set up on Government Hill, this fine hotel has an excellent old-time island ambience. The original stone and brick of the town house is exposed in places and there are patterned tiles and Tiffany stained glass. There are 15 suites and rooms, some huge, with a magnificent setting overlooking the town and harbour (in the time-honoured tradition of traders), others tucked away at the back looking over the courtyard where there is a pool. Often a lively atmosphere in the cavernous backgammon bar and on the balcony restaurant (renowned around the island).

Villa Santana, Denmark Hill, Charlotte Amalie, t 776 1311, *info@villasantana.com*, *www.villa santana.com*. Villa Santana stands among the many private villas and homes of Denmark Hill and its seven rooms have plenty of charm, set in stone and wooden buildings from the 19th century. The rooms are smartly decorated, with lacquered wooden furniture. There is a pool and each of the rooms has a full kitchen.

Moderate

Island Beachcomber Hotel, Lindbergh Beach, PO Box 30579, t 774 5250, US t 1 800 982 9898, *www.st-thomas.com/islandbeach comber*. Set in a profuse tropical garden and looking out on to a very pleasant curve of sand on Lindberg Beach, quite close to the airport. It is lower-key than most of St Thomas's beach hotels. The 50 rooms are in simple two-storey blocks overlooking the pretty beachside bar. Some watersports. The airport runway is quite close, but the atmosphere is friendly.

Bolongo Bay Beach Club, 7150 Bolongo, t 775 1800, US t 1 800 74 CHARMS, *info@bolongo. com*, *www.bolongo.com*. The rooms at the Bayside Inn behind the main resort are simple but well priced. A variety of packages on offer (most guests are all-inclusive), but you can use the hotel facilities or just use the rooms as a base.

Bolongo's Inn at Villa Olga, t 775 1800, Frenchtown, t 774 1376, *www.bolongobay. com/villaolga*. A very informal spot, over- looking Hassel Island from the point just beyond Frenchtown. It is set behind an old holiday villa (now a restaurant). The rooms and pool stand stacked on the hillside, painted in a faintly alarming medley of canary yellows, pinks and sky blues. Good atmosphere with travellers who chat to one another over breakfast. Some of the rooms are *expensive*.

Sea Horse Cottages, PO Box 2312-1306, Estate Nazareth, t 775 9231. This is just above the beach at the southeastern corner of the island. There are 16 units in one- and two- bedroom configurations, in cottages and a small block, each with kitchenette, set in a pleasant tropical garden that descends the hill to the coast. There's a swimming pool, a small beach and easy snorkelling just a breath off the coast. Very relaxed atmosphere.

Galleon House, PO Box 6577, Charlotte Amalie, t 774 6952, US t 1 800 524 2052, *info@ galleonhouse.com*, *www.galleonhouse.com*. This has cracking views of the red roofs of Charlotte Amalie. There are 14 comfortable rooms, a pool and a central dining terrace where guests take breakfast.

Danish Chalet Inn, PO Box 4319, Charlotte Amalie, t 774 5764, US t 1 877 40 PALMS, *www.danishchaletinn.com*. This is a home away from home, where there are 10 rooms with plenty of modern comforts (air-con, TV, VCR, phone) in a private house high up overlooking the town; some share baths. Friendly atmosphere.

The Miller Manor, PO Box 1570, Charlotte Amalie, t 774 1535, *www.millermanor.com*. An inexpensive choice, with the faded elegance of a town house and a fantastic view of the bay. It has 24 passable rooms.

Island View Guest House, PO Box 1903, Charlotte Amalie, t 774 4270, US t 1 800 524 2023, *info@islandviewstthomas.com*, *www.islandviewstthomas.com*. High up the hill, perched 500ft above the harbour, there are 15 rooms with comfortable furnish- ings and a variety of shared and private bathrooms.

Inexpensive

At a pinch, if you are down to your last few dollars, go to the marina and ask a yacht owner if you can sleep in a berth on board while the yacht is not on charter; some owners are prepared to allow this in exchange for a few hours' work.

Eating Out

As a developed island, St Thomas has a grander variety of restaurants than others, and so you can eat anything from 'contempo- rary exotic' and even 'passionate' cuisine through to wholesome local rice 'n' peas. Many menus are solidly American – burgers and steaks – but literally anything, no matter how exotic, can be imported, so you will find fine French fare as well as typical Caribbean seafood and fish. You might also consider spending the evening over in St John (a 20min ferry crossing, till late), which also has some good restaurants.

Categories are arranged according to the price of a main dish (excluding lobster and steak): expensive = US$20 and above; moderate = between US$10 and $20; inexpensive = US$10 and below.

A 10% or 15% service charge will be added to your bill, for your convenience... 'Tipping is not a city in China...'

Expensive

Craig and Sally's, Frenchtown, t 777 9949. Most of the best independent restaurants are in and around Charlotte Amalie, some of them in Frenchtown, where you'll find this charming restaurant. There is an intimate air among the columns, drapes, quiet opera and classical music, and, though it is set indoors, it has trelliswork walls and murals of Caribbean scenes. An eclectic menu with tastes drawn from around the world, presented with artistic flair – salmon medal- lions grilled and topped with fresh scallop *ceviche* or a grilled swordfish on a bed of blueberry basmati rice in *chipotle*-mango compound butter. Award-winning wine list, with bottles stacked against the walls.

Hervé's, Government Hill, t 777 9703. A very pleasant setting, a sleek dining room with black chairs and red and white tablecloths, looking out on the lights of St Thomas through large windows. You dine on cuisine that is 'classical French' and 'contemporary American'. Also varied – start with tender Bay scallops or warm smoked quail and continue with black sesame-crusted tuna in a ginger-raspberry sauce or grilled lamb chops stuffed with spinach and served with Montrachet and pine nuts on a chilled pear purée.

Hotel 1829, Government Hill, t 776 1829. This restaurant is well thought of around the island and has a very pleasant setting for excellent international fare touched with the Caribbean and Asia. You dine in the air-conditioned interior or on the delightful veranda. Start with their crispy parsnip fritters served with crème fraiche and smoked salmon and then try the *coquilles St Jacques*, served with lobster and shrimp in a light cream sauce with white wine and chives.

Agavé Terrace, Point Pleasant Resort, t 775 4142. A delightful open-air setting on a deck high above the east coast of the island and looking out towards the lights of St John and the BVI. The menu is strong Caribbean seafood with lobster served in different ways and, of course, grilled fresh fish.

Virgilio's, between Main and Back Streets, t 776 4920. This ever-popular spot serves classic Italian dishes in a small, but brisk and lively dining room hung to the roof with paintings, framed posters and Tiffany-style stained-plastic windows. Eggplant *parmigiana*, followed by pastas and meat and vegetarian dishes. There is an extensive wine list and it is worth going just for the cappuccino, to which is added a secret recipe of eleven ingredients including Galliano, Bailey's and Kahlua.

Havana Blue, Morning Star Beach Resort, t 715 2583. A new restaurant offering Pacific rim, Cuban and Latin America inspired dishes with exotic spices and tangy sauces. Favourites include grouper encrusted with red chile and avocado, seared Thai tenderloin and duck lettuce cups.

Old Stone Farm House, Mahogany Run, t 777 6985. In the walls of an old estate house from centuries past, which have been restored into a quaint, elegant setting, with wooden floors and antique furniture. International cuisine: a blackened salmon *quesadilla* to start, followed by the house speciality, three-day mango Asian duck with seared plantains and hearts of palm in a ginger plum wine sauce. Sushi is also available on a daily basis. (At the *moderate* end of this category.)

Oceana Restaurant and Wine Bar, Villa Olga, beyond Frenchtown, t 774 4262. A charming setting among the old stonework and wood and metal balconies of an old villa, with a view onto the sea. Fresh seafood and prime aged steaks. There's also a tasting table of tapas-style appetizers, and cheery American-style service. (At the *moderate* end of this category.)

Moderate

Alexander's Café, Frenchtown, t 776 4211. Austrian food in a plush, air-conditioned black-and-white dining room with exposed beams and decorated with Alpine scenes – *würst*, *Nürnberger Rostbraten*, *schnitzel* and pastas from farther afield. *Lunch and dinner, closed Sun.*

Alex's Bar and Grill, next to Alexander's Café, Frenchtown. Serves simpler meals to music and the television; grilled honey-mustard shrimp and club sandwiches, with a lively crowd at the bar.

Fagioli Ristorante, Waterfront, Charlotte Amalie, t 777 8116. Hearty Italian fare right across the road from the water's edge in downtown Charlotte Amalie, where you sit in a courtyard under brightly coloured parasols or inside where wine bottles stand stacked against the walls. Pastas, pizzas, *calzoni* and more.

Hook, Line and Sinker, on the dock, Frenchtown, t 776 9708. A typical, cheery Caribbean waterfront restaurant. You sit at bench seats on a covered wooden deck with a view onto the marina. Simple fare, burgers, fried fish and steaks.

Cuzzins, Back Street, Charlotte Amalie, t 777 4711. For something a little more West Indian, an air-conditioned lounge with brick walls, popular for local food in prodigious quantities – curried and stewed meats (chicken, conch, mutton and goat) accompanied by bewildering local vegetables.

Gladys' Café, Royal Dane Mall, Charlotte Amalie, t 774 6604. In all the mayhem of the downtown alleys, you will find a very nice stopping-point for breakfast, lunch or afternoon tea. Cool and air-conditioned, set in the old warehouse: *pasta primavera* with sautéed conch, lots of sandwiches and vegetarian dishes.

Off the Hook, Red Hook, t 775 6350. Set on a tin-roofed, double-level deck looking out onto the lagoon of Vessup Bay and the marina with an easygoing atmosphere. Euro-Caribe cuisine, including excellent fish and seafood bought fresh on the dock that day: some of the specialities include Caribbean Lobster creole and yellowtail snapper wrapped in banana leaf.

Randy's Bistro, Al Cohen's Plaza, t 775 5001. Fresh seafood from a creative menu that changes daily. Large selection of wines.

Inexpensive

Percy's Bus Stop, Charlotte Amalie. Found across from the waterfront in town. Situated aboard a No.12 London bus, somehow re-routed on its journey to Piccadilly Circus. Red tablecloths and a single decorative flower, plus simple West Indian fare, stew chicken or conch.

Bill's Texas Pit BBQ, t 776 9579. Two strategically placed snackwagons on the waterfront in downtown Charlotte Amalie and Red Hook. If you do not want to spend too much and don't mind dining out of a polystyrene box on your knees, you can get an excellent batter chicken or ribs swimming in barbecue sauce, set in a pile of coleslaw. *Open Tues–Sat.*

Bars and Nightlife

Pretty much any drink or spirit is available in St Thomas, but you will also find their locally brewed (well, in St Croix, anyway) beer, Blackbeard Ale, a bitter. The bottle comes with a little note from the man himself, from his journal, saying that his men would start plotting if they were allowed to remain sober for too long.

The jazz has just begun to reappear after the hurricane (check the papers and tourist magazines, *see* p.515). Otherwise you might try one of the small town hotels in Frenchtown – Blackbeard's or 1829, for example – where the bars sometimes have piano players. And if you want to go dancing, there are places open, usually at weekends. After you've gone at it too much on Friday and Saturday, you can join the crowd of other sybarites recovering on Sapphire Beach on Sunday afternoon.

Epernay Champagne Bar, Frenchtown. An excellent bar to start the evening with (whether you decide to eat nearby or not): hip chicks and executives gather after work for sushi and goat's cheese.

Coconut's, Charlotte Amalie. One of several lively bars downtown.

Green House, down at the waterfront, Veteran's Drive, Charlotte Amalie, t 774 7998. At this ever-cheery, ever-heaving night bar and restaurant, every night is happy hour.

Hard Rock Café, on the waterfront at International Plaza, Charlotte Amalie, t 777 5555. This is just like other Hard Rocks around the world, if that's your thing.

Duffy's Love Shack, Red Hook Plaza, t 779 2080. Bamboo rattan interior, tables out on the tarmac, lots of exotic cocktails and Jimmy Buffet music – and the theme is *2001* if you order a 'Love Shack Volcano'. All quite fun. Some food, dancing later on; on Wednesday ladies drink free.

East End Café, Red Hook. This bar can also be fun.

Warehouse, Red Hook. A rumbustious white crowd hangs our here where a sign reads *'A Poor Man's Bar; No Pets; No Dirtbags'*; there's pool, pinball, loud rock music and a load of beer.

New Old Mill, Crown Mountain Rd. A jazz bar and reggae club open from Wednesday to Saturday.

Sib's on the Mountain, on the Mafolie Estate high above Charlotte Amalie. Gathers a young crowd at weekends.

XO Bistro, Red Hook Plaza, behind Duffy's Love Shack. This wine and champagne bar is a neat little place, very popular with locals and little known to tourists. Some say it's *the* place to be on Friday nights.

Originally, the town was known as 'Tap Hus' (roughly translated as 'rum shop'), but in 1730 the Danes renamed it after the wife of their King Christian V. As well as the name, many Danish buildings also remain in Charlotte Amalie. The town is built over three main hills: Government Hill, Denmark Hill and Frenchman's Hill. The heartland of Charlotte Amalie, though, is down below, in the tight alleys of brick and plaster trading warehouses, some of them from the 18th century. These still buzz with trade: Palm Passage, Drake's Passage and King Christian Walk. As in all West Indian islands, the main **market** in the middle of the town sells fruit and vegetables, mainly on Friday and Saturday mornings, to the St Thomians who dare venture that far into town.

At the other end of Main St (formerly Dronningens Gade, where you can find a yellow arched building that was the birthplace of Camille Pissarro, father of French Impressionism), there is a small cluster of monumental buildings around **Emancipation Park**: the huge classical-fronted post office and the once-grand Grand Hotel (it used to be the social centre of the island, but now it is mainly shops). Close by is the dark red **Fort Christian**, built in 1672 when the Danes first arrived, which stands on the waterfront guarding the bay. In its time, it has been the Governor's house, the garrison and recently the prison, police station and courts. It is now home to the **Virgin Islands Museum** (*open Mon–Fri 9–noon and 1–5; adm free*) and the underground cells have displays of the simple island existence of the Arawaks and the planters' and traders' sumptuous life when St Thomas was in its prime. Over the road is the island **Legislature** (*open Mon–Fri 8–5*), formerly the Danish barracks, a grand structure from the 1870s that is dressed up in lime green, where the 15 US Virgin Island Senators do their business. You can listen in on a session in the gallery if you want.

On the hillside above the park, aloof from all the trading activity on the waterfront, is **Government House** (*open Mon–Fri 8–5; adm free*), a three-storey building with pretty wrought-iron balconies that was built in 1867 for the Danish colonial council and is now the official residence of the islands' Governor. Only the wooden-floored and formal entrance lobby can be visited, but you can see the names of the early Danish governors and their American counterparts and some Royal Danish porcelain, including the writing set with which Governor van Scholten signed the proclamation for the abolition of slavery in the Danish islands.

At the top of the **99 Steps** (actually there are 103 of them at present, made of nice old yellow brick), you will find **Haagensen House**, a delightful old St Thomian town house which dates probably from the 1830s and has a fantastic view over the town, looking straight down Crystal Gade, the first street with glass windows. Outside it has a traditional red roof and green pointing on cream clapboard and there are louvres on the windows and French windows to encourage the breeze. Inside, you will see mahogany and cane furniture, a wonderful Spanish porcelain water filter in the pantry (the water was filtered through coal pebble and sand) and old island prints, including reproductions by Camille Pissarro.

At the top of **Government Hill**, you come to what is known as **Blackbeard's Tower**, an extremely fine lookout, where the pirate was supposed to have lived around 1700. He was an extremely violent man – he would occasionally shoot one of his sidekicks to keep the others on their guard – and he liked to adopt an especially demonic appearance when going into battle by burning fuses in his hair. He was eventually killed in a shootout with the British Navy in 1718. On Crystal Gade, you will find the **St Thomas Synagogue**, a reconstruction of the original which dates from 1833, with a sand floor, local mahogany benches and Ark.

On the western outskirts of the town, you come to **Frenchtown**, the original settling point of a group of immigrants from the island of St Barthélemy in the Leewards, who first came over in 1852. Their descendants form a distinct community on the island (there have been more recent influxes of immigrants, too): some remain in Frenchtown and work as fishermen; others have become very influential and own some of the most valuable land on the north side. Beyond Sub Base, the original Navy base and now a marina, you will find the island power plant and the desalination plant, which gives island water its slightly disinfected taste.

At the opposite end of town is the **Yacht Haven**, St Thomas's main yachting marina, and close by is the West India Company Dock, where you will find the **Havensight Mall**, another agglomeration of tourist shops in long warehouses. If the hustle gets too much, you might take a ride up the hill, in a bubble-car ski lift of all things, to **Paradise Point**, another shopping centre, for a fine sunset view and and excellent banana daiquiri. You can arrange a personalized tour of Charlotte Amalie, conducted by a guide with a special knowledge of its history, through the **Historic Walking Tour** (**t** 774 9605).

Around the Island

The island of St Thomas is highly developed all around. The hills above Charlotte Amalie are covered with homes to their summits and, wherever you go on the island, you are not far from a residential area. Near the top of the central range is **Drake's Seat**, the vantage point supposedly used by Sir Francis Drake in his privateering days in the 1580s. Where the old English sailor had henchmen to scour the magnificent view across to the BVI for ships, today's visitors will find T-shirt vendors and a man with a donkey for your photographic delectation. At the actual summit is Mountain Top, where there is another cracking view of Magens Bay and the BVI. Oh, and another shopping centre for when the view palls.

Worth a visit in this area is the **St Peter Greathouse Estate and Gardens** (**t** 774 4999), where you can see countless examples of tropical plants – cacti, water plants, tropical crops (including 20 species of bananas), flowering trees and ornamental flowers like heliconia and Indian head ginger. There are 200 species in all alongside a small aviary, a nature trail and an iguana and Caribbean turtle sanctuary. The great house has been modernized and is surrounded by decks and lookouts, from where there is an excellent view of Magens Bay.

The southeast of the island is built up with condominiums and vacation homes that take advantage of the beaches in that area. **Coral World Ocean Park** (*tours available on request; adm expensive*) is an underwater world complex at Coki Beach in the east of the island, with good displays – a walk-down observatory 15ft underwater, a mangrove lagoon, stingray pool, excellent aquaria and a predator tank where sharks and tarpons patrol. Heading back towards Charlotte Amalie, you will find **Tillett Gardens**, an artists' retreat where there are galleries and studios with work as varied as screen printing and glass work.

At the west end of St Thomas is the **Reichhold Centre for the Arts** (*University of the Virgin Islands*, **t** *693 1559, www.reichholdcenter.com*), the island's main venue for the performing arts with a full programme of classical and contemporary music, dance and theatre. From the remote bays of the north coast around Bordeaux there are magnificent views of the islands of Culebra and Vieques with Puerto Rico beyond.

St John

First appearances are enough to reveal that St John is altogether different from St Thomas. Unlike its larger neighbour, where houses line the hillsides to their very summits, St John is mostly green and forested. You can only get there by boat and it sets the tone for the island. As you make the short crossing over the Pillsbury Sound to the island, the pressurized tempo of St Thomas will evaporate and St John will welcome you with a nonchalant calm.

St John has taken a different path from the other Virgin Islands since 1956, when Laurence Rockefeller and his Jackson Hole Preserve Corporation granted about half of the island to the National Parks. That part of St John has remained undeveloped since then and so much of the land is now undisturbed forest. The National Park has opened up the forests with walking trails and holds seminars on the natural life of the island. The development that is there is really only in two clusters, around Cruz Bay in the west and Coral Bay in the east.

St John still has a unique atmosphere; there is an easy small-island charm with the upbeat activity of a seafront holiday resort. And yet all the comforts of modern America are within a whisper (or a short trip by car ferry to St Thomas). The islanders joke that St John is really a part of the BVI and, in some ways, it feels more similar to them than to St Thomas. There is a close-knit community, with its large proportion of expatriates, and generally they welcome the tourists and the yearly invasion of 'snow-birds' (migrant winter residents) graciously.

Cruz Bay, the capital and principal but not quite only settlement, has just a few streets which are centred on the harbour and clamber up the hillside above the bay. The waterfront has a feel of a modern Caribbean playground – neat and tidy with little complexes of shops and restaurants and day trippers shifted around in safari buses – but there are lots of bars which come alive at night and over the hill there is a robust local community. On the eastern shores, after crossing the uninterrupted stretches of green, you will find the only other settlement, Coral Bay, where there is another small community, hillsides of private villas and some cool and easy water-front haunts. It is not hard to imagine how life was here 50 years ago when the islanders travelled everywhere by donkey on small trails cut out of the forest.

St John

N

2 km
1 mile

Tortola

Great Thatch

St John

Hansen Bay

Fort Berg

Coral Bay

Coral Bay

Estate
Annaberg

Waterlemon
Cay

Leinster
Bay

Estate
Concordia

Salt Pond
Bay

Mary's Point

Maho Bay Camps &
Harmony Resort

Francis Bay

Maho Bay

Lameshur
Bay

Bordeaux
Mountain

Cinnamon
Bay

St John
National Park

Cinnamon Bay
Campground

Centerline Rd

Reef Bay

Trunk
Bay

Hawksnest
Bay

Caneel Bay

Caneel Bay

Caribbean Sea

Windward Passage

Henley Cay

U.K.
U.S.

Lovango Cay

Solomon Bay

Estate Lindholm

Cruz
Bay

Great
Cruz Bay

Gallows Bay Point Bay

Frank Bay

Cruz Bay

St Thomas

Pillsbury Sound

Best Beaches

Trunk Bay: St John's answer to Magens Bay on St Thomas, with mounds of blinding white sand backed by palm trees. There are changing rooms, a snack bar, a hire shop, lifeguards and a snorkelling trail through the corals, where you will be surrounded by parrotfish and tangs.

Cinnamon Bay: East of Trunk Bay, rimmed with the softest sand and has a snack bar and changing rooms attached to the Cinnamon Bay Campground.

Maho Bay and **Francis Bay**: The next coves along, with excellent sand. Francis Bay has good snorkelling. Both bays have a superb view out over the other islands.

Salt Pond Bay and **Lameshur Bay**: Off the beaten track on the south coast, where there are few people, calm water and good sand. Take a picnic and drinks if you plan to stay for the day.

Solomon Beach: A 20-minute walk along the coastline from Mongoose Junction. Naturism has been known here (though it's illegal). No facilities, so take what you need in the way of drinks and food.

Caneel Bay: The hotel has a number of small beaches within the grounds, though access is restricted over land.

Gibney or **Oppenheimer Bay**: West of Trunk Bay, a small and charming strip of sand (quite difficult to find, down wooden steps), secluded and completely without facilities. Nearby is another couple of thin strips of sand in Hawksnest Bay, where you can usually be alone.

Offshore cays: Include Henley Cay (out from Caneel Bay) and Lovango Cay (further out), both worth the visit for their sands. Off Leinster Bay in the north is Waterlemon Cay, a short ride out of Francis Bay.

All may be quiet today, but once St John was as much a hive of plantation activity as the rest of the Caribbean islands. Two hundred years ago, the slopes were cut with terraces for the sugar cane. In 1733 St John saw one of the Caribbean's most successful slave rebellions, in which the Africans revolted and held out for over nine months, successfully beating off attempts by Danish and British troops to put them down. When they were eventually defeated by French soldiers brought in from Martinique, many preferred to commit suicide by jumping off the cliffs at Mary Point rather than allow themselves to be returned to slavery. Just a few plantation ruins remain, throttled by the jungle.

As on all the islands, the vast majority of St John's income derives from tourism. Over half a million tourists visit the island each year, the majority on day trips from the cruise ships in St Thomas. Things are developing on the island, too. You will see people cutting into the green of the interior as plots of land are reclaimed around the outside of the National Park, and ever more villas and private homes spring up on the small stretches of available private land.

Today's population of around 5,000 is less than that in the island's plantation heyday. Nowadays, the island is tranquil, favoured by a few writers and recluses and by campers (St John goes out of its way to provide a nature-based holiday for those who want it, and the campsites are often booked up well in advance). The desperation

Getting There

St John t (1 340–)

By Sea

It is one of the pleasures of St John that it can really only be reached by sea. Ferries can be caught in St Thomas from downtown Charlotte Amalie (about six times a day on Transportation Services, t 776 6282) and from Red Hook in East End (hourly on Transportation Services). You can also visit from Tortola in the BVI, with three or four sailings a day on Inter-Island Ferries, t 776 6597, departing West End terminal. There are even ferries to Jost van Dyke (a couple of days a week, on Inter-Island Ferries).

Getting Around

By Bus

There is a scant bus service, leaving Cruz Bay every hour or so and crossing to Coral Bay.

By Taxi

If you can persuade a taxi driver to take you, taxi rates, for two people, are as follows: Cruz Bay to Trunk Bay – $9, to Cinnamon Bay – $11, to Annaberg – $18, to Coral Bay – $18. You may find that somebody hops onto your ride and shares the price. A two-hour tour of the island by taxi will cost $30.

Hitch-hiking

Hitching a ride is not that easy on St John.

Car Hire

When you are out driving, you should watch for safari buses and water delivery trucks on the steep bends. Jeeps are popular here and daily rates start at around $50. Remember to drive on the left. Companies include:

Avis, Cruz Bay, t 776 6374.

Cool Breeze Car Rental, Cruz Bay, t 776 6588, *www.coolbreezecarrental.com*.

Delbert Hill Jeep and Auto, Cruz Bay, t 776 6637.

L & L Jeep Rental, Cruz Bay, t 776 1120, *www.bookajeep.com*.

St John Car Rental, Cruz Bay, t 776 6103, *www.stjohnusvi.com/car-rental*.

Spencer's Jeep Rentals, Cruz Bay, t 693 8784.

Tourist Information

There is a website devoted to St John at *www.st-john.com*.

Tourist Office, Cruz Bay, PO Box 200, St John, t 776 6450. Found opposite the ferry dock.

National Park Service, opposite Mongoose Junction, Cruz Bay, t 776 6201. Has a visitors' centre with an orientation video, bookshop and other information. *Open 8–4.30.*

Friends of the Park, t 779 4940, *www. friendsvinp.org*. Holds a great variety of interesting workshops and educational excursions during the winter season.

Virgin Islands National Park, PO Box 7789, St Thomas VI 00801. For more information, you can write to this address.

Medical Emergencies

In a medical emergency, contact the DeCastro Clinic in Cruz Bay, t 776 6252.

Watersports

Watersports are usually handled by the hotels but there are plenty of outside operators:

Adventures in Paradise, t 779 4527, *www. bookstjohn.com*.

Cruz Bay Watersports, t 776 6234, *info@divestjohn, www.divestjohn.com*.

Low Key Watersports, Cruz Bay, t 693 8999, *lowkey@viaccess.com, www.divelowkey.com*.

Day Sails

Cinnamon Bay, t 776 6462, *www.motoryacht cinnamonbay.com*. Motor yacht available.

Connections of St John, t 776 6922, *connectvi@ worldnet.att.net, www.connectionsstjohn.com*.

Ocean Runner, t 693 8809, *www.ocean runner.vi*. A powerboat.

Wayward Sailor, t 776 6922, *capt.phil@ waywardsailor.net*.

Deep-sea Fishing

Can be arranged through the above watersports companies or in Red Hook on St Thomas.

Kayaking

Kayak Safaris, t 792 5794, *www.kayaksafaris. com*. Kayak excursions accompanied by a fully-crewed yacht with sleeping quarters.

Virgin Islands Kayaks Tours, t 779 2155. Kayak tours of the Marine Sanctuary.

Wind N Surfing Adventures, Cinnamon Bay and Coral Bay, **t** 776 6330, *windsurf@viaccess.com*. Good for windsurfing and kayaking.

Scuba Diving

Favourite dive sites include the reefs and cays to the north of the island, Eagle Shoal to the south, Ten Fathom Pinnacle and even the steamship *Rhone* off Salt Cay in the British Virgin Islands. Contact the watersports companies above. Also try:

Snuba, Trunk Bay, **t** 693 8063, *www.visnuba. com*. This company will take you on a guided underwater swim with air pumped from the surface.

Snorkelling

Particularly good in Haulover Bay, Leinster Bay and on Waterlemon Cay. In Salt Pond Bay, you may be lucky and see a turtle in the sea grass.

Other Sports

Hiking

A number of activities are arranged: the Bird Walk from the National Park Office in Cruz Bay, **t** 776 6201, *www.nps.gov/viis*, the Reef Bay hike from the Cinnamon Bay Campground, **t** 776 6330, and others which are self-guided, like the Snorkel Trail in Trunk Bay, Annaberg, and the Petroglyph Trail. The guides are well-versed in island flora, fauna and history. A popular hike leads from Centerline Road in the middle of the island over to Reef Bay, from where they arrange a trip back by boat to save you the walk. Day hikes may include picnics and snorkelling breaks. Contact the National Park Office for details.

Horse-riding

Carolina Stables, **t** 693 5778. Will take you on guided tours through the island's blanket of forest and to hidden coves where you can ride along the sand.

Tennis

There are courts in the hotels as well as four public courts in Cruz Bay.

Where to Stay

St John t (1 340–)

There is a small selection of hotels on St John, mostly concentrated around Cruz Bay. There are also a couple of campsites, if you want to see the National Park from close up. The camping is by no means that 'rustic': you stay in permanent 'tents', with raised floors, canvas walls and netting at either end, or wooden cabins with mosquito screens and a central area, with washrooms and concessionary shops. Hikes, watersports and even environmental lectures are laid on. These resorts do get booked up well in advance, so you'll need to reserve early for the winter season. Government tax: 8% on all hotel bills.

Another option is to consider taking a **villa**, of which there are plenty on the island. Try:

Viva or Caribbean Villas, **t** 776 6152, US **t** 1 800 338 0987, *www.caribbeanvilla.com*.

VI Vacations, PO Box 1747, **t** 779 4250, *viva@vivacations.com*, *www.vivacations.com*.

Windspree Vacation Homes, 7 Freemans Ground, **t** 693 5423, US **t** 1 888 742 0375, *info@windspree.com*, *www.windspree.com*.

Luxury–Expensive

Caneel Bay, PO Box 720, **t** 776 6111, US **t** 1 877 273 2931, *caneelbay@worldnet.att.net*, *www.caneelbay.com*. Set on the magnificent sweep of Caneel Bay, with rooms ranged along the waterfront overlooking Pillsbury Sound and St Thomas. Amid lawned expanses and superb manicured gardens, the restored stone estate buildings lend the hotel an elegant and stately air, but there is also plenty of activity in the way of watersports. With weights room, tennis pro, children's centre and two good restaurants.

Gallows Point Resort, PO Box 58, **t** 776 6434, US **t** 1 800 468 3750, *information@gallows pointresort.com*, *www.gallowspointresort. com*. A collection of suites set in striking villas, built in clapboard with louvres and tin roofs, and found on the clifftop just out of Cruz Bay (a walk or a drive from the beach), surrounded by fine greenery. The suites are individually decorated; they are quite spacious, very comfortable and their balconies have a fine view of the other islands. Pool and swimming area down below. They have full kitchens, but there is a central restaurant for dinner.

Estate Lindholm, PO Box 1360, **t** 776 6121, *lindholm@viaccess.com*, *www.estate lindholm.com*. A very friendly inn with a fantastic setting in an old estate house with views stretching to St Thomas beyond. Pretty walkways meander among soursop, mango and pomegranate trees to the 11 very comfortable rooms set in modern blocks behind. Large balconies with rocking chairs.

Harmony Resort, contact 20–27 Estate Concordia, **t** 693 5855, *www.harmony-studios.com*. Separated from Maho Bay, but benefiting from the same facilities. The setting is charming; there are breezy and comfortable cottages ranged on the hillside, linked by wooden walkways and hidden among the profuse greenery. Kitchenettes and balconies; watersports facilities.

Moderate

Garden by the Sea Bed and Breakfast, Cruz Bay, PO Box 149, **t** 779 4731, *info@garden bythesea.com*, *www.gardenbythesea.com*. You are guaranteed a warm reception at this charming bed and breakfast with just three rooms. It overlooks an inland lagoon with pretty decks set in magnificent greenery. The rooms are extremely comfortable, with elephant bamboo beds and muslin netting, Japanese fountains and garden bathrooms, but you will find that you spend time in the central sitting area with the other guests.

Maho Bay Camps, PO Box 310, St John 00831, **t** 776 6240, US res **t** 1 800 392 9004, *mahony@maho.org*, *www.maho.org*. As the name suggests, they are set in Maho Bay, with a lacework of paths linking the tents to the facilities and beach.

Concordia Eco-Tents, 20–27 Estate Concordia, **t** 693 5855, *www.concordia-eco-tents.com*. On the south coast, this sister resort to Harmony offers multi-level tents with kitchens and private shower rooms, set in drier vegetation with a fantastic view over the east end of St John and the BVI.

Cinnamon Bay Campground, PO Box 720, **t** 776 6330, US **t** 1 800 539 9998, *www.cinnamon bay.com*. This is set at sea level in the forest. Cottages and tents and simple cooking facilities, and a restaurant, too.

Inexpensive

St John Inn, PO Box 556, **t** 693 8688, US **t** 1 800 666 7688, *info@stjohninn.com*, *www.stjohninn.com*. Takes a rather more aloof view from the hillside over a bay behind Cruz Bay. Friendly with quite simple rooms, some with share baths.

Inn at Tamarind Court, Cruz Bay, PO Box 350, St John 00831, **t** 776 6378, US **t** 1 800 221 1637, *tamarind@worldnet.att.net*, *www.tamarind court.com*. Twenty rooms in modern concrete, lime green and pink blocks, with bright décor and air-con. There is often a crowd gathered at the charming courtyard bar and restaurant, where you sit in the shade of a huge flamboyant tree. Some studios and some well-priced single rooms, with cable TV and housekeeping.

Hansen Bay Campground, **t** 693 5033 (or enquire at Miss Vie's snack shack, *see* 'Eating Out' below). On the wiggly peninsula beyond Coral Bay. Isolated and quiet.

Eating Out

St John has quite a good variety of places to eat for a small island (perhaps worth investigating on an evening out from St Thomas). As well as the more formal dining rooms of the big hotels, you will find lively restaurants in Cruz Bay and some easygoing haunts around Coral Bay in the east. The larger restaurants will accept credit cards. Service charge runs at 10–15%. **Categories** are arranged according to the price of a main dish: expensive = US$20 and above; moderate = between US$10 and $20; inexpensive = US$10 and below.

Expensive

Asolare, Northshore Rd, **t** 779 4747. This has the top position for cuisine and particularly for its setting: you dine sitting on wicker-backed chairs on a screened veranda made of stone high above Cruz Bay, with a fantastic view across to St Thomas. The fare is Thai-Asian cuisine and a few continental dishes: try *Namtok* salad (rare beef tenderloin with roasted rice crumbs in lemongrass, coriander and mint).

Tage, Cruz Bay, **t** 715 4270, *www.tagestjohn.com*. Run by one of the island's best-known chefs. Ted Robinson's ambitious fusion menu includes such creations as sauté of rock lobster medallions, roasted day-boat scallops, pear and fennel-arugula salad with champagne truffle vinaigrette, breast of chicken stuffed with Black Forest ham, roasted tomato *aioli*, and more. *Closed Sun.*

Stone Terrace Restarant, Cruz Bay, t 693 9370. A delightful restaurant with excellent international cuisine, set not on a stone terrace as it happens, but a tile one, above a quiet road. You eat at neat tables inside or out on the veranda. Thai curry chicken tortilla handrolled in coconut curry sauce followed by grilled salmon with a tomato tapenade and a yellow pepper purée.

La Tapa, Cruz Bay, t 693 7755. Set in a charming old local house, right in the middle of the town, with open doors, a small patio and a lively atmosphere. Well worth stopping by for tapas (*4.30–6.30*): *pâté maison*, *bruschetta* and home-made *mozzarella di bufala*. More substantial fare later on.

Zozo's Ristorante, Cruz Bay, t 693 9200. Italian fare set in an elegant air-conditioned setting, decorated with clay tiles and Italian scenes. Home-made lobster ravioli, stuffed veal chops and Italian wines.

Paradiso, Mongoose Junction II, t 693 8899. A pretty dining room with a hardwood floor and tall shutters. New American cuisine: pan-seared day-boat scallops served with truffles and balsamic vinegar or an Asian barbecued yellowfin tuna with sticky rice and a ginger-leek vinaigrette.

Moderate

Morgan's Mango, Cruz Bay, t 693 8141. A charming and very lively restaurant set on a fairy-lit white, pink and turquoise terrace with a friendly tree growing through it. The long menu is New World and there are some Argentinian plates among dishes drawn from across the Caribbean, so as well as a 14oz steak with *chimi-churri* sauce, you can expect Anegada lobster cakes, Cuban citrus chicken and spicy voodoo snapper. There is a long cocktail menu and in season it is worth reserving. Some entertainment and an occasional tango presentation.

Café Roma, Main St, Cruz Bay, t 776 6524. Serves Italian food in a pretty air-conditioned dining room upstairs, with a mural of an Italian scene: Venetian shrimp in lemon and garlic and a multiplicity of pastas and pizzas.

Lime Inn, Leomon Tree Mall, Cruz Bay, t 776 6425. A breezy terrace in electric green with trelliswork and tin roof. American style, with all-you-can-eat shrimp on Wednesdays.

Shipwreck Landing, Coral Bay, t 776 8640. Has a mixed menu; you eat on a wooden deck overhung by palms and sprays of bougainvillea, right across from the sea. Chicken *teriyaki* or Mexicali, lime butter *mahi-mahi* or burgers and sandwiches, plus daily pasta and fish specials.

Miss Lucy's Restaurant, Friis Bay, t 693 5244. A deck dressed up in pink right on the waterfront, it serves excellent Caribbean fish.

Inexpensive

Hercules Paté Delight, Cruz Bay, t 776 6352. Local fare including *patés* (elsewhere known as patties) of course, or otherwise heavyweight West Indian dishes.

Joe's, opposite the Post Office, Cruz Bay. Still cooking simple, barbecued fare as he has for 20 years.

Miss Vie, beyond Coral Bay. They say that Miss Vie makes the very finest conch fritters, but she'll also cook up a mean West Indian supper. Very rustic and fun.

Bars and Nightlife

St John can get surprisingly lively and, at the weekend, you will find Cruz Bay buzzing past midnight. Some of the bars put on bands. Wharfside Village is the busiest area.

Beach Bar, Cruz Bay, t 693 8834. Sunday Jazz Jam 4–7pm, with performers from across the world.

La Tapa, Cruz Bay. Good starting point in the middle of town.

Woody's Seafood Saloon, Cruz Bay. Have an early evening drink here.

Larry's Landing, Cruz Bay. All about beer, TV and pool: 'No one under 18, No pets allowed'.

Duffy's Love Shack, Cruz Bay. The bar of St Thomas fame, very lively when it gets going.

The Lime Inn, Cruz Bay, t 776 7425. Fairy-lit and brightly coloured, can be quite lively and has a band a couple of times a week.

Skinny Legs, Coral Bay. Try here for TV and beer.

Sea Breeze, Coral Bay. A rumbustious crowd.

suffered by the rebellious slaves seems as far away as the mercantile mayhem of St Thomas.

Beaches

St John has some magnificent beaches. Between the forested fingers of the coast-line, the water in the coves is crystalline and, on a sunny day, it will glow in the richest shades of turquoise. There is even a passable strip right in town. The most accessible beaches are located along the switchback meanderings of the northern coast. They are distinctly more secluded than the beaches on St Thomas, but this does not prevent crowds building up on the more popular ones, particularly if a cruise ship crowd is in. *See* 'Best Beaches', p.526.

St John National Park

The 13,000 acres of the St John National Park are managed from the office in Cruz Bay (*see* 'Tourist Information', p.527), where you can get information, along with films and maps, at the Visitors' Centre, opposite Mongoose Junction. The park is cut and crossed with about 20 walking trails (*see* 'Hiking', p.528), which pass through the full variety of St John's terrain, from the mangroves on the shoreline at Leinster Bay, where you may see gallinules and a mangrove cuckoo among the leafy sprouts, to the lusher vegetation on the upper mountainsides. Many species of plants in the forest are marked. Some 5,600 acres of the National Park are offshore, covering reefs and marine life. On the offshore islands, you can see frigatebirds and the usual boobies and pelicans.

Cruz Bay

Cruz Bay, the miniature capital of St John, is a more than typically cheery West Indian waterfront town set on a west-facing bay just a few miles across the Pillsbury Sound from St Thomas. The houses scattered on the hillside tumble down to the waterfront, where a couple of pint-size pastel-painted arcades have sprung up to catch the day trippers.

You are quite likely to arrive at the ferry dock, from where you will walk straight out into a bandstand where the taxi drivers like to sit. Off to the right is **Wharfside Village**, a small shopping complex; a little further away to the left is **Mongoose Junction**, where a very pretty network of walkways and stairs leads you to more shops. In between the two there is a cluster of restaurants and bars. Behind here, up the hill, you pass into a more local St John. The small island **museum** (*open Mon–Fri 9–5*) is downstairs in the public library as you go up the hill. Alongside the St Johnian schoolchildren, you can discover old-time St John through prints and the descriptions of their slave revolt in 1733.

Around the Island

In its plantation days, the slopes of St John were completely covered in sugar cane, but since the early 19th century the land has been left, and so the island is now carpeted with 50ft-high jungle. Just a few mill ruins poke out from beneath the over-growth. To drive along the north coast, follow the bay past Mongoose Junction, where the road starts to switchback, clambering up the slopes and sweeping down into the successive bays. On each headland there is a view of the other Virgins. At Mary Point is a ravine called **Minna Neger Ghut**, where the last survivors of the slave rebellion in 1733 are thought to have jumped to their deaths. Eventually, you come to the best-preserved and most accessible of the estate ruins at **Estate Annaberg** (*open in daylight hours, no guides; adm free*), a former sugar plantation with displays showing the process and describing the buildings.

Centerline Road carves a path into the forested hills, wiggling over the impossibly steep slopes and passing beneath **Bordeaux Mountain**, St John's highest peak. From **Coral Bay Overlook** there is a superb view of the islands to the northeast, looking along Sir Francis Drake Passage towards Virgin Gorda about 20 miles away. From here, the road descends towards St John's only other settlement at **Coral Bay**, a light smat-tering of houses around the harbour (though increasing madly at the moment) with an easygoing atmosphere in the waterfront bars and restaurants. Coral Bay was the first area settled by the Danes, and **Fort Berg**, the dilapidated fort on the point, dates from 1717, the year they arrived. Beyond the town, roads lead both south around the coast and to the eastern tip; these areas are mainly residential.

St Croix

St Croix (pronounced *St Croy*) is the largest of the Virgin Islands. Unlike the hillier islands of St Thomas and St John, St Croix has stretches of flat and fertile land between its hills and so historically it was agricultural. Once, its 84 square miles were divided up into more than 200 plantations, most of them growing sugar. In the 1960s agriculture was overtaken by tourism and industry as the main source of revenue.

But tourism in St Croix is not as intensive as in St Thomas, and you can still find deserted beaches on the island. The streets of Christiansted, though very attractive, do not have the pressure-cooker effect of Charlotte Amalie. Things are more low-key here, but you will find some surprisingly good places to stay and eat, including some with genuine Caribbean character, particularly around the towns. The island's name is French (a straight translation of Columbus's original name for it, Santa Cruz), but this is one of the few legacies of the short French ownership in the 17th century. The island was bought by the Danes in 1733 after they had established themselves in St Thomas.

From time to time, St Croix has been the senior island of the three US Virgin Islands, because of its successful plantation economy and because it had the largest popula-tion (presently about 55,000). The Governor resided here in the 19th century and it was in Frederiksted on St Croix that Governor von Scholten declared that the slaves should be freed in 1848. In the 20th century, the island's agricultural importance declined, while St Thomas, already a famous harbour, became an important naval base and then boomed with the tourist industry. Only recently have the Cruzans started to catch up with their neighbours.

Best Beaches

Buck Island: St Croix's best beach is actually on an offshore island, a couple of miles from the coast at the east end. The Buck Island underwater life is particularly good – there is an enormous reef of seafans, and antlers of staghorns teem with angelfish in shimmering yellow, blue and green. A snorkelling trail guides you through all this. The island is a National Park and concessionaires make the tour out there, about 45 minutes' sail each way, for the day or half a day (*about $35 for a half-day, $50 for a full day*).

Protestant Cay: The closest beach to downtown Christiansted is on the small island a couple of minutes' swim off the waterfront, or an expensive $3 ferry ride. Watersports equipment is available here.

Beauregard Bay: Site of the Buccaneer Hotel, to the east of town, a small, palm-backed strand, where there are chairs and facilities (*a fee for outsiders*) as well as a beach bar.

Shoy Point: A perfect half-moon curve of luscious sand. There are no facilities and you have to find your way down through the trees, but it is a superb, quiet sun trap.

Chenay Bay: Its calm shallow water makes it good for children; also has facilities, hammocks and watersports.

Cramer Park Beach: At the eastern tip of the island on the north side. Popular with Cruzans so it fills up at weekends. There is a changing room, but take drinks, a picnic and snorkelling gear to see the underwater life.

Isaac's Bay: On the other side of the point and even more isolated, where the snorkelling is even better. The best way to get to this beach is from the eastern end of Jack's Bay, though you must walk down there.

Grapetree Bay: On the south shore at the eastern end, a secluded strip of sand where the waves get up sometimes.

Sandy Point: A national Wildlife Refuge at the western tip of the island, where the sand comes ashore in mounds; quite isolated, and you are advised to be careful about locking your car and leaving belongings unattended. Take food and drinks. In season (May to July), leatherback turtles make their way up the beach here at night to lay their eggs.

Cane Bay: Here the palm-backed sand comes and goes, but the reef remains, giving superb snorkelling. Jewelfish glint among the coral heads and striped sergeant majors cruise around on patrol.

St Croix has a mixed community – as well as the original Cruzans, who are mainly of African descent, a large number of Puerto Ricans have made their way onto the island over the last hundred years, escaping the poverty of the larger island. There are also many 'down-islanders' and there is even a small community of Cruzans of Danish descent. This is the strongest remnant of the colonial legacy and, although it is not very strong, one commentator claimed that a week among the Cruzans was like a tropical version of a tortured Ibsen play! Generally speaking, the Cruzans of all descents are reserved.

St Croix

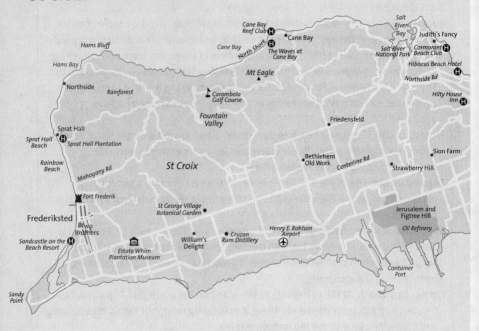

It is not entirely a happy community, as shown most recently by the looting and racial problems that followed Hurricane Hugo's incredible destructiveness in 1989, when 90% of the Cruzans were left homeless. About 20% of the population moved off the island after the hurricane and some have returned since. On a lighter note, there is little love lost between the St Thomians and the Cruzans, who consider St Thomas overdeveloped, traffic-ridden and stressful.

Christiansted, the capital, and Frederiksted (once the more important town because of its better harbour) are traditional West Indian waterfront towns, where the arched walkways can transport you back to the days of clippers and ocean-going trading ships, and wharves heaving with outgoing rum barrels and incoming tea chests and bales of cloth. They have been well restored and they have undoubted Caribbean charm.

Beaches

There are some excellent beaches in St Croix. The main ones have some development, but there are many charming and isolated coves tucked in between them. If you want to find a secluded spot to yourself, it is worth asking around or simply taking side-roads and tracks down to the sea. The snorkelling is good and many reefs are close to shore. All beaches are public, though if you want to use a hotel's deck chairs or changing facilities, you may well be charged (up to $5). All the watersports are available on the island. *See* 'Best Beaches', p.533.

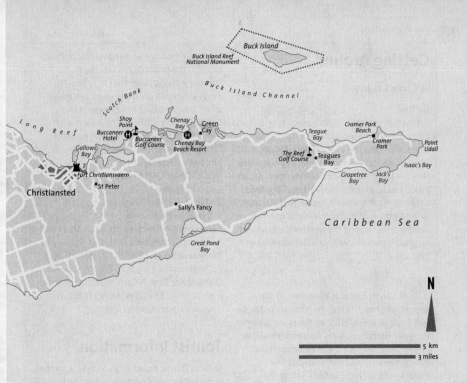

Christiansted

With its waterfront walkways, slab paving stones and arched Danish-era buildings and storage houses, Christiansted is an alluring harbour town that rings with echoes of another age. The inevitable invasion of air-conditioned boutiques and fast-food halls that makes it a modern trading town has been kept out of sight – neon signs must not protrude far beyond the original façades – and so you have the impression that a colonial official in serge with gold epaulettes might round the corner at any minute. But instead of clippers at anchor, the harbour is ranged with yachts and from time to time the seaplane belly-flops into the bay.

The town was laid out by the Danes when they arrived in 1734 and is named in honour of King Christian VI. It is protected by a large barrier reef, on which the waves break a few hundred yards out from the shore. Any potential invading force would have had to negotiate the reef and then face unformidable **Fort Christiansvaern** (*open Mon–Fri 8–4.45, Sat and Sun 9–4.45; adm, which also admits you to the Steeple Building*). Nobody did and so the yellow fort never saw action, but it is pleasant to visit (it seems that the walls were used mainly to lock the soldiers in at night rather than keep invaders out). It was started in 1733, with stones brought from Denmark as ballast, and since 1878, when it was abandoned by the military, it has functioned variously as a police station and courthouse. Now part of the Christiansted National Historic Site, it contains a military museum. The fort's guns have a good view over **Protestant Cay**, an island hotel just a few hundred yards out to sea. It takes its name

Getting Around

St Croix t (1 340–)

By Bus

A system of local VITRAN buses runs between the two main towns, priced $1 per ticket, but these are supplemented by share-taxis which run the same routes, leaving when they are full or the driver has the urge. You can pick them up at the supermarkets. They tend not to stray off the main routes, so if you want to get to the east end of the island or off the beaten track (around the rainforest area, for example), then you will have to hitch-hike or take a taxi.

By Taxi

These can be found at the hotels, at the airport, on Church Street in Christiansted or by Fort Frederik in Frederiksted. Rates are set by the government and cabs are not metered, so it is sensible to check the price beforehand. Typical fares: from Christiansted to the airport – $13, to Frederiksted – $20, to the north coast – $20.

Taxi drivers will willingly take you on an island tour – many are well-informed – for about $35 per hour. Contact:

St Croix Taxi Association, at the airport, t 778 1088.
Antilles Taxi Service, Christiansted, t 773 5020.

By Guided Tour

St Croix Safari Tours, t 773 6700, *safaritours@ stcroixtours.com*, *www.stcroixtours.com*. Tours can also be made in tourist safari buses (about $20), if you can bear the embarrassment. They depart at about 10am from Christiansted.

Hitch-hiking

Because of the limited local bus service on St Croix, you may be tempted to try your hand at hitch-hiking. Unfortunately, you may end up waiting a long time.

Car Hire

Cars are readily available, but come at a price, starting at $45 or $50 a day plus insurance (you can sometimes find reduced offers in the promotional literature). Most companies will deliver the car to you. The roads in St Croix are quite good, certainly when compared with elsewhere in the Caribbean. Remember to drive on the left.

Hire firms include the big international companies, which have an office at the airport and town, and local firms:

Avis, t 778 9365, US t 1 800 331 1084, *www.avis.com*.
Budget, t 778 9636, US t 1 888 227 3359, *budget@viaccess.com*.
Centerline Car Rentals, t 778 0450, US t 1 888 288 8755, *ccrlrss@aol.com*.
Mongoose Scooter Rental, 6B Hospital St, Christiansted, t 719 2525. Scooters available.
Olympic Ace Rent-A-Car, Christiansted, t 773 8000, US t 1 888 USVICAR, US t 1 878 4227, *www.stcroixcarrentals.com*.

Tourist Information

St Croix Tourist Board: Queen Cross St, in the market square, Christiansted, PO Box 4538, t 773 0495.
Information office: at the Henry E. Rohlson Airport.
Information office: On the pier, Frederiksted, t 772 0357.

There are websites devoted to St Croix at *www.st-croix.com*, *www.visitstcroix.com* and *www.virginislandvacation.com*.

Media

St Croix produces a pink island guide, *St Croix This Week*, with details of current events and helpful hints on the watersports and shops and even how to invest in a dream vacation or local real estate. You will find some informative signboards scattered around Christiansted and flyers advertising water-sports and restaurants pop up everywhere you go. There are plenty of American newspapers available on the island.

Medical Emergencies

Go to the Governor Juan F. Luis and Community Health Centre in mid-island, t 778 6311. The general emergency number is t 911.

Watersports

Most watersports can be arranged through the hotels, though there are plenty of independent operators around the island. Wetbikes are for hire if you want to scoot around among the yachts at anchor, and water-skiing is also easily arranged. If you wish to go parasailing, you can get airborne in Christiansted practically without wetting your feet.

General watersports operators include:

St Croix Watersports, Hotel on the Cay, t 773 7060.

Mile Mark Watersports, t 773 2628, *milemark charters@yahoo.com*, *www.milemark watersports.com*.

Day Sails

There are plenty of organized cruises which start out from St Croix, all of which are good fun (many go to Buck Island).

Captain Big Beard's Adventure Tours, t 773 7977, *www.bigbeards.com*. On the catamaran *Renegade* and the *Buck Island Flyer*.

Diva, t 778 4675, *www.buckisland-diva.com*. Personalized trips with a maximum of six on board at a go.

Mile Mark Charters, t 773 2628.

Shabeen, t 773 7185, *www.shabeencharters. com*. Smallish group trips.

Deep-sea Fishing

This is quite well-organized in St Croix, with fleets of sleek cruisers in which to ply the deep for 6ft marlin, sailfish and wahoo. A full day costs around $600; a half-day from $400.

Capt Pete's, Christiansted, t 773 123, *www.stcroixfish.com*.

Catch 22, Green Cay Marina, t 778 6987.

Lisa Ann Charters, Green Cay Marina, t 773 3712.

Kayaking

Caribbean Adventure Tours, t 778 1522, *www.stcroixkayak.com*.

St Croix Adventure Tours, Kingshill, t 773 4599, *www.tourcarib.com*.

Virgin Kayak, north shore, t 778 0071, *www.stcroix.com/virginkayak*.

Scuba Diving

The island is almost completely ringed by barrier reefs, and there are endless dive sites, some of which drop off just a few hundred yards from the shore. The island is particularly well known for its soft-coral life. There is an excellent wall off the north coast between Christiansted and Hams Bay in the west: the Salt River drop-off starts in 20ft of water, dropping to thousands, as with the Cane Bay dropoff (from 35ft). Frederiksted has good corals and offshore at Buck Island is another popular spot.

Many of the hotels offer dive packages and it is also easy to fix up lessons if you wish to learn. A single-tank dive costs from $50.

Cane Bay Dive Shop, on the north shore and in Frederiksted, t 773 9913, t 1 800 338 3843, *canebay@viaccess.net*, *www.canebayscuba.com*.

Dive Experience, Christiansted, t 773 3307, t 1 800 235 9047, *divexp@viaccess.net*, *www.divexp.com*.

Diverse Virgin, *www.diversevirgin.com*. An alliance of seven St Croix dive shops.

SCORE V. I. Divers, Christiansted, t 773 6045, t 1 877 773 6045, *score@viaccess.net*, *www.scorevi.com*.

Snorkelling

The best snorkelling areas are listed under 'Best Beaches', p.533. Buck Island has underwater guided trails for snorkellers.

Windsurfing

The best winds are at the eastern end, off Chenay Bay and Teague Bay. Contact the watersports operators or go through the hotels, who also have small sailing boats, sunfish and hobie cats.

Other Sports

Golf

Carambola Golf Course, north shore, t 778 5638, *www.golfvi.com*. 18 holes. Green fees $129.

Buccaneer Golf Course, t 714 2100, *www.the buccaneer.com*. 18 holes. Green fees $80.

The Reef Golf Course, eastern Teague Bay, t 773 8844. A 9-hole course.

Hiking

Ay-Ay Ecotours, t 277 0410, *eco@viaccess.net*.

Caribbean Adventure Tours, t 773 1989.

St Croix Environmental Association, t 773 1989, *www.stcroixenvironmental.com*. Leads a number of guided hikes in the Salt River National Park, the rainforest and at the East End.

Horse-riding

Paul and Jill's Equestrian Stable, Sprat Hall Estate, Frederiksted, t 772 2880, *reservations@paulandjills.com*, *www.paulandjills.com*. For a ride through the diminutive rainforest or around old-time St Croix, the land of the windmills.

Tennis

There are courts in practically every hotel on the island. Some have a tennis professional who can give lessons. If your hotel has no courts, just stop by one that does and pay the small fee.

Where to Stay

St Croix t (1 340–)

Like St Thomas, St Croix has a good variety of hotels. For those who want a beachfront resort there are plenty to choose from, but there is also a good selection of smaller inns, both on the beach and with antique (and mock-antique) charm, set in the older Danish buildings.

Small Inns of St Croix, *info1@smallinnsstcroix.com*, *www.smallinnsstcroix.com*, has a number of charming places on its books, some of which are listed below. There are few inexpensive places to stay in St Croix.

USVI government tax of 8% is levied on all hotel bills and you can expect a service charge as well.

Villa rental can be arranged through:

CPMI (Caribbean Property Management and Investments), PO Box 26160, Gallows Bay, t 778 8782, US t 1 800 496 7379, *cpmistx@aol.com*, *www.enjoystcroix.com*.

Island Villas, 3025 Estate Friendsthar, Suite 3, t 773 8821, US t 1 800 626 4512, *carphil@viacess.net*, *www.stcroixislandvillas.net*.

Vacation St Croix, PO Box 26157, t 778 0361, US t 1 877 788 0361, *vacationstx@viaccess.net*, *www.vacationstx.com*.

Luxury–Very Expensive

Buccaneer Hotel, Gallows Bay, PO Box 25200, t 712 2100, US t 1 800 255 3881, *mango@thebuccaneer.com*, *www.thebuccaneer.com*. The Buccaneer hotel, probably the most elegant on the island, is set just outside Christiansted in 300 acres of rolling grounds which descend to a string of private beaches. It is large, with 150 rooms around the central estate house of coral rock, but elegant and comfortable in an older Caribbean style.

Cormorant Beach Club and Hotel, 4126 La Grande Princesse, t 778 8920, US t 1 800 548 4460, *info@cormorant-st.croix.com*, *www.cormorant-st.croix.com*. A smaller retreat (just 38 double rooms) with modern Caribbean island comfort set on the beach to the north of Christiansted. It has everything you could want for the luxurious escape – sumptuous high-pastel rooms with their own balconies and a view of the ocean, afternoon tea and no telephones. And when you feel like emerging from your seclusion, there are watersports on the windy beach right outside and for the evenings a charming restaurant looking out through the palms.

Chenay Bay Beach Resort, PO Box 24667, near Christiansted, t 773 2918, US t 1 800 548 4457, *chenaybay1@att.net*, *www.chenaybay.com*. A comfortable hotel on a quiet and calm beach. There are 50 prettily decorated rooms in quite simple cottages set in a horseshoe around a grassy garden. Air-conditioning, TV, telephone, kitchenette and balcony.

Hibiscus Beach Hotel, west from Christiansted, 4131 La Grande Princesse, t 773 4042, US t 1 800 442 0121, *hibiscus@viaccess.com*, *www.1hibiscus.com*. A small assembly of two-storey blocks with pretty gingerbread trimmings that stand among the palm trees. There are 37 very attractively decorated rooms with all mod cons and comforts (cable TV, phones and air-conditioning), each with a balcony or terrace. Very nice atmosphere, particularly when you're dozing in a hammock hung between the palm trees.

Expensive
The Waves at Cane Bay, PO Box 1749, Kingshill, t 778 1805, US t 1 800 545 0603, *ry1805@ viaccess.net, www.canebaystcroix.com*. Comprises 12 large rooms in two blocks and a villa, standing right on the sea on the north coast. Comfortable self-contained accommodation with all you need to look after yourself (kitchens and a screened porch with a view), but a very friendly atmosphere downstairs.

Cane Bay Reef Club, PO Box 1407, Kingshill, t 778 2966, US t 1 800 253 8534, *cbrc@ viaccess.net, www.canebay.com*. Has nine suites in a modern block on the waterfront. It is brightly decorated, with full kitchens and balconies looking out onto the waves that crash on the volcanic shoreline. With a very low-key and friendly air, it's a good escape.

Moderate–Inexpensive
Sprat Hall Plantation, a couple of miles north of Frederiksted, PO Box 695, t 772 0305, US t 1 800 843 3584, *sprathall.vi@ worldnet.att.net, travel.to/sprathall*. The estate house, in which three rooms are decorated with period furniture, including four-posters, dates from the mid-1700s. Sprat Hall stands in open grounds just in from the coast, where there is a private beach and bar. Small but friendly, just 12 rooms and suites, some with kitchens, but a fine antique dining room with Caribbean home cooking.

Inn at Pelican Heights, just north of Christiansted, 4201 Estate St John, t 713 8022, US t 1 888 445 9458, *flaue@viaccess.net, www.innatpelicanheights.com*. Just six rooms and suites around a house in a residential area, with library and fantastic views over the coastline. All facilities – full kitchens and a communal pool. Friendly but private atmosphere.

Sandcastle on the Beach Resort, PO Box 1908, Frederiksted, t 772 1205, US t 1 800 524 2018, *onthebeach@virginislands.net*. This resort has 20 units in a concrete block that stands above the beach as well as some suites in newer villas. the latter are set around a pool in a garden. There are some kitchens. Large gay clientele.

Pink Fancy Hotel, 27 Prince St, Christiansted, t 773 8460, US t 1 800 524 2045, *info@ pinkfancy.com, www.pinkfancy.com*. A little way from the centre of town, the Pink Fancy is set in an old town house with arched brick foundations and a clapboard upper storey, louvred windows and shutters. As the name suggests, it is painted pink, but the interior of the 13 rooms is decorated with brazil wood in keeping with the antique style. They have all the modern comforts you need, though, including kitchens: the hotel serves breakfast but has no restaurant.

The Danish Manor, 2 Company St, Christiansted, St Croix 00820, t 773 1377, US t 1 800 524 2069, *danishmanor@ islands.com, www.danishmanor.com*. Right in the middle of town, the Danish manor has a nice courtyard with exposed brick and stone and 34 rooms that give onto the pool and explosive greenery. Friendly atmosphere and a lively restaurant.

Mount Victory Campgrounds, Creque Dam Road (Rt. 58), t 772 1651, *www.mtvictory camp.com*. Five tent structures built from local hardwood recovered from trees downed by hurricanes. Each tent is furnished with two hand-crafted teak beds, fresh linen, an equipped kitchenette, gas stove and cold water sink – all cooled by the tradewinds. The bathhouse has an open roof with hot showers and there's a group campfire area for cooking. Rates from $60 per night; up to two children per cottage free. Short walk to the beach.

Eating Out

There's no shortage of restaurants in St Croix. Many of the restaurants here are set in the pretty town houses and warehouses along the waterfront in Christiansted. If you are staying at the eastern end of the island, it's worth making the effort to get to Frederiksted. St Croix's second town has a different feel and it is worth investigating the bars and restaurants, perhaps for an early evening drink at one of the beach bars and then dinner.

Restaurants accept credit cards and most charge service at 10%.

Categories are arranged according to the price of a main dish: expensive = US$20 and above; moderate = US$10–$20; inexpensive = US$10 and below.

Expensive

Bacchus, Queen Cross St, Christiansted, t 692 9922. Contemporary combination of old favourites, like seafood cocktail, alongside more imaginative entrées such as pasta with shrimp, scallops and oysters with a garlic and chive cream sauce. House specialities include local lobster and fish, rack of lamb, and home-made bread pudding with a creamy rum sauce. Great place to mingle with the Cruzians. *Closed Mon.*

Kendrick's, Quin House, King Cross St, Christiansted, t 773 9199. In the delightful, historic setting of an old Christiansted courtyard, Kendrick's offers excellent innovative international fare – tastes are garnered from around the world: start with the pan-seared Thai shrimp served with onion-cucumber relish on coconut-infused rice and follow with a roasted pecan-crusted pork loin with ginger mayonnaise. Or have a pasta dish.

Moderate

Café Savant, Hospital St, Christiansted, t 713 8666. Set on the road headed out of town to the east just beyond the fort. A hip spot: music, bright décor and a fusion of cuisines from all over – Mexican and Thai to add to the Caribbean offerings.

Tivoli Gardens, Queen Cross and Strand St, Christiansted, t 773 6782. You eat on a breezy veranda surrounded by white trellis work and hung with greenery. Try chicken Tivolese, in tomato sour-cream sauce, or one of the many steaks and fresh fish.

Tutto Bene, Company St, Christiansted, t 773 5229. A lively Italian café, popular with locals and visitors alike, set in a brightly coloured dining room. Some Caribbean touches in otherwise straight Italian fare: fried home-made mozzarella followed by a *pesce del giorno*, or a fettucine shrimp.

Bombay Club, King St, Christiansted, t 773 1838. A popular spot around town at lunch and for dinner, set in the air-conditioned vaults of an old townhouse. Not Indian cuisine as the name might imply, but international fare including conch chowder followed by fajitas, ribs, burgers and sandwiches, or steaks.

Café Christine, Apothecary Hall Courtyard, Company St, Christiansted, t 712 1500. A good lunchtime stopover in town, a French café and art gallery set above a pretty courtyard.

Le St Tropez, Limetree Court, King St, Frederiksted, t 772 3000. An open-sided dining room built of brick, stone and wood, with palms outside in the courtyard garden. The cuisine is French – even *cuisses de grenouille persillées* (frogs' legs) as a starter, followed by the *magret de canard* or a host of fresh fish dishes. Charming and intimate feel.

The Blue Moon, Strand St, Frederiksted, t 772 2222. Set in the interior of an old trading house on Strand Gade on the bayfront. A changeable daily menu with local seafood and international dishes. There is piano and jazz entertainment sometimes, to go with the pictures of musicians on the walls.

Pier 69, King St, Frederiksted, t 772 0069. This ever-popular place consists of a courtyard with parasols and a bar boat set inside, with music at the weekends.

Duggan's Reef, Teague Bay, t 773 9800. Very popular with the locals, so it is a fun place for a meal out. It has a cracking setting on a breezy terrace looking offshore to Buck Island. There are some Caribbean dishes such as conch fritters but mainly international fare including lobster pasta, flying fish and burgers.

Cheeseburgers in Paradise, East End Rd, t 773 1838. An international-style snack bar which is set in a pretty tin-roofed shack by the roadside heading east from Christiansted. Excellent cheeseburgers, of course, also sandwiches and salads. Popular with a local white crowd.

South Shore Café, south of Routes 62 and 624 intersection, t 773 9311. A delightful breezy setting above the Great Salt Pond near the south shore, where you dine beneath coloured trelliswork and hanging sangria bottles. Mediteranean fare and seafood with some vegetarian dishes.

Inexpensive

Singh's Fast Food, top end of King St (by the Anglican Church), Christiansted. For the best *roti* and takeaway chicken.

Motown, Strand St, Frederiksted, t 772 9882. For something a little more West Indian, try this place situated in one of the old warehouses of Frederiksted. Excellent West Indian fare: shrimp or conch in butter sauce, or curried or stewed goat.

Villa Morales, on Route 70 just out of the town, Frederiksted, t 772 0556. Also serves good West Indian fare – 'Latin and local' – in a modern house just off the main road. Lots of seafood served with rice 'n' beans and johnny cake, and some heftier dishes such as roast pork, boil fish and fungi, even goat stew.

Junie's, Peter's Rest (near the Seventh-Day Adventist church and the Hovensa oil refinery), t 773 7077. Plastic tablecloths, huge anthuriums and loud music; stew fish, chicken or curried shrimp with a tonnage of ground provisions.

Bars and Nightlife

Many of the restaurants and the beach cafés on the island double as bars for an evening drink, and often they put on live bands, too. There are also some lively bars on the waterfront in Christiansted, where the yachties crawl ashore for a beer; others are hidden away in the arches (you will have to look quite carefully as you are stumbling around town). A number of the hotels stage steel-band shows and live music, particularly jazz; ask around.

Stixx Hurricane Bar, Pan Am Pavilion, Christiansted, t 773 5157. A good place to start the evening.

Bar at the Comanche Hotel, Comanche Walk, Strand St, Christiansted, t 773 0210. A mellow bar and a good place for an early-evening drink listening to the piano player.

Parrot's Perch, above Columbian Emeralds, Christiansted. Has a variety of karaoke, Latin music and live bands.

Pier 69, Frederiksted. A cheery haunt for a daytime stopover.

Lost Dog, King St, Frederiksted. Set in a stone warehouse; there are video games and a juke box, and T-shirts and a surfboard on the wall. Lots of beer.

Mt Pellier Domino Club. A rum shop hidden away in the rainforest. The big feature of the bar is the drinking pig: you hand the pig a can and it cracks it, slurps it and spits the can out again (they don't give it real beer of course: non-alcoholic beer only, please). This is a second-generation drinking pig. You can see the grave of the original drinking pig, Buster, at the bar.

Divi Carina Bay Resort. A casino.

Beach Bars

Chenay Beach Bar. A popular haunt: a simple, open-sided bar where you can retreat for a beer and a snack after a sailboard trip taming the waves, or rehydrate after lying in the sun.

Cane Bay Beach Bar. Has a charming setting on a deck across from the waves; snacks and substantial platters of fresh fish and steaks.

Changes in L'Attitude, just north of Frederiksted. Has facilities and good snorkelling, plus burgers, fries, sandwiches and salads.

Rainbow Beach Club. Set on the best stretch of sand, and probably the liveliest, with volleyball and crowds at the weekend. It serves salads, burgers and cocktails for a view of the Green Flash.

Sunset Grill, Rainbow Beach. You can get local fare including conch fritters and fried fish with a salad, and lots of frozen drinks.

from the French era when only Catholics could be buried on the mainland, and so Protestants were buried here. It is mostly referred to as the Hotel on the Cay, and is supposed to be the setting for Herman Wouk's classic novel about the nightmarish life of a Caribbean hotelier, *Don't Stop the Carnival* (*see* p.510).

Back on the mainland, newly arrived captains would first check in to the **Old Danish Customs House** before unloading. It was built in the 1750s, and the staircase, a suitably imposing entrance for the captains, was added in 1851. The National Park Service has its offices here. Next stop was the **Old Scale House** (weighing scales still in place), built in 1856, where they would measure their cargo.

Beyond the Old Danish West India and Guinea Company Warehouse, which the company used as its headquarters from 1749 (now the post office), is the **Steeple Building**, a Lutheran church constructed in 1735 (the steeple itself was added in 1794). Today it houses the **National Park Museum** (*open Mon–Fri 9–4; adm includes fort*), where you can see exhibits of Indian artefacts, architecture, religion and urban black history.

On King St (Kongens Tvaergade), you will find **Government House**, with its arcaded veranda and red sentry box. It was originally two private homes set around a garden, joined together by Governor van Scholten in the 1830s. The staircase at the entrance leads to the main hall, now redecorated with chandeliers and mirrors like those under which the islanders danced 150 years ago (the Danes took the originals with them when they left in 1917, but gave some others back to the islands in 1966). Today, the buildings house the offices of the Virgin Islands Government.

In the Caravelle Arcade, in the centre of town, you will find the **St Croix Aquarium and Marine Education Centre** (*t 773 8995, www.stxaquarium.homepage.com; adm*), which is well worth a visit. There is a series of small aquaria which are brought alive by Lonnie Kaczmarsky, who will tell you stories of the dentist shrimp (which cleans the teeth of other fish without them eating him), sponge crabs which disguise themselves with sponges and then eat them if they cannot find a meal, and the importance of mangrove swamps, where so many fish start their lives. He takes guided snorkelling tours. There is a Discovery Room for children.

Those looking to score a few duty-free bargains will find the main shopping streets just behind the waterfront, around **King St and King's Alley**, in the old trading houses. Another echo of the old West Indies (from before the age of the supermarket) can still be seen in the covered **market** (*trading Mon–Sat*), which has been there in one form or other since 1735. A few Cruzans have stalls selling ground provisions to other islanders.

Around the Island

St Croix's 84 square miles were once divided into about 180 sugar plantations, and the windmills used to crush the cane (now without sails and growing steadily more dilapidated) seem to be on every hilltop around the island. From them there are splendid views across the island and often as far north as the other Virgin Islands, grey stains on the horizon 40 miles to the north. There is an organized driving tour of the island, the St Croix Heritage Trail, for which you can get brochures and maps at the tourist offices.

Travelling west from Christiansted on the north shore road, you pass **Salt River**, a mangrove bay where Columbus put in for water in 1493, and then you follow the grassy slopes of the coastline. Eventually, you come to **Cane Bay**, where the road twists and drops into small coves forested with palm trees that are cut into the northern cliffs. The views are spectacular. Finally, the road turns inland past Fountain Valley to the Centerline Road. All over the island, you see the ruins of plantation buildings poking out of the undergrowth.

The **Centerline Road** runs west from Christiansted to the town of Frederiksted, mostly in a direct straight line across the centre of the island. As it leaves Christiansted, it passes close to St Croix's small industrial area, the Hovensa Oil Refinery on the south coast, and the aluminium plant. The road eventually passes Henry E. Rohlson Airport, which was once named after another Caribbean luminary, Alexander Hamilton, who came to St Croix from Nevis as a boy and grew up in Christiansted before leaving for North America in the 1760s.

North of Centerline Road, you approach the **St George Village Botanical Gardens** (*open daily for guided tours, 9–4; adm*) through an alley of royal palm trees, and emerge into 16 acres of neatly tended gardens that were once a plantation estate, and, before that, an Arawak village. Some colonial buildings around the great house have been restored and, on the various trails, you will find many Caribbean favourites marked: the bulbous sandbox tree (the pods of this spiky-barked tree were used to hold sand that was then sprinkled on ink to stop it smudging); the kapok tree with spikes on its trunk; the autograph tree (you can write on its leaves); the St Croix agave; and the dildo cactus, named for its shape. There is an orchid house and a collection of all the plants in St Croix that are endangered.

Sugar cane was the source of St Croix's wealth for many years and the crop blanketed the land as late as 1966. It is gone now, but the distillation of rum has continued, with imported molasses, at the **Cruzan Rum Distillery** (*t 772 0799; open daily 9–11.30 and 1–4.15; adm free*), just off Centerline Road to the south. A half-hour guided tour will lead you among the vats of distilling molasses, where the smell will have you teetering on the walkways. Some rum is bottled here for sale in the USVI, but most is exported. Tours finish with a snifter in the bar.

A couple of miles farther along the road is the **Estate Whim Plantation Museum** (*open Mon–Sat 10–4; adm exp*), which will cast you back to the days of plantation splendour, when planter Mr McEvoy lived in this oval house with the air of a church, surrounded by a small moat. It has been restored and refitted with period furniture, the huge bedroom at one end with a four-poster and a planter's chair with extended arms, and the sumptuous dining room at the other. In the dungeon-like outhouses, you can see the tools of all the island artisans – the cooper, the logger, the wheelwright, the joiner and the blacksmith – and also a history of slavery and field work.

St Croix's second town is **Frederiksted**, set on the west coast, 17 miles west of Christiansted. Founded in 1751, Frederiksted has always been important because of its open harbour, where large ships were able to dock. Nowadays, the traffic is mostly cruise ships, but even a hundred years ago, liners were passing by; in 1887 Lafcadio

Hearn stopped off in the town en route for Martinique, describing it in his *Two Years in the West Indies*. To him it had 'the appearance of a beautiful Spanish town, with its Romanesque piazzas, churches, many-arched buildings peeping through breaks in a line of mahogany, bread-fruit, mango, tamarind and palm trees'. The town, much of which was rebuilt after it was burned in a riot in 1878, was well known for its elaborate West Indian gingerbread architecture.

The pretty arches are still along the waterfront, but the feel of the Spanish town has gone. Frederiksted has its own life separate from the east end of the island (it is a popular day out for the locals on Sundays) and it has been developing recently with a series of new malls and restaurants. There are many very pretty buildings and there have been efforts recently to restore them.

As usual, the harbour is watched over by a fortress, **Fort Frederik**, now rundown. Named after the Danish King Frederik V, it was constructed in 1752 to encourage the settlement of the town (it was also a refuge in times of trouble). It was here in 1848 that Governor van Scholten made his announcement that he was abolishing slavery in the Danish islands, against the orders of his king. It also had a curious role in that it was the first fort to recognize, unofficially, the young nation of the United States on 25 October 1776. The glory of the official recognition went to St Eustatius, a dozy island now but a very important port at that time, about three weeks later (*see* pp.425–6). There are exhibitions of hurricanes and of the transfer of the Virgin Islands to the USA (with a photocopy of the US$25 million cheque). Opposite the cruise-ship pier close by is the **Old Customs House**, where the duty would be paid on the incoming and outgoing cargo. From here, **Strand Gade** runs past a line of old stone warehouses with arched walkways above the pavement.

A mile out of **Frederiksted**, towards the north coast of the island, is St Croix's miniature 'rainforest'. It is not wet enough to be a real rainforest, but the vegetation is different from the rest of the island and, as you drive along Mahogany Rd, the creepers and lianas will reach down to grapple with you. Orchids perch and ferns explode in the upper branches, just beneath the 100ft canopy, and you may see a hummingbird flit by. There are a number of roads leading from the top of West End Rd into the forest (many are unpaved and so it's best to go by jeep), and there are endless footpaths if you wish to walk. In the forest, you will find St Croix LEAP (Life Experience Achievement Programme), which has a wood mill and craft shop selling products made from local timber.

The **eastern end** of St Croix is drier and less lush than the west. It is becoming steadily built up with housing estates and holiday condominium complexes and there are some fun restaurants and beach bars. The beaches are worth a visit (some busy, others secluded), but otherwise all you will see among the windmill cones and the modern villas are a few goats and the dildo cactus. Point Udall is the easternmost point in the United States (unless you include the Aleutian Islands in Alaska).

Puerto Rico

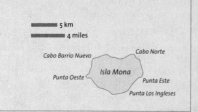

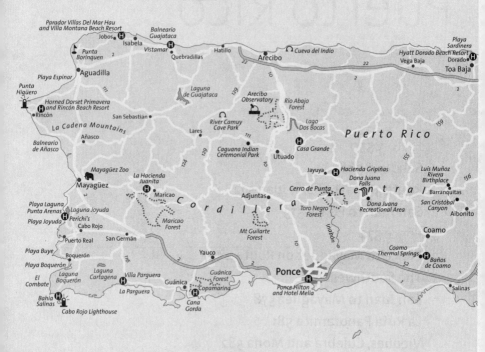

Caribbean Sea

Highlights

1 Wander the cobbled 18th-century streets of Old San Juan

2 Visit the 18th-century Hacienda Buena Vista coffee farm near Ponce, then the ultra-modern Arecibo Observatory

3 Take a kayak trip onto the bioluminescent lagoon in Vieques to see the ghostly glow of fish as they scatter beneath you

Puerto Rico

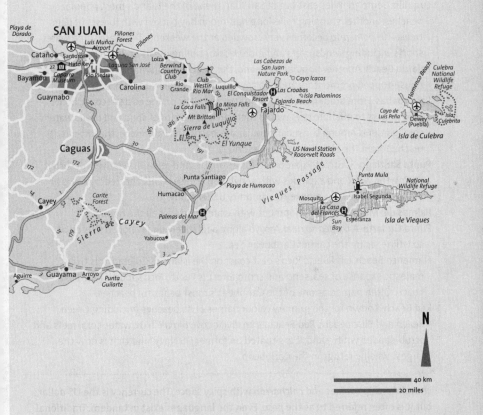

Atlantic Ocean

By American law, the Puerto Rican flag must always fly side-by-side with the Stars and Stripes. Puerto Rico is a Latin American island and so certain themes – music, dance, manners and political pride – run strongly through life on the island, but for the last hundred years, Puerto Rico has been owned by the USA. The result is an extraordinary overlay of America on this Latin Caribbean island.

The duality runs throughout Puerto Rican life. Side-by-side you will see air-conditioned high-rise buildings and tiny wooden West Indian shacks, pristine neon-lit shops and chaotic Caribbean markets, dog stands and *kioskos*,

Best Beaches

Condado and **Isla Verde**: These two famous strips are crowded and highly developed. Carolina Beach (Isla Verde) and Escambrón Beach (Condado) recently became the first Blue Flag beaches in the Americas; between the two is the Ocean Park area, popular with students and a gay crowd.

Piñones: Heading east the action evaporates and the skyscrapers turn to palm trees in this more remote area, where the Atlantic waves barrel in on to golden-red sand.

Luquillo: Some 30 miles east out of San Juan is one of the island's most popular beaches, another stunning mile-long half-moon bay backed with forests of palm trees. This *balneario* becomes very crowded at the weekend. There are some watersports, including windsurfers and more *kioskos* selling meals and snacks.

Fajardo Beach: Another popular *balneario*, this beach has dramatic views to a lighthouse-topped promontory and healthy patches of coral in its calm waters.

Las Croabas: From among the fishing shacks and villas on the eastern coast, boats take visitors to offshore cays where there are good strips of sand and underwater coral gardens. Among the most popular are Icacos and Palominos; the latter is reached from the El Conquistador Resort.

Punta Santiago: South of Fajardo, this long strip of sand remains relatively deserted during the week and explodes with activity on the weekend. The nearby cay is an off-limits refuge for a monkey community under study.

Palmas del Mar: A huge development with watersports for all the family.

Punta Guilarte: A *balneario* near Arroyo along a relatively undeveloped stretch of coastline facing the calmer Caribbean Sea.

Flamenco Beach: Off Puerto Rico's east coast on the island of Culebra, this truly majestic expanse of sea, sand and scrub forest is Puerto Rico's fourth Blue Flag beach. Often named as one of the Caribbean's most beautiful beaches.

Red Beach: Known for the primary colour names of its beaches (including Green Beach and Blue beach). Red Beach is an idyllic cove of pale blue water, coral reefs and scrub-shaded white sand. It is situated on former US Navy land that is now the largest wildlife refuge in the Caribbean.

chocolate-chip cookies and *chicharrón* with spicy sauce. The currency is the US dollar, but it is often referred to as the *peso*. Even the languages exist in tandem. Traditional Spanish is the tongue of the Puerto Rican legislature and of the poor country man, but much of daily life takes place in English. Businesslike American order has been imposed on the Latin Caribbean chaos.

Puerto Rico is the smallest (3,352 square miles) and most easterly of the four major islands in the Greater Antilles and it lies about 1,000 miles southeast of Miami, between the larger island of Hispaniola and the archipelago of the Virgin Islands. It is oblong in shape, about 100 miles from end to end by about 35 from north to south. It seems much larger though; like many of the mountainous Caribbean islands, the interior is very rough. Just a thin band of coastal plain runs around the Cordillera Central, a cumulus of peaks that rise to over 4,000ft, mostly clad in thick rainforest. In the northwest of the island, there is an odd geological phenomenon in the karst

Caja de Muertos Islet: Generally, the south coast has more mangrove-lined coves than long strips of sand; thus, beachgoers often head to the lovely mini-beaches on offshore cays and islets. Caja de Muertos, reached by charter boat, offers back-to-back beaches, a snorkelling trail, and a hilltop lighthouse.

Caña Gorda Beach: A narrow strip of beach adjoining Guánica Forest; boats regularly take visitors out to the magical cay nicknamed Gilligan's island.

El Combate: Near the southwestern tip of the island, a beach idyll lined with fishermen's shacks on the shore and their boats in the jade-coloured water. A perfect view of the sunset. You can also find deserted sun traps around the *salinas*, the salt flats.

Playa Boquerón: This magnificent curve is one of the best known on the island – ever popular at the weekend and less crowded during the week. Backed by a forest of palms, the 3 miles of sand gently slope away into the warm, limpid water.

Playa Buye: Beach beauty in miniature, this cove lies just south of Puerto Real, where fishing boats lie at anchor.

Playa Joyuda: Here the seafront is developed, so you can hire a windsurfer or bask on the thin beach before retreating inside for another piña colada.

Balneario de Añasco: A long and lovely curve of beach shaded by coconut palms. Camping is offered at this *balneario*.

Córcega: At Rincón, the calm waters and unending sand make this an ideal beach for families, bathers and beachcombers.

Punta Higüero: The beaches around and north of this point are world-renowned among surfers and windsurfers. Beautifully formed waves often top 20ft in the winter months.

Playa Espinar: Close to Aguada. Half a mile of white sand and gentle water.

Crashboat: Named for an old US Air Force pier, this protected beach has the best bathing and snorkelling on the island's northwest peninsula.

Jobos: A partially protected bathing and surfing beach, this and other beaches in the Isabela region provide a wide variety of watersports opportunities.

Playa Sardinera: Like most of the bathing beaches along the north coast, this popular *balneario* is protected by offshore rocks that were once sand dunes.

country, a conglomeration of hill-sized pimples and sinkholes shaped by aeons of water dripping through the limestone rock. The climate varies across the island – on the Atlantic coast in the north it is wetter and cooler than across the mountains. In the southwest, the country is hotter and savannah-like in places. Different crops and fruits, such as aloe and pineapple, grow there.

There are about 3.5 million Puerto Ricans on the island, of whom about one-third live in and around San Juan, the capital, which lies towards the eastern end of the north coast. The islanders have a mixed ancestry, a blend of the early Spaniards and the original Arawak Indians (some towns in the centre of the island have distinctly Amerindian names) and then Africans. Over the centuries, migrants from all over Europe and the Caribbean have added to the mix, followed in the 20th century by the Americans. Puerto Rico has a population noticeably whiter than the other Latin Caribbean islands.

Traditionally, Puerto Rico has had a rural economy, but that has changed over the last 50 years as the island has been encouraged to develop an industrial base. American firms have invested heavily (with considerable tax breaks) in Puerto Rico. With all the input from the States, it has one of the highest standards of living in the Caribbean. Unlike most Caribbean islands, the houses in Puerto Rico are built in concrete now. The material benefits of the American connection are clear.

Even with all the pharmaceutical and manufacturing concerns, tourism is still one of the most important industries on the island. It is very well organized. If you like a high-pressure vacation – a mugged-by-sunshine holiday with day-long beach activity and Vegas-style entertainment to keep you busy in the evenings – there are plenty of places on offer. But Puerto Rico is big enough for mass tourism not to swamp local life. Those who prefer to travel more independently and adventurously will find some superb Caribbean retreats. The hilltop towns of the Cordillera and offshore islands of Vieques and Culebra are charming and show the Spanish Caribbean at its most rural and laid-back.

History

The native Tainos called Puerto Rico Borinquen, which was supposed to mean 'Land of the Noble Lord'. These Arawak Indians, who had come up from South America along the island chain, were the most advanced of the Indian tribes who had lived on the island (the Archaics and the Igneris were hunter-gatherers who had come to the island as fishermen). Their skin was copper-coloured and they had long, dark hair. They lived in thatched huts in villages, around a ceremonial area called a *bateye*, a few of which can still be seen, where they would dance and play games with balls and shuttlecocks.

Columbus was the first European to come to Puerto Rico, on 19 November 1493, as he worked his way along the islands back to Hispaniola on his second voyage to the New World. He named it San Juan Bautista (St John the Baptist). Travelling with him was a man called Juan Ponce de León, who was to return as the first governor of the island in 1508. In 1511 the island was given the name of Puerto Rico (Rich Port).

Immediately the European settlers arrived, the 30,000 Taino Indians were divided among them and set to work as slaves in the hunt for gold. Inevitably there was a revolt. The Indians were soon defeated and retreated to the hills or fled the island. Ponce de León himself set off on his quest for the Fountain of Youth. He died in Havana of wounds received while exploring Florida and his body was returned to Puerto Rico. Eventually, it was placed in San Juan Cathedral.

By the late 1500s, the mines were exhausted and the few remaining Spaniards made a hard living out of cultivating sugar, cotton, ginger and indigo. They suffered the usual natural scourges of the Caribbean, including disease and hurricanes. They also were visited periodically by the canoe-borne Caribs from down-island, who would make lightning raids (5,000 attacked them in 1525). And then another human scourge put in an appearance in the middle of the 16th century: pirates. These men arrived with gold in mind, too – Spanish gold – or, if they could not find that, any loot they could lay their hands on.

Suggested Itinerary

In two weeks, you can spend time in San Juan, where there are some excellent small hotels and guest houses that use the best of their settings in old San Juan buildings, and then take off to tour the coast, as well as one of the offshore islands. You might even fit in a quick visit to the Virgin Islands.

From San Juan head east, to the eastern beaches and natural parks such as the El Yunque rainforest and Las Cabezas. A visit to either Vieques or Culebra is a must. Both have small-island charm but, if you choose Vieques, make sure to visit the phosphorescent bay. Back on the mainland, Ponce is a pretty town and is worth a quick look; from here head for the southwest coast, to Boquerón or perhaps Cabo Rojo, both seaside towns where the Puerto Ricans themselves take their holidays. From here, it is a short ride up into the mountains, along the *ruta panoramica*, where there are two superb *paradors* hidden away in the rainforest – the Hacienda Gripiñas and Hacienda Juanita. It is worth tailoring your trip around any festivals in the countryside. Ask at the tourist board.

Puerto Rico was a strategic port and the pirates infested its waters, trying to capture Spain's Central American riches as they were shipped back to Europe. Funded from Mexico, San Juan was fortified in defence against them. Perhaps the most famous pirate to attack the island was Sir Francis Drake. He made it into the harbour past the guns of El Morro and set the Spanish ships alight, but was bombarded in his turn – legend says he was forced to retire when a cannonball tore through his cabin, mortally wounding Jack Hawkins. The Dutch had a crack in 1625 and burned the town as they were forced out.

Meanwhile, the island was neglected by Spain, and the islanders took to smuggling. Officially, the Puerto Ricans could trade with no ships except those from Spain – but at one stage, not a single Spanish ship called for seven years, so they carried on brisk illegal trade in tobacco, ginger and cattle with other Caribbean islands. At one stage, Puerto Rico was nearly given to Britain in exchange for Gibraltar.

It was not until 1765 that the Spanish king sent an envoy to develop the island. Alejandro O'Reilly advised that sugar should become the main agricultural crop as in the other Caribbean islands and the trading laws be amended, and Spaniards should be encouraged to settle here. Within a few years, the ships of the new American Republic were doing a brisk legal trade.

As the 19th century progressed, the political scene became more important. The Puerto Ricans were granted citizenship of Spain in 1809 during the Napoleonic Wars and rights were accorded with a more liberal Spanish constitution in 1812. Steadily a Puerto Rican island identity crystallized and the struggle for autonomy began, encouraged by the wars of independence in South America. Spain started to clamp down in 1825, and sent over a series of ruthless military governors, later called the 'Little Caesars'. One governor even banned goatee beards because they were emotive of revolution. In 1856, the reformer Betances was exiled for his anti-colonial views. Encouraged by the revolution in the Dominican Republic in 1862, he and other exiles plotted revolution in Puerto Rico and Cuba.

On 23 September 1868, their first uprising came in the town of Lares in the north-west of the island and the Republic of Puerto Rico was declared. But the colonial authorities responded quickly, crushing the revolt at San Sebastian. It is remembered as the Grito de Lares (the Cry of Lares) and became symbolic of the struggle for inde-pendence. On 22 March 1873, slavery was abolished in Puerto Rico.

Politically the Puerto Ricans divided into two camps: the autonomists, who wanted independence, and the conservatives, who wished to remain connected with Spain, but with increased self-government. Their hope was that a new Republican govern-ment in Spain would grant them autonomy without a war. Their wish was granted and, on 28 November 1897, the Puerto Ricans were finally allowed to govern them-selves. They elected their own Lower House and half the Senate. The governor was appointed from Spain, but his powers were restricted.

But it was not to last for long. Within nine months, the Americans had invaded as part of the Spanish–American War. The campaign lasted 17 days. In December of that year, after four centuries as colonial masters, the Spaniards handed Puerto Rico to the Americans at the Treaty of Paris. Initially, the Puerto Ricans were hopeful that American intervention and severance from Spain would improve their political status, but it steadily became clear that the USA wanted to keep the island and would impose its political will. The Jones Act of 1917 granted the Puerto Ricans American citizenship and an elected bicameral legislature, but still the key administrative posts were appointed from the US government. Political struggle was by no means dormant for long. There were attacks on the government and, in 1937, 19 people were killed at an *Independentista* rally when police fired on the crowd.

On 5 August 1947, Harry Truman signed the bill that created the Commonwealth of Puerto Rico, ratified by the islanders themselves in 1952. As in the USA, the govern-ment is divided into executive, judicial and legislative branches. There are two houses of parliament, a 51-member House of Representatives and a 27-member Senate. The Governor is elected for four-year terms in line with the elections on the mainland.

The island does not pay taxes to the Federal Bank in the same way as a State of the Union and consequently has no representation in Congress. The elected Resident Commissioner, Luis Fortuño, has observer status – more of a lobbying role. The island also receives financial support in grants for public works, the universities and food stamps ('pan' cheques).

Today the politics of Puerto Rico are dominated by the status of the island with regard to the USA and there are two main possibilities (the desire for independence has faded into insignificance). The majority of the voters swing between maintaining the Commonwealth status and becoming the 51st State of the Union. The governing party is the Popular Democratic Party, led by Governor Aníbal Acevedo Vilá. Elections are next due in 2008.

Beaches

Puerto Rico's hundreds of miles of coastline have a great variety of beaches – from protected coves on the southwestern shore where the snorkelling is excellent to the busy, people-packed, golden sand strands in San Juan and the surfing beaches at the northwestern tip of the island. Perhaps the best beaches, though, are on the offshore islands of Vieques and Culebra, where the sand is white and undeveloped and the reefs are good. Going to the beach is a popular day out at the weekend among the Puerto Ricans and the government has developed some of the more popular spots with *balnearios*. These public beaches have changing rooms with lockers, lifeguards, a car park and usually a small restaurant (*open Tues–Sun 9–5; adm usually a dollar parking and 50¢ entrance*). Some also have sites where you can pitch a tent for a minimal fee. *See* 'Best Beaches', pp.548–9.

Flora and Fauna

Puerto Rico has the full variety of Caribbean wildlife, from the coral reefs that skirt the island and the coastal mangrove swamps to rainforest at 4,000ft. In El Yunque and the rough mountains of the Cordillera, you will see trees that soar and explode into canopy at 100ft, tangled with lianas and creeping vines, montane forests of extraordinarily lush ferns and palms, and on the upper slopes stunted elfin forest where mosses fur the prehistoric-looking tree bark.

In the heights, you might see the endangered Puerto Rican parrot, lizard cuckoos, warblers and screech owls – and hummingbirds, tiny delicate creatures with a metabolic rate so high that they must fly all day to keep up their intake of nectar. In the lower mountains, among Puerto Rico's manmade inland lakes, you will see kestrels and hawks on the hunt, cruising on the spirals of rising air and casting a drilling eye over the undergrowth, and in the flatlands, the cattle egret standing around, dumbstruck and mournful.

There are mangrove swamps all around the coastline, where you will see crabs with their eyes out on stalks, surprised to see you perhaps. These monstrously tangled waterways are refuge to hundreds of different birds, including the exotic green-backed heron and the purple gallinule. You might also see a mockingbird or a whistling duck. On the offshore islands, you will come across boobies, solitary pelicans and maybe even a red-billed tropicbird with an 18-inch tail.

Puerto Rico has the usual roll call of Caribbean reptiles, including lizards and iguanas, but the one the islanders think most fondly of is the coquí, an indigenous tree frog who you will hear singing every evening. *Eleutherodactylus portoricensis* is about 1 inch long with smooth and almost transparent skin, and he disappears into moist and cool hideouts during the day. His local name derives from his dual peep, sung loudest after rain – an immediately recognizable 'co-quí co-quí co-quí!'

There are around twenty Forest Reserves (*see* pp.573, 577, 578, 581, 582), of which the best known (also one of the closest to San Juan) is **El Yunque** (*see* p.572). Other mountain parks a little more off the beaten track are: the **Carite Forest Reserve**, in the Cayey mountains south of Caguas, the **Toro Negro Forest**, just east of Adjuntas in the centre of the island (this park contains the mountain Cerro de Punta, Puerto Rico's highest peak) and **Río Abajo Forest**, in the karst country south of Arecibo. If you would prefer somewhere less hilly, you could try the coastal mangrove swamps, for instance at **Guánica Forest**, on the south coast to the west of Ponce, which has extensive birdlife, or **Piñones Forest**, just a stone's throw out of San Juan to the east.

Getting There

Puerto Rico t (1–)

By Air

From Europe

The only direct scheduled flights from Europe to San Juan are with Iberia, Spain t 90 24 00 500, UK t 0845 601 2854, *www.iberiaair lines.co.uk*, from Madrid. A number of charter operators (including Condor out of Germany, Germany t (810) 233 7130, *www.condor.de*) do fly the route. Another alternative is to make a connection in Miami.

From the USA

Puerto Rico is a domestic destination for US airlines and an American Airlines hub: American Airlines, t 1 800 433 7300; American Eagle, t 1 800 433 7300; US Airways, t 1 800 428 4322; United Airlines, t 1 800 241 6522; and Delta, t 1 800 221 1212, all run frequent flights from Miami and many other US cities (including Atlanta, Baltimore, Boston, Dallas and Orlando).

From Other Caribbean Islands

San Juan is very well served from the Caribbean and South America by: BWIA, t 1 800 538 2942 (from Trinidad, Antigua and Barbados); American Eagle, t 1 800 433 7300; Air Jamaica, t 1 800 523 5585. Local airlines include LIAT, t 787 791 0800, whose flights to and from the Eastern Caribbean terminate here – direct services from the Virgin Islands, Anguilla, St Kitts, Antigua and beyond – and many other smaller airlines, such as Air St Thomas, t 787 791 4898, US t 1 800 522 3084, and Cape Air, t 1 800 352 0714.

Puerto Rico has the same entry requirements as the USA.

Getting Around

By Bus

There is an extensive network of *públicos* (Ford vans, marked with P or PD), that run to and from the central plaza in each town. Travelling like this works, though it can take a while, because you may have to take successive *públicos* from one town to the next (their beat is not usually longer than two or three towns).

The system is typically West Indian and services are quite frequent, but do not work to any recognizable schedule; *públicos* leave when they are full or when the urge takes the driver. You can flag them down on the roadside to let you on, and shout to get off. Service is more limited at the weekend. Travelling in them is fun because there is the latest salsa music to sing along to and you will get to know your fellow passengers fairly well. Destinations are marked on the windscreen.

The *público* terminals in San Juan for journeys around the island are at the Luis Muñoz Marin International Airport and at the Plaza del Mercado (at the end of metropolitan bus routes 1 and 2) in Río Piedras. The metropolitan area of San Juan is served by air-conditioned buses known locally as *guaguas* (pronounced 'wahwah'). From Old San Juan (Plaza Colón and the harbour area), you can get to Bayamón, Cataño, Country Club and Río Piedras (close to the Plaza del Mercado *público* terminal). The fare is 25¢; exact change only. Wait at the yellow posts (*paradas*). *Guaguas* run every 20–30 minutes until around 10pm.

If your feet get tired within Old San Juan itself, you might consider using the little safari buses (*free*) that run a circular route around the area.

A word of warning: if you want to get to and from the airport by bus, the *guagua* drivers will sometimes not let you aboard with luggage – so you are forced to go by taxi.

By Taxi

Taxis are readily available at the airport, at all the hotels and in areas like the dock in Old San Juan. You can avoid being over-charged by using one of the white *taxis turísticos* which follow a set fare schedule. For example, the fare from the airport to Isla Verde is $8; these fixed rates apply only from the Luis Muñoz International Airport or the cruise ship piers in Old San Juan. Between and beyond the tourism areas, taxi rates are metered and include two pieces of luggage.

By Ferry

Ferries operate within San Juan harbour. Aqua Expresso links San Juan to Hato Rey and

Cataño, every half-hour, 6am–10pm. From Fajardo on the east coast you can reach the offshore islands of Vieques (*generally three times a day, crossing 1 hour*) and Culebra (*generally twice a day, crossing 1 hour*).

Ferries are rarely full, but you can reserve on t 787 863 0852, *www.prtourism.com/ferries*.

By Air

There are small airstrips dotted around Puerto Rico. Flights can be caught from Isla Grande Airport in Condado or from San Juan International Airport to: Ponce, Mayagüez, Palmas del Mar, Fajardo and the offshore islands of Vieques and Culebra.

By Guided Tour

Island tours can be arranged to the principal sights – a day's excursion to El Yunque and Luquillo or over to Ponce, for instance. Most companies will pick you up and deliver you to your hotel. Contact:

Castillo Tours and Travel Services, t 787 728 2297.

Rico Suntours, t 787 722 2080.

Tour Co-op of Puerto Rico, t 787 762 7155, t 787 725 6245, *www.toursofpuertorico.com*.

United Tour Guides Co-op, t 787 723 5578.

Car Hire

Car hire is really the best way to see the island for the independent traveller and there is a limitless supply of them in Condado and Isla Verde. Although you can get a good price out of season, prices are high over the winter. Most companies will deliver and pick up rental cars for you. Driving is on the right and, although speed limits are indicated in miles per hour, distances are in kilometres. US licences are valid for three months. UK licences are valid, as are international licences. If you wish to travel around the island, in the Cordillera or around the less populous south coast, it is essential to have a good map and these can usually be provided by the hire company. Road signs are not brilliant, but the roads themselves are good. Small cars start at around $50 per day inclusive of insurance in the winter, mileage unlimited.

Hire companies include:

Afro, Ponce de León, t 787 724 3720.

Avis, t 800 874 3556.

Budget, t 787 791 0600, t 1 800 527 0700.

Charlie, t 787 728 2418, t 1 800 289 1227, *www.charliecars.com*.

L & M, Ashford Av, San Juan, t 787 791 1160.

National, t 787 791 1805.

Target, Baldorioty Av, Santurce, t 787 728 1447, US t 1 800 934 6457, *info@targetrentacar. com, www.targetrentacar.com*.

Tourist Information

Abroad

The official website and the best information for Puerto Rico is to be found at *www.prtourism.com*, and its associated site at *www.travelandsports.com*.

The Commonwealth of Puerto Rico Tourism Company can be contacted at:

Canada: 41–43 Colbourne St, Suite 301, Toronto, Ontario M5E 1E3, t 1 800 667 0394.

UK: There is no office in the UK, but there is a toll-free number that routes through to Spain, where receptionists speak good English, t 0800 898 920.

USA: Puerto Rican Tourism Co., 575 Fifth Av, 23rd Floor, New York, NY 10017, t (212) 599 6262, t 1 800 223 6530;
W. Cahuenga Bd, Suite 405, Los Angeles, t 1 800 874 1230;
901 Ponce de Léon Bd, Suite 101, Miami, t 1 800 815 7391.

In Puerto Rico

The island is dotted with information offices. Outside the capital, each major town has an information bureau in the *Alcaldía*, the Town Hall, on the main plaza (*open weekdays*). You'll find tourist offices at the following locations:

San Juan: La Princesa, Box 4431, Old San Juan Station, PR 00905–4431, t 787 721 2400.
La Casita, near Pier 1 on the cruise-ship dock in Old San Juan, t 787 722 1709.

International Airport: t 787 791 1014.

Condado: Next to the Condado Plaza Hotel, t 787 723 3135.

Ponce: 291 Las Caobos Av, Paseo del Sur Plaza, Suite 3, t 787 863 0465.

You can get information about the **Paradores** at La Princesa, Old San Juan 00905, t 787 721 2400, US t 1 800 443 0266.

Emergencies

In a medical emergency, you can contact the 24-hour emergency rooms at Ashford Memorial Community Hospital at 1451 Ashford Av, t 787 721 2160, or the San Juan Health Centre, 200 De Diego Avenue, t 787 725 0202. Ambulances can be reached on t 787 343 2550.

You are advised to have extensive **medical cover**, because charges for treatment in Puerto Rico are high. To contact the **police**, the emergency number is t 911; the central number is t 787 343 2020.

Language

English is widely spoken in the tourist areas of Puerto Rico, but if you venture off the beaten track into the country, you will find it very useful to speak Spanish. It is also worth requesting an English-speaking guide in some places if you need one.

Media

The Tourism Company publishes a quarterly guide, *Qué Pasa*, www.qpsm.com, with listings of current events as well as the hotels and restaurants. If you are driving and want to listen to the latest salsa music, tune in to Sal Sol on 98.5 FM, or Z93 on 93.7 FM.

Money and Banks

The **currency** of Puerto Rico is the US dollar, but it is often known as the peso. Quarters are called pesetas and cents centavos. Traveller's cheques and credit cards are widely accepted in the tourist areas, but out in the country, you will need to pay in cash. Small notes are useful for this as well as for tipping (the usual dollar or 15%). **Banks** are open Mon–Fri 8.30–2.30.

Shopping

Shoppers will find endless hunting grounds in Puerto Rico, and with there being no sales tax it is quite good sport. Individual shops and even malls are often found in the big hotels, but they are thickest on the ground in Old San Juan.

Most shops open Mon–Sat 9–6 and will accept credit cards quite happily.

Telephone Code

The IDD code for Puerto Rico is t 1 787, which is followed by a seven-digit island number. All calls, even those made within Puerto Rico itself, must now be prefixed by t 787. Some numbers, mainly mobiles, are prefixed with t 939 instead. Freephone numbers are prefixed by t 800.

There is an international telephone exchange on Baldorioty de Castro in Miramar. Alternatively, most hotels will put calls through for you for a price.

Festivals

January *Fiesta de la Calle de San Sebastian.* A very popular event in which the street is crammed with costumed locals dancing, singing, drinking and generally making whoopee.

December *Christmas.* Puerto Rican towns are strung end to end with fairy lights and coloured tinsel over the Christmas period often with a life-size nativity scene in people's front gardens.

Festival of the Innocents. The most spectacular and riotous event over the Christmas period, which takes place in the small town of Hatillo, near Arecibo, on 28 December. Groups of men (mainly) dress in suits of brightly coloured ruff-like material, wearing ghostly masks, and spend the day driving around the country on decorated floats. In the afternoon, they converge on the town square, where they bounce their vehicles from side to side until they nearly tip over. Well worth a visit for a riot of colourful excess.

Fiestas Patronales

Most towns in Puerto Rico celebrate their saint's day in a week-long blow-out of Masses, feasts, candle processions with statues, masked street parades and music centred on the plaza. These are fun to attend, and you will certainly be included in the activities if you are around.

The daytime parades are a riotous procession of *veijantes* (masked figures) and *diabolos* dancing in ghoulish, brightly coloured costumes, and everywhere the streets are alive with impromptu *kioskos* and games: a favourite is a crank-up merry-go-round where you bet on tin horses.

February Mayagüez (2nd). A very spectacular celebration in honour of La Virgen de la Candelaria.

March Lares, San Jose (19th).

May Arecibo, San Felipe Apostol (1st).

June Barranquitas, San Antonio de Padua (13th).

July Culebra, La Virgen del Carmen (17th). Loíza, Santiago. One of the best known on the island (25th). Fajardo, Santiago (25th).

August Adjuntas, San Joaquin and Santa Ana (21st).

September Jayuya, Nuestra Señora de la Montserrate (3rd). Utuado, San Miguel Arcangel (29th). Cabo Rojo (29th).

October Yauco, Nuestra Señora del Rosario (7th).

November Aguadilla (4th).

December Humacao (8th). Ponce (16th).

Watersports

Watersports depend mainly on the hotels and their concessionaires. All sports, water-skiing, parasailing, outings in small sailing craft, pedalos or jetskis are easily arranged in the major tourist areas of Condado and Isla Verde, and in the major resorts of Dorado (20 miles west of San Juan) and Fajardo in the east, which is a very popular getaway at the weekend.

If you travel further afield, sports become less available, though you will find operators on most of the popular beaches at the weekends.

Day Sails

There are endless excursions, usually out of the marinas in Fajardo (they normally offer transfers from hotels in San Juan), which will take you for a day's sailing and snorkelling, with a stop on an isolated beach for a picnic.

Caribbean School of Aquatics, t 787 728 6606, *www.saildiveparty.com.*

Castillo Watersports, San Juan, **t** 787 726 5752, *irene@coqui.net, www.caribead.com/castillo.*

Catamaran Spread Eagle II, t 787 887 8821, *www.snorkelpr.com.*

In other towns, ask at the hotels or see the tourist literature.

Deep-sea Fishing

The northern shore of Puerto Rico drops away to 6,000ft within a couple of miles, and there are some extremely fine waters. Cast for white and blue marlin, wahoo and sailfish and perhaps you could improve on one of Puerto Rico's many world records. You can set off from the Club Náutico in San Juan, with one of the following:

Benitez Deep Sea Fishing, Fernández Juncos Av, San Juan, **t** 787 723 2292, *www.mike benitezfishing.com.*

Caribbean Outfitters, Cangrejos, **t** 787 396 8346, *www.fishinginpuertorico.com.* A boat for six people costs around $650 for a full day's sail.

Snorkelling and Diving

Fajardo and its islands have the best of the reefs and sandbars. The reefs teem with schools of grunt and solitary graceful angelfish and butterflyfish. At La Parquera in southwest Puerto Rico is 'The Wall', which offers some of the best diving in the Caribbean. Contact:

Akuasport, San Juan, **t** 787 754 3363, *akuasport@caribe.net, www.akuasport.com.*

Boquerón Dive Shop, t 787 851 2155, *dive@coqui.net, home.coqui.net/dive.*

Caribbean School of Aquatics, Condado, **t** 787 728 6606, *www.saildiveparty.com.*

Mundo Submarino, Laguna Gardens Shopping Centre, Isla Verde, **t** 787 791 5764, *www.mundosubmarino.com.*

Parguera Divers, t 787 899 4171, *divepr@caribe.net, www.pargueradivers.com.*

Surfing

Popular in the northwest, around Aguadilla, Aguada and Rincón, where the wind and waves often provide high sport. Hire is around $20 per hour for a board and instruction is available through all the main beaches.

Windsurfing

Popular all over the island, particularly in Condado Lagoon. Rental equipment is easily found. Try:

Sun Rider Watersports, t 787 721 1000 ext. 2699.

Other Sports

Golf

There are 21 courses in Puerto Rico, some of them attached to the big hotels. Try:

Luis Ortiz, on the outskirts of San Juan, t 787 786 3859.

Berwind Country Club, Río Grande, t 787 876 3056. An 18-hole course. Open to the public at varying times, so it is best to ring before arriving.

Westin Rio Mar, Río Grande, t 787 888 8815. An 18-hole course. Ring before arriving.

Dorado Resort, t 787 796 1234. There are a number of courses here.

Wyndham El Conquistador Resort, t 787 863 6784. There are 27 holes here.

Palmas del Mar Resort, t 787 852 6000. Has an 18-hole course.

Punta Borinquen, Aguadilla, in the northwest, t 787 890 2987.

Hiking

There are endless possibilities in the mountainous interior of the island. Most national parks have trails, with the best hiking is in El Yunque National Forest. You can struggle up switchback paths in the mountains, taking a quick dip in the waterfalls, or stalk pelicans and tropicbirds in the mangrove swamps. The parks are coordinated by the Natural Environment Resources Department, PO Box 5887, San Juan 00906, t 787 724 3724.

More than 20 companies arrange nature and adventure tours. A complete list is available from the tourist office. Or try:

AdvenTours, Luquillo, t 787 889 0251.

Aventuras Tierra Adentro, San Juan metro, t 787 766 0470.

Copladet Nature & Adventure Travel, San Juan metro, t 787 765 8595.

Encantos Ecotours, San Juan metro, t 787 272 0005.

Yokahú Kayak Trips, Fajardo, t 787 604 7375.

Horse-riding

You might prefer to ride through the mountains or to gallop through the breakers.

Hacienda Carabalí, t 787 889 5820. For rides around Luquillo.

Palmas del Mar, t 85787 2 6000. Try this large horse-riding centre in the southeast of the island.

Pot-holing

Puerto Rico's underground rivers have carved out some extremely impressive cave systems in the limestone rock. There are tame, trolley-borne tours on offer but, if you are a keen spelunker, then you might want to check out the lesser-known caverns with an independent party.

Puerto Rico Speleological Society, PO Box 31074, 65th Infantry Station, Río Piedras, Puerto Rico 00929.

Aventuras Tierra Adentro, t 787 766 0470. Caving and climbing outings with experienced guides.

Tennis

Courts proliferate around the tourist hotels, though it may be difficult to get one in winter. If the hotel you are staying in does not have one, they can usually arrange it elsewhere. Otherwise, try:

San Juan Central Park, off Route 2, t 787 722 1646.

Spectator Sports

Baseball is the favourite spectator sport in Puerto Rico, as in the other Latin Caribbean islands of Cuba and the Dominican Republic. The season runs over the winter months here, from October to April, and some Puerto Rican sportsmen in the major leagues return here to play. There are stadia in San Juan, Santurce, Caguas, Ponce, Mayagüez and Arecibo. You are quite likely to see softball being played as well.

Another very popular sport in the Latin Caribbean islands is **cockfighting**. There is an organized and rather plush *gallera* in Isla Verde but, if you go to a *gallera* in a country town, you will see all the frenzied passion of a local tournament, where pride as well as money ride on the result. The sport is cruel and often ends with one of the birds being killed.

Usually held Saturday and Sunday afternoons.

Where to Stay

Puerto Rico t (1–)

Puerto Rico has something to suit every taste. It is well known for the large glitzy casino hotels along the coast in San Juan, but behind these you will find smaller, more personable inns.

There is a range of small hotels and guest houses set in San Juan's charming old buildings to suit most budgets. And away from the city there are some unexpected gems (particularly the luxurious Horned Dorset Primavera on the west coast), both in the resort towns on the seafront and also in the mountains, where some of the charming *paradors* (see section in *www.prtourism.com*) use the best of the old Puerto Rican plantation estate settings.

You might also want to try the **Small Inns of Puerto Rico**, part of the Puerto Rico Tourism and Hotel Association, **t** 787 725 2901, **t** 787 725 2913, *eperez@prhta.com*, *www.prtourism.com*.

If you are travelling around the island, it is useful to have the comprehensive list of hotels in *Qué Pasa*, the tourist brochure.

A government tax of 7% is applied to all paradors (11% in hotels with a casino, 9% in those without) and the service charge is 10–15%.

All except the smallest hotels accept credit cards.

Old San Juan

Very Expensive

Gran Hotel El Convento, 100 Calle Cristo, PO Box 1048, **t** 787 723 9020, *elconvento@aol.com*, *www.elconvento.com*. Set in the heart of the old city opposite the cathedral, this hotel is in a former 17th-century Carmelite convent which has been completely refitted. Downstairs it retains an atmospheric air with old beams, wall tapestries and chequerboard tile floors and a pleasant courtyard with trees and a café. The rooms, with an air of mock antiquity but actually very comfortable and modern (certainly more so than they were originally, when they were the former occupants' cells), are ranged around the arcaded balconies on the upper floors. A stylish retreat right in the centre of town.

Moderate

Gallery Inn, 204 Calle Norzagaray, Puerto Rico 00901, **t** 787 722 1808, *reservations@ thegalleryinn.com*, *www.thegalleryinn.com*. Another charming retreat, set around the interior courtyards of three Old San Juan houses and so-called because it is a working artists' studio. Ten comfortable rooms and suites around five brick-laid courtyards, everywhere with sculptures and profuse with greenery, all linked by a network of stairways. You may enjoy the buzz of artists at work, or you can lock yourself away in the isolation of your suite. (There are special 'Portrait Packages' in which your room is free if you commission a bust.) Outsiders are permitted to view the gallery area.

Hotel Milano, 307 Calle Fortaleza, **t** 787 729 9050, US **t** 1 877 729 9050, *www.coqui.net/ hmilano*. A small hotel set in a large 19th-century building, now neatly redone. The rooms are simple but comfortable and there's a rooftop terrace with harbour views.

Inexpensive

Hotel Plaza de Armas, just off the Plaza de Armas in the centre of Old San Juan, **t** 787 722 9191, *www.iphhoteles.com*. A good place to rest your head in the very heart of the town. Simple fan-ventilated rooms with share or private bathrooms and a busy air.

Condado and Isla Verde

Luxury–Very Expensive

Ritz Carlton, 6961 State Road, 187 Isla Verde, **t** 787 253 1700, US **t** 1 800 241 3333, *www.ritzcarlton.com*. A large hotel, more elegant than most of the big resorts on the city's oceanfront, less than ten minutes from the international airport. From the architecture outside to the furnishings inside, there's no mistaking this is a Ritz Carlton. But take a closer look and you will see the unmistakable imprint of Puerto Rico – in the art on the walls, the dishes on the menus, the martini bar with 70 different rums, the 2,000 cigars in the humidors, and the lobby opening on to the gardens that stretch to the pool, spa, beach and the ocean. The guest rooms have all the luxury amenities for which the chain is known, including three telephones with dual lines and data-port, bathroom scales and robes.

Expensive

The Water Club, 2 Tartak Street, Isla Verde, Puerto Rico 00979, **t** 888 265 6699, *www.waterclubsanjuan.com*. Puerto Rico's first urban boutique hotel when it opened in 2001, The Water Club retains its trendy status today. Located on the beach near the international airport, the small hotel has a clubby atmosphere and an austere décor of minimalist white softened with waterfalls and clever lighting. The 84 guest rooms feel more like bedrooms at home than hotel rooms, and yet all have the full range of facilities. On the open-air roof is a fitness centre, a small swimming pool and whirlpool, a sushi bar and a magnificent view of the beach and city – spectacular at sunset. The rooftop bar, Wet, is the place to be seen for San Juan's young sophisticates. Tangerine@Liquid is one of San Juan's best restaurants.

Wyndham El San Juan Hotel and Casino, 6063 Isla Verde, **t** 787 791 1000, US **t** 1 800 468 2818, *www.wyndham.com*. Has a similar humming quality as it towers above the beach. Pith-helmeted guards greet you as you pass into the massive elaborate foyer of dark-stained wood, imitation gas lamps and chandeliers. Huge lounging area and pool outside with swim-up bar, and then the superb sand. The rooms are high luxury, down to the third telephone in the bathroom. Ten restaurants, bars, clubs and casino on the premises.

Moderate

Hostería del Mar, 1 Tapia St, Ocean Park, Puerto Rico 00911, **t** 787 727 3302, *hosteria@caribe.net*, *www.prtourism.com*. Seventeen rooms in a block set behind a charming beachfront restaurant with louvred windows on sticks. Rooms are comfortable, with wicker furniture, TVs, mostly air-conditioned but some fan-ventilated (some with balconies, some with kitchenettes). Sunning deck upstairs and watersports right outside.

Numero Uno, on the beach at 1 Calle Santa Ana, Ocean Park, Puerto Rico 00911, **t** 787 726 5010, *roma@caribe.net*. Not far down the excellent strip of sand is a friendly guest house set in an old family villa. There are just eight rooms with private baths, air-conditioning and fans, and a library and TV room. All meals served on the deck next to the pool, where the guests meet at 7pm for a drink before dinner. Mixed crowd.

Tres Palmas, 2212 Park Bd, Puerto Rico 00913, **t** 787 727 4617, **t** US 1 888 290 2076, *trespalm@coqui.net*, *www.trespalmasinn.com*. Eight rooms and three simple apartments in a Spanish revival-style villa across the road from the sea. Air-con, TV and fridge, quite simple.

Casa de Playa Beach Hotel, 86 Av Isla Verde, Puerto Rico 00979, **t** 787 728 9779, US **t** 1 800 916 2272. A good place to stay if you want to be right on the beach in Isla Verde without spending an absolute fortune. There are twenty comfortable rooms with air-conditioning, phones and cable TV, flowery décor and wooden furniture; outside a restaurant and beachfront bar behind the palms.

El Canario Inn, 1317 Ashford Av, **t** 787 722 3861, US **t** 1 800 533 2649, *canariopr@aol.com*, *www.canariohotels.com*. A charming little hotel with just 25 rooms and a lush garden courtyard, offering excellent value.

Inexpensive

Green Isle Inn, 36 Calle Uno, **t** 787 726 4330, US **t** 1 800 677 8860, *reservations@greenisleinn.com*, *www.greenisleinn.com*. With 17 rooms.

Casa Mathieson Inn, 14 Calle Uno, **t** 787 726 4330, US **t** 1 800 677 8860, *reservations@casamathieson.com*, *www.casamathieson.com*. Sister property to the Green Isle.

Hotel Olimpo Court, Miramar, **t** 787 724 0600. Comfortable hotel; home of the Chayote Restaurant.

East of San Juan

Luxury

Wyndham El Conquistador Resort and Country Club, 1000 Conquistador Av, Fajardo, **t** 787 863 1000, US **t** 1 800 468 8365, *www.wyndham.com*. A large resort, with extensive sports and meeting facilities, restaurants, a large spa complex, and plenty of entertainment laid on for guests. The resort is set on the hillside above the north-eastern tip of the island with rooms and apartments scattered all around. The main house is spectacularly decorated with murals. There's an offshore island with beach, watersports facilities and horse-riding.

Expensive

Palmas del Mar, PO Box 2020, Humacao, Puerto Rico 00792, **t** 787 852 6000, *info@palmasdelmar.com*, *www.palmas delmar.com*. If you are one for a large resort, with facilities like golf, beach-bound watersports, tennis, horse-riding, a multiplicity of restaurants and even an outdoor movie theatre all in the one complex, then go for this one. Country club atmosphere, with rooms, suites, villas or apartments linked by shuttles.

Río Grande Plantation, PO Box 6526, Loíza Santurce, Puerto Rico 00914, **t** 787 887 2779, *rgplantation@riograndeplantation.com*, *www.riograndeplantation.com*. Good-value rooms in different styles on 40 acres of old plantation in the foothills of the El Yunque rainforest, on a river bend. Sumptuous suites with kitchenettes and cable TV, pleasant gardens. Some weddings and events, but a good place from which to explore.

Moderate

Hotel La Familia, Las Croabas, PO Box 21399, Puerto Rico 00738, **t** 787 863 1193, *peniro@ hotellafamilia.com*, *www.hotellafamilia.com*. Located in the Las Croabas area, with 35 air-conditioned rooms, a swimming pool and sun deck, beaches and watersports not far off. No restaurant, but plenty of places around.

Fajardo Inn, just outside Fajardo, PO Box 4309, Puerto Real, Puerto Rico 00740, **t** 787 860 6000, *info@fajardoinn.com*, *www.fajardo inn.com*. A small and comfortable bed and breakfast with nine rooms (clean and air-conditioned with TVs) and long, shady colonial verandas. Personal service; a good stopover.

Inexpensive

Anchor's Inn, Route 987, **t** 787 863 7200, *www.anchorsinn@libertypr.net*. Rooms are simple but comfortable and the restaurant, though touristy, serves excellent *criolle* and international cuisine.

Ponce

Expensive

Ponce Hilton and Casino, **t** 787 259 7676, **t** 1 800 445 8667, *www.hilton.com*. International comfort, good service and the full range of facilities, including a casino and golf course.

Moderate

Hotel Meliá, Plaza Degetau, PO Box 1431, **t** 787 842 0260, **t** 1 800 742 4276, *melia@coqui.net*, *home.coqui.net/melia*. For a little more Caribbean style and charm try this one, situated in the historic area in the centre of Ponce. It keeps some of the old-time feel of the town in the period foyer and courtyard, though the comfortable rooms are modern. It has managed to poach one of the best chefs on the island from the Hilton. He now runs his own restaurant, Marks, attached to the hotel.

Inexpensive

Hotel Belgica, 122 Villa, **t** 787 844 3255. Situated in a large town house with wrought-iron balconies.

Hotel El Tuque, Km 220.1 R42, Ponce, **t** 787 290 2000. Next to a water park.

Hotel Colville, Av Muñez Riviera at the corner of Las Américas, **t** 787 843 1935. The least expensive place to stay in town, with pleasant simple rooms.

Baños de Coamo, **t** 787 825 2239, US **t** 1 877 797 3434, *www.banosdecoamo.com*. This *parador* is just off the San Juan–Ponce road (Route 153). The *baños* are the hot springs that attracted so elegant a crowd in the 19th century. They have lost most of their refinement now – the rooms are sparse and functional – but there are still one or two fine buildings around the courtyard, and the dining room has been restored nearly to its former elegance. Not a bad stop if you are travelling through.

The Southwestern Corner

In the southwestern corner of the island, you will find a number of seaside resort towns with small and friendly hotels. These are popular with the Puerto Ricans at the weekends and in the holidays (prices tend to rise for the summer months rather than in the winter season).

There are plenty of villas and houses for rent in the Boquerón area, t 787 851 4751.

Expensive

Copamarina Beach Resort, PO Box 805, Guánica, Puerto Rico 00653, t 787 821 0505, USA t 1 800 468 4553, *www.copamarina.com*. A pleasant beachfront hotel where there are 69 rooms in quite attractive, red-roofed blocks laid out around a lawned garden of palms. There is a freshwater pool, tennis courts and watersports available on the reasonable beach right out front, or the (better) public beach nearby.

Moderate

Villa Parguera, PO Box 273, Parguera, PR 00667, t 787 899 7777, *elshop@ elshop.com*, *www.villaparguera.com*. This *parador* is the nicest place to stay on the south coast, overlooking the lagoon and the mangrove islands where the holiday houses stand on stilts. The 63 rooms are in two-storey blocks with balconies giving on to a palm garden and the pool. There is no beach, but you can find sand just a boat-ride away.

Posada Porlamar, PO Box 405, Parguera, PR 00667, t 787 899 4015. A *parador* found along the waterfront. Simpler, but has air-conditioned, comfortable rooms in a cabin. There is no restaurant, but the 18 rooms have kitchenettes.

Inexpensive

Wildflowers Inn, 113 Calle Manoz Rivera, Boquerón, t 787 851 1793. The best place by far to stay. Spacious, high-ceilinged rooms packed with antiques.

Parador Oasis, in the centre of San Germán, off Highway 2, PO Box 144, PR 00683, t 787 892 1175. Set in an old town house, with a colonial foyer furnished with ornate woodwork and wicker-backed rocking chairs. The dining room overlooks the pool, as do some of the 50 rooms. Another agreeable stopover for the setting and the friendly crowd. No longer an official parador.

Parguera Guest House, opposite the Porlamar, Parguera, t 787 899 3993. This is probably the most comfortable of the guest houses in the streets behind the waterfront. Double rooms, all with private bath and air conditioning.

Pargomar, Parguera, t 787 899 4065. Three simple, air-conditioned rooms.

Estancia La Jamaca, Km 3.9 Rt. 304, La Parguela, t 787 899 6162. Nice gardens, near the waterfront restaurants.

Parador Boquemar, Boquerón, PO Box 133, PR 00622, t 787 851 2158, US t 1 888 634 4343, *www.boquemar.com*. A modern block in the centre of the town. The 63 air-conditioned rooms are fitted out with televisions and fridges and balconies that overlook the swimming pool.

Muelle Guesthouse, Av José de Diego, Boquerón, PO Box 150, Puerto Rico 00622, t 787 254 2801. In the centre of town, with four simple and adequate apartments and two studios.

Bahia Salinas Beach Hotel, near the Cabo Rojo Lighthouse, PO Box 1329, Cabo Rojo, PR 00623, t 787 254 1212, *bahiasal@caribe.net*, *www.pinacolada.com/abahiahome*. Lies in isolation and peace on the salt flats. All rooms have two verandas looking out to sea, from which to view spectacular sunsets. Now a *parador*.

Perichi's, PO Box 16310, Route 102, Playa Joyuda, PR 00623, t 787 851 3131, US t 1 800 435 7197, *perichi@tropicweb.com*. A most comfortable *parador*. The service is personal and friendly and there is a popular restaurant downstairs. Twenty-two rooms with balconies and a pool.

Costa del Sol Hotel Punta Arenas, t 787 851 5196. Eleven rooms decorated simply, with air-conditioning and TVs.

The Northwest

The area around Rincón and Isabel has seen considerable development in recent years.

Very Expensive

Horned Dorset Primavera, PO Box 1132, Rincón, Puerto Rico 00677, t 787 823 4030, *horned*

dorset@relaischateaux.fr, www.horned
dorset.com. This is the exception, and is one
of the most elegant hotels on the island. The
24 suites, most of which stand on the
seafront in Spanish revival-style buildings,
are furnished with tile floors, brass fittings,
louvred windows and doors, and four-poster
beds. The bathrooms are laid with marble
and each suite has a balcony with a view
onto the garden or to the sea horizon. The
main house has the grace and finery of the
old Spanish colonial days. Above,
approached by the 'embracing' staircase, is
the restaurant, one of the best on the island,
with chequerboard floor, wrought-iron
lamps and candles. Downstairs are the
classical balustrades of the terrace, just
above the waves, together with the rarefied
air of a country house in the drawing room
and library, where Proust and the New
Yorker magazine will keep you busy. Quite
isolated, but ideal if you're happy to lock
yourself away. One of the Caribbean's few
Relais et Châteaux.

Expensive

Rincón Beach Resort, Anasco, t 787 589 9000.
Family comfort in a laid-back style, with
landscaped surroundings.

Rincón of the Seas-Grand Caribbean Hotel,
t 787 823 7500, www.rinconoftheseas.com.
Visually stunning grounds and a grand lobby
on prime beachfront overlooking Mona
Island and the famed Rincón sunsets.

Villa Montaña Beach Resort, Isabela, t 787 872
9554, www.villamontana.com. Set along the
Atlantic Ocean in beautiful gardens and. Has
an impressive list of activities on offer.

Moderate

Hotel El Faro, Aguadella, t 787 882 8000. Large
and spacious with many amenities, well-
kept grounds and pools. Good food along
with friendly, efficient service.

Parador Villas del Mar Hau, Isabela, t 787 872
2627. Set on a beautiful beach; a good option
for the whole family.

Villa Antonio, PO Box 68, Rincón, Puerto Rico
00677, t 787 823 2645. North of Mayagüez
you will find this passable parador beach
hotel. The hotel itself is modern and air-
conditioned and the cottages and

apartments are comfortable if a little uninspiring, but they give right onto a fine
brown-sand beach.

Lazy Parrot Inn, PO Box 430, Rincón, 00677,
t 787 823 5654, t 1 800 294 1752, lazyparrot
inn@juno.com, www.lazyparrot.com. In
Rincón itself. Seven rooms, each with TV,
refrigerator and bath, and its own art gallery
selling local crafts.

Vistamar, on a hilltop off Route 113,
Quebradillas, t 787 895 2065, US t 1 888 339
6226, hotelera.naco@codetel.net.do
www.paradorvistamar.com. On the north
shore, a parador situated in a modern block,
with comfortable rooms.

Inexpensive

Ocean Front Hotel, Isabela, t 787 872 0444.
Well situated, overlooking Jobos Beach, with
cheerful, comfortable rooms and an eclectic
dining menu.

Sandy Beach Inn and Restaurant, Rincón, t 787
823 1146. Great views, friendly service and
good food.

Inland

Moderate–Inexpensive

La Hacienda Juanita, on Route 105, PO Box 777,
Maricao, Puerto Rico 00606, t 787 838 2550,
US t 1 800 443 0266, juanita@caribe.net,
www.hacienda.juanita.com. Set in the original estate house of a coffee plantation. Very
much a mountain and forest escape – no TV
or phones; 21 rooms, some with antique
furniture and others simpler, set in the
estate buildings around the main house,
where there is a superb veranda for your
meals and chairs swinging from the ceiling
for ruminating in afterwards. The hotel is
still family-run and the restaurant produces
some excellent home cooking – a really good
spot to relish local cuisine. Quite low-key,
with real isolation; there are about thirty
species of birds for the enthusiast to spot,
some trails.

Hacienda Gripiñas, PO Box 387, PR 0064, t 787
828 1718, gripinas@excite.com, www.
haciendagripinas.com. One of the loveliest
spots on the island. The inn isset in a
charming wooden West Indian house,
formerly the estate house of a coffee planta-

tion, built in 1853. There is a superb veranda overlooking the explosive tropical flora where you can take an early-evening cocktail in time-honoured Caribbean style. The 19 rooms are in the main house and an extension – many have the gracious atmosphere of the planters' days. It is high in the mountains and so it can get quite cold at night (the pool is freezing in the winter).

Casa Grande, PO Box 616, Utuado, PR 00761, **t** 787 894 3939, US **t** 1888 343 2272, *tarzan@coqui.net*, *www.hotelcasagrande. com*. Set on a former coffee plantation. The main house stands on the hillside with the wooden cabins on stilts containing the 18 rooms strung out beneath it. Lost in the rainforest, the inn is private and quiet, another good retreat from the city.

Eating Out

Puerto Rico, and particularly its capital San Juan (which is both a large city and the centre of the tourist industry), has a grand variety of places in which to eat out, with endless styles – Spanish, Chinese, seafood and *nouvelle* – and as many settings – sophisticated dining rooms, waterfront fish restaurants, milk bars and local *fondas*.

The hotels tend to have international and continental menus and, of course, as Puerto Rico is a part of America, there are endless burger bars. You will find the service slightly snappier than in much of the Caribbean. Restaurants accept credit cards and service runs at 10–15%.

Categories are arranged according to the price of a main course: expensive = $25 and above; moderate = $15–25; inexpensive = $15 and below.

It would be a pity to ignore Puerto Rican food itself, which can be quite heavy; the Puerto Ricans are hearty eaters. Main course is often a thick soup or a stew, such as *asopao*, which is made with pork, chicken or seafood. You also get a mound of rice in *arroz con pollo* (chicken or another meat with rice cooked in coconut). To accompany it, you will have *mofongo*, battered spiced plantain, or *arroz con habichuelos*, rice and beans (*cristianos y morros* are white and black beans). *Lechón asado*, roast suckling pig, is a popular dish

(and the best is to be had around the area of Cayey in the southeast), and otherwise seafood and goat meat are often used.

The Tourism Company has a system of recommended local restaurants around the country called *Mesones Gastronómicos*, at which you will find reliably prepared Puerto Rican cuisine.

Snacks are also very popular in Puerto Rico and you will see *kioskos* at the roadside all over the island (there is a string of them at the roadside in Luquillo). They sell a bewildering variety of snacks – seafood appears in crabsticks, or deep-fried crab with yucca which is then presented to you in a sea-grape leaf, and you will find lobster and chicken tacos. *Alcapurrias* are meat or crab fritters and traditional Caribbean codfish also comes frittered as *bacalao*. *Pinchos* are kebabs of chicken, pork or shark, served with a thick tomato sauce and a lump of bread. *Chicharrón* are pieces of fried pork rind like outsize pork scratchings. Sweet potato and banana are often fried, too.

Cheese is often used to best advantage. Try a *sorullo*, a sugared cheese roly-poly. *Picadillos* are meat patties and *empanadas* and *pasteles* are made with fried cassava dough inlaid with meat or raisins and beans. A locally brewed (light) beer is *Medalla*. It is always worth seeking out locally grown Puerto Rican coffee, which a hundred years ago was exported all over the world.

San Juan and the Suburbs

San Juan has no shortage of excellent new restaurants, many of them concentrated in a few blocks of Old San Juan, where they are housed in renovated historic structures that add to the charm of a night out.

Expensive

Barú, 150 San Sebastián Street, **t** 787 977 5442. Very popular Old San Juan bar and restaurant. Creative, non-traditional Latin/Mediterranean cuisine in an artsy atmosphere with hand-painted wall murals.

Chayote, 603 Miramar Avenue. Modern, warmly lit setting in the basement of Olimpo Court Hotel in Miramar. The décor features large chayote, a Caribbean vegetable. Caribbean and international fare with creative tastes and presentation. A favourite of San Juaneros.

Il Perugino, 105 Cristo Street, Old San Juan, **t** 787 722 5481. This award-winning restaurant, set in a beautiful colonial home in Old San Juan, serves outstanding Italian cuisine and a comprehensive Italian wine list.

Pikayo, 299 De Diego Avenue, **t** 787 721 6194. One of island's most elegant restaurants, situated in the Museum of Puerto Rican Art in Santurce. Food as art – Puerto Rican, American, seafood – by the island's most famous chef.

Compostela, 106 Condado Avenue, **t** 787 724 6088. Just south of Condado, Compostela has long been known as the island's best restaurant for Spanish food.

Tangerine@Liquid, The Water Club, 2 Tartak Street, Isla Verde, **t** 888 265 6699/787 728 3666, *www.waterclubsanjuan.com*. An avantgarde restaurant in San Juan's leading boutique hotel by the beach. Outstanding cuisine and dramatic presentations.

Ramiro's, 1106 Magdalena, **t** 787 721 9049. Offers 'creative cuisine' – Spanish and international fare delivered in neat *nouvelle* form in an elegant, carpeted dining room with wooden panelling, candles and mockantique chairs. The atmosphere is calm and subdued as you tuck into lobster in anisette and cilantrillo sauce, or buffalo, lamb and venison in a three-pepper sauce.

La Chaumière, 367 Calle Tetuán, **t** 787 722 3330. In Old San Juan itself, a small and attractive dining room. French cuisine, fine style and seamless service.

Dragon Fly, 364 Calle Fortaleza, **t** 787 977 3886. With the same ownership as the Parrot Club, and situated right next door, Dragon Fly offers a fusion of Latin and Asian cuisine. The flank steak is grilled and served with a timbale of banana and the lamb with a mint and pineapple mojo.

Ajilli Mojilli, Condado, San Juan, **t** 787 725 9195. An excellent restaurant for local cuisine, popular for its food and an edgily trendy atmosphere. *Mofongo* filled with shrimp or seafood, or chicken breast in an orange, lemon and almond sauce. The dining room, which is attached to the Condado Lagoon Hotel, is air-conditioned and modern and a

little characterless, and the service can be somewhat disdainful.

Moderate

The Parrot Club, 363 Calle Fortaleza, **t** 787 725 7370. A lively mix of Latin and American, in true Puerto Rican fashion ('taste exciting food, *charlar* (chat) and *tomarse un buen drink*'), in a bright yellow, orange and blue setting in the middle of Old San Juan. Seared *rodaballo* simmered *a guiso latino de almejas con longaniza*, potatoes and black beans, or *nuestra famosa* blackened tuna in a dark rum sauce and orange essence, *yuca mash y viandes*. Live music and a loud crowd.

Al Dente, Recinto Sur, in Old San Juan, **t** 787 723 7303. Set in a very pleasant dining room of arches, white walls and mannequins. The fare is Italian, including pumpkin linguini in basil and olive oil followed by *pollo alla Contandina*, chicken sautéed in white wine. There is a clutch of lively and good restaurants among the bars on Calle San Sebastian (*see* below).

Amadeus, **t** 787 722 8635. A relaxed retreat, with an arty crowd. Try the fried dumplings with guava sauce or chicken breast stuffed with escargots, mushrooms and parsley.

El Patio de Sam, **t** 787 723 1149. Another haunt popular with the locals, set in an attractive town house with a Puerto Rican coquí frog chirruping in the waterfall. It attracts a fun crowd, particularly at the weekends, and serves good food – lobster tail broiled or scampied, or *mofongo de mariscos*.

La Mallorquina, Calle San Justo, **t** 787 722 3261. Something of an institution in the city ever since it was built in 1848. It has seen generations of San Juañeros deep in political discussion over a meal (the broken vase in the corner is witness to a flared temper apparently). Nowadays, the visitors tend to be tourists and the service a little brisk, but you get a good local meal in historic surroundings. The house speciality is *asopao*, or you might try various seafoods cooked in wine.

La Casita Blanca, 351 Tapia St, **t** 787 726 5501. One of the most entertaining restaurants on the island. This is a brightened-up version of a Puerto Rican *fonda*, set in the *barrio* (the ghetto). You feel that you have come into someone's home when you arrive – you sit either outside in the courtyard, under the guinep trees, or indoors on foldaway chairs at tables with bright plastic table cloths. The waiters wear neckerchiefs and the place is generally hip. Appetizers – codfish or sugary corn fritters – arrive in a banana leaf and you eat them with *mariada*, a local mix of wine, rum, mavi and fruit juices. Follow up with goat stew or fish dishes and finish with coffee and their own additive (with rum and cinnamon). Well worth a visit for its novel atmosphere and some of the best local food.

Che's, Calle Coaba, Isla Verde, t 787 726 7202. A popular Argentinian restaurant set in a large dining room in Isla Verde: *churrasco* and *parillada Argentina*.

Inexpensive

La Bombonera, Calle San Francisco. The best café and a popular gathering point, particularly after Mass on Sundays. Past the pastries section at the entrance you can sit at the long bar on round stools or at the bench tables along the walls. Busy, and full of waiters in red coats storming around tending to singles reading the paper, doting lovers and noisy families. Try local dishes or an omelette, with superb lemonade served in crushed ice.

Café Berlin, Plaza Colón, t 787 722 5205. Part art gallery, part vegetarian café (plus some meat dishes); plenty of pastries and freshly squeezed juices.

Butterfly People, Calle Fortaleza, t 723 2432. After inspecting the butterfly designs, you can grab a salad or a grilled platter in a courtyard hung with greenery.

Hard Rock Café. There's even one of these, set around a charming San Juañero courtyard, if that's your thing.

Around the Island

You will find good local *fondas* everywhere in the country, though they will not usually provide gourmet dining.

However, the Tourist Board sponsors a list of restaurants called the *Mesones Gastronómicos* which are located throughout the island. There are about 40 of them and they are listed in *Qué Pasa*.

Rosa's Sea Food, Fajardo, t 787 863 0213. In an ugly concrete house, but serves good local food – shrimp, crayfish as well as steak or BBQ chicken Rosa style.

Anchor's Inn, on the road to Las Croabas, Fajardo, t 787 863 7200. Don't be put off by the touristy atmosphere; the seafood is excellent (especially the fish soup) and the *mofongo* (mashed plantain with pork, lobster or chicken, served in traditional wooden goblets) is really rather hard to beat.

El Ancla, in the Playa area, south of Ponce, t 787 840 2450. You can eat seafood, including the house speciality, red snapper stuffed with lobster. *Open daily, main dish $15.*

Mark's, near the main city square, Ponce, t 787 284 6275 (*expensive*). One of Puerto Rico's top restaurants. In 1996, award-winning chef Mark French left a job at the nearby Hilton to start up on his own. Local cuisine takes on a gourmet air (try fried plantain *tostones* with caviar and cream cheese as a starter). Meals are pricey (around $30 for a main course), and it's a good idea to book, as the restaurant fills up with foodies from across the island.

Pito's, along the coast, west of Ponce, t 787 841 4977 (*expensive*). A waterfront restaurant which collects a lively crowd at weekends, when they tuck into seafood and Spanish fare. You can eat under parasols on a deck above the Caribbean Sea. If you are a seafood-lover, try shrimp in white wine sauce with linguini ($17). There's occasional live music to spice up the party mood.

Perichi's, Playa Joyuda, t 787 851 3131. North of Boquerón, a good seaside *meson gastronómico* with good lobster specialities.

Tony's, Playa Joyuda, t 787 851 2500. A little further on from Perichi's, has the reputation for serving some of the best fish and seafood on the island, though the service is brusque. *Main courses around $15.*

El Bohío, Playa Joyuda, t 787 851 2755. Also stands on the waterfront and serves local food and seafood.

Hacienda Juanita, a little inland, near Maricao, t 787 838 2500. A romantic old coffee plantation homestead, now a family-run hotel. Here you'll find really top-notch local cooking – the sort of home-made fare that doesn't make it to the menus of touristy establishments. The Sunday buffet lunch on the long, wooden verandahs has become a local institution.

Horned Dorset Primavera Hotel, Rincón, t 787 823 4030 (*very expensive*). For gourmet meals, undoubtedly the best place to go is this hotel's restaurant, which combines chic, heady luxury and laid-back charm. Menus change frequently, but you may encounter chilled leek soup, duck *confit* with grilled vegetables or a tangy lemon pie.

The Lazy Parrot Inn, Rincón, t 787 823 5654. Offers a tasty selection of grilled and barbecued dishes.

Bars and Nightlife

San Juan

Old San Juan's bars may be frequented by cruise-ship tourists by day, but they are more local at night when the San Juañeros venture outside to take the evening air in a promenade (or its car-borne equivalent, in which they cruise around, stereo blaring).

The liveliest street in Old San Juan (one long traffic jam in the late evening) is Calle San Sebastián, where there are cocktail bars alongside more raucous drinking and dancing bars. The larger hotels in Condado and Isla Verde have discotheques, sometimes cabarets.

Nono's, Calle Christo, corner San Sebastián. A lively crowd gathers here, many for beer and a game of pool.

Shannan's Pub, 496 Calle Bori, off Route 1, Río Piedras. One of the best bars in the city, an Irish theme bar with a very lively crowd at the weekend – videos, sleek chicks in black and cool guys.

Lazer Disco, in old San Juan. Brick and glass decor UV-lit, with salsa, merengue and rap.

Carli Café Concierto, 206 Tetuán St, Banco Popular Building, t 787 725 4927. Criollo food by day, Mediterranean and international cuisine at night. *Live jazz Wed–Sat from 8.30pm.*

Nuyorican Café, 312 San Francisco Street, t 787 977 1276. Café-theatre with live music, theatrical performances and poetry readings. *Live salsa band Fri nights at 10pm, Charanga on Sat after 10pm.*

Parrot Club, 363 Fortaleza Street, t 787 725 7370. Background jazz and gathering hole

for young professionals. *Live Latin music Tues, Thur and Sat 8.30–11pm.*

Pier 10, Fernandez Juncos Avenue. Entertainment complex with a club, The Maze, and large hall, The Arena, where young adults congregate on weekends to hear DJ and trance music.

Santurce

Plaza del Mercado, Canals Street. The traditional open-air atmosphere here attracts large crowds, particularly on Thursday and Friday evenings.

Ocean Park

Dunbar's, McLeary Street. A popular local bar and restaurant, especially packed on Thursday and Friday evenings.

Condado

Beach Bum, Ashford Avenue. A good place for rock, reggae and DJs, and just hanging out.

Isla Verde

Wet at The Water Club. Techno music for young sophisticates.

Club Babylon, Wyndham El San Juan Hotel. The best hip hop, house and rock for a dressed-to-the-hilt crowd.

El Chico Bar, Wyndham El San Juan Hotel. Salsa and merengue are featured.

Shots Sports Bar & Grill, Isla Verde Mall. Live music on weekends.

Tito Puente Amphitheatre, Hato Rey. A friendly, safe outdoor setting for jazz, reggae and other groups.

Luis A. Ferré Performing Arts Center, Santurce. Largest facility of its kind in Caribbean with extensive schedule of classical concerts, Casals Festival, pop music, Broadway shows, theatre and dance.

José Miguel Agrelot Coliseum, Hato Rey. New coliseum seating 18,000, hosting international performers.

Ponce

Ponce is pretty quiet at night, but some bars are worth a detour.

Paradise Café, Calle Major. Live music at the weekend.

Café 149, Paseo Arias. A pool bar and drinker's hangout.

There is usually a ranger's hut in the parks, where you might get information to help you get the best out of the natural life. Their services are free of charge. They also publish information (usually) in both Spanish and in English. For more information, contact the Natural Resources Department, PO Box 5887, San Juan 00906, **t** 787 724 3724, *www.drnapr.com*. Information on El Yunque can be obtained on **t** 787 888 1880.

San Juan

The capital of Puerto Rico captures best the duality of this American-Caribbean island. Side-by-side here, you will see charming Spanish colonial town houses and modern glass-fronted offices, West Indian shanties and massive air-conditioned tourist hotels.

Since it was founded in 1520, San Juan has expanded from a little collection of shacks huddled together for protection near the point at El Morro into a massive metropolis. It crept along the peninsula and over to the mainland and then splurged around the lagoons and beaches into suburbs, eventually becoming a city of over a million. It has its own university, a huge international airport and is the top financial centre of the whole Caribbean area.

The seven blocks of **Old San Juan**, which have recently been restored to their original state as an 18th-century Spanish colonial city, are one of the most charming spots in the Caribbean. Among the steep and narrow alleys, you will see the old gas lanterns and cast-iron balconies and louvred windows. The houses are painted in bright colours, cut with white door-frames and window sills.

The whole of Old San Juan is surrounded by massive defensive walls 30ft thick and studded with lumbering fortresses. *Garitas*, little stone sentry boxes perched above the sea, run around the town. The streets are laid with adoquines, cobblestones of a rich blue-grey colour that were brought out as ballast in the ocean-going ships. They speak of the days when the island was the 'Rich Port' of its name and San Juan a very wealthy harbour town. At its less crowded moments, the colonial city has such an aura of history that you might expect to see a bearded merchant or a cleric in flowing vestments swish past.

Despite its slightly tourist-precious air, Old San Juan is fun because it is also a living city, with banks and bookshops, business people and domino players, and when there are not too many cruise trippers around, it has real charm. After dark, the islanders promenade, and the bars and restaurants come alive as crowds of young Puerto Ricans loiter around the nightclubs. One of the most special things about the town are the inner courtyards: they are usually surrounded by arches and the internal steps are decorated with beautiful patterned tiles. Unfortunately, they are mostly behind closed doors; some museums and restaurants are set around courtyards and these are worth a look, but if you see an open door it is well worth the risk of peeking inside.

On the western point of the peninsula is **San Felipe del Morro** (*morro* means 'headland'), a fortress and a half (**t** *787 729 6960; open daily 9–5, a small historical museum and video shows for the studious visitor; adm, children free*). Its walls, 20ft thick, rise from the sea to a height of 140ft, and inside it contains a network of tunnels, dungeons and bastions on six levels. On the uppermost level, the cannon were placed on runners so that they could get a better angle of fire. Construction began in 1540 and it was not completed until 1783. Sir Francis Drake was one of the first to attack it in 1595, and it was last shelled by the Americans in 1898.

One of the few buildings older than El Morro is the crenellated **Casa Blanca** (*t* 787 725 1454; *open Tues–Sun 9–noon and 1–4.30*), built in 1521 as the Ponce de León family home, which it remained for the next 250 years. It was eventually restored as a museum of island life in the early colonial days, with old wooden furniture, including a throne, and arms, not all original, but pleasant enough to view. Another is **La Fortaleza** (*t* 787 721 7000; *hourly tours Mon–Fri in English and Spanish, 9–3.30; adm free*), which overlooks San Juan bay from the top of the city walls. This mansion (the 'fortress' that was originally built here in 1532 as a defence against Carib Indians has long been swallowed up by plaster walls) is the official residence of the Governor of Puerto Rico. It sells itself as the 'oldest executive mansion still used as such in the Western Hemisphere', but for all the tourist twaddle, it is a pleasant visit to see the corridors of power and ceremonial rooms. Both have good gardens.

Another pillar of the Spanish establishment was **San Juan Cathedral** on Calle Cristo (*t* 787 722 0861; *open daily 8.30–5, Sun till 2pm*), a grand Spanish colonial church dressed in beige with white stucco and topped with three red and white cupolas. It was begun in 1521, but the first thatch-roofed building had to be rebuilt after a hurricane. There is a marble tomb containing the remains of Ponce de León himself, brought here in 1913. Check the mouth of St Pius in the glass case at the back.

When León's remains were originally returned to Puerto Rico, he was buried in his family chapel, the **San José Church** on the Plaza San José, a little north of the Cathedral (*closed for restoration at the time of writing*). The chapel is of medieval design, its domes supported by coral rock walls and Romanesque arches, and laid with ochre tiles. In the centre of the plaza, where young San Juañeros like to loiter at night, stands a statue of Ponce de León, built from cannon captured during an unsuccessful attack on San Juan by the British in 1797. Behind here is the old **Dominican Convent**, where two cool floors of arched cloisters surround an inner courtyard. Built in 1523 by Dominican friars, it has offered sanctuary to besieged citizens and pious besiegers (the Earl of Cumberland in 1598) and, until 1966, it was the headquarters of the US Army Antilles Command. Now, once again, it has a more peaceful mission as home to exhibits of modern art. Next to the convent on Calle San Sebastian is the **Pablo Casals Museum** (*t* 787 723 9185; *open Tues–Sat 9.30–4.30; adm free*), dedicated to the cellist who came live in Puerto Rico in 1957 – as well as hearing recordings of his concerts, you will see his favourite cellos. Close by is the **Plaza del Quinto Centenario**, an open square dedicated to the last five centuries of Puerto Rican culture. The striking totem pole at its centre, the **Totema Tellurica**, represents a soil core of Puerto Rican history. Just beyond here is the vast and surprisingly attractive **Cuartel de Ballajá**, a former military barracks now brightly restored to a more peaceful mission, as the home of the **Museum of the Americas** (*t* 787 724 5052; *open Tues–Sun 10–4*), which illustrates American culture over the centuries, and mounts other revolving exhibitions. A short walk away, at the corner of Norzagay and MacArthur is the **San Juan Museum** (*t* *787 724 1875; open Tues–Sun 8.30–4; recommended donation $1*), where there are exhibitions of Puerto Rican art and an audiovisual presentation of the history of San Juan.

Back in the heart of town is the **Plaza de Armas**, once the parade ground and now an open piazza with fountains and bandstands, cafés and department stores. Originally it was larger, to accommodate military manoeuvres, but it became San Juan's central square. On the northern side is the **Alcaldía** (City Hall), a copy of the City Hall in Madrid. Started in 1609 and completed in 1789, it has an attractive staircase and coral rock arches and was the nucleus of San Juan social life; now it contains a tourist information desk, a gallery and offices. Calle Luna has the oldest recorded whorehouses in the Americas.

Just south of here on Calle Cristo are two more museums set in San Juan's charming 18th-century town houses: the **Centro Nacional de Artes Populares y Artesanías**, with exhibits of island crafts (*t* *787 722 0621; open Wed–Sun 10–5; adm free*), and the **Casa del Libro** (*t* *787 723 0354; open Tues–Sat 11–4.30*) with exhibits of the art of printing and bookbinding, and a library of books, including some from the 15th century. The small shop is a treasure trove of unusual souvenirs, such as prints made with 15th-century woodblocks. Across the way, you will find the tiny, ornate **Capilla del Cristo**, where behind a grille a silver altar commemorates the apparently miraculous survival of a rider who supposedly plunged off the cliff on a round-the-city horse-race. You get a good view over the harbour and the city beyond from **Parque de las Palomas** (pigeon park, with special nesting holes), but do not go too close to the edge or you could end up in **La Princesa** prison, 50ft below. It is no longer a jail, but is used as the offices of the Puerto Rico Tourism Company.

If you walk down the hill beneath the city walls, you come to the dock in San Juan Bay, where the vast gleaming cruise ships tie up before they each offload their thousand-odd passengers. Behind the Customs building and coastguard station on the headland is **El Arsenal** (*t* *787 724 5949; open Wed–Sun 9–4.30*), the old Spanish naval base, where revolving art exhibitions are staged in the three galleries.

Back up top, Calle Fortaleza is full of shops and bars (one claims, erroneously, that the piña colada was invented there) and runs the full length of Old San Juan from La Fortaleza itself to **Plaza Colón** (Columbus Square), where a statue commemorates the explorer, at the entrance to the colonial city.

Just above the Plaza Colón, the eastern extent of Old San Juan is guarded by another fortress, **El Fuerte Castillo de San Cristóbal** (*t* *787 729 6960; open daily 9–5, tours in Spanish and English; adm*), a vast and lumbering affair worthy of its counterpart on the western point of the peninsula. Completed in 1678, it is a classic piece of 17th-century military architecture, with five bastions, each of which had to be captured before the main keep could be taken. Its 27 acres are a maze of ramparts, tunnels and arches, bristling with cannon, overlooking the Atlantic approaches.

Just outside the northern city walls beneath San Cristóbal, you will see another side of Puerto Rico. The rundown area of **La Perla**, with its wooden shacks and forests of television aerials, is an alter ego to neat and tidy Old San Juan. You are advised to be careful if you go there.

As you travel farther east, you come to a more modern Puerto Rico in the white, pillared and domed **Capitol**, the seat of the island legislature (Senate and House of Representatives; *t 787 721 6040; open daily, guided tours by appointment*). Started in 1925, the Capitol contains the Puerto Rican Constitution in an urn. Inside, the elaborate dome, friezes depict Puerto Rican history.

San Juan Suburbs

Soon after you pass the Capitol, the hotels and the expressways begin to appear and you cross from the peninsula on to the mainland. On the Atlantic waterfront is the high-rise **Condado** strip, where a range of humming factory hotels jostle for beach space, and fast-food joints and designer shops muscle in on Ashford Avenue beneath them. A few miles farther along the coast, through the continuing suburbs, you come to Ocean Park and Isla Verde, lines of luxury hotels and high-rise condominiums set on excellent beaches. These two strips are developed to bursting point, and you can expect canned music, cable television and Vegas-style entertainment.

Across the Condado Lagoon, where kayaks and windsurfers skim back and forth, you come to the business/residential districts of **Miramar** and **Santurce**, with the grand, walled homes of San Juan's wealthy. Among the industrial estates on the shores of the San José lagoon are the shanty towns where the poorest San Juañeros live.

Renovations in Santurce have transformed the district into an important centre for the arts. The **Luis A. Ferré Centro de Bellas Artes** is the largest performing arts facility in the Caribbean. Distinguished by sculptures and a large pavilion, the centre stages popular and classical concerts, dance and theatre productions. One block away, a handsome neoclassical building has been converted into the **Museum of Puerto Rican Art** (*229 De Diego Avenue, t 787 977 6277, open Tue–Sun, hours vary; adm*). The permanent exhibition showcases centuries of Puerto Rican art. There are changing international exhibitions as well as an outdoor sculpture garden and one of the city's best restaurants. If your preference is for contemporary Puerto Rican works, visit the **Museum of Contemporary Art** (*Ponce de León Avenue, corner R. H. Todd, t 787 977 4030, open Tues–Sat 10–4, Sun 12–5*), housed in a lovely two-storey brick building.

Following Highway 1 south out of Santurce, you come to **Hato Rey**, the business capital of Puerto Rico. On the **Golden Mile**, you will see the glass-fronted head offices of the corporations and banks that operate on the island. Nearby is the suburb of **Río Piedras**, home of the **University of Puerto Rico**, its faculty buildings scattered around the distinctive clock tower. In the **University Museum** (*t 787 764 0000; entrance on Avenue Ponce de León; open Mon–Fri, hours vary*) there are exhibitions of contemporary sculptures and paintings from Puerto Rico and from Latin America.

South of here at the bus terminal is the **Plaza del Mercado**, San Juan's biggest market, where tropical fruit and vegetables are shipped in from the countryside and stacked in colourful piles on the tables and where the Puerto Ricans haggle.

Further on to the south are the **Botanical Gardens** (*t 787 767 1710; open daily 9–6; adm free*), 200 acres that are peaceful and green after the mayhem of the city. Among the walks and waterways is an endless variety of palm (from the tall spiked royal palm to the scratchy sable), 60ft bamboos, an orchid garden and everywhere Puerto Rican lovers. The entrance is on the south side of the intersection of Route 1 and Route 847 (hard to spot).

West of Hato Rey (also a 75c ride on the ferry across the bay from Old San Juan), you come to the suburb of **Cataño** and the vast **Bacardi Rum Plant**, on Route 888 (*t 787 788 8400, www.casabacardi.org; open Mon–Sat 8.30–5.30; adm free*), where after descriptions and some family and rum history (you will learn about the Bacardi Bat), you whizz through the factory and its rich smell of rum and molasses. At the end, you can claim a free daiquiri, of course. On Route 2 travelling towards Bayamón are the ruins of **Caparra**, the island's oldest settlement, founded in 1508 by Ponce de León, but only used for 10 years before the pioneers decamped for Old San Juan. A small museum, the **Museum of the Conquest and Colonization of Puerto Rico** (*t 787 781 4795; open Tues–Sat 9–4; adm free*), has about as many excavated artefacts on view as there are words in its title.

Route 3 – East of San Juan

Driving east on the north coastal route 187 beyond Isla Verde, you come to Piñones, where there is a forest reserve in the mangroves with a boardwalk and a coastal bike path. Here you can hope to see herons (green-backed and tricoloured), pelicans digesting a meal and crabs holding their arms across their bodies as though they were broken. Boats can be fixed up at the Cangrejos Marina on the Laguna Torrecilla. From here, you pass palm-backed sand beaches and mangrove for 6 miles (10km) before turning inland and eventually coming to **Loíza**. The area has a strong African influence and is best known for its church, Iglesia San Patricio, built in 1645, and its saint's day festival, dedicated to Santiago Apostol (July, see 'Festivals', p.557).

Luquillo, 35 miles (56km) outside the capital, is best known for its beach, a mile-long strip backed with more palm trees, which is very popular with the San Juañeros at the weekends. Visible from the beach is the **Sierra de Luquillo**, a 3,000ft mountain range with a mantle of rainforest, where the Atlantic winds stack in vast rainclouds and then go at it hammer and tongs, dropping as much as 200 inches of rain a year. **El Yunque** (the Anvil) is a spectacular rainforest, where the air fizzes with mist and rain among 100ft trees, and exotic birdlife (60 species) flits among the perfectly formed ferns, scratchy sierra palms and the tabanuco trees, which seeps a sap smelling like Vicks (see 'Flora and Fauna', p.553). The rainforest is home to the endangered Puerto Rican parrot, and if the squawking was not enough, the forest also rings with the dual tone of millions of tiny tree frogs (*coquís*).

El Yunque is a popular place to visit and you can get information at the **El Portal Tropical Forest Center** (*t 787 888 1810; open daily 9–5; adm*) on Route 191. A number of concrete trails have been laid in the forest to give you a close-up view of the intricate beauty of the individual plants – tiny orchids the size of a cent coin – and panoramic views as far as the coast. The trails, which are well maintained, start from Route 191 or 186, and include **El Yunque**, **Mt Britton** and the relatively easy 8 miles of **El Toro**, also known as the Tradewinds. Take a pair of training shoes (or better) for the slippery rocks, and waterproofs if you do not want to get too wet. There are two waterfalls worth the detour, **La Coca Falls**, not far into the park and **La Mina Falls**, which are more remote (approach from the Palo Colorado Recreation Site). The locals drink the water, but it is better to take your own, to be absolutely safe.

Back down below the mountains, Route 3 continues from Luquillo Beach to **Fajardo** at the northeastern tip of the island, a sleepy town around a typical paved plaza. On the coast a few miles away (Playa de Fajardo), you will still see the town's traditional side – fishermen from the fleet of small boats selling their catch on the beach – but the bay between here and Las Croabas has also become a major tourist centre, with three marinas and ranges of villas perched on the hills above. You can hire boats to reach the tiny offshore cays where the snorkelling and diving are excellent. La Playa is also the ferry terminal for the islands of **Vieques** and **Culebra**.

At the northeastern tip of the island is **Las Cabezas de San Juan Nature Park** (*t 787 722 5882, weekends t 787 860 2560, www.fideicomiso.com; open at weekends only, unless you can claim to be a group; call to reserve; adm*), with the central visitors' centre set in an old lighthouse, El Faro (the park also goes by this name). It is quite tame; you are guided along forest paths and boardwalks that give you a close-up view of the mangroves. There is also a phosphorescent lake in the park which is well worth a visit (*see* 'Vieques', p.583).

Turning south, the road passes Roosevelt Roads, a former US Naval Base, **Playa de Humacao** and Humacao itself (turn off on Route 30 for a trip back through the mountains to **Caguas** and eventually San Juan) before it disappears south into the cane-covered hills to **Yabucoa** and the south coast. Arroyo, Guayama and Aguirre are sleepy, rural and waterfront towns where the old wooden buildings around the plaza have been encrusted with concrete suburbs. At Salinas, Route 3 meets Route 1, which continues to the city of Ponce.

San Juan to Ponce

Two freeways (tollway Route 52 and untolled Route 1) carve a way up into the mountains south of San Juan en route for the Caribbean coast and 15 miles (24km) out of the capital they meet at **Caguas**. Named after an old Amerindian chief, the city is set in the massive foothills of the Cordillera Central. From here, Route 172 switchbacks up into the mountains to be swallowed by tunnels of bamboos and ferns. Both the main roads cross the Panoramic Route near **Cayey**, where the land is dotted with small private tobacco plantations and drying sheds, and then descend to the south coast, from where they head west towards Ponce.

Back up in the hills on Route 153 is the town of **Coamo**, established in 1579, the third oldest on the island. The old church and the town houses of its former splendour can

Latin Heritage and the American Legacy

In places, Puerto Rico can seem exactly like America itself. Kids wear jeans, trainers and T-shirts and cruise around in large gas-guzzlers, spending their evenings in drive-in cinemas and fast-food joints. Buses cost a quarter, 'Exact fare only please'. The billboards scream at you – 'Buy Buick!' and 'Drink Bud!' – it's just that the models have Puerto Rican faces.

For all the superficial change, beyond the coconut suntan oil on Condado Beach and the glass-fronted skyscrapers of Hato Rey and the coastal factories, once you are out into the country, Puerto Rico becomes far more like the other Caribbean islands, and stateside USA seems to belong to another age. In the country towns, the islanders pass the time of day chatting on the plaza, surveyed calmly by the local church, or wait patiently to sell their fruits at a roadside stall. And in the evenings, they promenade and take the night air.

And for all the changes that America has brought, the Latin heritage also rings clear in modern Puerto Rican life. Besuited executives wilt as soon as they emerge from their air-conditioned offices, so many islanders prefer to wear the *guayabera*, a square-tailed, pleated long shirt. Cotton *guayaberas* are worn instead of a suit; pineapple fibre is for more formal evening occasions. You will certainly hear the bustling and compulsive rhythms of salsa blaring in the street and the macho poise and swagger is all too evident. The country is strongly Catholic – there are convents, monasteries and even one or two shrines where the Virgin Mary has appeared to the faithful. The Caribbean-wide desire for a jump-up expresses itself in the week-long *fiestas patronales*, in which each town celebrates its saint's day.

still be seen set around the classic plaza. There is a small **museum** in the inner courtyard of one of the houses on the plaza, with a display of family life a hundred years ago, but Coamo is best known for its **thermal springs** just south of the town. They were used by the Arawaks and are thought to have been visited by Ponce de León in his search for the Fountain of Youth. They became popular as a resort in the 19th century but fell into disrepair, and are now a *parador*, with the spring water brought to the pool at 44°C.

Ponce

Ponce (pronounced *Pon-tsé*, with pursed Spanish vowels) is Puerto Rico's second city and it is situated across the Cordillera on the southern coast of the island. It was founded in the late 17th century and is thought possibly to have taken its name from the first governor of the island, Ponce de León, or otherwise from his great-grandson (presently the source of raging academic controversy). The city may be only an hour and a bit's drive from the capital nowadays, but 50 years ago, the journey of 70 miles was daunting; the 200,000 Ponceños have always been cut off from the capital. They have a proud tradition (and an idiom of speech) all of their own and they refer to their city as *la Perla del Sur* (the Pearl of the South).

There have been changes, however, in traditional island life. The role of the family, traditionally an extended collection of uncles, aunts and grandparents, has taken a turn for the nuclear, and romantic old gents lament the demise of the serenade, impossible now that she lives on the 13th floor.

Another issue that has changed with the American presence is the feeling of being Puerto Rican. Perhaps more than any other American minority, the Puerto Ricans are Puerto Rican first and American second. In the 19th century, there was a strong desire for independence on the island, but this was killed with the uninvited arrival of the American army. The island was made a Commonwealth of the United States. The issues still remain – streets and plazas are still named after the Independentistas of the 19th century and many Puerto Ricans are voluble in political discussion – but, with the easing of the relationship with the USA and the material benefits that the association has brought, the desire for independence has faded and it is hardly considered a practical solution now. In a recent vote, the Independentistas polled just 3%.

As citizens of the USA, the Puerto Ricans can move to the mainland if they want to (Puerto Rico is a crowded island and emigration acts as a pressure valve). There are large communities of Puerto Ricans all over the States, particularly in New York, where there are supposed to be more Puerto Ricans than in San Juan. Many of these 'Neoyorkinos', as they are known, maintain close links with their island.

For their part, the Americans have pumped huge amounts of money into the island, in investment and also in healthcare, food stamps, unemployment benefit and tax concessions. The island is strategically important and for years they maintained huge military bases there. Puerto Rico has some of the best schools in the Caribbean.

As you come to the outskirts on the freeway, you pass the old clapboard shanties alongside new residential villas, and a plethora of sports stadia and drive-in fast-food joints, eventually coming to the centre of the town, where the old plastered and wooden buildings are embellished like wedding cakes with streetfront pillars with recessed balconies, and intricate latticeworks of wood and iron.

Plaza Central

The heart of the city is the old Plaza Central, where the Ponceños gather by day in the shade of the neatly trimmed fig trees and promenade in the evenings. It is guarded on one side by the Cathedral of Our Lady of Guadeloupe, a 17th-century Spanish creole church (designed by Puerto Rican architects who had studied in Spain) with classical pillars and devotional statues, topped with rounded silver towers.

On the plaza is Ponce's most famous sight, the **Parque de Bombas**, a striking red and black wooden structure with towers and arched windows, which was built in 1882 for an agricultural fair held on the plaza. There is old fire-fighting equipment on display, including hand-pulled tanks, in which the water pressure was built up by the movement of rushing to the scene of a fire. Discover why the heroes of Polvorin were court-martialled. The **Ponce Museum of History** (*t 787 844 7071; open Wed–Mon 9–5; adm*) is set in two attractive houses that have been joined together on Calle Isabel.

The story of Ponce is told in Amerindian artefacts and its literary, commercial and agricultural prowess are illustrated in documents and pictures.

The renowned **Ponce Museum of Art** (*t 787 848 0505; open daily 10–5; adm $3*) on Avenue Las Americas has over 1,000 paintings and 400 sculptures on view (among them the best collection of European art in the Caribbean). The Puerto Rican artists exhibited include Jose Campeche (1751–1809) and Francisco Oller (1833–1917), along with Latin Americans Murillo and Rivera, and Reubens, Velásquez and Gainsborough.

Around the Plaza

As in many Puerto Rican coastal towns, the plaza is a few miles from the coast. On the shoreline itself is Playa de Ponce, a collection of old brick warehouses and more modern storage areas. The La Guancha Boardwalk is a popular gathering place with lovers and families in the evenings and weekends. From here, you can take a trip out to the mile-long Caja de Muertos, a rough and rocky protrusion a few miles offshore, so named for its coffin-like shape. (*For current information phone t 787 721 5495*.) It is a popular destination for a day out with the locals, for its beaches, reefs and guided nature walks through the island's dry terrain.

Like many West Indians, the wealthy Ponceño traders built their mansions on the hill above the town. The hillside community is called **El Vigia** (the lookout) because they would watch for merchant ships approaching the harbour, and no doubt any other interlopers who appeared. The outsize cross that dominates the town has replaced a wooden one that guided the ships to the right part of the coast. The **Castillo Serrallés** (*t 787 259 1774; open Tues–Thurs 9–5, Fri–Sun 9.30–5.30; adm $3*) is probably the most sumptuous of these mansions and now open to the public. It was built in 1933 as a family home (on the proceeds of the local rum, Don Q), in Spanish revival style (which has Moorish influences) in a grand hillside garden. A lovely indoor courtyard leads to a wood-panelled living room and library and an extraordinary medieval dining-room. Downstairs in the kitchen are the original fridges, stoves and massive sinks.

Behind the town is the **Tibes Indian Ceremonial Center** (*t 787 840 2255; open Tues–Sun 9–4; adm $2*), an Amerindian site discovered in 1974. An Arawak village of thatched *bohíos* has been reconstructed; as have some *bateyes*, stone-lined ceremonial grounds used for sports (using a shuttlecock or a ball), dancing and inhaling hallucinogens (cajoba seeds). Among the skeletons unearthed by the archaeologists were decorated ceramic pots, axe heads and *zemies* (ceremonial idols).

The **Hacienda Buena Vista** (*about 7 miles/11km north out of Ponce on Route 10; t 787 722 5882, t 787 284 7020 weekends; open Fri–Sun; they do not accept casual callers, so reserve; adm $5*) is a restored coffee and corn plantation from the late 19th century, a time when Puerto Rico produced some of the most famous coffee in the world, drunk in coffee houses as far afield as Paris and Vienna. You can see original machinery restored and working: pulping, fermenting, rinsing, drying and husking the coffee berries. The whole complex is driven by a network of waterways – collected from a waterfall at the top and channelled for 200 yards to the estate, where it is sluiced off to run the different machines (waterwheels, crushers and turbines). Not a pint of the water is wasted as it is all channelled back to a waterslide where it is frothed up and dropped into a communal bath, the 19th century's answer to the Jacuzzi. Among the exhibits at the estate house museum are a dripstone (to provide cool and clean drinking water) and stencils that were used to mark up the bags of coffee beans.

Ponce to Mayagüez on Route 2

The southwest coast of Puerto Rico is the driest part of the island, but inland the mountains manage to support coffee (now almost gone) and the traditional Caribbean crop, sugar cane. Route 2 follows the southern coastline, in the shadow of the vast Cordillera (past small fishing villages where the houses stand on stilts at the water's edge and vendors sell oysters at the streetside), and then cuts inland into the hills and the Spanish colonial hill towns.

Guánica sits on the waterfront among the cactus and mangrove forest. The beaches are placid nowadays, but they saw action in July 1898 when a force of 16,000 American troops landed there and began a 17-day campaign (called 'a picnic' by one journalist) that culminated in the surrender of Puerto Rico to America. Just south of here is the **Guánica Forest Reserve**, where ornithologists will have a field day, so to speak, among the rocky scrubland. The 1,600 acres have been designated a 'World Biosphere Reserve' by UNESCO and are part of the US National Forest network. The reserve is home to about half of the species to be found on Puerto Rico. Among the knotted guayacan trees (*lignum vitae*, a wood so hard it was used to replace metal propeller shafts and ball bearings) you will see bullfinches, hummingbirds and possibly even the guabairo or whippoorwill, a bird that was thought to be extinct for 80 years, but which was found on the reserve in the 50s. There are trails in the park and rangers to help you on your way. A popular day's trip off the south coast is to **Gilligan Island**, for the reefs and the iguanas.

Farther along Route 116 is the resort town of **Parguera**, which has sprung up around an old fishing village. It is a lively holiday spot, popular among the Puerto Ricans themselves, who have built cabins on stilts above the water, and there are many cafés and small places to stay. Just west of Parguera, among the coastal mangrove swamps, is a well-known phosphorescent bay, though reports say that it has lost much of its luminescence (there is an excellent bay on Vieques). Not far from this spot is the famous dive site known simply as The Wall, a relatively recent find which offers some of the best diving in the Caribbean.

San Germán

San Germán is the oldest settlement on Puerto Rico after San Juan and one of the island's most charming Spanish colonial towns. It had to be moved a number of times to be safe from the Caribs and pirates in the 16th century but it settled here in the foothills of the Cordillera in 1573. Today the town has 30,000 inhabitants and a university.

The central streets of old San Germán remain intact, running parallel and enclosing a series of paved plazas lined with trees, above which the old white colonial buildings stand proudly in the sun and the town houses from the coffee era display their elaborate gabling. The **Porta Coeli Church** (meaning 'Heaven's Gate', *t 787 892 5845; open Wed–Sun 9–noon and 1–4*) was built in 1606 by Dominican friars, and is one of the few examples of Spanish Baroque architecture in the Caribbean. It stands above the Parque de Santo Domingo, an old marketplace, and is approached by brick steps. Inside the wooden beams and ceiling are thought to be original, though the balcony is not. Statues and paintings from the 19th century are on view. It is really more of a museum of religious art than a working church, as Mass is celebrated only three times a year.

The Southwest

The remote Cabo Rojo district in the southwestern corner of the island is the driest area of Puerto Rico and has long been known as a vacationers' spot because of the beaches. Puerto Real on the coast was once the principal harbour for merchandise offloaded for this part of the island and it is still an important fishing area. The seaside villages here have an easy, holiday air and you will find stalls selling clams and oysters at the roadside.

Boquerón is just such a place. It is well known for its *balneario* (many say it is the best beach on the island) but less known for the **Boquerón Nature Reserve**, which includes two swamp areas, the Laguna Boquerón and the Laguna Cartagena. Boardwalks run through the mangrove, where you can expect to see plenty of birds sporting spiked haircuts and glaring plumage – including ducks, herons, pelicans and the purple gallinule. At the southwestern tip of the island, where there are sandy salt pans once used by Ponce de León, is the Cabo Rojo lighthouse, built on the 100ft clifftops by the Spaniards a century ago. This area was a favourite pirate haunt in the 17th century, used by the Spaniard Roberto Cofresi.

North of Boquerón, you pass the other resort town of **Playa Joyuda**, which is stretched along the seafront in a long string of restaurants and villas. There is a good beach just out of the town, which continues into Punta Arenas. Offshore is a tiny island, **Isla de Ratones**, nothing more than a beach and a few casuarina pines. It can be visited by arranging a boat in the town. Inland, Laguna Joyada is designated as a wildlife reserve. Continuing north, you come to Puerto Rico's third town of Mayagüez.

San Juan to Mayagüez

The north coast, running west from San Juan, is the most developed area of the island. Routes 2 and 22 eventually emerge from the sprawl of suburban San Juan and cruise the 80 miles to the northwestern corner at Rincón, bypassing resorts, towns and factories. They follow the coastal plain, 5 miles broad, in the shadow of the mountains – minor roads labour tortuously up into these forested hills of 1500ft, known as karst country, where the rainwater has carved a landscape of sharp pinnacles and caverns out of the limestone rock.

Bayamón has been all but swallowed up by the ever-encroaching San Juan, but it seems that modernity has already arrived anyway in the form of shopping malls and the Alcaldía, a massive space-age construction of glass and yellow beams that seemingly hovers above the road. One of the island's finest artists, Francisco Oller (1883–1917), came from here. Local arts and crafts are on show at the **Museo Francisco Oller** in the old Alcaldía (*open Mon–Fri 8–4*), along with Arawak figurines.

The beaches around **Dorado** have been developed as a tourist resort – the ¼ mile waterslide at Cerromar being the next most appealing feature after the sand – though the town itself retains something of the sedated feel it had before the tourists arrived. Farther down the coast, by 15 miles (24km), Vega Baja is set among fertile grounds that once riffled with sugar cane.

Arecibo, set on a bay 50 miles west of San Juan, was founded in the late 16th century and is now home to about 80,000 people. It was named after an Arawak Indian chief, Aracibo, whose tribe used a cave, the **Cueva del Indio**, a few miles west of the town, for their ceremonies. There are petroglyphs visible on the cave walls. Arecibo is one of the industrial centres of Puerto Rico – pharmaceutical companies established themselves here during 'Operation Bootstrap', the American investment programme, in the 1940s.

In the mountains 15 miles (24km) south of the town is the **Arecibo Observatory** (Interactive Visitor Center, *t 787 878 2612; open Wed–Fri 12–4, Sat–Sun 9–4; adm*), which houses the largest radio telescope in the world – a 20-acre dish that fits neatly into a karst sinkhole 1,300ft across, the sort of place where James Bond might end up on a bad day (in fact, he did in one film). Radar and radio waves bounce off the dish and are collected by the huge triangular measuring gear slung 600ft above the bowl, and then analyzed by the batteries of computers in the buildings nearby. The observatory, run by Cornell University, was responsible for discovering, among other things, the first pulsars and quasars.

Route 10 leads across the island to Ponce via Utuado and Adjuntas, the heartland of the *jíbaro*, the self-reliant Puerto Rican farmer who cuts a living out of the mountains and cultivates the fertile ground of the rainforest. About 8 miles (13km) west of Utuado is the **Caguana Indian Ceremonial Park and museum** (*t 787 894 7300; open daily 8.30–4.30; adm free*), towered over by mountain peaks. The stone-lined playing fields (called *bateyes*) were built about 800 years ago by the Arawaks for their ballgames and religious ceremonies. It is a bit sad and empty because the activity is long gone, but the gardens are pleasant to walk in.

For a close up of the **karst country**, a sea of forested cones, take the minor roads south and west of Arecibo to the forest reserves of **Río Abajo** on Route 621, where you will see the forest at its richest (you can also get a boat trip on **Lago Dos Bocas** from nearby) and to **Lago Guajataca**, on Route 446 to the west.

The karst cones are mirrored below ground by a series of sinkholes and caverns. The limestone base of this area has been eroded over the millennia by acidic water, and all the dripping has created stalactites, stalagmites and caves. Rivers emerge momentarily in the base of a sinkhole and then disappear again underground. It is one of the largest cave systems in the Americas.

The **River Camuy Cave Park** (*t 787 898 3100; open Wed–Sun 8.30–3.30; adm $10*), on Route 129, puts all of this on view in a regimented way, with bilingual lectures followed by a trip in a little trolley bus and then a walk, strictly monitored to keep you on the concrete path (you are asked not to touch anything because human oils quickly destroy aeons of work on the limestone by dripping water). You wind down the overgrown walls of a sinkhole into the depths of the karst to a cavern 170ft high, where mighty and bulbous stalactites continue to drip and stalagfruitcakes of goo below rise to meet them at a speed of about an inch per million years. You will see the 'witch', complete with a drip on the end of her nose, and you will even discover the secret of curving stalactites. The underground Río Camuy can be seen crashing through the base of the Tres Pueblos sinkhole. You may have to wait up to an hour for a place on a tour. The **Cueva de Camuy** (*t 787 898 2723; open daily 9–5; adm*) is a different venture on Route 486, where there are go-carts and horses to keep you amused as well as a cave.

The town of **Lares**, perched on the hillside at the southern edge of karst country, has a special place in the Puerto Rican soul. The *Grito de Lares* (the Cry of Lares), a revolt which many feel was the first expression of Puerto Rican national consciousness, took place here in 1868. When liberals such as Betances were expelled from the island in 1867 by the Spaniards, from their exile they tried to rally the Puerto Ricans. Their plans were rumbled, but they captured Lares and declared the Republic of Puerto Rico. Their first crack at independence was short-lived, because they were defeated the next day when they advanced on the nearby town of San Sebastián. The 'cry' is celebrated every year by *Independentistas* on 24 September. An obelisk in the town square commemorates the heroes of the revolt.

Back on the coast, Route 2 hits the west coast at Aguadilla, spread along the seafront. Christopher Columbus is supposed to have landed between here and Añasco on his second voyage in 1493. The controversy over exactly where continues, each town claiming the honour. The waves can get up in this area and **Rincón**, backed by the massive foothills of La Cadena mountains, is a popular surfing spot. The world championships were held here in 1968 and 1988.

Fifteen miles south of here is **Mayagüez** (pronounced '*majjawezz*'), Puerto Rico's third town, an industrial centre and important port. Rebuilt after an earthquake in 1917, Mayagüez now has a population of around 100,000 and is dotted with modern blocks, but it still pulses around the traditional square, the Plaza Colón, where Columbus and the classical Alcaldía (Town Hall) face one another through the trees. In the outskirts, you will see the factories that process over 50 per cent of the tuna fish eaten in the USA.

The gardens of the **Tropical Agricultural Research Station** (*t 787 831 3435; open Mon–Fri 7–4; adm free*) are attached to the University of Puerto Rico and are sited on a former plantation in the north of the town, on Route 65. Tropical plants from all over the world are neatly set out. Check out the smells of the leaves – cinnamon, citrus and clove – and oddities such as the cannonball tree (with fruit like wooden cannonballs and yet the most ephemeral flowers that die at dusk), the Panama canoe tree and pink torch ginger.

At **Mayagüez Zoo** (*t 787 834 8110; open Wed–Sun 8.30–4; adm*) a little north of town on Route 108, the animals' compounds are laid out in a garden of tropical exuberance. There is a new open compound for African animals; other sections were being renovated at the time of writing.

La Ruta Panoramica – West to East

The Panoramic Route follows a tortuous path along the chain of mountains in the Cordillera Central, running for a hundred miles (as the crow flies, though he might have some difficulty over these mountains). Starting at Mayagüez, the road climbs quickly into the hills, often touching heights of 3,000ft and passing close to the island's highest peak, the Cerro de Punta. It crosses the main San Juan–Ponce road near Cayey and then descends to Yabucoa on the southeastern coast. The vistas are quite spectacular; with just a small turn in the road whole new valleys and views of the coast can open up. There are also some strategically placed lookout towers. Some days, you will find yourself in the clouds at this height, but whatever the weather, the flora is as exuberant and stunning as the views. The open road will often be swallowed up in a tunnel of foliage: strangled mahogany, bamboos, sierra palms, mango trees, coffee plants and 30ft tree ferns of luminescent green, as powerful a colour as the nighttime glow of the fireflies. The Ruta Panoramica is marked (though the route numbers vary along the way) and it takes a minimum of a couple of days to cover the ground at leisure. You could take far longer over it, stopping along the way at the mountain *paradors*.

From Mayagüez, the road climbs into traditional coffee country around the town of Maricao. The **Maricao** and (a little further east) **Mt Guilarte Forest Reserves** are two of the lesser-known and less developed reserves on the island, but there are trails that will lead you among the mahogany, tabanuco and trumpet trees of the forest (ask around because many are unmarked and you may decide to take a guide). Woodpeckers, cuckoos and hawks as well as the more delicate hummingbirds live in the luxuriant trees.

At Adjuntas, the Ruta Panoramica joins the main Ponce to Arecibo road for 5 miles (8km) before turning east to the **Toro Negro Forest Reserve**, where a path leads from the road up Cerro de Punta, at 4,390ft the highest peak on the island. On a clear day, you can see for 50 or 60 miles, beyond the coasts of the island. Unfortunately, you will find that you are not alone up there, because there are some communications antennae on the peak. Many rivers rise in this area and there are plenty of waterfalls and rock pools beneath them in which to swim. The Inabón River, (difficult to find; take ropes) thrashes out a ravine for itself heading south from the reserve. The Doña Juana Falls in the **Doña Juana Recreation Centre** are 200ft high. Most of the trails in the forest are unmarked and so you should ask directions.

Thirty-five miles (56km) farther on, you come to the towns of **Aibonito**, the highest town on the island, and **Barranquitas**, birthplace of the 19th-century Puerto Rican leader Luís Muñoz Rivera. The **San Cristóbal canyon** is a spectacular river ravine that runs between the two towns. Its sides are almost sheer and in places they plummet for 500ft, but they are still infested with tropical growth. There are two easy descents (though you will have to ask because they are not marked). From Aibonito, go north on Route 725 and after three miles descend on a path to a 100ft waterfall on a rocky face. Outside Barranquitas on Route 156, you can climb down into the other end of the ravine among the riotous mosses and greenery.

Not far after crossing the main San Juan–Ponce Expressway (Route 52), you come to the **Carite Forest Reserve**, a 6,000-acre reserve in the Sierra de Cayey, where 50 species of birds live, including hummingbirds and the Puerto Rican tanager. There are waterfalls and a small pool called Charco Azul about 10 yards across where the water is a strong blue colour. Just next to the reserve, high on Route 134, you will find a friendly mountain stopover and retreat at **Las Casas de la Selva**. The estate is on 1,000 acres of former coffee and banana plantation which has now been replanted with mahogany and teak in a sustainable forestation project. There are organized walks on old mule trails to rock pools, with guides to explain bird life and medicinal uses of plants, a library in which to chill out and some simple rooms. Ring in advance (*t* 787 721 3148). From here, the road descends to the southwestern coast at Yabucoa and returns to the tourist world at Palmas del Mar.

Vieques, Culebra and Mona

There are a number of islands off the coasts of Puerto Rico. To the east lie **Vieques** and **Culebra** and a scattering of sand-rimmed cays, midway between Puerto Rico and the Virgin Islands, to which they are geologically related. You can fly or take the ferry from Fajardo. In some ways, these islands are the best of the Spanish Caribbean, with undeveloped slow-time, Latin Caribbean life and yet with all the service and supplies of the larger island nearby. **Mona** stands out on its own, 50 miles off the west coast, halfway between Puerto Rico and the Dominican Republic.

Vieques

Vieques (pronounced '*Bee yay kess*') lies 7 miles from the eastern shore of Puerto Rico and is 25 by 5 miles, larger than Culebra. With 9,000 inhabitants and about as many horses, it is a good example of a small Spanish Caribbean island, easygoing and well worth a visit. The island's local nickname is Isla Nena, which means 'little girl'. There is an easy, unexpected tranquillity about Vieques – most of the time.

As for **beaches**, Vieques has some of Puerto Rico's finest. On a coastline of 60 miles, there are about 40 of them, which makes it all the more surprising that the island is not developed. The reason is a connection with the military, which appropriated the east and west ends of the island in the Second World War. The western end was used

Getting There

Vieques t (1–)

There are many daily flights from San Juan (both the international airport and Isla Grande), St Thomas, St Croix and Fajardo (from where the flight is good value).

Contact Vieques Air Link, t 787 741 8331 on-island, and t 787 722 3736 in San Juan, toll free t 1 888 901 9247, *valair@coqui.net*, *www.tld. net/users/val-air*; or Isla Nena Air, t 787 741 1577, t 1 866 208 1130.

The ferry ride from Fajardo, t 787 863 0705, is also very good value at just a few dollars.

Getting Around

Públicos will take you around the island, or you can go by taxi, t 787 741 2318.

For car rental contact:
Island Car Rentals, t 787 741 1666.
Martineau Car Rental, t 787 741 0087.
Vieques Car Rental, t 787 741 1037. Offers jeep rentals, too.

Tourist Information

There is a helpful tourist office on the northern side of the plaza in Isabel Segunda, t 787 741 5000, toll free t 1 800 866 7827. There is a website devoted to Vieques at *www. enchanted-isle.com*. You can also find plenty of information on *www.vieques-island.com*.

Sports

Snorkelling is best off Esperanza and there are reefs in Hidden Bay and Blue Bay. Scuba diving can be fixed up through Centro, t 787 781 8086, and Blue Caribe Kayak Center, t 787 741 2522, *bluecaribe@aol.com*. Other sports operators, most of whom do luminescent bay trips, include Blue Lagoon Kayak Shop, t 787 741 0025, *bluelagoonkayaks@aol.com*, and Aqua Frenzy Kayaks, t 787 375 2625. For mountain bike tours, contact La Dulce Vida, t 787 435 3557. Anglers should contact the Caribbean Fly-Fishing Company, t 787 741 1337.

Where to Stay

Vieques t (1–)

There is only one large hotel in Vieques. Most are guest houses or small inns, with personal service and an easygoing atmosphere, along with well-stocked libraries. If you wish to hire a villa, contact Vieques Villa Rentals, 494 Calle Gladiolas, Esperanza, Puerto Rico 00705, t 787 741 0549, *www.viequesvillarentals.com*, or Rainbow Realty, Box 6307, Vieques, PR 9019, t 787 741 4312, *rainbowrealty@hotmail.com*.

Government tax on hotel rooms is levied at 9% and service is usually 10%.

Luxury

Martineau Bay, Route 200, Vieques, PR 00765–9800, t 787 741 4100, t 787 741 4105,

for bunkering ordnance and the eastern tip, in Camp García, as a bombing range. When the US Navy finally packed up and left in 2003, the entire eastern side was declared a **National Wildlife Refuge**, creating overnight the largest wildlife sanctuary in the Caribbean; control was handed over to the US Fish and Wildlife Service.

Most of refuge has not yet been officially opened to the public, nor has the government revealed its plans for the future of Vieques. But that has not restrained speculation – helped by the lavish attention it has received in glossy travel magazines – that Vieques is on the verge of becoming the next hot Caribbean destination. Given its present lack of infrastructure and the very limited hotel base, the transformation is not likely to happen anytime soon.

A trip to **Mosquito Bay**, one of Vieques' three phosphorescent bays, is one of the most extraordinary sights in the Caribbean. The bioluminescence arises from a chemical reaction in microscopic protozoa living in the water, which glow when they are

US toll free **t** 1888 687 6044, *www. martineaubay.com*. The only upscale place on the island, set on a series of passable beaches on the north shore. The 156 large air-conditioned and glass-fronted rooms and suites are set in angled blocks that overlook the sea and Puerto Rico in the distance and they are finished with Mexican hardwood and elegant furniture – baths have a through view to the sea. At the hotel's heart is the Great House, with the main dining room, and next to it the main pool and grill restaurant. Other facilities to keep you occupied include a spa, children's and teens' club, weights room and tennis court.

Expensive

The Inn on the Blue Horizon, just outside Esperanza, PO Box 1556, PR 00765, **t** 787 741 3318, *www.enchanted-isle.com/blue horizon*. A delightful, very low-key inn set on a small cliff and the sea on the southern shore of the island. Their excellent dining room Blue Macaw (*see* below) is popular with visitors, but it is kept separate from the rooms, of which there are just nine. They are in the main house, which is covered in sprays of bougainvillea and in cottages standing in a grassy, savannah-like garden which look down to a pool on the clifftop. Very comfortable and quiet; a perfect, secluded escape.

Hix Island Houses, PO Box 372, Vieques 00765, **t** 787 741 2302, *hixisle@coqui.net*, *hixisland house@tropicweb.net*. Seven, individual self-catering apartments set in extremely stylish

buildings – bare concrete walls and magnificent views over the south of the island and beyond. An excellent retreat.

Moderate

Hacienda Tamarindo, Route 996, km 4.5, Barrio Puerto Real, **t** 787 741 0420, *www.enchanted-isle.com/tamarindo*. An informal 16-room hotel with an open-air dining room, which enjoys panoramic views of the Caribbean.

Crow's Nest Guest House, above Isabel Segunda, PO Box 1521, **t** 787 741 0033, *lizodell@coqui.net*, *www.enchanted-isle.com/crowsnest*. Overlooking the countryside, a friendly guest house, with 14 self-catering rooms in a variety of configurations and sizes around a modern villa. There is a pool, a bar with a view, and a restaurant which specializes in steaks and seafood.

Inexpensive

Sea Gate Guest House, above Isabel Segunda, PO Box 747, **t** 787 741 4661. Set in a modern house above town, there are 16 brightly painted rooms in cottages (some with their own kitchens) set in a very pretty hillside garden, each with tropical artwork on the walls and a view from their balcony. The owner is President of the Vieques Humane Society and she has a number of dogs on the property. Very welcoming.

La Finca Caribe, PO Box 1332, PR 00765, **t** 787 741 0495, *lafinca@merwincreative*, *www.lafinca.com*. Just six very simple rooms in a rustic wooden house set in a pretty

moved. They shine in weird bright-green whorls and clouds as you move through the water, or as you kick and splash. You will see fish dart away ahead of you (huge mantas are known to glide by, too), and if you flick the water with your canoe paddle, you can set off a bright-green arc of spray. Launch trips can be arranged (the motor makes an impressive trail), but it is best to go by canoe, which can be arranged through Island Adventures (**t** 787 741 0720, *biobay@biobay.com*, *www.biobay.com*), who have well-informed guides.

Beaches

Sun Bay, often written Sombe, just east of Esperanza, is the best known of the island's beaches and has public facilities. You can hire watersports equipment here and in Esperanza. Other beaches, many of which have taken on the colours of military-speak, are in eastern section of the island. Enter by the gate on Route 997 and

tropical garden high in the hills in the centre of the island. Very quiet and a young clientele. No phones or TVs; books and mountain-biking instead.

Tradewinds, Esperanza, PO Box 1012, **t** 787 741 8666, *tradewns@coqui.net*, *www.enchanted-isle.com/tradewinds*. The nicest inn in Esperanza, with 11 rooms, each with terra-cotta floors and decorated with bright floral furnishings.

Posada Vistamar, Esperanza, **t** 787 741 8716. Five simple rooms, both air-conditioned and fan-ventilated; also good local fare in the dining room.

Le Chateau Esperanza, Calle Robles, Esperanza, **t** 787 741 8722. Aka Chateau Relaxo, very simple rooms in a large concrete building at the back of town.

Eating Out

Expensive

Blue Macaw, at the Inn on the Blue Horizon just out of Esperanza, **t** 787 741 3318. Fine 'World' cuisine is served on a balcony decorated in tropical colours, attached to a villa with a view down to the sea. Leaning towards fresh seafood. Start with black-pepper-seared sea scallops or jumbo blue crab in fresh lemon and garlic and follow with a tandoor-seasoned chicken with caramelized leeks and noodles, or a roasted sea bass fillet with mango-coconut crêpes.

Café Media Luna, 351 Antonio G. Mellado, Isabel Segunda, **t** 787 741 2594. Well-hip two-storey cafe and bar on a street corner in the heart of town. Lots of Latin music and jazz, occasional concerts. Dishes from all over: Thai shrimp in coconut ginger sauce with steamed sticky rice or a seared duck breast in orange dust.

Moderate–Inexpensive

Bananas, along the Malecon across from the waterfront, Esperanza, **t** 787 741 8700. A busy and cheery joint set on a pretty fairy-lit terrace on the street front so you can watch the world pass by, with caesar salads, grilled fish, burgers and steaks.

Chez Shack, in the back country on Route 995, **t** 787 741 2175. Simple setting with a tin roof and concrete floor dressed up with pink and electric green paint. Gets wild on their busy night – BBQ and live music

The Patio, on the main road leading west out of Isabel Segunda, **t** 787 741 6381. Hardcore Puerto Rican fare served indoors or out on a terrace right by the traffic (the only place to be for the local Viequenses). Shrimp, fish or chicken, with bashed plantains and peas and rice.

The Trade Winds, 107-C Flamboyan St, Esperanza, **t** 787 741 8666. Seafood and American favourites.

Posada Vista Mar, Esperanza. Simple but good fish and local food.

Taverna Espanola, Isabel Segunda. Simple décor, good paella and *asopao*.

you will come to a sign to **Red Beach** – roads lead off this to **Barracuda** and **García** beaches – and then half a mile beyond here, you will come to a turning leading to the best beach on the island, **Secret** or **Hidden Beach**. Farther on is a cracking bay called **Blue Beach**. Finally, in the far northwest of the island is another good beach, **Green Bay**, which is approached by the airport road.

Around the Island

The main town (and ferry arrival point) is **Isabel Segunda**, on the north coast, a typically pleasant and dozy Latin Caribbean town with just a few nice old buildings with small verandas and tall, louvred doors. On the plaza is a bust of Simon Bolivar, El Libertador, who came to the island in 1816. Overlooking the town is a fort, the last built (unfinished) by the Spaniards, in 1843, and restored to its intended original state. It now contains a **museum** (*adm*), which exhibits moments from throughout the island's history, from El Hombre de Ferro, an 'archaic' hunter-gatherer who used no ceramics, through Taino pottery, with more recent examples of domestic architecture and artefacts such as an 8ft saw. There are photocopies of excellent old Caribbean maps. The **Punta Mulas Lighthouse** has exhibits of lighthouses in Puerto Rico, and some history, including Columbus and Amerinidan life, with some of their vomit spatulas on view. As you'd expect, the views from the lighthouse are spectacular.

Along the south coast, you will come to the only other settlement, **Esperanza**, a growing settlement of villas and guest houses. The main road, the Malecón, runs along the rocky shoreline, paved on one side and the other lined with bars and restaurants, where Viequenses and visitors can be found liming and taking the evening air. Beyond Esperanza there are a number of small hotels and guest houses before the road peters out.

Route 995 leads back to the north coast through the highest and greenest section of the island. It arrives at the airport, from where you can see Mosquito Pier on the northwest coast. The pier was built in the Second World War as a reserve port for the British Navy.

Culebra

An amoebic seven miles by four, Culebra rises lazily from the water in a range of low scrubby hills, surrounded by its satellites, a host of rocks and cays. Around them stretches a series of spectacular coral reefs. Life is peaceful for the 2,000 Culebrans, most of whom live around the main bay, **Ensenada Honda**, in the south of the island. On its western edge is the only settlement of **Dewey** (the name comes from an admiral who served here, but generally the town is known locally as Puebla, which actually means 'town'). Just a few wooden houses and the odd grocery shop remain among the encrustation of concrete. Dewey is none too attractive, particularly as so many of the newer houses are surrounded by large chain-link fences.

Like Vieques, Culebra used to occupied by the US Navy, but they left in 1975. Not a lot happens on the island now: a few fishermen work from the bays, there are a few small hotels and guest houses, and once-domestic animals wander around the scrub. One of the main excitements is the arrival of the ferry. There is a sleepy atmosphere; it's a tropical island idyll, Spanish-style.

Seeking out the **wildlife** can be rewarding. Four species of sea turtle come to the beaches to nest – they crawl up the sand at night, dig a hole with their back flippers in which they lay their eggs, and then scoop the sand back over them before disappearing back into the sea. You might have to stay up most of the night, but if you get a chance to see the giant leatherback laying its eggs between April and July, it is well worth it. The best beaches are Resaca and Brava on the north shore. Talk to the watersports shops to arrange a guide. In the flatlands around the coast and the mangrove swamps, you might come across such characters as the sandwich tern or the black-and-white sooty tern, the red-billed tropicbird or red-footed booby. Culebra has an

Getting There and Around

Culebra t (1–)

The 'sporting' runway at Culebra is served by the same **airlines** that serve Vieques, but also try the locally based charter Air Culebra, **t** 787 268 6951, US **t** 1 888 967 6623, *airculebra@sprynet.com*, *www.airculebra.com*. **Car rentals** are available with Coral Reef Car Rental, **t** 787 742 0055, and Jerry's Jeeps, **t** 787 742 0587. Publico vans are available also.

Tourist Information

Information and assistance can be obtained from the Tourist Office in the Alcaldía (Town Hall) in Dewey. There is a website devoted to the island at *www.culebra-island.com*. The town does come alive once a year, during the *fiesta patronal* on 17 July.

Watersports

A few watersports (**windsurfing**, **sailing** and **snorkelling**) can be arranged through Ocean Safari, **t** 787 379 1973, who run day trips to secluded beaches. *Tanamá* is a glass-bottom boat, **t** 787 505 6776, *tanama@culebra-island.com*. **Diving** among the excellent coral reefs, where deep-blue angelfish glide and groupers pout, can be fixed up through the Culebra Divers, **t** 787 742 0803, *www.culebradivers.com*, and Culebra Dive Shop, **t** 787 742 0566, *www.culebradiveshop.com*, which also has **kayaks** for hire.

Where to Stay

Culebra t (1–)

Club Seabourne, PO Box 357, Culebra 00775, **t** 787 742 3169, *www.gobeach.com/culebra1* (*expensive–moderate*). Fifteen brightly decorated units in the main house and cottages which stand scattered across a gently sloping hillside near the southern tip of the island. The central area is fairy-lit and has a screened-in dining room and a pretty pool deck. Quiet and pleasant atmosphere.

Costa Bonita Resort Villas, **t** 787 742 3000, *www.costabonitaresort.com* (*moderate*).

Culebra's new hotel is located on the bay and its balconies enjoy spectacular sunsets.

Culebra Beach Villas, Flamenco Beach, **t** 787 742 0319, *orlando@culebrabeach.com*, *www.culebrabeach.com* (*moderate*). The three-storeyed wooden-clad villa at the eastern end of Flamenco Beach. Comfortable rooms in different categories, all with full kitchens. Right on the sand, with a beach bar.

Villa Fulladoza, **t** 787 742 3576, *fulladoza@culebra-island.com*, *www.fulladoza@culebra-island.com* (*inexpensive*). Sits on the lagoon just outside town, seven units all with full kitchens, in two pink and blue buildings above a wooden deck on the waterfront. Very quiet, book exchange, phones, no TV, not even a bar.

Mamacitas, **t** 787 742 0090, *www.mamacitaspr.com* (*inexpensive*). A riot of pastel colours, sitting right on the Channel. The five brightly decorated rooms are comfortable. Right in the centre of town.

Palmetto Guest House, Culebra, 00775, **t** 787 742 0257, *www.palmettoguesthouse.com* (*inexpensive*). A private villa with five simple rooms downstairs, with private bathrooms but share kitchen and sitting area with VCR.

Eating Out

Mamacitas, Dewey, **t** 787 742 0090 (*expensive–moderate*). The liveliest restaurant on the island, with colourful tables standing under a tin roof on a deck right on the canal in town. Dishes are cooked fresh and rubbed off the menu when they run out. Jerk chicken or catch of the day. Mexican fare at lunchtime. Lively bar in the evenings.

Dinghy Dock, **t** 787 742 0233 (*expensive–moderate*). On a deck on the lagoon heading out of town, with the tables right on the waterfront looking across the inky-black water to the yachts. Again, dishes served fresh until they run out: sautéed kingfish *filet* or *churrasco* steak or pasta.

El Caobo, on Luis Muñoz Marin – ask for Tina's, **t** 787 742 3235 (*inexpensive*). Set in the backstreets of the new area of town, a classic West Indian restaurant, with a tin roof, trellis and a lino floor, TV wittering in the background. Rice and peas with chicken or fish, or steak with onion.

extensive wildlife refuge, which includes all its offshore rocks. Inland you may see a large iguana, a sort of 4ft armoured lizard.

There are some spectacular beaches on Culebra, particularly on the north shore. The best known of these is **Flamenco Beach**, a cracking strip of bright white sand set in enormous bay (now a Blue Flag beach). *Públicos* run regularly from town, particularly at weekends. There are some facilities and a camping area. Other beaches worth visiting are **Resaca** and **Zoni** on the east coast. You might also consider a trip over to one of Culebra's 23 satellites – **Pirate's Cay** in Ensenada Honda, **Luis Peña** and **Culebrita**, which has four beaches and a tidal pool for swimming in. Fix it up through a watersports office and remember to arm yourself with a picnic and snorkelling gear.

Mona

Mona Island is the remotest of them all – 50 miles from Puerto Rico and further from civilization; an oval 25 square miles surrounded by coral reefs which make excellent diving. Mona is administered by the Department of Natural Resources (*t 787 722 1726 on Puerto Rico*) as a reserve and is deserted except for passing fishermen and the lighthouse keeper. There are a few animals, descended from the stock once farmed here but now running wild. A number of tour companies organize trips to the island; try Acampa (*San Juan Metro, t 787 706 0695*) or Mona Aquatica (*Cabo Rojo, Boquerón, t 787 851 2185*).

The Dominican Republic

14

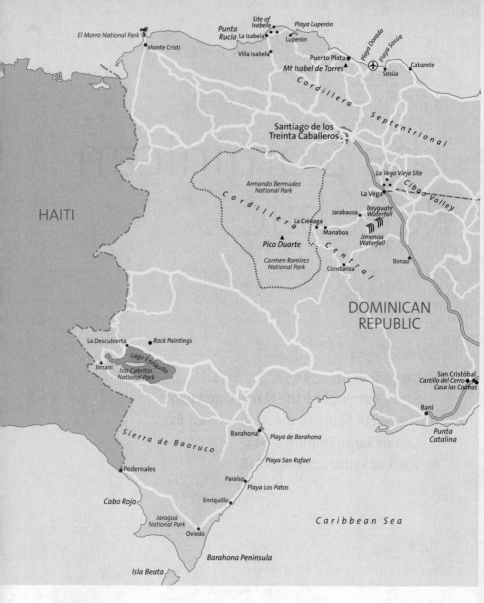

Highlights

1 Wander the historic district of Santo Domingo, the oldest city in the New World

2 Dance merengue with the Dominicans, if you dare, in any town on a Saturday or Sunday night

3 Take a trip to the Samaná Peninsula, with its superb beaches fringed by thousands of palms

4 Glide a windsurfer across the bay at Cabarete on the north coast

The Dominican Republic

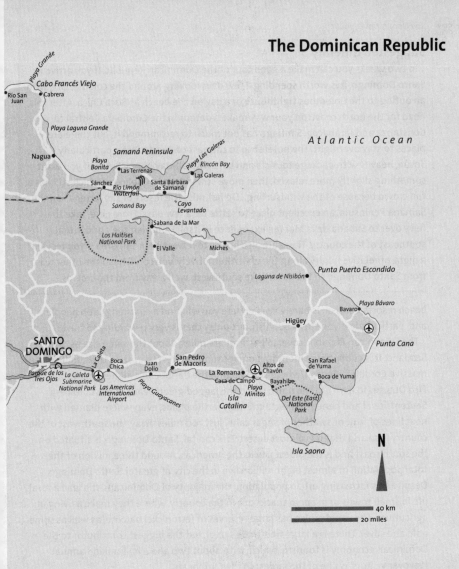

Hispaniola is the second-largest island in the Caribbean (after Cuba) and it is shared by two countries, each with a surprisingly different heritage. In the east is the Spanish-speaking Dominican Republic, a bustling Latin American nation. In the western third of the island is the press of Haiti, a country unlike anywhere else in the world. Here there are echoes of France, but also reverberations of Africa that are the strongest of any Caribbean country.

The Dominican Republic is one of the poorest of the Caribbean countries, but even a quick walk down to the Avenida del Puerto beneath the colonial city in Santo Domingo, where the Dominicans take the evening air, will show you that it is also one of the liveliest. The country is large, and so beyond the coastal encrustation of

Suggested Itinerary

In two weeks you can make a good tour of the Dominican Republic. If you arrive in Santo Domingo, it is worth spending a few days looking around the colonial city, with an outing to the Columbus Lighthouse or a day on the beach at Boca Chica. After this, head for the north coast: on your way make a detour in the Cordillera Central to Constanza and Jarabacoa. Santiago has not much to recommend it, but there are places to stay overnight. The hotel strip to the east of Puerto Plata, particularly Sosúa, heaves with package tourists and bars with all-day happy hours; if you want something slightly more relaxed, then move straight on to Cabarete (which still has a fun crowd because of the windsurfing). Do not miss the resort of Las Terrenas on the Samaná Peninsula, an excellent place to settle for a few days. From here, take the ferry over to Sabana de la Mar (an experience in itself) and visit the agricultural southeast of the country. There are also hotels to retreat to in this area if you feel like a night of relative luxury along the way. Alternatively, you could head the other way from Santo Domingo to the desert-like southwest, well away from the crowds.

beach resorts, tourism is barely visible. Here you will find a charming Latin people and, particularly if you speak Spanish, a country that is very rewarding to travel.

The Dominican Republic covers 18,750 square miles, about the same size as Scotland. It is cut by three mountain ranges running west to east. In the middle is the massive Cordillera Central, where you will find the Caribbean's highest mountain, Pico Duarte (10,417ft). In the north stand the jagged green peaks of the Cordillera Septentrional and beneath them extremely fertile plains, everywhere planted with neat lines of fruit or swathes of sugar cane. Just 100 miles away, the southwest of the country is so arid that it is almost desert. The capital, Santo Domingo, is situated on the south coast and is the oldest city in the Americas. Around three million of the total population of almost eight million live in the city of greater Santo Domingo. Despite this increasing urban population, the majority of Dominicans still lead a rural life in small towns or in *bohío* shacks out in the country, where they make a living in agriculture. The country also has large reserves of ferronickel bauxite, as well as some gold and silver. There is a large free-trade sector, but the biggest contributor to the Dominican economy is tourism, which, with about two and a half million annual stayover visitors, is one of the largest in the Caribbean.

The Dominican heritage is both Latin and Caribbean. The women are flamboyant and the men macho here; men will strike a matador's pose as a woman walks by, or maybe just grab her and dance in the road. Life is demonstrative and incessantly lively. Music is everywhere. After dark, the tree-lined streets come alive as people take the evening air and the portable stereos strike up with the latest sounds of merengue and bachata, the two national rhythms. A look at the faces will show what a vibrant and thorough mix the Dominicans are. In colour they range from white (about 15%) to pure African (about 15%), but the majority of the Dominicans are somewhere in between, and occasionally you will see clear Arawak Indian features. There is not much overt colour prejudice, but it is clearly a social advantage to have a lighter colour. There is, however, a certain racism against the estimated 700,000

Haitians. The prejudice goes a long way back and there is not much love lost between the two countries. Haitians are currently being blamed for bringing Aids and malaria.

The Dominican Republic is extremely poor (one recent estimate puts two-thirds of the country on the poverty line) and this is immediately visible if you venture beyond the enclave of the tourist hotels into the country or into the outskirts of Santo Domingo. There have been considerable efforts to improve island infrastructure over the past few years, with new roads and large amounts spent on the electrical network, but if you travel around the island you should still expect power cuts and water shortages (resort hotels tend to have their own generators). Many Dominicans express their frustration by trying to escape to the USA.

Visitors get a good deal in the Dominican Republic. Tourism is often package tours to all-inclusive hotels and they are considerably less expensive than on most Caribbean islands. As an independent traveller, it is possible to combine a tourist's beach-based holiday with travel to the towns of the interior to discover the flamboyant style of Dominican life. There are some surprisingly cool hangouts in the beach towns – Las Terrenas and Cabarete (renowned for windsurfing) – and some mountain retreats, as well as the small but attractive colonial glory of the oldest city of the New World.

History

Columbus discovered 'Quisqueya' on his first voyage, reaching the north coast of the island on 5 December 1492, as he sailed down from the Bahamas. He named it Hispaniola, 'Little Spain', and he chose it as the headquarters of the Spanish Empire in the Americas. On his second voyage in 1493, he established the first Spanish settlement in the New World with a thousand colonists. Initially, they settled the north coast (the foundations can be seen at La Isabela near Luperón), but the site proved to be unhealthy and so they moved to the south coast, nearer to the gold mines.

Columbus was not a great administrator and in 1502 he was recalled to Spain in disgrace, but his son Don Diego oversaw the expansion of the Spanish Empire from the glorious city of Santo Domingo. The conquistadors and colonizers set out from here: Hernán Cortés departed for his invasion of Mexico, Ponce de León went to settle Puerto Rico, and Diego Velázquez to Cuba. But as the gold in Hispaniola dried up and the mines of Colombia and Peru were discovered, Santo Domingo gradually lost its lustre. It remained the official capital of the Spanish dominions, but the colonists simply moved on and eventually the island was eclipsed, ignored by Spain.

In the late 1500s, buccaneers moved into the remote northwestern part of Hispaniola (see **Haiti**, 'History', p.631), managing to hang on despite repeated Spanish attempts to root them out. Finally, at the Treaty of Ryswick in 1697, the Spaniards acknowledged their presence and ceded the western third of the island to France. Over the next hundred years, Saint Domingue, as the French part of the island was known, became the archetypal West Indian sugar factory, the richest colony in the world. In the east, Santo Domingo languished.

It was the fall of the French colony that was to stir the torpor of Santo Domingo. In 1793, Saint Domingue was involved in a civil war as the slaves rose up in rebellion. The Spaniards stepped in on the side of Toussaint and the slaves, but then soon found

Best Beaches

Punta Rucia: In the remote area between the Haitian border and Puerto Plata, you will find secluded bays, close to Columbus's La Isabela. There are hotels in the area.

Playa Luperón: Better known, set on a wide bay with excellent golden sand and palm trees with a hotel to retreat to in the heat of the midday sun.

Cofresi: A mile-long strand with a number of villas, relatively untainted despite being so close to Puerto Plata. Visited mostly by locals at the weekend.

Playa Dorada: The beaches and hotels really get going as you head east from Puerto Plata. The beach in the town itself is disappointing but, three miles to the east, you will find a superb strand, now developed with hotels, active and busy with all the watersports. Officially the hotels each have their strip of beachfront on the two miles of sand and palms. You can negotiate with the concessionaires for a windsurfer or a waterskiing trip.

Playa Sosúa: A crescent curve of mounded white sand brushed by more palms. It is a very busy beach and, inevitably, you will be accosted to buy a wood carving, a T-shirt or any number of other exotic services. There are bars around the whole length of the beach. Watersports are available. There are other smaller coves with fantastic sand and less of a crowd close by.

Cabarete: Nine miles further along the coast, this is best known for its winter-season winds, which blow off the Atlantic with such force that they held the 1987 windsurfing world championships here. It is a very laidback and friendly town strung along miles of excellent, light-coloured sand, where you can hire a sailboard.

Playa Grande, **Playa la Preciosa** and **Cabo Francés Viejo**: Between Río San Juan and Cabrera. Picture-postcard Caribbean: white sand and palms and ridiculously blue sea. Facing on to the Atlantic, so the waves are big and the undertow is strong.

Samaná Peninsula: There are some good beaches here, though not many near to the town of Samaná itself. The best are on the northern shore, where they run seemingly endlessly east and west from Playa Las Terrenas. Watersports are available at the hotels. It is well worth exploring because you will find superb, deserted strands,

themselves without an ally as Toussaint switched sides to the French. In 1801 he invaded Santo Domingo and the whole of Hispaniola was in his hands.

In 1809, with the help of the British, the Spaniards conquered the Haitians in the eastern part of the island and the colony was restored to Spanish colonial rule. But, following the lead of other colonies on the South American mainland, the creole Dominicans started an independence movement to drive out the Spanish officials. In 1821 they succeeded and the eastern part of the island became independent. It was not to last. In 1822, under General Boyer, the Haitians in their turn occupied the new country, unifying the whole island under the name of Haiti. Some of the Dominicans welcomed him (slavery was abolished), but the occupation fostered a spirit of Dominican nationality and an underground independence organization, *La Trinitaria*, was formed, led by Duarte, Sánchez and Mella. In 1843 Boyer was ousted from power in Haiti in a coup, and then on 27 February 1844 the Dominican rebels took their chance, storming the Ozama fortress and freeing the Dominican Republic once again.

including Playa Coson (though it is slated for development). You can find transport in Sánchez. Buses run to Las Galeras at the northeastern tip of the peninsula. The beach is OK, and there are places to get a drink or a meal. The best beach in the area is Playa de Rincón, which is reached by boat from the town.

Cayo Levantado: An islet off the southern shore of the Samaná Peninsula, 6 miles east of the town of Samaná; take a boat from the quay (RD$100 return), or from the beach opposite the island. Watersports and scuba diving are available here and there is a restaurant.

Miches to Punta Cana: The beaches run in an almost continuous stretch, interspersed occasionally with coral cliffs. An occasional hotel breaks the isolation, but access to the beach is often reserved for guests only. The waves can be quite big as they come straight in off the Atlantic, so be careful when you swim but, if you want untouched sands to walk, you will find 20 miles of them here.

Bayahibe Beach: A strip of stunning white sand lapped with gentle waves and fringed with palms, with bar and restaurant for a drink when the going gets too hot.

Playa Catalina: A fantastic beach on an uninhabited island offshore opposite La Romana. Trips (*expensive*), which include a visit to a natural, sand-bottomed swimming pool in the sea on the way, are easily arranged.

Embassy Beach: In Juan Dolio, with palms and snack bars and waves that roar in between two arms of coral rock.

Playa Guayacanes: Gentler, quieter spot where there is a hotel and restaurant to retreat to.

Boca Chica: About 20 miles east of Santo Domingo, this is the busiest of all the beaches, particularly at the weekends when Dominicans stream out of the capital. It is noisy, with hundreds of portable stereos blaring out the latest merengue.

Playa Los Patos and **Playa San Rafael**: West of Santo Domingo beaches are few. The coastline is mostly rocky till the Barahona Peninsula, where the white sands resume.

Eagles Bay Beach: An excellent beach with no development in the far southwest in the Jaragua National Park.

This early independence set the pattern for Dominican politics, which have swung between a state of ineffective liberal democracy and the extreme of repressive dictatorship. During the latter periods, dictatorial rule was maintained by terror tactics; in the Trujillo era earlier this century, many died in office at the hands of assassins. In the chaos, the USA has decided to step in to maintain order more than once.

The Trinitaria found themselves ousted from power almost immediately in 1844 and for the next forty-five years the power swung between two self-appointed generals, Buenaventura Báez and Pedro Santana. Santana even invited the Spaniards back in to administer the country in 1861, but the colonizers were forced out in a violent campaign, culminating in the Restoration of 16 August 1865.

The Americans also were beginning to show an interest. In the 1870s, the US Senate failed to pass a bill for the annexation of the country by just one vote. By 1907, having reneged on its foreign debts, the bankrupt Dominican Republic was placed in the receivership of the USA. In 1916, after an invasion of Haiti the previous year, the

Some Advice

To get the best out of the Dominican Republic, it is essential to speak at least some Spanish. English is enough in the tourist areas, but if you go off the beaten track, you will find few people who understand it.

It is a good idea to lock your bags when you send them into the aeroplane hold. Once beyond the airport, you are unlikely to encounter any trouble. However, you will definitely come across hustlers, particularly in downtown Santo Domingo. They are persistent and quite persuasive, and have a whole inventory of drugs and services on offer. Most of them are also tricksters. If you want to be sure of a guide's reliability, go through the tourist office. You will not be hustled that much beyond the tourist towns, though you may find yourself surrounded by a crowd of inquisitive children. Unfortunately, travellers who venture out and about are at the mercy of unscrupulous traders and so you will find yourself outrageously overcharged for snacks, drinks and bus fares. It is, of course, haphazard, but this practice has become quite widespread over the last few years as tourism on the island has increased.

Do not drink unpurified tap water. It is quite easy to get hold of purified water in the main towns (most cheap hotels have it), but in the more remote regions, you will have to stock up. Drinks bought on the street are dodgy because they will not be made from purified water. Key words are *filtrada* and *purificada*. There are sometimes power cuts in the Dominican Republic, so you may want to take a flashlight or candles. Spare batteries are easily available. Remember that the water supply will probably be cut off too. Tourist hotels usually have their own generating system. Mosquito coils are available and make life a bit more comfortable. You may consider using a mosquito net (available in Santo Domingo). It is a good idea to have a room with a fan or air-conditioning in the summer months because the nights can be hot.

Women travellers may find themselves the centre of some macho attention, usually verbal but occasionally tactile. You are advised not to make long journeys alone or to go to the downtown areas alone at night. All white foreigners are *gringos* to some of the Dominicans, and so you may find that you get some odd reactions.

The authorities take a very hard line with drugs, and suspects are liable to find themselves in an unpleasant Dominican jail for a few weeks before they think about a trial (there is no system of bail here either).

Prostitution is pretty big in the Dominican Republic (there is considerable sex tourism) and so single men particularly will find themselves approached by *aviones*, as they are known (often with some pretty surprising tactile introductory lines). The country is very poor and so it is inexpensive. Apart from all the weird and wonderful strains of clap you could catch, the island is rife with HIV.

Americans occupied the country, staying for the next eight years. Some Dominicans resisted the occupation, but others welcomed the stability it would bring after years of turbulent internal politics. There were many improvements in island infrastructure – roads, schools, sanitation and public health – but there was a brooding political resentment at the military rule and eventually, in 1924, the Marines left.

Within a few years, another despot was in control. Rafael Leonidas Trujillo, the army chief of staff, had himself elected in a rigged ballot in 1930. His 30 repressive years in power are still remembered with horror and bitterness. It is true that he turned the economy round to begin with, but the price was ruthless dictatorship. The country became his personal fiefdom, a police state. Trujillo himself was responsible for the disappearance of thousands of people. He renamed Santo Domingo Ciudad Trujillo in his own honour, and helped himself to a personal fortune estimated at one billion dollars. Finally, in 1961, he was assassinated and the country was plunged into chaos. Fearful of another Cuba, the Americans took it upon themselves to invade again in 1965.

Next year, Joaquín Balaguer, once a moderate associate of Trujillo, was overwhelmingly elected President in what seemed like a vote for peace. He was re-elected twice, but was ousted in the elections of 1978 (only after he returned ballot boxes that had been stolen, under pressure from the USA). He was elected once again in 1994, taking his sixth presidency at the age of 86. He even stood for election again in 2000, as a blind nonagenarian, but although he was respected, he was by then regarded as too old. As in many Caribbean islands, politics is a source of considerable dispute and sometimes erupts into violence in the streets, so it is best to avoid the cities in the run-up to election time, occurring once every four years. The last elections were held in August 2004 and were won by the Dominican Liberation Party (PLD). The president of the country is Leonel Fernandez.

The economy of the Dominican Republic is based on the export of nickel, bauxite and gold and agricultural products including sugar, coffee, tobacco and cocoa and some fruit. In the towns there are many free-trade zones making clothes, shoes, textiles and cigars for the export market, but the largest sector is tourism, which has been the principal industry and primary foreign income earner since 1984.

Beaches

There are miles and miles of beach in the Dominican Republic, many of them developed with hotels or condominiums and with every conceivable watersport on offer, but in remoter areas you will find seemingly endless stretches of sand that are completely deserted. Beaches with hotels tend to be well-kept and sprayed to get rid of sandflies but, off the beaten track, remember to take insect repellent. You are advised to watch your possessions closely. See also 'Best Beaches', pp.594–5.

Flora and Fauna

The Dominican Republic has rainforests, lowlands, deserts and coastal swamplands (and at Lago Enriquillo, a lake three times saltier than the sea at over a hundred feet below sea level). On the barren ('bald') plains near the summits of the Caribbean's highest peaks, the vegetation is stunted, 'dwarf forest' of ferns and grasses, but this soon descends into pines and then into the dripping, tangled rainforest. Among the buttressed mahogany trees, infested with lianas and creeping vines, you will see rufous-throated solitaires, the greater Antillean elaenia and the Hispaniolan parrot, the green cotorra. Lower down, you will also come across the Hispaniolan woodpecker, a noisy character, and plenty of hummingbirds, including the Hispaniolan emerald and the tiny *zumbadorcito*, one of the tiniest birds in the world.

In the coastal areas, you will find many of the Caribbean's most elegant birds, including ibises, herons and flamingos and the magnificent frigatebird, as well as terns, todies – red and green plumage and a long, straight bill – and turnstones.

The National Tree is the mahogany, which you will see lining the roadside in some places (for example around Higüey). Other trees include *lignum vitae*, or tree of life, and satinwood, with a grain so fine that it is used in veneers. The coconut palms are endless and the towns are decorated with *ceiba*, or kapok, and many species of flowering tree, like the flaming poinciana, the flamboyant. The Dominican Republic has suffered considerable deforestation as people have moved into the hills to chop wood for burning and for cultivation. Efforts have been made to improve the situation.

Island fauna is more limited, though there are numerous reptiles, from tiny lizards crawling upside down on the ceiling, thankfully catching mosquitos, to iguanas and crocodiles. You might meet the odd vast spider, the size of a man's hand: a tarantula.

There are 16 National Parks in the Dominican Republic, the six main ones being the two in the Cordillera Central, Los Haitises on Samaná Bay, the Parque Nacional del Este (National Park of the East), Jaragua in the southwest and Isla Cabritos on Lago Enriquillo. There has been considerable growth in adventure and eco tourism in the last few years in the Dominican Republic. Entry to a National Park costs RD$50 if you travel independently, but it is probably best to go on some sort of tour. You are supposed to check with the National Parks office (*Avenida Independencia 359, Santo Domingo, t 472 4204*) and travel with an official guide. Alternatively, you can access the National Parks with various tour operators (*see* below, pp.600–601 and p.605).

Los Haitises is the second largest area of karst mountains in the world. There are excellent caves with birds and bats, mangroves and small islands and beaches. The National Park of the East is tropical and subtropical forest, with mangroves on the coastal fringes where endangered manatees and bottle-nosed dolphins live. There are trips to Saona Island, for the birds and beaches. Jaragua is remote and undeveloped, but has a large population of flamingos on Oviedo Lagoon. Directly west of Santo Domingo, almost to the Haitian border, is Lake Enriquillo, an inland saltwater lake about 21 miles in length and 90ft below sea level. In the centre of the lake is Goat Island National Park (Parque Nacional Isla Cabritos), a reserve that is designed to protect the native American crocodile. From the village of La Descubierta, the island is half an hour by boat and has 62 species of birds and reptiles. Companies that arrange tours to the National Parks include Emely Tours (*t 566 4545, info@emelytours.com.do, www.emelytours.com*).

Santo Domingo

The capital of the Dominican Republic, Santo Domingo (called La Capital by the Dominicans themselves), is the oldest city in the New World. In the early 1500s, it was the seat of the Viceroys of the Americas, replete with fittingly glorious coral-stone

Getting There

Dominican Republic t (1 809–)

By Air

The main airport is at Santo Domingo, about 18 miles east of the city itself (internal flights leave from Herrera Airport in the west of the city). Most of the charter flights (there are about 60 charter airlines in total) to the tourist resorts of the north coast fly into Puerto Plata or Punta Cana in the east. There is a departure tax in the Dominican Republic of US$20, which is usually included in the price of the airline ticket.

From Europe

There are regular flights to Santo Domingo from Madrid (with the national carrier Iberia), where connections can be made from the major cities in Europe. Air France flies from Paris and TAP from Lisbon.

From the USA

There are direct links every day to Santo Domingo, Puerto Plata, La Romana and Punta Cana from Miami, New York, New Jersey and other gateways (Delta, JetBlue, US Airways, USA 3000, Continental, Northwest and American Airlines), with connecting flights from other US cities. Other cities with direct links are Boston, Atlanta and Detroit.

From Other Caribbean Islands

There are numerous daily flights to Santo Domingo from San Juan (American Airlines, American Eagle, Caribbean Sun, and LIAT) and also from Curaçao (Aeropostal). Occasional services link the city to Sint Maarten, Martinique and Guadeloupe (Air Caraibes), Kingston and Montego Bay (Air Jamaica), and to Santiago in the east of Cuba. There are also plenty of links to South America, including Caracas, Lima, Bogotá, Buenos Aires and Chile.

There are direct flights to Puerto Plata and Punta Cana from Miami and New York, and also from San Juan (daily service by American Airlines). There is also a link to Grand Turk and Providenciales in the Turks and Caicos Islands. Santiago is served twice daily from San Juan and La Romana is served daily from San Juan, too, mainly for guests at Casa de Campo.

From Haiti

There are occasional flights from Port-au-Prince. There are overland links with Haiti through Caribe Tours, Av 27 de Febrero, t 221 8223, t 221 8225. The terminal in Haiti is at Rue Clerueaux et Gabart in Pétionville, t 257 9379.

Entry Regulations

Visitors from Denmark, Finland, Greece, Iceland, Israel, Lichtenstein, Norway, Japan, Argentina, Ecuador and Peru among others can enter the Dominican Republic on a valid passport and can stay for 90 days without a visa. Citizens of Belgium, Canada, France, Holland, Jamaica, Portugal, the USA, Germany, Spain, Canada, Switzerland, Netherlands, Italy, Poland, Portugal, France, Monaco, Mexico, Surinam, Britain and its dependencies must purchase a tourist card on arrival. This costs US$10 and is valid for 60 days (it can be renewed twice at no further cost). You must surrender it when you leave.

Getting Around

By Bus

The Dominican Republic has a very extensive transport system, on which you can reach anywhere from Santo Domingo within the day. At the top end of the range, you will get the pleasure of your own seat in an air-conditioned bus with Bruce Lee videos to keep you amused. Lower down the scale, buses can be a bit ramshackle and the sobriety of the drivers is not all that dependable. They tend to be fairly crowded, so you will get to know your fellow passengers pretty well. The back row of the bus, the source of all gossip, is known as *la cocina* (the kitchen). The other alternative is to travel by *motoconcho*, or motorbike taxi, which with their constant rasp are a prominent feature of Dominican life.

Within Santo Domingo (and other towns), the quickest method of transport is the crowded ***públicos***, or share taxis. Actually private cars, they run along the main drags, picking up and setting down passengers as required. Fares are 5 pesos generally. You can also take the yellow public buses that run fixed routes, also 5 pesos, but it can be a long wait as there are no schedules.

The cities of the Dominican Republic are linked by **coach** service, with up to five daily runs to the north coast by each company. Most routes originate in Santo Domingo. Coaches leave according to a schedule from a terminus, or the main plaza in a smaller town. There is a system of reservations, but this is not all that reliable. To be sure of a seat, join the queue about an hour before departure. In large towns like Santiago and Puerto Plata, buses terminate in the suburbs or on the ring road on the outskirts of town, but in smaller towns they usually stop in the main street.

Caribe Tours, depart from Avenida 27 de Febrero (corner Leopoldo Navarro), not far northwest of the colonial city, t 221 4422, Puerto Plata t 586 4544, Sosúa t 571 3808.

Metrobus, leave from the corner of Avenida Winston Churchill and Hatuey, Santo Domingo, t 566 7126/29. Has the smartest and most comfortable buses, with on-board snacks and videos (also in Puerto Plata, t 586 6161/6062).

Guaguas are privately operated minibuses which run between the towns, picking up passengers in the villages on the way. These are the loudest, most crowded and best fun of all, particularly if you join in when they sing along to the latest merengue and salsa on the stereo. You will see the best side of Dominican life here, cooped up with the shopping and the chickens. *Guaguas* run local routes and tend to leave when all the seats and any room in the aisles have been filled, starting about 6am and running until dusk and beyond. Out in the country just hail them down; in town go to the plaza. In Santo Domingo, buses headed west depart from the Parque Independencia, but most leave from Parque Enriquillo at the intersection of Avenida Duarte and Calle Caracas, north of the colonial city. Listen out as they drive around the square shouting for passengers. You can catch a bus from here to the airport. Fares are low: Santo Domingo to Boca Chica costs RD$12, to Santiago RD$55 and to Higuey RD$60. One problem with *guaguas* can be the drivers, many of whom drive as fast as their engines will take them and some of whom have been known to drink. Take your chances. Another problem, thankfully restricted to the tourist areas of the north coast, is an almost constitutional habit of overcharging foreigners (in places as much as five times what the locals pay for the same trip). If this annoys you, all you can do is find out what the going rate is before getting to the bus stop and then stick to your guns. Alternatively, practise swearing and cursing in Spanish. Between the smaller towns the local *guagua* will often be a pick-up truck, brimful of Dominicans along with their produce and animals.

By Taxi

Taxis are available in the tourist areas and at the airports. They are expensive in comparison with local transport. They are also unmetered, so be sure to arrange the price beforehand (rates are fixed in hotels, but you can bargain if you want). The going rate for a trip from Las Américas International Airport to downtown Santo Domingo (about 18 miles) is about US$29 (RD$870). Taxi firms include Aero Taxi, t 685 1212, and Taxi Anacaona, t 530 4800. *Motoconchos* have become a vital feature of Dominican life and they are popular as taxis. Fares are good, but you should fix the price before setting off.

Hitch-hiking

Hitching works adequately around the Dominican Republic, though you might be expected to sub the driver. Women passengers will often be offered the front seat. This is generally politeness rather than a way to get to know you better.

By Guided Tour

Organized tours will take you to all the recognized sights and beaches as well as for night-time excursions around Santo Domingo. Hotel front desks can arrange them for you (and you will be picked up there), or you can go to the tour companies direct. Contact:

Apolo Tours, Puerto Plata, t 586 6610, *p.brugal@verizon.net.do*. Guides take you up the mountain by cable car.

Caoba Tours, Puerto Plata, t 571 1530, *caoba.tours@verizon.net.do*.

Caribero Tours, t 686 3712, *www.caribero.com*.

Hola Tours, t 473 4323, *www.holatours.com*.

Metro Tours, Santo Domingo, t 544 4580, *metro.tours@verizon.net.do*, *www.metro tours.com.do*.

Outback Jungle Safari, Puerto Plata, t 244 4886, *rhino@verizon.net.do*, *www.outback safari.com.do*. You might try their tours for a trip into the country.

Prieto Tours, Santo Domingo, t 685 0102, *prieto.tours@verizon.net.co*, *www. prieto-tours.com*.

Tropical Tours, Casa de Campo, La Romana, t 556 5801, *ttours.sa@verizon.net.do*.

Turinter, Puerto Plata, t 686 4020, *incoming@ turinter.com*, *www.turinter.com*.

Car and Bike Hire

In such a large country, it is convenient to have the freedom of travelling by hire car. Your licence is valid for 90 days. Driving in the Dominican Republic is mainly on the right and can be quite an experience. In town, it is chaotic, with cars and buses nosing for position and generally ignoring the unspoken rules that govern driving elsewhere. On the country roads, it can be downright dangerous as all the same manoeuvres are performed at high speed. The main roads are good – most of the main roads leading to and from the capital are now toll roads – but in remoter areas, the surfaces will often be quite rough. Leave plenty of time if you are going off the beaten track. There are not that many petrol stations in the remoter areas of the country. All in all you might prefer to go by bus.

Insurance is not usually comprehensive and some companies will expect you to pay the first US$500 of a claim against you. Rates start at US$40 per day for a small car. You will have to leave a hefty deposit. Contact:

Avis, Av Republica de Colombia Esq. Monumental, Los Peralejos, t 331 5000, *www.avis.com*.

Budget, John F. Kennedy, Santo Domingo, t 567 0177, toll free t 1 800 527 0707, *budget@ verizon.net.do* (also at the airport); Avenida L. Ginebra, Puerto Plata, t 586 4433.

Dollar, t 221 7368, Santo Domingo, *www. dollar.com.do*.

Hertz, 454 Av Independencia, Santo Domingo, t 221 5333.

Honda, t 567 1015, *hondarentcar@ verizon.net.do* (also in La Romana).

National, Puerto Plata, t 549 8303, *national.dr@ grupoambar.com*, *www.nationalcar.com*. Also offices at the airport.

Nelly, 654 Av Independencia, Santo Domingo, t 508 0088, toll free t 1 800 526 6684; Av Santa Rosa, La Romana, t 556 2156.

Remax, North Coast Car Rental, Puerto Plata, t 571 2101, 571 2406, *remax.coast@verizon. net.do*, *www.remaxnorthcoast.com*.

Thrifty, Hotel Hispaniola, Santo Domingo, t 686 0133.

You will find it easy to hire a **motorcycle** or a moped in any of the tourist areas. If you do get one, be extremely careful to lock it up, and make sure it is kept behind closed doors at night. In the remoter areas, away from the most dangerous traffic, a motorbike is probably the best method of travel. However, do not take any risks with larger vehicles. Drive defensively and always be ready to get off the road should the situation require it. Usual hire costs are from at least US$35–50 a day.

By Air

Finally, another option is to travel across the Republic by air, since there are a number of airstrips around the country which are capable of taking small aircraft; in the western suburbs of Santo Domingo is Herrera Airport, t 567 3900, and there are also strips in Santiago, Puerto Plata, Cabo Rojo, La Romana, Casa de Campo, Punta Cana, Barahona and Samaná at Las Terrenas and Portillo.

Aerodomca, t 567 1195, *reservations@ aerodomca.com*.

Air Century, Aeropuerto Internacional de Herrera, t 566 0888, t 567 2705, *air.century@ verizon.net.co*. Small-aircraft charters.

Servicios Aeros, t 683 8020. Internal flights.

Bavaro Sun Flight, t 685 8101. Charters.

Caribair, Avenida Luperón, t 542 6688. Charters.

Tourist Information

Abroad

The official website of the Secretariat of Tourism is at *www.dominicana.com.do* while *www.hispaniola.com* has quite a lot of general information about the country. You can also find plenty of reviews of restaurants, hotels and tours at *www.debbiesdominicantravel. com*. There is a good regional website for independent travellers at *www.samana.com*. Also try *www.dr1.com* and *www.drpure.com*.

Canada: 2080 Rue Crescent, Montreal, Quebec, H3G 2B8, t (514) 499 1918, t 1 800 563 1611, *montreal@sectur.gov.do*;
26 Wellington Street, Suite 201, Toronto, Ontario, Canada M5E 1T3, t (416) 361 2126, *toronto@sectur.gov.do*.

Spain: Calle General Yague 4, Puerta 12, 28020 Madrid, t 91 417 7375, *espana@sectur.gov.do*.

UK: The Dominican Republic Tourist Board, 18–22 Hand Court, High Holborn, London WC1 6JF, t (020) 7242 7778, *inglaterra@sectur.gov.do*. Brochures can be ordered from the English section of *www.hispaniola.com*.

USA: 136 East 57th St, Suite 803, New York, NY 10022, t (212) 588 1012, t 1 888 374 6361, *newyork@sectur.gov.do*;
248 NW Lejeune Rd, Miami, Florida 33126, t (305) 444 4592, t 1 888 358 9594, *miami@sectur.gov.do*;
561 West Diversey Parkway, Suite 214, Chicago, IL 60614 1643, t (773) 529 1336/7, t 1 888 303 1336, *chicago@sectur.gov.do*.

In the Dominican Republic

The main tourist information centre in the Republic is on Avenida Mexico (at the corner with Avenida 30 de Marzo) in Santo Domingo, t 221 4660, *sectur@verizon.net.do*, where you will find helpful staff.

There is a helpful kiosk at the airport and offices are also found at:
Long Beach, Puerto Plata, t 586 5000/3676.
Santiago, t 582 5885.
Jarabacoa, t 574 6189.
La Romana, t 550 6992.
Higüey, t 554 2672.
Samaná, t 538 2332.
Barahona, t 524 3650.
Boca Chica, t 523 5106.
Santo Domingo's colonial zone, t 682 0185 ext. 1321. *Open 8–3*.

Embassies and Consulates

British Embassy, Av 27 de Febrero No. 233, Edif. Corominas Pepin, 7mo, Piso, Santo Domingo, t 472 7111.

Canadian Embassy, 30 Máximo Gómez, Santo Domingo, t 685 1136.

US Embassy, César Nicolás Penson in central Santo Domingo, t 221 2171.

Emergencies

In an emergency, you can contact the **Policia Turistica** (Politur) in Santo Domingo on t 221 4660 ext. 285/286/287, or Puerto Plata on t 586 2331. Few police speak English, and so if the problem is not urgent, it might be best to contact the tourist authorities/hotel.

In a **medical** emergency, there are 24-hour casualty rooms available in Santo Domingo, Clínica Abreu, on Avenida Independencia, t 688 4411, or Clínica Gomez Patiño, Avenida Independencia 701, t 685 9131, and in Puerto Plata, Grupo Medico Dr Bournigal, t 586 2342. A general emergency number is t 711.

Media

The Dominican Republic's leading newspaper is the Spanish daily *Listin Diario*. English-language papers include *Hispaniola Business*, the *Santo Domingo News* and *Touring*, which include plenty of tourist information and listings of current events. American newspapers and magazines make their way down within a few days and are available in the Santo Domingo bookshops.

Money and Banks

The **currency** of the Dominican Republic is the peso (RD$), divided into 100 centavos. At present, it stands at US$1 = RD$30 (about RD$40 = £1) and this rate makes travel quite cheap in the Republic. Most banks have exchange facilities for dollars into pesos. The authorities are strict about changing pesos back into dollars and it is not that easy (it is theoretically possible, up to a small amount, at the airports or at the Banco de Reservas in Santo Domingo, on presentation of a recent exchange receipt, and your passport).

You are quite likely to be accosted in the street by someone whispering furtively, 'dollars, dollars, I change 100 for 1500', and flicking through a wad of notes. The best advice is to say no: their rate is not that much better than the official one and you always run the risk of their sleight of hand and quick turn of speed.

Credit cards are widely accepted by hotels, tourist restaurants, travel agents and the car-hire firms. Outside these areas, you will be given a blank look if you flash your plastic at somebody. Take pesos in small denominations.

Banks open Mon–Fri 8.30–3.30, with an extra stint on Saturday morning for foreign exchange, 8–noon.

Museums and Churches

Most museums are captioned in both Spanish and English and generally admission is about RD$10. In certain places, as a mark of respect, men are not allowed to enter in shorts (at the cathedral, however, there is usually somebody on hand to lend you a pair of tracksuit bottoms for a few pesos).

Shopping

With a long siesta over lunchtime, shops open Mon–Sat 8.30–noon and 2.30–6.30. Dominicans will usually expect you to bargain, not only in the markets.

You can buy duty-free goods in US$ inside the free zones, some of which are at Las Atarazanas in the colonial district of Santo Domingo, Centro de Los Héroes and the airport. Goods must be bought a couple of days in advance; they will be given to you once you are past the ticket barrier at the airport.

Telephone Code

International and local calls can usually be arranged by hotel receptionists, but you may find it easier to go to the telephone company offices, open daily 8am–10pm or midnight, depending on the size of the town. Verizon is the most widespread. The IDD code for the Dominican Republic is **t** 1 809. Dialling into the country is far easier than dialling out.

Maps and Books

The Dominican Republic's most famous book is *Enriquillo*, by Manuel de J. Galvan, which tells the story of the Taino nobleman who took to the hills and waged a guerrilla war against the Spaniards in the 1520s. He is something of a national hero. Sumner Welles's *Naboth's Vineyard* (Arno Press; 1972) gives an excellent view of the country in the 1920s. Samuel Hazard wrote an enlightening account of the island in *Santo Domingo Past and Present with a Glance at Hayti*, published in 1873. Although there are some factual errors, it is interesting reading because it was written at a time when the Dominicans were considering joining the United States. A Dominican-American author well worth looking out for is Julia Alvarez, for *¡Yo!* and particularly for *In the Time of Butterflies* about life under Trujillo.

Festivals

As befits a Catholic country, many of the Dominican festivals are based on church celebrations. However, as well as religious processions, the Dominicans make sure to get a week or so's dancing out of a festival. Apart from the major dates in the Christian festival calendar, each town also celebrates the day of its patron saint (with an associated blow-out) in its *fiesta patronal*. These start with a Mass in the early morning and continue with street games, horse races and sports such as running and shinning up a waxed pole (*palo encebao*), even bull-fighting, and later dancing. In remoter areas, the celebrations can have a strong trace of Dominican *santería*, similar to Haitian voodoo, in which drums produce such a relentless rhythm that the dancers go into a trance.

January *Our Lady of Altagracia* (21st). Patron saint of the Dominican people, when Dominicans visit their families.
  Independence Day. Carnival parades.
February *Carnival.* Celebrated over the weekend nearest to 27 February.
April/May *Fiesta de Palo.* A big drum- and music-based festival, in which the *novena* is celebrated over the nine days that run up to the *Fiesta de la Sanctissima Cruz* on 3 May.
August *Restoration Day* (16th). Marks the Dominican liberation from Spain in 1865.

Fiestas Patronales

A list of the upcoming *fiestas patronales* can usually be winkled out of the tourist offices. It is well worth attending if you hear of one happening.

June Puerto Plata, San Felipe (5th).
  Sosúa, San Antonio (13th).
  San Pedro de Macoris, San Pedro Apostol (29th).
July Santiago, Santiago Apostol (22nd).
  San Cristóbal, San Cristóbal (25th).

August La Vega, Nuestra Señora de Antigua (15th).

September Constanza, Nuestra Señora de las Mercedes (24th).

October Barahona, Nuestra Señora del Rosario (4th).

Boca Chica, San Rafael (24th).

December Samaná, Santa Barbara (4th).

Watersports

Watersports gravitate around the tourist centres. The larger hotels usually have them on offer (anything from parasailing to banana boat rides), but as an outsider you may not be allowed into the hotel compound. If you are travelling independently, the best bet is to go to the more offbeat areas such as Sosúa, Cabarete and Las Terrenas. Boca Chica, the favourite with the Dominicans themselves, has most sports on offer, too, though it gets very crowded.

Deep-sea Fishing

Trips out on the hunt for magnificent 10ft marlin in the Mona Channel can be arranged from Boca de Yuma, which holds a fishing tournament each year in June. The fishing is also good off the north coast in the region of Monte Cristi, where they hold a couple of yearly competitions. Try:

Club Andres, Boca Chica, t 685 4940.

Puerto Plata, t 586 1121.

Sailing

For small sailing craft, two-person hobie cats and sunfish, you will depend on the hotels, but if you wish to charter a larger yacht, you can go to the marinas at Boca Chica. Or contact:

Sailing Club of Santo Domingo (Club Nautico de Santo Domingo), at La Romana and at Boca de Yuma in the far southeast, t 685 4940.

Scuba Diving

Diving was late developing in the Dominican Republic compared to other islands in the Caribbean, but that has changed. Now, all the major centres have PADI-certified dive operators. There are reefs off all sides of the coast, many of which can be reached by snorkellers. Diving reefs include Catalina Island and Bayahibe near La Romana, and there are wrecks on the reefs off Monte Cristi and near Miches. There is a marine park near the airport at La Caleta (make arrangements in Boca Chica). Visit *www.dominican-diving.com* or contact:

Aqua Dive, Hotel Castello Beach, Calle Portillo, Las Terrenas/Samana, t 240 6616.

Casa Daniel Swiss Diving School, Calle Principal, Bayahibe, t 833 0050.

Dive Samaná, Las Galeras, t 538 0001.

Dominican Adventure Dive Center, Abraham Lincoln Av, Santo Domingo, t 565 9771.

Hippocampo Dive Centre, Julio Arseno, Los Charamicos, Sosua Beach, t 571 4437, *www.hippocampo.com*.

Mundo Submarino, Santo Domingo, t 566 0430. Another useful contact in the capital, they arrange trips for trained divers and sailing and snorkelling excursions.

Northern Coast Aquasports, Sosúa, t 571 1028, *northern@verizon.net.do, www.northern coastdiving.com*.

Puerto Plata, t 586 1121. A general watersports operator for diving and deep-sea fishing.

Samaná Tourist Services, Samaná, t 538 2332.

Treasure Divers, Boca Chica, t 523 5320, *treasuredivers@hotmail.com*.

Windsurfing and Kiteboarding

These are extremely good in the Dominican Republic. You can pick up a board in most places on the north and east coasts, but all standards of windsurfers can enjoy Cabarete, just a few miles east of Sosúa, where there is a strong windsurfing and kiteboarding scene. The winds run across the bay, slightly onshore, and several hundred yards out there is a reef where you can sail the waves. Note that winds are at their highest in the early part of the year. You may want to look at the portal for kiteboarding in Cabarete: *www.cabarete kiteboarding.com*. Hire is about US$50 daily for all equipment, proportionally less for the week.

All the companies are along the beach strip, but you can contact:

Carib BIC Centre, t 571 0640, *info@carib wind.com, www.caribwind.com*. With BIC equipment. Kiteboarding tuition, too.

Fanatic Windsurf Centre, t 571 0861, *fanatic@ verizon.net.do, www.fanatic-cabarete.com*.

Other Sports

Golf

There are courses in all the main resort towns (Playa Dorada, Bavaro, four at Casa de Campo, Sosúa, Cabarete, Samaná) and the main cities, Santo in Santo Domingo, Santiago and Bonao.

Hiking and Mountain-biking

Walkers will not generally find anything organized, except occasionally by the National Parks Service (*see* 'Flora and Fauna' p.598). However, if you are prepared to rough it a bit, the parks can provide excellent hiking.
Bikes & More, Sosúa, **t** 571 3661, *www.carib beanbiketours.com*. Offers bike tours but also river tubing, deep-sea fishing and historical tours.
Iguana Mama, t 571 0908, **t** 1 800 849 4720, *info@iguanamama.com, www.iguanamama. com*. An excellent company which offers off-the-beaten-track tours both on foot and by bike (from a single day's outing to a hard-core, 10-day tour that takes you across the whole island). They are based in Cabarete but their tours go all over the island.

Horse-riding

Possible in a number of resorts throughout the island. Try:
Adventure Horseback Riding, on the north coast, **t** 571 0816, *info@dominicanadventures. com, www.dominicanadventures.com*.

Polo

The Dominican Republic must be one of the only places in the world where you can hire polo ponies (at Casa de Campo).

Tennis

Courts are everywhere. Once again, go to a nearby hotel.

Spectator Sports

The Republic's national sport (if you don't include dancing) is **baseball**; some of the Dominicans play in the national leagues in the States, returning home to winter in the warmth, where they keep their eye in with the local teams during the season from October to February. There are stadia in Santo Domingo, Santiago, Puerto Plata, La Romana and San Pedro de Macoris (from where there are four teams).

Another very popular spectator sport is **cockfighting**, particularly in the country areas (*see* 'Martinique', p.259). The Gallera Santo Domingo is about 7 miles from the city.

Last but not least, if you get a chance to see a Dominican **wrestling** match, do go, because you'll find it is a great spectacle. The fervour is extraordinary and is matched only by the suspension of disbelief.

Where to Stay

Dominican Republic t (1 809–)

The Dominican Republic has a full range of hotels: large, self-contained resorts of international-standard luxury set on glorious sand, through to the smaller, more personal beach clubs; and in the mountains, small, hillside retreats. If you are travelling the island, you will probably spend some time in the capital, Santo Domingo, where you will find restored colonial palaces as well as guest houses in the colonial town. The Dominican Republic offers well-priced package tours at the moment and, with a bit of shopping around, independent travellers will find some very good prices in the off-beat tourist resorts. In the larger tourist hotels, you can pay with credit cards and in US dollars with cash or traveller's cheques, but in more local hotels, you will have to pay in pesos. A government tax of 8%, a room tax of 5% and a service charge of 10% is added to all bills.

Santo Domingo

Expensive

Renaissance Jaragua Hotel and Casino, Malecón, 367 Av George Washington, **t** 221 2222, US **t** 1 800 352 4354, *www. renaissancehotels.com*. The hotels in Santo Domingo are not near to the beaches, but if you want high Caribbean comfort in glitzy pink right in the city, try here. There are three restaurants, a casino, a club, tennis courts and 300 rooms in high pastel décor with cable television.

Santo Domingo Hotel, Malecón, Av Independencia y Av Abraham Lincoln, **t** 221 1511, US **t** 1 800 877 3643, *www.hotelsantodomingo. com.do*. A slightly more Dominican version of the international standard fare: the hotel was decorated by the Dominican designer Oscar de la Renta and there are echoes of another era in the arches, dark-stained louvres and palms in the courtyard. It is very much a modern hotel though, with the 215 rooms all in one block and with a special floor devoted to business travellers. It is low-key; they serve afternoon tea; there is no discotheque, nor a casino, but they do have two restaurants and a swimming pool.

Hilton Santo Domingo, 500 George Washington Av, **t** 238 5059, *www.hilton caribbean.com/santodomingo*. A new 21-floor hotel located on the Malecon, the city's oceanfront drive. It anchors a mixed-use complex that includes retail shops, a cinema, restaurants, entertainment areas and the city's largest casino. All guest rooms have high-speed Internet access, speaker-phones, and cable television. Among its facilities are a health club, restaurant and pool bar.

Hostal Nicolás de Ovando, 2975 Calle las Damas, **t** 685 9955, *h2975@accor-hotels.com*, *www.sofitel.com*. Listed as a World Heritage site by UNESCO, the hotel was recently converted into a luxury hotel. It is set in the palace of a 16th-century governor – from the days when Santo Domingo was a gracious viceregal capital. The rooms are placed around three charming tiled courtyards, each surrounded by colonnades. Within, the hallways are inlaid with dark mahogany beams and hung with tapestries and paintings on exhibit. There are 45 rooms, some dressed up in colonial grandeur (rooms at the rear above the new Avenida del Puerto are quite noisy).

Moderate

Hispaniola, Av Independencia y Av Abraham Lincoln, **t** 221 7111, *res@pwmonline.com*, *www.hotelhispaniola.com*. Sister hotel of the Santo Domingo (across the road), slightly more upbeat. The Hispaniola is also a modern town hotel with 165 rooms in a block, but it has a nice feel. Bar, casino and cable TV to keep you in touch.

Hamaca Coral by Hilton, 26 Duarte Av, PO Box 2973, Boca Chica, Santo Domingo, **t** 523 4611, *www.coralbyhilton.com*. A comfortable hotel set on a good strip of sand. Rooms in blocks, but all the expected requisites for a break are there.

Don Juan Beach Resort, Boca Chica, **t** 523 4511, *h.donjuan@verizon.net.do*, *www.caei.com/ djbr*. As the name suggests, life centres around the beach and night-time activity. The 124 rooms are in a block above the pool within spitting distance of the sand, where there is every watersport imaginable, and entertainment. Quite a few package tourists but a lively hotel.

Inexpensive

Hostal Nicolás Nader, 151 Calle Luperón, Esquina Duarte, **t** 687 6674, *www.nader enterprises.com*. A smaller and quieter, but equally gracious, palace – another charming retreat from the bustle of the town. Set around an interior courtyard, with arches and mahogany beams. Just 10 rooms, furnished in dark colonial style but with air conditioning. No restaurant, but simple food available and a lively bar.

Sofitel Hotel Frances, Calle Las Mercedes, Esquina Meriño, **t** 685 9331, US **t** 1 800 221 4542, *h2137@accor-hotels.com*. Set around a very pretty courtyard of coral stone, the 19 stylish rooms lead off the wrought-iron balconies upstairs.

Hotel Palacio, 106 Calle Duarte, **t** 682 4730, *palacio@verizon.net.do*, *dominican-rep.com/ hotel-palacio*. Old town house restored with elegant stone and brick work outside and Spanish tile and rafter ceilings inside, but modern comforts and fittings. A little dark inside, but it has pleasant courtyards.

Hotel Conde de Penalba, Calle el Conde, **t** 688 7121, *condepenalba@verizon.net.do*, *www.condepenalba.com*. A touch frumpy but it does have the advantage of being right on the main square in the colonial city, in a pretty building. Some of the rooms over-look the square from attractive wrought-iron balconies.

Antiguo Hotel Europe, Old City, t 285 0005, www.antiguohoteleuropa.com. This renovated hotel preserves its original 1930s architecture, with characteristic wrought-iron balconies and 52 rooms decorated in antique style. There are two bars and a restaurant overlooking the San Francisco Monastery. The 52 rooms and suites are decked out in mahogany furniture, with cable television.

La Casona Dorada, Avenida Independencia, t 221 3535, casona.dorada@verizon.net.do. Just outside the colonial zone, set in a restored colonial villa from the last century and now redecorated to plush modern comfort. There are 22 air-conditioned rooms with modern wooden furniture and a palm-courtyard with a pool at the front.

La Gran Mansion Guest House, 26 Calle Danae, t 682 2033. Eleven simple rooms with private baths, cafeteria.

Don Paco Guest House, 6 Calle Duarte, Boca Chica, t 523 4816. There are plenty of guest houses along the strip, many of them a bit sultry, but you will find 10 clean and comfortable rooms at this friendly place.

Caribe Sol, Calle Rafael, Boca Chica, t 523 4010. Contact these people if you would prefer to rent an apartment.

Hotel Aida, Calle Espaillat, t 685 7692. Simple but recommended.

The Central Mountains

Hotel Pinar Dorado, on the road towards Constanza, Jarabacoa, t 574 2820, hotel pinardorado@verizon.net.do (inexpensive). Has a charming courtyard restaurant filled with flowers, opposite a modern block with rooms.

Santiago

A couple of decent options are listed below, but if you want somewhere even cheaper to stay there is a clutch of small and very simple hotels around the Plaza Valero.

Moderate–Inexpensive

Hodelpa Gran Almirante, slightly out of town on the Av Estrella Sadhalá, t 683 1000, granalmirante@hodelpa.com, www.hodelpa. com. The smartest hotel in Santiago, modern, comfortable and air-conditioned

with a good restaurant and café, pool, cable TV, massage parlour and executive floor. The service is good, but it's a bit characterless.

Hodelpa Centro Plaza, 54 Calle del Sol, t 581 7000, www.hodelpa.com. Right in the centre of the town on one of the main shopping streets. Also modern in style, with 71 rooms, but it boasts a fine view of the town from its dining room on the top floor.

The North Coast

Expensive

Gran Ventana, PO Box 22, Puerto Plata, t 320 2111, sales@vhhr.com, www.vhhr.com. A large hotel with rooms in blocks around a pool and leading down to the beach. All bright colours and Mediterranean style. All the sports; dining on the breezy terrace to the sound of a band.

Azzurro Club Estrella by Starz, Cabarete, t 571 0808, US toll free t 1 800 472 3985, info@ starzresorts.com, www.starzresorts.com. The best of the all-inclusive resort-style hotels that are creeping into town. There are 164 rooms in blocks around a grassy garden and pool. Lots of activities, right on the beach.

Casa Colonial Beach and Spa, Playa Dorada, Puerto Plata, t 320 3232, reservascc@vhhr. com, www.vhhr.com. The north coast's first all-suite boutique hotel, with 50 elegant suites, two gourmet restaurants and a large spa. It combines the Old World charm of its colonial architecture with modern comforts and tasteful, contemporary décor. Stunning details include coralline stonework, mahogany wood floors and cathedral ceilings. The suites, all with balconies, have Italian marble floors, fine furnishings, Frette linens, a stocked minibar, high-speed Internet access, safe, and flat-screen television. On the third floor, which overlooks the Caribbean, is an outdoor rooftop pool with four Jacuzzis. The spa is equipped with 10 indoor treatment rooms and three ocean-front gazebos for outdoor treatments. A gym with Cybex equipment and personal trainers is also available.

Moderate–Inexpensive

Orquideria del Sol, Punta Rucia, Estero Hondo, t 583 2825. West of Puerto Plata, this small and friendly place overlooks the beach through a garden of orchids, as suggested by the name.

Hotel Mountain View, Calle José Eugenio Kunhardt, Puerto Plata, **t** 586 4093. In the residential part of town. Simple, clean rooms, restaurant, pool, cable TV. A good stopover if you are passing through.

Playa Naco Golf and Tennis Resort, Playa Dorada, **t** 320 6226, US **t** 1 888 339 NACO, *sales@naco.com.do*, *www.naco.com.do/ playanaco*. If you would like to stay on the beach itself, you can try this resort, where there is a variety of one- and two-bedroom apartments.

Dorado Naco Resort, Playa Dorada, **t** 320 2019. A large timeshare hotel like the Playa resort above. You can use the facilities of either; there are five restaurants, nine bars, all modern comforts, including a good stretch of beach with all the watersports.

Victoria Resort, Playa Dorada, PO Box 22, **t** 320 1200, *sales@victoriahoteles.com*, *www. victoriahoteles.com*. Also has a certain style: the main house stands above the lake and pool, finished with Spanish colonial trimmings and classical motifs. In spirit the hotel is more modern, with high-pastel decoration in the rooms and wicker furniture.

Hotel Waterfront, 1 Calle Dr Rosen, Sosúa, **t** 571 2670, *h.waterfront@verizon.net.do*, *www. hotelwaterfront.com*. A good alternative which has more of a resort feel, in a block above a pool with a good dining room right on the cliffs.

Tropix Hotel, Sosúa, **t** 571 2291, *info@tropix hotel.com*, *www.tropixhotel.com*. The best place to stay in town with just 10 rooms overlooking the pool behind the main house, set in a cool tropical garden. There is a communal kitchen, with a daily breakfast menu on offer if you do not want to cook and outside is the barita, an honour bar in a breezy clapboard house under the fishtail palms. Laid-back and well away from the hustle of the town, a charming place to stay.

El Magnifico Condominiums, Cabarete, **t** 571 0868, *hotel.magnifico@verizon.net.do*, *www.hotelelmagnifico.com*. Eleven apartments with a lot of style – classic, Caribbean, Art Deco and Picasso – in a small but very pretty compound overflowing with tropical flowers at the eastern limits of the town. Mostly weekly rentals, but if you're passing they might let you in for a couple of days if there are free rooms. Bedrooms are large; it's a family-style resort.

La Punta Hotel, Cabarete, **t** 571 0897, *lapunta@verizon.net.do*, *www.hispaniola. com/punta*. Twelve sleek and modern one-bedroom apartments in blocks above a pool among the palm trees on the point of the name. Fan-ventilated and self-catering, though there is a good restaurant.

Cabarete Beach Houses, Calle Principal, Cabarete, **t** 571 0744, *www.cabaretebeach houses.com*. Right on the main beach in town, this has 28 rooms with private bathrooms and either fans or air-conditioning and a beachfront deck restaurant; half-board plan only.

Ocean Breeze, Cabarete, **t** 571 0656, *www. oceanbreezecabarete.com*, US **t** 1 800 524 7610. An excellent place to stay, on the quiet outskirts of town to the east. Just eight comfortable and modern rooms, with a couple of apartments, each of which has a balcony set above a garden and pool. Very calm ambience, offering a bed and breakfast package.

Inexpensive

El Rancho del Sol, La Isabela, **t** 543 8172. Just outside the gates of the Parque Nacional Historico La Isabela, a villa with eight air-conditioned rooms in blocks, just above a passable beach on a well protected bay. There's a pool and tennis court, and breakfast is served on the upstairs balcony.

La Yola, Luperón. Try this guest house which is on the outskirts of the town near the beach.

Hostal Jimessón, 41 John F. Kennedy, Puerto Plata, **t** 586 5131. The 22 modern rooms are simple; the nicest thing about this hotel is really the 19th-century foyer – wood-panelled and tiled, with rocking chairs, antique mirrors and a collection of clocks and gramophones.

Latin Quarter Hotel, Malecón Esquina Carolina, Puerto Plata, **t** 586 2588. Has standard air-conditioned rooms, a restaurant and a bar.

Pension Anneliese, Calle Dr Rosen, Sosúa, **t** 571 2208, *analise.pension@verizon.net.do*.

Ten comfortable rooms in one large villa, with a bar and pool out in the garden. Friendly reception.

Casa María, Cabarete. Holiday villa on the streetside. Five very simple fan-ventilated rooms, with breakfast available.

The Samaná Peninsula

Villas in Las Terrenas can be arranged through **Immobilaria Rene**, t 240 6429, *lasterrenas@verizon.net.do*.

Expensive–Moderate

Gran Bahía By Occidental, opposite Cayo Leventado, PO Box 2024, Santo Domingo, t 538 3111, US t 1 800 858 2258, *www. occidentalhotels.com*. Beyond Samaná on the south coast, you will find an unfeasibly smart and elegant retreat here, a few miles east of the town itself, opposite Cayo Leventado. The hotel is an extraordinary compendium of turrets, triangular eaves, awnings and balconies, all trimmed with very pretty white gingerbread and balustrades. In the great house is a foyer with a fountain and tiled floor; upstairs the rooms are extremely attractive. Small beach, but trips to Cayo Leventado are available. A gracious air of the old-time Caribbean.

Hotel Bahía las Ballenas, Playa Bonita, t 240 6066, *b.lasballenas@verizon.net.do*. A delightful hotel with thatched-roofed cottages ranged around a pool and garden, just across from the fantastic beach. The rooms are large and decorated in earthy colours, ochre and terracotta offset with bright greens and blues. There's a good French restaurant.

Hotel Atlantis, Playa Bonita, t 240 6111, *hotel. atlantis@verizon.net.do, www.atlantisbeach-hotel.com*. A curious resort which has been here for over 20 years. Eighteen rooms (most fan-ventilated) in a meandering series of villas and cottages with columns, arches and balustrades all dressed up in white stucco. French restaurant. Quiet.

Club Bonito, along the beach track, Las Galeras, t 538 0203, *club.bonito@ verizon.net.do, www.club-bonito.com*. A stylish-looking building dressed in earthy terracotta, with balconies overlooking the palm-thatched gazebos around the pool,

through the palms of tall trunks to the sea. Large rooms with bamboo beds, balconies and Haitian paintings. Air-conditioning, fans and phones. Very comfortable.

Villa Serena, Las Galeras, t 538 0000, *vserena@verizon.net.do, www.villaserena. com*. Also stylish, but architecturally completely different: a gingerbread house with green wriggly tin roofs, balustrades and tall French windows. Inside, the 21 rooms are cool and tiled, some with four-poster beds.

Inexpensive

Hotel Tropic Banana, Paseo Maritimo West, Las Terrenas, t 240 6110, *hotel.tropic@erizon. net.do*. A hotel which has held hip sway over the town for about 25 years. There are about 30 rooms scattered in small blocks around a grassy palm garden and pool, but the heart of the hotel is the main house, where the hip chicks and pig-tailed windsurfers loiter listening to a local band in the afternoon and evening. Comfortable rooms furnished in rattan, with a veranda for taking it easy after action on the beach (tennis and scuba diving) or in the bar. Bed and breakfast.

Las Cayenas Hotel, slightly out of town to the west, Las Terrenas, t 240 6080. Set in an old plantation-style house. Some stylish rooms upstairs, a nice restaurant on a deck and a friendly, quiet air.

Hotel Los Pinos, 23 Calle Portillo, Las Terrenas, t 240 6168, *hotellospinos@verizon.net.do*. Six rooms in neat cottages set in a pretty garden across from the beach at the eastern edge of town. There's a pretty restaurant out front.

Coyamar, Playa Bonita, t 240 5130, *peter@ coyamar.com*. A small resort dressed up in bright colours, 10 rooms in a couple of villas in a tropical garden. Small pool and a bar under the palm trees.

Tropical Lodge Hotel, Avenida Marina, Santa Barbara de Samaná, t 538 2480, *juan.felipe@ verizon.net.do, www.samana.net*. There are not many hotels in the town of Samaná itself but you can find a comfortable room here, in a modern villa set into the hillside on the Malecón, at the eastern edge of the town. Seventeen rooms, good restaurant, good library to keep you occupied.

L'Aguada Tropical, Santa Barbara de Samaná, t 257 3339. Simpler rooms, just above the Tropical Lodge.

El Marinique Resort, on the west side of the beach, Las Galeras, t 538 0262, *office@ elmarinique.com*, *www.elmarinique.com*. Four fan-ventilated cabanas in a pretty garden; simple, nice and clean. Friendly atmosphere.

Hotel L'Aubergine, Las Terrenas, t 240 6167. Simple hotel near the beach; four rooms with hot and cold water, plus restaurant with a seafood speciality.

Khannes, Las Terrenas, t 240 6187. Here you can stay simply and cheaply while in the town.

Hotel Dinny, Las Terrenas, t 240 6113. Found on the beach, simple but functional.

Cotubanama, Santa Barbara de Samaná, t 538 2557. Just up from the Malecón. Clean and comfortable, if simple. Private baths and a good French restaurant.

South Coast East of Santo Domingo

Luxury–Expensive
Casa de Campo, PO Box 140, La Romana, t 523 3333, *www.casadcampo.com*. A huge estate with 900 rooms and villas, in landscaped grounds with golf courses (there are four), tennis courts, and set on cliffs overlooking the sea. The rooms are luxurious, designed by Dominican designer Oscar de la Renta. Buses shuttle the length and breadth of the complex, racing you from villa suburb to the beach and from the massage clinic to the hilltop restaurants at Altos de Chavón.

Moderate
Club Dominicus, Bayahibe, t 562 6000. The biggest hotels in the town, offering all-inclusive packages with all the sporting facilities.

Inexpensive
Hotel Bayahibe, Bayahibe, t 707 3684. Small and with more style, better for independent travellers. Close to the beach, simple rooms in a pleasant setting around a courtyard.

East Coast
The east coast, from Bavaro to Punta Cana, has seen unprecedented development in the last decade and now boasts the largest room count in the country. There are a few independent hotels, but most are large resorts belonging to well-known international, all-inclusive hotel chains. Below are two of the better choices.

Luxury
Punta Cana, Punta Cana, t 221 2262, US toll free t 1888 442 2262, *ventas@puntacana.com*, *www.puntacana.com*. Probably the best on the eastern tip. A huge development, much of it along the rocky shoreline either side of the beach. All the sports: scuba diving, horse-riding, golf. It has some smart new villas with interiors by Oscar de la Renta, who is among the celebrities who own homes here. The resort has a marina, a fabulous Club House, seven restaurants, eight bars, four pools and a spectacular, ocean-front 18-hole Peter Dye golf course.

Expensive–Moderate
Barcelo Bavaro Beach Resort, PO Box 1, Higüey, t 686 5797, *www.barcelo.com*. Set on a magnificent mile-long sweep of impeccable sand backed along its entire length by palm trees. All watersports; pools, golf and plenty of evening entertainment. You will have a good, active beach holiday here even if you do not see much of Dominican life.

South Coast West of Santo Domingo
There are few hotels to the west of Santo Domingo, but you will find guest houses in the towns.

Moderate
Barahona Beach Club, Barahona, t 524 1111. A few miles beyond the town of Barahona, a complex of suites and apartments with watersports, horse-riding and tennis.

Casa Bonita, in the hills of Bauruco, t 472 3939, *poli@casabonitadr.com*, *www.casabonitadr. com*. Twelve palm-thatched rooms above the beach, a few miles beyond Barahona. Very quiet but friendly and secluded.

Inexpensive
Hotel Guaracuyá, Barahona, t 233 0748. Close to town, a small and simple hotel with its own beach.

Eating Out

Like dancing, eating out is a favourite pastime in the Dominican Republic and the islanders savour it as they dine out with their families in the evenings. The food is heavy by most standards and many of the meals are centred around a meat stew with a salad. Starters are *sopa* (soup) or *chicharrones*, crispy pork rind or chicken pieces that are served with a spicy dip. *Sancocho* is a thick stew made with seven or more different meats and vegetables, including yucca, plantain and potato, steeped in herbs, and other favourites include *mondongo*, a stew made with tripe, *mofongo*, plantain mashed with spices and garlic, and *mang*, boiled plantain flattened with meat or egg. *Pescado con coco* (fish with coconut sauce) is a traditional dish in the Samaná Peninsula. *Locrio* is similar to paella, rice and meat or possibly seafood, which is good in the Dominican Republic. *Arepa* is a sweet cake served with the main course. Finally, for a filling local meal, try *arroz con pollo* (rice and chicken) with fried plantains on the side. The Republic grows its own coffee in the northern mountains, which is good. During the day, it is drunk as espresso, in tiny plastic cups; cafés are an important part of Dominican city life.

The Dominicans make the best of their fruits, which grow in profusion in the island and end up in ice creams and drinks served in the small bars open on to the street. *Jugos* are drinks made from fresh fruit, water, sugar and crushed ice: extremely refreshing. *Bastidas* are a milkshake version of the drink, the best of their kind in the Caribbean. *China* or *naranja* (orange) is exceptionally good; other fruits include *chinola* (passion fruit), *lechosa* (papaya) and *zapote* (melon).

The Dominicans brew a number of beers; Presidente is an excellent, light-coloured lager beer, while Quisqueya is a slightly darker brew. Rum can be white, the traditional tipple and mixing drink; *dorado* (gold); or *añejo*, which is aged in the barrel and usually drunk as a liqueur.

Restaurants

There are literally thousands of restaurants, cafés, local bars and ice-cream halls in the Dominican Republic. Part of the pleasure is simply to wander until you find one you like the look of. As you walk, you get the idea that entertainment is probably the country's biggest industry. Santo Domingo has an extraordinary variety of restaurants in both style – gourmet, seafood, Italian, Argentinian – and setting: in the old colonial palaces of the Alcázar, modern villas and in open-fronted cafés along the Malecón. The Dominicans like to go out in the colonial city (rather than live there) and so there are plenty of stopping points for when you tire of the sightseeing. Just off the Cathedral Square, at the very foot of El Conde, you come to a paved alleyway set with tables and chairs that have spilled out of restaurants. In restaurants outside the hotels, if you do not pay by credit card, you must pay in Dominican pesos. Restaurant **price categories** are arranged according to the price of a main course: expensive = RD$200 and above; moderate = RD$100–$200; inexpensive = RD$100 and under.

Santo Domingo

Expensive

Caribbean Blue, Calle Hostos 205, **t** 685 5162. A delightful restaurant set in an old colonial *palacio* with tables in the covered courtyard among the palms and under the bare coral-rock wall and arches. A hip atmosphere, with quiet jazz and Latin music and waiters in long *guayaberas*. *Croqueta de cangrejo* (crab croquettes) with a passion-fruit tartar and a basil coulis followed by *manzana miel salmon* (apple-honey salmon) with an oriental coleslaw and orange vinaigrette or traditonally prepared *chillo a la leña*: grouper cooked in a wood-fired oven. The oven, around which they have built their kitchen, is reckoned to date from 1540.

Cantabrico, Avenida Independencia 54, **t** 687 5101, *www.restaurantcantabrico.com.do*. Set in a formal, air-conditioned dining room with paintings and stained-wood skirtings on Calle Independencia. The cuisine is Spanish with a long seafood menu; try a crayfish brochette or a *parille de mariscos*, a seafood platter.

Reina de España, Cervantes 103, **t** 685 2588. Set in a private villa with a subdued and elegant air. Steak and seafood specialities but excellent *costillitas de cordero Don Seve*, lamb prepared in delicate peppermint sauce. Long Spanish wine list.

Vesuvio, Avenida George Washington 521, **t** 221 3333. Ever popular, right on the Malecón, glass-fronted and modern. The dining room is decorated with colourful friezes of tropical fruits and fish. You start with a cocktail about the size of a swimming pool and set about the huge menu of Italian and international food; try stuffed queen conch cannelloni with pink béchamel sauce or *veal scalopina au poivre vert*.

Don Pepe, Calle Santiago, at the corner with Calle Pasteur, **t** 686 8481. Also set in a converted suburban villa. It is a bit stuffy and formal, presided over by major-domos in tuxedos, but it serves renowned international fare: *cochinillo* or suckling pig and variations on the vast crabs that are on view as you come in through the door. There is also a good wine cellar.

La Bricciola, Calle Arzobispo Meriño 152, **t** 688 5055. An open-air dining room in a courtyard among the palms and cloistered arches (and an air-conditioned lounge), formerly a private house in the colonial city. Italian fare with lots of fish, including some exotic offerings like grilled breaded cuttlefish.

Aqua, Av Gustavo Mejía Ricart 106, **t** 541 8761. Nouvelle cuisine, sushi and ceviche bar. Risotto and ravioli are among the specialities.

Neptuno's Club Restaurant, Av Duarte 12, Boca Chica, **t** 523 4703, *www.neptunosclub.com*. Great setting on the beach. Noted for fresh seafood.

Outback Steakhouse, Av Winston Churchill, Acrópolis Center, **t** 955 0001. In case you're hungry for a good steak.

Season's, Roberto Pastoriza 14, **t** 412 2655. New and creative cuisine, Dominican and international, and a good selection of wines.

Moderate

El Conuco, Calle Casimro de Moya 152, **t** 686 0129, *www.elconuco.com.do*. At the opposite end of the scale, full of the joys of life and with a riotously informal air. 'Conuco' means 'country' and the theme is current throughout the restaurant, as is obvious

immediately you walk under the rustic thatch roof and palm supports. Huge pestles and mortars, pitchforks, loofahs, *lechones* and fishtraps adorn the walls, between the *cibaeño campesino* (farmer's sayings) on wooden plaques. And the menu is farmers' food, dressed up a little for the capital – all the tripe dishes you can imagine and some a little less of an adventure, for example *chicharrones de pollo* (deep-fried chicken) or *filete de rez con longos*. It's a fun place: when the waiters have had enough, they turn the music up, grab their instruments and dance instead.

Mesón Bari, at the corner of Calle Salome Ureña. A lively joint in the heart of the colonial city. It is the favourite gathering point of Santo Domingo's writers and artists on a Friday night, so the diet consists of philosophy, gossip and beer as much as creole food; *lambi guisado* and *bistek empanado*.

Café Bachata Rosa, La Atarazana, opposite the Alcázar de Colón. Celebrates the famous Dominican *bachata* singer Juan Luis Guerra (whose picture hangs all over the walls). Grab a plate of local meat with white rice and red beans.

Mesón de Jamón (or is it Muséo de Jamón, with so many haunches hanging from the ceiling?), La Atarazana, opposite the Alcázar de Colón. Has ham dishes, of course, but also tasty tapas.

Pat'e Palo, La Atarazana 25, opposite the Alcázar de Colón, **t** 687 8089, *www.patepalo. com*. Named after the celebrated one-legged pirate, serving international fare. Flamed *brochette*, steaks and fish with chips or rice and peas.

Italos, Calle Los Locutores, **t** 541 7883. Italian fare with a good atmosphere.

Crazy Fish, Calle Roberto Pastoriza, **t** 540 1492. Chinese and Japanese fare.

Inexpensive

You can find very local meals at one of hundreds of *comedors* around the city. These are family kitchens that open up to all-comers. Your average plate of rice 'n' beans is also known as *la bandera* (national flag) because it is an unofficial national dish. Finally, you might consider a snack next to the obelisk on the Malecón, where you sit in a rocking chair as they cook your *chimichurri* (a spicy sausage burger). For other inexpensive options try:

Lumi's Park, Abraham Lincoln 809, t 540 4755. The best *mofongo* in town, with fresh fruit soft drinks. Fast food Dominican style.

Ananda's, Calle Casimiro de Moya 7, t 682 4465. More options for non-meat eaters include Ananda's and Ojas, both of which serve a huge variety of tropical vegetables and fruits in Dominican sauces.

Ojas, Calle Gazcue, t 682 3940. Vegetarian fare (*see* 'Anandas' above).

Santiago

Expensive

El Café, just off Calle 5, near esquina Texas, Santiago, t 587 4247. The most elegant restaurant in Santiago. The cuisine is French and international: almond sea bass in a sauce of almond, lemon, parsley and butter, whisky lobster and some unlikely and exotic meats. The candlelit dining room is subdued, presided over by tuxedoed waiters, with some piano entertainment.

El Pez Dorado, Calle del Sol at the Parque Colón, Santiago, t 582 4071/2518. Seafood and fish mainly, with a few oriental dishes thrown in, too. Set in a plush, air-conditioned dining room with wicker furniture. Shrimps *chofan* (cooked in flavoured rice), sea bass in a white wine sauce or sweet and sour grouper.

Camp David Ranch, Santiago, t 276 6400. Set high on the hillside outside the city with a superb view over Santiago and Moca. International fare.

Paparazzo, Calle Mauricio Alvarez, Los Colegios, t 582 6578. Fusion and creative Dominican selections.

Moderate

Il Pasticcio, Calle 35, Av Del Llano, t 582 6061. Excellent Italian fare.

Puerto Plata

There are a few nice restaurants in the town of Puerto Plata if you would like to go out to dinner. The eastern end of the Malecón is very lively and there are lots of good, simple stop-ins there.

Expensive

De Armando, Calle Separación, t 586 3418. In the centre of town, set in an old wooden house which has been refitted and enclosed with glass to make it air-conditioned. You still take cocktails on the veranda, though, in an inside gazebo. The decor is pink and luxurious and the fare international. Try *cordero al vino*, lamb cooked in a wine sauce, or sea bass with shrimps and clams. Some entertainment with a *perico ripiao* (string) band.

Acuarela Garden Café, Profesor Certad 3, t 586 5314. Set in a wonderfully cool garden in the middle of the city. You sit at wicker-backed chairs in a traditional-style house with French windows and fans whirring overhead, looking onto the tropical plants. Long seafood menu, Thai shrimp followed by Duck Delight or Basil Chicken. Hip air, walls covered with works of modern art.

Moderate

Café Cito, San Felipe 29, t 586 7923. Courtyard setting under banana trees and a mango tree with an open-sided bar. Grilled fish and chicken dishes to go with jazz and blues music.

Aguacate Bar, San Felipe. In the same garden as Cito (*see* above), also has a very nice setting under trees, bamboo and thatch. Mexican dishes, pasta and sandwiches.

Sosúa

There are beach bars almost along the whole length of Sosúa Beach and any of them make a good daytime hangout.

Expensive–Moderate

La Puntilla de Piergfiorgio. An Italian restaurant with a charming setting on the clifftops, where iron garden chairs and tables sit on terraces around a gingerbread house. Specialities include cannelloni beef in béchamel sauce and 'Spanish ravioli'. The 'therapy to happiness...'

On the Waterfront, Calle Dr Rosen, t 571 2670. Also an excellent setting on the cliff's edge, where there is an excellent view of the sunset. Try sea bass *meunière* in butter, lemon and parsley, or grouper Almendra cooked with cream, brandy and almonds. Also lots of steaks.

Restaurant Atlàntico, Los Charamícos, **t** 571 2878. Enjoys an excellent position on the Charramícos side of the town, with a lovely view of the palms and activity of Sosúa Beach. It is set on its own veranda, with rafters, wooden seats and tables, and a tree growing in the middle. The menu is French and strong on seafood. Specials vary according to the catch of the day, but there are often *gambas* (shrimps) flambéed in various liqueurs, or a paella.

Moderate

White House, Calle Allejo. Italian café with sandwiches and pasta, on a corner in the middle of town.

El Toro, Calle Pedro Clisante. If steaks are your thing, then there's plenty to get your teeth into here. Thatch-covered open terrace with wicker chairs. Steak by the ounce.

Inexpensive

Mama Mia's, Calle Dr Rosen. Italian food; great thin-crust pizza.

Tanja's Pastry, (quite a long way down) Calle Pedro Clisante, **t** 571 3515. A very good spot for all-day cakes and coffee; they do nice sandwiches, too.

Cabarete

Cabarete has a surprising clutch of beach bars and restaurants where you might easily find yourself willing to linger, escaping the sun during the day and relaxing over a meal in the evenings.

Expensive–Moderate

Otra Cosa (often called **La Punta** after the hotel where it's based), **t** 571 0897. Set on a very small and pretty deck on the point of the name, slightly to the east of the town. Very pleasant with a lovely view of the sea. French menu and short but good selection of wines. *Pavé de chillo* (grouper), *frais au beurre citronné* or a *filet de boeuf* in Roquefort. Finish up with a *tarte tatin*.

La Casita de Papy (Don Alfredo), on the beach (no phone). Very pretty setting downstairs on the sand or upstairs on a deck looking into the palm fronds. Fresh is the word: huge fresh tropical fruit juices and then fish

cooked to order, lobster served flambéed in a sauce *Pastis Papy*.

Inexpensive

Ristaurante Típico Mercedes, in the backstreets west of town, **t** 571 0247. A simple local setting, on a concrete terrace with plastic tablecloths, has the best in local food. Their blackboard menu might feature *cangrejo* (crab), *camarones* (prawns), *mondongo*, *mofongo* and *merengue*.

Judith's, on the main road. In an orange concrete house, more *comida típica*, lots of rice and beans and plantain.

Samaná Peninsula

In Las Terrenas on the Samaná Peninsula there are plenty of simple places to eat, but if you want a more formal meal, you are probably best off going to one of the hotels. The **Tropic Banana** (*see* 'Where to Stay', p.609) has a pretty setting under palms and you can expect a good meal at **Atlantis** in Playa Bonita (*see* 'Where to Stay', p.609). The hotels often double as bars, too. There are some good cafés overlooking the Malecón in Samaná town.

Moderate–Inexpensive

La Salsa, west along the beachfront. A superb Caribbean beach setting, with a cosy, palm-thatched deck right on the seafront. Low-coloured lights and a French menu: *poulet à l'ananas* to go with Celia Cruz, Neil Young, Kassav, John Lee Hooker and the gentle wash of the waves.

La Capannina, opposite waterfront. Italian Ristorante and Bar, with palm thatch. *Calamari fritti* or *carpaccio di dorado*.

Paco Cabana. A beach bar in the heart of town. Fish or meat dishes if you want but also sandwiches and lots of fruit drinks.

Las Bellenas, at the end of Playa Bonita Beach. Restaurant and beach club named after the whales seen off the peninsula. The deck is brightly coloured and there's *cuisine creole*, crab creole or Samaná's national dish: fish in coconut sauce.

La Mata Rosada, on the Malecón in Samaná town, **t** 538 2388. The nicest place to eat is this French restaurant: *caropaccios* followed by a long fish and seafood menu.

Café de Paris, also in Samaná town, t 538 2488. Salads and crêpes served all day, or you can just loiter over endless drinks.

Jardín Tropical, in Las Galeras. There are not many places to eat out in Las Galeras, but this one is nice. Serving French and international fare, on a pretty terrace decorated with colourful Spanish colonial tiles. Barbecue, spaghetti and local fare, fish or *lambi criollo*.

South Coast East of Santo Domingo

In Boca Chica, you will find a long string of snack bars and beach restaurants specializing in fish and seafood, both sides of the beachfront road. Further east, the village of Altos de Chavón above Casa de Campo also has a number of restaurants.

Expensive

Casa del Río, Altos de Chavón. Probably the smartest place, from which you get a superb view of the river in the evening, floodlit below. All very atmospheric and mock-medieval, with French cuisine. Caribbean lobster roasted and baked in vanilla vinegar broth with glazed *chapote* squash or lamb loin in orange marmalade and pastry. Take a constitutional walk on the battlements.

Moderate

Café del Sol, Altos de Chavón. For something simpler and rather less expensive; pizza and salads.

Big Sur, on the beach east of Altos de Chavón, in Bayahibe. The best restaurant here, a tin-roofed deck with a sandy garden out front and Italian fare. There are also plenty of *comedors* if you fancy local Dominican fare.

Papa Jack's, Altos de Chavón. A fun bar, with a drinking crowd settled downstairs and a gallery upstairs.

Bars and Nightlife

Although you'll find dedicated bars and discothèques in large towns such as Santo Domingo, much of the time the bars and restaurants double up along the beach and within hotels, so you'll find them anywhere you go. There are a number of discothèques in Samaná town, which gets quite lively at the weekends,

Santo Domingo

Just as there are hundreds of restaurants in Santo Domingo, the bars seem to go on forever. Following El Conde down to the colonial city you will find lots of bars and *heladerías* (ice-cream parlours).

Rita's Café, t 688 9400. Set in the restored surroundings of the oldest part of town.

Casa de Teatro, Calle Arzobispo Meriño, t 689 3430. Popular with students and young professional Dominicans, in the old colonial city. Busiest on a Monday.

Doubles, Calle Arz. Meriño 154, t 688 3833. Also in the venerable streets, next to the restaurant La Bricciola (*see* 'Eating Out', above).

Beer House, Avenida Winston Churchill, Arcadas, t 683 4804. Popular with the Dominican youth, a (not necessarily beer) bar that collects a lively crowd early on in the evening.

Trío Café, Avenida Abraham Lincoln, t 412 1722. Another one to try.

Bistro de Paris, Avenida Abraham Lincoln, t 683 4473.

Praia, Av Gustavo Mejía Ricart, t 540 8753.

Discos

If you feel like watching the Dominicans at it, dancing the merengue (and maybe even having a go yourself), you could try out the popular clubs. They usually have a cover charge of RD$50–150 (which often includes a drink) and many have a ladies' night on Thursdays.

Bella Blu, Avenida George Washington, t 689 2911. All glass, pillars and palms, attracting a slightly older crowd.

Guacara Taina, Avenida Abraham Lincoln, t 533 1051. A popular club in a natural cave.

Club Monaco, t 562 6615.

Meson de la Cava, Av Mirador del Sur, t 533 2818, *www.mesondelacava.com*. A large restaurant/nightclub on several levels, inside a cave.

Santiago

Francifol, Calle del Sol, t 971 5558. Stylish bar.

Tribeca, t 724 5000. A popular drinking haunt.

palaces and among them the earliest cathedral, university and hospital in the New World (the oldest surviving building dates from 1503). From here, the conquistadors departed on their expeditions to conquer the mainland and to settle the other islands. But the glory was eclipsed within a couple of generations as the riches of the Spanish Main were revealed and the administrators moved there. In 1562 much of the town was destroyed in an earthquake and by 1586, when Sir Francis Drake had taken a share (25,000 ducats to be precise), it was in ruins and it never really recovered. Today the colonial city has been restored and the streets retain some of their former splendour. It is listed by UNESCO and as you wander around, beneath the wrought-iron lamps and balconies and the coral stone walls covered with bougainvillea, it is not hard to imagine how it was nearly five centuries ago.

There is little that is glorious about Santo Domingo outside this immediate area, though. It is a working city of about three million people; the streets teem with lottery-ticket vendors, fruit-sellers and the endless traffic. Away from the city centre, along the lively Malecón on the seafront, are prosperous-looking villas set in tree-lined boulevards and the high-rises of the country's well-to-do. Beyond this screen of prosperity, in the ever-expanding shanties, are some of the Caribbean's poorest slums.

The Colonial City

The centrepiece of the colonial city is the **Alcázar de Colón** (*open daily 9–5; adm*), a two-storey, coral-stone palace with recessed arches, for 60 years the seat of the Spanish Crown in the Caribbean. It was constructed in 1510 by Don Diego Columbus, son of the discoverer, during his tenure as Viceroy, reputedly without the use of a single nail (doors and windows turned on pivots sunk into the walls). It was restored in 1957 with stone from the original quarry and period 16th- and 17th-century pieces, including outsize earthenware water-carriers and pint-size chairs. It is a nice place in which to pass the time of day, beneath the gargoyles and 17th-century tapestries and amid such viceregal paraphernalia as leather- and velvet-covered travelling trunks.

La Atarazana is opposite the Alcázar and runs down to the river beneath the square. In the 16th century, the eight buildings housed the royal armoury, the customs house and the official warehouses of old Santo Domingo; they have a similar role today in as much as they are stuffed with duty-free goods shipped in for sale. In the last building, you will find the **Museum of Marine Archaeology** (*open daily 9–5; adm*), with relics from wrecks that have foundered on the island's coasts: the *Guadeloupe*, the *Tolosa* and the *Concepción*. You'll also discover about life on board ship in the 17th century, including why the poop deck is so-called. You will find idyllic courtyards in which to rest in the Atarazana when you are gorged with buying and strolling the historic streets, museums and galleries, and there are a couple of bars. The oldest surviving building in the Americas, the **Casa del Cordón**, is just up the hill from the Alcázar, on the corner of Calle Emiliano Tejera and Calle Isabel la Católica. Built in 1503, it is named after the cord of the Franciscan order that is carved in stone above the lintel. Today it is the Banco Popular, but they permit tours during working hours.

South of the Alcázar, by the **Calle de Las Damas** (where the court ladies would take the evening air in colonial times), you come to the **Capilla de Nuestra Señora de los**

Remedios, a recently restored 16th-century chapel. Opposite is the **Museo de las Casas Reales** (*open daily 9–6; adm*), in former times the palace of the Governors and the Captains General, with some of the finest exhibits of the Spanish colonial heritage in the Dominican Republic, including handblown glass, armour and weapons. There are also reconstructions of Columbus's voyages and his ships.

Across Calle las Mercedes is the monumental **Panteón Nacional**, with an eternal flame to the heroes of the Republic, including the assassins of Trujillo. The building dates from 1714 and was a Jesuit monastery. The Calle de las Damas continues south, lined with attractive old palaces, until it reaches the old fortress of the colonial city, the **Fortaleza Ozama** (*open Tues–Sun 9–6*) on the banks of the river. Its heart is the Torre del Homenaje (the Tower of Homage), a minor colossus with walls 4ft thick, where for centuries prisoners were held. Nearby there is a good art gallery and café in which to sit, located in an alley, the **Plaza Toledo**, which is named after the wife of Bartholomew Columbus. You can see the works of the Dominican painters Alberto Ulloa, Freddy Javier and Martos García. Off the Calle de las Damas is the **Casa de Bastidas**, which has a pleasant courtyard where you can go to recover from the fray.

Not far off is **Parque Colón** (Columbus Square), where a statue of the explorer stands pointing to the horizon surrounded by arched walkways and coral-stone town buildings. On the south side is the **Catedral de Santa María la Menor** (*open Mon–Sat 9–6*), the first cathedral in the New World, which was built between 1523 and 1540. It is squat and not particularly magnificent, but has an attractive conglomeration of styles, with friezes and statues and gracefully curved roofs of rusty dark rock. Its grandeur lies in its status as the Catedral Primada de América (the senior cathedral in the Americas). Sir Francis Drake had no fitting respect for it in 1586, and used it as a place to hole up during his raid, chipping off the nose and hand of Bishop Bastidas's statue in a fit of anger. For a long time, it was also one of the many supposed resting places of Columbus (there are other claims from Seville and Cuba). He was supposed to have been brought here by his daughter-in-law in 1544, many years after he died. His next journey was in 1796, when the whole of Hispaniola was ceded to France – he was apparently moved to the cathedral in Havana so that he would remain in Spanish soil – and then in 1898 he was supposedly taken back to Seville. However, in 1877 Padre Francisco Billini discovered a small crypt containing some ashes. He declared them the ashes of Columbus. Now he has been moved (or may not have been, according to whose version of history you credit) a few miles east to El Faro, the huge lighthouse dedicated in 1992. With its columns and vaulted ceilings, the cathedral is pretty inside and you can see a huge mahogany throne and gold- and silverware from across the centuries. Diagonally opposite is the **Palacio de Borgella**, built during the Haitian occupation of 1822–44, and seat of the Dominican Congress until 1947, when it moved to the Palacio Nacional.

The main street of old Santo Domingo is **El Conde**, which leads west from the Parque Colón towards the Parque Independencia. This is an unashamedly modern shopping street, but turn off it and you will find endless other ruins and monuments. Some are modern, but many will cast your mind back to the glorious days of the 16th century. Now in ruins, the **Hospital Iglesia di San Nicolás de Barí** was the first hospital in the New World; also dating from 1510 is the **Convento de los Dominicos**, which once housed the first university founded here in 1538. On Calle Padre Billini, you will find the **Convento de Santa Clara**, a refuge for the Clarissa Sisters, dating from 1522, and the **Museum of the Dominican Family** (*open daily 9–6; adm*), with exhibits of the good life in the 19th century. In the Puerta de la Misericordia, you will find the old refuge of the city dwellers during hurricanes, and the spot where Mella initiated the revolt against Haitian occupation in 1844.

El Conde itself is a lively pedestrian precinct, usually teeming with people out promenading, sitting in the cafés and browsing the shops, which are among the city's best. At its western limit is the **Parque Independencia**, a major terminus for local transport and the official centre of the country (from where all distances are measured; there is even a bar called Kilometro Zero). On the square itself, behind the crumbled city wall and one of the old city gates, the **Puerto del Conde**, is a **mausoleum** constructed in 1976. Inside, you will see an eternal flame and a monument to the 1844 Independence leaders, Duarte, Mella and Sánchez.

The Modern City

The modern city of Santo Domingo lies to the north and west of the Parque Independencia, leading off in broad streets lined with trees where the villas stand back from the endless parade of motorbikes and the red and blue share taxis. The **Malecón** (the sea promenade, officially called Avenida George Washington) has an avenue of *palma cana* on the seafront between the occasional obelisk, and is one of the nicest spots in town. The road has recently been extended to the east, beneath the walls of the colonial city and along the Ozama River. The whole strip comes alive at dusk when the Dominicans take the evening air, walking up and down past the hundreds of portable stereos blaring out merengue. Unfortunately, many people seem to take the air in Toyota convertibles and so it becomes one big traffic jam, but it is fun to be a part of. The Malecón is particularly lively during Carnival and the merengue festival (*see* opposite), when the parades go by.

Another scene of Dominican mayhem is the **Mercado Modelo**, to the north of the colonial city on Avenida Mella (another major shopping street). It is one of the main Santo Domingo markets.

The **Plaza de Cultura**, on the Avenida César Nicolás Penson, is the site of a number of museums. The **Museum of the Dominican Man** has excellent exhibits from Taino life and more recent Dominican lives like those of the cane-cutters and modern carnival players. The **Museo Nacional de Historia y Geographica** (*open Tues–Sun 10–5; adm*) has more Arawak Indian exhibits and also Trujillo memorabilia. You will also find the **Galería de Arte Moderna**, the **Teatro Nacional** (the National Theatre and home of the Symphony Orchestra) and the **Bibliothéca Nacional** (National Library).

The **Palacio Nacional** (*t 686 4771; adm free, by appointment only*), just to the north-west of Parque Independencia on Calle Dr Delgado, is an imposing, mock-classical edifice of rose marble that might well have come from 17th-century Europe. In fact, it was built in the 1940s and for a while it was the home of the Congress of the Dominican Republic. It is guarded, but visitors are permitted inside by guided tour.

Merengue

Merengue – bright, lively and bustling, the perfect upbeat Latin music – is a way of life in the Dominican Republic. The Dominicans take music with them everywhere on noisy portable stereos, and you will see even two-year-olds moving to a beat, developing their sense of rhythm. The buses are like mobile discotheques and it is not unusual to find that the passengers sing along. Most popular merengue is produced on modern instruments now, but you will certainly still see the traditional three-piece band of the *perico ripiao*, made up of a drum, an accordion and a *güira* (a cheese grater scratched with a metal stick or a soul comb) and sometimes a *bajo* (a sit-on bass-box with metal teeth that the player thrums). Leading merengue singers are Juan Luis Guerra y 440, famed for his classic songs, Rubby Perez, Sergio Vargas, Fernando Villalona, Sin Fronteras, Toño Rosario and Los Hermanos Rosarios and, most popular for their (incredibly fast) dance music, Coco Band and La Banda Gorda.

An annual Merengue Festival is held in Santo Domingo in the last 10 days of July. There are three main stages for the bands on the Malecón, but the radio stations and the drinks companies set up their own stalls there, too. It is one of the year's liveliest events, a week's blowout of dancing, drinking and local food in the capital. If you cannot make that, there are endless discotheques, even in the smallest Dominican towns. After an evening's promenading around the town square, the locals end up there. Friday, Saturday and particularly Sunday nights are most popular.

Another sound to make a hit recently is bachata, once poor man's music but now more widely listened to. It has a wailing, often plaintive sound, though it's still excellent to dance to. The leading performers are Antony Santos, Raulin Rodriguez, Joe Veras, Luis Vargas, Zacharias Ferreiras and Luis Seguras among others. Puerto Rican salsa has also gained popularity as Dominican bands in the States such as Los Sabrosos have begun to play it.

In the northwest of town, you will find a quiet retreat from the mayhem of Santo Domingo, the kempt botanic violence of the **Jardín Botánico Nacional** (*open daily 9–5; adm*), at the top end of Avenida Sir Winston Churchill. More than 200 species of palm are on display and there is also a Japanese garden, as well as an orchid pavilion. Train and boat rides are available in the company of screaming Dominicans. To the northeast of here is the **Parque Zoológico** (*open daily 10–6; adm*): 10 acres of landscaped gardens above the river, where you will find dromedaries roaming, more miniature train rides and a vast aviary. 'Después del Puente' – on the other side of the River Ozama – you will find the immense **Faro a Colón** (the Columbus lighthouse), a monumental construction in the shape of a cross that was dedicated in the discoverer's honour during the 500th anniversary celebrations in 1992. It contains a lighthouse with an 80-mile radius and a laser that can throw a cross up into the Santo Domingo sky. Columbus made what was possibly his final journey when his ashes were brought to a chapel in the lighthouse. His white marble, wedding-cake-style tomb is at the heart of the cross and is guarded by soldiers in white.

The idea of a lighthouse was first mooted in the 19th century, but this particular design was submitted for a 1929 competition by a student of architecture from

Manchester, J. Gleave. Construction was undertaken by Trujillo but was abandoned until it was taken up again by Balaguer in 1987. It is a vast structure, built mostly of concrete with small stained-glass windows, and it contains a number of museums about marine and New World history. Also try the shipwreck museum.

A little farther out along the coast is the **Parque de los Tres Ojos** (the three 'eyes', four in fact), limestone sinkholes with pools. In the caves there are some impressive stalactites and stalagmites. From here, the Avenida de las Américas, lined with the flags of all the American nations, leads along the south coast to Boca Chica.

Santo Domingo to the North Coast

The road from Santo Domingo to Santiago and the north coast runs beneath the Cordillera Central, the Republic's largest mountain range, and then into the fertile Cibao Valley before rising again into the hills of the Cordillera Septentrional on the north coast. From the road, you will see huge plantations of citrus, pineapple and banana alongside cattle pastures and the plots of the subsistence farmers cut into the deep brown earth, with their small clapboard and thatched *bohíos* right by the side of the road. The town of **Bonao**, halfway to Santiago, has recently been transformed by the discovery of mineral deposits (nickel and bauxite) and the arrival of the mining industry, an overlay of modernity on the traditional town centre.

The road is good to **Constanza**, which is unexpectedly home to a small community of Japanese, brought here by Trujillo. It's a small and lazy town which stands among the pineforests at 2,000ft. A short distance off the main road is **Jarabacoa**, a friendly town with a population of about 40,000. These valleys are cooler than the coast so they have become the favoured retreat of the Dominican wealthy. At this height, they cultivate different crops, including tomatoes, onion, garlic, apples, peaches and even strawberries, many of which are flown out to the USA and even Europe.

Two waterfalls (*saltos*) can be visited from here: **Jimenoa**, a 70ft cascade into a rock-pool about 4 miles through the plantations and about 10 minutes' walk along an irrigation canal, and **Bayguate**, about 6 miles from the town. There is white-water rafting on the the Río Yaque de Norte and canyoning on the Río Jimenoa. A popular picnic, dancing and general gathering place is at the junction of the two rivers at the bottom of town. There is occasionally frost up here and so a swim in the water is pretty invigorating. Out of Constanza, you can visit the **Aguas Blancas**, a run of two waterfalls a few miles south of the town. Jarabacoa is also the dropping-off point for an ascent of **Pico Duarte**, at 10,416ft the island's highest peak, lost in the Bermúdez and Ramírez National Parks. The mountain has only recently been called after Duarte, the Independence hero. Before that, it knew a spell as Pico Trujillo after the dictator, but for most of its history, it has been known simply as Pico la Pelona (the bald mountain) because of the barren plains around the top. A bust of Duarte has been placed at the summit. The usual route passes Monabao and La Ciénaga, via Casa Tabalone, through the changing vegetation of palms and tangled rainforest to pines and ferns and diabolic dwarf growth. It is possible to hike, without the use of mountaineering gear, but you need to be reasonably fit. Take food for four days and warm clothing for the evenings (there are wooden cabins en route). Arrange a permit (*RD$75*) and a guide (*RD$125 a day*) and make sure to inform the National Park staff at La Ciénaga.

A number of wealthy towns draw their prosperity from the fertile Cibao Valley, the breadbasket of the Republic that sits between the two Cordilleras. The people are renowned for their pride and the area is referred to jokingly by Dominicans from elsewhere as the 'Republic of Cibao'. As you descend into the Cibao Valley, you come to **La Vega**. For a spectacular view, climb to the top of the Santo Cerro (just north of the town). Nearby are the ruins of Columbus's original settlement of Vega Real (Royal Valley), which was abandoned for the present site after an earthquake.

Santiago de los Treinta Caballeros

Santiago (population about 500,000) is the Dominican Republic's second city and quite a change from the mayhem of the capital. The romantic-sounding 'St James of the 30 noblemen' is set on the banks of a river gorge, inland where it was less vulnerable to attack, and it has a stately and confident air. There are some grand town houses from the 19th century, when Cibao agriculture was the engine of the Dominican economy. The city is generally bypassed by tourists, but a traveller may enjoy the pace of life here after the capital, before rejoining the fray on the north coast. You will not be pestered by hustlers in Santiago.

A striking and rather ugly 200ft **obelisk** stands above the town, commemorating the heroes of the Restoration of 1844, when the Dominican Republic forced out the Haitian occupation (it was originally built by Trujillo in honour of himself). There is an excellent view from the top. The **Museo del Tabaco**, on Calle 30 de Marzo, tells the story of tobacco, historically, as used by the Taino Indians (who thought the plant had magical properties), pirates, slaves and smugglers, and from cultivation to cigars. In the town centre is the **Museo de Arte Folklorico**, set in an elegant old town house, which exhibits local arts and crafts as well as the '*lechones*', the mischievous imps who pop up during the Santiago carnival. Fans of ruins will enjoy the old **colonial ruins** at Jacagua in the north of the city.

As you head northwest along the Cibao from Santiago towards the Haitian border, the land becomes steadily more arid. The town of **Monte Cristi** is known as '*Estamos muriendo de sed*' ('we are dying of thirst'), because it is so very dry and windswept.

The North Shore to the Amber Coast

The 150 miles of coastline from Monte Cristi to the Samaná Peninsula contain the bulk of the island's tourist industry. You will come across vast factory hotels arranged in complexes, but in other places you will still find stretches of palms and beaches extending as far as the eye can see, offset with the glorious blue of the reef-protected sea. There has been considerable building all along the coast and this is set to continue. Northeast of Monte Cristi (the northwesterly point of the country), beyond the cacti and the salt pans, is the **Parque Nacional Monte Cristi**, on a point that sticks into the sea like a pimple. Here you will find an undeveloped reserve that has extensive birdlife, including oystercatchers, ruddy turnstones, plovers and seabirds. Cayo Cabrito just offshore takes its name from the goats that were left there to graze (there are many places around the Caribbean called *cabrit*, which means 'goat').

The coastline is remote from the road for several miles as you head east (although you can get to the beach at Punta Rucia), but you can turn north to **Luperón**, with a few streets of elegant Dominican buildings, where the countryside begins to get a little bit greener. At **La Isabela**, which is going through the early stages of tourist development, you will find the **Parque Nacional Historico La Isabela** (*adm*), the remains (now purely archaeological) of Columbus's first settlement. The pattern of houses remains visible in low walls, including the Casa del Almirante (Columbus's own house) with a chapel and tower attached. There is also a museum (mainly in Spanish) which illuminates the settlement and has early Spanish artefacts, such as spurs, stirrups, coins and rings. Just before Puerto Plata is **Cofresi**, named after a buccaneer (he got about a bit: there is another town named after him on the west coast of Puerto Rico), which is popular at the weekends with the Dominicans.

Puerto Plata

The 'Silver Port', founded at the beginning of the 16th century, lies on the Atlantic coast in the shadow of the Cordillera Septentrional. At the western end of the Malecón (so long that it never becomes busy, though people do collect at the eastern end), you will find the **Fortaleza de San Felipe** (*open daily 9–4; adm*), a lumbering brute that was built in 1577 to defend the town from pirates. They managed to take the place over eventually and so Spain sacked it in 1605. Puerto Plata now has a faded charm in its many elaborate wooden gingerbread houses and Spanish plazas. Tourists are well known here, but they have not swamped the local life. **Playa Dorada**, a few miles through the cane fields to the east of Puerto Plata, is the main tourist area. It is a gaggle of modern hotels all collected together in a little complex.

The **Amber Museum**, 61 Calle Duarte (*t 586 2848; open Mon–Sat 9–5; adm*), has a series of exhibits about the origins and mining of amber, with pieces containing prehistoric creepy-crawlies on show, in an elegant old town house. There is a sales room with amber jewellery on sale. At the **Brugal Rum Distillery**, on the Avenida Colón (*open Mon–Fri 9–12 and 2–5*), a tour will take you through the Republic's second industry (for years the backbone of the economy), from cane-cutting to rum punch, with samples to taste if you have not already had enough from the fumes. One of the stranger sights in the Caribbean is a cable car (*teleférico; working Thurs–Tues 8–5 but summer season restricted*) that runs from behind the town to the summit of **Mt Isabel de Torres** (2,600ft), from where the view is magnificent, when it is not in cloud. There are botanical gardens and a restaurant at the top.

Puerto Plata to Samaná

The town of Sosúa splits into two halves: **El Batey**, the tourist area in the east with restaurants shoulder-to-shoulder and buzzing nightlife; and the more Dominican part, **Los Charámicos**, separated by a mile-wide bay.

Amber and Larimer

The Dominican Republic possesses one of the world's largest reserves of amber, a semi-precious gem. Amber is not a stone, but petrified sap from trees that grew on the earth 50 million years ago. It has been known as a 'touchstone' in the past because of its static qualities. The word 'electricity' derives from the Greek for amber, *elektron*. The featherweight gem varies from an almost transparent variety that has undergone the least chemical reaction, through the familiar yellow and amber colour to a deep red (the price increases with the depth of colour). Value is increased further by wisps of blue smoke within it, gases that were caught as the sap formed in the old rainforests millions of years ago. Most exquisite (and most expensive) are pieces in which leaves and insects have been caught. There are three main mining areas in the Republic, the largest at Cotui in the Cibao, in the mountains just south of Puerto Plata on the north coast, and at El Valle close to Santo Domingo.

Several museums exhibit amber, including Joyas Criollas at the Plaza Criolla, and the Amber Museums in Santo Domingo and in Puerto Plata. There are pieces for sale in these places as well as in any tourist shop you might go into. It is possible to visit the amber mines, though you will have to do much of the organizing yourself. The best place to start is at the museums. It is illegal to export unpolished amber.

Larimar, or Dominican turquoise, is unique to the Dominican Republic. It is a very hard, semi-precious stone, slightly lighter in colour than other turquoise, and it is mined in the southwestern corner of the country. You will find examples of jewellery made from larimar in all the tourist shops and markets.

Leave the town and you soon come to **Cabarete**, which is strung along the coastal road just by a huge bay of buff-coloured sand. Cabarete, which has seen a great deal of development in recent years, is renowned for windsurfing and kiteboarding, and so it attracts a fun, active crowd who spend the day on the waves and the evenings in the beach bars and restaurants. Beyond Cabarete the endless beaches begin, all of them undeveloped. The coastal road leads through the local towns of Río San Juan and Cabrera down to the town of Nagua, towards the Samaná Peninsula. This is a poor area of the country, as you can see by the houses, which are made of wattle and daub (mud and wood) and with the stems of palm fronds.

The Samaná Peninsula

North and slightly east of Santo Domingo, the Samaná Peninsula is one of the most beautiful parts of the island. Its mountains, some like eggbox limestone hillocks as in the Cockpit Country in Jamaica, are cut by swathes of light green coconut palm and deep green pine trees, and the small clapboard *bohíos* of the Dominicans are painted in pastel washes of pink or purple. In Samaná Bay you will see the fishermen standing in their flat-bottomed boats and casting their fishing nets. There are spectacular beaches, mainly on the north side of the peninsula (not in the town of Samaná itself).

Columbus appeared in the bay in 1493, but was met by such a volley of arrows from the local inhabitants (probably Caribs from down-island on a raid against the Tainos) that he named it 'Golfo de las Flechas'. The original town of Samaná was populated by escaped American slaves who came to the free island of Haiti in the early 19th century. There are Protestant churches in the area (in a strongly Catholic country) dating from this time. As such a well-protected anchorage, the town was also sought by the Americans as a possible naval base in the area.

Today **Samaná** is an ugly concrete infestation along a four-lane seafront boulevard (the old wooden houses were destroyed in the name of tourism development that was destined but has yet to take off). The odd-looking aqueduct in the bay was supposed to lead to a hotel on the offshore island, but that, too, was never built. However, if there is no charm in the town, the people make it extremely lively and great fun. The Báhia de Samaná is the winter home of up to three thousand **humpback whales**, who come here to mate and to give birth at the Silver Bank in January and February. Trips taking several hours can be arranged in town, for a minimum number of people (*expensive*). You will see babies piggy-backing and the adults making whale-style whoopee, splashing their tails or jumping clean out of the water. There have been problems recently with the noise of the engines interrupting the whales' highly sensitive hearing (letting sharks come in and steal the young) and so some boats will not go too close.

In the hills above Samaná (on the road to Las Terrenas), you can visit the **Río Limón Waterfall**, which falls 160ft in a number of chutes. **Las Terrenas** itself lies on the north coast of the peninsula and is a very low-key resort town with an easy air and some small and hip places to stay, on what are some of the country's best beaches. Barely any package tourists make it over there, so it is the best resort on the island for the independent traveller. There is not much to do, but there are watersports.

To the south and west of Sanchez is **Los Haitises National Park**, an area of karst limestone and coastal mangrove swamps. It includes also a number of small offshore cays inhabited by hawks, pelicans, noddies and roseate terns. Deeper in the swamps, you will see the ungainly jacana, with overlong toes that help it walk over water-lilies, and herons and ibises. You can arrange a trip from Samaná.

East of Santo Domingo

Headed east from Santo Domingo on the Avenida de las Américas, you first come to **Boca Chica**, just past the airport, a hotel strip set on a good beach that becomes very crowded and noisy at the weekends as the Dominicans escape in droves from the capital. At **La Caleta**, you can see an Arawak burial site. You then pass by **San Pedro de Macoris**, which is known for its free-trade zones, its baseball team, its carnival and its 'Cocolas', migrant workers whose ancestors came from Tortola in the British Virgin Islands early last century to cut sugar cane.

Beyond **La Romana**, an agricultural town, is the famous and very expensive resort Casa de Campo, where there is a whole host of hotels, villas, golf courses and polo pitches. Set high on a river bend, **Altos de Chavón** is a Spanish medieval clifftop town built of rusty coral rock, everywhere festooned with bougainvillea and sprays of hibiscus, and inhabited by a colony of artists. Its heart is the **Iglesia St Stanislaus**, and all around are aged cobbled alleys and streets. There is even an amphitheatre, where Frank Sinatra and Julio Iglesias have sung in recent years. And yet, there is something slightly wrong about Altos de Chavón. Somehow there is an unruly Gothic air to the medieval idyll; it is slightly overdone, very neat and really rather twee. It comes as no surprise to find that it was all designed in 1978 and that Frank Sinatra actually inaugurated the amphitheatre. There is a free bus service from Casa de Campo. The presence of an art school means that there are also some art galleries.

Beyond here is the **National Park of the East**, which contains much of the V-shaped point of land and the island of Saona off the southern shore. The western entrance to the park is at Bayahibe, which until recently was a dozy fishing village and is now seeing the beginnings of tourism. There are paths that cross the park, but you will need to find a guide to lead you along them. On the south coast is Catalina Bay, a phosphorescent bay where the water glows in green luminescent whorls as you drag your fingers through it. In the park, you may see lizard cuckoos and orioles, while on the coast you can spot oystercatchers and other seabirds, such as pelicans and magnificent frigatebirds. Access to the eastern side of the park is through the little town of **San Rafael de Yuma**, where you will find the restored house of Ponce de León, who lived here for three years before he moved on to settle Puerto Rico in 1508. The road reaches the coast at **Boca de Yuma**, a tranquil fishing village.

About 20 miles (32km) northeast of La Romana, lost in the cattle and sugar cane flats of the southeast, is the genuine 16th-century town of **Higüey**, which is known for having the sweetest oranges in the country. A charming church lies at its centre, the **Basílica de Nuestra Señora de la Merced**, supposedly erected on the site of a battle in which the early Spaniards fended off the Caribs. It had long been a place of pilgrimage and then in the 1950s the massive new church was built. The monumental **Basílica de Nuestra Señora de Altagracia** (the patron saint of the Dominican Republic) is built of concrete and shaped like a 200ft pair of hands held in prayer. Pilgrims arrive on 21 January and 16 August.

Beyond Higüey, the countryside becomes wilder: *campesinos* ride around on their horses, people live in simple palm-thatch *bohíos*, and in places there are Haitian *bateys* (small villages). But then in **La Otra Banda**, you will notice a rash of pretty and brightly coloured houses with gingerbread decoration. Originally populated with Canary Islanders, it is now a popular place for wealthy returning Dominicans.

East of Higüey, you reach the coast at **Punta Cana** and **Bavaro**. In recent years, this area has transformed itself into the country's largest resort zone. And more is on the way, with the development of Capa Cana, a kind of mega-resort fronting 5 miles of beach. There are plans for a 500-berth marina, three new golf courses and a Mediterranean-style seaside village with a residential community of 5,000. The sands here continue to the northeast almost uninterrupted for the 30 miles (50km) to Laguna Nisibón. You should be careful when swimming because of the Atlantic currents. Beyond Miches, you enter wild farming country and eventually come to the sleepy town of Sabana de la Mar, from where you can get a ferry across to the Samaná Peninsula.

West of Santo Domingo

The southwestern corner of the Dominican Republic (or simply 'The South' as it is known) is the remotest area of the country and in places it is barren and desert-like, though this does, of course, mean that the sun is more reliable than on the north coast. There's not a great deal of organized tourism in the region (though there are some recent developments in Barahona) and so it's a good place to come to get a view of local Dominican life. As you get closer to the frontier with Haiti, you should expect the army activity to increase: you will be stopped and you may also be subject to searches.

Taking the Carreta Sanchez out of Santo Domingo you come to **San Cristóbal**, most infamous for being the birthplace of Trujillo. During his life, he built it up with a grandeur that befitted his status as dictator: take a look at the plaza, the ornate church and his mausoleum (although he is not buried there: his remains were taken to France). **Casa las Coabas**, his family home, overlooks the town from a hill. It has fallen into disrepair now, but it is due for restoration. Also being renovated is the **Castillo del Cerro**, another of Trujillo's palaces, a monstrous over-elaborate affair on a nearby summit. Despite the ongoing restoration work, you can visit for a small fee. Also worth a visit are caves at **El Pomier**.

Passing through endless cane fields you come to the prosperous town of **Baní**, birthplace of Máximo Gómez, a hero of the Cuban Independence movement, and eventually to **Barahona**, an industrial but nonetheless sleepy town. The countryside in this area turns to barren hills covered with prickly pear and organ-pipe cactus trained into fences. From here, one road runs south into the V-shaped **Barahona Peninsula**, passing through poor fishing villages like Enriquillo and Oviedo, with excellent beaches, before heading north to the town of Pedernales on the Haitian border. It was from the Baoruco Mountains that Enriquillo led his guerrilla campaign against the Spaniards in the 1520s.

The **Jaragua National Park** lies in the southwestern tip of the peninsula: 500 square miles of cactus plains, sea and discoloured limestone shoreline. You will see pelicans and terns on the coastline. The park is remote, so visitors should go well-prepared. Go by jeep and be sure to take plenty to eat and particularly to drink if you are going off the beaten track. Note that **Beata Island**, off the southern tip, has excellent birdlife, too.

From Barahona a road inland leads towards Jimaní on the Haitian border. The town is close to **Lago Enriquillo**, a saltwater lake that lies 140ft below sea level. **Isla Cabritos** (Goat Island, after the livestock left to forage there) is a national park in the centre of the lake. The five-mile-long island is dry and scrubby but supports an extremely wide variety of wildlife, including alligators and iguanas. Among the birds that live on the island are flamingos, clapper rails and roseate spoonbills. You can usually get permission to go to the lake at the park office in **La Descubierta**, a hot and desolate town (you should also request permission in the National Parks Office in Santo Domingo before you set off; alternatively, take a tour with Roi Caiman, see 'Flora and Fauna'). If you make the trip, make sure to stock up on food and drink, which is not that easily found in the remote areas beyond Barahona. About half a mile before La Descubierta there are **Arawak petro-glyphs** carved on a cliffside. In the town is a *balneario*, a freshwater swimming pool.

Haiti

Haiti

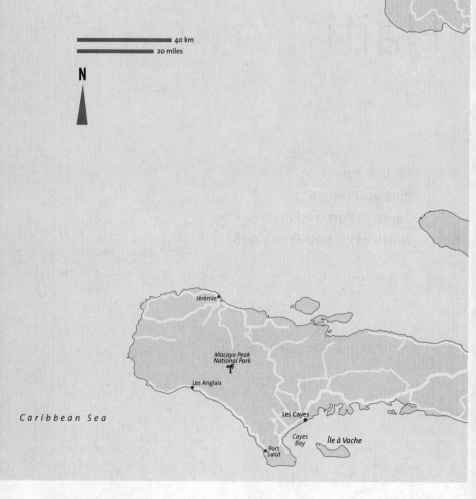

40 km
20 miles

N

Jérémie

Macaya Peak
National Park

Les Anglais

Les Cayes

Caribbean Sea

Cayes
Bay

Île à Vache

Port
Salut

Highlights

1 Tramp up to the Citadelle outside Cap Haïtien, a mountaintop fortress so
large that it could garrison 10,000 men for a year without resupply
2 Attend a voodoo ceremony and see initiates, driven by drums, possessed by
their guardian spirits
3 Shop for Haitian art

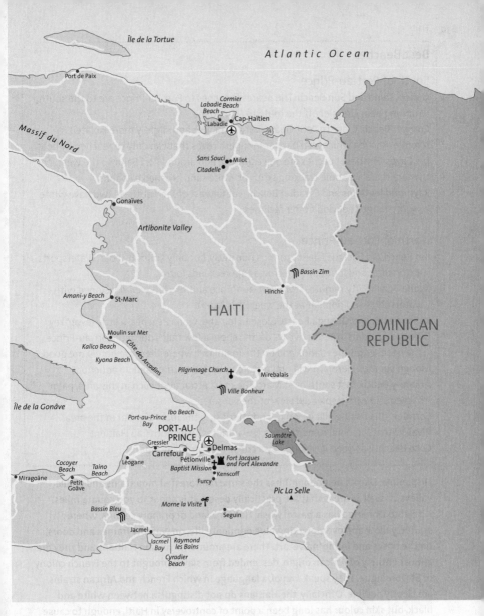

The rhythms and reverberations of Africa echo more strongly in Haiti than in any other Caribbean country – in the speech and the faces, in the sheer effervescence of its people, and in the spiritual world and the relentless beat of African drums. Haiti, which staged the Caribbean's only successful slave rebellion, fighting for its independence in 1804, is the oldest black republic in the world.

Haiti was originally an Arawak name for the island and supposedly meant 'mountainous land' (a good guess at translation, if nothing else, because the island has three vast mountainous ranges). Haiti has the western third of the island of

Best Beaches

South of Port-au-Prince

Guilou, Taino and **Sun Beach**: The nearest beaches to Port-au-Prince are to the south, running near Gressier off the route to Miragoâne.

Cocoyer Beach: Close to Petit Goâve. Very attractive and slightly more isolated.

Jérémie: An area which also has some superb coves that can only be reached by boat.

Les Cayes: The best beaches are on Île à Vache and around Port Salut to the west, where there are some cracking strips of white sand brushed by palms.

Raymond les Bains and **Cyradier Beach**: Not far east of Jacmel, these two have white sand, though they don't offer facilities.

North of Port-au-Prince

Ibo Beach: On Cacique Island, 30mins ride away, but only 5mins by boat. Watersports are on offer and it pulls in the crowds at weekends (*adm*).

Kyona Beach: Fifty minutes from Port-au-Prince and, like Ibo, well-developed with watersports and popular at the weekends (*adm*).

Kalico Beach and **Ouanga Beach**: Close to Ibo and Kyona Beaches; a little lower-key.

Côte des Arcadins: A series of cays off the shore a few miles north of Port-au-Prince. The beaches on the islands and on the mainland, where there are hotels, are good.

Moulin sur Mer: Here you will find restored plantation ruins and an aqueduct.

Amani-y Beach: Just south of St Marc. The most attractive beach in this area, palm-backed and with a splendid view of the sunset.

Cormier: This fishing village, on the north coast, is the most popular in the area.

Rival: With its colonial ruins, this is a few minutes' walk from Cap Haïtien.

Coco Beach: Has been developed by a cruise-line company (*adm*).

Hispaniola. Like its neighbour it has the same rainforested mountains and fertile valleys, as well as areas that are practically desert. It is about 10,700 square miles.

If Santo Domingo has a pastel wash, Haiti is a land of primary colours, where scarlet, yellow and overpowering blue dominate life, on window frames and doors, on the buses and in the 'naïve' art. There are around 7.5 million Haitians and they are almost entirely of African origin, descended from slaves brought to the French colony of St Domingue. They speak *kreyol*, a language in which French and African strains are clearly audible. Officially, the Haitians do not distinguish between white and black, but skin colour has long been a point of controversy in Haiti, enough to cause massacres and political violence.

There is grinding poverty – Haiti is the poorest country in the western hemisphere. As in many Caribbean countries, the people are poorly dressed, but here they are also poorly fed. You will see fifty children clamouring at the only standpipe for miles around, collecting water which they take home balanced on their heads in vast plastic buckets. Out in the country, they go to church if they can afford shoes.

Politics has also been hard on the Haitians. Over the last two centuries, they have seen endless internal strife as a succession of corrupt dictators jockeyed for position and then administered with a brutal disregard for their population's pitiable situation. Despite a desire for stability among the people themselves, it seems a forlorn hope that the situation should improve radically in the near future. On the international scene, Haiti has been embattled from the beginning, shunned as a stronghold of black magic and, most recently, as the original source of AIDS. The Haitians were blacklisted by the USA until the USA freed her own slaves.

For all this, though, the people maintain an undefiable optimism and they are certainly not resigned in their poverty. The country has an irrepressible spirit, and they escape their drab physical existence in many ways. The most notorious is the religious cult of voodoo (*see* pp.646–7), but the islanders also express themselves in vibrant traditions of naïve art and a lively street culture. Get out into the streets of Port-au-Prince and you will soon see. Haiti seems to have taken all the strains essential to Caribbean life and amplified them to a blare. And, unlike so many Caribbean countries which have a hang-up about their colonial past, Haiti has no problem about its national identity.

Haiti is hardly a tourist destination, though it has the beaches and the reliable winter sun, but the joy of Haiti lies well behind the screen of palms and coconut oil. It is a thoroughly rewarding place to travel in, though it can be very tiring and at times of political difficulties it can be dangerous.

History

Columbus discovered Haiti on 5 December 1492 on his first voyage to the New World, as he sailed east from Cuba. His ship, the *Santa Maria*, was wrecked there. He was forced to leave the crew behind and so, after building them a fort, La Navidad (Christmas), with the wood from the ship, he left the 40 men with instructions to discover gold of which they had heard reports and which Marco Polo had reported as 'inexhaustible' (Columbus thought he had discovered Japan). When he returned a year later, the men were all dead.

A hundred years after this, as the colony of Hispaniola was languishing, pirates and sea rovers began to creep into the inaccessible northwestern corner of the island. They holed up on the island of Tortuga, fortifying themselves so that they were almost impossible to winkle out. Often they would disappear on jaunts around the Caribbean as mercenaries, but when there was peace, they made their way over to the remote areas of the mainland to kill cattle, which they smoked over a frame called a *boucan*. They came to be known as the *boucaniers*, or buccaneers.

The buccaneers were mostly French (English pirates had a similar hideout in Port Royal, Jamaica) and eventually, at the Treaty of Ryswick in 1697, the Spaniards ceded the western third of the island to the French Crown. Over the next century, St Domingue became the richest colony in the world, supplying sugar, coffee and indigo to France in a fleet of 700 ocean-going ships. With annual exports worth $40 million, it was far more prosperous than any of the American colonies, and its capital, Cap Français, was called the Paris of the New World. The regime was as brutal as it was successful. The 500,000 slaves were treated with abominable cruelty: the planters flogged them close to death for the most minor offence and some were buried alive.

With so many slaves, and internal rivalries between the whites, those of mixed race and free blacks, the colony was a virtual powder keg sparked off by the French Revolution. The National Assembly in Paris granted those of mixed race political rights, but the whites would not let it happen in reality in the colony and so the rebellions started. The mixed-race Ogé and Chavannes, who made a call to arms, were publicly broken on the wheel.

Rebellion and Revolution

These events were overtaken in August 1791, when the first major black rebellion took place. It was initiated by Boukman, a voodoo *houngan*, who gave instructions to torch the northern plains with the call of a conch shell and with the voodoo drums. The slaves pillaged and burned, subjecting the white slave owners to the tortures they had undergone themselves. The few who escaped fled to Cap Français and left the country, many settling in eastern Cuba. Over the three years of the rebellion, the northern part of the colony was devastated and the lines were drawn for civil war between the blacks in the north and the mixed-race dominated south. The French colonial authorities were powerless to intervene.

The rebel leader in the north was the remarkable Toussaint L'Ouverture (called so either because of an opening he created in a battle or for the gap between his teeth), who sided with the French Republicans after they abolished slavery in 1793. Toussaint had educated himself with the sanction of his white master (whom Toussaint helped to escape during the 1791 rebellion) and he entered the rebel army as a herb doctor. His skill as a military man, supposedly learned from a book about Alexander's campaigns, soon became clear, and by 1796, he was the undisputed leader of the former slaves in the north. He then showed his brilliant colours as a politician and he administered his country humanely, ending the massacres and managing to restore some of St Domingue's former prosperity. He was the unofficial governor of a colony that was independent from France in all but name.

But when he tried to introduce a constitution that allowed the country autonomy and appointed him governor for life, it was too much for Napoleon, who wished to re-establish his power in the Americas. In 1801 Bonaparte despatched an army of 34,000 men, led by his own brother-in-law Leclerc, with instructions to subdue the slave armies and to retake the colony for France. It was an unsuccessful campaign and Leclerc's soldiers died like flies from disease (in all over 100,000 European soldiers died trying to take Haiti back, a huge number in those days). Leclerc treated with Toussaint and, during a dinner to discuss the affairs of the colony, had him seized and deported to France. Toussaint's final words on departure from St Domingue were: 'In overthrowing me, they have cut down in St Domingue the trunk of the tree of black liberty. It will shoot up again through the roots, for they are numerous and deep.' Toussaint was held in a castle in the Jura mountains, ill-fed and without warmth. His letters to Napoleon went unanswered and within a year he was dead.

The blacks did not revolt immediately, but they buried their arms rather than turn them in. In May 1802, the Convention in Paris reintroduced slavery and the blacks rose up against the French once more. More whites were massacred, and the French Army, decimated by disease and guerrilla war, evacuated. On 1 January 1804, Jean Jacques Dessalines tore the white strip out of the *tricolore*, and proclaimed the independent black Republic of Haiti in the northern half of the island.

Dessalines was a tyrant, but he started to rebuild the economy, forcing the former slaves back to their plantations. Ever fearful of an attack by the French to retake the colony, he maintained a large army, introducing into Haitian society a traditional power which continues even today. But soon he became unpopular, particularly with the mixed-race Haitians, and he was assassinated in 1806.

His death led to civil war again between the mixed-race south, under General Pétion, and the black north, which adopted Henry Christophe as its leader. As leader of Haiti, Christophe, a megalomaniac and an immense man in size and energy, wished to show that the first black republic was as capable as any European power. He had himself crowned king (Dessalines had made himself an emperor in imitation of Napoleon) and he built a magnificent palace worthy of any European kingdom at Sans Souci near Cap Haïtien in the north of the island. Nearby, his Citadel is one of the most extraordinary feats of engineering in the world. But his reign was also tyrannical and, in 1820, as armies closed in on him, he committed suicide by shooting himself with a silver bullet. He was buried in the Citadel. After his death, the two sides of the country were united again, under the southern General Boyer.

Boyer treated with France, who finally accepted Haitian Independence at the price of 150 million French francs as compensation (later reduced to 60 million). He also invaded Santo Domingo, which had just won Independence from Spain. He governed well for 15 years but then fled the country after an uprising in the black north.

In the 72 years between Boyer's flight in 1843 and 1915, Haiti saw 22 heads of state, most of whom left office by violent means. Some tried to improve the infrastructure of the country, but the aspirations of the early leaders foundered with a succession of corrupt and self-seeking dictators. Rivalry continued between the whites and the mixed-race élite and the blacks, who dominated the army, flaring up from time to time in politically motivated massacres. In the fields, the Haitian peasants suffered a continuing poverty, scraping barely enough food from the soil to survive. In 1915, after the dismemberment of President Guillaume Sam, the Americans invaded the country, concerned by the influence of the German community in the country at the time of the First World War. There followed 19 years of heavy-handed administration. It brought considerable development in roads, sanitation and in schools, but the Haitians opposed it with a nationalist movement which erupted increasingly in violence. In 1930, Haiti was flourishing and they wanted independence again. In 1934 the Marines left.

The mixed-race élite had come to prominence again during the American occupation and it was not long before internal political troubles started along the traditional lines. Until the accession of François Duvalier in 1957, and since the deposition of his son in 1986, Haiti has suffered the political turmoil it has always faced.

The Duvaliers

The Duvalier regime was another brutal chapter in Haitian history, in which the country was hijacked by a ruthless despot who then arranged to hand over power to his son. It was characterized by repression, particularly through 'Papa Doc's' private militia, the notorious *tontons macoutes* (meaning 'uncle knapsack', which comes from a character in Haitian folklore who carries off children in the middle of the night). Father and son amassed vast personal fortunes from the Haitian national coffers.

François Duvalier, a doctor and union leader and a member of Haiti's emerging black middle class, was elected president at the age of 50 in 1957. For the first few years in his 14-year rule, 'Papa Doc' terrorized the country, consolidating power and rooting out potential rivals in the army, the Church and the mixed-race élite. A shrewd manipulator, he ensured that there was no organized resistance to his regime. He was also a practising vodunist; his *lwa* was Baron Samedi, guardian of cemeteries and a harbinger of death. Thousands of Haitians died in his regime. He had the constitution changed in 1964 so he could be elected president for life; he remained so until his death in 1971.

As his son, Jean Claude, then 19 years old, took over, there was initially some political liberalization and there was also foreign investment as the regime became less isolationist. But the status quo was maintained by the usual terror tactics and, once again, the poorest Haitians benefited little. Haiti was the poorest country in the western hemisphere. Many Haitians took their chance and tried to get illegally into the USA. Corruption ran rife. In the face of this poverty, 'Baby Doc' lavished an estimated US$7 million dollars of national money on his wedding in 1980.

In the early 1980s, he cracked down on any liberalization and the new political parties were banned. Riots broke out as the regime began to founder in 1984, and by late 1985, the country was in open revolt. Eventually, in what was known as Operation Deschoukay, the regime collapsed on 6 February 1986 and 'Baby Doc' fled the country for France. The country lurched from one ineffectual government and political crisis to the next until Jean-Bertrand Aristide, a priest and leader of the Lavalas Party, was elected in a landslide victory in December 1990. He introduced radical changes, but his government soon foundered on the inertia of military and neo-Duvalierist power and eventually he was deposed in a coup, led by certain sections of the army. The coup provoked international condemnation and resulted in the imposition of an embargo by the Organization of American States. Other nations suspended aid and froze government assets.

After many attempts, Aristide was finally able to return in late 1994, sponsored by the USA, to serve the rest of his term of office. This was facilitated by US military back-up and later by UN troops. On his return to power, Aristide began to downscale the role of the army and police force within Haiti, which ultimately resulted in the breakdown of law and order. He remained in power until 2003, when opposition to his regime led Haiti to the brink of civil war. Once again the US and the UN stepped in. Aristide was ousted and Gerald Latortue, a Haitian businessman living in Florida, was picked to head the government until stability could be established and new elections held. Unfortunately, Haiti's political problems continue to rumble on.

There seems to be a general will among the people for internal stability, but for the moment, with endless suspicions of corruption and involvement in drug-trafficking at the highest levels and the unpredictable activities of the rival security forces and traditional political power-blocs, it is impossible to say what will be the outcome. The future is by no means bright. Many Haitians are still trying to escape to the USA.

The economy is in a mess: inflation is running out of control and three-quarters of the population of Haiti is reckoned to be on the breadline. The majority are subsistence farmers, but many work in the coffee industry. The low wages make a certain amount of industry possible, including the manufacture of some electronic goods, shoes and baseballs. The usual Caribbean mainstay, tourism, has fallen off because of the political problems. For the same reason, mineral resources remain untouched. The literacy rate in Haiti is 48%.

Torrential rains in 2003–2004 added to the troubles, causing severe flooding. Entire villages were swept away and thousands of people died. While the trickle of tourists continues, visitors should be aware that Haiti's infrastructure is largely shattered, after years of turmoil and neglect. A number of new hotels and restaurants have opened in recent years, but Haiti's security situation may prove cause for concern.

Beaches

Haiti has a full range of beaches, from strips of idyllic white sand to secluded coves which you can only reach by rowing boat, and with the political trouble they have become generally deserted. The more popular beaches, if they are owned by a hotel or have been developed by a cruise ship company, will charge an entrance fee. You will find most watersports available here. You can also go further afield and discover fishing villages on idyllic half-moon coves. Remember to take all you need: picnic, mosquito repellant, water and snorkelling gear. *See* 'Best Beaches', p.630.

Flora and Fauna

The 'mountainous land' of Haiti is extremely fertile, particularly in the well-watered heights of the northern and southern massifs, each of which has developed unique flora. The nearest park to Port-au-Prince is in the hills above Kenscoff: **Morne la Visite** lies between Furcy and Seguin, and in the lush montane forests you will find parrots and parakeets and the Hispaniolan hummingbird. Similar vegetation and birdlife can be found at the western end of the peninsula, at the remote **Macaya Peak National Park**. Take everything you will need if you go exploring here.

At **Saumâtre Lake** near the Dominican border, you will see crocodiles and extensive birdlife, including flamingos and jacanas with rebellious toes and an embarrassing splurge on their faces. Across the cactus plains in the centre of the island where the hawks and hummingbirds hover, the **Massif du Nord** has more rich red earth and precipitous slopes which can be treacherous after rain. There is considerable deforestation in Haiti as the islanders chop down trees for burning. If you go out into the country, you will see the charcoal pits in which the Haitians prepare their fuel.

There is little organized about the national parks in Haiti, though there is sometimes a ranger's hut available. Take all you need in the way of food and water and a four-wheel-drive car. You should get permission in Port-au-Prince before you visit the parks, through ISPAN (Institut pour la Sauvegarde du Patrimoine National), PO Box 2484, 86 Av John Brown in Port-au-Prince, **t** 222 5286.

Some Advice

Because of the political unrest, there is very little tourism in Haiti at the moment. There are hardly even any hustlers any more. However, it is a fascinating country in which to travel, even allowing for the fact that it is quite hard work.

A traveller in Haiti will soon become familiar with the word *blanc* (white), which the islanders will say at every turn. It is not a racist insult: although it means 'white', all foreigners in Haiti are referred to as *blanc*, even black visitors. It is a cross between an exclamation and a greeting to a stranger (if a Haitian wants to insult you, he will do it with a babble of incomprehensible expletives in Haitian *kreyol*). There is no reason to feel threatened by the word *blanc*, but it may not be a request for you to stop and talk. You are quite likely to be shouted at in the street, but this is not always with malicious intent: more often than not, it is a humorous quip in the Haitian street-theatre (though it can still be a little disconcerting to find that the whole road collapses in raucous laughter).

Dollar, on the other hand, is definitely a request for money, and you sometimes get the idea that this is the first word that a Haitian child learns. White travellers, who must have money to have got to Haiti in the first place and are therefore all assumed to be rich, will find themselves surrounded by crowds of kids requesting a dollar, or five. The best advice is not to give in to their demands, even though they are quite persistent. It is important to distinguish between the hustlers who nobble you at the gates of your hotel and in downtown Port-au-Prince (making a reasonable living out of it), and the genuinely poor countryman to whose life the donation of a dollar would make an appreciable difference. Inevitably, you will find yourself habitually overcharged by taxi drivers and traders. Set the price before and bargain.

As in any city, you are advised to be aware when in Port-au-Prince (watch your pockets in public places). Violence in Haiti tends to be political and surfaces at election time and in occasional *coups d'état*. Consider getting out of town then, though trouble is not generally directed at foreigners.

Women do not usually suffer sexual harassment in Haiti. You are advised not to drink the water in Haiti, or to buy the iced drinks off the streets, sold from the tricycles with a box of concentrates on the front. Stick to soft drinks and coconuts. Purified water (Culligan is an accepted term for purified water) is easily available in the shops. The electrical supply in Haiti is hopeless. Expect it to be off for most of the day and to come on at any time between 6 and 8pm. When visiting Haiti, you should take a preventative medicine against malaria. There is a problem with venereal diseases, most notably with HIV.

Lastly, photography is something of a problem in Haiti. It can be quite entertaining as all the Haitians dive for cover at the sight of a camera. If you look too determined, they will remonstrate with you and tell of their soul being stolen. The odd Haitian has been known to sell his soul for a few dollars – take your choice. If you go ahead without paying, expect to be screamed at and cursed in *kreyol* and for the whole street to collapse in giggles again.

Getting There

Haiti t (509–)

By Air

The main airport, t 246 0642/4105, is 13km from the capital Port-au-Prince, on the north side of Delmas. A taxi into town costs about US$20; a cheaper alternative is to take a taptap. Occasional flights fly into Cap Haïtien on the north coast, where you can get a taxi through Metrotaxi, t 262 4672. A departure tax of US$25 is usually payable in dollars.

From Europe

Air France, t 222 5926, has a weekly flight from Paris. From other cities in Europe, you will need to change planes, which is most convenient in Miami, though it is possible through Guadeloupe (*see* p.283) and even overland from the Dominican Republic (*see* p.599).

From North America

There are direct links to Haiti from Miami and sometimes New York, with flights on American Airlines, t 226 0100, t 249 0311, and Lynx Air (Ft. Lauderdale). Air Canada, t 246 0441/2, flies once a week from Montreal.

From Central America

Copa Panama, t 223 2326/27, offers flights from Panama City.

From Other Caribbean Islands

Many links have been cut due to recent troubles, but Air Caraibes flies from Martinique and Guadeloupe twice a week. Caribinter, t 250 2304, flies from Santo Domingo and sometimes from Cuba and Jamaica. Cap Haïtien on the north coast is linked nearly every day to the Turks and Caicos Islands.

From the Dominican Republic

There are two points of entry on the Haitian border with the Dominican Republic, at Jimani in the south and Ouanaminthe in the north. There is a daily bus service from Santo Domingo with Caribe Tours, Angle rue Clerueaux et Gabart, Pétionville, Haiti, t 257 9379. Check locally for more details.

Getting Around

By Bus

Around Port-au-Prince you can take *camionettes*, like small taptaps, which run specific routes through the town, picking up and setting down where you please. They have no timetable, but they run frequently from dawn until dusk, less frequently after that. One ride costs 2 gourdes. Otherwise take a *publique*, recognizable by the red cloth tied to the rear-view mirror. These pick up any passenger and the driver decides who to let off first. If you want to get up to Pétionville, flag down a *publique* on Av John Brown, which leads from Place du Marron Inconnu, or catch it earlier down by the Marché de Fer.

Taptaps run the length and breadth of the country. If you are on a long journey, you may find it more comfortable to ride in one of the more regular buses, though these can be crowded enough. Once again, they leave when they are full (ask around for the next one to leave). Jacmel and Cap Haïtien are quite well-served; other towns have only a couple of services a day. Get to the bus stop early. If you are going to a beach, ask the driver to drop you off. Buses going south and west leave from behind the customs building, towards the waterfront from the Marché de Fer. If you are going north, you leave from the top of Bd

Port-au-Prince

The capital of Haiti is tucked deep into the southeastern corner of Haiti's huge bay and is backed by the mountains of the southern peninsula. It was founded in 1749, and became the capital of the new republic in 1806. It has a population of 1.8 million.

The small commercial area downtown is set out in a gridiron plan of unattractive streets, scattered at intervals with venerable churches, gingerbread mansions, a few

Jean Jacques Dessalines. Fares are generally pretty cheap.

By Taxi

Taxis are available at the airport and at major hotels and restaurants. They are not always in the best condition, but usually get you home. They are unmetered and rates are officially set by the government, so you should establish the price (don't forget to bargain) and make sure of the currency before you set off on the journey.

Taxi drivers would be happy to take you on a **tour** for about US$15 per hour, though not all speak English. You will probably get the run-around, and be taken only to the galleries where the driver gets a commission on your purchase, so be firm if there is a place you particularly want to visit. The Association des Chauffeurs Guide, 18 Bd Harry Truman, can be contacted on t 222 0330, or Nick's Taxis on t 257 7777.

Hitch-hiking

Hitch-hiking is not recommended.

Car Hire

This is an alternative option, but not one to be taken lightly because it comes with certain hazards. Driving in town is chaotic, and on the country roads, it can also be dangerous as larger vehicles have little sympathy for cars. Officially driving is on the right. Drivers are permitted to use a licence from home for the first three months. It is best to use the large international firms (**Avis**, t 246 2696; **Budget**, t 246 0554; **Hertz**, t 246 0700), most of which have offices both at the airport and in town. Renting by the week rather than by the day will bring the price down. Cars are available at around US$40–45 per day, plus insurance, through the hotels and at the airport.

By Air and Sea

The easiest way to reach Cap Haïtien is to fly, though Haiti's air service has a stop-start history, so check schedules in advance. It's relatively inexpensive and flights leave daily from the Aeroport Civile. Airlines include: **Caribinter**, t 250 2304, Cap t 262 3701. **Mission Aviation**, t 246 3993. **Tropical**, t 256 3626-9.

You may be able to hitch a ride on the old boats plying between the ports with produce.

Tourist Information

Abroad

There is not very much tourism in Haiti at the moment because of the political situation, and there are no tourist boards around the world. You might get some information by contacting the embassies. There is a website devoted to tourism in Haiti at *www.haiti tourisme.com*. As you would expect, many of the sites are more social and political than tourist-based, but you will find some information on *www.disoverhaiti.com* and some at *www.haitiguide.com* and *www.haitifocus.com*. **France**: Ambassade d'Haiti, 10 rue Théodule Ribot, 75017 Paris, t 42 47 63 78.

In Haiti

Because travel in Haiti is not that easy, tour companies make useful contacts. Hotel managers are also well informed. Haiti's many missionaries may be helpful in remote areas. **Agence Citadelle**, Place du Marron Inconnu, t 223 5900, t 222 5900, *citagen@haitiworld. com*, *www.agencecitadelle.com*. Tour group. **Chatelain Tour**, t 223 2962. Another tour group. **Secrétairerie d'État au Tourisme**, 8 rue Légitime, Champ de Mars, Port-au-Prince,

---

glass-fronted structures and large classical official buildings. The human activity is immeasurable – vendors stand three deep on the pavement and there is a constant rush of traffic – and the street theatre is ever-present. Clustered around the town centre are the *cités*, the poorest shanties you will see in the Caribbean, where the stoves light up long before dawn as families prepare their cassava bread. On the hill, aloof from the bustle of Port-au-Prince, is the capital's prosperous alter ego, Pétionville. Here, villas sit in stately calm behind 10ft walls and wrought-iron gates.

t 223 5631/2143, *tourisme@set-haiti.org*. The office is in front of the French Embassy.
Voyages Lumiere, **t** 249 6177/ 557 0753, *voyageslumiere@haitelonline.com*, *www.voyagelumierehaiti.com*. Tour agency.

Embassies and Consulates
British Embassy, Hotel Montana, PO Box 1302, Port-au-Prince, **t** 257 3969.
Canadian Embassy, Edifice Banque Nova Scotia, Delmas 18, **t** 223 2358.
Dominican Embassy, Hotel El Rancho, 121 rue Panamericaine, Pétionville, **t** 257 1208.
US Embassy, near the waterfront, bd Harry Truman, Port-au-Prince, **t** 223 5511.

Emergencies
In a **medical** emergency, you should contact the Hôpital Canapé Vert, rue Canapé Vert, Port-au-Prince, **t** 245 1052, **t** 223 0984. If you are having problems, most hotels have an English-speaking doctor on call.
Police: t 114.
Ambulance: t 118.

Language
Strangely, the official language in Haiti is French. You will find that in the towns, you'll be able to get by on your French, but in the country, it is not that widely understood. English is understood in the tourist hotels, and Spanish can also be useful, as many Haitians are fluent in the language. Around 90% of the Haitians communicate in *kreyol*, an extraordinary mixture of French and African that has grown into a new language. Of all the French creoles in the Caribbean (there are others in the French Antilles), this is the hardest-baked and it is certainly not easily comprehensible if you know French. You will notice expressions written in *kreyol* on the taptaps and daubed on the walls. There is a different spelling system from the official French, but if you read it out loud, you will sometimes be able to make out the French meaning by the way it sounds.

Money and Banks
The official currency of Haiti is the gourde. The currency was introduced by King Christophe at the beginning of the 19th century, when he supposedly made the gourde or calabash (a large fruit with a hard exterior that can be used as a bowl) into the currency, slowly introducing notes to replace them. The name remains. The exchange rate used to be fixed at 5 gourdes to the US dollar, and, although this is no longer the case, five gourdes is still referred to for ease as a '*dollar haitien*' (H$). If you go off the beaten track, you should get hold of some gourdes.

At present, the rate stands at US$1 = 36–38 gourdes, although obviously this is subject to fluctuation. You should bring either US dollars or euros with you; other currencies such as sterling can be changed, but at a very poor rate.

The US dollar is not really legal currency beyond the tourist hotels and restaurants, which can accept traveller's cheques and credit card bills in dollars. You will be approached in the streets by characters flicking a wad of notes. Dealing on the street is not illegal but it is not recommended. However, businesses that deal in foreign goods need hard currency to buy in their products, so they have been known to buy dollars at a preferential rate. Carry around plenty of small change. **Banking hours** are Mon–Fri 9–1.

Telephone Code
The IDD code for Haiti is **t** 509, followed by a seven-figure national number. You only need

---

The heart of the town is centred around the imposing **Palais National**, a vast white pile with classical columns and cupolas, which was the former home of President Duvalier and the seat of the government. Built in 1918, it is guarded and is not accessible to the public.

Across the square is the statue of the **Marron Inconnu** (the unknown maroon soldier), a runaway slave with a machete who is blowing into a conch horn, raising the slaves to rebellion.

to dial the seven-digit number when within Haiti itself.

Maps and Books

Haiti has quite a literary tradition of its own and has inspired plenty of books by writers from other countries. One of the country's earliest literary sons was Alexandre Dumas, author of *The Three Musketeers* and *The Count of Monte Cristo*. The Cuban Alejo Carpentier wrote a magical representation of life under Christophe, including the building of the Citadelle, in *A Kingdom of this World*.

In the 1930s, the Haitians re-evaluated their culture and their African heritage much as other Caribbean writers did. Perhaps the best novel from this period was about Haitian peasant life, called *Les Gouverneurs de la Rosée*, by Jacques Roumain. It was published posthumously in 1944 (Heinemann put out a translation under the name *Masters of the Dew*). Other works by Roumain include *La Montagne Ensorcelée*. Another excellent author of the period was Jacques Stephen Alexis, who wrote a number of novels, including *Compère Général Soleil*, *Romancero aux Étoiles* and *L'Espace d'un Cillement*. More modern, *The Beast of the Haitian Hills*, by the brothers Philippe and Pierre Marcalin, tells a fatal tale of peasant and voodoo life.

The Trinidadian historian C. L. R. James treated the subject of the Haitian revolution in *The Black Jacobins*, an angry and extremely powerful book that was first published in 1938. *From Dessalines to Duvalier* by David Nicholls is an excellent history of Haiti for those who would enjoy a detailed account of the country since the rebellion and Independence.

Many books look at the sensational side of Haitian life and mystery, of which the most famous is probably *The Magic Island* by W. B. Seabrook, published in 1929. An authoritative and scholarly view can be found in Alfred Métraux's *Le Vaudou Haïtien*. The American anthropologist Zora Neale Hurston's work *Tell my Horse* describes a visit to Haiti in the 20th century and tells some stories of voodoo. A more recent and frightening tale of a scientist's explorations into the supernatural is told in Wade Davis's *The Serpent and the Rainbow*.

Graham Greene's novel *The Comedians* describes the oppressive life under 'Papa Doc' Duvalier in the 1960s. The inspiration for the hotel is the Oloffsen in the southeast of town. At one time, this book was banned in the country. Brian Moore's *Another Life* tells a story similar to that of Aristide in fictional form. Two recent travel books are *Best Nightmare on Earth*, written by Herbert Gold (Grafton; 1991) and *Bonjour Blanc* by Ian Thomson (Hutchinson; 1992).

Audubon, the great bird artist who was the inspiration for all the Audubon birding societies, was from Haiti.

Shopping

Few visitors leave Haiti without buying a piece of art. It is available everywhere and often for very little cost, but if you want to make a serious investment in art, you should visit one of the established art galleries (*see* more on Haiti Art, p.645).

A visit to see the famous murals by the early masters in the Episcopal church is a good place to start and should be on every visitor's must-see list. The place to shop for art is the affluent hillside town of Pétionville, which is packed with galleries.

Just east of the Palais National is the **Place des Héros de l'Indépendance**, or Champ de Mars, an open park where other national heroes are commemorated – Toussaint L'Ouverture, Jean-Jacques Dessalines, Christophe and Pétion. The bunker-like **Musée National** (*open Mon–Fri 10–2 or 3.30; adm*) is also on the square and contains national treasures like the pistol with which Christophe shot himself and the *cloche de la liberté*, rung by Toussaint himself at Ennery. The crown of Emperor Faustin I is on display and there is even an ancient 13ft anchor, supposedly from Columbus's *Santa Maria*, which was wrecked off the island in 1492.

Festivals

Each town and village has its *fête patronale*, in honour of their patron saint. For forthcoming celebrations, ask around.

1 January *Haitian Independence Day*. Also known as *Jou d'lan*, at which time wreaths are laid at the statue of the Marron Inconnu in Port-au-Prince.

January–February *Carnival*. This is the principal festival in the Haitian calendar and celebrations take place every Sunday, beginning on Epiphany (6 Jan) and culminating on Mardi Gras just before Lent. Costumed dancers fill the streets, all strutting in time to ra-ra bands and following the bandwagons (articulated lorries stacked with speakers).

Watersports

Haiti is not very well organized for sports, but it is possible to find some opportunities for watersports, such as windsurfing and sailing, through the beach hotels. Try the beach hotels north of the capital, particularly those at Ibo and Kyona beaches. There is a marina at Ibo Beach where you can fix up a deep-sea fishing trip.

Boat Hire

Kopan Boat, located on the Côte des Arcadins, **t** 246 1896.

Scuba Diving and Snorkelling

There is a superb coral reef at Sand Cay out in Port-au-Prince harbour (it is also good for snorkelling). The other main reefs are on the island of Gonâve in the bay, a half-hour boat trip from the hotels. Labadie on the north coast has good snorkelling.

Other Sports

Miniature Football

In the Haitian streets, you will also see an entertaining version of this game, played with five a side and a goal 2ft high. It is very skilful and fun to watch.

Tennis

Courts can be fixed up through the hotels.

Spectator Sports

On land there are few sports on offer. If you have the stomach for a **cockfight** after Sunday lunch, then you can go to a *guaguère* and watch the frenzy of the audience and the two poor battling cocks.

Where to Stay

Haiti t (509–)

There are a few hotels and guest houses in the centre of Port-au-Prince, but most of the best places to stay are off the road leading to Pétionville or in Pétionville itself. Haiti is not blessed with many traditional Caribbean beach hotels, but there are some wonderful creole town houses. Few visitors mean prices are fairly low at present. An energy tax is often levied and service is usually charged at 10%.

Port-au-Prince and Pétionville

Expensive–Moderate

El Rancho, PO Box 71, rue José de San Martin, just off the Panaméricaine, **t** 257 2080/4, *elrancho@haitiworld.com*. Three miles from the city centre, perched on the hillside above the plain, with a terrace for tea and dinner overlooking the swimming pools and

Close by is the **Musée d'Art Haïtien du College St Pierre** (*t 222 2510; open Mon–Fri 9.30–1.30, Sat 9.30–12.30; adm free*) in which many of the country's finest works of art are displayed. De Witt Peters' Centre d'Art was moved here. The exhibitions change, but there are often paintings by Hector Hippolyte, Sénèque and Philome Obin. You will find other permanent exhibits of Haitian art in the Episcopalian **Cathédrale de la Ste-Trinité**, where the apse was painted by Obin, Benoit, Bazile and Leveque. Scenes from the birth of Christ to the Crucifixion are represented in the bright colours of the naïve school.

dip-and-sip bar. There's a touch of colonial Spain in the arches and orange roof tiles and some rooms have sumptuous décor, with massive mahogany furniture and local works of art. Also has tennis courts, a masseur, a casino and dancing (*Fri*).

Visa Lodge Hotel, Route des Nîmes, Port-au-Prince, t 250 1561/1377. Popular with businessmen; in an industrial area by the airport, it has a gym and two restaurants.

Moderate

Montana Hotel, PO Box 523, rue F. Cardozo, t 257 1920/1, *hmontana@aol.com*. A modern town house with spectacular views over the city and the bay beyond. There are 120 rooms, a tennis court, gardens and a glorious swimming pool.

Villa Créole, PO Box 126, Pétionville, t 257 1570/1, *villacreole@aol.com*, *www.villacreole.com*. A particularly nice, elegant retreat just beyond El Rancho. You are luxuriously cocooned from the excesses of Haitian life on the balcony – large poolside veranda and restaurant, tennis courts and comfortable rooms, recently upgraded.

Hotel Kinam, Place St Pierre, in the centre, t 257 6525, *kinam@haitiworld.com*. With excellent prices, this is set in an old, restored town house, and the rooms, neat with white tiles and wicker furniture, have been added in mock-gingerbread blocks beside the swimming pool. The restaurant is also good, with a French and creole menu (or a *menu léger*): *poulet djon-djon* or *cabrit boucane* (grilled goat) in *sauce 'ti malice*.

Hotel Oloffson, PO Box 260, rue Capois, Port-au-Prince, t 223 4000/4101, *oloffsonram@globelsud.net*. Not far from the city centre, this was once one of the Caribbean's classic hotels, a magnificent gingerbread town house, tin-roofed, turreted and dripping in luxurious fretwork. Made famous by Graham Greene as the setting for *The Comedians*, the building has since deteriorated through lack of maintenance. The bar and balconies, overlooking the gardens above the town, collect an interesting crowd and serve excellent rum punch. Rooms in the main house are decorated with antiques; more modern ones are in a block behind.

Le Plaza, rue Capois, Champs de Mars, t 223 9282. In the town centre, to the east of Place des Héros, with blocks around a pool in a garden festooned with tropical plants. It is mainly used by businessmen.

Inexpensive

Villa Kalawes, 99 rue Grégoire, t 257 0817. Just out of the town on the road to Kenscoff.

Coconut Villa Hotel, Delmas 19, Port-au-Prince, t 246 0712, *coconutvillahotel@prodigy.net*. Located near the town centre, it has 50 air-conditioned rooms and large furnished apartments with cable television. Facilities include bar and restaurant, swimming pool, racquetball court, generators and treated water. Continental breakfast is included in rate. Children under 12 stay free with parents. Nearby are banks, shops, restaurants and cinemas.

South of Port-au-Prince

Inexpensive

Hotel Florita, Rue du Commerce, Jacmel, t 288 2805, *hotelflorita@yahoo.fr*. Dating from 1888 and full of character, this hotel is the former home of Selden Rodman, who wrote the classic books on Haitian art.

Cap Lamandou, Jacmel, t 288 9898, *caplamandouhotel@aol.com*. A new hotel located

The main thoroughfare in Port-au-Prince is the **Boulevard Jean-Jacques Dessalines**, a little closer to the waterfront, where the vendors line the street. Each person has their beat and in the covered walkways in front of the buildings you will find music vendors with elaborately arranged stacks of cassettes, tables of sweets and cigarettes, and watchmenders and moneychangers fanning a wad of notes. Trade becomes more and more hectic as you approach the **Marché de Fer**, where the vendors stand three-deep, women standing in line, their arms slung with towels and a huge basket of soap and

out on the headland overlooking the Jacmel Bay in the area called La Saline. Has a pool but no beach.

Jaclef Plaza Hotel, Cyvadier, t 288 9700. Located on the road to the coast, just before Cyvadier Beach, a short distance from Jacmel, with a pool but no beachfront.

Cyvadier Plage Hotel, Cyvadier, short distance out of Jacmel on the road to the coast, t 288 3323, *contact@hotelcyvadier.com*. Has a pool and a lovely beachfront on a sandy bay.

Guy's Guest House, 52 Grand' Rue, Jacmel, t 288 3241. Clean and popular.

North of Port-au-Prince

On the coast to the north of the capital are a number of hotels in an area called the Côte des Arcadins, where Haitians go for weekend breaks, either at the hotels or their villas.

Expensive–Moderate

Moulin sur Mer, t 222 1918, t 278 6700, *info@moulinsurmer.com*, *www.moulin surmer.com*. The smartest, on the coast in the grassy expanse of an old plantation. The house, which has five rooms with antique furniture, dates from the 1750s. (There is a private museum worth a visit, and a mule-driven sugar-cane mill.) Another 40 rooms are set in gingerbread blocks painted in red and white running down to the waterfront, all with air-conditioning, fans and screened balconies, with tile floors and large wooden double beds. On the shaded beach is a nice restaurant with classical columns, with a fantastic view of the Île de Gonâve.

Inexpensive

Wahoo Bay Club & Resort, t 223 2940/53, *www.wahoobay.inhaiti.com*. An active resort, also set right on the excellent beach, where

there are sports laid on for the guests. Twenty-four reasonably comfortable rooms, with air-conditioning or fans, and wicker furniture.

Kaliko, t 246 2592. Another nice, small resort, where there are 55 rooms set in rondavels on gradually descending ground on a forested hillside above the beach. There are two rooms per rondavel, and the décor is white with murals on the walls. There is a charming beach-club atmosphere (though it is not usually full, of course), with the pool and restaurant just above the sand, among the casuarina pines and palm trees.

Ouanga Bay, t 547 3207. Forty rooms in a block on the waterfront. Quiet, with some sports facilities.

Cap Haïtien

Moderate

Roi Christophe, PO Box 34, t 262 0414/0514. An oasis of calm in the gridiron of streets in the centre of town, set in a charming old colonial mansion with faded rustic gentility, with tall doors and nice wicker furniture on black and white floor tiles. There is a swimming pool and an interior courtyard with shaded gardens surrounding most of the hotel.

Mont Joli, PO Box 12, t 262 0300. A trusty stopover on the hilltop above Cap Haïtien, where the terraces overlook the town and bay. There are 54 rooms and a swimming pool.

Cormier Plage Hotel, PO Box 70, t 223 5900, t 262 1000. About 5 miles west of the Cap, this has 30 rooms which are scattered along the seafront, shaded by a screen of trees. The hotel restaurant is good, especially for locally caught seafood.

flannels on their heads, or seated in front of rebellious piles of tropical fruits. The Marché de Fer (the iron market) itself is magnificent and seems to cover whole acres with its iron columns and huge riveted arches. Its corrugated tin roofs are painted red as in all Caribbean markets. Erected by President Hyppolite in 1889, it looks a bit odd with its minarets – originally it was intended for India. But, around it, the human endeavour is uniquely Haitian. Expect to be accosted at every turn; most of what you are offered will not be much good, but who knows, you could pick up a bargain.

Inexpensive

Les Jardins de L'Océan, 90 bd de Mer Carénage, t 262 1169, t 553 4270. Just a few simple but clean rooms set in a modern villa that stands above the town and the shoreline at the northern end of town. Good French fare and a nice reception.

Brise de Mer, on the waterfront, t 262 08 21/26. Cheap, simple and mostly clean. Set in a pretty hundred-year-old house that was once a family home, it still has pictures, verandas and period furniture, within a nice garden.

Eating Out

Though the colonial connection was severed almost two centuries ago, the Haitians maintain a sympathetic link with the French in their treatment of food, and Haitian creole cooking is excellent. They use the fish and the seafood of the Caribbean and cover them with strong creole sauces – lobster and *lambi* swim in thick and spicy oil and the traditional Caribbean chicken comes crisp and flavoured with lime or coconut. The French expatriate community makes sure that there is plenty of traditional French cuisine, too, and you will even be offered snails and frogs' legs. Haiti's fertile hills produce all the Caribbean vegetables, including plantain and breadfruit, which are served at all creole tables, and fruits, from pineapple to papaya, which turn up in delicious ice creams and sorbets. Even in the few small places in downtown Port-au-Prince the food is good – traditional Caribbean cook-ups with rice 'n' peas or *tassot* (dried and grilled chicken or pork) – as are the barbecued roadside snacks, though these are best avoided for a few days unless you think that your stomach is up to it. The local beer, Prestige, is quite

drinkable. Prices are mostly listed in Haitian dollars (H$). **Categories** refer to the price of a main dish: expensive = US$20 and above; moderate = US$10–20; inexpensive = US$10 and under.

Expensive

The smartest restaurants around the capital are in Pétionville. Beyond Port-au-Prince, you are dependent on the hotels for all but the simplest meals.

Chez Gérard, 17 rue Pinchinat, near Place St Pierre, t 257 1949. Set in its own profuse tropical garden. Start at the bar, in leather armchairs, and then move on to tables set out on terraces beneath columns and arches for French and creole fare: poached red snapper or duck in green pepper sauce followed by chocolate marquise. *Closed Sun*.

La Souvenence, 8 rue Gabart, t 257 7688. Try this one for gourmet French dishes.

Les Cascades, 73 rue Clerveaux, t 257 7589. Take cocktails upstairs, before descending to the waterfalls and tropical greenery to dine. The French menu offers lots of seafood; try scallops topped with shrimp or veal in a creamy ginger sauce. *Closed Sun*.

Moderate–Inexpensive

La Voile, 32 rue Rigaud, t 257 4561. Also French.

Coin des Artistes, 59 rue Panaméricaine, t 257 2400. Offers seafood and Haitian dishes in a nice courtyard setting. A gathering point for Bohemian Haitians, often with music.

Tiffany Restaurant, bd Harry Truman, Bicentenaire 12, t 222 0993. Downtown in the Cité de L'Exposition, a mixture of international and Haitian dishes.

Aux Cosaques, 8 av Christophe, t 245 4236. One of very few restaurants in downtown Port-au-Prince, serving good Haitian fare.

The **Oloffson Hotel** at the head of rue Capois is something of an institution in the city, and a good place to retreat for a rum punch. Both hotel and punch were made famous by Graham Greene, who used the setting for his novel *The Comedians*, about life in Haiti under 'Papa Doc'. The hotel also attracts a transient crowd of journalists and researchers, so there is often good company. There are plenty of pictures to buy on the walls and the occasional show of Haitian dancing. It's worth a visit just to see the building, a gingerbread masterpiece – though, unfortunately, it is beginning to deteriorate through lack of maintenance.

Around Port-au-Prince

Removed from all of the activity of downtown Port-au-Prince, on the cooler heights of the mountainside, **Pétionville** is stately. The large hotels and fine restaurants, which are set in lovely gardens, have a magnificent view of the town and the bay beyond from 1,500ft. The buildings are grand, but there is not much to see here. There is a beautiful forested valley, where the lianas creep and the trees block out the sun. Leave the town by way of the rue Borno.

The **Barbancourt Rum Distillery** (*t 255 7303; free tasting, bottles from US$5*) is on the road to Kenscoff, set in a mock Teutonic castle. The family has been distilling rum on the island since 1765. You are invited to sit on the veranda, surrounded by vast rum

Haitian Art

Another of Haiti's most vibrant traditions is that of 'naïve' art. It is unique, and has a simple, almost childlike style, usually without the use of perspective, and invariably using very bright primary colours. As well as on canvas, it appears all over the island: in churches, on the taptaps and in a profusion of politically inspired murals, and for the recent election. Catholicism, the *lwas* of the voodoo world and rural Haitian life are typical themes in Haitian painting.

Haitian naïve painting became known outside the country when the American teacher De Witt Peters came to Haiti in the early 1940s. The form had been frowned on initially by the Haitian élite, who tended to look to French culture for their inspiration, but Peters recognized the extraordinary flavour of the primitivists and helped the artists to develop their skills by setting up the Centre d'Art, which provided materials for the painters and sponsored them. The school produced the likes of Philomé Obin, Hector Hyppolite (a voodoo *houngan*), Bazile, Dufont, Benoit and later Lafortune Félix. Sculptors were also encouraged, and Liautaud, Brierre and Jasmin Joseph became famous.

There are many places to view and to buy Haitian art. It can literally be bought by the yard and you will even be approached in the street by people clutching their latest masterpiece, but the galleries, both downtown and in Pétionville, contain the best (and most expensive) works. You can buy at the renowned **Centre d'Art** (*t 222 2018*) in the Musée d'Art Haïtien on the Champ de Mars (58 rue Roy) and the **Carlos Jara Gallery**, 28 rue Armand Holly, Pacot (*t 245 7164*). In Pétionville there is a selection of galleries, including the **Mapou Galerie** at 8 rue Panaméricaine (*t 257 6430*), and the **Galerie Nader** at 50 rue Grégoire (*t 257 5602*), both of which have a good selection.

Selden Rodman has written a number of histories of Haitian art. He described the growth of the primitive school in *Haiti: The Black Republic* (published 1954) and later wrote *The Miracle of Haitian Art* (published 1974). His most recent book, published in 1988, is *Where Art is Joy – Haitian Art: The First Forty Years*.

There is also a strong tradition of arts and crafts on the island and, if you go to the Marché de Fer, you will be inundated with offers of gaudy religious paintings, mahogany work and ghostly faces in shawls made of leather. The best place to go for ironwork and for metal sculptures is an alleyway which leads off avenue John Brown as you leave Port-au-Prince for Pétionville.

puncheons and cane-crushing gear, tasting their 19 varieties of flavoured rums – hibiscus, apricot, coffee, mango, coconut.

Ten miles beyond Pétionville, and 3,000ft higher up into the cultivated slopes, you come to **Kenscoff**, another retreat with an excellent climate (take a jersey if you stay there) and more superb views. The fruit and vegetable market held every Friday seems to be limitless. There is a handicraft centre and a café at the nearby Baptist Mission, the **Mountain Maid** (*open 8–5*), which sells excellent woodwork at good prices. Fort

Voodoo

Voodoo is an essential part of Haitian life, but one that is little understood outside the country – with sensationalized stories of frenzied drumming, dancing and sacrificial black magic ceremonies, it is one of the sources of the country's mystery and its bad PR. In fact, voodoo (*vodun* in Haitian *kreyol*) is a religion (a system of beliefs at least), in which the spiritual world is inhabited by *lwas*, spirits who can have a direct effect on human life. There is no overall voodoo theology, complete creed of beliefs or order of service, and the spirits will be different in different parts of the country. The saying has it that 90% of Haitians are Catholic, but 99% of them believe in voodoo.

Voodoo started on the slave plantations as a form of escape and celebration, in which some of the spirits from Africa were invoked, but over the years, many have taken on noticeably Catholic characteristics; other new spirits were discovered in Haiti. Good and evil are not so clear cut as in the monotheistic religions. Spirits can be angry or content and will bring happiness and good luck if treated well, but they can also be capricious. Over the years, it has been used as a political weapon and denied as quackery and superstitious nonsense. However, voodoo runs very deep in Haitian society. It is one of the strongest expressions of the Haitian spirit.

The principal *lwa* is Papa Legba, the guardian of doors, gates, roads and crossroads, who acts as a sort of go-between for the believers and their other *lwas*. Erzulie is a female *lwa* and resembles the Virgin Mary, as well as being the spirit of love. Damballa, on the other hand, is the spirit of water and so he can send rain enough to provide for the crops, but when angry, he will cause destruction in floods. Others include Papa Zaca, the father of agriculture; Ogun, the spirit of war; the well-known top-hatted Baron Samedi; who watches over cemeteries; and spirits who control the livelihoods of fishermen, hunters or tradesmen, such as Agwé, the spirit of the sea and fishermen. Christian deities are acknowledged, but they are far more remote than these spirits, except Erzulie, of course. Each spirit has its favourite colour, often white or grey, but sometimes red, and animals that are sacrificed to them must be of that colour.

The voodoo ceremony itself takes place in a *hounfort*, a building with an altar and an area of beaten earth where the dancing takes place. It is held to honour a *lwa* or sometimes to ask the *lwa* to pronounce on a problem. It begins with a ritual very similar to Catholic liturgy, but then the drumming strikes up (on drums of different

boffins will enjoy the ruins of **Fort Jacques** and **Fort Alexander**, with their thousands of cannonballs. Beyond Furcy is the **Morne La Visite National Park** and east of there is Haiti's highest mountain, **Pic la Selle**.

Gonâve Island lies in the bay off the capital, with mountains that rise up to a height of 2,500ft and some superb coral reefs. It is 30 miles long and skirted with mangrove swamps, where you can come across herons, clapper rails, roseate spoonbills and the occasional flamingo.

sizes, carved out of mahogany, with a skin stretched over the top and held taut with vast pegs) and the dancing begins. A *lwa* will reveal him or herself to the *houngan* (the nearest thing to a priest) and the particular rhythms of that *lwa* will be played. Libations and offerings of food are made, and a *véver*, a patterned symbol, is drawn on the ground with cornmeal or with ash to appease the specific *lwa*. Eventually, if the conditions are right, the *lwa* may come and 'mount' a dancer, who will then go into a trance, sometimes screaming and flailing around, often intoning predictions. The first *lwa* to mount a voodoo initiate becomes their guardian angel for life.

There is another side to Haitian spiritual life, connected to voodoo, in which magic can be used in curing an illness or warding off evil spirits or to change the course of events. An illness might be the act of a *lwa*, and so the sick person would seek the advice of the *houngan* or perhaps a *bocor* (a sorcerer), to find out why. Some cures will resemble old wives' brews; others have more sinister ritual. The sorcerer has a powerful hold over his devotees, but the final arbiter is his success. Many *bocors* are also '*docteurs feuilles*', practitioners of traditional medicine, who use local plants for their cures.

One of the most sensational aspects of Haitian life is that of zombies, of which evidence exists, and which make fascinating and ghoulish stories. Supposedly a person is fed a potion which makes their metabolic rate drop so low that they appear to be dead. After they are buried, the administrator of the poison will then dig them up, restoring them to full physical capacity, but keeping their mind in limbo. The zombie is then transported to the other end of the country and used as a slave. Try *The Serpent and the Rainbow*, by Wade Davis (Simon & Schuster), about an anthropologist who investigated the story of zombies, which makes an interesting read.

Voodoo ceremonies generally take place according to a calendar and to celebrate special events. You will hear the drumming blow on the still night air, and if you are driving around at these times, you may well see streams of people heading for the local *hounfort*. It is very difficult for a white stranger to attend a local voodoo ceremony. Unless your contacts are very good, the best you can really hope for are the various shows that admit foreigners. These are impressive sights nonetheless, though it is difficult to tell how authentic they are. It is easy, however, to attend the pilgrimages at the Saut d'Eau (*see* p.650), where believers clean themselves in a waterfall, and the Plaine du Nord, where a much darker ceremony takes place around a mud pool.

South of Port-au-Prince

Travelling 2½ hours in a taptap will get you over to **Jacmel** on the south coast of the island. Founded in 1698, it has a few magnificent old gingerbread town houses that remain from its glorious days as a coffee port a century ago, but its trade was cut off by Duvalier in the 1950s and it has decayed. You will find the usual Haitian press, particularly around the iron market. In the hills west of the town is the **Bassin Bleu**, a triple waterfall where each cascade drops into a rockpool. You will be told the legend of a goddess who combs her hair with a golden comb but vanishes with the approach of humans. You are advised to take a guide (you would be lucky to get away without one) and they will encourage you to go by horse.

On the northern side of the peninsula, where the rugged landscape has a rare physical beauty, you pass through **Léogane**, supposedly the city of the Arawak Queen Anacoana who ruled at the time of the Spaniards' arrival, and then climb into hills of banana and coffee plantations before descending into **Miragoâne**. Off the road to Les Cayes is a **lake** where birdwatchers can spot many of the great Caribbean shorebirds: magnificent frigatebirds, blue herons, white ibises and ungainly purple gallinules with overlong toes.

The road crosses over the mountains, passing the *cailles* and the wattle and daub shacks of the small Haitian farmers, and then skirts the south coast and comes to **Les Cayes**, situated on a large fertile agricultural plain. **Île à Vache** sits in the bay about 30 minutes from the town. You can hire a motorboat to get there for the day.

From Les Cayes the increasingly rough road crosses back over to the north coast towards the town of **Jérémie**, its coffee wealth now diminished, where the old colonial-style buildings stand in faded grandeur. The town was the home of the father of Alexandre Dumas, the author.

North of Port-au-Prince

The main road to the north and Cap Haïtien runs along the coast as far as the town of St Marc, from where it descends into the Artibonite Valley, flooded in places to create ricefields, but dry enough in others for cacti to line the hills. At **Gonaïves**, just under a hundred miles from the capital, Dessalines proclaimed Independence in 1804. From here, the main road climbs to over 2,000ft into the extraordinarily lush hills of the Massif du Nord.

There are two waterfalls inland north of Port-au-Prince. Closest to the city is the **Ville Bonheur** waterfall, southwest of Mireblais (also the scene of a very popular pilgrimage for the Haitian Catholics and *vodunistes* each year on 16 July, in memory of an appearance of the Virgin Mary). The '*saut d'eau*' is made up of several streams that cascade 100ft onto rocks in a maelstrom of spray. More remote from the capital is the **Bassin Zim**, close to the town of Hinche, where two cascades tumble 100ft out of the thickest rainforest.

The **Cap**, as Haiti's second city is known, lies on the north coast about 150 miles from Port-au-Prince. In French colonial days, Cap Haïtien was the island's capital

Taptaps

Taptaps are the brightly decorated buses that you see barging their way through the traffic in Port-au-Prince or chasing from one town to the next, loaded to the gunwales. They take their name from the old lorries, whose engines would labour over the hills with a *tap-tap-tap*, but now they can be anything from a Mitsubishi van with a cage on the back to a vast 7-ton Mack lorry with multiple horns and flashing lights.

The decorations on the cage are all-important and make the buses look a bit like old circus or gypsy caravans. The basic wooden frame on the back is often red, but it is carved in graceful sweeps, with curves and cresting waves. It is embellished with stars and diamonds in red, gold and green, kiss curls and unwinding squiggles. Along each side you will see a *kreyol* maxim, often religious, lit by a stream of coloured flashing bulbs: '*Pran courage fre la Tribilation*', '*A Koua Bon*' ('*Béni Soit L'Eternel Nissan*' looks a bit odd). There is often a biblical scene painted on the bonnet.

Clearly there are more normal-looking buses around, but these coloured ones are very popular and are a sort of Haitian street art. You can get a large lorry on longer journeys (as a foreigner, you might be offered the front seat: take it because it gets pretty crowded in the back), but within the towns, there are smaller versions on the back of pick-ups, cages with whirligig fans on the front, coloured plastic windows and loud compas music on the stereo, making the whole thing like a mobile discotheque. Be careful walking through the traffic in Port-au-Prince, otherwise you might look up and receive a final sacrament as you are run over by a bus screaming '*Dieu te Bénisse!*'

(called Cap Français), a city so illustrious that it was known as the 'Paris of the Antilles' (as was St Pierre in Martinique later on). Some of the grand buildings remain, but most were destroyed in the slave rebellions in the 1790s. Later it became a successful port once more. Isolated from Port-au-Prince, it always had an independent attitude, but this was too much for 'Papa Doc' Duvalier, who cut it off and let it fall into decay. Today it has a population of around 100,000.

Close by is the town of **Milot**, from where Christophe ruled his northern kingdom. His magnificent palace, the **Sans Souci**, was built in 1813 above the town, and was supposed to rival Versailles. It was partly destroyed in an earthquake in 1842 and the marble floors of the galleries are gone, but the design of the palace can be seen in the surviving walls and the last of the yellow plaster remains in places.

But Christophe's most lasting monument stands at the top of a mountain, 3,000ft above the town. The **Citadelle** (*open till 5pm; adm includes Sans Souci*) broods like a vast colossus on the peak of Mt Bonnet à l'Evéque, a tropical Gormenghast. It is a two-hour walk in the heat of the Caribbean sun to get there, and yet every stone that was used to build it was carried up between 1804 and 1817. The whole population of the north was involved, about 200,000 people, of whom an estimated 20,000 died. Their megalomaniac leader Christophe just mixed their blood into the mortar. When it was completed, he was supposed to have impressed visiting dignitaries with the loyalty of his troops by marching them into the abyss. The walls are more than 100ft high and 30ft thick in places, arrow slits (for cannon) were 4ft wide, there were 365

The Saut d'Eau

The saint's day of Our Lady of Mt Carmel is 16 July and each year it sees a huge gathering of the faithful at the normally slumberstruck village of Saut d'Eau. The Virgin appeared in a palm tree near a waterfall (the meaning of the French '*saut d'eau*') about a century and a half ago. The faithful go for the same reasons as any Catholic pilgrim: to honour the Virgin. Some are on a vow, some come to make a request; some are there out of guilt, others because it is fashionable. In the way of the West Indies, they go also for the party. The faith is not in doubt (this is a country where the president is a Catholic priest), but in Haiti the spiritual rhythms beat rather differently from elsewhere in the Catholic world. Saut d'Eau is also a voodoo pilgrimage and the waterfall the central feature.

The mix of the two religions is a historical thing, from the days when newly arrived slaves were permitted to worship in church. Ostensibly they prayed to the Catholic divinity, but behind the façade they continued to worship their West African gods, equating them with the Catholic saints. The Virgin Mary's equivalent is Erzulie, the spirit of love, and many people go to Saut d'Eau particularly to ask Erzulie for a change in their love lives.

At the festival, you can recognize the familiar elements of any Catholic pilgrimage. The faithful place dedicatory candles by the waterfall, whispering prayers, and carry pictures of the Virgin. But, of course, there is a parallel, different significance: the candles are placed at particular trees – at a kapok to honour Damballa – and the different *lwas* are invoked until some people enter trances (beforehand they hold crossed candles high towards the church to get God's permission to invoke the spirits).

Next morning, Mass is celebrated to honour the Virgin. Each year, the local Catholic bishop denounces the mix of voodoo and Christianity. There have often been possessions in the church and the vodunists sometimes actually come inside with their drums and play, causing fights to break out.

cannons, weighing 5 tons each, and 250,000 cannonballs – 10,000 soldiers could hold out here for a year. The Citadelle is so vast that it makes the mountain on which it squats look square from 20 miles. From Milot you can walk the 4–5 miles and 3,000ft, or you can take a horse. If you have a car, you can drive to within half a mile. **Bois Cayman**, also near the town, is reputedly where the slaves would meet at the time of their rebellions two hundred years ago.

If you explore the northwestern peninsula, one of the least touched parts of Haiti, you will find no restaurants or guest houses. Stock up with food and drink in Gonaïves or Port de Paix and take extra fuel as there are no petrol stations between the two towns. Roads (tracks) are rough, particularly after rains, and many of the villages are linked to the road by footpath. It is possible to visit **Île de la Tortue**, the old stronghold of the buccaneers. Life is very basic there, too.

Cuba

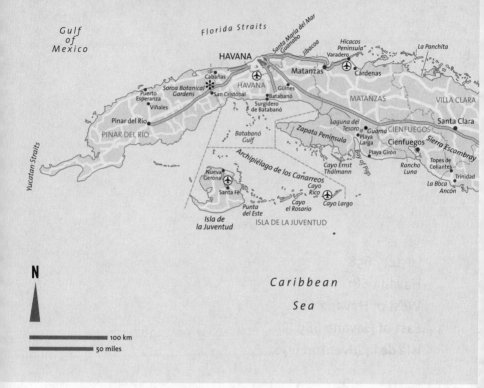

Highlights

1 Explore the 16th- and 17th-century streets of Old Havana
2 Follow the Hemingway trail, from his house at Finca Vigía to his favourite restaurants and bars in Old Havana
3 Visit the Muséo de la Revolución in Havana for an earnest and hefty dose of Communist self-appraisal
4 Enjoy salsa in a club or in a *casa de la trova*, or witness cabaret in all its energetic glory at Tropicana in Havana

Cuba is a magnificent anachronism. The region's largest island takes everything Caribbean to the logical conclusion, from perfect beaches and fine scenery to rich culture and cuisine. Yet politically it remains an enigma – like nowhere else on earth, let alone the Caribbean: the last relic of state socialism, a Communist outpost moored 90 miles south of Key West, Florida.

Presiding over 11 million people is a seemingly invincible leader, Fidel Castro, variously described as *el lider máximo*, *el comandante*, *el jefe*, or simply *El*. After several years of struggle, he defeated an archetypal Latin dictator, Fulgencio Batista, on the first day of 1959. Since then, Castro has squared up against 10 US presidents and has shown no indication of loosening his grip on the country. In the 21st century, Cuba's

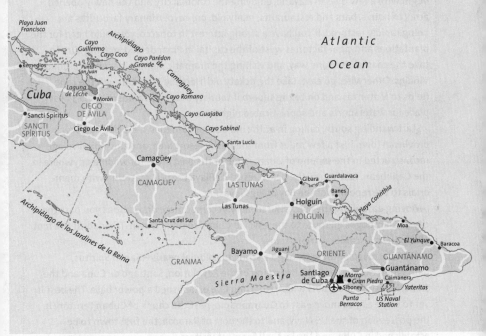

Cuba

Playa Juan
Francisco

Archipiélago

Cayo
Guillermo
Cayo Coco

Cayo Parédon
Grande

Punta
San Juan

Remedios

Cuba

Laguna
de Léche
Morón

Cayo Romano

Cayo Guajaba

Sancti Spíritus

CIEGO
DE ÁVILA

Ciego de Ávila

Cayo Sabinal

SANCTI
SPÍRITUS

Santa Lucía

Atlantic

Ocean

Camagüey

CAMAGUEY

LAS TUNAS

Gibara

Guardalavaca

Banes

Archipiélago de los Jardines de la Reina

Santa Cruz del Sur

Las Tunas

Holguín

HOLGUÍN

Playa Corinthia

Moa

El Yunque

Baracoa

Bayamo

Jiguani

ORIENTE

GUANTÁNAMO

GRANMA

Sierra Maestra

Santiago
de Cuba

Morro
Gran Piedra

Siboney

Guantánamo

Caimanera

Yateritas

Punta
Berracos

US Naval
Station

geopolitical status as ideological thorn in the side of America, and hence theoretically off-limits to US tourists, means it differs from all the other Antilles.

Each year, tens of thousands of Americans circumvent Washington's tight economic embargo and discover – along with a couple of million other tourists – an island that has spent getting on for half a century in a curious suspension. The character of the island remains very different from that of its neighbours – though, with every luxurious new or refurbished hotel that opens, the tourist experience becomes closer to that in the rest of the region.

The surge in tourism to Cuba is a source of considerable concern to other Caribbean islands. On the map, and from the perspective of smaller neighbours, Cuba looks like an alligator, a large and threatening predatory beast that might switch its tail and lunge at the smaller creatures in its wake. And so it might, economically at least. When Washington finally agrees to allow US citizens to visit Cuba freely, there could be a seismic shift in Caribbean vacation patterns. Many of the tourists upon whom the smaller islands depend could choose instead to go to the republic that, until the Revolution, was the obvious Caribbean destination for Americans – it is the nearest island to the US and offers the widest range of experiences.

The corollary is that other nationalities could find themselves dispossessed. In the past decade, millions of British, Italian and Spanish tourists, plus visitors from Canada and Mexico, have helped, in Castro's words, 'Save Cuba' after the economic

Suggested Itinerary

If you have just a couple of weeks in Cuba, the best way to divide your time is to begin with a few days in Havana, enjoying the colonial city and the newly opened array of hotels, bars and restaurants; many old, pre-revolutionary favourites are being rapidly restored. If you have a strong interest in tobacco, you could head for the plantations and cigar factories west of the capital in Pinar del Río, making sure to take the coastal road one way, and visiting the dramatic mountain scenery around Viñales. Otherwise, go east. Take the rickety old 'Hershey' train through the cane fields to Matanzas and on to the superb if touristy beach at Varadero, Cuba's best place for watersports and sophisticated nightlife.

Start wending south, calling in at the old port of Cárdenas, a typically drowsy provincial town just a few miles from the flashy resort area, and the Indian village reconstructed in the swamp of Guamá: one of the best areas for wildlife anywhere in the Caribbean. Just south, the beach resort of Playa Larga is scattered with memorials to the repelling of the Bay of Pigs invasion.

Moving east along the coast, the scenery becomes more dramatic as you pass the city of Cienfuegos en route to the jewel in Cuba's colonial crown: Trinidad, at the foot of the Sierra Escambray mountains.

If time allows, continue through a string of colonial pearls – Sancti Spíritus, Camagüey, Holguín – to the heartland of the Revolution, Santiago de Cuba and the Sierra Maestra mountains where Fidel and Che established a power base. The best is yet to come as you move east to Guantánamo, past the chunk of Cuban territory in the possession of the US Navy, and to the port of Baracoa: the first town to be established in Cuba, and the last call for most visitors.

calamity that followed the collapse of Communism. When the big US tour operators move in, they could easily outbid other nationalities – who will take up the empty spaces vacated on the other islands. For the whole Caribbean, an awful lot hinges on relations between Castro and US President Bush.

Havana has become the most dynamic city in the Caribbean. Even so, Communism, Cuban-style, still pervades life in the capital and everywhere in the island: in the rhetoric of the seemingly invincible leader, Fidel Castro, in the hideous post-revolutionary buildings, and in a sinister state bureaucracy that does not permit political diversity. Yet beneath this Communist overlay the typical themes of the Hispanic Caribbean ring through, in the beaches and palms, in the relentless salsa music and the easygoing, multi-racial population.

Seven hundred and fifty miles from east to west, and averaging around 60 miles in width, Cuba is as large as all the other Caribbean islands put together. Its 44,000 square miles make it about the same size as England or Pennsylvania. The island lies at the mouth of the Gulf of Mexico in the northwest of the Caribbean, just south of the Tropic of Capricorn.

Cuba is as beautiful as anywhere in the Caribbean. It has three magnificent mountain ranges: in the west, the Sierra de los Organos; the Sierra Escambray in the centre; and the Sierra Maestra in the southeast. In between, the undulating plains are immensely fertile. Seeds seem to explode in the rich red-brown earth, growing into the swathes of sugar cane, citrus fruit and the tobacco for which Cuba is celebrated. And wrapped around the island are some of the best beaches in the world.

Of Cuba's 11 million people, one-fifth live in and around Havana, the capital, in the northwest of the island. As in the other former Spanish Caribbean colonies, the population has a range of complexions from blackest African to European blond. The mix is thorough, and the skin tone of the average Cuban is a rich coffee colour. Although a certain draining of colour still takes place as you move to more privileged areas of society, there is little overt racial discrimination: one notable social achievement of the Revolution has been to reduce ingrained racism. The position of women in Cuban society may have been improved considerably by the Revolution, but the Latin tradition of machismo remains with the Cuban men (they joke that the best thing that the Spanish did for them is the *mulatta*, a Cuban girl with the looks of a Spaniard, who can move like an African).

Standards of healthcare and education have increased dramatically since the Revolution. Even during the cataclysmic economic decline that took place in the early 1990s, social provisions remained among the best in Latin America. The achievements, art and rhetoric of the Revolution, are spelt out everywhere: billboards that offer a choice between Socialism and death accompany the traveller on the highways of Cuba, though the thoughts of Lenin have become an endangered ideological species. Cubans still refer to one another as *compañero* and *compañera* (comrade). Che Guevara, the ultimate revolutionary icon, has lost none of his lustre here. This 'Knight without flaw and without fear' stares benevolently out on the Cubans, exhorting them to fulfil their social duties. Schoolchildren still promise eternal loyalty to Che and the Revolution, vowing to 'die in a hail of bullets like Che' should the need for martyrdom arise. The Cuban state makes much of the handy collusion between Che, Communism and the Revolution, which blurs into a trinity with many religious overtones in what is to all intents and purposes a secular state.

Even though Cuba has been ideologically isolated for more than a decade, since the Soviet Bloc collapsed, the leadership has been reluctant to soften state Socialism. Limited liberalization began in the mid-1990s to relieve the boiling tensions in a nation brought to its knees by the superpowers. Cuba had been hammered by the removal of Soviet support, coupled with a vengeful economic embargo imposed by the United States, Cuba's natural trading partner.

The streets of Havana provide plenty of evidence that a nation widely regarded as being on its economic and political deathbed has made a remarkable recovery. Yet Castro retains a personal grip on the island that is the envy of many a tyrant. The people are solidly nationalistic and many of them, even now, have a genuine affection for their leader who carved out a position for the island in defiance of the 'colossus in the north'.

There is an ambivalence to the United States on the part of the Cubans themselves. State-sponsored anti-American propaganda is everywhere, amplified by a strong streak of Latin pride which wants to stand up to the overbearing attitude of the United States. Each successive tightening of the economic blockade has served to

Best Beaches

Playas del Este: The closest of the beaches to Havana which are strung out over 20 miles of the northern coastline of Havana province.

El Mégano and **Santa María del Mar**: Good strips of crystalline sand; Santa María is the busier of the two.

Boca Ciega and **Guanabo**: Farther east along the Vía Blanca, the northern coastal freeway; these are the most developed beaches.

Jibacoa: Idyllic bays where the snorkelling is particularly good; a new all-inclusive resort is proving popular.

Varadero: At 12 almost uninterrupted miles, this is one of the longest beaches in the Caribbean: a supreme strand, up to 40 yards wide and mounded with satin-smooth granules of sand that trickle through your toes. It is built up and very popular, mostly with foreigners. All the usual watersports are on offer, together with evening fun in the bars and clubs. It's about 100 miles from Havana and 20 from Matanzas.

La Panchita and **Playa Juan Francisco**: The northern coastline of Villa Clara province is not developed and it is off the beaten track anyway, but among the mangrove swamps you will find small beaches with fishing villages and offshore there are more idyllic sands on the cays.

La Tinaja and the **XI Festival Beach**: North of the remote town of Morón in Ciego de Avila province, on the Punta de San Juan.

Cayo Coco, **Cayo Guillermo** and **Cayo Paredón Grande**: In contrast, the islands of the Archipiélago de Camagüey have been chosen for development. Money was poured in during the 1990s, including a new airport on Cayo Coco that makes it easy to get out to the superb sands and coral reefs. It's now just 15mins as opposed to 90mins from Ciego de Avila Airport, and new charter flights to Ciego de Ávila are feeding the expanding resort areas on the Cayos. During a flare-up in the 90s, Cayo Coco was the target of a feeble attack by anti-Castro Cuban exiles from Florida, but no impact was made upon the high-grade resort.

Cayo Guajaba and **Cayo Sabinal**: Can be reached for the day from Santa Lucía.

Santa Lucía: Another 10 miles of idyllic, palm-backed sand with 20 miles of brilliant off-shore coral reefs; good for snorkellers as well as scuba divers. The area is built up, with a marina and hotels with watersports. Of all the island's resorts, this is the most isolated from real Cuban life and culture. As you head east from Santa Lucía, the beaches are undeveloped and do not have facilities, so take food and water.

Guardalavaca: This is a relatively compact concentration of hotels around an attractive, curving bay where the seas can get rough at times.

Don Lino: Here you will find a small cove with the beginnings of a large-scale development. Windsurfing and snorkelling gear is available to rent.

Playa Corinthia: A few miles west of Moa, this is one to try for swimming. Beyond here there is no discernible beach to Baracoa, a place that makes the claim of being the location of Columbus's first landfall; historians generally place it much further west, at Gibara near Holguín.

Yateritas: Round the eastern tip of the island, popular with the locals.

Punta Berracos, **Daiquirí** (where the drink of the same name was invented a century ago) and **Siboney**: Somewhat scruffy beaches with facilities on the approach to Santiago de Cuba from the east.

Playa Mar Verde: The first of a string of attractive but undeveloped beaches strung out west from Santiago de Cuba.

Playa Sevilla: Some big developments are under way.

Marea del Portillo: One of the first developments on the south side of the island, and showing its age, but nevertheless an attractive arc of beach; very popular with Canadians.

Santa Cruz del Sur: There are fewer beaches on the protected southern shore of the island. Much of the shoreline is mangrove swamp, impenetrable forest of the sort that the cruiser *Granma* encountered when it came ashore in 1956 (near Las Coloradas). If you are dying for a beach in Camagüey, instead of going north, you might try going south through the hill and cattle country to Santa Cruz del Sur, where there is an attractive strand and offshore cays and reefs.

La Boca and **Ancón**: Close to Trinidad, each with hotels nearby.

Rancho Luna: Near the mouth of Cienfuegos Bay.

Playa Girón and **Playa Larga**: Backed with sea-grape and palms and shelving very gently into the water.

Cayo Ernst Thálmann: Offshore; you will find more sun-bleached sand and water the colour of aquamarine.

Puerto Esperanza: The mountainous area to the west of Havana has fewer beaches, though you will find some attractive bays that are enclosed by lumbering headlands.

Island Beaches off the South Coast

There are two main archipelagos off the south coast of Cuba, with hundreds of islands, cays and sandbars.

Isla de la Juventud: With so many good beaches to choose from on the mainland, you would not come here merely to sunbathe: there are many good diving opportunities on this, Cuba's largest offshore island. There are a couple of black-sand beaches on the north coast, a few miles east of the capital, Nueva Gerona; the best, though, are the beaches on the south coast, at Playa Larga and Punta del Este.

Cayo Largo: A series of subsurface reefs and sandbars that just break the waves runs east from Isla de la Juventud, past the undeveloped Cayo Avalos and Cayo el Rosario to this island, which has been developed as a tourist resort. The island is nearly all beach and the water is stunningly blue: you can go to any bit of 15 miles of sand between Playa Sirena in the southwest and Playa Tortuga in the northeast.

Archipiélago de los Jardines de la Reina (the Gardens of the Queen): Another 100-mile string of islands and barrier reefs teeming with tropical fish, off the province of Ciego de Ávila.

unite Cubans behind their regime. They would certainly not like to see their island return to its pre-revolutionary state as a corrupt unofficial colony of Washington.

Revolutionary Cuba has always had something of a siege mentality. Not without good reason: the failed Bay of Pigs action of 1961 is merely the most notable example of US action against Cuba. There have been plenty of other attacks on the country's leader, and some on its industry, too. The army and police, instruments of state security, have frightening power. Most visitors, though, remain unaware of political tensions. Cubans have an explosive vitality that filters into everyday life. Foreigners can expect to be treated with kindness, respect and genuine interest; hustling is, however, rife in tourist areas, and instances of robbery and muggings have increased.

Music is a national pursuit, and you will hear the compulsive rhythms of rumba, son and salsa, blasting out of ancient loudspeakers, or played by impromptu bands at the street corner and in the bandstands in town squares. Four centuries of Spanish heritage also ring clear in Cuban life. In the centres of colonial towns, you will find plazas overlooked by beautiful churches and old houses with wrought-iron balconies. Trinidad is the most celebrated town, but Sanctí Spíritus and Remedios are equally atmospheric and less touristy. Old Havana is both stunning and decrepit: a square mile of colonial palaces and colonnaded streets.

It is perfectly possible to have a typical Caribbean sun, sea and sand holiday here. Though it is at the primitive end of the Caribbean tourism league, Cuba has the resorts and beaches, 10-mile strips in places with idyllic offshore cays – but for the traveller who wants to explore beyond the coconut oil and jet skis, there is a stimulating and increasingly vibrant island waiting just beyond the beach. As the island climbs back towards its rightful place as *de facto* Caribbean supremo, there could not be a better time to visit Cuba.

History

Columbus landed in Cuba on his first voyage to the New World, touching the eastern end of the island on 27 October 1492 as he sailed south from his first landfall in the Bahamas. Confidently he sent off emissaries to find the Imperial court of Japan (he presumed he had discovered the East Indies), but all they found were 50 Arawak huts. He explored the south coast on his second voyage in 1494, but he never accepted that Cuba was an island.

Columbus was proved conclusively wrong in 1508 when Cuba was first circumnavigated by Sebastian de Ocampo, whose son Diego sent Spanish settlers from Santo Domingo in 1511. The conquistador Diego de Velázquez arrived with 300 men, to be met by the Arawak chief Hatuey, originally from Hispaniola, who roused the Indians into resistance. Hatuey besieged the Spaniards in their fort for three months, but was betrayed and captured. He was offered salvation if he became a Christian, but apparently he preferred not to go to heaven, fearing that it was full of Spaniards. Hatuey's name lives on in Cuba as the country's first revolutionary and on the country's leading beer. His people were wiped out within 50 years; just a few Amerindian features can be seen in the faces in the Baracoa region in the extreme east.

Velázquez founded seven *villas*, or fortified towns, most of which sit along the southern shore of the island from Baracoa to Batabanó, the original site of the capital, Havana. Cuba was eventually to become one of the jewels in the Spanish Crown, but initial development was slow. Without the precious metals found elsewhere in the Spanish colonies, the settlers could do little besides grow tobacco and cure hides. They were also constantly at the mercy of pirate raids. Sir Francis Drake besieged Havana in 1586 without success, but the likes of Henry Morgan and Montbars the Exterminator held whole towns to ransom. Their main target, though, was the yearly *flota*, the fleet that transported the combined riches of Central and South America back to Spain. Once the order was given that it would assemble in Havana harbour, the town grew rapidly in importance, becoming capital in 1589. In 1628, Piet Heyn, at the head of the Dutch West India fleet, captured the entire *flota* and its treasure worth millions within 100 miles of the city.

Havana became one of the three richest and finest Spanish colonial cities, alongside Mexico City and Lima. Spain officially maintained a monopoly of the trade and the merchants became incredibly wealthy; their magnificent houses may still be seen. Away from the city, the country languished, involved mainly in small agriculture, and making a bit on the side through smuggling. It was not until a British invasion in 1762 that the island was opened up to traders of all nations. The economy boomed.

The British introduced sugar, a crop that was to change the face of the island to this day (Cuba is still one of the world's largest exporters of sugar). At the end of the 18th century, when the rule of law in France's richest colony, St Domingue (now Haiti), collapsed, Cuba became the main sugar island in the West Indies. Slaves were needed in their thousands to cultivate the cane. Over the next hundred years, Cuba developed one of the world's most brutal slave regimes. The unfortunate Africans were worked for as much as 19 hours per day, seven days a week. One in ten died each year, and as many as a quarter would be ill at any time. Despite the abolition of slavery in most other Caribbean islands by 1848, the practice continued in the Spanish colonies until 1886. The industry was run on mutual fear, with the call 'Remember Haiti!' as a reminder of what would happen in a slave rebellion. The Torre de Iznaga, a slave watchtower near Trinidad, was the tallest building when it was built in 1820.

After Independence spread rapidly through South America and Mexico at the beginning of the 19th century, Cuba was the last remaining 'Jewel in the Spanish Crown'. There was anti-colonial unrest and an Independence movement began to crystallize, calling for the abolition of slavery. The Cubans rebelled in 1868, led by the landowner Carlos Manuel de Céspedes. Now celebrated in a thousand street names, Céspedes freed his slaves and then armed them. There followed 10 bitter years of war against the Spanish authorities. Céspedes died in 1874, but his movement was carried on by men such as Antonio Maceo and Máximo Gómez, whose vast statue stands on the Malecón in Havana. In 1878, after 200,000 people had died, a truce was drawn up, but within two years, the Cubans had rebelled again under Calixto García, and this time were brutally crushed.

The Spanish sent 250,000 troops to control the population, numbering one million, but fighting broke out again in 1895. This insurrection was inspired by José Martí, a

respected writer and Cuban nationalist. Martí was killed in an ambush in the early
stages of the revolt before he had fired a shot, but he is still considered the hero of
Cuban Independence. Martí is revered by Communists and anti-Communists alike,
and you will see his bust in every town on the island. The whole country rose up
against the colonial authorities. By 1897, the rebels had forced the Spaniards to
concede autonomy, but by now they were set to fight for complete Independence. The
following year, however, the Americans stepped in, officially because their warship,
the USS *Maine*, was blown up in Havana harbour (by whom, it was never discovered).
Ostensibly led by Theodore Roosevelt – though some say he arrived after the battle
was over – the Americans defeated the last of the Spanish troops at San Juan Hill on
the outskirts of Santiago de Cuba. They would not even allow the Cuban rebels the
pleasure of accepting the Spanish surrender. In 1899, the Treaty of Paris gave the
Americans possession of Cuba and Puerto Rico in the Caribbean, and the other
Spanish territories of Guam and the Philippines. After a long, bitter struggle against
colonial power, Independence was denied to the Cubans at the last minute.

The Americans installed the government, invested heavily and reserved the right to
intervene in Cuban affairs 'to preserve its Independence'. As José Martí had warned
when he spoke of 'historical fatalism', the Americans were in control: it would now be
impossible to escape their influence. Cuba became a US colony in all but name.

For the next 30 years, the Cuban Republic was headed by corrupt and ineffectual
leaders. In the 1930s, the regime degenerated into dictatorship and gangsterism.
General Gerardo Machado, elected in a landslide vote in 1924, was ousted in a coup in
1933, led by the army's chief of staff Fulgencio Batista. He held the reins of power for
over a decade, before his nominated successor was defeated in a 1944 election that
brought Ramón Grau San Martin to power, the man whom Batista had deposed.

Batista moved to Miami, while Cuban society descended into a kind of corrupt
anarchy. He returned to fight the 1952 election but, when support looked insufficient,
he seized power in a military coup. Throughout the 1950s, he exercised a ruthless and
brutal grip on the country. The economy was performing well, bringing wealth to
some in the capital, but the lot of the average Cuban was pitiful. Unemployment was
about 50%, and nearly a quarter of the population suffered from malnutrition.

The Revolution

The starting date of the Revolution, as officially chronicled, was 26 July 1953. A
bespectacled lawyer, Fidel Castro, led an attack by 130 young men and women upon
the highly fortified Moncada garrison in Santiago. Militarily the assault was an abject
failure: most of the rebels were rounded up and tortured or killed. Castro survived
and, at his subsequent trial, made his mark with a five-hour indictment of the Cuban
system that has become known as the 'History Will Absolve Me' speech. He was
sentenced to 15 years in jail, but his revolt had caught the imagination of the Cuban
people. After 20 months, he was released and went into exile in Mexico. Here, he
launched the revolutionary 26 July Movement (M-26-7), which devoted itself to the
overthrow of the Batista regime – and was joined by an Argentinian doctor, Ernesto
'Che' Guevara.

On 25 November 1956, 82 rebels sailed from the Mexican port of Tuxpan to Cuba in the yacht *Granma*, now on display outside the Museum of the Revolution in Havana. They barely made land, and lost most of their equipment during a chaotic disembarkation. Within a month, they had been ambushed by Batista's troops. Only a dozen of them were left to make their way through the Sierra Maestra, the mountains in the southeast of the island. Crucially, two of the survivors were Guevara and Castro. They began to pick off military outposts and build support. Steadily their numbers swelled. Supported by underground movements in the cities, who in turn were rallied to general strikes by the guerrilla radio station, *Radio Rebelde*, the insurrection gained ground geographically and politically. In May 1958, Batista put 10,000 men into the Sierra Maestra to defeat the rebels, still numbering only 300, but the assault failed and many of the soldiers went over to the guerrillas. The morale of the Batista regime was broken. As the Revolution spread west, government troops refused to fight. It was only a matter of time before the regime collapsed. In the early hours of 1 January 1959, Batista fled the country. Castro accepted the surrender of the Moncada garrison that he had stormed so unsuccessfully five years earlier, and on 8 January, the 31-year-old lawyer entered the capital in triumph.

Fidel Castro

The world's longest-serving political leader, Dr Fidel Castro Ruz has ruled Cuba since his M-26-7 Movement swept the Batista regime out of the country as the year 1959 dawned. Even after more than four decades of what has been a turbulent, repressive regime, this charismatic leader still commands the admiration and respect of many. Increasingly, it must be said, these are people outside rather than inside the country; his political stamina and consummate skills are envied by other leaders, who line up to meet him at international events. Within Cuba, his achievements in welfare are becoming less and less significant amongst a young population eager for increased freedom and economic opportunity. But all Cubans recognize that he has carved out a path of Cuban self-respect and independence, in defiance of José Martí's 'historical fatalism', the inescapable dominance of the USA. Just across the Florida Straits, of course, Castro is despised by many of the Cubans in exile. Many Americans regard him as a harbinger of the Communist scourge and would therefore like to see him toppled. The CIA is known to have made several inept attempts on his life using exploding cigars and *femmes fatales*; you can witness some of the more absurd bids to kill him at the Ministry of the Interior Museum in Havana. Castro uses each attempt to destabilize Cuba to vilify the overbearing 'colossus in the north'.

Fidel still appears in his battle fatigues and cap when he addresses his people, but they have the lustrous sheen of good-quality material nowadays. The five-hour speeches and rapturous applause from half a million people have also gone, but he remains an impressive speaker, who will hold forth eloquently and persuasively without notes for an hour or more. The main topic of political conversation for the past decade has been the succession. Likely contenders have come and gone. For many Cubans – most of whom have never known any other leader – life without the ever-present Fidel is difficult to imagine.

The M-26-7 movement assumed control of the country. The new government began sweeping educational and agricultural reforms. They ran a huge literacy campaign, in which students left school to spend a year living and working in the country, cutting illiteracy to 4%, the lowest in Latin America. The casinos and brothels that made Havana famous were closed down. There were immediate agricultural reforms, with a limit of 1,000 acres placed on private landholdings, followed by further nationalization of foreign banks and businesses. Such moves understandably alienated the USA, whose interests in Cuba by then amounted to close on $1 billion.

The USA reacted by sponsoring the Bay of Pigs invasion attempt by Cuban exiles in 1961. The government in Havana had been expecting an attack. Castro oversaw the defence personally and defeated it with ease. The Cubans rallied behind him. And so began the US trade embargo which has gradually tightened ever since. Besides prohibiting direct trade between the two countries, Washington operates draconian controls against companies in other nations that deal with Cuba.

Forced to look elsewhere for oil and other basic supplies, Cuba turned east. Initially there was little evidence of Communist inclination on the part of Fidel Castro; his actions were portrayed as straightforwardly nationalist and anti-imperialist. But two days after the Bay of Pigs attack in 1961, he proclaimed the Revolution to be a socialist one. Later in the year, as the press was muzzled and promised elections were shelved, he said that he was a Marxist-Leninist and would be until the day he died (a date that, for some Americans, cannot come soon enough). Other political groups that had worked independently of him for change in Cuba were silenced. Soviet aid and trade began to replace the US connection, much to Washington's concern.

In October 1962, the situation flared up once more with the Cuban missile crisis, as grippingly depicted in the film *Thirteen Days*. Reconnaissance photography by US spy planes revealed that the Soviet Union sought to maximize the value of its strategic outpost in the western hemisphere by beginning to install nuclear missiles in Cuba. Kennedy sent out the US Navy to intercept the shipment and threatened nuclear war unless the missiles were taken back to the USSR. Without consulting Castro, the two superpowers eventually agreed that the missiles would be withdrawn by the Soviet Union if the USA agreed not to invade the island. At one stage, the possibility of 'exchanging' West Berlin for Cuba was discussed between Washington and Moscow.

When Communism failed to deliver the optimistic early dreams of the Revolution, the plans of Che Guevara – by now in charge of economic development – for rapid industrialization had to be revised. Sugar remained the island's economic base, but it became clear that the moral incentive of working for the state alone were not enough to encourage the Cubans into high productivity. The state became increasingly dependent on a highly favourable trade deal with the USSR, whereby sugar was sold to the Eastern Bloc at inflated prices and oil shipped to Cuba at an artificially low rate. This ultimately amounted to a subsidy of $10 per person per day.

With the backing of the biggest country on earth secure, Cuba's social revolution could get under way. Basic foodstuffs were made available at minimal prices, and free education became the right of every child. The improvement in healthcare was little short of miraculous: Cuba eradicated the diseases of poverty that had afflicted much of the population under Batista. 'Microbrigades' were sent out to provide housing for the rapidly expanding population; even with several well-publicised mass departures from Cuba, there are currently twice as many people living on the island than in 1959. There are people in Cuba who still live in thatched *bohío* huts, but only by choice.

The life support provided to Cuba by the Soviet Union followed the USSR into oblivion. In three years from 1992, living standards plunged as much of the country ground to a halt. With huge debts, no foreign exchange and a moribund economy, many of the achievements of the Revolution dissipated: ambulances had no fuel, schools had no pencils and paper, while the people had ration coupons but nothing on which to spend them. The transport system, already shaky, more or less collapsed.

Castro's response was typical of the guile that has kept him in power for so long. In August 1993, he suddenly decreed that, henceforth, it would be legal for Cubans to hold and use US dollars (previously, a two-year jail term was the norm for any ordinary citizen found with a $10 bill). As the wily president expected, Cuban exiles in the US started sending funds to family members still on the island. These remittances were despatched via circuitous routes to evade the US economic blockade, and the recipients had little choice but to spend the cash in government 'dollar shops'. This move provided much-needed foreign exchange, but it also established a two-class society. The dissatisfaction felt by much of Cuba's youth built up into open dissent, which in August 1994 erupted in Havana for the first time since the Revolution.

As police and troops struggled to contain the protestors, Castro addressed the crowd and announced that no attempt would be made to restrain anyone seeking to leave the island. In the following days, flotillas of home-made rafts set off from the coast near Havana, heading north towards Florida. Once in international waters, boats operated by Miami Cubans were waiting to pick up the refugees and take them to safety in the USA. Washington's long-standing commitment to give automatic citizenship to any Cuban who set foot in America meant that President Clinton had around 20,000 new arrivals on his hands. He was forced to negotiate with Castro to stem the tide. Many of the emigrés ended up back in Cuba, in a temporary holding camp at the US naval base of Guantánamo Bay. Washington rescinded the policy of automatic citizenship, and settled on expanding legitimate departures from Cuba.

In 1999, Castro scored another publicity coup with the case of Elián González, the young boy who was plucked from a raft drifting in the Florida Straits after the death of his mother and the other adults attempting to escape. Relatives in Miami sought custody of the boy, but the US courts insisted that he should be returned to his father in Cuba. At the end of 2000, though, hopes that the incoming US president would pursue warmer relations with Havana were dashed. Traditionally, both Democrat and Republican presidential candidates had been hawkish on Cuba in the hope of securing the important Florida vote for the Electoral College, which ultimately selects the winner. When George W. Bush beat Al Gore by a few hundred votes in a painfully long, drawn-out process, it signalled to future contestants that the exile vote was crucial. Once again, Cuba found itself to be an extension of US domestic politics.

In the run-up to the 2004 US presidential election, one of the candidates announced he would end the ban on tourism, thus flooding Cuba with American tourists. But the Democrat challenger, John Kerry, was soundly beaten and the anti-Castro hawks in the White House prevailed. Facing up to George W. Bush, Fidel Castro remained as belligerent as ever; shortly before the election, he announced that the US dollar would no longer be an acceptable form of payment; tourists who paid in American dollars would be subject to a tax of 10%, avoidable only by using 'convertible' pesos (CUC), the so-called 'hard peso', worth exactly US$1. This was intended to yield a short-term financial windfall for the Castro government, but its longer-term effects could reduce the appeal of Cuba to both foreign tourists and investors.

Castro's regime remains untroubled by election results on the island. Even as the Revolution celebrates middle age, Cuba is still under the authoritarian control of the Communist Party, headed by the Central Committee and ultimately the Politburo. Castro is president of both.

With the exception of the tobacco farms and tourism, industry is mostly state-controlled, though there are now a number of joint ventures with companies from abroad and many of the farms have passed into cooperative control. Cuba was one of the world's largest sugar producers, but the harvest has fallen dramatically over the last few years. Yet the Cuban economy as a whole appears to have turned the corner and is enjoying steady growth, largely thanks to tourism, though much of this comprises low-margin mass-market packages. Sometimes regarded by the Cubans as trivial and demeaning, tourism has imposed severe strains on society. Yet it is helping the country to recover from apparent economic calamity.

Politically, Cuba has shown little inclination to move with the changes in the post-Communist world. There has been no talk of the Communist Party relinquishing ultimate control. But economic liberalization means that everyone is an entrepreneur now. The vitality that seems so naturally Cuban is returning to the island.

Beaches

All the other Caribbean islands are watching the unravelling saga of relations between Washington and Havana with trepidation, because they realize how much they stand to lose when US citizens are once again permitted to visit Cuba. Many of the best beaches in the Caribbean are ringed around the coastline.

Cuba is relatively flat, at least when compared to other Caribbean islands. The 1,200 or so offshore cays have produced coastlines that slope gently into the sea, the softest sand and superb coral reefs. Around 50 of the beaches (playas) have facilities and hotels for the thousands of Cubans who pour out of the cities in trucks at weekends. Others have been developed with tourist hotels and watersports facilities. Yet you do not need to stray too far from the beaten track to find idyllic strands, tucked between the 'dark teeth' of the coral coastline and the shoreline mangrove swamps.

By law, all beaches in Cuba are public. Topless bathing is banned in theory, but is widely practised by tourists. See also 'Best Beaches', pp.656–7.

Flora and Fauna

Cuba, like many Caribbean islands, is extremely beautiful and it has a grand variety of flora, varying from thick mountain forest through the extraordinarily fertile plains

Coping with Cuba

Outside the established tourist network, life in Cuba can be wearing. A fearsome bureaucracy hampers an overloaded system. If your time is short, Cuba can be infuriating, particularly when it comes to travel. From the end of July into August and over the Christmas period, when the Cubans themselves like to go on holiday, things are yet more hectic. Fortunately for those with cash to spend, the scarcity of transport can be overcome by resorting to hard-currency-only flights and buses.

Even so, you will need a fair amount of patience. Meal times can be frustrating in the last bastion of state-socialist catering; sometimes, the simplest plate of food can take an hour to arrive. In the course of a few years, the amount of restaurants has rocketed with the arrival of *paladares*: private restaurants that can occasionally serve some exceptional food (but, equally often, quite dismal dishes). In towns and cities, it is easy to pick up snacks and drinks along the street, though these may not match your idea of good fast food. If you prefer to self-cater, markets in each town can supply a range of fruit and vegetables. On the main highways, there are also plenty of roadside vendors.

Queueing is something of a way of life in Cuba. Sometimes you have to queue to buy a ticket and then queue again to collect your purchase. The Cubans themselves are inured to the practice and simply wait patiently (it can be three or four hours outside a state-run restaurant sometimes). If you have to queue, check that you are at the back by asking '*Último?*' or, if you are addressing a woman, '*Última?*' (it means 'last in line') and then take your place. If you are travelling independently, take some good books to Cuba to while away time spent in queues. They will be gratefully received when you have finished reading them (English is the second language taught in Cuban schools). Altogether, it may be easier to be a package tourist.

Cuba remains reasonably safe, though the economic decline combined with the rise in tourism means that foreigners are becoming targets for robberies more frequently. Be careful after dark in Havana, and anywhere that is crowded with tourists. Hustling has started up in Cuba and you can now expect to be accosted around the tourist areas much as you would elsewhere in the Caribbean. You will be offered a variety of services or simply asked for money. Often, hustlers can be very persistent. Begging is also on the increase.

Women should have no problem in Cuba other than the occasional over-attentive local: harassment can be verbal, but is rarely physical. Plenty of Cuban men see foreign women as a potential ticket out of the country (Cuban women regard foreign men in the same way), so you may receive a proposal as well as a proposition. A 'wedding ring' can be a convenient defence against a persistent man.

Lastly, the Cubans place restrictions on photography. In particular, be careful not to take pictures in the presence of uniformed personnel or around industrial or military installations; this includes happy snaps of Cuban sugar factories and any old forts which have aerials sticking out of them. These restrictions may seem absurd in the 21st century, but the regime has keen memories of US attempts to wreck the sugar industry and destabilize the island.

Getting There

Cuba t (53–)

By Air

From the UK

The history of air links between the UK and Cuba has not been a happy one. Until 1991 there were no direct flights between London and Havana. Then an occasional charter using a clapped-out Ilyushin 62 began operating from Stansted. Gradually the national airline Cubana, t 733 4949, www.cubana.cu, has expanded and it now flies twice a week from London Gatwick to Holguin and on to Havana. You can also fly non-stop between Heathrow and Havana on Air Jamaica, and Virgin Atlantic now operate direct flights between Gatwick and Havana. Many British travellers reach the island on charter flights from Gatwick, Manchester and Glasgow, landing at Cuba's resort airports (primarily Varadero, Cayo Coco and Holguin) on airlines such as Monarch, Britannia and Thomas Cook. Incidentally, British Airways suspended its Cuba flights in 2001. A departure tax (equivalent to US$25) is payable in cash on departure from Cuba.

From the Rest of Europe

Many airlines connect Europe and Cuba including Air France from Paris, Iberia and Air Europa from Madrid, LTU and Condor from Germany, Air Europe from Milan and Martinair from Amsterdam. Many of these airlines offer prices from London. Cubana flights are from Copenhagen, Milan, Paris, Rome and Madrid.

From the USA

Once upon a time, Miami to Havana was the world's busiest international air route. Now, there are just a couple of daily departures on semi-clandestine flights, which are neither widely advertised nor available to most American citizens; to circumvent the economic embargo, they have to fly via a third country, usually the Bahamas, Jamaica or Mexico. US Treasury Department regulations are destined to prevent Americans from visiting the island except in specified personal or professional circumstance. Non-American visitors intending to travel to Cuba from the

USA must obtain a Tourist Card (£15) in advance, which most agencies specializing in travel to Cuba can obtain easily.

From Canada

There are scheduled flights between the major Canadian gateways and Cuba on both Cubana and Air Canada: in addition, several charter flights link the two countries.

From Other Caribbean Islands

The most frequent links from Havana are with Kingston, Jamaica and Nassau, Bahamas. In addition there are charters linking Havana and Varadero with the Caymans, Santo Domingo and Montego Bay. There are some services from the Dominican Republic to Santiago.

From Latin America

Services from Latin American countries include flights from Cancún, Mérida and Mexico City; Caracas; San José; Bogotá; Buenos Aires; and Lima.

Getting Around

If you like your transportation to be well planned, then you should perhaps select a different destination. Travelling around the island is one of the main problems – or joys – of a visit to Cuba. Much of the transport infrastructure crumbled with the economic collapse of the early 1990s, and although services are improving you can still expect to find problems booking seats or arriving at approximately the right hour (or day). Because Cuba is such a large island, this can be stressful in the extreme if you have a tight schedule. And unlike elsewhere in the Caribbean, playing the irate foreigner with officials will cut little ice here. If nothing else, though, most transport is relatively cheap and convivial.

By Bus

Tourists are encouraged to travel on **Viazul** buses, t 781 1413, www.viazul.com, a network of air-conditioned buses, a fleet of convertible-peso only buses with fares around double those on normal long-distance buses. The spine of the network runs from Havana to

Santiago de Cuba, with detours to Varadero and Trinidad.

On other journeys, you can also join Cubans on the buses (known locally as *guaguas*) run by the state-controlled **Astro Enterprise**. Services are either long-distance (*Interprovincial*), or run between the towns within a province (*Intermunicipal*). They serve a number of different terminals in each town, often some distance apart. Interprovincial services (usually aboard large and decrepit ex-Mexican buses) link the major cities of Cuba. Foreigners can buy their way onto most of these services with convertible pesos; in Havana there is a special ticket office at the Interprovincial terminal in Havana, near the Plaza de la Revolución (on the Avenida Rancho Boyeros, t 7879 2456); elsewhere foreigners usually get a fast track to the front of the queue and are expected to pay in convertible pesos (CUC).

Intermunicipal *guaguas* (pronounced 'wah-wah') link the towns within a province, for a fare of a few pesos; convertible pesos will not usually be expected. These buses tend to be rattly old European models, donated by communities in Spain or Italy when they have reached the end of their natural lives. Though they're uncomfortable and crowded, they are one of the best exposures to Cuban life. With luck, you might just get a seat.

To guarantee a seat, and often a speedy journey, on journeys of 25–100 miles (40–160km) seek out a *colectivo* (a long-distance share taxi, sometimes also called a *maquina*). These take up the overspill from the bus network. The average *colectivo* is a grand old Cadillac or Pontiac built some time before 1959 and lovingly preserved. They usually park outside the bus station and depart when they are full, or when the urge takes the driver. Prices are roughly three times the fare by bus. You can also rent the entire car and persuade the driver to take you further afield, as an unofficial taxi, at a price.

By Passenger Truck or 'Camel'

Another option is the passenger truck, plying a fixed route and offering the chance to stand up in the back for about the same as the bus fare. This is all part of the Cuban experi-

ence, though you may elect to do it simply because of the shortage of buses.

Urban transport offers the most telling insights into the state of the Cuban economy. The largest unit of mass transit in Havana and some other cities is the 'Camel', an enormous humped vehicle hauled by a gruff old tractor unit. The flat fare for these is just 20 centavos. These are supplemented by local *guaguas* on fixed routes (the fare will be around 50 centavos, exact change only), and some smaller and more expensive 'microbuses' (fare around one or two pesos). In smaller towns, the only form of transport may be a horse towing a carriage crowded with passengers and their possessions. The usual flat fare for this form of transport, known as a *coche* or *caleza*, is one peso. Some drivers, though, have identified the higher spending power of foreigners and will demand convertible pesos.

By Taxi

The other form of motorized urban transport is, of course, the taxi, of which there are three basic types. Official '*turistaxis*' are available in all the tourist areas, and these charge fares in convertible pesos. **Local taxis** are popularly known as *los incapturables*, because supply for these 'peso taxis' far exceeds demand. These two official kinds of taxi are supplemented by almost anyone who owns a motor vehicle of any kind. You can flag down any car and request a ride, and more often than not the driver will be prepared to reach a mutually agreeable price.

The same technique applies if you want to rent a car for the day.

By Train

Cuba's rail network is pretty impressive, at least in theory. Lines run the length of the country, with branches to the north and south. Travelling by train can give another good introduction to Cuban society as well as offering a relatively flexible method of travel. You are supposed to buy tickets through the convertible peso organization Ferrotur, though for short journeys this is not worth the time, trouble or money. Long-distance services such as Havana–Santiago must be booked through the official channels; expect the trip to cost CUC$45 and to take anything up to 16 hours.

Most long-distance services arrive at and depart from Havana's central railway station, on the southern edge of the colonial city. Foreigners buy tickets in convertible pesos from the Ferrotur ticket office at the far end of the platforms on the north side of the station. Matanzas is served four or five times daily from the station at Casablanca, across the water from the colonial city; this is Cuba's only electric railway, known as the Hershey line because it runs through the former plantations of the US confectionery company of that name; it is highly erratic.

Hitch-hiking

At the bottom of the transport hierarchy is the hitch-hiker; Cuba is the only place on earth where this practice is regulated by the state. Some towns still have an official hitching point, where travellers register their destination with an official in curious yellow trousers who wields a clipboard. Any state or private vehicle that passes is required to stop (tourists are not). He or she then instructs the driver to fill up the vehicle with hitchers, who pay a few pesos – usually less than the equivalent bus fare – for the ride. For women, Cuba is one country where hitch-hiking is more or less guaranteed to be safe.

Car and Bike Hire

Car rental in Cuba gives independence of travel, but it is not cheap and it is dangerous. Cuban driving is fairly typical of the Caribbean, but the roads are worse. The main highway is the *autopista*, running from Pinar del Río in the west, past Havana and along to Santa Clara, where it dissolves into the older *Carratera Central*, which straggles down to Santiago and beyond. The road surfaces are dreadful, the signposting is poor and the lighting non-existent. Other motor vehicles are rare on Cuban roads, but in their stead you find a motley selection of pedestrians, cyclists, farm machinery and animals.

You could get lucky and rent a car on the spur of the moment, but advance booking is preferable. It is possible to book one before you fly and pick it up at Havana airport. Your home driving licence is valid.

The main hire firm in Cuba is **Havanautos**, which has offices in all the major tourist

hotels and the airports, but competition has increased significantly over the past few years with companies such as **REX** gaining in reputation. Prices begin at around CUC$50 per day for the smallest, cheapest Mexican-built Nissan. Insurance adds $5–10 per day on top. Fuel is now relatively easily available, for hard currency only, at any of the growing number of Cupet service stations. Most of these are open 24 hours.

In the 1990s, Cuba became a nation of **cyclists**. More than a million Chinese bicycles were imported, and despite the increasing affluence of the 21st century, these are still ridden recklessly all around the island. It is possible to rent them in tourist areas, but serious cyclists should bring their own machines.

By Air

For long journeys, flying might be an appealing alternative, though frequent delays and cancellations make flying just as unpredictable an experience as other ways of getting around the island. Fares are low by international standards, such as US$100 for the Havana–Santiago hop of over 500 miles.

The alternative to the national carrier Cubana (statistically the most dangerous airline in the world) is Aerocaribbean **t** 7879 7524, *www.aero-caribbean.com*, which flies between the major tourist destinations.

Tourist Information

Abroad

Promotion of Cuba abroad is patchy, with a scattering of official tourist offices; elsewhere, you must rely upon the Cuban Embassy.
Canada: Canada: 1200 Bay St, Suite 305, Toronto, Ontario, M5R 2A5, **t** (416) 362 0700, *www.gocuba.ca* ;
440 Boul. Rene Leveque Ouest, Bureau 1105, Montreal, Quebec, H2Z 1V7, **t** (514) 875 1004.
UK: 1st Floor, 154 Shaftesbury Avenue, London, WC2H 8JT, t(020) 7240 6655, *www.cuba travel.cu*.

In Cuba

On the island itself, **Cubatur** runs information desks in tourist hotels, but these mainly sell tickets for organized trips. The best source of information is almost always local people.

Communications

The IDD **telephone code** for Cuba is **t** 53. The Cuban telephone system is struggling to keep pace with the rest of the world, despite many lines now being connected to a modern, digital network which operates in isolation from the rattly old Cuban telephone system (barely touched since the Revolution). This 'normal' network is chaotic: try, try again. There are a few old payphones (taking centavo coins), but these rarely work. A number of phones are now operated by phonecard, either peso or convertible peso. Buying and using a convertible peso phonecard will work out far cheaper than operator-assisted calls, especially those from hotels. If you plan to have a long conversation with someone abroad, get them to call you straight back; hotel receptionists are used to this and do not seem to mind, even if you are not staying there.

For political reasons, Cuba has been very slow to get **online**; the government is rather sensitive about the uncontrolled flow of information. While a few tourism enterprises have websites, these are often not functioning. Though the number of public Internet access points is growing (many post offices have them), be prepared for relatively high prices.

Embassies and Consulates

British Embassy, 702/4 Calle 34, a handsome villa in Miramar, **t** 7204 1771; open Mon–Fri 8–3.30.

Canadian Embassy, 518 Calle 30, Miramar, Havana, **t** 7204 2516; open Mon–Thurs 8.30–5, Fri 8.30–2.

Because it has no diplomatic relations with Cuba, the United States has no official Embassy in Cuba. The US Interests Section (USINT) represents American citizens in Cuba, and operates under the legal protection of the Swiss government. You'll find it at Calzada, Vedado, between L and M streets, **t** 7833 3551; open Mon–Thurs 8.30–5, Fri 8.30–4.

Media

As a rule, Cuban newspapers are of the Pravda school of journalism: neither interesting nor enlightening. *Granma*, the

official government paper (named after the boat in which Fidel arrived in Cuba from Mexico), is published daily. There is not much hard international news. Its English-language sibling is *Granma International*, which trills the triumphs of Communism. Among the other local journals are *Trabajadores* (Workers), the trade union paper, and *Juventud Rebelde* (Rebel Youth).

Foreign news magazines, which are sold in some hotels, are the most reliable source of printed news.

Medical Emergencies

Cuba's medical services are generally good, and minor treatment will routinely be given free to foreigners at local clinics. If you are given a prescription, you may have find it difficult to track down a pharmacy with the required drugs in stock. Should you require extensive medical attention while in Havana, the main clinic for foreign patients is the **Cira García Clinic**, on Avenida 20 in Vedado (**t** 732 9501). Treatment here is expensive, and payment is expected in convertible pesos.

Money and Banks

The currency of Cuba is the peso (symbol $), which is divided into 100 centavos. Officially, the **exchange rate** is US$1 = 21 pesos. For the purposes of visitors the official currency is the **convertible peso** (CUC), introduced in 1995 as a Cuban form of tourist currency. Its value is pegged to the US dollar.

The US dollar's status as an official currency in Cuba was was withdrawn in November 2004 as a protest against US trade sanctions. Many businesses and individuals continue to request and accept payment in US dollars, though in general everything previously payable in hard currency is now payable in convertible pesos. To complicate currency matters further, euros are increasingly accepted at some of the larger tourist resorts.

In terms of changing your foreign currency to convertible pesos, using *cadecas* (short for *casas de cambio*) tends to be simpler and quicker than using banks. Though most visitors won't need copious amounts of standard pesos, these can be useful for simple public transport, fruit stalls and small shops, especially outside the capital and tourist areas.

Tipping used to be discouraged, but it is gradually becoming more common. A gratuity will be readily accepted, but since US citizens do not visit the island in significant numbers the Cubans have not yet developed a tradition of adding 15% to every check. Rounding up the bill will usually suffice.

Because of Cuba's reactions to US-imposed restrictions, you should not take America brands of **traveller's cheques** (other brands are normally accepted). Changing traveller's cheques into convertible pesos is easily done at *casas de cambio* and hotels (expect to pay higher commission at the latter). Since November 2004, an additional 10% charge is added when changing US dollar traveller's cheques. If you intend to use credit cards, again be aware that those issued by US banks are unlikely to be accepted. The larger cities have a few ATMs but they do not always work. In theory, you can withdraw cash with your cards at banks (show your passport), but in practice not all cards are accepted.

Shopping

Visitors to Cuba are warmly encouraged to spend, spend, spend. Many hard-currency shops are stocked with imported goods. Although there are some good **duty-free** deals, when you compare the prices with those at home (e.g. rum, whisky, Caribbean rums and musical hardware), the contents are mostly tourist souvenirs taking in varying degrees of tackiness. The best buy here, of course, is cigars (*see* p.684). You will find there is little of interest in the local shops except for those keen to snap up some bargain-priced Cuban music on vinyl. Cuban clothes are hardly in the vanguard of fashion. A browse in the bookshops (*librerías*) will occasionally turn up Cuban classics.

Maps and Books

There are many histories of Cuba written in English, of which the most monumental is *Cuba or The Pursuit of Freedom*, by Hugh Thomas. This ends with the Revolution, but there are plenty of other books with which to pick up the threads. One of the most readable is *Cuba Libre: Breaking the Chains?* by Peter Marshall. Tad Szulc's *Fidel: A Critical Portrait* gives a very detailed and well-researched account of the Cuban leader, and is both an informative and easy read. The other great revolutionary figure, Che Guevara, was the subject of several biographies in 1997, the 30th anniversary of his death. The best of these is *Che Guevara: A Revolutionary Life* by Jon Lee Anderson, massive and finely researched.

One of the most celebrated Cuban writers is Nicolás Guillén, author of among others *Patria o Muerte*. Alejo Carpentier was a Cuban journalist and writer, author of *El Reino de este Mundo* (*A Kingdom of this World*), about the Haitian revolution, and other works that have influenced Latin American authors. Ernest Hemingway lived for 20 years on the island and is remembered for his Nobel Prize-winning *The Old Man and the Sea*, which gives the most poignant picture of a poor fisherman's life in 1950s Cuba. *Our Man in Havana* is another classic by Graham Greene, in which the vacuum-cleaner salesman Wormold gets in a pickle as his ring of fictional agents starts to take on a disturbing life of its own. It was first published in 1958, shortly after which Cuba's story became stranger than fiction.

The cartographic void that existed in Cuba for three decades after the Revolution is now being filled, and reasonable maps of the island and its cities are available in hotels, petrol stations and hard-currency shops.

Festivals

Much to the relief of the Habañeros, the annual Carnaval returned to the capital a few years ago. After several years of suspension because of economic privation, it has returned bigger and brighter than ever before. Other public holidays tend to commemorate revolutionary and historical moments.

January *Anniversary of the Victory of the Revolution*. At this time Fidel often appears to a crowd of hundreds of thousands in the Plaza de la Revolución in Havana, though on significant anniversaries he is likely to be found in Santiago (the next will be the 45th, in 2004).
Birthday of José Martí (28th).

Feb/March *Carnival*. The brightest and liveliest event in the Cuban year was always traditionally held around the holiest date in the revolutionary calendar, 26 July. This was not to commemorate Fidel's first strike against the Moncada garrison; rather, his attack in 1953 was carried out under cover of carnival. The end of July was chosen to mark the completion of the sugar harvest. This still holds in various places outside the capital, and it is possible to hear Fidel speak during this time (usually in Santiago). However, in Havana the celebrations are now much earlier, spread across three weekends each February or March. In Varadero, there is a winter carnival staged for the tourists, which takes place during the second week in February. It is worth going to if you are around.

19 April *Bay of Pigs Victory*.

8 October *Death of Che Guevara*.

November *Festival of the classical arts* in Havana. *Festivities*. The capital enjoys yet more festivities on 14–16th November, with some carnival-like celebrations.

December *Landing of the* Granma (2nd). *Latin American film festival*.

Watersports

Availability of watersports in Cuba is patchy. Equipment may sometime be of a poor quality or even non-existent. However, **water-skiing** is popular in Cuba and easy to arrange.

Boat Hire

It is difficult to find small sailing craft, not least because many of them sailed off one-way to Florida in the 1994 exodus, and the authorities are keen to avoid losing any more. The best selection is to be found in Playas del Este, Varadero, Cayo Coco, Playa Santa Lucía and the offshore islands.

Day Sails

Day sails are limited, but available through the Hemingway Marina, west of Havana (at Calle 248, Santa Fe) and at Varadero. Out on Cayo Largo, you can take a boat trip to Cayo Avalos or Cayo Rosario, for snorkelling and a picnic.

Deep-sea Fishing

Popular in Cuba, and you can take a launch out into the Gulf Stream and cast for blue, white or black marlin, yellowfin tuna, sailfish or wahoo. Again, try the Hemingway Marina. The other principal resorts also have boats equipped for offshore fishing and for deep-sea trips, including the Playas del Este, Varadero, Playa Santa Lucía, Guardalavaca, Santiago de Cuba and on the Isla de la Juventud. Sailing is cheap compared with most Caribbean islands. You can reckon on CUC$250 to charter a boat for the whole day, but do not expect the same standards as you might find around, for example, the US Virgin Islands.

Scuba Diving

Scuba divers will find some superb reefs off Cuba. Whole forests of black coral, sponges and gorgonians fur the submarine walls and the sloping dropoffs, and in the shallow sandy bottoms between the islands schools of tropical fish dip and dart in unison, while single angelfish float and lobsters and crabs scuttle. On the north coast, scuba dives can be arranged at the tourist resorts and instruction is available. On the protected south coast there are stunning underwater landscapes in the cays of the two archipelagos – between the Isla de la Juventud (go to the Colony Hotel) and Cayo Largo there are supreme reefs with crystalline water, good also for snorkelling, and the cays of the Jardines de la Reina are yet more beautiful and remote. Underwater photographic equipment is also on hand at the bigger dive shops.

Other Sports

Hiking

This is not an organized activity in Cuba. In some ways, this is a boon: there are no crowds or over-hiked trails. From other points of view, particularly if you like to have good map and a fair idea of where you are going, it is a pain. The Sierra Maestra in the southeast of the island is the best territory for getting good and lost, which is partly why the rebels chose it as their first battleground. The Escambray Mountains, between Santa Clara and Trinidad, are more accessible.

Horse-riding

It is possible to set up horseback outings along the beach or into the hills in many of the resorts; it is popular with the Cubans and so there are plenty of stables.

Inland Fishing and Hunting

This is possible in the right season, for anything from quail and snipe to wild boar and even an alligator if you so desire. Book through **Cubatur**; the resorts will provide guides, boats and weapons.

Tennis

Courts are attached to most of the larger hotels and in the resort areas.

Spectator Sports

In Cuba, these are mostly so cheap that they are almost free, even though standards are high. In relation to its population, Cuba is the most successful sporting nation at the Olympics. It is well worth taking time out to watch a Cuban game of **baseball** during the October–April season – there are stadia all over the island. The best venue is the Latino Americano stadium in the south of Havana, home ground to Industriales. Admission is less than 5 pesos. In the back streets you will see a scaled-down version of baseball played by children in which they are not allowed to run, which is quite fun to join in. You will also see games of **dominoes** being played quickly and demonstratively in the town squares (dominoes is popular all over the Caribbean).

Where to Stay

Cuba t (53–)

Whether you are travelling independently or as part of a package, the accommodation picture in Cuba is better than it has been for decades. Standards in the package hotels have improved markedly, while independent travellers now have the choice of finding a room in a *casa particular* (private home) – a great way to get to know the Cubans. Many of the island's hotels were built before the Revolution. The sheer magnificence of a building like the Hotel Nacional at the foot of La Rampa in Havana gives an idea of the opulence and splendour (their decadence aside) of the hotels of Cuba in the 40s and 50s. The exterior remains magnificent, if in decay, but the hotel has a very different atmosphere now. You might do better to select one of the newly restored hotels in the old part of town, or indeed to choose to spend much less by staying with a family. Nowadays, there is more choice than there has ever been in Havana, and in the leading resorts; several hotels have recently been built in joint ventures with foreign companies, bringing styles and fittings to which westerners are more accustomed. Outside the tourist areas, though, rooming with a family becomes all the more appealing because the regular hotels are distinctly unappetizing: awkwardly located, shabby and with questionable facilities. Throughout the island, though, tourist hotel rooms are usually air-conditioned with private bath. In Havana, most will have a television showing American films and usually providing access to CNN.

If you don't book a room in advance, some locals (including hotel employees) may assure you that all the hotel beds are taken, but this is often a plot to get you to stay in a private house. Finding a hotel room is most difficult in the Cuban summer holiday season (July and Aug) and over the winter (Dec, Jan and Feb).

Unusually for the Caribbean, single travellers can expect a reduction of about a third on the double-room rate. It is also possible to camp while travelling around the island and many towns have well-equipped campsites where you can stay for a couple of CUC pesos, tent and facilities included.

So far, very few hotels in Cuba have their own websites, though most come under the wing of a marketing group and feature briefly on their respective group website. Only individual hotel websites are featured below.

Old Havana

In the past few years, several old colonial buildings have been converted into stylish hotels in and around Old Havana, making these the obvious choice for travellers on any budget. The remaining hotels in colonial Havana date principally from the late 19th and early 20th century.

Expensive

Hotel Santa Isabel, Plaza de Armas, t 7860 8201, *www.hotelsantaisabel.cu*. An opulent choice, set in a brilliant location right at the heart of the old city. Much of the fabric of the original Palacio de los Condes de Santaventa, complete with an ancient iron elevator, has been retained, but the Hotel Santa Isabel nevertheless boasts modern facilities in its 17 rooms and 10 suites, as well as a cool and restful bar that offers a handy retreat from the heat of the day. It is pricey, but it's worth it – not least for the chance of meeting cigar aficionado Jack Nicholson – he stays here on his frequent visits to Havana.

Hotel Florida, on the corner of Calle Obispo and Calle Cuba, t 7862 4127. A relatively recent conversion, with 25 rooms ranged around a lovely, breezy courtyard in a 19th-century mansion. Again, it is worth stopping off for a drink or meal if you are just passing by. You are just a few feet away from one of the busiest thoroughfares in Old Havana, yet it possesses an extraordinary feeling of peace in the city.

NH Park Central, Calle Neptuno, on the northern side of the main square, t 7860 6627, *www.nh-hotels.com*. This is one of the few locations in the old part of town that can offer online facilities. The rooms are modern and well-furnished, if somewhat lacking in character; but the hotel is probably most enticing for its superb rooftop swimming pool, which is reserved for the use of its guests.

Hotel Raquel, Calle Amargura, t 7860 8280, *www.hotelraquel.cu*. Set in a building from 1905, this is one of the excellent Habaguanex chain's most charming properties. It has 25 lovely rooms and a bright lobby with a stained-glass roof. You might not expect to find a kosher-style restaurant in a Cuban hotel but the Raquel is in the heart of Old Havana's former Jewish Quarter.

Palacio O'Farrill, Calle Cuba 102–8, t 7860 5080, *www.hotelofarrill.cu*. This 38-room hotel opened in 2002 in a neoclassical palace – the name comes from an early owner, Don Ricardo O'Farrill, a Cuban with – as you might guess – Irish origins. Décor on each of the three floors reflects a different century.

Moderate

Hostal Los Frailes, Calle Teniente Rey, t 7862 9383, *www.hostallosfrailes.cu*. The designers did not have to look far for a theme for this 19th-century former mansion of a Marquis: close by is the Convent of St Francis of Assisi, and 26-room Los Frailes successfully conveys simple monastic beauty and tranquility – but with comfort, not austerity. There's a delightful courtyard, the mini-suites have balconies but note that the ground floor bedrooms are windowless.

Hotel Beltran de Santa Cruz, Calle San Ignacio 411, t 7860 8330, *www.habaguanex.com*. Although this 18th-century house – built by a celebrated Count – was painstakingly restored and opened as a hotel in 2002, most of the other properties in the vicinity haven't been so lucky and are very run down. It's still a good choice, and arty Plaza Vieja is nearby.

Hotel Park View, Calle Colon, t 7861 3293, *www.hotelparkview.cu*. Dating from 1928, this was once one of central Havana's premier hotels. Like so much else, the Park View fell into decline but was rescued recently. With a lobby bar and a top floor restaurant, it's not a bad choice.

Inexpensive

Hostal Valencia, 53 Calle Officios, t 7867 1037, *www.hostalvalencia.cu*. Established, small and friendly, set in an old colonial palace with a courtyard surrounded by two stories of balconies with lamps and balustrades. The dozen rooms and suites are named after the provinces of Spain, some decorated in older style with louvres and tiled floors. The café-restaurant is worth visiting even if you are staying elsewhere.

El Meson de la Flota, Calle de los Mercaderes 257, t 7863 3838, *www.mesondelaflota.cu*. With an old nautical theme and fine nightly flamenco performances in the downstairs restaurant, this is a five-room Spanish-influenced inn.

Hotel Caribbean, 164 Prado, down towards the Malecón, t 7860 8233. Budget travellers congregate at this ever-reliable hotel. Once you actually find the place (unmarked from the outside, but just north of the corner of Calle Colón), it proves a friendly and comfortable base for the independent traveller, with clean rooms, some of them looking out on to the Prado itself.

Vedado District, Havana

Not far off are the large, imposing hotel blocks that were erected in the decades before the Revolution in the district of Vedado.

Expensive

Hotel Nacional de Cuba, corner of O and 21, t 873 3564. Set in one of Havana's most sumptuous and magnificent neocolonial buildings. The foyer is very elegant with colonnades and old Cuban tiles and fine old lifts, looking onto an attractive courtyard with palm trees. This massive place has 483 rooms, all with minibar, telephone and television and some antique décor. Quite smart and comfortable, it has executive floors with business facilities, though the online connections are neither fast nor reliable.

Tryp Habana Libre, La Rampa, corner of L and 23, t 7834 6100. The former Havana Hilton, taken over by the revolutionaries, which stands tall at the top of La Rampa. There is a fantastic view of the city, over Old Havana and the harbour, from the Turquino Bar on the top floor. Entertainment is provided.

Hotel Presidente, Calle Calzada and G, t 755 1801. Farther into the Vedado district, a taxi ride or a long walk from the centre of the town. Has a certain style, with awnings on the outside and a foyer with marble floors, chandeliers and huge vases. Even the rooms have a grander feel than elsewhere, though they are not that large. There is a good bar on the top floor and a swimming pool.

Habana Riviera, Paseo and Malecón, t 7836 4051. On the coast, a tall, ugly block with a similar feel to the Habana Libre, with pool and cabaret.

Moderate

Hotel Victoria, corner of 19 and M, t 7833 3510. The most comfortable place to stay in the Vedado district, close to the commercial centre of the town, this is probably the best hotel for business travellers; business facilities are available. There's also a pool.

St John's, Calle O, t 32 9531. With a top-floor music bar, but somewhat lacking in charm.

Inexpensive

Colina, on L and 27, t 7836 4071. Reliable, if not over-exciting

Hotel Vedado, Calle O 244, t 7836 4072. Don't expect architectural delights or overmuch charm from the Vedado, built in 1952. However, prices are reasonable and the location – near the Malecón – very good.

Pinar del Río Province

Moderate

Moka, Carretera de Candelaria Km 51, t 8277 8601. Tastefully integrated into the surrounding forest – the Moka has trees growing up through the roof – this 26-room hotel just above the village of Las Terrazas is quiet, friendly, and an excellent base for nature-lovers.

Hotel Los Jazmines, Carretera de Viñales km23.5, t 879 6205. Superb view of the valley from up above. There are about 70 newly upgraded rooms and a pool and a good restaurant upstairs.

La Ermita, Carretera de la Ermita km2, Viñales, t 879 6072. On the other side of the town from Los Jazmines, 18 rooms, also with a pool and a good view from the hillside.

Inexpensive

Hotel Pinar del Río, José Martí, Pinar del Río, t 8275 5070. A textbook example of the accommodation in almost all the provincial capitals: a 136-room hotel with a swimming pool and nightclub, on the edge of town, utterly devoid of character and seemingly based on a (flawed) design imported direct from Bulgaria. But at least the price is reasonable.

Villa Aguas Claras, t 827 8426. With pleasant grounds and a rustic restaurant, this is a good base for exploring the Viñales Valley.

East of Havana

In the **Playas del Este**, you can find beach hotels, though they tend to be full of package tourists and they become very booked up at the weekends when the *Habañeros* escape from the capital. At **Jibacoa**, accommodation is restricted to people on all-inclusive packages.

Club Atlantico, Avenida de las Terrazas, Santa María del Mar, **t** 797 1085 (*moderate*). Probably the best in Santa María, with 20 rooms. The local **Intur** office is situated here (they can help find you a room).

Villa Armonia Tarara, Calle 9na, Tarara, **t** 796 1526. A good family choice on Tarará Beach with a collection of pleasant villas. Less than 20mins from Havana.

Matanzas Province

There are numerous hotels in Varadero and, naturally, many of those are set on the town's magnificent beach. Most of them are large, but they are well spaced and the design evokes a relaxed feel with large pools and tropical gardens laid out between the buildings and the beach. There are some smaller hotels set back from the shore for those who do not require beachfront space. At the top of the range are the newest joint-venture developments towards the far end of the peninsula.

Expensive

Hotel Melia Las Américas, Autopista Sur km7, Varadero, **t** 4566 7600. Vast in size, this has over 400 rooms ranged around a cool and pleasant central area with fountains and greenery, and all the modern conveniences down to the video and minibar. There is a large pool and palm-thatch restaurant just above the beach. If you are not on a package holiday it may sometimes be difficult to get a room.

Paradisus Varadero, Punta Frances, **t** 4566 8700. A relatively luxurious all-inclusive with 429 rooms (standard or junior suites) with sea or garden views. Well-maintained with lush gardens, excellent pools and friendly staff. Good for families, though the main buffet is rather ordinary: you'll need to book the (better) restaurants well in advance.

Tryp Peninsula Varadero, Punta Hicacos, **t** 4566 8800. Another fine all-inclusive with beautiful grounds located in the Punta Hicacos Natural Park towards the eastern tip of the peninsula. You may well have to queue for the dependable (if unchanging) buffets.

Moderate

Club Tropical, Avenida Primera at Calle 22, Varadero, **t** 4566 7145. A mid-range resort hotel in the more densely packed southwest of the peninsula. There are 142 rooms in all, but staff are quite friendly, some entertainment in the evenings and right in town.

Sol Palmeras, Carretera de las Morlas, Varadero, **t** 4566 7009. With rooms as well as a number of bungalows set around the lawned gardens above the beach. All the watersports to keep you occupied by day, quieter in the evenings.

Inexpensive

There are some cheaper options in the centre of Varadero. Budget travellers will, however, look in vain for private rooms in Varadero; try the city of **Matanzas** instead.

Hotel Pullman, Av Primera at Calle 49, Varadero, **t** 4561 2702. A little inland, this is friendly and has just 15 rooms.

Dos Mares, Av Primera at Calle 53, Varadero, **t** 4561 2702. Offers small but comfortable rooms.

Villa la Mar, Avenida 3ra, **t** 4561 3910. Surrounded by lush gardens and only metres from the beach. Well-located for bars and restaurants.

Mar del Sur, Ave 3ra and Calle 30, **t** 4561 2246. Spread over several buildings, offering both hotel rooms and apartments.

Villa Playa Larga, Playa Larga, Zapata Peninsula, **t** 4559 7294. Less comfortable, and as faceless as any post-Revolutionary import from Bulgaria.

Villa Playa Girón, Playa Girón, Zapata Peninsula, **t** 4559 4110. On the coast with 190 rooms in concrete *cabañas*, one of which has been left, collapsed, since it was shelled in the abortive 1962 Bay of Pigs invasion. It does have a good swimming pool, and some entertainment.

Archipiélago de los Canarreos

Expensive–Moderate

Hotel El Colony, Isla de la Juventud, **t** 4539 8282. On a superb beach in the southwest of the island, about 25 miles from Nueva Gerona, with 77 rooms looking over the sea, pool, bars, nightclub and watersports.

Sol Pelicano, Cayo Largo del Sur, t 454 8333. A good choice with above-average food and service and free transport to beautiful Playas Paraiso and Sirena.

Sol Cayo Largo, Cayo Largo del Sur, t 454 8260. Don't be put off by a somewhat chaotic front desk – this 296-room all-inclusive has pleasant grounds, a good pool and tasty (and surprisingly varied) food.

Inexpensive

Villa Isla de la Juventud, on the road out of Nueva Gerona towards Santa Fe, Isla de la Juventud, t 6132 3290. There are 20 rooms, and a swimming pool.

Rancho el Tesoro, a little farther out of Nueva Gerona, Isla de la Juventud, t 6132 3657. Thirty-nine air-conditioned rooms; its present refurbishment is likely to push the price up.

Cienfuegos Province

Moderate

Pasacaballo, Carretera a Rancho Luna km22, on the heights above the harbour mouth, t 9 6212. Has a pool and a good view, but is 15 miles south of the town.

Rancho Luna, 10 miles out of Cienfuegos on the same road, t 4 8120. Has cabins on a good beach.

Boutique La Unión, Calle 31, Cienfuegos, t 432 551 020. La Union is a modern hotel with 49 rooms including 13 suites. Its Venus Negra terrace boasts an amazing view of the city and the bay.

Trinidad

In Trinidad, the *casa particular* (private room) network is the most highly developed in Cuba, with a range from cheap and nasty rooms in unattractive parts of town to handsome villas where you have the run of the place.

Moderate

Club Ancón, t 419 6120. On the nearby beaches. Unexciting.

Brisas Trinidad del Mar, t 419 6500. This all-inclusive on Playa Ancon has an unusual stepped design with the lobby, pool, restaurants and entertainment areas on the top floor of the building. There are several restaurants and a snack bar.

Las Cuevas Motel, Finca Santa Ana, t 419 6133. The only vaguely central place, sits on the hill above the town.

Costasur, t 419 6174. Also on the beaches, about six miles out of the town.

Ciego de Ávila Province

Moderate–Inexpensive

Hotel Ciego de Ávila, Ciego de Ávila, t 3322 8013. Large, in the north of the town, with pool, a bar and a night club,

Hotel Santiago Habana, Calle Honorato del Castillo, Ciego de Ávila, t 3322 5703. In the centre of the town; noisy but handy.

Carrusel Morón, Morón, t 335 2230. Actually a mile south of the town of that name, this standard four-storey concrete monstrosity has one bonus: it is a training establishment for the hospitality industry, so you may find service is a bit sharper than usual.

Camagüey and the Archipiélago de Camagüey

Melia Cayo Coco, Jardines del Rey, t 3330 1180 (*moderate*). On Cayo Coco's Las Coloradas beach, this Melia is not for families with young children (it's strictly over-18s only). Those rooms overlooking the lagoon are the nicer of the resort's 62 rooms. If you tire of the buffet, reserve well in advance for the Italian or (for steak lovers) Lagoon restaurants.

Gran Hotel, in the centre of town at Maceo 67, Camagüey, t 3329 2093 (*moderate*). One of the clear winners, a newly refurbished 18th-century mansion with 72 pleasant and comfortable rooms.

Hotel Colón, t 3228 3368 (*moderate*). Benefiting from a much needed facelift, the centrally-located Colón's best selling point is a charming antique dark-wood lobby bar. Request a room looking on to the patio – they're smaller but generally quieter.

Villa Cojimar, Cayo Guillermo, t 3330 1712 (*moderate*). Villa-style blocks with 212 rooms in total, located on a lovely beach.

Club Amigo Mayanabo, Playa Santa Lucía, t 3236 5168 (*moderate*). An all-inclusive on Santa Lucía beach.

Holguín Province

In Holguín itself, the downtown outlook is bleak, unless you go for a private room.

Moderate

Pernik, Av Jorge Dimitrov and Av XX Aniversario, Holguín, t 2448 1011. On the edge of town, large (200 rooms), but with a good pool, restaurant and friendly atmosphere. Where the locals gather for evening entertainment.

Hotel Guardalavaca, Guardalavaca, t 243 0529. This 220-room hotel is set on the stunning Guardalavaca beach, with plenty of watersports.

Don Lino Villa, Guardalavaca, t 20433. Smaller, has good *cabañas* and watersports.

Inexpensive

Villa El Bosque, Av Jorge Dimitrov, Holguín, t 2448 1012. Seventy cabins and a pool.

Hotel Mirador de Mayabe, five miles southeast of Holguín, t 2442 2160. Twenty-four rooms and a cracking view of the valley; pool and nightclub.

Bayamo

In Bayamo, the options have improved hugely in the last few years.

Moderate–Inexpensive

Royalton Hotel, on Parque Céspedes, Bayamo, t 2342 2290. Small and beautifully restored.

Carrusel Sierra Maestra, Carretera Central Km 1.5, t 2342 7970. Not a bad second choice in the city.

Villa Carrusel El Yarey, just off the highway near Jiguaní, Bayamo, t 2342 7256. For some fresher air, you might consider staying at this villa, where 14 rooms are dressed up as country dwellings.

Santiago de Cuba

Expensive

Casa Granda, on the west side of Parque Céspedes, t 2268 6600. If location is important to you, then this is the only address in town. Newly restored, the building is an attractive early 20th-century *palacio* with a busy atmosphere. Its 55 rooms have gone up in price, but if you are on a tight budget and decide to treat yourself just once during your trip, then this is the place to do it.

Meliá Santiago de Cuba, Av de las Américas, t 2268 7070. The flashiest hotel Santiago has to offer, startlingly modern and decorated in the three colours of the Cuban flag. It's the tallest building on the island outside the capital, with 290 rooms and good business facilities. The irritating thing about it is the distance from the centre of town: about two miles.

Moderate–Inexpensive

Las Américas Hotel, Av de las Américas, t 2264 2011. With 64 rooms, this has the same problem as the Meliá, being a bit of a way out. However, it does have a pool and also entertainment.

Villa San Juan, Carretera a Siboney km1, t 2268 7200. Recently changed its name from the Motel Leningrado. The new name is better suited to this villa, which is in a leafy suburb on the edge of town. There are 32 simple rooms.

Rancho Club, high on the hill, on Altos de Quintero, t 2263 3202. To be avoided if you don't have a car, despite the good views, because of the difficulties of getting into town.

Hotel del Balcón del Caribe, near the airport and the Morro fortress on the point, t 2269 1544. If you are catching a flight, you might consider trying this hotel. It has a pool, but is inconveniently far out of town if you plan to use it as a base from which to visit Santiago.

Club Bucanero, t 2268 6363, *www.hotel bucanero.com*. If you're after a beach hotel, the Bucanero is set on a small cove cut into the coastline, with watersports and a swim-up bar.

Hacienda El Caney, Calle Marquetí 2, Repto Las Flores, t 2264 1368. A small hotel in a verdant fruit-growing region with a swimming pool, bar and Cuban restaurant.

Guantánamo Province

In Baracoa, the local people have tuned in to budget travellers' desire for cheap and cheerful accommodation – there are plenty of *casas particulares*.

Moderate–Inexpensive

Hotel Guantánamo, Plaza Mariana Grajales, Guantánamo, **t** 2138 1015. Absolutely standard; a mile or two north of the city centre.

The Hotel Caimanera, Caimanera, **t** 219 9414. A second, much more intriguing choice 12 miles south. Poking into Guantánamo Bay, it seems to be more an exercise in propaganda than a commercial venture; it rarely attracts significant numbers of visitors, yet it is a smart new place within sight of the US naval base that occupies the territory to the south.

Hotel El Castillo, Baracoa, **t** 214 5164. Has two dozen rooms ranged around a decent pool, and its high location gives good views over the town and mountains.

Rusa, on the Malecón, Baracoa, **t** 2140 3011. Cheaper; this once belonged to a Russian woman ('*Rusa*' in Spanish) named Mima Rubenskaya.

Eating Out

Thanks to the proliferation of Cuban restaurants in places like London, New York and Los Angeles, you can enjoy far better Cuban food in Kensington or Greenwich Village than on the island itself, but the Republic is catching up. The last few years have seen Cuba rescued from its status as gastronomic wasteland and transformed to a place where the potential from the land and sea is beginning to be realized. Not only are there many more places to eat, but many of them actually serve decent meals at reasonable prices. The two dynamics that have been responsible for this happy state of affairs are products of the rise in tourism. Foreign investors have pushed up standards of dining in the big hotels, which has forced other places to improve. The other force is the creation of *paladares*: small, privately run restaurants offering good home-cooked food (and, it must be said, some poor home-cooked food in rather too many places). Faced with increased competition on two fronts, state restaurants were obliged to pull their gastronomic socks up.

This happy state of affairs applies in Havana, Varadero and those other places where the tourists congregate. Elsewhere, the menu is not quite so appetizing: at the hotel restaurants in outlying areas, it can be a frustrating wait for even the simplest meal. The menu too is often frustrating, because you will find that many of the dishes are simply not available.

The Cubans like to start their meals with fresh fruit; it gets the gastric juices working, they say, though supply is somewhat erratic. In Cuban cooking, outside the finest *criollo* restaurants, the standard meal comprises chicken, rice and beans, perhaps with one or two tropical veg; plantain is the favourite. Sometimes pork is substituted for chicken. This diet gets quite heavy on the stomach (especially if you sample crocodile meat, a speciality at Guamá). Only in the top Havana restaurants will you find menus employing seafood and fish with more adventurous sauces. Vegetarians are not likely to enjoy a terribly happy time, since the concept of voluntarily not eating meat is not an easy one for the average Cuban to grasp.

Coffee – referred to jokingly as 'American' if you go for sloppy continental-style dishwater – is usually drunk by Cubans as espresso. The most entertaining places to drink it is in bars on the street. Some upmarket coffee bars, Cuba's answer to Starbucks, are beginning to appear on the streets of Havana. The Coppelia is the local ice-cream parlour, usually marked by a queue; there is often a hard-currency counter with no queue.

To find a *paladar*, look around for signs advertising them, or ask other travellers; any locals you consult are likely to take a few (CUC) pesos' commission from their recommendation, which will be added to your bill. You should be especially circumspect about any offers on the street.

The 'official' restaurants described below are arranged according to the price of a main dish: expensive = CUC$20 and above; moderate = CUC$10–$20; inexpensive = CUC$10 and under. Service is not charged officially, but tipping is becoming the norm.

Havana

Expensive

Turquino Bar, on the top floor of the Tryp Habana Libre Hotel (*see* p.674), **t** 7834 6100. A good place to start any evening, with a cocktail. It gives a fantastic view of the city as the sun goes down.

Floridita, corner of Montserrate and Obispo, t 867 1299. The top address in Old Havana, a low-lit salon hung with velvet curtains and trimmed with chrome. Ernest Hemingway's chair is roped off in a corner; the writer used to kick off each evening here with a daiquiri or several. The restaurant specializes in fish and seafood – try the giant Hemingway plate of lobster, shrimp and fish in garlic sauce – and, of course, daiquiris, as drunk by Hemingway himself. Unfortunately cashing in on its celebrity, the high prices are not justified by either quality or quantity.

El Patio, Plaza de la Catedral, t 867 1034. This restaurant is worth coming to for the setting alone: a lovely view across the cobbled square from beneath the arches and stained-glass windows; *langosta enchilado* and *lonjas de pavo al jugo*, sliced roast turkey. There is a café downstairs on the patio itself.

La Cecilia, on 5th Avenue between 110 and 112, Miramar, t 204 1562. The best restaurant in Miramar, offering international fare and good food and service.

La Divina Pastora, Castillo del Morro, Casablanca, t 860 8341. This place, offering a fantastic view over the Malecón and the buildings of Havana, specializes in seafood such as *camarones al ajillo* (shrimp in garlic).

Moderate

Bodeguita del Medio, Calle Empredado and Cuba, t 867 1374. Yet another famed spot on the Hemingway trail, where he downed post-prandial *mojitos*. Customers are encouraged to sign their names on the wall, as drunken writers have since the 1940s. Ask about the chair (the upside-down one on the ceiling). Hearty creole food, *pierna de puerco asado rollo* or cooked *en su jugo*, is served at not-unreasonable prices.

La Torre, in the edificio Fosca on Calle 35, Vedado, t 553 089. The best of the restaurants in Vedado, at least for the view, with reliable Cuban and international fare.

1830, on the waterfront just over the bridge from Vedado, on the Malecón, t 553 090. Set in a small and attractive *palacio* with tables inside and out. Cuban and international fare; service average.

Papa's, at the Hemingway Marina in the west of Havana, t 204 1150. Predictably named, serves Cuban and international fare including seafood. The walls are decorated with murals of the undersea world.

Fiesta, Hemingway Marina, t 2041150. A varied menu means you can choose between Spanish and Cuban dishes as well as international fare. There's also a good club at the marina if you fancy a spot of dancing.

La Terraza, at Cojimar, to the east of Havana, t 559 486. This restaurant offers mainly fish and seafood dishes.

Los Doces Apostoles, Castillo del Morro, Casablanca, t 863 8295. Serves Cuban cuisine.

Inexpensive

Restaurant Hanoi, Av Brasil 507 and Bernaza, t 867 1029. The menu has nothing to do with Vietnam: standard Cuban dishes of rice, beans and fish are served in pleasant surroundings.

Don Giovanni, Calle Tacon, t 871 1027. A simple Italian restaurant, set in restored colonial rooms.

Varadero

Varadero offers perhaps even more choice and value than Havana. Competition between hotels and restaurants has caused prices to be cut and standards to be raised. The greatest concentration of choice is close to the bridge from the mainland. If you prefer to spend a little less and be more at the centre of things, you could try the Parque Josoné: a walled park on the east of the main strip, with statues among the palms and a lake where you can take out a boat.

Expensive

Las Américas, Av Las Américas, t 663 850. If money is no object, begin an evening here, a beautifully tiled and breezy terrace approached by a tiny stairway. Downstairs in the restaurant, you can sit in magnificent surroundings on antique chairs, while dining on rum shrimp, or Dakota chicken marinated in apple and lemon, while the waves thunder below.

Moderate

El Retiro, Parque Josoné, **t** 667 228. Set in an old family house with the paintings still hanging and international fare.

Dante's, Parque Josoné, **t** 667 738. An Italian restaurant serving some of the tastiest pizzas in Cuba.

La Campana, Parque Josoné, **t** 667 228. Here you'll find creole fare, served in an old house on the hill.

El Bodegón Criollo, Avenida Playa at Calle 40, **t** 667 784. Set in a breezy coral-rock house. This is an offshoot of Havana's Bodeguita del Medio, complete with graffiti all over the walls. Local fare as the name suggests: *bistec de cerdo grille* and *picadillo a la criollo*.

Mi Casita, Avenida Playa between Calle 11 and 12, **t** 613 787. A pretty spot, set in a coral-rock villa with paintings and antique furniture. Set international menu of fish, lobster or chicken.

Las Brasas, not far from Mi Casita, **t** 612 407. Somewhat cheaper, this serves creole fare: *lonjas de cerdo al jugo*, roast pork chops in a natural sauce, or *pollo en salsa*.

Cienfuegos

Moderate–Inexpensive

1819, Av Prado, **t** 514 514. Superbly preserved, in an old town house on the Prado. The cuisine is Cuban.

Mandarín, near the above. Serves some surprisingly plausible Cantonese dishes.

Covadonga, Calle 37, **t** 519 642. Specializes in paellas and seafood.

Trinidad

Moderate–Inexpensive

Trinidad Colonial, Calle Maceo 55, **t** 419 3873. Serves international fare.

El Mesón del Regidor, Calle Simón Bolívar 424, **t** 419 3654. Creole and Spanish food.

Holguín

Moderate–Inexpensive

La Floresta. As you head farther east, you will become more and more dependent on the hotels, but you can try this place, which serves creole food.

El Laurel. Again, creole food.

Santiago de Cuba

Expensive–Moderate

La Cecilia, **t** 229 1889. Sister to the Havana Restaurant, serving international food.

El Zunzun, **t** 2264 1528. In a lovely colonial building.

El Cayo. For seafood.

El Morro. Cuban creole.

La Casa de Rolando, **t** 2235 6156. Cuban creole.

Baracoa

The best alternative to the average restaurant at **El Castillo** is one of the expanding number of *paladares*.

Archipiélago de los Canarreos

On Cayo Largo, you will be dependent on hotel dining rooms or barbecues. On the Isla de la Juventud the possibilities are better.

Moderate

El Avión, Nueva Gerona, Isla de la Juventud. A fun restaurant, where meals are served in the fuselage of an old airliner.

Restaurante El Dragon, on the main drag, Calle 39, Isla de la Juventud. Better food.

Bars and Nightlife

Havana

La Bodeguita del Medio, Empedrado 207, **t** 867 1374. A bar on the Hemingway trail.

Hotel Sevilla, Trocadero and Prado, **t** 860 8560. Where *Our Man in Havana* drank.

Copa room, Hotel Riviera, Paseo and Malecón, **t** 33 4051. A jazz bar.

Varadero

Bars and snack bars have proliferated all over town, but most of the club action is in the west. Clubs include:

Cueva del Pirata, Autopista Sur km11, **t** 561 3829. The entry charge covers a cabaret and dancing.

Tuxpan, Carretera Las Américas, **t** 566 7560. Club in a hotel.

Kastillito, between Calle 49 and 50, **t** 561 3888. On some nights, the $10 admission covers all the alcohol you can consume.

Hotel Internacional, Av Las Américas, **t** 566 7038. Hotel with a cabaret.

where sugar cane (*guarapo*) and tobacco sprout from the rich brown earth, to the dry cactus flats and the coastal mangrove swamps that are home to endless birds and reptiles. Cubans maintain, probably correctly, that the island has the richest flora and fauna in the Caribbean. Of the 60 species of palm, the royal palm is the most magnificent – 100ft tall, with an explosive bush and a topmost spike – and it is the national tree. Other palms include the *barrigona*, rather rudely called the *palma puta* because it looks pregnant, the traveller's tree that opens like a fan, and the stunted fossil palm, recently almost extinct. Cuban forests were once an excellent source of hardwoods, including mahogany, teak and ebony, of which some still grow. There are many flowering trees, such as the African tulip tree and the flamboyant, which explodes into scarlet bloom in summer. There is one that grows wooden pineapples on its branches.

Real pineapples grow on spiky plants at ground level; they are just one of the many Cuban fruit crops, some of which are exported. You will also see huge citrus orchards of orange, lemon, lime and grapefruit and more exotic fruits such as soursop, mango and guava. The white mariposa, the butterfly flower, is Cuba's national flower.

Cuba has a greater variety of animals than other Caribbean islands, with a range of reptiles from 12ft crocodiles (you can see them in the Zapata Peninsula, where they are farmed for their meat), tank-like iguanas, endless lizards and geckos, down to the tiny almiqui, a shrew-like reptile found only in Cuba. There are 14 species of snake, but none of them is poisonous. Rodents include the agouti and the jutia. There is the odd wild boar, introduced by the Spanish as meat in buccaneer days. In the coastal waters, there are five species of turtle and the occasional endangered manatee or sea cow.

Insects include nearly 200 species of butterfly and hand-sized tarantulas which will give you a bit of a fright. (Mosquitoes are widespread, and while they are not malarial, there is a danger of dengue fever if you are bitten.)

The zunzuncito hummingbird is the world's smallest bird, and one of Cuba's 380 local and migratory species. In the forests are solitaires, owls and parrots, and on the plains there are hawks and the mournful-looking cattle egrets that keep a daytime vigil with the grazing cattle. Vultures gather in small, ominous groups by the roadside. The Cuban trogon, with its green, red, white and blue colouring, is the national bird. Around the shore, you will see single pelicans diving and magnificent frigatebirds soaring, seeking other birds to prey on; in the swamps are herons that stand on one leg waiting to strike for food, and flocks of flamingos that strut in unison.

Havana

Cuba's capital, La Habana, lies on the northern shore of the island, towards the western end, about 90 miles across the Gulf Stream from Key West in the USA. Its population of just over two million makes it by far the largest city in the Caribbean. The city was founded in 1514 as San Cristóbal de la Habana, but diametrically across the island at present-day Batabanó; after five years, it shifted to a magnificent natural harbour on the north coast. Havana's importance grew as it became the principal port for the Spanish Main. Ships put in here, their last stop before the Atlantic crossing back to Europe. By 1558, the small collection of coral-stone buildings and palm thatch *bohíos* had become the capital of Cuba. Heading west from the harbour along the Malecón (the Embankment, or sea wall), you will see the city's history mapped out before you, from the stunning colonnaded courtyards of 16th-century *palacios* in Old Havana, past the stately 19th-century colonial edifices of Habana Central and the vast and luxurious Art Deco palaces thrown up in the 30s and 40s in Vedado, to the imposing ferro-concrete monstrosities that followed the Revolution. The city seems steeped in decay. Initially, the Revolution set about correcting the economic imbalance between Havana and the rest of Cuba, which meant putting a higher priority on developing the country than on maintaining the capital. The state discouraged farmers from moving into shanty towns as they have on the outskirts of most other Caribbean capitals, and there has been little cash available in recent years.

Old Havana

Habana Vieja is by far the most beautiful town in the Caribbean, a view shared by UNESCO, which designated Old Havana as a city of world heritage. It is an egg-shaped area of a square mile, comprising glorious colonial palaces ranged in lines along narrow alleys and around handsome plazas. Behind the grey façades of coral rock, embellished with wrought-iron balustrades and stained-glass windows, you will discover idyllic interior courtyards, forested in greenery and overlooked by cloistered walkways. On the cobbled streets and in the colonnades, you can almost imagine the merchants of the 17th century clattering past in their carriages. You can wander for days.

Much of the old city is in distressing disrepair. The stucco and plasterwork has crumbled, and in places, whole façades are shored up with timber spars and scaffolding. Gradually restoration is taking place, mostly with help from European organizations.

A few sections remain of the old city wall. This was started in 1633 to keep out the plague of pirates and freebooters who were roving the islands at that time, but it was not completed until over a century later, in 1767. You may hear a cannon fired at 9pm each day from the San Carlos fort across the harbour, which once warned the citizens to return to the safety of the city walls. To protect Havana from sea attack, a chain was slung across the entrance of the harbour.

The oldest part of Havana is the **Plaza de Armas**, where the city's first Mass was said in November 1519, in the shade of an old ceiba (silk cotton) tree and where the neoclassical **Templete** has stood since 1754. Murals by the French artist Vermay commemorate the event. The most sought-after hotel in town, Hotel Santa Isabel, occupies the former Palacio de los Condes de Santovenia. From here, you can see the tiny Giraldilla, Havana's symbol, a statue of a woman holding a cross, who stands atop the tower of the **Castillo de la Real Fuerza** (*open daily 9–5; adm*). Constructed between 1538 and 1542, la Fuerza is Cuba's oldest surviving fortress. As a tourist attraction, though, it is challenged: the CUC$1 admission charge takes you around a selection of uninteresting rooms which double as dismal art galleries.

At the centre of the Plaza de Armas, surrounded by the royal palms of Cuba, stands a statue of Carlos Manuel de Céspedes, the father of Cuban Independence and hero of the 1868 War of Independence. But his old adversaries still dominate the square

Havana

CASABLANCA

Fortaleza de la Cabaña

Castillo del Morro

Canal de Entrada

Entenada de Atarés

OLD HAVANA

Castillo de San Salvador de la Punta

Statue of Máximo Gómez

Palacio del Segundo Cabo
Palacio del Segundo Cabo
Templete
Mesón de la Flota
Castillo de la Fuerza
Museo Numismático

Museo de la Revolución
Palacio de la Artesanía
Museo de la Revolución
Gramna Memorial
Museo Nacional de Bellas Artes

AV CARLOS M. CÉSPEDES (AV DEL PUERTO)

Catedral de San Cristóbal
Museo de Arte Colonial
Palacio de los Capitanes Generales

PLAZA DE LA CATEDRAL
PLAZA DE ARMAS

Iglesia y Convent de San Francisco

Parque Martí

Capitolio

Convento de Santa Clara

Iglesia de Nuestra Señora de la Merced

Casa Natal de José Martí

Central Train Station

CENTRO

Parque Maceo

PASEO DE MARTÍ (PRADO)

MALECÓN

AV DE ITALIA

PADRE VARELA (BELASCOAIN)

PADRE VARELA (BELASCOAIN)

AV SIMÓN BOLÍVAR (REINA)

MÁXIMO GÓMEZ (MONTE)

AV SALVADOR ALLENDE (CARLOS III)

CALZADA DE INFANTA

CALZADA DE INFANTA

SOLEDAD

VEDADO

Castillo de San Lázaro

Hotel Nacional

Havana Libre Hotel

Coppelia

RAMPA (23)

Universidad de la Habana

Hospital General Calixto García

Estadio Juan Abrahantes

Castillo del Príncipe

MALECÓN

PRESIDENTES

LÍNEA

PASEO

Interprovincial Bus Terminus

AV RANCHO BOYEROS

PLAZA DE LA REVOLUCIÓN

Statue of José Martí

AV CARLOS M. DE CÉSPEDES

Nacional Teatro

Cementerio Cristóbal Colón

1km
1/2 mile

N

Cigars

Bill Clinton was barely out of office when, during a stopover at Heathrow airport, he nipped into the duty-free shop to buy Cuban cigars. It is an ironic twist that the world's most accomplished capitalists prefer cigars made in one of the last vestiges of Communism. Despite the years of economic privation, cigars such as Monte Cristo, H. Upmann and Davidoff are the most celebrated in the world.

The tobacco plant cannot be mass-cultivated like sugar; it is best tended by an individual farmer, and many of Cuba's plantations are still in private hands. West of Havana, you will see the tobacco fields and the distinctive *vegas* (drying sheds) – clapboard buildings with shaggy thatch or more modern aluminium roofs – where the leaves are hung over bamboo spars to dry. Then they are baled up according to age and the position on the plant on which they grew and sent off to the factories.

A tour of a cigar factory can be intriguing; visits are easily arranged, and cost a few pesos (CUC). The cigar maker stretches out the leaves, cuts the youngest to size and holds it in his (or, since the Revolution, her) open hand, placing two slightly older leaves with stronger flavour on top. Offcuts and tobacco shavings are then packed in the centre and the cigar is hand-rolled. It gets its shape between boards in a vice, pressed for 20 minutes, turned and pressed again. On removal, it is cut at one end for length. Then the outer cover, the tenderest leaf, is rolled around the exterior (this leaf is slit down the middle and the cigars are rolled alternately left and right). The mouthpiece is sealed with a touch of glue and the label slipped on. The cigars are sent off to be packed, between thin layers of cedar wood to keep them dry, or in a palm leaf if they are for local consumption. The cigar makers are kept amused and informed by a lector, who reads from the newspaper as they work. In some factories in Pinar del Río and Havana, their day is also enlivened by tourists.

What happens to the cigars after manufacture is an interesting topic. A foreigner will be constantly assailed by people – mostly young men – whispering that they can sell you cigars. You will be assured that their brother/cousin/friend works in the factory, and can supply cigars at far below the official price. If you show interest, you will be led to a dwelling and shown the goods. Although this is unlikely to be a dangerous move, it is not a sensible way to buy cigars. There is a flourishing black-market trade in second-rate cigars sporting first-rate boxes and labels. You may be told that the box seal will be broken for you, but that you will then have to buy the contents. Even if the cigars are genuine, the contents are likely to have deteriorated, having been kept in warm conditions rather than in a humidor. And if you try to take cigars out of the country, they are very likely to be confiscated if you are unable to produce an official receipt. (All luggage is X-rayed on the way into and out of Cuba.)

The problem with buying legally, from hard-currency stores, is that service is poor and the choice is often absurdly limited. You might as well wait until you are in the airport's duty-free shop, where, although prices are no different, the range of cigars and care taken of them is about as good as you will find anywhere in Cuba itself.

Note that despite the flourishing black market in Cuban cigars in America, it is illegal to import them to the United States.

around him in the massive **Palacio de los Capitanes Generales**, seat of the Spanish colonial government. Today this huge palace, which was built between 1772 and 1776, is home to the **Museo de la Ciudad** (*open daily 9.30–6.30; adm*), the museum of Havana City, dedicated to the history of Cuba. On view are relics of the splendour of colonial days, mementoes of 20th-century Cuban triumphs as well as archaeological and folklore collections. There is a statue of Columbus in the cloistered courtyard. The colonnaded **Palacio del Segundo Cabo**, which stands next to the museum and was built in the same period, is occupied by the Ministry of Culture, but you are permitted to go into the inner courtyard. There are one or two cafés on the square.

A number of other gracious old *palacios* look onto the square and onto the nearby Calle Obispo, including the **Méson de la Flota**, the **Palacio Intendencia** – now the Letras Cubanas Publishing House – and **La Casa del Agua**, where until recently you could get stone-filtered water in metal beakers for 5 centavos, but are more likely now to be offered a plastic bottle of mineral water for a peso (CUC). There is also the old university bell, an old pharmacy and herb shop, dressed up as it would have been in the 19th century, and the **Casa de Las Infusiones**, where you can stop for a vanilla or lemon tea. The **Casa de la Obra Pia**, or 'house of charity' (*open Tues–Sat 10.30–5.30, Sun 9.30–12.30; adm*), is set in a 17th-century town house with a delightful courtyard and has an exhibition of 18th-century and 19th-century furniture. Downstairs there is a room devoted to Cuban journalist Alejo Carpentier.

On the Calle Oficios, which runs south from the Plaza de Armas, you will find the old **Monte Piedad** (the pawn shop), now the **Museo Numismático**, with Cuban notes and coins on display. A much more intriguing place is the **Museo de Automóvil** (*open daily 9–6.30; adm*), with some of Cuba's stately old motor cars on view. These include a 1902 Cadillac, Al Capone's 1924 Packard and the lime-green Chevrolet Bel Air saloon driven (apparently ineptly) by Che Guevara. The **Plaza de la Catedral**, just northwest of the Plaza de Armas, is another cobbled square enclosed by stunning colonial balconies and colonnades. At its head stands the baroque **cathedral** itself, originally built by the Jesuits in 1704, with towers of different size. Though it is dedicated to the Virgin Mary, it is usually known as the Columbus Cathedral: the bones of Christopher Columbus were reputed to have spent some years here between 1796 and 1898, brought from Santo Domingo and then taken to Seville. The cathedral offers a marvellous respite from the heat and noise of Havana, but its opening hours are erratic. The rest of the square was built in the first half of the 18th century. Directly opposite the cathedral is the **Museo de Arte Colonial** (*open Mon and Wed–Sat 10.30–5.30, Sun 9.30–12.30; adm*), where there are exhibits of 19th-century furniture and carving. Check out the washstand. In the square, you will see a shocked-looking face built into one of the walls. It is in fact a postbox, Cuba's oldest.

Old Havana is studded with colonial masterpieces: churches, seminaries, convents and old family *palacios*. A third stunning square is the **Plaza Vieja**, to the south of the Plaza de Armas. Look out for the **Palacio de la Artesanía** on Avenida Tacón, the **Palacio del Arsobispo de la Habana** on Calle Chacón, the old **Convento de Santa Clara** on Calle Sol, now restored, and the nearby **Iglesia de Nuestra Señora de la Merced**.

Most of the Revolutionary memorabilia occupies the open space between Calles Zulueta and Montserrate, parallel to the Prado, a boulevard with raised gardens and wrought-iron street lamps where Cuban gents congregate to read the paper and foreigners inevitably get nobbled by the hustlers. As you walk south from the Máximo Gómez statue at the harbour mouth, you come first to a tank that was involved in the Bay of Pigs battle, and then the former presidential palace, where Batista only just escaped an attack by 40 students in March 1957 by hiding in a lift. The palace has been turned into the **Museo de la Revolución** (*open Tues–Sun 10–5; adm*). On three richly decorated floors, it gives a detailed history of Cuba from the arrival of the Spaniards to the Revolution and beyond, covering moments such as the conquistadors and the suicide in 1951 of the opposition politician Eduardo Chíbas as he addressed the nation on the radio. The main celebration, though, is the minutely chronicled Revolution and Cuba's achievements since then. Conflicts such as the Bay of Pigs, and the 'October Crisis' (as the 1962 Cuban Missile Crisis is called) are given prominence, as are comprehensive statistics about enhanced health and education since 1959. On the ground floor, you'll find the *Sala de Che* (Che's room). The caskets that brought the remains of the rebel with a cause, and his fellow revolutionaries, back from Bolivia take pride of place, but other curiosities include one of Che's socks. You may seek relief from the relentless ideological battering by admiring the exquisite décor, created by Tiffany of New York; the Room of Mirrors was Cuba's response to a similar salon in the Palace of Versailles, and is equally impressive. Outside, the cabin cruiser *Granma*, which brought the rebels to Cuba in 1956, sits behind a glass screen, surrounded by relics of revolution.

Just east of the museum is Havana's leading cigar factory, the vast and fascinating **Real Fábrica de Tabacos La Corona** (*open Mon–Sat 10–1.30*). Heading south, the modern building next in line from the former presidential palace is the **Museo Nacional de Bellas Artes** (National Art Museum; *open Thurs–Mon 10–5; adm*), with Cuban rooms and works by foreign artists including Goya, Velázquez, Rubens and Turner. At the top of the slope is the most imposing building in Havana: the **Capitolio** (*open daily 8–5; adm*), a grand edifice designed in the style of the US Capitol in Washington. It was built by the Henderson Corporation to house the old Cuban House of Assembly. After remaining closed for years, it is now open to visitors and constitutes one of the most remarkable sights in the city. While much of Cuba was going hungry in the years between 1929 and 1932, Machado spared no expense in constructing this vast marble confection. A 24-carat diamond is embedded in the floor at the centre, marking the spot from which all distances in Cuba are measured.

From here, you can continue south towards Havana's grand old Central Train Station. Over the road at Calle Cuba 314 is the **Casa Natal de José Martí** (*open Tues–Sat 9–5; adm*), where Cuba's Independence hero was born. It traces his perambulations in exile and gives a strong impression of the man whose image is everywhere in Cuba.

The western side of the Parque Martí, and the Capitolio, marks the transition to Central Havana, which dates from the 19th century. This is where you will find most of the capital's shopping streets. It is also an exhilaratingly busy area.

Vedado

As you travel west from Central Havana, you pass through rundown residential streets, but soon these open out into **Vedado** district. Built in the 1930s and 1940s, the huge Art Deco palaces and villas are a reminder of just how luxurious and rich Havana was at that time. The best view of all is from the top of the **Havana Libre Hotel**, formerly the Havana Hilton.

The central street is Calle 23, better known as **La Rampa**, which runs from the Malecón up towards the Cementerio Colón. At the foot of La Rampa are all the airline offices. As you ascend, you find the **Coppelia** ice-cream parlour on your right and the Havana Libre Hotel on your left. In the southern area of Vedado, between Avenidas Rancho Boyeres and Céspedes, you will find the the vast open space of the **Plaza de la Revolución**. It is dominated by a New Age statue of José Martí and a 380ft **obelisk** (*open daily 9–5; adm exp*), a masterpiece of supremely ugly concrete architecture – but nevertheless one of the city's leading tourist attractions. The ground floor is taken up by an exhibition of Revolutionary glories, while the lift to the top yields spectacular views across the Caribbean's largest city. The square comes into its own when hundreds of thousands collect there to hear Fidel speak, usually at the New Year celebrations. Beyond here are the headquarters of the Cuban Communist Party, not open to the public.

The **Cementerio Cristóbal Colón** is a vast acreage of imposing mausolea and marble statuary set around an octagonal chapel. Among the graves of the martyred revolutionaries there are areas dedicated to the particular professions. It was in a speech outside the cemetery that Castro declared the Revolution a socialist one in 1961 – commemorated with a relief which bears one of only two three-dimensional images of Fidel anywhere on the island.

Cabaret

There are cabarets all over the island, many of them in the tourist hotels, but the most spectacular of them all is the Tropicana (*t 267 0110, www.cabarettropicana.com; best to reserve; closed Mon*). Set in the outskirts of the capital, it has changed surprisingly little since Havana was at its sleaziest in the 1950s. It is a show of hundreds of dancing girls (and a few men), who appear from everywhere, on catwalks, on trapezes, descending out of trees...

Voluptuous matriarchs act as '*commeres*', whose main job seems to be spurring on their cohorts of thrusting beauties to feats of dancing and athletic daring. In unison 30 of them strut around the stage high-kicking, skirts flailing, head-dresses quivering and cascading, thighs up to their ribs, scrunching up their noses at moments of high exertion. A familiar salsa pulse drives them on, backed by relentless African drums. It is a celebration of bodies as only the Latin Americans know how.

Around CUC$150 will be enough to get two people to and from your hotel, a ringside view of the action and a couple of drinks, which is probably cheaper than it was in the 1950s.

One unusual attraction in the western district of Miramar is the pavilion, Calle 28 between Avenidas 1 and 3, holding the **Maqueta de la Capital** (model of the city; *open Tues–Sat 10–5.30; adm*). The extraordinarily detailed model gives you an excellent overview; it is colour-coded by date, so you can trace the development of the city.

Outside the Centre

Across the harbour mouth from Old Havana is Casablanca, where you can climb to the 56ft **statue of Christ**. Getting to the distinctive Morro lighthouse is tricky because much of the intervening land is occupied by the military; you may find it easier to catch one of the many buses through the tunnel beneath the mouth of Havana harbour. The Morro itself is dominated by a lumbering **fortress** built to guard the approaches to the harbour. Beyond here, you come to the suburb of **Cojímar**, the setting of Hemingway's *The Old Man and the Sea*. It was once a fishing village, but now most of the fishermen have moved to more comfortable houses and it is only just possible to imagine a marlin's huge tail and backbone discarded on the beach. A bust commemorates the writer. The hero of *The Old Man and the Sea* is said to reside in Cojímar, and any local will point you in the direction of Gregorio Fuentes. He looks remarkably well considering he claims to be 100 years old.

Altogether more interesting is Hemingway's house, **Finca Vigía** ('lookout farm'; *open Mon and Wed–Sat 9–4, Sun 9–12.30; only open when it is not raining, to prevent visitors churning up the turf*), in the suburb of San Francisco de Paula, southeast of Havana. The writer ('Ernesto' to the Cubans) lived here in the 40s and 50s. It is maintained exactly as he left it in 1960. The walls are lined with hunting trophies and you can see his typewriter at chest height (he wrote barefoot standing up) and the sad record of his decreasing weight in the bathroom (he was dying from cirrhosis and eventually shot himself in 1961 in the USA). Because of previous thefts by avid souvenir collectors, visitors are now restricted to looking in through the windows and doors. The small estate stands on a cliff and has an excellent view looking north from the garden. The Hemingway Marina, situated five miles west of the capital, is Hemingway's only in name and in that it reflects his love of sport fishing.

South of Havana itself is the **Parque Lenin**, just outside the Havana ring road, a huge area of parkland with lakes, an amusement park, art galleries, a spiral aquarium and a massive, blinding-white bust of Lenin himself. There are also stables to hire horses, a diminutive train to ride, and in the evening you may like to visit the drive-in cinema (*autokine*), if you can get hold of a car. There is a railway terminal in the park, reached from Cristina station in the south of Havana. The park gets busy at the weekends, when the Habañeros pour out of the city. Close by to the south are some **Botanical Gardens**, with an effusion of Caribbean flora, and **Expocuba**, a series of pavilions that illustrate the country's successes in industry and social progress.

West of Havana

The province of Pinar del Río occupies the western tip of Cuba and, with the Sierra de los Organos (which seems to collect rainclouds) along its northern shore, it is both beautiful and fertile. It is here that Cuba's finest tobacco is grown. Among the royal palms and the karst limestone outcrops, the hills are smothered in bright green plantations and dotted with aluminium and shaggy-roofed *vegas*, the tobacco-drying houses. If you drive out to the west of the island, make sure to travel on the northern coastal route between Cabañas and Puerto Esperanza, either outbound or on your return. It's much slower, but much more scenic than the *autopista*.

In the hills north of San Cristóbal are the botanical gardens of **Soroa**, with a walkway through Cuba's explosive vegetation. The garden, which covers a hillside, was built by a Spaniard in memory of his daughter who had died in childbirth. As well as 'mother-in-law's tongue' and the 'elephant's foot' tree from Mexico there is an **orquideario** (*open daily 8.30–12 and 1.30–4 for guided tours; best in November and December; adm*), where most of the island's 250 varieties of orchid (including the extraordinary 'Queen's shoe') are on view. There is a waterfall nearby.

The city of **Pinar del Río**, 110 miles from Havana, was once nicknamed Cinderella because it was so poor. Since then, it has grown on the back of the tobacco industry. You can visit any number of cigar factories, or the **Museo del Tabaco**, in the west of town, on Calle Ajete, where there is an illustration of the industry from seed to cigar. Among numerous museums is the **Museo Provincial de Historia** on Calle José Martí (*open Tues–Sat 2–6, Sun 9–1; adm*), with displays of Cuban life.

North of Pinar del Río, the **valley of Viñales** showcases an extraordinary geographical phenomenon in its karst mountain outcrops, once the supports of a vast plain which collapsed through water erosion millions of years ago. (Called *mogotes* here, they appear similar to the Burren in west Ireland and the 'haystack mountains' of South China.) The verandah of the Motel Los Jazmines (*see* 'Where to Stay', p.674) presents one of Cuba's most attractive views, where these vast neolithic fruit cakes soar from the lush tobacco fields. The *mogotes* are laced with cave systems where the Guanahatabeyes – cave-dwelling Indians who were Cuba's earliest inhabitants – lived and where you can take boat trips. West of Pinar del Río the mountains subside.

East of Havana

Beyond the beaches of Playas del Este to the east of Havana and past the drilling heads of Cuba's oil industry, you come to the city of Matanzas, set on a deep bay about 80 miles from the capital. You can also make the journey by the 'Hershey train', which departs four or five times each day from Casablanca station, on the eastern side of Havana's harbour. Besides being the only electric railway line in Cuba, it is also one of the most scenic rides – much of it through startling gone-to-seed sugar plantations that once belonged to the Hershey Corporation.

Matanzas, which takes its name from a massacre (perhaps of Spaniards, but more likely of bloodstock), was founded in 1690. The city did not really develop until the 19th century, when it became immensely wealthy through the sugar industry. It became a Cuban leader in matters cultural and is full of grand old buildings from the period, including the **cathedral** and others ranged around the **Parque Central** and the

Teatro Sauto, built in 1863. It comes across as a gentler town after the bustle of the capital. Here horse-drawn carriages still provide the main form of public transport. The **Museo Farmacéutico** (*open Mon–Sat 10–5, Sun 10–12; adm*) is on the Parque Central (officially the Plaza de la Libertad) and has an original display of old wives' remedies and medicinal plants. Nearer the waterfront, you will find the provincial museum in the **Palacio de Junco** (*open Tues–Fri 10–12 and 1–6, Sat 1–9, Sun 8.30–12; adm*), a beautiful mansion built by a sugar planter in the 19th century.

Matanzas is the gateway to **Varadero**, Cuba's premier resort: a 12-mile-long beach known as the Hicacos Peninsula, itself is as large as many Caribbean islands. Varadero is devoted to sun, sea and sand vacations, with watersports by day and exotic cabaret and clubs by night. The town, which consists mainly of high-rise and beachfront blocks interspersed with pretty coral rock houses and wooden villas from pre-revolutionary days, is strung out along the peninsula. The best-known house is some way beyond the main resort: the **Du Pont family vacation home**, a Spanish-revival villa, now an expensive restaurant, but with some rooms left in their original state. There is a bar on the rooftop with an impressive view of the area. **Parque Josoné** is a modest sort of pleasure garden, usually frequented by tourists, with a scattering of cafés.

The town of **Cárdenas**, not far south of Varadero, is a backwater of a port where very little ever happens – and it remains largely untouched by the tourist race. Its sleepy nature gives a good idea of rural Cuba. It is known, rather grandly, as the 'City of Flags' because the Cuban flag was first raised here in 1850, in a failed insurrection. It was also the birthplace of José Echevarría, a militant student leader who was killed by the Batista regime in March 1957. A **museum** (*open Tues–Sat 9.30–12 and 1–6; Sun 9.30–12*) of Cárdenas's commercial and revolutionary tradition has been created in his home on the street now named after him. More recently, Cárdenas has become celebrated as the home town of Elián González, the young boy who was rescued after his mother and other adults were drowned in a doomed escape attempt in 1999.

As you travel south from the provincial capital, you pass through the endless cane-fields, the source of Matanzas's wealth, and across the drowsy agricultural heartland of Cuba. On the southern seaboard of Matanzas province is the swamp of the Zapata Peninsula, the largest expanse of wilderness in Cuba and probably in the whole of the Caribbean. It attracts a huge variety of wildlife, particularly birds. The set-piece tourist attraction here is **Villa Guamá**, an inland 'Indian village' resort built of palm-thatch *bohíos* and decorated with sculptures by Rita Longa. You approach it from the highway on a long, leisurely boat ride. Nearby is a **crocodile farm**, best visited at feeding time in the early evening. Note, however, that the biggest concentration of mosquitoes in Cuba regards the nightly arrival of visitors as a feeding frenzy.

Just to the south, on the coast itself, is the place renowned among the Cubans for being the site of the 'First major defeat of Imperialism in Latin America': the **Bay of Pigs**. Fidel himself returned to the battlefield in April 1961 to repel the landing by Cuban exiles. It is a proud piece of post-revolutionary history, with memorial stones positioned along the route to honour those who died. In the resort of **Playa Girón**, the main attraction is a **museum** (*open daily 9–12 and 1–5; adm*) devoted to the repulsing of the invasion force. You can't miss the British Sea Fury fighter.

The city of **Cienfuegos** is 40 miles east of Playa Girón. It is set on an almost land-locked bight on the south coast of the island. Cienfuegos is an industrial and port town, with a population of 100,000 and a large naval base. It is also the venue for the biggest nuclear power installation in Cuba, begun, but never actually completed, by Soviet scientists. In the city centre there are some elaborate old Spanish colonial buildings, including the **cathedral** with its octagonal cupola and the **Tomas Terry theatre** on the square of the Parque Martí. The waterfront Prado is uninspiring, but you can follow it south to the hilarious and elaborate folly of **Valle Palace**, a zany conglomeration of the styles of the three religions of Christianity, Judaism and Islam.

Trinidad

A further 50 miles east of Cienfuegos, along a spectacular coastal road that winds over the headlands thrown off by the peaks of the Sierra Escambray, you come to the extraordinary and charming town of Trinidad. The 21st century appears to have had no impact on the town, one of the original seven Spanish *villas*, making it prime tourism territory. Trinidad has been restored entirely to its early 19th-century glory: cobbled streets, Spanish colonial town houses, wrought-iron street lamps, cannon at the street corners with muzzles buried in the ground to stop the carriage wheels clipping the walls. Two hundred years ago, Trinidad was one of Cuba's richest trading ports and its fleets would sail as far afield as Brazil and the Baltic. Today the narrow streets may be festooned with telephone wires, but they still retain an antique ambience, overlooked by wrought-iron balconies and pastel-coloured plaster façades. The cannon still makes themselves useful, too, defending the stone-work from wayward lorry wheels. Like Old Havana, Trinidad is on UNESCO's World Heritage list.

The town is one of Cuba's oldest and was founded by Diego Velásquez in 1514. In 1518, Hernán Cortés embarked on his conquest of Mexico from a house on the beautiful central square, the Plaza Martí. The site is now occupied by the **Museo de Archueología Guamuhaya** (*open Tues–Sun 9–5; adm*), which has a lacklustre display of pre-Columbian Indian life, including burial pots. Diagonally opposite, set in a pretty town house, is the **Museo de Arquitectura de Trinidad** (*open Tues–Sun 9–5; adm*), which illustrates the development of Trinidad's buildings and their embellishments through pictures, including the pineapples that crop up all over the town. Look out for the ingenious 18th-century steambath and the toilets with a communicating door between men's and women's – and then see which side you can lock it from. The **Museo Romantico** (*open Tues–Sun 8–5; adm*) is also on this square, a classically beautiful colonial palace set around a courtyard, stuffed with elaborate furniture and with marvellous views from the upstairs windows; at the start of 2001 it was closed indefinitely for refurbishment, much to the chagrin of all the newly married couples in the province of Sancti Spíritus, who traditionally pose for photographs here. The **Museo de la Lucha Contra Bandidos** (*open Tues–Sun 9–5; adm*) tells the story of the struggle against counter-revolutionaries, and provides superb views of the city, Caribbean and surrounding hills from the tower.

The **Torre de Iznaga** is a reminder of Trinidad's other career as a centre of sugar. This folly stands a few miles out of the town on the road to Sancti Spíritus, the provincial capital. It was originally built as an observation tower for plantation overseers to watch the slaves.

Above Trinidad, straddling the three provinces of Villa Clara, Cienfuegos and Sancti Spíritus are the mountains of **Sierra Escambray**, Cuba's central mountain range, where immensely fertile peaks and valleys reach up to 3,000ft in places. The northern slopes are covered in tobacco plantations and their shaggy drying-houses. The highest summit is Pico San Juan (3,800ft) just northwest of Trinidad on the south coast. A trip to **Topes de Collantes** makes a good day out from Trinidad: the views are magnificent. The **Soledad botanical gardens** are east of Cienfuegos; here you can see 60 sorts of palm among the 2,000 species of plant in the pleasant parkland. Look out for the 'pineapple tree'.

Trinidad to Santiago de Cuba

In the centre of the island, directly north of Trinidad, is the city of **Santa Clara**, the capital of Villa Clara province. The city has a population of 200,000 and is the home of one of Cuba's four universities. Although it has become quite industrialized, the city still supports a tradition of agriculture, with sugar-cane flats interspersing its fields of maize, beans and yuca (cassava) as well as ranches of cattle.

Santa Clara is also central to the triumph of the Revolution, a role emphasized in 1997 when the remains of Che Guevara were re-buried at an enormous mausoleum on the edge of the city. It was quite natural that Santa Clara should be chosen as the location for the revolutionary's final resting place: it was here, in December 1958, that he commanded the decisive victory against Batista's troops. The site of the battle has been turned into one of Cuba's oddest museums, the **Tren Blindado** (*site open to visitors at any time; wagons open Tues–Sat 9.30–12 and 3–6, Sun 9–12*), an armoured troop train that stands derailed at the site where it was stormed by the revolutionaries. The exhibits are set inside the old wagons.

Northeast of Santa Clara is one of Cuba's most atmospheric old towns, peacefully off the tourist circuit. **Remedios** was the old provincial capital until it was struck by a terrible fire in 1692, yet it has preserved much of its 17th-century architecture. The town's main square, dominated by the handsome **Parroquia de San Juan Bautista de Remedios**, is dreamily beautiful.

The province of **Ciego de Ávila** is mainly agricultural, with more sugar-cane flats and pineapple plantations. Its capital, the city of Ciego de Ávila, is quiet and a little lack-lustre, and is only really visited because it happens to lie on the main east–west road and railway line. A more pleasant place to visit goes by the unlikely name of **Morón**, which has the atmosphere of a 19th-century country town. If you wish to fix up a shooting trip, you can do so on the **Laguna de Leche** and in the swamps north of the town. It is now the gateway to the massive **Cayo Coco** development on one of Cuba's largest offshore islands. A 20-mile-long causeway leads northwards from Morón to Cayo Coco, with links extending to neighbouring islands. The development of the resort, which took place in the early 1990s, was personally overseen by Fidel Castro himself. The resort has proved to be a success, particularly with European visitors, despite feeling isolated from the rest of the country.

The city and province of **Camagüey** comprise altogether a better prospect. The city of Camagüey, originally called Puerto Principe, was one of Cuba's earliest settlements, established on the coast in 1514, but moved inland to save it from pirate raids. Today, it is Cuba's third largest city and it sits on the plain among the canefields and cattle ranches. Camagüey boasts many old Spanish colonial buildings, among them the **Teatro Principal**, **La Soledad** church and the 18th-century **Palace of Justice**. The large earthenware pots which you can see all around the city were used for storing and keeping water cool, and have become the symbol of the province.

There are two museums bearing the name of Ignacio Agramonte, a hero of the Cuban War of Independence who was born here in Camagüey. The **Museo Ignacio Agramonte**, the provincial museum, is set in a magnificent building on the Avenida de los Mártires and depicts local history and the many moves the town has made. The **Museo Casa Natal de Ignacio Agramonte** (*open Mon and Wed–Sat 10–5*) gives a more personal view of the rebel leader's life and achievements in the charming house where he was born.

Holguín and Granma provinces straddle the island as it widens towards the south-eastern tip. They consist mainly of agricultural plains, rising into the foothills of the Sierra Maestra on the south coast. **Holguín**, a small colonial town with three main squares surrounded by an infestation of concrete, is scattered in the lee of a large hill, the Loma de la Cruz, from where the views are magnificent. The **Museo de Ciencias**

Music

Within an hour of arriving in Cuba, you will discover how central music is to life in the republic. Where most Caribbean islands have a rhythm of their own, Cuba has several, most notably **salsa**. Cuban salsa is distinctly Latin, but differs from the salsa of Puerto Rico, which has been influenced by the Neoyorkeñans (Puerto Ricans living in New York). Salsa grew out of son, with a guitar and a guiro (washboard) and heavy drum backing. Other Cuban rhythms include **rumba**, **danzón** and **cha-cha-cha**. All of these are preferable to the endless renditions of 'Guantanamera' (meaning 'Girl from Guantánamo'). You will hear the tune bashed out relentlessly and often tune-lessly in tourist spots throughout the island. This is an example of yet another style, the **guajira**.

Every Cuban town has a music scene that appeals to the whole age range. It may comprise a band made up of a few old gents bashing out tunes in the town square, or performances may take place within a *casa de la trova* (literally 'house of the trouba-dours', in practice a state-sponsored hall where bands play and rum is consumed, both with considerable gusto).

Carnival is making a comeback as economic circumstances improve; Havana's re-appeared in 1997, after being cancelled for years because cash was so tight. If your visit coincides with a festival, look out for the wind-up organs that play old son rhythms. Cuban **jazz** is also excellent, and you might just catch groups such as Irakere while you are in town. There is an increasing amount of dismal Western pop, too, but fortunately the real Cuban thing shines through.

Carlos de la Torre (*open Tues–Sun 9–6; adm*) is set in a fine colonial house on Calle Maceo and has displays of Cuban animals from crustaceans to mammals, including an exhibit of the rare manatee.

Beyond the town are the beaches and resorts around Guardalavaca on the north coast. **Gibara** lays claim to be Columbus's landfall on the island in 1492, when he thought he had discovered Japan. In **Banes**, 12 miles inland from Guardalavaca, there is the excellent **Museo Indocubano** (*open Tues–Sat 12–6, Sun 2–6; adm*), with an extensive collection of Siboney and Taino artefacts, including their illustrated pottery and descriptions of their ceremonies.

The capital of Granma province is **Bayamo**, one of Cuba's oldest towns, founded by Diego Velázquez in 1513. The church of **San Salvador** is one of the oldest buildings in Cuba. The town was also the home of Céspedes, who initiated the Cuban War of Independence here in 1868 by freeing his slaves and providing them with arms against the Spaniards. He is remembered in the Parque Céspedes and the **Museo Casa Natal de Carlos Manuel de Céspedes** (*open Tues–Fri 9–4.30, Sat and Sun 9–12.30; adm*), a colonial house on Calle Maceo, which tells of his life and struggle. The **Museo Nico López** (*open Tues–Sun 9–5*) tells the story of the Bayamo people who staged a rebellion in 1953 to coincide with the Moncada garrison attack. The province is named after the boat in which the revolutionaries sailed from Mexico, which in turn, is named after the grandmother of the previous American owner of the vessel. **Las Coloradas** has a concrete memorial to the landing.

Santiago de Cuba

In Oriente province, 60 miles east of Bayamo, is Cuba's second city, Santiago de Cuba. The town sits on the edge of a massive harbour, where the Sierra Maestra mountains tumble down to the south coast. It holds a special place in the panoply of modern Cuba as the spiritual home of the Independence movement and also of the Revolution. Independence heroes, such as Céspedes and José Martí, are buried in the city. The Moncada Barracks, where Castro made his first attack in 1953, have become a shrine to the Revolution. Castro returns to speak here often, usually in the summer celebrations around 26 July each year.

Santiago de Cuba is the island's third oldest city. It was founded in 1513 by Diego Velásquez, and for 40 years it was the colony's capital. Some buildings survive from the earliest period (among them is the oldest building on the island, Velásquez's palace), but the town's charming atmosphere comes from all the 19th-century town houses, with their wrought-iron balconies and shuttered windows, that line the steep streets and stepped alleyways. You will find it an excellent city to wander in, more compact and less overwhelming than Havana.

Santiago has a complex heritage as refugees have fled here in floods from every conflict in the islands nearby. A strong French heritage dates from the influx of 30,000 planters who fled St Domingue at the time of the Haitian Revolution in 1791. In addition, there is a substantial community from elsewhere in the Caribbean –

particularly from Jamaica, due south of Santiago. The city centre is **Céspedes Square**, set on the hill a few hundred yards above the harbour. It is one of the finest squares in all the Hispanic world. On its southwest corner is the house of Diego Velásquez, built in around 1514. Recently restored, it is a charming house with balconies set around inner courtyards. It is now home to the **Museo de Ambiente Histórico Cubano** (*open Mon–Sat 9–5, Sun 9–1*), although at the beginning of 2001 it was closed for restoration. On the south side is the **cathedral**, first built on this site in 1524, though the imposing edifice has been enlarged since then.

To the east of the square, past the famous Santiago Casa de la Trova (one of the best in Cuba) is the **Bacardi Museum** on Pío Rosado (*open Mon–Sat 10–8; adm*), a splendid 19th-century mansion built by the founder of the rum dynasty. It is now Cuba's closest equivalent to the Victoria and Albert Museum in London, and houses a fine collection of 19th-century artefacts and art.

The national hero José Martí is buried in a vast concrete mausoleum in the **Santa Efigenia cemetery** to the west of the town. As the spiritual home of the Revolution, Santiago has plenty of museums dedicated to the armed struggle in the 1950s. The most famous is, of course, the **Moncada Barracks**, restored (with all its bullet holes) as it was after the attack on 26 July 1953. Like many of Batista's barracks, it has been turned into a school, but there is a small and interesting museum on the assault (*open daily 9–5; adm*) off the Avenida de los Libertadores. Nearby is the **Parque Histórico**, site of the hospital where Castro was tried after the attack, and where he delivered his five-hour speech asserting 'history will absolve me'. Close by, you can also visit the Hotel Rex, where the rebels ate their last meal before the doomed attack.

Farther out of town to the south is the great bulk of the **Morro** fortress, rising several hundred feet above the sea, built on the point at the harbour mouth in 1643. Within, it houses the **Museo de la Piratería** (*open daily 9–5; adm*), where exhibits of pistols, cutlasses and maps illustrate the tale of Caribbean piracy, including an assault on the Morro fortress itself by Henry Morgan in 1662. There are supreme views from here along the south coast and up into the mountains above the town. On the road leading east out of the town, towards the south-coast beaches, is **Siboney farm**: yet another museum on the assault on the Moncada Barracks. It was from here that Castro's rebels set out to storm the garrison. The route into town is dotted with memorials.

Soon after, you come to one of Cuba's most curious parks as outsize pterodactyls and brontosauri in concrete appear around you in the 'Dinosaur Park' or the **Valle de la Prehistoria** (*adm*). North of here is the nature park of **Gran Piedra**, set around the 4,000ft mountain of the same name, where you can walk among the explosive vegetation of the Sierra Maestra. The area gets crowded at weekends, when the Santiagueros pour out of the city to get here. On a clear day, you can see the Blue Mountains of Jamaica 80 miles to the south.

The remote and thinly populated province of Guantánamo runs from Santiago to the eastern tip of the island. The capital, also called **Guantánamo**, is not an attractive town and is known locally as the hometown of the woman celebrated in the song 'Guantanamera'. Nowadays it is better known for the US naval base at Guantanamo

Bay, location of notorious Camp X-Ray. The base was leased by the USA in 1902 and the Americans pay a handsome US$2,000 each year for the pleasure. You are not allowed near it, but can get a view from the hills above.

The road continues along the south coast and then cuts into the mountains to the north coast and the city of **Baracoa**. Despite its somnolent ambience, this port with 60,000 inhabitants is perhaps the most alluring town in the whole of Cuba. Established in 1510, it is certainly Cuba's oldest Spanish colonial town. Steeped in history, it is surrounded by fine scenery, including the magnificent plateau of **El Yunque**, the table mountain which dominates every view. In the central square, where the locals gather to play dominoes, is a statue of Cuba's first rebel, the Indian Hatuey. The town is guarded by a series of forts, of which one, **Matachín**, has been turned into a **museum** of Baracoa history (*open Tues–Sat 9–5, Sun 9–1; adm*).

Isla de la Juventud

Sixty miles south of the mainland, in the bay made by the alligator's tail (in the west of Cuba), is the flat 'Isle of Youth'. Discovered in 1494 by Columbus, it was a pirate haunt for several hundred years. Until 1978 it was known as the 'Isle of Pines', but the government changed the name to one felt to be more socialistically uplifting. The main town is **Nueva Gerona**, in the north of the island. Good roads run to the southwest and southeast coast, where there are fine beaches, but much of the country in the south is swampland. There are regular flights to the island from Havana, costing as little as $20 each way; you could alternatively travel by catamaran (retired from the Mediterranean) from Surgideno de Batabanó, south of Havana.

Up until 1999, the Isla de la Juventud had a population of about 70,000 and an exciting, youthful atmosphere to go with its name: students, many of them from African countries, came to take courses here. Since the collapse of the Soviet Union, the cash has dried up and the last few overseas students have left. The island has returned to its former existence, as a remote and relaxed alternative to the mainland, like some of the sleepier islands elsewhere in the Caribbean. Increasingly, tourists are taking over from students. The island is surrounded by reefs for excellent scuba diving, and the fishing, one of the islanders' main occupations, is good, too. There are caves to explore in the east of the island.

Easily the most intriguing tourist attraction is the **Presidio Modelo** (*open Tues–Sat 9–5, Sun 9–1; adm*), the former high-security prison with its five round cell blocks, where Castro and his fellow rebels did a stint after the Moncada garrison attack. Most of the prison has been converted into a school, but part has been preserved as it was when Castro was imprisoned here.

Cayo Largo, at the other end of the archipelago, has been developed exclusively as a tourist resort. If you want to spend a few days uninterrupted in the relentless pursuit of beach lounging and watersports, this place is as good as any in Cuba – except for the interruptions caused by numerous charter flights carrying day trippers from the mainland. If you feel the need for greater isolation, you can go even further afield and be even more remote in the nearby cays of **Cayo Rico** and **Cayo Pájaros**.

Jamaica

17

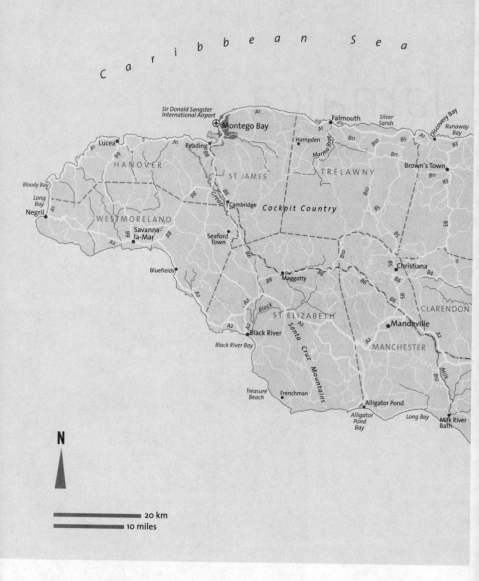

Highlights

1 Watch for the Green Flash from the cliffs at Negril on the western tip of the island
2 Catch a world-famous reggae artist playing to a home crowd of a few thousand
3 Admire the view from Firefly, Noël Coward's house
4 Try out a Jerk Centre

Jamaica

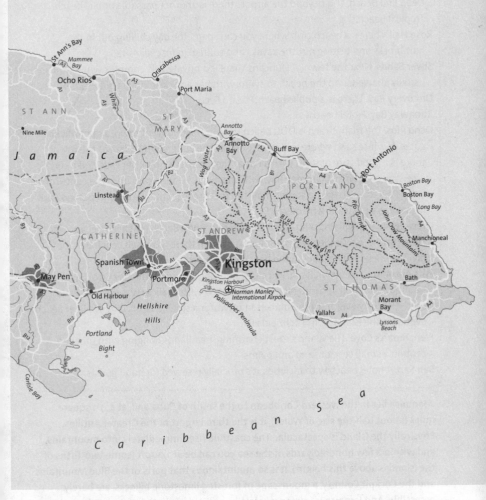

Everyone has an image of Jamaica: the island idyll of palms and beaches, a hedonist's paradise of rum, reefers and reggae rhythm, a land of plantation houses and fantastically beautiful tropical gardens. Jamaica is all these things. Although often considered to be a little threatening, Jamaica is among the liveliest of all the islands, its allure the strongest of all the former British Caribbean islands.

Best Beaches

Montego Bay: The popular public beaches are Doctor's Cave Beach and Cornwall Beach (well known for its beach parties), both popular with the locals, lively and usually crowded, with changing facilities and a small admission charge. There are bars where you can get a drink to cool you off and watersports can be arranged there. At the end of Kent Avenue, beneath the airport run-in, is a small strip of sand, Dead End Beach, and beyond the airport there is another passable public beach, Tropical Beach.

Rose Hall: There's a beach club where you can spend the day chilling out in the hammocks and testing out the kayaks and sunfish (*adm expensive*).

Silver Sands: Near the town of Duncans there is a private villa complex where you are usually allowed in to the beach to swim, with bar and changing facilities (*adm*).

Discovery Bay: There is a public beach, Puerto Seco.

Runaway Bay: Hotel beaches.

Ocho Ríos: The main beach is UDC beach right in the middle of town, a magnificent curve of white sand where you can try out all the watersports. West of the town there is a good strip of sand with a bar at the foot of Dunn's River Falls and a very nice strip of sand at Mammee Bay, with snack bar. Headed east from the centre of Ocho Ríos town there are some small and pretty coves cut into the cliffs: Shaw Park Beach has a pleasant strip of sand.

Oracabessa: You will find a hip spot called James Bond Beach (so called because Ian Fleming's house, Goldeneye, is not far off), where there is a small beach bar and facilities. Beyond Oracabessa the beaches peter out.

Port Antonio: In the town itself, you can go to Navy Island off the bay, Errol Flynn's old haunt, where there is an attractive strip of sand with shallow water. Call up and catch the ferry over from the market in town, for a small charge. Jamaica Reef Beach overlooks the island from Titchfield Hill.

Frenchman's Cove: The island's most charming: headlands hanging with greenery contain a small cove of sand and palms.

San San: A hotel beach with facilities, it's officially reserved for hotel guests.

Jamaica lies in the western Caribbean to the south of Cuba and, at 4,411 square miles (about half the size of Wales), it is the third largest of the Greater Antilles. Physically the island is spectacular. The coastline rises immediately into mountains, and within a few hundred yards of the sea you can be at 1,000ft (some two-fifths of the island is above this height). It is so mountainous that parts of the Blue Mountains and the Cockpit Country, a moonscape of forested limestone hillocks, are barely accessible. And Jamaica is immensely fertile, particularly in the east and along the north coast, where you could almost expect a pencil to take root.

On a map Jamaica may look as though it languishes like a turtle, but nothing could be further from the truth when it comes to the Jamaicans themselves. Almost 3 million Jamaicans live on the island (probably more than this number live elsewhere in the world). The streets are something of a theatre as the Jamaicans shout and quip

Dragon Bay: Some facilities.

Winnifred Beach: Lots of bars and activity at weekends.

Boston Bay: Big waves whipped by the trade winds roll in from the east and surfers get out and do their stuff occasionally. There is a good strip of sand at the head of the bay and, of course, you can grab a jerk chicken or pork for lunch.

Long Bay: Here there's a fishing village and a lovely deserted stretch of sand. There are no watersports here, of course, just coconut palms and sand.

Lyssons Beach: The beaches along the southeastern coastline tend to be brown sand and the water a little muddy, but there is a passable stretch of sand here.

Kingston: The local favourite beaches are Fort Clarence, where there is an admission charge, so many Jamaicans prefer to go to Hellshire, where the mounded sand is backed with endless wooden snack huts – check out the curious-looking beach chairs made of driftwood. Some people go just for the fish or lobster and bammy, which is cooked to your order. These beaches are quite hard to reach (buses from the parade). There are dark-sand beaches on the Palisadoes Peninsula, but an excellent day out is to catch a ferry over to Port Royal and then hire a boat to take you over to Lime Cay, where the snorkelling is excellent, or Maiden Cay, which is no more than a sand bar. There's little or no shade on either cay, so sunblock is essential.

Alligator Pond Bay: This fishing village in Manchester Parish has a reasonable strip of sand.

Treasure Beach: This small resort area has brown sand but two good beaches in Frenchman's Bay and Great Bay and there are facilities and bars in the hotels.

Bluefields Bay: A very natural stretch of shallow water with trees lining the shore.

Negril: An almost uninterrupted 5 miles of golden sand running north from the roundabout at the centre of the town (south of here it is nearly all 'ironshore' cliffs). It is good to walk or, if that seems too energetic, there are hip places to loiter and wait for the Green Flash at sunset. There are beach concessionaires who will arrange most watersports.

Bloody Bay: There is another wide curve of sand, steadily being developed. Beyond here you will find other tiny inlets with lovely sand.

with one another. Markets, from downtown Kingston to the three or four people selling fruit at the roadside in the country, are mayhem. The Jamaicans do not suffer authority or formality gladly (queuing died soon after the British left) and they are very forward; some stop you to give advice or to say hello, others to hustle you.

You are likely to be accosted in the main tourist areas – Jamaica has always been exuberant and at times slightly rough, but the reports that call it unsafe are ill-founded, as long as you take advice and use as much care as you would in any economically poor country. One solution to the problem is never to leave the compound of your hotel, but this is to miss out on the best of Jamaica, which you will find in the local villages beyond the resorts. Occasionally, the fervour spills over into violence, but this is rarely directed against foreigners. Avoid Kingston at election time when political tensions are at their highest.

Suggested Itinerary

You can make a good tour of Jamaica in ten days or two weeks; this will give you some time in the well-known tourist resorts as well as a look at something more Jamaican, the magnificent interior of the island and some of the inland activities such as river bathing and rafting. Whether you arrive in Kingston or in Montego Bay, you can follow the coastline. Stay a few days either in Montego Bay or Ocho Rios, until you get the urge to look beyond the beaches and bars. Go east to Port Antonio, a charming and laidback town in the far east, the lushest and most strikingly fertile area of the island. From here, you can make your way over to the southern side of the island via the Blue Mountains, where there are now inns and guest houses in all price ranges, and then drop down into Kingston. The capital will also show you the Jamaicans' Jamaica – check out the markets downtown and make a ferry trip over to Port Royal. From here, you should head west to the sleepy towns of Treasure Beach and Black River, where the Jamaicans themselves take their holidays. Leave enough time for Negril, which is a tourist town with a difference – great for a few days' 'hanging out' waiting for the sunset and the flight home.

Jamaica became independent from Britain on 6 August 1962, but the echoes of three centuries of British colonial rule still ring through. Churches and Georgian great houses were constructed by the planters in the style of buildings at home. Jamaica has moved on since Independence, but many British institutions remain in creolized form, including the Westminster model of democracy, and the belts, peaked caps and serge trousers of uniformed policemen.

And yet things are never quite as they seem: a very strong African element underpins the British façade. Jamaican marching bands may wear scarlet tunics with trimmings of gold braid, but their movements are not the clipped and formal procession of the British – they have a rhythmic swagger that is Jamaican. Cricket is still played in whites, but it has developed its own, typically West Indian expression and is now thrown back at the English with a vengeance.

Many visitors to Jamaica go for the sun, sea and the ganja, but beyond the beach Jamaica has a special appeal which over the centuries has attracted men as diverse as Henry Morgan, Errol Flynn and Noël Coward. The British have had a love affair with the island for centuries. Tropical paradise or tricky destination, Jamaica offers the most romantic liaison with the Caribbean.

History

There are thought to have been 100,000 Arawaks living on Jamaica when Columbus arrived on 5 May 1494, on his second voyage. He went to investigate reports of gold on Xamayca, as the Indians called the island and which supposedly translates as 'the land of Wood and Water'. To him it was the 'fairest isle that eyes ever beheld; the land seems to touch the sky...' But there was no gold and so he left. It was another nine years before he returned, on his fourth voyage, washed up here after exploration of the Central American coast, this time unintentionally. His ships were worm-eaten and they sank off St Ann's Bay; the admiral was stranded there for a year before he was rescued (two of his sailors braved the high seas and hostile Indians in a canoe and paddled to Hispaniola, from where they fetched him).

The Spaniards first came to Jamaica to settle in 1510 and to begin with they used the island to supply the senior colony on Hispaniola (now the Dominican Republic). Colonization was a failure, but it succeeded in wiping out the Arawak Indians within a hundred years. The Spaniards worked the Indians as slaves, tortured them to death and even killed them for sport. The Indians also died like flies from European diseases. The Spaniards' first settlement, Sevilla la Nueva, was on the north coast, near St Ann's Bay, but it proved to be an unhealthy spot, so the town was moved to the south coast. St Jago de la Vega (now Spanish Town) became their principal settlement. The colonists planted crops, but their main occupation was farming pigs for their fat and hides.

The colony was neglected in favour of Havana and the settlements on the mainland coast and faced regular attack by pirates in which hard-won wealth could disappear overnight. Jamaica languished for 150 years until the British arrived in 1655. Little remains of Spain's influence now, apart from a few names, but in the hills the *cimar-róns*, later known as the maroons (slaves armed and set free by the Spaniards to attack the British), were to have an effect on Jamaican life until the 19th century.

On capturing the island in the heartland of the Spanish Indies, the English immediately fortified Port Royal, which soon became a base for the buccaneers, who would come here to repair their ships and sell their loot. In time of peace these 'brethren of the coast' could not be officially sanctioned because they trod too fine a line between freebooting and piracy but, when the islands were at war, they were an invaluable fighting force. Port Royal, the richest and most decadent town of its age, received its comeuppance in 1692 when it was destroyed in an earthquake (*see* p.725).

Some Advice

Particularly as a new arrival, you will be accosted by taxi drivers, higglers (street vendors), hustlers and the occasional Rent-a-dread on the street in Kingston and around the beaches in the main tourist areas. You will be asked to buy goods and then offered a whole inventory of services. Until you get a tan or learn to 'give them the eye', they can be quite persistent.

While travelling in Jamaica, take the same precautions you would in the cities of any foreign country, and be wary. Do not flash a full wallet around or hang an arm with a bracelet out of a bus window. You are advised not to walk around downtown Kingston alone after dark. If you wish to go to an area you think might be dodgy, you can always get a Jamaican to go with you.

The Jamaican authorities strongly disapprove of illegal drugs and they nobble offenders from time to time (there are quite a few foreigners serving time in Jamaica for drug possession). In practice, you will be offered almost anything by the beach hustlers, from a single spliff to a hunnerd-weight of cullyweed, along with other drugs, including cocaine and crack, dropped in en route from South America. Buying and consuming proscribed drugs is against the law and the risks are obvious.

Pirates continued to plague the coasts of the island, though, until about 1720, and the likes of Charles Vane, Blackbeard (a natty dresser who would go into battle with lit fuses in his hair), 'Calico' Jack Rackham (supposedly called so because of his penchant for calico underclothes) and his women pirates Anne Bonney and Mary Read, would use the bays along the coast to drink captured rum and to refit their ships before setting off again on the high seas.

But at the same time, Jamaica was growing into Britain's wealthiest colony in the West Indies. The island became a massive sugar factory and for a while Jamaica was the largest sugar producer in the world. The planters and merchants at any rate enjoyed immense wealth and they built their great houses on the estates and town houses in the capital. The whole venture depended on a massive workforce, made up of slaves from Africa, shipped in to the market in Kingston. The slaves were subjected to brutal treatment in what was already a cruel age and the estates were run on the basis of mutual fear. The planters maintained their law with a rod of iron and with a liberal use of the whip, while always living in the fear that the slaves would rebel, which from time to time they did.

Some slaves ran away to the mountains and joined the communities of maroons, hunting pigs and planting a few crops, and occasionally descending from the hills at night to attack the plantations, torching the fields and stealing cattle. They settled in townships in the Cockpit Country and in the mountains of the east, and became expert at defending themselves from the raiding parties sent out against them. They fought a guerrilla war and would disguise themselves with jungle foliage, ambushing the routes through the hills and then filtering away into the forest. Led by men such as Cudjoe, Accompong and Cuffee (and the female maroon Nanny, one of Jamaica's national heroes), they eventually forced the government to sue for peace, and in 1739 the maroons were granted an area of land to themselves, in what is now Trelawny parish, where they would be left undisturbed. In return, they promised to cease hostilities against the plantations and to hunt and return runaway slaves. A treaty was also made with the maroon leader Quao in the Blue Mountains in the east.

The maroons were quiet for half a century, but the slaves themselves revolted. Tacky's Rebellion took place in 1760 when a band of Coromantee slaves broke into a fort and stole arms and ammunition, attacked a few plantations and then took to the hills. Tacky was killed by one of the maroons who had been called out against them, and his followers committed suicide rather than surrender, but revolts broke out all over the island and it was months before the old order was reimposed.

In 1795, when the French Revolution had an explosive effect on the French colony of St Domingue, and the slaves took over the country in open revolt, a second maroon war broke out in Jamaica. This time 300 of them held out against 4,500 trained troops and militia, once again waging a guerrilla war against the government and torching estates. Tracker dogs were brought from Cuba to find them and the maroons knew their time was up. Under the terms of the treaty they should have been allowed to settle elsewhere on the island, but the majority were deported to Nova Scotia and then eventually shipped to Sierra Leone.

At the end of the 18th century, the Abolitionist movement, led by men such as William Wilberforce, was born in Britain, and despite the objections of the West Indian planters, the slave trade from Africa was banned in 1808. Slave laws were passed in Britain but the planters refused to institute them. Unrest continued on the island and Jamaica erupted in another massive revolt in 1831. It was led by Sam 'Daddy' Sharpe, who has since become another of Jamaica's national heroes. He was hanged for his action, but it was enough for Parliament in London to force the Emancipation Act for all the West Indian islands in 1834. There was a period of 'apprenticeship' for four years, in which the slaves were tied to the plantations, but in 1838 the slaves were set free unconditionally.

They left the estates and took plots of land where they could find them, turning to subsistence agriculture. With the help of Baptists, Methodists and other missionaries, who had sided with the slaves against the planters, they formed free villages. For their part, the planters fared badly, despite waves of immigrant workers (East Indians mainly, but also some voluntary Africans), and the sugar industry, now competing with islands which still had slavery, steadily declined.

The pressure for political change came soon after the slaves were freed. Their cause was adopted by men such as the mixed-race lawyer George William Gordon and the preacher Paul Bogle. Matters came to a head under Governor Eyre and in 1865 there was a rebellion in Morant Bay in the southeast of the island, led by Bogle. The riot was put down brutally. The blame for it was laid at Gordon's door and he was hanged. Bogle was hunted down and he was tried in Morant Bay, where he was sentenced and hanged in the arch of the Court House where his rebellion had taken place. Statues of him stand at the Court House today and in National Heroes Park. Eyre was recalled and dismissed from the colonial service, but his last act was to get the Jamaican Assembly to vote for its own demise and give power to the Colonial Office in London. In 1872 the capital was removed from Spanish Town to Kingston.

In the 20th century, as the original plantocracy declined, more black and mixed-race Jamaicans began to be elected to the local assemblies and to enter the civil service. Changes were particularly influenced by another Jamaican national hero, Marcus Mosiah Garvey.

Garvey was born in St Ann's Bay in 1887 and as a young man he travelled around the Americas. Seeing the desperate poverty in which blacks were living everywhere, he resolved to unite the African race to better their situation in the white-ruled world. In 1914 he founded the Universal Negro Improvement Association, which by the 1920s had become an international movement, with offices all over the Americas, in African countries, and even as far off as Australia. They were all linked by the newspaper the *Negro World*. The UNIA ran businesses and banks and a shipping line, the Black Star Line (after the White Star Line), in competition with the whites. There was even an aim to go 'back to Africa', to create a model state in which blacks could be proud.

Garvey became a champion of blacks everywhere because he brought pride and self-respect in a way that had never been possible under colonial rule, but he was generally disliked by the white establishment and in 1922 he served a jail term in the

Jamaican Music – Ska, Reggae and Dancehall

Visitors joke that the Jamaicans switch the roll of their gait as they walk down the street, passing each successive shop and its stereo system. This is not far from the truth, as music is played everywhere, constantly, and almost always at high volume. Buses are like mobile discotheques, usually audible before they come into view, and out in the country you can see a stack of speakers higher than the bar that has the stereo. Like so much Caribbean music, Jamaican songs have a strong element of satire, and singers will often address topical issues in their lyrics.

Mento was a lively dance rhythm and it lasted for many years in the early part of the 20th century. Bands played accoustic guitars, a ukelele, a fiddle and a boomer box (a sit-on box with metal teeth) and their lyrics were often jokingly rude about life and love. In the early 1960s, with the arrival of the electric sound system, Jamaican music began to evolve very quickly: mento was overtaken by **ska**, a riotous and often compulsive beat, and after a few years this developed into the slow and heavy drum and bass rhythms of **rocksteady** and **rub-a-dub**. Like the steel pans of Trinidad, these sounds came from the yards of downtown Kingston and were disapproved of initially by the authorities, but they are an elemental expression of Jamaica and unique in their inventiveness.

Reggae, which speeded up rocksteady again and introduced the chaka-chaka lilt to the rhythm, developed in the late 60s as singers like Jimmy Cliff and Bob Marley and the Wailers began to have their success on the island. It was not until around the time of his death in May 1981 that Bob Marley and more generally reggae gained international fame. Other leading reggae groups and singers include Toots and the Maytals, Burning Spear, Third World, Black Uhuru, Peter Tosh and Gregory Isaacs. And abroad, among the large expatriate Jamaican community in Britain, reggae groups, including Steel Pulse and Aswad, flourished.

The mid-80s and early 90s were dominated by another rhythm, **dancehall**, a compulsive and monotonous rap grafted on to a hard reggae beat. Its rhythm makes it danceable, but like all Jamaican music it is the lyrics, often rude or controversial,

States for supposed fraud. He returned to Jamaica in 1927 and set out aims for a political party in 1929. In 1935 he moved his offices to London. Though his movement was eclipsed after his death in London in 1940, his remains were flown back in triumph to Jamaica in 1964. He was proclaimed the country's first national hero soon afterwards.

Pressure for political change grew ever stronger in the 1930s, in the wake of the Depression. There were riots all over the Caribbean in 1938 and, soon after, the Jamaican trade unions and then political parties were born. The two leaders who emerged were the flamboyant Alexander Bustamante, later leader of the Jamaica Labour Party (JLP) and Norman Manley of the People's National Party (PNP). In 1944 adult suffrage for all Jamaicans was introduced, the first in the Caribbean, and in 1957 cabinet government and full internal autonomy were granted. In a referendum put to them by Bustamante in 1961, the Jamaicans decided not to remain in the West Indies Federation, and within the year they had taken Independence, the first British Caribbean island to do so, on 6 August 1962.

that make it so popular. Dancehall addressed the issues of the day, anything from sex to corruption (a fair dose of the former, which are known as slack songs), although they are nigh incomprehensible unless you can understand patois. There are singers (who tend to be slower and more melodic) and DJs, who rap their lyrics to a number of established rhythms (cherry-o, satta, taxi). Leading DJs include Beenie Man, Bounty Killa, Capleton and Babycham. Singers include Tony Rebel, who often addresses cultural issues, and Beresford Hammond, who is big on love ballads. Recently the scene has begun to change again. Through the efforts of Irie FM, culture reggae has undergone a revival and Jamaica is beginning to sound a little more as it did in the 70s. Many of the heavyweight DJs have softened up their lyrics. The biggest singers on the island at the moment are Elephant Man, Wayne Marshall and T.O.K. Some of the top Dancehall women are Tanya Stevens and Lady Saw.

The highlight of the Jamaican music calendar is Reggae Sumfest (*www.reggaae sumfest.com*), which takes place every July or August in Montego Bay, a six-day bonanza of reggae, featuring individual singers, dancehall and American R&B acts. It is a fun event, more like a day at the races than a concert in the European style, with games being played at the rumshops and stalls that line the back of the concert area. Reggae artists from all over the world come to it and they each play a set of a couple of songs, so you see about 20 performers in a night. It usually gets started at about 10pm and goes on until dawn, and beyond. Sting, a similar but smaller one-night show, takes place every Boxing Day in Portmore, on the outskirts of Kingston.

You get a good idea of Jamaican music from just wandering around the streets of Kingston, but to see it Jamaican-style you have to get out into the concerts and clubs; ask around, but your best bet is probably in Kingston or Negril. You may find a world-famous band playing to a crowd of just a few hundred. (The tourist hotels often play calypso, which comes from Trinidad and Barbados at the other end of the Caribbean.) During the day, you can listen to non-stop reggae on Irie FM (105.5 or 107.7). Any club or record shop will sell you cassettes of the latest tunes.

After Independence, politics continued to be dominated by these two men, who also later became Jamaican national heroes. The Jamaican Parliament, set up following the Westminster model, is made up of a 60-member House of Representatives, elected every five years, and a smaller Senate, to which members are appointed on the advice of the Prime Minister and leader of the opposition. The country remains within the Commonwealth and the Queen is represented by the Governor General, at present Sir Howard Cooke. The judicial system is based on British law and the highest court of appeal is the Privy Council in London.

Until recently, the PNP, now led by P. J. Patterson, and the JLP still dominated Jamaican politics, but in early 1996 a third party, the National Democratic Movement, was formed. Led by Bruce Golding, who came from the JLP, it held its own with about 15% of the vote. Elections in Jamaica tend to be somewhat traumatic, despite efforts to calm them in recent years, and they are always hard, if not entirely honourably, fought. The 1980 election was extremely bloody (500 people died) and it returned the

JLP, led then and still by Edward Seaga, with a massive majority. He followed monetarist policies that reversed the decade of left-inclined government from the PNP under Michael Manley (son of Norman Manley). In 1989, Michael Manley was re-elected on a less radical ticket than before, and then the PNP was re-elected in 1993, 1997 and 2002, with P. J. Patterson at its head. Elections are next due in 2006.

The Economy

There are three important sectors of the Jamaican economy: the mining and export of bauxite and its derivative, alumina, which makes aluminium; tourism, which is the largest earner of foreign exchange – in 2004 Jamaica had almost 2.5 million tourists, with an earning of US$1.41 billion; and agriculture, which is the largest employer at around 35% of the workforce (about half of Jamaica's population lives in rural areas) and contributes about 10% of GDP. Export crops include sugar, bananas, coffee and cocoa. The best-known unofficial export earner in Jamaica is, of course, marijuana, and at one stage this was thought to top all others.

Beaches

There are innumerable excellent beaches on Jamaica, from the seemingly endless strand at Negril with its fantastic view of the sunset, to the tight bays in the east where the mountains tumble into the sea around you. There are secluded beaches where you will be alone and there are active beaches with all the watersports to keep you busy.

Though all beaches are officially public below the high-water mark (you can swim in from the open sea), many Jamaican beaches are effectively private because there is limited access over land. This guarantees some privacy on your hotel beach, but it limits exploration of the beaches around the island. Some hotels allow people from outside to use their facilities for a small fee. There are, of course, public beaches in Jamaica which are usually lively. The Jamaicans are far too modest (in public, about their bodies at any rate) to go nude on the beach, but several of the resorts do have designated nude beaches.

See 'Best Beaches', p.700–1.

Inland Bathing and River-rafting

Perhaps unexpectedly, some of Jamaica's best bathing is inland, in the river rock pools, often beneath waterfalls. Some rivers even disappear in the limestone caverns and flow underground, emerging in a pool. If you go off the beaten track, ask around, because the locals will know where the best spots are. It is better not to swim after rain because the mud will have been stirred up.

Somerset Falls at Hope Bay (near Port Antonio) are a little tame (*adm*). Preferable, though difficult to get to, are **Reach Falls**, inland from Manchioneal, 20 miles beyond Port Antonio, a series of pools, a stunning waterfall and a cave (*adm free*). If you go into the John Crow Mountains to **Ginger House** south of Port Antonio, there is a cascade and rock pool called Jupiter. At **Upton** above Ocho Ríos (ask around), you will find good swimming and rapids at Spanish Bridge.

Rastafari and Revival

Jamaica has a mind-boggling proliferation of religions – Anglicans, Presbyterians, Congregationalists, Methodists and Moravians, Baptists and Seventh Day Adventists, as well as Muslims, Jews and lesser-known faiths such as the Baha'i. Many of these religions were introduced by missionaries in colonial times, others adapted by the slaves from their African beliefs, but perhaps the best known outside the country is the Rastafarian religion. It is known for its dreadlocks and reggae music and also for its connection with its sacrament ganja (there are many opportunist pseudo-rastas around the tourist areas in Jamaica), but it is less appreciated for the quiet and peaceful ideals that its true adherents follow, in fear of Jah (God).

Rastafari was born in the 1930s at the time of the crowning of Haile Selassi as King of Ethiopia, after the Ethiopian War. Rastafarians consider Haile Selassi Ras (prince) Tafari (to be feared), the King of Kings, Lord of Lords, the Conquering Lion of Judah. Haile Selassie died in 1975, but is still revered by the rastas, who do not believe that he is dead. The rastas consider themselves brought to 'Babylon' by the white man (they think of themselves as one of the lost tribes of Israel), and their aim is eventual return to Africa.

There are different rasta sects, but as a rule, genuine rastas are gentle people who follow their avowed beliefs of 'peace and love'. They are vegetarians, and many are herbalists living in the mountains; some are teetotal and do not smoke tobacco. They do regard ganja as sacred and the 'chalice' (pipe), as it is known, is supposed to bring wisdom.

There are a number of semi-religious sects in Jamaica, part Christian, part animist, with a view of the spirit world not dissimilar to the voodoo of Haiti. The best-known are Pukumina (also written pocomania), and Revival Zion, which believe in the Holy Trinity, but also invoke spirits from the worlds beyond direct human experience. Kumina is more purely African and its adherents also invoke spirits, particularly those of ancestors. These sects are particularly strong in the countryside and some involve ceremonies with drumming and dancing to drums, with the eventual possession of one of the participants by the spirits. Quite a lot of Jamaicans believe in deads and duppies (the ghosts of people who have died but who are not at peace), some of whom remain in conflict with the living over issues dating from their lifetime. Obeah is another system of beliefs in which individuals are able to affect the outcome of their lives with the use of spells and specially prepared potions.

Irie Beach is a lovely daytime stopover high in the hills above Ocho Ríos, where the White River runs through a gulley, cool green water sluicing over rocks and into pools; there's sunbathing, bar and snacks (*adm*).

The **YS Falls** in St Elizabeth Parish are an extremely impressive series of seven falls with rockpools and a spacious garden. There are quite a lot of tourists, but it's supremely beautiful; you ride to them by trolley bus through fantastic Jamaican countryside (*adm*). There are also some superb falls off the beaten track at **Maggotty** and at the **Black River Gorge** near Apple Valley.

Flora and Fauna

From its wet and mountainous northeast corner, where the jumble of the John Crow Mountains and Blue Mountains soars to thousands of feet, Jamaica's stunningly beautiful countryside descends through dwarf and montane forest, where mahogany and mahoe trees are grappled by creeping vines, lianas and ferns; through hilltop coffee and spice plantations, where you will see overgrown telephone wires and fences; headed west through the immensely fertile banana and yam plots in the rich red earth of the Central Mountain range; and so down on to the sugar flats that ring the coast in the west. Jamaica has an amazing variety of geography. In the south and southwest of the island, the rainfall is low (by Jamaican standards), and you will find savanna and scrub country. But then there are also huge areas of swampland covered with mangroves.

If you are not accustomed to the tropics, the plant life is almost bewildering. The national tree of Jamaica is the blue mahoe, and the national flower, which also grows on a tree, is the *Lignum vitae* (the wood of life). There are endless palms, from the magnificent royal palm, which grows to over 100ft, to the typical seafront coco palms that lean out over the beach into the sunset. Jamaica has many botanical gardens, some of them left to decline into riotous growth, but most worth visiting even for botanical novitiates (they are excellent for escaping the hustle and bustle of the towns for a while). They were set up in order to encourage Jamaica's agricultural development as most of the food crops were brought in to the island, from the breadfruit shipped by Bligh to the mango from the south seas. The Jamaicans all keep flowering gardens too, so you will constantly see bougainvillea and hibiscus reaching out into the road. Even the traditional farmer's hedge, made with quick-stick (called so because it takes from just a cutting placed in the ground), comes out in a riot of lavender blooms.

With the extraordinary variety of terrain and vegetation comes an equal diversity of bird life, with over 250 species seen during the year – 25 of these are endemic and about half are migratory. In the heights, you may hear the mournful solitaire, or see the Jamaican eleania or the Blue Mountain vireo and a handful of warblers. In the lower mountains are hosts of grackles and grassquits, the Jamaican euphonia and woodpecker and two rare parrots, yellow-billed and black-billed. The Jamaican nightingale sings at dawn and sunset. You will also see hummingbirds, including the Jamaican national bird, the doctorbird, or red-billed streamertail, whose forked tail is about twice as long as its emerald green body. The smallest bird on the island is the tiny vervain or bee hummingbird. The Jamaican tody, called robin redbreast, is odd because it lays its eggs at the end of a 2ft underground tunnel. Among the lilies and aerial roots of the mangroves in the morasses are gallinules and green-backed herons, and whistling ducks. Offshore, you may see sooty and noddy terns.

The animal life is not so varied, though there are many reptiles, ranging from the crocodiles of the Black River swamp and the Jamaican boa (rarely seen), which grows up to 15ft in length, to the tiny lizards that find their way all over the walls and the ceiling. The whistling toad is the second-largest tree frog in the world and there are many other varieties to be heard chirruping at different altitudes. The iguana was

Getting There

Jamaica t (1 876–)

By Air

The main airport for tourist arrivals in Jamaica is the Sangster International Airport in Montego Bay, which serves the resort towns of Negril, Montego Bay, Runaway Bay and Ocho Ríos. If you are travelling on to Port Antonio or to Kingston itself, you should fly to the Norman Manley Airport just outside Kingston. Long-haul scheduled flights often make a stop at both airports. The national carrier is Air Jamaica. You need an onward or return ticket to get into the country and there is a departure tax of J$1000.

From Europe

Direct flights to Jamaica from Europe include British Airways and Air Jamaica from London and Martinair from Amsterdam. If flight timings are not convenient, flying via Miami is a serious option. There are also plenty of charter flights from Britain (Airtours and Monarch) and from Germany and Switzerland, some of which offer flight-only tickets.

From the USA

There are direct scheduled flights to Montego Bay (and often to Kingston) on Air Jamaica from Atlanta, Baltimore, Fort Lauderdale, Los Angeles, Miami (plenty each day, also on American Airlines), Newark, New York (several flights daily, also American Airlines), Orlando, Philadelphia and Tampa (on Northwest Airlines). US Airways fly from Charlotte and Philadelphia, and TWA from St Louis.

From Canada

There is a daily scheduled service on either Air Jamaica or Air Canada from Toronto to Kingston, sometimes stopping at Montego Bay, and a multitude of charter flights including Canada 3000 and Air Transat.

From Other Caribbean Islands

Air Jamaica has recently made Montego Bay its Caribbean hub, with connections to Antigua, Barbados, St Lucia, the Turks and Caicos, and Nassau. There are flights most days from Grand Cayman on either Air Jamaica or Cayman Airways to Nassau in the Bahamas, and to Havana in Cuba on Cubana (there are also charter flights from Montego Bay to Cuba). There are links with Sint Maarten, Antigua and Barbados, Port of Spain in Trinidad (almost daily on BWIA) and Curaçao and Bonaire (several times a week on Air Jamaica). Most connections from South America are made in Miami, from where there are plenty of flights each day, but there are some direct links to Kingston as well.

Getting Around

By Bus

The Jamaicans have complained bitterly about their **bus** system (minibuses and larger) for the past few years as, particularly in Kingston, it has become very slow, crowded and hot. However, it is possible to get almost anywhere in Jamaica on a bus, eventually, and it will give you excellent exposure to Jamaican life. Buses are fairly noisy (if not because of the people, then because of the relentless pulse on the stereo) and, if you are sitting, you may find that a 'standee' will hand you their bag to hold.

Check the fare as you get on, though you may not actually hand over the money until later in the journey. In the country, flag buses down from the side of the road with a frantic wave.

You will also find that **share taxis**, often referred to as 'robot' taxis because they are seemingly driven by automatons, run the same routes for the same fare.

Hitch-hiking

Hitch-hiking in Jamaica is usually a bit slow, but is worth chancing if you're on for an adventure. To signal to a driver wave your arm vigorously.

By Taxi

Taxis are readily available in Jamaica, through any hotel lobby if you cannot find one yourself, which is pretty unlikely around the tourist areas. Steel yourself to run the gauntlet of drivers touting for business as you emerge from the airport. The Tourist Board sets a standard fare, posted in JUTA taxis and quoted in both US and Jamaican dollars. With the others, bargain. Taxis are not usually metered in Jamaica and so you are advised to settle the fare before you set off. All licensed taxis have the red PPV plates. Some restaurants will send a car to pick you up and return you to your hotel if you ask.

By Air

You can fly to a number of towns on the island. There are regular scheduled flights between Kingston (Tinson Pen Airport) and Montego Bay and the other tourist areas. Contact Air Jamaica Express, toll free **t** 1 888 FLY AIRJ, *www.airjamaicaexpress.com*, who have offices in Montego Bay, Kingston and Port Antonio. The return fare from Kingston to Montego Bay is US$150 per person.

By Guided Tour

Jamaica is very well served with organized tours – there is endless information in the hotel lobbies. These take in many of the sights mentioned in the text and are an easy way to get around for those without transport. Many of the **taxi** drivers make good tour guides if you wish to take a ride to the local sights or up into the hills. Any hotel lobby will find a driver for you and the price is reasonable when divided between four.

Tour companies include:

Blue Mountain Bicycle Tours, **t** 974 7493, *info@bmtoursja.com, www.bmtoursja.com*. You could try a downhill bicycling tour, which is fun and a good way to see the Jamaican countryside: start at nearly 6,000ft in the Blue Mountains in rainforests and run for 17 miles down to a waterfall.

Caribic Vacations, Montego Bay, **t** 953 9895. Standard island tours.

Cockpit Country Tours, **t** 979 0308.

Forsythe's, Montego Bay, **t** 952 0394. Standard island tours.

Galaxy Tours, Kingston, **t** 925 1492. Cycling tours.

Glamour Tours, Montego Bay, **t** 979 8207. Standard island tours.

Island Hopper Helicopter Tours, Ocho Rios, **t** 974 1285. Call a couple of days in advance for helicopter tours of the island.

JUTA, Negril, **t** 957 9197; Port Antonio, **t** 993 2684. Standard island tours.

Sunventure Tours, **t** 960 6685, *sunventure@hotmail.com, www.sunventure tours.com*. Can arrange personalized tours for individuals or groups, including hiking, historical, caving, architectural and coffee farm tours.

Tourwise, Ocho Rios, **t** 974 2323. Standard island tours.

Car and Bike Hire

The Jamaicans joke that you buy the car each time you hire one because it's so expensive. However, if you can afford it, it is well worth having one to explore the mountain roads and the successive headlands and bays along the coastline. There are plenty of hire cars available, but it is still a good idea to arrange it a few days ahead in season.

The Jamaicans are pretty awful drivers and the roads are notorious for being pot-holed. Avoid driving in downtown Kingston except for sport. The traffic is generally chaotic and the Jamaicans perform some remarkable manoeuvres in their constant hurry. Driving on the high roads is correspondingly more dangerous, as all the same manoeuvres are performed at high speed.

The country is not that well signposted, so take a good map, easily available from petrol stations, the hire companies and the Tourist Board. Driving happens, mainly, on the left. Finally, watch out for goats and cows.

A driving licence from home is acceptable, minimum age 25. Take a credit card for the hefty deposit. There are many hire companies, with a variety of different contracts – read yours. The Jamaica U-Drive Association represents a number of car-hire companies with a standard code of business and rates. You can get their list at the Tourist Board offices. Reckon on daily rental of at least US$70 plus charges for the smallest car for a single day with reductions for a week's hire. There are other smaller, local enterprises which offer lower rates. Remember that car-rental companies will deliver to you, though if you are in another town there may be a delivery charge.

All the big hire companies have offices at the Montego Bay airport:

Bargain, Kingston and Norman Manley
Airport, toll free **t** 1 888 991 2111.
Budget, Montego Bay airport, **t** 952 3838.
Caribbean, Ocho Ríos, **t** 974 2513; Montego Bay
airport, **t** 952 0664.
Derren's, Port Antonio, **t** 974 7726.
Eastern Rent-a-Car, Port Antonio, **t** 993 3624.
Hertz/Elite, Montego Bay airport, **t** 952 4250.
Island, Montego Bay airport, **t** 952 5771, toll
free **t** 1 800 892 4581; Ocho Ríos, **t** 974 2334;
Kingston, **t** 926 8861; Norman Manley
Airport, **t** 924 8075.
Rite Rate Rent-a-Car, Negril, **t** 957 4667.

For the very brave and for pot-hole dodgers,
there are **mopeds and motorbikes** for hire in
all the tourist areas. Drive defensively, and be
prepared to get off the road in a hurry. Make
sure to get hold of a helmet somehow. They
are quite expensive, at around US$30 a day for
a motorbike and $12 for a bicycle.
Abe's, Ocho Ríos, **t** 974 1008.
Kool Bike Rental, Negril, **t** 957 9224.
Kryss Bike Rental, Montego Bay, **t** 940 0476.
Quality Bike Rental, Montego Bay, **t** 979 3531.
Tropic Ride Car & Bike Rental, Montego Bay,
t 952 7096.
Tyke's Bike Rental, Negril, **t** 957 0388.

Tourist Information

Abroad

The Jamaica Tourist Board has a website at
www.visitjamaica.com. Other websites with
information about the island include
www.jamaica-irie.com, *www.jamaicans.com*,
www.seejamaicacheaply.com, *www.
jamaicaway.com*. Some entertainment news
can be found at *www.bashment.com* (a 'bash-
ment' is a party or an event in Jamaican).
Canada: 1 Eglington Av East, Suite 616 Toronto,
Ontario M4P 3A1, **t** (416) 482 7850, toll free
t 800 465 2624, *jtb@jtbcanada.com*.
UK: 1–2 Prince Consort Rd, London SW7
4BZ, **t** (020) 7224 0505, *jtbtuk@
compuserve.com*.
USA: The JTB can be contacted on a toll-free
number at **t** 1 800 233 4582, or by email at
jamaicatrvl@aol.com. There are offices at:
1320 South Dixie Highway, Suite 1101, Coral
Gables, Florida 33146, **t** (305) 665 0557.

In Jamaica

You will find a number of small octagonal
tourist information booths around the main
towns, with helpful staff. There are offices in:
Kingston: Tourist Centre, Knutsford Bd, New
Kingston, **t** 929 9200.
Montego Bay: Near Cornwall Beach, PO Box 67,
t 952 4425; in Sangster Airport, **t** 952 2462.
Ocho Ríos: Ocean Village Shopping Centre,
close to Turtle Beach, **t** 974 2570.
Port Antonio: City Centre Plaza, **t** 993 3051.

Embassies and Consulates

British High Commission, 26 Trafalgar Rd,
Kingston 10, New Kingston, **t** 926 9050.
Canadian High Commission, 3 West Kings
House Rd, New Kingston, **t** 926 1500–7.
US Embassy, Jamaica Mutual Life Centre
Building, 2 Oxford Rd, New Kingston,
t 929 4850.

Media

The principal Jamaican newspaper is the
Daily Gleaner, released in the morning.
The same company, a formidable Jamaican
institution, puts out the tabloid the *Star* in
the afternoon, daily except Sundays. Other
papers include the *Sunday Herald*, and the
Observer, also published daily. The Jamaican
tourist publications are quite good, with
current events as well as advice on shopping
opportunities.

Medical Emergencies

In a medical emergency, you may find that
there is a doctor on call to the larger hotels.
If not, contact the University Hospital in
Kingston, at Mona Campus in the east, **t** 927
1620; the Cornwall Regional Hospital in
Montego Bay, in Mt Salem behind the main
town, **t** 952 5100; MoBay Hope Medical Centre
in the Half Moon Shopping Centre in Rose
Hall, **t** 953 3649; and in Port Antonio, the
General Hospital on Naylor's Hill, **t** 993 2646.

Money and Banks

The currency of Jamaica is the Jamaican
dollar (J$), which fluctuates on the interna-
tional exchange. At present, the **exchange rate**
is about US$1 = J$65 or £1 = J$115. Tourist activi-
ties tend to be linked with the US dollar, which

is also accepted as legal tender on the island. Hotel and hire bills can be paid with a credit card or traveller's cheques, as can shopping bills in the tourist areas and in the shops in Kingston. It is often better to use Jamaican dollars in restaurants and bars because you will usually be offered a very unfavourable rate of exchange. The going rate for tipping is 10–15%.

You will certainly need some Jamaican dollars for getting about on the buses and for a patty and a skyjuice at the roadside. There are foreign exchange desks in most hotels, at airports and in many banks. Occasionally, you will be offered a black market rate on the streets. This is usually about 10% better than the bank rate and invariably quicker, but it is illegal and comes with attendant risks. Keep your exchange receipts if you want to change Jamaican dollars back into another currency on departure.

Banking hours are Mon–Thurs 9–2 and Fri 9–4.

Shopping

Hours are Mon–Sat 10–6, but if you are looking to score duty-free bargains, you will find that hours in hotel boutiques and in-bond warehouses are extended. Few shops open for Sunday trading, except at Christmas.

Telephone Code

The IDD code for Jamaica is t 1 876, followed by a seven-digit number. On-island, you should prefix a '1' if you are dialling long-distance or to mobile phones; for local calls dial the seven digits.

Maps and Books

Two early travelogues of Jamaica are Lady Nugent's *Journal of Residence in Jamaica 1801–3* and Matthew 'Monk' Lewis's *Journal of a West Indian Proprietor*, written in 1834 and published after his death at sea on his return from the West Indies.

Andrew Salkey's *A Quality of Violence* looks into the life of a Jamaican village during a drought at the start of the 20th century. Roger Mais also wrote books about Jamaican country life. His best-known book is *The Hills*

are Joyful Together. Also look out for V. S. Reid. John Hearne's excellent short book *Voices under the Window* gives a very colourful idea of the mercurial nature of the Jamaicans in the frenzy of the crowd.

There is some good contemporary literature coming out of Jamaica, including *Bake Face*, short stories by Opal Adisa Palmer, and collections by Olive Senior, *Summer Lightning* and *The Arrival of the Snake Woman*; also *Mint Tea* by Christine Craig.

Anthony Winkler has written three excellent books which cut straight to the heart of 20th-century Jamaican life: *The Painted Canoe*, *The Lunatic* and, most recently, *The Great Yacht Race*. Margaret Cezair-Thompson's *A True History of Paradise* paints a detailed portrait of middle-class life in the 1970s. Jamaican poets include Lorna Goodison and Mervyn Morris. A good magazine of current Jamaican culture is the *Jamaica Journal*, which is available in big bookstores.

Herbert G. de Lisser has put some of Jamaica's traditional tales into novels in *Morgan's Daughter*, *The White Witch of Rose Hall* and *Psyche*.

If you can track down a copy of *How to Speak Jamaican* by Ken Maxwell, read it. *Jamaica Labrish* will give you a chance to read some of the late Louise Bennett's hysterical machine-gun poetry at a gentler pace, and the *How to be Jamaican Handbook* takes a chuckling look at all aspects of Jamaican life and love, from the north coast hustler to the ICI (a higgler for the 1990s).

Festivals

January *Maroon Festival*. Held annually at Accompong.

February *Pineapple Cup*. The Montego Bay Yacht Club holds the annual Miami to Mo Bay Yacht Race.

March *Annual fishing tournament*. Port Antonio.

April *Carnival Week*. Celebrations all over the island, but particularly in Kingston.

August *Reggae Sumfest*. The biggest music festival of the year is now held in Montego Bay, a gathering for rastas and reggae fans from all over the world.

Regatta. The Royal Jamaican Yacht Club on the Palisadoes Peninsula outside Kingston holds a regatta.

August 6 *Independence Day*. Celebrations take place, with parades and marching bands in the National Stadium in Kingston. It's all a bit staid but quite fun. At about this time, as well as at Christmas and at Easter, you will find many concerts staged, many by big-name Jamaican musicians.

September and early October *Marlin fishing tournaments*. Held in Montego Bay and Discovery Bay.

Mid-October *Annual fishing tournament*. Port Antonio.

Twice a year *National Dance Theatre Company performances*. Well worth attending. See the Jamaica Tourist Board's website for exact dates.

Watersports

Watersports are laid on by all the beach hotels in Jamaica, either in-house or through beach concessionaires. If watersports are important to you, you should check carefully before you select a particular hotel. Independent travellers can sometimes hire equipment at a hotel, but usually they will have to go to the watersports shops on the larger public beaches.

The full range of watersports is on offer in Jamaica, from a ride in a stately pedalo or on a trusty wetbike to a high-speed ride on an inflated sausage, parasailing, or an evening cruise to catch the sunset. Small sailing boats are available through the general operators, as is waterskiing.

In Montego Bay, the best beach for watersports is Cornwall Beach, but some are also available at Doctor's Cave Beach.

Negril Beach is probably the best on the island for watersports. General operators include:

Resort Divers, Ocho Ríos, t 974 5338.
Resort Divers and Watersports, Montego Bay, t 952 4285. All main watersports, plus diving and deep-sea fishing.
Lady G'Diver, Port Antonio, t 715 6044.
Wild Thing, Negril Beach, t 957 9929.

Day Sails

Day and half-day trips, usually taking in some snorkelling and a picnic stop, are available through the hotels in the major resort areas. There are lots of silly, mock-piratical excursions also on offer, so if you are in the mood for an afternoon of rum-soaked fun and tee-ree-ree, you can fix these through any hotel.

Calico, Montego Bay, t 952 5860, *www.calico sailingcruises.com*. Departs daily from Pier 1. Day sails.
Heave Ho Charters, Ocho Ríos, t 974 5367. What it sounds like.
Rapsody Tours, Montego Bay, t 979 0102. For a day, sunset or disco cruise.
Red Stripe Cruising, Ocho Ríos, t 974 2446. Day sails.

Deep-sea Fishing

Possible in all the resorts, but reckoned to be at its best off Port Antonio in the east. *See* 'Festivals' for tournaments. Fish inhabiting the waters off the Jamaican north shore include kingfish and sailfish with a fin like a sail, as well as wahoo and tuna. Contact:

Semper Fi, Port Antonio, t 997 7926.
Striker and Neptune, Negril, t 957 4401.

River-rafting

Another classic tourist activity (but nonetheless good fun). Some companies offer torch-lit night-time cruises. Rafting takes place on several rivers:

Great River, Lethe, near Montego Bay, t 912 0020, *lethe@cwjamaica.com*, *www.lethe-jamaica.com*.
Martha Brae, near Falmouth, t 952 0889, *rafting@montego-bay-jamaica.com*.
Río Grande, near Port Antonio, winding up at Rafter's Rest, t 993 5778. Best of all but expensive. Wear a bathing suit because when you have finished your rum punch you'll be expected to dive in.
White River Valley Tours, in the hills east of Ocho Ríos, t 917 3375. Offers tubing, riding and hiking.

Sailing

Keen sailors will find themselves taken on as crew during the friendly weekend regattas (*see* 'Festivals', above). There are yacht clubs in

Kingston (Royal Jamaica Yacht Club, Palisades Park, **t** 924 8685) and Montego Bay (Montego Bay Yacht Club, Freeport, **t** 979 8038).

Scuba Diving

Jamaica is surrounded by offshore reefs, furred with sponges and corals, where tropical fish play and barracuda stalk their lunch. The reefs are supposed not to be in the best condition because they have been stripped for their corals, but some are now protected and there are still enough around the north-coast resorts to keep divers occupied.

The major operators of the Jamaica Association of Diver Operators work under PADI specifications – you must show your certification – and most can provide instruction. Some smaller operators do not. Underwater photographic equipment is for hire at the bigger rental companies.

A two-tank dive costs around US$75. Most companies offer free pick-up from your hotel. Glass-bottom boats are available on most beaches, too, for a trip to a nearby reef. Contact:

Buccaneer Scuba Club, Morgan's Harbour Hotel, Port Royal, Kingston, **t** 924 8140, *buccaneer@cwjamaica.com.jm*.

Captain's Watersports, Montego Bay, **t** 956 7050, *captains@n5.com.jm*.

Jamaqua Dive Centre, Runaway Bay, **t** 973 4845, *webedivin@jamaqua.com*, *www.jamaqua.com*.

Lady G'Diver, Port Antonio, **t** 715 6044, *ladygdiver@cwjamaica.com*, *www.geocities.com/ladygdiver2000*.

Mobay Undersea Tours, Montego Bay, **t** 940 0659.

Negril Scuba Centre, Negril Beach Club, **t** 957 4425, *neg.scuba.centre@cwjamaica.com*, *www.jamaica-irie.com/negrilscubacenter*.

Resort Divers, Montego Bay, **t** 940 1183, *resdiv@bigfoot.com*, *www.resortdivers.com*; Ocho Rios, **t** 974 5338.

Wild Thing, Negril, **t** 957 4944.

Windsurfing

Windsurfing is a popular activity in Jamaica and is available all over the island. Connoisseurs say the best beach for the sport is Burwood Beach, a public stretch of sand beyond Trelawny Beach just outside Falmouth.

Other Sports

Golf

There are many golf courses in Jamaica:

Caymanas Golf and Country Club, near Kingston, **t** 922 3386.

Constant Springs Golf Club, near Kingston, **t** 924 1610.

Half Moon, Montego Bay, at the hotel east of the town, **t** 953 2211. Luxuriant and well-kept; green fees expensive.

Mandeville Course, **t** 962 2403. The oldest in the Caribbean supposedly, with 18 tees that play to nine greens.

Negril Hills Golf Club, outside Negril on the road towards Savanna-la-Mar, **t** 957 4638.

Ritz-Carlton's White Witch Course, **t** 953 2204. Has established a good reputation for itself and has a good restaurant in the clubhouse.

Sandals Golf Club, Upton, near Ocho Rios, **t** 975 0119.

SuperClubs Breezes Hotel, Runaway Bay, **t** 973 7319.

SuperClubs Golf Club, Ironshore, near Montego Bay, **t** 953 3681.

Tryall, beneath the Tryall resort, 15 miles west of Montego Bay, **t** 956 5681. Set out on the coast.

Wyndham Rose Hall, east of Montego Bay, **t** 953 2650.

Hiking and Biking

Walkers are not really that well served for a country as magnificent as Jamaica but there are some good new places opening up. The country offers a huge variety, in the scrubby bush of the Hellshire Hills, around the Cockpit Country southeast of Montego Bay, and on the trails of the Blue Mountains in the east. The Blue Mountain Peak is usually climbed very early in the morning, so that you are at the 7,402ft summit at dawn, with the best chance of seeing Haiti and the Sierra Maestra in Cuba. However, there are many other trails in the Blue Mountains. As well as the organizations below, try the guest houses and small hotels in the Blue Mountains themselves. If you do go to the Blue Mountains, you should wear ankle-length boots and take a woolly jersey because it gets cold high up. Also take a waterproof, because somehow it always seems to rain.

Blue Mountain Tours, Ocho Ríos and Port
  Antonio, **t** 974 7073.
Forestry Dept, 173 Constant Spring Rd, Blue
  Mountains, **t** 924 2667. For information and
  a few ideas.
Jamaica Conservation Department Trust,
  www.greenjamaica.org. Has cottages and
  offers hiking tours in the Blue Mountains.
Sunventure Tours, Blue Mountains, **t** 960
  6685, *sunventure@hotmail.com*,
  www.sunventuretours.com.
Valley Hikes, Port Antonio, **t** 993 7267, *valley*
  hikes@cwjamaica.com. Guided hikes into the
  Río Grande Valley.

Horse-riding and Polo

If you wish to go horse-riding, for anything
from a beach canter at dawn to a day-long
trek through the plantations in the Jamaican
highlands, there are stables in all the main
towns. Riding out costs roughly J$250 per
hour. You are advised to call a couple of hours
before arriving to book the horses. Contact:
Bonnie View Hotel, Port Antonio, **t** 993 2752.
  Rides into the mountain foothills.
Chukka Blue, Blue Hole, Hanover, **t** 990 9166.
Chukka Cove Farm, near Ocho Ríos, **t** 972 2506.
  Polo is quite big in Jamaica, and here you
  can hire polo ponies or get a refresher
  course if you haven't hit a nearside forehand
  for a while.
Good Hope Estate, Falmouth, **t** 610 5798.
Hooves Limited, Ocho Ríos, **t** 972 0905,
  www.jamaica-irie.com, hooves@cwjamaica.
  com. Offers guided tours through the
  countryside on well-trained horses.
Rocky Point Stables, Montego Bay, **t** 953 2286.

Spectator Sports

These include **cricket**, which is something of
a national preoccupation. You will see it played
in the streets (join in), yards, country roads, on
the beaches and in Kingston at Sabina Park
(well worth going to a match if there is one
on). The only time when the radios stop
playing dancehall music is for the cricket
commentary. Even the hustlers are magnani-
mous if the West Indies are winning.
Horse-racing is popular in Jamaica and you
will find details of coming meetings in the
local press. The only racetrack, to the west of
Kingston, is Caymanas Park.

Tennis

There are courts at most of the hotels and if
not the sport can easily be arranged through a
front desk.

Where to Stay

Jamaica t (1 876–)

Jamaica has a superb, wide-ranging selection of hotels, which use the best of the
island's dramatic coastline and interior. Some
are extremely expensive and luxurious, but
there is something for everyone in Jamaica.
You will find secluded mountain retreats, plantation houses and classic laid-back beachfront
spots tucked in between the larger resorts –
excellent stops if you are travelling the island.
Jamaica is also the Caribbean leader in all-
inclusive hotels and these offer a full range
too, with à la carte dining and champagne in
the Jacuzzi through to the activity-led fun-
factories of times past.

Chances are your hotel will be booked in a
package, but you can also reserve direct, or
book through the Jamaica Reservation Service,
1320 South Dixie Highway, Suite 1180, Coral
Gables, FL 33146, Jamaica **t** 953 6841, USA toll
free **t** 1 800 JAMAICA, Canada **t** 1 800 432 7559,
sales@jrstours.com, www.jrstours.com. A
number of companies will help with booking
smaller and more remote hotels, or will
arrange an itinerary for you around the island.
For hotels in Mandeville and along the south
coast, contact Countrystyle, **t** 962 3725, **t** 962
7758, *countrystyle@cwjamaica.com*, which
specializes in 'community tourism' (village
tours and the like) and is a valuable resource
for general information about the area.

Most hotel rates are quoted in US dollars –
you can pay with credit cards and traveller's
cheques in all hotels. A General Consumption
Tax of 15% is levied on all purchases and hotel
bills. Some hotels also charge 10% for service.

Individual **villa rental**, with anything from a
studio to seven bedrooms on offer, can be
arranged through JAVA, the Jamaica
Association of Villas and Apartments, based in
Ocho Ríos, PO Box 298, Pineapple Place, **t** 974
2508, *javavillas@aol.com, www.villasinjamaica.*
com. They can be contacted in the USA at 1501
West Fullerton Av, Chicago, IL 60614.

For listings of individual hotels in Jamaica, *see* pp.722–3 for Kingston, pp.728–31 for the east, pp.736–40 for the south coast and Negril, and pp.746–51 for the north coast.

Eating Out

Once the staple diet of the plantation slaves, ackee and saltfish is now the Jamaican national dish. Ackee is the yellow fruit of the ackee tree from Africa, which cooks and tastes like scrambled egg, and salt fish is salted cod, originally imported as food for the slaves.

Other classic Jamaican dishes include curry goat, brown stew chicken and rice 'n' peas, cooked in coconut milk. Good use is made of the Caribbean vegetables – pepperpot is a thick soup based on callaloo; popular traditional vegetables are breadfruit and plantain and the many roots, such as yam and eddoe. Fruits – soursop, sweetsop, coconut, mango, pawpaw and pineapple – are served at breakfast, as midday thirst-quenchers and in the ice creams at dinner. Many restaurants will offer you Jamaica's own Blue Mountain coffee, considered by many to be the best in the world. It rounds off a dinner well.

In hotel dining rooms, you are likely to come across international-style fare (with the occasional Jamaican buffet), but some are becoming more adventurous, and there is a greater variety on offer within the hotels now. You have to go outside the hotels or go local to get good Jamaican food.

Jerk centres (*see* p.732) are well worth the visit, and an excellent lunchtime snack is a patty and a soft drink, rounded off with plantain tart or a coconut cake. A proliferation of snack bars and restaurants has opened up along the roadside over the last few years and so there are plenty of stopovers for lunch.

Some restaurants and the occasional hotel dining room require a jacket and occasionally a tie for dinner. Credit cards can be used in the larger restaurants. There is a General Consumption Tax of 15% and many restaurants also charge service.

Price categories throughout the chapter are arranged according to the price of a main course: expensive = J$500 and above,

moderate = between J$300 and $500, inexpensive = J$300 and below.

For listings of individual restaurants in Jamaica, *see* pp.723–4 for Kingston, p.731 for the east, pp.740–1 for the south coast and Negril, and pp.751–4 for the north coast.

Bars and Nightlife

Entertainment in the hotels is varied – in some places, it owes nothing to Jamaica, and is as packaged as the holiday that gets you there (wet T-shirt competitions, pot-belly contests, fire-eating, and limbo competitions that nobody wins because they all fall over backwards).

However, there are some quite good combos who will serenade you at dinnertime. There are good discotheques in some of the larger and more sophisticated hotels, and there is often a lively crowd at the all-inclusives if you can get in for the evening.

The clubs are fun and worth a visit to see the Jamaicans themselves at play, though you should be slightly wary in some areas of Montego Bay and Kingston about going in alone. You can always get a Jamaican to go with you.

There are plenty of venues for concerts around the island – keep an eye on the papers because sometimes world-famous reggae bands will play a gig in a small club. And there are limitless bars around the island, from the hillside setting of plantation house restaurants or a local rumshop to the cliffs and beachside bars of Negril, where the crowds gather to watch the sunset with almost religious adoration.

The national brew of Jamaica is Red Stripe beer, though you will also find many imported beers. Appleton is the best-known rum – the smoothest is Appleton Gold, but the most popular among the Jamaicans is Appleton Overproof, a white rum. John Crow Batty, the most fearsome in strength, is not sold in shops.

For listings of individual bars and clubs in Jamaica, *see* p.724 for Kingston, p.731 for the east, p.741 for the south coast and Negril, and p.754 for the north coast.

thought to be near extinction, but some have been sighted in the Hellshire Hills up to 7ft long. The few rodents include jutia, but this is rare. Manatees, lumbering great walrus-like creatures without tusks, are occasionally sighted in Milk River on the south coast, and turtles come to the island. Some terrapins live in the rivers.

Kingston

Jamaica's capital, a sprawling city of over 1.5 million people on the south coast, is the hub of the Jamaicans' Jamaica. It is the political, cultural and business centre of the island and it buzzes with the most vibrant and vigorous of Jamaican life. Downtown on the Parade the press is incessant as the busmen shout and the higglers tout their wares; goats wander oblivious and the traffic bobs and weaves; everywhere is the deafening rap of dancehall; an occasional policeman in dark serge trousers and a peaked cap tries to keep order. All the extremes of Jamaican life are there: the poor urban shanties, the markets in the downtown area, the grand old institutions in the few remaining Victorian buildings close by, the gleaming air-conditioned offices of New Kingston and the fortified villas that take a cool view of it all from the Kingston mountainsides.

The city owes its birth to the death of Port Royal in the earthquake of 1692 (*see* p.725). The new city was originally laid out on a gridiron pattern and within a few years it was the commercial and social centre of the island. Hundreds of ships would put in to Kingston's magnificent harbour and the city grew as the traders built themselves wooden townhouses to match the splendour of the estate houses in the country. Kingston became the capital of the island in 1872. Another earthquake struck in 1907, killing 800, and much of the Old Town was destroyed – stone and brick buildings by the quake itself, wooden ones by the fires from escaping gas. Modern Kingston is not an attractive city as far as its buildings are concerned.

The **waterfront**, once the heart of the town, is quiet now that the big passenger liners and the freight ships no longer call. The docks are in decay and a few characters 'lime' on the Boulevard. Just off the waterfront is the **Victoria Crafts Market**, where the Kingstonians sell their tourist souvenirs, straw hats and wooden carvings, and among them one or two finer pieces. The **National Gallery** at the foot of Orange St (*t 922 1561; open Mon–Thurs 10am–4.30pm; adm*) is well worth a look. There is a very impressive display of Intuitive paintings as well as wood carvings by Mallica 'Capo' Reynolds and work by the sculptress Edna Manley.

King St, one of Kingston's main shopping streets, leads from the waterfront up to the Parade, from where the Market spills out into the road. This is the heartland of the downtown area and it is mercantile mayhem. Outside the shops of King St, watchmenders, clothes vendors and sweet and cigarette salesmen tout their wares from countless stalls and from blankets laid out on the pavement. This is '*ben dung*' (bend down) plaza at its best – the higglers generally prefer to lay their wares out on the ground than use tables and so you literally have to '*ben dung*'. Periodically the higglers are cleared off the street and told to go back into the market buildings, but they always come back because they prefer it here and trade is better.

The **Parade**, called so because the colonial soldiers would parade here, is officially called William Grant Park. It is the terminal for Kingston's bus system – yet more chaos. The hawkers tout iced drinks from their handcarts with a shout of 'Bag-juice!, Box-drink!' and the busmen practically kidnap you to put you on their bus (your intended destination seems only a secondary consideration). The small square, a park shaded by trees where more limers hang out among the statues of famous Jamaicans, is overlooked by the Ward Theatre on the north side, a wedding-cake affair which was built after the 1907 earthquake.

East of the downtown area, which has become run down since many of the businesses moved to New Kingston in the 1960s, you will find a few of the attractive timber-frame buildings with which Kingston was originally built. **Headquarters House** was the seat of Parliament in the 20th century. Once used by the military (hence the name), it was actually built in the 18th century by a merchant, Thomas Hibbert. Next door is the modern **Gordon House**, the present seat of the Jamaican Parliament, where the representatives and senators do their business. Further east, on South Camp Rd, is the **Sabina Park** cricket stadium, where the international tests are played. To the west of the Parade are some of Kingston's poorest shanty towns, including Trench Town, immortalized by Bob Marley. It would be unwise to go there without a guide.

Back on Duke St, you pass the Gleaner Building and come to **National Heroes Park** (t 922 0620; open Mon–Sat 8.30–4; adm free), which was dedicated following Independence in 1962. There are monuments to Paul Bogle and George William Gordon, champions of the poor in the 19th century, and to Nanny the Maroon and Sam Sharpe. The graves of Marcus Mosiah Garvey, founder of the UNIA, and the fathers of modern Jamaican politics, Norman Manley and Alexander Bustamante, are also there. Simon Bolivar, El Libertador, the hero of South American independence, who stayed in exile in Jamaica, is remembered here as well. On East St is the **Institute of Jamaica**, which has a natural history museum.

The buses run up Slipe Rd from the Parade towards **New Kingston**, the commercial centre of the modern capital. Knutsford Boulevard is the principal street, with the shops and banks. On Hope Rd is the classical **Devon House** (gardens open daytime and evenings until 10pm; Devon House open Tues–Sat 9.30–4.30; adm to the tour of the house), set in gardens of palms and flowering trees. This huge wooden house with louvred balconies, parquet flooring throughout and very attractive palm-patterned silk wallpaper was built in 1881 for Jamaica's first black millionaire and it has been restored as a museum, furnished with period antiques. It's quite touristy as well as popular with the Jamaicans themselves, but worth a look, particularly for the craft shops, Norma's on the Terrace restaurant, and the gourmet patties and exotic-flavoured ice creams on sale in the stables.

In a large area of parkland just up from here are **Jamaica House**, built in the 1960s as the residence of the Prime Minister, now just his office, and **Kings House**, the

Kingston

To the Blue Mountains (A3)

SKYLINE DRIVE

GRANTS PEN RD

BARBICAN RD

JACK'S HILL RD

DUNROBIN RD

RED HILLS RD

SPRING ROAD

WATERLOO ROAD

EAST KING'S HOUSE RD

BARBICAN RD

BARBICAN

Kings House

Bob Marley Museum

HOPE ROAD

Liguanea Plaza

To the Blue Mountains (B1)

GORDON TOWN ROAD

Hope Zoo

Hope Botanical Gardens

Coconut Park

Jamaica House

CONSTANT SPRING ROAD

Devon House

HOPE ROAD

NEW KINGSTON

OLD HOPE ROAD

PAPINE

EASTWOOD PARK ROAD

Half Way Tree

MAXFIELD AV

British High Commission

TRAFALGAR

ST LUCIA AV

ROAD

WELLINGTON DRIVE

MONA HEIGHTS

RUTHVEN RD

CHELSEA AV

KNUTSFORD BOULEVARD

OLD HOPE ROAD

MONA ROAD

Mona Reservoir

University of the West Indies

GROVE RD

HALFWAY TREE ROAD

OXFORD RD

MANNING

BELMONT RD

RIPON RD

TOM REDCAM AV

National Stadium

LYNDHURST RD

US Embassy

EARL

PENNINGTON

Long Mountain

ROUSSEAU RD

RETIREMENT RD

CALEDONIA AV

MOUNTAIN VIEW AVENUE

SLIPE ROAD

MARESCAUX RD

CAMP ROAD

Up Park Camp

DEANERY ROAD

MOUNTAIN VIEW GARDENS

TRENCH TOWN

LYNDHURST RD

ARNOLD RD

HEROES CIRCLE

National Heroes Park

MERRION RD

ST ANDREW KINGSTON

JONES TOWN

Sabina Park

SOUTH CAMP ROAD

WATERLOO RD

UPPER ELLESTON

NORTH ST

DUKE ST

JOHN ST

NORTH ST

CHARLES ST

PASSMORE TOWN

CHARLES ST

ORANGE ST

UPPER KING ST

BEESTON ST

BEESTON ST

SUTTON ST

Gordon House

Headquarters House

EAST QUEEN ST

WINDWARD ROAD

SPANISH TOWN RD

W QUEEN ST

BECKFORD ST

THE PARADE

EAST ST

LOWER ELLESTON ROAD

VICTORIA AV

TOWER ST

TEMPLE LA

KING ST

MARK LA

JOHN ST

TOWER ST

Water Lane

Victoria Craft Market

HARBOUR ST

PORT ROYAL ST

National Gallery

Port Royal Ferry Pier

Kingston Harbour

N

Palisadoes Peninsula

Airport

1 km

1/2 mile

Getting Around

There are a number of **bus** terminals in Kingston, including the Parade (downtown), Half Way Tree, Cross Roads, Barbican and Papine. In town the buses will stop only at official stops. The fare is J$6–12. Buses run until 10pm. There is a bus service (roughly every half-hour) from the airport to the Parade, downtown. Buses to towns on the north coast leave from downtown Kingston, west along Beckford St from the Parade. For Spanish Town and Mandeville, go to the station at Half Way Tree. The different rest stops en route from the capital are known for their different snacks. At Old Harbour (going west) there is fry fish and bammy; at Melrose Hill (near Mandeville) the popular meal is roast yam and salt fish; and at Friendship Gap the popular snack is fry chicken.

The **ferry** to Port Royal leaves Pier 2 on the Kingston waterfront about four times a day, fare J$20.

Art Galleries

There is a lively art scene in Jamaica and in Kingston there are a number of good galleries.
Bolivar Bookshop and Gallery, 1D Grove Road, **t** 926 8799.
Contemporary Art Centre, 1 Liguanea Av, Kingston 6, **t** 927 9958.
Frame Centre Gallery, 10 Tangerine Place, **t** 926 4644.
Hi-Qo, 19 Spanish Court, **t** 926 4183.
Mutual Life Gallery, Mutual Life building, Oxford Rd.
National Gallery of Art, 12 Ocean Bvd, **t** 922 1561
Things Jamaican, Devon House, 26 Hope Road, **t** 929 6602.

Where to Stay

Kingston **t** (1 876–)

Expensive

Jamaica Pegasus, Knutsford Bd, **t** 926 3690, *jm.pegasus@cwjamaica.com, www.jamaica pegasus.com*. A high-rise hotel directed at business people: international standards of accommodation and good business facilities if little atmosphere.
The Courtleigh Hotel & Suites, Knutsford Bd, **t** 929 9000, *courtleigh@cw.com, www. courtleigh.com*. The second of the three high-rise business hotels at the bottom of Knutsford Bd: excellent facilities but no Caribbean atmosphere.
Hilton Kingston Hotel, Knutsford Bd, **t** 926 5430, *www.hilton.com/hotels/kinhitw*. Another high-rise business hotel, with everything you would expect from this well-known chain.

Moderate

Morgan's Harbour Hotel, Port Royal, **t** 967 8075, **t** 967 8280, *mharbour@kasnet.com*. Within a shout of town (a short ferry ride across the harbour), Morgan's is built into the old colonial brickwork of Naval Dockyard, a short walk to the east of the town itself. There are 40 air-conditioned and fan-ventilated rooms, decorated with Jamaican wood furniture and set in a shaded, sandy garden with a pool and seafront bar – some rooms have superb views over Kingston and to the hills beyond. There is a marina and some watersports. The hotel is conveniently close to the international airport.
Mayfair Hotel, 4 West Kings House Close, **t** 926 1610–2, *mayfair@in-site.com, www. in-site.com/mayfair*. Next to the Governor-General's residence, this charming 32-room hotel is set in the midst of a residential area and within easy reach of the main thoroughfares Hope Rd and Trafalgar Rd. Guests stay either in the main building or in converted houses across the road, each with its own garden. There are weekly poolside barbecues and an English pub, popular with the locals. The homey atmosphere makes it particularly comfortable for long stays.
Hotel Four Seasons, 18 Ruthven Rd, **t** 929 7655, US and Canada **t** 1 800 448 8355. An Edwardian town house with additions. The hotel is quite large, with 76 rooms, some decorated in bright, modern Caribbean style. The interior of the dining room, with its panelled walls and dark, sumptuously thick carpets, is a little unlikely for the Caribbean; you can also eat out on the breezy veranda.

There's no pool, but the front desk will arrange for you to go to one.

Indies Hotel, 5 Holborn Rd, **t** 926 2952, *indies@ discoverjamaica.com*. Just 15 rooms in blocks behind a small town house with a pretty foyer with wooden floor and tray ceiling. The rooms, each one with TV, air-con and phone, lead off a peaceful courtyard festooned with golden palm and colourful crotons. They are comfortable though quite basic. All meals are available in the restaurant. Some *inexpensive* rooms.

Knutsford Court Hotel, **t** 929 1000, *sales@knutsfordcourt.com*, *www.knutsfordcourt.com*. A modern, air-conditioned 180-room hotel with restaurant, kitchen facilities and swimming pool. Same owners as Courtleigh Hotel.

Christar Villas, Hope Rd, Liguanea, **t** 978 3933, *christar@n5.com.jm*, *www.christarvillashotel.com*. Good if you don't need to be near the New Kingston business district, and within walking distance of shopping centres, restaurants and the cinema. Thirty-two comfortable rooms and a pool.

Inexpensive

Holborn Manor Guest House, Holborn Rd, **t** 929 3070. A popular stopping-off point in town for younger travellers. There are 10 fairly basic but clean rooms with private bath, now gentrified to the point of having telephones and some televisions. There is a friendly atmosphere; home-cooked breakfast is included.

Eating Out

Expensive

Red Bones Blues Café, 21 Braemar Av, **t** 926 4006, **t** 926 3480. A romantic and pricey spot with an inventive and flavourful 'nouvelle-Jamaican' menu. Dine indoors or on the garden patio. Try the sautéed nuggets of lobster and shrimp served in a cream sauce or the julienne of shrimp and chicken served in a herb sauce on a bed of fettucine, and finish with their home-made bread pudding.

Akbar, Holborn Rd, **t** 926 4006, **t** 926 3480. Serves excellent Indian food and has a popular lunchtime buffet during the week. Their tiny boutique is good for an interesting post-meal browse.

Guilt Trip, Orchid Village, 20 Barbican Rd, **t** 977 5130. Laid-back and open late, this is set on a terrace with latticework walls and a wooden roof hung with greenery, overlooking a lawn and fountain. The fare is international with a distinctly Jamaican twist: try the pimento-stuffed chicken breast or roasted snapper fillet in a passion-fruit cream. And the desserts are magnificent; there is also a bakery on the premises, which specializes in cakes, so afternoon tea is particularly popular here.

The Devonshire, Devon House. Dine on verandas overlooking an inner courtyard with a small forest of greenery and a lily pond. Try the roast suckling pig and island coconut lobster; lots of steaks too.

Norma's on the Terrace, Devon House, **t** 968 5488, **t** 920 8976. Light, sophisticated and tasty fare for lunch and dinner. The garden setting is a cool and relaxing oasis. Try a flame-roasted corn-fed chicken with mashed and seasoned sweet potatoes and follow with a novel variation on an *apfelstrüdel*, made with tropical *otaheite* apple.

Moderate

Grog Shoppe, Devon House, **t** 929 7027. Something of the Port Royal of the 1680s still exists in this old brick warehouse building – the guests behave rather better now, though. There is an easy mix of visitors and some locals here. After you have tucked into a list of exotic and colourful cocktails (their names taken from some sensational moments in Jamaica's history, including Devon Duppy and the White Witch), you will be served local Jamaican callaloo and hot pot, as well as Blue Mountain burgers and steaks. It's a pleasant spot with tables inside under a ship's figurehead or a fairy-lit mango tree.

Heather's, Haining Rd, **t** 960 7739, **t** 926 2826. Tables set on a terrace beneath a mango tree. It's popular with expats, who cluster here for a drink and sometimes a plate of food after work: a long menu includes seafood and fish specialities, cottage pie and burgers, and even bangers and mash.

The Hot Pot, Altamont Terrace, **t** 929 3906. A much more Jamaican affair, set in a courtyard under umbrellas. It serves trusty if odd-sounding Jamaican food in large portions – anything from *gungo* soup or beef balls to the less worrisome steam fish and fricassee chicken, all with rice 'n' peas.

The Pantry, Dumfries Rd, **t** 929 4149. At lunchtime, you might try for Jamaican fare: soup and a plate of fried rice or a sandwich. In the evening, they serve mackerel rundown, chicken in sweet potato or an ackee pizza.

Indies Pub, Holborn Rd. Draws a crowd after work and at lunchtime, when it is popular with New Kingston businesspeople. Simple chicken and fish with chips, or a pizza.

Jamrock Sports Bar & Grill, Knutsford Bd, **t** 754 4032. This does a roaring trade with the yuppy set who work in the business district. Burgers, pizza and Jamaican fare are on order in this noisy and lively eatery, which also has big-screen TVs for sporting events. Quite a scene after work and at the weekends.

Eden Restaurant, Constant Spring Rd, just above Half Way Tree, **t** 926 3051. There are a few exclusively vegetarian restaurants around Kingston – this one offers lunch and dinner until 8pm. *Closed Sat – they are Seventh-Day Adventists.*

The Fish Place, 136 Constant Spring Road, **t** 924 4063. Select your fish, which is cooked to order, then dine inside or out. A new and very popular restaurant.

Susie's Bakery and Coffee Bar, Southdale Plaza, **t** 968 5030. Salads, pastries, a great coffee menu and Lebanese goodies such as chicken and beef kibbie by the Lebanese owner. Also has takeouts. Very sociable spot.

Inexpensive

Chelsea Jerk Centre, Chelsea Av, New Kingston, **t** 926 6322. There are several jerk centres in town, but this is the most popular. You can buy chicken or pork doused in hot pepper sauce. *Closed Sun.*

Peppers, Upper Waterloo Rd, **t** 969 2421. Another good jerk centre, and popular bar.

Tastee, branches all over Kingston. Don't leave without tasting a Jamaican beef patty, a spicy version of the Cornish pastie. This chain has been making them in exactly the

same way for over 30 years and is acknowledged as the best patty place.

Brick Oven, Devon House. Has lobster, vegetable and chicken patties at lunchtime.

Jici Patties, with branches all over Jamaica. Specializes in Jamaican meat dishes or shrimp turnovers.

Bars and Nightlife

Bars

Jamrock Sports Bar & Grill, Knutsford Bd. A great place to start any evening in Kingston. The lively bar and restaurant is filled with Kingston's 'beautiful people', who stop in for an after-work drink that lasts till 11pm.

Carlos Café, Belmont Rd. One of many haunts which are part bar, part restaurant and part café too, frequented by Kingstonians; this one gathers a lively crowd of drinkers and diners under its awnings and umbrellas.

Guilt Trip (also known as Colin's), Orchid Village, 20 Barbican Rd. Caters to the more sophisticated and often female crowd.

Peppers, Upper Waterloo Rd. A bar and jerk centre popular with preppy drinkers.

Chaser's Café, Barbican Rd. An animated bunch hang out drinking and generally make whoopee.

Harry's Bar, Constant Spring Rd. A hip crowd gathers here to listen to alternative music.

Priscilla's, Constant Spring Rd. At this roof-top bar the atmosphere is more relaxed and less of a 'scene' than at Harry's across the road.

Clubs

Asylum Nightclub, Knutsford Bd. Has a colourful dancehall night on Thursday and nostalgic 80s night on Wednesday.

Mingles, Courtleigh Hotel. Good for dancing.

Countryside Club, Eastwood Park Rd. A popular venue for late-night drinking and dancing and soca concerts.

Cuddy'z, New Kingston Shopping Centre. A new nightspot belonging to cricket star Courtney Walsh. Finger food, drinks, dancing.

Music

Grog Shoppe, Devon House. Jazz lovers can come here for weekly live music.

Red Bones Blues Café, 21 Braemar Av. Jazz.

official residence of the Jamaican Governor-General. You can visit the grounds by appointment (*t 927 6424*). The red, green and black house at 56 Hope Rd is the old Tuff Gong recording studio, where Bob Marley lived and recorded. It is now the **Bob Marley Museum** (*t 927 9152; open Mon–Sat 9.30–4.30; adm*); you can see his golden and platinum disks, album covers, press clippings and the 'Shot Room' where an attempt was made on his life. The tour culminates with 20 minutes of your favourite track on the video. At the top of Old Hope Rd are the **Hope Botanical Gardens** (*open daily 8.30–dusk; adm free, tip guides*), which were established in 1881. The vast lawns are lined with royal palms, and bougainvillea explodes in colourful blooms. The 150 acres are a good retreat from the noise of downtown Kingston, as well as a favoured spot for Jamaican limers, picnickers and lovers. Guides are available to point out the many plants such as bottle brush and pimento (which goes into jerk seasoning). **Hope Zoo** has a few lacklustre exhibits including Jamaican crocodiles and American owls and parrots. At the top end of Hope Rd is the Mona Campus of the University of the West Indies on an old sugar estate at the foot of the Blue Mountains, where the old aqueducts and some stone buildings are still visible.

Port Royal

At the tip of the Palisadoes Peninsula, past the Royal Jamaica Yacht Club and Norman Manley Airport, is the settlement of Port Royal. The peninsula almost encloses the bay, making the harbour one of the best in the Caribbean. The British fortified it immediately after they arrived in 1655. Very soon it became a haunt for the buccaneers, who had been driven out of the island of Tortuga off Hispaniola. These men were possessed in their hatred of the Spaniards, the dominant power in the region, and were useful as an unofficial army for the governor.

They brought back vast piles of loot from their attacks on Caribbean shipping and land raids on Cuba, Hispaniola and the Spanish Main. Port Royal was the sorting station for it all and it quickly became the richest town in the area. Grog by the shipload, silks from the east, chests of jewels and gold and silver were auctioned off by the returning buccaneers, who then gambled and drank and generally made whoopee until the money ran out and they had to go off again to find more. It became a commercial centre where the inhabitants wore the latest fashions from London, and artisans, including ivory-turners, pewterers and potters, gathered around the trade. The town was also full of pimps and prostitutes and, at its height in the 1680s, there was one ale house to every 10 inhabitants. In the opinion of one man, 'this place has been one of the lewdest in the Christian world, a sink of all filthiness and a mere sodom'.

When it came, a few minutes before noon on 7 June 1692, the earthquake seemed like divine retribution, as 2,000 people died in three minutes. Fort Charles sank 3ft, whole streets of the 'Gilded Hades' slid into the sea, fissures opened in the ground and a tidal wave threw a ship into the middle of the town. Some continued drinking and others started to loot the shops and cut the gold off the dead. Another 2,000 were dead of disease in a few days. One Lewis Galdy had quite a story to tell, after being swallowed up by the earth and then thrown out again into the sea as another shock came. His tomb, with his story on the stone, is in the graveyard of St Peter's Church. Next to it is the simple grave of three children who died in the earthquake in 1692 but whose bodies were preserved under a falling wall. They were discovered by marine archaeologists and were buried in 1992.

The merchants rebuilt their town, but in 1703 a fire destroyed it again and the last of the inhabitants moved off to Kingston. The area remained a naval base, where Horatio Nelson served at the time of the American War of Independence. **Fort Charles** was his base and you can still visit it today, with its castellated ramparts and cannon and a fantastic view of the Kingston mountains. It is dozy and quiet and has been left high and dry due to sedimentation (once ships could tie up to its walls, but it is now inland). There is a small **Maritime Museum** in the fort (*t 967 8438; open daily 10–5*) with descriptions of Port Royal in its heyday and some artefacts recovered during excavations of the town.

Beyond the fort is the **Giddy House**, once a Royal Artillery store, which lurched to its present position in the earthquake of 1907. The old naval hospital building, an early cast-iron section building built in 1818, was badly damaged in Hurricane Gilbert and the Museum of Historical Archaeology that it contained had to be closed.

A visit to Port Royal is a good day out from Kingston. Although the town is, in fact, quite rundown, it provides a welcome respite from the hustle of Kingston. After the few sights and a meal of fried fish and bammy, you can take a trip to one of the offshore cays or across to Port Henderson.

The East of the Island

Into the Blue Mountains

The Blue Mountains rise behind Kingston as steeply as a theatre curtain and as soon as you leave the town you will be surrounded by countryside, winding up into the mountains. The A3 or Junction Rd goes via Half Way Tree and Constant Spring and then up to **Castleton** and over to the north coast at Annotto Bay. Set either side of the road at Castleton are some **Botanical Gardens** that date from 1869, set in 39 acres in the dramatic, incredibly fertile (and pretty wet) Wag River Valley. The plants are marked and there are guides who will explain the 35 palms among the 60ft explosions of bamboo and point out the lair of the trap-door spider (sealed watertight and lined with silk).

The main entrance to the Blue Mountains is from Papine at the top of Old Hope Rd, along the magnificent cleft of the Hope River Valley. If you take the left fork just after the Blue Mountain Inn the road winds gradually up to **Irish Town**, a typically laid-back and charming village, and then to **Newcastle**, one of the barracks of the Jamaican Defence Force, its buildings stacked top to toe down the hillside. The road leads over the parade ground and when they are parading the traffic is held up. Just above here, beyond the Gap Café, you come to the Hardwar Gap which leads to the northern side

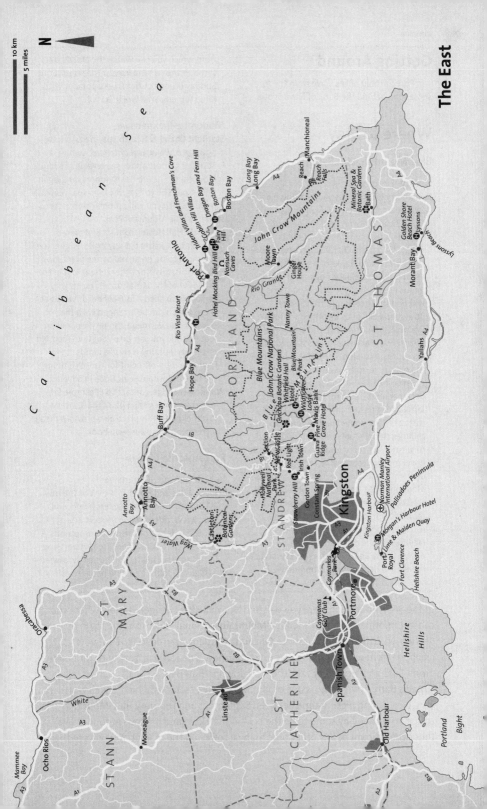

Getting Around

In **Port Antonio** buses leave from the foreshore road behind the Bank of Nova Scotia.

Where to Stay

Blue Mountains t (1 876–)

Luxury–Expensive

Strawberry Hill, just beyond Irish Town on the Irish Town road (coming from Kingston), t 944 8400, *strawberryhill@islandoutpost. com*, *www.islandoutpost.com*, UK t 0800 169 5884, USA t 1 800 OUT POST. Scattered over the summit and flanks of a 3,100ft hill among the camelback ridges and outrageous greenery of the Blue Mountains, you will find these cottages. The area of Strawberry Hill once belonged to Horace Walpole, gothic novelist and son of the British Prime Minister, and is named after his estate in London. The hotel, built when the old Great House was destroyed during Hurricane Gilbert in 1988, has been designed in the best romantic colonial Jamaican style: the clinker-laid wooden cottages have white louvred windows, tray ceilings, shingle roofs, wooden floors and furniture, and some four-poster beds, with novel modern touches, including Jamaican dancing scenes and even illustrations from Madonna's *SEX* book in one cottage – and the comforts are modern. There are just 18 rooms (studios up to four-bedroom cottages, some with kitchens), one with facilities for the disabled. There is an infinity pool, a sauna and an Aveda spa. Everywhere there are balconies with stunning views

from which you can watch the clouds track through the banana leaves. The sumptuous Sunday brunch buffet is very popular with Kingstonians. Well worth a visit.

Moderate–Inexpensive

Starlight Chalet & Health Spa, in St Andrew, t 969 3116, *www.starlightchalet.com*. Situated 5,000ft above sea level in the Blue Mountains. The inn has 17 rooms ranging in price from $66 to $225. It offers spa treatments which you will probably need after a hike to Blue Mountain Peak.

Whitfield Hall Hostel, contact 8 Armon Crescent, Kingston 6, t 927 0986. Higher in the mountains, on an old coffee plantation at 4,000ft, this is another retreat lost in the grandeur of the Jamaican peaks. It's very remote (you need a four-wheel drive to get there, which can be arranged with the number above); meals can be prepared on request, but you can take your own food. No electricity: lighting is by gas lamps. It is a favourite drop-off point for those climbing the Blue Mountain Peak. Book in advance.

Wildflower Lodge, contact 10 Ellesmore Rd, Kingston, t 926 5874, t 929 5394. Close to Whitfield Hall, this place also provides meals on request. Make sure you book.

Port Antonio t (1 876–)

Very Expensive–Expensive

Trident Villas and Hotel, just east of the town, PO Box 119, t 993 2602, *trident@infochan. com*, *www.tridentvillas.com*, US t 404 237 4608. This is one of the most sumptuous spots on the island. There are 12 rooms and 14 cottages set neatly in luxuriantly lawned gardens of palms and pine hedges with

of the Blue Mountains. Here you will find Hollywell Park Ranger Station, where you can get information about the **Blue Mountain National Park**. From the town of Section, you can reach the remote **Cinchona Gardens**, started in 1868 to grow cinchona from which quinine was extracted, now a peaceful retreat with rhododendrons, lilies and orchids, or take the road down to Buff Bay.

Mavis Bank (*tours daily*) is one of Jamaica's coffee factories, which is well worth a visit, best during picking time between September and February. Blue Mountain coffee is reckoned by some to be the best in the world and it retails at four or five times the amount of any other pure arabica coffee on the market. You will see the roaming peacocks and doves, all on a dramatic ledge of pitted volcanic cliffs. The rooms are exquisitely decorated – tiled, with stained-wood panelling and solid furniture in the black and white colour scheme that runs throughout the resort. Ventilation is mainly by fan and sea breeze here, though there is air-conditioning, and each room has its own veranda. There is a charming and very private beach in its own protected inlet, and some sports, including windsurfing, dinghy sailing, scuba and tennis; there's some luxury accommodation, particularly the magnificent Imperial Suite.

Moderate

Hotel Mocking Bird Hill, PO Box 254, **t** 993 7267, *mockbrd@infochan.com*, *www.hotel mockingbirdhill.com*. Standing high on the hillside a few miles to the east of Port Antonio, this has a magnificent view, nearly 180 degrees wide. The stark concrete of the villa belies the relaxed air and eco-friendly philosophy of the place. The 10 rooms, with locally made bamboo furniture, pretty floral decorations, balconies and hammocks, are set in 6 acres of forest crisscrossed by paths and scattered with benches. The dining room is on a very attractive balcony and offers exceptional home-made fare: jams, mayonnaise and breads, including rye, sunflower, coconut, even cheese breads, baked in their own solar oven. And inventive Jamaican dishes are served with vegetables from Mocking Bird Hill's own organic garden. It is an extremely peaceful spot and you will be looked after well.

Goblin Hill Villas, San San, contact 11 East Av, Kingston 10, **t** 925 8108, **t** 993 7443, *info@ goblinhill.com*, *www.totalcaribbean.com/*

goblinhill, US **t** 1 800 472 1148. This has 28 one- and two-bedroom villas in a 12-acre hilltop setting of charming gardens. Goblin Hill is run more as a villa resort than as a hotel and so there is no central restaurant. The villas have maid service and all meals can be provided, though there are full kitchens if you want to look after yourself. The rooms are comfortable and fan ventilated, on a split level or on two floors, all with patios and many with fantastic views, with air-conditioning in the bedrooms and king-size beds. There are no TVs in the villas, but there is a central TV room. Quite a few families come to the resort so there is a children's play area and some activity programmes. There is a charming bar, where you sit on fan-backed wicker chairs, on a stepped deck that twines around a huge fig tree.

Fern Hill Club, San San, PO Box 26, **t** 993 7374, *fernhill@cwjamaica.com*, *www.fernhill hotel.com*. Thirty-one rooms and suites in villas high on the hill above San San. The appearance is striking – white-painted villas with sharply pointed shingle roofs stand out starkly against the greenery of the beautifully forested hillside. The brightly decorated rooms have TV, fan and air-con, plus some Jacuzzis, two pools and tennis courts; the beach down below is reached by shuttle and offers watersports. The central great house, with a restaurant serving international and Jamaican fare, has a magnificent view of the coastline and mountains around. Friendly, but rather quiet.

Frenchman's Cove, PO Box 101, Port Antonio, **t** 993 7270, *cdegagne@wiband.ca*, *www .frenchmanscove.com*. Set in a magical cove and lush tropical valley just a few miles to the east of Port Antonio, Frenchman's Cove is

'cherry berries' come in from the field, thrown into water to remove the 'floaters', and then pulped and sweated for a few days. Once they have been dried, by laying them out on to concrete barbecues, they are husked and 'rested' for a few weeks as 'dry parchment' and then hulled of another layer of skin. Finally, they are sized and packed in barrels and bags or sometimes roasted and ground. The **Blue Mountain Peak** itself is Jamaica's highest (7,402ft) and the ascent can be made in seven hours from Abbey Green. The mountains are often lost in cloud and mist in the day, and so, to get the best chance of a clear view, you should aim to reach the peak soon after dawn, when you might be able to see as far as Cuba and Haiti. On the way down, you will pass a hotel with an illustrious history – among other luminaries, Winston Churchill stayed here. There are 17 villas with one to three bedrooms set on the hillsides around a Great House, where there are also rooms and suites. There is a delightful beach. *At the top end of this price category.*

Inexpensive

De Montevin Lodge, 21 Fort George St, Titchfield Hill, PO Box 85, **t** 993 2604. Fifteen rooms in the three storeys of the red-painted brick house; a couple have their own cast-iron filigree balconies. The wooden stairs and door surrounds, and the large number of pictures of the British Royal family, create a Jamaican home atmosphere. Rooms have fan ventilation; all meals are available.

Ivanhoe's, Queen St, Titchfield Hill, **t** 993 3043. Fifteen inexpensive rooms in a modern extension, with plush décor, ceiling fans and hot and cold water, attached to a traditional wooden Jamaican house; all meals are available.

Draper San, Drapers, **t** 993 7118, *carla-51@cw jamaica.com*. To the east of Port Antonio, you will find a very small and simple guest house sitting in a pretty garden plot on the roadside in Drapers village, within earshot of the waves in the bay below. It's friendly, with just six rooms, a sitting area and kitchen; Italian food is cooked to order.

The Holiday Home, King St, **t** 993 2882. Set in a traditional wooden house with nine rooms and a nice balcony where meals are served. The walls are a bit thin; there are some private baths, with cold water only.

Rio Vista Resort and Villas, St Margaret's Bay, PO Box 4, **t** 993 5444, *riovistajamaica@rio vistajamaica.com, www.riovistajamaica.com*. A few miles to the west of town, this resort has just a few one- and two-bedroom cottages, with magnificent views over the Río Grande river valley or over the sea. The rooms are brightly decorated in white and they are fan-ventilated; with satellite TV and maid service.

Port Antonio to Kingston **t** (1 876–)

Heading east from Port Antonio, you come to Boston Bay, where villas with rooms to rent are steadily springing up, and then to Long Bay, which has become quite a popular stopover on the 'backpack' circuit.

Rooms in private houses are available there, though most are not registered with the Tourist Board.

Inexpensive

The Chalet, Long Bay, no tel. In a modern building above the beach.

Coconut Isles, Long Bay, **t** 913 7818. In modern building above the beach.

Morant Villas, Morant Bay, **t** 982 2418/9. Officially recommended.

Golden Shore Beach Hotel, Windward Drive, PO Box 8, Lyssons, St Thomas, **t** 734 0923/4. Has a bit more style for excellent value. It is on a lovely beach, quiet but with the occasional weekend crowd. The rooms are fairly basic but clean, some with air-con, some fans; all rooms have private baths, but some have only cold water. You sleep to the wash of the waves. There is a bar under the palms, with meals available (order by 6pm).

Whispering Bamboo Cove, Morant Bay, St Thomas, **t** 982 1788. A 10-room inn on the southeast coast of Jamaica with a

through elfin growth, stunted grasses, knee-high trees and lichens, and then into montane woodland, still swirling in cloud, where the ferns and orchids sit in the upper branches and trees reach tall to catch the sunlight. (For a tour, *see p.712.*)

Annotto Bay to Port Antonio

The main road from Kingston emerges on the north coast at **Annotto Bay**. This area remains undeveloped and you will see some 'natural' Jamaican life as you drive through. The coast road east follows the magnificent coastline beneath the massive and beautiful foothills of the Blue Mountains. **Buff Bay** (in name only) is now a faded

restaurant, meeting facilities and satellite television. A quiet place to hang out.

Eating Out

Blue Mountains

The hotels (*see* p.728) also provide food.

Blue Mountain Inn, on the road to Gordon Town from Kingston, **t** 927 1700 (*expensive*). The most formal and smartest restaurant around Kingston. It sits in a vast cleft in the mountains. The interior is dressed up as a drawing room, carpeted in red with black beams and white walls, and there's a magnificent view of the river from here and from the vine-covered terrace, where you can take coffee to the rush of the river water. The menu is international: start with an ackee quiche and follow with lobster bathed in mint and ginger sauce. Jackets are required.

Port Antonio

There are few places in which to eat in Port Antonio. If you want to dine out, you will have to go to the hotels (*see also* pp.728–31).

Trident Villas, **t** 993 2602 (*expensive*). Enjoy a six-course candlelit set dinner of very fine West Indian and continental fare in a subdued and elegant setting.

Norma at the Marina, at the new Port Antonio Marina, **t** 993 9510 (*expensive*). Run by the well-known restaurateur, Norma Shirley, who also has Norma's in Kingston, Negril, and Coral Gables, serving refined Jamaican cuisine.

Hotel Mockingbird Hill, Mille Fleurs, **t** 993 7267, **t** 993 7134 (*expensive*). The dining room is set on a charming veranda and offers innovative cuisine using the best of the exotic Jamaican fruits and vegetables: carpaccio of tropical fruits or ackee soufflé followed by a soup (combinations such as tomato and sweet potato) and then an ital rundown or chicken in June plum sauce. The three-course menu has a choice for each course (and always includes a vegetarian dish).

Golden Happiness (*moderate*). A new Chinese restaurant in town.

Tri-Me (*inexpensive*). Another excellent stopover for a stew fish or fry chicken.

Roadside braziers (*inexpensive*). You can pick up a barbecued chicken leg from the people cooking on braziers on the roadside all around town.

Boston Bay

Boston Bay is the home of jerk. There are three or four centres on either side of the road – **Sufferer's Jerk Centre**, **Mickey's Jerk Centre**, **Shaggy's Jerk Centre** and, a little down the road, **Fuzzy's Jerk Centre**. You sit on open-air terraces amid the barbecues. Chicken and pork, occasionally other meats, are chopped (hacked to bits) to order and served with a festival roll and a beer.

Bars and Nightlife

Port Antonio

Rafter's Rest, at the bottom of the Río Grande. A good bar.

Crystal Nightclub. The latest local favourite.

Huntress Marina, the harbour. A good restaurant bar.

Roof Club, West St. A wild and hip spot which is well worth checking out.

---

parish town, with its old buildings in decay, and **Hope Bay** is a small fishing village best known for the **Somerset Falls** (*open daily 10–5; adm*) just above the town: there are falls, pools and a swimmable channel. Soon afterwards, the road crosses the **Río Grande**, Jamaica's largest river, and best known for river-rafting since Errol Flynn joined the banana growers who shipped their fruit downriver on bamboo rafts.

Port Antonio

Port Antonio is the capital of Portland parish. Both the town and its parish are charming and spectacular, among the most beautiful places on the island. The town's heyday is clearly past, for the moment at least, as the grand old buildings show in their distressed decay, but its setting, on the point between two bays and with vast and fertile mountains behind it, makes Port Antonio incomparable. Once it was described as the 'most exquisite port on earth'.

Port Antonio was a Spanish settlement and, although it was laid out in 1723, it remained a sedate coastal town until the late 1880s, when it became the centre of the banana trade and exploded into prosperity. By the start of the 20th century, it was the most important town on the north coast. Tourists poured in from the USA and the place was so popular that there was a 400-room hotel, three storeys high with verandas on all sides, an Italian orchestra to play at mealtimes and a massive ball-room. In the winter season, it was patronized by the likes of Rudyard Kipling. As the banana trade failed in the 1930s, so did the hotel and with it the tourist trade in Port Antonio. The town received a fillip in the 1950s with the arrival of the film star Errol Flynn. He bought Navy Island in the West Harbour and the glamour returned with his parties, to which guests like Bette Davis and Ginger Rogers came.

The most attractive area of the town, where you will find the classic Caribbean timber-frame houses with gingerbread fretwork and wrought-iron filigree, is on the point between the two bays, or '**Titchfield Hill**'. The remains of Fort St George, a few embrasures and some mean-looking cannon on rollers, have been turned into a

Jerk

Jerk is a special Jamaican way of barbecuing seasoned meats slowly over a wood fire set in the ground. The technique was supposedly developed by the maroons, runaways who lived in the mountains in the 18th century, who would cure meat for sale. Traditionally, they would kill early in the week and cook the meat in an underground oven for a couple of days before taking it to market on Friday or Saturday. Nowadays the fresh meat is seasoned with a marinade (of as many as 20 spices, including peppers, scallions, pimento and ginger) and then it is cooked over a pit on slats of green pimento wood, which itself increases the flavour. Meat is 'jerked' all over the island now, but the home of jerk is Boston Bay, beneath the John Crow Mountains in Portland parish in the east, where the maroons lived. There are a number of shacks at the roadside, where they start to cook early in the morning – don't arrive after about 4pm or it will all be gone.

Jerk Centres are among the best local Jamaican restaurants. Despite their name, they are not for the socially ungainly, but a place where you order jerk (pork, chicken, spare ribs, sausage, fish and even lobster), which you eat with a special sauce and with a festival, a sweet fried dumpling, or a slice of dense hard-dough bread. As you order, the cook will suddenly pull out a machete before you and proceed to chop the food into bite-size pieces and throw it onto a piece of paper. You will then be asked if you want hot pepper sauce. Jerk seasoning is already pretty spicy, so try one tiny dash on a corner of the meal on your first time out – Jamaican hot pepper sauce can be a vicious and searing scourge and has a habit of affecting everything edible for miles around.

school. The centre of the town itself is the clocktower at the head of West St, and not far from here you will find **Musgrave market**, always worth a visit, but particularly active on Thursdays and Saturdays. The view from the **Bonnie View Hotel** is superb. Port Antonio is still the main shipping port for bananas, and you will see the huge Jamaica Producers banana boats in harbour a couple of times a week.

Around Port Antonio

Above Port Antonio, between the Blue Mountains and the John Crow Mountains, is the maroon settlement of **Moore Town**. In the 18th century, the Windward maroons occupied this area and they are supposed to have lived in Nanny Town, beneath the Blue Mountain Peak. They were forced out of the town by the British in 1730, but in 1739 they signed a treaty allowing them to live in peace. Legends grew up around the place and around their leader Nanny, who was supposed to have supernatural powers. Locals say that the spirits of the maroons still inhabit the area. Nanny's reputation was such that he became a national heroine of Jamaica in 1975. It is possible to visit the town, but it is worth remembering that it is much like any other remote Jamaican town nowadays. **Bump Grave**, opposite the school, is supposed to contain the remains of Nanny.

Close by there are some waterfalls: **Nanny Falls**, a short distance from the town, and **Jupiter Falls**, lost in the densest greenery, with a rockpool where you can swim. Ask around for directions. **Nonsuch Caves** (*open daily 9–5; adm*) are made up of nine chambers in Athenry Gardens up in the hills behind Port Antonio, with walkways and lighting to let you see the stalactites and stalagmites (shapes include a woman with a basket on her head, organ pipes and an owl). The gardens have a magnificent view of the town from above.

Port Antonio Round to Kingston

Back on the coast the main road leads east out of Port Antonio, passing through small villages and some of Jamaica's expensive villas until you reach the **Blue Hole**, a limestone sinkhole with patches of hot and cold water fringed with palm trees and coloured a beautiful shade of royal blue. There is a bar and restaurant (*adm free if you go to the restaurant*). Beyond Boston Bay, home of jerk (*see* 'Jerk', opposite), the road follows the rugged southeast coast to **Reach Falls** (*adm*), a couple of miles up into the hills and well worth a visit, as the river cascades 25ft into a rockpool.

From here, you pass into the parish of St Thomas and to the tip of the island. Inland is the town of **Bath**, Jamaica's favourite resort two centuries ago because of the hot and cold springs, and home to the second-oldest botanical gardens in the western hemisphere (now dilapidated). At the **Bath Fountain Hotel** (*t 982 2132*), you can have a dip in the waters, which are supposed to have curative properties.

On the south coast, **Morant Bay** is the capital of the parish and the site of the famous 1865 rebellion, after which over 400 people were executed, including Paul Bogle and George William Gordon, who were hanged outside the town hall. The road follows the coast from Morant Bay through Yallahs and on to the capital.

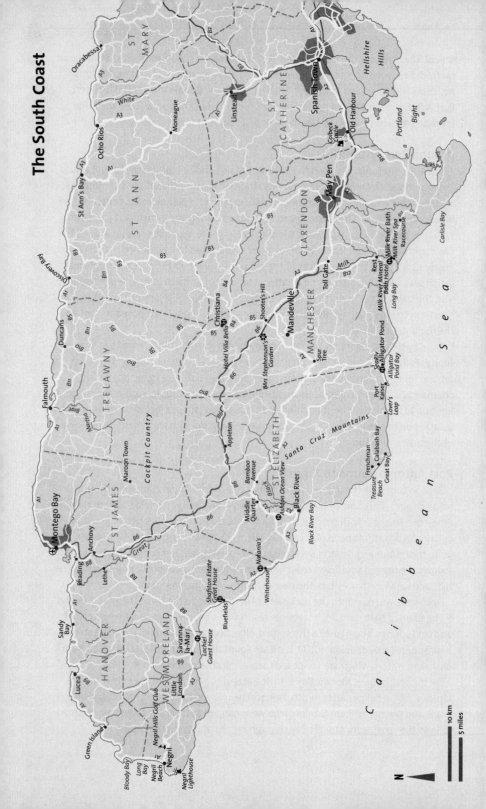

The South Coast

N

10 km
5 miles

The South Coast and Negril

Spanish Town

West of Kingston by 12 miles, across sugar flats and swamps, is **Spanish Town**, the capital of Jamaica for over three centuries until 1872, except for a brief interlude (1755–8) when the Kingston merchants managed to force through a bill moving the capital to their home town. The town has a few remnants of its former glory and magnificence – a cluster of old-time stone and timber buildings around a square of elegant and monumental colonial edifices – but it has mushroomed recently with suburbs, mostly modern villas. It is worth a quick look as you are driving through. Nearby, in the village of White Marl, you will find the **Taino Museum**, which chronicles the lives of the Arawak Indians.

Santiago de la Vega was laid out by the Spaniards when they moved here from the north coast in 1523, but there is nothing left of the original plaza in the central square of Spanish Town. The Georgian architecture and the iron railings around the park give the square a distinctly British feel and it was the social hub of Jamaica during colonial times. The **Rodney Memorial**, sculpted by John Bacon, commemorates Admiral George Rodney following his victory at the Battle of the Saints off Guadeloupe in 1782 (widely reckoned to have saved Jamaica from invasion). Opposite is the **Court House**, which was burned down in the 1980s and is no more than a façade now. On the east side of the square, the colonnaded building with wooden upper storeys and a balcony is the former **House of Assembly**, where Jamaica's elected representatives met until the British Commonwealth Office took over government of the island in 1866. Now it houses the Parish Council Offices. Opposite it stands **Old King's House**, built in 1762, which was the official residence of the island's governor. The proclamation of the Abolition of Slavery was read from the building, but it was burned down to its façade in 1925. In the overgrown courtyards there is a lacklustre series of exhibits at the Jamaican People's Museum of Craft and Technology: examples of architectural techniques and old-time household utensils.

Look out for the **Cathedral Church of St James**, head of the diocese of Jamaica, on Barrett St. It was built in 1714 on the site of an original Spanish church, but there are commemorative tablets from the earliest English settlers to Jamaica. Beyond this rarefied square with its colonial echoes, Spanish Town is a busy Jamaican town, partly industrialized, partly fading timber businesses and homes.

Spanish Town to Negril

Past the massive ruins of 17th-century **Colbeck Castle** near Old Harbour you come to the town of **May Pen**. There are many Pens in Jamaica – the name refers to a farm-stead where animals were kept. At Toll Gate, you can take the turning to the south coast, along the meandering Milk River with its pastures and canefields, past a village called Rest, eventually coming to the **Milk River Hotel & Spa** (**t** 902 4657), where the highest levels of natural radioactivity in the world occur in the water – about 50 times the radioactive levels of Baden-Baden. The water comes out of the ground at

Getting Around

In Negril, buses leave from near the roundabout at the southern end of the beach, over the bridge from the crafts market. In Mandeville, they leave from beneath the church on the main square.

Where to Stay

Kingston to Mandeville t (1 876–)

There is nowhere good to stay in Spanish Town, so you are advised to stay in Kingston.

Milk River Hotel & Spa, t 902 4657 (*inexpensive*). This building is a genuine old Jamaican red-tin-roofed affair with gingerbread pickings, louvres, screens and cooling vents; the 17 rooms are authentically decorated and comfortable, with TV, phone, fan and Bible in each. The baths downstairs are free while you are staying at the hotel. It sees mainly a Jamaican crowd who come to take the spa waters, so it is an amusing place.

Mandeville t (1 876–)

Moderate

Mandeville Hotel, 4 Hotel St, PO Box 78, **t** 962 2460, *manhot@cwjamaica.com*, *www. mandevillehotel.com*. The most comfortable place to stay in town: it's set in its own enclave just off the town square. The building is modern but the hotel has an unhurried air about it. There are 60 well-decorated rooms (some of them suites) with TV, phone and fan, with a bar (called the Manchester Arms) downstairs and a pool in the pleasant gardens.

Hotel Villa Bella, Christiana, in the hills to the north of Mandeville, PO Box 473, **t** 964 2243, *villabella@cwjamaica.com*, *www.jamaica-southcoast.com/villabella*. A nice retreat. The style of the décor harks back to the '50s; the building is modern, but there is a gracious air of times past in the drawing room and on

the veranda, where an old sign says: 'Ring twice for ice water, three times for the maid'. Well-kept, comfortable rooms upstairs.

Inexpensive

Astra Country Inn, Ward Av, **t** 962 3725, *country style@cwjamaica.com*. A friendly, family-run hotel just outside the town centre. It has 15 comfortable, clean rooms upstairs in the villa and in modern blocks behind; it's also a good source of information about the area. In need of refurbishment.

Kariba Kariba, Atkinson Close, **t** 962 8006, *kariba@cwjamaica.com*. One of a number of guest houses in the area around Mandeville. Here, you'll find five rooms and suites with bathrooms and a restaurant.

Mandeville to Negril t (1 876–)

The area to the west of Mandeville, running from Treasure Beach up to Black River and on to Bluefields, has some charming small, typically Jamaican guest houses and some inns off the beaten track.

Expensive

Jake's, Treasure Beach, **t** 965 0635, *jakes@ cwjamaica.com*, *www.islandoutpost.com*, UK **t** 0800 169 5884, US **t** 1 800 OUT POST. The most stylish place to stay in the area: this is a hip retreat on the cliffs of Treasure Beach, with a superb view across the sea to the sunset. Jake's is quite rustic, with adobe buildings marooned in a sea of tall wild grass, but its colours give it plenty of style. The cottages are painted rich red and mauve, turquoise and tangerine. There are 10 rooms and 22-bedroom villas, with muslin nets and fans (anyone who insists on air-con would not be right for this place), and solar-heated water. Behind the tin-roofed gingerbread terrace, with its bar and sitting area, is a scattering of parasols and upturned cable barrels to eat on; Jamaican fare is adapted a little for the European palate. And just above the sea is a

120°F and the spa is popular for its supposed healing powers. Not far from here, the town of **Racecourse** has a large East Indian population, who stage very colourful festivals at Divali and Hosay.

Mandeville, the capital of Manchester Parish, is set in mountainous uplands at 2,000ft, which gives it a cooler climate than the rest of Jamaica. In British days,

meandering, tile-studded swimming pool with Adirondack chairs strategically positioned for watching the waves. There is a small beach. You will probably need to book in advance in the winter season.

Sandals Whitehouse, Whitehouse Beach, t 800-SANDALS, *www.sandals.com*. Located on a beach in the southwestern corner of Jamaica, an area that has seen little tourist development. It has 360 rooms, including 54 suites, a variety of dining options and a spa. All arranged in villages of Italian, Dutch and French design. *All-inclusive*.

Moderate

Treasure Beach Hotel, t 965 0110–3, *www. treasurebeachjamaica.com*, US t 1 800 330 8272. A traditional beachfront resort hotel, with a relaxed atmosphere. There are 36 modern and very comfortable rooms in small blocks ranged along a palm-dotted hillside around a large main block with dining room and bar. They look over the pool and garden and a brown-sand beach.

Sunset Resort Villa, Calabash Bay, t 965 0143, *srv@sunsetresort.com*, *www.sunsetresort. com*, US t 1 801 487 8127. There are 12 rooms, all with private patio, air-con and satellite TV, and a couple with kitchens (but there is also a restaurant serving international cuisine). Palm-thatch gazebos offer the finest view of the sunset. Some *moderate* rooms.

Inexpensive

The Golden Sands Motel, Frenchman's Bay, t 965 0167. An ugly concrete construction on the golden-brown sand. There are three buildings in fact, with 20 simply decorated rooms, some with private kitchen. Cold water is laid on, and so, if there are enough people, is a restaurant; it's excellent value with a funny transient crowd.

Four M's Cottage, Frenchman's Bay, t 965 0131. A six-room hotel with restaurant on the beach near the Golden Sands Motel.

SeaRivs Resort, Alligator Pond, on the road to the Kaiser port, t 962 7265. This is the one place to stay in the area. The building is a modern concrete villa which, if you don't mind the isolation, makes a passable stopover, with 20 reasonable rooms at a good price. Fans and phones, no TVs, and a nice section of dark-sand beach, usually all to yourself.

Waterloo Guest House, Black River, t 965 2278. In Black River itself, this is a characterful colonial Jamaican house with five fan-ventilated rooms in the rickety main house and 16 with air-con and TV in a new block behind. It has a swimming pool.

Ashton Ocean View Great House and Hotel, Black River, PO Box 104 Luana, t 965 2036. Just to the north of the town. It is set in an old estate house which commands a magnificent view over the countryside around. It has been modernized and painted oddly in white and turquoise, but shades of the old plantation style return in the lacquered wooden floor, the rugs, the wooden interior walls and louvred day rooms. There are 24 rooms, 11 of these in the tin-roofed main building, which has less atmosphere. Rooms have fan and air-con, phone and TV.

Natanias's, Bluefields, t 963 5342, *info@ natanias.com*, *www.natanias.com*, US t 1 508 432 3114. If you are passing through Bluefields, this is an excellent guest house just up from Whitehouse. There are 16 rooms in a modern wooden house with huge walkaround balconies, rooms with wooden furnishing and louvred windows. Good central area and a small secluded beach; very quiet, but friendly.

Shafston Estate Great House, Bluefields, t 955 8081, *frank.shafston@cwjamaica.com*, *www.shafston.com*. Has a superb setting high on the hills above the town (village) of Bluefields at the end of an impossibly rickety road. There are 10 extremely basic rooms, with shared bathrooms with cold water only,

---

Mandeville was a hill station, to which the colonial authorities and the planters would retreat in the heat of the summer (in those days, nobody lay on the beach because the heat was thought to be degenerative). It was even laid out like a village green, with the Georgian court house and the parish church standing opposite one another across the open square. Nowadays they stand rather oddly aloof among all

but the place has the unforgettable aura of an old Jamaican estate house and a veranda from which you can admire a hazy horizon that stretches from Whitehouse to Savanna-la-Mar. Not everyone's cup of tea, it's firmly on the backpacker circuit. *All-inclusive.*

Negril t (1 876–)

Long renowned for its pleasure-seeking and sensual way of life, Negril has excellent and easygoing places to stay, on both sides of town (the beach and the cliffs). The laid-back style has also been updated and repackaged for the 21st-century man and woman, in some very expensive all-inclusive hotels. But the most stylish of the small hotels in Negril are really the ones on the cliffs, where you will find palm-thatched wooden cabins with louvres and ceiling fans, set in charming and abundant jungle-like gardens, with magnificent views over the cliffs to the sea.

Luxury–Very Expensive

The Caves, West End Road, **t** 957 0270, *thecaves@islandoutpost.com, www.island life.com*, UK **t** 0800 169 5884, US **t** 1 800 OUTPOST. Another of Island Outpost's chic boutique hotels, this is the most stylish place to stay in Negril and a seaside home away from home to members of the music, film and fashion jet set. Its boldly coloured rooms sit ranged along the clifftop among dry tropical greenery, each large and well decorated, and set in stone and wood cottages with thatched roofs, with huge windows to take in the best of the sea view. Stylishly bohemian and very private.

Couples Swept Away, Norman Manley Bvd, **t** 957 4061, *couplesresorts@couples.com, www.couples.com*. The most complete sports-oriented resort in Jamaica, if not the Caribbean, with 10 tennis courts, a fully-equipped gym, two racquet courts, squash court, aerobics centre, Olympic-size swimming pool, unlimited golf, yoga sessions,

watersports and more. Large, attractively furnished rooms; five restaurants.

Catch a Falling Star, PO Box 22, **t** 957 0390, *catcha99@hotmail.com, www.negril.com/cfsmain.htm*. This is a similar hideaway on the cliffs, a few one- and two-bedroom cottages linked by stone-lined, sandy paths in a garden of crotons, sea grape and flamboyant trees. There are hammocks on the cool verandas and a Jacuzzi in the garden; rooms are louvred and screened. It's peaceful, set around a central house and small gym. Breakfast (no other meals) is served right on the spectacular cliffs.

Grand Lido, PO Box 88, **t** 957 5010, **t** 957 5145, *www.super-clubs.com/Glido*, UK **t** (01749) 677200, US **t** 1 800 859 SUPER. This has taken the all-inclusive concept upmarket, packaging sheer luxury, with 24-hour room service and champagne at the flick of a finger. It still has the brisk air and the constant activity and entertainment of the all-inclusive and it is quite a large resort, with 200 rooms set on excellent beaches; as always with Superclubs, there is a nudist area (well tucked away). The grounds are lovely and the rooms very comfortable: all have TVs, fan ventilation and air-con; many have an excellent view of the magnificent sweep of Bloody Bay. There is plenty to keep you busy: a beauty parlour, watersports and Jacuzzis, nine bars, a games room, a library and afternoon tea.

Hedonism II, PO Box 25, **t** 957 5200, **t** 957 3636, *www.superclubs.com*, UK **t** (01749) 677200, US **t** 1 800 859 SUPER. The most original of the all-inclusive hotels at the top end of the beach. It calls itself the naughtiest club in town and has been offering an adult playground now for over 20 years, with the slogan 'Be Wicked for a Week!' The resort allows couples and groups, but encourages singles in an endless catalogue of hedonistic activities: bar open 19 hours a day, nudes and prudes beaches, watersports, diving, trapeze and juggling instruction, wet T-shirt

the chaos of the Jamaican market and the taxi men touting for business. The area around the town calls itself the feeding tree (the Jamaican equivalent of the bread-basket) and you will see the neatly tended lines of green crops offsetting the orange of the rich Jamaican earth – there are also endless stalls at the roadside selling

competitions, body-painting lessons (yours or somebody else's), singalong piano bar, drink and dance till you drop, mirrors on the bedroom ceiling, breakfast served until late. There is an à la carte restaurant for the evening. You may be put in a room with a stranger if you arrive as a single. It's pricey but a riot for a weekend or a couple of days during a trip around the island.

Expensive

Tensing Pen Village, PO Box 13, **t** 957 0387, US **t** (216) 546 9000, *tensingpen@cwjamaica. com*, *www.tensingpen.com*. Twelve very quiet and secluded rooms, in stone and wooden cottages, on paths that meander through wonderful greenery of sea grape and bougainvillea, right on the cliff edge. Rooms are fan-ventilated with ice chests, four-posters and louvred French windows giving on to a balcony; no TVs. The charming central house, under a huge fig tree, has a library, sitting area and a small kitchen.

Sunset at the Palms Resort, PO Box 118, **t** 957 5350, **t** 957 5360, US **t** 1800 382 3444, *www.sunsetatthepalms.com*. Fifty unusual African-looking cabins on stilts set in superb lawns and tropical gardens. There is a meandering pool with a swim-up bar and an easygoing atmosphere. The 86 rooms, some louvred and fan-ventilated, others with air-con and TV, all have a balcony and make a very comfortable retreat. There's tennis and a fitness centre, and the beach is just five minutes' walk away. All-inclusive.

Idle a While, **t** 957 9566, *info@idleawhile.com*, *www.idleawhile.com*. A small and stylish beachfront hotel with a very friendly staff. Guests can use the facilities at nearby Swept Away resort.

Moderate

Banana Shout, **t** 957 0384, *bananashout@ yahoo.com*, *theone.negril.com/bananashout*. On the cliffs, this also has real charm – rooms overlook the sea or the tropical profu-sion of a garden, where hummingbirds flit around the lily ponds. There are 10 rooms in villas and cottages, with dark wooden furniture, screens and louvres, decorated with Haitian art. All rooms are fan ventilated and have kitchens (no restaurant, though breakfast can be ordered). Simply walk down the steps cut in the cliffs for a swim.

Coco La Palm, Norman Manley Bd, **t** 957 4227, *cocolap@cwjamaica.com*, *www.cocolapalm. com*. Five, two-storey buildings with large junior suites set around a pool in a lush garden in a quiet corner of Negril's famous Seven Mile Beach. There is an annexe with moderate sized rooms The hotel's terrace restaurant has an idyllic setting on the beach. Two pools, with watersports available from the vendor next door. Family-owned and operated; popular with Europeans.

Rockhouse, PO Box 24, **t** 957 4373, *rockhouse hotel@cwjamaica.com.jm*, *www.rockhouse hotel.com*. Twenty villas, seven studios and nine standard rooms in a garden setting on the cliffs, with a wonderfully relaxed atmosphere. Accommodation is very comfortable, with four-posters and muslin netting, outdoor showers with hot and cold water, and a slightly surreal pool bar down on the cliffs.

Jackie's on the Reef, **t** 957 4997, *jackiesonthe reef@hotmail.com*, *www.harlem-ontime. com/features/jackie*. Set beyond the Lighthouse on the cliffs, Jackie's is billed as Jamaica's only holistic spa and offers guests a very new-agey menu of spa treatments – past life regression, reiki, etc. Accommodation is in seven spartan rooms in the main building, each with an open-air (yet private) bathroom. The organic menu is delicious, and Jackie, a transplanted American in her 60s, is a fascinating host.

Inexpensive

Lighthouse Park, **t** 957 4491. Just south of Negril Lighthouse there are cabins, cottages and tent sites – the tent sites are very cheap.

cashews and strings or bags of whatever fruits are in season. In the 1950s the area suddenly became the centre of the Jamaican bauxite industry, but the town still has a stately air and many Jamaicans have returned from abroad and built themselves retirement homes here.

Roots Bamboo, on the beach, **t** 957 4479. The very simple double rooms have private bath and porch, giving on to the lush beachside garden. There's not much atmosphere, but it has a restaurant and bar, and some very cheap tent sites.

Ms Gloria, also known as 'Barry's Place', **t** 957 4741. Has just a few plain rooms on the beach.

Eating Out

Mandeville

Moderate–Inexpensive

Hungry Jack's, **t** 962 0648. A good spot for local fare, such as curry goat and a stewed chicken with ground provisions.

Grove Court, opposite the Court House on the Square, **t** 962 0855. Local fare.

Four Points Restaurant, Northern Caribbean University on the outskirts of town, **t** 625 2238. Serves decent vegetarian meals.

Astra Country Inn, Ward Av. The restaurant here serves Jamaican health food and fresh-squeezed juices.

Negril

Negril has literally hundreds of restaurants and snack bars along its roadsides. There is no really smart and formal restaurant (except the à la carte restaurants in the all-inclusives – to go there just for a meal, you would have to buy an evening pass, for two), but there are many beach bars which serve drinks and snacks by day and then turn into lively bars and restaurants by night. A few of the restaurants offer a pick-up service.

Expensive

Rockhouse, West End Road, **t** 957 0557, www.rockhouse.com. The hotel's restaurant on a terrace overlooking the sea. Has an eclectic menu popular with tourists and town folks as well as hotel guests.

Norma's at Sea Splash, Sea Splash Resort, **t** 957 4041/968 5488; www.seasplash.com/norma.htm. The latest restaurant of Norma Shirley's, who is known for her sophisticated Jamaican fusion cuisine.

Lemon Grass, a new restaurant at Couples Swept Away. Serves Thai specialities.

Moderate

Kuyaba, **t** 957 4318. On a meandering wooden deck right on the sand of Negril beach, under a pointed thatch roof. The name means 'heaven' in the Arawak Indian language and, with its candlelight and serene seaside ambience, it's about as close as Negril's got. It serves simple fare by day and then in the evening more adventurous cuisine – snapper stuffed with orange and shrimp in a coconut sauce. Take advantage of the free pick-up service.

Margueritaville's, **t** 957 4467, www.margueritaville.com. You'll see their brightly painted bus cruising the Boulevard offering free transportation to the bar and grill. The menu includes fajitas, burgers, pizzas and sandwiches, as well as Jamaican specialities like a large escoveitched whole fish (head and all, fried and dressed with a peppery vinegar and onion sauce).

The Hungry Lion, **t** 957 4482. Set in a forested tropical courtyard across the road from the cliffs, this is a charming and original restaurant, with bright yellow walls and sprays of bougainvillea, benches and tables under a tin roof, and a fountain. Exotic natural foods and juices are a speciality – eggplant parmesan followed by lobster in lemon butter or kingfish in coconut milk – served by hip waiters. It is quite small and popular, so it fills up quickly; get there early. *Dinner only.*

Sweet n' Spicey, town centre, and a second one on West End Road. Good Jamaican cuisine.

Samsara Hotel, West End Road, **t** 957 4395. If you want to splurge, the Samsara does a mouthwatering lobster thermidor.

There are a number of unlikely-sounding but entertaining things to do around Mandeville. **Mrs Stephenson's garden** (*t 962 2328; adm*), on the northern outskirts of the town near New Green, is interesting to visit, even for those who are novices, botanically speaking. She has 50 species of orchids as well as such flowers as the

LTU Pub, **t** 957 0382. An interesting menu, featuring a selection of Austrian and German dishes. Good food and great value.

Lighthouse Inn, **t** 957 4052. At the far end of town, beyond the Lighthouse, this inn sits on a deck beneath trees garlanded with fairy lights. Enjoy the conch or any number of fish steaks, pepper shrimp and other Caribbean combinations including ginger chicken. Free pick-up service.

Paradise Yard Café, on the road to Savanna-la-Mar, **t** 957 4006. Another restaurant with great Caribbean style, in a wooden building among the trunks of royal palms. You sit at benches and tables on open terraces, in a proper yard of beaten earth, eating foreign and authentic Jamaican food – *enchiladas*, *jambalaya*, *callaloo alfredo* and *fricassee*, or the speciality, rasta pasta: red (tomatoes), gold (ackee) and green (green peppers).

Inexpensive

Cosmo Seafood, **t** 957 4784, **t** 957 4330. Praised for their specialities. Here you are supposed to get the best conch in town.

Erica's, quite a long way down on the cliffs. Here you are assured the finest lobster in town (served, among other ways, in butter, lime and garlic).

Three Sisters Restaurant, about half a mile inland on the Sav road. For an excellent local meal, you should try this place, in an old wooden house that looks a bit like a church. Real Jamaican dishes (oxtail, brown stew chicken, tripe beans and peppered steak) are presented at tables with bright tablecloths and plastic roses, and served with a tonnage of ground provisions; also juices. *Closed in the evening.*

Chicken Lavish, close to the town centre. As well as chicken (curried or sweet and sour), they also serve steam fish. You can dine on the covered terrace enclosed by a white picket fence, or order a takeaway.

Serious Chicken, West End Rd. Here you'll find the inimitable Roy and Felix, in a colourful

bamboo and thatch construction at the corner of Summerset Road.

Bars and Nightlife

Negril

Negril has a multitude of bars and clubs along its 10 miles or so of seafront. Besides the beach bars there are plenty of spots on the cliffs where you can spend the day chilling out until the great highlight of the day, watching the sunset. Negril is known for its music – ask around, or consult the papers or the posters nailed to the telegraph poles, to find out who's playing. The main live reggae venues are **Kaiser's Café**, **Waves** and **MX3**.

Rick's. A popular venue for watching the sunset – worth trying once though it does involve buying drinks with tokens and it can get pretty packed, because tourists are bussed in for the event, by which time you might feel compelled to jump 40ft into the water below.

LTU Pub. If you want something a little less crowded, try this place a couple of hundred yards further on; still lively at times, but with fewer lobster-red tourists and more locals.

Margueritaville. The place to sample exotic-flavoured frozen margaritas. It hosts daytime beach parties on holiday weekends which attract a large Jamaican crowd from as far away as Kingston.

Pickled Parrot, perched on the cliff. Another popular daytime hangout, this is a shingle-roofed gazebo and platforms on the cliff edge with the waves crashing beneath; it offers drinks and simple meals all day long, satellite TV, swings and a waterslide.

Alfred's Ocean Palace, on the beach. Can get particularly lively.

De Buss, on the beach. Last resting place of a pink and green double decker that washed up here, perhaps in the 1960s, and is now decrepit to the point of collapse; it's a bar with occasional live music and a jerk centre.

ortanique (an indigenous cross-fertilized citrus fruit), the stag-horn fern and pig-tailed anthurium. Not far off at Shooter's Hill, in the shadow of the huge bauxite plant, you will find the **Pickapeppa Sauce Factory** (**t** 603 3441; *visit by arrangement*), the source of the pungent concoction that the Jamaicans dash liberally on their food.

The **ALCAN aluminium factory** is also an interesting experience: you see the rich red Jamaican earth conveyed (3.5 miles on a conveyor belt), slurried with caustic soda, pressure cooked in liquid digesters until it becomes sodium aluminate, passed over with succulents, purified and heated to become alumina trihydrate and finally heated in a kiln, ending up as a white powder, aluminium oxide. (If this all sounds a bit much, you see it on film anyway.)

Finally, **Marshall's Pen** is a charming and peaceful spot, a classic 200-year-old Jamaican great house set in gentle hills, once a coffee plantation and now a farm for Jamaican red poll cattle. Bird-watching tours and private visits to the house, which is still lived in, are available if you arrange it in advance (best to contact through the Astra Hotel).

Following the main road west out of Mandeville, you descend to the plains of St Elizabeth at Spur Tree. The views are fantastic, as they are on the south coast at **Lover's Leap**, a 1,600ft drop sheer into the sea from the Santa Cruz Mountains. The story goes that two slave lovers were chased here by an ardent planter who fancied the girl, and they jumped to their death rather than be split up.

On the road to Black River is **Bamboo Avenue**, one of Jamaica's best-known sights. It is certainly impressive, a three-mile tunnel of bamboo, still mostly complete, which creaks constantly in the breeze. At **Middle Quarters**, you will find vendors at the road-side selling bags of 'swims' (shrimps cooked in pepper sauce).

Black River itself is a faded and rundown Jamaican town on the south coast, but one which was clearly prosperous at the start of the 20th century as there are magnificent gingerbread houses decaying on the waterfront. It made its wealth through exporting dyes – indigo and logwood, which were used in jeans. You can take boat-trips into one of Jamaica's two swamps called the **Great Morass** (the other being in Negril). Tendrils hang like curtains from the extended families of mangrove trees, and great blue herons and jacanas or purple gallinules creep and strut around. You may also see a crocodile flop into the water and cruise lazily away, or pose for a photograph. These crocs are tame enough to be moved around in the water for the best shot. There are three or four daily tours, starting at the dock in town; contact South Coast Safaris, **t** 965 2513, or St Elizabeth Safari, **t** 965 2374.

A few miles down the coast to the east is **Treasure Beach**, a lovely, laid-back seaside town stretched along a series of passable beaches. It is only gradually developing, with the arrival of greater numbers of tourists in recent years, though it has a charming feel when compared to the resort towns on the north coast. The Jamaicans themselves like to go on holiday there.

The coastal road continues through drowsy towns and plains in the shadow of huge forested mountains, to Bluefields, from where Henry Morgan set off to sack Panama in 1670, and then to **Savanna-la-Mar**. The town of Sav-la-Mar, as it is known, is run-down and tatty. Once it was a thriving port, exporting sugar from Frome, but its position on the coast has not always been a blessing as it is scourged by storms – in 1912, a schooner ended up in the main street.

Negril and Around

Twenty miles further on, you come to the western tip of the island and the resort town of **Negril**, which stretches north and south along 7 miles of spectacular beach and 4 miles of ironshore cliffs. The town's well-known hippy history is all but over now that the big players of Jamaican tourism have muscled in on the beachfront space (it has even been gentrified to the point of having a golf course), but it still has a laid-back and easygoing air.

Negril was a pirate haunt, and the crews of corsairs would lie in wait for ships en route from the Spanish Main to Havana. 'Calico' Jack Rackham and his disguised women companions Anne Bonney and Mary Read were captured here in 1720, while on a rum blow-out. They were taken off to Spanish Town and found guilty of piracy, robbery and felony. Rackham was executed and then 'hung out to dry' (in an iron frame) on Rackham Cay off Port Royal, but the two women, who were renowned for being just as fierce as their male counterparts, pleaded pregnancy and were jailed.

The town remained a backwater until a road was built in 1959 and hippies began to wash up here. They rented space on the floor in the local houses and enjoyed the magic mushroom omelettes, the weed, the palm-backed beach and the sunsets. Hanging out is still the main pastime here, on the beach by day and in the bars by night (some quite good bands play in the music parks in Negril). There are not really any sights in Negril, unless you wish to visit the **lighthouse** at the southern end of the West End Rd (south from the roundabout), though you can visit the **Great Morass**, a vast swamp behind the Norman Manley Boulevard, where there are herons and other waders among the mangroves.

Bloody Bay, off the road to Montego Bay, takes its name from the whales that were beached and cut up here, or possibly from pirate battles of centuries past. The road northeast to Montego Bay follows the magnificent coastline, skirting the bays and clambering over lumbering headlands to **Lucea**, the capital of Hanover Parish, which is set on a wide harbour overlooked by cliffs. The clock on the court house in the town was sent here by mistake (it was supposed to have been sent to St Lucia), but the residents kept it and built a special tower, complete with cupola that resembles a German helmet, donated by a German plantation owner. There is a small but worthwhile museum in the town, the **Hanover Museum** (*open Mon–Fri; adm*), in the former workhouse and police station, with displays of historical artefacts of the area since Arawak times – a zemi, an Arawak canoe, coins (quotties, gills, bobs and bits), an orange rinder, a floor brush made from a coconut and a coconut oil lamp called a kitchen bitch.

The North Coast

The north coast of Jamaica is legendary as a tourist destination, the favoured haunt of Britons such as Winston Churchill and Noël Coward, and royal families from all over. The villas of the rich and famous have dotted the hillsides since the 1930s.

Caribbean Sea

Coyoba Resort & Club
Half Moon Club
Ritz-Carlton Rose Hall
Sandals Royal Caribbean
Royal Reef Hotel
Sir Donald Sangster International Airport
Ironshore Relax Villa
Rose Hall Great House
Greenwood
Falmouth
Silver Sands
Montego Bay
Jamaica Safari Village
Rock
Duncans
Sandy Bay
Round Hill Hotel
Reading Reef Club
A1
B11
B10
B5
Tryall Club
A1
Reading
Rockland Bird Feeding Station
Orange River Ranch
Hampden
Good Hope
B10
Anchovy
Good Hope
B11
HANOVER
Lethe
ST JAMES
Great
TRELAWNY
B5
B8
Belvedere Plantation
B6
Cambridge
Maroon Town
Windsor House & Caves
B10
Cockpit Country
B5
WESTMORELAND
Croydon in the Mountains
B8
Seaford Town
Quick Step
B5
Accompong
B6
B10
B5
Apple Valley
Christiana
Bluefields
Maggotty
Appleton
B6
B4
YS Falls
B6
Maggotty Falls
MANCHESTER
N
Middle Quarter
ST ELIZABETH
B6
A2
A2
Black
Shooter's Hill

10 km
5 miles

Today's tourists fly into Montego Bay by the jumbo-load; it is the main airport for the north of the island.

Montego Bay

Situated in the northwest of the island, Montego Bay, or Mo Bay, as it is usually known, is Jamaica's second city. Mo Bay is also Jamaica's tourist heartland; its coastline has become encrusted with humming factory-like hotels for miles and the beaches are awash with lobster-red trippers sizzling in coconut oil. Rude boys joust on their jet skis and higglers apply their high-pressure selling techniques from the roadside. Downtown it is mayhem as the goats and boys pushing handcarts compete for road space and relentless horns and shouts of 'Bag-juice!' interrupt the pulse of dancehall music. Old-time Montego Bay looks on from its Georgian stone buildings and timber houses as it has done for two centuries.

The bay was first named by Columbus for its favourable winds, the 'Golfo de Buen Tiempo', but when the Spaniards settled the area it came to be called Manteca after the butter or pig fat that was its trade. Development was slow because of the maroons in the mountains, but in the 18th century there was big business in sugar ('Monk' Lewis thought it the prettiest town in Jamaica), and then in bananas in the

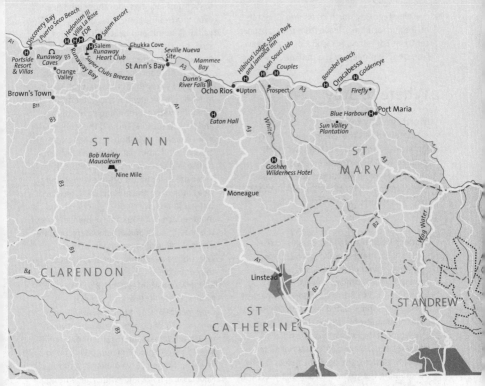

19th century. The latest boom, tourism, began in 1906 with the opening of Doctor's Cave Beach.

The centre of the town itself is **Sam Sharpe Square**, still occasionally called Charles Square, as it was originally known. Sam Sharpe, now a Jamaican national hero, was hanged here, near where his statue stands. His 1831 rebellion went far further than his intended sit-down strike – plantations were torched and riots continued for months – but it speeded the eventual end of slavery. In one corner of the square is the **Cage**, once used as a lock-up for slaves out after curfew at 3pm and drunks or sailors in the town after their curfew at 6pm.

The **St James Parish Church** is behind the square, an imposing structure straight out of England with arched windows and a mahogany interior, which was first erected in 1778. Montego Bay's town **market** (as opposed to the craft market) is on Fustic St, down at the end of Railway Lane, and it is well worth a visit to see the traditional way of buying ground provisions West Indian style. Headed north from the downtown area you come to the main tourist drag on **Gloucester Avenue**, known as the Hip Strip, a mile-long strip of all-day cafés, mid-range package hotels and tourist shops. Modern Mo Bay has spread all over the hills that are the backdrop to the Old Town and along the coastlines for several miles east and west. The surrounding countryside

Getting Around

In Montego Bay, north-coast and Kingston buses and local taxis leave from the transport centre at Barnett St. In Ocho Ríos, buses leave from the terminal near the market.

Where to Stay

Montego Bay t (1 876–)

Montego Bay is the leading resort area in Jamaica and you will find the town itself studded with huge tower blocks of hotel rooms. Farther afield, tucked away in their own coves, are some of the Caribbean's most luxurious resorts.

Luxury

Round Hill Hotel and Villas, 8 miles to the west of Montego Bay, PO Box 64, **t** 956 7050–5, *roundhill@cwjamaica.com*, *www.roundhilljamaica.com*, UK **t** (020) 7730 7144, US **t** 1 800 424 5500. The smartest and most sophisticated resort on the island. The pineapple of traditional West Indian welcome is the leitmotif of the hotel's elegant décor. Round Hill has 27 villas set in hillside gardens; the pool, the blocks (each containing the 36 private rooms), the central foyer and the dining room are ranged around an amphitheatrical slope, with the private bay below them, where there is a beach protected by an offshore reef. Redesigned by Ralph Lauren, the décor uses traditional Jamaican styles, with white louvred screens and latticework offsetting the dark blue and dark green colours of the awnings. Round Hill is elegant but also relaxing, managed by staff who have been here for years. Watersports and a number of other activities are available if the library

palls. The resort has just added a health spa to its list of facilities – for those who need even more pampering.

Tryall Golf, Tennis and Beach Club, PO Box 1206, **t** 956 5660, *info@tryallclub.com*, *www.tryallclub.com*, US and Canada **t** 1 800 336 4571. Another enclave of low-key high luxury lies a few miles further west. The great house, an elegant conglomeration of buildings with overhanging eaves, terraces and balustrades, set around the stone shell of an old plantation house, stands on the crest of a hill amid palm trees, with the golf course and the sea stretching before it. There are 47 very comfortable rooms and 55 villas ranged on the hills behind (these are self-contained, with pools, gardeners and maid service, but you can use the facilities of the hotel). Scuba and other watersports are available, plus tennis and golf; otherwise laze around over lunch and afternoon tea on the veranda.

The Half Moon Montego Bay, 8 miles east of Montego Bay, PO Box 80, **t** 953 2211, *hmooners@infochan.com*, *www.halfmoon. com.jm*, US **t** 1 800 237 3237. A sumptuous resort, set in manicured gardens and buildings of old colonial grandeur, giving on to a lovely half-moon curve of beach. A motif of Neoclassical black and white runs through the resort, from the atrium of the great house to the chequerboard floors and classical columns of many of the rooms. Half Moon is a large hotel (and it does get quite full): there are 340 rooms in all, with 39 swimming-pools, 13 tennis courts and four squash courts, a children's entertainment centre, plenty of watersports (jet skis excluded), plus stables and a golf course. The rooms are set in low blocks attached to the main house; there are also huge suites on the seafront and villas around the grounds.

is dotted with the remnants of 18th-century Jamaica in the plantations and their great houses, some of them restored or turned into hotels. Many of the places mentioned below can be visited on the endless tours arranged from Montego Bay.

South of Montego Bay

The **Rockland Bird Feeding Station** (*t 952 2009; open daily 2.30–5; adm*) in Anchovy, three miles south of Reading, is open to the public in the afternoon, when a stream of

Ritz-Carlton Rose Hall, east of Montego Bay, t 953 2204, *www.ritzcarlton.com*. A concrete monolith that boasts service like none other on the island. An impressive health club and spa, luxurious rooms, traditional English afternoon tea and staff trained to satisfy guests' every whim. Luxury, American-style. Amenities include several excellent restaurants, a fabulous White Witch golf course, tennis facilities and a popular children's programme.

Expensive
Coyaba Resort and Club, Little River, east of Montego Bay, t 953 9150, *coyaba@n5.com.jm*, *www.coyabajamaica.com*. A small beach resort in contemporary Caribbean style, with tall blocks standing over a pool above the beach. There are 50 very comfortable rooms, with terracotta tiles and mock antique furniture; each has a balcony. Life centres on the beach, however, where there is a bar and a deck stretching out into the shallow water towards a reef. Dining takes place in the pretty, vine-covered restaurant or above the beach itself. There's a fitness centre, watersports and the Polo Lounge, a panelled bar with a lively local scene on a Friday night. *All-inclusive packages available.*

Moderate
The Reading Reef Club, Reading, PO Box 225, Reading Post Office, t 952 5909, *rrc@n5. com.jm*, *www.montego-bay-jamaica. com/jhta/reefclub*, US t 1 800 223 6510. This sits on the waterfront across the bay a little out of the town, and is quiet and well off the beaten tourist trail. There are just 28 rooms in three villa-style blocks set in an attractive garden of traveller's palms and heliconia, and the resort stands around a pool on a pleasant if slightly pebbly beach. The rooms

are brightly decorated and furnished with wicker; all have ceiling fans as well as air-con and some have balconies looking out on to the sea. There are some suites. The friendly bar has a wonderful view and, above it, the restaurant serves fine international and Caribbean food, including curried lobster and catch of the day as well as pastas. There is a dive shop on the premises and snorkelling right offshore.

Moderate
The Relax Villa Resort, 26 Hobbs Av, White Sands Beach PO, t 952 7218, *relaxresort@ cwjamaica.com.jm*, US and Canada t 1 800 742 4276. Close to the airport, in a couple of modern blocks set in the tropical gardens of a hillside estate. It's friendly and well run, with large rooms and (one-, two- and three-bedroom) apartments, all of them comfortably decorated in bright white and pastel colours, with balconies, air-con and fans, TVs, etc. The beaches are not within walking distance but are easy to get to by car or taxi. Pick-up from the airport is offered and car hire is available at a reasonable price. It's a good place to start your holiday.

Inexpensive
Ocean View Guest House, Sunset Bd, just above the airport, t 952 2662. Perhaps the friendliest stopover in the area. There are 12 rooms, some air-conditioned and some with fan ventilation. Inexpensive meals are cooked to order and served in the busy central area (where there's a TV and some books), or under parasols on the veranda at the front. There is no pool, but a washroom you can use if you've been to the beach before flying out late in the day.
Ridgeway Guest House, just up the hill from the airport roundabout, t 952 270. Rooms

Jamaica's colourful birdlife heads in for feeding – hummingbirds including the vervain, the Jamaican mango and the doctor bird. You might even get one to sit on your finger while it feeds (*see* 'Flora and Fauna', p.710). You can also see warblers, tanagers and the yellow and black Jamaican oriole on the short walks in the forest.

High in the hills as the name would suggest, **Croydon in the Mountains** (*t 979 8267; open Tues–Wed; adm*) is a working plantation off the road to Cambridge. After a tour of the grounds, where you can see a number of exotic fruits, including strains of

and self-contained apartments with fans and air-con, and meals cooked to order.

El Greco Resort, Queen's Drive, PO Box 1624, **t** 940 6116, *elgreco@n5.com*, *www.elgreco jamaica.com*. Adjacent to the Air Jamaica building, this was originally built for residential use. The spacious one- and two-bedroom apartments have fully equipped kitchens and comfortable living rooms with balconies. There is a pool and two tennis courts. A lift down to Gloucester Avenue will put you in touch with the town, the beach and shops.

Montego Bay to Ocho Ríos **t** (1 876–)

Very Expensive–Expensive

Good Hope Country House, Falmouth, **t** 610 5798, **t** 610 5798, *info@goodhope.com.jm*, *www.goodhope.com.jm*. Set in a restored 18th-century estate house overlooking a fantastic stretch of Trelawny countryside, a patchwork of rich red-brown earth and orchards, against a backdrop of the Cockpit Country. Built of stone and wood, with huge windows and breezy louvres, the house has original antique furniture, planters' chairs, vast glass hurricane lamps, four-poster beds and commodes, all on the original floor of wild orange wood. There are only 10 bedrooms, scattered around the main house, the garden buildings and stables, and so Good Hope never seems full. There is a pool and tennis court, and you can take a ride on horseback through the valley beneath the house – or you can simply watch from the drawing room or the veranda as the view alters constantly with the changing light of the day. Ideal for the lazy life among old Jamaican plantation elegance. Good Hope works as a villa rather than a hotel – you cannot take a simple room, so you will need to get together with friends.

FDR (Franklyn D. Resort), Runaway Bay, PO Box 201, **t** 973 3067, *fdr@infochan.com*, *www.fdrholidays.com*. A resort devoted especially to children, with the slogan 'A giant step for kid kind'. The package is all-inclusive here, but the activity is centred mainly around taking the children off your hands. A 'girl Friday' puts them through their paces at finger painting, tiny tots' computer programming, kiddies disco technique or simply runs them around until they tire out so that you can busy yourself with more important things like windsurfing and sitting at the pool bar. She also cooks and babysits for you. It has 67 modern, high-pastel suites. The same company has opened a similar resort, **FDR Pebbles** (**t** 617 2500, *pebbles@fdrholiday.com*), in Trelawny, where the emphasis is on family-friendly adventure and 'learning as well as fun'.

Hedonism III, Runaway Bay, **t** 973 4100, *www.superclubs.com*. A wild and crazy adult all-inclusive just off the main road in Runaway Bay, where pretty much anything goes. Not for the timid.

Moderate

Royal Reef Hotel, Greenwood, **t** 953 1700, *royalreef@cwjamaica.com*, *www.royal-reef.com*. On the Montego Bay/Trelawny border, the Royal Reef has 19 comfortable air-conditioned rooms with hairdryers and satellite TV. The atmosphere is welcoming and quiet. Greenwood Great House (once the summer home of Elizabeth Barrett Browning) is nearby and well worth a quick tour.

Portside Resort and Villas, Discovery Bay, PO Box 42, **t** 973 2007. A small and concentrated cluster of pointy-topped villas in the town

pineapple – bullhead, natty, cowboy, Natal queen and smooth cayenne – you can see how coffee is grown and harvested (pulping, fermenting, drying, hulling, selecting, roasting and eventually grinding and brewing). For a plantation visit with a twist, head for the Montpelier Plantation in the hills west of Montego Bay, where you can swing through the treetops on a harness system of traverse cables and pulleys. The canopy tour is run by Chukka Blue Adventure Tours (**t** 953 5619, *info@chukkablue.com*, *www.chukkablue.com*).

overlooking Discovery Bay. They vary in size from one bedroom to five; you can cater for yourself or use the central hotel facilities. The central dining room is right on the waterfront and the resort has its own beach, next to the main Puerto Seco Beach. Cooks are available.

Runaway Bay HEART Hotel, Runaway Bay, PO Box 98, **t** 610 5798. Set in a stately house surrounded by extensive, well-tended gardens a short way in from the coast, this has the feel of old Jamaica. There are 20 comfortable rooms with balconies, air-con and phones, but no TVs. A shuttle takes you to the beach. The service is energetic and enthusiastic if a little raw, as most of the staff are drawn from the hotel training school. It is a quiet and fun place to stay.

Inexpensive

Salem Resort, Salem, **t** 973 4256. A slightly unfortunate position right on the road in Salem, east of Runaway Bay, but offers comfortable rooms with TVs and balconies in a modern block at reasonable prices; meals are available.

Ocho Ríos to Port Maria t (1 876–)

Ocho Ríos has put in a late bid as Jamaica's leading tourist centre (it used to be a sleepy fishing village), but it has a string of good beaches, and there are some excellent hotels in the town, plus a string of restaurants, bars and clubs to keep everyone occupied in the evening.

Luxury–Very Expensive

The Jamaica Inn, PO Box 1, **t** 974 2514, US res **t** 1 800 243 9240, *jamminn@infochan.com*, *www.jamaicainn.com*. Two miles from the centre of the town is one of Jamaica's most elegant hotels. Its setting is magnificent,

enclosed in its own pretty bay, with a fantastic stretch of sand between small headlands. The old white and Wedgwood-blue estate house has a gracious colonial air, echoed in the old plantation style of the columns and balustrades, and louvred doors and fantail coolers above them. Each impeccably decorated room looks out on to the sea from an external living room on its own colonnaded balcony. There is a pool and some watersports (kayaks and sunfish) if you are feeling active, or the library and Scrabble if the desire should pass. Just 45 rooms and a certain formality (a jacket and tie are required in the winter season) but friendly: the staff recognize guests who return year after year.

Goldeneye, Oracabessa, **t** 975 3354, *golden eye@islandoutpost.com*, *www.island outpost.com*, UK **t** 0800 169 5884, US **t** 1 800 OUT POST, *reservations@island*. Ten rooms set in the original villa and in the gardens surrounding Ian Fleming's estate, Goldeneye, where he wrote many of his James Bond novels (his bulletwood desk is still in one of the rooms). The main house is now decorated in Asian style and each room has an impressive outdoor bathroom, enclosed in a wall of bamboo, where you shower beneath banana trees. Situated on cliffs, there are tiny coves just below for swimming. A hip retreat, very private (each of the cottages is self-contained, with cook, butler and housemaid).

Sans Souci Resort and Spa, PO Box 103, **t** 994 1206, *info@sansoucijamaica.com*, *www.san soucijamaica.com*. All but hidden in an explosively fertile Jamaican garden, Sans Souci is a modern version of the luxury that the name implies. It lies 4 miles beyond the town centre and the 70 rooms with balconies stand on the hillside above the

Seaford Town is the home of the descendants of German families who arrived in 1835. The community has become inbred and many have emigrated, but the blond features and blue eyes of the 200 or so that remain are clearly visible, even if they hold themselves more like Jamaicans when they dance.

Passing the village of Maggotty the road and railway come to **Appleton Sugar Estate** (*adm and rum-tasting on offer in the reception area*), set in swathes of cane that make Jamaica's most famous rum. During working hours, there is a tour of the

hotel spa, with its swimming pool and work-out area, around the point from the beach, where most watersports are available. *All inclusive.*

Expensive

Couples, PO Box 330, east of Ocho Ríos, **t** 974 4271, *couplesresort@couples.com*, *www.couples.com*. Here you will find an action-packed regime of daytime water-sports and other essential activities like massage and pool volleyball. Everything happens in pairs here, from the swimming-pool loungers to the cocktails (the bar is open all day of course). Breakfast and lunch are buffets, but dinner is *à deux*, à la carte. You must arrive in a man–woman couple, which may well put you right off the place! *All inclusive.*

Shaw Park Beach Hotel, PO Box 17, **t** 974 2552, *shawparkbchhtl@cwjamaica.com*, *www.shawparkhotel.com*, UK **t** (020) 7581 4094. This centres on an Edwardian-style villa, with wooden panelling and solid furni-ture, that stands above a protected cove with an excellent beach, where a number of watersports are available, including glass-bottomed boat trips, windsurfing, sunfish and scuba diving. Its 118 rooms and suites are comfortable and modern and all have a balcony or terrace with air-conditioning, phones and a view across the sea; most of the rooms have TVs. The waterfront terrace provides a lovely setting for dinner; there's evening entertainment and Ocho Ríos town is not too far off.

Moderate

Hibiscus Lodge Hotel, 83 Main St, Ocho Ríos, PO Box 52, **t** 974 2676, *mdoswald@cwjamaica.com*. Stands in very pretty gardens on the clifftops in town. The pool, some of the rooms, the dining room and bar (where the chairs are slung from the ceiling) are all set on stepped terraces on the cliffside itself, shaded by tropical greenery and a huge almond tree (from which the restaurant takes its name). It is quite private and has a friendly atmosphere and charming setting. There is snorkelling down below in the daytime, and some entertainment in the evenings. Rooms are comfortable if not luxurious.

Ocean Sands Resort, 14 James Av, Ocho Ríos, **t** 974 2605, *oceansands@cwjamaica.com*, *www.oceansandsresorts.com*. Another good option in the middle range, this offers excel-lent value for money. The small hotel is in a simple modern block above its own small strip of sand and shallow water out to the reef, and it has a friendly, quite homey atmosphere. There are 28 pretty pastel-decorated rooms, all with tiled floors, tele-phones and air-con or a fan (some with balconies), overlooking the pool and the restaurant which sit above the sea on a deck. Some evening entertainment.

Pier View Apartments, PO Box 134, Ocho Ríos, **t** 974 2607. A short walk from the Ocho Ríos Bay Beach and set right in the centre of town, you will find a small number of slightly cheaper rooms here. The rooms are cheaper than the suites and they are set in two modern blocks above a crammed garden. All have TV, air-con and fan and most have balconies; some suites have kitchens. No pool or dining room, but all the restaurants are close by. Some *inexpen-sive* rooms.

Inexpensive

James Avenue, at the lower end of the market, is a good area to find inexpensive accommodation.

---

distillery, which produces 10 million litres of rum each year in the column stills and the oak barrels of the cool storage house. You might be lucky and get a tour of the sugar factory itself, where the canes are crushed on conveyors and the liquid is boiled and then granulated in a centrifuge.

Not far off are **YS Falls** (**t** 634 2454; *open daily; adm exp*), some of Jamaica's most beautiful waterfalls. En route, you can concentrate on the spectacular scenery, open fields like parkland with isolated trees where Jamaican red poll cattle graze the luxu-rious grass. There are bars at the reception area and at the falls themselves, where you

Marine View Hotel, 9 James Av, Ocho Rios, t 974 5753. The building is uncompromisingly concrete, with pink, white and grey décor, but the large tiled rooms are available at good rates (the cheapest are the ones with ceiling fans). There is a pool and a restaurant where you can get meals throughout the day.

Hummingbird Haven, PO Box 95, t 974 5188. Just up from the White River on the main road, this is a garden retreat set in 6 acres of forested hillside, near the beach. There are a few simple cabins and endless tent sites. A restaurant is nearby but there are also limited cooking facilities available; it's a friendly stopover for travellers.

Tamarind Great House, t 994 0817. Inland (look for the turn-off to Sun Valley Plantation), the Tamarind overlooks a fertile valley of farmland and fruit groves. A stunning view awaits from this newly built 10-bedroom 'great house' run by an English couple who are eager to share their love of the island with guests. Ask them to take you to Crescent Waterfall for a refreshing dip in the cool waters and buy a bottle of home-made pimento liqueur before you leave.

Goshen Wilderness Resort, lost in the country to the south of Ocho Rios (signed off the White River Road). Very basic accommodation (cabins and tent space) and a serene atmosphere. Recently sold; so enquire locally before setting out.

Eating Out

Montego Bay

Montego Bay has a good selection of restaurants, in and outside the hotels, some of them in very elegant surroundings. Eating out is pretty expensive though, so you may want to go local some of the time.

Expensive

Marguerite's Seafood by the Sea, Gloucester Av, t 952 4777. The finest seafood restaurant in town. The large menu features fresh Caribbean fish, shrimp and lobster, pasta dishes and steaks. For the best view and most intimate atmosphere, request a table outside on the deck or on the Almond Terrace and listen as the waves crash to the rocks below. Diners get free entry to Margueritaville next door, a restaurant by day that transforms into a disco at night. Complimentary pick-up from most hotels. *Dinner only.*

Town House, Gloucester Avenue, t 952 2660. Recently, the restaurant abandoned its location in a historic mansion in the old part of town and moved to the 'hip strip' – the main drag of restaurants and nightlife in Montego Bay. The menu is international with some Jamaican flavours: red snapper is served as a papillotte, cooked in a cheese, wine and lobster sauce, and Jamaican chicken curry is served with breadfruit, ackee and plantain.

Akbar, t 979 0113. Serves the same spicy Indian cuisine as the original in Kingston and is a favourite with the locals.

Moderate

The Houseboat, t 979 8845. A fondue restaurant, an unlikely concept for the Caribbean, but an original one and actually quite fun. The houseboat itself sits on the lagoon in the Freeport area and you ride across to it on a small hand-drawn ferry floating on oil barrels. There are three courses, all of them fondues: cheese sauce and wine to begin with, into which you dip Jamaican hard-

can swim. In recent years the 2,000-acre site has expanded to become one of Jamaica's main tourist attractions.

North of this area is the **Cockpit Country**, a weird landscape of shaggy hillocks like 300ft haystacks. They were carved into their regular, egg-box shape by water action as it fell on the limestone plateau. Even today, the Cockpit Country is very remote country: two centuries ago, it was the maroon heartland, and in the south is the infamous area known by soldiers as the 'land of the look-behind' – it was so treacherous that they would apparently ride back to back on their horses. The maroons held out

dough bread; then the meats and vegetables – steak, chicken, shrimp and plantain – with Béarnaise, spicy tomato and teriyaki sauces and mango chutney; and finally, a chocolate fondue, made of local Jamaican chocolate, into which you dip fresh Caribbean fruits. Take a constitutional on the upper deck and admire the lights of the Bogue Hills.

The Pelican, Gloucester Av, t 952 3171. An ever-popular spot for a trusty Jamaican meal (and some more regular international fare). It is set in a modern and aggressively air-conditioned room, with quick service, but it pulls a lively crowd of Jamaicans and tourists and you can get a curry goat or a brown stew with rice cooked in coconut milk. Locals will tell you they serve the best malted milk-shakes in town and their Sunday breakfast of ackee and saltfish has become something of an institution.

Tapas, Gloucester Av, t 971 1921. A tiny restaurant on the patio of the chef's home, overlooking the sea and Gloucester Avenue. The Mediterranean-inspired menu features fresh seafood, unusual dishes like steak marinated in coffee and, of course, tapas. *Dinner only.*

The Groovy Grouper Beach Bar & Grill, Gloucester Avenue, t 9528287. Good local cuisine with an emphasis on seafood. You can dine on the decks by the beach from 11am until well into the evening when the last person leaves.

Guangzhou, Gloucester Av, t 952 6200. Serves reasonably priced Chinese dishes.

The Brewery, t 940 2433. Another popular grill and bar with a lively weekend trade.

Ritz-Carlton Rose Hall, t 953 2204. Afternoon tea here is an elegant option that is fast becoming popular with Montego Bay's 'ladies who lunch'.

Inexpensive

There are endless bars which double as simple eateries along Gloucester Avenue, offering burgers, salads and sandwiches, usually with music, sometimes a live band. Many of these restaurants stay open all day. There are plenty of stalls around the downtown area for a lunchtime patty.

Smokey Joe's, a little alley off St James's St, t 952 1155. If you want to go a little more local, try lunch at this downtown dingy dining room. Delicious pumpkin soup is followed by curry goat and rice 'n' peas or a fish platter and a Red Stripe.

Pork Pit, t 952 1046, Gloucester Av, opposite Aquasol. A classic among jerk centres and something of an institution. It serves excellent jerk – chicken and pork, some 'spear ribs' and sausage – which is hacked to pieces before you, tossed into a basket and thrust through the small window. You eat at picnic tables, mitigating the effect of their electrifying jerk sauce with a festival roll, yam or sweet potato. Also on offer are some Jamaican standards: steam fish and rice 'n' peas.

Island Grill, Harbour St. Has good local fast food including fish steamed in foil, grilled chicken sandwiches and pumpkin and callaloo rice.

Juici Patties, St James St in the middle of town. Mo Bay's answer to the Tastee original and quite good. The island-wide chain is known for its Jamaican turnovers.

Montego Bay to Ocho Ríos

Moderate–Inexpensive

Far Out Fish Hut, Greenwood, t 954 7155. Cooks fish, conch and lobster to order in a thatched hut by the sea. Seating is outside and in the open so best at night when the temperature drops. If you're in a hurry, call ahead to order.

here (*see* 'History', p.704), in settlements where the villages of Accompong, Maroon Town and Quick Step are today, descending to attack the plantations at night. The maroons, who still have some autonomy and self-government, celebrate their treaty with the British each year on 6th January in Accompong.

Montego Bay to Ocho Ríos

Rose Hall Great House (*t* 953 2323; *open daily 9–6; adm exp*) is Jamaica's most famous great house, an imposing Georgian mansion that stands on the hillside

Glistening Waters, Main Street, Falmouth, t 954 3229. You can get a tasty conch and a beer: sit on a breezy wooden deck at the waterfront surrounded by deep-sea fishing boats. It serves a good conch as a starter and then wholesome Jamaican food: chicken or fish with a heap of coleslaw and coconut-flavoured rice. You can see the phosphorescence in the bay from here and the restaurant has a boat in which you can take a tour of the lagoon.

Time 'n Place, near the Trelawny Beach Hotel, t 954 4371. A charming bar and restaurant, thatch-covered bamboo shacks with a sandy floor and festooned with greenery, right on the waves. Burgers, seafood and fries.

Ocho Rios

Ocho Rios has only a few good restaurants outside the hotels.

Expensive

Evita's, t 974 2333. The most pleasant restaurant, for its setting high above the lights of Ocho Rios, in a charming old 1860s house. You enter through an arbour of four-poster bedposts. You can dine outside on a vine-hung veranda, or in the attractive wooden interior with its stained-wood floor and louvres. The fare is Italian, including dishes from a classic fettucine Alfredo to a Fra Diavolo, but there are also some Caribbean–Italian combinations – pasta escovicha and lasagne rastafari.

Passage to India, upstairs in Soni's Plaza, Main St, t 795 3182. A good local Indian restaurant.

Toscanini's, Harmony Hall Art Gallery just outside town, t 975 4785. Popular for its Italian dishes and garden setting. It is the best restaurant in the Ocho Rios area and one of the best in Jamaica, operated by a brother-sister team. The menu, based on fresh products, is changed daily for lunch and dinner.

The Almond Tree, 83 Main St, t 974 2813. A very sympathetic setting at the Hibiscus Lodge Hotel, on the main street of Ocho Rios. You dine on a terrace high above the sea, with gingerbread fretwork surrounded by greenery and a huge almond tree. Pumpkin soup is followed by snapper or kingfish in coconut and then a volley of tropical fruit ice creams. *At the lower end of expensive.*

Café Aubergine, on the main road to Kingston at Moneague, t 973 0527. Although the service at this restored 18th-century carriage house can be slow, the imaginative French and Italian meals like crayfish Provençale and flame-roasted suckling pig are worth the wait. A truly unique setting and ambience. *Open Wed–Sun; reservations highly recommended for dinner.*

Moderate

Many of the bars in the town double up as restaurants, and so you can take a drink and look at the menu before you decide whether to eat.

Spring Garden Café, Ocho Ríos Bypass Road, t 795 3149. Specializes is seafood, available in a variety of preparations for conch, crab, lobste and shrimp. There are vegetarian dishes as well. Inside and outside seating and ample parking space.

Bibibips, t 974 8759. A bar with a reliable kitchen set beneath a tin-roofed TV-bar that has a balustraded seating area on the clifftop just behind a car park; the menu is plain and wholesome Jamaican food.

Hard Rock Café. You might think that it was just another over-imaginative T-shirt, but in fact there really is a Hard Rock here. It offers simple fare, such as grilled fish and shrimp fettucine, and a long list of cocktails, which

10 miles east of Montego Bay. Built in the 1770s, Rose Hall has been restored to its former splendour as the most illustrious manor on the island, with mahogany floors and panelling, chandeliers, period antiques and some very attractive silk wallpaper painted with tropical birds and palm trees. But Rose Hall is most famous for the legend of its mistress Annie Palmer, who came here in 1820. A renowned beauty, feared as a black magician, she is supposed to have got through three husbands (by poisoning, by stabbing and then pouring boiling oil into his ears, and by strangling) and innumerable lovers, including slaves, whom she simply killed when she was

you can take around the waterfall, or sip while making use of the pool table.

Duble V. For something a little more Jamaican, try one of the two jerk centres: this one is very touristy and lunch comes complete with MC accompaniment, loud music and embarrassing dancing competitions.

Ocho Ríos Jerk Centre, near the 'roundabout' to Kingston, **t** 974 2549. This is a much more low-key spot, also popular with the locals after work.

White River Ranch Bar Restaurant & Games, on the edge of Ocho Ríos in an open shed, **t** 974 6932. Home cooking of local specialties, such as steamed fish, chicken and chips and fried rice.

Coconuts on the Bay, Fisherman's Point, **t** 975 0064. An Ocho Ríos standby for light fare and snacks, with a new location by the cruise ship pier.

Inexpensive

On weekend evenings, people sell 'pan-chicken' at the roadside in Ocho Ríos.

The Blue Cantina, Main St, **t** 974 2430. A modest dining room famous for its tacos and Mexican-Jamaican food.

The Mug, west of the town near St Ann's Bay. Popular with the locals, in a rustic setting at the water's edge. It attracts a fun crowd, particularly on a Wednesday.

Bars and Nightlife

Montego Bay

The major gathering point is along Gloucester Avenue.

Walter's. Has a garden bar with television (you can keep up with the NFL at most bars in the area), popular with tourists; you can sit inside or in the open air under parasols.

Brewery. Another busy watering hole; the air-conditioned lounge bar has leather benches, stained wood and brass.

Margueritaville. Probably the liveliest spot. Popular Kingston DJs spin every Saturday night and there is a live one-man band in the rooftop bar. The 110ft waterslide is open every day (when the dancefloor is converted into a restaurant) and on special nights.

Blue Beat, Gloucester Avenue, **t** 952 4777, *www.margaritavillecaribbean.com*. A new martini bar and jazz club by the same owners of Margueritaville (above). A multi-million dollar project, Blue Beat features state-of-the-art lighting and sound equipment with live jazz for hours nightly. New talent, as well as established musicians, are hosted. Light Asian and Caribbean cuisine is served each night.

Pier One, near the centre of the downtown area. A very lively bar, particularly on Fridays, when it will often double as a dance venue.

Ocho Ríos

Ocho Ríos is upbeat and so, outside the hotels, where there are plenty of shows, you will find a string of bars and clubs.

The Cocktail Lounge, Jam Palace, Main St. An easygoing upstairs bar with a loud crowd.

Little Pub. You can often hear loud rock music and there are shows in the evening.

Roof Club, St James's Av. A locals' club with an open-air lounge and rooftop terrace where you will hear the latest sounds on the Jamaican scene, as well as some more traditional reggae.

Wicky-Wacky Club. For something a little more sultry, such as a dose of Jamaican go-go dancing.

White River Reggae Park. Occasional concerts.

Amnesia, Main Street. DJ, reggae, drinks and dancing.

bored with them. She was eventually murdered in her bed. There is a bar and restaurant downstairs in the barrel-vaulted cellar, with photographs taken by visitors in which mysterious faces appear. There is apparently no evidence for the legend, but an amusing version was written up by H. G. de Lisser in his *White Witch of Rose Hall*.

Another magnificent plantation great house, **Greenwood** (**t** *953 1077, www.green woodhouse-jamaica.com; open daily 9–6; adm*), sits high on the hillside 4 miles farther on, also comanding a magnificent view over the coastline. Built in the late 1700s, it was a home for many years of the Barrett family, from which the poet Elizabeth

Barrett Browning was descended, and it is still lived in. On view are musical instruments, including wind-up organs and an excellent polyphon, the old carriages and portraits and the Barrett family library. The view from the veranda is so broad that you can see the curvature of the earth.

On the coastal road, on the fringes of a mangrove swamp, the **J. Charles Swaby Swamp Safari** (*t 954 3065; open Mon–Sat 9–4*) makes for a slightly odd experience. It is really a small zoo, with snakes, iguanas and some birds, but it is best known for its crocodiles, which lurk in the mangroves with huge diabolic and toothy smiles. This was the film location for James Bond's lucky escape from a sticky marooning in *Live and Let Die*, when he used crocodiles as stepping stones. Unfortunately, the stuntman, Ross Kananga (who owned the farm), did not fare so well on an earlier take of the shot: he fell in and had to have 193 stitches.

Just down the road is the town of **Falmouth**, capital of Trelawny Parish and site of some of the finest Georgian architecture on the island. The town was founded in 1790 and for a time was the busiest port on the north coast, but the sugar trade declined and the town faded with it. Nowadays Falmouth is a fairly ordinary Jamaican town, best known for its market on Wednesdays, in which goods are brought from abroad for distribution to shops all over the western part of the island.

The main road passes **St Peter's**, the parish church (supposedly a direct copy of the church in Falmouth in Cornwall in England) and then heads through the centre of the town, turning at the red-tin-roofed market building and a large roundabout, a tank which was once the town's water supply. From here, you can glimpse the older area of town, well worth a look, where some of the original Georgian buildings are still standing, with verandas supported on stilts, reaching out over the pavement, and timber-frame upper storeys on stonework bases. Some have recently been restored. Look out for the huge **court house**, and **Market St**, with the post office and the Methodist manse. On the point the fort is tired and dilapidated, its barracks now a school. Just east of Falmouth is a phosphorescent lagoon at **Rock**. You can arrange a trip from the deck restaurant, Glistening Waters: it is best seen on a moonless night when there has been no rain (the outflow of the Martha Brae dissipates the microscopic protozoa which emit light when stirred). South of here on the fringes of the Cockpit Country are the **Windsor Caves** where, conducted by torchlight, you will see rock formations in the shape of a hand and of Moses. If you're in luck, the guide might even play a tune for you on the stalactites.

For the next 20 miles the main road to Ocho Ríos and Kingston runs inland and then skirts the coastline, which is lined with endless snack bars, fruit stalls and rum shops, until it comes to Discovery Bay. This is named after Columbus's arrival here in 1494 (so the history runs, though some dispute the point of landing). He is commemorated in **Columbus Park** (*adm free*), a small museum park with a few artefacts at the roadside. At first, it seems a little unadventurous but in fact it is worth a good look because it gives an excellent overview of Jamaican agricultural and industrial history. **Runaway Bay** takes its name from another moment in Jamaican history, when the last Spaniards gathered in 1655 before making a break for Cuba 90 miles to the north. The seven miles of the **Runaway Caves** (*open daily 9–5*) have been used by other runaways – slaves and pirates – and latterly by disco-goers. They are firmly on the tourist trail (yet more carvings for sale), but merit a visit for a swim in the Green Grotto and to see the extraordinary and alarmingly long, snake-like, thigh-thick fig-tree roots which have made their way down into the caves in search of water.

Inland, beyond the stunningly fertile areas of the Orange Valley, **Brown's Town** has a cut-stone and wood church, which stands opposite a classic Caribbean iron market, to which the local farmers bring their produce from the hills around. At Nine Miles, seemingly lost in the Jamaican interior, you will find the **Bob Marley Mausoleum** (*adm; no cameras*), on a hillside in the town of his birth, now behind a huge chain-link fence and barbed wire. The mausoleum itself is made of grey marble and is adorned with gifts and dedications sent to the singer. You'll be hustled like mad and told all sorts of tall stories.

Back on the coast, you pass between the site of **Nueva Sevilla**, the first Spanish settlement of 1510 (where a few remains are still visible), and **Seville Great House**, which stands high on the hill; built in 1750, the original wattle and daub walls still exist beneath the plaster. It houses an exhibit called Maima-Seville, commemorating the many influences that have contributed to Jamaica today (Arawak Indian, European and African) with a video presentation. A little farther on is the town of **St Ann's Bay**, capital of the parish of St Ann. It is the birthplace of Marcus Garvey, the Jamaican national hero and founder of the UNIA (*see* 'History', p.705) and he is remembered with a statue in front of the town library. Seven miles farther along the coast you come to the resort town of Ocho Ríos, announced by a small fortress (don't bother to investigate – it contains the local sewage plant) and the enormous bauxite shipping station just before the town.

Ocho Ríos

Ocho Ríos, or 'Ochi' as it is often known, is Jamaica's second tourist town, about 70 miles over the hill from Kingston and the same from Montego Bay. It is another busi-nesslike tourist town that was created in the 1960s from a tiny fishing village on a magnificent beach. It is a little ugly and has developed completely without plan, but it is business as usual as two or three cruise ships call in some days and the tourists come in droves. Ocho Ríos has some of the island's best beaches and a couple of Jamaica's smartest hotels as well as a string of high-pressure fun-factory resorts. The name, which looks as though it might come from 'eight rivers' in the vicinity, is more likely a corruption of Las Chorreras, meaning waterfalls or spouts, of which there were many coming off the hills that rise immediately behind the town. Ocho Ríos has no real centre, apart from the clocktower, or perhaps the new entertainment and shop-ping complex called **Island Village** (*t 888 VILLAGE, www.islandvillageja.com*), situated at the entrance to the cruise ship pier. Such unashamed tourism and lack of heritage make Ocho Ríos feel a little soulless at times, but, of course, that doesn't mean you don't get a good holiday there.

In the hills south of Ocho Ríos, the village of **Walkerswood** (*t 800 827 0769, www.walkerswood.com*) has a cooperative, well-known for its excellent and extensive range of Jamaican food products. Begun two decades ago as a simple effort to provide employment for the villagers, it has grown into a multi-million dollar enterprise, employing over 100 people and exporting its products round the world. There is a guided tour for visitors, and the opportunity to buy the likes of canned ackee, jerk seasoning, rundown sauce and sorrel chutney.

Dunn's River Falls (*open daily 8–5; start at the bottom and buy another carving at the top; adm*) is probably Jamaica's most famous sight, a series of waterfalls that tumble 600ft from top to bottom. It is a bit of a rigmarole as you have to join a conga of other tourists, holding hands and clearly dicing with death as you edge gingerly up among the relentless two- and three-foot cascades, but it is a quite beautiful and surprising feature and if you take it all with a pinch of salt it can be quite fun. Wear rubber-soled shoes and prepare to get soaked. Nearby, at **Dolphin Cove** (*t 974 5335, www.dolphincovejamaica.com; open daily 8.30–5.30*), you can swim with dolphins, pet sting rays and sharks and follow a nature trail. Admission, which includes entrance to Dunn's River Falls, is expensive, but worth it for a once-in-a-lifetime experience (dolphin encounters by reservation only).

The road to Kingston leads south out of town from the roundabout up into the mountains towards Moneague. As it climbs, the road passes through **Fern Gully**, an absurdly fertile chasm three miles long where the vegetation makes a tunnel over the road and only angled shafts of sunlight penetrate to the gulley floor. Creepers and lianas tangle and many of Jamaica's 500 varieties of fern explode in the upper branches of the trees. Until a few years ago, the gulley was alive with fireflies at night, but now the petrol fumes have killed them off.

There are a number of gardens on the hills above Ocho Ríos. **Coyaba River Garden and Museum** (*t 795 0907; adm*) is set in a cleft shaded by huge cedar trees. You take a guided tour among the waterfalls and streams, where you will see impatiens (or Busy Lizzie), Poor Man's Orchid (on the cloven-leafed bauhinia tree) and many palms such as the makali palm, with fronds shaped like fans. The museum gives a quick view of St Ann's Parish since Arawak times – old maps, quaint colonial pictures and more recent island life. The **Shaw Park Botanical Gardens** (*t 974 2723; open daily 8–5*) are also laid out on a hillside, where two rivers run down into multi-layered lily ponds. Here, you will see a stunning range of ornamental tropical plants including heliconias, ginger lilies and red shrimp plants.

Ocho Ríos to Port Maria

Heading east from Ocho Ríos, over the White River (good swimming if you follow it up on the backroads, including Irie Beach, *see* p.709), you come to the **Prospect Plantation** (*open daily 10.30–3.30; adm*). There are three daily tours of its grounds, where many of Jamaica's plantation crops are set out on view, including cassava, banana, coffee and, of course, sugar cane. See how unripe ackee was used for soap in old-time Jamaica. Horseback rides are available into the mountains. Close by is **Harmony Hall**, a very pretty, turreted estate house from the 19th century which has been restored with gingerbread fretwork and tray ceilings. Now it houses a restaurant, gallery and craft shop; upstairs there are paintings by artists who have worked in the island and by the Jamaican 'Intuitives'. There are displays of crafts from around the Caribbean and temporary exhibitions and regular craft fairs. Downstairs is Toscanini Restaurant.

On the hill above the town of Port Maria is Noël Coward's house **Firefly** (*adm; video and tour*), chosen with customary discernment because from its 1,000ft vantage point it has perhaps the finest view in the whole of the Caribbean. The view takes in the Blue Mountains to the south and the northern coastline where the successive headlands outreach one another into the Caribbean Sea. Coward lived here for the last 23 years of his life until he died in 1973 (the same site was chosen by Henry Morgan 300 years before him: his old kitchen is still standing and now contains a café and gift shop, with Noël Coward paintings transferred onto T-shirts and baseball caps of all unlikely things). Noël Coward is buried in the garden under a simple marble tablet. The house has been restored as he left it, with his musical scores, records, crockery as used by the Queen Mum on a visit, and some paintings still on view.

Author Ian Fleming, creator of the character James Bond, lived on the coast nearby (at Oracabessa) from 1946 until his death in 1964, in a house called **Goldeneye**. The name James Bond was borrowed from the cover of a book by one of Jamaica's other renowned birdwatchers, an ornithologist this time, the author of *The Birds of the West Indies*. The house is now a hotel. Also nearby is the James Bond Beach Club (*t 975 3663, www.islandjamaica.com; open Tue–Sun; adm*), a beach and entertainment complex with watersports facilities and a restaurant.

Following the coastal road farther east, you come to **Port Maria**, the capital of St Mary Parish, which sits on a stunning bay but has little to recommend it. The island in the bay, Cabarita Island, is named after the Spanish word for goat: animals were let loose here so that sailors would have a supply of fresh meat in the early days of Caribbean exploration. Some way inland on a rickety road is **Sun Valley Plantation** (*t 995 3075; three tours each weekday, 9, 11, 3; adm*), a working banana plantation. A two-hour nature tour includes the history of the plantation and takes you through the cultivation of a number of tropical plants and trees and their uses in herbal medicine. On Mondays, visitors can watch coconut water being bottled.

The Cayman Islands

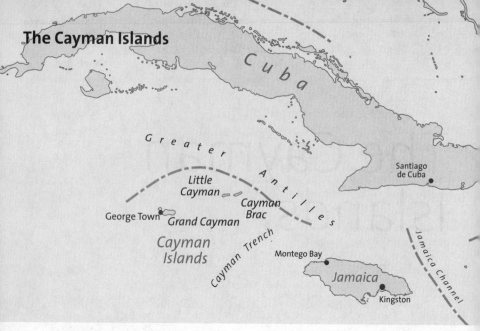

The Cayman Islands

Cuba

Greater Antilles

Santiago de Cuba

Little Cayman

Cayman Brac

George Town

Grand Cayman

Cayman Islands

Cayman Trench

Montego Bay

Jamaica

Kingston

Jamaica Channel

Highlights

1 Dive Bloody Bay Wall off Little Cayman, encrusted with corals
2 Swim among tarpon and barracuda in Tarpon Alley, or see them being fed nightly at the Wharf Restaurant on Grand Cayman
3 Swim with rays at Stingray City off Grand Cayman

The tiny Cayman Islands are well known globally as an offshore banking centre, the official home to massive corporations, but they are equally celebrated among diving fiends as having some of the finest coral grounds in the Caribbean. Successfully managed, the two industries have combined to make the Cayman Islands the most prosperous islands in the Caribbean for their size.

The three Cayman Islands, often collectively referred to simply as 'Cayman' (with the emphasis on the second syllable), lie in the western Caribbean, northwest of Jamaica and south of Miami and Cuba. They are the coral-encrusted summits of a submarine mountain range (around them the slopes descend to the Bartlett Deep and the Cayman Trough, at 3,500 fathoms the deepest water in the Caribbean). The islands are in two groups, separated by 89 miles of sea. In the south is Grand Cayman, where the capital George Town is situated. Its two partners are to the northeast: Cayman Brac and Little Cayman are just five miles apart.

No point on Cayman rises to more than 140ft, and so they do not have the rainfall and the luxurious greenery of other Caribbean islands. They are covered mainly in a tangle of scrubby forest and mangrove swamps, with superb beaches along some of the coasts. There is not much wildlife on land, just the ubiquitous Caribbean goat and a few indigenous iguanas (though there are endemic parrots on Grand Cayman and

Cayman Brac). Turtles still visit the islands, but the marine crocodile, from which the name 'cayman' comes, is no longer seen. Venture beneath the waterline, though, and the natural life is amazing. The Cayman Islands have a stunning variety of corals, sponges and tropical fish in excellent, clean water.

There are about 24,000 Caymanians in a current population of 40,000 and they are some of the most approachable people in the Caribbean. Most live in the towns of Grand Cayman; Cayman Brac has a population of about 1,600 and Little Cayman just 115. About half the islanders have a mix of African and European blood: you will come to recognize the familiar orange-red of the Caymanian hair. Caymanian English is easy to understand; if you hear a different patois, it is probably Jamaican. Unlike other Caribbean islands, there is no hustling and very little crime in Cayman. The islands are strongly influenced by the USA: home-delivery pizzas; massive, petrol-guzzling cars; satellite television; cheery American restaurants; and the occasional desperate-looking person power-walking their way along the West Bay Road in the midday heat. In places, Grand Cayman looks as though it is in danger of becoming an outsized shopping precinct.

The Cayman Islands package is very slick. The islands are hardly cheap, but what they offer they do well. It's ideal for high-pressure executives who want comfort on call and a by-the-hour, percentage return on their leisure time (if you begin to feel out of touch, you can always hire a cellular phone and call the broker). You can even take an extra-curricular course in the advantages of offshore banking in the Caymans. However, Seven Mile Beach in Grand Cayman is an ideal vacation destination, and elsewhere on the islands you can still experience a slow and gentle pace of life ideal for a break from the humdrum.

In September 2004, Grand Cayman suffered one of the worst hurricanes in its history, causing enormous damage across the island. Her sister islands of Cayman Brac and Little Cayman were spared the worst of the winds. The airport resumed normal operations within a matter of months, as did many of the hotels and tourist attractions. By winter 2005–6, even those hotels and businesses that were worst hit expect to be fully restored. Nonetheless, you should check with the tourist board before finalizing your plans.

History

As Columbus passed Cayman Brac on his fourth voyage in 1503, he saw 'two very small and low islands, full of tortoises, as was the sea all about' and it was the animals that gave their name to the islands. Columbus called them the Tortugas after the turtles, but a while later they became known as Los Lagartos (from 'alligators'); eventually the name Caymanas stuck, taken from the crocodiles and iguanas seen there. The first reference to Grand Cayman was by Portuguese sailors, who called it Cayo Manos when they passed in 1526.

Initially, Little Cayman became a stopover for its reliable supply of fresh water and the easily available food, the iguanas and turtles (the latter will stay alive for weeks if laid on their backs). The islands were also convenient hideouts for pirates. It was not until the invasion of nearby Jamaica in 1655 that the islands were settled. Supposedly

Getting There

Cayman Islands t (1 345–)

By Air

Most flights go into Grand Cayman (from where local connecting flights can usually be taken on the same day to Cayman Brac or Little Cayman). Contact:

Cayman Airways: Grand Cayman t 949 2311, *www.caymanairways.com*; Cayman Brac t 948 2535; USA and Canada t 1 800 422 9626. The national carrier. Departure tax is included in the ticket price.

From Europe

British Airways have a direct service three times weekly from London Gatwick. Otherwise you can connect in Miami.

From the USA

The main centre for flights to the Cayman Islands is Miami, from where five or six flights originate each day (Cayman Airways, Continental Airlines, US Airways, Delta Airlines, American Airlines/American Eagle and Northwest). Other direct links, some of them stopping at Miami, include Atlanta, Baltimore, Charlotte, Chicago, Houston, Memphis, Orlando, Seattle, New York and Tampa.

From Other Caribbean Islands

There are five flights a week from Kingston, Jamaica (on either Air Jamaica or Cayman Airways), sometimes stopping in Montego Bay.

Getting Around

By Air

For flying between the different Cayman Islands, contact:

Cayman Airways, Grand Cayman t 949 2311, US t 1 800 422 9626, *customerrelations@ caymanairways.net*, *www.caymanairways. com*. The Cayman Islands' national carrier provides a Twin Otter service for regular hopper flights between Grand Cayman, Cayman Brac and Little Cayman.

By Bus

In **Grand Cayman**, a bus service emanates from George Town, departing from next to the public library on the main square and running until dusk. Green and yellow-striped minibuses run along the main Seven Mile Beach strip to West Bay in the north of the island, where most of the Caymanians live, and purple-striped ones serve the eastern end of the island. There are stops along the route, but hail them madly anyway.

In **Cayman Brac**, the bus stop signs are for school buses and not for adults. If you stick out your thumb, the few cars that pass will probably pick you up.

By Taxi

There is an abundance of taxis in Grand Cayman: if there is not one to hand, simply wander into the foyer of the nearest hotel. Fares are fixed by the government: airport to George Town – US$12, mid-way up Seven Mile Beach – US$11, West Bay (top of Seven Mile Beach) – US$16, Spanish Bay Reef – US$28, Bodden Town – US$35, Rum Point – US55, East End – US$60, Turtle Farm – US$26, Links – US$16, Marriott – US$10.

Hitch-hiking

With the exception of the Seven Mile strip on Grand Cayman, hitch-hiking is quite a reliable way to get around the islands. Elsewhere on Grand Cayman, and also on Cayman Brac, you will find that the Caymanians sometimes stop even without your having to flag them down.

By Guided Tour

On Grand Cayman, taxi drivers would be happy to take you on an island tour, with up to five people in the cab. You should reckon on an hourly rate of US$30. Tours are also available by bus through the following companies:

Majestic Tours, Grand Cayman, t 949 7773, *www.majestic-tours.com*.

Tropicana Tours, Grand Cayman, t 949 0944, *www.tropicana-tours.com*.

Car and Bike Hire

Cars are readily available for hire. Driving is on the left. Everything in Cayman proceeds at a stately pace, the driving included, which is something of a relief after other Caribbean islands. There are so many cars on Grand Cayman that turning right can actually be a bit of a problem because it takes so long for a gap to appear in the traffic.

To drive on Grand Cayman you need a local driving licence (issued by the hire firm on presentation of your normal licence, price US$7.50) and a credit card or cheque deposit. Hire charges are better value for a week's rental. Rates start at US$30 for the smallest car, with charges on top.

Grand Cayman

Andy's Rent-a-Car, t 949 8111, *info@andys.ky*, *www.andys.ky*.

Avis Cico, t 949 2468, US **t** 1 800 228 0668, *avisgcm@candw.ky*, *www.aviscayman.com*.

Coconut Car Rentals, t 949 4370, US **t** 1 800 262 6687, *coconut@candw.ky*, *www.coconutcarrentals.com*. Good rates.

Dollar, t 949 4790, *dollar@candw.ky*.

Soto's 4x4 Jeep Rentals, t 945 2424, US **t** 1 800 625 6174, *sotos4x4@candw.ky*, *www.sotos4x4.ky*. For Jeep rental.

Scooters and **motorbikes** are easy to get hold of and are a very good way of getting around. Rates are around US$25–30 per day; driving licence required. **Bicycles** are available through the same companies for about US$15 per day (the only hill on the Cayman Islands is at the east of Cayman Brac). Contact **Soto's Scooters, t** 945 4652.

Cayman Brac

B&S Motor Venture, t 948 1646, *rock@candw.ky*, *www.bandsmv.ky*. For scooters and bikes.

Brac Rent-a-Car, t 948 1515, *scotlaud@candw.ky*, *www.bracrentals.com*.

Little Cayman

Hire cars are available through McLaughlin Car Rentals, **t** 948 1000, *littlecay@candw.ky*, located within walking distance of the airstrip. All of the hotels seem to have **bicycles** available for hire, and these are quite adequate if you are going to stick to the southwestern corner of the island, where all the hotels are situated.

Tourist Information

Abroad

One website devoted to Cayman tourism is at *www.caymanislands.ky*, and you can also get information at *www.caymansonline.com*.

Canada: Earl B. Smith Travel Marketing Consultants, 234 Eglington Av East, Suite 306, Toronto, Ontario, Canada M4P 1K5, **t** (416) 485 1550.

UK: Cayman Islands Department of Tourism, 6 Arlington St, London SW1A 1RE, **t** (020) 7491 7771.

USA: 3 Park Ave, 39th Floor, New York, NY 10016, **t** 212 889 9009.

Suite 920, One Lincoln Centre, Butterfield Rd, Chicago, IL 60181, **t** 630 705 0650.

Trenton Bldg, 8300 NW 53rd St, Miami, Fl 33166, **t** 305 599 9033.

Two Memorial City Plaza, 820 Gessner, Suite 1335, Houston, TX 77024, **t** 713 461 1317.

In the Cayman Islands

Write to the Cayman Islands Department of Tourism at Regatta Business Park, Leeward Two, West Bay, George Town, Grand Cayman, British West Indies, **t** 949 0623.

There is an information desk at the airport and at the cruise-ship terminal when a ship is in town.

Emergencies

There is a good hospital on Hospital Rd in George Town, **t** 949 8600, but first try the reception at your hotel as there may well be a doctor on call.

In emergencies, dial **t** 555 (ambulance) or **t** 911 (police).

Media

Tourist magazines on the Cayman Islands include *Key to Cayman* yearly, *Destination Cayman*, *What's Hot in Cayman* monthly, and the Cayman Airways in-flight magazine, *Horizons*. The local newspaper is the *Caymanian Compass*, published on weekdays with a weekend section on Fridays.

Money and Banks

The currency of the Cayman Islands is the Cayman Islands dollar, which is fixed to the

USA dollar at a rate of CI$1 = US$1.25. It comes as a bit of a surprise to find that the greenback is worth just 80 Cayman cents, but business is booming in the Cayman Islands. US dollars are also valid and are accepted everywhere anyway, so you might not even see the local money. Prices are often quoted in both currencies.

All major credit cards are accepted around the islands, in the hotels, restaurants and shops, as are traveller's cheques. Tipping runs at 10–15%, usually added to your bill by the restaurants and hotels.

Banks open Mon–Thurs 9–4, Fri 9–4. Cayman National Bank in town is open on Saturday mornings.

Shopping

Open 9–5 and usually closed on Sundays. Duty-free shopping is plentiful.

Telephone Code

The IDD code for the Caymans is **t** 1 345, followed by a seven-digit number. On the island, dial all seven digits.

Festivals

April *Cayfest.* A showpiece for island culture, including craft and culinary displays on the theme of old-time island life.
Family week. Cayman Brac.
Fishing tournament.

May *Batabano.* A carnival held over a weekend in which the islanders and visitors dress in themed costumes and shuffle-step through the streets of George Town.

October *Pirates Week.* The big event in the Caymanian calendar: a swashbuckling affair of fake eye patches and tee-ree-ree. Choreographed invasions amuse the tourists, but the evenings are enjoyed by tourists and locals alike in the bars. Ring **t** 949 5078.

Watersports

You can fix up anything from nitrox nightdiving to a ride on a bouncy banana, pedalo or jetski. The best area is Seven Mile Beach in Grand Cayman.

Day Sails

Very popular, these can also be arranged through the watersports shops and the many small boat operators. Typically these will include snorkelling and lunch or a sunset cruise, and some of them make a visit to Stingray City (*see* below). Most companies offer transport from your hotel.

Fantasea Tours–Don't Even Ask, Grand Cayman, **t** 949 2182, *fantasea@candw.ky*. Catamaran trips.

Jolly Roger, Grand Cayman, **t** 949 7245, *jolroger@candw.ky, www.jollyrogercayman. com*. An afternoon of rum-soaked fun on the mock pirate boat.

Stingray City Trips

A trip to Stingray City from Grand Cayman is the ultimate in tourist junkets, but entertaining nonetheless. In fact, there are two stingray cities: both are sandy sections of sea bed in the North Sound: one lies in 15ft of water and the other rises to within 3ft of the surface. The stingrays were first attracted here when fishermen came to clean their catch and threw the fish innards into the water. Now they know they will be offered food and so they are friendly to humans. Stand in the water and you will see the grey shadows cruise by on the bottom of the sea, first circling and then touching you; some pass between your legs, or flare their wings against you as they sniff for food. Trips, costing from US$35 per person, can be arranged with any of the general watersports operators, or through one of the local (and cheaper) companies in Coconut Plaza. For some reason, they are all called Ebanks, but you can choose from:

C+G, t 947 4049.

Captain Marvin, t 947 4590.

Frank's, t 947 5491.

Deep-sea Fishing and Bonefishing

Casting for tuna and wahoo or 6ft marlin is another popular day out on the high seas, and the Cayman Islands have a host of sleek vessels. Rates are US$600–1000 for a full day for six people, US$300–450 for a half-day. Try the following Grand Cayman companies:

Bayside Watersports, t 949 3200, *bayside@ candw.ky, www.baysidewatersports.com*.

Black Princess Charters, t 949 0400, *princess@candw.ky, www.fishgrandcayman.com*.

The fishing off Little Cayman is excellent, as is the bonefishing in the shallow flats; contact the hotels to make arrangements.

Glass-bottomed Boats

For those who don't want to dive, there's **Atlantis Submarine**, t 949 8383, *cayman@res.atlantisadventures.com, www.atlantisadventures.com*. The submarine leaves from South Church St, just down from the museum, Grand Cayman, and trips are quite expensive, starting at about US$72, but the guides are informative and knowledgeable. On some trips, divers outside the sub talk to you through headsets and describe the marine life. You get a deeper tour in the three-man Atlantis submersibles which dive the wall down to 1,000ft; this allows you to visit the odd wreck or hang between huge barrel sponges and turtles, with lamps to illuminate the corals as the sunlight fades. Price about US$450 per person.

Scuba Diving

See also p.774 for more general information about diving in the Cayman Islands. There is a website devoted to the subject at *www.divecayman.ky*. There are about 40 dive outfits on the islands. Divers should have a 'C' card or take a resort course (about US$75), available with most dive shops. Some outfits even specialize in older-guy instructors or blonde-waif instructresses for your maximum diving pleasure. Instruction is available in a number of different languages. Dive shops usually offer a two-dive outing each morning (prices from US$65) and a single-tank dive in the afternoon (about US$40). The average price for a night dive is US$40. Any equipment you need is charged on top. The island also has a decompression chamber, t 949 4324.

The first outing of the day is often at 8am in Grand Cayman; the plethora of operators means that there is often a race for the good dive sites.

Grand Cayman

The following operators are large and well established:

Bob Soto's Reef Divers, t 949 2871, US t 1 800 BOB SOTO, *bobsoto@candw.ky, www.bobsotodiving.com*.

Fisheye Diving, Seven Mile Beach, t 945 4209, *info@fisheye.com, www.fisheye.com*.

Large operators have all the facilities, but they take out large groups of divers, sometimes on double-decker dive boats. However, these crowds are usually broken down into groups of eight or ten, each with a dive-leader. If you would prefer a more personalized trip on a smaller boat, you might want to go with one of the smaller operators, who also have the advantage of a certain flexibility. They may well be able to visit a particular dive site for you. Contact:

The Cayman Marine Lab, t 916 0849, *marlab@camdw.ky, www.caymanmarinelab.com*. Run by a trained marine biologist who gives a lecture each day in between the dives.

Dive Tech/Turtle Reef Divers, Cobalt Coast area next to the turtle farm, t 949 1700, *divetech@candw.ky, www.divetech.com*.

Divers Down, West Bay Rd, t 945 1611, *diversdown@diversdown.net, www.diversdown.net*.

The following two operators work from slightly out-of-the-way hotels, but they are very friendly:

Sunset Divers, South Church Street, south of George Town, t 949 7111, US t 1 800 854 4767, *reservations@sunsethouse.com, www.sunsethouse.com*.

Cayman Diving Lodge, Seaview, t 949 7560, *info@divelodge.com, www.divelodge.com*.

Cayman Brac

The scuba diving here is even better than that in Grand Cayman; divers' groups have taken to leaving painted driftwood signs to record their trip and general satisfaction. Contact:

Brac Aquatics, t 948 1429, *bracdive@candw.ky*.

Reef Divers, Brac Reef Beach Resort, t 948 1323, *www.bracreef.com*.

Divi Dive & Photo, Tiara, West End, t 948 1553, *comments@diviresorts.com*.

Little Cayman

Here, you'll find the best scuba diving of all. There are a number of dive operators on the

island, each attached to accommodation.
Contact:

Southern Cross Club, t 948 1098, *info@southern
crossclub.com, www.southerncrossclub.com.*
Little Cayman Beach Resort, t 948 1033,
www.littlecayman.com. Has a photographic
centre.
Paradise Villas, t 948 0001, *diving@paradise-
divers.com, www.paradisevillas.com.*

Snorkelling

Excellent in all three islands. In **Grand
Cayman**, there are reefs off the south coast
and in the northeast, though you should be
careful of the currents here. Some of the best
snorkelling is at Cemetery Beach at the
northern end of Seven Mile Beach, Eden Rock
and Devil's Grotto south of George Town, and
at Soto's Reef. On **Cayman Brac**, there is excellent snorkelling opposite the old Buccaneer
Inn, close to the airport, and west of there
towards Stake Bay. On **Little Cayman**, snorkel
off the north shore in Jackson's Bay, directly
opposite the road that crosses the island.

Windsurfing (and Small Sailing Boats)

You can hire equipment at many of the
hotels and watersports shops along Seven
Mile Beach in Grand Cayman. The best winds,
though, are out at the East End. Try:

Don Foster's Watersports, t 945 5132.
Sailboards Caribbean, t 949 1068. Has a
MISTRAL concessionary.

Other Sports

Golf

There is also minigolf, on West Bay Road, by
the Hyatt Hotel, Grand Cayman.
Brittania Golf Club, Hyatt Regency Hotel,
Grand Cayman, **t** 949 8020, *www.britannia
golfclub.com.* This course can be played as a
9-hole, full-length course or an 18-hole
course with par-3 holes (using the same fair-
ways and greens; played on alternate days of
the week). You can also play a third course,
designed for the short-hitting Cayman ball.
Book well in advance.
Links Safehaven, West Bay Road, Grand
Cayman, **t** 949 5988, *proshop@safehavenltd.*

com. The low-lying, sandy land lends itself to
a links course; 18 holes and par 71.

Hiking

The Cayman Islands National Trust arranges
a number of walking tours around Grand
Cayman: George Town, West Bay and Bodden
Town. They also have a guided tour of the
bush in the middle of the island, the Mastic
Trail, run by Silver Thatch Tours, **t** 916 0678,
silver@hotmail.com.

Horse-riding

For a horseback ride along the beach, call:
Honeysuckle Beach Trail Rides, Barkers, **t** 916
5420, *twoodenhorsepower@hotmail.com,
www.caymanhorseridingtour.com.*
Horse Back in Paradise with Nicki, Barkers
Beach, *nikiride@candw.ky, www.cayman
horseriding.com.* It's expensive.
Pampered Ponies, Barkers, **t** 945 2262.

Tennis

There are plenty of tennis courts on
Grand Cayman.

Where to Stay

Grand Cayman t (1 345–)

The majority of the hotels are along the five
miles of Seven Mile Beach to the north of
George Town; they range from simple but quite
expensive guest houses to the height of luxury.
Many offer diving packages. There is very little
cheap accommodation in Cayman so you might
prefer to stay in a self-catering or 'efficiency'
apartment in one of the many condominium
complexes. These have some common facilities
such as watersports and a pool, but no restaurant or bar. All hotels add a government tax of
10% and usually a service charge of 10%. Hotel
room rates are usually listed in US$.

Luxury

Hyatt Regency Hotel, PO Box 1588, West Bay
Rd, **t** 949 1234, US **t** 1 800 223 1234, *hyatt@
candw.ky, www.hyatt.com.* This is the most
luxurious place to stay on the island. It is large
(236 rooms), modern and very neat, decorated
in plush Caribbean pastel, with echoes of the

colonial era in its mock-classical columns and tall Georgian-style windows. The atmosphere is quite upbeat, with a dip-and-sip bar, watersports across the road on the beach and low-calorie *cuisine naturelle* in one of the four restaurants.

Westin Casuarina Resort, PO Box 30620, t 945 3800, US t 1 800 WESTIN 1, *salesing@candw.ky, www.westincasuarina.com*. Equally extravagant but right on the sand along an excellent part of the beach. It has 343 rooms ranged over five floors, north and south wings adorned in mock-classical airs and graces (including a cloistered walkway leading to the restaurants), pointed in a shade of light blue that matches the Caymanian sea. There is an attractive pool, surrounded by profuse greenery, set above the beach where all the watersports are on offer. The rooms, cool and carpeted, have all the requisites for a luxurious stay: TVs, air-con and fans, coffee-makers and minibars; most of them have balconies, too.

Ritz-Carlton Grand Cayman, West Bay Rd, Seven Mile Beach, t 945 7489, *www.ritzcarlton.com*. Set to open in December 2004, the hotel was so badly damaged by the hurricane of September 2004, that it had to be rebuilt. It is now scheduled to open in October 2005, and when it does, the 365-room resort will raise the bar for all hotels in the Cayman Islands. The resort's 144 acres stretch from sea to sea and includes an unusual nine-hole golf course by Greg Norman; two restaurants by highly regarded chef Eric Pipert of New York's Le Bernardin; La Prairie Spa and much more.

Very Expensive–Expensive

Beach Club Colony, Seven Mile Beach, PO Box 903, t 949 8100, US t 1 800 482 DIVE, *bchclub@candw.ky, www.caymanresorthotels.com*. Unlike the luxury pastel palaces, this resort has a low-key, more West Indian atmosphere, with that classic Caribbean beach-club feel. The 41 rooms look down from balconies or give straight onto the sands; right in the middle stands the central house, with the resort's restaurant and bar set out on an attractive, brick-pillared terrace that catches the breeze. The rooms

are comfortable but not sybaritic, equipped with telephone, air-con and TV.

Moderate

Sunset House Hotel, just south of George Town, PO Box 479, t 949 7111, US t 1 800 854 4767, *sunset@candw.ky, www.sunsethouse.com*. Very popular in the early evening, as the name would suggest. Its blocks of rooms, the pool and restaurant and a palm-thatch bar fringe the ironshore coastline and the reefs begin close by. All 59 rooms are comfortable, with telephones and air-con, some with fans.

Cayman Diving Lodge, PO Box 11, t 947 7555. If you are happy in the isolated southeast of the island, this place offers just 17 rooms and a very easygoing atmosphere, just above the beach. Plenty of sports facilities are available at an all-inclusive rate.

Erma Eldemire's Guest House, south of George Town, PO Box 482, t 949 5387, *tootie@eldermire.com, www.eldemire.com*. This is the best of the few reasonably priced places to stay. It offers three apartments (with kitchens) and nine simple double rooms; there's a common kitchen for breakfast and a sitting area, as well as a verandah.

Villas, Condominiums, Apartments

Condominium complexes vary much less in price than the hotels. There are also plenty of villas for rent. Try contacting the following organizations or, alternatively, book through your nearest Department of Tourism reservations office.

Calypso Cove Apartments, t 949 3730. Inexpensive apartments.

Cayman Villas, PO Box 681, t 945 4144, US t 1 800 235 5888, *cayvilla@candw.ky, www.caymanvillas.com*. An agency for condo rentals.

Lacovia Condominiums, PO Box 1998, t 949 7599. These eminently comfortable condominiums occupy an excellent spot on Seven Mile Beach. On offer are 45 apartments in a variety of configurations up to three-bedroomed suites.

Victoria House, PO Box 30571, t 945 4233, US t 1 866 422 9626, *victoria@candw.ky, www.victoriahouse.com*. Has just 25 rooms, with a friendly atmosphere. The building was badly damaged in the hurricane of September 2004; the owners expect to be up-and-running by the 2005–6 winter season, but check in advance.

Villas of the Galleon, PO Box 1797, **t** 945 4433, *vogcay@candw.ky*, *www.villasofthegalleon.com*. There are 74 one-, two- and three-bedroom units, all pleasantly decorated in white and bright pastel, some right on the beach, all with a view of the sea.

Cayman Brac **t** (1 345–)

Expensive–Moderate

Divi Tiara Beach Resort, PO Box 238, **t** 948 1553, US **t** 1 800 367 3484. The hotel has 70 rooms ranged in blocks ranged behind the seafront, as well as four time-shares. There is an attractive bar area on a deck under the trees just above the excellent powder-soft sand where hammocks hang among the palms. Facilities include tennis courts, a pool, Jacuzzis, watersports and snorkelling. Diving packages available.

Brac Reef Beach Resort, PO Box 56, **t** 948 1323, US **t** 1 800 327 3835. *bestdiving@reefseas.com*, *www.bracreef.com*. Not far from the Divi Tiara Resort but slightly smaller (40 rooms) and quieter. Modern, comfortable rooms, with fans, TVs and air-con, are set in blocks that overlook a sandy garden with a tangle of sea-grape trees. There is a reasonable beach and some sports on offer – including diving, of course.

Brac Caribbean Beach Resort, **t** 948 2265, US **t** 1 800 791 7911, *bracarib@candw.ky*, *www.brac-caribbean.com*. Condominiums.

Turtle Nest, West End Rd, **t** 948 2697, *the tnest@candw.ky*, *www.thenest.com*. A beachfront guest house with fresh water swimming pool and restaurant. Rooms have phone and television. Weekly rates include a free seventh night.

Little Cayman **t** (1 345–)

Very Expensive

The Southern Cross Club, **t** 948 1099, US **t** 1 800 899 2582, *info@southerncrossclub.com*, *www.southerncrossclub.com*. The most stylish place to stay on Little Cayman, this stands on a sandy stretch of shoreline nearly opposite Owen Island. There are just 12 spacious rooms, furnished in breezy and bright Caribbean fabrics and louvred for fan-ventilation (there is also air-con), set in double bungalows scattered loosely around the garden. There is a central clubhouse with a freshwater pool and sunning deck. The plan includes all meals.

Expensive

Pirate's Point, **t** 948 1010. Occupies its own small stretch of beach to the west of the Village. Ten rooms are set in cottages (only four of them air-conditioned) in a garden overgrown with sea-grape trees, palms and casuarina pines. You will be well looked after in the dining room. Meals are part of the all-inclusive package; some diving and fishing packages are available.

Little Cayman Beach Resort, **t** 948 1033, US **t** 1 800 327 3835, *lcbr@candw.ky*, *www.littlecayman.com*. This is a busier, resort-style hotel, situated on a private stretch of beach just down from the Village. The 32 rooms stand in two-storey blocks either side of the central garden and sitting area. There's a pool and an open-air bar, with steps down on to the passable beach. Rooms are large and comfortable, with all modern comforts, such as air-con, fans and TVs. There are the usual sports including diving and fishing, kayaks and sea cycles and a tennis court. There are also eight suites attached to the hotel.

Paradise Villas, PO Box 30, **t** 948 0001, *iggy@candw.ky*, *www.paradisevillas.com*. A bit more reasonably priced, on the seafront close to the airstrip in the Village. There are 12 villas built in pink and white wood with balconies overlooking the sea. The smallish rooms are furnished in pastel tones and have fans and air-con. There's a freshwater pool and watersports.

Conch Club Condos, Blossom Village, **t** 800 327 3835, *info@conchclubcondominiums.com*, *www.conchclub.com*. Try here if you prefer to stay in an apartment rather than a hotel.

The Club Condos, Little Cayman, **t** 948 1033, *bestdiving@reefseas.com*, *www.theclubat littlecayman.com*.

Eating Out

Grand Cayman

As Grand Cayman has developed over the last 20 years, so too has a wide range of restaurants. These range from successful local ventures serving West Indian food, and tiny local Caymanian restaurants in the back streets of George Town, to gourmet establishments with celebrity chefs from the USA, imported dial-a-pizza parlours and burger joints. There are also restaurants specializing in Italian, French, Mexican and Chinese food. Much of the hotel food is imported, but there is generally good local seafood: spiny lobster, conch or turtle (farmed on Grand Cayman). Make sure you reserve tables in winter, when there will be a waiting list of up to three days in the more popular restaurants. Restaurant bills are steep in Cayman and most restaurants, except the smaller local ones, do add a 15% service charge on top. Prices are usually quoted in Cayman dollars. The **price categories** used here are as follows: expensive = CI$20 and above; moderate = CI$12–CI$20; inexpensive = CI$12 and under.

Expensive

The Grand Old House, South Church St, **t** 949 9333, *www.grandoldhouse.com*. Set in a charming old gingerbread town house on the shoreline, with tables ranged on the two-tier screened veranda and on the waterfront itself, where they are hung with fairy lights. The menu is international with some variations on a traditional Caribbean theme. Start with a conch *ceviche* in a mild tomato, cilantro and key lime marinade and then try their delectable potato-crusted tuna in a lemon butter sauce or a turtle steak if you dare. There is a long wine list of good quality. *Closed Sun.*

Hemingway's, Hyatt Regency Beachfront Suites, **t** 945 5700. For an elegant and intimate meal out, where you dine in a formal dining room or out on the terrace through the French windows. The menu is international; *cuisine naturelle* dishes include good poached salmon with Sicilian beans.

The Wharf Restaurant, George Town, **t** 949 2231. Ever popular and quite large, the tables scattered between the brightly lit terraces and the covered veranda leading down to the shoreline. Enjoy the Caribbean and international fare, and the tarpon feeding at nine each evening (though the fish seem happy to swim for you at any time).

The Restaurant at Rum Point, **t** 947 9412. All dressed up with brightly painted fish on the walls, starfish chairbacks and outrageously bright tablecloths.

The Lighthouse, at Breakers on south coast main road, **t** 947 2047. Catch the breeze off the sea as you dine on the wooden terrace here to the roar of the waves breaking on the reef. There is a lengthy wine list to accompany the menu based around Italian and seafood dishes. Flash-fried calamari followed by pasta specialities or a yellow-fin tuna seared very rare with sesame, greens, pickled ginger and wasabi.

Moderate

Deckers 269, West Bay Road, next to the Hyatt Regency, **t** 945 6600. Centred on an old English double-decker bus, which acts as the bar, the fare is American Bistro in style, with wings, ribs, steaks and pizzas. Lively.

Cracked Conch, West Bay, **t** 945 5217. Next to Turtle Farm and Tortuga Rum Store. Specializes in seafood; good conch chowder.

The Tree House, West Bay Road, near the junction of Eastern Av, **t** 949 2893. Sit under the eponymous tree (and breadfruit and guinep trees) in a mock-rustic setting evocative of the South Seas, and dine on Caribbean and international fare.

Inexpensive

Eats Crocodile Rock Café, Cayman Falls Plaza, West Bay Rd, **t** 945 5288. A traditional American diner which is quite a good place for breakfast or for burgers and pizzas.

Lone Star Bar and Grill, **t** 945 5175. Just outside the entrance to the Hyatt. Serves Tex-Mex food.

Corita's Copper Kettle, in the centre of town, **t** 949 2696. For something a little more West Indian, head here for some of the best basic island fare: fritters and callaloo followed by conch burger or chicken and chips liberally dashed with hot pepper sauce (beware).

Champion House II, Eastern Av, George Town, t 949 7882. If you feel like a late-night jerk, you can come here for simple West Indian fare and, of course, Jamaican jerk chicken.

Cayman Brac

Moderate–Inexpensive

Captain's Table, Brac Caribbean Beach Village, t 948 1418. You should certainly try here.

Aunt Sha's Kitchen, near the turning to West End, t 948 1581. This is a local eatery; the dining room is on a terrace dressed in pink, and the constant roar of breakers provides the soundtrack to your meal. Fried kingfish and curried chicken are served with coleslaw or rice 'n' peas.

La Esperanza Bar and Restaurant, on the north coast, t 948 0531. Here you will get an equally good West Indian meal at tables right on the water's edge: fish, chicken or shrimp followed by a key lime pie.

Edd's Place, West Bay, t 948 0364. Local and international fare.

Little Cayman

Each of the hotels has its own dining room and most of them offer a meals-inclusive package. You can also get them to make you a picnic if you are going to take off for the day.

The Hungry Iguana, Iguana Court, t 948 0007, (*moderate–inexpensive*). This is a gathering place for Little Cayman residents. The main room is part American diner and part bar, with bench seats along one side and a long high bar down the other, serving Caribbean and American lunches and dinners, burgers and salads, fresh catch lightly grilled or blackened, some pizzas and occasional barbecues under the trees above the beach.

Bars and Nightlife

Grand Cayman

Cayman has recently begun to brew its own beer, Stingray, which is quite dark and bitter for a Caribbean brew, not really what you would expect and probably best avoided. However, there are lighter beers available: all the American ones, as well as Red Stripe from Jamaica and Carib from Trinidad. The big name on the Caymanian cocktail list at the moment is the Mudslide, made with vodka, Kahlua and Bailey's Irish Cream, if you think you can bear it. The main nights out tend to be Wednesday and Friday. On Sundays, Grand Cayman is dead. There are plenty of bars around the island, some of which have superb waterfront settings. Those on the cliffs to the south of the town tend to be popular with the locals for sundowners after work.

My Bar @ Sunset House, Sunset House Hotel, South Church St, t 945 1383. With liberal palm thatching, on a walled terrace; mainly attracting an expat crowd.

Paradise Bar & Grill, South Church St, t 945 1383. Sit under parasols on the waterfront terrace. This place can be quite lively at sunset, when there is a happy hour, which attracts a nice mix of locals and tourists. It also has a sandy platform just off the road for a bit of daytime lounging in the sun.

Durty Reid's, Red Bay Plaza. An all-American bar in the eastern outskirts of town, with big-screen TV and walls covered with pictures of the US Marines.

Over The Edge, Bodden Town, t 947 9568. A slightly dark and dingy bar-discotheque with a pool table and juke box; it does have a terrace over the waterfront.

Lone Star Bar & Grill, West Bay Road, close to the Hyatt, t 945 5175. This can get pretty rowdy in the evening. It is set in a wooden cabin, its walls covered in T-shirts (left by satisfied customers no doubt). TVs hang from the roof, visible from all angles and playing continuously, so you can catch up on the NFL.

Legendz, Cayman Falls Mall, t 945 3001. A themed bar which honours such 20th-century heroes of popular culture as James Dean, Marilyn Monroe, Elvis and Jimi Hendrix; their portraits on the walls jostle with the fluorescent décor and slender metal furniture for your attention.

Passione Restaurant & Lounge @ The Links, Safehaven, t 945 4234. Chill out over their jazz happy hour every Friday.

Club Inferno. Dancing at weekends. Restaurant serves local food.

Jungle, Trafalgar Place. A good nightclub.

DJs Café, Coconut Place. Fun for dancing.

two soldiers by the name of Walter and Bowden came to Grand Cayman (their names are still evident in the Caymanian names Watler and Bodden). In 1670 the Spaniards gave up Jamaica and the Cayman Islands to Britain at the Treaty of Madrid. This did not make the islanders any safer, though, as they were still harassed by the Spaniards and roving bands of pirates who still put in occasionally.

The settlers farmed cotton and turtles (as many as forty turtling ships would set out from Kingston in the season) and they became wreckers – taking what they could find from the ships that foundered on Cayman's treacherous reefs. Wrecks still happen, but salvage laws tend to be rather stricter nowadays.

In 1802 the population on Grand Cayman had climbed to 933, of whom just over half were slaves until Emancipation in 1834. Cayman Brac and Little Cayman were only settled permanently in 1833. By the start of the 20th century, there were 5,000 Caymanians, and without employment on the islands, the men went to sea to make a living. They were renowned for their seamanship and were in particular demand by National Bulk Carriers of New York.

For three centuries, the Cayman Islands were administered as a part of Jamaica, but on 4 June 1960, as the Jamaicans prepared for Independence, the Caymanians seceded, preferring instead to become a Crown Colony directly dependent on the UK. Today the Cayman Islands are administered by the representative of Queen Elizabeth, Governor Bruce Dimwiddy, who presides over the eight-strong Executive Council. The Governor is in charge of defence, foreign affairs, police and internal security. Elections to the 18-member Legislative Assembly take place every four years and are next due in 2009. Alongside tourism, the central pillar of the Cayman economy is offshore finance, and among the reams of tourist bumph, you will find brochures on how to invest in the islands. They are basically tax free (though visitors will find themselves paying a 10% government tax on their hotel room) and the handling of money is made as easy as possible (no direct taxation, laws of confidentiality, absence of exchange controls, teams of lawyers and accountants to handle it all, good communications). The islands are famous for it and they have attracted over 500 banks and 30,000 companies to register there. Hardly any even have an office; they are simply a plaque on the wall.

Grand Cayman

George Town

The Cayman Islands' capital is on a broad bay in the southwest of Grand Cayman. The nucleus is almost entirely a modern town, with streets of smart glass-fronted offices and air-conditioned shopping malls, but there are a number of very pretty timber buildings from old-time Cayman dotted around. Nothing remains of the 'Hogstyes' that gave the town its original name, before it was called after King George III at the beginning of the 19th century. The remains of the town's original defence, **Fort George**, just a few waist-high walls, lie on the shore just north of the

Grand Cayman

Caribbean Sea

Grand Cayman

North Sound

Geographic features and locations:

Barkers Head
Conch Point
Spanish Bay
North West Point
West Bay
Turtle Farm
Hell
Calypso Cove Apartments
Morgan's Harbour
Salt Creek
Governor's Creek
Victoria House
Seven Mile Beach
The Ritz Carlton
Villas of the Galleon
Safehaven
Coconut Plaza
Westin Casuarina Resort
Beach Club Colony
Lacovia Condominiums
Hyatt Regency Hotel
Britannia Golf Course
George Town
Sunset House Hotel
Smiths Cove
Eldemire's Guest House
Cayman Islands National Museum
Pull-and-be-Damned Point
South Sound
Crawl Bay
Prospect Fort
Owen Roberts International Airport
Jetty
Spott's Bay
Little Pedro Point
Pedro Castle
Old Jones Bay
Bodden Town
Moon Bay
Joe Conyer Bay
Betty Bay Point
Heritage Beach
Frank Sound
Blow-holes
White Sand Bay
Cayman Diving Lodge
East End
CHURCH AV
South Channel
Sparrow-hawk Point
East End Channel
Coconut Point
Long Channel
Colliers Channel
Tortuga Club
Great Beach
Little Bluff Bay
Old Man Bay
North Side
The Channel
Elizabeth II Botanic Park
Little Sound
Water Cay
Finger Cay
Rum Point
RUM POINT DRIVE
Booby Point
Rum Point Channel
Main Channel
Big Channel

N

8 km
5 miles

Best Beaches

The Caymanians ask you not to wander around the town in your bathing costume; nudity and toplessness are illegal but, if you are determined, you may find somewhere right off the beaten track to strip off.

Seven Mile Beach: The centre of the island's tourism, home to the majority of the hotels, watersports and diving operations, its gently shelving sands extend from just north of George Town up the west coast to West Bay. It is marginally less crowded at the northern end, though even here, it's almost entirely built up. Signs on the road indicate paths down to the beach between the hotels. Facing west, Seven Mile Beach has one of the finest views of the sunset anywhere, with a good chance of seeing the Green Flash.

Smiths Cove: A favourite with the Caymanians, a small cove a mile or so south of town.

Spott's Bay: Not far east of George Town, a passable public beach, with mounded, steeply sloping sand, sunshades and hammocks.

East End (**Heritage Beach** or **Pirate's Beach**): Isolated sun traps hidden behind bushes of sea grape at the end of sandy tracks.

Rum Point: Set among casuarina pines that roar on the breeze, looking out onto the North Sound, with water that's clear and shallow for a hundred yards offshore. Now quite smart and expensive, with a restaurant, a bar and a snack bar as well as a watersports shop. You can reach Rum Point on a ferry from the Hyatt Hotel.

Kaibo at **Cayman Kai**: A small beach, also with a bar; palms, simple fare, hammocks and picnic tables, and a view over the sand onto the lagoon.

---

cruise-ship terminal and main dock. Close by is the **Emslie Memorial Church**, built in the 1920s on the site of an earlier church.

Inland you come to the **main square**, a small park with lawns and trees surrounded by a cluster of official buildings. A statue of James Manoah Bodden, Cayman's first national hero, stands in the park. Perhaps the prettiest building is the public library, which stands on the eastern side of the square; across from here is yet another shop.

Back on the waterfront, just down from the cruise-ship dock, the **Cayman Islands National Museum** (*open Mon–Fri 9–5, Sat 10–4*) is set in the Old Courts Building, one of the island's finest traditional buildings. Built some time in the middle of the 19th century, with a solid lower storey and a wooden upper, it has served variously as post office, jail and library as well as the courthouse. The excellent museum has various displays showing the natural history and cultural heritage of the islands: geological exhibits include unique Cayman stones, displays of seafaring life, fragments of wattle and daub structures, tiny coins called quotties, and also an audiovisual presentation.

Leaving the town centre you soon arrive in the suburbs, modern concrete houses enclosed within chain-link fences, with satellite dishes sitting in the garden. Scattered among them are a few older houses, invariably neat, with wraparound verandas where bench seats hang from the ceiling on chains, set in yards full of pretty blooms surrounded by white picket fences.

Scuba Diving in the Caymans

Scuba-diving in the Cayman Islands is some of the best in the Caribbean. Cayman is known particularly for its 'walls': the islands are surrounded by a few miles of sand and reefs and then, suddenly, the sea bed drops almost sheer to 20,000ft. Visibility is superb in the Cayman Islands, often over 100ft.

There are caverns, pinnacles and underwater ravines, all of them encrusted with a vast array of corals, sponges and gorgonians: corals like tufts of shaggy white wool, thin tube sponges and vast barrel sponges, the jigsaw patterns of purple seafans standing against the tide, and deep down the fingers of the black corals. Single damselfish pout, and shimmering schools of bar jacks and blue tangs dip and dart in unison in your exhaled bubbles. Camouflaged crabs eye you with suspicion from their hide, and little red and white banded coral shrimps tangle their spindly feet and antennae. Tiny, shy seahorses lunge to find the cover of the coral; starfish flip as they move. At **Stingray City** in the North Sound, you can cavort with tame rays 5ft across; at **Tarpon Alley** you will see tarpon and grey reef sharks.

There are reefs on all sides of Grand Cayman, but most popular is the **North Wall** off the north shore. **Cayman Brac** is less well known than Grand Cayman, but if anything the diving is even better there. The main sites are around the West End. In Little Cayman, when the weather is good and the channel is not too rough, the diving is better still at **Jackson Bay** and **Bloody Bay** on the north shore. The wall here starts at 18ft below sea level. There are plenty of wrecks off the Cayman Islands, the best known being the *Balboa* off George Town.

The Cayman Islands have strict laws for the protection of their reefs and fish, and there is zoning to encourage regeneration of fish and coral life. Spearfishing and setting traps are prohibited; there are strict rules about anchoring. You are not allowed to take any corals or sponges, dead or alive. However, many of the diving outfits have underwater photography equipment for E6 slide photographs and video, so you can keep them on film at least. If you happen across any buried treasure, then you'll have to work out an agreement with the Cayman government, because all wrecks and hoards officially belong to the Crown.

For details of scuba-diving operators and tours in the Cayman Islands, *see* 'Scuba Diving', p.765.

North of George Town into Hell

West Bay Road runs north straight out of the town, tracking behind the tourist development on Seven Mile Beach, to the old settlement of West Bay. **Seven Mile Beach** is not actually seven miles long (more like five and a half). Either side of the road there are shopping malls, restaurants and bars dotted among the endless hotels and condominium complexes. Many of the Caymanians themselves live in **West Bay**, in the north; their ancestors moved to this area when they were emancipated in the 1830s. It gets jokingly referred to as the 'Republic of West Bay'. **Hell** is a small moonscape surrounded by mangrove and the occasional frangipani. It looks like petrified cake mix, a series of grey pinnacles whipped up by some diabolic chef. It is in fact limestone 'cliff-rock' that has been eroded unevenly (through former wave action), leaving a pitted and scarred stony mess. It is called Hell because the sharp points appear like the flames of hell turned to stone. You can send a postcard from the postbox, which will be stamped 'Hell'.

At the northwestern point, you will come to the **Turtle Farm** (*open daily 9–5; adm*), a farm and research station that breeds the green sea turtles. You can see almost the whole life-cycle of the turtle in the farm. They start as eggs, white and very slightly larger than ping-pong balls; these hatch after about 60 days of incubation in a heated room. Hatchlings are transferred through the series of tanks as they increase in size, about a foot across at one year, 80lbs in weight by the time they are five years old. They can grow as large as 6–7ft long and reach 200–600lbs. Around 40% of the turtles are released into the wild each year, but most only make it into soup. They are butchered at four or five years old. Unfortunately, it is not possible to see the most interesting part of the turtle's life cycle, the very beginning, when the female turtles crawl up onto the beach to lay their eggs; it usually happens at night and so all you see are their tractor-like tracks in the sand next morning. Females each lay an average of five times between May and October. The sex of turtle hatchlings depends on the temperature in the nest: a particularly hot spring will bring more females and a cold one more males.

Other rarer and endangered turtles, including loggerheads, hawksbills and ridleys, are also on view in the farm and there is a small menagerie of iguanas and alligators. In the café, an excellent series of displays illustrates Cayman history and the use of turtleshell over the ages, dating back to Roman times; from the Renaissance, it was used in Europe as decorative inlay on furniture and in combs, fans and brushes. It was even thought to ward off disease and so made into linings for bathtubs.

Attached to the Turtle Farm is a new marine theme park called **Boatwain's Beach**, which is presently under construction (due to be completed January 2006). The park will have a nature trail, a large saltwater lagoon where visitors can swim with turtles and other marine life, and the Caymanian Heritage Street complete with artisans.

East from George Town

In the eastern part of George Town is a small wildlife park, **Cardinal D's Park** (*adm*). There is a walkway leading past a lagoon and through some gardens, where you will see indigenous Cayman birds and animals as well as some from overseas: emus, American wild turkeys, toucans, parrots, macaws and the Cayman blue iguana. It's great for children; buy a bag of feed and the ducks, turtles and fish will race over.

Heading east from George Town, you come to **Bodden Town**, the island's only other town, and the first capital. In the country, you will see grazing cattle and their eternal companions, the cattle egrets. A road skirts the shoreline at the east end of the island and in the scrub you may spot the rare Cayman iguana. On the south shore, look out for **blow-holes** cut into the ironshore, blowing like whales with the incoming waves.

In the heart of the Cayman scrub, off the road linking the north and south shores, you will find the **Queen Elizabeth II Botanic Park** (*adm*). There is a visitors' centre, from which lead a number of walks. A mile-long trail cuts through the Cayman bush (Cactus County, Bull Thatch Bend and Epiphyte Woodland), where you will see iguana

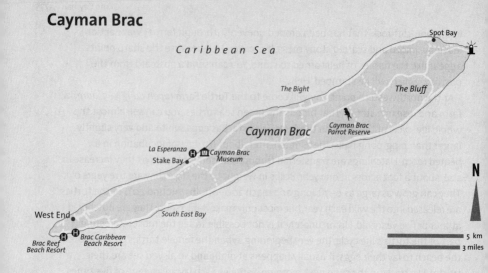

Cayman Brac

Caribbean Sea

Spot Bay

The Bight

The Bluff

Cayman Brac
Parrot Reserve

Cayman Brac

La Esperanza
Stake Bay

Cayman Brac
Museum

West End

South East Bay

5 km

3 miles

Brac Reef
Beach Resort

Brac Caribbean
Beach Resort

N

habitat, water holes with buttonwood trees, and plants (with informative labels) such as agave and 'duppy bush', so called because its leaves shimmer in the moonlight, and Cayman's various epiphytes and orchids.

Cayman Brac

Ask a 'Bracker' and you'll be told that success has gone to their heads in Grand Cayman. Cayman Brac, they say, keeps the easygoing tranquillity that Grand Cayman had 20 years ago, before there were any hotels along Seven Mile Beach. It is true that Cayman Brac is far quieter and calmer: there are just a couple of hotels and a few villas and none of the buzz or the endless traffic of Cayman.

Cayman Brac is 12 miles long and about a mile wide. It takes its name from its cliff (*brac* means 'cliff' in Gaelic), a central core of limestone that extends along the middle of the island. The island rises gradually from the west, achieving a vertiginous 140ft in the northeast, the highest point in the Cayman Islands. There are a number of caves in the limestone, none that exciting. The island is scrub- and cactus-covered, but can be surprisingly lush in the wet season.

Beaches

There are no great beaches in Cayman Brac. Most of the shoreline is rocky and the only place with any sand is in the southwest where the hotels are. There is a small public beach just east of the hotels, with mounded sand and swimming protected by the offshore reef. For the limited watersports, you are dependent on the hotels.

Around the Island

A road runs along the coastline, on the stretches of low-lying land either side of the raised central *brac*. The main settlements are at the west end, around the airport, and at Stake Bay, where you will find the island administrative buildings and the small **Cayman Brac Museum** (*open Mon–Sat 9–12 and 2–4, Sun 2–4*). This has two rooms of artefacts gathered from around the island, from domestic items such as garden tools and *yobbas* (water storage bowls) to ancient-looking communications paraphernalia and an early ice-making machine driven by kerosene. Other exhibits tell the romantic story of Brac's connection with the sea.

On the *brac* itself (reached on the central island road) you can walk in the **Cayman Brac Parrot Reserve**, on a path cut into the central bush with annotated trees and plants: mango, hemlock and liquorice, and the 'dildo' cactus, covered in spikes. If you are lucky, you might disturb a pair of Brac parrots, which will fly away twittering and screeching. Following the track beyond here to the eastern end of the island, past thatch palms and agave (originally used for making rope) and a few small plots of farmed land, you come to the top of the *brac*. There are lighthouses (old and new) and, curiously, two Portaloos, at the time of writing anyway.

Little Cayman

Five miles west of Cayman Brac is Little Cayman, a dozier, more isolated and less developed island even than the Brac. It is just 10 miles long, about one mile wide and makes it to a massive 40ft in elevation. The scrub- and mangrove-covered land is relieved by salt ponds and inland lagoons. At its most popular, when the island was frequented as a source of fresh water, the population reached 400, but nowadays it is inhabited by just over 100, most of whom are involved with the tourism business. The place is barely developed: electricity reached the island only in 1990; there is only one policeman, one petrol pump and one bank, which is open only for a few hours a week. The population of birds is far greater than that of humans and around the ponds on the south coast you will find boobies, ducks and stilts, and flights of magnificent piratical frigatebirds, which puff out their huge red gullets when courting. There are

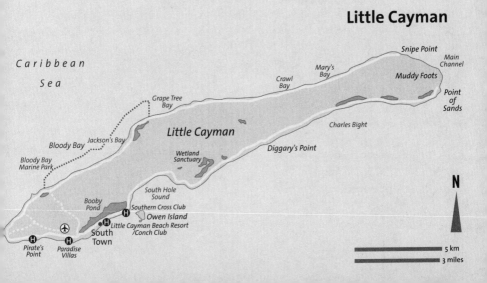

Little Cayman

around 2,000 iguanas on the island, but unfortunately they have a potentially fatal habit of sunning themselves on the road.

Beaches

The beaches around the hotels in the southwest are passable, though there is quite a lot of turtle grass just offshore. There is good sand on **Owen Island** and a reasonable beach at **Point of Sands** at the east end of the island looking out to Cayman Brac.

Around the Island

The only area in Little Cayman that can be described as a settlement is in the southwest, the cluster of houses that make up the 'Village', as it is usually known. Officially, it is called **South Town**, but this does not imply another town on the island as there is none. Elsewhere, there is just the occasional house or hotel dotted along the shoreline, mainly on the south coast of the island. The grass airstrip is close to the town. It is quite entertaining watching the flights come in and go out. The plane has to cross the main (only) road to get to the terminal building and it is kick-started out of a wheelbarrow.

A road (tarmacked in places, but mostly dirt trail) rings the island just in from the coast. As you head east from the Village you pass between the hotels on the shoreline and the **Booby Pond** inland, a lagoon fringed with mangrove where boobies and frigatebirds roost and nest. At the western end there is a house with a veranda from which you can view the birds through a telescope. Further up on the south coast, you come to **Tarpon Lake**, where a boardwalk leads out into the lagoon. On the north coast is **Bloody Bay**: some say it was so called because of the blood on the beach after a conflict between the British and Spaniards but the beach may also have gained its name from whalers who came here to butcher their catch.

The Bahamas

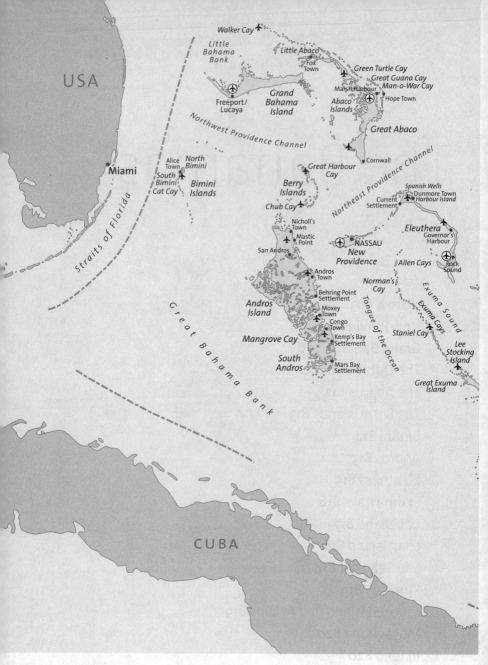

Highlights

1 Sail the bluest waters in the West Indies around the Out Islands of the Bahamas

2 Scuba dive with sharks

3 Go deep-sea fishing off Bimini, the haunt of Hemingway

THE

BAHAMAS

Atlantic

Ocean

N

100 km
50 miles

Arthur's Town
Cat Island
Bight Settlement
Old Bight Settlement
Port Howe
Cockburn Town
Dixon's Settlement
Long Bay Settlement
San Salvador

Rum Cay
Stella Maris
Port Nelson

Moss Town
George Town
Little Exuma Island
Long Island
Deadman's Cay
Clarence Town

Crooked Island
Landrail Point Settlement
Colonel Hill Settlement

Ragged Island Range

Crooked Island Passage

Long Cay
Bight of Acklins
Spring Point

Mayaguana
Abraham's Bay Settlement

Duncan Town

Acklins Island

Caicos Passage

Turks and Caicos Islands (UK)

North Caicos
Grand Caicos
East Caicos

Little Inagua
West Caicos
Grand Turk

Great Inagua
Matthew Town
Lake Rosa

The Bahamas are favourite subjects for satellite photographers – 700 emerald-green islands and cays scattered over 100,000 square miles of absurdly blue sea. The water is gin-clear, glistening over the banks of sand that stretch for miles and miles. In places, you must walk hundreds of yards into the sea to get as deep as your waist. The activity is there too – the reefs are superb and make bewildering diving, and the fishing and sailing are world-renowned. Since Columbus first made land in 1492, these cays have been plied by generations of pirates and gun-runners, and more recently rum- and drug-runners.

For the purposes of tourism, the islands are divided into three separate groups. Cable Beach and Paradise Island are on the senior island of New Providence at the heart of the Bahamas, where the capital Nassau is situated. To the north is Freeport/Lucaya on Grand Bahama island, a complete resort area that has sprung up from a barren and virtually uninhabited island 30 years ago. The 697 other islands are known as the Out Islands. These are less developed and mostly far gentler in their lifestyle, so they make for an ideal isolated island break. The only problem is choosing which to visit. They include islands such as Bimini, the Abacos, Eleuthera, the Exumas and Andros.

Named by the Spaniards after the '*baja-mar*' (the shallow sea) in which they lie, the Bahamas are not geographically part of the Caribbean. These splinters and fragments of land stretch from just north of the Greater Antilles (Haiti and Cuba), across the Tropic of Capricorn, and up alongside the coast of Florida, separated from the USA only by the 50 miles of the Gulf Stream. In all there are about 3,000, if you include the rocks, fringing reefs and the ribbons of sand that just make it above the surf.

The Bahamas are low-lying, coral limestone outcrops that sit on top of the Great Bahama Bank (stretching from Bimini to Cat Island and Ragged Island) and the Little Bahama Bank (in the north, with Grand Bahama and the Abacos). Most do not make it above 50ft; the highest point among them is 206ft, on Cat Island. They are not really that lush and are mostly covered with scrub and wispy casuarina pine trees. There are many inland lakes, usually salt water. Altogether the islands cover about 5,380 square miles.

The 300,000 or so Bahamians do not consider themselves West Indians. They have a long-standing association with the USA, and this is clearly audible in their voices: there is an American drawl on the West Indian English. Most of the islanders are of African descent, but in contrast with most other Caribbean islands, white Bahamians (informally known as 'Conkie Joes') make up a high 15% of the population. One or two communities have remained determinedly white since they arrived here as loyalists in the late 1700s. There is also a large number of expatriates resident in the islands.

The Bahamas were a colony of Britain until they took their Independence in 1973 and the connection with Britain still rings clear in parts of Bahamian life. You will actually come across garden fêtes here. The parliamentary system is based on the British model and the policemen are recognizable in their uniforms of black serge and red stripe, complete with white helmet. But of course the Bahamians have also been strongly influenced by the States. The cars, many of them left-hand drive even though the Bahamians drive on the left, are big American cruisers, and, though they have trouble in the tight streets of Nassau, a quick look at Freeport will show them more at ease on the boulevards of the recent development there.

Traditionally, commerce has come from outside the islands, as the Bahamas are not fertile. The Bahamians have muddled along, scraping a living from the land, but there have been successive waves of prosperity, many of them brought by wars or carried on the wrong side of the law. The monuments to the different eras are visible in

Suggested Itinerary

If you are travelling independently around the Bahamas it will probably be necessary to spend some time in Nassau (most flights arrive there). To see the best side of the Bahamas you must get beyond here but, if you need to change planes (or mailboats) in Nassau, there are good bars and restaurants to occupy you while you wait. Two weeks gives enough time to see a variety of the Bahamian islands. Start with a trip to one of the more developed Out Islands, perhaps Harbour Island or North Eleuthera or to the lovely cays off the Abacos. Great Exuma is also worth a visit – from here you can reach the superb Exuma Cays.

If you cannot persuade a yachtsman to take you on down to the other islands you may have to return to Nassau and set off again, but the further south you go from here, the more remote the islands become.

For a taste of small-island life, try Andros, Cat Island, Long Island or San Salvador. Another option, to help you see as much as possible, is to fly in or out of the Bahamas through Bimini, Eleuthera or the Abacos.

Nassau, from the early stone and timber houses of the Bahamian gun-runners on the hill to the Nassau mansions that have been built on the prosperity of Prohibition and most lately tourism.

The Bahamas have a highly developed tourist industry and the islands see over five million tourists a year, most of whom arrive by cruise ship (as many as 10 a day can call at Nassau). About two-thirds of the work force are employed in tourism one way or another and some 70% of GNP is derived from the industry. The Bahamas offer an extraordinary variety to the visitor. In the traditional centres, you can take in glitz and gambling in the vast, brightly coloured palaces of Cable Beach and Freeport, while just a few nautical miles away are the idyllic castaway cays of the Out Islands.

History

The recorded history of the New World begins on one of the Bahamian islands. On 12 October 1492, after more than a month at sea sailing into the unknown, Columbus made land on the island of Guanahani – and named it San Salvador or 'Holy Saviour'. He landed with the banners of Ferdinand and Isabella and immediately claimed the island for Spain, greeted by no doubt awestruck native islanders, the Lucayan Indians. They were fascinated by the bells and mirrors that Columbus gave them in return for food, beads and the gold ornaments that they wore through their noses. It was the gold that attracted his attention, and the Indians explained that it came from the south. Soon afterwards, Columbus sailed off to search for it, touching other islands before leaving Bahamian waters and heading for Cuba.

The Lucayans (an Arawak tribe) had inhabited the Bahamas for around 500 years before the arrival of the Europeans, living off fish and turtles and growing a small amount of cassava. Columbus noticed scars on their bodies, received in raids by the Carib Indians from the islands farther south. The Lucayans numbered around 40,000 when the Spaniards first came to the Bahamas, but within 40 years, none remained; they had all been transported off the island to work in the gold mines in Hispaniola.

The Bahamas, rejected as *islas inutiles* (useless islands), were simply left alone by the Spaniards for the next hundred years, avoided because the *baja mar* was a treacherous sea in which to sail. Many ships were to founder over the next four centuries and 'wrecking' became one of the principal Bahamian industries in an otherwise barren place. There are even stories of the islanders putting out false lighthouses to lure passing ships onto the reefs. Others were more open about their profligacy. Pirates discovered the islands in the 16th century and they would lie in wait for the Spanish *flota*, the yearly fleet which collected in Havana harbour and set off into the Gulf Stream for Spain, loaded with the riches of the Spanish Main. Just as they are today, the coves and bays were the perfect hideaways for small sailing vessels.

The first British interest in the island came in one of the many royal grants, which involved chunks of uninhabited land being handed out as favours in the courts of Europe. Charles I granted the Bahamas to Sir Robert Heath in 1629, in addition to the Carolinas on the American mainland, just as the French king granted other islands a few years later. Settlement was another matter, and it was not until 20 years later that the first serious attempt was ventured from Bermuda. Religious troubles, mirroring the disputes in England itself, led a group of Puritans under the governor William Sayle to leave Bermuda in 1648 for the Bahamas, settling an island that they called Eleuthera (from the Greek word for 'freedom'). The colony had difficulties from the start, and most of the settlers returned to Bermuda, but it was at this time that Sayle discovered by accident a fine harbour on another island, which he called New Providence.

New Providence soon became the important island in the group, and the pirates and privateers swarmed to it in the late 1600s. Pirates like Charles Vane and Blackbeard, Benjamin Hornigold and Jack Rackham with his two women companions, Anne Bonney and Mary Read, made their way up here from Port Royal in Jamaica and from the Virgin Islands. Working for the British as 'privateers' or on their own account, they looted any Spanish ship or settlement they could find and returned with their loot to Nassau. In revenge, the Spaniards sacked the town four times in 25 years. The town flew the British flag, but it was almost completely lawless, and so, in 1717, the British sent out a governor to bring it under control. When he arrived, Woodes Rogers was popular, with the merchants and pirates alike, but within months he had stopped piracy, persuading the freebooters to become privateers only in time of war, and hanging those who did not want to give up the trade.

And so the Bahamas took shape, muddling through in times of peace, but flourishing as an entrepôt when there was a war. In the American War of Independence, the 3,000 Bahamians did not side openly with the rebelling mainland colonists, but there was an undercover trade of arms and gunpowder through the islands. Some took to the seas as privateers on the hunt for American shipping. Nassau was captured in 1766 by the colonist fleet and all the island's military supplies shipped off to the colonies.

Following the war, the population of the islands trebled as 8,000 loyalists fled for the Bahamas, setting up cotton estates on the Out Islands, which prospered for a

Diving

Washed by currents on all sides, the Bahamas have superbly clear waters with excellent diving. The corals and fish are basically the same as in other Caribbean islands, but there are more of certain fish and some corals are able to grow larger here. There are shallow reefs on the slopes close to shore off some of the islands; canyons and pinnacles that rise close to the water's surface; and walls, where the Bahama banks drop sheer down to the deep ocean floor – the resting-place of many wrecks that were beyond the famed Bahamian 'wreckers'. 'Blue holes' are a curious feature – they are cylindrical holes up to 200ft across which descend to 90ft below the surface of the sea. In a strong tide, they can generate a vortex as water is sucked in and out from below.

Visibility is excellent, often over 100ft, and it reveals fantastic landscapes of corals: gorgonians like vast fans standing among the fingers and branches of fur-covered corals, bouquets of flower corals and layers of carpet anemone. The fishlife is bewildering. You will come across single rays cruising and groupers loitering, or stopping off at cleaning stations to have their teeth picked by shrimps. Luxuriously coloured angelfish twitch as they glide past and trumpetfish hang vertically beneath the surface of the water.

Diving is available at all the main centres and there are some spectacular reefs right off Nassau itself (these have been used in a number of film sets). If you go farther afield into the Out Islands, there is excellent variety. Off the eastern coast of Andros is the third-largest barrier reef in the world, where the colours of the corals and sponges are supreme. Off the Abacos and Eleuthera, wreck dives include the wrecks not only of ships, but of two trains that went down while they were being transported. You could also take a ride in the tidal race at Current Cut off Eleuthera. Lessons are available in all the resorts.

Shark diving has become popular in the Bahamas over the past few years. There are about ten dive shops that offer it. Divers line up, led into place by guides, and then watch as a chain-mailed feeder appears with a bucketful of frozen fish. The sharks arrive, knowing they're in for a free meal, nuzzling and bumping the feeder. Understandably, it is quite closely controlled, but it is still an interesting sight to see these creatures in their element. They are phenomenally graceful and move almost like space-ships, hovering as they collect food and then flicking their tail in slow motion to move off, sometimes straight at you.

while. To work the plantations they brought slaves, whose descendants form the majority of today's Bahamian population. As their plantations failed, the white settlers left the islands, simply leaving the slaves to fend for themselves. Emancipation was declared in 1833.

In the American Civil War, Nassau saw another wave of prosperity as blockade runners made the dash over to the coast of the States with boatloads of arms. It lasted just four years and then the islands were eclipsed again, and so the Bahamians continued to scrape a living growing sisal and fruits, and collecting sponges from the sea bed. Prohibition in the States, from 1920 to 1933, turned the wharves of Nassau into a forest of bootleg barrels and casks waiting for the run across to Florida in fast boats. It took a few years before the coastguard could hope to catch them. The tradition was revived for a while recently as the islands were used as a stopover on the drugs trail from South America, for shipment of marijuana and cocaine, but now the DEA and Royal Bahamas Defence Force is better equipped to deal with it.

The Bahamian tourist industry has mushroomed over the last 40 years, to the point today where there are ten times as many visitors each year as the entire population of the islands. After the Second World War, Hog Island was sexily renamed Paradise Island and it exploded with hotels. Freeport was conceptualized in the 50s and then appeared in the 'pine barren' of Grand Bahama. Bahamians flooded into the centres from other islands to get a piece of the action. Tourism, the mainstay of the economy, is worth over a billion dollars annually and employs over two-thirds of the workforce. Other industries include offshore finance and agriculture, fishing and some light industry in Freeport on Grand Bahama. There is still visible poverty in certain parts of the Bahamas, but the situation is better than in most Caribbean islands, and far better than it was 40 years ago. Considerable money is invested in the country by expatriates who have built houses in estates like Lyford Cay outside Nassau and increasingly throughout the islands.

Traditionally the colonial Bahamas were administered by a small group of mainly white Bahamians called the 'Bay Street Boys', but after the Second World War their predominance came to an end. Universal suffrage did not come until 1962 when their power began to be shared with the Bahamian blacks. Independence was achieved on 10 July 1973. For many years, the Bahamas were led by the charismatic leader of the Progressive Liberal Party, Sir Lynden Pindling, despite occasional scandals implicating him in corruption. He was finally ousted in 1992. The country is now led by the Hon. Perry Christie of the Progressive Liberal Party. The country is a member of the British Commonwealth and is headed by a Governor General, Ivy Dument.

New Providence

The island of New Providence is small (just 21 by 7 miles), but it has always been the hub of Bahamian life. It lies in the northern area of the islands and is the site of the Bahamian capital, Nassau. Two-thirds of the Bahamas' population, 170,000 people, live on New Providence, most of them in Nassau, which has flourished periodically over the centuries as an entrepôt because of its magnificent harbour.

The island is the engine room of Bahamian tourism, and the three main resort areas now see as many as 1.25 million tourists a year. You can see the successive generations of hotels, each one fading as a newer and more exciting one is built. The old colonial houses on the hill, which are now old-time hotels of 'character', were overtaken in the 1930s by Art Deco piles and in the 50s by high-rise hotels downtown. The newest and most exciting are the pastel palaces on Cable Beach, the cabarets and gambling halls with their acres of slot machines.

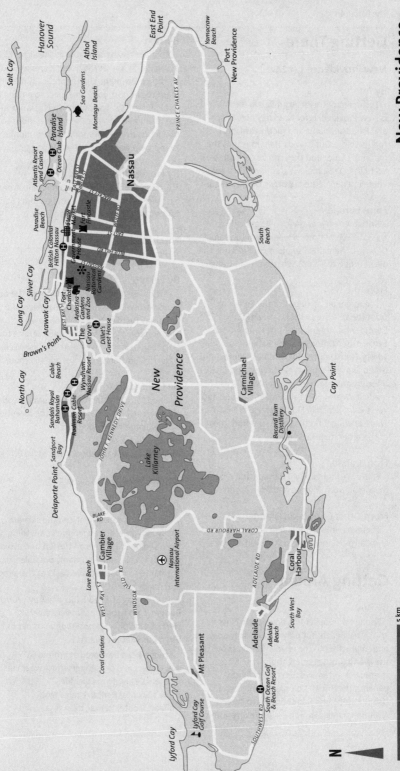

New Providence

Hanover Sound

Salt Cay

Athol Island

East End Point

Sea Gardens

Paradise Island
Ocean Club Island

Atlantis Resort
and Casino

Montagu Beach

Yamacraw Beach

Port
New Providence

PRINCE CHARLES AV

Paradise Beach

British Colonial
Hilton Nassau

Nassau

Silver Cay

Government House
Straw Market

Fort
Fincastle

South Beach

Long Cay

Arawak Cay

WEST BAY ST

Fort
Charlotte

Ardastra
Gardens and Zoo

Nassau
Botanical
Gardens

Brown's Point

The
Grove

Dillet's
Guest House

New
Providence

North Cay

Cable
Beach

Wyndham
Nassau Resort

Carmichael
Village

Cay Point

Sandals Royal
Bahamian

Radisson Cable
Beach Resort

JOHN F. KENNEDY DRIVE

Delaporte Point
Sandport
Bay

Lake
Killarney

Bacardi Rum
Distillery

BLAKE
RD

CORAL HARBOUR RD

Coral
Harbour

Love Beach

Gambier
Village

WEST BAY ST

FIELD RD

Nassau
International Airport

ADELAIDE RD

WINDSOR

Adelaide

ADELAIDE RD

Coral Gardens

Mt Pleasant

South West Bay

Adelaide Beach

Lyford Cay
Golf Course

South Ocean Golf
& Beach Resort

SOUTHWEST RD

Lyford Cay

N

5 km

3 miles

Getting There

New Providence t (1 242–)

By Air

The main centre for air arrivals in the Bahamas is New Providence, for Nassau, Cable Beach and Paradise Island, and for onward local flights to the Out Islands. Bahamasair is the national carrier and they can be contacted on US t 1 800 222 4262, *www.bahamasair.com*. There is a departure tax of $15 from Nassau.

From Europe

British Airways and Virgin Atlantic fly to Nassau several times a week from London Gatwick. There are also plenty of links from all over Europe to Miami, where you can transfer.

From the USA

The major air carriers into the Bahamas from the USA are Delta, US Airways, Continental, American Airlines and American Eagle; other airlines include Bahamasair, Trinity, Gulfstream, Spirit Airlines, Hooters Air, Island Express, JetBlue, Northwest and Chalk International. Connections for Nassau can be made in Miami, Fort Lauderdale, Orlando and West Palm Beach in Florida and also New York. There are direct flights to Nassau from most of the other major US cities.

From Canada

There are flights on Air Canada and charters to Nassau from Toronto and from Montreal.

From Other Caribbean Islands

There are links to Providenciales in the Turks and Caicos Islands and to Kingston, Jamaica.

Getting Around

By Bus

Endless minibuses link downtown Nassau and Cable Beach, but only occasionally does one run further to the residential areas out on the island (until about 6.30pm). The Nassau terminal is at the western end of Bay St, beneath the British Colonial Beach Resort. Use the stops and flag them down; fare $1. A minibus circles Paradise Island every 30mins.

By Taxi

Taxis are always available at the airport, along Bay St and at the hotels. Fares are fixed by the government and theoretically metered. From the airport, you can expect to pay $15 to Cable Beach, $22 to downtown Nassau, and $27 (includes $2 toll) to Paradise Island. If you hire a taxi by the hour for a trip around the island, negotiate a rate of around $45.

By Horse-drawn Carriage

Around the town itself, you might just prefer to travel by horse-drawn carriage. Tours $20 for two adults; $10 for children.

Hitch-hiking

Hitch-hiking is illegal.

By Ferry

Ferries run across the harbour from the dock in downtown Nassau to Paradise Island for $3.
Bahamas Fast Ferries, t 323 2166, *www. bahamasferries.com*. Scheduled service to Harbour Island as well as to Spanish Wells, North Eleuthera and Governor's Harbour.

By Guided Tour

Island tours, visiting the few sights beyond Nassau, can be booked through the reception of most large hotels, or directly:
Happy Tours, t 323 5818.
Majestic Tours, t 322 2606, *www.majestic holidays.com*.
Tropical Travel Tours, t 322 3802.

Car and Bike Hire

Car rental is convenient and the cars are easily available, but expensive at anything from $50 per day. Drive on the left and avoid downtown Nassau if humanly possible. The big-name companies have desks at the airport and major hotels.
Avis, West Bay St, **t** 326 6380, *www.avis.com*.
Budget, t 377 7405, *bracnas@batelnet.bs*.
Hertz, t 377 8684, *sidmac@bahamas.net.bs*.
Virgo Car Rental, t 394 2122.

Scooters can be rented at around $28–35 per day. Drivers and passengers must wear crash helmets by law. Firms include:
Bowe's Scooter Rental, t 326 8329.
Holiday Scooter Rental, t 322 3552.

Tourist Information

Abroad

The main Bahamas Tourist Office website is at *www.bahamas.com*.

Canada: 1130 Sherbrooke St West, Suite 750, Montreal, Quebec H3A 2M8, **t** 1 800 667 3777; 121 Bloor St East, Suite 1101, Toronto, Ontario M4W 3M5, **t** (416) 968 2999, *aadderle@ bahamas.com*.

UK: Parkway House, Suite 301, Sheen Lane, East Sheen, London SW14BlS, **t** (020) 8878 5569, *btogfd@bahamas.com*.

USA: 150 East 52nd St, 28th Floor North, New York, NY 10022, **t** (212) 758 2777, *vbrown@ bahamas.com*;
8600 W. Bryn Mawr Av, Suite 820, Chicago Illinois 60631, **t** (312) 693 1500, *astuart@ bahamas.com*;
3450 Wilshire Bd, Suite 208, Los Angeles, California 90010, **t** (213) 385 0033, *jjohnson@ bahamas.com*.

In New Providence

In New Providence itself, there are tourist information booths at Nassau International Airport: in arrivals, **t** 377 6806; and departures, **t** 377 6782. In downtown Nassau, there is an office at Rawson Square on Bay St, **t** 322 7801.

Media

There are two daily newspapers published in Nassau: the *Nassau Guardian*, which comes out in the morning, and the evening *Tribune*. A wide selection of US dailies is flown in on the day of release. There is a proliferation of tourist literature, where some quite useful information is hidden. *What to Do* mainly contains adverts about jewellery and watches, along with such essential advice as to which perfume might be best suited to your sign of the zodiac, but you will find a little practical advice thrown in, too. There are also a couple of dining magazines.

Medical Emergencies

Contact the Princess Margaret Hospital on Shirley St, Nassau, **t** 322 2861.

Money and Banks

The Bahamian dollar and the US dollar, set at par with one another, are both valid currencies in the Bahamas. You may receive change in either currency or even both, including Bahamian $3 and 50¢ notes, though these are nearly finished now. You are usually best off exchanging money in the banks, but hotels will change money at a slightly worse rate. **Traveller's cheques** and **credit cards** will be accepted almost everywhere in the hotels, restaurants and shops. If you go off the beaten track, however, take cash with you. Personal cheques are not readily accepted.

Tipping runs at a high 15%. In Nassau, the **banks** keep hours of Mon–Fri 9.30–3 (until 5pm on Fri).

Shopping

Shops open Mon–Sat 9–5 generally, but they often close one afternoon in the week.

Telephone Code

It is possible to direct-dial telephone to and from the major Bahamian islands. The IDD code is **t** 1 242, which is followed by a seven-digit number.

Festivals

Sailing regattas are some of the liveliest events. As well as races, there are onshore parties with barbecues and jump-ups.

December/January *Junkanoo*. Celebrated at the turn of the year, with masquerades out in the streets on 26 December and 1 January against a backdrop of Bahamian goombay.

June onwards *Goombay*. A wider series of cultural events as well as carnival parades through the streets.

10 July *Independence Day*.

12 October *Discovery Day*.

Watersports

Nassau offers a full gamut of watersports and most hotels have **windsurfers** on offer to guests. Otherwise, go to the concessionaires on Cable Beach or Paradise Island, where you can arrange **parasailing**, **jetskiing** and **waterskiing** or a more stately ride on a **pedalo**. You can keep children quiet with a ride on an **aqua-sausage** for a high-speed view of the harbour. Many hotels have sailing **dinghies**.

Canoeing

Canoeing at Lake Nancy, just off J. F. Kennedy Drive, **t** 323 3382. Lake Nancy's clear, shallow waters are home to lots of bird life.

Day Sails

There are endless yacht tours on offer, for an outing of snorkelling, boozing and dancing.
Bahamian Queen, **t** 393 2973.
Calypso, **t** 363 3333, *www.paradiseislandferry terminal.com*.
Flying Cloud, Paradise Island Ferry Dock, **t** 363 4430, *flyingcloud@bahamas.net.bs*, *www.flyingcloud.com*.
Island World Adventures, **t** 363 3333, *sales@islandworldadventures.com*, *www.islandworldadventures.com*.
Nassau Yacht Haven, **t** 393 8173.
Seahorse Sailing Adventure, **t** 363 5510, *www.seahorsesailingadventures.com*.
Sea Island Adventures, **t** 325 3910, *seaisle@ bahamas.net.bs*, *www.seaisl.com*.
Powerboat Adventures, East Bay Street, **t** 393 7116, *www.powerboatadventures.com*.

Deep-sea Fishing

Easily arranged through the marinas, or contact:
Born Free Charters, **t** 393 4144, *bornfree@coral wave.com*, *www.bornfreefishing.com*.
Chubasco, **t** 327 8148.

Underwater Adventures

Atlantis Submarine, **t** 356 3842.
Seaworld Explorer, Moses Plaza, Bay Street, **t** 356 2548, *shorex@batelnet.bs*. A semi-submarine, which glides over the Nassau Sea Gardens while you sit in comfort.
Hartley's Undersea Walk, Nassau Yacht Haven, East Bay Street, **t** 393 8234, *hartleys@ batelnet.bs*, *www.underseawalk.com*. Sealed helmet; safe for all ages and non-swimmers.
Underwater Wonderland, Nassau Yacht Haven, **t** 322 8234, *www.underseawalk.com*. Same as Hartley's Undersea Walk, above.
Dolphin Encounters, Blue Lagoon Island, **t** 363 1003, *info@dolphinencounters.com*, *www.dolphinencounters.com*.

Scuba Diving

For general information, *see* p.785. Dive shops on the island include:

Bahama Divers, East Bay St, **t** 393 1466, *www.bahamadivers.com*.
Dive Dive Dive, Smuggler's Rest Resort, **t** 362 1401, *www.divedivedive.com*.
Nassau Scuba Center, Ranfurly Drive, Coral Harbour, **t** 362 1964, *info@divenassau.com*, *www.divenassau.com*.
Stuart Cove's Dive South Ocean, **t** 362 4171, *info@stuartcove.com*, *www.stuartcove.com*.

Other Sports

Golf

Fees are $30–35.
Cable Beach Hotel, **t** 327 6000.
Paradise Island, on the eastern end, **t** 326 3926.
South Ocean Golf Club, southwest, **t** 326 4391.

Horse-riding

Horses are available if you would like to explore the pine-barren interior of New Providence or take a canter along the beach.
Happy Trails, **t** 362 1820. $25 per hour.

Tennis

There are plenty of tennis courts in the hotels and these are often free for hotel guests. If you are travelling independently, you can try the hotels (fee usually around $10 per hour).

Where to Stay

New Providence t (1 242–)

Nassau, Cable Beach and Paradise Island is the largest resort area in the Bahamas, and in all it has nearly 8,000 rooms, in hotels ranging from the most modern, massive, pastel-pink palaces of Cable Beach, through the tower-block hotels of the 70s and early 80s to small and comfortable guest houses, the family homes of the 19th century, built 'on the hill' in Nassau. If you feel like splashing out, you'll find the Caribbean's most expensive hotel room (almost a whole floor in fact, complete with robot servant and thunderstorm light-show) in the Marriott-Crystal Palace on Cable Beach – a snip at $25,000 a night, but you'll be pleased to hear that they'll throw it in free if you are a high roller on the casino downstairs ($100,000 stake). There is a 6% government tax on hotel rooms and there are various supplementary energy and service charges.

Luxury

One and Only Ocean Club, on the north side of Paradise Island, t 326 2501, UK t (01491) 411 222, US t 1 888 528 7157, *www.oceanclub.com*. The most elegant resort on the two islands and the finest setting. There are 109 rooms (and villas) on either side of the charming main courtyard laid with coral flagstones, sprouting with small palms, a fountain and pool and gingerbread trimmings. In the luxuriant gardens are the tennis courts and swimming pool, and a walkway leading down to the resurrected French cloister. All mod cons, cable TV, beach nearby.

Sandals Royal Bahamian Spa Resort and Offshore Island, Cable Beach, t 327 6400, US t 1 800 543 4300, *sandals@grouperbatenet.bs*, *www.sandals.com*. Probably the most attractive of the large hotels on Cable Beach, with its neoclassical façade dressed up in Nassau pink. There are 405 rooms and villas linked by coral paving stones in the manicured garden, with private beach. Satellite TV, health spa, weights room and cabaret.

Expensive

British Colonial Hilton Nassau, 1 Bay St, t 302 9032, *www.hilton.com*. The most distinctive and pleasant of the island's large hotels. The British Colonial building towers above Nassau itself and its multiple wings look out onto the harbour on one side and onto Bay St on the other. There are nearly 300 rooms which are comfortable and have all the conveniences you could need.

Wyndham Nassau Resort & Crystal Palace, Cable Beach, t 327 6200, UK t 0800 221 222, US t 1 800 222 7466, *www.marriotthotels. com*. If you like all the activity of a humming casino hotel on the beach, you can try this huge complex, with its five towers of pastel pink, lavender and fuchsia. It is vast, as bright inside as out, with 860 rooms, eight restaurants, 24-hour room service, endless activities, waterslide, beached ship bar.

South Ocean Golf and Beach Resort, t 362 4391, *sales@southoceanbahamas.com*, *www.southoceanbahamas.com*. Set in its own grand and luxurious landscaped gardens on the south coast of the island, the South Ocean resort has 230 rooms ranged in wings around the central great house. There are plenty of sports (there is a golf course) and watersports, including diving, on the beach just across the road. Country-club luxury; the hustle of Nassau is miles away.

Graycliff Hotel, West Hill St, Nassau, t 322 2796, *www.graycliff.com*. Set in one of Nassau's magnificent old town houses: downstairs is the restaurant, but on the creaking wooden floors upstairs, behind the breezy screened balconies, and in the explosive walled garden are 14 sumptuous rooms – including Hibiscus, Jasmine and Mandarino, all dressed up in traditional colonial style. Elegant atmosphere.

Moderate

Buena Vista Hotel, Delancy St, Nassau, t 322 2811. Set in an old colonial town house. There are just a few rooms upstairs, comfortable and decorated in old style.

Casuarinas of Cable Beach, PO Box CB-1322, West Bay Street, Nassau, t 327 7921, US t 1 800 327 3012, *casuarinashotel@bahamas. net.bs*, *www.casuarinashotel.com*. Well priced if you want to stay at the quieter end of Cable Beach. It is a bit pre-fab, but friendly. The rooms are set around the pool and gardens, with air-con and satellite TV.

Orange Hill Beach Inn, West Bay St, t 327 7157, *info@orangehill.com*, *www.orangehill.com*. A charming and very low-key hotel, untypical for the up-beat Bahamas. The 32 air-conditioned rooms are quite simple (some have kitchenettes, others full kitchens and all have televisions), standing in a modern block above the pool and garden, just across the road from the beach. But it is the main house with its bar and restaurant which is fun, where everyone meets, to read, swap diving stories and watch videos.

Dillet's Guest House, t 325 1133, *dillets@ batelnet.bs*, *www.islandeaze.com*. A family-owned, 70-year-old Bahamian home converted into a 7-room bed and breakfast. Set on an acre of gardens with hammocks, and walking distance from the beach and main attractions. Rooms have bath, air-con, sitting areas and cable TV. Some have cooking facilities. There is a garden pool,

Internet café and art studio and a resident artist. Home cooked meals and afternoon tea are available on request.

Inexpensive

The tourist desk at the airport is a good source of information on cheap accommodation.

Parthenon Hotel, West St, Nassau, t 322 2643. Just out of the downtown area of Nassau, has 18 neat and clean rooms.

Diplomat Inn, 4 Delancy St, Nassau, t 325 2688. A nice old town house on the hill. Kitchen available and bar.

Mignon Guest House, Market St in central Nassau, t 322 4771. Has just a few air-conditioned rooms.

Eating Out

There are some good restaurants to be found, and you should look beyond the hotels, which tend to serve standard international fare. Like so many other things in the Bahamas, there is a West Indian lilt, but the accent is also distinctly American. There are the familiar fast-food restaurants, such as McDonald's and KFC, but also a strong influence from the American South – you will even find *grits* here. The top restaurants serve gourmet food, ingredients imported from the States, as well as local fish and seafood, but traditional Caribbean dishes are readily found – rice 'n' peas is peas 'n' rice here – and the Bahamians do a mean seasoned chicken. Goat and tropical vegetables find their way in from the Out Islands and are then served up curried and stewed. *Souse* is a watery stew in which you will find vegetables and odd-looking parts of animals, e.g. 'pig foot'. And the Bahamians make good use of seafood, of the lobsters and crabs (stoned crab and cracked conch), and of the fish that they trawl in the shallows and haul out of the deep, from grouper to kingfish. *Kalik*, named after the cowbells that are used in the carnival processions, is the beer of the Bahamas and it is quite good: light and quite bitter for a lager, always served chilled.

Nassau has the largest selection of restaurants (many of the best local Bahamian eateries are 'behind the hill'). Most restaurants add service at 15%. **Categories** are arranged according to the price of a main dish:

expensive = US$20 and above; moderate = US$10–20; inexpensive = US$10 and under.

Expensive

Café Matisse, Bank Lane (behind Parliament Square), t 356 7012, *www.cafe-matisse.com*. Homemade pasta, pizza, seafood, *filet mignon*, and great desserts can be enjoyed in a charming historic house built in 1800s with a courtyard in the heart of downtown Nassau for outdoor dining. Smart attire required. *Closed Sun and Mon*.

Dune, One & Only Ocean Club, t 363 2501. The outstanding restaurant of highly-acclaimed chef Jean-George Vongerichten with creative French-Asian fusion cuisine in a blissful setting by the sea. The dining room is dressed in dark venge wood against white with an open kitchen; you can also eat outside on the wraparound terrace.

Churrascaria, Graycliff Hotel. West Hill St, t 302 9150. Sip a refreshing Caipirinha cocktail as you begin your Brazilian-style gastronomic tour. Gaucho waiters serve you a variety of chicken and meats, slow-roasted on a giant hearth spit. The grand salad bar offers fish appetizers and pasta and bean dishes, along with wine from the world-class cellars.

Graycliff Restaurant, West Hill St, Nassau, t 322 2796. A magnificent setting in an old town house, it serves probably the finest food in Nassau. Before the meal, you take cocktails in the drawing room, to a piano accompaniment, and then you move into one of the three dining rooms, candlelit with huge windows and polished wooden floors and tables. The menu is French: Dover sole *à la ciboulette* or grilled spiny lobster *aux deux sauces*. The wine list is like a Bible, and to follow you can have a brandy or try an aged Caribbean rum.

Buena Vista, Delancy St, Nassau, t 322 2811. A restaurant also set in a West Indian town house with a large and airy dining room. The cuisine is French and the menu long, including Bahamian fish and seafood in creole style, fillet of red snapper in honey mustard and venison and pheasant '*Grande-mère*'.

Sun and..., Lakeview Drive, off East Bay St, Nassau, t 393 1205. Set in a modern villa. The tables stand around the courtyard garden, overlooking the fountain and ornamental pool. The menu is French and continental with some Bahamian dishes; try *tournedos rossini* with Madeira truffle sauce or roast duck with raspberry sauce. *Closed Mon.*

Moderate

Green Shutters, 48 Parliament Street, Nassau, t 325 5702. A pub-style restaurant and saloon bar with studded leather seats and hunting-scene table mats. Bangers and mash and fish 'n' chips as well as burgers. Quite a lively drinking crowd in the early evening.

The Shoal, Nassau St by the Texaco garage, Nassau. A classic West Indian setting – an air-conditioned dining room with thick carpets and formica on the walls. And the best in local food: Bahamian broiled craw-fish, or stew-fish and johnny cake, all washed down with a Kalik beer.

The Poop Deck, Nassau Yacht Haven, East Bay Street, t 393 8175. One of Nassau's hotspots for conch chowder and seafood, set on a large veranda overlooking the marina. It's new sister, The Poop Deck West (West Bay Street, Sandyport, t 327 3325) has the same casual, friendly atmosphere.

Café Johnny Canoe, Nassau Beach Hotel, Cable Beach, t 327 3373. Colourful and comfortable with indoor/outdoor casual dining from burgers to roast chicken, including Bahamian classics such as cracked conch and grouper. Dessert speciality is rum cake.

Conch Fritter, Marlborough Street, t 323 8778. Conch fritters and other Bahamian dishes, as well as hamburgers, in a noisy, friendly tropical atmosphere. You can watch satellite TV with your meal or at the bar.

Clay Oven, West Bay St, t 325 2525. Wide selection of Indian cuisine and vegetarian dishes.

Inexpensive

If you want to go more local, you can find some superb and authentic Bahamian take-away food in small shacks in Nassau. You should be quite careful at night if you go 'over the hill'. The thing to have is a conch snack: cracked conch (beaten and then covered in batter), which usually comes swimming in tomato sauce and with chips. Try:

Dirty's, Boyd Rd, Nassau.
Bamboo Shack, Nassau St, Nassau.
Johnson's, Shirley St, Nassau.

Bertha's Go-go Ribs, Mackey St, Nassau.
Stalls, near the Crystal Cay Bridge.
Fish Fry at Arawak Cay, t 323 2227. Dozens of stalls offering conch to aficionados.

Bars and Nightlife

You will find that many of the bars around Nassau get filled up with sunburnt tourists making whoopee, so if you want something a bit more sophisticated, perhaps a cocktail in colonial surroundings, you might be best off in one of the smarter restaurants. There are, however, a good many local bars, too.

There are discotheques, cabaret shows and casinos in the large hotels on Paradise Island and Cable Beach.

Poop Deck, above the marina on East Bay St, Nassau. There is a boozy early evening scrum here, gathering a lively crowd of tourists and some locals.

Hammerheads, East Bay St. Hip chicks and dudes in sunglasses (a permanent fixture, it seems, even at night) gravitate around here.

Deep End, Marlborough. Keep cool with light beer and MTV.

Candles Wine Bar, Paradise Island, t 363 4536. Open until sunrise.

Friday's Soon Come, East Bay St, t 328 3088. Bahamian fare plus Atkins-friendly and children's menus. Live entertainment.

Hard Rock Café, Charlotte St, t 325 7625, *www.hardrock.com.*

Clubs

If you feel like going dancing, you can try the following spots:

Waterloo, East Bay St, Nassau. The best club, with bars and a dancefloor set around a pool and garden with statues and balustrades. It attracts an easy mix of ages.

Club 601, 601 East Bay St, Nassau.
The Bomb, Elizabeth Av, Nassau.
The Zoo, West Bay St, Nassau.

Beach Bars

Traveller's Rest, on the West Bay Rd. A pleasant place for hanging out with a view of the sea through the sea grape and palm trees.

Montagu Beach Bar, east of town. Very popular with the locals at the weekends.

With all the cruise ships and straw-hat vendors, Nassau has a pretty fearsome tourist race, but there is a more sophisticated side to it, too. There are good restaurants and a large expatriate crowd. And there are a few more noticeably 'West Indian' parts of the island – 'over the hill' in Nassau and in outlying towns on the island.

Nassau

The capital of the Bahamas has always centred on its harbour as the source of its prosperity. Large ocean-going ships and local boats have always put in here, and then occasional waves of pirates, gun-runners and rum-runners have traded in the port, bringing extra prosperity while the good times lasted. The old waterfront buildings look on to Bay St, where the commercial buzz still continues, now driven by shiploads of cruise-trippers – *hackers* tout their goods in the street (usually offering to braid your hair nowadays or sell you a conch shell) and the warehouses contain air-conditioned boutiques with cut-price bargains. You will even hear the cruise liners calling their passengers by blowing their foghorns. The inhabitants of Nassau are not always very forthcoming, but most will oblige if you approach them. You should be careful about your valuables.

Settled in 1666, the city was originally called Charles Town, but it was renamed Nassau after William III of Orange Nassau. The town divides into three areas: the commercial district down by the waterfront with its colonnaded warehouses; the colonial mansions and the large town houses built by the merchants, set back from the activity on top of the ridge; and the area 'over the hill', where the inhabitants of Nassau live in streets of clapboard and now modern concrete houses – an extremely lively part of Nassau life.

The commercial hub of the city is still **Bay St**, an outsize shopping precinct as it always has been, running parallel to the waterfront, just a short walk from the cruise-ship dock. At its heart is the **straw market** (constructed on the site of the traditional market building in 1974), with endless stalls selling anything from rush matting to a straw hat, carvings and beads to plait into your hair. Its activity is infectious and the saleswomen are persuasive – more mercantile mayhem.

Not far down Bay St, close to the cruise-ship wharf and Rawson Square, is the traditional heart of the Bahamas government in **Parliament Square**, where a statue of Queen Victoria sits surrounded on three sides by neoclassical buildings dressed up in Nassau pink. Here, you will find the Bahamas **House of Assembly**, the old Treasury and Supreme Court. Taking Parliament St out of the square, you come to an octagonal building, which once was the town prison, decommissioned in 1879 and now the Nassau **public library**. The alcoves with the books were the original cells. The *surreys* (horses and traps) that you see everywhere are tourist taxis.

The **National Historical Museum**, occupying the Bahamas Historical Society building on Elizabeth Av, houses a collection of paintings, photographs and maps from Bahamian history, starting in Arawak times, through pirates and loyalists. The **Queen's staircase** leads to the top of the cliff to **Fort Fincastle** (*open daily 9–5; adm free*), built

> **Best Beaches**
>
> **Lighthouse Beach**: Within a shout of downtown Nassau, on the western esplanade leading out of town. Crowded but close.
>
> **Paradise Beach**: A ferry-ride over on Paradise Island, this is another active beach on the west of the island (*adm*). Alternatively, if you want to be a little less crowded, there is a beach farther round on the northern shore.
>
> **Cable Beach**: A bus-ride away, west of town, with all the sporting activities on offer.
>
> **Delaporte Point** and **Love Beach**: Beyond the Cable Beach area.
>
> **Orange Hill Beach**: Runs about a half mile along the coast, before Love Beach.
>
> **Travellers' Rest**: A small beach in front of the island's best-known beach bar.

in 1793 with the shape of a ship's prow. It is now restored and has a commanding view and a few hefty cannon that were never used. The view is better still from the watertower nearby.

Farther along the ridge, where many of Nassau's finest old stone town houses with louvred verandas were built in the 19th century (among them the attractive restaurant Graycliff), you will come to **Government House**, a neoclassical mansion built in 1801 and dressed in Nassau pink, now the residence of the Governor General. On the stairs leading down to the street is a statue of Columbus.

Near the toll bridge leading over to Paradise Island is another lively bit of Bahamian life: the **market**, where fruit vendors sit and conch salesmen extract the animal from its shell. Fruits and ground provisions are shipped in from the Out Islands and sold here on the dock. The mail boats also dock here.

There is not much to see on **Paradise Island** (*toll costs 25¢ for walkers, theoretically, and $1 for cars*) itself unless you are a student of the tourist industry; the best reason to go over is for the beaches. However, the island, which was called Hog Island until 1961, is quite pretty and some of the hotels are set in attractive grounds. The one sight to aim for is the **Cloisters** in Versailles Gardens (near the Ocean Club in the east of the island), where a walkway of stairs and statuary leads down to a 14th-century cloister that has ended up thousands of miles from its monastery in Lourdes.

Around the Island

Leaving downtown Nassau to the west you reach the seafront on the Western Esplanade. To the left is the lumbering **Fort Charlotte** on the hill (*open daily; adm free*), built at the beginning of the 19th century; it once manned a fearsome 42 cannon, but they never fired a shot in anger.

Behind the fortress are the **Nassau Botanical Gardens** (*t 323 5975; open daily 9–4.30; adm*), where trails lead through the 16 acres of flowering trees and shrubs, a cactus garden, and past ponds of tropical fish to a grotto. Nearby the **Ardastra Gardens** (*t 323 5806; open daily 9–5; adm*) show off the Bahamian national birds, the pink flamingos, to their best advantage when they perform a bit of precision marching at the orders of their drill sergeant. In the 5 acres of tropical luxuriance there is an aviary of birds and a few animals.

Cable Beach is called so because the Bahamas' first cable link to Florida was made from here, along the magnificent stretch of sand. It is the Bahamas' most built-up resort area, ever-increasing since hotels first appeared here in the 1950s. Travelling further west, you pass many expensive private houses and other condominium developments before reaching **Lyford Cay** on the western tip of the island, an exclusive and extremely rich housing estate mainly peopled by expatriates. It is private.

The south of the island is less densely populated, though there are a few local Bahamian towns like **Adelaide** that the tourism race seems to have passed by. Some were settled by emancipated slaves, others by Africans who were being transported on Spanish slave ships caught by the British Navy after the abolition of the slave trade in 1807. In the east of the island is the **Retreat** (*t 323 1317; tours Tues–Thurs; adm*), the headquarters of the Bahamas National Trust, where there are some 200 species of palms and other exotic plants in the five acres of garden.

Grand Bahama

The tourist area of Freeport/Lucaya is unlike anything else in the Caribbean or the Bahamas. It is visibly American in style, with wide tree-lined boulevards and spacious suburbs, satellite dishes and air-conditioned supermarkets. Freeport/Lucaya is run by a company, the Grand Bahama Port Authority.

The island of Grand Bahama itself is the fourth largest of the Bahamian islands and, with 44,000 inhabitants, its city Freeport has become the second largest in the country. But 50 years ago none of the Freeport/Lucaya area existed. The resort was simply dreamt up and created in the early 1960s.

Best Beaches

Silver Point Beach and **Xanadu Beach**: Located in Lucaya (Xanadu is a little further west), these are the most developed and the best for watersports (*see p.798–9* for companies).

Williams Town: South of Freeport, a cracking beach beyond the tourist hotels, a superb suntrap with casuarina trees down to the sand and with excellent snorkelling and swimming. There are no jet skis or windsurfers for hire there, but you can get a drink and a snack in the town.

Mather Town Beach: Just to the east of Lucaya, a stunning stretch that runs for miles.

Barbary Beach: The other side of the Lucayan Waterway, with yet more perfect white sand and isolation.

Taino Beach: In Lucaya, just west of Smith's Bay. Good snorkelling, with shade and facilities.

Gold Rock Beach: Can be reached from the Lucayan National Park (no facilities).

Fortune Beach: Off Midshipman Road, south of the Garden of the Groves.

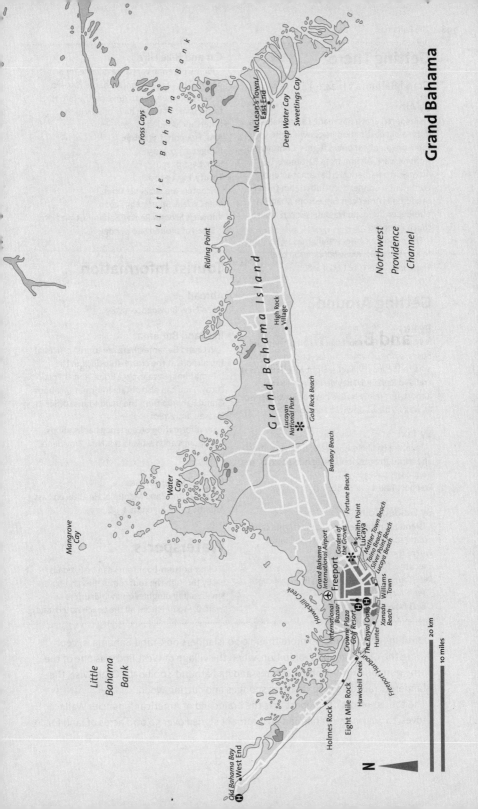

Grand Bahama

Little Bahama Bank

Cross Cays

Little Bahama Bank

McLean's Town
East End

Deep Water Cay

Sweetings Cay

Riding Point

Grand Bahama Island

High Rock
Village

Northwest
Providence
Channel

Gold Rock Beach

Lucayan
National Park

Water
Cay

Barbary Beach

Mangrove
Cay

Fortune Beach

Smiths Point
Lucaya
Mother Town Beach
Taino Beach
Silver Point Beach
Lucaya Beach

Grand Bahama
International Airport

Garden of
the Groves

Freeport

International
Bazaar

Williams
Town

Hawksbill Creek

Crowne Plaza
Golf Resort

The Royal Oasis
Hunter
Xanadu
Beach

Little
Bahama
Bank

Holmes Rock

Eight Mile Rock

Hawksbill Creek

Freeport Harbour

Old Bahama Bay
West End

N

10 miles
20 km

Getting There

Grand Bahama t (1 242–)

By Air

Freeport/Lucaya has made Grand Bahama quite a big destination in its own right, so there are plenty of direct flights: Continental from Newark, AirTran from Baltimore, US Airways from Charlotte, Bahamasair and Continental Connection/Gulfstream from Ft. Lauderdale, American Eagle from Miami. A number of flights to Nassau (see p.788) also touch Freeport.

The national carrier is Bahamasair, US t 1 800 222 4262, www.bahamasair.com. There is a departure tax of $18.

Getting Around

By Bus

Within the Freeport/Lucaya area, there are buses, some of which run beyond the central area to the local villages: Eight Mile Rock, West End and East End. They do not run to the airport, but many hotels have a shuttle service as well as buses down to the beach.

By Taxi

Taxis are easily found in the tourist centres and through hotel lobbies. To hire a taxi by the hour costs $25–30.
Freeport Taxi, t 352 6666.

By Guided Tour

Island tours to the island's few sights can be arranged (again through any hotel lobby, where they will pick you up):
Executive Tours, t 352 8858.
Reef Tours, t 373 5880, www.portlucaya.com/ reeftours.
C & G Travel & Tours, t 351 3366.

Car and Bike Hire

Plenty of rental **cars** are available for a deposit and a steep rental charge ($55–70 per day). Remember to drive on the left. Hire firms, some of which have offices in the hotels, include:
Avis, Freeport, t 352 7666.
Budget, t 377 7405.
Star, t 352 9325.
Thrifty, t 352 9300.
Scooters are available from:
Mac Cycle & Sports, t 352 2629.
Knowle's Scooter Rental, Bahamia, t 351 2481.
Steep at around $40 per day.

Tourist Information

Abroad

See 'New Providence', p.789.

In Grand Bahama

In Grand Bahama, there are tourist offices at the airport, at the cruise-ship dock, in the International Bazaar, t 352 8044, and at Port Lucaya. You can also obtain information about Grand Bahama from the main tourist office in Nassau, t 322 7801.

For information on currency, banks, shops, telephones and festivals, see 'New Providence', p.789.

Medical Emergencies

Contact the Rand Memorial Hospital on East Atlantic Drive, Freeport, t 352 6735.

Watersports

Glass-bottom-boat tours can be fixed up easily through the tour companies and hotels. Small sailing **dinghies** and **windsurfers** are available to hire from all the beach hotels, and

Until 1955 there were no more than 1,000 islanders on Grand Bahama, except during the Civil War and Prohibition, when the village of West End was one of the prime gun- and rum-running centres, and had around 400 boats. Otherwise, the islanders scraped a living catching sponges and cutting wood.

The tourist resort of Freeport was the brainchild of American financier Wallace Groves, to whom the Bahamian government signed over 50,000 acres of land for

there's **jetskiing** and **parasailing** at Our Lucaya Resort. Major watersports operators outside the hotels include:

Executive Tours, t 352 8858.

Forbes Charter and Tours, t 352 9311.

Ocean Motion, Our Lucaya, **t** 374 2421.

Paradise Watersports, t 373 4001, *pwsports@batelnet.bs*.

Reef Tours, t 373 5880, *www.portlucaya.com/reeftours*.

Deep-sea Fishing

There are a number of boats for hire in which you can trawl the fishing grounds off the island. Renting a boat with tackle and bait for half a day comes out at $400, while a full day's hire is $650.

Sailing

Sailors will find plenty of marinas on Grand Bahama. **Yacht** tours can also be arranged with the big operators, anything from a day's roistering with rum punch in hand to a hard day's yachting:

Jolly Roger, **t** 373 3923.

Pat and Diane Fantasia Tours, **t** 373 8681, *www.snorkelingbahamas.com*.

Scuba Diving

Sun Odyssey, t 373 4014, *karen@sunodysseydivers.com, www.sunodysseydivers.com*.

UNEXSO (Underwater Explorer's Society), Lucaya Marina, **t** 373 1244, *info@unexso.com, www.unexso.com*.

Xanadu Undersea Adventures, t 352 3811, *xanadu@batelnet.bs, www.xanadudive.com*.

Snorkelling

There is fine snorkelling to be had in many places along the south coast, but it is particularly good at Peterson Cay, to the east of the resort areas, **t** 352 5438.

Other Sports

Golf

Crowne Plaza Golf Resort and the **Ruby** courses, close to the International Bazaar area, **t** 350 7000.

Fortune Hills Golf Course, t 373 4500.

Lucayan Golf and Country Club, t 373 1066. Set around Lucaya.

The Reef, Our Lucaya Beach & Golf Resort, **t** 373 1066. Designed by Robert Trent Jones Jnr.

Horse-riding

Pinetree Stables, Beachway Drive, Freeport, **t** 373 3600. You can expect to canter in the surf along Grand Bahama's fantastic beaches. *Closed Mon.*

Tennis

Tennis courts are widely available in the hotels and often free to hotel guests. Some hotels will let visitors use the courts anyway, for a fee (commonly $10/hr).

Where to Stay

Grand Bahama t (1 242–)

Expensive

Crowne Plaza Golf Resort & Casino, in Freeport, across the road from the International Bazaar, *reservations@crowneplazagrandbahamas.com, www.theroyaloasis.com*, **t** 350 7000. If you like a large and active resort, then this low-rise place is likely to appeal. There are 965 rooms in two locations (in the Tower and the Country Club), five dining rooms, multiple Jacuzzis, golf, nightclub and, of course, a massive casino.

development as a duty-free port in 1955, with agreements over tax exemptions for 35 years. Industry came – oil refining and bunkering. As tourism boomed, the company began to build hotels on the island's magnificent beaches and Freeport/Lucaya took off. The resort sells itself on the ticket of a truly all-mod-cons cure for your woes – endless watersports by day, and gambling, glitz and cabaret at night.

The Westin & Sheraton at Our Lucaya Beach and Golf Resort, t 373 1444, www.westin.com/ourlucaya, www.sheraton.com/ourlucaya. This massive complex, in a good location just across from the Port Lucaya Marketplace, includes the 738-room Westin (*expensive*) and the 475-room Sheraton (*moderate*) with Caribbean-style rooms and suites, 14 restaurants, a spa and fitness centre, golf, tennis courts, four pools, watersports, children's camp and casino.

Moderate

Port Lucaya Resort and Yacht Club, PO Box F-42452, t 373 6618, vacation@coralwave.com, www.portlucayaresort.com. Overlooking its own marina, a series of two-storey buildings surrounds the Olympic-size swimming pool, Jacuzzi and landscaped gardens.

Pelican Bay at Lucaya, next to Port Lucaya Marketplace, t 373 9550, pelicanb@batelnet.bs, www.pelicanbayhotel.com. Almost 200 whimsically appointed guest rooms and suites with balconies, hot tubs and a pool bar. Sits on the lagoon but not far from the beach. There is also plenty of scope for activities, including safaris and ocean kayaking.

The Bell Channel Inn, PO Box F-3817, t 373 2673, caribdiv@grouper.batelnet.bs. Thirty-two comfortable air-conditioned rooms with TV in a modern block in the town area.

Inexpensive

Royal Islander, near the International Bazaar, PO Box F-42549, t 351 6000.

Eating Out

There is a quite a variety of restaurants in Freeport/Lucaya (many in the International Bazaar, of course). There are also a number of places to eat out on the beaches during the day. Remember that service at 10–15% will be added to your bill. **Categories** are arranged according to the price of a main dish: expensive = US$20 and above; moderate = US$10–20; inexpensive = US$10 and under.

Expensive

The Stoned Crab, Taino Beach, t 373 1442. A popular restaurant on the seafront with a breezy terrace and an air-conditioned dining room beneath a pyramid roof. Lobster *al pesto* and other exotic seafood creations. A pleasant place for a dinner for two.

Ruby Swiss, near the International Bazaar, t 352 8507. Has a subdued, candlelit setting in a modern building. The menu is European: seafood *fettuccine au Pernod* or coconut-fried shrimp.

Pier One, on stilts in Freeport Harbour, t 352 6674. Popular. Seafood and fish specialities.

Ferry House, Pelican Bay at Lucaya, t 373 1595. Subdued setting outlined in fairy lights, with windows overlooking the lagoon. French, Asian and Caribbean combine into artful dishes by chef/owner.

Moderate

Outrigger's, Smith's Point, t 373 4811. Here you can get a well-priced beachside meal, scorched conch or steamed grouper.

Inexpensive

Mama Flo's White Wave Club, Smith's Point. The best of island food: a classic rum shop, serving fried fish and chicken dinner.

Chicken Nest, West End, t 346 6440. Excellent chicken.

Sunset Village, in Eight Mile Rock, West End. Rows of huts along the shore sell drinks and food. Local plates for $10 are filled with chicken, ribs or fish, plus rice 'n' peas, plantain and all the local favourites.

Around the Island

There are very few sights on the island, but in Freeport you will definitely come across the **International Bazaar**, an odd conglomeration of buildings in imitation of styles from all over the world, from a Japanese arch of welcome to a Turkish bazaar. You can eat and shop here. It feels a little odd and soulless, but most people do not worry because they have come here on the hunt for bargains. Occasionally, there is some entertainment. The real centre of the town of Freeport is **Churchill Square**, near the Port Authority Building; this is also the best spot for buying groceries if you are catering for yourself.

There is a botanical garden in the area. The **Garden of the Groves** (*t 352 4045; open Thurs–Tues 10–5; adm*) is set in 12 acres of Bahamian greenery laced with lagoons and streams and with a hanging garden at the entrance. The plant species are named.

The **Dolphin Experience**, where you can cavort with several bottlenose dolphins who are kept in captivity while being studied, is now in Sanctuary Bay. Learn about dolphin communication. They are eventually to be let back into the wild if they wish to go. **Port Lucaya** is a resort area with hotels, marina and shopping complexes.

Beyond Freeport to the east, you come into the pine barren, endless pine forest with just a few local towns which are a bit more typical of the rest of the Bahamas and where you can usually get a meal or a drink. At the **Lucayan National Park and Caverns**, trails lead through the scrub to a couple of limestone sinkholes, Ben's Cave and Burial Mound Cave. Beyond the park, you come to the old **Gold Rock missile tracking station**, the first down-orbit of Cape Canaveral, and eventually the road comes to McLean's Town at the east end.

To the west of Freeport is Hawksbill Creek, the centre of Grand Bahama industry, a container transhipment port and ship repair yard. The town of **Eight Mile Rock** is strung along eight miles of coral shoreline and you will see some of the attractive old Bahamian homes that were here before the recent concrete development. At **West End**, you can still see the remnants of the old warehouses and decaying piers from the days of Prohibition, where the boats tied up before making the dash over to the coast of Florida loaded up with liquor.

The Out Islands

The Out Islands comprise the Bahamian out islands and their hundreds of cays and sandbars that barely make it above the waves. They leave the casinos and cabarets of New Providence and Grand Bahama far behind, offering instead a more traditional Bahamas landscape: pretty, well-kept houses painted in bright colours and topped with shingle roofs, set amid gardens of tropical flowers and surrounded by white picket fences.

Though the houses are mostly built in concrete now, in the remoter islands you may still just see poorer clay houses with thatched roofs and little ovens built away from the main building. In the most barren areas, the topsoil is so thin that it is unable to support much growth. Here the islanders have developed a system of planting deep in holes in the ground, by making a kind of compost in there in which they plant. Traditionally self-sufficient and more remote from the capital than the few miles of sea would imply, the Out Islands are now populated in many cases with older folk, as the younger generations have gone off to Nassau in search of work.

Scattered in splinters and shards over the *baja mar*, most of the islands stretch no more than 100ft from the sea. Many are just a couple of miles wide, but they can

Getting There

The Out Islands t (1 242)

By Air

Most of the Out Islands are served by once- or twice-daily flights from Nassau (the Abacos are also served from Freeport), but a few have direct flights from the US mainland: Marsh Harbour and Treasure Cay (both in the Abacos) have flights from Miami, Fort Lauderdale, Orlando, Tampa and also West Palm Beach; Governor's Harbour (Eleuthera) and Bimini are served from Miami and Fort Lauderdale; George Town in the Exumas from Miami, Fort Lauderdale and Key West; and Andros from Miami. It is possible to charter a plane to almost any of the Out Islands from Florida. Airlines include:

American Eagle, US and Bahamas **t** 1 800 433 7300, **t** 367 2231.

Bahamasair, US **t** 1 800 222 4262, **t** 367 2095, *www.bahamasair.com*. Flies from Nassau to about twenty different islands dotted around the archipelago. The more isolated islands are served only a couple of times a week, though most have a daily service. Hotels usually have a connecting motorboat if you need to make a hop to an offshore cay. All flights are routed via Nassau so, if you wish to travel from one Out Island to another, you will find that you have to return to the capital.

Gulfstream, US **t** (305) 871 1200, **t** 1 800 688 7225, *www.gulstreamair.com*.

Chalk's Ocean Airways, US **t** (305) 373 1120, US **t** 1 800 424 2557, *reservations@flychalks.com*, *www.flychalks.com*. A seaplane service, which links the coast of Florida (Watson Island off Miami and Fort Lauderdale), with several points in the Bahamas, including Paradise Island and Bimini. Charters are also available.

There are a number of air charter companies that fly light planes ideally suited for a short hop down the islands. Contact:

Calypso Air, *www.calypsoair.com*. To Marsh Harbour and Treasure Cay.

Congo Air, **t** 377 8329.

Lynx Air, **t** 1888 596 9247, **t** 954 772 9808, *info@lynxair.com*, *www.lynxair.com*.

By Sea

Inter-island ferries connect destinations within the Abacos. A complete list is available from the Out Islands Promotion Board.

Albury's Ferry, **t** 242 365 6010. Daily sailings between Marsh Harbour and Hopetown.

Green Turtle Ferry, **t** 242 365 4128. Daily sailings between Green Turtle and Treasure Cay.

Abaco Adventures Ferry, **t** 242 365 8749. Several sailings each week from Treasure Cay to Guana Cay, Man-O-War and Hope Town.

Mail boats do a weekly run from Nassau to an island with the mail, the stores, and any locals heading home, accompanied by their goats and chickens. Spaces on mail boats are offered on a first-come, first-served basis and they leave from Potter's Cay docks in downtown Nassau, close to the bridge over to Paradise Island, **t** 393 1064. The boats are fun to travel on, though they can take anything up to 24hrs to reach their destination. Typical one-way fares are: Nassau to the Abacos – about $35, Grand Bahama – $50, Andros – $30, South Andros – $30, Bimini – $40, the Exumas – $40–45, Cat Island – $40, Rum Cay – $35, San Salvador – $35, Mayaguana and Inagua – $50.

You might consider hitching a lift on a **yacht** by turning up at the marina and asking around.

There are ports of entry for sailors in the following islands:

The Abacos: Green Turtle Cay, Marsh Harbour, Sandy Point, Treasure Cay, Walker's Cay.

Berry Islands: Chub Cay, Harbour Cay.

Bimini: Alice Town, at any marina facility.

Andros: Congo Town, Fresh Creek, San Andros.

Eleuthera: Governor's Harbour, Harbour Island, Hatchet Bay, Cape Eleuthera, Rock Sound.

Exuma Cays: George Town.

Cat Island: Cat Cay Club at Government Dock.

Long Island: Stella Maris.

San Salvador: Cockburn Town.

Mayaguana: Government Dock.

Getting Around

By Bus and Hitch-hiking

There are rarely any **buses**, but you can often catch a pick-up. Activity tends to centre around the arrival of the boat or the plane and so there are usually people around.

Alternatively, **hitch**. If you walk, people will often stop to offer you a lift. It is polite to offer something towards petrol, though it usually won't be accepted. People tend to walk or go by boat as much as by car.

By Taxi

Taxis, either boats or cars, are usually available at all the main airstrips. If not, ask around and one will either be found or you will be offered a lift by someone going your way.

The taxi drivers often also operate as **tour guides** around the islands and will be happy to take you out for about $25 per hour for a full car.

Car, Boat and Bike Hire

Hire cars and boats are available in the larger resorts and tend to be expensive, as are scooters. Bicycles are also on hire in many places. If you can't find a hire company, the hotels will usually be able to help you. Firms in the Abacos and Exuma Cays are:
The Abacos, t 366 0332. Bikes and golf carts.
A & P Auto Rentals, Marsh Harbour, t 367 2655.
The Bike Shop, Hope Town, t 366 0292.
Exuma Cays, Exuma Transport, t 336 2101.
Rental Wheels, Marsh Harbour, t 367 4643.
Wendals Bicycle Rentals, Treasure Cay,
    t 365 8687.

Tourist Information

Information on the Out Islands can be found at *www.bahama-out-islands.com*. You can also contact the main tourist office in Nassau, t 322 7801, or the Bahama Out Islands Promotion Board, at Cornerstone One, 1200 South Pine Island, Suite 750, Plantation, FL 33324, t 954 475 8315, *info@boipb.net, www.boipb.net*. It has around 75 hotels in the Out Islands on its books. Local tourist offices are:
The Abacos, Percy Harbour Building, Marsh
    Harbour, t 367 3067, *www.go-abacos.com*.
    The website has plenty of local information.
Andros Tourist Office, t 242 368 2286.
Bimini Tourist Office, t 242 347 3529.
Cat Island Tourist Office, t 242 332 2112.
Eleuthera: Governor's Harbour, t 332 2142;
    Harbour Island, t 333 2621.
Exuma Cays: t 336 2457.

For information on telephone codes, etc, *see* 'New Providence', p.789.

Media

The Out Islands issue a destination guide, which contains a number of feature articles and some practical information on local transport and accommodation.

Money and Banks

In the Out Islands, you may find that the bank only opens for a few hours a couple of times a week, particularly in the smaller islands. For information on currency, *see* 'New Providence', p.789.

Festivals

April *Out Islands Regatta*. Local boats and
    crews vie with one another in the Exumas.
April–June *Abaco Regatta*. Open to all-comers.
May *The Long Island Regatta*.
June onwards *Goombay*. The festival begins in
    June and runs throughout the summer
    months, interspersing carnival and
    cultural events.
July *Independence Day* (10th).
    Green Turtle Cay Regatta.
    All Eleuthera Regatta.
August *Andros Regatta*.
October *Discovery Day* (12th).
    North Eleuthera Regatta. Coincides with
    Discovery Day.
December/January *Junkanoo*. The main
    festivities colour the streets of Nassau and
    Freeport (*see* p.789), but smaller events are
    mounted in the Out Islands.

Watersports

In those smaller islands that do not offer fully-fledged watersports outfits, contact the largest resort on the island for information, such as the Rum Cay Club on Rum Cay, or Club Med in San Salvador.

Deep-sea Fishing

The Abacos: You can arrange deep-sea fishing
    at the following outfits, with rates at around
    $600 for a full day:

Donna Sands, Great Guana Cay, **t** 365 5195, *www.donnasands.com*.

Green Turtle Cay Club, **t** 365 4271, *www.greenturtleclub.com*.

Seagull Cottages, Elbow Cay, **t** 366 0266, *www.seagullcottages.com/fishing*.

Bimini: Deep-sea fishing is the biggest sport on the island. For Bimini's fishing tournaments, *see* p.840. Marinas on the island include:

Bimini Big Game Fishing Club, **t** 347 3393, *biggame@janics.com, www.bimini.big-game.club.com*.

Blue Water Resort, **t** 347 3166, *www.bimini undersea.com*.

Weech's Bimini Dock, Alice Town, **t** 347 3290.

Kayaking

Abaco Outback Tours, **t** 477 5682, *abacoout back@oii.net*. Full-day excursions, with snorkelling gear and picnic lunch.

Sailing

There are facilities on most of the islands, and sailing is the main sport on the Abacos.

The Abacos

Abaco Bahamas Charters, Hope Town.

The Moorings, Marsh Harbour, *moorings-conchinn@oii.net*.

Sunsail, Marsh Harbour. Big bareboat operator.

Scuba Diving

The Abacos

Abaco Beach Resort Dive Centre, Marsh Harbour, **t** 367 4646, *info@abacodive, www.abacodive.com*.

Brendal's Dove Centre, Green Turtle Cay, **t** 365 4411, *brendals@grouper.batelnet.bs, www.brendal.com*.

Dive Abaco, Marsh Harbour, **t** 367 2787.

Walker's Cay Undersea Adventure, **t** 353 1252, *shkrodeo@batelnet.bs, www.walkerscay.com*.

Berry Islands

Chub Cay Undersea Adventures, US **t** (305) 763 2188.

Bimini

Bill and Nowdla Keefe's Undersea Adventure, **t** 347 3079, *info@bimini undersea.com, www.biminiundersea.com*.

Andros

Seascape Andros, **t** 369 0342, *relax@ seascapeinn.com, www.seascapeinn.com*.

Small Hope Bay, **t** 368 2014, *shbinfo@small hope.com, www.smallhope.com*.

Eleuthera

Romora Bay Club, Harbour Island, **t** 333 2325, *www.romorabay.com*.

Spanish Wells Dive Centre, **t** 333 4238.

Valentine's Dive Center, Harbour Island, **t** 333 2080, *dive@valentinesdive.com, www.valentinesdive.com*.

Exuma Cays

Exumas Dive Centre, **t** 336 2390, *exuma dive@batelnet.bs*.

Minns Watersports, **t** 336 3483.

Cat Island

Cat Island Dive Center, **t** 342 3053, *info@greenwoodbeachresort.com, www.greenwoodbeachresort.com*.

Long Island

Stella Maris, **t** 338 2051, *smresort@batelnet. bs, www.stellamarisresort.com*.

San Salvador

Riding Rock Inn, **t** 331 2631, *info@ridingrock. com, www.ridingrock.com*.

Crooked Island

Pittstown Point Landings Hotel, **t** 344 2507, *info@pittstownpointlandings.com, www.pitstownpointlandings.com*.

Windsurfing

Ask around, as windsurfers and a limited range of other watersports are on offer through a number of hotels.

Other Sports

As with watersports, most opportunities for playing 'dry' sports are arranged through the hotels and resorts. Details of any hotel sporting facilities are provided in the descriptions under 'Where to Stay', below.

You will often find **tennis courts** in the hotels, charging on average about $10 per hour, though hotel guests may be able to play for free.

You can play **golf** at Treasure Cay Resort on The Abacos, **t** 367 2570, and at the new Four Seasons Hotel, **t** 336 6800, in the Exumas.

Where to Stay

The Abacos t (1 242–)

Expensive–Moderate

Abaco Beach Resort and Boat Harbour, Marsh Harbour, PO Box 511, t 367 2158, US t 1 800 468 4799, *info@abacoresort.com*, *www.abaco beachresort.com*. The most upbeat and active, with 80 rooms in blocks above the pool and a passable beach, with tennis, watersports, boat hire and evening entertainment.

Regattas of Abaco, Marsh Harbour, PO Box 486, t 367 0148, US t 1 800 322 7757, *rentals@ regattas-of-abaco.com*, *www.regattas-of-abaco.com*. A low-key resort with the 68 villas hidden in the hibiscus, casuarina pines and palms between the sea of Abaco and Marsh Harbour. Villas, dressed up in high Caribbean pastel, are well equipped, with full kitchens and terraces. All the watersports are on offer and there is a central pool.

Hope Town Hideaways, Hope Town, t 366 0224, *enquiries@hopetown.com*, *www. hopetown.com*. A small collection of villas set amid a supreme garden full of tropical blooms. Comfy, with complete kitchens and a deck at the front. A suitably excellent hideaway.

Schooner's Landing Resort, Man O' War Cay, t 365 6072, *schoonerslanding@abacoinet. com*. Individually decorated units offer views out over the ocean and the large freshwater pool; some have lofts with bunk-beds. Besides fully equipped kitchens there are outdoor barbecues.

The Walker's Cay Hotel and Marina, Miami t 954 763 6025, US t 1 800 954 763 6025, *info@walkerscay.com*, *www.walkerscay.com*. Set on its own 100-acre island, it's particularly popular for deep-sea fishing, for which it holds many records. There are 62 rooms and two restaurants and the island has its own airstrip for easy access. Also scuba diving, tennis and a friendly crowd passing through the marina.

Moderate

Moorings Conch Inn Resort and Marina, Marsh Harbour, PO Box 434, t 367 4000. Fifty-six rooms in a sandy palm garden. Quite simple but comfortable enough and with a friendly crowd passing through; air-conditioned. A pool and all the sports are available nearby.

Sea Spray Resort and Marina, White Sound, Elbow Cay, a 20min ferry ride from Marsh Harbour, t 366 0065, *seasprayres@oii.net*, *www.seasprayresort.com*. You will find isolated beach-club comfort here, set between the Sea of Abaco and the Atlantic. Just a few clapboard villas in pretty pastel colours overlooking the beach.

Abaco Inn, Elbow Cay, t 366 0133, US t 1 800 327 0787, *info@abacoinn.com*, *www.abacoinn. com*. A small retreat just out of Hope Town. There are 14 rooms, standing amid the windswept greenery above the beach, each with a hammock on its private terrace. Swimming pool, tennis and watersports. Rooms have a full kitchen.

Hope Town Harbour Lodge, Hope Town, t 366 0095, US t 1 800 316 7844, *harbourlodge@ abacoinet.com*, *www.hopetownlodge.com*. There are 18 rooms in this house, dressed in pastel grey and pink, with lovely views over the harbour, and in cottages on the Atlantic shore. Good beach, friendly and fun atmosphere.

Club Soleil Resort, Hope Town, t 366 0003, *info@clubsoleil.com*, *www.clubsoleil.com*. An appealing retreat. Just six rooms with pastel decoration, minibar, television and video, and outside a pool with sun decks surrounded by flowers.

Guana Sunset Beach Resort, PO Box AB 20474, t 365 5133, *guanabeach@guanabeach.com*, *www.guanabeach.com*. A retreat on an isolated cay off the main island. Just 15 rooms standing above the beach (all seven miles of it), with windsurfers and small sailboats on offer.

Green Turtle Club and Marina, Green Turtle Cay, t 365 4271, US t 1 800 327 0787, *info@ greenturtleclub.com*, *www.greenturtleclub. com*. A low-key, club-style hotel on the waterfront. The hotel rings with colonial echoes in the decoration and hardwood floors and dark-stained antique-style beds and overhead fans. Rooms and villas look over the harbour, but there are beaches a few minutes' walk away. A trusty retreat.

Bluff House Beach Hotel, Green Turtle Cay, t 365 4247, *bluffhouse@oii.net*, *www.bluff house.com*. Stands above the sea and beach on a cliff: 25 air-conditioned rooms in a block and in suites and villas. Tennis, pool and bar and a library with a view.

New Plymouth Club and Inn, New Plymouth, t 365 4161, t 800 688 4752. A charming place to stay, in one of New Plymouth's picture-postcard town houses. The atmosphere of the inn fits the colonial elegance of the building itself. Low-key and comfortable in an enchanting gingerbread setting. Nine rooms in old-time Bahamian style; some sports, beaches nearby, and a congenial atmosphere centred on relaxing on the pool terrace or at the Galleon Bar.

Inexpensive

Ambassador's Inn Hotel, Marsh Harbour, PO Box 484, t 367 2022, *abrandhh@batelnet.bs*. A classic West Indian pre-fab with air-conditioned comfort. Six rooms.

The Berry Islands t (1 242–)

Great Harbour Cay Club, t 367 8005, US t (313) 689 1580, US t 1 800 343 7256, *www.great harbourmarina.com* (*luxury–expensive*). Sixteen rooms set in beachfront villas. The hotel also services the passing yachts so there is plenty of activity and an easygoing feel. Sports for non-sailors include tennis, a 9-hole golf course and bicycles.

Chub Cay Club, t 325 1490, US t 1 800 662 8555, *chubcay@batelnet.bs*, *www.chubcay.com* (*expensive–moderate*). Also sees a number of yachts passing through. There are 15 rooms overlooking the swimming pool. Also with tennis and, of course, excellent fishing and scuba diving.

Bimini t (1 242–)

Expensive–Moderate

Bimini Big Game Club, Alice Town, North Bimini, PO Box 669, t 347 3391, US t 1 800 737 1007 *reservations@biminibiggame.com*, *www.biminibiggame.com*. The most modern and comfortable hotel, on the sheltered shore. There are 56 rooms overlooking the central pool in the courtyard. Scuba diving, and endless fishing packages.

Moderate–Inexpensive

Bimini Blue Water Resort, Alice Town, PO Box 601, t 347 3166, t 800 688 4752, *info@ biminiundersea.com*, *www.biminiunder sea.com*. Traditional island charm with an attractive old timber-frame house and an ocean view towards Miami and the sunset. There are 12 air-conditioned rooms in suites and in a cottage. Close to all the activity of the town.

The Compleat Angler, Alice Town, t 347 3122. Offers the best in Bimini charm, with just a few rooms in one of the island's classic buildings. The interior is lined with wood and the walls are strung with nauticalia (along with the exhibits of the Hemingway Museum). Rooms are quite simple, with a couple of good bars downstairs, which can get quite lively, and evening entertainment in season.

Weech's Bimini Dock & Apartments, at the south end of North Bimini, t 347 3028. Cheaper air-con rooms, located on the dock.

Brown's Hotel, just up from the seaplane terminal, t 347 2227. The cheapest deal of all.

Andros t (1 242–)

Expensive

Emerald Palms by the Sea, South Andros, PO Box N-9520, t 369 2661, US t 1 800 835 1018. One of the Bahamas' more luxurious hotels. High Caribbean comfort on the five-mile, palm-backed oceanfront; just 20 rooms with four-poster beds and muslin netting. A fine restaurant. Sports on offer include tennis, windsurfing, small sailing boats and scuba diving, or simply sunning by the freshwater pool with a book from the library.

Small Hope Bay Lodge, Fresh Creek, t 368 2014, US t 1 800 223 6961, *shb@smallhope.com*, *www.smallhope.com*. A charming small hotel, the classic Caribbean retreat, special-izing in scuba diving. There are only 20 rooms, built of local coral rock and island pine wood, each of which overlooks the sand and the sea. The atmosphere is extremely low-key, particularly as most people have been out diving all day and are building up their strength for the following day's activity. There is an all-inclusive rate.

Cargill Creek Lodge, Fresh Creek, **t** 368 5129, US **t** 1 800 942 6799. Specializing in fishing, with a fleet of boats to take you out to the deep waters and the bone-fishing flats. They also offer scuba diving, a pool and a central sunning area. The air-conditioned rooms look out to sea and have televisions.

Tiamo Resort, **t** 357 2489, *www.tiamoresorts. com*. This award-winning nature resort in undeveloped South Andros Island is about as far as you need to go to get away from it all. Eleven rustic bungalows set on a white-sand beach that is accessible only by boat. Palm-shaded hammocks, good food from the restaurant, and great snorkelling, kayaking and diving.

Moderate

Andros Lighthouse Yacht Club, Fresh Creek, **t** 368 2305, *relax@androslighthouse.com*, *www.androslighthouse.com*. Centred around sailing, it has a small marina. There are 20 rooms and villas on the beach. Watersports include scuba diving and fishing. Restaurant overlooking the marina.

Andros Island Bonefish Club, Fresh Creek, **t** 368 5167, *androsbonefish@batelnet.bs*, *www.androsbonefishing.com*. With all-inclusive packages for fishermen.

Cool Breeze Cottages, Mangrove Cay, **t** 369 4465. Just four cottages on the beach.

Conch Sound Resort Inn, in Nicholl's Town near San Andros, PO Box 23029, **t** 329 2060. It is a bit pre-fab but friendly and the most comfortable place to stay. Just six rooms with satellite television and ceiling fans or air-con.

Andros Beach Hotel, Nicholl's Town, **t** 329 2582. A place to retreat, with 24 simple rooms on a superb strip of sand. Sports include scuba diving and, of course, fishing.

Inexpensive

Donna Lee's Motel, Nicholl's Town, **t** 329 2194. Twelve rooms within a short walk of the beach.

Chickcharnie Hotel, Fresh Creek, **t** 368 2025. On the waterfront; eight rooms and a restaurant.

Bonefish Bay Club, South Andros, **t** 369 1443.

Rahming Bonefish Lodge, South Andros, **t** 369 1608.

Eleuthera t (1 242–)

Luxury

Pink Sands Resort, PO Box 87, **t** 333 2030, *reservations@islandoutpost.com*, *www.island outpost.com*. Named after the east-coast beach above which it sits, Pink Sands is an exquisite hotel. The delightful cottages are ranged along the ridge overlooking the sea and in the tropical gardens, while the tables of the dining room hide in the explosive greenery around the pool. An excellent atmosphere of informal luxury, in a hip and charming hotel. Some watersports are available.

Expensive

Runaway Hill Club, near Dunmore Town, PO Box EL-27031, **t** 333 2150, US **t** 1 800 327 0787, *www.runawayhill.com*. Charming, with 10 rooms set in a traditional Bahamian house. In its own garden, it is nice and quiet and isolated from the buzz, if that's what you want.

The Landing, Harbour Island, **t** 333 2707, *tbarry@batelnet.bs*, *www.harbourisland landing.com*. A charming traditional house with 7 rooms.

Moderate

Coral Sands Hotel, near Dunmore Town, **t** 333 2320, US **t** 1 800 468 2799, *coralsands@ batelnet.bs*, *www.coralsands.com*. Stands on three miles of pink sand beach; 33 rooms and a number of suites and apartments. Charming setting and an easy, relaxed air.

Romora Bay Club, just a short walk from Pink Sands Beach, PO Box 146, **t** 333 2325, US **t** 1 800 327 8286, *info@romorabay.com*, *www. romorabay.com*. An active hotel, offering diving and other watersports. There are 37 rooms with air-conditioning and ceiling fans, and a central area with a dining terrace slung with greenery.

Valentine's Resort and Marina, Dunmore Town, PO Box 1, **t** 333 2142, US **t** 1 800 327 0787, *info@valentinesresort.com*, *www. valentinesresort.com*. A busy town hotel where yachtsmen gather. It is a neat inn, with cottages gathered around an old town house and its tropical garden courtyard.

The marina is right over the road and there is evening entertainment in season.

Cove Eleuthera, Gregory Town, PO Box 1548, **t** 335 5142, **t** 800 552 5960, *info@thecove eleuthera.com, www.thecoveeleuthera.com*. Twenty-eight rooms dressed up in Caribbean pastel colours and white rattan furniture. Pool, tennis and a restaurant.

Rainbow Inn, Hatchet Bay near Gregory Town, **t** 335 0294, US **t** 1 800 688 0047, *vacation@ rainbowinn.com, www.rainbowinn.com*. Set on an expanse of white-sand beach, lost among the palm trees. There's surfing when the waves are up and tennis, or a pool bar if you are feeling lazy.

Moderate–Inexpensive

Cigatoo Resort, Governor's Harbour, PO Box 86, **t** 332 2343, US **t** 1 800 688 4752. Has 26 rooms in a modern block and a restaurant. Some sports on the superb beach.

Laughing Bird Apartments, Governor's Harbour, PO Box EL 25076, **t** 332 2012, US **t** 1 800 688 4752, *ddavies@batelnet.bs*. Comfortable rooms, scuba diving and tennis.

Inexpensive

Tingum Village, Harbour Island, **t** 333 2161. Twelve simple rooms in cottages, a bar and dining room. The restaurants have some good kitchens.

Hilton's Haven Motel, Governor's Harbour, **t** 334 2216. Simple rooms in a modern block, with a restaurant and a lively bar.

Exuma Cays **t** (1 242–)

Most of the hotels in the Exumas are on Great Exuma in the far south, where a clutch of small resorts lies along the seashore of George Town and Elizabeth Harbour. Those that are not on the beach have shuttle buses to ferry you around.

Luxury

Four Seasons Great Exuma at Emerald Bay, PO Box EX-29005, Great Exuma, **t** 336 6800, US **t** 1 800 332 3442, *reservations.exu@four seasons.com, www.fourseasons.com*. Set on 470 acres, surrounded by a new golf course and overlooking the perfect waters of Emerald Bay. The colonial-style main building forms the centrepiece of the resort, which features a large spa treatment centre, two pools, a kids' club, watersports desk and tennis courts. The rooms feature the full range of luxury fittings and facilities.

Very Expensive–Expensive

Higgins Landing, Stocking Island, PO Box Ex 29146, **t** 357 0008, *stockisl@aol.com, www.higginslanding.com*. One of the loveliest settings in the islands, with rooms in cottages built of clapboard and furnished with mock Caribbean antiques and each with a large balcony to take in the best of the magnificent views. A charming spot, with an ecologically sound philosophy.

Coconut Cove, Elizabeth Harbour, **t** 336 2659, *www.exumabahamas.com/coconutcove*. Its 11 rooms are set around a pretty courtyard, with a restaurant and bar on a wooden deck overlooking the blue harbour. Air-conditioned rooms with TV.

Staniel Cay Yacht Club, **t** 335 2024, *info@staniel cay.com, www.stanielcay.com*. Situated on its own island, Staniel Cay, about halfway along the string of the Exuma Cays. The hotel, with just six rooms in cottages, sees plenty of passing yachts and so it has a lively crowd at times. Diving and fishing available and simple isolation. All-inclusive rate. Sailors who want to stop in for dinner should contact the kitchen well in advance.

Moderate

Club Peace and Plenty, Great Exuma, PO Box 29055, **t** 336 2551, US **t** 1 800 525 2210, *ppclub@batelnet.bs, www.peaceandplenty. com*. Old-time Bahamian charm in a pretty pink building, with 35 rooms set around a courtyard and looking onto the water. It is named after the ship that brought colonists here in 1783, and the name conveys the hotel's theme: it's quiet and comfortable, if a little faded, with air-conditioning, but no TVs or telephones.

Peace and Plenty Beach Inn, Elizabeth Harbour, **t** 336 2250, US **t** 1 800 525 2210, *ppbeach@ batelnet.bs, www.peaceandplenty.com*. More modern; 32 bright and breezy rooms with white tiles, pastel decoration and wicker chairs – air-con, telephones, TV in the rooms, right above the beach. Lively restaurant and bar.

Regatta Point, on its own peninsula just out of George Town, PO Box 6, **t** 336 2206, US **t** 1 800 688 0309, *www.regattapointbahamas. com*. This is secluded but still within a shout of all the activity of the town, if you can call it that. The few apartments have fully equipped kitchens, with balconies looking through the palms.

Two Turtles Inn, George Town, PO Box EX-29251, **t** 336 2545, *www.twoturtlesinn.com*. A pleasant spot, with 14 air-conditioned rooms round a stone courtyard.

Inexpensive

Marshall's Guesthouse, George Town, PO Box 29027, **t** 336 2081.

Cat Island **t** (1 242–)

Fernandez Bay Village, **t** 342 3043, US **t** 305 792 1905, *catisland@fernandezbayvillage.com*, *www.fernandezbayvillage.com* (*expensive–moderate*). The smartest hotel on the island. It's classic castaway stuff, set on its own magnificent beach. Rooms are set in villas overlooking the sea through casuarina pines, with full kitchen facilities, though there is a restaurant, too. Some watersports are available. Very low-key, but ideal for an escape.

Greenwood Beach Resort, **t** 342 3053, **t** US 1 800 688 4752, *info@greenwoodbeachresort. com*, *www.greenwoodbeachresort.com* (*moderate–inexpensive*). Twenty rooms set on a superb eight-mile stretch of sand, embellished with palm-thatch parasols and a dining room on the beach.

Orange Creek Inn, **t** 354 4110, *www.orange creekinn.com* (*inexpensive*). Simple rooms looking over one of the island's magnificent beaches at Orange Creek.

Long Island **t** (1 242–)

Cape Santa Maria Beach Resort, **t** 338 5273, US **t** 1 800 663 7090, *www.capesantamaria.com* (*expensive*). One of the best places to stay, with six cottages, a clubhouse and a good restaurant. The complex fronts a four-mile stretch of white beach. All rooms have fans and air-con, but no phone or TV. Offers free

beach equipment, also snorkelling gear, sailboards and bikes.

Stella Maris Resort Club, PO Box LI 30105, **t** 359 8236, US **t** 1 800 426 0466, *info@stellamaris-resort.com*, *www.stellamarisresort.com* (*moderate*). Sixty rooms and self-catering units in low pre-fab buildings scattered around a sandy garden of pines and palms. There are three pools, a bar and dining room in the central area, which can get lively because the property has a marina, too. Windsurfing, sailing, fishing and diving are on offer and you can hire cars from them to explore the island.

Thomson Bay Inn (*inexpensive*). Simple rooms.

San Salvador **t** (1 242–)

Club Med, **t** 331 2000, *www.clubmed.com* (*expensive*). Not everybody's cup of tea, but if it's your thing, you can try it.

Riding Rock Inn, on the beach north of Cockburn Town, **t** 331 2631, US **t** 1 800 272 1492, *info@ridingrock.com*, *www.ridingrock. com* (*moderate*). With 24 air-conditioned rooms and villas around the freshwater pool, dining room and bar; tennis, full diving operation and fishing.

Ocean View Villas, Cockburn Town, via the Batelco operator **t** 323 4911 (*inexpensive*). A smaller option with kitchenettes.

Rum Cay **t** (1 242–)

You can stay at the **Rum Cay Club**, Port Nelson, which is expensive, or you can save pennies at **Dolores**.

Crooked Island and Acklins **t** (1 242–)

Pittstown Point Landings, Landrail Point, **t** 344 2507, US **t** (513) 732 2593, *info@pittstown pointlandings. www.pittstownpointlandings. com* (*moderate–inexpensive*). Twelve rooms set on a magnificent beach (one of a number on the island). It is very low-key, with an honour bar and huts on the beaches where you cook up your own catch at lunchtime. Boating, snorkelling and scuba.

Mayaguana **t** (1 242–)

Baycaner Resort, **t** 339 3605. Sixteen rooms.
Mayaguana Inn Guest House, **t** 339 3065.

Inagua t (1 242–)

There are a couple of inexpensive guest houses in Matthew Town, one mile from Great Inagua airstrip, both of which are simple, with a dining room and beach nearby.

Morten Main House, t 339 1267. Six rooms.

Walkine's Guest House, t 339 1612. Five rooms.

Eating Out and Bars

Aside from the restaurants and bars listed below, the main sources of sustenance are the hotels and inns, most of which have dining rooms. See 'Where to Stay', above, for details.

The Abacos

Moderate–Inexpensive

Mangoes, Marsh Harbour, **t** 367 2366. Has a charming setting on the harbour water-front, where you dine on the veranda or in the air-conditioned interior. Local and international fare such as crawfish and pizzas.

Wally's, Queen Elizabeth Drive, Marsh Harbour, **t** 367 2074. Has a good setting, in a classic gingerbread house. Bahamian food and some concessions to continental style; try seafood fritters followed by catch of the day in a local sauce. Lively; sometimes live music in the evenings.

Bayview on the Water, Marsh Harbour, **t** 367 3738. A good setting on a pink and green deck above the harbour. Seafood and steaks.

Jib Room, across the harbour, **t** 367 2700. Also popular; known for its rib night on Wednesdays.

Golden Grouper, Dove Plaza, Marsh Harbour, **t** 367 2301. A popular spot for a local meal, including a stew or a souse.

Cap'n Jack's, Hope Town Harbour, **t** 366 0247. On the waterfront in a bright pink and white house. International dishes and a sailing crowd can be found, alongside ribs, wings and fritters as well as more substantial platters. Some entertainment at the weekends.

Harbour's Edge, Elbow Cay, **t** 366 0087. Another popular gathering place, where you can get a game of pool and a wetsuit for your beer. Local fare, but some concessions to stateside burgers and steaks. Some entertainment at the weekends.

Captain's Table, in the New Plymouth Inn, Green Turtle Cay, **t** 365 4161. Come here for a fine meal. Start off with cocktails at the bar and then retreat to the dining room for grilled local catch, crawfish or rack of lamb with local vegetables, served up in an old-time Bahamian setting.

Roosters Rest, Great Guana Cay, east of New Plymouth, **t** 365 4066. Good local food: souse or a stew goat as well as cracked conch.

Laura's Kitchen, near ferry dock, Green Turtle Cay, **t** 365 4287. Bahamian specialities – perhaps a plate of peas 'n' rice with shrimps.

The Berry Islands

Tamboo Club, **t** 367 8203. Attached to the Great Harbour Cay Club Hotel (see above), this is probably the best bet for a meal; you dine out on the waterfront on ribs and chicken dishes.

Basil's Bar and Restaurant, Great Harbour Cay. Catches a crowd of yachties making whoopee at either the very beginning or the end of their trip. Burgers, snacks and plenty of beer.

Bimini

You will find a string of restaurants and bars in Alice Town in North Bimini, none of them that cheap. Elsewhere, you will be dependent on the hotels.

Moderate

Red Lion Pub, **t** 347 3259. You sit in a wooden-walled dining room, where a lively crowd collects, boozing and watching the television while they tuck into baked turtle or a platterful of shrimps in fluffy batter.

Fisherman's Paradise. A classic West Indian restaurant, air-conditioned, modern and a liming point for a few locals. Chicken or fish.

The Sand Bar, **t** 347 3277. Lower-key and good for a beer or two; set in a small shack with sand on the floor.

The Compleat Angler, **t** 347 3122. The bar is excellent, particularly when they have live music: then the whole town stops in for a beer and a dance.

Andros

Moderate–Inexpensive

Lilley's Bar, Nicholl's Town. A local favourite.

Andros Lighthouse Yacht Club, Fresh Creek, t 368 2305, *relax@androslighthouse.com*, *www.androslighthouse.com*. Dine in the restaurant overlooking the marina.

Land Crab Restaurant, North Andros, t 329 4172. A local meal – you can pick up some peas 'n' rice or a curry goat.

L & M Restaurant, Congo Town, South Andros, t 369 2655. Local dishes.

Eleuthera

Moderate

Ma Rubi's, at the Tingum Village, Harbour Island. Rubi Percentie cooks the best when it comes to local food: sample her excellent conch fritters, or grilled lobster and shrimp.

Harbour Lounge, Harbour Island, t 333 2031. On the waterfront.

Spanish Wells Yacht Haven, Spanish Wells, t 333 4255. Overlooks the harbour side of the island and has its own bar and dining room. Fishing and scuba-diving trips depart from the dock below.

The Reach, Harbour Island. A favourite stop with passing yachtfolk, located on the waterfront opposite Valentine's.

Inexpensive

Angela's Starfish Restaurant, Harbour Island. Come here for local seafood.

Willy's Tavern, Harbour Island. The atmosphere in the bar is quite fun; drop in for a beer or a cocktail.

Gusty's, Harbour Island, t 333 2165. With sand strewn on the floor, this is a local bar where you can get a beer and catch up on the latest sports news on the satellite television.

Seagrapes, Harbour Island, t 554 5041. There's a discotheque here, and you may occasionally catch a live band playing, too.

Buccaneer Club, New Bond St, Governor's Harbour, t 332 2000. The Buccaneer offers lunch or dinner out in the open air; the cuisine is local Bahamian. *Closed Sun.*

Haven Restaurant and Bakery, Governor's Harbour, t 334 2155. Good for a local meal of grilled fish or curry goat.

Exuma Cays

The best food is really in the hotels. It's worth trying the dining rooms at the **Peace** and **Plenty** and also **Coconut Cove** (*see* 'Where to Stay', above), but you will also find one or two good local eateries.

Moderate–Inexpensive

Runaway Bay, Rolleville, t 345 6279. A new restaurant set on a long powdery beach. Serves grouper fingers, conch fritters, lobster salad and other Bahamian dishes.

Eddie's Edgewater Restaurant and Bar, George Town, t 336 2050. A classic West Indian bar and restaurant where you will find all the variations on conch and local catch with peas 'n' rice.

Sam's Place, George Town, t 336 2579. On an upstairs deck above the harbour, quiet but pleasant, burgers and local fish and seafood.

Silver Dollar, George Town, t 336 2615. There is occasionally a band at this place, which collects domino players in the evenings.

Stocking Island Beach Club, Stocking Island. Will keep you topped up with beer and rum punch while you spend the day lazing around in the sun. Very popular.

Big D's Conch Spot Restaurant, Steventon. Local conch specialities.

Cat Island

Pilot Harbour Restaurant, at the beach resort overlooking the harbour, t 342 4066 (*moderate–inexpensive*). Try some grilled local fish in creole sauce.

San Salvador

Driftwood Bar & Lounge, Riding Rock Inn, Cockburn Town, t 331 2631.

Halem Square Club, Cockburn Town. Here, you can get some conch fritters and a lobster platter and live music at the weekends.

Rum Cay

Kaye's Bar, next to the pier in Port Nelson, t 331 2816. Good local fare.

Ocean View. Local specialities.

Crooked Island and Acklins

Gibson's Lunchroom, t 344 2020. You'll find this place at Landrail Point.

Mayaguana

Reggie Satellite Lounge, in the guest house, t 339 3749. A popular bar.

stretch for a hundred miles. On their sheltered coastlines the beaches are superb; they descend gently into shallows of warm and crystal-clear water, rising again as sandbars a few hundred yards offshore before descending into deep green or blue. Flying over them, the views are fantastic; back on land, you can walk for miles and hardly see a soul.

As travellers begin to look beyond the glitz and high-rise tourism of Nassau and Freeport/Lucaya, the Out Islands are steadily beginning to open up. A few of the islands have developed around their pretty waterfront towns and there are a few small and very low-key retreats on isolated cays, ideal for a break from the humdrum in wonderful, seemingly uncharted territory.

But besides the superb natural surroundings and the gentle island lifestyle, certain islands have gained renown for their sports: Bimini is known for its deep-sea fishing, and the Abacos and the Exumas have superb sailing. Andros has recently gained a reputation as a dive-site.

Some of the Out Islands, particularly the Abacos, were hit hard by the hurricane of September 2004. Check that your hotel is up-and-running before finalizing plans.

The Abacos

In the northeast of the Bahamian archipelago are the Abaco Islands and their offshore cays, stretched in a 140-mile curve around the east of Grand Bahama. They have a population of over 11,000 and outside the two major resorts of Nassau and Freeport they are the most developed area of the Bahamas. There are two main areas, each served by an airport, to which a string of smaller islands is linked by water taxi: Marsh Harbour in the south with nearby Hope Town on Elbow Cay; and farther north Treasure Cay and Green Turtle Cay. Walker's Cay, which has its own airstrip, is a self-contained resort 10 miles off Little Abaco Island in the far northwest of the island group. The Abacos are very popular with sailors and have about half of the 60 marinas in the Bahamas.

Marsh Harbour, long the site of a lumbering industry as well as the Abacos's traditional lifeline of shipbuilding, is the third largest town in the Bahamas. As well as building ships, the islanders traditionally helped to destroy them with their other invisible industry, 'wrecking', in which they would clean up after passing ships had been washed onto the reefs. Eventually, things were regularized when the lighthouse at Hope Town was built in the 1830s, despite the islanders' best efforts at sabotage. The east coast of Great Abaco (in the south) is fringed by a string of cays, many of which were settled, along with the mainland, by loyalists following the American War of Independence. These islands are still the focus of much of Abaco life. Abaconian 'loyalty' came to the fore once again as the Bahamas headed towards Independence in 1973, when there was a movement to remain part of Britain rather than go along with Nassau.

Marsh Harbour is set on a north-facing cove about midway down Great Abaco. It is a modern town and has local shops and tourist restaurants and there are many vacation villas around the area. Above the town stand the yellow turrets of the house of Dr Evans Cottman, author of *Out Island Doctor*. From here, ferries will take you out to the other islands. There is a tourist information office in the Percy Archer building in town. There are two underwater parks off the Marsh Harbour area, at Sandy Cay in the south and at Fowl Cay next to Man O' War Cay.

Elbow Cay and its very attractive settlement of **Hope Town** are easily reached from Marsh Harbour. There is a charming and slow atmosphere here, with pretty clapboard houses and gardens festooned with blooms and surrounded by white picket fences. Hope Town is best known for the 120ft pink and white lighthouse that stands above the town. The **Wyannie Malone Historical Museum**, restored as it was in the 19th century, gives a good idea of the old-time life of the Abaconians right down to the rocking chair and the broom-making press. There are bicycles and golf carts for hire to explore the ribbon of land that leads north and south of the town.

Man O' War Cay has a slightly unreal feel about it, untypical of the Bahamas. The small community of 250 is almost entirely white; until Independence, the islanders would demand that black Bahamians left the island at sundown. They are proud and polite, and their island, one of the traditional boat-building areas of the Abacos, is clearly prosperous. No alcohol is sold on the island and there is just one hotel and a couple of places to eat. You will still see some of the traditional hulls taking shape in the dockyards. Offshore, Sandy Cay is an excellent spot for snorkelling.

Great Guana Cay, with a population of 100 or so, is visited principally for its fantastic seven miles of beach, where there is excellent swimming and snorkelling, and for its drink, the Guana Grabber, a concoction of rums and juices. You can also swim with the dolphins.

Back on the main island, about 30 miles northeast of Marsh Harbour is the resort area of **Treasure Cay** and the surrounding settlements. Despite the name, which implies an island, it is set on a peninsula of Great Abaco, overlooking a wonderful three-mile beach. A couple of miles offshore is **Green Turtle Cay**, two miles by four, where the town of New Plymouth is situated. The cay is characterized by more clapboard houses with gingerbread fretwork set in flowering gardens, and on the ocean shore another superb beach. The **Albert Lowe Museum** is in a Victorian home in the town and it traces the history of the island back to the loyalists. Model boats built by Albert Lowe himself are on view alongside works by his artist son, Alton. There are Boston Whalers in which you can explore the smaller islands around.

Walker Cay, the most northerly point in the Bahamas, has been a game-fishing haunt since 1939.

The Berry Islands

The Berry islands are scattered over 40 miles of the Great Bahama Bank to the northwest of Nassau, en route from the capital to the American mainland and a regular stop-off for cruise ships and yachts. A population of shorebirds (noddies and terns) and just 500 people is scattered across the islands, mainly living in Bullock's

Harbour on Great Harbour Cay in the north. Many of the islands are private estates (Wallace Groves of Freeport fame owns Little Whale Cay). There are airstrips in Great Harbour Cay and Chub Cay. Scuba diving in the nearby Tongue of the Ocean is superb, while Chub Cay offers excellent fishing.

Bimini

The string of the Bimini Islands, famed as the game-fishing capital of the world, are the westernmost of the Bahamian islands and they lie a bare 50 miles from down-town Miami. In between the two is the Gulf Stream, which has carved out its path over the millennia, and it is here that the biggest marlin and giant tuna are to be found. In the past the islands have been rich and raw; drug money poured through at one stage not long ago (Bimini is one of the traditional staging posts en route to the States), and it would become quite riotous as fishermen, fresh from the day's fight on the seas, would return and booze at night. Bimini is the setting of the novel *Islands in the Stream* by Ernest Hemingway, who visited often in the 30s. It is all a bit tamer now, and it is a pretty nice spot for a few days, though it is expensive. It can get quite lively at the weekends when the Florida vacationers drop in for a break.

South Bimini was one of Ponce de León's stop-offs on his hunt for the Fountain of Youth, and he supposedly came here in 1513 before discovering Florida. The northern island is the main fishing haunt. The inner coastline around **Alice Town** is furred with marinas, and all the bars are inland. Most of the islanders live in **Bailey Town** on the King's Highway leading north. A superb white-sand **beach** runs along the west coast of the island. You will find watersports at the **Anchorage** and, if you want to be a little more isolated, you can go to **Paradise Beach** and **Radio Beach** farther north. There is a **museum** (*adm free*) devoted to Hemingway inside the Compleat Angler Hotel; the walls are hung with pictures of the great man showing off his catches and there are illustrations and excerpts from *The Old Man and the Sea* as well as general fishing memorabilia. Cays to the south of Bimini include **Gun Cay** and **Cat Cay**, a private club, founded in the 1930s. There is a bank in Alice Town (*open Mon–Fri 9–1*). There are also many marinas on the islands.

Deep-sea fishing is obviously the biggest sport on the island, but Bimini also holds a host of fishing tournaments through the year (*see* below). Scuba diving is also growing in popularity; dive sites include the reef to the west of the island and a wreck known as 'the concrete ship' (*see* 'Watersports', p.804).

Bimini Fishing Tournaments

Among Bimini's famous fishing tournaments are the **Hemingway Billfish Tournament** (*March*) and the **Championship Billfish Tournament** (*April*), both of which are part of the Bahamas Billfish Championship. In the summer, the Bimini Big Game Fishing Club holds the **Blue Marlin Tournament** (*June*), followed closely by the **Jimmy Albury Blue Marlin Tournament** (*July*). Two all-fish tournaments are held in August and there are competitions to catch wahoo in November.

Andros

At 100 miles by 40, Andros is the largest island in the Bahamas, and it has a population of 8,400, the third largest. It lies just 20 miles from New Providence, across the Tongue of the Ocean, a 6,000ft trench that cuts into the Great Bahama Bank. The island is flat and crossed in places by 'bights' (channels), and inland there are many 'blue holes'. It is so low that parts of it are mangrove flats, forested swamp impenetrable except to terns, whistling tree ducks, the island's 6ft iguana and the island gremlin, the *chickcharnie*. This tiny character supposedly has three fingers, three toes, red eyes and hangs upside-down in trees, and he has been attributed with a mischievous turn of mind if you do not believe in him. The island was first settled by loyalists who grew cotton, though later sponges and sisal (for rope) were the mainstays of the economy. In recent years, the government has encouraged agriculture and farming of livestock on Andros. The settlements are scattered along the east coast, alongside superb, pristine beaches. There are airports at both San Andros and Andros Town on the northern island, at Moxey Town on Mangrove Cay and in Congo Town on the southern island.

A mile off the island's eastern shore the sea floor drops sheer for 6,000ft into the Tongue of the Ocean. On its submarine 'wall' is the third largest barrier reef in the world, 140 miles of corals and sponges plied by surgeonfish, soldierfish and angelfish. Scuba diving is possible at a number of resorts on the island (*see* p.804) and windsurfers and limited other watersports are available through the hotels. Bone-fishing, casting in the shallow sandy flats, is reputed to be amongst the best in the world around Andros.

Eleuthera

Eleuthera was the first of the Bahamas to be settled when the band of Eleutherian Adventurers arrived in 1648, escaping religious persecution in Bermuda and England. They called their island Eleutheria after the Greek word for freedom. The settlement was quickly overtaken by New Providence (about 50 miles to the west), but Eleuthera has flourished steadily, helped by an influx of loyalists in the 1780s, making a living from agriculture and the sea. Today, Eleuthera is among the most developed of the Out Islands with regard to tourism.

The island is 100 miles long and barely more than 2 miles wide, and on its sheltered side the beaches and sandbars stretch for tens of miles into the jade-green water. On the ocean side, the waves barrel in, and are big enough to surf on. Eleuthera is quite fertile, traditionally a farming area, nowadays mainly producing pineapples and tomatoes, though you will still see grain silos along the road.

There are three airstrips: North Eleuthera which serves the north of the island and the offshore islands of Harbour Island and Spanish Wells, Governor's Harbour which serves the centre of the island, and Rock Sound for the south. Make sure to get off at the correct one because it can be a 100-mile drive to the other end of the island.

Harbour Island, with its inhabitants the 'Brilanders', was once the second most prosperous place in the Bahamas after Nassau, but the docks are quiet now compared to when the shipbuilding industry was at its height. **Dunmore Town** is a pretty village that lines the protected shore of the island; sugary pink gingerbread houses sit snug behind the white picket fences as they always have, only now they are accompanied by satellite dishes. Some of the hotels are set in these old antique houses and so they are quaint and comfortable. The islanders are laid-back, and only too happy for you to join in their musings. The famous **Pink Beach**, miles of sand a delicate shade of pink, is on the ocean side of the island.

Nearby is another offshore island, **Spanish Wells**, which is almost as picturesque, and has the beaches to match Harbour Island, but it has a different feel altogether. The islanders are among the richest in the Bahamas because of the fishing industry. They fish mainly for lobster or crawfish, sailing off for three weeks at a time in their refrigerated boats, scouring the Bahamian waters as far south as Cuba, reaping vast profits. They reappear and make whoopee back home before setting off again a couple of weeks later. But the island, just three miles long and less than a mile across, has an atypical feel for the Bahamas because there are very few black faces. Until quite recently, black Bahamians, even the doctor, would be asked to leave the island at sunset.

On the main island of **North Eleuthera**, you can visit Preacher's Cave, where the early settlers are supposed to have worshipped. **Current Cut** is a popular dive at the change of the tide because the water races through it at around seven knots. Heading south past Gregory Town, a fishing village, you come to the '**Glass Window**' (named after a natural bridge that has collapsed), where the difference between the ocean and the protected leeward coast is most clearly visible. At **Hatchet Bay** there is a more extensive underground cave system, which culminates in a clifftop 70ft above the sea.

Governor's Harbour is another tired town of timber houses set around the curve of Cupid's Bay. **Rock Sound** is the largest settlement on Eleuthera and a good place to stock up, but still little more than a cluster of fading gingerbread houses gathered above the bay. Not far off is one of Eleuthera's famous 'Blue Holes', an inland lake connected to the ocean deep underwater.

Watersports (windsurfers, dinghies and water-skiing) and tennis courts are available through the hotels, which will often allow outsiders to use their equipment if it is available. Scuba divers can check out the tidal race at Current Cut and explore the wreck of the train that was on its way to Cuba on the Devil's Backbone reef off the north coast of the island.

Exuma Cays

The 350 or so Exuma cays are strung out over more than 100 miles of magnificent sea, starting 50 miles from Nassau and heading southeasterly towards Great Exuma and Little Exuma in the south, where most of the population lives. Most are uninhabited and some, just sandbars, disappear with the 1ft tides. Others, like Allen's Cay, are just home to a crowd of iguanas. In the string of islands Staniel Cay, Farmer

Cay and Black Point each have a marina and a small yacht club, with limited sports facilities. You may hear stories about Norman's Cay, which was used as a smuggling base by cocaine barons until it was raided by the DEA. All that remains are a few buildings, rusting cars with bullet holes and an airstrip.

The airstrip is at Moss Town, 10 miles north of the main settlement, on Great Exuma in the south, the largest island and home to most of the 3,500 population (of which about one third have the name Rolle). A few people live on Staniel Cay, situated midway up the chain. The islands have some small agriculture, but the main industry is tourism. Getting around is easy as there are plenty of taxis for hire.

The Exumas are famed for their sailing and the islands see quite lively crowds on yachts during the winter season. The Out Islands Regatta, held each year in April, pits traditional Bahamian sailing vessels against one another, and the whole of Georgetown comes alive with open-air parties in the evenings. **Elizabeth Harbour** is a magnificent stretch of stunning blue water seven miles by two and rimmed with classic Bahamian beaches. It is well worth hiring a Boston whaler to explore it. Alternatively, take a ride over to **Stocking Island**, where you will find a beach bar and miles of deserted sand. There are also excellent snorkelling grounds. Exuma is also known for its bone-fishing, on the huge expanse of knee-to-waist-deep water on the sheltered leeward coast of the island. The **Exuma Land and Sea Park** is based around Warderick Wells Cay.

George Town is set around a lagoon on one side and on the magnificent Elizabeth Harbour. There is a scattering of houses around the one-way ring road, a local market and a straw market under the trees near the neoclassical, pastel-pink government building. Across the harbour you can see a tall obelisk on Stocking, erected to guide ships in to load up with salt in the 19th century. They would fly flags or burn fires on it when there was salt for sale. There are a few other small settlements and isolated private villas on Great Exuma, and across the bridge to Little Exuma you will find the Ferry, home of Gloria Patience, alias Shark Lady, who sells shark-teeth necklaces made from her own catches when out fishing.

Cat Island

Cat Island is a sliver of land, 45 miles by 1 on average, that lies northwest–southeast, across the prevailing ocean winds, ribboned on both coasts by pristine beaches. Named after the British sea captain Catt, the island has a line of cliffs (at 206ft, **Mt Alvernia** is the highest in the Bahamas) and it is fertile, as the walls and the derelict houses of its former plantation prosperity show at a glance. But if it was developed for cotton and sisal a century ago, Cat Island is one of the least developed of the Bahamian islands today. Old-time Bahamian life continues here, where there are small plantations cut out of the hillside, and traditions such as *obeah*, the West Indian magic, of which you will still see the signs hanging in the trees.

There are three airstrips on Cat Island: near Port Howe in the south; by Fernandez Bay in the centre; and the main airstrip, which is in the north at Arthur's Town.

Arthur's Town is the most populous settlement on the island, and it is much the same as when Sidney Poitier grew up here. It is the commercial centre, but there is not much to see. You are best to set off along the island where you will find the traditional Bahamian thatch-roofed cottages and their outdoor ovens set in the tropical gardens.

The Bight is a large cove with two seafront villages (New Bight and Old Bight) linked by a stunning beach. **Pigeon Bay Cottage** is the ruin of a 19th-century estate house nearby, and on top of Mt Alvernia above the town is the **Hermitage**, a monastery built in miniature by Father Jerome, who also designed many of the Bahamian churches, including the Augustinian monastery on New Providence. He came to live as a hermit on Cat Island in his last years. To the south of the Bight the road passes the **Deveaux Mansion**, an impressive ruined plantation house, and heads towards Columbus Point and the small town of **Port Howe**, famed as a wrecking town in years past. Hawks Nest Creek, in the southwest, has a large number of herons. You will find that hire cars and sports, including tennis, diving and deep-sea fishing, are available through the few hotels on the island.

Long Island

Long Island, which stretches southeast from the tip of the Exuma Cays and cuts the Tropic of Cancer, is 57 miles long and 4 wide at most. In the north are rugged headlands and at the southern tip of the island the hills subside into salt flats. There are over 40 small communities, many of them of white Bahamians or 'Conkie Joes', scattered along its virtually undeveloped western coastline of reefs and beaches. The largest settlements are Deadman's Cay, midway down the island, and Clarence Town, set on a beautiful harbour farther south. The main airstrips are at Stella Maris, in the north, and Deadman's Cay. Though some of the 3,500 islanders work in the tourist industry, most are involved with fishing and farming. The produce, much of which is grown in fertile 'pot holes' in the limestone ground, is sold to the government and shipped out on the weekly boat to Nassau.

The **beaches** around the Stella Maris Inn and up to the north of the island at Cape Santa Maria are spectacular and they have some of the best of the Bahamas' superbly clear water. Travelling south you will see that the island is littered with the walls and the ruins of former plantation prosperity. **Deadman's Cay** is the best place for provisions. **Clarence Town**, which is still the island capital, is dominated by two of Father Jerome's churches (see 'Cat Island', above). St Paul's Anglican Church was topped when he turned Catholic and constructed St Peter's Catholic Church.

San Salvador

San Salvador takes its name (the Saviour) from Columbus's first landfall in the New World on 12 October 1492. Just 12 miles by 5, San Salvador is out on its own, a little farther into the Atlantic than the other islands, and historians decided that the spot that the Indian inhabitants called Guanahani was the best site for Columbus's island (in the meantime it had become known as Watling's Island, the lair of a pirate). Just as there are other islands that dispute the claim, so there are four sites on the island that vie for the title of the first bay where Columbus put in and you will see several monuments commemorating them. Long Bay with its simple white cross is the most favoured.

For all the controversy, the island is inhabited by only a few hundred people; it has seen little development and feels much like the other Out Islands. It is mainly flat, with a series of inland lakes, and offshore reefs that the Navigator had to avoid. The island's one airstrip is just north of the main village of Cockburn Town (pronounced 'Co'burn'). There is a spectacular view of the island from the 160ft **lighthouse** on Dixon Hill in the northeast. On the hill above the south coast is '**Watling's Castle**', supposedly the pirate's lookout. In fact, it is one of the plantation houses owned by the American loyalists who settled the island in the late 1700s.

A few sports are available through the Riding Rock Inn, including a tennis court, scuba diving with three boats, and a darkroom for film shot on the dives. There are also marina facilities.

Rum Cay

About 35 miles from San Salvador is Rum Cay, another former pirate haunt surrounded by spectacular reefs. It was supposedly Columbus's second island stop, which he named after the Virgin Mary. Just 10 miles by 4 and with a population of under 100, it is perhaps the most slumberstruck and friendliest island of them all. **Port Nelson**, the only village, is hidden among the palms on the southeast coast and the island is fringed with supreme sand. Apart from piracy, salt manufacture was the only industry. The **reefs** are as magnificent as they are dangerous for shipping; a shipload of rum that foundered here gave the island its name, and you can make a superb dive to the **HMS *Conqueror***, wrecked in 1861, which lies in just 25ft of water. There are marina facilities at the head of the harbour. Watch out for the wild boars. The Rum Cay Club has its own airstrip. Other than that, you are dependent on the mail boat. Watersports can also be arranged through the club.

Crooked Island and Acklins

About 300 miles southeast of Nassau, Long Cay, Crooked Island and Acklins enclose on three sides the stunning Bight of Acklins, where crystal-clear water slips onto sandbars and palm-lined beaches. The population of the Crooked Island district (only 500 on Crooked Island and 600 on Acklins) is far lower now than it was a century ago when the islands were a major port of call. Life here today is gentle and friendly. Long Cay has about 20 inhabitants, most of whom are fishermen by trade.

The twice-weekly flight from Nassau touches both major islands: Colonel Hill on Crooked Island and Spring Point on Acklins. There is a twice-daily boat link from one island to the other across The Going Through, the strait that divides Lovely Bay and the Ferry (Crooked Island). The reefs are superb and scuba diving can be arranged through the Pittstown Point Landings Hotel on Crooked Island. Bone-fishing in the bay is also excellent.

Mayaguana

Mayaguana is rarely visited except as a stopover for yachts headed south to the Caribbean. And then only for shelter in Abraham's Bay, the capital village on the south coast, because there are no organized facilities here. Life is extremely slow for the 600 or so islanders, many of whom have left because there is no work other than farming. There is a twice-weekly flight to Inagua.

Inagua

Most southerly of the Bahamas, Great Inagua is just within sight of Cuba to the south, about 60 miles across the Old Bahama Channel. The island is remote, over 350 miles away from the bustling centre of Nassau, and less than 1,000 people live there. Its remoteness and size (at 35 miles by 25 it is the third largest of all the Bahamas) have led it to become the last resort of a large colony of birds, including spoonbills, ducks and, most spectacular, pink flamingos; an estimated 60,000 of these birds, which now survive in just a few places in the Americas, are protected in the **Inagua National Park**, set around Inagua's inland lakes. Trips can be arranged through the Bahamas National Trust (*Nassau t 323 1317*).

The traditional industry on this low, windswept island is salt manufacture, and miles of brilliant white salt flats of the Morton Salt Company make up the second largest in the world. The main town is Matthew Town in the southwest, where the airport is located for the twice-weekly flights to Nassau. You might also be able to arrange a ride on the ships belonging to the Morton Salt Company, based in Port Canaveral, Fort Lauderdale.

The Turks and Caicos Islands

20

Alexander Resort
Grace Bay

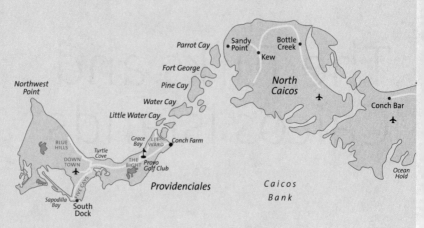

Parrot Cay

Sandy Point • Bottle Creek

Kew

Fort George

North Caicos

Pine Cay

Northwest Point

Water Cay

Conch Bar

Little Water Cay

BLUE HILLS

Turtle Cove

Grace Bay

LEE WARD

Conch Farm

DOWN TOWN

THE BIGHT

Provo Golf Club

Ocean Hold

FIVE CAYS

Providenciales

Caicos Bank

Sapodilla Bay

South Dock

West Caicos

N

20 km
10 miles

Highlights

1 Dive the ocean walls, which drop from twenty feet to six thousand in the blip of a depth sounder

2 Walk the miles and miles of Grace Bay beach on Providenciales

3 Get dropped off on a deserted cay for a day of being a castaway

The Turks and Caicos Islands

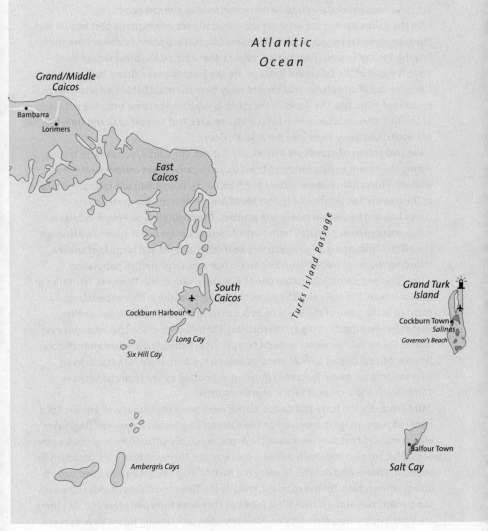

Atlantic Ocean

Grand/Middle Caicos

Bambarra

Lorimers

East Caicos

South Caicos

Cockburn Harbour

Long Cay

Six Hill Cay

Turks Island Passage

Grand Turk Island

Cockburn Town

Salinas

Governor's Beach

Ambergris Cays

Balfour Town

Salt Cay

The Turks and Caicos Islands stick out like a spur at the southeastern tip of the Bahamian archipelago. They remained almost unknown for centuries, but are now very popular with divers for their pristine corals and extensive fish life, and there is also a steadily increasing trade in traditional Caribbean tourism. Like the Bahamas, the islands are set in the shallows, but here the skies are so clear and the sea is so intensely turquoise that it all appears almost surreal.

TCI, as they are often known, are made up of eight main islands and a host of tiny cays situated about 575 miles southeast of Miami and 100 miles north of Haiti, with a total land area of about 192 square miles. They stand in two separate groups, both scrub-covered limestone outcrops that rise no more than 250ft and in many places are close enough to sea level to be mangrove swamp and salt ponds.

On the Caicos Bank in the west are the Caicos Islands, of which the best known and most developed is Providenciales. The name Caicos is supposed to derive from the Spanish for 'cay' (*cayos*). Twenty-two miles farther east, on the other side of the 7,000ft depth of the Columbus Passage, are the Turks Islands – Grand Turk and Salt Cay – the cap of an outcrop that eroded away from the main Bahamian archipelago millions of years ago. The 'Turks' in the name is supposed to come from the red dome of the Turk's head cactus, which looks a bit like a fez. Not far east of Grand Turk, the sea floor drops away sheer into the Atlantic Ocean.

The two groups of islands are historically distinct. The Caicos Islands were settled during the American Revolution by Loyalists , who came to cut cotton plantations, while the Turks Islands were settled much earlier, by Bermudian salt rakers. The bulk of the country's population of 15,000 are of African descent, the descendants of slaves brought by the salt rakers and planters. The population on Providenciales is supplemented by expatriates from North America, Europe and Hispaniola. Although the official language is English, you will hear other accents and languages spoken, including strains of French-sounding creole from the large Haitian population.

The Turks and Caicos Islands are one of five remaining British Overseas Territories in the Caribbean. You still catch the occasional glimpse of the British imperial regalia paraded in the guise of the Royal Turks & Caicos Islands Police Force, but as the islands develop (particularly Providenciales), the influence of the USA resounds ever louder. The islands' economy rests on two principal industries: tourism and offshore finance. Annual tourist arrivals stand at around 190,000, while TCI's status as an international tax haven is steadily growing, supported by the Financial Services Commission and a cadre of financial professionals.

Until recently, the Turks and Caicos Islands were never really that well known. For a hundred years, an igloo appeared on the national flag because a colonial flagmaker, who presumed that they were near the Arctic, reputedly mistook their symbol, a pile of salt, for an igloo and kindly added a doorway. But their isolation is an attraction for some, and those who do visit, to enjoy the islands' magnificent beaches and superb diving, often return. For the moment, most of the Turks and Caicos Islands still retain the tranquil feel of the British West Indies as they were forty odd years ago. But there are signs everywhere, especially on Providenciales, proclaiming future development.

History

A theory that enjoys some credibility with historians is that Columbus in fact made his original landfall in the New World on Grand Turk, rather than on San Salvador in the Bahamas). If it was not Columbus himself, then the first visitor to the islands was probably Ponce de Léon, who is supposed to have dropped by in 1512, while on his quest for the Fountain of Youth. At any rate, there were Arawak Indians living on the islands at the time of their arrival (the oldest archaeological site in the Bahamian archipelago lies on Grand Turk) and their thousands of years of peace were destroyed

Best Beaches

Providenciales

Grace Bay: The whole north coast of Providenciales. The barrier reef lining the coast breaks the incoming surf to create calm, crystal-clear water. Despite the presence of several dozen hotels and condominium developments, there is still plenty of peaceful, pristine sand for long strolls.

Erebus Beach (at the mouth of Turtle Cove Pond), **Smith's Reef** and the **White House Beach** (off Penn's Road in the Bight): These offer the most accessible snorkelling.

Leeward Beach (at the top end of Grace Bay): Secluded beaches with small cliffs and stone jetties, accessible by various roads and paths in the Leeward district.

Sapodilla Bay Beach: Towards South Dock, this is an anchorage for visiting yachts; it sports warm, shallow waters and an escape from the resort 'crowd'.

Taylor Bay Beach: West of Sapodilla Bay, overlooking the Caicos Banks to the south.

Malcolm Roadstead: On the island's northwest shore, a short ride from Blue Hills Settlement. Accessible with a four-wheel-drive vehicle via a foray through hills and bush, the spectacular two-mile beach and excellent snorkelling are worth the trip. Tiki huts provide shade and an interesting picnic spot.

Islands East of Providenciales (West to East)

Little Water Cay: Rare and endangered Turks and Caicos rock iguanas waddle to meet your boat and there is an interpretative nature trail. Plenty of opportunity for beach-combing on vast stretches of sugar-white sand.

Pine Cay: A two-mile expanse of simply stunning silky sand shelving gradually into the shallows. The Meridian Club (*t 946 5128*) is a private resort; you can get lunch there (if you contact them in advance and they are not too full).

Parrot Cay: A former favourite with pirates, fringed with white coral sand and washed by azure sea. Home to the Parrot Cay Hotel; you need permission to go to the island.

North Caicos: Miles and miles of wild sand, much of it protected from the Atlantic swell by offshore islands and reefs.

Middle Caicos: Mudjin Harbour. A photographer's dream: the harbour envelops breathtaking views of coastal bluffs, caves and cove-enclosed beaches. A vacation community is planned overlooking the beach and a nature trail runs along the cliffs.

South Caicos: Minutes from the airstrip, on the northern side of the island, there are idyllic curves where the waves clap and hiss: vast stretches of utterly uninhabited beach (take a picnic and snorkelling gear if you wander off there for the day).

Grand Turk: The leeward shore is edged by one long beach: Governor's Beach, running south from Cockburn Town, is a popular picnic and party spot. Pillory Beach is a wide stretch near the Guanahani Beach Resort, where Columbus is thought to have landed. There are hotels dotted along the central shore where you can get drinks and watersports gear, but there are miles of sand to tread; this is also a good spot to see the Green Flash at sundown.

Salt Cay: Jagged ironshore embraces sandy coves on the eastern side of the island, while a gorgeous white beach hems the entire northern shore.

within a few decades by the Europeans, who rounded up and shipped out to work in Spanish gold mines in Hispaniola to the south. With the population gone, the islands had nothing to offer the Spaniards and so they were left alone for the next couple of centuries. However, they were a convenient stopover for the buccaneers from the island of Tortuga off Hispaniola, and so pirates used the bays to lie in wait for shipping. It was not until 1678 that permanent settlers returned. Over the summer, Bermudians came to rake salt from the inland ponds on Grand Turk, Salt Cay and South Caicos, a commodity in demand as a preservative in the North American states.

The Spaniards complained that the settlers would drop the salt business all too readily the minute there were ships around to plunder, and so they staked their claim and occupied the islands in the 1710s. France invaded during the American War of Independence but the islands were returned to Britain by 1783. After the war, Loyalists from the southern states of the USA were granted land in the islands and they established sea island cotton and sisal estates in the uninhabited Caicos Islands. In 1799, both groups of prosperous islands were annexed to the Bahamian government. Subjection to Bahamian control caused great dissatisfaction and eventually in 1848 the islands were granted internal self-government led by a president who answered to Jamaica. But the estates and the salt industry failed and most of the planters left (you can still see ruins poking out of the undergrowth in many places), and so in 1873, after many years of financial difficulty, the islanders voted to annexe themselves to Jamaica, under whose control they remained until 1959. When, in 1962, Jamaica took its Independence, the Turks and Caicos were handed back over to the Bahamas. At that point, the islands became a separate Crown Colony and, after the Bahamas became independent, a Governor was appointed for the islands. The islands became internally self-governing in 1976 with a legal system based on the centuries-old common law of England.

As the islands are a Crown Colony of Britain, they are administered by a Governor, His Excellency James Poston, in conjunction with an Executive Council (partly elected, partly appointed) and a 13-member Legislative Council. The British Governor, Chief Secretary and Attorney General retain responsibility for foreign affairs, internal security, defence and offshore finance. The primary political parties are the Progressive National Party (PNP) and the People's Democratic Movement (PDM). The present leader is Chief Minister Hon. Michael E. Misick, representing the PNP. The next elections are due to take place in 2007.

The islands struggled financially in the 20th century and the economy has only really picked up in the last few years with the development of tourism and the offshore finance industry. The salt industry has finished, but some income is generated from the export of conch and lobster.

Beaches

For their soft ivory sand, lack of crowds and backdrop of extraordinarily powerful blue sea, the Turks and Caicos beaches reign supreme. In fact, along the vast majority of the islands' estimated 200 miles of pristine beach, often only accessible by boat, there is often complete isolation. See 'Best Beaches', p.825.

Getting There

Turks and Caicos t (1 649–)

By Air

Providenciales is the main airport of entry into the Turks and Caicos. There are also international airports on Grand Turk, North Caicos, and South Caicos, and domestic airports on all inhabited islands except West Caicos and East Caicos. Domestic air service is provided to all of the inhabited islands on a daily basis. There is a departure tax of US$35, usually included in the ticket.

From Europe

British Airways runs direct flights from London Heathrow on Sunday and Monday, and other flights via Nassau in the Bahamas. You can also go via Miami.

From North America

American Airlines, t 946 4948, t 1 800 433 7300, flies twice daily from Miami and daily from New York. Delta Airlines flies daily from Atlanta. US Airways, t 941 5837, has a daily service from Charlotte and Ft. Lauderdale, plus a Saturday flight from Philadelphia. In high season, scheduled and charter flights leave from a number of North American destinations, including Boston, Chicago, Detroit, New York, Montreal and Toronto. Lynx Air International, t 888 LYNX AIR, t 1888 596 9247, info@lynxair.com, www.lynxair.com, flies between Providenciales, Grand Turk and Fort Lauderdale.

From the Bahamas and Other Caribbean Islands

Connections to Providenciales can be made via Nassau and Grand Bahamas via Bahamasair, US t 1 800 222 4262, www.bahamasair.com, and SkyKing, t 941 KING, king@tciway.tc, www.skyking.tc. There are also flights from Montego Bay on Air Jamaica. Flights are available on Air Turks and Caicos, t 941 5481, www.airturksandcaicos.com, Global Airways, t 946 7093, SkyKing and InterIsland Airways, t 946 5481, www.interislandairways.com, to other Caribbean destinations, including the Dominican Republic, Haiti, Puerto Rico and Cuba. You may be able to charter one of the InterIsland planes.

Getting Around

By Bus

The Gecko Shuttle Bus, t 232 7433, www.thegecko.com, is a new service designed for tourists, providing regular transportation between the Grace Bay and Turtle Cove areas. The service runs daily 11–10, every 30mins. Check on the website for fares.

By Taxi

Taxis work on fixed rates and are expensive (ensure the price before you set off).
Four Corners, Grand Turk, t 946 2239.
Hillside Taxi, Grand Turk, t 231 0934.
Nell's Taxi, Provo, t 941 3228.
Paradise Taxi, Provo, t 941 3555.
Provo Taxi & Bus Group, Provo, t 946 5481.
Tina's Taxi, Provo, t 941 3999.

By Guided Tour

On Providenciales, contact the following to arrange **island tours**:
Island's Choice Taxi Service, t 941 0409.
Majestic Tours, t 946 4181. Combines flights to the other islands with guided ground tours.
Provo Taxi Association, t 946 5481.

Car and Bike Hire

Cars and **scooters** are available for hire on the major islands. Rates start at US$40 per day for a small car. Remember to drive on the left. A licence from home is valid, but a government tax of $15 is levied on all cars hired and $5 on motorbikes. In **Provo**, contact:
Avis, Provo Airport, t 946 4705, reservations@avis.tc, www.avis.tc.
Hertz/Contour Rental, t 941 5718.
Budget Rent-A-Car, t 946 4079, budget@provo.net, www.provo.net/budget.
Provo Fun Cycles and Autos, t 946 5868, provofuncycles@provo.net, www.provo.net/provofuncycles.
Provo Rent-A-Car, t 946 4475, rentacar@provo.net, www.provo.net/rentacar.
Rent-A-Buggy, t 946 4158, reservations@tciway.tc, www.rentabuggy.tc.
Scooter Bob's, t 946 4684, scooter@provo.net, www.provo.net/scooter. Scooters as well as jeeps, motorbikes and bicycles.
Tropical Auto Rentals, t 946 5300, www.provo.net/tropicalauto.

Turks & Caicos National Car Rental, Airport Plaza, **t** 946 4701, *tcnational@provo.net*.

On **Grand Turk**, contact:

Dutchie's, t 946 2244. Car hire.

Tropical Auto Rental, t 946 5300. Car rentals.

On the **other islands**, enquire at the hotels or airport.

Between the Islands

As with buses in the West Indies, you will find that the islanders say 'good morning' when they board the small planes which link the chain of islands from Providenciales to North Caicos, Middle Caicos, South Caicos and Grand Turk. (Occasional services go to Pine Cay and Salt Cay.) Scheduled daily flights are offered by SkyKing, **t** 941 5464, *www.skyking.tc*, and Turks and Caicos Airways, **t** 946 4255, **t** 946 4438, with chartered services available from InterIsland Airways, **t** 946 4623, *fly@tciway.tc*, *www.interislandairways.com*, and Provo Air Charter, **t** 946 5578. If you cannot get a seat, ask around; you may well find that someone is chartering a plane and wants other passengers to share the cost.

Tourist Information

Abroad

There is a website dedicated to the Turks and Caicos Islands at *www.turksandcaicos tourism.com*. You can also find some useful information at *www.turksandcaicos.tc*. Take a look at *www.provo.net* as well, a website devoted specifically to the main tourist island of Providenciales. Another useful website is *www.tcimall.tc*.

For tourist offices abroad, contact:

Canada: R. R. 2 Bancroft, Ontario, K0L 1C0, **t** 613 332 6472.

UK: MKI, Mitre House, 66 Abbey Rd, Enfield, Middlesex EN1 2RQ, **t** (020) 8350 1017, *mki@ttg.co.uk*.

USA: 2715 East Oakland Park Blvd, Suite 101, Ft. Lauderdale, FL 33306, **t** 954 568 6588, *tcitrsm@bellsouth.net*;

60 East 42nd Street, Suite 2817, New York City 10165.

There is a general freephone number for the USA: **t** 1 800 241 0824.

In the Turks and Caicos

On the islands, contact the Turks and Caicos Tourist Board at the following offices:

Grand Turk: Front St, PO Box 128, Grand Turk, **t** 946 2321, *tci.tourism@tciway.tc*. Open *Mon–Thurs 8–4.30, Fri 8–4*.

Providenciales: Stubbs Diamond Plaza, **t** 946 4970.

Media

Times of the Islands is a full-colour magazine published quarterly, containing some features on local culture, ecology, lifestyle and development and offering advice for sun-worshippers and investors alike. There is a free monthly visitor's guide called *Where, When, How Providenciales* (*www.wherewhenhow.com*) as well as a similar publication produced quarterly for Grand Turk and Salt Cay. There are two newspapers, the *Free Press* (issued bi-weekly) and the *Turks and Caicos News* (issued fortnightly). *Sand, Sea, Serenity* is a new publication with interesting articles, dining information and a directory.

Medical Emergencies

There is a good choice of health care services available in the Turks and Caicos, especially on **Providenciales**. In a medical emergency, you can call an ambulance on **t** 999 or **t** 911, or contact the M. B. S. Group Medical Practice on Leeward Highway, **t** 946 4242/4222/5252. There is a hospital on **Grand Turk, t** 946 2333, and an air ambulance service is available to the USA and Nassau.

Money and Banks

The official currency of the Turks and Caicos is the US dollar, though some smaller local coins are issued. Major credit cards and traveller's cheques are usually accepted in any tourist area. If you go off the beaten track or to one of the less inhabited islands, you should take sufficient cash.

Banks are open Mon–Thurs 8.30–2.30, Fri 8.30–4.30.

Telephone Code

The IDD code for the Turks and Caicos Islands is **t** 1 649 followed by a seven-figure island number. Telephoning within the island, dial the seven digits.

Shopping

Opening hours are Mon–Sat 9–5.30, usually with a long Caribbean lunch-break. Shops on **Providenciales** include:

Bamboo Gallery, Market Place. Here you'll find Caribbean paintings.

Caicos Conch Farm. Shells to take home.

Greensleeves and **Paradise Gifts**, at Central Square. Offer some locally made handicrafts.

Hotel boutiques. These often carry a selection of resort wear, postcards and sundries.

Maison Creole, next to Ports of Call. For crafts.

Ports of Call, across from the Allegro Resort. Provo's largest shopping complex, with the atmosphere of an old Caribbean seaside town. You can browse an ever-increasing collection of retail shops and restaurants.

Royal Jewels and **Goldsmith Duty Free Shops**. Duty-free outlets selling liquor, jewellery, perfume and Cuban cigars.

Tourist Shoppe, Central Square. For T-shirts.

Unicorn Bookstore, Market Place. Videotapes and books about the islands.

The Saltmills, Grace Bay. Large shopping complex in the new Village at Grace Bay, billed to become the new town centre of the Grace Bay area.

Festivals

Local island festivals include sailing and boat races, beauty pageants, local bands and a chance to sample native dishes. As a British Crown Colony, the islands recognize many of the official British celebrations, including the Queen's Birthday in June.

January *Junkanoo Jump Up*, on New Year's Day, Grand Turk and Provo.

May *South Caicos Regatta*. Held at the end of the month.

June *Fun in the Sun*. Held on Salt Cay.
Queen's Birthday.
Conch Carnival, Grand Turk.

July *Provo Music and Cultural Festival.*
North Caicos Festarama.
Deep-sea fishing tournament. Draws in sports fishermen from across the US and the Caribbean for a two-week orgy of deep-sea fishing and parties.

August *Cactusfest.* Held at the end of August in Grand Turk.

Watersports

You can rent watersports equipment at the major hotels, including **windsurfers**, **sailboats**, **kayaks** and **sea cycles**.

Day Sails

Day trips by boat to nearby cays and islands are offered on **Providenciales** by:

Beluga, t 946 4396, *sailbeluga@tciway.tc*.

J & B Tours, Leeward Marina, t 946 5047, *jill@jbtours.com*, *www.jbtours.com*.

Sail Provo, t 946 4783, *sailprovo@tciway.tc*, *www.sailprovo.com*.

Silver Deep, t 946 5612, *silverdeep_dean@tciway.tc*, *www.silverdeep.com*.

Tao Charters, t 231 6767, US t 1 800 645 1179 *tao@provo.net*, *www.provo.net/tao*.

Salt Cay Tours, t 946 6904, *www.saltcay.org/saltcaytours*.

Sun & Fun Sports/Sea Doo, t 496 5724.

Fishing

Quite popular, either close to the shore for feisty reef fish, including those in the much-prized snapper and grouper families, or over the deep-sea channels, where you might hook a yellow tuna or a marlin. There is an annual international billfishing tournament in July. Most of the above day-sailing companies offer deep-sea fishing trips.

Bone-fishing, casting in the shallow flats, is also extremely popular and can be arranged through the same companies, or through:

Bonefish Unlimited, t 946 4874, *bonefish@provo.net*, *www.provo.net/bonefish*.

Catch The Wave, t 941 3047, *catchthewave@tciway.tc*, *www.tcimall.tc/catchthewave*.

Gwendolyn Fishing Charters, Provo, t 946 5321, *gwendolyn@provo.net*, *www.fishingtci.com*.

Hatteras Sakitumi, t 946 4065, *sakitumi@provo.net*, *www.provo.net/sakitumi*.

Hook'em Fishing Adventures, Turtle Cove Marina, Provo, t 231 3586, *www.hookem.tc*.

J & B Tours, Leeward Marina, t 946 5047.

Sand Dollar Cruising, t 946 2018, t 946 5238, *sanddollar@tciway.tc*.

Sea Captivations, t 946 1407.

Silver Deep Fishing Charters, Provo, t 946 4526.

Turkoise Excursions, t 946 5379, *www.turkoiseexcursions.com*.

Scuba Diving

Divers return each year to the submarine walls (which drop sheer) around Grand Turk, at North West Point in Providenciales and at West Caicos. Elsewhere, pinnacles of coral are surrounded by an expanse of sand and ravines plied by flotillas of tiny fish and scoured by a barracuda, with even the odd coral-encrusted anchor offshore. Beds of soft corals are near the surface and lower down are forests of gorgonians and black coral. Lobsters scrabble on the sea bed and, above them, groupers and yellowtail snapper hang out with vibrant blue butterfly fish and the odd long, thin trumpet-fish. Turtles cruise by and, in winter, migrating humpback whales travel the Columbus Passage. The Grand Turk Wall starts in 35ft of water in places and has overhangs to explore just below the lip. Off Providenciales, there are fish of all kinds, particularly impressive on the wall at the North West Point, where there are ravines, undercuts and chimney tunnels. Other good dive sites include West Caicos, where stingrays, loggerhead turtles, hammerhead sharks and even whales have been seen, and South Caicos, pretty much virgin territory.

Divers must present certification cards, but if you haven't dived before, it's easy to arrange introductory courses. Providenciales has a recompression chamber, t 946 4242. Dive operators are often run out of the hotels, and also cluster around Turtle Cove in Providenciales.

Art Pickering's Provo Turtle Divers, Turtle Cove, t 946 4232, US t 1 800 833 1341, *provo turtledivers@provo.net, www.provo turtledivers.com.*

Caicos Adventures, Turtle Cove, t 941 3346, *divucrzy@tciway.tc, www.caicos adventure.com.*

Dive Provo, Turtle Cove, t 946 5040, US t 1 800 234 7768, *diving@diveprovo.com, www.dive provo.com.*

Flamingo Divers, Turtle Cove, t 946 4193, US t 1 800 204 9282, *flamingo@provo.net, www.provo.net/flamingo.*

Ocean Vibes, Turtle Cove, t 231 6636, *ocean vibes@tciway.tc, www.oceanvibes.com.*

Ocean Haven, South Caicos, t 946 3444, *divesouth@tciway.tc, www.oceanhaven.tc.*

Blue Water Divers, Grand Turk, t 946 2432, *mrolling@tciway.tc, www.grandturks cuba.com.*

Oasis Divers, Grand Turk, t 946 1128, US t 1 800 892 3995, *oasisdiv@tciway.tc, www.oasis divers.com.*

SeaEye Diving, Grand Turk, t 946 1407, *cl@tciway.tc, www.seaeyediving.com.*

Salt Cay Divers, Salt Cay, t 946 6906, *scdivers@tciway.tc, www.saltcaydivers.tc.* Here you can dive the wreck of the *Endymion*, an 18th-century British warship.

There are also two **live-aboard dive boats** based in Turks and Caicos waters:

Sea Dancer, US t 305 669 6237, US t 1 800 932 6237, *dancer@peterhughes.com, www.peter hughes.com.*

Turks & Caicos Aggressor, US t 1800 348 2628, *aggressor@provo.net, www.turksandcaicos aggressor.com.*

Underwater Adventures

Undersea Explorer, t 231 0006, *caicostours@ tciway.tc.* A semi-submarine with tours from Turtle Cove Marina in Provo. *Tours daily at 10am, 2pm and 4pm; adm adults $39, children $29, inc. transport from most hotels in the Grace Bay area.*

Other Sports

Cricket

You will occasionally see cricket matches played by the local teams.

Golf

Provo Golf Club, near the hotels in northeast Providenciales, t 946 5991. An 18-hole championship golf course cut into the scrubland, recently rated as one of the ten best in the Caribbean. Also a driving range.

Horse-riding

Provo Ponies, t 241 6350, *camille@tciway.tc.* Offers morning and afternoon beach and trail rides for all levels.

Phillip Outten, t 941 3610, *phillipoutten@ tciway.tc.* Guided rides, trail rides, pony rides and sunset rides. Riding lessons can be arranged; all ages welcome.

Tennis

Courts are available at many of the hotels. Check at the reception desk.

Where to Stay

Turks and Caicos t (1 649–)

Providenciales is the primary destination in the Turks and Caicos and offers a more typical Caribbean holiday package than its sister islands, strong on watersports and organized relaxation, with some entertainment thrown in. It has developed fairly recently, with a selection of modern resorts, smaller hotels, guest houses, condominiums and private villas.

Grand Turk is quieter and more low-key. Lodging choices include small resorts and hotels, restored Bermudian homes serving as inns and some villa units. Especially worth recommending are some fine old creole coralstone houses with shuttered windows and wooden balconies that have been turned into guest houses. They all have a familiar, friendly atmosphere and you quickly get to know the managers and other guests.

On the **smaller islands**, there is little choice of accommodation. Hotels add a 7% government tax and charge service at 10% or 15%.

Caicos Islands

Luxury

Parrot Cay Resort, t 946 7788, *parrot@ tciway.tc, www.parrot-cay.com*. A private island resort with 58 rooms in villas ranged around the sandy garden. Each has a deck with a view across the incredibly blue sea. The design is clean and sleek (some colonial touches offset with white), with four poster beds hung with muslin and terracotta tiles. A hideaway for the stars, with all they need to pamper them including a Shambala spa.

Meridian Club, Pine Cay, t 946 5128, US t 1 800 331 9154, *www.meridianclub.com*. Very exclusive, with 12 sumptuous suites on a stunning two-mile crescent of blinding sand with palm-thatch parasols. Watersports, pool, tennis court, cocktail bar and an elegant restaurant for a five-course dinner; birdwatching trips to inland lakes or simply seclusion; quite a discerning crowd.

Grace Bay Club, PO Box 128, Providenciales, t 946 5757, US t 1 800 946 5757, *gracebay@ tciway.tc, www.gracebayclub.com*. On a magnificent strip of sand on the huge Grace Bay, this elegant Spanish revival palace has balustrades, terracotta floor tiles and rounded roof tiles, set among palmetto and coconut palms. The 21 suites have fully equipped kitchens, large living areas, televisions, VCR, safes, washer/dryer, etc. There's a pool, tennis courts, some watersports, one- and two-bedroom suites and penthouses. Attached is the excellent Anacaona Restaurant (*see* p.833).

Point Grace, Grace Bay, Providenciales, t 946 5096, US t 1888 682 3705, *pointgrace@ tciway.tc, www.pointgrace.tc*. The 32 suites carry a Caribbean theme; some are in cottages with balconies of traditional gingerbread fretwork and shingle-tiled roofs. They centre on the pool and there is a pleasant feel of a modern 'resort' which gives onto the fantastic beach. The dining room is in Grace's Cottage, which has tables on the veranda and outside in the gardens.

The Palms, Grace Bay, Providenciales, t 946 8666, US t 1 866 877 7256, *info@gopalms. com, www.thepalmstc.com*. The latest lavish resort to grace Grace Bay. There are 72 two- and three-bedroom suites with vaulted ceilings, marble floors, mahogany four-poster beds, Roman-style baths, broadband access, iPod docking stations, DVD/CD players and ocean-view terraces. The eight penthouse suites come with Jacuzzi, butler and chauffeur service. The infinity pool is bordered by circular cushioned sun pods for that perfect tan, while the spa has an outdoor meditation area and eight treatment rooms built of hand-cut coral stone. Six tented cabanas in an adjacent garden provide a different setting for treatments. Pan-Asian tropical cuisine is served at Parallel23, the resort's signature restaurant with an open kitchen equipped with a wood-burning oven, wok station and tandoori oven. Plunge, the poolside restaurant, offers light fare from around the world.

Very Expensive

Ocean Club Resorts, Grace Bay, Providenciales, t 946 5461, US t 1 800 457 8787, *oceanclb@ caribsurf.com, www.oceanclubresorts.com*. A condo complex with considerable Caribbean style, including large screened balconies and views down the fantastic beach. Apartments are very comfortable, fully equipped with tropical-coloured decorations and furnishings; some common facilities including two pools, a beachside bar and grill and also an excellent restaurant, the Gecko Grille.

Expensive

Miramar Erebus Inn, Turtle Cove, Providenciales, PO Box 238, t 946 4240, US t 1800 323 5655, *erebus@tciway.tc*, *www. erebus.tc*. One of the most comfortable of the more traditional-style hotels, which perches on the cliff above Turtle Cove, from where the bar and pool have excellent views. There are 25 neat and comfortable rooms, tennis courts, fitness centre, restaurant and shuttle to the beach.

Sibonné, Providenciales, t 946 5547,US t 1 800 223 9815, *sibonne@provo.net*, *www.sibonne. com*. Making the most of its prime spot on Grace Bay, the charming hotel is U-shaped to open directly onto the beach. Its 25 rooms surround a garden courtyard; each has a balcony. Has dive facilities and a seafront restaurant serving European cuisine.

Treasure Beach Villas, Grace Bay, Providenciales, t 946 4325, *treasurebeach@ tciway.tc*. Quiet and well priced; 18 fully equipped units right by an excellent snorkelling reef. Common facilities include a pool and tennis courts.

Allegro Resort and Casino, on the 12-mile, northside beach, Providenciales, t 946 5555, US t 1800 858 2258, *www.allegroresorts.com*. All-inclusive; offering the full range of sports, dining, entertainment and activities.

Moderate–Inexpensive

Turtle Cove Inn, Providenciales, t 946 4203, US t 1 800 887 0477, *turtlecoveinn@provo.net*, *www.turtlecoveinn.com*. Another small and low-key resort. It has 32 simple but comfortable rooms overlooking the Turtle Cove marina, with all the dive shops around, plus several good restaurants (Tiki Hut Bar & Grill and Aqua Bar and Terrace) and shuttle to the beach.

Airport Inn, Provo, t 941 3514, *airportinn@ provo.net*, *www.provo.net/tcnational*. Perhaps the cheapest option on Provo, with 18 rooms.

Pelican Beach Hotel, North Caicos, t 946 7112, *pelicanbeach@tciway.tc*. Stands on miles of

sand. It is quiet, with a restaurant and bar, and 14 passable rooms.

Ocean Beach, North Caicos, t 946 7113, *www. turksandcaicos.tc/oceanbeach*. Just 10 rooms with cane furniture set in a sandy garden just across from the beach.

JoAnne's B & B, North Caicos, t 946 7301, *joannesbnb@tciway.tc*, *www.turksandcaicos. tc/joannesbnb*. Four rooms off Whitby beach in the north; friendly and easygoing.

Blue Horizon Resort, Middle Caicos, t 946 6141, *bhresort@tciway.tc*, *www.bhresort.com*. Four studio cottages with fantastic views over Mudjin Harbour Beach, screened porches, kitchens and living/dining areas.

Dreamscape Villa, Bambarra Beach, Middle Caicos, t 946 6175, *www.middlecaicos.com*, *eagle@tciway.tc*.

Taylor's Guest House, Middle Caicos, t 946 6161.

South Caicos Ocean Haven, t 946 3444, t 946 3446, *divesouth@tciway.tc*, *www.ocean haven.tc*. A quiet and very comfortable place to stay, with 22 rooms on a superb strip of sand and others on the waterfront.

Mae's B & B, Tucker's Hill, South Caicos, t 946 5207. Three rooms.

Grand Turk and Salt Cay

Very Expensive–Expensive

Windmills Plantation, Salt Cay, t 946 6962, US t 1 800 822 7715, *plantation@saltcaysite.com*, *www.windmillsplantation.com*. Set on two and a half miles of superb beach is a fantastic retreat on an already secluded island. The eight rooms and suites are arranged around a central bar and pool area, each decorated in bright Caribbean pastels with period antiques and reproduction furniture made with Costa Rican mahogany. Some watersports.

Osprey Beach Hotel, Cockburn Town, Grand Turk, t 946 1453, t 946 2817, *sraker@tciway.tc*, *www.ospreybeachhotel.com*. A modern block, with 28 nicely decorated rooms looking over the sea on the Caribbean side.

Moderate–Inexpensive

Salt Raker Inn, Cockburn Town, t 946 2260, *sraker@tciway.tc*, *www.saltraker.com*. One of the most charming hotels on Grand Turk, on historic Duke St. Some of the 12 rooms are set in a classic seafarer's home with wooden walls and floors; others are in suites around the very attractive garden with palms, palmetto and sprays of bougainvillea. Rooms are equipped with air-conditioning, cable TV and a fridge, in old Caribbean style and atmosphere.

Turks Head Inn, Cockburn Town, t 946 2466, *turkshead@tciway.tc, www.grandturk. com*. On the shore road in town. Another haunt with historic West Indian style, circa the 1840s. There are seven rooms, of which the best are the four upstairs, featuring some antique furniture and a balcony with a superb sea view. Excellent bar and covered restaurant.

Island House, Cockburn Town, Grand Turk, t 946 1519, *ishouse@tciway.tc, www. islandhouse-tci.com*. Eight suites in a Mediterranean-style house with a view over the North Creek towards the sea. Friendly and personable atmopshere.

Mount Pleasant Guest House, Salt Cay, t 946 6927, US t 180 289 5056, *mtpleasantinfo@ yahoo.com, www.turksandcaicos.tc/mt pleasant*. Eight air-conditioned rooms with televisions in a newly refurbished historic inn, offering horseback riding, bicycles, on-site dive facilities and a restaurant with gourmet dining, bar and lounge.

Eating Out and Bars

Seafood is the great speciality in the islands, including lobster (in season), conch and local fish, which are brought in straight from the seas. Remember that almost everything else is imported by boat or plane and the full menu may not always be available. Ask about daily specials. On Provo, dining has changed significantly over the past few years. With the explosive growth of high-end hotels and villas has come a proliferation of restaurants with experienced, well-trained chefs.

As noted before, the Turks and Caicos Islands are not cheap. Nonetheless, there are also plenty of enjoyable dining rooms in the low-key inns. Besides such specialties as conch 'n' grits, boiled fish with johnnycake and turtle stew, islanders are fond of spicy fried chicken,

jerk pork, *souse* and stewed beef, and almost all native meals are accompanied by peas 'n' rice, macaroni and cheese and potato salad.

Nightlife is fairly limited and includes local bands playing traditional island **music** at bars and restaurants (ask when and where at your hotel), Providenciales' **casino**, Port Royale, at the Allegro Resort, and some **nightclubs**. Don't miss strolling the beach at night: stargazing is extraordinary, and it is quite safe, although standard safety precautions should be taken.

Categories are arranged according to the price of a main dish: expensive = US$20 and above; moderate = US$10–20; inexpensive = US$10 and under.

Providenciales

Expensive

The best dining is in the hotels and there are plenty to choose from. Try **Grace's Cottage** at Point Grace and **Anacaona** at Grace Bay Club. Both have lovely settings: the one around a Caribbean-style gingerbread cottage, and Anacaona under South Seas-like pointed palm thatch roofs. Some other Grace Bay Hotel restaurants to try are **Bay Bistro**, t 946 5396, *baybistro@tciway.tc*, at Sibonne Beach Hotel, for fine dining beachside; **Coyaba**, t 946 5186, *coyaba@provo.net*, at Coral Gardens, one of the more elegant restaurants with an eclectic, Caribbean menu; **Mango Reef**, t 946 8200, at Royal West Indies Resort, for fine French cuisine at affordable prices; and **Simba**, t 946 5588, *info@turksandcaicosclub.com*, at the Turks & Caicos Club, popular for seafood and Caribbean cuisine.

Gecko Grill, Ocean Club Plaza, t 946 5885. The 'flavors of the world with an island twist' are served in an 'Art Gecko dining room oozing with tropical sophistication' or out on the patio, with thousands of twinkling lights in the surrounding trees. Well-stocked bar, excellent wine list, monthly Gourmet Club.

Moderate–Inexpensive

Tiki Hut Cabana Bar & Grill, Turtle Cove Inn, t 941 5341. Lively dockside dining on Black Angus beef, gourmet pizza, fish and pasta.

Baci Ristorante, dockside in Turtle Cove, t 941 3044. Southern Italian cuisine, veal dishes, pasta and nightly specials.

Bambooz Bar & Grill, at The Saltmills, t 941 8146. Casual meals, pizza and snacks for the whole family. Happy hour, pool, wide-screen televisions, theme nights, music.

Magnolia Wine Bar and Restaurant, overlooking Turtle Cove, t 941 5108. Light international cuisine with island touch; extensive wine list. Good for sunsets.

Banana Boat Caribbean Grill, Turtle Cove Marina, t 941 5706. On a bright and breezy wooden deck hung with nauticalia. Easy atmosphere, featuring Black Angus, fresh fish, Caribbean cuisine and excellent tropical drinks. Every Tuesday is Seafood Night, with 12 types of seafood prepared three ways, punctuated with live local entertainment.

Caicos Café, Grace Bay, t 946 5278. Next to the Ports of Call complex. Chef Perrik prepares fresh grilled fish, steak, lamb and chicken.

Hey Jose's Cantina, in Central Square on the Leeward Highway, t 946 4812. Very popular meeting place; hardly a romantic setting, but a lively crowd and Mexican food in a modern air-conditioned dining room.

Bugaloo's on the Beach, after the turn to Blue Hills from Leeward Highway. A small building surrounded by shiny pink conch shells. Bugaloo's tangy conch salad couldn't be fresher: the conch are pulled from the water, shelled and diced to order.

Gilley's Restaurant, Leeward Marina, t 946 5094. An especially romantic place to dine in the evenings. Reliable seafood and local fare.

Dora's Restaurant and Bar, Leeward Highway, t 946 4558. Good island seafood and native dishes in a modern concrete building. Open all day and night. Often a crowd. Monday and Thursday seafood buffet.

Barefoot Café, Ports of Call, t 946 5282, *barefootcafe@provo.net*. Conch is the speciality, especially on Monday night, plus Caribbean selections; *fajitas* on Thursday. Bagels, fresh baked pastries and ice cream.

Calico Jack's, Ports of Call, t 946 5129. International cuisine, seafood, pastas and local dishes in a casual setting. Live music, singing, dancing on a Friday night.

Coco Bistro, t 946 5369. Mediterranean cuisine at tables set in a coconut grove.

Danny Buoy's Irish Pub & Restaurant, t 946 5921. About as authentic an Irish pub as is possible in the tropics, with traditional Irish

cuisine, imported draft beers, and Provo's own Turks Head beer. Pool and darts on Fridays; island music on Saturdays. Big screen for sports during the week.

Hole in the Wall Bar & Restaurant, Old Airport Road, t 941 4136. Jerk and other Jamaican specialities and island fare. Shuttle service to most hotels.

West Indian Roti Shop, Leeward Highway, t 941 5959. Roti or dhall puri; chicken, beef, duck curry; vegetarian; West Indian and daily specials.

North and South Caicos

Ocean Beach Hotel, Whitby Beach, North Caicos, t 946 7113. Excellent food; book first.

Club Titters, Bottle Creek, North Caicos, t 946 7316.

Pappa Grunt's Seafood House, Whitby Plaza, North Caicos, t 946 7301.

Muriel's Restaurant, North Caicos, t 946 3535.

Pond View Restaurant and Bar, North Caicos, t 946 3276. Offers good and wholesome local fare: fish and two tropical veg.

Ocean Haven Sunset Bar and Restaurant, South Caicos, t 946 3444. Generous portions of southern-styled fish, lobster and conch.

Eastern Inn, Stamers St, South Caicos, t 946 3301. Close to the harbour; local fish and chicken.

Grand Turk

Most of the small inns have good kitchens, turning out some international food, but mostly good local fare.

Water's Edge, Duke St, t 946 1680. A concrete house, dressed up into a very attractive restaurant right above the waves, decorated with coloured lights and palm trees; international fare including pastas and steaks.

Lilian Chicken Inn, t 946 2155. Traditional fare.

Regal Begal, Hospital Rd, t 946 2274. Their cracked conch is not to be missed.

Turks Head Inn, t 946 2466. The best place to catch up on local gossip and enjoy after-dinner guitar and piano music.

Nookie Hill. Attracts a young crowd; there's some dancing, too.

Town Tigers. Try this out if you fancy watching a bit of dominoes and politics in action.

Arawak Inn & Beach Club, t 946 2277, *www.arawak.com*. On Governor's Beach.

The Turks

Grand Turk

Grand Turk (about six miles by one) is the seat of government (population 6,000) and site of the nation's capital at **Cockburn Town**, situated on the sheltered leeward coast. Overlooking the waterfront are some classic, Bermudian-style West Indian buildings, timber-framed houses with louvred windows and gingerbread verandas. Among them are the official government buildings, guarded by a couple of cannons. In a restored building at Guinep House, you will find the **Turks and Caicos National Museum** (*t 946 2160*). Besides displays of natural history and human heritage (Taino Indian, Spanish, African and Bermudian), the major exhibit is what is thought to be the oldest shipwreck in the Americas, a caravel which sank on Molasses Reef as early as 1513. A shop offers a wide selection of books, maps and island handicrafts.

Behind the waterfront are the old *salinas* (salt flats) and the residential districts of the island, which, despite the satellite dishes, retain an old-time Caribbean feel. Many buildings have walled courtyards meant to keep wandering donkeys from dining on the foliage. The attractive island **church** and its graveyard are in the middle of the town pond. A venerable **lighthouse**, more than 140 years old, awaits restoration at the northern tip of the island. Beyond Government House (called Waterloo because it was built in 1815) is a former US airbase to which the astronaut John Glenn was welcomed back to land after the first voyage into space. The southern tip of the island is where some historians believe that Columbus made his first landfall in 1492.

Salt Cay

Seven miles southwest of Grand Turk is Salt Cay, another of the original salt-raking settlements and just three and a half square miles. The industry is defunct, but the sun still does its work and you will be aware of blinding-white expanses of sea salt, studded by old windmills. There are just 300 islanders, centred around Balfour Town, a a peaceful, tidy, idyllic village, where pastel-painted homes and pretty walled gardens line the streets. In the past, whaling helped to support the economy – humpback whales are frequently spotted off the west coast during migration. The island is a UNESCO World Heritage Site.

The Caicos Islands

South Caicos to Little Water Cay

The Caicos Islands were traditionally the more agricultural of the two groups of islands. They had a few prosperous plantation years in the late 1700s, boasted a sisal plantation in the 1900s and produced a variety of fruits and vegetables, especially in fertile North Caicos. **South Caicos** (population 1,220) was once the centre of commercial activity, for the collection of salt and its fine natural harbour. AKA 'the Big South', it was also the first island to have a commercial airstrip. Now, it retains a slow, old-time atmosphere, but continues to be the centre of the islands' fishing industry.

East Caicos is uninhabited, save a few roaming donkeys and cattle, but it was once the site of a large sisal plantation complete with a railway and cattle farm. There is a supreme beach (17 miles long) along the north coast. **Middle** or **Grand Caicos** is the largest island in the group, and the least inhabited (population 270). Of the three settlements, Conch Bar is the largest and home to the island's airstrip. Nearby, you'll find Village Cave with its network of tunnels and caverns. It boasts four species of bat and was once mined for guano. Tours are available; enquire at the airport. There are a number of pre-Columbian archaeological sites, including a Lucayan Indian ball court.

Separated by a channel in the west, **North Caicos** has a few more inhabitants (1,300) in the villages of Bottle Creek, Sandy Point, Whitby and Kew. The lush island is known for its agriculture and its wildlife. Attracting a higher annual rainfall than the other islands, the land is fertile enough to grow a variety of fruits and vegetables, including custard apples, sapodilla, papaya, mangoes, bananas, sweetsop, tamarind, pigeon peas, tomatoes, corn and pumpkin. 'North' is bustling with birds and the country's largest flock of flamingos roosts at Flamingo Pond near Kew. You can visit a superb example of loyalist plantation ruins at Wade's Green, featuring a courtyard and jail.

On the cays strung out between North Caicos and Provo are two islands that are now getaway retreats: **Parrot Cay** and **Pine Cay**, each fringed by a fantastic beach. The silken sands continue through **Water Cay** and **Little Water Cay** to the tip of Providenciales, and are the perfect spots for a 'deserted island' experience.

Providenciales and West Caicos

Providenciales is the centrepiece of tourist development and has shot from a tiny and barely inhabited backwater to a resort island with a population of 15,000. The hotels are mostly strung along the northern shore and its fantastic beach. The main town, which has the banks, shops and offices, is just north of the airport. Tourist centres include **Turtle Cove**, where there is a small cluster of hotels, restaurants and shops around a marina, and the **Grace Bay 'Gold Coast'**, which features the resort hotels, a variety of restaurants and the Ports of Call shopping complex. Recently, a large number of condominium projects have been initiated along the Grace Bay Beach. Beyond the golf course, you come to **Leeward** (*t 946 5000, info@leeward-provo-tci.com, www.leeward-provo-tci.com*), a resort area, including a marina hotel and 'town square' to complement the ambitious residential sales programme under way.

In the far northeast tip of the island is the **Caicos Conch Farm** (*t 946 5330; guided tours available for $6/person, Mon–Fri 9–3*). It was established in 1984 to grow conch commercially, from eggs to adult (a four-year life cycle). It has a current inventory of 1.5 million conch at each and every stage and is the only such facility in the world. The shop features unique gifts and souvenirs. Conch meat has long been a staple food in the Caribbean and turns up on the islands under various guises in conch salad, conch fritters, conch chowder and 'cracked conch'.

West Caicos is uninhabited for now, except by passing flamingos. That will all change with the development of a resort and residential community, anchored by a marina and a Ritz Carlton Hotel. Around 90 per cent of the island will remain an official nature reserve. There is a stunning beach in the northwest and superb diving.

Index

Main page references are in **bold**. Page references to maps are in *italics*.

Also available from Cadogan Guides...

France

France
Brittany
Côte d'Azur
Corsica
Dordogne & the Lot
Gascony & the Pyrenees
Loire
Normandy
Provence
Short Breaks in Northern France
South of France

Italy

Italy
The Bay of Naples and Southern Italy
Bologna and Emilia Romagna
Central Italy
Italian Riviera and Piemonte
Lombardy and the Italian Lakes
Northeast Italy
Rome Venice Florence
Sardinia
Sicily
Tuscany
Tuscany, Umbria and the Marches
Umbria

Spain

Spain
Andalucía
Bilbao and the Basque Lands
Granada Seville Córdoba
Northern Spain

Greece

Greece
Athens and Southern Greece
Crete
Greek Islands

The UK and Ireland

EnglandIreland
Ireland
London–Paris
London Markets
Scotland
Scotland's Highlands and Islands
Southwest Ireland

Other Europe

Portugal
Madeira & Porto Santo
Malta, Gozo & Comino

The City Guide Series

Amsterdam
Barcelona
Bruges
Brussels
Dublin
Edinburgh
Florence
London
Madrid
Milan
Paris
Prague
Rome
Venice

Flying Visits

Flying Visits Central and Eastern Europe
Flying Visits France
Flying Visits Germany
Flying Visits Ireland
Flying Visits Italy
Flying Visits Mediterranean
Flying Visits Scandinavia
Flying Visits Spain
Flying Visits Switzerland

Cadogan Guides are available from good bookshops, or via **Littlehampton Book Services**, Faraday Close, Durrington, Worthing, West Sussex BN13 3RB, **t** (01903) 828800, **f** (01903) 828802; and **The Globe Pequot Press**, 246 Goose Lane, PO Box 480, Guilford, Connecticut 06437–0480, **t** (800) 458 4500/**t** (203) 458 4500, **t** (203) 458 4603.

Thoroughly researched for family entertainment, hotels and restaurants, *take the kids Florida* is your passport to a relaxing, fun-filled holiday.

'a godsend' – *the sunday times*

take the kids

FLORIDA and

Melanie Dakin

WALT DISNEY World.
RESORT IN FLORIDA

CADOGANguides

CADOGANguides
well travelled...*well read*